Making Arguments about Literature

A COMPACT GUIDE
AND ANTHOLOGY

Making Arguments about Literature

A COMPACT GUIDE
AND ANTHOLOGY

John Schilb
Indiana University

John Clifford
University of North Carolina at Wilmington

BEDFORD/ST. MARTIN'S   Boston • New York

For Bedford/St. Martin's
Executive Editor: Stephen A. Scipione
Production Editor: Bridget Leahy
Production Supervisor: Jennifer Wetzel
Senior Marketing Manager: Jenna Bookin-Barry
Editorial Assistant: Amy Hurd
Copyeditor: Michaela Dodd
Text Design: Geri Davis, The Davis Group, Inc.
Cover Design: Terry Govan Design
Cover Art: Soon-Ae Tark, *Pink*
Composition: Stratford Publishing Services, Inc.
Printing and Binding: Quebecor World Kingsport

President: Joan E. Feinberg
Editorial Director: Denise B. Wydra
Editor in Chief: Karen S. Henry
Director of Marketing: Karen Melton Soeltz
Director of Editing, Design, and Production: Marcia Cohen
Managing Editor: Elizabeth M. Schaaf

Library of Congress Control Number: 2004107882

9   8   7   6   5
f   e   d   c   b

For information, write: Bedford/St. Martin's, 75 Arlington Street, Boston, MA 02116
(617-399-4000)

ISBN: 0–312–43147–3
EAN: 978–0–312–43147–1

Acknowledgments

Diane Ackerman. "Plato: The Perfect Union." From *A Natural History of Love* by Diane Ackerman. Copyright © 1994 by Diane Ackerman. Reprinted by permission of Random House, Inc.

Sherman Alexie. "Capital Punishment." From *The Summer of Black Widows* by Sherman Alexie. Copyright © 1996 by Sherman Alexie. Reprinted by permission of Hanging Loose Press.

Acknowledgments and copyrights are continued at the back of the book on pages 949–53, which constitute an extension of the copyright page. It is a violation of the law to reproduce these selections by any means whatsoever without the written permission of the copyright holder.

As with Making Literature Matter, we dedicate this book to our wives. May our relationships with them never be compact, always expanding.

Preface for Instructors

Making Arguments about Literature began as a compact version of our already existing book *Making Literature Matter*. We assume that if you are examining this book, your course aims to integrate literary study and composition. *Making Literature Matter* was our response to literature anthologies that failed to deliver the substantial writing instruction they often promised; *Making Arguments about Literature* is, at least in part, our response to people who wanted *Making Literature Matter*'s substantial advice on writing, without quite as much literature. In the process of preparing this book, though, as we read what reviewers had to say, we came to believe that this shorter book would be even more useful to instructors if it included more advice on writing and rhetoric than its predecessor. Accordingly, *Making Arguments about Literature* offers not only a compact and flexible anthology of literature, but also a complete (if brief) text on argument, with argumentation presented as civil, reasoned inquiry through which writers persuade their audience that their interpretations are sound.

Making Arguments about Literature consists of three parts, the first of which deals extensively with the student's writing and with the process of arguing about literature. In explaining this process to students, we put forth various principles and discuss them at length, showing in particular how to turn personal responses into persuasive analyses. We define key terms of argument, including *claim*, *issue*, *audience*, *evidence*, and *warrants*. We discuss fallacious reasoning. We identify concerns that literary critics typically address. We analyze how each of the main literary genres poses special demands for the student who writes about them. We show how to conduct and document research, including how to use electronic sources. In addition, we provide numerous examples of written arguments. These include a model of what we call *weighted comparison*, as well as two kinds of research paper: one that situates a literary work in context, and one that uses a literary work as a springboard for examining related social issues. Throughout this first section, we emphasize concrete practice, guiding students through the analysis of specific literary works. Furthermore, every chapter in Part One concludes with a Summing Up box that provides a quick reference to the chapter's key points.

An important stage in making arguments about literature is getting ideas about a particular text in the first place. We find that students are most likely to achieve rhetorical invention if they can compare the text they are studying with another on the same topic. Therefore Part Two presents literary works in 15 thematic clusters. The topics of these groupings are issues relevant to students' lives, including Losing Innocence, Responding to Teachers, and Community Justice. In addition, many of these clusters stimulate thinking by juxtaposing classic and contemporary texts. Special clusters demonstrate how to work with (1) authors in depth, (2) critical contexts, (3) cultural contexts, and (4) "re-visions," or different retellings of a literary work. Every work in Part Two is followed by questions for discussion and writing. Moreover, as each cluster proceeds, we raise questions that help students compare the pieces it includes.

Part Three consists of even more literature, presented as an anthology of individual works. Specifically, this section includes 14 stories, 45 poems, 2 plays, and 6 essays, organized by genre. In many literature textbooks, a "gallery" such as this fails to say much (or anything) about the works' authors. We, however, provide a biographical headnote in each case, believing that students will appreciate having such information. In another departure from standard practice, we follow each selection with questions about the work. Again, as in Part Two, we think these questions stimulate critical inquiry, alerting students to issues they might ponder with classmates and pursue in their papers. Together, Parts Two and Three offer hundreds of prompts for discussion and writing, repeatedly enabling students to practice the rhetorical strategies explained in Part One.

Finally, we present an appendix that identifies and demonstrates contemporary critical approaches to literature. This section is ideal for instructors who wish to introduce their students to various current "schools" of literary theory, such as feminism, reader response theory, and post-colonial perspectives. The appendix uses these methods to analyze a particular short story, and then invites students to try them out on another piece of short fiction.

An instructor's manual, *Resources for Teaching* MAKING ARGUMENTS ABOUT LITERATURE, is also available. It includes sample syllabi, suggestions for teaching argument and literature, and commentary on every literary selection in the book. Additional resources can be found on the companion Web site at bedfordstmartins .com/argumentsaboutlit.

Acknowledgments

In working on this compact edition, we have again benefited greatly from the insight and diligence of the staff at Bedford/St. Martin's. As usual, we are especially indebted to our editor, Steve Scipione, and to the company's president, Joan Feinberg. We are also grateful for the assistance of Denise Wydra, Karen Henry, Karen Melton Soeltz, Jenna Bookin-Barry, Kevin Feyen, and Amy Hurd. As she did with *Making Literature Matter*, Bridget Leahy deftly guided *Making Arguments about Literature* through the production process. Thanks, too, to Janet E. Gardner of the University of Massachusetts at Dartmouth for contributing most of the section on research, and to Joyce Hollingsworth for her extensive work on the instructor's manual. John Clifford would like to thank both his chair, Chris Gould, for arranging a leave to complete *Making Arguments about Literature*, and Chris and Forrest Williamson, who generously allowed John and his wife to live and work under idyllic conditions in their beautiful home at East Chop overlooking Martha's Vineyard Sound.

Our conceptualization of this book was aided, too, by the comments of the following reviewers: Anna-Marie Alessa, MiraCosta College; Susie Crowson, Del Mar College; Richard Grande, Penn State University; Christopher A. Healy, University of Louisiana at Lafayette; Joseph S. Horobetz, Northern Virginia Community College; Tamara Kuzmenkov, Tacoma Community College; Miles S. McCrimmon, J. Sargeant Reynolds Community College; Kelly A. O'Connor-Salomon, Black Hills State University; Michelle Stewart, Mount San Jacinto College; Trey Strecker, Ball State University.

Contents

PART TWO
Thematic Clusters of Literature

PART THREE
A Gallery of Literature

15. A Gallery of Plays　733

16. A Gallery of Essays　877

APPENDIX: Making Arguments Using Critical Approaches　919

Making
Arguments

1

What Is Literature? What Is Argument?

> Art lives upon discussion, upon curiosity, upon variety of attempt, upon the exchange of views and the comparison of viewpoints.

This observation is from an 1895 essay called "The Art of Fiction" by the American novelist, short-story writer, and critic Henry James. James's own "art" was chiefly literature, and he produced a great deal of it. But we take his statement as also referring to the ways in which *readers* of literature find it meaningful. James implies that a literary work becomes especially significant for its readers when they can share and test their analyses of it. James himself welcomed this "exchange of views," this "comparison of viewpoints," and we hope that you will as well. Throughout our book, we refer to this process as *making arguments about literature.* When you engage in this activity, you don't just express your personal response to a text. You also try to persuade an audience that you are analyzing the text thoughtfully. While an argument involves real or potential disagreements, you need not treat it as a war. Rather, see it as a civilized effort aimed at making your ideas plausible. When you argue about literature, you carefully reason with others, helping them to grasp how a certain text should matter to them.

To help you learn and practice this art of persuasion, we present a number of literary works, including short stories, poems, plays, and essays. We also offer many suggestions for constructing arguments about such texts, whether your audience is your own classmates, your teacher, or other people. So, here at the outset, we want to explain briefly (1) how we are using the term *literature;* (2) why people read literature; (3) how to approach the literature in this book productively; and (4) what we mean when we emphasize *arguing* about it.

How Have People Defined Literature?

Asked to define *literature,* most people would say that it encompasses poetry, fiction (short stories as well as novels), and plays. But limiting the term's scope to these genres can be misleading, for it is rooted in everyday life. Often literary works employ ordinary forms of talk, although they may play with these expressions and blend them with less common ones. Moreover, certain words or

3

expressions may function as symbols in ordinary speaking and thinking as well as in literary works. For example, even people who aren't poets, fiction writers, or playwrights have little trouble associating things like shadows, evening, and darkness with death. In addition, in their everyday lives people put literary genres into practice. Perhaps you have commented on certain situations by quoting a song lyric or citing words from a poem, story, or play. Surely you are poetic in that you use metaphors in your everyday conversations. Probably you are often theatrical as well, acting out various kinds of scripts and performing any number of roles. Most likely you engage in storytelling, too, no matter how little fiction you actually write. Imagine this familiar situation: You are late for a meeting with friends because you got stuck in traffic, and now you must explain to them your delay. Your explanation may well become a tale of suspense, with you as the hero racing against time, against the bumper-to-bumper horde. As writer Joan Didion has observed, "We tell ourselves stories in order to live." Almost all of us spin narratives day after day because doing so helps us to frame our lives meaningfully.

You may admit that literature is grounded in real life and yet still tend to apply the term only to written texts of fiction, poetry, and drama. But this tendency is distinctly modern, for the term *literature* has not always been applied so restrictively. *Literature* was at first a characteristic of *readers*. From the term's emergence in the fourteenth century to the middle of the eighteenth, *literature* was more or less a synonym for *literacy*. People of literature were assumed to be well read.

In the late eighteenth century, however, the term's meaning changed. Increasingly it referred to books and other printed texts rather than to people who read them. At the beginning of this shift, the scope of literature was broad, encompassing nearly all public writing. But as the nineteenth century proceeded, the term's range shrank. More and more people considered literature to be imaginative or creative writing, which they distinguished from nonfiction. This trend did take years to build; in the early 1900s, literature anthologies still featured essays as well as excerpts from histories and biographies. By the mid-1900s, though, the narrower definition of literature prevailed.

This limited definition has become newly vulnerable. From the early 1970s, a number of literature faculty have called for widening it. In 1979, for instance, a National Endowment for the Humanities–Modern Language Association institute entitled "Women's Nontraditional Literature" applied the term *literature* to genres that had not been thought of as such. Participants studied essays, letters, diaries, autobiographies, and oral testimonies. To each of these genres, women have contributed much; in fact, the institute's participants concluded that a literature curriculum slights many works by women if it focuses on fiction, poetry, and drama alone.

Of course, even within these three categories, the term *literature* has been selectively applied. Take the case of novelist and short-story writer Stephen King, whose books have sold millions of copies. Despite his commercial success, a lot of readers—including some of his fans—refuse to call King's writing literature. They assume that to call something literature is to say that it has artistic merit, and for them King's tales of horror fall short.

Yet people who use the term *literature* as a compliment may still disagree about whether a certain text deserves it. Plenty of readers do praise King's writing as literature, even as others deem it schlock. In short, artistic standards differ. To be sure, some works have been constantly admired through the years; regarded as classics, they are frequently taught in literature classes. *Hamlet* and other plays by William Shakespeare are the most obvious examples. But in the last twenty years, much controversy has arisen over the *literary canon*, those works taught again and again. Are there good reasons why the canon has consisted mostly of works by white men? Or have the principles of selection been skewed by sexism and racism? Should the canon be changed to accommodate a greater range of authors? Or should literary studies resist having any canon at all? These questions have provoked various answers and continued debate.

Also in question are attempts to separate literature from *nonfiction*. Much nonfiction shows imagination and relies on devices found in novels, short stories, poems, and plays. The last few years have seen the emergence of the term *creative nonfiction* for essays, autobiographies, histories, and journalistic accounts that use evocative language and strong narratives. Conversely, works of fiction, poetry, and drama may center on real-life events. An example is Bharati Mukherjee's short story "The Management of Grief," which serves as the basis for a sample research paper on page 618. Although its characters are fictional, the story concerns an actual disaster, the 1985 bombing of an Air India plane. To be sure, some people argue that literature about real events is still "literary," because it inspires contemplation rather than action. This view of literature has traditionally been summed up as "art for art's sake." The notion brushes aside, however, all the poems, novels, short stories, and plays that encourage audiences to undertake certain acts. For example, Sherman Alexie's "Capital Punishment" is a poem obviously designed to spark resistance to the death penalty. Even a work of literature that is not so conspicuously action oriented may encourage its readers to change their behavior or thinking.

In our book, we resist endorsing a single definition of *literature*. Rather, we encourage you to review and perhaps rethink what the term means to you. At the same time, to expand the realm of literature, we include several essays in addition to short stories, poems, and plays. We also present numerous critical commentaries as well as various historical documents. Throughout the book, we invite you to make connections among these different kinds of texts. You need not treat them as altogether separate species.

Why Read Literature?

People have studied literature for all sorts of reasons. You may be surprised to learn that in the late 1800s, English departments in American colleges taught Shakespeare's plays mainly by having students trace the origins of particular words he used. His plots, characters, and themes received little attention. Today, by contrast, most Shakespeare classes consider these things important; they are not content to use his plays as a springboard for dictionary research. In fact, literary history can be seen as a history of changing responses to literature. Nevertheless, if you were to ask several people today why they read literature, probably you would get several common answers. The following are some we have heard. As we enumerate them, compare them with what you might say.

One common reason for reading literature has to do with seeming sophisticated. Since the eighteenth century, people have sought to join cultural elites by proving their familiarity with literature. Read Shakespeare's plays, their thinking goes, and then you can impress high society by quoting him. The desire to raise one's status is understandable. Still, this motive is rarely enough to sustain a person's interest in literature. Frankly, we hope you find other reasons for reading it. At the same time, we invite you to analyze how knowledge of literature has served as *cultural capital*: that is, as a sign of a person's worth. In coining the term *cultural capital*, sociologist Pierre Bourdieu suggested there is something wrong when a society makes literature a means of achieving status. Do you agree?

Another common reason for reading literature has to do with institutional requirements. Millions of students read literature simply because they have to take courses in it. Probably Roland Barthes, the French critic, had this situation in mind when he wryly defined *literature* as "what gets taught in schools." Barthes was being provocatively reductive; if pressed, perhaps he would have conceded that people read literature outside school, too. Across the United States, college graduates and others meet regularly in book discussion groups, studying literature together. Even if you are taking this course only because you must, the obligation may turn out to be enjoyable. When required to read literature, students have found value in it. While inevitably they end up preferring some works to others, they learn that literature provides them with pleasures and insights that they had not anticipated. Stay open to the possibility that you will find it much more than a waste of time.

Still another popular reason for reading literature is, in fact, the enjoyment it provides. Quite simply, lots of people find the experience entertaining. They may revel in literature's ability to render human existence concretely. They may delight in its often eloquent and evocative language. They may like finding all the various patterns in a literary text. They may prize the moments when literature makes them think, laugh, or cry.

People have also turned to literature because, as scholar and critic Kenneth Burke has noted, it serves as "equipment for living." Perhaps you have found that a certain story, poem, play, or essay helped you understand your life and conduct it better. Of course, even readers who look to literature for guidance may have different tastes. While some readers prefer literature that reflects their own lives, others like it most when it explores situations they have not lived through or pondered. "When it's the real thing," critic Frank Lentricchia suggests, "literature enlarges us, strips the film of familiarity from the world; creates bonds of sympathy with all kinds, even with evil characters, who we learn are all in the family."

Some people *dislike* literature because they find it too vague and indirect. They resent that it often forces them to figure out symbols and implications when they would rather have ideas presented outright. Perhaps you wish the speaker in James Wright's poem (p. 728) had made clear why his observations prompted him to criticize himself. But in life, truth can be complicated and elusive. In many ways, literature is most realistic when it suggests the same. Besides, many readers—perhaps including you—appreciate literature most when it resists simple decoding, forcing them to adopt new assumptions and learn new methods of analysis. Indeed, throughout this book we suggest that the most interesting and profitable conversations about literature are those in which the issues are not easily resolved.

We hope that any literature you read in this book strikes you as "equipment for living." If a particular selection leaves you cold, try at least to identify and review the standards by which you are judging it. Even if you like a piece, think about the values you are applying to it. Probably these will grow clearer to you in class debates, especially if you have to support your own view of a text.

If any of the selections in this book puzzle you, keep in mind that you need not read in isolation, relying solely on yourself. If you have trouble understanding a literary work, try consulting other readers. In the course you are taking, you will have plenty of chances to exchange insights with your classmates and teacher. All these people are resources for your thinking. Encourage them to see you as a resource, too.

Often, the process of reading literature is collective in another sense. Consciously or not, you may compare the text you are focused on with those you have previously read. By recalling your experience with other texts, you grow more able to identify typical features of the present one, along with ways it is distinctive. Because such comparisons are useful, we seek to encourage them throughout this book. This is why we group texts together and invite you to compare works within each cluster.

Still another good way to ponder a literary work is to write about it. Again, do not feel obliged to churn out a polished, profound analysis of the text right away. If reading literature is best seen as a process, so too is writing about it. To begin your study of a work, you might freewrite in a notebook or journal. Then you might try extended drafts in which you experiment with sustained analysis. Only later might you attempt a whole formal paper on the text, aiming to show others that you have arrived at a solid, credible view of it. In each of these activities, your thinking might be helped by class discussions. Perhaps classmates will even be able to give you direct feedback on your writing, including the freewriting you have just done.

In your course, you will read many of the literary selections we present. Naturally, we hope that you will find them emotionally engaging as well as thought-provoking. Moreover, we hope the course helps you become a more learned and thoughtful reader of whatever literature you read later. But we have yet another goal. With the texts we present, the background information we provide, the questions we raise, and the assignments we suggest, we seek to help you become a more thoughtful and effective writer.

Probably you have already taken courses that required you to write a great deal. On your own, perhaps you have enjoyed writing poems, short stories, plays, essays, or other kinds of texts. Actually, almost everyone does some kind of writing outside of school, whether it's merely a letter or a full-fledged essay. Nevertheless, you may hesitate to call yourself a writer out of a belief that your writing is often flawed. Yet everyone brings strengths to the act of writing, and we hope this course helps you recognize yours. While obviously the course is a chance for you to improve as a writer, believing that you deserve to be called a writer is an important step in your growth.

What Is Argument?

Our writing assignments are designed to help you reflect on the literature you read. Although these assignments are varied, mostly we encourage you to argue about literature. We do so for three reasons. First, the term **argument** refers to a kind of talk as well as a kind of writing; thus, focusing on this term can help you relate your own written work to discussions in class. Second, you will read a work of literature with greater direction and purpose if you are working toward the goal of constructing arguments about it. Finally, when you argue, you learn a lot, because you have to ponder things you may have taken for granted as well as things unfamiliar to you.

Specifically, *arguing* is a process in which you identify a subject of current or possible debate; you take a position on that subject; you analyze why you view the subject the way you do; and you try to persuade others that your view is worth sharing or is at least reasonable. Often the process of arguing is not straightforward. Just when you think you have decided how you feel about a subject, class discussion may lead you to change your position or shift to a completely different topic. Whatever the case, to argue well means to engage in self-examination. Also, it means attending to the world around you: especially to the ways that other people think differently from you.

For many, *argument* is a negative term. Perhaps it makes you think of unpleasant shouting matches you have been in or witnessed — times when people have bitterly disagreed with one another and refused to compromise. Almost everyone has experienced arguments of this sort. Moreover, they are a kind of argument that the media promote. On talk radio, hosts as well as callers are often brutally argumentative, mixing strong opinion with outright insult. Similarly, television's political talk shows regularly become sheer quarrels; on *Crossfire*, *The McLaughlin Group*, and *The Capital Gang* panelists fall again and again into nasty, noisy debate. Spats are even more spectacular on daytime talk shows like Jerry Springer's, which invite friends and family members to clash in public on such high-voltage topics as "You Stole Him from Me and I Want Him Back!" On occasion, the participants turn from words to fists. No wonder many people see argument as fierce competition, even as a form of war.

Although many people view argument as war, we encourage you to argue in a more positive sense. In any meaning of the term, to *argue* is to disagree with others or to set forth a view that you suspect not everyone holds. But argument need not be a competition in which you aim to prove that only you are right. For one thing, at times you might collaborate with someone else in arguing a position. Also, in an argument you can concede that several views on the subject are possible, even as you develop your own position. You are in fact more likely to persuade your audience if you treat fairly opinions other than yours. Furthermore, successful arguers establish common ground with their audience; they identify and honor at least some of the beliefs that their readers or listeners hold.

Keep in mind, too, that participants in an argument ought to learn from one another. If you take seriously other people's responses to your position, you will find yourself reexamining why and how you express that view. As we have already noted, you may even change your mind. Above all, we hope you will see argument as *inquiry*, a process in which you think hard about your beliefs rather than just declare them.

SUMMING UP

• Literature encompasses poetry, fiction, and plays—but may also encompass other genres, such as nonfiction essays. (pp. 3–5) This book does not endorse a single definition of literature, but encourages you to review and perhaps rethink what the term means to you.

• People have studied literature for pragmatic reasons but often come to value it as a source of pleasure and as "equipment for living." (pp. 5–7)

• The *literary canon*—works taught again and again as great art—is nowadays being re-evaluated. (p. 5)

• Understanding literature involves collaboration with other readers and comparison with other texts. (p. 7)

• Thinking about literature is enhanced and clarified by writing about it. (p. 7)

• Making *arguments* about literature is a process. You identify a subject of debate, take a position on the subject, analyze why you view the subject this way, and try to persuade others that your view is worth sharing or at least reasonable. (pp. 8–9)

• The most effective arguments about literature involve inquiry, not rancor and battle. (p. 8)

2

Developing Arguments about Literature

Responding to Four Poems about Work

As we discuss the process of arguing about literature, we mention arguments that might be made about the following set of four poems, each of which features a speaker reflecting on his or her work experience. Also, we stress how useful it can be for you to **compare** these texts. Indeed, we continue to emphasize comparison in subsequent chapters. As you read each poem, take a few moments to reflect on the questions we ask after each one, perhaps jotting down your responses to keep in mind as you read the rest of the chapter.

Three of the poems in this set are by contemporary writers. The first poem, however, is from the eighteenth century. It is a famous one by William Blake (1757–1827), who, though dismissed by many of his contemporaries as eccentric and even mad, is now regarded as a major figure in British Romanticism. Besides being a writer, Blake was a painter and engraver, lavishly illustrating his own editions of his poems. These volumes included his 1789 collection *Songs of Innocence*, where "The Chimney Sweeper" first appeared.

WILLIAM BLAKE
The Chimney Sweeper

When my mother died I was very young,
And my father sold me while yet my tongue
Could scarcely cry " 'weep! 'weep! 'weep! 'weep!"
So your chimneys I sweep, and in soot I sleep.

There's little Tom Dacre, who cried when his head,   5
That curled like a lamb's back, was shaved: so I said
"Hush, Tom! never mind it, for when your head's bare
You know that the soot cannot spoil your white hair."

And so he was quiet, and that very night,
As Tom was a-sleeping, he had such a sight!   10
That thousands of sweepers, Dick, Joe, Ned, and Jack,
Were all of them locked up in coffins of black.

And by came an Angel who had a bright key,
And he opened the coffins and set them all free;
Then down a green plain leaping, laughing, they run,   15
And wash in the river, and shine in the sun.

Then naked and white, all their bags left behind,
They rise upon clouds and sport in the wind;
And the Angel told Tom, if he'd be a good boy,
He'd have God for his father, and never want joy.   20

And so Tom awoke; and we rose in the dark,
And got with our bags and our brushes to work.
Though the morning was cold, Tom was happy and warm;
So if all do their duty they need not fear harm.   [1789]

THINKING ABOUT THE TEXT

1. Blake wrote his poem at a time when many children in London indeed labored in filth as chimney sweepers and were even sold by family members for this service. What are possible counterparts to such child workers today?

2. The speaker of the poem tells us a dream related to him by Tom, another chimney sweeper, which the speaker proceeded to interpret. Is the poem more about Tom, or more about the speaker, or about both of them equally?

3. Tom's dream is a religious vision. To what extent do you think Blake himself endorses it?

4. At the end, the speaker seems resigned to his lot, but what's *your* view of it? How inclined are you to agree with the last line: "So if all do their duty they need not fear harm"?

The next poem is by Stephen Dunn (b. 1939). In addition to being Trustee Fellow in the Arts and Distinguished Professor of Creative Writing at Richard Stockton College of New Jersey, Dunn is a much-published poet. In 2001 he won the Pulitzer Prize for his sixteenth book of verse, *Different Hours*. The following poem is from an earlier collection, *Work and Love* (1981).

STEPHEN DUNN
Hard Work
1956

At the Coke plant, toting empties
in large crates to the assembly line,
I envied my friends away at camp,
but the money was good
and hard work, my father said,   5
was how you became a man.
I saw a man for no special reason
piss into a coke bottle
and put it back onto the line.
After a while I, too, hated   10
the bottles enough to break some
deliberately, and smile
and share with the other workers
a petty act of free will.
When I came home at night my body   15
hurt with that righteous hurt
men have brought home for centuries,
the hurt that demands
food and solicitation, that makes men
separate, lost.   20
I quit before the summer was over,
exercised the prerogatives of my class
by playing ball all August
and spent the money I'd earned
on Barbara Winokur, who was beautiful.   25
And now I think my job
must be phased out, a machine must
do it, though someone for sure
still does the hard work of boredom
and that person can't escape,   30
goes there each morning
and comes home each night
and probably has no opportunity
to say who he is
through destruction, some big   35
mechanical eye watching him
or some time and motion man
or just something hesitant, some father
or husband, in himself.   [1981]

THINKING ABOUT THE TEXT

1. Evidently the speaker in this poem is recollecting a job he held several years ago. What may have provoked him to remember it now?

2. He indicates that, in part, he took the job in obedience to his father's notion that "hard work . . . / was how you became a man." What meanings of *manhood* does this poem touch on? What possible definitions of *hard work*?

3. On the job, a fellow worker and eventually the speaker himself rebelled "through destruction." In what ways, if any, have you witnessed or done the same sort of thing at work?

4. Although at first the speaker refers to his vandalism as "a petty act of free will," later in the poem he seems to mourn the lost "opportunity" for such "destruction." How do you explain this apparent change in attitude?

The next poem is by Dorianne Laux (b. 1952), a native of Maine whose ancestry includes Irish, French, and Algonquin Indian strands. This selection comes from her second collection of poetry, *What We Carry* (1994). Laux's other volumes include *Awake* (1990) and *Smoke* (2000), as well as a book coauthored with Kim Addonizio, *The Poet's Companion: A Guide to the Pleasures of Writing Poetry* (1997). Like the speaker in the poem, Laux has been a sanatorium cook, gas station manager, maid, and donut holer. Presently she is a professor of creative writing at the University of Oregon.

DORIANNE LAUX
What I Wouldn't Do

The only job I didn't like, quit
after the first shift, was selling
subscriptions to *TV Guide* over the phone.
Before that it was fast food, all
the onion rings I could eat, handing   5
sacks of deep fried burritos through
the sliding window, the hungry hands
grabbing back. And at the laundromat,
plucking bright coins from a palm
or pressing them into one, kids   10
screaming from the bathroom and twenty
dryers on high. Cleaning houses was fine,
polishing the knick-knacks of the rich.
I liked holding the hand-blown glass bell
from Czechoslovakia up to the light,   15
the jewelled clapper swinging lazily
from side to side, its foreign,

A-minor ping. I drifted, an itinerant,
from job to job, the sanatorium
where I pureed peas and carrots   20
and stringy beets, scooped them,
like pudding, onto flesh-colored
plastic plates, or the gas station
where I dipped the ten-foot measuring stick
into the hole in the blacktop,   25
pulled it up hand over hand
into the twilight, dripping
its liquid gold, pink-tinged.
I liked the donut shop best, 3 AM,
alone in the kitchen, surrounded   30
by sugar and squat mounds of dough,
the flashing neon sign strung from wire
behind the window, gilding my white uniform
yellow, then blue, then drop-dead red.
It wasn't that I hated calling them, hour   35
after hour, stuck in a booth with a list
of strangers' names, dialing their numbers
with the eraser end of a pencil and them
saying hello. It was that moment
of expectation, before I answered back,   40
the sound of their held breath,
their disappointment when they realized
I wasn't who they thought I was,
the familiar voice, or the voice they loved
and had been waiting all day to hear.   [1994]   45

THINKING ABOUT THE TEXT

1. Make a list of the jobs you've had, and compare your list with the speaker's. To what extent have your work experiences been similar?

2. The speaker seems to move chronologically through her work history. What, if anything, do some of her jobs have in common? What does the fact that she "liked the donut shop best" say about her?

3. Although the speaker begins by referring to "The only job I didn't like," she postpones explaining it until she abruptly returns to it and spends the poem's last eleven lines on it. What is the effect of the delay? Again, what does her dislike of this particular job say about her?

4. What would you say to someone who argued that the speaker deserves no sympathy at the end because telemarketers are a nuisance?

The next poem is by Maura Stanton (b. 1946), a professor of creative writing at Indiana University, Bloomington, who has published collections of short stories as well as verse. Her volumes of poetry include *Snow on Snow* (1975), *Tales of the Supernatural* (1988), *Life Among the Trolls* (1998), and *Glacier Wine* (2001). The following selection first appeared in *Atlantic Monthly* and then became part of Stanton's second book of poems, *Cries of Swimmers* (1984).

MAURA STANTON
Shoplifters

I'd smoke in the freezer
among the hooked beefsides,
wondering about the shoplifters
who wept when the manager's
nephew tugged them to his office.   5
He made me search the women.
I found twenty cans of tuna fish
under the skirt of a mother whose son
drowned in a flash flood out west.
Now he haunted her,   10
begging for mouthfuls of fish.
Candles fell from a nun's sleeves.
She meant to light the route
for tobogganists on the convent hill.
Two old sisters emptied beans   15
from their big apron pockets,
claiming they cured rheumatism.
Soon I recognized snow
drifting across faces at the door,
watching in the round mirrors   20
the way hands snatched out
unhesitatingly at onions.
In the mirrors everyone stole,
buttoning coats again, looking
once over their shoulders   25
while eggs bulged in a mitten
or salt sifted from their hems.
Did they think me an angel
when I glided in my white uniform
down the soap aisle, preventing   30
some clutch of fingers?
An old man I caught last year
stuffing baloney down his trousers
lived alone in a dim bedroom.
The manager said cupcake papers   35
blew across his floor—

hundreds, yellow, white & pink.
Now he peers through the window,
watching me bag groceries
for hours until my hands sweat.   [1984]   40

THINKING ABOUT THE TEXT

1. This poem seems to be about not only shoplifters but also the speaker's attitude toward them. Does her attitude change, or does it seem consistent throughout the poem? Support your answer with specific details.
2. How much do *you* sympathize with the shoplifters depicted here? Again, note details that affect your attitude toward them.
3. What, if anything, do the shoplifters have in common?
4. In what ways is this poem about acts of watching? What moral problems do these acts raise?
5. The poem ends with the speaker's hands sweating. Why do you suppose Stanton chose to end with this particular image?

A WRITING EXERCISE

Once you have read the four poems as a group, write brief responses to at least two. You might jot down things you especially notice about them, feelings they evoke in you, and questions you have about them. You might also note your own work experiences that they lead you to recall. With each poem, write for ten minutes without stopping. Again, this useful exercise is usually called freewriting.

THE ELEMENTS OF ARGUMENT

We turn now to specific elements of argument. An argument involves six basic elements. When you argue, you attempt to **persuade** an **audience** to accept your **claims** regarding an **issue** by presenting **evidence** and relying on **warrants**. The boldfaced words are key to this book; we mention them often. Here we explain what we mean by each, beginning with *issue* and then moving to *claims*, *persuasion*, *audience*, *evidence*, and *warrants*. Throughout our discussion, we refer to the poems by Blake, Dunn, Laux, and Stanton.

Issues

An **issue** is something about which people have disagreed or might disagree. Even as you read a text, you can try to guess what features of it will lead to disagreements in class. You may sense that your own reaction to certain aspects of the text is heavily influenced by your background and values, which other students may not share. Some parts of the text may leave you with conflicting ideas or mixed feelings, as if half of you disagrees with the other half. At moments like these, you come to realize what topics are issues for you, and next you can urge the rest of your class to see these topics as issues, too.

An issue is best defined as a question with no obvious, immediate answer. Thus, you can start identifying issues by noting questions that occur to you as you read. Perhaps this question-posing approach to texts is new for you. Often readers demand that a text be clear, and they get annoyed if it leaves them puzzled. Of course, certain writing ought to be immediately clear in meaning; think of operating instructions on a plane's emergency doors. But the value of a literary work often lies in the work's complexities, which can lead readers to reexamine their own ways of perceiving the world. Also, your discussions and papers about literature are likely to be most useful when they go beyond the obvious to deal with more challenging matters. When your class begins talking about a work, you may feel obliged to stay quiet if you have no firm statements to make. But you can contribute a lot by bringing up questions that occurred to you as you read. Especially worth raising are questions that continue to haunt you.

In the case of William Blake's "The Chimney Sweeper," one possible issue concerns its ending. From Tom's dream of the chimney sweepers' release, the speaker concludes that "if all do their duty they need not fear harm." Should readers accept this interpretation, or is there a better way of understanding both the dream and the sweepers' grueling daily life? A possible issue with Stephen Dunn's "Hard Work" concerns its numerous references to manhood. To what extent are the ideas and feelings expressed in the poem indeed gender-specific? An issue related to Dorianne Laux's poem has to do with its form. Though the speaker begins by referring to "The only job I didn't like," she waits until the end of the poem to elaborate on the job. What conceivably is the effect of postponing such details? An issue concerning Maura Stanton's poem involves the speaker's attitude toward the shoplifters. To what extent does she sympathize with them?

You may feel unable to answer questions like these. But again, you achieve much when you simply formulate questions and bring them up in class. As other students help you ponder them, you will grow better able to explore issues through writing as well as through conversation.

You are more likely to come up with questions about a text if you do not assume that the text had to be written exactly the way it was. For every move the writer made, alternatives existed. Blake might have presented his own interpretation of the dream more directly instead of having his poem's speaker be another chimney sweeper. Dunn might have consistently referred to all humanity instead of referring so much to men. Laux might have immediately provided details of the unpleasant job. Stanton might have had her poem's speaker express clearer judgments about the shoplifters. When you bear in mind writers' options, you grow more inclined to explore why they made the choices they did and what the effects of those choices may be.

You will recognize writers' options more easily if you compare their texts with others. As we have said, we invite comparison throughout this book. For instance, Blake's mention of an angel is more apt to strike you as a calculated decision if you note Stanton's use of this figure. In Blake's poem, Tom dreams of an angel who frees him and other chimney sweepers. At least within Tom's dream, then, the angel is real. In Stanton's poem, the speaker wonders if would-be shoplifters saw her as an angel when she stopped them from stealing. This text, then, depicts at most a *metaphorical* angel. Of course, in both cases we can ultimately see the angel image as a projection of human hopes. Nevertheless, Blake's poem first confronts us with an angel's literal presence, whereas Stanton's poem does not.

Next we identify ten kinds of issues that arise in literature courses. Our list will help you detect the issues that come up in your class and discover others to bring up in discussions or in your writing. The list does not include every kind of issue; you may think of others. Moreover, you may find that an issue can fit into more than one of the categories we name. But when you do have an issue that seems hard to classify, try nevertheless to assign it to a single category, if only for the time being. You will then have some initial guidance for your reading, class discussions, and writing. If you later feel that the issue belongs to another category, you can shift your focus.

1. Issues of fact.   Rarely does a work of literature provide complete information about its characters and events. Rather, literature is usually marked by what literary theorist Wolfgang Iser calls "gaps," moments when certain facts are omitted or obscured. At such times, readers may give various answers to the question, What is happening in this text? For instance, Dunn's poem "Hard Work" does not specify the speaker's present circumstances. Although we learn some of the thoughts he has "now," we do not know what in his current life prompted him to recall a job he had back in 1956. Of course, readers tackle questions of fact only if they suspect that the answers will affect their overall view of a text. Imagine a reader who believes that Dunn's speaker recalls his 1956 job because he also hates his present one. Imagine a second reader who supposes the speaker's recollection is a result of current insecurities about his masculinity. How might these two readers see the whole poem differently because of their different assumptions?

2. Issues of theme.   You may be familiar with the term **theme** from other literature courses. By *theme* critics usually mean the main claim that an author seems to be making with his or her text. Sometimes a theme is defined in terms of a single word — for example, *work* or *love*. But such words are really mere topics. Identifying the topics addressed by a text can be a useful way of starting to analyze that text, and later in Part One we list several topics that currently preoccupy literary studies. A text's theme, however, is best seen as an assertion that you need at least one whole sentence to express.

With many texts, an issue of theme arises because readers can easily disagree over what the text's main idea is. In literature classes, such disagreements often occur, in part because literary works tend to express their themes indirectly. Readers of Stanton's poem may give several different answers to the question, What is Stanton ultimately saying? Perhaps some readers will take her to imply that our dislike of crime often conflicts with our sense of the criminal's physical or emotional neediness. Other readers may conclude that her poem is much more than a list of petty crimes and instead is a call for recognizing how isolated many human beings are.

If you try to express a text's theme, avoid making it a statement so general that it could apply to an enormous number of works. Arguing that Stanton's theme is "Refrain from quickly judging others" hardly gets at the details of her poem. On the other hand, do not let the text's details restrict you so much that you wind up making the theme seem relevant only to a tiny group. If you argue that Stanton's theme is "Store employees shouldn't let managers make them spy on customers," then the many readers who are *not* store employees will wonder why they should care. In short, try to express themes as midlevel generalizations. With Stanton's poem, one possibility is "When people do wrong out of desperation, we may sympathize with them, but our compassion may leave us feeling conflicted rather than purely angelic." A statement like this seems both attentive to Stanton's specific text and applicable to a large portion of humanity. Of course, you are free to challenge this version of Stanton's theme by proposing an alternative. Moreover, even if you do accept this statement as her theme, you are then free to decide whether it is a sound observation. Identifying a theme is one thing; evaluating it is another.

Sometimes an author will appear to state the theme explicitly in his or her text. Such moments are worth studying as you try to determine what the theme is. For instance, you may believe that Blake's theme is his concluding line: "So if all do their duty they need not fear harm." Yet a poem's author may not share the views of its speaker; perhaps Blake disagrees with the chimney sweeper's declaration. Recognize, too, that a theme ties together various parts of a text. Focusing on a single passage, even if it seems thematic, may lead you to ignore other passages that a statement of theme should encompass. With Blake's poem, someone may argue that the last line does *not* state the theme, for it neglects the hard, dirty labor that these children must perform.

Often you will sense a work's theme but still have to decide whether to state it as an **observation** or as a **recommendation**. You would be doing the first if, for example, you expressed Stanton's theme as we did above: "When people do wrong out of desperation, we may sympathize with them, but our compassion may leave us feeling conflicted rather than purely angelic." You would be doing the second if you said Stanton's theme is "One should consider criminals' circumstances rather than automatically condemn them." Indeed, when they depict a theme as a recommendation, people often use a word like *should*. Neither way of expressing a theme is necessarily better than the other. But notice that each way conjures up a particular image of the author. Reporting Stanton's theme as an observation suggests that she is writing as a psychologist, a philosopher, or some other analyst of human nature. Reporting her theme as a recommendation suggests that she is writing as a teacher, preacher, manager, or coach: someone who is telling her readers what to do. Your decision about how to phrase a theme will depend in part on which of these two images of the author you think appropriate.

You risk obscuring the intellectual, emotional, and stylistic richness of a text if you insist on reducing it to a single message. Try stating the text's theme as a problem for which there is no easy solution. This way you will suggest that the text is, in fact, complex. For instance, if you incorporate into Stanton's theme the idea that "our compassion may leave us feeling conflicted," you position yourself to address various elements of her poem.

Also weigh the possibility that a text is conveying more than one theme. If you plan to associate the text with any theme at all, you might refer to *a* theme of the text rather than *the* theme of the text. To be sure, your use of the term *theme* would still have implications. Above all, you would still be suggesting that you have identified one of the text's major points. Subsequently, you might have to defend this claim, showing how the point you have identified is indeed central to the text.

Issues of theme have loomed large in literary studies. We hope that you will find them useful to pursue. But because references to theme are so common in literary studies, students sometimes forget that there are other kinds of issues. As you move through this list, you may find some that interest you more.

3. *Issues of definition.* In arguments about literature, issues of **definition** arise most often when readers try to decide what an author means by a particular word. Look at the ending of Dunn's poem, where the speaker suggests that his present-day counterpart holds back from rebelling at work because of "some father / or husband, in himself." What, conceivably, does Dunn mean here by *father* and *husband*? Evidently we are to consider more than these figures' official family roles, associating such men with particular qualities. But which? Perhaps Dunn wants us to see fathers and husbands as horribly domineering patriarchs, who inhibit us from engaging in worthwhile revolt. Perhaps Dunn respects these figures and wants us to see them as enforcing a desirable prudence. Or perhaps Dunn is ambivalent toward them, believing they blend tyranny with wisdom.

An issue of definition looms especially when a word or phrase appears to shift meaning as the text proceeds. A good example is the very title of Dunn's poem, "Hard Work." When this term first appears in the poem itself, it seems to refer to arduous physical labor; at least, this is what the speaker's father seems to have had in mind when declaring that "hard work . . . / was how you became a man." Later in the poem, though, comes a reference to "the hard work of boredom," which associates the term *hard work* with a tedium that seems mostly psychological. We can even identify the main subject of the poem as sons' struggles to fit their fathers' standards of manhood, in which case *hard work* takes on yet another sense.

4. *Issues of symbolism.* In literary studies, an issue of **symbolism** is often a question about the meaning and purpose of a particular image. Blake's poem is filled with evocative images, including soot, a lamb, white hair, black coffins, an angel, a green plain, a river, the sun, nakedness, clouds, and the dark. What do you usually associate with each? What new associations, if any, does the poem prompt you to make? An issue of symbolism is also involved if you find yourself wondering whether some element of a text is symbolic in the first place. At the

start of Dunn's poem, the speaker reports that his job was "toting empties." In what ways might this mention of emptiness relate to other things in the text?

5. *Issues of pattern.*   With issues of **pattern**, you observe how a text is organized. More precisely, you try to determine how certain parts of the text are related to other parts of it. But keep in mind the meaning and purpose of any pattern you find, especially since readers may disagree about the pattern's significance. Also ponder the implications of any moment when a text *breaks* with a pattern it has been following. Disruptions of a pattern may be as important as the pattern itself.

Many poems exhibit patterns in their rhymes and stanza lengths. Blake's poem is six stanzas, with four lines each. In each of the first four stanzas, the first two lines rhyme, and the next two lines rhyme in a different way. The last two stanzas slightly break with this pattern. They feature what literary critics term **off-rhymes**. In stanza 5, "wind" does not exactly rhyme with "behind." In stanza 6, "work" does not exactly rhyme with "dark," and the same goes for "harm" and "warm." Worth considering, then, is the relation between the form and content of these last stanzas. What about their ideas might have led Blake to make their rhymes a bit awkward?

Another common pattern in literature is **repetition**. Perhaps you have noticed already that the speaker of Laux's poem "What I Didn't Like" refers often to acts performed with hands as she recites her work history. She remembers "handing / sacks of deep fried burritos through / the sliding window, the hungry hands / grabbing back." She recalls "plucking bright coins from a palm / or pressing them into one." She "liked holding the hand-blown glass bell / from Czechoslovakia up to the light." At the sanatorium, she "scooped"; at the gas station, she "dipped the ten-foot measuring stick / into the hole in the blacktop, / pulled it up hand over hand." What do you think Laux aims to convey with this chain of references? Even when repetition is easy to detect, readers may have different ideas about its function. The issue then becomes not so much whether the author is repeating words but how this repetition contributes to the work as a whole.

Stanton's poem also refers many times to acts of touching. Such acts are committed by the shoplifters, including those whose "hands snatched out / unhesitatingly at onions." In addition, the manager's nephew "tugged" the would-be thieves and made the speaker "search" them. Furthermore, much to her distress, she found herself "preventing / some clutch of fingers." Continuing this pattern right to the end, the poem concludes with the speaker's acknowledgment that "my hands sweat." Yet while Stanton and Laux resort to a rather similar pattern, perhaps it functions differently in their respective poems. What do you think?

Again, just as important to consider is any divergence from a pattern. Toward the end of her poem, for example, Laux moves away from an emphasis on touching. The job that Laux's speaker enjoyed most left her "alone in the kitchen"—that is, without human contact. But next we learn that the job she hated most did not involve touching at all. Rather, she telephoned people, "dialing their numbers / with the eraser end of a pencil." If any holding occurred on the job, it was done by the people she called, who disturbed her when they responded with "held breath." What do you conclude from the poem's climactic shift in *this* direction?

A text's apparent oppositions are also patterns to be debated. An example in Laux's poem is the opposition that the speaker establishes when she notes her most favorite and least favorite jobs. In one respect, these jobs resemble each other: both deemphasize the human touch. How, then, do you explain the speaker's quite different attitudes toward them? Maybe the key difference is that the phone job cruelly frustrated people who longed for human warmth.

6. *Issues of evaluation.*   Consciously or unconsciously, **evaluation** always plays a central role in reading. When you read a work of literature, you evaluate its ideas and the actions of its characters. You judge, too, the views you assume the author is promoting. Moreover, you gauge the artistic quality of the text.

Specifically, you engage in three kinds of evaluation as you read. One kind is *philosophical*: you decide whether a particular idea or action is wise. Another kind is *ethical*: you decide whether an idea or action is morally good. The third kind is *aesthetic*: you decide whether parts of the text, or the work as a whole, succeed as art. Another reader may disagree with your criteria for wisdom, morality, and art; people's standards often differ. It is not surprising, then, that in the study of literature issues of evaluation come up frequently.

As we suggested earlier, philosophical differences may arise when Blake's speaker claims, "So if all do their duty they need not fear harm." Some readers may like his attitude, others may accuse him of being too passive, and others may disagree with his view but feel that a child can perceive only so much. Different ethical judgments may arise as readers contemplate the society evoked by the poem. While few readers approve of all child labor, some may condone certain uses of it. And even those readers who would ban it may disagree about what kind of economy best prevents it. Some may look to capitalism for salvation, while others may condemn capitalism as the most exploitative of all economic systems. Finally, different aesthetic judgments are possible as readers decide the artistic value of Blake's poem. Some readers may simply be stirred by the poignancy of the chimney sweepers' life. Others may enjoy the poem's interplay of images. Still others may find the poem interesting chiefly because its speaker is a child, so that we must guess what the poem's adult author really believes. Meanwhile, another group of readers may dislike the poem for the very same reasons.

Sometimes you may have trouble distinguishing the three types of judgments from each other. Philosophical evaluation, ethical evaluation, and aesthetic evaluation can overlap. Probably all three operate in the mind of a reader who disagrees with the chimney sweeper's concluding view, believes that Blake shares that view, and therefore dislikes the whole poem. Keep in mind, however, that you can admire many aspects of a literary work even if you disagree with ideas you see the author promoting. Again, someone may relish the imagery of "The Chimney Sweeper" regardless of its author's thinking.

If you disputed the artistic value of Blake's poem, you would be challenging countless admirers of it. Increasingly, though, the status of Blake's poem and other literary classics is being questioned. Many scholars argue that literary studies have focused too much on white male authors. They refuse to assume that Blake's works are great and universally relevant; they criticize the long neglect of women and minority authors. Yet other people continue to prize more well-known writers such as Blake. The result is ongoing debate about whose works should be taught in the classroom.

7. *Issues of historical and cultural context.*   Because works of literature are written by people living in particular times and places, issues of **historical and cultural context** arise. Eventually these works may engage a wide variety of readers, including members of much-later generations and inhabitants of distant lands. Yet these works often continue to reflect the circumstances of their creation. You can tell just by the title of Blake's poem "The Chimney Sweeper" that he wrote at a time when a certain form of child labor was more common in England than it now is. With this fact in mind, you might address the question, To what extent does the situation described in this poem apply to more than just chimney sweepers? Although the poems of Dunn, Laux, and Stanton seem much closer to the present, you can examine from a historical perspective the specific aspects of contemporary life that each of these texts mentions. For example, Dunn's poem explicitly notes that a certain kind of assembly-line job in 1956 no longer exists nowadays. Therefore, you might address the question, What contemporary forms of "hard work" does Dunn conceivably have in mind as he looks back to the 1950s? Meanwhile, phone jobs like the one mentioned in Laux's poem have proliferated, especially now that computers enable salespeople to ring potential customers easily. Therefore, an issue to address is, To what extent does Laux's poem suggest that this kind of job is the wave of the future?

We provide some background for each literary work we present, thereby helping you begin to situate it historically and culturally. In Chapter 8, "Writing a Research Paper," we explain how to keep putting literature in context, especially by doing research in the library and on the World Wide Web. For now, we want to emphasize that contextualizing a work involves more than just piling up facts about its origin. In the study of literature, often issues of historical and cultural context are issues of *relevance*. The questions become, *Which* facts about a work's creation are important for readers to know? and *How* would awareness of these facts help readers better understand the work? For instance, while readers can inform themselves about a particular author's life, they may disagree about the extent to which a given text by that author is autobiographical.

Perhaps you like to connect a literary work with its author's own life. Since all three of the contemporary poems we have been discussing use the first person ("I"), you may feel that they strongly invite you to make such a link. Yet you are almost always engaging in a debatable move when you assert that a work is thoroughly autobiographical. Among other things, you risk overlooking aspects of the text that depart from the author's own experiences, impressions, and beliefs. Like the three contemporary poems, certain texts do seem windows into the author's life. We are not urging you to refrain from ever making this connection. Rather, we are pointing out that whatever links you draw may be the subject of debate.

It is also important to note that the term *history* can be defined in various ways. When you refer to a work's historical context, you need to clarify what you have in mind. After all, you may be examining one or more of the following: (1) the life of the work's author; (2) the time period in which it was written; (3) any time period mentioned within the text; (4) its subsequent reception, including responses to it by later generations; (5) the forms in which the work has been published, which may involve changes in its spelling, punctuation, wording, and overall appearance.

8. *Issues of genre.* So far we have been identifying categories of issues. Issues of **genre** are *about* categorization, for they involve efforts to determine what *kind* of text a particular work is. If you were asked to identify the genres of the works by Blake, Dunn, Laux, and Stanton, you might logically call each a poem. But you do not have to stop there. You can try to classify each poem more precisely, aiming for a term that better sums up its specific content and form. Issues of genre often arise with such further classification. And as you come up with more exact labels for the poems, other readers may label them differently. Because Blake's speaker is obviously trying to soothe the distress that he and his friend Tom feel as chimney sweepers, you may see the poem as an act of self-consolation. Meanwhile, a number of readers may be more inclined to see the poem as a sermon, with Blake using the speaker to exemplify and advance his own religious views. Still others may see the poem mainly as social criticism, believing that Blake scorns a world in which child laborers accept their lot. You may find that two or more labels for the poem are appropriate, in which case you must decide whether they are *equally* so. Much of the time, issues of genre are issues of priority. Readers debate not whether a certain label for a work is possible but whether that label is the best.

9. *Issues of social policy.* Many works of literature have been attempts at social reform, exposing defects of their cultures and encouraging specific cures. A famous example is Upton Sinclair's 1906 novel *The Jungle;* by vividly depicting horrible working conditions in Chicago's stockyards, it led the meat processing industry to adopt more humane practices. Even when a work of literature is not blatantly political or seems rooted in the distant past, it may make you conscious of your own society's problems and possible solutions to them. Yet you and your classmates may propose different solutions and even disagree about what is a problem in the first place. The result is what we call issues of **social policy**.

Sometimes your position on a current issue of social policy will affect how you read a certain work. If you have been interrupted by telephone pitches at dinnertime and have welcomed various states' efforts to limit these, you may empathize immediately with the people called in Laux's poem. Similarly, your view on whether religion should play a central role in contemporary American society may affect your response to Blake's text. Even if current issues of social policy do not influence your original reading of a work, you can still use the work to raise such issues in your writing or in class discussion. Imagine discussing

Stanton's poem "Shoplifters" at a police convention. What policies might the poem be used to promote there?

10. Issues of cause and effect.   Issues of **causality** are common in literary studies. Often they arise as readers present different explanations for a certain character's behavior. Remember that even the speaker in a poem can be thought of as a character with motives worth analyzing. You can pursue questions like these: Why does Blake's chimney sweeper draw the conclusion he does? Why does Dunn's speaker recall a job he held back in 1956? Why was Laux's speaker especially disturbed by her phone job? Why do the hands of Stanton's speaker "sweat"?

These questions can be rephrased to center on the author. For example, you can ask why Blake has his speaker end by affirming "duty." Actually, if you look back at all the questions we have brought up in discussing the various types of issues, you may see that most can be phrased as questions about the author's purposes. But keep in mind your options. You may not find it useful to focus on authorial intention in a given case. Often you will be better off sticking with one of the other types of issues. Or you may prefer to turn a question about authorial intention into a question about authorial effect. For instance, how should readers react when Blake has his speaker defer to "duty"? You can address questions like this without sounding as if you know exactly what the author intended.

Claims

You may not be used to calling things you say or write *claims*. But even when you utter a simple observation about the weather — for instance, "It's beginning to rain" — you are making a claim. Basically, a **claim** is a statement that is spoken or written in the hope that it will be considered true. With this definition in mind, you may start noticing claims everywhere. Most of us make lots of them every day. Furthermore, most of our claims are accepted as true by the people to whom we make them. Imagine how difficult life would be if the opposite were the case; human beings would be perpetually anxious if they distrusted almost everything they were told.

At times, though, claims do conflict with other claims. In a literature course, disagreements inevitably arise. Again, try not to let disagreements scare you. You can learn a lot from encountering views other than yours and from having to support your own. Moreover, exciting talk can occur as your class negotiates differences of opinion.

Recall that we defined an *issue* as a question with various debatable answers. *Claims*, as we will be using the term, are the debatable answers. For examples of claims in literary studies, look back at our explanations of various kinds of issues. Along the way, we mentioned a host of claims: that the conclusion reached by Blake's speaker is misguided but understandable; that Dunn's speaker feels insecure about his masculinity; that Laux's speaker disliked her phone job because it meanly disappointed people seeking contact; and that Stanton's theme is that our compassion may leave us feeling torn. These claims are debatable because in each case at least one other position is possible.

Not every claim is a firm, sweeping generalization. In some instances, you may want to *qualify* a claim of yours, which involves expressing the claim in words that make it less than absolute. The terms available for qualifying a claim are numerous. You might use words such as *perhaps, maybe, seems, appears, probably,* and *most likely* to indicate that you are not reporting a definite fact. Similarly, words such as *some, many, most,* and *several* allow you to acknowledge that your claim is limited in scope, applicable to just a portion of whatever you are discussing.

In literature classes, two types of claims are especially common. To criticize Laux's choice of images is to engage in **evaluation**. To identify the main ideas of her poem is to engage in **interpretation**. Conventionally, interpretation is the kind of analysis that depends on hypotheses rather than simple observation of plain fact. Throughout this book, we refer to the practice of interpreting a work or certain aspects of it. Admittedly, sometimes you may have trouble distinguishing interpretation from evaluation. When you evaluate some feature of a work or make an overall judgment of that work, probably you are operating with a certain interpretation as well, even if you do not make that interpretation explicit. Similarly, when you interpret part of a work or the text as a whole, probably you have already decided whether the text is worth figuring out. Nevertheless, the two types of claims differ in their emphases. When you attempt to interpret a work, you are mostly analyzing it; when you attempt to evaluate the work, you are mostly judging it.

In class discussions, other students may resist a claim you make about a literary work. Naturally, you may choose to defend your view at length. But remain open to the possibility of changing your mind, either by modifying your claim somehow or by shifting completely to another one. Also, entertain the possibility that a view different from yours is just as reasonable, even if you do not share it.

In much of your writing for your course, you will be identifying an issue and making one main claim about it, which can be called your **thesis**. Then, as you attempt to support your main claim, you will make a number of smaller claims. In drafts of your paper, welcome opportunities to test the claims you make in it. Review your claims with classmates to help you determine how persuasive your thinking is. You will be left with a stronger sense of what you must do to make your paper credible.

Persuasion

As we have noted, argument is often associated with arrogant insistence. Many assume that if two people are arguing, they are each demanding to be seen as correct. At its best, however, argument involves careful efforts to persuade. When you make such an effort, you indicate that you believe your claims, even if you remain open to revising them. You indicate as well that you would like others to agree with you. Yet to attempt **persuasion** is to concede that you must support your claims if others are to value them.

The art of persuasion has been studied for centuries under the name of **rhetoric**. Today, often the term *rhetoric* is used negatively: politicians accuse one another of indulging in "mere rhetoric," as if the term meant deceptive exaggeration. But human beings habitually resort to persuasion; hence, rhetoric deserves more esteem. Besides, only in modern times has rhetoric not been regarded as a central part of education. In ancient Greece and Rome as well as in Renaissance Europe, rhetoric was an important academic subject. It was viewed, too, as a body of thought that people could actually put to use, especially in the realm of public affairs. Much of the advice we give you about writing looks back to this history. Over and over, we convey to you principles drawn from the rhetorical tradition.

As you have probably discovered on many occasions, it can be hard for you to sway people who hold views different from yours. Not always will you be able to change their minds. Yet you may still convince them that your claims are at least reasonable. Moreover, the process of trying to persuade others will force you to clarify your ideas, to review why you hold them, and to analyze the people you aim to affect.

Audience

When you hear the word **audience**, perhaps you think first of people attending plays, concerts, movies, or lectures. Yet *audience* also describes readers, including the people who read your writing. Not everything you write is for other people's eyes; in this course, you may produce notes, journal entries, and even full-length drafts that only you will see. From time to time in the course, however, you will do public writing. On these occasions, you will be trying to persuade your audience to accept whatever claims you make.

These occasions will require you to consider more than just your subject matter. If you are truly to persuade your readers, you must take them into account. Unfortunately, you will not be able to find out everything about your audience beforehand. Moreover, you will have to study the ways in which your readers differ from one another. Usually, though, you will be able to identify some of their common values, experiences, and assumptions. Having this knowledge will strengthen your ability to make a case they appreciate.

In analyzing a work of literature, you may try to identify its *implied reader:* that is, the type of person that the work seems to address. Remember, too, that people may have read the work in manuscript or when it was first published. Finally, the work may have had innumerable readers since. Often we ask you to write about a text's effect on you and to compare your reaction with your classmates'.

Evidence

Evidence is the support that you give your claims so that others will accept them. What sort of evidence you must provide depends on what your audience requires to be persuaded. When you make claims during class discussions, your classmates and instructor might ask you follow-up questions, thereby suggesting what you must do to convince them. As a writer, you might often find yourself having to guess your readers' standards of evidence. Naturally, your guesses will be influenced by any prior experiences you have had with your audience. Moreover, you may have opportunities to review drafts with some of its members.

When you make an argument about literature, the evidence most valued by your audience is likely to be details of the work itself. Direct quotations from the text are an especially powerful means of indicating that your claims are well grounded. But when you quote, you need to avoid seeming willfully selective. If you merely quote Dunn's reference to "hard work" of lifting crates without acknowledging his later phrase "the hard work of boredom," you may come across as distorting his poem. In general, quoting from various parts of a text will help you give your readers the impression that you are being accurate.

If you make claims about the historical or cultural context of a work, your evidence may include facts about its original circumstances. You may be drawn to the author's own experiences and statements, believing these shed light on the text. But again, use such materials cautiously, for not always will they seem strong evidence for your claims. Even if the author of a text explicitly declared what he or she was up to in writing it, people are not obliged to accept that declaration as a guide to the finished work. Some people may feel that the author's statement of intention was deliberately misleading, while others may claim that the author failed to understand his or her own achievement.

Another kind of evidence for your arguments about literature is your **ethos**. This is a traditional term in rhetoric; it refers to the image of you that your audience gets as you attempt to persuade. Actually, there are two kinds of ethos. One is the image of you that your audience holds even before you present your analysis. Often your audience will not know much about you beforehand. In general, this kind of ethos plays a role when the speaker or writer has a prior reputation. When Secretary of State Colin Powell gives a speech, he can expect much of his audience to start off trusting him, since millions of Americans admire him already as a retired army general.

Even if you are not well known, the second kind of ethos may greatly influence how people respond to your argument. This is the image of you that your audience develops in hearing or reading your actual words. To secure your audience's trust, you ought to give the impression that you are calmly and methodically laying out your claims as well as your reasons for them. Making concessions to views different from yours is also a good strategy, indicating that you aim to be fair. On the other hand, if your presentation is disorganized or your tone self-righteous, you may put your audience on guard. You may come across as someone not committed to serious inquiry.

Warrants

Of all the elements of argument, **warrants** may be the least familiar to you. You have heard of search warrants and arrest warrants, documents that indicate the police are justified in searching a place or jailing a person. More generally, warrants are the beliefs that lead people to call certain things evidence for their claims. Imagine that you have just made a claim to your classmates and are now trying to support it. Imagine further that your listeners are reluctant to call your supporting information *evidence*; they want you to explain why you do so. In effect, your audience is asking you to identify your warrants: that is, the assumptions that make you think the information you have given reinforces your case. Throughout this book, we use the terms *warrants* and *assumptions* interchangeably.

Let's say you claim that when Stanton's speaker refers twice to the mirrors that revealed shoplifting, she is concerned as well about the image of *herself* that her policing of them "reflects," for she can be accused of insensitivity to their circumstances. Asked to provide evidence for your claim, you might point out the following things: (1) that her repetition of the mirror reference suggests troubled thoughts lurk within her; (2) that mirrors can be associated with *self*-reflection; (3) that at other moments in the poem, the speaker notes the shoplifters' desperate conditions; and (4) that the poem ends with an image of her hands sweating, which implies feelings of guilt. But then you may be asked for your warrants, the assumptions that lead you to see your evidence as support for your claim. Some of your assumptions might be about literature itself: for instance, that repetition in a poem is significant; that the final image of a poem is also important; and that characters are most interesting when they express emotions indirectly. Some of your assumptions might be about human nature: for example, that people often sweat when they feel ashamed. Some of your assumptions might be about specific historical periods and cultures: for instance, that contemporary American society often sees mirrors as devices for revealing the self. Often literature classes are most enlightening when students discuss with one another their assumptions about literature, about human nature, and about particular times and places. If your classmates differ in their assumptions, that may be because they differ in the ways they grew up, the experiences they have had, the reading they have done, and the authorities that have influenced them.

Once you state your warrants for a claim you are making, your audience may go further, asking you to identify assumptions supporting the warrants themselves. But more frequently you will have to decide how much you should mention your warrants in the first place. In class discussion, usually your classmates' and instructor's responses to your claims will indicate how much you have to spell out your assumptions. When you write, you have to rely more on your own judgment of what your audience requires. If you suspect that your readers will find your evidence unusual, you should identify your warrants at length. If, however, your readers are bound to accept your evidence, then a presentation of warrants may simply distract them. Again, reviewing drafts of your paper with potential readers will help you determine what to do.

LITERATURE AS ARGUMENT

Much of this book concerns arguing *about* literature. But sometimes literary works can be said to present arguments themselves. In some of the works we have included, certain characters make claims, often in debate with one another, while other works give the impression that the author is arguing for a certain position. Admittedly, not all works of literature are best seen as containing or making arguments, but occasionally, you will find that associating a literary text with argument opens up productive lines of inquiry. Moreover, as you argue about literature, arguments *within* literature can help you see how you might persuade others.

For an example of such arguments, let us turn to the following poem. Written around 1652, it is by John Milton (1608–1674), a poet who played a leading role in England's Puritan revolution. Seeking to make dominant their own version of Christianity, the Puritans executed King Charles I and installed their leader, Oliver Cromwell, as head of state. Milton wrote "When I consider how my light is spent" while working as an official in Cromwell's government. This is an autobiographical poem and refers to Milton's growing blindness, which threatened to prevent him from serving both his political leader and his religious one, God.

JOHN MILTON

When I consider how my light is spent

When I consider how my light is spent,
    Ere half my days in this dark world and wide,
    And that one talent which is death to hide
Lodged with me useless, though my soul more bent
To serve therewith my Maker, and present   5
    My true account, lest He returning chide;
    "Doth God exact day-labor, light denied?"
I fondly ask. But Patience, to prevent
That murmur, soon replies, "God doth not need
    Either man's work or His own gifts. Who best   10
    Bear His mild yoke, they serve Him best. His state
Is kingly: thousands at His bidding speed,
    And post o'er land and ocean without rest;
    They also serve who only stand and wait."   [c. 1652]

The speaker does not actually spell out his warrants. Consider, however, his reference to Christ's parable of the talents (Luke 19:12–27). In the ancient Middle East, a *talent* was a unit of money. In the parable, a servant is scolded by his master for hoarding the one talent that his master had given him. By telling this story, Christ implies that people should make use of the gifts afforded them by God. For the speaker in Milton's poem, the parable has a lot of authority. Evidently he feels that he should carry out its lesson. In effect, then, the parable has indeed become a warrant for him: that is, a basis for finding his blindness cause for lament.

Who, exactly, is the speaker's audience? Perhaps he is not addressing anyone in particular. Or perhaps the speaker's mind is divided and one side of it is addressing the other. Or perhaps the speaker is addressing God, even though he refers to God in the third person. Given that the speaker is answered by Patience, perhaps he means to address *that* figure, although Patience may actually be just a part of him rather than an altogether separate being.

At any rate, Patience takes the speaker for an audience in responding. And while Patience does not provide evidence, let alone warrants, Patience does make claims about God and His followers. Furthermore, Milton as author seems to endorse Patience's claims; apparently he is using the poem to advance them. Besides pointing out how God is served, Milton suggests that God ought to be served, even if God lets bad things happen to good people like Milton.

Every author can be considered an audience for his or her own writing, but some authors write expressly to engage in a dialogue with themselves. Perhaps Milton wrote his poem partly to convince himself that his religion was still valid and his life still worth living. Significantly, he did not publish the poem until about twenty years later. Yet because he did publish it eventually, at some point he must have contemplated a larger audience for it. The first readers of the poem would have been a relatively small segment of the English population: those literate and prosperous enough to have access to books of poetry. In addition, a number of the poem's first readers would have shared Milton's religious beliefs. Perhaps, however, Milton felt that even the faith of this band had to be bolstered. For one thing, not every Protestant of the time would have shared Milton's enthusiasm for the Puritan government. Recall that this regime executed the king, supposedly replacing him with the rule of God. Milton's words "His state / Is kingly" can be seen as an effort to persuade readers that the Puritans did put God on England's throne.

Most works of literature do not incorporate each element of argument we have discussed. Rarely do they feature arguments that do everything: acknowledge an audience, specify an issue, articulate claims, and carefully support these claims with substantial evidence and identified warrants. When characters argue, typically they do so in dramatic situations, not the sort of circumstances that permit elaborate debate. Also, traditionally literature has been a way for authors to make their own arguments indirectly: that is, to persuade with characterization, plot, and image rather than with straightforward development of claims. Do register the "gaps" as well as the strengths of any argument you find in a literary work. If the argument seems incomplete, however, a more drawn-out argument may have made the work less compelling.

Investigating Topics of Literary Criticism

To generate ideas about a literary text, try considering how it deals with **topics** that have preoccupied literary studies as a profession. Some of these topics have interested the discipline for many years. One example is work, a common subject of the poems by Blake, Dunn, Laux, Stanton, and Milton. Traditionally, literary studies has also been concerned with the cluster topics in Part Two, which in general are family relations, teaching and learning, love, justice, and mortality. Moreover, the discipline has long called attention to topics that are essentially classic conflicts: for example, innocence versus experience, free will versus fate or determinism, the individual versus society, nature versus culture, and eternity versus the passing time.

Over the last few years, however, literary studies has turned to several new concerns. For instance, quite a few literary critics now consider the ways in which literary texts are often *about* reading, writing, interpretation, and evaluation. Critics increasingly refer to some of the following subjects in their analysis of literature:

+ Traits that significantly shape human identity, including gender, race, ethnic background, social class, sexual orientation, cultural background, nationality, and historical context;
+ Representations of groups, including stereotypes held by others;
+ Acknowledgments — or denials — of differences among human beings;
+ Divisions, conflicts, and multiple forces *within* the self;
+ Boundaries, including the processes through which these are created, preserved, and challenged;
+ Politics and ideology, including the various forms that power and authority can take; acts of domination, oppression, exclusion, and appropriation; and acts of subversion, resistance, and parody;
+ Ways that carnivals and other festivities challenge or preserve social order;
+ Distinctions between what's universal and what's historically or culturally specific;
+ Relations between the public and the private; the social and the personal;
+ Relations between the apparently central and the apparently marginal;
+ Relations between what's supposedly normal and what's supposedly abnormal;
+ Relations between "high" culture and "low" (that is, mass or popular) culture;
+ Economic and technological developments, as well as their effects;
+ The role of performance in everyday life;
+ Values — ethical, aesthetic, religious, professional, and institutional;
+ Desire and pleasure;
+ The body;
+ The unconscious;
+ Memory, including public commemorations as well as personal memory.

If you find that a literary text touches on one of these topics, try next to determine how the work specifically addresses that topic. Perhaps you will consider the topic an element of the text's theme. In any case, remember that by itself, a topic is not the same as a theme. While a topic can usually be expressed in a word or short phrase, a theme is a whole claim or assertion that you believe the text makes.

Actually, the topics we have identified may be most worth consulting when you have just begun analyzing a literary text and are far from establishing its theme. By using these topics, you can generate preliminary questions about the text, various issues you can then explore.

To demonstrate how these topics can stimulate inquiry, we apply some of them to the following poem, "Night Waitress." It is from the 1986 book *Ghost Memory*, by the late American poet Lynda Hull (1954–1994). Hull had been

developing an impressive career in literature when she died in a car accident.
This poem is also about work, the speaker being the night waitress of the title.

LYNDA HULL

Night Waitress

Reflected in the plate glass, the pies
look like clouds drifting off my shoulder.
I'm telling myself my face has character,
not beauty. It's my mother's Slavic face.
She washed the floor on hands and knees   5
below the Black Madonna, praying
to her god of sorrows and visions
who's not here tonight when I lay out the plates,
small planets, the cups and moons of saucers.
At this hour the men all look   10
as if they'd never had mothers.
They do not see me. I bring the cups.
I bring the silver. There's the man
who leans over the jukebox nightly
pressing the combinations   15
of numbers. I would not stop him
if he touched me, but it's only songs
of risky love he leans into. The cook sings
with the jukebox, a moan and sizzle
into the grill. On his forehead   20
a tattooed cross furrows,
diminished when he frowns. He sings words
dragged up from the bottom of his lungs.
I want a song that rolls
through the night like a big Cadillac   25
past factories to the refineries
squatting on the bay, round and shiny
as the coffee urn warming my palm.
Sometimes when coffee cruises my mind
visiting the most remote way stations,   30
I think of my room as a calm arrival
each book and lamp in its place. The calendar
on my wall predicts no disaster
only another white square waiting
to be filled like the desire that fills   35
jail cells, the old arrest
that makes me stare out the window or want
to try every bar down the street.

When I walk out of here in the morning
my mouth is bitter with sleeplessness.   40
Men surge to the factories and I'm too tired
to look. Fingers grip lunch box handles,
belt buckles gleam, wind riffles my uniform
and it's not romantic when the sun unlids
the end of the avenue. I'm fading   45
in the morning's insinuations
collecting in the crevices of buildings,
in wrinkles, in every fault
of this frail machinery.   [1986]

A WRITING EXERCISE

After you read "Night Waitress," do a ten-minute freewrite in which you try
to identify how the poem relates to one or more of the topics mentioned
on page 32. You might also find it helpful to compare this poem about work
to the poems by Blake, Dunn, Laux, Stanton, and Milton on pages 10 to 16
and 30.

We think that several of the topics now popular in literary studies are relevant
to Hull's poem. Here are a few possibilities, along with questions that these topics
can generate:

Gender.   The speaker alludes to conventional roles through which men
and women relate to each other. When the speaker declares that "at this hour the
men all look / as if they'd never had mothers," she indicates that women have often
played a maternal role for men. Furthermore, she implies that often women have
been the primary caretaker of their sons. (Notice that she makes no reference to
fathers.) What is the effect of this attention to women as mothers of men? In most
of the poem, the speaker refers to men as potential lovers. Yet even as she suggests
she would like a sexual relationship with a man, she suggests as well that she has
had trouble establishing worthwhile attachments. Why has she had such difficulty, do you think? Does the problem seem due to her personality alone, or do
you sense larger forces shaping her situation? Notice, too, that the poem refers to
the factory workers as male, while the woman who speaks is a waitress. To what
extent does American society perpetuate a gendered division of labor?

Ethnic background.   Near the start of the poem, the speaker refers to her
"mother's Slavic face" and points out that her mother served "the Black
Madonna," a religious icon popular in Central European countries like the
Czech Republic and Poland. What is the effect of these particular ethnic references? To pursue this line of inquiry, probably you will need to do research into
the Black Madonna, whether in a library or on the Internet.

Social class.   In part, considering social class means thinking about people's
ability to obtain material goods. When the speaker compares her ideal song to

"a big Cadillac," she implies that she doesn't currently possess such a luxurious car. At the same time, she is expressing her desire for the song, not the car. Why might the first item be more important to her right now? Social class is also a matter of how various workplaces are related to one another. This poem evokes a restaurant, factories, refineries, and bars. How are these settings connected as parts of American society? Think, too, about how you would label the social class of the various occupations the poem mentions. What would you say is the social class of a waitress? To what classes would you assign people who work in factories and refineries? Who, for the most part, are the social classes that have to work at night?

Sexual orientation. The speaker of "Night Waitress" seems heterosexual, an orientation often regarded as the only legitimate one. Because almost all societies have made heterosexuality the norm, a lot of people forget that it is a particular orientation and that not everyone practices it. Within literary studies, gay and lesbian critics have pointed out that a literary work may seem to deal with sexuality in general but may actually refer just to heterosexuality. Perhaps "Night Waitress" is examining heterosexuality as a specific social force. If so, how might the speaker's discontent be related to heterosexuality's influence as a particular institution? Keep in mind that you don't have to assume anything about the author's sexuality as you pursue such a question. In fact, heterosexuality may be a more important topic in Hull's poem than she intended.

Divisions, conflicts, and multiple forces within the self. The poem's beginning indicates that the speaker experiences herself as divided. The first four lines reveal that she feels pride and disappointment in her mirror image: "telling myself my face has character, / not beauty." Later she indicates that within her mind are "remote way stations" that she visits only on occasion. Furthermore, she seems to contradict herself. Although she initially refers to her room as "a calm arrival," she goes on to describe that place negatively, as empty and confined. Early in the evening, she seems sexually attracted to the man playing the jukebox ("I would not stop him / if he touched me"), but by morning her mood is "not romantic" and she is "too tired / to look" at the male factory workers. What may be the significance of these paradoxes?

Boundaries. In the first line the speaker is apparently looking at a window, and later, she reveals that at times she feels driven to "stare out the window" of her room. What should a reader make of these two references to such a common boundary? When the speaker observes that the men in the restaurant "do not see me," she indicates that a boundary exists between them and her. Do you think she is merely being paranoid, or do you suspect that the men are indeed ignoring her? If they *are* oblivious to her, how do you explain their behavior? Still another boundary explored in the poem is the line between night and day. What happens when the speaker crosses this line? What can night, day, and the boundary between them signify? You might also consider what the author of a literary work does with its technical boundaries. Often a poem creates boundaries in its breaks between stanzas. Yet "Night Waitress" is a continuous, unbroken text; what is the effect of Hull's making it so? At the same time, Hull doesn't always respect sentence boundaries in her lines. At several points in the poem, sentences spill over from one line to another. This poetic technique is called **enjambment**; what is its effect here?

Politics and ideology.   When, in referring to the jukebox man, the speaker declares that "I would not stop him / if he touched me," she can be taken to imply that often male customers flirt with waitresses. How might flirtation be seen as involving power, authority, and even outright domination? Do you see the poem as commenting on such things? Earlier we raised issues of social class; these can be seen as political issues, too. How would you describe a society in which some people have "a big Cadillac" and others do not?

Carnivals and other festivities.   Although the poem does not refer to a "carnival" in any sense of that word, it does mention bars, which today are regarded by many people as places of festive retreat from work. What adjectives would you use to describe the speaker when she says that sometimes she wants "to try every bar down the street"?

Distinctions between what is universal and what is historically or culturally specific.   Try to identify anything that is historically or culturally specific about this poem's setting. Certainly the word *Slavic* and the reference to the Black Madonna indicate that the speaker has a particular background. You might also note her description of the restaurant, her use of the Cadillac as a metaphor, and her mention of the "factories" and the "refineries" that "are squatting on the bay." Although a wide range of places might fit these details, the poem's setting does not seem universal. Indeed, many readers are attracted to literature *because* it deals with specific landscapes, people, and plots. Nevertheless, these same readers usually expect to get some larger, more widely applicable meanings out of literature even as they are engaged by its specific details. Are you inclined to draw general conclusions from "Night Waitress"? If so, what general meanings do you find in it? What sorts of people do you think might learn something about themselves from reading this poem?

Relations between the public and the private, the social and the personal. The speaker of "Night Waitress" works in a very public place, a restaurant. Yet she seems to feel isolated there, trapped in her own private world. How did she come to experience public life this way, do you think? Later, she initially seems to value her room as a private retreat, calling it a "calm arrival," but then she describes it as a place so lonely that it leads her to "stare out the window or want / to try every bar down the street." How, then, would you ultimately describe the relations between the speaker's public life and her private one? In addressing this issue, probably you need to consider whether the speaker's difficulties are merely personal or reflect a larger social disorder. When, at the end of the poem, she refers to "this frail machinery," is she referring just to herself, or is she suggesting that this phrase applies to her society in general? If she is indeed making a social observation, what do you sense are the "faults" in her society? Who else might be "fading"?

Relations between "high" culture and "low" culture. Although the speaker does not identify the "songs / of risky love" playing on the jukebox, surely they are examples of what is called low, mass, or popular culture. Just as a lot of us are moved by such music when we hear it, so the jukebox player and the cook are engaged by it. In contrast, the poem itself can be considered an example of high culture. Often poetry is regarded as a serious art even by people who don't read it. In what ways, if any, does this poem conceivably resemble the songs it mentions? Given that author Lynda Hull is in essence playing with combinations of words, can we compare her with "the man / who leans over the jukebox nightly / pressing the combinations / of numbers"? (Actually, *numbers* has been a poetic term; centuries ago, it was commonly used as a synonym for the rhythms of poems.)

The role of performance in everyday life. The most conspicuous performer in this poem is the cook, who "sings words / dragged up from the bottom of his lungs." But in everyday life, people often perform in the sense of taking on certain roles, even disguising their real personalities. Do you see such instances of performing in this poem? If so, where? Notice that the speaker wears a uniform; can that be considered a costume she wears while performing as a waitress?

Religious values. The speaker clearly refers to religion when she recalls her mother's devotion to the Black Madonna, behavior that involved "praying / to her god of sorrows and visions." And although that god is "not here tonight," the speaker's description of waitressing has ritualistic overtones reminiscent of religious ceremonies. When she says, "I bring the cups. / I bring the silver," she could almost be describing preparations for Communion. In fact, she depicts the cook as wearing a religious emblem: "On his forehead / a tattooed cross furrows, / diminished when he frowns." What do you make of all this religious imagery? Might the speaker be trying to pursue certain religious values? Can she be reasonably described as looking for salvation?

Desire and pleasure. The speaker explicitly mentions the word *desire* when she describes the emptiness she feels in her room, a feeling of desolation "that makes me stare out the window or want / to try every bar down the street." These lines may lead you to believe that her desire is basically sexual. Yet when the speaker uses the words *I want* earlier in the poem, she expresses her wish for "a song that rolls / through the night like a big Cadillac." Here, her longing does not appear sexual in nature. Is the speaker referring to at least two kinds of desire, then? Or do you see her as afflicted with basically one kind?

The body. A notable feature of this poem is its attention to body parts. The speaker mentions her "shoulder," her "face," her mother's "face," her mother's "hands and knees," the cook's "forehead," his "lungs," her "palm," the "way stations" of her "mind," her "mouth," the factory workers' "fingers," and their "belt buckles." At the same time, the speaker never describes any particular body as a whole. What is the effect of this emphasis on mere parts? Does it connect in any way to the speaker's ultimate "fading"?

Memory.   Already we have noted the speaker's reference to her mother at the start of the poem. In what way, if any, is it significant that she engages in recollection? What circumstances in her life might have prompted the speaker to look back at the past?

A WRITING EXERCISE

We have applied several topics from our list to Lynda Hull's poem "Night Waitress." Now see how you can apply topics from the list to another poem about work in Part One. Try to come up with several questions about the poem you choose, referring to topics on our list. Then select one of the questions you have formulated, and freewrite for ten minutes in response to it.

SUMMING UP

+ When you argue, you attempt to *persuade* an *audience* to accept your *claims* regarding an *issue* by presenting *evidence* and relying on *warrants.*

+ The art of *persuasion* — of changing people's minds, of convincing them that claims are reasonable — has been studied for centuries under the term of *rhetoric.* (pp. 26–27)

+ The term *audience* applies to the people who read your writing. If you are to persuade them, you must take into account their common values, experiences, and assumptions, not just focus on your subject matter. (p. 27)

+ An *issue* is something about which people have disagreed or might disagree. Defined as questions with no obvious, immediate answers, ten kinds of issues that arise in literature courses are those of (1) fact, (2) theme, (3) definition, (4) symbolism, (5) pattern, (6) evaluation, (7) historical and cultural context, (8) genre, (9) social policy, and (10) cause and effect. (pp. 16–25)

+ *Claims* are the debatable answers to an issue. In literature classes, two common types of claims are those of interpretation and those of evaluation. (pp. 25–26)

+ *Evidence* is the support that you give your claims so that others will accept them. When you make an argument about a literary work, your readers expect you to support your case with details in the text and to convince them by methodically laying out your claims as well as your reasons for them. (pp. 27–28)

(continued on next page)

- ***Warrants*** **are the beliefs that lead people to call certain things evidence for their claims.** The terms *warrants* and *assumptions* are more or less interchangeable. (pp. 28–29)

- **Some literary works can be said to present arguments themselves.** Certain characters make claims, often in debate with one another, and other works indicate that the author is arguing for a certain position.

- **To generate ideas about a literary text, consider how it deals with** ***topics*** **that have preoccupied literary studies.** (pp. 31–38) Remember, however, that a topic, which can usually be expressed in a word or short phrase, differs from a theme — a whole claim or assertion that you think the literary work makes.

| 3 |

Writing an Argument

In Chapters 4 through 7, we discuss how to write about each of the four literary genres featured in this book. Here, however, we suggest how to write about a literary work of any genre. To make our advice concrete, we trace what one student did as she worked on a writing assignment for a course much like yours. The assignment was given to a class that had been reading and discussing several poems about work, including the poems we included in Chapter 2. Each student chose a single poem from the syllabus and wrote a 600-word argument paper on it for a general audience. We focus on the writing process of a student named Abby Hazelton.

Ultimately, Abby chose to write about William Wordsworth's "The Solitary Reaper." In his own day, Wordsworth (1770–1850) was poet laureate of England, and he continues to be regarded as a major British Romantic poet. He and fellow poet Samuel Taylor Coleridge collaborated on *Lyrical Ballads* (1798), a collection of verse that became a landmark of Romantic poetry. In his preface to the second edition two years later, Wordsworth famously defined *poetry* as "emotion recollected in tranquillity," contended that it should draw on "common life," and called for it to incorporate "language really used by men." Like many other Romantics, Wordsworth celebrated scenes of nature and country life, while deploring the increasing spread of cities. "The Solitary Reaper" appeared in his 1807 *Poems in Two Volumes*.

Before examining Abby's writing process, read Wordsworth's poem.

WILLIAM WORDSWORTH
The Solitary Reaper

Behold her, single in the field,
　　Yon solitary Highland Lass!
Reaping and singing by herself;
　　Stop here, or gently pass!
Alone she cuts and binds the grain,

5

40

And sings a melancholy strain;
O listen! for the Vale profound
Is overflowing with the sound.

No Nightingale did ever chaunt
   More welcome notes to weary bands   10
Of travellers in some shady haunt,
   Among Arabian sands:
A voice so thrilling ne'er was heard
In spring-time from the Cuckoo-bird,
Breaking the silence of the seas   15
Among the farthest Hebrides.

Will no one tell me what she sings? —
   Perhaps the plaintive numbers flow
For old, unhappy, far-off things,
   And battles long ago: 20
Or is it some more humble lay,
Familiar matter of to-day?
Some natural sorrow, loss, or pain,
That has been, and may be again?

Whate'er the theme, the Maiden sang   25
   As if her song could have no ending;
I saw her singing at her work,
   And o'er the sickle bending; —
I listen'd, motionless and still;
And, as I mounted up the hill,   30
The music in my heart I bore,
Long after it was heard no more.   [1807]

Once she chose to write about Wordsworth's poem for her paper, Abby engaged in four sorts of activities: (1) exploring, (2) planning, (3) composing, and (4) revising. As we describe each, keep in mind that these activities need not be consecutive. Abby moved back and forth among them as she worked on her assignment.

Exploring

As you read a literary work, you are bound to interpret and judge it. Yet not all reading is **critical reading**, which involves carefully and self-consciously analyzing various aspects of a text, including its meanings, its effects, and its treatment of typical elements of its genre. When you read a work critically, you also note questions it raises for you — issues you might explore further in class discussion and writing. Indeed, critical reading is a process of self-reflection. During this process, you monitor your own response to the text and try to identify why you see the text the way you do.

Perhaps you assume that literature contains hidden meanings that only an elite group of readers can spot. This is a common belief, but most people are quite capable of analyzing a literary work, especially if they know certain strategies for getting ideas about it. In rhetorical theory, these strategies are called *methods of invention.* Here we list some that Abby used, including a few strategies that we have mentioned already. Try out any that are unfamiliar to you, even as you first read a text. Again, critical reading does not require divine inspiration. The following techniques have helped many a mortal:

1. *Make predictions as you read a text, guessing how it will turn out.*   If you wind up being surprised, fine. You may gain several insights into the text and into yourself as you reflect on the ways in which the text defies your expectations. Even if the text proceeds as you anticipated, making predictions about it is worthwhile, for at least you will have considered its possible lines of development.

2. *Read the text more than once.*   You greatly increase your chances of getting ideas about it if you do. The first time around, you may be preoccupied with following the plot or with figuring out the text's basic meaning. Only by looking at the text repeatedly may you notice several of its other aspects, including features that really stir your thoughts. Given the busy schedule of a college student, you may be tempted to read a work just once before your class discusses it. But a single reading may leave you with relatively little to say, whereas multiple readings may give you several ideas to share.

3. *Note whatever changes of mind you go through as you read and reread the text.*

4. *Describe the audience that the author apparently had in mind, and note features of the text that support your image of its implied audience.*   At the same time, consider how real readers of the text—past, present, and future—might react to it and why they might respond so. Also reflect on your own response to the text, noting anything in your own life that affects your reading of it.

5. *Read at least part of the text aloud, even if you are alone.*   Doing this will give you a better sense of how the text manipulates language.

6. *Consciously focus on the text's content and on its form.*   If you can focus on both content and form at the same time, fine, but many readers have trouble paying attention to the two simultaneously. In this case, deliberately alternate your focus first on content and then on form. This way you increase your chances of noticing things that the text is saying and doing.

7. *Consult a dictionary when you come across words in the text that you do not understand.*   Keep in mind that a text may make a familiar word ambiguous, leaving you with the impression that the author is attaching more than one meaning to it. An example might be Dunn's use of the words *hard work,* which seem to take on various definitions as his poem proceeds. Furthermore, a text may define a commonly used word in a way unfamiliar to you. As we noted earlier, an example would be Milton's use of the word *fondly,* which in his time

meant "foolishly," not "affectionately." If you suspect that a writer is using a common word in what for you is an uncommon way, turn to a dictionary to check the word's possible meanings.

8. *Note patterns within the text.*   At the same time, pay attention to elements of the text that appear to threaten its unity — for instance, apparent contradictions or digressions.

9. *Try to identify the text's most important word, image, or scene.*   At the same time, consider how to justify your choice.

10. *Identify moments where the text makes a significant shift in meaning, imagery, tone, plot, narrator, or point of view.*   These moments may very well occur at typographic breaks in the text. In a poem, for example, significant changes may occur when one stanza ends and another begins. Similarly, a play may change significantly as it moves from scene to scene. Short stories and essays may also engage in important shifts as they go from paragraph to paragraph. But you may find turning points anywhere in the text, so do not look solely at its obvious moments of transition.

11. *Mark passages in the text that strike you as especially memorable.*   These passages would include any that you might quote in a paper about the text.

12. *Aim to complicate the views you take of characters in the text.*   If you tend to see a character as thoroughly mistaken, evil, or "sick," look for potentially redeeming qualities of that person. Similarly, if you tend to see a character as thoroughly good, look for qualities that suggest the person is less than perfect. Furthermore, consider whether you or the author are inclined to stereotype people. Note, too, any ways in which the characters fail to fit stereotypes.

13. *Raise questions about the text even as you read.*   For help, you can turn to our list of ten different types of issues (pp. 18–25). In effect, the list indicates some aspects of the text that might be especially worth pondering. Recall that these include the following:

- Facts obscured or absent in the text
- The text's theme
- Possible definitions of key words in the text
- The symbols it employs
- Its patterns
- Evaluations that might be made in response to it
- Its historical and cultural context
- Its genre
- Its relevance to current political debates
- Causes and effects of its characters' behavior; the author's aims and effects

14. *Note whether and how the text addresses topics of particular interest to professional literary critics today.*   (For a discussion of such topics, refer to the last section of Chapter 2, pp. 31–38.)

15. Think about the writer's alternatives—things the writer could have done and yet didn't do. Then, imagine that the writer had pursued these alternatives. How would the effect of the text have been different?

16. Consider whether and how the text itself features elements of argument. (Refer back to pp. 29–30 in Chapter 2.)

17. Compare the text with others on the same subject. So far, we have encouraged you to compare various poems about work. Going beyond the world of literature, you might compare whatever text you are focusing on to certain films, television shows, songs, advertisements, and articles in newspapers and magazines.

18. Discuss the text with your instructor, your classmates, and other people you know. If differences emerge between their views and yours, try to identify the exact issues at hand, as well as the possible reasons for those differences. Perhaps you will talk about the text with people who have not read it at all. If so, note the questions these people have about the text. Note, too, what you find yourself emphasizing as you describe the text to them.

You can also develop and pull together your thoughts about a text by informally writing about it. And the sooner you plunge into the rhythms of composing, the more comfortable you will feel producing a full-length paper. Your informal, **preliminary writing** can take various shapes. The following are just some of the things you might do.

1. Make notes in the text itself. A common method is to mark key passages, either by underlining these passages or running a magic marker through them. Both ways of marking are popular because they help readers recall main features of the text. But use these techniques moderately if you use them at all, for marking lots of passages will leave you unable to distinguish the really important parts of the text. Also, try "talking back" to the text in its margins. Next to particular passages, you might jot down words of your own, indicating any feelings and questions you have about those parts. On any page of the text, you might circle related words and then draw lines between these words to emphasize their connection. If a word or an idea shows up on numerous pages, you might circle it each time. Furthermore, try cross-referencing, by listing on at least one page the numbers of all those pages where the word or idea appears.

2. As you read the text, occasionally look away from it, and jot down anything in it you recall. This memory exercise lets you review your developing impressions of the text. When you turn back to its actual words, you may find that you have distorted or overlooked aspects of it that you should take into account.

3. At various moments in your reading, freewrite about the text for ten minutes or so. Spontaneously explore your preliminary thoughts and feelings about it, as well as any personal experiences the text leads you to recall. One logical moment to do freewriting is when you have finished reading the text. But you do not have to wait until then; as you read, you might pause occasionally to freewrite. This way, you give yourself an opportunity to develop and review your thoughts about the text early on.

4. *Create a "dialectical notebook."*   So named by composition theorist Ann Berthoff, it involves using pages of your regular notebook in a particular way. On each page, draw a line down the middle to create two columns. In the left column, list various details of the text: specifically, words, images, characters, and events that strike you. In the right column, jot down for each detail one or more sentences indicating *why* you were drawn to it. Take as many pages as you need to record and reflect on your observations. You can also use the two-column format to carry out a dialogue with yourself about the text. This is an especially good way to ponder aspects of the text that you find confusing, mysterious, or complex.

5. *Play with the text by revising it.*   Doing so will make you more aware of options that the author rejected and give you a better sense of the moves that the author chose to make. Specifically, you might rearrange parts of the text, add to it, change some of its words, or shift its narrative point of view. After you revise the text, compare your alternative version with the original, considering especially differences in their effects.

A WRITING EXERCISE

Do at least ten minutes of freewriting about Wordsworth's poem, keeping it nearby so that you can consult it if you need to. In particular, try to raise questions about the poem, and consider which of these may be worth addressing in a more formal paper.

Here is an excerpt from Abby's freewriting:

```
    I see that this poem consists of four stanzas, each
of which is eight lines long. But these stanzas have dif-
ferent emphases. The first stanza is a series of com-
mands. The speaker tells people to "Behold," "Stop here,
or gently pass," and "listen." The second stanza mainly
describes the reaper. The third stanza is basically a
bunch of questions. The fourth is the speaker's recollec-
tion of his experience in general. So I could write a
paper about how this poem changes as it moves along and
why the stanzas shift in emphasis. But one problem with a
paper like that is that it might get me bogged down in
mechanically moving from stanza to stanza. I don't want
that to happen. Another thing I could do is answer one of
the speaker's own questions, which are about what kind
of song the reaper is singing. Evidently this "Highland
```

Lass" is using a Scottish dialect that he doesn't understand. But I'm just as ignorant as he is about the song.
I guess I'm more likely to contribute some analysis of
my own if I come up with a question myself. I'm struck
by the fact that he doesn't give us much sense of the
reaper's song. There's no way that a printed poem could
convey the reaper's tune, but still. And the words are
foreign to the speaker. But I'm surprised that he doesn't
make a little effort to convey at least some of the
song's lyrics even if they're foreign words that he might
hear wrong or misspell. How can I as a reader join him in
experiencing the beauty of her song if I don't learn any
of its words? I wonder if we're supposed to see the poem
as being more about the speaker than about the reaper.
More specifically, maybe we're supposed to be a little
disturbed that he's a British intellectual who is making
a spectacle out of a foreign woman from the working
class. At any rate, he seems bent on controlling this
experience even as he invites us to share it. Another
question for me is, Why does he shift from present tense
to past tense in the last stanza? This change is really
curious to me. I don't see anything earlier on that prepares me for it. First, we're led to believe that the
speaker is observing the reaper right then and there,
but at the end he speaks as if this occurred in the past,
though maybe the recent past. This inconsistency in the
time frame makes me think that in some important way the
overall poem is about time. At any rate, I'm drawn to
the inconsistency because it's so blatant. If I wrote
about it, I might still devote a paragraph to each stanza,
but I'd be starting with the last one and referring back
to the others in order to explain that stanza. What I
still have to figure out, though, is what exactly the poem
is saying about time when it makes the shift of tense.

Freewriting enabled Abby to raise several questions. At the same time, she
realized that her paper could not deal with everything that puzzled her. When
you first get an assignment like hers, you may fear that you will have nothing
to say. But you will come up with a lot of material if, like Abby, you take time

for exploration. As we have suggested, it's a process of examining potential subjects through writing, discussion, and just plain thinking. One of your challenges will be to choose among the various issues you have formulated. At the end of the above excerpt from her freewriting, Abby is on the verge of choosing to analyze the poem's shift of tense in its final stanza. For her, this shift is an interesting change from a pattern, the poem's previous uses of present tense. Abby has not yet decided how to explain this shift; at the moment, it remains for her a mystery. But her paper would achieve little if it focused just on aspects of the poem that are easy to interpret. Though Abby has more thinking to do about the poem's shift of tense, it seems a promising subject for her precisely because it puzzles her.

Planning

Planning for an assignment like Abby's involves five main activities:

1. Choosing the text you will analyze;
2. Identifying your audience;
3. Identifying the main issue, claim, and evidence you will present;
4. Identifying particular challenges you will face and warrants you will use;
5. Determining how you will organize your argument.

Abby considered several poems before choosing one for her paper. She settled on Wordsworth's for five reasons. First, it was a text that left her with plenty of questions. Second, she believed that these questions could be issues for other readers. Third, she felt increasingly able to *argue* about the poem—that is, to make and support claims about it. Fourth, she believed that she could adequately analyze the poem within the assignment's word limit. Finally, Wordsworth's poem drew her because she had heard about the Romantic movement in English literature and was curious to study an example of it.

Faced with the same assignment, you might choose a different poem than Abby did. Still, the principles that she followed are useful. Think about them whenever you are free to decide which texts you will write about. With some assignments, of course, you may need a while to decide which text is best for you. And later, after you have made your decision, you may want to make a switch. For example, you may find yourself changing your mind once you have done a complete draft. Frustrated by the text you have chosen, you may realize that another inspires you more. If so, consider making a substitution. Naturally, you will feel more able to switch if you have ample time left to write the paper, so avoid waiting to start your paper just before it is due.

To determine what your readers will see as an issue and to make your claims about it persuasive to them, you need to develop an audience profile. Perhaps your instructor will specify your audience. You may be asked, for example, to imagine yourself writing for a particular group in a particular situation. If you were Abby, how would you analyze "The Solitary Reaper" for an orchestra wanting to know what this poem implies about music? Even when not required of you, such an exercise can be fun and thought-provoking for you as you plan a paper.

Most often, though, instructors ask students to write for a "general" audience, the readership that Abby was asked to address. Assume that a general audience is one that will want evidence for your claims. While this audience will include your instructor, let it also include your classmates, since in class discussions they will be an audience for you whenever you speak. Besides, your class may engage in peer review, with students giving one another feedback on their drafts.

If your audience is indeed supposed to be a general group of readers, what can you assume about their prior knowledge? You may not be sure. Above all, you may wonder how familiar your readers already are with the text you are analyzing. Perhaps your teacher will resolve your uncertainty, telling you exactly how much your audience knows about the text. Then again, you may be left to guess. Should you presume that your audience is totally unfamiliar with the text? This approach is risky, for it may lead you to spend a lot of your paper merely summarizing the text rather than analyzing it. A better move is to write as if your audience is at least a bit more knowledgeable. Here is a good rule of thumb: assume that your audience has, in fact, read the text but that you need to recall for this group any features of the text that are crucial to your argument. Although probably your paper will still include summary, the amount you provide will be limited, and your own ideas will be more prominent.

When you have written papers for previous classes, you may have been most concerned with coming up with a thesis. Maybe you did not encounter the term *issue* at all. But good planning for a paper does entail identifying the main issue you will address. Once you have sensed what that issue is, try phrasing it as a question. If the answer would be obvious to your readers, be cautious, for you really do not have an issue if the problem you are raising can be easily resolved.

Also, try to identify what *kind* of issue you will focus on. For help, look at our list of various types (pp. 18–25). Within "The Solitary Reaper," the speaker raises an issue of fact: he wants to know what sort of song the reaper is singing. But as someone writing about Wordsworth's poem, Abby wanted to focus on another kind of issue, which she decided is best regarded as an issue of pattern. More precisely, she thought her main question might be, What should we conclude from the inconsistency in pattern that occurs when the final stanza shifts to past tense? To be sure, Abby recognized that addressing this issue would lead to issues of theme and of cause and effect, for she would have to consider why Wordsworth shifts tenses and how the shift relates to his overall subject.

Now that she had identified her main issue, Abby had to determine her main claim. Perhaps you have grown comfortable with the term *thesis* and want to keep using it. Fine. Bear in mind, though, that your thesis is the main *claim* you will make and proceed to support. And when, as Abby did, you put your main issue as a question, then your main claim is your answer to that question. Sometimes you will come up with question and answer simultaneously. Once in a while, you may even settle on your answer first, not being certain yet how to word the question. Whatever the case, planning for your paper involves articulating both the question (the issue) and the answer (your main claim). Try actually writing both down, making sure to phrase your main issue as a question and your main claim as the answer. Again, Abby's main issue was, What should we conclude from the inconsistency in pattern that occurs when the final stanza shifts to past tense? After much thought, she expressed her main claim this way:

```
One possible justification for the shift to past tense is
that it reminds us of the speaker's inability to halt the
passage of time. He would like to freeze his encounter
with the reaper, keeping it always in the present. But as
the shift in tense indicates, time goes on, making the
encounter part of the speaker's past. Perhaps, therefore,
the poem's real subject is the idea that time is always
in flux.
```

Audiences usually want evidence, and as we noted earlier, most arguments you write about literature will need to cite details of the work itself. Because direct quotation is usually an effective move, Abby planned to elaborate her claim by citing several of Wordsworth's references to time. Remember, though, that you need to avoid seeming willfully selective when you quote. While Abby expected to quote from Wordsworth's last stanza, she also knew she had to relate it to earlier lines, so that her readers would see her as illuminating the basic subject of the whole poem. In particular, she looked for language in the first three stanzas that might hint at the speaker's lack of control over time, thereby previewing the last stanza's emphasis.

Often, to think about particular challenges of your paper is to think about your warrants. Remember that warrants are assumptions; they are what lead you to call certain things evidence for your claims. Abby knew that one of her warrants was an assumption about Wordsworth himself—that he was not being sloppy when he shifted tenses in his last stanza. Rarely will your paper need to admit all the warrants on which it relies. Most of the time, your task will be to guess which warrants your readers do want stated. Abby felt there was at least one warrant she would have to spell out—her belief that the poem's verb tenses reveal something about the speaker's state of mind.

To make sure their texts seem organized, most writers first do an **outline**, a list of their key points in the order they will appear. Outlines are indeed a good idea, but bear in mind that there are various kinds. One popular type, which you may already know, is the **sentence outline**. As the name implies, it lists the writer's key points in sentence form. Its advantages are obvious: this kind of outline forces you to develop a detailed picture of your argument's major steps, and it leaves you with sentences you can then incorporate into your paper. Unfortunately, sentence outlines tend to discourage flexibility. Because they demand much thought and energy, you may hesitate to revise them, even if you come to feel your paper would work better with a new structure.

A second, equally familiar outline is the **topic outline**, a list in which the writer uses a few words to signify the main subjects that he or she will discuss. Because it is sketchy, this kind of outline allows writers to go back and change plans if necessary. Nevertheless, a topic outline may fail to provide all the guidance a writer needs.

We find a third type useful: a **rhetorical purpose outline**. As with the first two, you list the major sections of your paper. Next, you briefly indicate two things for each section: the effect you want it to have on your audience, and how you will achieve that effect. Here is the rhetorical purpose outline that Abby devised for her paper.

INTRODUCTION

The audience needs to know the text I'll discuss.	I'll identify Wordsworth's poem.
The audience must know my main issue.	I'll point out that the poem is puzzling in its shift of tenses at the end.
The audience must know my main claim.	I'll argue that the shift to past tense suggests that the poem's real subject is the inability of human beings to halt the passage of time.

ANALYSIS OF THE POEM'S FINAL STANZA

The audience needs to see in detail how the final stanza's shift to past tense signals the speaker's inability to control the passage of time.	I will point out not only the shift of tense but also other words in the last stanza that imply time moves on. I will note as well that music is an especially fleeting medium, so the reaper's song was bound to fade.

ANALYSIS OF THE PRECEDING STANZAS

To accept that the passage of time is the poem's real concern, the audience must see that the preceding stanzas hint at this subject.	I will analyze the first three stanzas in turn, showing how each implies the speaker is frustrated over his inability to control time.

CONCLUSION

The audience may need to be clearer about what I consider the ultimate <u>tone</u> of the poem.	I will say that although the poem can be thought of as a warm tribute to the singing reaper, the final emphasis on the passage of time is pessimistic in tone, and the speaker winds up as "solitary" as the reaper.

For your own rhetorical purpose outlines, you may want to use phrases rather than sentences. If you do use sentences, as Abby did, you do not have to write all that many. Note that Abby wrote relatively few as she stated the effects she would aim for and her strategies for achieving those effects. Thus, she was not tremendously invested in preserving her original outline. She felt free to change it if it failed to prove helpful.

Composing

Composing is not always distinguishable from exploring, planning, and revising. As you prepare for your paper, you may jot down words or whole sentences. Once you begin a draft, you may alter that draft in several ways before you complete it. You may be especially prone to making changes in drafts if you use a computer, for word processing enables you to jump around in your text, revisiting and revising what you have written.

Still, most writers feel that doing a draft is an activity in its own right, and a major one at that. The next four chapters present various tips for writing about specific genres, and Chapter 8 discusses writing research papers. Meanwhile, here are some tips to help you with composing in general.

Title

You may be inclined to let your **title** be the same as that of the text you discuss. Were you to write about Wordsworth's poem, then, you would be calling your own paper "The Solitary Reaper." But often such mimicry backfires. For one thing, it may lead your readers to think that you are unoriginal and perhaps even lazy. Also, you risk confusing your audience, since your paper would actually be about Wordsworth's poem rather than being the poem itself. So take the time to come up with a title of your own. Certainly it may announce the text you will focus on, but let it do more. In particular, use your title to indicate the main claim you will be making. With just a few words, you can preview the argument to come.

Style

Perhaps you have been told to "sound like yourself" when you write. Yet that can be a difficult demand (especially if you are not sure what your "self" is really like). Above all, the **style** you choose depends on your audience and purpose. In writing an argument for a general audience, probably you would do best to avoid the extremes of pomposity and breezy informality. Try to stick with words you know well, and if you do want to use some that are only hazily familiar to you, check their dictionary definitions first.

At some point in our lives, probably all of us have been warned not to use *I* in our writing. In the course you are taking, however, you may be asked to write about your experiences. If so, you will find *I* hard to avoid. Whether to use it does become a real question when you get assignments like Abby's, which require you chiefly to make an argument about a text. Since you are supposed to focus on that text, your readers may be disconcerted if you keep referring to yourself. Even so, you need not assume that your personal life is irrelevant to the task. Your opening paragraph might refer to your personal encounters with the text, as a way of establishing the issue you will discuss. A personal anecdote might serve as a forceful conclusion to your paper. Moreover, before you reach the conclusion, you might orient your readers to the structure of your paper by using certain expressions that feature the word *I*: for example, *As I suggested earlier, As I have noted, As I argue later.* In general, you may be justified in saying *I* at certain moments. When tempted to use this pronoun, though, consider whether it really is your best move.

In a paper, the expressions *I think* and *I feel* are rarely effective. Often writers resort to such phrasing because they sense they are offering nothing more than their own opinion. The audience may view such expressions as indications of a weak argument or limited evidence. You might make the claim more persuasive by avoiding *I think* and *I feel* and by qualifying it through words such as *probably, possibly, maybe,* and *perhaps.* If you believe that you have little evidence for a claim you want to make, take time out from writing and go back to exploring your ideas. If you can, come up with additional means of support.

Arguments about literature are most compelling when supported by quotations, but be careful not to quote excessively. If you constantly repeat other people's words, providing few of your own, your readers will hardly get a sense of you as an author. Moreover, a paper full of quotation marks is hard to read. Make sure to quote selectively, remembering that sometimes you can simply paraphrase. When you do quote, try to cite only the words you need. You do not have to reproduce a whole line or sentence if one word is enough to support your point.

When summarizing what happens in a literary work, be careful not to shift tenses as you go along. Your reader may be confused if you shift back and forth between past and present. We suggest that you stick primarily to the present tense, which is the tense that literary critics customarily employ. For example, instead of saying that the speaker *praised* the lass, say that he *praises* her.

Introduction

Many writers aim to impress their audience right away. You may be tempted, then, to begin your paper with a grand philosophical statement, hoping your readers will find such an **introduction** profound. Often, however, this approach results in broad, obvious generalities. Here are some examples:

> Society doesn't always appreciate the work that everyone does.

> Over the centuries, there has been a lot of literature, and much of it has been about work.

> William Wordsworth was a great British Romantic poet.

As writing theorist William Coles points out, statements like these are mere "throat-clearing." They may lead your audience to think that you are delaying, not introducing, your real argument. Rather than beginning your paper with such statements, try mentioning the specific text you will analyze. Start by making assertions about that text.

Usually, your introduction will identify the main issue that you will discuss. Perhaps you will be able to assume that your audience is already aware of this issue and sees it as important. Abby felt that her audience would wonder, as she did, why Wordsworth shifts to the past tense. Sometimes, however, your introduction will need to set out your issue at greater length. It will need to identify the issue as a significant question with no obvious answer.

A classic way to establish the importance of an issue is to show that other critics have grappled with it or wrongly ignored it. You may, however, get assignments in your course that do not push you to consider what previous critics have said. An alternative method of establishing your issue's significance is personal anecdote. By describing how the issue came to matter to you, you may persuade your readers to see it as mattering to them. If you do not want to be autobiographical, you have at least one other option. You can show that if your issue is left unaddressed, your readers will remain puzzled by other key aspects of the text you are discussing.

Development

When you write a paper, naturally you want the parts of each sentence to hang together. But make sure, too, that each sentence connects clearly to the one before and the one after. Smooth transitions from one paragraph to the next encourage your reader to follow the **development** of your argument. Certain words can help you signal relations between sentences. Here are just a few examples. Each could appear at the beginning of a sentence, where it would indicate how that sentence relates to the one before.

- Numerical order: *first, second, third*, etc.
- Temporal order: *then, next, earlier, previously, before, later, subsequently, afterward*
- Addition: *also, in addition to, furthermore, moreover, another*
- Degree: *more/less important, more/less often*
- Effect: *thus, therefore, as a result, consequently, hence, so*
- Opposition: *but, yet, however, nevertheless, still, even so, by contrast, on the contrary, conversely, on the other hand*

- Exemplarity: *for example, for instance*
- Emphasis: *indeed, in fact*
- Restatement: *that is, in other words*
- Specificity: *specifically, more precisely, in particular*

Do not fall into the habit of relying on *and* as a connective. As a means of linking sentences or of bridging ideas within them, *and* may seem a safe choice; besides being a common word, it looks too little to cause trouble. Nevertheless, as a connective *and* is often vague, failing to show how words actually relate. Note the following sentence:

The speaker loves the reaper's song, and he does not know what it is.

The word *and* does little to fuse the sentence's two halves. A more precise way to connect the halves would be with language that shows their relation to be contrast:

The speaker loves the reaper's song, *but* he does not know what it is.

Whatever the merits of this revision, it is more coherent than the sentence using *and*, which hardly conveys relation at all. Also, if your paper constantly uses *and* or any other particular word, your prose may come across as monotonous.

The word *and* often becomes a prime means of transition in papers that mostly just summarize plots of texts. Presumably, though, your goal in a paper is to *analyze* whatever text you are discussing, not simply outline it. If you see that you are using *and* a lot in your writing, consider the possibility that you are, in fact, summarizing more than analyzing. In our experience, writers are most apt to lapse into plot summary toward the middle of their paper. At that point, they may grow tired of developing and keeping track of their own ideas. The easiest thing to do then is to coast, simply paraphrasing their chosen text line by line. Pause in your writing from time to time to see if you have lapsed into this practice. Remember that you can analyze details of a text without sticking to their original order.

How coherent a paper seems depends in part on the length of its paragraphs. Usually, a paragraph should be at least three sentences long. When readers confront one very short paragraph after another, they are apt to feel that they are seeing random, fragmented observations rather than a well-organized argument. Of course, paragraphs can also be too long. Readers have trouble following the structure of one that runs a full page. If you find yourself writing a lengthy paragraph, stop and check to see if there is any place in it where starting a new paragraph makes sense.

Emphasis

Many people assume that academic writing consists of long, dense statements. Furthermore, they assume that such prose is virtually unreadable. Whether or not they are right about the kind of writing favored in college, your own readers may get tired and lost if each of your sentences seems endless. On the other hand, your writing may strike your readers as choppy if each sentence contains just a few words. Usually, your papers will be most effective if you vary the lengths of your sentence for **emphasis**. In any paper you write for your course, aim for a mixture of sentence lengths, blending long, medium, and short.

But in any of your sentences, use only the amount of words you need to make your point. For example, do not resort to sixteen words when eight will suffice. Your readers are likely to become impatient, even bored, if your prose seems padded. Also, they may doubt your credibility, suspecting that you are pretending to have more ideas than you do.

Perhaps you fear that if you economize with your language, all your sentences will wind up short. But a concise sentence is not always brief; a sentence can be long and yet tightly edited, with every word in it deserving a place. Another possible fear has to do with writer's block. You may worry that you will have trouble getting words down if you must justify every single one of them. A good solution is to postpone editing for a while, perhaps even waiting until you have finished a draft. Simply remember that at some point you should review whatever you have written, looking for words you might trim.

Your sentences will have more impact if you use active rather than passive verbs. To grasp the difference, read the following two sentences:

> In the final stanza, tenses are shifted by the speaker.

> In the final stanza, the speaker shifts tenses.

Certainly both sentences are grammatical. The second, however, is more concise and dynamic. That is because it uses the active form of the verb *to shift* and indicates right away the agent performing the action. The first sentence uses the passive form, *are shifted by*. The word *is* can serve as a tip-off: passive verbs always feature some version of *to be*.

Passive verbs are not always bad. Sometimes a sentence will work better if it uses one. We can even envision a situation where our first sample sentence would perhaps make more sense. Imagine that up to this point, the writer has repeatedly referred to the "you." Imagine, too, that the writer had left off mentioning the speaker several paragraphs back. By making the "you" the grammatical subject of the sentence, the writer can maintain consistency, whereas suddenly switching to "the speaker" might throw readers off. Usually, however, passive verbs are unnecessary and counterproductive. Make them an exception, not the rule.

Usually, a sentence will seem better paced if you keep the main subject and verb close together. When several words come between subject and verb, readers may have trouble following along. This pair of sentences illustrates what we mean:

> The speaker, hoping to make other people abandon all motion and gaze at the reaper, commands them to "Behold her."

> Hoping to make other people abandon all motion and gaze at the reaper, the speaker commands them to "Behold her."

Neither sentence is bad. But the first forces the reader to slow down right in the middle, since it puts several words between subject and verb. By keeping them together, the second sentence flows more.

Sentences are easier to read when they include at most one negative expression: words such as *not, never, don't,* and *won't.* On the other hand, a sentence is often hard to follow when it features several negatives. Look at the following pair of examples:

> Not able to halt the passage of time, because no human being ever can, the speaker does not stick to the present tense.

> Because, like other human beings, he cannot halt the passage of time, the speaker shifts to the past tense.

While the first sentence is grammatically correct and makes a logical point, its blizzard of negatives will confuse many readers. The second sentence makes basically the same point, but because it minimizes negatives, it is easier to read.

A point can have greater or less emphasis depending on where you place it. If you want to call attention to a paragraph's main idea, try beginning the paragraph with it. In any case, most likely your readers will assume that a paragraph's opening sentence is important. Usually they will pay special attention to its last sentence, too. Therefore, try not to fill either of these slots with relatively trivial points. Also, remember that you may obscure an important idea if you put it in the middle of a paragraph. There, the idea will have trouble getting the prominence it deserves.

Conclusion

You can always end your paper by summarizing the argument you have made. In fact, many readers will welcome a recap. Yet a conclusion that merely restates your argument risks boring your audience. Therefore, try to keep any final summary brief, using your **conclusion** to do additional things.

For example, the conclusion is a good place to make concessions. Even if you have already indicated ways in which people may reasonably disagree with you, you may use the close of your paper to acknowledge that you have no monopoly on truth. Your conclusion is also an opportunity for you to evaluate the text you have been discussing or to identify questions that the text still leaves in your mind. Consider as well the possibility of using your conclusion to bring up some personal experience that relates to the text. Yet another option is to have your conclusion identify implications of your argument that you have not so far announced: How might people apply your method of analysis to other texts? What, in effect, have you suggested about how people should live? What image have you given of the author that you have been discussing?

You might also end your paper by indicating further research you would like to do. Admittedly, this sort of conclusion is more typical of the sciences and social sciences. Literary critics tend to conclude their arguments as if there is nothing more they need to investigate. But if you do suggest you have more work to do, your readers may admire you for remaining curious and ambitious.

Further Suggestions for Developing an Argument about a Work of Literature

1. *Avoid long stretches of mere plot summary.*   Short stories and plays spin tales. So do many poems and essays. But if you are writing about a literary work that is narrative in form, don't spend much of your paper just summarizing its narrative. Developing a genuine argument about the work involves more than recounting its narrative. Assume that your reader knows the basic plot and needs only a few brief reminders of its key elements. Keep in mind that your main agenda is to put forth, explain, and support a *claim* about the text—your answer to some question you raise about it. In your paper, you will develop your main claim by making a series of smaller points. Try to begin each of your paragraphs with one of these subclaims, using the rest of your paragraph to elaborate and provide evidence for it. Don't begin a paragraph simply by recording a plot incident, for doing so is liable to bog you down in sheer summary. You can also avoid this trap by writing about how the work you are analyzing is *constructed*. Make observations about specific methods that the author uses to present the story, including techniques of organization and characterization. Linger on some of the author's specific language, exploring possible definitions of particular words.

2. *Be cautious about relating the work to its author's life. Don't write as if you have firm knowledge of the author's intentions. At moments, you can acknowledge to your reader that you are guessing about them.*   Sometimes a certain character within a work will express the author's own views. But don't simply assume that a particular character speaks for the author. Even the *I* of a first-person poem may differ significantly from its creator. True, many literary works are at least somewhat autobiographical, based on one or more aspects on the author's life. Nevertheless, even works that are largely autobiographical may not be entirely so. Besides, knowledge of the author's life won't always help you figure out his or her text. William Wordsworth may have derived "The Solitary Reaper" from a personal encounter, but we must still interpret the particular poem he proceeded to write. Therefore, be cautious about linking a work to the author's own circumstances. Such connections can be legitimate, but the more you push them, the more you may ignore the work's exact design. You also risk neglecting the author's artistic achievement. Not everyone who hears a reaper sing could turn this event into a poem!

Much of what you write about a literary work will reflect your understanding of its author's intentions. Needless to say, you can't peer into the author's mind. Rather, you'll make hypotheses about the author's aims. Your reader will assume you're speculating about these without being told. Even so, sometimes you may want to admit you're guessing at what the author thought. Acknowledging this is fine, but take care to explain why your guesses are logical. Sometimes you'll suspect that the author would object to your view of the text. Feel free to acknowledge such possible disagreements. In fact, many theorists argue that a literary work may differ from how its author sees it. They refuse, therefore, to treat the author as an absolute authority on the work. D. H. Lawrence's advice was "Trust the tale, not the teller." Do you think Lawrence was right? Even if you do, you must show how *your* interpretation of a text manages to make sense of it.

3. *Feel free to concede that your analysis of the work isn't the only reasonable one.*   You can develop your main claim about a literary work partly by noting and addressing ways in which other readers may disagree with you about it. Bear in mind, though, that you will annoy your own audience if you come across as dogmatic. Be as fair as you can to views different from yours. Actually, your readers will appreciate it if at times you concede that yours isn't the only reasonable interpretation of the work. For example, while offering your own explanation of a character's behavior, you can admit that other accounts of it are possible. You can even specify one or more of these alternatives. Of course, you would still try to make a case for *your* explanation, perhaps by saying why it's *more plausible* or *more helpful* than its rivals. But speak of these competitors with respect, instead of just dismissing them with scorn.

Sample Student Paper: First Draft

The following is Abby's first complete draft of her paper. Eventually, she revised this draft after a group of her classmates reviewed it and after she reflected further on it herself. For the moment, though, read this first version, and decide what you would have said to her about it.

```
Abby Hazelton
Professor Ramsey
English 102
4 March —
                     The Passage of Time in
                    "The Solitary Reaper"
    William Wordsworth, one of the most famous writers in
the movement known as British Romanticism, liked to write
about beautiful features of the countryside. In his poem
"The Solitary Reaper," the speaker enthuses over a girl
who sings as she works in the fields. Yet although he is
enraptured by her "melancholy strain," he is unsure what
it is about because she is using a Scottish dialect that
he cannot understand. By contrast, the subject of the
poem itself seems much clearer. The very title of the
poem refers to the singing girl, and the subsequent lines
repeatedly praise her song as wonderfully haunting. Nev-
ertheless, the poem has puzzling aspects. Many readers
```

are likely to wonder if they are supposed to find the speaker guilty of cultural and class superiority when he, as a British intellectual, treats a Scottish peasant girl as a spectacle. Another issue, the one I focus on in my paper, arises when the final stanza shifts to past tense. In the first three stanzas, the speaker uses present tense, as if he is currently observing the singer whom he describes. In the concluding stanza, however, the speaker uses verbs such as "sang," "saw," and "listen'd," as if he is <u>recalling</u> his encounter with her. How can we explain this inconsistency? One possible justification for the final shift to past tense is that it reminds us of the speaker's inability to halt the passage of time. Even though he would like to freeze the encounter, time goes on. Perhaps, therefore, the poem's real subject is the idea that time is always in flux. Indeed, even before the final stanza, the speaker betrays an awareness that he can't bend time to his will.

Simply by virtue of the shift to past tense, the last stanza indicates that time goes on despite the speaker's wishes. But other elements of this stanza convey the same notion. Recalling his experience of the girl's singing, the speaker reports that he was "motionless and still," yet in the very next line he admits that he eventually moved: "I mounted up the hill." When the speaker says that "The Maiden sang / As if her song could have no end-ing," the words "As if" are significant, implying that the song did end for him in reality. Similarly, the poem itself has to end at some point. In fact, it concludes with the words "no more," which stress that the singer and her song now belong to the speaker's past. Only in his "heart," apparently, can he retain them. Furthermore, the medium of print can never convey the sound of music. In fact, prior to recording technology, music was the most fleeting of media, its notes fading with each new moment. By seeking to transmit music, the speaker ensures that he will wind up being frustrated by time.

     Even if the final stanza's shift of tense is jarring,
the first three stanzas give hints that the speaker will
end up defeated by time. Significantly, the poem's very
first word is "Behold." In issuing this command, the
speaker evidently hopes that other people will abandon
all motion and gaze at the singer, basking in her song.
The speaker reinforces this call for paralysis with the
command that begins line 4: "Stop here." Yet, as if
acknowledging limits to his control, he adds "or gently
pass!" Besides referring to other human beings, these
commands seem directed at time itself. The speaker hopes
that time, too, will "Stop" and "Behold." Even at this
point in the poem, however, he realizes that time is
inclined to "pass," in which case he hopes that it will
at least move on "gently."
     The second stanza is chiefly concerned with space.
Comparing the girl's song to other sounds, the speaker
ranges from "Arabian sands" to "the seas / Among the farthest Hebrides." In the third stanza, however, he focuses
again on time. Trying to determine the subject of the
song, he expresses uncertainty about its time frame. He
wonders whether the song concerns "old, unhappy, far-off
things / And battles long ago" or instead deals with
"Familiar matter of to-day." Moreover, even if he suspects the song's subject is "Some natural sorrow, loss,
or pain," he is unsure whether this experience of despair
is confined to the past ("has been") or will reoccur
("may be again"). Whichever of the possibilities he
raises is true, the speaker is clearly limited in his
ability to figure out the song's relation to time. In
other words, he cannot force time into a meaningful pattern, let alone prevent its passing.
     By the end of the poem, the speaker seems as "soli-
tary" as the reaper. In addition to losing his experience
with her as time moves on, he is isolated in other ways.
Throughout the poem, actually, we don't see him in the
company of others. His opening "Behold" is directed at no

one in particular. Furthermore, we can't be sure he is
speaking to actual passers-by or, rather, to the poem's
hypothetical future readers. Nor, for all his praise of
the singer, does he apparently talk to her. Rather, he
gives the impression that he keeps at a distance. Even if
he did try to converse with the reaper, he himself would
still be "solitary" in the sense of failing to understand
her language and failing to communicate her song to his
readers. He does not even bother trying to reproduce some
of the song's words. Therefore, despite the speaker's
enchantment over the reaper, this poem is ultimately pessimistic. The speaker is left only with his memories of a
wonderful experience. He has lost the experience itself.

Revising

Most first drafts are far from perfect. Even experienced professional writers
often have to revise their work. Besides making changes on their own, many of
them solicit feedback from others. In various workplaces, writing is collaborative,
with coauthors exchanging ideas as they try to improve a piece. Remain open to
the possibility that your draft needs changes, perhaps several. Of course, you are
more apt to revise extensively if you have given yourself enough time. Conversely,
you will not feel able to change much of your paper if it is due the next day. You
will also limit your ability to revise if you work only with your original manuscript,
scribbling possible changes between the lines. This practice amounts to conser-
vatism, for it encourages you to keep passages that really ought to be overhauled.

You may have trouble, however, improving a draft if you are checking many
things in it at once. Therefore, read the draft repeatedly, looking at a different
aspect of it each time. A good way to begin is to outline the paper you have written and then compare that outline with your original one. If the two outlines differ, your draft may or may not need adjusting; perhaps you were wise to swerve
from your original plan. In any case, you should ponder your departures from
that plan, considering whether they were for the best.

If, like Abby, you are writing an argument paper, here are some topics and
questions you might apply as you review your first draft. Some of these considerations overlap. Nevertheless, take them in turn rather than all at once.

Logic

- Will my audience see that the issue I am focusing on is indeed an issue?
- Will the audience be able to follow the logic of my argument?
- Is the logic as persuasive as it might be? Is there more evidence I can
  provide? Do I need to identify more of my warrants?
- Have I addressed all of my audience's potential concerns?

Organization

- Does my introduction identify the issue that I will focus on? Does it state my main claim?
- Will my audience be able to detect and follow the stages of my argument?
- Does the order of my paragraphs seem purposeful rather than arbitrary?
- Have I done all I can to signal connections within and between sentences? Within and between paragraphs?
- Have I avoided getting bogged down in mere summary?
- Will my conclusion satisfy readers? Does it leave any key questions dangling?

Clarity

- Does my title offer a good preview of my argument?
- Will each of my sentences be immediately clear?
- Am I sure how to define each word that I have used?

Emphasis

- Have I put key points in prominent places?
- Have I worded each sentence for maximum impact? In particular, is each sentence as concise as possible? Do I use active verbs whenever I can?

Style

- Are my tone and level of vocabulary appropriate?
- Will my audience think me fair-minded? Should I make any more concessions?
- Do I use any mannerisms that may distract my readers?
- Have I used any expressions that may annoy or offend?
- Is there anything else I can do to make my paper readable and interesting?

Grammar

- Is each of my sentences grammatically correct?
- Have I punctuated properly?

Physical Appearance

- Have I followed the proper format for quotations, notes, and bibliography?
- Are there any typographical errors?

We list these considerations from most to least important. When revising a draft, think first about matters of logic, organization, and clarity. There is little point in fixing the grammar of particular sentences if you are going to drop them later because they fail to advance your argument.

As we noted, a group of Abby's classmates discussed her draft. Most of these students seemed to like her overall argument, including her main issue and claim. Having been similarly confused by the poem's shift of tense, they appreciated the light that Abby shed on it. They were impressed by her willingness to examine the poem's specific words. They especially liked her closing analogy between the reaper and the speaker himself. Nevertheless, the group made several comments about Abby's paper that she took as suggestions for improvement. Ultimately, she decided that the following changes were in order.

1. *She should make her introduction more concise.*   The first draft is so long and dense that it may confuse readers instead of helping them sense the paper's main concerns. This problem is common to first drafts. In this preliminary phase, many writers worry that they will fail to generate *enough* words; they are hardly thinking about how to restrain themselves. Moreover, the writer of a first draft may still be unsure about the paper's whole argument, so the introduction often lacks a sharp focus. After Abby finished and reviewed her first draft, she saw ways of making her introduction tighter.

2. *She should rearrange paragraphs.*   After her introduction, Abby discussed the poem's last stanza in more detail. Then she moved back to stanza 1. Next, just before her paper's conclusion, she analyzed stanzas 2 and 3. Abby thought that the structure of her paper moved logically from the obvious to the hidden: the poem's last stanza emphasized the passage of time, and the earlier stanzas touched on this subject more subtly. Yet Abby's method of organization frustrated her classmates. They thought her paper would be easier to follow if, after the introduction, it moved chronologically through the poem. For them, her discussion of stanzas 2 and 3 seemed especially mislocated. Though she had positioned this discussion as her paper's climax, her classmates did not sense it to be her most significant and compelling moment of insight. Most important, they believed, were her comments on the *final* stanza, for that seemed to them the most important part of Wordsworth's poem. In other words, they thought the climax of the paper would be stronger if it focused on the climax of the poem. Abby hesitated to adopt her classmates' recommendation, but eventually she did so. When you read her final version, see if you like her rearrangement of paragraphs. Sometimes, though not always, a paper about a literary work seems more coherent if it does follow the work's chronological structure. And papers should indeed build to a climax, even if readers disagree about what its content should be.

3. *She should reconsider her claim that "the poem is ultimately pessimistic."* Abby's classmates thought this claim did not fully account for the poem's last two lines: "The music in my heart I bore, / Long after it was heard no more." While they agreed with her that the words "no more" emphasize that the singer has faded into the past, they disagreed that her song is lost as well, for it remains in the speaker's "heart." They noted that Abby had acknowledged this fact, but they felt she had done so too briefly and dismissively. In addition, one student encouraged her to think about poetry and music as ways of keeping memories alive. More specifically, he suggested that the speaker of "The Solitary Reaper" is Wordsworth himself, who is using this poem to preserve his memory of an actual encounter. After studying the poem again, Abby decided her classmates' ideas had merit, and she incorporated them into her revision. Of course, such advice is

not always worth heeding. Still, writers should accept the invitation to look more closely at whatever text they are analyzing.

Recognizing and Avoiding Fallacies

Although arguments presented in literary texts are often not logical, your arguments about these texts should be. Readers do not expect a lyric poet, for example, to present cogently reasoned arguments to her lover, nor a lament for the lost passions of youth to be anything but subjective. But different kinds of writing have different conventions. What works in poetry probably will not be appropriate in an argument. The kinds of serious arguments you are expected to create cannot be successful using heartfelt emotion alone. When writing about literature, shaky thinking might cause your audience to dismiss your ideas. Your claims and the assumptions behind them should be clear and reasoned. If they are not, you might be committing a **fallacy**, a common term for unsound reasoning.

In the next few paragraphs, we discuss several typical fallacies. Some of them are especially relevant to literary studies, and for all of them we provide examples related to "The Solitary Reaper." We don't want you to brood over this list, seeing it as a catalogue of sins to which you might fall prey. If you constantly fear being accused of fallacies, you might be too paralyzed to make claims at all! In our discussion of fallacies, we also identify circumstances in which your audience might *not* object to a particular fallacy. In addition, we suggest how a writer might revise such claims to be more persuasive. Indeed, the main value in studying fallacies is to identify ways you might develop arguments more effectively.

One of the most common fallacies, ***ad hominem*** (Latin: "toward the man"), is probably the easiest to commit because it is the hardest to resist. Instead of doing the hard work of analyzing the claim and the evidence, we simply ignore them and attack the character of the person making the argument. Instead of trying to figure out what is going on in a complex work of literature, we say, "How can you take seriously a poem about love written by a manic depressive who commits suicide?" It is best to focus on the message, not the messenger.

A related fallacy, **begging the question** (a kind of circular reasoning in which the statement being argued is already assumed to have been decided) is also involved in this example since it is assumed (not proved) that unstable poets canot have cogent insights about love.

In writing about "The Solitary Reaper," a classmate of Abby's ignored whatever argument the poem is making and focused on Wordsworth's credibility as an observer: "British intellectuals have been either romanticizing or degrading country people for centuries. Whatever Wordsworth thinks about the 'Highland lass' is almost certainly wrong." First of all, the narrator of the poem should not be automatically equated with the poet. When they write, poets and fictional writers construct personae that may or may not reflect their own views. Secondly, attacking Wordsworth is a fallacy for several reasons. It first has to be demonstrated that the poet is a British intellectual, that intellectuals have consistently misrepresented rural people, and that the narrator has done so in this particular case. The student's safest strategy is to revise her claim so that it deals with the words in the text, not her view of the poet's credibility.

Professional historians, mathematicians, and philosophers usually cite other professionals working in their field; that is, they **appeal to authority** to bolster their credibility. Disciplinary knowledge is created by a community of scholars that cite the ideas of its members as evidence for their claims. The warrant is that recognized authorities know what they're talking about. Quoting them is persuasive. But not completely: appeals to authority can also be fallacious. Literary critics, like other thinkers, often disagree. Just citing an expert does not conclusively prove your claim. A classmate of Abby's, for example, quotes a critic, Ian Lancashire, who says that the narrator "transcends the limitations of mortality," but the student does not give his own reasons or his own evidence for thinking this way. This appeal to critical authority without giving reasons or evidence is a fallacy because a sound argument would at least have to consider other critics. An argument is a reasoning process in which claims are supported, not simply asserted, even if from an expert.

A related fallacy from authority involves using quotations from unreliable sources. Although it is often a valuable tool, students sometimes use the Internet uncritically. If you went to the search engine *Google* and entered Wordsworth's "The Solitary Reaper," you would quickly find Ian Lancashire's essay; and since he is a professor at the University of Toronto with many publications on this and other Romantic topics, citing him is appropriate. But some of the commentators noted by the *Google* search are students, perhaps English majors who have written a paper for a course on the Romantic poets. Using them as authorities would damage your judgment and credibility.

Equally harmful to the soundness of your argument is to rely too heavily on personal experience as evidence for your claim. Personal experience can sometimes be compelling and authoritative. Feminist and postcolonial critics (see the Appendix, pp. 919–47) have successfully used their own experiences with discrimination to create cogent arguments. But they rarely rely exclusively on personal experience. Instead they blend relevant experience with textual and critical specifics. Telling your readers that "The Solitary Reaper" is factually flawed because you never saw harvesters work alone when you worked on your uncle's farm would be a fallacy.

Actually, the previous example of using personal experience as authority is also unsound because the personal sample is too small to warrant a reasonable conclusion. It is hard to convince your audience if you claim too much based on limited experience. A student arguing that "The Solitary Reaper" demonstrates that field workers are melancholy would be committing a **hasty generalization** fallacy. Simply claiming less would improve the argument. In fact, this student eventually changed the focus of her argument by doing research on other poems by Wordsworth, finding several which deal with young women in nature. Using "She Dwelt among Untrodden Ways" and "She Was a Phantom of Delight," the student argued that Wordsworth is so enraptured by the natural world that he often blurs the boundaries between people and nature.

Another common fallacy is *post hoc ergo propter hoc* (Latin: "because of this, then that"). Few of us escape this error in cause and effect. Many superstitions probably began because of this fallacy. A man breaks a mirror and bad luck follows. Did the mirror cause the bad luck? Logic says no, but the next day he breaks a leg, and a week later his car is stolen. The coincidence is often too tempting to resist. Does smoking marijuana lead to hard drugs? Logic says no, since you could argue just as plausibly that almost anything (carrots, beer, coffee) that comes before could be said to cause what comes after. Unless a clear, logical link between the two events is demonstrated, you might be accused of the *post hoc* fallacy.

In writing about "The Solitary Reaper," you might want to argue that "the melancholy strain" the traveler heard caused him to have a deeper appreciation for the beauty and mystery of rural people. But perhaps the narrator held such an opinion for a long time, or perhaps this is just one of dozens of such encounters that the poet remembers fondly. A sounder argument would focus on the cause and effect that does seem to be in the text: the mystery of the song's content adds to the emotional response the poet has.

Most of us commit a version of the **intentional fallacy** when we defend ourselves against someone we offended by saying, "That's not what I meant. It was just a joke." The problem arises because we are not always able to carry out our intentions. Perhaps our language is not precise enough, or perhaps our intention to be sincere or honest or witty gets mixed up with other intentions we have to sound intelligent, confident, or impressive. Students are often surprised when teachers tell them that a writer's stated intentions cannot be taken as the final word on a poem's meaning. "Wordsworth knows the poem better than anyone else" is an understandable retort. But that might not be the case. Wordsworth might not be the most astute reader of his own work. And he may not be fully aware of all that he intended. A student would be committing an intentional fallacy by arguing that "The Solitary Reaper" is written in the language used by the common man because Wordsworth says so in his "Preface to *Lyrical Ballads*." While this student should be commended for doing extra research, another student might point out that "Vale profound," "plaintive number," and "humble lay" seem conventionally poetic. Like others, this fallacy is easily revised by claiming less: "Most of 'The Solitary Reaper' is written in simple diction to approximate the language used by ordinary people."

When you try to destroy someone's argument by ignoring their main point and focusing on something marginal, you are attacking a **straw man**. The student who argues that we should dismiss Wordsworth's credibility as an observer because of "his absurd declaration that 'a voice so thrilling ne'er was heard' " is committing the straw man fallacy. While it is probably true that the song he hears is not the most thrilling in the history of the world, this is hardly Wordsworth's main point. Writers gain more credibility if they deal with a writer's strongest or main claim.

A favorite tactic of traditionalists trying to hold the line against change, the **slippery slope** fallacy is used to claim that if we allow one thing to happen, then slipping into catastrophe is just around the corner. If we don't prevent students from wearing gangsta rap fashions, gangs will eventually roam the hallways; if we allow the morning-after pill, sexual anarchy will follow. A small step is seen as precipitating an avalanche.

The following claim by a student anticipates something that simply is not logically called for: "Although Wordsworth probably means well, his praise for the 'Highland Lass' is a dangerous move since she is probably illiterate and full of rural biases and superstitions. His failure to discriminate will lead to loss of judgment and standards." Again, claiming less improves the argument: Wordsworth is less interested in the content ("Whate'er the theme") than in the "music in my heart," an emotional response that we hope doesn't carry over into his views on medicine, engineering, and economics.

We are all guilty at times of the fallacy of **oversimplification** — of not seeing the inevitable complexity of things. At the risk of committing a hasty generalization ourselves, it is probably the case that your instructor will be impressed if you look for complexity in literary texts and in your arguments. Seeing complexity is a consequence of hard thinking. There are rarely two sides to a question. More likely, there are a dozen plausible and reasonable perspectives. The cliché that the truth often appears in shades of gray rather than in than black and white gets at the idea that simple solutions are often the result of shallow thinking.

Complexity is not what the following claim reveals: "'The Solitary Reaper' is a poem about a traveler who hears a young girl 'singing by herself' and like a catchy ad, the tune stays with him." Being exposed to other viewpoints in class discussions and in peer-group revision can help this student avoid oversimplifying the experience Wordsworth has, one that touches on issues of mortality, the mysteries of emotional response, the purpose of poetry, and the power of the natural world. When Henry David Thoreau, the author of *Walden*, urged his contemporaries to live simply, he was talking about their lifestyles, not their thinking.

Non sequitur is a general catch-all fallacy that means "it does not follow." Some principle of logic has been violated when we make a claim that the evidence cannot support. In "The Solitary Reaper," it does not follow that because the Highland Lass "sings a melancholy strain," she herself is sad. She could be happy, absent-minded, or simply bored. Perhaps the song is a conventional ballad typically sung by workers to pass the time. Revising this fallacy, like many of the others, involves setting aside time in the revision process to look again at your claims and the assumptions behind them, carefully and objectively making a clear connection between your thesis and the evidence you say supports your claim.

Sample Student Paper: Revised Draft

Here is the new version of her paper that Abby wrote. Again, decide what you think of it.

```
Abby Hazelton
Professor Ramsey
English 102
11 March —
                 The Passage of Time in
                 "The Solitary Reaper"
     In William Wordsworth's poem "The Solitary Reaper,"
the speaker enthuses over a girl who sings as she works
```

in the fields. Throughout the poem, his rapture is evident. Yet in the last stanza, he makes a puzzling move, shifting to past tense after using present tense in the previous three stanzas. No longer does he seem to be currently observing the singer he describes; rather, now he seems to be recalling his encounter with her. One possible justification for this shift in tense is that it reminds us of the speaker's inability to halt the passage of time. Even though he would like to freeze the encounter, time goes on. Perhaps, therefore, the poem's real theme is that time is always in flux. Indeed, even before the final stanza, the speaker betrays an awareness that he can't bend time to his will.

Significantly, the poem's very first word is "Behold." In issuing this command, the speaker evidently hopes that other people will abandon all motion and gaze at the singer, basking in her song. The speaker reinforces this call for paralysis with the command that begins line 4: "Stop here." Yet, as if acknowledging limits to his control, he adds "or gently pass!" Besides referring to other human beings, these commands seem directed at time itself. The speaker hopes that time, too, will "Stop" and "Behold." Even at this point in the poem, however, he realizes that time is inclined to "pass," in which case he hopes that it will at least move on "gently."

The second stanza is chiefly concerned with space. Comparing the girl's song to other sounds, the speaker ranges from "Arabian sands" to "the seas / among the farthest Hebrides." In the third stanza, however, he focuses again on time. Trying to determine the subject of the song, he expresses uncertainty about its time frame. He wonders whether the song concerns "old, unhappy, far-off things / And battles long ago" or instead deals with "Familiar matter of to-day." Moreover, even if he suspects the song's subject is "Some natural sorrow, loss, or pain," he is unsure whether this experience of despair is confined to the past ("has been") or will reoccur ("may be again"). Whichever of the possibilities he raises is true, the speaker is clearly limited in his ability to figure out the song's relation to time. In other words, he cannot force time into a meaningful pattern, let alone prevent its passing.

Simply by virtue of the shift to past tense, the last stanza indicates that time goes on despite the speaker's wishes. But other elements of this stanza convey the same notion. Recalling his experience of the girl's singing, the speaker reports that he was "motionless and still," yet in the very next line he admits that he eventually moved: "I mounted up the hill." When the speaker says that "The Maiden sang / As if her song could have no ending," the words "As if" are significant, implying that the song did end for him in reality. Similarly, the poem itself has to end at some point. In fact, it concludes with the words "no more," which stress that the singer and her song now belong to the speaker's past. Only in his "heart," apparently, can he retain them.

This situation seems to leave the speaker as "solitary" as the reaper. Throughout the poem, actually, we don't see him in the company of others. His opening "Behold" is directed at no one in particular. Furthermore, we can't be sure he is speaking to actual passersby or, rather, to the poem's hypothetical future readers. Nor, for all his praise of the singer, does he apparently talk to her. Rather, he gives the impression that he keeps at a distance. Even if he did converse with the reaper, he himself would still be "solitary" in the sense of failing to understand her dialect and failing to communicate her words to his readers. As things stand, he is apparently unable or unwilling to reproduce any of the song's lyrics. Just as important, the medium of print can never convey the sound of music. In fact, prior to recording technology, music was the most fleeting of

```
media, its notes fading with each new moment. By seeking
to transmit music, the speaker ensures that he will wind
up being frustrated by time.

     Yet perhaps the singer and her song are preserved in
more than just the speaker's "heart." It can be argued
that they are also preserved by the poem, if only to a
limited extent. More generally, we can say that litera-
ture is a means by which human beings partially succeed
in perpetuating things. This idea seems quite relevant to
"The Solitary Reaper" if we suppose that the speaker is
the poet himself and that he actually witnessed the scene
he describes. If we make such assumptions, we can see
Wordsworth as analogous to the speaker. After all, both
engage in commemorative verbal art. Because time passes,
the "strains" that Wordsworth and the singer produce in
their efforts to preserve time are bound to be "melan-
choly." Still, their art matters, for through it they can
imaginatively "reap" experiences that would otherwise
fade.
```

To us, Abby's revision is more persuasive and compelling than her first draft. In particular, she has nicely complicated her claim about the poem's "pessimism." Nevertheless, we would hesitate to call this revision the definitive version of her paper. Maybe you have thought of things Abby could do to make it even more effective. In presenting her two drafts, we mainly want to emphasize the importance of revision. We hope, too, that you will remember our specific tips as you work on your own writing.

Writing a Comparative Paper

Much writing about literature *compares* two or more texts. After all, you can gain many insights into a text by noting how it resembles and differs from others. Throughout this book, therefore, we cluster texts, encouraging you to trace similarities and differences within each set. For instance, the chapters in Part One repeatedly present clusters that treat various aspects of work. At the moment, we offer suggestions for writing a comparative paper, a task you may be assigned in your course.

To aid our discussion, we ask you to reread Wordsworth's "The Solitary Reaper" and then read the following poem, which is by the contemporary American poet Ted Kooser (b. 1939). Though born in Iowa, Kooser has spent much of his life in Nebraska. There he has not only produced several volumes of poetry but also worked for an insurance company, from which he eventually retired as vice president. This selection is from Kooser's book *Weather Central* (1994).

TED KOOSER
Four Secretaries

All through the day I hear or overhear
their clear, light voices calling
from desk to desk, young women whose fingers
play casually over their documents,

setting the incoming checks to one side,   5
the thick computer reports to the other,
tapping the correspondence into stacks
while they sing to each other, not intending

to sing nor knowing how beautiful
their voices are as they call back and forth,   10
singing their troubled marriage ballads,
their day-care, car-park, landlord songs.

Even their anger with one another
is lovely: the color rising in their throats,
their white fists clenched in their laps,   15
the quiet between them that follows.

And their sadness — how deep and full of love
is their sadness when one among them
is hurt, and they hear her calling
and gather about her to cry.   [1994]   20

A class like yours sensed value in comparing Wordsworth's poem with Kooser's. So the students proceeded to brainstorm lists of specific similarities and differences — something you might do to start analyzing texts you bring together. For these two poems, the class came up with the following comparisons:

SIMILARITIES

"Reaper" and "Secretaries" both have titles that refer to
    women at work.
Both poems describe women <u>singing</u> at work.
The speakers in both poems "hear or overhear" the singing
    rather than being its direct audience.
In general, the speakers in both poems seem alone or
    detached as they observe their subjects.

Both speakers seem to find beauty in the people they
    observe.
Both speakers refer to sorrow: the speaker of "Reaper"
    detecting "a melancholy strain," the speaker of "Sec-
    retaries" noting "sadness."
Both poems use fairly simple language for their time
    period.

DIFFERENCES

The speaker of "Reaper" observes one woman; the speaker
    of "Secretaries" four.
The reaper is literally singing; the secretaries only
    metaphorically so.
The speaker of "Reaper" is referring to a particular
    event of singing, whereas the speaker of "Secre-
    taries" describes singing that occurs daily.
"Reaper" is set in the countryside; "Secretaries" in an
    office.
The woman in "Reaper" seems to sing to herself, whereas
    the women in "Secretaries" sing to one another.
The speaker of "Reaper" cannot understand the singer's
    words, but the speaker of "Secretaries" seems to know
    what the women are singing about.
The speaker of "Reaper" refers consistently to the
    woman's singing, but the speaker of "Secretaries"
    gives more attention to the four women's "calling,"
    using that word in the first and last stanzas.
While each stanza of "Reaper" ends with a period, the
    first two stanzas of "Secretaries" end with sentences
    that spill over into the next sentences.
"Reaper" ends by focusing on the speaker's "heart," but
    "Secretaries" ends with an expression of heartfelt
    sympathy by the women whom the speaker has been
    observing.

As you plan your own comparative paper, lists such as these can help you
organize your thoughts. To be sure, this class did not immediately think of all the
similarities and differences it ended up noting. Usually, going beyond obvious

points of comparison is a gradual process, for which you should give yourself plenty of time. Similarly, once you have made lists such as the above, take time to decide which similarities and differences truly merit your attention. At most, only a few can be part of your paper's main issue and claim.

Unfortunately, many students writing a comparative analysis are content to put forth main claims such as these:

```
There are many similarities and differences between "The
    Solitary Reaper" and "Four Secretaries."
While "The Solitary Reaper" and "Four Secretaries" have
    many similarities, in many ways they are also dif-
    ferent.
While "The Solitary Reaper" and "Four Secretaries" are
    different in many ways, they are similar in others.
```

Several problems arise with these common methods of introducing a comparative paper. For one thing, they give the reader no preview of the specific ideas to come. Indeed, they could have been written by someone who never bothered to read the two poems, for any two texts are similar in certain ways and different in others. Furthermore, these sorts of claims leave no meaningful and compelling way of organizing the paper. Rather, they encourage the writer to proceed arbitrarily, noting miscellaneous similarities and differences on impulse. More precisely, claims such as these fail to identify the *issue* driving the paper. Why compare Wordsworth's and Kooser's poems in the first place? Comparison is a means to an end, not an end in itself. What important question is the writer using these two texts to answer? In short, what's at stake?

A more fruitful approach, we think, is to write a *weighted* comparative analysis — that is, an argument chiefly concerned with *one* text more than others. When professional literary critics compare two texts, often they mainly want to answer a question about just one of them. They bring in the second text because they believe that doing so helps them address the issue they are raising about their key text. True, a good paper can result even when you treat equally all texts you discuss. But you are more apt to write a paper that seems purposeful and coherent if you focus basically on one work, using comparisons to resolve some issue concerning it.

Sample Comparative Paper

The following paper by student Marla Tracy demonstrates weighted comparative analysis. The author refers to Wordsworth's "The Solitary Reaper" as well as Kooser's "Four Secretaries," but she is mainly concerned with Kooser's poem. She brings up Wordsworth's poem not to do comparison for its own sake but to address a question she has about Kooser's text.

Marla Tracy
Professor James
English 12
23 February —

When Singing Is Not Singing

In Ted Kooser's poem "Four Secretaries," the speaker
praises the "singing" of the title characters, whose
voices he listens to as they perform their daily clerical
duties nearby. His admiration for the music of women
workers has precedent in poetry. In William Wordsworth's
"The Solitary Reaper," a poem from the early nineteenth
century, the speaker glories in the tune that a Scottish
country girl produces as she "cuts and binds the grain."
But whereas the reaper of Wordsworth's poem really does
sing, such is not the case with Kooser's secretaries.
When the speaker in Kooser's poem refers to their "singing," he is being metaphorical. Given that he more or
less imagines the women's singing, what should we conclude? We may be tempted to see the poem as chiefly
exposing the speaker's own warped mind. But a more plausible interpretation is that the speaker reveals how the
secretaries really interact. Though his reference to
their "singing" is figurative, his imaginative use of
the word enables him to convey the sensitivity they show
one another.

Some elements of Kooser's poem do encourage readers
to see it as a psychological case study of the speaker.
Rather than mind his own business, he clearly likes to
"hear or overhear" the secretaries' conversations and
thus seems at least a bit nosey. Perhaps he is even
indulging the power of observation typically granted a
boss. (Kooser has been an insurance executive, and maybe
the poem is about his own office.) At the same time, the
speaker can be thought emotionally detached, especially
when he reports the women's occasional sadness, notes
that they console one another, and yet apparently does
not offer them comfort himself. Moreover, he risks

seeming sadistic when he declares that "their anger with one another / is lovely," for here he appears to find beauty in their pain. His claim that the women are "singing," then, can be considered another sign that his own idiosyncrasies are the poem's main concern.

Ultimately, though, the poem seems much more about the secretaries than about the speaker. If the speaker has quirks, they are rather understated; throughout the poem, his tone remains calm. Again, Wordsworth's "Solitary Reaper" provides an instructive contrast, for its speaker puts his emotions blatantly on display. Besides declaring that the reaper's song is "welcome," "thrilling," and "plaintive," he beseeches passers-by to "Behold her" and "tell me what she sings." Compared with Wordsworth's speaker, Kooser's is fairly reticent, focusing on the secretaries' behavior rather than his own personal passions.

The speaker admits that the secretaries are "not intending / to sing." Indeed, this phrase spills over from the second to the third stanza, thereby emphasizing the speaker's confession. At the same time, the speaker's claim that they are in some sense "singing" enables him to consider the various possible actions that this word can entail. In fact, because "singing" here is metaphorical rather than literal, the poem can more easily raise an issue of definition: What do we <u>want</u> "singing" to mean?

The speaker answers this question by focusing largely on the interplay of the women's voices. In the first stanza, he describes their "light voices calling / from desk to desk"; in the third, he observes that "they call back and forth." With these references to "calling," the speaker defines and praises "singing" as the vocal building of relationships. Perhaps Kooser even wants us to think of the "call and response" tradition of African American religious music, which helped keep that community together during years of oppression. In any case, the poem's emphasis on the social nature of singing

differs yet again from the focus of "The Solitary
Reaper," where singing is a solo affair.

Of course, Kooser's fourth stanza complicates the
poem's emphasis on the secretaries' emotional bonds. By
noting that sometimes the secretaries experience "anger
with one another," the speaker seems to put their feeling
of community in question. But "the quiet" mentioned in
the stanza's last line seems merely a typical pause in
a song, not the ceasing of it. While the singing of
Wordsworth's reaper is eventually "no more," the singing
of these secretaries seems bound to resume. Furthermore,
anger can be considered another form of emotional commitment. Often, people are angry with someone precisely
because they expect a lot from that person. Actually,
when the speaker asserts that "Even their anger with one
another / is lovely," perhaps "lovely" here means "full
of love," a phrase that the speaker subsequently uses to
describe the secretaries' "sadness."

However we interpret the wording of the fourth stanza,
the poem's basic drift is clear. It ends with a concrete
image of the secretaries' bonding. More specifically,
three of the secretaries comfort the fourth. Rather than
make her "cry" alone, they join her in her tears, reminding us that "singing" in this poem is collective.

Marla gains much from comparing Kooser's poem with Wordsworth's. By
bringing up "The Solitary Reaper" in her first paragraph, she establishes that
"Four Secretaries" belongs to a poetic tradition, while also pointing out this contemporary text's distinctiveness (its references to "singing" are metaphorical). In
paragraph 3, she contrasts Kooser's speaker with Wordsworth's to reinforce her
claim that Kooser's poem is more about the secretaries. In paragraphs 5 and 6,
she contrasts the two poems again, as part of her argument that "singing" in
Kooser's poem is an ongoing social relationship. Clearly, though, Marla focuses
her paper on Kooser's poem, not both. By concentrating chiefly on "Four Secretaries," she enables herself to develop a logical analysis, whereas focusing on both
poems would encourage her to wander through various similarities and differences at random.

Perhaps you know the advice usually given about how to organize a comparative paper. Traditionally, writers aiming to compare two texts learn of two
options: (1) discuss one text and then move to the other, comparing it with the
first; (2) discuss the texts together, noting each of their similarities and differences

in turn. Both of these alternatives make sense and provide a ready-made structure for your paper; either can result in a coherent essay. Still, a weighted analysis such as Marla's — an analysis that focuses on one text more than another — is more likely than either of the alternatives to seem the logical evolution of a pointed claim.

SUMMING UP

* Writing an argument about a literary work involves *preliminary writing, exploring, planning, composing,* and *revising.* (pp. 41–56 and 61–64)

* *Preliminary writing* draws on several kinds of tactics. These may include commenting in the text's margins; note-taking; freewriting; creating a "dialectical notebook"; and playfully revising the text. (pp. 44–45)

* *Exploring* requires you to read the work critically, noting questions it raises for you. Does the text confirm your predictions about it? Does rereading it change your mind about it? What are its audience, content, and form, including its key moments and patterns? Does the text present an argument? How does it compare to other texts? What do other readers — including your classmates and teacher — think about it? (pp. 41–47)

* *Planning* combines several activities. These include selecting a text to write about; envisioning your audience; identifying your main issue, claim, and evidence as you anticipate challenges to them; deciding what warrants to use; and determining how you will organize your argument. (pp. 47–51)

* Keep in mind the following tips when you are *composing* a draft.

Come up with a title that previews your main claim. (p. 51)

Indicate the text you are analyzing, as well as your main issue and claim, at the beginning of your paper. (pp. 52–53)

Accommodate your style to your audience and purpose. (p. 52)

Try to signal relations between sentences; vary your sentence lengths; use active verbs; keep grammatical subjects and verbs close together; avoid shifting tenses. (pp. 54–56)

Quote selectively. (p. 52)

You may briefly summarize your argument in the conclusion of your paper, but you may also: make concessions; evaluate the work you have analyzed; identify questions you still have; bring up a relevant personal experience; identify implications of your argument; indicate further research you want to do. (p. 56)

(*continued on next page*)

┌───┐

────────────────── **SUMMING UP** ──────────────────

- *Revising* **is a process.** Read your draft repeatedly, looking at a different aspect of it each time, in particular its logic, organization, clarity, emphases, style, grammar, and physical appearance. (pp. 61–64)

- **Avoid long stretches of mere plot summary.** (p. 57)

- **Be cautious about relating the work to its author's life, and be alert to fallacious reasoning in your arguments and those of others.** (pp. 57–58 and 64–67)

- **Feel free to concede that your analysis of a literary work is not the only reasonable interpretation of it.** (p. 58)

- **Favor** *weighted* **comparisons if you are writing a paper that compares two or more literary works.** (pp. 70–73)

└───┘

4

Making Arguments about Stories

Short stories can be said to resemble novels. Above all, both are works of fiction. Yet the difference in length matters. As William Trevor, a veteran writer of short stories, has observed, short fiction is "the art of the glimpse; it deals in echoes and reverberations; craftily it withholds information. Novels tell all. Short stories tell as little as they dare." Maybe Trevor overstates the situation when he claims that novels reveal everything. All sorts of texts feature what literary theorist Wolfgang Iser calls "gaps." Still, Trevor is right to emphasize that short stories usually tell much less than novels do. They demand that you understand and evaluate characters on the basis of just a few details and events. In this respect, short stories resemble poems. Both tend to rely on compression rather than expansion, seeking to affect their audience with a sharply limited number of words.

Short stories' focused use of language can make the experience of reading them wonderfully intense. Furthermore, you may end up considering important human issues as you try to interpret the "glimpses" they provide. Precisely because short stories "tell as little as they dare," they offer you much to ponder as you proceed to write about them.

In discussing that writing process, we refer often to the three stories that follow. The stories tell of the work that a healthy person does as he or she encounters someone physically suffering. The first story, "The Use of Force," is by a writer more known for his poetry, William Carlos Williams (1883–1963). Even as he produced literature, Williams served as a doctor in his hometown of Rutherford, New Jersey, as well as in the nearby city of Paterson. The story presented here, which appeared in Williams's 1938 collection *Life along the Passaic River*, is one of several based on his medical work during America's Great Depression. The second selection, "A Visit of Charity," is by a pioneer of the modern American short story, Eudora Welty (1909–2001), who spent most of her life in her hometown of Jackson, Mississippi. This particular piece appeared in Welty's first collection, *A Curtain of Green and Other Stories*, published in 1941. The final story, "The Gift of Sweat," is by a contemporary American writer, Rebecca Brown (b. 1956). It is the lead-off piece in her 1994 book *The Gifts of the Body*, a sequence of short stories narrated by a woman who does housekeeping for people with AIDS—a kind of service work that Brown, too, has done.

79

WILLIAM CARLOS WILLIAMS
The Use of Force

They were new patients to me, all I had was the name, Olson. Please come down as soon as you can, my daughter is very sick. When I arrived I was met by the mother, a big startled looking woman, very clean and apologetic who merely said, Is this the doctor? and let me in. In the back, she added. You must excuse us, doctor, we have her in the kitchen where it is warm. It is very damp here sometimes.

The child was fully dressed and sitting on her father's lap near the kitchen table. He tried to get up, but I motioned for him not to bother, took off my overcoat and started to look things over. I could see that they were all very nervous, eyeing me up and down distrustfully. As often, in such cases, they weren't telling me more than they had to, it was up to me to tell them; that's why they were spending three dollars on me.

The child was fairly eating me up with her cold, steady eyes, and no expression to her face whatever. She did not move and seemed, inwardly, quiet; an unusually attractive little thing, and as strong as a heifer in appearance. But her face was flushed, she was breathing rapidly, and I realized that she had a high fever. She had magnificent blond hair, in profusion. One of those picture children often reproduced in advertising leaflets and the photogravure sections of the Sunday papers.

She's had a fever for three days, began the father and we don't know what it comes from. My wife has given her things, you know, like people do, but it don't do no good. And there's been a lot of sickness around. So we tho't you'd better look her over and tell us what is the matter.

As doctors often do I took a trial shot at it as a point of departure. Has she had   5
a sore throat?

Both parents answered me together, No . . . No, she says her throat don't hurt her.

Does your throat hurt you? added the mother to the child. But the little girl's expression didn't change nor did she move her eyes from my face.

Have you looked?

I tried to, said the mother, but I couldn't see.

As it happens we had been having a number of cases of diphtheria in the   10
school to which the child went during that month and we were all, quite apparently, thinking of that, though no one had as yet spoken of the thing.

Well, I said, suppose we take a look at the throat first. I smiled in my best professional manner and asking for the child's first name I said, come on, Mathilda, open your mouth and let's take a look at your throat.

Nothing doing.

Aw, come on, I coaxed, just open your mouth wide and let me take a look. Look, I said opening both hands wide, I haven't anything in my hands. Just open up and let me see.

Such a nice man, put in the mother. Look how kind he is to you. Come on, do what he tells you to, he won't hurt you.

At that I ground my teeth in disgust. If only they wouldn't use the word   15
"hurt" I might be able to get somewhere. But I did not allow myself to be hurried
or disturbed but speaking quietly and slowly I approached the child again.

As I moved my chair a little nearer suddenly with one catlike movement
both her hands clawed instinctively for my eyes and she almost reached them too.
In fact she knocked my glasses flying and they fell, though unbroken, several feet
away from me on the kitchen floor.

Both the mother and father almost turned themselves inside out in embarrassment and apology. You bad girl, said the mother, taking her and shaking her
by one arm. Look what you've done. The nice man . . .

For heaven's sake, I broke in. Don't call me a nice man to her. I'm here to
look at her throat on the chance that she might have diphtheria and possibly die
of it. But that's nothing to her. Look here, I said to the child, we're going to look
at your throat. You're old enough to understand what I'm saying. Will you open it
now by yourself or shall we have to open it for you?

Not a move. Even her expression hadn't changed. Her breaths however were
coming faster and faster. Then the battle began. I had to do it. I had to have a
throat culture for her own protection. But first I told the parents that it was
entirely up to them. I explained the danger but said that I would not insist on a
throat examination so long as they would take the responsibility.

If you don't do what the doctor says you'll have to go to the hospital, the   20
mother admonished her severely.

Oh yeah? I had to smile to myself. After all, I had already fallen in love with
the savage brat, the parents were contemptible to me. In the ensuing struggle
they grew more and more abject, crushed, exhausted while she surely rose to
magnificent heights of insane fury of effort bred of her terror of me.

The father tried his best, and he was a big man but the fact that she was his
daughter, his shame at her behavior and his dread of hurting her made him
release her just at the critical times when I had almost achieved success, till I
wanted to kill him. But his dread also that she might have diphtheria made him
tell me to go on, go on though he himself was almost fainting, while the mother
moved back and forth behind us raising and lowering her hands in an agony of
apprehension.

Put her in front of you on your lap, I ordered, and hold both her wrists.

But as soon as he did the child let out a scream. Don't, you're hurting me.
Let go of my hands. Let them go I tell you. Then she shrieked terrifyingly, hysterically. Stop it! Stop it! You're killing me!

Do you think she can stand it, doctor! said the mother.   25

You get out, said the husband to his wife. Do you want her to die of diphtheria?

Come on now, hold her, I said.

Then I grasped the child's head with my left hand and tried to get the
wooden tongue depressor between her teeth. She fought, with clenched teeth,
desperately! But now I also had grown furious — at a child. I tried to hold myself
down but I couldn't. I know how to expose a throat for inspection. And I did my
best. When finally I got the wooden spatula behind the last teeth and just the

point of it into the mouth cavity, she opened up for an instant but before I could see anything she came down again and gripped the wooden blade between her molars. She reduced it to splinters before I could get it out again.

Aren't you ashamed, the mother yelled at her. Aren't you ashamed to act like that in front of the doctor?

Get me a smooth-handled spoon of some sort, I told the mother. We're going through with this. The child's mouth was already bleeding. Her tongue was cut and she was screaming in wild hysterical shrieks. Perhaps I should have desisted and come back in an hour or more. No doubt it would have been better. But I have seen at least two children lying dead in bed of neglect in such cases, and feeling that I must get a diagnosis now or never I went at it again. But the worst of it was that I too had got beyond reason. I could have torn the child apart in my own fury and enjoyed it. It was a pleasure to attack her. My face was burning with it. 30

The damned little brat must be protected against her own idiocy, one says to one's self at such times. Others must be protected against her. It is a social necessity. And all these things are true. But a blind fury, a feeling of adult shame, bred of a longing for muscular release are the operatives. One goes on to the end.

In the final unreasoning assault I overpowered the child's neck and jaws. I forced the heavy silver spoon back of her teeth and down her throat till she gagged. And there it was — both tonsils covered with membrane. She had fought valiantly to keep me from knowing her secret. She had been hiding that sore throat for three days at least and lying to her parents in order to escape just such an outcome as this.

Now truly she was furious. She had been on the defensive before but now she attacked. Tried to get off her father's lap and fly at me while tears of defeat blinded her eyes. [1938]

EUDORA WELTY
A Visit of Charity

It was mid-morning — a very cold, bright day. Holding a potted plant before her, a girl of fourteen jumped off the bus in front of the Old Ladies' Home, on the outskirts of town. She wore a red coat, and her straight yellow hair was hanging down loose from the pointed white cap all the little girls were wearing that year. She stopped for a moment beside one of the prickly dark shrubs with which the city had beautified the Home, and then proceeded slowly toward the building, which was of whitewashed brick and reflected the winter sunlight like a block of ice. As she walked vaguely up the steps she shifted the small pot from hand to hand; then she had to set it down and remove her mittens before she could open the heavy door.

"I'm a Campfire Girl. . . . I have to pay a visit to some old lady," she told the nurse at the desk. This was a woman in a white uniform who looked as if she were cold; she had close-cut hair which stood up on the very top of her head exactly like a sea wave. Marian, the little girl, did not tell her that this visit would give her a minimum of only three points in her score.

"Acquainted with any of our residents?" asked the nurse. She lifted one eyebrow and spoke like a man.

"With any old ladies? No—but—that is, any of them will do," Marian stammered. With her free hand she pushed her hair behind her ears, as she did when it was time to study Science.

The nurse shrugged and rose. "You have a nice *multiflora cineraria*° there,"   5
she remarked as she walked ahead down the hall of closed doors to pick out an old lady.

There was loose, bulging linoleum on the floor. Marian felt as if she were walking on the waves, but the nurse paid no attention to it. There was a smell in the hall like the interior of a clock. Everything was silent until, behind one of the doors, an old lady of some kind cleared her throat like a sheep bleating. This decided the nurse. Stopping in her tracks, she first extended her arm, bent her elbow, and leaned forward from the hips—all to examine the watch strapped to her wrist; then she gave a loud double-rap on the door.

"There are two in each room," the nurse remarked over her shoulder.

"Two what?" asked Marian without thinking. The sound like a sheep's bleating almost made her turn around and run back.

One old woman was pulling the door open in short, gradual jerks, and when she saw the nurse a strange smile forced her old face dangerously awry. Marian, suddenly propelled by the strong, impatient arm of the nurse, saw next the sideface of another old woman, even older, who was lying flat in bed with a cap on and a counterpane° drawn up to her chin.

"Visitor," said the nurse, and after one more shove she was off up the hall.   10

Marian stood tongue-tied; both hands held the potted plant. The old woman, still with that terrible, square smile (which was a smile of welcome) stamped on her bony face, was waiting. . . . Perhaps she said something. The old woman in bed said nothing at all, and she did not look around.

Suddenly Marian saw a hand, quick as a bird claw, reach up in the air and pluck the white cap off her head. At the same time, another claw to match drew her all the way into the room, and the next moment the door closed behind her.

"My, my, my," said the old lady at her side.

Marian stood enclosed by a bed, a washstand and a chair; the tiny room had altogether too much furniture. Everything smelled wet—even the bare floor. She held on to the back of the chair, which was wicker and felt soft and damp. Her heart beat more and more slowly, her hands got colder and colder, and she could not hear whether the old women were saying anything or not. She could not see them very clearly. How dark it was! The window shade was down, and the only door was shut. Marian looked at the ceiling. . . . It was like being caught in a robbers' cave, just before one was murdered.

"Did you come to be our little girl for a while?" the first robber asked.   15

---

multiflora cineraria: A house plant with brightly colored flowers and heart-shaped leaves.
counterpane: Bedspread.

Then something was snatched from Marian's hand—the little potted plant.

"Flowers!" screamed the old woman. She stood holding the pot in an undecided way. "Pretty flowers," she added.

Then the old woman in bed cleared her throat and spoke. "They are not pretty," she said, still without looking around, but very distinctly.

Marian suddenly pitched against the chair and sat down in it.

"Pretty flowers," the first old woman insisted. "Pretty—pretty . . ."　　　　20

Marian wished she had the little pot back for just a moment—she had forgotten to look at the plant herself before giving it away. What did it look like?

"Stinkweeds," said the other old woman sharply. She had a bunchy white forehead and red eyes like a sheep. Now she turned them toward Marian. The fogginess seemed to rise in her throat again, and she bleated, "Who—are—you?"

To her surprise, Marian could not remember her name. "I'm a Campfire Girl," she said finally.

"Watch out for the germs," said the old woman like a sheep, not addressing anyone.

"One came out last month to see us," said the first old woman.　　　　25

A sheep or a germ? wondered Marian dreamily, holding on to the chair.

"Did not!" cried the other old woman.

"Did so! Read to us out of the Bible, and we enjoyed it!" screamed the first.

"Who enjoyed it!" said the woman in bed. Her mouth was unexpectedly small and sorrowful, like a pet's.

"We enjoyed it," insisted the other. "You enjoyed it—I enjoyed it."　　　　30

"We all enjoyed it," said Marian, without realizing that she had said a word.

The first old woman had just finished putting the potted plant high, high on the top of the wardrobe, where it could hardly be seen from below. Marian wondered how she had ever succeeded in placing it there, how she could ever have reached so high.

"You mustn't pay any attention to old Addie," she now said to the little girl. "She's ailing today."

"Will you shut your mouth?" said the woman in bed. "I am not."

"You're a story."　　　　35

"I can't stay but a minute—really, I can't," said Marian suddenly. She looked down at the wet floor and thought that if she were sick in here they would have to let her go.

With much to-do the first old woman sat down in a rocking chair—still another piece of furniture!—and began to rock. With the fingers of one hand she touched a very dirty cameo pin on her chest. "What do you do at school?" she asked.

"I don't know . . ." said Marian. She tried to think but she could not.

"Oh, but the flowers are beautiful," the old woman whispered. She seemed to rock faster and faster; Marian did not see how anyone could rock so fast.

"Ugly," said the woman in bed.　　　　40

"If we bring flowers—" Marian began, and then fell silent. She had almost said that if Campfire Girls brought flowers to the Old Ladies' Home, the visit would count one extra point, and if they took a Bible with them on the bus and read it to the old ladies, it counted double. But the old woman had not listened, anyway; she was rocking and watching the other one, who watched back from the bed.

"Poor Addie is ailing. She has to take medicine — see?" she said, pointing a horny finger at a row of bottles on the table, and rocking so high that her black comfort shoes lifted off the floor like a little child's.

"I am no more sick than you are," said the woman in bed.

"Oh, yes you are!"

"I just got more sense than you have, that's all," said the other old woman, nodding her head.

"That's only the contrary way she talks when *you all* come," said the first old lady with sudden intimacy. She stopped the rocker with a neat pat of her feet and leaned toward Marian. Her hand reached over — it felt like a petunia leaf, cling-ing and just a little sticky.

"Will you hush! Will you hush!" cried the other one.

Marian leaned back rigidly in her chair.

"When I was a little girl like you, I went to school and all," said the old woman in the same intimate, menacing voice. "Not here — another town . . ."

"Hush!" said the sick woman. "You never went to school. You never came and you never went. You never were anything — only here. You never were born! You don't know anything. Your head is empty, your heart and hands and your old black purse are all empty, even that little old box that you brought with you you brought empty — you showed it to me. And yet you talk, talk, talk, talk, talk all the time until I think I'm losing my mind! Who are you? You're a stranger — a perfect stranger! Don't you know you're a stranger? Is it possible that they have actually done a thing like this to anyone — sent them in a stranger to talk, and rock, and tell away her whole long rigmarole? Do they seriously suppose that I'll be able to keep it up, day in, day out, night in, night out, living in the same room with a ter-rible old woman — forever?"

Marian saw the old woman's eyes grow bright and turn toward her. This old woman was looking at her with despair and calculation in her face. Her small lips suddenly dropped apart, and exposed a half circle of false teeth with tan gums.

"Come here, I want to tell you something," she whispered. "Come here!"

Marian was trembling, and her heart nearly stopped beating altogether for a moment.

"Now, now, Addie," said the first old woman. "That's not polite. Do you know what's really the matter with old Addie today?" She, too, looked at Marian; one of her eyelids dropped low.

"The matter?" the child repeated stupidly. "What's the matter with her?"

"Why, she's mad because it's her birthday!" said the first old woman, begin-ning to rock again and giving a little crow as though she had answered her own riddle.

"It is not, it is not!" screamed the old woman in bed. "It is not my birthday, no one knows when that is but myself, and will you please be quiet and say noth-ing more, or I'll go straight out of my mind!" She turned her eyes toward Marian again, and presently she said in the soft, foggy voice, "When the worst comes to the worst, I ring this bell, and the nurse comes." One of her hands was drawn out

45

50

55

from under the patched counterpane—a thin little hand with enormous black freckles. With a finger which would not hold still she pointed to a little bell on the table among the bottles.

"How old are you?" Marian breathed. Now she could see the old woman in bed very closely and plainly, and very abruptly, from all sides, as in dreams. She wondered about her—she wondered for a moment as though there was nothing else in the world to wonder about. It was the first time such a thing had happened to Marian.

"I won't tell!"

The old face on the pillow, where Marian was bending over it, slowly gath- 60 ered and collapsed. Soft whimpers came out of the small open mouth. It was a sheep that she sounded like—a little lamb. Marian's face drew very close, the yellow hair hung forward.

"She's crying!" She turned a bright, burning face up to the first old woman.

"That's Addie for you," the old woman said spitefully.

Marian jumped up and moved toward the door. For the second time, the claw almost touched her hair, but it was not quick enough. The little girl put her cap on.

"Well, it was a real visit," said the old woman, following Marian through the doorway and all the way out into the hall. Then from behind she suddenly clutched the child with her sharp little fingers. In an affected, high-pitched whine she cried, "Oh, little girl, have you a penny to spare for a poor old woman that's not got anything of her own? We don't have a thing in the world—not a penny for candy—not a thing! Little girl, just a nickel—a penny—"

Marian pulled violently against the old hands for a moment before she was 65 free. Then she ran down the hall, without looking behind her and without looking at the nurse, who was reading *Field & Stream* at her desk. The nurse, after another triple motion to consult her wrist watch, asked automatically the question put to visitors in all institutions: "Won't you stay and have dinner with *us*?"

Marian never replied. She pushed the heavy door open into the cold air and ran down the steps.

Under the prickly shrub she stooped and quickly, without being seen, retrieved a red apple she had hidden there.

Her yellow hair under the white cap, her scarlet coat, her bare knees all flashed in the sunlight as she ran to meet the big bus rocketing through the street.

"Wait for me!" she shouted. As though at an imperial command, the bus ground to a stop.

She jumped on and took a big bite out of the apple.   [1941] 70

REBECCA BROWN
The Gift of Sweat

I went to Rick's every Tuesday and Thursday morning. I usually called before I went to see if he wanted me to pick up anything for him on the way. He never used to ask me for anything until once when I hadn't had breakfast and I stopped at this place a couple blocks from him, the Hostess with the Mostest, to get a cinnamon roll and I got two, one for him. I didn't really think he'd eat it because he was so organic. He had this incredible garden on the side of the apartment with tomatoes and zucchinis and carrots and he used to do all his own baking. I also got two large coffees with milk. I could have eaten it all if he didn't want his. But when I got to his place and asked him if he'd had breakfast and showed him what I'd brought, he squealed. He said those cinnamon rolls were his absolute favorite things in the world and he used to go to the Hostess on Sunday mornings. He said he'd try to be there when they were fresh out of the oven and get the best ones, the ones from the center of the pan, which are the stickiest and softest. It was something he used to do for himself on Sunday, which was not his favorite day.

So after that when I called him before I went over and asked if he wanted anything, he'd still say no thanks, and then I would say, "How about the usual," meaning the rolls and coffee, and he'd say he'd love it.

So one morning when I called and asked him if he wanted "the usual" and he said he didn't, I was surprised.

He said, "Not today!" He sounded really chirpy. "Just get your sweet self over here. I got a surprise for you."

I said OK and that I'd see him in a few. I made a quick cup of coffee and downed the end of last night's pizza and went over. I was at his place in half an hour.

I always knocked on the door. When he was there he'd always shout, "Hello! Just a minute!" and come let me in. It took him a while to get to the door but he liked being able to answer it himself, he liked still living in his own place. If he wasn't at home I let myself in and read the note he would have left me—that he had an appointment or something, or if there was some special thing he wanted me to do. Then I would clean or do chores. I used to like being there alone sometimes. I could do surprises for him, like leave him notes under his pillow or rearrange his wind-up toys so they were kissing or other silly things. Rick loved surprises.

But this one morning when I knocked on the door it took him a long time to answer. Then I heard him trying to shout, but he sounded small. "Can you let yourself in?"

I unlocked the door and went in. He was in the living room on the futon. It was usually up like a couch to sit on, but it was flat like a bed and he was lying on it.

I went over and sat on the floor by the futon. He was lying on his side, facing away from me, curled up. His knees were near his chest.

"Rick?" I said. I put my hand on his back.

He didn't move, but said, "Hi," very quietly.

"What's going on?" I said.

He made a noise like a little animal.

"You want me to call your doc?"

He swallowed a couple of times. Then he said, "I called UCS. Margaret is coming over to take me to the hospital."

"Good," I said, "she'll be here soon."

5

10

15

"Yeah," he said. Then he made that animal noise again. He was holding his stomach. "I meant to call you back," he said, "to tell you you didn't need to come over today."

"That's OK, Rick. I'm glad I'm here. I'm glad I'm with you right now."

"I didn't feel bad when you called." He sounded apologetic. "It was so sudden."

"Your stomach?"   20

He tried to nod. "Uh-huh. But everywhere some."

He was holding the corner of his quilt, squeezing it.

"I was about to get in the shower. I wanted to be all clean before you came over. It was so sudden."

"Oh, Rick," I said, "I'm sorry you hurt so much."

"Thank you."   25

"Is there anything I can do before Margaret gets here?"

"No." He swallowed again. I could smell his breath. "No thank you."

Then his mouth got tight and he squeezed the quilt corner, then he was pulsing it, then more like stabs. He started to shake. "I'm cold," he said.

I pulled the quilt over most of him. It had a pattern of moon and stars. "I'm gonna go get another blanket," I said.

"Don't go," he said really fast. "Please don't go."   30

"OK," I said, "I'll stay here."

"I'm so cold," he said again.

I touched his back. It was sweaty and hot.

I got onto the futon. I slid on very carefully so I wouldn't jolt him. I lay on my side behind him. I could feel him shaking. I put my left arm around his middle. I slipped my right hand under his head and touched his forehead. It was wet and hot. I held my hand on his forehead a couple of seconds to cool it. Then I petted his forehead and up through his hair. His hair was wet too. I combed my fingers through his wet hair to his ponytail. I said, "Poor Rick. Poor Ricky."

He was still shaking. I pulled my body close to him so his butt was in my lap   35 and my breasts and stomach were against his back. I pressed against him to warm him. He pulled my hand onto his stomach. I opened my hand so my palm was flat across him, my fingers spread. He held his hand on top of mine, squeezing it like the quilt. I could feel the sweat of his hand on the back of mine, and of his stomach, through his shirt, against my palm. I could feel his pulse all through him; it was fast.

I tightened my arms around him as if I could press the sickness out.

After a while he started to shake less. He was still sweating and I could feel more wet on the side of his face from crying.

When Margaret came we wrapped his coat around him and helped him, one on either side of him, to the car. Rick hunched and kept making noises. I helped him get in and closed the door behind him while Margaret got in the driver's side. While she was fumbling for her keys I ran around to her and asked her, "You want me to come with you?"

She said, "You don't need to. We'll be OK."

Rick didn't say anything.   40

I leaned in and said, "Your place will be all clean when you come back home, Rick."

He tried to smile.

"I'll call you later," said Margaret. She put her hand up and touched the side of my face. "You're wet," she told me.

I touched my face. It was wet. "I'll talk to you later," I said to her.

"I'll see you later, Rick," I said.   45

He nodded but didn't say anything. His face was splotched. Margaret found her keys and started the car.

I went back into his apartment. When I closed the door behind me I could smell it. It was a slight smell, sour, but also partly sweet. It was the smell of Rick's sweat.

I started cleaning. I usually started in the kitchen, but as soon as I set foot in there and saw the kitchen table I couldn't. I turned around and stood in the hall a second and held my breath. After a while I let it out.

I did everything else first. I stripped the bed and put a load of laundry in. I vacuumed and dusted. I dusted all his fairy gear, his stones and incense burners and little statues and altars. I straightened clothes in his closet he hadn't worn in ages. I untangled ties and necklaces. I put cassettes back in their cases and reshelved them. I took out the trash. I did it all fast because I wanted to get everything done, but I also wished I could stretch it out and still be doing it and be here when he came home as if he would come home soon.

I cleaned the bathroom. I shook cleanser in the shower and sink and cleaned   50
them. I sprayed Windex on the mirror. When I was wiping it off I saw myself. My face was splotched. My t-shirt had a dark spot. I put my hands to it and sniffed them. They smelled like me, but also him. It was Rick's sweat. I put my hands up to my face and I could smell him in my hands. I put my face in my hands and closed my eyes. I stood there like that a while then I went to the kitchen.

What was on the kitchen table was this: his two favorite coffee mugs, his and what used to be Barry's. There was a Melitta over one full of ground coffee, all ready to go. There were two dessert plates with a pair of cinnamon rolls from the Hostess, the soft sticky ones from the center of the pan.

I thought of Rick going down there, how long it took him to get down the street, how early he had to go to get the best ones. I thought of him planning a nice surprise, of him trying to do what he couldn't.

Rick told me once how one of the things he missed most was Sunday breakfast in bed. Every Saturday night he and Barry would watch a movie on the VCR in the living room. They'd pull the futon out like a bed and watch it from there and pretend they were at a bed-and-breakfast on vacation. Rick would make something fabulous and they'd eat it together. That was when he was still trying to help Barry eat. After Barry died Rick started going to the Hostess, especially on Sundays, because he had to get out of the apartment. He used to go to the Hostess all the time until it got to be too much for him. That's about the time I started coming over.

I sat at the table he'd laid for us. I put my elbows on the table and folded my hands. I closed my eyes and lowered my head and put my forehead in my hands. I tried to think how Rick would think, I tried to imagine Barry.

After a while I opened my eyes. He'd laid the table hopefully. I took the food he meant for me, I ate.   55
                                                                          [1994]

A WRITING EXERCISE

Once you have read the three stories, write your reaction to them off the top of your head, spending at least ten minutes on each. For each story, note any personal experience affecting your response as well as one or more questions that you have about the story even after you have finished reading it. Remember that question-posing is a good way to prepare for a formal paper on the story, enabling you to identify issues worth writing about at length.

Students' Personal Responses to the Stories

Here is some freewriting that students did about the three stories you have just read.

Alison Caldwell on Williams's "The Use of Force":

    I can understand why the doctor got furious at the
    girl. He was asking her to open her mouth for her own
    good, and she started physically attacking him. On the
    other hand, I can sympathize with the girl. I can remem-
    ber being scared of doctors when I was that young. I
    dreaded having to get various shots. The girl in the
    story is probably not used to seeing doctors in the first
    place, so this one is bound to seem especially frighten-
    ing to her. I can sympathize with her parents, too,
    because they only want what's best for their daughter and
    they're doing everything they can to assist the doctor. I
    was kind of shocked to see the doctor fuming with anger
    at them. Of course, his reaction to them is one of the
    interesting things about this story, along with the
    strange respect that he feels in a way for the girl. I
    guess the biggest issue for me is what we're to make of
    the doctor's sort of identification with the girl even as
    he gets mad at her and she strongly resists him. There's
    some connection between these two characters that I need
    to figure out. I notice that at the end her eyes are

"blinded" and not long before he's possessed by a "blind fury." Probably I should explore this particular similarity more.

Monica Albertson on Welty's "A Visit of Charity":

I'm not sure which character I should be sympathizing with in Welty's story. Right away I disliked the girl because she wasn't really interested in seeing the old women. I don't know why the story is called "A Visit of Charity," since she just wanted to get more points. And yet I have to admit that when I was younger I was sort of like her. I remember one time that my church youth group had to sing Christmas carols at an old folks' home, and I was uneasy about having to meet all these ancient men and women I didn't know, some of whom could barely walk or talk. It's funny, because I was always comfortable around my grandparents, but I have to confess that being around all those old people at once spooked me a little. I smiled a lot at them and joined in the singing and helped hand out candy canes afterward. But I couldn't wait to leave. Once I did, I felt proud of myself for going there, but I guess I also felt a little guilty because I didn't really want to be there at all. So, maybe I'm being hypocritical when I criticize the girl in Welty's story for insensitivity. Anyway, I expected that Welty would present in a good light any old women that Marian encountered, just to emphasize that Marian was being unkind and that it's really sad for people to have to live in a retirement home (or senior citizens center or whatever they're calling such places nowadays). And yet the two old women she meets are cranky and unpleasant. Even the receptionist doesn't come off all that good. If I were Marian, I probably would have left even sooner than she did! Maybe Welty didn't want us to sympathize with anyone in the story, and maybe that's OK. I tend to want a story to make at least some of the characters sympathetic, but maybe it's unfair of me to demand that.

Still, I'm wondering if I'm not appreciating Welty's
characters enough. When the two old women argue, should
we side with one of them, or are we supposed to be bothered by them both? Are we supposed to think any better of
the girl by the time she leaves? The apple she eats immediately made me think of the Adam and Eve story, but I
don't know what I'm supposed to do with that parallel.

Jon Pike on Brown's "The Gift of Sweat":

The narrator's tone in this story is very quiet, very
matter-of-fact and understated, but the story moved me
all the same. I can't help feeling sorry for poor Ricky,
who seems to be dying from AIDS and wanted to give the
narrator a really good breakfast in return for the work
she's done for him and the friendship she's given him.
But I think the story is mostly about the narrator's
helplessness, especially when Ricky is taken off to the
hospital and she's left with nothing directly to do for
him. I think it's interesting that we're not told right
away what she seeks in the kitchen. Instead, she tells
about how she thoroughly cleaned Ricky's apartment, as if
that was the only way she could think of to help him at
this point. When she finally reveals that what's in the
kitchen is the breakfast he has prepared for her, I wonder why she the sight of it originally disturbed her and
even made her leave the room, plunging herself into her
cleaning work. It's as if she couldn't bear taking this
"gift" from him when he risked his health to get it for
her. I wonder, though, why the story is called "The Gift
of Sweat" rather than "The Gift of Breakfast." Maybe it's
because the breakfast is the result of Ricky's sweat, in
the sense that he physically struggled to prepare it. In
the same way, the narrator sweats as she cleans the
apartment. So which is more important, the similarities
between these two people or their differences?

Before any of these students could produce a full-length paper on the story
they freewrote on, they had to do more writing and thinking. Yet simply by jotting

down some observations and questions, they provided themselves with seeds of a paper. Compare your thoughts to theirs. To what extent did you react to the stories as they did? In what ways, if any, did your responses differ from theirs? What would you say to them if they were your classmates, especially as they proceeded to write more developed arguments?

The Elements of Short Fiction

Whether discussing them in class or writing about them, you will improve your ability to analyze stories like Williams's, Welty's, and Brown's if you grow familiar with typical elements of short fiction. These elements include plot and structure, point of view, characterization, setting, imagery, language, and theme.

Plot and Structure

For many readers, the most important element in any work of fiction is **plot**. As they turn the pages of a short story, their main question is, What will happen next? In reading Williams's story, probably you were curious, as the narrator is, to know whether the girl is concealing an infected throat. In reading Welty's story, quite possibly you wanted to know how Marian's visit to the rest home would turn out. In reading Brown's story, most likely you hoped to learn why Rick was unable to let the narrator into his home. Furthermore, if a friend unfamiliar with Williams's, Welty's, and Brown's stories asked you what each was about, probably you would begin by summarizing their plots.

A WRITING EXERCISE

In one or two sentences, summarize what you take to be the plot of Welty's story. Then read the following three summaries of her plot, which were written by three other students. Finally, list a few similarities and differences you notice as you compare the three summaries with one another and with yours.

> *Jerry's summary:* A girl visits an Old Ladies' Home just so she can add some points to her record as a Campfire Girl. Much to her dismay, she encounters two roommates who fight a lot with each other, and their unpleasantness eventually causes her to flee.
>
> *Carla's summary:* A young girl named Marian who starts off basically interested in only herself is forced to consider the suffering of old people when she spends time with two old women at a retirement home. Eventually she leaves in fear and disgust, but as she leaves she eats an apple, which implies that she is no longer as innocent as she was and that she is maybe a little more prepared to acknowledge what goes on in the wider world.
>
> *Matt's summary:* A really insensitive girl meets two old women, and though in many respects she is put off by both of them, she can't help being intrigued by the one who is sick in bed. Maybe she becomes

more aware of mortality at this point, but if so she has trouble facing it
and in the end runs away.

To an extent, the students point out different things. For instance, only Carla
mentions the apple, and only Matt observes that Marian is momentarily interested in the bedridden woman. Also, these two students are more willing than
Jerry is to speculate about Marian's final state of mind. At the same time, Carla's
summary ends on a slightly more upbeat note than Matt's. She emphasizes that
Marian has perhaps become more open-minded, while Matt concludes by pointing out that Marian nevertheless flees.

Any summary of Welty's story will be somewhat personal. It is bound to
reflect the reader's own sense of who the story's main characters are, which of
their actions are significant, how these actions are connected, and what principles these actions illustrate. Were you to compare summaries with Jerry, Carla,
and Matt in class, each of you might learn much from discussing experiences and
beliefs that influenced your accounts.

Even so, you do not have to treat every summary of Welty's story as merely
subjective. Probably some accounts of it are more attentive than others to actual
details of Welty's text. If a reader declared that Marian loves visiting the Old
Ladies' Home, many other readers would rightfully disagree, pointing out that
Marian dashes off. If you discussed Welty's story with Jerry, Carla, and Matt, the
four of you would probably consider which summary of it is best. Furthermore,
probably each of you would argue for your respective candidates by pointing to
specific passages in Welty's text. Ultimately, you might still prefer your own summary. On the other hand, you might wind up adopting someone else's, or you
might want to combine aspects of various summaries you have read.

Jerry's, Carla's, and Matt's summaries do have some features in common,
indicating that there are certain basic things for you to consider when you examine a short story's plot. For example, plots usually center on human beings, who
can be seen as engaging in actions, as being acted upon, or both. In recounting the
plot of Welty's story, each of the three students focuses on Marian. Furthermore,
each describes her as acting (she "encounters," "flees," "spends time," "leaves,"
"eats," "meets," "runs away") *and* as being affected by other forces (the "un-
pleasantness" of the old women "causes her to flee"; she is "forced to consider"
their pain; she is "put off" as well as "intrigued"). Also, most short stories put characters into a high-pressure situation, whether for dark or comic effect. To earn the
merit points she desires, Marian has to contend with the feuding roommates.

Besides physical events, a short story may involve psychological developments. Each student here points to mental changes in Welty's heroine. According to Jerry, Marian experiences "dismay." According to Carla, she "starts off
basically interested in only herself" but perhaps becomes "a little more prepared
to acknowledge what goes on in the wider world." According to Matt, she starts
off "really insensitive," perhaps grows "more aware of mortality," yet then "has
trouble facing it." Many stories do show characters undergoing complete or partial conversions. Meanwhile, a number of stories include characters who stick to
their beliefs but gain a new perspective on them.

Jerry, Carla, and Matt connect Marian's visit to the rest home with her subsequent behavior. Like most plot summaries, in other words, theirs bring up relations of cause and effect. The novelist and short-story writer E. M. Forster refers to cause and effect in his famous definition of plot. To Forster, a plot is not simply one incident after another, such as "the king died and then the queen died." Rather, it is a situation or a whole chain of events in which there are reasons *why* characters behave as they do. Forster's example: "The king died, and then the queen died of grief."

Writers of short stories do not always make cause and effect immediately clear. Another possible plot, Forster suggests, is "The queen died, no one knew why, until it was discovered that it was through grief at the death of the king." In this scenario, all of the characters lack information about the queen's true psychology for a while, and perhaps the reader is in the dark as well. Indeed, many short stories leave the reader ignorant for a spell. For instance, only near the conclusion of her story does Welty reveal that prior to entering the rest home, Marian had put an apple under the shrub. Why does the author withhold this key fact from you? Perhaps Welty was silent about the apple because, had she reported it right away, its echoes of Eve might have overshadowed your interpretation of the story as you read. Worth considering are issues of effect: what the characters' behavior makes you think of them and what impact the author's strategies have on you.

When you summarize a story's plot, you may be inclined to put events in chronological order. But remember that short stories are not always linear. Often they depart from strict chronology, moving back and forth in time. Consider the following opening sentences, both of which deal with a funeral ceremony. They come from two of the stories featured in this book, William Faulkner's "A Rose for Emily," reprinted in Chapter 13, and Andre Dubus's "Killings," reprinted in Chapter 9:

> When Miss Emily Grierson died, our whole town went to her funeral: the men through a sort of respectful affection for a fallen monument, the women mostly out of curiosity to see the inside of her house, which no one save an old manservant—a combined gardener and cook—had seen in at least ten years.

> On the August morning when Matt Fowler buried his youngest son, Frank, who had lived for twenty-one years, eight months, and four days, Matt's older son, Steve, turned to him as the family left the grave and walked between their friends, and said: "I should kill him."

Probably Faulkner's opening makes you wonder why Emily Grierson kept people out of her house. Probably Dubus's opening makes you wonder how Frank died and whom Steve means by "him." Eventually the authors do answer these questions by moving their stories back in time. Faulkner presents episodes in Emily's life, returning only at the end of the story to the time after her death. Dubus spends much of his story's first half on flashbacks that inform you about Frank's murder; then, Dubus returns to the present and shows Matt's effort to avenge his son. Many literary critics use the term **discourse** for a text's actual ordering of events. Chronologically, Emily Grierson's funeral comes near the end of Faulkner's short story. Yet it appears at the beginning of his discourse. Chronologically, Frank's funeral is sandwiched between several events. Yet it is the start of Dubus's discourse.

Alice Adams, author of many short stories, offers a more detailed outline of their typical **structure**. She has proposed the formula **ABDCE**: these letters stand for **action**, **background**, **development**, **climax**, and **ending**. More precisely, Adams has said that she sometimes begins a story with an action, follows that action with some background information, and then moves the plot forward in time through a major turning point and toward some sort of resolution. Not all writers of short stories follow this scheme. In fact, Adams does not always stick to it. Certainly a lot of short stories combine her background and development stages, moving the plot along while offering details of their characters' pasts. And sometimes a story will have several turning points rather than a single distinct climax. But if you keep Adams's formula in mind, if only as a common way to construct short stories, you will be better prepared to recognize how a story departs from chronological order.

The first paragraph of Welty's story seems to be centered on *action*. Marian arrives at the Old Ladies' Home and prepares to enter it. Even so, Welty provides some basic information in this paragraph, describing Marian and the rest home as if the reader is unfamiliar with both. Yet only in the second paragraph do you learn Marian's name and the purpose of her visit. Therefore, Welty can be said to obey Adams's formula, beginning with *action* and then moving to *background*. Note, however, that the second paragraph features *development* as well. By explaining to the receptionist who she is and why she is there, Marian takes a step closer to the central event, her meeting with the two roommates. The remainder of the story keeps moving forward in time.

Williams's story "The Use of Force" begins with a paragraph that establishes the *background* to the narrator's visit. Nevertheless, the paragraph is brief and the background slight, with the narrator acknowledging that "They were new patients to me, all I had was the name, Olson." Then we are quickly plunged into *action*, as the narrator starts to describe his experience at the Olson house. Even as the story proceeds, we continue to receive some background information, as when the narrator tells us of an outbreak of diphtheria at the child's school. Yet, for the most part, we sense *development* as the narrator wages an increasingly violent struggle to open the child's mouth.

Brown's story "The Gift of Sweat" begins with two paragraphs mostly devoted to background. They tell you about the arrangements between the narrator and Rick prior to the particular day that will be the story's focus. With the opening words of her third paragraph—"So one morning when I called"— Brown signals that she has spent the previous two on background material. Now, she implies, she will turn to developing the story's main situation.

What about *climax*, Adams's fourth term? Traditionally, the climax of a story has been defined as a peak moment of drama appearing near the end. Also, it is usually thought of as a point when at least one character commits a significant act, experiences a significant change, makes a significant discovery, learns a significant lesson, or perhaps does all these things. With Welty's story, you could argue that the climax is when Marian asks Addie her age, meets with refusal, sees Addie crying, and tries to bolt. Certainly this is a dramatic moment, involving intense display of emotion resulting in Marian's departure. But Welty indicates, too, that Marian here experiences inner change. When she looks on Addie "as though there was nothing else in the world to wonder about," this is "the first time such a thing had happened to Marian."

Adams's term *ending* may seem unnecessary. Why would anyone have to be reminded that stories end? Yet a story's climax may engage readers so much that they overlook whatever follows. If the climax of Welty's story is Marian's conversation with tearful Addie, then the ending is basically in four parts: the plea that Addie's roommate makes to Marian as she is leaving; Marian's final encounter with the receptionist; Marian's retrieval of the apple; and her escape on the bus, where she bites into the apple. Keep in mind that the ending of a story may relate somehow to its beginning. The ending of Welty's "A Visit of Charity," for instance, brings the story full circle. Whereas at the start Marian gets off a bus, hides the apple, and meets the receptionist, at the conclusion she rushes by the receptionist, recovers the apple, and boards another bus. However a story ends, ask yourself if any of the characters has changed at some point between start and finish. Does the conclusion of the story indicate that at least one person has developed in some way, or does it leave you with the feeling of lives frozen since the start? As Welty's story ends, readers may have various opinions about Marian. Some may find that she has not been changed all that much by her visit to the home, while others may feel that it has helped her mature.

A common organizational device in short stories is **repetition**. It takes various forms. First, a story may repeat various words; in Williams's story, for example, the word "look" appears again and again. Second, a story may involve repeated actions. In Welty's story, the two roommates repeatedly argue; Marian travels by bus at beginning and end; and the receptionist consults her wristwatch both when Marian arrives and when she leaves. Third, a story may echo previous events. In Brown's story, the narrator mentions her earlier visits to Rick and his past trips to the Hostess. Of course, in various ways a story's current situation will be new. In Brown's story, Rick's present condition makes his trek to the Hostess a big step for him, and he winds up in pain.

Point of View

A short story may be told from a particular character's perspective or **point of view**. Probably you have noticed that Williams's and Brown's stories are written in the **first person**; each is narrated by someone using the pronoun *I*. With every first-person story, you have to decide how much to accept the narrator's point of view, keeping in mind that the narrator may be psychologically complex. How objective does the narrator seem in depicting other people and events? In what ways, if any, do the narrator's perceptions seem influenced by his or her personal experiences, circumstances, feelings, values, and beliefs? Does the narrator seem to have changed in any way since the events recalled? How reasonable do the narrator's judgments seem? At what moments, if any, do you find yourself disagreeing with the narrator's view of things?

Not every short story is narrated by an identifiable person. Many of them are told by what has been traditionally called an **omniscient narrator**. The word *omniscient* means "all-knowing" and is often used as an adjective for God. An omniscient narrator is usually a seemingly all-knowing, objective voice. This is the kind of voice operating in the first paragraph of Welty's story. There, Marian is described in an authoritatively matter-of-fact tone that appears detached from her: "Holding a potted plant before her, a girl of fourteen jumped off the bus in front of the Old Ladies' Home." Keep in mind, though, that a story may primarily rely on an omniscient narrator and yet at some points seem immersed in a character's perspective. This, too, is the case with Welty's story. Consider the following passage about Marian:

> Everything smelled wet — even the bare floor. She held on to the back of the chair, which was wicker and felt soft and damp. Her heart beat more and more slowly, her hands got colder and colder, and she could not hear whether the old women were saying anything or not. She could not see them very clearly. How dark it was! The window shade was down, and the only door was shut. Marian looked at the ceiling. . . . It was like being caught in a robbers' cave, just before one was murdered.

The passage remains in the third person, referring to "she" rather than to "I." Nevertheless, the passage seems intimately in touch with Marian's physical sensations. Indeed, the sentence "How dark it was!" seems something that Marian would say to herself. Similarly, the analogy to the robbers' cave may be Marian's own personal perception, and as such, the analogy may reveal more about her own state of mind than about the room. Many literary critics use the term **free indirect style** for moments like this, when a narrator otherwise omniscient conveys a particular character's viewpoint by resorting to the character's own language.

First-person singular narration and omniscient narration are not the only methods for telling a story. For instance, William Faulkner's "A Rose for Emily" (in Chapter 13) is narrated by "we," the first-person plural. Even more striking is the technique that Pam Houston uses in her short story "How to Talk to a Hunter" (Chapter 13). The story seems to be narrated from an unnamed woman's point of view, but she avoids the word *I* and instead consistently refers to *you*. While Houston's method is unusual, it serves as a reminder that short stories can be told in all sorts of ways.

Throughout this book, we encourage you to analyze an author's strategies by considering the options that he or she faced. You may better understand a short story's point of view if you think about the available alternatives. For example, how would you have reacted to Welty's story if it had focused on Addie's perceptions more than on Marian's? With Williams's or Brown's story, how would you have felt if the narrator had been omniscient?

A WRITING EXERCISE

Choose a passage from Williams's, Welty's, or Brown's story and rewrite it from another point of view. Then exchange your rewritten passage with a classmate's response to this assignment. Finally, write a paragraph analyzing your classmate's revision. Specifically, compare the revision with the original passage that your classmate chose, noting any differences in effect.

Characters

Although we have been discussing plots, we have also referred to the people caught up in them. Any analysis you do of a short story will reflect your understanding and evaluation of its **characters**. Rarely does the author of a story provide you with extended, enormously detailed biographies. Rather, you see the story's characters at select moments of their lives. To quote William Trevor again, the short story is "the art of the glimpse."

A WRITING EXERCISE

Choose any character from the three stories featured here. Off the top of your head, jot down at least five adjectives you think apply to that character. Next, exchange lists with a classmate. When you look at your classmate's list, circle the adjective that surprises you most, even if it deals with another character. Finally, write a brief essay in which you consider how applicable that adjective is. Do you agree with your classmate that it suits the character he or she chose? Why, or why not?

You may want to judge characters according to how easily you can identify with them. Yet there is little reason for you to read works that merely reinforce your prejudices. Furthermore, you may overlook the potential richness of a story if you insist that its characters fit your usual standards of behavior. An author can teach you much by introducing you to the complexity of people you might automatically praise or condemn in real life. If you tend to admire home-care providers, Brown's portrayal of one can be thought-provoking for you, since this particular provider is not sure what to do with the breakfast that Rick has set out in his kitchen. You may be tempted to dismiss the roommates in Welty's story as unpleasant, even "sick"; in any case, take the story as an opportunity to explore *why* women in a rest home may express discontent.

One thing to consider about the characters in a story is what each basically desires. At the beginning of Welty's story, for example, Marian is hardly visiting the Old Ladies' Home out of "charity," despite that word's presence in the story's title. Rather, Marian hopes to earn points as a Campfire Girl. Again, characters in a story may change, so consider whether the particular characters you are examining alter their thinking. Perhaps you feel that Marian's visit broadens her vision of life; then again, perhaps you conclude that she remains much the same.

Reading a short story involves relating its characters to one another. In part, you will be determining their relative importance in the story. When a particular character seems to be the story's focus, he or she is referred to as the story's **protagonist**. Many readers would say that the doctor is the protagonist of Williams's story, Marian is the protagonist of Welty's, and the home-care worker is the protagonist of Brown's. When the protagonist is in notable conflict with another character, the latter is referred to as the **antagonist**. In Williams's story, the child seems to assume this role, since the narrator winds up fighting her. To be sure, the relationship between a protagonist and an antagonist may show nuances worth exploring. For example, Williams's narrator does not simply hate his patient. Rather, he wants to help her, and he grudgingly admires her stubbornness while harboring scorn for her parents.

Even a seemingly minor character can perform some noteworthy function in a story. Take Brown's character Margaret, who is apparently the narrator's supervisor. On the surface, Margaret seems much less important to the story than the narrator and Rick do. For one thing, Margaret's appearance is brief: she arrives, she exchanges some words with the narrator, and then she drives off with Rick. Before she goes, though, Margaret points out that the narrator is sweaty, and thus she makes the reader aware of this fact. Furthermore, Brown uses Margaret to put the narrator in a psychologically complex situation. Once Margaret takes Rick away, the narrator must figure out how to express her concern for him, which she ultimately does by thoroughly cleaning his home. On the whole, Margaret is more a plot device than a fully developed personality. Nevertheless, she merits study if only as an example of author Brown's craft.

In many short stories, characters are allies or enemies. But as the story proceeds, they may alter their relationships, forging new bonds or developing new conflicts. Although Welty's Marian initially finds both roommates unpleasant, she grows more conscious of the tension *between* them, and then for a moment she sympathizes with Addie. It is possible, too, for one character to be ambivalent about another, feeling both drawn and opposed to that person. We have already suggested that such is the case with Williams's narrator as he struggles with the child. One might argue, too, that the two roommates in Welty's story have a love-hate relationship, needing each other's company even as they bicker. As perhaps you have found in your own experience, human relationships are often far from simple. Works of literature can prove especially interesting when they suggest as much.

What power and influence people can achieve have often depended on particular traits of theirs. These include their gender, social class, race, ethnic background, nationality, sexual orientation, and the kind of work they do. Because these attributes can greatly affect a person's life, pay attention to them if an author refers to them in describing a character. For instance, in Brown's story, the narrator indicates her gender as she recalls how she lay down with pain-stricken Rick: "I pulled my body close to him so his butt was in my lap and my breasts and stomach were against his back." But would the story be significantly different if she were a man? Perhaps. Certainly it is interesting that she has become a caretaker of what was formerly the home of a male couple. Also, note that the physical position described in the quoted passage is that of mother with fetus. In fact, just before the passage, the narrator addresses Rick as if he were her child, changing his name to "Ricky." Remember, too, that for many people, Mother is the original Hostess with the Mostest. Still, you may feel that we are making too much of gender here. If so, what would you point to in arguing that view?

Typically, characters express views of one another, and you have to decide how accurate these are. Some characters will seem wise observers of humanity. Others will strike you as making distorted statements about the world, revealing little more than their own biases and quirks. And some characters will seem to fall in the middle, coming across as partly objective and partly subjective. On occasion, you and your classmates may find yourselves debating which category a particular character fits. One interesting case is Welty's character Addie. Look again at the speech in which she berates her roommate:

> "Hush!" said the sick woman. "You never went to school. You never came and you never went. You never were anything—only here. You never were born! You don't know anything. Your head is empty, your heart and hands and your old black purse are all empty, even that little old box that you brought with you you brought empty—you showed it to me. And yet you talk, talk, talk, talk, talk all the time until I think I'm losing my mind! Who are you? You're a stranger—a perfect stranger! Don't you know you're a stranger? Is it possible that they have actually done a thing like this to anyone—sent them in a stranger to talk, and rock, and tell away her whole long rigmarole? Do they seriously suppose that I'll be able to keep it up, day in, day out, night in, night out, living in the same room with a terrible old woman—forever?"

Some may argue that this speech is merely an unreasonable rant, indicating Addie's dour mood rather than her roommate's true nature. (For one thing, contrary to Addie's declaration, the roommate must have been born!) Yet it can also be argued that Addie shrewdly diagnoses her situation. Perhaps statements like "you never were born," "your head is empty," and "you're a stranger" are true in a metaphorical sense.

Setting

Usually a short story enables readers to examine how people behave in concrete circumstances. The characters are located in a particular place or **setting**. Moreover, they are shown at particular moments in their personal histories. Sometimes the story goes further, referring to them as living at a certain point in world history.

As the word *sometimes* implies, short stories vary in the precision with which they identify their settings. At one extreme is Tim O'Brien's "The Things They Carried," featured in Part Three. The story's place and time are clearly defined: The action occurs in the fields and jungles of South Vietnam during the United States's military involvement there. On the other hand, the setting of Williams's "The Use of Force" is much less exact. Most of the action occurs in the Olsons' kitchen, but we get practically no details of it. Mainly we learn that "it is warm," while the rest of the house can be "very damp." And though the Olsons are evidently from the working class, the text does not situate them within a particular region or era. Even when a story's setting is rather vague, certain details may seem historically or geographically specific. Brown's story says little about Rick's apartment and events in the larger world, but since he has AIDS, the time frame can be no earlier than the 1980s.

Short stories differ as well in the importance of their setting. Sometimes, as with "The Use of Force," location serves as a mere backdrop for the plot. At other times, the setting can be a looming presence. When Welty's character Marian visits the Old Ladies' Home, we get her vivid impressions of it. Even when a story's setting seems ordinary, it may become filled with drama and meaning as the plot develops. For most people, a kitchen is a mundane place, but there Brown's narrator must decide whether to accept the breakfast that Rick has assembled.

Stories may focus on one site and show it changing over time. This is the case with Faulkner's "A Rose for Emily" (Chapter 13), in which Emily's town comes to view her differently over the years. Of course, a story may take place in more than one setting, and when it does, the differences between its various sites may be notable. In Nathaniel Hawthorne's story "Young Goodman Brown" (featured in Part Three), the title character must figure out how to relate everyday life in his village to his experiences one night in a forest, where various citizens of his town appear as demons.

One way of analyzing characters is to consider how they accommodate themselves—or fail to accommodate themselves—to their surroundings. The two roommates in Welty's story are evidently frustrated with living in the Old Ladies' Home, and they take out this frustration on each other. In Brown's story, the narrator's cleaning of Rick's home may leave you with mixed feelings. When, in his absence, she strips his bed, washes his laundry, vacuums his floor, dusts his objects, straightens his clothes, stores his cassettes, removes his garbage, and scrubs his bathroom, she is certainly caring for him. At the same time, her actions signify that he has lost all privacy. Though it is his own apartment, she has taken charge.

A WRITING EXERCISE

To become more aware of how setting may function in a short story, write a two- to three-page description of a setting you associate with someone you know. Choose a particular room, building, or landscape in which you have seen that person. In your description, use details of the setting to reveal something about his or her life.

Imagery

Just like poems, short stories often use **imagery** to convey meaning. Sometimes a character in the story may interpret a particular image just the way you do. Some stories, though, include images that you and the characters may analyze quite differently. One example is the apple in Welty's story. Whereas Marian probably views the apple as just something to eat, many readers would make other associations with it, thinking in particular of the apple that Adam and Eve ate from the Tree of Knowledge in Eden. By the end of Welty's story, perhaps Marian has indeed become like Adam and Eve, in that she has lost her innocence and grown more aware that human beings age. At any rate, many readers would call Marian's apple a **symbol**. Traditionally, that is the term for an image seen as representing some concept or concepts. Again, probably Marian herself does not view her apple as symbolic; indeed, characters within stories rarely use the word *symbol* at all.

Images may appear in the form of metaphors or other figures of speech. For example, when Marian enters the Old Ladies' Home, she experiences "a smell in the hall like the interior of a clock." Welty soon builds on the clock image as she describes the receptionist checking her wristwatch, an action that this character repeats near the end. Welty's whole story can be said to deal with time and its effects, both on the old and on the young.

Images in short stories usually appeal to the reader's visual sense. Most often, they are things you can picture in your mind. Yet stories are not limited to rendering visual impressions. They may refer and appeal to other senses, too. In Brown's story, the narrator is struck by how Rick's sweat smells. Similarly, Welty's young heroine notes the odor of the hall.

A WRITING EXERCISE

Write a brief essay in which you analyze how a particular advertisement uses imagery. The ad may come from any medium, including a newspaper, a magazine, television, or radio. What specific associations do you make with the ad's imagery? Why do you think the advertiser used it? Would you say that this use of imagery is successful? Why, or why not?

Language

Everything about short stories we have discussed so far concerns **language**. After all, works of literature are constructed entirely out of words. Here, however, we call your attention to three specific uses of language in stories: title, predominant style, and dialogue.

A story's **title** may be just as important as any words in the text. Not always will the relevance of the title be immediately clear to you. Usually you have to read a story all the way through before you can sense fully how its title applies. In any case, play with the title in your mind, considering its various possible meanings and implications.

A WRITING EXERCISE

Write a brief essay in which you focus on Williams's, Welty's, or Brown's story and examine how the title relates to the actual text. Consider the writer's alternatives. If you choose to discuss Welty's "A Visit of Charity," you may find it helpful to think about this famous passage from the New

Testament: "And now abideth faith, hope, charity, these three; but the great-est of these is charity" (I Corinthians 13:13). You may also want to look up the word *charity* in a dictionary.

Not all short stories have a uniform **style**. Some feature various tones, dialects, vocabularies, and levels of formality. Stories that do have a predominant style are often narrated in the first person, thus giving the impression of a presid-ing "voice." Brown's story "The Gift of Sweat," with its matter-of-fact, conversa-tional tone, comes across as an anecdote that someone is relating to a friend.

Dialogue may serve more than one purpose in a short story. By reporting var-ious things, characters may provide you with necessary background for the plot. In Welty's story, it's only from the roommates' fragmentary remarks that Marian — and the reader — can learn anything about their lives up until now. Also, by saying certain things to one another, characters may advance the plot. When, in Brown's story, suffering Rick says to the narrator "please don't go," she winds up in a physical intimacy with him that they may not have had together before. Actually, dialogue can be thought of as action in itself. Try to identify the particular kinds of acts that characters perform when they speak. For instance, Rick's "please don't go" can be labeled a plea.

Another plea occurs when the mother in "The Use of Force" begs her daughter to open her mouth for the narrator: "Such a nice man. . . . Look how kind he is to you. Come on, do what he tells you to. He won't hurt you." Just a bit later, though, the narrator scolds the mother herself: "For heaven's sake, I broke in. Don't call me a nice man to her." To the narrator, no longer are the girl's par-ents his partners; instead, he feels contempt for them. Indeed, dialogue may function to reveal shifts in characters' relations with one another.

Theme

We have already discussed the term **theme** on pages 18 to 20. There, we identified issues of theme as one kind of issue that comes up in literary studies. At the same time, we suggested that term *theme* applies to various literary genres, not just short stories. Later, in Chapters 5, 6, and 7, we examine theme in con-nection with poems, plays, and essays. Here, though, we consider theme as an element of short fiction. In doing so, we review some points from our earlier dis-cussion, applying them now to the three stories you have just read.

Recall that we defined the theme of a work as the main claim it seems to make. Furthermore, we identified it as an assertion, proposition, or statement rather than as a single word. "Charity" is obviously a *topic* of Welty's story, but because it is just one word, it is not an adequate expression of the story's *theme*. The following exercise invites you to consider just what that theme may be.

A WRITING EXERCISE

Here we list possible statements of theme for Williams's, Welty's, and Brown's stories. Choose one of these stories, and rank the statements listed for it, placing at the top whatever sentence you think most accurately expresses the story's theme. Then, in two or three pages, explain your reasoning, referring at least once to each statement you have ranked. Propose your own statement of the story's theme if none of those listed seem adequate to you.

Statements of Theme for Williams's "The Use of Force"

1. Force against people is justified when it is used to halt disease.
2. Though we like to think doctors are kind, they may actually scorn us.
3. Doctors should be especially sensitive when their patient is a child.
4. Children are capable of stubborn fury.
5. The desire to help may be met with resistance.
6. Working-class life is different from the life of middle-class professionals.
7. We should cooperate with doctors, even if they seem threatening to us.
8. People may secretly admire those who resist them.
9. All of us are "blind" in one way or another.
10. The cure may be worse than the disease.

Statements of Theme for Welty's "A Visit of Charity"

1. Be nice to old people, for many of them have it tough.
2. None of us can escape the passage of time.
3. Searching for merit points is incompatible with a true spirit of charity.
4. Everyone has to give up dreams of innocence and paradise, just as Adam and Eve did.
5. Although we are tempted to repress our awareness of mortality, we should maintain that awareness.
6. We should all behave charitably toward one another.
7. We can tell how charitable we are by the way we treat people we find strange or irritable.
8. Old age homes need to be made more pleasant, both for the residents and for their visitors.
9. Whenever we become strongly aware of mortality, we tend to repress that awareness, thus robbing ourselves of any benefit we may gain from it.
10. Young people are capable of showing interest in others, if only for a moment, but for better or worse they're basically self-centered.

Statement of Theme for Brown's "The Gift of Sweat"

1. We should be compassionate toward people with AIDS.
2. Even when we sympathize with others, we may not be sure how to help them.
3. Simple acts, such as cleaning and eating, may be ways of coping.

4. We should give one another a lot more gifts.

5. Gifts may take various forms.

6. Live life to the fullest, for it is the greatest gift of all.

7. We may feel guilt as well as gratitude in accepting a person's gift.

8. Risking one's health may be worthwhile.

9. Sweat is a sign of our humanity.

10. We may do more for people when we accept *their* work rather than work *for* them.

Think about the other points we made when we discussed theme in Chapter 2. To see how these apply to short fiction, we can start by relating each point to the stories by Williams, Welty, and Brown.

1. Try to state a text's theme as a midlevel generalization. If you were to put it in very broad terms, your audience would see it as fitting a great many works besides the one you have read. If you went to the opposite extreme, tying the theme completely to specific details of the text, your audience might think the theme irrelevant to their own lives.

The phrase "the moral of the story" suggests that a story can usually be reduced to a single message, often a principle of ethics or religion. Plenty of examples can be cited to support this suggestion. In the New Testament, for instance, Jesus tells stories — they are called *parables* — to convey some of his key ideas. In any number of cultures today, stories are used to teach children elements of good conduct. Moreover, people often determine the significance of a real-life event by building a story from it and by drawing a moral from it at the same time. These two processes conspicuously dovetailed when England's Princess Diana was killed in a car crash. Given that she died fleeing photographers, many people saw her entire life story as that of a woman hounded by media. The moral was simultaneous and clear: thou shalt honor the right to privacy.

It is possible to lose sight of a story's theme by placing too much emphasis on minor details of the text. The more common temptation, however, is to turn a story's theme into an all-too-general cliché. Actually, a story is often most interesting when it *complicates* some widely held idea that it seemed ready to endorse. Therefore, a useful exercise is to start with a general thematic statement about the story and then make it increasingly specific. With "The Gift of Sweat," for example, you might begin by supposing that the theme is "We should do whatever we can for sick people." Your next step would be to identify the specific spin that Brown's story puts on this idea. How does her story differ from others on this theme? Note, for instance, that Brown's narrator evidently wants to help sick people right from the beginning of the story, whereas other stories might trace how a character gradually becomes committed to charity. Also, not every story about helping sick people would emphasize sweat and cleaning as Brown's does. With these two observations and others in mind, try now to restate our version of Brown's theme so that it seems more in touch with the specific details of her text.

2. *The theme of a text may be related to its title.* It may also be expressed by some statement made within the text. But often various parts of the text merit consideration as you try to determine its theme.

In our discussion of a short story's language, we called attention to the potential significance of its title. The title may serve as a guide to the story's theme. What clues, if any, do you find in the three story titles in this chapter — "The Use of Force," "A Visit of Charity," and "The Gift of Sweat"? Of course, determining a story's theme entails going beyond the title. You have to read, and usually reread, the entire text. In doing so, you may come across a statement that seems a candidate for the theme because it is a philosophical generalization. Nevertheless, take the time to consider whether the story's essence is indeed captured by this statement alone.

3. *You can state a text's theme either as an observation or as a recommendation.* Each way of putting it evokes a certain image of the text's author. When you state the theme as an **observation**, you depict the author as a psychologist, a philosopher, or some other kind of analyst. When you state the theme as a **recommendation** — which often involves your using the word *should* — you depict the author as a teacher, preacher, manager, or coach. That is, the author comes across as telling readers what to do.

As we have noted, stories are often used to teach lessons. Moreover, often the lessons are recommendations for action, capable of being phrased as "Do X" or "Do not do X." The alternative is to make a generalization about some state of affairs. When you try to express a particular story's theme, which of these two options should you follow? There are several things to consider in making your decision. First is your personal comfort: do you feel at ease with both ways of stating the theme, or is one of these ways more to your taste? Also worth pondering is the impression you want to give of the author: do you want to portray this person as a maker of recommendations, or do you want to assign the author a more modest role? Because Brown has helped people with AIDS, you may want to state the theme of her story as a prescription for physical and spiritual health. Yet maybe Brown is out to remind her audience that home-care providers have human frailties; hence, expressing her theme as an observation may be the more appropriate move.

4. *Consider stating a text's theme as a problem.* That way, you are more apt to convey the complexity and drama of the text.

We have suggested that short stories often pivot around conflicts between people and conflicts within people. Perhaps the most interesting stories are ones that pose conflicts not easily resolved. Probably you will be more faithful to such a text if you phrase its theme as a problem. In the case of Brown's story, for example, you might state the theme as follows: "When we try to help people, we may find ourselves resisting the gifts they want to give us because our guilt over their suffering interferes with our ability to accept things they do for us."

5. *Rather than refer to* the *theme of a text, you might refer to* a *theme of the text, implying that the text has more than one.* You would still be suggesting that

you have identified a central idea of the text. Subsequently, you might have to defend your claim.

Unlike the average novel, the typical short story pivots around only a few ideas. Yet you need not insist that the story you are analyzing has a single theme; in fact, even the shortest piece of short fiction may have a number of them. Besides, your audience is apt to think you nicely open-minded if you suggest that the theme you have discovered is not the only one. We believe, for example, that Brown's story has at least two themes. One is that people with AIDS deserve more understanding, appreciation, and attention than many of them now get. A second theme is that care of the ill may involve more than helping them keep their life "clean"; it may also mean sharing their "sweat," by making bodily contact with them and accepting whatever they achieve in their pain. Although we are labeling each of these ideas *a* theme of Brown's story rather than *the* theme of it, we are still making strong claims. To use the term *theme* at all implies that we are identifying key principles of the text. You might disagree with our claims about Brown's themes, and if you did, we would have to support our position in order to change your mind.

Perhaps the biggest challenge you will face in writing about short stories is to avoid long stretches of plot summary. Selected details of the plot will often serve as key evidence for you. You will need to describe such moments from the story you are discussing, even if your audience has already read it. But your readers are apt to be frustrated if you just repeat plot at length. They will feel that they may as well turn back to the story itself rather than linger with your rehash. Your paper is worth your readers' time only if you provide insights of your own, *analyzing* the story rather than just *summarizing* it.

To understand what analysis of a short story involves, let's return to Alison Caldwell, whose freewriting on "The Use of Force" you read earlier. Assigned to write an argument paper about a short story, Alison decided to focus on Williams's. She realized that for her paper to be effective, she had to come up with an issue worth addressing, a claim about that issue, and evidence for that claim. Moreover, she had to be prepared to identify the warrants or assumptions behind her evidence.

For most writing assignments, settling on an issue will be your most important preliminary step. Without a driving question, you will have difficulty producing fresh, organized, and sustained analysis. For her paper on "The Use of Force," Alison chose to address an issue that she had raised in her freewriting: What's the most important connection between the narrator and the child? Ultimately, she saw this as an issue of pattern because she would have to identify, analyze, and rank in order of importance whatever sets of words link the two characters. Again, building on her freewriting, Alison thought in particular about the narrator's closing reference to the child's "blindness." In her paper, she came to argue that "blindness" was the most important similarity between these two people. She realized, of course, that she would have to explore various possible meanings of the term, especially since neither character was literally blind. To a certain extent, then, she would have to address an issue of definition, even as the issue of pattern remained her key concern. Moreover, she felt obliged to justify her emphasis on the narrator's final words. You will see that in her paper she states her warrant for taking them as evidence. The narrator's concluding reference to "blindness" is significant, she contends, because the last words of a character often are. To be sure, Alison also assumed that Williams was deliberate rather than arbitrary in having the narrator speak this way at the end.

A paper about a short story need not explicitly mention the elements of short fiction we have identified. Nevertheless, thinking of these elements can help you plan such a paper, providing you with some preliminary terms for your analysis. Alison perceived that her paper would be very much about two characters who on the surface are protagonist and antagonist but who actually have features in common. Also, the paper would attend much to the story's ending. It would deal as well with a particular symbol, blindness.

When you plan a paper about a short story, keep in mind that you are more apt to persuade readers if you include quotations from the text you discuss. Before you attempt a complete draft, copy in your notebook any words from the story that might figure in your analysis. Alison, for example, was pretty sure that her paper on "The Use of Force" would incorporate the narrator's final words, "tears of defeat blinded her eyes," as well as his interesting declaration that "I had already fallen in love with the savage brat, the parents were contemptible to me." Yet, as with plot summary, quoting should be limited, so that the paper seems to be an original argument about the story instead of a mere recycling of it. Alison sensed that practically every sentence of Williams's story could be quoted and then plumbed for meaning. At the same time, she realized that she should quote only some words rather than all.

Sample Student Paper: Final Draft

Here is Alison's final draft of her paper about "The Use of Force." As you read it, keep in mind that it emerged only after she had done several preliminary drafts, in consultation with some of her classmates as well as her instructor. Although Alison's paper is a good example of how to write about a short story, most drafts can stand to be revised further. What do you think Alison has done well in her paper? If she planned to do yet another version, what suggestions would you make?

```
Alison Caldwell
Professor Stein
English 1A
November 3, —
            Forms of Blindness in "The Use of Force"
     In William Carlos Williams's story "The Use of
Force," the narrator is a doctor frustrated by one of his
patients, a young girl who refuses to let him determine
```

if her throat is infected. After violently struggling
with the child, he finally manages to pry open her mouth
and does find her tonsils diseased. In an important
sense, therefore, the child is the narrator's antagonist,
over whom he eventually triumphs. Yet throughout the
story, the narrator seems to identify with the child,
almost as if she is his secret self or double. At the
same time, we readers must decide which of her characteristics he shares most. To answer this question, we should
consider the narrator's very last words, which seem significant just because they serve as his conclusion. After
his victory over the girl, he reports, "tears of defeat
blinded her eyes." These final words suggest that he,
too, has been "blind," in various senses of the term.
Most important, his anger at the child has obscured for
him her humanity. Even at the end, perhaps, he does not
fully "see" the limits of his compassion.

To understand the narrator's identification with the
child, we should note his relationship with her parents.
Though her mother and father are allies in his fight
against her, he feels increasing scorn for them. When the
mother says to the child "He won't hurt you," the narrator must conceal his "disgust." Later, he openly snarls
at the mother: "For heaven's sake, I broke in. Don't call
me a nice man." Although the child accuses the narrator
of "killing me," he is actually homicidal toward her
ineffective father: "I wanted to kill him."

With the child, the narrator has a different relationship. At several moments, he is negative about her,
too. When she resists his effort to open her mouth with a
wooden tongue depressor, he gets "furious," even though
he realizes that he is angry at a mere girl. Eventually,
his wrath becomes so intense that "I could have torn the
child apart in my own fury and enjoyed it." Nevertheless,
his anger is mixed with admiration. The child's sheer
force of resistance makes him think highly of her. After
he triumphs, he admits to himself that "She had fought

valiantly to keep me from knowing her secret." More important, midway through the story he contrasts her quite favorably with her parents: "I had already fallen in love with the savage brat, the parents were contemptible to me. In the ensuing struggle they grew more and more abject, crushed, exhausted while she surely rose to magnificent heights of insane fury of effort bred of her terror of me."

The narrator's identification with the child is not simply one person's respect for another. In various ways, he comes to resemble her. For example, both find her parents unhelpful as allies. If she shows "insane fury of effort," he feels "my own fury." She violently resists him; he violently attacks her. If "her face was flushed," eventually he feels a "pleasure" in combat with her that leaves his face "burning." Perhaps the narrator finds the child compelling precisely because they mirror each other.

But which of their similarities is most important? By announcing at the end that the girl has been "blinded," the narrator invites us to suppose that he has been "blind" as well and to believe that this is their most noteworthy connection. Significantly, the narrator wears glasses, which the girl knocks off. Literally, he lacks clear vision. For much of the story, though, the narrator has been "blind" in that he lacks the opportunity to see what disease lurks behind the girl's mouth. His earnestly repeated use of the word "look" suggests what a struggle it is for him to view his patient's secret. After proposing to the parents that "we take a look at the throat first," he pleads with the girl to "open your mouth and let's take a look at your throat." When she refuses, he begs her to "let me take a look," "Just open up and let me see." He even resorts to the word "look" as he tries to reassure her: "Look, I said opening both hands wide, I haven't anything in my hands." Once he gets more exasperated with the child, he uses the word "look" more

sternly: "Look here, I said to the child, we're going to
look at your throat."

Yet the narrator seems "blind" in a psychological
sense, too. As he intensifies his attack on the girl, he
tells himself that he is doing so for her own and society's good: "The damned little brat must be protected
against her own idiocy, one says to one's self at such
times. Others must be protected against her." At some
point, though, he realizes that his rationalizations protect himself. In reality, he comes to acknowledge, he has
been driven by "a blind fury" which leads him to a "final
unreasoning assault." Here, the word "blind" refers to
obsession with victory, regardless of its human consequences. For the narrator, helping the girl becomes less
crucial than conquering her.

Nevertheless, the narrator doesn't seem "blind" as he
looks back on his own conduct. Notice that he tells the
story in the past tense, which means that he is analyzing
how he behaved on a previous occasion. As he reviews what
he did and felt when he visited the Olsons, he comes
across as remarkably candid about his own base motives.
We readers do not have to infer that he acted mainly out
of "a blind fury"; he himself informs us of this fact. If
anything, we may conclude that he is now a man of vision,
bursting with true insights about himself.

We need not accept all of his self-analysis, however.
By acknowledging his more negative feelings, he may win
points with us for honesty without really changing his
behavior or mindset. Even as he notes his "blind fury,"
for example, he concludes that "One goes on to the end,"
as if humanity in general would inevitably have acted as
he did. When he makes this fatalistic declaration, he may
be protecting himself yet again by refusing to see ways
in which he must still take personal responsibility.

Perhaps he is using a strategy that many middle-class
professionals have used when confronted with lower-class
suffering. Although Williams provides few details of the

Olsons' life, clearly they belong at best to the working class. Their house can get "very damp," they seem unused to doctors, and the narrator points out that the mother is "clean," as if she might well have been living in filth. The narrator is not blatantly prejudiced against the lower classes. After all, he has responded when the Olsons' summoned him. But he seems disposed to think of the parents as stupid, and his concern about their daughter stems in part from his effort to stop a diphtheria outbreak. His tone of ironic wisdom in telling the story is consistent with a basic detachment from such people. By summarizing his visit to the Olsons with the world-weary statement "One goes on to the end," he may still be "blinding" himself to the possibility of forming a genuine bond with this specific family.

SUMMING UP

- Short stories require you to understand and evaluate them on the basis of just a few details and events.

- Think carefully about the title, and its possible meanings and implications.

- The elements of short fiction include *plot* and *structure, point of view, characterization, setting, imagery, language,* and *theme.*

- *Plot* and *structure* are closely related, with plots usually centering on human beings and their actions, and structure often following the ABCDE formula (action, background, development, climax, ending). (pp. 93–97)

- *Points of view* vary and include first-person, second person, and omniscient. (pp. 97–98)

- As you analyze and evaluate the *characters* in a short story, consider these questions:

    What does each character desire?

    How do the characters, even minor characters, relate to each other?

    Can you identify a protagonist and an antagonist?

(continued on next page)

— SUMMING UP —

How are the characters' lives affected by traits such as gender, class, race, ethnicity, nationality, sexuality, and occupation?

Can you trust the accuracy of the views the characters have of one another?

How does the characters' dialogue function—does it provide background, advance the plot, reveal shifts in characters' relations, or what?

• *Setting* **provides a context for actions.** One way of analyzing characters is to consider how they do or do not accommodate themselves to their surroundings. (pp. 101–102)

• *Images* **appeal to the reader's senses—usually the visual sense—and may appear in the form of metaphors and other figures of speech.** (pp. 102–103)

• **The** *theme* **of a short story is the main claim it seems to make, best identified as an assertion, proposition, or statement.** In your writing, try to state the theme as a midlevel generalization, either as an observation or as a recommendation, or as a problem. (pp. 104–109)

• **In writing an argument about a short story, remember to formulate an issue worth addressing.** (pp. 108–109)

5

Making Arguments about Poems

Some students are put off by poetry, perhaps because their early experiences with it were discouraging. They imagine poems have deep hidden meanings that they can't uncover. Maybe their high-school English teacher always had the right interpretation, and they rarely did. This need not be the case. Poetry can be accessible to all readers.

The problem is often a confusion about the nature of poetry, since poetry is more compressed than prose. It focuses more on connotative, emotional, or associative meanings and conveys meaning more through suggestion, indirection, and the use of metaphor, symbol, and imagery than prose does. Poetry seldom hands us a specific meaning. Poetic texts suggest certain possibilities, but the reader completes the transaction. Part of the meaning comes from the writer, part from the text itself, and part from the reader. Even if students are the same age, race, religion, and ethnicity, they are not exact duplicates of each other. All of them have their own experiences, their own family histories, their own emotional lives. If thirty people are reading a poem about conformity or responsibility, all thirty will have varying views about these concepts, even though there will probably be commonalities. (Our culture is so saturated with media images that it is nearly impossible to avoid some overlap in responses.)

In a good class discussion, then, we should be aware that even though we might be members of the same culture, each of us reads from a unique perspective, a perspective that might also shift from time to time. If a woman reads a poem about childbirth, her identity as a female will seem more relevant than if she were reading a poem about death, a more universal experience. In other words, how we read a poem and how significant and meaningful the poem is for us depends both on the content of the poem and our specific circumstances. Suppose you are fourteen when you first read a poem about dating; you would likely have very different responses rereading it at nineteen, twenty-five, and fifty. We read poems through our experiences. As we gain new experiences, our readings change.

That is one reason that it is important to respond in writing to your first reading. You want to be able to separate your first thoughts from those of your classmates; they too will be bringing their own experiences, values, and ideas to the discussion. In the give-and-take of open discussion, it may be difficult to remember what you first said. Of course, the point of a classroom discussion is not simply to defend your initial response, for then you would be denying yourself the benefit of other people's ideas. A good discussion should open up the poem, allow you to see it from multiple viewpoints, and enable you to expand your perspective, to see how others make sense of the world.

This rich mixture of the poet's text, the reader's response, and discussion among several readers can create new possibilities of meaning. Even more than fiction or drama, poetry encourages creative readings that can be simultaneously true to the text and to the reader. A lively class discussion can uncover a dozen or more plausible interpretations of a poem, each backed up with valid evidence both from the poem and the reader's experience. You may try to persuade others that your views about the poem are correct; others may do the same to you. This negotiation is at the heart of a liberal, democratic education. In fact, maybe the most respected and repeated notion about being well-educated is the ability to empathize with another's point of view, to see as another sees. Reading, discussing, and writing about poetry can help you become a person who can both create meaning and understand and appreciate how others do. This is one important way literature matters.

We have chosen six poems about work — about the joys and sorrows, the satisfactions and frustrations of physical labor. Some people might think of poets as intellectuals far removed from the experiences of the working class, but this is not the case. Indeed, many poets were themselves brought up in working-class homes and know firsthand the dignity and value of such work. Even among poets who do not themselves toil with their hands, few lack the imaginative empathy that would allow them to write perceptively about firefighters and factory workers, cleaning women and mill workers. These six poems are especially relevant today when physical work is becoming less and less a reality among middle-class Americans. Poems that matter are poems about real life — about love and death, about pain and loss, about beauty and hope. These six poems about work are about all of these and more.

The first poem, "In Creve Coeur, Missouri," is by Rosanna Warren (b. 1953), a contemporary poet and scholar who teaches at Boston University. Charles Fort (b. 1951), the author of "We Did Not Fear the Father," is an African American poet who grew up in New Britain, Connecticut, taught in the South for a number of years, and now lives and teaches in Nebraska. His poem first appeared in *The Georgia Review*. Philip Levine (b. 1928) grew up in Detroit. Much of his poetry, including "What Work Is," recalls his youth in his native city, where he worked as a laborer in Detroit factories. Mary Oliver's (b. 1935) "Singapore" appeared in *House of Light* (1992). She has won a Pulitzer prize for her poetry. "Blackberries" is by Yusef Komunyakaa (b. 1947), who has become known for exploring various aspects of African American experience; the poem is from *Magic City* (1992). Edwin Arlington Robinson's "The Mill" is the oldest poem in the cluster. Robinson (1869–1935) is considered the first major poet of twentieth-century America.

ROSANNA WARREN

In Creve Coeur, Missouri

Only in Creve Coeur
would an amateur photographer
firebug snap a shot so
unconsolable: fireman bent low

over the rag of body held   5
like impossible laundry pulled
too soon from the line, too pale,
too sodden with smoke to flail

in his huge, dark, crumpled embrace.
He leans to the tiny face.   10
Her hair stands out like flame.
She is naked, she has no name.

No longer a baby, almost
a child, not yet a ghost,
she presses a doll-like fist   15
to his professional chest.

Her head falls back to his hand.
Tell us that she will stand
again, quarrel and misbehave.
He is trying to make her breathe.   20

Strong man, you know how it's done,
you've done it again and again
sucking the spirit back
to us from its lair of smoke.

We'll call it a fine surprise.   25
The snapshot won a prize
though it couldn't revive *her*
that night in Creve Coeur.   [1993]

CHARLES FORT

We Did Not Fear the Father

We did not fear the father as the barber who stood
like a general in a white jacket with a green visor cap.
For six long days he held a straight razor like a sword
until his porcelain-chrome chariot became a down-home chair.
The crop-eared son learned to see how the workingman's   5

day job after the night shift filled the son's small pockets
with licorice, filled the offering plate, and paid for the keeper
who clipped our grape vines under his own pageant.

We did not fear the father as landlord in our three-story tenement
who took charge of four apartments and the attic dwellers.   10
We searched each corner of the dirt cellar for a fuse box
while he broke out plasterboard upstairs with a sledgehammer.
We peeled out paper from wire mesh and read the headline news
a century old before he lifted us like birds into our bunk beds.

We did not fear the father until he entered the tomb of noise   15
for his night job, shaping molten steel into ball bearings
as we stared into the barbed grate where he stood
before the furnace sending smoke into the trees.
Fear became the eight-hour echo and glow inside his skull,
the high-pitched metal scraping our ears as our provider   20
left the factory floor with oil and sawdust inside his mouth
and punched out as fermented daylight burned his eyes.
We did not fear our father until he stooped in the dark.   [1999]

PHILIP LEVINE
What Work Is

We stand in the rain in a long line
waiting at Ford Highland Park. For work.
You know what work is — if you're
old enough to read this you know what
work is, although you may not do it.   5
Forget you. This is about waiting,
shifting from one foot to another.
Feeling the light rain falling like mist
into your hair, blurring your vision
until you think you see your own brother   10
ahead of you, maybe ten places.
You rub your glasses with your fingers,
and of course its someone else's brother,
narrower across the shoulders than
yours but with the same sad slouch, the grin   15
that does not hide the stubbornness,
the sad refusal to give in to
rain, to the hours wasted waiting,
to the knowledge that somewhere ahead
a man is waiting who will say, "No,   20
we're not hiring today," for any

reason he wants. You love your brother,
now suddenly you can hardly stand
the love flooding you for your brother,
who's not beside you or behind or   25
ahead because he's home trying to
sleep off a miserable night shift
at Cadillac so he can get up
before noon to study his German.
Works eight hours a night so he can sing   30
Wagner, the opera you hate most,
the worst music ever invented.
How long has it been since you told him
you loved him, held his wide shoulders,
opened your eyes wide and said those words,   35
and maybe kissed his cheek? You've never
done something so simple, so obvious,
not because you're too young or too dumb,
not because you're jealous or even mean
or incapable of crying in   40
the presence of another man, no,
just because you don't know what work is.   [1991]

MARY OLIVER
Singapore

In Singapore, in the airport,
a darkness was ripped from my eyes.
In the women's restroom, one compartment stood open.
A woman knelt there, washing something
        in the white bowl.   5

Disgust argued in my stomach
and I felt, in my pocket, for my ticket.

A poem should always have birds in it.
Kingfishers, say, with their bold eyes and gaudy wings.
Rivers are pleasant, and of course trees.   10
A waterfall, or if that's not possible, a fountain
        rising and falling.
A person wants to stand in a happy place, in a poem.

When the woman turned I could not answer her face.
Her beauty and her embarrassment struggled together, and   15
        neither could win.
She smiled and I smiled. What kind of nonsense is this?
Everybody needs a job.

Yes, a person wants to stand in a happy place, in a poem.
But first we must watch her as she stares down at her labor,   20
    which is dull enough.
She is washing the tops of the airport ashtrays, as big as
    hubcaps, with a blue rag.
Her small hands turn the metal, scrubbing and rinsing.
She does not work slowly, nor quickly, but like a river.   25
Her dark hair is like the wing of a bird.

I don't doubt for a moment that she loves her life.
And I want her to rise up from the crust and the slop
    and fly down to the river.
This probably won't happen.   30
But maybe it will.
If the world were only pain and logic, who would want it?

Of course, it isn't.
Neither do I mean anything miraculous, but only
the light that can shine out of a life. I mean   35
the way she unfolded and refolded the blue cloth,
the way her smile was only for my sake; I mean
the way this poem is filled with trees, and birds.   [1992]

YUSEF KOMUNYAKAA
Blackberries

They left my hands like a printer's
Or thief's before a police blotter
& pulled me into early morning's
Terrestrial sweetness, so thick
The damp ground was consecrated   5
Where they fell among a garland of thorns.

Although I could smell old lime-covered
History, at ten I'd still hold out my hands
& berries fell into them. Eating from one
& filling a half gallon with the other,   10
I ate the mythology & dreamt
Of pies & cobbler, almost

Needful as forgiveness. My bird dog Spot
Eyed blue jays & thrashers. The mud frogs
In rich blackness, hid from daylight.
An hour later, beside City Limits Road   15
I balanced a gleaming can in each hand,
Limboed between worlds, repeating *one dollar.*

The big blue car made me sweat.
Wintertime crawled out of the windows.　　　　　　　　20
When I leaned closer I saw the boy
& girl my age, in the wide back seat
Smirking, & it was then I remembered my fingers
Burning with thorns among berries too ripe to touch.　　　[1992]

EDWIN ARLINGTON ROBINSON
The Mill

The miller's wife had waited long,
　　　The tea was cold, the fire was dead;
And there might yet be nothing wrong
　　　In how he went and what he said;
"There are no millers any more,"　　　　　　　　　　5
　　　Was all that she had heard him say;
And he had lingered at the door
　　　So long that it seemed yesterday.

Sick with fear that had no form
　　　She knew that she was there at last;　　　　　　10
And in the mill there was a warm
　　　And mealy fragrance of the past.
What else there was would only seem
　　　To say again what he had meant;
And what was hanging from a beam　　　　　　　　15
　　　Would not have heeded where she went.

And if she thought it followed her,
　　　She may have reasoned in the dark
That one way of the few there were
　　　Would hide her and would leave no mark:　　　20
Black water, smooth above the weir
　　　Like starry velvet in the night,
Though ruffled once, would soon appear
　　　The same as ever to the sight.　　　　　　　[1920]

A WRITING EXERCISE

Look again at the Topics of Literary Criticism (p. 32), selecting one that
seems promising as an interpretive lens through which to view the six work
poems in this cluster. Freewrite for a few minutes on all six, but don't worry if
your topic doesn't seem to fit all the poems. A later exercise will eventually
ask you to pick the three poems that work the best.

A Student's Personal Responses to the Poems

The following are selections from the response journal of Michaela Fiorucci, a nineteen-year-old sophomore from Cape May, New Jersey, who chose to focus on boundaries—on the various divisions we set up between ourselves and other people, such as income, race, gender, sexual preference, and religion. It seemed to her an interesting way to talk about work since Michaela had observed barriers of all kinds between workers at her job at the university.

As an explorative strategy, Michaela did some freewriting on the six poems, hoping to discover an argument about boundaries that might fit at least three of the poems. The following are selections from her response journal.

In "In Creve Coeur, Missouri," there are the obvious boundaries between life and death, between the firefighter and the girl, between the photograph and reality, but I think the biggest boundary is between an acceptance of what is actually the case--that the little girl is dead--and the poet's desire for another reading of the photo. Since the boundary between life and death cannot be crossed by imagination or desire, she must admit the stark reality of the firefighter's failure.

In "We Did Not Fear the Father," the poet begins with a division between his father as a normal man and his own image of him as a general in a chariot. Mostly there is the father's separation from the family during his day job, his night job, and his landlord job. In the last stanza we can see the real separation that the poet has been leading up to--the separation of the father as he enters "the tomb of noise" where he might lose his health. The boundary the poet really fears is between a robust and a "stooped" father, between his protection and his loss.

Although the boundary in "What Work Is" seems to be between those who know what hard work is and those who don't, the narrator shifts his focus when he thinks he sees his brother in line, waiting for work. The most significant boundary in the poem is emotional intimacy or honesty. The poet laments our inability to cross that psychological boundary.

In "Singapore," there is a clear boundary between the middle-class American tourist and the cleaning lady, so much so that at first the narrator says, "Disgust argued in my stomach." The cleaning woman also seems to believe in a barrier and continues to work in a steady way. The narrator finally sees beauty in her dedication to her work. When the narrator does see beauty in her work habits, it helps close the barrier between them. There are also the issues of boundaries between fantasy and reality and between a world of pain and logic and one with birds and rivers. But at the end these boundaries also seem to be closing.

In "Blackberries," the young boy seems to be living in a rural paradise, beyond the city boundaries, outside the usual urban and suburban environment. He lives in a land of bird dogs, jays, thrashers, and mud frogs. He makes comparisons between blackness and light that seem to anticipate the economic boundary that appears in the last stanza, the one between the poor boy and the rich kids in the car. It is this division between the children in air conditioned comfort and the narrator on the outside looking in that seems to be the main point of this poem. Some boundaries cause us pain.

"The Mill" tells the sad story of a miller who could not see a boundary between himself and his job. When he tells his wife "there are no millers any more," he is really saying that his life is over; he has no reason to live. And so he crosses the boundary between life and death. Tragically, his wife also has difficulty seeing herself outside her role as wife and housekeeper, and so she also crosses that ultimate boundary. She does so, however, in a completely different way: she drowns herself, so no one will know. She passes through life's boundary without leaving a trace.

After reading these six brief freewrites to her response group, Michaela decided that "Blackberries, "Singapore," and "The Mill" were the most promising.

Michaela still didn't have a focus, but she liked the idea that boundaries, like walls, sometimes serve a purpose and sometimes they don't. She remembered a discussion of Robert Frost's "Mending Wall" from another course that focused on negotiating the walls we build between us. Her professor liked this idea since it helped her considerably narrow the concept of boundaries.

After reviewing her freewriting, Michaela wrote the following first draft and read it to her response group. She then discussed with her instructor her plans for a revision. Her instructor made a number of specific and general comments. After reading her first draft, what feedback would you give Michaela? Her revision appears at the end of the chapter.

Sample Student Paper: First Draft

Michaela Fiorucci

Mr. Hardee

English 102

Boundaries in Robinson,

Komunyakaa, and Oliver

Although most sophomores I know at school value their privacy, they also want to create intimate relationships. It is often hard to reconcile these two impulses. Most middle-class students are lucky enough to have their own rooms, private enclaves against annoying sisters and brothers, intrusive mothers and fathers. But a room is also more than a physical boundary; it is also a symbolic assertion of identity. It says, "I'm separate from others, even within the closeness of the family." Such a commitment to physical privacy might be innocent enough, but it does contain dangerous seeds, especially when extended beyond the home to neighborhoods. When different ethnic groups want boundaries between them, it is no longer innocent. When the upper classes need to be separated from workers because they see each other as radically different, a dangerous boundary has been erected.

It would be reductive, however, to say all boundaries need to be erased. Edwin Arlington Robinson's "The Mill" is a good example of the dangerous consequences of a missing boundary. The poem narrates the sad story of a farm couple who commit suicide--the husband because he

feels useless, the wife because she can't imagine life
without her husband. During my first few readings, I was
struck by the lack of communication between the couple.
He must have been depressed for a long time, but it seems
they never discussed his feelings. Keeping an emotional
distance from others was probably a typical part of the
way men and women dealt with each other a hundred years
ago. It was a boundary not to be crossed. Apparently he
could not say, "I feel terrible that I am going to lose
my job." And his wife accepts his reticence, even though
he might have been having second thoughts as he "lingered
at the door." Clearly this is a boundary that should have
been breached. But after several readings I began to
realize that the boundary that should have been established wasn't--the idea that a person's value or worth is
synonymous with their identity is dehumanizing. And it
probably isn't something that just happened in the past.
Nor is the equally dehumanizing idea that a wife is nothing without her husband. When the miller's wife decides
to "leave no mark" by jumping into the pond, she is
admitting she is not a worthwhile person by herself. Both
identify totally with a role that in my view should only
be one aspect of a complex human life. The final barrier
she crosses, from life to death, is symbolically represented in the poem as a feminine domestic gesture: she
doesn't want to leave a mess. The boundaries of person
and occupation should be made clear; the arbitrary boundaries between genders should not.

When the narrator in "Blackberries" claims that he is
"Limboed between two worlds," he means the rural paradise
of "Terrestrial sweetness" and "rich blackness" he temporarily lives in versus the commercial, urban work that
"made him sweat." He has constructed a boundary between
the ancient picking of berries and the technology of
automobiles, between a natural closeness with nature and
the artificial "Wintertime crawled out of the windows."
Even though the narrator is only ten, he senses the

sensual joys of being one with nature. He seems to reject
"old lime-covered / History" in favor of "mythology,"
which seems to suggest a conscious rejection or maybe
repression of the contemporary world. But this boundary
cannot stand. He needs the outside world to survive, and
when the car approaches, it is the modern world and all
its pluses and minuses that draw near. When he looks in
he sees "Smirking" children; he sees class prejudice,
hierarchy, and economic reality. The smirkers of the
world are in charge. This realization dissolves the protective boundary around his garden of Eden, and he feels
physical pain. But really he feels the pain of initiation, the pain of having to cross a boundary he wanted to
delay as long as possible. Although we can sympathize
with the young narrator, he would probably have fared
better by not making his boundary so extreme.

The narrator in Mary Oliver's "Singapore" at first
sees a significant boundary between herself as a middle-
class traveler and a cleaning woman washing a toilet. It
is a separation we might all make, given our socialization to see this kind of physical labor is degrading.
College-educated people in America have a tendency to see
themselves as distinct from workers. For most, a woman
washing something in a compartment is beyond the pale, a
clear indication that the woman is other. But Oliver does
have some conflicting ideas since she says a "Disgust
argued in my stomach." Since we are also socialized to be
tolerant and open-minded, she knows she shouldn't think
this way. And since she is also a writer with ideas about
how poems should "always have birds in it," she looks
harder at the cleaning woman, finally seeing in her face,
in her hair, and in the way she works slowly, "like a
river," the positive aspects she probably wants to find.
Oliver does not simply accept the boundaries that her
culture constructs but negotiates with herself, eventually seeing that "light can shine out of a life" even
where we do not expect it. In the woman's careful folding

and unfolding of her blue work cloth and in her smile,
Oliver eclipses the social boundary and ends up with a
life affirming vision "filled with trees, with birds."

The Elements of Poetry

Speaker and Tone

The voice we hear in a poem could be the poet's, but it is better to think of the speaker as a sort of poetic construction—perhaps a **persona** (mask) for the poet or perhaps a complete fiction. The speaker's tone or attitude is sometimes difficult to discern. It could be ironic or sentimental, joyful or morose, or a combination. In "In Creve Coeur, Missouri," for example, we can get at the tone of the speaker by noticing the ironic comment in the town's name (broken/sad heart). Content is not always a reliable guide to tone, since writers can be trying to be satiric. But as with Swift's essay "A Modest Proposal," in which he suggests that babies be cooked and eaten to relieve the famine in Ireland, we use our own moral sense to figure out that he could not really be suggesting such a monstrously aberrant solution. So too in the content of this poem we sense a bitter irony in the opening stanzas that changes to images ("rag of body," "tiny face") that directly suggest the speaker's sadness. But her description of a static photo becomes a kind of narrative as the speaker sees in the position of the child in the firefighter's "huge, dark, crumpled embrace" a glimmer of hope. Using the present tense, the speaker imagines the child's "head falls back to his hand," giving us the possibility that "she will stand / again." The strength and professionalism of the firefighter give the poet confidence and pride and change her bitter irony and sadness to hope for a miracle. But in the final stanza, she must move from wishing for "a fine surprise" to the harsh realization that, regardless of the artistic quality of the photo, finally and irrevocably a child died in a place called broken heart.

A WRITING EXERCISE

Each of the poems in this cluster has a distinctive tone. Sometimes the narrator speaks in the first person; sometimes, in the third person as an observer. Compare the tone of the narrators in Charles Fort's or Mary Oliver's poem to the tone of Edwin Arlington Robinson's "The Mill," noting if it is easier to sense the narrator's tone when *I* or *we* is used.

Diction and Syntax

In "We Did Not Fear the Father," we initially assume that "fear" in the first line carries the usual negative **denotation** of anxiety, but the image that follows—the "general in a white jacket with a green visor"—doesn't seem threatening. In line three, "razor" and "sword" might cause concern, but that quickly dissolves under the positive **connotations** of "chariot" and "down-home chair." Except for the similes and metaphors, throughout the first stanza the diction and syntax seem almost colloquial and straightforward, mostly with the usual subject-verb-object pattern. The second half of the first stanza is also filled with positive connotations ("licorice," "offering plate," and "grape vines") that continue to undercut the worrisome "fear" of the first line.

But Fort repeats "We did not fear the father," this time referring to him not as barber but as landlord. Again the narrator's syntax and diction belie any threat. On the contrary, the poetic simile "lifted us like birds" suggests a gentle and strong provider.

In the last stanza, he again repeats the opening phrase but adds the simple but critical "until." Now we anticipate that there might actually be a reason for "fear" in its usual denotation. But again we see the father at work. Now as factory worker, "shaping molten steel ball bearings." The diction becomes more menacing ("barbed grate," "glow inside his skull," "metal scraping our ears," "punched out," "burned his eyes"). Now we are prepared for the simple declarative sentence: "We did not fear our father until he stooped in the dark." The poignant image of the father "stooped" dramatically clarifies the meaning of the ambiguous "fear": the children fear that his hard work has seriously weakened their general. Fort is actually fearful for his father and, of course, by extension fearful that his protector will be taken from him.

WRITING EXERCISE

Compare the diction and syntax in "Singapore" and "Blackberries." How do the denotation and connotation of the words convey the poet's attitude? How does the syntax?

Figures of Speech

When we use figures of speech, we mean something other than the words' literal meaning. In the first sentence of "Singapore," Mary Oliver writes that a "darkness was ripped from my eyes." This direct comparison is a **metaphor**. Had she been more indirect, she might have written "it was like a darkness . . . ," a common literary device called a **simile**. Poets use metaphors and similes to help us to see in a fresh perspective. Comparing love to a rose encourages us to think differently about love, helping us to see its delicate beauty. Of course, today that comparison is no longer novel and can even be a cliché, suggesting that a writer is not trying to be original and is settling instead for an easy comparison. When Robert Burns wrote "my love is like a red, red rose" over two hundred years ago, it was a fresh comparison that excited new ways of looking at love. Indeed, some thinkers, like the contemporary American philosopher Richard Rorty, think that metaphors can change our ways of looking at the world. Our thinking about time, for example, might be different if we didn't think with linear metaphors about the past being behind us and the future up ahead. What if, like some American Indian languages, we used a circular metaphor, having just one day that constantly repeated itself? Would our perceptions of time change?

What if Mary Oliver had begun her poem by saying that a misunderstanding was corrected, instead of "a darkness was ripped from my eyes"? Her metaphor is not only more dramatic and memorable but more suggestive. Darkness deepens the idea of lack of knowledge, suggesting not only intellectual blindness but a host of negative connotations that readers might associate with the dark. Fresh metaphors can be expansive and illuminating. They help us understand the world differently.

Oliver creatively uses metaphors and similes throughout "Singapore." "Disgust argued" is an interesting metaphor or perhaps a personification, where her stomach is given the ability to argue. Oliver interrupts her observation of the cleaning woman in the third stanza to make a comment on the function of poetry itself, claiming that poems should have birds, rivers, and trees in them. Is she suggesting metaphorically that poems should be pleasant? Is that the only thing birds, rivers, and trees suggest to you?

She returns to the woman, and they exchange glances. Apparently Oliver is struggling with her own socialization that sees this kind of physical labor as demeaning. She directly describes the woman's "scrubbing and rinsing" but then returns to similes, describing her work as "like a river" and her hair "like the wing of a bird." These comparisons seem for a moment to clarify the event for Oliver, helping her see this seemingly oppressive job positively. Amazingly, she wants the woman actually to become a bird and "rise up from the crust and the slop and fly."

But she reminds us in the final stanza that she isn't really expecting that kind of physical miracle; instead, she wants to remind us that how we describe the woman working controls how we feel about her. If we see the folding and unfolding of her wash cloth metaphorically, then we might see her differently; we might see her natural dignity, her beauty, and how her "light" was able to illuminate Mary Oliver's "darkness."

Although students often seem perplexed when professors find hidden **symbols** in poems, writers rarely plant such puzzling images deep in the recesses of their texts. The best symbols grow naturally out of the meaning-making process that readers go through. In the context of a particular poem, symbols are usually objects that can stand for general ideas. And like metaphors and similes, they suggest different things to different readers. The whale in *Moby-Dick*, for example, can be read as a symbol for implacable evil or perhaps the mysteries of the universe. The glass unicorn in *The Glass Menagerie* is often read as a symbol for Laura's fragility, but it might also suggest her uniqueness or maybe her isolation from real life. In "Singapore," the specific event of the poet watching a woman washing a toilet could be symbolic of anything we find unpleasant or strange or alien. And the whole event, including her eventual understanding, could easily be an **allegory** or extended symbol for the necessity for all of us to transcend our cultural socialization to understand other cultures and other attitudes toward working.

WRITING EXERCISE

Look at several of the poems in this cluster, noting the metaphors, similes, symbols, and allegories that you notice. Do they enhance the meaning of the poem? Do they help you see the situation in a fresh way?

Sound

The English poet Alexander Pope hoped that poetry's **sound** could become "an echo to [its] sense," that what the ear hears would reinforce what the mind understands. To many people, **rhyme** is the most recognizable aspect of poetry. The matching of final vowel and consonant sounds can make a poem trite or interesting. The now-familiar rhyming of "moon" and "June" with "swoon" suggests a poet that will settle for a cliché rather than do the hard work of being fresh. Rhyme, of course, is pleasing to the ear and makes the poem easier to remember, but it also gives the poem psychological force. Most contemporary poets choose not to rhyme, preferring the flexibility and freedom of free verse. But sound is still a high priority.

In Philip Levine's "What Work Is," for example, sound is used in subtle ways to reinforce meaning. Poets use *alliteration,* for example, to connect words near each other by repeating the initial consonant sound. A variation, *assonance,* repeats vowel sounds. Levine focuses on the shifting meaning of work, claiming first that "You know what work is" and then in the last line that "you don't know what work is." Levine begins by talking about the difficulties of physical labor and concludes by noting the difficult work of emotional intimacy. He creates patterns of sound that prepares us for this shift. A number of words are repeated: *work, stand, know, waiting, rain, long, love, sad, ahead, man, wide, not,* and *because,* as well as the phrase "You know what work is." And a number of words are alliteratively connected:

> forget, foot, feeling, falling, fingers
>
> someone, shoulders, same sad slouch, stubbornness, sad
>
> wasted waiting, wants, somewhere
>
> brother beside, behind
>
> works, worst, wide, words
>
> never, not

Although these sounds probably affect readers unconsciously, they do prepare us for a shift from people waiting for a job to the job of brotherly love. The repeated sounds connect both halves of the poem. Note the way *stand* first means being in line but later ("you can hardly stand / the love") connects with a brotherly bond. Similarly, *shift* first describes restless behavior in line but later the night job of the sleeping brother. The word *long* also fits this pattern, as it initially means the length of the line and later refers to the duration of their relationship: "How long has it been since you told him / you loved him." In these and other ways, Levine uses sound to enhance meaning.

WRITING EXERCISE

Note the use of alliteration in "In Creve Coeur." How might this and other sound devices enhance meaning?

Rhythm and Meter

Many poets in the early twentieth century chose to have their poems rhyme. Edwin Arlington Robinson's "The Mill" employs a typical **rhyme scheme** in which in each stanza the last words in lines 1 and 3 sound the same and the last words in lines 2 and 4 sound the same. We indicate such a pattern with letters — abab. The second half of the first stanza would then be cdcd and so forth.

Rhythm in poetry refers to the beat, a series of stresses, pauses, and accents. We are powerfully attuned to rhythm, whether it is our own heartbeat or the throb of the bass guitar in a rock band. When we pronounce a word, we give more **stress** (breath, emphasis) to some syllables than to others. When these stresses occur at a regular interval over, say, a line of poetry, we refer to it as **meter**. When we scan a line of poetry, we try to mark its stresses and pauses. We use ´ to indicate a stressed syllable and ˘ for an unstressed one. The basic measuring unit for these stressed and unstressed syllables in English is the **foot**. There are four usual feet: *iambic, trochaic, anapestic,* and *dactylic.* An **iamb** is an unstressed syllable followed by a stressed one, as in "the woods." Reversed we have a **trochee**, as in "tiger." An **anapest** contains three syllables that are unstressed, then unstressed, then stressed, as in "When the blue / wave rolls nightly / on deep Galilee." The reverse, the **dactyl**, can be heard in the Mother Goose rhyme, "Pussy cat, / pussy cat / where have you / been?" If you look at the first four lines of "The Mill" again, you can hear a regular beat of iambs:

> The mill / er's wife / had wait / ed long,
> The tea / was cold, / the fire / was dead
> And there / might yet / be noth / ing wrong
> In how / he went / and what / he said:

Depending on the number of feet, we give lines various names. If a line contains one foot, it is a **monometer**; two is a **dimeter**; three a **trimeter**; four a **tetrameter**; five a **pentameter**; six a **hexameter**; seven a **heptameter**; and eight an **octometer**. So Robinson's lines are iambic tetrameter. Most lines in Shakespeare's sonnets are iambic pentameter, or five iambs.

Note the punctuation in Robinson's poem. When a line ends with a comma, we are meant to pause very briefly; when a line ends with a period (end stop), we pause a bit longer. But when there is no punctuation (line 7), we are meant to continue on until the end of the next line. This is known as *enjambment.* These poetic techniques improve the sound and flow of the poem and enhance the thoughts and feelings that give poetry its memorable depth and meaningfulness.

A WRITING EXERCISE

Finish marking the rhythm and meter of "The Mill." Why do you think the poet chose these patterns rather than free verse? Does the rhyme add to the poem's somber, rather grim conclusion?

Theme

Some readers are fond of extracting **theme statements** from poems, claiming, for example, that the theme of "Blackberries" is the loss of innocence or that "What Work Is" is the emotional reticence of men. In a sense, these thematic observations are plausible enough, but they are limiting and misleading. "Blackberries" certainly seems to have something to do with the interruption of a certain view about physical labor, but the significance for each reader might be much more specific, having to do with the noble savage, the Garden of Eden, hierarchy in society, with the arrogance of the rich, with sensitivity, cruelty, and dignity. Reducing a complex, ambiguous poem to a bald statement robs the poem of its evocative power, its mystery, and its art.

Some critics stress the response of readers; others care only for what the text itself says; still others are concerned with the social and cultural implications of the poem's meaning. There are psychoanalytic readers who see poems as reflections of the psychological health or illness of the poet; source-hunting or intertextual readers want to find references and hints of other literary works hidden deep within the poem. Feminist readers may find sexism, Marxists may find economic injustice, and gay and lesbian readers may find heterosexual bias. Readers can and will find in texts a whole range of issues. Perhaps we find what we are looking for, or we find what matters most to us.

This does not mean that we should think of committed readers as biased or as distorting the text to fulfill their own agenda, although biased or distorted readings are not rare. In a literature course, readers are entitled to read poems according to their own interpretations as long as they follow the general convention of academic discourse. That is, it is possible to make a reasonable case that "Blackberries" is really about rejecting contemporary technology in favor of rural life. The reason that some themes sound more plausible than others is that these critics marshal their evidence from the text and their own experience. Usually the evidence that fits best wins: if you can persuade others that you have significant textual support for your theme and if you present a balanced and judicious persona, you can usually carry the day. Poems almost always have several reasonable themes. The critic's job is to argue for a theme that seems to make the most sense in relation to the support. Often the same evidence can be used to bolster different themes because themes are really just higher-level generalizations than the particulars found in the text. Critics use the concrete elements of a poem to make more general abstract statements. In "Blackberries," for example, the same textual support could be used to support the theme of the cruelty of children or the more general notion of an initiation in a class-conscious culture or the even more general idea of the inevitable loss of innocence.

WRITING EXERCISE

What are some possible themes introduced in "The Mill"? How might the theme change if read from the context of gender? Culture? Economics? Psychology?

Sample Student Paper: Revised Draft

Michaela Fiorucci

Mr. Hardee

English 102

Negotiating Boundaries

Although most college students value their privacy, they also want to create intimate relationships; it is often hard to reconcile these two impulses. Most middle-class students are lucky enough to have their own bedrooms, private enclaves against annoying sisters and brothers, intrusive mothers and fathers. But such boundaries are more than physical barriers; they are also a symbolic assertion of identity. They say, "I'm separate from you even within the closeness of our family." Such a commitment to physical privacy might be innocent enough, but it does contain dangerous seeds, especially when extended beyond the home to neighborhoods. When different ethnic groups want boundaries between them, it is no longer innocent. When the upper classes want to be separated from workers because they see each other as radically different, a dangerously undemocratic boundary has been erected. Boundaries clearly serve a protective function, but unneeded ones can also prevent us from helping and understanding each other. Writers like Edwin Arlington Robinson, Yusef Komunyakaa, and Mary Oliver understand that we must negotiate boundaries, building them when they increase privacy and self-worth and bridging them when human solidarity can be enhanced.

It would be reductive to say that boundaries are either good or bad, since their value depends so much on context. Robinson's "The Mill" is a good example of the dangerous consequences of a failure to cross a boundary that should not exist and then a failure to establish a boundary where one should exist. The poem narrates the sad story of a farm couple who commit suicide--the husband because he feels useless, the wife because she can't

imagine life without her husband. A contemporary reader
is struck by the lack of communication between the couple.
He must have been depressed for a long time, but it seems
they never discussed his feelings. Keeping such an emotional boundary between husband and wife was probably
typical of the way men and women dealt with each other
one hundred years ago. Apparently it was a constructed
barrier that few could cross. He simply could not bare
his heart by saying, "I feel terrible that I am going to
lose my job." And his wife accepts his reticence, even
though he might have been having second thoughts as he
"lingered at the door." Clearly this is a boundary that
should have been breached. The time for their solidarity
was before he kills himself, not after.

After several readings it is clear that the boundary
that should have been established wasn't. The miller is
the victim of the demeaning idea that a person's worth is
synonymous with his or her occupation. When his job disappears, so must he. Although Robinson's tone is flat, we
sense his frustration with the inevitability of this grim
tragedy, one that is compounded by the equally dehumanizing idea that a wife cannot exist without her husband.
When the miller's wife decides to "leave no mark" by
jumping into the pond, she is admitting that she is useless outside her matrimonial role. Both identify with a
role that should only be one aspect of a complex human
life. The final barrier she crosses, from life to death,
is symbolically represented in the poem as a feminine
domestic gesture: she doesn't want to leave a mess. She
continues as a housewife even in death. The boundaries
between a person and occupation should be clear, but the
arbitrary boundaries between husbands and wives should
continue to be eradicated.

When the ten-year-old narrator in "Blackberries"
claims that he is "Limboed between two worlds," he means
the rural paradise of "Terrestrial sweetness" and "rich
blackness" he temporarily lives in versus the commercial

urban world that seems to make him anxious. He has constructed a boundary between the ancient task of picking
berries and the modern technology of automobiles, between
a closeness with nature and the artificial air-condition-
ing of the car. Although the narrator enjoys being one
with nature, he seems to be cutting himself off from the
realities of the world. He seems to reject "old lime-
covered / History" in favor of "mythology," which seems to
suggest a conscious rejection of the present. But this is
a boundary that cannot stand. He needs the outside world
to survive financially, and so when the car approaches,
it is the modern world and all its complexity that draws
near. When he looks into the car, he sees "smirking children"; he sees class prejudice, hierarchy, and economic
reality. The smirkers of the world are in charge. It is
this realization that dissolves the protective boundary
around his Garden of Eden; consequently, he feels physical pain, but it is really the pain of initiation into
reality that he feels. He must now cross a boundary he
tried to delay. Although we can sympathize with the young
narrator, like the couple in "The Mill," he would have
been better off not making his boundary so extreme.

The narrator in Mary Oliver's "Singapore" also imagines that she sees a significant boundary, here between
herself as a middle-class traveler and a cleaning woman
laboring over a toilet. It is a separation we might all
make, given our socialization in America to consider this
kind of physical labor as degrading. College-educated
people have a tendency to see themselves as distinct from
the working class. For many, a woman washing an ashtray
in a toilet bowl is beyond the pale, a clear indication
that the woman is Other. But Oliver does not simply give
into her cultural conditioning; she contests the boundary, asserting that a "Disgust argued in my stomach."
Since part of our democratic socialization is also to be
tolerant and open-minded, Oliver knows that she shouldn't
stereotype workers. And since she is also a writer with

ideas about how a poem should "always have birds in it," she looks hard at the cleaning woman, finally seeing in her face, in her hair, and in the way she works, slowly "like a river," the positive aspects of the woman that most of us would probably miss.

Oliver does not simply accept the boundaries that her culture constructs. Instead, she negotiates internally, eventually seeing that a "light can shine out of a life" even where we would not expect it. In the woman's careful folding and unfolding of her blue work cloth and in her smile, Oliver sees a beauty that helps her eclipse a social boundary, ending with a life-affirming vision "filled with trees, with birds." Such an insight does not come easily to us because we usually accept our given cultural boundaries. The miller and his wife are tragically unequipped to bridge the divide between them. Likewise, the boy in "Blackberries" is unable to sustain his fantasy boundaries. Oliver's traveler, however, struggles to negotiate boundaries and is thereby able to increase human solidarity even across class structures and cultures.

SUMMING UP

- The elements of poetry include *speaker* and *tone, diction* and *syntax, figures of speech, sound, rhythm* and *meter,* and *theme.*

- **Identify the speaker and tone.** The voice we hear in a poem is often a *persona* — that is, a "mask" that could be the poet's real voice or a complete fiction. Paying áttention to the speaker's tone — that is, his or her attitude — illuminates a poem's meaning.

- **Be aware of the complexities of *diction* and *syntax.*** In poetry, the connotations or emotional and personal associations of the diction — word choice — often suggest more than the literal meaning of the words. Poetry is more compressed and indirect than prose, so meaning is often suggested through connotation, metaphor, and imagery, and is seldom finite. The order of the words — syntax — can be varied and experimented with to amplify and complicate meaning.

(continued on next page)

◆ **Major figures of speech include *metaphor* and *symbols*.** A metaphor is a dramatic direct comparison—"Love is a rose," "Faith is a sea"—poets use to help readers see and think differently and creatively. Symbols suggest more general ideas. They reinforce or extend the poem's possible meanings, and rarely point in one direction.

◆ ***Sound, rhythm,* and *meter* work together to give a poem psychological force.** How a poem sounds is often overlooked, perhaps because modern poems often do not rhyme. *Alliteration,* for example, connects words and enhances meaning. As in music, rhythm adds to the meaning of poetry, encircling the thoughts and feeling that give poetry depth and meaning.

◆ **Don't expect a poem's *theme* to be straightforward or clear-cut.** Strong poems are rich, complex, and often ambiguous. Theme statements such as " 'What Work Is' is about the emotional reticence of men" are often misleading and limiting. Although plausible enough, a number of other ideas are certainly possible. Be wary of reducing a poem's theme to a bold statement that robs the poem of its evocative power.

◆ **Arguing successfully that your interpretation is worth considering depends largely on the validity of your evidence.** Poems almost always have several reasonable themes. We can, however, argue strongly for a theme if we can support our claim. The critic who can present the best evidence for a particular theme in a balanced and judicious way is often the most persuasive.

6

Making Arguments
about Plays

Most plays incorporate elements also found in short fiction, such as plot, characterization, dialogue, setting, and theme. But unlike short fiction and other literary genres, plays are typically enacted live, in front of an audience. Theater professionals distinguish between the written *script* of a play and its actual *performances*. When you write about a play, you may wind up saying little or nothing about performances of it. When you first read and analyze a play, however, try to imagine ways of staging it. You might even research past productions of the play, noting how scenery, costumes, and lighting—as well as particular actors—were used.

Because a play is usually meant to be staged, its readers are rarely its only interpreters. Theater audiences also ponder its meanings. So, too, do cast members; no doubt you have heard of actors "interpreting" their parts. When a play is put on, even members of the backstage team are involved in interpreting it. The technical designers' choices of sets, costumes, and lighting reflect their ideas about the play, while the director works with cast and crew to implement a particular vision of it. No matter what the author of the script intended, theater is a collaborative art: All of the key figures involved in a play's production are active interpreters of the play in that they influence the audience's understanding and experience of it. Therefore, you can develop good ideas when you read a play if you imagine yourself directing a production of it. More specifically, think what you would say to the actors as you guided them through their parts. As you engage in this thought experiment, you will see that you have options, for even directors keen on staying faithful to the script know it can be staged in any number of ways. Perhaps your course will give you and other students the chance to perform a scene together; if so, you will be deciding what interpretation of the scene to set forth.

To help you understand how to write about plays, we will refer often to the two one-act plays that follow. Both works explore relations between women. The first play, *The Stronger*, had its stage debut in 1889. Its author, the Swedish playwright August Strindberg (1849–1912), is widely acknowledged as a founder of modern drama. Throughout his career, Strindberg experimented with theatrical styles. For this particular play about an encounter between two actresses, he

138

unconventionally chose to have one character speak and the other remain silent. The second play, Susan Glaspell's *Trifles*, premiered in 1916 with the author and her husband, the novelist George Cram Cook, in the cast. Glaspell (1876–1948) is best known for her association with the Provincetown Players, which was considered avant-garde in its day. Glaspell and Cook had founded the company a year earlier while vacationing in Provincetown, Massachusetts. Since its debut, the play has continued to be performed and read, in part because it is a compelling detective story as well as an analysis of female relations.

AUGUST STRINDBERG
The Stronger

Translated by Elizabeth Sprigge

CHARACTERS

MRS. X, *actress, married*
MISS Y, *actress, unmarried*
A WAITRESS

SCENE: *A corner of a ladies' café [in Stockholm in the eighteen eighties].° Two small wrought-iron tables, a red plush settee, and a few chairs.*

Miss Y is sitting with a half-empty bottle of beer on the table before her, reading an illustrated weekly which from time to time she exchanges for another.

Mrs. X enters, wearing a winter hat and coat and carrying a decorative Japanese basket.

MRS. X: Why, Millie, my dear, how are you? Sitting here all alone on Christmas Eve like some poor bachelor.

Miss Y looks up from her magazine, nods, and continues to read.

MRS. X: You know it makes me feel really sad to see you. Alone. Alone in a café and on Christmas Eve of all times. It makes me feel as sad as when once in Paris I saw a wedding party at a restaurant. The bride was reading a comic paper and the bridegroom playing billiards with the witnesses. Ah me, I said to myself, with such a beginning how will it go, and how will it end? He was playing billiards on his wedding day! And she, you were going to say, was reading a comic paper on hers. But that's not quite the same.

A waitress brings a cup of chocolate to Mrs. X and goes out.

MRS. X: Do you know, Amelia, I really believe now you would have done better to stick to him. Don't forget I was the first who told you to forgive him. Do you remember? Then you would be married now and have a home. Think how happy you were that Christmas when you stayed with your fiancé's

---

Addition to scene bracketed. First mention of Miss Y and Mrs. X reversed. [Translator's note]

people in the country. How warmly you spoke of domestic happiness! You really quite longed to be out of the theatre. Yes, Amelia dear, home is best — next best to the stage, and as for children — but you couldn't know anything about that.

Miss Y's expression is disdainful. Mrs. X sips a few spoonfuls of chocolate, then opens her basket and displays some Christmas presents.

MRS. X: Now you must see what I have bought for my little chicks. *(Takes out a doll.)* Look at this. That's for Lisa. Do you see how she can roll her eyes and turn her head. Isn't she lovely? And here's a toy pistol for Maja.° *(She loads the pistol and shoots it at Miss Y who appears frightened.)*

MRS. X: Were you scared? Did you think I was going to shoot you? Really, I didn't think you'd believe that of me. Now if *you* were to shoot *me* it wouldn't be so surprising, for after all I did get in your way, and I know you never forget it — although I was entirely innocent. You still think I intrigued to get you out of the Grand Theatre, but I didn't. I didn't, however much you think I did. Well, it's no good talking, you will believe it was me . . . *(Takes out a pair of embroidered slippers.)* And these are for my old man, with tulips on them that I embroidered myself. As a matter of fact I hate tulips, but he has to have tulips on everything.

Miss Y looks up, irony and curiosity in her face.

MRS. X *(putting one hand in each slipper)*:   Look what small feet Bob has, hasn't he? And you ought to see the charming way he walks — you've never seen him in slippers, have you?

Miss Y laughs.

MRS. X: Look, I'll show you. *(She makes the slippers walk across the table, and Miss Y laughs again.)*

MRS. X: But when he gets angry, look, he stamps his foot like this. "Those damn girls who can never learn how to make coffee! Blast! That silly idiot hasn't trimmed the lamp properly!" Then there's a draught under the door and his feet get cold. "Hell, it's freezing, and the damn fools can't even keep the stove going!" *(She rubs the sole of one slipper against the instep of the other. Miss Y roars with laughter.)*

MRS. X: And then he comes home and has to hunt for his slippers, which Mary has pushed under the bureau . . . Well, perhaps it's not right to make fun of one's husband like this. He's sweet anyhow, and a good, dear husband. You ought to have had a husband like him, Amelia. What are you laughing at? What is it? Eh? And, you see, I know he is faithful to me. Yes, I know it. He told me himself — what *are* you giggling at? — that while I was on tour in Norway that horrible Frederica came and tried to seduce him. Can you imagine anything more abominable? *(Pause.)* I'd have scratched her eyes out if she had come around while I was at home. *(Pause.)* I'm glad Bob told me about it himself, so I didn't just hear it from gossip. *(Pause.)* And, as a matter of fact,

Maja: Pronounced Maya.

Frederica wasn't the only one. I can't think why, but all the women in the Company° seem to be crazy about my husband. They must think his position gives him some say in who is engaged at the Theatre. Perhaps you have run after him yourself? I don't trust you very far, but I know he has never been attracted by you, and you always seemed to have some sort of grudge against him, or so I felt. *(Pause. They look at one another guardedly.)*

MRS. X: Do come and spend Christmas Eve with us tonight, Amelia — just to show that you're not offended with us, or anyhow not with me. I don't know why, but it seems specially unpleasant not to be friends with you. Perhaps it's because I did get in your way that time . . . *(slowly)* or — I don't know — really, I don't know at all why it is.

Pause. Miss Y gazes curiously at Mrs. X.

MRS. X *(thoughtfully)*:   It was so strange when we were getting to know one another. Do you know, when we first met, I was frightened of you, so frightened I didn't dare let you out of my sight. I arranged all my goings and comings to be near you. I dared not be your enemy, so I became your friend. But when you came to our home, I always had an uneasy feeling, because I saw my husband didn't like you, and that irritated me — like when a dress doesn't fit. I did all I could to make him be nice to you, but it was no good — until you went and got engaged. Then you became such tremendous friends that at first it looked as if you only dared show your real feelings then — when you were safe. And then, let me see, how was it after that? I wasn't jealous — that's queer. And I remember at the christening, when you were the godmother, I told him to kiss you. He did, and you were so upset . . . As a matter of fact I didn't notice that then . . . I didn't think about it afterwards either . . . I've never thought about it — until *now! (Rises abruptly.)* Why don't you say something? You haven't said a word all this time. You've just let me go on talking. You have sat there with your eyes drawing all these thoughts out of me — they were there in me like silk in a cocoon — thoughts . . . Mistaken thoughts? Let me think. Why did you break off your engagement? Why did you never come to our house after that? Why don't you want to come to us tonight?

Miss Y makes a motion, as if about to speak.

MRS. X: No. You don't need to say anything, for now I see it all. That was why — and why — and why. Yes. Yes, that's why it was. Yes, yes, all the pieces fit together now. That's it. I won't sit at the same table as you. *(Moves her things to the other table.)* That's why I have to embroider tulips, which I loathe, on his slippers — because you liked tulips. *(Throws the slippers on the floor.)* That's why we have to spend the summer on the lake — because you couldn't bear the seaside. That's why my son had to be called Eskil — because it was your father's name. That's why I had to wear your colours, read your books, eat the dishes you liked, drink your drinks — your chocolate, for instance. That's why — oh my God, it's terrible to think of, terrible! Everything, everything came to me from

in the Company: Translator's addition.

you — even your passions. Your soul bored into mine like a worm into an apple, and ate and ate and burrowed and burrowed, till nothing was left but the skin and a little black mould. I wanted to fly from you, but I couldn't. You were there like a snake, your black eyes fascinating me. When I spread my wings, they only dragged me down. I lay in the water with my feet tied together, and the harder I worked my arms, the deeper I sank — down, down, till I reached the bottom, where you lay in waiting like a giant crab to catch me in your claws — and now here I am. Oh how I hate you! I hate you, I hate you! And you just go on sitting there, silent, calm, indifferent, not caring whether the moon is new or full, if it's Christmas or New Year, if other people are happy or unhappy. You don't know how to hate or to love. You just sit there without moving — like a cat° at a mouse-hole. You can't drag your prey out, you can't chase it, but you can out-stay it. Here you sit in your corner — you know they call it the rat-trap after you — reading the papers to see if anyone's ruined or wretched or been thrown out of the Company. Here you sit sizing up your victims and weighing your chances — like a pilot his shipwrecks for the salvage. *(Pause.)* Poor Amelia! Do you know, I couldn't be more sorry for you. I know you are miserable, miserable like some wounded creature, and vicious because you are wounded. I can't be angry with you. I should like to be, but after all you are the small one — and as for your affair with Bob, that doesn't worry me in the least. Why should it matter to me? And if you, or somebody else taught me to drink chocolate, what's the difference? *(Drinks a spoonful. Smugly.)* Chocolate is very wholesome anyhow. And if I learnt from you how to dress, *tant mieux!*° — that only gave me a stronger hold over my husband, and you have lost what I gained. Yes, to judge from various signs, I think you have now lost him. Of course, you meant me to walk out, as you once did, and which you're now regretting. But I won't do that, you may be sure. One shouldn't be narrow-minded, you know. And why should nobody else want what I have? *(Pause.)* Perhaps, my dear, taking everything into consideration, at this moment it is I who am the stronger. You never got anything from me, you just gave away — from yourself. And now, like the thief in the night, when you woke up I had what you had lost. Why was it then that everything you touched became worthless and sterile? You couldn't keep a man's love — for all your tulips and your passions — but I could. You couldn't learn the art of living from your books — but I learnt it. You bore no little Eskil, although that was your father's name. *(Pause.)* And why is it you are silent — everywhere, always silent? Yes, I used to think this was strength, but perhaps it was because you hadn't anything to say, because you couldn't think of anything. *(Rises and picks up the slippers.)* Now I am going home, taking the tulips with me — *your* tulips. You couldn't learn from others, you couldn't bend, and so you broke like a dry stick. I did not. Thank you, Amelia, for all your good lessons. Thank you for teaching my husband how to love. Now I am going home — to love him.

Exit. [1907]

---

cat: In Swedish, "stork." **tant mieux:** French for "so much the better."

SUSAN GLASPELL
Trifles

CHARACTERS

GEORGE HENDERSON, *county attorney*

HENRY PETERS, *sheriff*

LEWIS HALE, *a neighboring farmer*

MRS. PETERS

MRS. HALE

SCENE: *The kitchen in the now abandoned farmhouse of John Wright, a gloomy kitchen, and left without having been put in order — the walls covered with a faded wall paper. Down right is a door leading to the parlor. On the right wall above this door is a built-in kitchen cupboard with shelves in the upper portion and drawers below. In the rear wall at right, up two steps is a door opening onto stairs leading to the second floor. In the rear wall at left is a door to the shed and from there to the outside. Between these two doors is an old-fashioned black iron stove. Running along the left wall from the shed door is an old iron sink and sink shelf, in which is set a hand pump. Downstage of the sink is an uncurtained window. Near the window is an old wooden rocker. Centerstage is an unpainted wooden kitchen table with straight chairs on either side. There is a small chair down right. Unwashed pans under the sink, a loaf of bread outside the breadbox, a dish towel on the table — other signs of incompleted work. At the rear the shed door opens and the Sheriff comes in followed by the County Attorney and Hale. The Sheriff and Hale are men in middle life, the County Attorney is a young man; all are much bundled up and go at once to the stove. They are followed by the two women — the Sheriff's wife, Mrs. Peters, first; she is a slight wiry woman, a thin nervous face. Mrs. Hale is larger and would ordinarily be called more comfortable looking, but she is disturbed now and looks fearfully about as she enters. The women have come in slowly, and stand close together near the door.*

COUNTY ATTORNEY (*at stove rubbing his hands*):   This feels good. Come up to the fire, ladies.

MRS. PETERS (*after taking a step forward*):   I'm not — cold.

SHERIFF (*unbuttoning his overcoat and stepping away from the stove to right of table as if to mark the beginning of official business*):   Now, Mr. Hale, before we move things about, you explain to Mr. Henderson just what you saw when you came here yesterday morning.

COUNTY ATTORNEY (*crossing down to left of the table*):   By the way, has anything been moved? Are things just as you left them yesterday?

SHERIFF (*looking about*):   It's just about the same. When it dropped below zero last night I thought I'd better send Frank out this morning to make a fire for us — (*sits right of center table*) no use getting pneumonia with a big case on, but I told him not to touch anything except the stove — and you know Frank.

COUNTY ATTORNEY: Somebody should have been left here yesterday.

SHERIFF: Oh—yesterday. When I had to send Frank to Morris Center for that man who went crazy—I want you to know I had my hands full yesterday. I knew you could get back from Omaha by today and as long as I went over everything here myself——

COUNTY ATTORNEY: Well, Mr. Hale, tell just what happened when you came here yesterday morning.

HALE *(crossing down to above table)*: Harry and I had started to town with a load of potatoes. We came along the road from my place and as I got here I said, "I'm going to see if I can't get John Wright to go in with me on a party telephone." I spoke to Wright about it once before and he put me off, saying folks talked too much anyway, and all he asked was peace and quiet—I guess you know about how much he talked himself; but I thought maybe if I went to the house and talked about it before his wife, though I said to Harry that I didn't know as what his wife wanted made much difference to John——

COUNTY ATTORNEY: Let's talk about that later, Mr. Hale. I do want to talk about that, but tell now just what happened when you got to the house.

HALE: I didn't hear or see anything; I knocked at the door, and still it was all quiet inside. I knew they must be up, it was past eight o'clock. So I knocked again, and I thought I heard somebody say, "Come in." I wasn't sure, I'm not sure yet, but I opened the door—this door *(indicating the door by which the two women are still standing)* and there in that rocker—*(pointing to it)* sat Mrs. Wright. *(They all look at the rocker down left.)*

COUNTY ATTORNEY: What—was she doing?

HALE: She was rockin' back and forth. She had her apron in her hand and was kind of—pleating it.

COUNTY ATTORNEY: And how did she—look?

HALE: Well, she looked queer.

COUNTY ATTORNEY: How do you mean—queer?

HALE: Well, as if she didn't know what she was going to do next. And kind of done up.

COUNTY ATTORNEY *(takes out notebook and pencil and sits left of center table)*: How did she seem to feel about your coming?

HALE: Why, I don't think she minded—one way or other. She didn't pay much attention. I said, "How do, Mrs. Wright, it's cold, ain't it?" And she said, "Is it?"—and went on kind of pleating at her apron. Well, I was surprised; she didn't ask me to come up to the stove, or to set down, but just sat there, not even looking at me, so I said, "I want to see John." And then she—laughed. I guess you would call it a laugh. I thought of Harry and the team outside, so I said a little sharp: "Can't I see John?" "No," she says, kind o' dull like. "Ain't he home?" says I. "Yes," says she, "he's home." "Then why can't I see him?" I asked her, out of patience. " 'Cause he's dead," says she. "*Dead?*" says I. She just nodded her head, not getting a bit excited, but rockin' back and forth. "Why—where is he?" says I, not knowing what to say. She just pointed upstairs—like that. *(Himself pointing to the room above.)* I started for the stairs, with the idea of going up there. I walked from there to here—then I says, "Why, what did he die of?" "He died of a rope round his neck," says she, and just went on pleatin' at her apron. Well, I went out and called Harry. I thought I might—need help. We went upstairs and there he was lyin'———

COUNTY ATTORNEY: I think I'd rather have you go into that upstairs, where you can point it all out. Just go on now with the rest of the story.

HALE: Well, my first thought was to get that rope off. It looked . . . (*stops; his face twitches*) . . . but Harry, he went up to him, and he said, "No, he's dead all right, and we'd better not touch anything." So we went back downstairs. She was still sitting that same way. "Has anybody been notified?" I asked. "No," says she, unconcerned. "Who did this, Mrs. Wright?" said Harry. He said it businesslike—and she stopped pleatin' of her apron. "I don't know," she says. "You don't *know*?" says Harry. "No," says she. "Weren't you sleepin' in the bed with him?" says Harry. "Yes," says she, "but I was on the inside." "Somebody slipped a rope round his neck and strangled him and you didn't wake up?" says Harry. "I didn't wake up," she said after him. We must 'a' looked as if we didn't see how that could be, for after a minute she said, "I sleep sound." Harry was going to ask her more questions but I said maybe we ought to let her tell her story first to the coroner, or the sheriff, so Harry went fast as he could to Rivers' place, where there's a telephone.

COUNTY ATTORNEY: And what did Mrs. Wright do when she knew that you had gone for the coroner?

HALE: She moved from the rocker to that chair over there (*pointing to a small chair in the down right corner*) and just sat there with her hands held together and looking down. I got a feeling that I ought to make some conversation, so I said I had come in to see if John wanted to put in a telephone, and at that she started to laugh, and then she stopped and looked at me—scared. (*The County Attorney, who has had his notebook out, makes a note.*) I dunno, maybe it wasn't scared. I wouldn't like to say it was. Soon Harry got back, and then Dr. Lloyd came and you, Mr. Peters, and so I guess that's all I know that you don't.

COUNTY ATTORNEY (*rising and looking around*): I guess we'll go upstairs first— and then out to the barn and around there. (*To the Sheriff.*) You're convinced that there was nothing important here—nothing that would point to any motive?

SHERIFF: Nothing here but kitchen things. (*The County Attorney, after again looking around the kitchen, opens the door of a cupboard closet in right wall. He brings a small chair from right—gets on it and looks on a shelf. Pulls his hand away, sticky.*)

COUNTY ATTORNEY: Here's a nice mess. (*The women draw nearer up center.*)

MRS. PETERS (*to the other woman*): Oh, her fruit; it did freeze. (*To the Lawyer.*) She worried about that when it turned so cold. She said the fire'd go out and her jars would break.

SHERIFF (*rises*): Well, can you beat the woman! Held for murder and worryin' about her preserves.

COUNTY ATTORNEY (*getting down from chair*): I guess before we're through she may have something more serious than preserves to worry about. (*Crosses down right center.*)

HALE: Well, women are used to worrying over trifles. (*The two women move a little closer together.*)

COUNTY ATTORNEY (*with the gallantry of a young politician*):   And yet, for all their worries, what would we do without the ladies? (*The women do not unbend. He goes below the center table to the sink, takes a dipperful of water from the pail, and pouring it into a basin, washes his hands. While he is doing this the Sheriff and Hale cross to cupboard, which they inspect. The County Attorney starts to wipe his hands on the roller towel, turns it for a cleaner place.*) Dirty towels! (*Kicks his foot against the pans under the sink.*) Not much of a housekeeper, would you say, ladies?

MRS. HALE (*stiffly*):   There's a great deal of work to be done on a farm.

COUNTY ATTORNEY: To be sure. And yet (*with a little bow to her*) I know there are some Dickson County farmhouses which do not have such roller towels. (*He gives it a pull to expose its full-length again.*)

MRS. HALE: Those towels get dirty awful quick. Men's hands aren't always as clean as they might be.

COUNTY ATTORNEY: Ah, loyal to your sex, I see. But you and Mrs. Wright were neighbors. I suppose you were friends, too.

MRS. HALE (*shaking her head*):   I've not seen much of her of late years. I've not been in this house — it's more than a year.

COUNTY ATTORNEY (*crossing to women up center*):   And why was that? You didn't like her?

MRS. HALE: I liked her all well enough. Farmers' wives have their hands full, Mr. Henderson. And then——

COUNTY ATTORNEY: Yes——?

MRS. HALE (*looking about*):   It never seemed a very cheerful place.

COUNTY ATTORNEY: No — it's not cheerful. I shouldn't say she had the home-making instinct.

MRS. HALE: Well, I don't know as Wright had, either.

COUNTY ATTORNEY: You mean that they didn't get on very well?

MRS. HALE: No, I don't mean anything. But I don't think a place'd be any cheer-fuller for John Wright's being in it.

COUNTY ATTORNEY: I'd like to talk more of that a little later. I want to get the lay of things upstairs now. (*He goes past the women to up right where steps lead to a stair door.*)

SHERIFF: I suppose anything Mrs. Peters does'll be all right. She was to take in some clothes for her, you know, and a few little things. We left in such a hurry yesterday.

COUNTY ATTORNEY: Yes, but I would like to see what you take, Mrs. Peters, and keep an eye out for anything that might be of use to us.

MRS. PETERS: Yes, Mr. Henderson. (*The men leave by up right door to stairs. The women listen to the men's steps on the stairs, then look about the kitchen.*)

MRS. HALE (*crossing left to sink*):   I'd hate to have men coming into my kitchen, snooping around and criticizing. (*She arranges the pans under sink which the lawyer had shoved out of place.*)

MRS. PETERS: Of course it's no more than their duty. (*Crosses to cupboard up right.*)

MRS. HALE: Duty's all right, but I guess that deputy sheriff that came out to make the fire might have got a little of this on. (*Gives the roller towel a pull.*) Wish I'd thought of that sooner. Seems mean to talk about her for not having things slicked up when she had to come away in such a hurry. (*Crosses right to Mrs. Peters at cupboard.*)

MRS. PETERS (*who has been looking through cupboard, lifts one end of towel that covers a pan*):   She had bread set. (*Stands still.*)

MRS. HALE (*eyes fixed on a loaf of bread beside the breadbox, which is on a low shelf of the cupboard*):   She was going to put this in there. (*Picks up loaf, abruptly drops it. In a manner of returning to familiar things.*) It's a shame about her fruit. I wonder if it's all gone. (*Gets up on the chair and looks.*) I think there's some here that's all right, Mrs. Peters. Yes—here; (*holding it toward the window*) this is cherries, too. (*Looking again.*) I declare I believe that's the only one. (*Gets down, jar in her hand. Goes to the sink and wipes it off on the outside.*) She'll feel awful bad after all her hard work in the hot weather. I remember the afternoon I put up my cherries last summer. (*She puts the jar on the big kitchen table, center of the room. With a sigh, is about to sit down in the rocking chair. Before she is seated realizes what chair it is; with a slow look at it, steps back. The chair which she has touched rocks back and forth. Mrs. Peters moves to center table and they both watch the chair rock for a moment or two.*)

MRS. PETERS (*shaking off the mood which the empty rocking chair has evoked. Now in a businesslike manner she speaks*):   Well I must get those things from the front room closet. (*She goes to the door at the right but, after looking into the other room, steps back.*) You coming with me, Mrs. Hale? You could help me carry them. (*They go in the other room; reappear, Mrs. Peters carrying a dress, petticoat, and skirt, Mrs. Hale following with a pair of shoes.*) My, it's cold in there. (*She puts the clothes on the big table and hurries to the stove.*)

MRS. HALE (*right of center table examining the skirt*):   Wright was close. I think maybe that's why she kept so much to herself. She didn't even belong to the Ladies' Aid. I suppose she felt she couldn't do her part, and then you don't enjoy things when you feel shabby. I heard she used to wear pretty clothes and be lively, when she was Minnie Foster, one of the town girls singing in the choir. But that—oh, that was thirty years ago. This all you want to take in?

MRS. PETERS: She said she wanted an apron. Funny thing to want, for there isn't much to get you dirty in jail, goodness knows. But I suppose just to make her feel more natural. (*Crosses to cupboard.*) She said they was in the top drawer in this cupboard. Yes, here. And then her little shawl that always hung behind the door. (*Opens stair door and looks.*) Yes, here it is. (*Quickly shuts door leading upstairs.*)

MRS. HALE (*abruptly moving toward her*):   Mrs. Peters?

MRS. PETERS: Yes, Mrs. Hale? (*At up right door.*)

MRS. HALE: Do you think she did it?

MRS. PETERS (*in a frightened voice*):   Oh, I don't know.

MRS. HALE: Well, I don't think she did. Asking for an apron and her little shawl. Worrying about her fruit.

MRS. PETERS (*starts to speak, glances up, where footsteps are heard in the room above. In a low voice*):   Mr. Peters says it looks bad for her. Mr. Henderson is awful sarcastic in a speech and he'll make fun of her sayin' she didn't wake up.

MRS. HALE: Well, I guess John Wright didn't wake when they was slipping that rope under his neck.

MRS. PETERS (*crossing slowly to table and placing shawl and apron on table with other clothing*):   No, it's strange. It must have been done awful crafty and still. They say it was such a—funny way to kill a man, rigging it all up like that.

MRS. HALE (*crossing to left of Mrs. Peters at table*):   That's just what Mr. Hale said. There was a gun in the house. He says that's what he can't understand.

MRS. PETERS: Mr. Henderson said coming out that what was needed for the case was a motive; something to show anger, or—sudden feeling.

MRS. HALE (*who is standing by the table*):   Well, I don't see any signs of anger around here. (*She puts her hand on the dish towel, which lies on the table, stands looking down at table, one-half of which is clean, the other half messy.*) It's wiped to here. (*Makes a move as if to finish work, then turns and looks at loaf of bread outside the breadbox. Drops towel. In that voice of coming back to familiar things.*) Wonder how they are finding things upstairs. (*Crossing below table to down right.*) I hope she had it a little more red-up up there. You know, it seems kind of *sneaking*. Locking her up in town and then coming out here and trying to get her own house to turn against her!

MRS. PETERS: But, Mrs. Hale, the law is the law.

MRS. HALE: I s'pose 'tis. (*Unbuttoning her coat.*) Better loosen up your things, Mrs. Peters. You won't feel them when you go out. (*Mrs. Peters takes off her fur tippet, goes to hang it on chair back left of table, stands looking at the work basket on floor near down left window.*)

MRS. PETERS: She was piecing a quilt. (*She brings the large sewing basket to the center table and they look at the bright pieces, Mrs. Hale above the table and Mrs. Peters left of it.*)

MRS. HALE: It's a log cabin pattern. Pretty, isn't it? I wonder if she was goin' to quilt it or just knot it? (*Footsteps have been heard coming down the stairs. The Sheriff enters followed by Hale and the County Attorney.*)

SHERIFF: They wonder if she was going to quilt it or just knot it! (*The men laugh, the women look abashed.*)

COUNTY ATTORNEY (*rubbing his hands over the stove*):   Frank's fire didn't do much up there, did it? Well, let's go out to the barn and get that cleared up. (*The men go outside by up left door.*)

MRS. HALE (*resentfully*):   I don't know as there's anything so strange, our takin' up our time with little things while we're waiting for them to get the evidence. (*She sits in chair right of table smoothing out a block with decision.*) I don't see as it's anything to laugh about.

MRS. PETERS (*apologetically*):   Of course they've got awful important things on their minds. (*Pulls up a chair and joins Mrs. Hale at the left of the table.*)

MRS. HALE (*examining another block*):   Mrs. Peters, look at this one. Here, this is the one she was working on, and look at the sewing! All the rest of it has been so nice and even. And look at this! It's all over the place! Why, it looks as if she didn't know what she was about! (*After she has said this they look at each other, then start to glance back at the door. After an instant Mrs. Hale has pulled at a knot and ripped the sewing.*)

MRS. PETERS: Oh, what are you doing, Mrs. Hale?

MRS. HALE (*mildly*):   Just pulling out a stitch or two that's not sewed very good. (*Threading a needle.*) Bad sewing always made me fidgety.

MRS. PETERS (*with a glance at door, nervously*):   I don't think we ought to touch things.

MRS. HALE: I'll just finish up this end. (*Suddenly stopping and leaning forward.*) Mrs. Peters?

MRS. PETERS: Yes, Mrs. Hale?

MRS. HALE: What do you suppose she was so nervous about?

MRS. PETERS: Oh — I don't know. I don't know as she was nervous. I sometimes sew awful queer when I'm just tired. (*Mrs. Hale starts to say something, looks at Mrs. Peters, then goes on sewing.*) Well, I must get these things wrapped up. They may be through sooner than we think. (*Putting apron and other things together.*) I wonder where I can find a piece of paper, and string. (*Rises.*)

MRS. HALE: In that cupboard, maybe.

MRS. PETERS (*crosses right looking in cupboard*):   Why, here's a bird-cage. (*Holds it up.*) Did she have a bird, Mrs. Hale?

MRS. HALE: Why, I don't know whether she did or not — I've not been here for so long. There was a man around last year selling canaries cheap, but I don't know as she took one; maybe she did. She used to sing real pretty herself.

MRS. PETERS (*glancing around*):   Seems funny to think of a bird here. But she must have had one, or why would she have a cage? I wonder what happened to it?

MRS. HALE: I s'pose maybe the cat got it.

MRS. PETERS: No, she didn't have a cat. She's got that feeling some people have about cats — being afraid of them. My cat got in her room and she was real upset and asked me to take it out.

MRS. HALE: My sister Bessie was like that. Queer, ain't it?

MRS. PETERS (*examining the cage*):   Why, look at this door. It's broke. One hinge is pulled apart. (*Takes a step down to Mrs. Hale's right.*)

MRS. HALE (*looking too*):   Looks as if someone must have been rough with it.

MRS. PETERS: Why, yes. (*She brings the cage forward and puts it on the table.*)

MRS. HALE (*glancing toward up left door*):   I wish if they're going to find any evidence they'd be about it. I don't like this place.

MRS. PETERS: But I'm awful glad you came with me, Mrs. Hale. It would be lonesome for me sitting here alone.

MRS. HALE: It would, wouldn't it? *(Dropping her sewing.)* But I tell you what I do wish, Mrs. Peters. I wish I had come over sometimes when *she* was here. I — *(looking around the room)* — wish I had.

MRS. PETERS: But of course you were awful busy, Mrs. Hale — your house and your children.

MRS. HALE *(rises and crosses left)*:   I could've come. I stayed away because it weren't cheerful — and that's why I ought to have come. I — *(looking out left window)* — I've never liked this place. Maybe because it's down in a hollow and you don't see the road. I dunno what it is, but it's a lonesome place and always was. I wish I had come over to see Minnie Foster sometimes. I can see now — *(Shakes her head.)*

MRS. PETERS *(left of table and above it)*:   Well, you mustn't reproach yourself, Mrs. Hale. Somehow we just don't see how it is with other folks until — something turns up.

MRS. HALE: Not having children makes less work — but it makes a quiet house, and Wright out to work all day, and no company when he did come in. *(Turning from window.)* Did you know John Wright, Mrs. Peters?

MRS. PETERS: Not to know him; I've seen him in town. They say he was a good man.

MRS. HALE: Yes — good; he didn't drink, and kept his word as well as most, I guess, and paid his debts. But he was a hard man, Mrs. Peters. Just to pass the time of day with him — *(Shivers.)* Like a raw wind that gets to the bone. *(Pauses, her eye falling on the cage.)* I should think she would 'a' wanted a bird. But what do you suppose went with it?

MRS. PETERS: I don't know, unless it got sick and died. *(She reaches over and swings the broken door, swings it again, both women watch it.)*

MRS. HALE: You weren't raised round here, were you? *(Mrs. Peters shakes her head.)* You didn't know — her?

MRS. PETERS: Not till they brought her yesterday.

MRS. HALE: She — come to think of it, she was kind of like a bird herself — real sweet and pretty, but kind of timid and — fluttery. How — she — did — change. *(Silence: then as if struck by a happy thought and relieved to get back to everyday things. Crosses right above Mrs. Peters to cupboard, replaces small chair used to stand on to its original place down right.)* Tell you what, Mrs. Peters, why don't you take the quilt in with you? It might take up her mind.

MRS. PETERS: Why, I think that's a real nice idea, Mrs. Hale. There couldn't possibly be any objection to it could there? Now, just what would I take? I wonder if her patches are in here — and her things. *(They look in the sewing basket.)*

MRS. HALE *(crosses to right of table)*:   Here's some red. I expect this has got sewing things in it. *(Brings out a fancy box.)* What a pretty box. Looks like something somebody would give you. Maybe her scissors are in here. *(Opens box. Suddenly puts her hand to her nose.)* Why —— *(Mrs. Peters bends nearer, then turns her face away.)* There's something wrapped up in this piece of silk.

MRS. PETERS: Why, this isn't her scissors.

MRS. HALE *(lifting the silk):* Oh, Mrs. Peters—it's——*(Mrs. Peters bends closer.)*

MRS. PETERS: It's the bird.

MRS. HALE: But, Mrs. Peters—look at it! Its neck! Look at its neck! It's all—other side *to.*

MRS. PETERS: Somebody—wrung—its—neck. *(Their eyes meet. A look of growing comprehension, of horror. Steps are heard outside. Mrs. Hale slips box under quilt pieces, and sinks into her chair. Enter Sheriff and County Attorney. Mrs. Peters steps down left and stands looking out of window.)*

COUNTY ATTORNEY *(as one turning from serious things to little pleasantries):* Well, ladies, have you decided whether she was going to quilt it or knot it? *(Crosses to center above table.)*

MRS. PETERS: We think she was going to—knot it. *(Sheriff crosses to right of stove, lifts stove lid, and glances at fire, then stands warming hands at stove.)*

COUNTY ATTORNEY: Well, that's interesting, I'm sure. *(Seeing the bird-cage.)* Has the bird flown?

MRS. HALE *(putting more quilt pieces over the box):* We think the—cat got it.

COUNTY ATTORNEY *(preoccupied):* Is there a cat? *(Mrs. Hale glances in a quick covert way at Mrs. Peters.)*

MRS. PETERS *(turning from window takes a step in):* Well, not *now.* They're superstitious, you know. They leave.

COUNTY ATTORNEY *(to Sheriff Peters, continuing an interrupted conversation):* No sign at all of anyone having come from the outside. Their own rope. Now let's go up again and go over it piece by piece. *(They start upstairs.)* It would have to have been someone who knew just the——*(Mrs. Peters sits down left of table. The two women sit there not looking at one another, but as if peering into something and at the same time holding back. When they talk now it is in the manner of feeling their way over strange ground, as if afraid of what they are saying, but as if they cannot help saying it.)*

Mrs. Hale (hesitatively and in hushed voice): She liked the bird. She was going to bury it in that pretty box.

MRS. PETERS *(in a whisper):* When I was a girl—my kitten—there was a boy took a hatchet, and before my eyes—and before I could get there——*(Covers her face an instant.)* If they hadn't held me back I would have—*(catches herself, looks upstairs where steps are heard, falters weakly)*—hurt him.

MRS. HALE *(with a slow look around her):* I wonder how it would seem never to have had any children around. *(Pause.)* No, Wright wouldn't like the bird—a thing that sang. She used to sing. He killed that, too.

MRS. PETERS *(moving uneasily):* We don't know who killed the bird.

MRS. HALE: I knew John Wright.

MRS. PETERS: It was an awful thing was done in this house that night, Mrs. Hale. Killing a man while he slept, slipping a rope around his neck that choked the life out of him.

MRS. HALE: His neck. Choked the life out of him. *(Her hand goes out and rests on the bird-cage.)*

MRS. PETERS *(with rising voice):* We don't know who killed him. We don't *know.*

MRS. HALE (*her own feeling not interrupted*):   If there'd been years and years of nothing, then a bird to sing to you, it would be awful — still, after the bird was still.

MRS. PETERS (*something within her speaking*):   I know what stillness is. When we homesteaded in Dakota, and my first baby died — after he was two years old, and me with no other then——

MRS. HALE (*moving*):   How soon do you suppose they'll be through looking for the evidence?

MRS. PETERS: I know what stillness is. (*Pulling herself back.*) The law has got to punish crime, Mrs. Hale.

MRS. HALE (*not as if answering that*):   I wish you'd seen Minnie Foster when she wore a white dress with blue ribbons and stood up there in the choir and sang. (*A look around the room.*) Oh, I *wish* I'd come over here once in a while! That was a crime! That was a crime! Who's going to punish that?

MRS. PETERS (*looking upstairs*):   We mustn't — take on.

MRS. HALE: I might have known she needed help! I know how things can be — for women. I tell you, it's queer, Mrs. Peters. We live close together and we live far apart. We all go through the same things — it's all just a different kind of the same thing. (*Brushes her eyes, noticing the jar of fruit, reaches out for it.*) If I was you I wouldn't tell her her fruit was gone. Tell her it *ain't*. Tell her it's all right. Take this in to prove it to her. She — she may never know whether it was broke or not.

MRS. PETERS (*takes the jar, looks about for something to wrap it in; takes petticoat from the clothes brought from the other room, very nervously begins winding this around the jar. In a false voice*):   My, it's a good thing the men couldn't hear us. Wouldn't they just laugh! Getting all stirred up over a little thing like a — dead canary. As if that could have anything to do with — with — wouldn't they *laugh*! (*The men are heard coming downstairs.*)

MRS. HALE (*under her breath*):   Maybe they would — maybe they wouldn't.

COUNTY ATTORNEY: No, Peters, it's all perfectly clear except a reason for doing it. But you know juries when it comes to women. If there was some definite thing. (*Crosses slowly to above table. Sheriff crosses down right. Mrs. Hale and Mrs. Peters remain seated at either side of table.*) Something to show — something to make a story about — a thing that would connect up with this strange way of doing it —— (*The women's eyes meet for an instant. Enter Hale from outer door.*)

HALE (*remaining by door*):   Well, I've got the team around. Pretty cold out there.

COUNTY ATTORNEY: I'm going to stay awhile by myself. (*To the Sheriff.*) You can send Frank out for me, can't you? I want to go over everything. I'm not satisfied that we can't do better.

SHERIFF: Do you want to see what Mrs. Peters is going to take in? (*The Lawyer picks up the apron, laughs.*)

COUNTY ATTORNEY: Oh, I guess they're not very dangerous things the ladies have picked out. (*Moves a few things about, disturbing the quilt pieces which cover the box. Steps back.*) No, Mrs. Peters doesn't need supervising. For that matter a sheriff's wife is married to the law. Ever think of it that way, Mrs. Peters?

MRS. PETERS: Not—just that way.

SHERIFF *(chuckling):*   Married to the law. *(Moves to down right door to the other room.)* I just want you to come in here a minute, George. We ought to take a look at these windows.

COUNTY ATTORNEY *(scoffingly):*   Oh, windows!

SHERIFF: We'll be right out, Mr. Hale. *(Hale goes outside. The Sheriff follows the County Attorney into the room. Then Mrs. Hale rises, hands tight together, looking intensely at Mrs. Peters, whose eyes make a slow turn, finally meeting Mrs. Hale's. A moment Mrs. Hale holds her, then her own eyes point the way to where the box is concealed. Suddenly Mrs. Peters throws back quilt pieces and tries to put the box in the bag she is carrying. It is too big. She opens box, starts to take bird out, cannot touch it, goes to pieces, stands there helpless. Sound of a knob turning in the other room. Mrs. Hale snatches the box and puts it in the pocket of her big coat. Enter County Attorney and Sheriff, who remains down right.)*

COUNTY ATTORNEY *(crosses to up left door facetiously):*   Well, Henry, at least we found out that she was not going to quilt it. She was going to—what is it you call it, ladies?

MRS. HALE *(standing center below table facing front, her hand against her pocket):* We call it—knot it, Mr. Henderson.

Curtain.   [1916]

A WRITING EXERCISE

Once you have read the two plays, write your reaction to them off the top of your head, spending at least ten minutes on each. Note any personal experiences affecting your response to each play. Note as well the questions you have about each, for one or more of these questions can serve as the basis for a paper of your own.

A Student's Personal Response to the Plays

Trish Carlisle was enrolled in a class that read and discussed both Strindberg's *The Stronger* and Glaspell's *Trifles*. Members of her class even performed these plays. Here is some freewriting that Trisha did about each of them:

>   Near the end of Strindberg's play, Mrs. X says that
> "at this moment it is I who am the stronger." But is she?
> I guess that depends on what Strindberg meant by "the
> stronger" when he gave his play that title. As I was
> reading, I started to think that the stronger woman is

actually the silent one, Miss Y, because she seems to have more self-control than Mrs. X does. I mean, Miss Y doesn't apparently feel that she has to make long, loud speeches in defense of her way of life. I can even believe that with her silence she is manipulating Mrs. X into getting fairly hysterical. Also, I guess we're to think that Amelia has managed to lure away Mrs. X's husband, at least for a while. Furthermore, we don't have to believe Mrs. X when at the end she claims that she has triumphed over Miss Y. Maybe people who have really succeeded in life don't need to proclaim that they have, as Mrs. X does.

Nevertheless, I can see why some students in this class feel that Mrs. X is in fact the stronger. If she has her husband back and wants her husband back, and if Miss Y is really without companionship at the end and has even lost her job at the theater, then probably Mrs. X is entitled to crow. Was Strindberg being deliberately unclear? Did he want his audience to make up their own minds about who is stronger? Maybe neither of these women is strong, because each of them seems dependent on a man, and Mrs. X's husband may not even be such a great person in the first place. If I were Mrs. X, maybe I wouldn't even take him back. I guess someone could say that it's Mrs. X's husband who is the stronger, since he has managed to make the two women fight over him while he enjoys his creature comforts. Anyway, Strindberg makes us guess what he is really like. Because he's offstage, he's just as silent as Miss Y is, although his wife imitates his voice at one point.

In a way, I feel that this play is too short. I want it to go on longer so that I can be sure how to analyze the two women and the man. But I realize that one of the reasons the play is dramatic is that it's brief. I might not be interested in it if it didn't leave me hanging. And it's also theatrical because Miss Y is silent even as Mrs. X lashes out at her. I wonder what the play would be

like if we could hear Miss Y's thoughts in a sort of
voice-over, like we find in some movies. It's interesting
to me that the play is <u>about</u> actresses. I wonder if these
characters are still "performing" with each other even if
they're not acting in a theater at the moment.

   <u>Trifles</u> is a clearer play to me because obviously I'm
supposed to agree with the two women that Minnie Wright
was justified in killing her husband. Glaspell steers all
our sympathies toward the two women onstage and Minnie.
I'm hazy about the offstage husband in Strindberg's play,
but Glaspell makes clear how we're to feel about the offstage Minnie. Meanwhile, the men in her play come across
as insensitive dummies. They're not really brutal or
mean, but they don't seem to understand or appreciate
women. Their wives seem a heck of a lot smarter about
women's daily lives than they are. Glaspell did keep me
guessing about how John Wright died. I figured early on
that his wife played a big role in his death, but I
didn't know exactly how she contributed to it. I liked
how slowly her motives were revealed; the use of the dead
bird as a prop must be very theatrical on a real stage.
At the end, I despised the men for thinking that their
wives were still just concerned with trivial things. A
lot of men I know would probably say that men today
aren't nearly as condescending as Glaspell's men are in
this play. But I think men today really are inclined to
consider women's interests as a bunch of trifles.

   I'm undecided, though, about whether women who kill
their husbands should go free if those husbands are
cruel. It's interesting to me that Minnie's husband evidently didn't beat her. Glaspell implies that Minnie is
more a victim of psychological abuse rather than physical
abuse. I realize that a woman out in the country couldn't
go to a counselor, but I think that she had more options
than Glaspell suggests. Why didn't Minnie just leave her
husband if he was so mean to her? Mrs. Hale seems to feel
guilty about not doing more to help Minnie, but can't we

expect Minnie to have tried to help herself? I guess I
wish that Minnie and her husband had been onstage so that
I could see better what they're really like. As things
stand, I feel that Glaspell is pushing me to accept Mrs.
Peters's and Mrs. Hale's interpretation and evaluation of
the marriage. I can imagine a second act to this play,
where we get to see Minnie thinking in her jail cell and
maybe even talking with some other prisoners about her
marriage. Of course, then I'd have to decide whether to
accept Minnie's own account of her marriage and her
explanation of why she killed her husband. In Glaspell's
play, there's some reference to the possibility that
Minnie has gone insane. If I saw Minnie and heard her
speak, I'd have to decide whether she's crazy and whether
her degree of sanity should even matter to me as I consider whether she should go free.

Trish's freewriting will eventually help her develop ideas for one of her major class assignments, a paper in which she has to analyze either Strindberg's play or Glaspell's. Compare your responses to the plays with hers. Did the same issues come up for you? How do you feel about the two plays' women characters? What, if anything, do you wish the playwrights had made clearer? What would you advise Trish to think about as she moved from freewriting to drafting a paper?

The Elements of Drama

You will strengthen your ability to write about plays like Strindberg's and Glaspell's if you grow familiar with typical elements of drama. These elements include plot and structure, characterization, stage directions and setting, language, and theme.

Plot and Structure

Most plays, like most short stories, have a **plot**. When you read them, you find yourself following a **narrative**, a sequence of interrelated events. Even plays as short as *The Stronger* and *Trifles* feature plots, though in their cases the onstage action occurs in just one place and takes just a little while. As with short fiction, the reader of a play is often anxious to know how the events will turn out. The reader may especially feel this way when the play contains a mystery that characters are trying to solve. In Strindberg's play, for example, Mrs. X is apparently bent on discovering what relation her husband has had with her friend, while the two women onstage in Glaspell's play attempt to figure out the circumstances of John Wright's death.

In summarizing these two plays, you might choose to depict each plot as a detective story. Then again, you might prefer to emphasize the characters' emotional conflicts as you describe how these plays proceed. In fact, there are various ways you can describe Strindberg's and Glaspell's plots; just bear in mind that your accounts should be grounded in actual details of the texts. However you summarize a play's **structure** will reflect your sense of which characters are central to it. How prominent in Glaspell's plot is Minnie Wright, would you say? Is she as important as the two women onstage? More important than them? Less important? Your summary will also reflect your sense of which characters have power. Do you think the two women in Strindberg's drama equally influence that play's events? In addition, your summary ought to acknowledge the human motives that drive the play's action. Why, evidently, did Minnie Wright kill her husband?

Summarizing the plot of a play can mean arranging its events chronologically. Yet bear in mind that some of the play's important events may have occurred in the characters' pasts. In many plays, characters learn things about the past that they did not know and must now try to accept. For example, several of the important events in *Trifles* take place before the play begins. By the time the curtain rises, John Wright has already tormented his wife, and she has already killed him. Now, onstage, Mrs. Hale and Mrs. Peters proceed to investigate how John Wright died. A summary of Glaspell's play could begin with the sad state of the Wrights' marriage, then move to the murder, and then chronicle the subsequent investigation. But you can also summarize the play by starting with the investigation, which is what the audience first sees. Only later would you bring up the past events that Mrs. Hale and Mrs. Peter learn about through their detective work.

A WRITING EXERCISE

List in chronological order the events referred to and shown in *The Stronger*. Start with the earliest event that Mrs. X mentions; end with the event that concludes the play. Next, choose from this list an event that apparently occurred before the characters appear onstage. Then, write at least a paragraph analyzing the moment when the audience is made aware of this event. Most likely the audience learns of the event from Mrs. X. Why do you think Strindberg has her announce it at this particular moment?

In discussing the structure of short stories, we noted that many of them follow Alice Adams's formula ABDCE (**action, background, development, climax,** and **ending**). This scheme, however, does not fit many plays. In a sense, the average play is entirely action, for its performers are constantly engaged in physical movement of various sorts. Furthermore, as we have been suggesting, information about background can surface quite often as the play's characters talk. Yet the terms *development, climax,* and *ending* do seem appropriate for many plays. Certainly the plot of *The Stronger* develops, as Mrs. X becomes increasingly hostile to Miss Y. Certainly the play can be said to reach a climax, a moment of great significance and intensity, when Mrs. X moves to another table and declares her hatred for Miss Y. The term *ending* can also apply to this play, although readers may disagree about exactly when its climax turns into its ending. Certainly Mrs. X is in a different state of mind at the play's last moment; at that point, she stops haranguing Miss Y and leaves, declaring that she will save her own marriage.

Like short stories, plays often use repetition as an organizational device. The characters in a play may repeat certain words; for example, trace the multiple appearances of the word *knot* in *Trifles*. Also, a play may show repeated actions, as when the men in Glaspell's drama repeatedly interrupt the two women's conversation. In addition, a play may suggest that the onstage situation echoes previous events; when the men onstage in *Trifles* utter obnoxious comments about women, these remarks make Mrs. Hale and Mrs. Peters more aware of the abuse that Minnie Wright's husband inflicted on her.

The Stronger and *Trifles* are both short one-act plays. But many other plays are longer and divided conspicuously into subsections. The ancient Greek drama *Antigone*, which appears in Chapter 15, alternates choral sections with scenes involving only two characters. All of Shakespeare's plays, and most modern ones, are divided into acts, which are often further divided into scenes. Detecting various stages in the action is easier when the play is fairly lengthy, as is the case with Lorraine Hansberry's *A Raisin in the Sun* (Chapter 11). But you can also break Strindberg's and Glaspell's one-act plays down into stages.

A WRITING EXERCISE

Outline either *The Stronger* or *Trifles*, breaking down its action into at least three stages. Write at least a couple of sentences describing each stage you have identified.

Characters

Many short stories have a narrator who reveals the characters' inner thoughts. Most plays, however, have no narrator. To figure out what the characters think, you must study what they say and how they move. Some characters say a great deal, leaving you with several clues to their psyche. Shakespeare's play *Hamlet*, for example, contains thousands of lines. Moreover, when Hamlet is alone onstage making long speeches to the audience, he seems to be baring his very soul. Yet despite such moments, Hamlet's mental state remains far from clear; scholars continue to debate his sanity. Thus, as a reader of *Hamlet* and other plays, you have much room for interpretation. Often you will have to decide whether to accept the judgments that characters express about one another. For example, how fair and accurate does Strindberg's Mrs. X seem to you as she berates Miss Y?

As with short stories, a good step toward analyzing a play's characters is to consider what each desires. The drama or comedy of many plays arises when the desires of one character conflict with those of another. Strindberg's Mrs. X feels that Miss Y has been a threat to her marriage, and while we cannot be sure of Miss Y's thoughts, evidently she is determined not to answer Mrs. X's charges. At the end of the play, the women's conflict seems to endure, even though Mrs. X proclaims victory. Many other plays end with characters managing to resolve conflict because one or more of them experiences a change of heart. Whatever play you are studying, consider whether any of its characters change. For example, is anyone's thinking transformed in *Trifles*? If so, whose?

The main character of a play is referred to as its **protagonist**, and a character who notably opposes this person is referred to as the **antagonist**. As you might guess without even reading Shakespeare's play, Hamlet is the protagonist of *Hamlet*; his uncle Claudius serves as his antagonist. Applying these terms may be tricky or impossible in some instances. The two women in *The Stronger* oppose each other, but each can be called the protagonist and each can be called the antagonist. *Trifles* also seems a challenging case. How, if at all, would you apply the two terms to Glaspell's characters?

In discussing the elements of short fiction, we referred to point of view, the perspective from which a story is told. Since very few plays are narrated, the term *point of view* fits this genre less well. While it is possible to claim that much of Shakespeare's *Hamlet* reflects the title character's point of view, he is offstage for stretches, and the audience may focus on other characters even when he appears. Also, think about the possible significance of characters who are not physically present. A character may be important even if he or she never appears onstage. In *The Stronger*, the two women's conflict is partly about Mrs. X's unseen husband. In *Trifles*, everyone onstage aims to discover what happened between two unseen people, Minnie and John Wright.

In most plays, characters' lives are influenced by their social standing, which in turn is influenced by particular traits of theirs. These may include their gender, social class, race, ethnic background, nationality, sexual orientation, and the kind of work they do. Obviously *Trifles* deals with gender relationships. Mrs. Peters and Mrs. Hale come to feel an affinity with Minnie Wright because they sense she has been an oppressed wife; meanwhile, their husbands scoff at women's obsession with "trifles."

A WRITING EXERCISE

Susan Glaspell's play *Trifles* depicts Mrs. Peters and Mrs. Hale covering up evidence to protect Minnie Wright. They seem to act out of loyalty to their gender. Do you feel that there are indeed times when you should be someone's ally because that person is of the same gender as you? What would you say to someone who is generally comfortable with alliances between women but less comfortable with alliances between men, since throughout history women have been oppressed by bands of men? Freewrite for fifteen minutes in response to these questions.

Stage Directions and Setting

When analyzing a script, pay attention to the **stage directions** it gives, and try to imagine additional ways that the actors might move around. Through a slight physical movement, performers can indicate important developments in their characters' thoughts. A good example is Glaspell's stage directions when Mr. Hale declares that "women are used to worrying over trifles." By having Mrs. Hale and Mrs. Peters "move a little closer together," Glaspell suggests that these two women *grow* closer because of Mr. Hale's scorn. As we have noted, Mrs. Hale and Mrs. Peters do seem to develop a kinship based on their common gender, and in turn they both seem increasingly sensitive to Minnie's plight.

You can get a better sense of how a play might be staged if you research its actual production history. Granted, finding out about its previous stagings may be difficult. But at the very least, you can discover some of the theatrical conventions that must have shaped presentations of the play, even one that is centuries old. Take the case of Sophocles' *Antigone* and Shakespeare's *Hamlet*, both of which appear in this book. While classical scholars would like to learn more about early performances of *Antigone*, they already know that it and other ancient Greek plays were staged in open-air arenas. They know, too, that, *Antigone's* Chorus turned in unison at particular moments, and that the whole cast wore large masks. Although the premiere of *Hamlet* was not videotaped, Shakespeare scholars are sure that, like other productions in Renaissance England, it made spare use of scenery and featured an all-male cast.

Most of the modern plays we include in this book were first staged in a style alien to Sophocles and Shakespeare, a style most often called **realism**. Realism marked, for example, the first production of Lorraine Hansberry's *A Raisin in the Sun*, reprinted in Chapter 11. When the curtain rose on that play's opening night in 1959, the audience saw a vivid re-creation of a shabby Chicago apartment. Indeed, when a production seems quite true to life, audiences may think it has no style at all. Nevertheless, even realism uses a set of identifiable conventions. That first production of Hansberry's play relied on what theater professionals call the *illusion of the fourth wall.* Although the actors pretended the "apartment" was completely enclosed, the set had just three walls, and the audience looked in. Similarly, an audience watching a production of *Trifles* is encouraged to think that it is peering into Minnie Wright's kitchen.

Some plays can be staged in any number of styles and still work well. Shakespeare wrote *Hamlet* back in Renaissance England, but quite a few successful productions of it have been set in later times, such as late-nineteenth-century England. Even modern plays that seem to call for realistic productions can be staged in a variety of ways. Note Strindberg's description of the setting for *The Stronger:* "A corner of a ladies' café [in Stockholm in the eighteen eighties]. Two small wrought-iron tables, a red plush settee, and a few chairs." Many productions of this play have remained within the conventions of realism, striving to make the audience believe that it is seeing a late-nineteenth-century Stockholm café. But a production of *The Stronger* may present the audience with only a few pieces of furniture that barely evoke the café. Furthermore, the production might have Mrs. X's husband physically hover in the background, as if he were a ghost haunting both women's minds. You may feel that such a production would horribly distort Strindberg's drama; a boldly experimental staging of a play can indeed become a virtual rewriting of it. Nevertheless, remember that productions of a play may be more diverse in style than the script would indicate.

A WRITING EXERCISE

A particular theater's architecture may affect a production team's decisions. Realism's illusion of the "fourth wall" works best on a proscenium stage, which is the kind probably most familiar to you. A **proscenium stage** is a boxlike space where the actors perform in front of the entire audience. In a proscenium production of *Trifles*, Minnie Wright's kitchen can be depicted in great detail. The performing spaces at some theaters, however, are "in the round": that is, the audience completely encircles the stage. What would have to be done with Minnie's kitchen then? List some items in the kitchen that an "in the round" staging could accommodate.

In referring to possible ways of staging a play, we inevitably refer as well to its setting. A play may not be all that precise in describing its setting; Strindberg provides set designers with few guidelines for creating his Stockholm café. More significant, perhaps, than the place of the action is its *timing*: Mrs. X finds Miss Y sitting alone on Christmas Eve. Yet a play may stress to its audience that its characters are located in particular places, at particular moments in their personal histories, or at a particular moment in *world* history. For example, *Trifles* repeatedly calls attention to the fact that it is set in a kitchen, traditionally a female domain. Furthermore, the audience is reminded that Minnie Wright's kitchen is in an isolated rural area, where a spouse's abuse and a neighbor's indifference can have devastating impact on a woman. Furthermore, as Mrs. Peters and Mrs. Hale explore Minnie's kitchen, they increasingly see its physical decline as a symptom of the Wrights' failing marriage.

You can learn much about a play's characters by studying how they accommodate themselves—or fail to accommodate themselves—to their settings. When Strindberg's Mrs. X can no longer bear sitting next to Miss Y, her shift to another table dramatically signifies her feelings. In *Trifles*, Mrs. Peters and Mrs. Hale are clearly interlopers in Minnie Wright's kitchen; they analyze its condition like detectives, or even like anthropologists. Increasingly they realize that they should have been more familiar with this kitchen—in other words, they should have been better neighbors for Minnie. Of course, much of the drama in Strindberg's and Glaspell's plays occurs because there is a single setting, which in both plays makes at least one character feel confined. Other plays employ a wider variety of settings to dramatize their characters' lives.

Imagery

When plays use images to convey meaning, sometimes they do so through **dialogue**. At the beginning of *The Stronger*, for instance, Mrs. X recalls "a wedding party at a restaurant," where "the bride was reading a comic paper and the bridegroom playing billiards with the witnesses." The play proceeds to become very much about divisions between husband and wife; moreover, the two women engage in a tense "game" that seems analogous to billiards. But just as often, a play's meaningful images are physically presented in the staging: through gestures, costumes, lighting, and props. For instance, perhaps the key image in *Trifles* is the dead bird wrapped in silk, which the audience is encouraged to associate with Minnie Wright. While Glaspell presents dialogue about the bird, the physical presence of the bird and cage props may make the audience more inclined to see the bird as a **symbol**, the term traditionally used for an image that represents some concept or concepts.

A WRITING EXERCISE

Imagine that you have been asked to stage a production of *The Stronger*. List the key props and gestures you would use to stress the meanings you find in the play. Then exchange lists with a classmate, and write a brief interpretation of each item on that classmate's list. Then, get your own list back and see whether the interpretations written there are what you wanted to convey.

Keep in mind that you may interpret an image differently than the characters within the play do. When Strindberg's Mrs. X refers to billiards, she may not think at all that she will be playing an analogous game with Miss Y. You, however, may make this connection, especially as the play proceeds.

Language

You can learn much about a play's meaning and impact from studying the **language** in its script. Start with the play's title. At the climax of Strindberg's play, for example, Mrs. X even refers to herself as "the stronger;" in Glaspell's play, the men and women express conflicting views about women's apparent concern with "trifles." Obviously both playwrights are encouraging audiences to think about their titles' implications. Yet not always will the meaning of a play's title be immediately clear. In her freewriting, Trish wonders how to define *stronger* and which of Strindberg's characters fits the term. Even if you think the title of a play is easily explainable, pause to see whether that title actually leads to an issue of definition.

In most plays, language is a matter of dialogue. The audience tries to figure out the play by focusing on how the characters address one another. At the beginning of Glaspell's play, the dialogue between Mrs. Peters and Mrs. Hale reveals that they do not completely agree about how to view Minnie Wright's situation:

MRS. PETERS: But, Mrs. Hale, the law is the law.
MRS. HALE: I s'pose 'tis. *(Unbuttoning her coat.)* Better loosen up your things, Mrs. Peters. You won't feel them when you go out.

Mrs. Hale's response seems half-hearted. Unlike Mrs. Peters, the wife of the county attorney, she seems more disposed to believe that Minnie's situation may justify sparing Minnie the force of the law. To bring up issues of definition again, you might say that Mrs. Hale subtly questions just what "the law" should be, whereas Mrs. Peters says only that "the law is the law." Furthermore, when Mrs. Hale advises Mrs. Peters to "loosen up your things," perhaps the playwright is suggesting that Mrs. Peters should also "loosen up" her moral code.

Remember that the pauses or silences within a play may be just as important as its dialogue. In fact, a director may add moments of silence that the script does not explicitly demand. In many plays, however, the author does specify moments when one or more characters significantly fail to speak. *The Stronger* is a prominent example: Miss Y is notably silent throughout the play, and as a reader you probably find yourself wondering why she is. Ironically, the play's absence of true dialogue serves to remind us that plays usually *depend* on dialogue.

A WRITING EXERCISE

Choose a moment in *The Stronger* when Miss Y notably fails to speak — perhaps one in which she makes a sound but does not utter words. Then, write a brief monologue for her in which you express what she may be thinking at that moment. Next, write a paragraph or two in which you identify what Strindberg conceivably gains by *not* having Miss Y speak at that moment.

Theme

We have already discussed **theme** in Part One, and here we will build on some points from our earlier discussion. A theme is the main claim — an assertion, proposition, or statement — that a work seems to make. As with other literary genres, try to state a play's theme as a midlevel generalization. If expressed in very broad terms, it will seem to fit many other works besides the one you have read; if narrowly tied to the play's characters and their particular situation, it will seem irrelevant to most other people's lives. With *The Stronger*, an example of a very broad theme would be "Women should not fight over a man." At the opposite extreme, a too-narrow theme would be "Women should behave well toward each other on Christmas Eve, even if one of them has slept with the other's husband." If you are formulating Strindberg's theme, you might start with the broad generalization we have cited and then try to narrow it down to a midlevel one. You might even think of ways that Strindberg's play *complicates* that broad generalization. What might, in fact, be a good midlevel generalization in Strindberg's case?

As we have noted, the titles of *The Stronger* and *Trifles* seem significant. Indeed, a play's theme may be related to its title. Nevertheless, be wary of couching the theme in terms drawn solely from the title. The play's theme may not be reducible to these words alone. Remember that the titles of Strindberg's and Glaspell's plays can give rise to issues of definition in the first place.

You can state a play's theme as an **observation** or as a **recommendation**. With Strindberg's play, an observation-type theme would be "Marriage and career may disrupt relations between women." A recommendation-type theme would be either the broad or narrow generalization that we cited earlier. Neither way of stating the theme is automatically preferable, but remain aware of the different tones and effects they may carry. Consider, too, the possibility of stating the theme as a problem, as in this example: "We may be inclined to defend our marriages when they seem threatened, but in our defense we may cling to illusions that can easily shatter." Furthermore, consider the possibility of referring to *a* theme of the play rather than *the* theme, thereby acknowledging the possibility that the play is making several important claims.

A WRITING EXERCISE

Write three different versions of the theme of *Trifles*: a version that is excessively broad, one that is a midlevel generalization, and one that is too narrow.
Then, exchange sheets with several of your classmates. (Your instructor may
have all the sheets circulated quickly through the entire class.) As a group,
select the best midlevel generalization. Be prepared to say why it is the best.

When you write about a play, certainly you will refer to the text of it, its
script. But probably the play was meant to be staged, and most likely it has been.
Thus, you might refer to actual productions of it and to ways it can be performed.
Remember, though, that different productions of the play may stress different
meanings and create different effects. In your paper, you might discuss how
much room for interpretation the script allows those who would stage it. For any
paper you write about the play, look beyond the characters' dialogue and study
whatever stage directions the script gives.

Undoubtedly your paper will have to offer some plot summary, even if your
audience has already read the play. After all, certain details of the plot will be
important support for your points. But, as with papers about short fiction, keep
the amount of plot summary small, mentioning only events in the play that are
crucial to your overall argument. Your reader should feel that you are analyzing
the play rather than just recounting it.

To understand more what analysis of a play involves, let's return to Trish
Carlisle, the student whose freewriting you read earlier. Trish was assigned to
write a 600-word paper about Strindberg's *The Stronger* or Glaspell's *Trifles*. She
was asked to imagine herself writing to a particular audience: performers rehears-
ing a production of the play she chose. More specifically, she was to identify and
address some question that these performers might have, an issue that might be
bothering them as they prepared to put on the play. Trish knew that, besides presenting an issue, her paper would have to make a main claim and support it with
evidence. Moreover, the paper might have to spell out some of the warrants or
assumptions behind her evidence.

Trish found both Strindberg's play and Glaspell's interesting, so she was not
immediately sure which one to choose. Because finding an issue was such an
important part of the assignment, she decided to review her freewriting about
each play, noting questions she had raised there about them. Trish saw that the
chief issue posed for her by *The Stronger* was, "Which character is the stronger?"
She also saw that, for her, *Trifles* was a more clear-cut play, although it did leave
her with the question, "Should women who kill their husbands go free if their
husbands are cruel?" Eventually Trish decided to focus on Strindberg's play and
the issue of how to apply its title. Much as she liked *Trifles*, she thought the issue
she associated with it went far beyond the play itself, whereas the issue she associated with *The Stronger* would enable her to discuss many of that play's specific
details. Also, she thought that performers of Strindberg's play would be anxious to
clarify its title, whereas performers of *Trifles* need not be sure how to judge the
Minnie Wrights of this world.

Nevertheless, Trish recognized that the issue "Which character is the stronger?" still left her with various decisions to make. For one thing, she had to decide what kind of an issue she would call it. Trish saw that it could be considered an issue of fact, an issue of evaluation, or an issue of definition. Although it could fit into all of these categories, Trish knew that the category she chose would influence the direction of her paper. Eventually she decided to treat "Which character is the stronger?" as primarily an issue of definition, because she figured that, no matter what, she would be devoting much of her paper to defining *stronger* as a term.

Of course, there are many different senses in which someone may be "stronger" than someone else. Your best friend may be a stronger tennis player than you, in the sense that he or she always beats you at that game. But you may be a stronger student than your friend, in the sense that you get better grades in school. In the case of Strindberg's play, Trish came to see that a paper focused on which character is *morally* stronger would differ from one focused on who is *emotionally* stronger, and these papers would differ in turn from one focused on which character is *politically* stronger, more able to impose his or her will. These reflections led Trish to revise her issue somewhat. She decided to address the question, "Which particular sense of the word 'stronger' is most relevant to Strindberg's play?" In part, Trish came up with this reformulation of her issue because she realized that the two women feuding in the play are actresses, and that they behave as actresses even when they are not professionally performing. Trish's answer to her revised question was that the play encourages the audience to consider which woman is the stronger *actress*—which woman is more able, that is, to convey her preferred version of reality.

When you write about a play, you may have to be selective, for your paper may not be able to accommodate all the ideas and issues that occur to you. Trish was not sure which woman in Strindberg's play is the stronger actress. She felt that a case can be made for Mrs. X or Miss Y; indeed, she suspected that Strindberg was letting his audience decide. But she decided that her paper was not obligated to resolve this matter; she could simply mention the various possible positions in her final paragraph. In the body of her paper, Trish felt she would contribute much if she focused on addressing her main issue with her main claim. Again, her main issue was, "Which particular sense of the word 'stronger' is most relevant to Strindberg's play?" Her main claim was that, "The play is chiefly concerned with which woman is the stronger actress, 'stronger' here meaning 'more able to convey one's version of reality.' "

Although a paper about a play need not explicitly mention the elements of plays we have identified, thinking about these elements can provide you with a good springboard for analysis. Trish saw that her paper would be very much concerned with the title of Strindberg's play, especially as that title applied to the characters. Also, she would have to refer to stage directions and imagery, because Miss Y's silence leaves the reader having to look at her physical movements and the play's props for clues to her thinking. The play does not really include dialogue, a term that implies people talking with each other. Nevertheless, Trish saw that there are utterances in the script she could refer to, especially as she made points about the play's lone speaker, Mrs. X. Indeed, a persuasive paper about a play is one that quotes from characters' lines and perhaps from the stage directions, too. Yet the paper needs to quote selectively, for a paper chock full of quotations may obscure instead of enhance the writer's argument.

Sample Student Paper: Final Draft

Here is Trish's final draft of her paper about *The Stronger*. It emerged out of several drafts, and after Trish had consulted classmates and her instructor. As you read this version of her paper, note its strengths, but also think of any suggestions that might help Trish make the paper even better.

```
Trish Carlisle
Professor Zelinsky
English 102
28 April ----
                Which Is the Stronger Actress
             in August Strindberg's Play?
     You have asked me to help you solve difficulties you
may be experiencing with August Strindberg's script for
The Stronger as you prepare to play the roles of Mrs. X
and Miss Y. These female characters seem harder to judge
than the three women who are the focus of Susan Glaspell's
play Trifles, the play you are performing next month.
Obviously Glaspell is pushing us to think well of Mrs.
Hale, Mrs. Peters, and Minnie Wright. The two women in
Strindberg's play are another matter; in particular, you
have probably been wondering which of these two women
Strindberg thinks of as "the stronger." If you knew which
character he had in mind with that term, you might play
the roles accordingly. As things stand, however, Strind-
berg's use of the term in his title is pretty ambiguous.
It is not even clear, at least not immediately, which
particular sense of the word stronger is most relevant to
the play. I suggest that the play is chiefly concerned
with which character is the stronger actress. In making
this claim, I am defining stronger as "more able to con-
vey one's version of reality."
     You may feel that Strindberg is clarifying his use of
the word stronger when he has Mrs. X bring up the word in
```

the long speech that ends the play. In that final speech, she declares to Miss Y that "it is I who am the stronger" and that Miss Y's silence is not the "strength" that Mrs. X previously thought it was. At this point in the play, Mrs. X is evidently defining stronger as "more able to keep things, especially a man." She feels that she is the stronger because she is going home to her husband, while Miss Y is forced to be alone on Christmas Eve. Yet there is little reason to believe that Mrs. X is using the word stronger in the sense that the playwright has chiefly in mind. Furthermore, there is little reason to believe that Mrs. X is an accurate judge of the two women's situations. Perhaps she is telling herself that she is stronger because she simply needs to believe that she is. Similarly, perhaps she is telling herself that she now has control over her husband when in actuality he may still be emotionally attached to Miss Y. In addition, because Miss Y does not speak and because Mrs. X sweeps out without giving her any further opportunity to do so, we don't know if Miss Y agrees with Mrs. X's last speech.

Since Mrs. X's final use of the word stronger is so questionable, we are justified in thinking of other ways that the term might be applied. In thinking about this play, I have entertained the idea that the stronger character is actually Mrs. X's husband Bob, for he has two women fighting over him and also apparently has the creature comforts that servants provide. But now I tend to think that the term applies to one or both of the two women. Unfortunately, we are not given many facts about them, for it is a brief one-act play and one of the major characters does not even speak. But as we try to figure out how Strindberg is defining the term stronger, we should notice one fact that we are indeed given: Each of these women is an actress. Both of them have worked at Stockholm's Grand Theater, although apparently Mrs. X got Miss Y fired from the company. Furthermore, Mrs. X engages in a bit of theatrical illusion when she scares

Miss Y by firing the toy pistol at her. Soon after, Mrs. X plays the role of her own husband when she puts her hands in the slippers she has bought for him and imitates not only his walk but also the way he scolds his servants. Miss Y even laughs at this "performance," as if she is being an appreciative audience for it. In addition, if Mrs. X is right about there being an adulterous affair between her husband and Miss Y, then those two people have basically been performing an act for Mrs. X. It is possible, too, that Mrs. X has not been quite so naive; perhaps she has deliberately come to the café in order to confront Miss Y about the affair and to proclaim ultimate victory over her. In that case, Mrs. X is performing as someone more innocent than she really is. On the other hand, Miss Y might be using her silences as an actress would, manipulating her audience's feelings by behaving in a theatrical way.

Because we do know that these women are professional actresses, and because Strindberg gives us several hints that they are performing right there in the café, we should feel encouraged to think that he is raising the question of which is the stronger actress. Of course, we would still have to decide how he is defining the term stronger. But if he does have in mind the women's careers and behavior as actresses, then he seems to be defining stronger as "more able to convey one's version of reality." Obviously Mrs. X is putting forth her own version of reality in her final speech, although we do not know how close her version comes to the actual truth. Again, we cannot be sure of Miss Y's thoughts because she does not express them in words; nevertheless, she can be said to work at influencing Mrs. X's version of reality by making strategic use of silence.

I realize that the claim I am making does not solve every problem you might have with the play as you prepare to perform it. Frankly, I am not sure who is the stronger actress. I suspect that Strindberg is being deliberately

ambiguous; he wants the performers to act in a way that
will let each member of the audience arrive at his or
her own opinion. Still, if you accept my claim, each of
you will think of yourself as playing the part of an
actress who is trying to shape the other woman's sense
of reality.

SUMMING UP

- **Consider the differences between page and stage.** Theater professionals distinguish between a play's written script and its actual performances, so consider how any play you are analyzing has been or
might be staged. Try to imagine yourself as its director, thinking about
how you would guide the actors through their parts. (p. 138)

- **The elements of drama include *plot* and *structure, characters,
stage directions* and *setting, imagery, language,* and *theme.***

- **The *plot* and *structure* of plays often resemble those of stories.** Like
short stories, plays often feature plot development, a climax, a significant ending, and repetitions of words and situations. (pp. 156–58)

- ***Characters* in plays function like characters in stories.** As such,
they can often be analyzed by asking the same questions (see Summing Up on pp. 113–14). A difference is that most plays lack a narrator and even a central point of view; you have to figure out the
characters' thoughts from dialogue and movement.

- **When analyzing a script, pay attention to its *stage directions*, and
imagine other ways that the actors might move around.** (pp. 159–61)

- **While some plays do not describe their *setting* precisely, others
stress that they are occurring in particular places or moments.** As
with short stories, you can learn much about a play's characters by
examining how they accommodate themselves — or fail to accommodate themselves — to their settings. (p. 161)

- ***Images* are often conveyed through words *and* stagecraft** — through
dialogue, gestures, costumes, lighting, and props. (pp. 161–62)

- **Most plays rely on dialogue as their most important *language*,**
making their audience figure things out from how the characters
address one another. Pauses or silences may be important as well.
(pp. 162–63)

(continued on next page)

┌─────────────────── **SUMMING UP** ───────────────────┐

- The *theme* of a play is the main claim — an assertion, proposition, or statement — that it seems to make. As when writing about short stories, try to state the theme as a midlevel generalization, either as an observation or as a recommendation. By specifically wording the theme as a problem, you may better convey the complexity and drama of the play.

- When you write about a play, remember to formulate an issue worth addressing, a claim about that issue, and evidence for that claim, besides preparing to identify your warrants. Keep in mind that you will refer to its script, but you might also discuss how much room for interpretation the script allows those who would stage it.

└──┘

7

Making Arguments
about Essays

Many readers do not think of nonfiction as a literary genre. They believe dealing with information and facts, science and technology, history and biography, memories and arguments is too ordinary, too far from traditional literary works such as sonnets, short stories, and plays. But what counts as literature is often more a matter of tradition and perspective than content, language, or merit. Many contemporary critics have noticed that definitions of literature are quite subjective, even arbitrary. We are told that literature must move us emotionally; it must contain imaginative, extraordinary language; it must deal with profound, timeless, and universal themes. If all of these claims are true of poems, stories, and plays, they might also be true of essays, autobiographies, memoirs, and historical writing.

Essays demand as much of a reader's attention as fiction, drama, and poetry. They also demand a reader's active participation. And, as with more conventional literature, the intellectual, emotional, and aesthetic rewards of attentively reading essays are significant.

Writing about essays in college is best done as a process, one that begins with a first response and ends with editing and proofreading. Author Henry David Thoreau once noted that books should be read with the same care and deliberation with which they were written. This is as true for essays as it is for complex modern poetry. One's understanding is enhanced by careful reading and a composing process that calls for a cycle of reading, writing, and reflecting. Few people, even professionals, can read a text and write cogently about it the first time. Writing well about essays takes as much energy and discipline as writing about other genres. And the results are always worth it.

The two essays here deal with women and work—more specifically, with the struggles of gifted African American women in a context of poverty and oppression. Both essays were originally speeches. "Many Rivers to Cross" by June Jordan (1936–2002) was the keynote address at a 1981 conference on "Women and Work" held at Barnard College in New York City. In the speech, Jordan recalls the suicide of her mother fifteen years earlier. Alice Walker's was given at a May 1973 conference on "The Black Woman: Myths and Realities" held at Radcliffe College in large part as a response to the 1965 Moynihan report that argued that women-headed families were a major cause of poverty among African Americans. Walker (b. 1944) made additions when it appeared in the May 1974 issue of *Ms.* and then in the essay collection *In Search of Our Mothers' Gardens: Womanist Prose* (1983).

JUNE JORDAN
Many Rivers to Cross

When my mother killed herself I was looking for a job. That was fifteen years ago. I had no money and no food. On the pleasure side I was down to my last pack of Pall Malls plus half a bottle of J & B. I needed to find work because I needed to be able fully to support myself and my eight-year-old son, very fast. My plan was to raise enough big bucks so that I could take an okay apartment inside an acceptable public school district, by September. That deadline left me less than three months to turn my fortunes right side up.

It seemed that I had everything to do at once. Somehow, I must move all of our things, mostly books and toys, out of the housing project before the rent fell due, again. I must do this without letting my neighbors know because destitution and divorce added up to personal shame, and failure. Those same neighbors had looked upon my husband and me as an ideal young couple, in many ways: inseparable, doting, ambitious. They had kept me busy and laughing in the hard weeks following my husband's departure for graduate school in Chicago; they had been the ones to remember him warmly through teasing remarks and questions all that long year that I remained alone, waiting for his return while I became the "temporary," sole breadwinner of our peculiar long-distance family by telephone. They had been the ones who kindly stopped the teasing and the queries when the year ended and my husband, the father of my child, did not come back. They never asked me and I never told them what that meant, altogether. I don't think I really knew.

I could see how my husband would proceed more or less naturally from graduate school to a professional occupation of his choice, just as he had shifted rather easily from me, his wife, to another man's wife — another woman. What I could not see was how I should go forward, now, in any natural, coherent way. As a mother without a husband, as a poet without a publisher, a freelance journalist without assignment, a city planner without a contract, it seemed to me that several incontestable and conflicting necessities had suddenly eliminated the whole realm of choice from my life.

My husband and I agreed that he would have the divorce that he wanted, and I would have the child. This ordinary settlement is, as millions of women will testify, as absurd as saying, "I'll give you a call, you handle everything else." At any rate, as my lawyer explained, the law then was the same as the law today; the courts would surely award me a reasonable amount of the father's income as child support, but the courts would also insist that they could not enforce their own decree. In other words, according to the law, what a father owes to his child is not serious compared to what a man owes to the bank for a car, or a vacation. Hence, as they say, it is extremely regrettable but nonetheless true that the courts cannot garnish a father's salary, nor freeze his account, nor seize his property on behalf of his children, in our society. Apparently this is because a child is not a car or a couch or a boat. (I would suppose this is the very best available definition of the difference between an American child and a car.)

Anyway, I wanted to get out of the projects as quickly as possible. But I was going to need help because I couldn't bend down and I couldn't carry anything heavy and I couldn't let my parents know about these problems because I didn't want to fight with them about the reasons behind the problems—which was the same reason I couldn't walk around or sit up straight to read or write without vomiting and acute abdominal pain. My parents would have evaluated that reason as a terrible secret compounded by a terrible crime; once again an unmarried woman, I had, nevertheless, become pregnant. What's more I had tried to interrupt this pregnancy even though this particular effort required not only one but a total of three abortions—each of them illegal and amazingly expensive, as well as, evidently, somewhat poorly executed.

My mother, against my father's furious rejections of me and what he viewed as my failure, offered what she could; she had no money herself but there was space in the old brownstone of my childhood. I would live with them during the summer while I pursued my crash schedule for cash, and she would spend as much time with Christopher, her only and beloved grandchild, as her worsening but partially undiagnosed illness allowed.

After she suffered a stroke, her serenely imposing figure had shrunk into an unevenly balanced, starved shell of chronic disorder. In the last two years, her physical condition had forced her retirement from nursing, and she spent most of her days on a makeshift cot pushed against the wall of the dining room next to the kitchen. She could do very few things for herself, besides snack on crackers, or pour ready-made juice into a cup and then drink it.

In June, 1966, I moved from the projects into my parents' house with the help of a woman named Mrs. Hazel Griffin. Since my teens, she had been my hairdresser. Every day, all day, she stood on her feet, washing and straightening hair in her crowded shop, the Arch of Beauty. Mrs. Griffin had never been married, had never finished high school, and she ran the Arch of Beauty with an imperturbable and contagious sense of success. She had a daughter as old as I who worked alongside her mother, coddling customer fantasy into confidence. Gradually, Mrs. Griffin and I became close; as my own mother became more and more bedridden and demoralized, Mrs. Griffin extended herself—dropping by my parents' house to make dinner for them, or calling me to wish me good luck on a special freelance venture, and so forth. It was Mrs. Griffin who closed her shop for a whole day and drove all the way from Brooklyn to my housing project apartment in Queens. It was Mrs. Griffin who packed me up, so to speak, and carried me and the boxes back to Brooklyn, back to the house of my parents. It was Mrs. Griffin who ignored my father standing hateful at the top of the stone steps of the house and not saying a word of thanks and not once relieving her of a single load she wrestled up the stairs and past him. My father hated Mrs. Griffin

5

because he was proud and because she was a stranger of mercy. My father hated Mrs. Griffin because he was like that sometimes: hateful and crazy.

My father alternated between weeping bouts of self-pity and storm explosions of wrath against the gods apparently determined to ruin him. These were his alternating reactions to my mother's increasing enfeeblement, her stoic depression. I think he was scared; who would take care of him? Would she get well again and make everything all right again?

This is how we organized the brownstone; I fixed a room for my son on the top floor of the house. I slept on the parlor floor in the front room. My father slept on the same floor, in the back. My mother stayed downstairs.

About a week after moving in, my mother asked me about the progress of my plans. I told her things were not terrific but that there were two different planning jobs I hoped to secure within a few days. One of them involved a study of new towns in Sweden and the other one involved an analysis of the social consequences of a huge hydro-electric dam under construction in Ghana. My mother stared at me uncomprehendingly and then urged me to look for work in the local post office. We bitterly argued about what she dismissed as my "high-falutin" ideas and, I believe, that was the last substantial conversation between us.

From my first memory of him, my father had always worked at the post office. His favorite was the night shift, which brought him home usually between three and four o'clock in the morning.

It was hot. I finally fell asleep that night, a few nights after the argument between my mother and myself. She seemed to be rallying; that afternoon, she and my son had spent a long time in the backyard, oblivious to the heat and the mosquitoes. They were both tired but peaceful when they noisily re-entered the house, holding hands awkwardly.

But someone was knocking at the door to my room. Why should I wake up? It would be impossible to fall asleep again. It was so hot. The knocking continued. I switched on the light by the bed: 3:30 A.M. It must be my father. Furious, I pulled on a pair of shorts and a t-shirt. "What do you want? What's the matter?" I asked him, through the door. Had he gone berserk? What could he have to talk about at that ridiculous hour?

"OK, all right," I said, rubbing my eyes awake as I stepped to the door and opened it. "What?"

To my surprise, my father stood there looking very uncertain.

"It's your mother," he told me, in a burly, formal voice. "I think she's dead, but I'm not sure." He was avoiding my eyes.

"What do you mean," I answered.

"I want you to go downstairs and figure it out."

I could not believe what he was saying to me. "You want me to figure out if my mother is dead or alive?"

"I can't tell! I don't know!!" he shouted angrily.

"Jesus Christ," I muttered, angry and beside myself.

I turned and glanced about my room, wondering if I could find anything to carry with me on this mission; what do you use to determine a life or a death? I couldn't see anything obvious that might be useful.

"I'll wait up here," my father said. "You call up and let me know."

I could not believe it; a man married to a woman more than forty years and   25
he can't tell if she's alive or dead and he wakes up his kid and tells her, "You figure it out."

I was at the bottom of the stairs. I halted just outside the dining room where my
mother slept. Suppose she really was dead? Suppose my father was not just being
crazy and hateful? "Naw," I shook my head and confidently entered the room.

"Momma?!" I called, aloud. At the edge of the cot, my mother was leaning
forward, one arm braced to hoist her body up. She was trying to stand up! I
rushed over. "Wait. Here, I'll help you!" I said.

And I reached out my hands to give her a lift. The body of my mother was
stiff. She was not yet cold, but she was stiff. Maybe I had come downstairs just in
time! I tried to loosen her arms, to change her position, to ease her into lying
down.

"Momma!" I kept saying. "Momma, listen to me! It's OK! I'm here and
everything. Just relax. Relax! Give me a hand, now. I'm trying to help you lie
down!"

Her body did not relax. She did not answer me. But she was not cold. Her   30
eyes were not shut.

From upstairs my father was yelling, "Is she dead? Is she dead?"

"No!" I screamed at him. "No! She's not dead!"

At this, my father tore down the stairs and into the room. Then he braked.

"Milly?" he called out, tentative. Then he shouted at me and banged around
the walls. "You damn fool. Don't you see now she's gone. Now she's gone!" We
began to argue.

"She's alive! Call the doctor!"   35

"No!"

"Yes!"

At last my father left the room to call the doctor.

I straightened up. I felt completely exhausted from trying to gain a response
from my mother. There she was, stiff on the edge of her bed, just about to stand
up. Her lips were set, determined. She would manage it, but by herself. I could
not help. Her eyes fixed on some point below the floor.

"Momma!" I shook her hard as I could to rouse her into focus. Now she fell   40
back on the cot, but frozen and in the wrong position. It hit me that she might be
dead. She might be dead.

My father reappeared at the door. He would not come any closer. "Dr. Davis
says he will come. And he call the police."

The police? Would they know if my mother was dead or alive? Who would
know?

I went to the phone and called my aunt. "Come quick," I said. "My father
thinks Momma has died but she's here but she's stiff."

Soon the house was weird and ugly and crowded and I thought I was losing
my mind.

Three white policemen stood around telling me my mother was dead. "How   45
do you know?" I asked, and they shrugged and then they repeated themselves.

And the doctor never came. But my aunt came and my uncle and they said she was dead.

After a conference with the cops, my aunt disappeared and when she came back she held a bottle in one of her hands. She and the police whispered together some more. Then one of the cops said, "Don't worry about it. We won't say anything." My aunt signalled me to follow her into the hallway where she let me understand that, in fact, my mother had committed suicide.

I could not assimilate this information: suicide.

I broke away from my aunt and ran to the telephone. I called a friend of mine, a woman who talked back loud to me so that I could realize my growing hysteria, and check it. Then I called my cousin Valerie who lived in Harlem; she woke up instantly and urged me to come right away.

I hurried to the top floor and stood my sleeping son on his feet. I wanted to get him out of this house of death more than I ever wanted anything. He could not stand by himself so I carried him down the two flights to the street and laid him on the backseat and then took off.

At Valerie's, my son continued to sleep, so we put him to bed, closed the door, and talked. My cousin made me eat eggs, drink whiskey, and shower. She would take care of Christopher, she said. I should go back and deal with the situation in Brooklyn. 50

When I arrived, the house was absolutely full of women from the church dressed as though they were going to Sunday communion. It seemed to me they were, every one of them, wearing hats and gloves and drinking coffee and solemnly addressing invitations to a funeral and I could not find my mother anywhere and I could not find an empty spot in the house where I could sit down and smoke a cigarette.

My mother was dead.

Feeling completely out of place, I headed for the front door, ready to leave. My father grabbed my shoulder from behind and forcibly spun me around.

"You see this?" he smiled, waving a large document in the air. "This am insurance paper for you!" He waved it into my face. "Your mother, she left you insurance, see?"

I watched him. 55

"But I gwine burn it in the furnace before I give it you to t'row away on trash!"

"Is that money?" I demanded. "Did my mother leave me money?"

"Eh-heh!" he laughed. "And you don't get it from me. Not today, not tomorrow. Not until I dead and buried!"

My father grabbed for my arm and I swung away from him. He hit me on my head and I hit back. We were fighting.

Suddenly, the ladies from the church bustled about and pushed, horrified, between us. This was a sin, they said, for a father and a child to fight in the house of the dead and the mother not yet in the ground! Such a good woman she was, they said. She was a good woman, a good woman, they all agreed. Out of respect for the memory of this good woman, in deference to my mother who had committed suicide, the ladies shook their hats and insisted we should not fight; I should not fight with my father. 60

Utterly disgusted and disoriented, I went back to Harlem. By the time I reached my cousin's place I had begun to bleed, heavily. Valerie said I was hemorrhaging so she called up her boyfriend and the two of them hobbled me into Harlem Hospital.

I don't know how long I remained unconscious, but when I opened my eyes I found myself on the women's ward, with an intravenous setup feeding into my arm. After a while, Valerie showed up. Christopher was fine, she told me; my friends were taking turns with him. Whatever I did, I should not admit I'd had an abortion or I'd get her into trouble, and myself in trouble. Just play dumb and rest. I'd have to stay on the ward for several days. My mother's funeral was tomorrow afternoon. What did I want her to tell people to explain why I wouldn't be there? She meant, what lie?

I thought about it and I decided I had nothing to say; if I couldn't tell the truth then the hell with it.

I lay in that bed at Harlem Hospital, thinking and sleeping. I wanted to get well.

I wanted to be strong. I never wanted to be weak again as long as I lived. I   65
thought about my mother and her suicide and I thought about how my father could not tell whether she was dead or alive.

I wanted to get well and what I wanted to do as soon as I was strong again, actually, what I wanted to do was I wanted to live my life so that people would know unmistakably that I am alive, so that when I finally die people will know the difference for sure between my living and my death.

And I thought about the idea of my mother as a good woman and I rejected that, because I don't see why it's a good thing when you give up, or when you cooperate with those who hate you or when you polish and iron and mend and endlessly mollify for the sake of the people who love the way that you kill yourself day by day silently.

And I think all of this is really about women and work. Certainly this is all about me as a woman and my life work. I mean I am not sure my mother's suicide was something extraordinary. Perhaps most women must deal with a similar inheritance, the legacy of a woman whose death you cannot possibly pinpoint because she died so many, many times and because, even before she became your mother, the life of that woman was taken; I say it was taken away.

And really it was to honor my mother that I did fight with my father, that man who could not tell the living from the dead.

And really it is to honor Mrs. Hazel Griffin and my cousin Valerie and all the   70
women I love, including myself, that I am working for the courage to admit the truth that Bertolt Brecht has written; he says, "It takes courage to say that the good were defeated not because they were good, but because they were weak."

I cherish the mercy and the grace of women's work. But I know there is new work that we must undertake as well: that new work will make defeat detestable to us. That new women's work will mean we will not die trying to stand up: we will live that way: standing up.

I came too late to help my mother to her feet.

By way of everlasting thanks to all of the women who have helped me to stay alive I am working never to be late again.   [1985]

ALICE WALKER
In Search of Our Mothers' Gardens

I described her own nature and temperament. Told how they needed a
larger life for their expression. . . . I pointed out that in lieu of proper channels, her emotions had overflowed into paths that dissipated them. I talked,
beautifully I thought, about an art that would be born, an art that would
open the way for women the likes of her. I asked her to hope, and build up
an inner life against the coming of that day. . . . I sang, with a strange quiver
in my voice, a promise song.

> —"Avey," Jean Toomer, *Cane*
> *The poet speaking to a prostitute who falls*
> *asleep while he's talking*

When the poet Jean Toomer walked through the South in the early twenties,
he discovered a curious thing: black women whose spirituality was so intense, so
deep, so *unconscious*, they were themselves unaware of the richness they held.
They stumbled blindly through their lives: creatures so abused and mutilated in
body, so dimmed and confused by pain, that they considered themselves unworthy even of hope. In the selfless abstractions their bodies became to the men who
used them, they became more than "sexual objects," more even than mere
women: they became "Saints." Instead of being perceived as whole persons, their
bodies became shrines: what was thought to be their minds became temples suitable for worship. These crazy Saints stared out at the world, wildly, like
lunatics—or quietly, like suicides; and the "God" that was in their gaze was as
mute as a great stone.

Who were these Saints? These crazy, loony, pitiful women?

Some of them, without a doubt, were our mothers and grandmothers.

In the still heat of the post-Reconstruction South, this is how they seemed to
Jean Toomer: exquisite butterflies trapped in an evil honey, toiling away their
lives in an era, a century, that did not acknowledge them, except as "the *mule* of
the world." They dreamed dreams that no one knew—not even themselves, in
any coherent fashion—and saw visions no one could understand. They wandered or sat about the countryside crooning lullabies to ghosts, and drawing the
mother of Christ in charcoal on courthouse walls.

They forced their minds to desert their bodies and their striving spirits sought   5
to rise, like frail whirlwinds from the hard red clay. And when those frail whirlwinds fell, in scattered particles, upon the ground, no one mourned. Instead,
men lit candles to celebrate the emptiness that remained, as people do who enter
a beautiful but vacant space to resurrect a God.

Our mothers and grandmothers, some of them: moving to music not yet
written. And they waited.

They waited for a day when the unknown thing that was in them would be
made known; but guessed, somehow in their darkness, that on the day of their
revelation they would be long dead. Therefore to Toomer they walked, and even
ran, in slow motion. For they were going nowhere immediate, and the future was

not yet within their grasp. And men took our mothers and grandmothers, "but got no pleasure from it." So complex was their passion and their calm.

To Toomer, they lay vacant and fallow as autumn fields, with harvest time never in sight: and he saw them enter loveless marriages, without joy; and become prostitutes, without resistance; and become mothers of children, without fulfillment.

For these grandmothers and mothers of ours were not Saints, but Artists; driven to a numb and bleeding madness by the springs of creativity in them for which there was no release. They were Creators, who lived lives of spiritual waste, because they were so rich in spirituality—which is the basis of Art—that the strain of enduring their unused and unwanted talent drove them insane. Throwing away this spirituality was their pathetic attempt to lighten the soul to a weight their work-worn, sexually abused bodies could bear.

What did it mean for a black woman to be an artist in our grandmothers' time? In our great-grandmothers' day? It is a question with an answer cruel enough to stop the blood.   10

Did you have a genius of a great-great-grandmother who died under some ignorant and depraved white overseer's lash? Or was she required to bake biscuits for a lazy backwater tramp, when she cried out in her soul to paint watercolors of sunsets, or the rain falling on the green and peaceful pasturelands? Or was her body broken and forced to bear children (who were more often than not sold away from her)—eight, ten, fifteen, twenty children—when her one joy was the thought of modeling heroic figures of rebellion, in stone or clay?

How was the creativity of the black woman kept alive, year after year and century after century, when for most of the years black people have been in America, it was a punishable crime for a black person to read or write? And the freedom to paint, to sculpt, to expand the mind with action did not exist. Consider, if you can bear to imagine it, what might have been the result if singing, too, had been forbidden by law. Listen to the voices of Bessie Smith, Billie Holiday, Nina Simone, Roberta Flack, and Aretha Franklin, among others, and imagine those voices muzzled for life. Then you may begin to comprehend the lives of our "crazy," "Sainted" mothers and grandmothers. The agony of the lives of women who might have been Poets, Novelists, Essayists, and Short-Story Writers (over a period of centuries), who died with their real gifts stifled within them.

And, if this were the end of the story, we would have cause to cry out in my paraphrase of Okot p'Bitek's great poem:

> O, my clanswoman
> Let us all cry together!
> Come,
> Let us mourn the death of our mother,
> The death of a Queen
> The ash that was produced
> By a great fire!
> O, this homestead is utterly dead

> Close the gates
> With *lacari* thorns,
> For our mother
> The creator of the Stool is lost!
> And all the young men
> Have perished in the wilderness!

But this is not the end of the story, for all the young women — our mothers and grandmothers, *ourselves* — have not perished in the wilderness. And if we ask ourselves why, and search for and find the answer, we will know beyond all efforts to erase it from our minds, just exactly who, and of what, we black American women are.

One example, perhaps the most pathetic, most misunderstood one, can pro-   15
vide a backdrop for our mothers' work: Phillis Wheatley, a slave in the 1700s.

Virginia Woolf, in her book *A Room of One's Own*, wrote that in order for a woman to write fiction she must have two things, certainly: a room of her own (with key and lock) and enough money to support herself.

What then are we to make of Phillis Wheatley, a slave, who owned not even herself? This sickly, frail black girl who required a servant of her own at times — her health was so precarious — and who, had she been white, would have been easily considered the intellectual superior of all the women and most of the men in the society of her day.

Virginia Woolf wrote further, speaking of course not of our Phillis, that "any woman born with a great gift in the sixteenth century [insert "eighteenth century," insert "black woman," insert "born or made a slave"] would certainly have gone crazed, shot herself, or ended her days in some lonely cottage outside the village, half witch, half wizard [insert "Saint"], feared and mocked at. For it needs little skill and psychology to be sure that a highly gifted girl who had tried to use her gift of poetry would have been so thwarted and hindered by contrary instincts [add "chains, guns, the lash, the ownership of one's body by someone else, submission to an alien religion"], that she must have lost her health and sanity to a certainty."

The key words, as they relate to Phillis, are "contrary instincts." For when we read the poetry of Phillis Wheatley — as when we read the novels of Nella Larsen or the oddly false-sounding autobiography of that freest of all black women writers, Zora Hurston — evidence of "contrary instincts" is everywhere. Her loyalties were completely divided, as was, without question, her mind.

But how could this be otherwise? Captured at seven, a slave of wealthy, dot-   20
ing whites who instilled in her the "savagery" of the Africa they "rescued" her from . . . one wonders if she was even able to remember her homeland as she had known it, or as it really was.

Yet, because she did try to use her gift for poetry in a world that made her a slave, she was "so thwarted and hindered by . . . contrary instincts, that she . . . lost her health. . . ." In the last years of her brief life, burdened not only with the need to express her gift but also with a penniless, friendless "freedom" and several small children for whom she was forced to do strenuous work to feed, she lost her health, certainly. Suffering from malnutrition and neglect and who knows what mental agonies, Phillis Wheatley died.

So torn by "contrary instincts" was black, kidnapped, enslaved Phillis that her description of "the Goddess" — as she poetically called the Liberty she did not have — is ironically, cruelly humorous. And, in fact, has held Phillis up to ridicule for more than a century. It is usually read prior to hanging Phillis's memory as that of a fool. She wrote:

> The Goddess comes, she moves divinely fair,
> Olive and laurel binds her *golden* hair.
> Wherever shines this native of the skies,
> Unnumber'd charms and recent graces rise. [My italics]

It is obvious that Phillis, the slave, combed the "Goddess's" hair every morning; prior, perhaps, to bringing in the milk, or fixing her mistress's lunch. She took her imagery from the one thing she saw elevated above all others.

With the benefit of hindsight we ask, "How could she?"

But at last, Phillis, we understand. No more snickering when your stiff, struggling, ambivalent lines are forced on us. We know now that you were not an idiot or a traitor; only a sickly little black girl, snatched from your home and country and made a slave; a woman who still struggled to sing the song that was your gift, although in a land of barbarians who praised you for your bewildered tongue. It is not so much what you sang, as that you kept alive, in so many of our ancestors, *the notion of song.*

25

Black women are called, in the folklore that so aptly identifies one's status in society, "the *mule* of the world," because we have been handed the burdens that everyone else — *everyone* else — refused to carry. We have also been called "Matriarchs," "Superwomen," and "Mean and Evil Bitches." Not to mention "Castraters" and "Sapphire's Mama." When we have pleaded for understanding, our character has been distorted; when we have asked for simple caring, we have been handed empty inspirational appellations, then stuck in the farthest corner. When we have asked for love, we have been given children. In short, even our plainer gifts, our labors of fidelity and love, have been knocked down our throats. To be an artist and a black woman, even today, lowers our status in many respects, rather than raises it: and yet, artists we will be.

Therefore we must fearlessly pull out of ourselves and look at and identify with our lives the living creativity some of our great-grandmothers were not allowed to know. I stress *some* of them because it is well known that the majority of our great-grandmothers knew, even without "knowing" it, the reality of their spirituality, even if they didn't recognize it beyond what happened in the singing at church — and they never had any intention of giving it up.

How they did it — those millions of black women who were not Phillis Wheatley, or Lucy Terry or Frances Harper or Zora Hurston or Nella Larsen or Bessie Smith; or Elizabeth Catlett, or Katherine Dunham, either — brings me to the title of this essay, "In Search of Our Mothers' Gardens," which is a personal account that is yet shared, in its theme and its meaning, by all of us. I found, while thinking about the far-reaching world of the creative black woman, that often the truest answer to a question that really matters can be found very close.

In the late 1920s my mother ran away from home to marry my father. Marriage, if not running away, was expected of seventeen-year-old girls. By the time she was twenty, she had two children and was pregnant with a third. Five children later, I was born. And this is how I came to know my mother: she seemed a large, soft, loving-eyed woman who was rarely impatient in our home. Her quick, violent temper was on view only a few times a year, when she battled with the white landlord who had the misfortune to suggest to her that her children did not need to go to school.

She made all the clothes we wore, even my brothers' overalls. She made all   30
the towels and sheets we used. She spent the summers canning vegetables and fruits. She spent the winter evenings making quilts enough to cover all our beds.

During the "working" day, she labored beside — not behind — my father in the fields. Her day began before sunup, and did not end until late at night. There was never a moment for her to sit down, undisturbed, to unravel her own private thoughts; never a time free from interruption — by work or the noisy inquiries of her many children. And yet, it is to my mother — and all our mothers who were not famous — that I went in search of the secret of what has fed that muzzled and often mutilated, but vibrant, creative spirit that the black woman has inherited, and that pops out in wild and unlikely places to this day.

But when, you will ask, did my overworked mother have time to know or care about feeding the creative spirit?

The answer is so simple that many of us have spent years discovering it. We have constantly looked high, when we should have looked high — and low.

For example: in the Smithsonian Institution in Washington, D.C., there hangs a quilt unlike any other in the world. In fanciful, inspired, and yet simple and identifiable figures, it portrays the story of the Crucifixion. It is considered rare, beyond price. Though it follows no known pattern of quiltmaking, and though it is made of bits and pieces of worthless rags, it is obviously the work of a person of powerful imagination and deep spiritual feeling. Below this quilt I saw a note that says it was made by "an anonymous Black woman in Alabama, a hundred years ago."

If we could locate this "anonymous" black woman from Alabama, she would   35
turn out to be one of our grandmothers — an artist who left her mark in the only materials she could afford, and in the only medium her position in society allowed her to use.

As Virginia Woolf wrote further, in *A Room of One's Own*:

> Yet genius of a sort must have existed among women as it must have existed among the working class. [Change this to "slaves" and "the wives and daughters of sharecroppers."] Now and again an Emily Brontë or a Robert Burns [change this to "a Zora Hurston or a Richard Wright"] blazes out and proves its presence. But certainly it never got itself on to paper. When, how-

ever, one reads of a witch being ducked, of a woman possessed by devils [or "Sainthood"], of a wise woman selling herbs [or root workers], or even a very remarkable man who had a mother, then I think we are on the track of a lost novelist, a suppressed poet, or some mute and inglorious Jane Austen. . . . Indeed, I would venture to guess that Anon, who wrote so many poems without signing them, was often a woman. . . .

And so our mothers and grandmothers have, more often than not anonymously, handed on the creative spark, the seed of the flower they themselves never hoped to see: or like a sealed letter they could not plainly read.

And so it is, certainly, with my own mother. Unlike "Ma" Rainey's songs, which retained their creator's name even while blasting forth from Bessie Smith's mouth, no song or poem will bear my mother's name. Yet so many of the stories that I write, that we all write, are my mother's stories. Only recently did I fully realize this: that through years of listening to my mother's stories of her life, I have absorbed not only the stories themselves, but something of the manner in which she spoke, something of the urgency that involves the knowledge that her stories — like her life — must be recorded. It is probably for this reason that so much of what I have written is about characters whose counterparts in real life are so much older than I am.

But the telling of these stories, which came from my mother's lips as naturally as breathing, was not the only way my mother showed herself as an artist. For stories, too, were subject to being distracted, to dying without conclusion. Dinners must be started, and cotton must be gathered before the big rains. The artist that was and is my mother showed itself to me only after many years. This is what I finally noticed:

Like Mem, a character in *The Third Life of Grange Copeland*, my mother   40 adorned with flowers whatever shabby house we were forced to live in. And not just your typical straggly country stand of zinnias, either. She planted ambitious gardens — and still does — with over fifty different varieties of plants that bloom profusely from early March until late November. Before she left home for the fields, she watered her flowers, chopped up the grass, and laid out new beds. When she returned from the fields she might divide clumps of bulbs, dig a cold pit, uproot and replant roses, or prune branches from her taller bushes or trees — until night came and it was too dark to see.

Whatever she planted grew as if by magic, and her fame as a grower of flowers spread over three counties. Because of her creativity with her flowers, even my memories of poverty are seen through a screen of blooms — sunflowers, petunias, roses, dahlias, forsythia, spirea, delphiniums, verbena . . . and so on.

And I remember people coming to my mother's yard to be given cuttings from her flowers; I hear again the praise showered on her because whatever rocky soil she landed on, she turned into a garden. A garden so brilliant with colors, so original in its design, so magnificent with life and creativity, that to this day people drive by our house in Georgia — perfect strangers and imperfect strangers — and ask to stand or walk among my mother's art.

I notice that it is only when my mother is working in her flowers that she is radiant, almost to the point of being invisible — except as Creator: hand and eye.

She is involved in work her soul must have. Ordering the universe in the image of her personal conception of Beauty.

Her face, as she prepares the Art that is her gift, is a legacy of respect she leaves to me, for all that illuminates and cherishes life. She has handed down respect for the possibilities — and the will to grasp them.

For her, so hindered and intruded upon in so many ways, being an artist has   45 still been a daily part of her life. This ability to hold on, even in very simple ways, is work black women have done for a very long time.

This poem is not enough, but it is something, for the woman who literally covered the holes in our walls with sunflowers:

> They were women then
> My mama's generation
> Husky of voice — Stout of
> Step
> With fists as well as
> Hands
> How they battered down
> Doors
> And ironed
> Starched white
> Shirts
> How they led
> Armies
> Headragged Generals
> Across mined
> Fields
> Booby-trapped
> Kitchens
> To discover books
> Desks
> A place for us
> How they knew what we
> *Must* know
> Without knowing a page
> Of it
> Themselves.

Guided by my heritage of a love of beauty and a respect for strength — in search of my mother's garden, I found my own.

And perhaps in Africa over two hundred years ago, there was just such a mother; perhaps she painted vivid and daring decorations in oranges and yellows and greens on the walls of her hut; perhaps she sang — in a voice like Roberta Flack's — *sweetly* over the compounds of her village; perhaps she wove the most stunning mats or told the most ingenious stories of all the village storytellers. Perhaps she was herself a poet — though only her daughter's name is signed to the poems that we know.

Perhaps Phillis Wheatley's mother was also an artist.

Perhaps in more than Phillis Wheatley's biological life is her mother's signa-   50 ture made clear.   [1974]

A WRITING EXERCISE

Read Jordan's "Many Rivers to Cross," jotting down your notes and comments in the margin. Consider your immediate reactions, and don't ignore personal associations. Then freewrite a response to her essay for ten minutes.

A Student's Personal Response

Isla Bravo wrote in her journal:

It was shocking to read about Jordan's mother's suicide in the first sentence of "Many Rivers to Cross." I expected the rest of the essay to be about only that one event, but she went on to talk about everything else that was going on in her life around that time first. It is hard to understand how she managed everything in her life. She is out of money and needs to find a way to improve her financial status in just three months. My family may not have everything we've ever wanted, but we've always done pretty well, and I never worried about where we lived.

Even though I have never had to struggle the way Jordan did, I can relate to her descriptions of her friends and neighbors. They all help her out the best they can when her husband leaves her and then when her mother dies. These are the people that she really appreciates in her life. They are the same kind of people that brought food to my parents when my grandmother died. These are the people that she loves and creates her own sort of family despite the fact that her father is so mean to her. These are people with whom she creates relationships that aren't defined by specific standards created by society.

When Jordan says that her mother's death may not be extraordinary, that maybe every woman watches someone die over and over, she is really talking about all the little things that can wear a lot of women down and cause their deaths a long time before they actually die. She can't even tell that her mother is dead because she's been wearing down for so long. The image of her mother looking

as if she was "just about to stand up" made me think of
my grandmother's funeral and how she looked like she was
sleeping rather than dead. For Jordan the image of her
mother in that sort of stasis is also an image of her
possible future. It is strange to think of someone whose
life has been so hard on them that their death doesn't
create a jarring difference.

  Jordan seems to be trying to keep herself from wearing down just like her mother at the end. Women are given
roles by society that prevent them from being able to
really enjoy their lives. She uses her other friends and
family as models for how to survive. She has a friend who
calms her down on the phone, a cousin that gives her advice in the hospital, and more that take care of her son
when she can't. Mrs. Griffin is a good example of the type
of person she wants to be. She has to work hard to avoid
becoming her mother. It seems as if she is motivated by
guilt because she wasn't able to help her mother when she
says, "I came too late to help my mother to her feet."
Even though it wasn't her fault that her mother put up
with so much, it certainly makes her determined to prevent
her life from ending up the same way her mother's did.

The Elements of Essays

First impressions are valuable, but writing intelligently about essays should
not be completely spontaneous. We can be personal and insightful, but persuading others about the validity of our reading takes a more focused and textually
informed presentation. The following discussion of the basic elements of the
essay is meant to increase your ability to analyze and write about essays. The elements include **voice**, **style**, **structure**, and **ideas**.

Voice

When we read the first few sentences of an essay, we usually hear the narrator's **voice**: we hear a person speaking to us, and we begin to notice if he or she
sounds friendly or hostile, stuffy or casual, self-assured or tentative. The voice
might be austere and technical or personal and flamboyant. The voice may be
intimate or remote. It may be sincere, hectoring, hysterical, meditative, or ironic.
The possibilities are endless.

We usually get a sense of the writer's voice from the **tone** the writer projects. In the first paragraph of Walker's essay, we get a sense of the speaker's voice through the informed and serious tone that she takes. We also sense some irony and anger especially when she asks, "Who were . . . these crazy, loony, pitiful women?" There also seems a note of lyrical sadness in her tone in paragraph 6: "Our mothers and grandmothers, some of them: moving to music not yet written. And they waited." Writing about such complex matters as racism and art, Walker's voice is equally complex. At times her tone is alternately angry ("When we have pleaded," paragraph 26); hopeful ("Therefore we must fearlessly pull out of ourselves," paragraph 27); thoughtful (paragraph 28); admiring (paragraph 29), and honestly self-reflective ("Only recently did I fully realize this," paragraph 38). And there are numerous examples of her employing a celebratory tone, especially when she discusses the matriarchal artists she so admires. The tone of her speculative conclusion is dramatic as she uses "perhaps" seven times, a rhetorically satisfying ending to an essay meant to be a moving argument about the ability of oppressed women to keep their artistic spirit alive. When we speak of a writer's persona, we mean a kind of performance mask or stance the writer assumes. Writers are trying to construct a persona that will serve their purposes. Voice and tone are techniques that help writers create a persona.

A WRITING EXERCISE

Read June Jordan's essay "Many Rivers to Cross," and make some notes about the voice you hear. Like Walker, Jordan is also concerned with injustice and racism. Is her tone angrier? More determined? And like Walker, Jordan employs the rhetorical technique of repetition to conclude her essay. How would you compare the effectiveness of repeating "I" with Walker's "perhaps"?

Style

We all have stylish friends. They look good. Their shoes and pants and shirts seem to complement each other perfectly. It's not that they are color-coordinated — that would be too obvious for them — it's something more subtle. They seem to make just the right choices. When they go to a party, to the movies, or to school, they have a personal style that is their own.

Writers also have **style**. They make specific choices in words, in syntax and sentence length, in diction, in metaphors, even in sentence beginnings and endings. Writers use parallelism, balance, formal diction, poetic language, even sentence fragments to create their own styles.

Review each of the two essays with an eye to comparing the styles of Walker and Jordan. Notice the interesting use of the colon in Walker's first sentence and the dramatic repetition of "so intense, so deep, so *unconscious*." Actually, Walker's first paragraph makes creative use of the colon and dash. She writes sophisticated, complex sentences, varying the usual subject/verb/object pattern. In the second and third paragraphs, she varies the length of her sentences with short questions and statements before returning in the fourth, fifth, and sixth paragraphs to a literary style employing metaphors ("exquisite butterflies"), similes ("like frail whirlwinds"), and analogies ("moving to music"). It is an impassioned style, moving, evocative, and committed. Filled with literary devices, rhetorical flourishes, and emotional honesty, Walker writes her own rules for how a persuasive essay works.

A WRITING EXERCISE

Note any literary techniques in Jordan's style. Focus especially on the last dozen paragraphs or so. Are her sentences as complex as Walker's? Is her style appropriate to her purpose? Explain.

Structure

The way essayists put their work together is not mysterious. The best writers create a **structure** to fit their needs. Most do not have a prearranged structure in mind or feel the need to obey the composition rules many students think they have to follow: topic sentence first and three examples following. Writers of essays aren't inclined to follow formulas. Essayists begin and end as they see fit; they give explicit topic sentences or create narratives that imply themes; they begin with an assertion and support it, or vice versa. Essayists are inventors of structures that fit the occasion and their own way of seeing the world. The thought of the essay significantly influences its structure. Like the relationship between mind and body, form and thought are inseparable.

Walker's essay is an argument and its structure is part of her persuasive intent. In "Literature as Argument" (p. 29), we note that writers sometimes specify an issue, make claims, and then explicitly support these claims with substantial evidence, hoping to persuade a particular audience. Most literary texts usually make arguments indirectly, but essays are often more direct. Walker directly uses personal experience in the service of her argument. Although students are sometimes taught that one's own experience is too subjective to persuade others, experienced writers like Walker and Jordan do use personal and literary experiences to call for certain changes in the attitudes of their readers.

In her first paragraph, Walker reveals some of her **assumptions** or warrants, especially the idea that black women were not aware of their capabilities, were "abused and mutilated," and were misread. After establishing common ground with her audience—that these women are the mothers and grandmothers of the speaker and her audience—Walker comes eventually to her thesis in paragraph 9, in which she asserts that these women were "not Saints, but Artists." After asking how these women kept their creativity from disappearing, she notes that African American women of her mother's generation found a way through song and other strategies to keep an artistic heritage alive in spite of the barriers they faced. Most of the essay then develops this idea more concretely.

Walker's essay does not use a thesis statement and then a point-by-point argument. Instead, she leads us into her main idea gradually, interweaving examples, letting one idea lead to another, coming back to ideas mentioned earlier, and developing them further. She ends by returning to her Phillis Wheatley example to make a connection to the deep past, as just one of the many ways she achieves coherence and unity in this quilt-like essay, sewn together with carefully crafted transitions.

A WRITING EXERCISE

As you read through Jordan's essay, describe the structure or organizing strategies that she uses. How does her extended personal narrative support her main idea?

Ideas

All writers have something on their minds when they write. That seems especially true when writers decide to put their **ideas** into a nonfictional form such as the essay. Of course, lots of ideas fill poems and short stories too, but they are usually expressed more indirectly. Although essays seem more idea-driven, this does not mean that as readers we have a responsibility to extract the precise idea or argument the writer had in mind. That may not even be possible since in the creative process of all writing, ideas get modified or changed. Sometimes a writer's original intention is significantly transformed; sometimes writers are not fully conscious of all their hidden intentions. Regardless, readers of essays are not simply miners unearthing hidden meanings; they are more like coproducers. And in creating that meaning, ideas are central.

"In Search of Our Mothers' Gardens" is an argument based on the idea that Walker's ancestors were not really the strange "crazy, loony, pitiful women" that Jean Toomer thought—not "exquisite butterflies" but artists "driven to a numb and bleeding madness by the springs of creativity in them for which there was no release." They could not do the work that was in their hearts and minds, and yet they managed to survive. They did so, Walker claims, through a psychological process Freud might call sublimation, by channeling their unacceptable creative drive into such acceptable ordinary paths as singing, quilting, and gardening. Phillis Wheatley is used as an example of an artist whose natural creativity was so thwarted that her health deteriorated as a result. And after reviewing her main ideas of heritage, love of beauty, and respect for the strength of her creative ancestors, Walker concludes with the speculation that perhaps the artistic tradition goes back even further than Wheatley, back to Wheatley's African mother and beyond.

A WRITING EXERCISE

Ideas are often more powerful and more dramatic when they seem to evolve as a result of personal experience and not simply from political beliefs or ideological conviction. There seems to be a considerable difference between starkly asserting that black women were not able to live up to their potential and enveloping that idea that Walker does here. What do you think are some ideas that June Jordan develops? Comment on the effectiveness of her extended narrative in enhancing her ideas.

Sample Student Paper: Final Draft

After writing journal entries and a freewrite, Isla planned her essay and then wrote a draft. She used responses from several students in a small-group workshop and from her instructor to help her revise her essay, sharpening her focus and supporting her claims more explicitly. Here is Isla's final version.

```
Isla Bravo
Ms. Hollingsworth
English 201
21 April —
                    Resisting Women's Roles
     June Jordan takes a strongly feminist stance against
the roles women are forced to contend with in her essay
"Many Rivers to Cross." She begins the essay from her
experience as a woman who has conformed to the social
expectations of a wife, daughter, and mother. Her commit-
ment to these roles have left her as a single mother who
is contending with an unwanted pregnancy, forced to care
for a dying mother and a belligerent father, and without
a place of her own to live or work. This essay is Jor-
dan's own testimonial to why women need to establish
their independence and not allow society to control their
lives. She makes this statement by exploring her own
defiance of society's conventions regarding the roles for
women as wife, daughter, and mother in an attempt to pre-
serve herself from the restrictions that destroyed her
mother.
     Women are expected by society to place their families
before their careers, and part of this sacrifice includes
aiding their husband's careers in lieu of their own. Jor-
dan portrays herself as an example of how this convention
is detrimental to a woman's ability to survive on her
own. Jordan sacrifices her own professional ambition to
her husband's pursuit of his career. The ensuing compli-
cations depict the limitations and perils of the idea
```

that women must always place their own careers behind their husbands. Rather than specifically condemn this social expectation, she provides an illustration of the destruction it can cause. Her own career is a secondary priority, subjugated to her roles as a supportive wife and mother, while her husband pursues graduate school in another city and has an affair with another man's wife. Jordan squanders a year of her life waiting for her husband's return and becomes "a mother without a husband, as a poet without a publisher, a freelance journalist without assignment, a city planner without a contract." She abides by the social conventions that insist she support her husband, and her life remains in stasis until he steps out of his own commitments. By living her life under the social guidelines for a wife, she allows herself to be exploited for her husband's convenience. Her needs are supplanted by her husband's, and his abandonment leaves her embarrassed and destitute.

Jordan's depiction of her parent's relationship illustrates the generational quality of these social conventions. Her parent's relationship foreshadows the potential outcome of her marriage if it continues. Her parents' relationship is wholly restricted to the typical gender roles they both inherit from society. Her mother subjugates her own life only to the needs of her husband, a sacrifice he expects from her. This historical relationship becomes clear when Jordan describes her father's response to her mother's fatal illness when she says, "I think he was scared; who would take care of him? Would she get well again and make everything all right again?" The fact that his concern was about his own life--"who would take care of him?"--makes it clear that their relationship revolved around only his own comfort. Jordan is desperate to prevent her own life from following this path.

Jordan's relationship with her father explores another aspect of the expectations placed on women by

society, that of a daughter. Jordan's father's reliance
on her mother for all of his comfort turns onto Jordan
when her mother is no longer able to fulfill these
duties. Jordan's role as his daughter, her most important
function, is dynamically portrayed when her father forces
her to check her mother's body to see if she is alive
because he is incapable or unwilling to do it himself. He
says to her, "I'll wait up here. . . . You call up and let
me know," only to yell at her inaccurate determination.
His anger appears to stem more from the disruption to his
own life rather than the loss of his wife; he is angry
rather than sad. He appears almost offended by her death
and his daughter's failure to provide him with the level
of comfort he craves for his life. His own expectations
for the superior role in the household have been created
by a male-dominated society and have been enforced by the
manner in which his wife seems to have fulfilled those
expectations as well. The role of a dutiful child is not
by itself destructive until it begins to take precedence
in this destructive manner. His expectation is that Jordan should take on the role of caregiver, waiting on him
despite any reluctance on her part and regardless of the
animosity that exists between them.

Jordan also defies social conventions by her unwill-
ingness to become a mother again to the new baby she's
carrying. She attempts to abort the child several times
until she finally does lose the baby. Jordan describes
the advice she receives from a friend in the hospital,
"Whatever I did, I should not admit I'd had an abortion
or I'd get her into trouble, and myself in trouble." The
possibility that Jordan does not want to be a mother to
another child is abhorrent to the social standards that
have formed her life and surroundings. Motherhood is the
expected career for a woman, and her choice to not have
another baby is a direct rejection of those standards.

As a woman in this particular culture, she has certain designated assignments of work that include being a

daughter, wife, and mother. She rejects a caretaker role for her father, her marriage has dissolved, and she has an abortion. These portrayals do not suggest a rejection of these roles in their entirety; rather, they explicitly show how they can become harmful if they force women into situations they might have avoided if not for these societal pressures. From this point, she is able to look toward her own career and her own needs. The role society imposes on her as a woman puts her in a position that deemphasizes her own ambitions and preferences. The end of her mother's life is the catalyst that forces her to fully recognize the restrictions that she has been living with and that her mother succumbed to until her death. Jordan says, "I came too late to help my mother to her feet. . . . I am working never to be late again." She wants to free herself from the limiting standards for women in society and hopefully free other women as well.

SUMMING UP

- **Essays (and nonfiction) use language as imaginatively and effectively as other genres of literature.** Essays should—like stories, poems, and plays—be read with care and deliberation and written about with as much energy and discipline. (p. 171)

- **The elements of essays include *voice*, *ideas*, *structure*, and *style*.**

- **In essays, *voice* is extremely important.** The writer's voice (which might be sincere, ironic, meditative, etc.) can convey the tone a writer projects. But even in essays, writers might assume a persona that serves their purposes. (pp. 186–87)

- **As in all genres, *ideas* are crucial, but they seem especially prominent in essays.**

- **The *style* and *structure* of essays often provide useful models for writers.** Noticing how essays are put together, how sentences and paragraphs follow one another logically, can lead to the writing of well-organized and stylish essays. (pp. 187–89)

(continued on next page)

─── SUMMING UP ───

- **Argumentative essays model effective ways to make arguments.** It is often valuable to analyze argumentative essays for the ways writers make claims about issues, the way they support their claims with evidence and their techniques for projecting a good image of themselves. (pp. 108–109)

8

Writing a Research Paper

You may imagine that writing a research paper for your English class is a significantly different, and perhaps more difficult, assignment than others you have had. Because more steps are involved in their writing (for example, additional reading and analysis of sources), research papers tend to be long-range projects. They also tend to be more formal than other kinds of papers because they involve integrating and documenting source material.

These differences, however, are essentially of magnitude and appearance, not of substance. Despite the common misconception (cause of much unnecessary anxiety) that writing a research paper requires a special set of knowledge and skills, it draws principally on the same kind of knowledge and skills needed to write other types of papers. A writer still needs to begin with an arguable **issue** and a **claim**, still needs to marshal **evidence** to defend that claim, and still needs to present that evidence persuasively to convince an audience that the claim has merit. The main difference between research papers and other papers that you will write for this course is that the evidence for a research paper comes from a wider variety of sources.

Writing about literature begins with a **primary research source**—the story, poem, play, or essay on which the paper is focused. In addition to this primary source, however, research papers call on **secondary research sources**—historical, biographical, cultural, and critical documents that writers use to support their claims.

Identifying an Issue and a Tentative Claim

Your first task in writing a research paper is to identify an issue that you genuinely want to think and to learn more about. The more interested you are in your issue, the better your paper will be. You may choose, for example, to write about issues of theme, symbolism, pattern, or genre, or you may prefer to explore contextual issues of social policy, or of the author's biography, culture, or historical period. Any of the types of issues described on pages 18–25 are potentially suitable for research. The type of secondary research materials you use will depend largely on the issue you choose to pursue.

First, read your primary source carefully, taking notes as you do so. If you work with the texts in this book, you will want to read the biographical and contextual information about the author and any questions or commentaries that follow the texts. Then ask questions of your own to figure out what really interests you about the literature. Do not look for simple issues or questions that can be easily answered with a few factual statements; instead, try to discover a topic that will challenge you to perform serious research and do some hard thinking.

Before you begin looking for secondary research sources for your paper, formulate a tentative claim, much like a scientist who begins research with a hypothesis to be tested and affirmed or refuted. Since this tentative claim is unlikely to find its way into your final paper, do not worry if it seems a little vague or obvious. You will have plenty of opportunities to refine it as your research proceeds. Having a tentative claim in mind — or, better still, on paper — will prevent you from becoming overwhelmed by the multitude of potential secondary sources available to you.

Rebecca Stanley, who wrote the research paper that begins on page 211, chose to write on Kate Chopin. After reading the three Chopin stories included in this book, she found herself wondering about the racial issues raised by "Désirée's Baby" (p. 569). She was horrified by the racism depicted by Chopin but also fascinated by Chopin's unusual and apparently sensitive treatment of the topic. Still, she knew that she lacked a clear sense of direction for her paper and would have to do more reading and thinking. On her second reading of the story (now that she was no longer concentrating on what would happen next), she began to notice how Chopin's vivid, descriptive language, especially her use of light and dark imagery, seemed to create a mood and comment on the theme of racism. She decided on a tentative claim: that there is a connection between the imagery in "Désirée's Baby" and Chopin's attitude towards race relations in her society. Clearly this claim would need refining, but it gave Rebecca a starting point as she headed to the library to begin her research.

Finding and Using Secondary Sources

Once you have your topic in mind and have sketched a tentative claim, begin looking for secondary research sources. Many different types of sources for literary research are available, and the types you will need will depend largely on the type of claim you choose to defend. If your issue is primarily one of interpretation — about the theme, patterns, or symbolism of the text, for instance — you will most likely need to consult literary criticism to see what has been said in the past about the literature you are discussing. If your issue concerns historical or cultural context, including issues of social policy, you may need to consult newspapers, magazines, and similar sorts of cultural documents. Some topics, like Rebecca's, might require several different types of sources.

Researching your project divides into two main activities. First, you will need to identify several secondary sources and construct a **working bibliography**—that is, a list of the materials you might use. Most researchers find it useful to record this working bibliography on a stack of note cards, with one entry per card containing all the pertinent information to help find the source and later to list it in the paper's bibliography, called the **Works Cited**. (Some researchers who have notebook-style computers prefer to bring them to the library and record their working bibliographies on a computer file instead of a collection of cards.) Once you have compiled a working bibliography, you will be ready to move on to the second stage: tracking down the materials you have identified, reading and evaluating them, and writing notes from (and about) them as a preliminary step to writing your own paper.

As you make note of potentially useful sources, it is important that you include in your working bibliography all of the information—including names, titles, publication information, and page numbers—that will eventually be needed for your Works Cited list. An explanation of the Works Cited format for each type of source (from books and articles to CD-ROMs and Web sites) begins on page 203. Acquaint yourself with this format before you begin compiling your working bibliography; otherwise, you may forget to record crucial information that you will need when you prepare the final version of your paper.

FINDING SOURCES IN THE LIBRARY

Not many years ago, for most people the word *research* was synonymous with hours spent in the library hunting for books and articles. For many students today, *research* has become synonymous with the Internet. We have quickly come to believe that "everything" is available online. When it comes to scholarly research on literary topics, though, this is simply not true. Many of the best and most reliable sources are still available only in old-fashioned print media. If you restrict yourself to sources available electronically—on the Internet, say, or in full-text articles on CD-ROMs—you do yourself a serious disservice as a researcher.

A good place to commence your research is your college or university library's computerized **catalog**. Be aware that scholarly books are often quite specialized, and that you may want to start with one or two fairly general titles to orient you before venturing into more sharply focused scholarship. Because Rebecca was interested in race relations in the South during Chopin's time, she searched the catalog using the very general key words *race relations* and *United States*, which turned up references to a number of books. Among the most interesting titles was Stetson Kennedy's *Jim Crow Guide*, which provided her with a good deal of useful information for her paper.

Perhaps an even better place than the library catalog to begin research for your paper is the ***MLA International Bibliography***, published each year by the Modern Language Association. Most college and university libraries carry both the CD-ROM and print versions of this work, which lists scholarly books and articles on a wide range of topics in literary criticism and history. The CD-ROM version is a powerful and flexible tool that allows a researcher to enter a topic or the name of an author or work of literature and then to see on-screen a list of books and articles addressing that topic. These references can be copied by hand, printed out, or downloaded to a floppy disk for your working bibliography.

The print version of the *Bibliography* is also useful, though you must understand its organization to use it efficiently. The bibliographic references are subdivided first by the nationality of the literature, then by its date of publication, then by the author and title of the work. To find information from this source for her paper, Rebecca first located the most recent edition of the *MLA International Bibliography*, moved to the section devoted to American literature, found the section on literature of 1800 to 1899, and finally moved to Kate Chopin and the specific story, "Désirée's Baby." If you find few or no references to your topic in an edition of the bibliography, try the editions for the previous few years. Chances are your topic will show up.

Sources of cultural information other than literary criticism and history can be found by using other excellent options widely available in college and university libraries. These include **InfoTrac**, a user-friendly electronic index of academic and general-interest periodicals including scholarly journals, magazines, and several prominent newspapers. Many researchers also like to use the *Readers' Guide to Periodical Literature* (available in both print and CD-ROM versions), the *Newspaper Abstracts*, and the many specialized indexes devoted to particular fields of study, from science, to history, to education. Let your topic lead you to the information sources that will be most valuable to you. Your reference librarians will be happy to tell you what is available in your particular library as well as how to use any of these books and databases.

EVALUATING SOURCES

Whatever method you use to locate your research materials, remember that not all sources are created equal. Be sure to allot some time for **evaluating** the materials you find. In general, the best and most reliable sources of information for academic papers are (1) books published by academic and university presses; (2) articles appearing in scholarly and professional journals; and (3) articles in prominent, reputable newspapers, such as the *New York Times* or the *Washington Post*. Many other types of sources — from CD-ROMs to popular magazines — may prove useful to you as well, but if you have any hesitation about the trustworthiness of a source, approach it with healthy skepticism. Also, the more recent your information, the better (unless, of course, you are doing historical research).

In general, basic questions you should ask of your sources include: (1) Is the information recent, and if not, is the validity of the information likely to have changed significantly over time? (2) How credible is the author? Is he or she a recognized expert on the subject? (3) Is the source published by an established, respectable press, or does it appear in a well-respected journal or periodical (the *Los Angeles Times* has more credibility than the *National Enquirer*, for example) or Web site (one supported by a university or library, for instance)? (4) Based on what you've learned about responsible argument, do the arguments in your source seem sound, fair, and thoughtful? Is the evidence convincing? Is the development of the argument logical?

You increase your own credibility with your audience by using the most credible research materials available to you, so do not just settle for whatever comes to hand if you have the opportunity to find a stronger source.

FINDING SOURCES WITH A COMPUTER

These days, reliable information is widely and conveniently available on CD-ROMs, many of which may be found in college and university libraries. These include texts of literary works (often with commentaries on these works), bibliographies and indexes to help you locate more traditional sources of information, and even the texts of historical and cultural documents. (For example, a CD-ROM about Robert Frost includes not only the texts of his poems but also critical commentaries, relevant source materials, biographical and autobiographical passages, and recordings of Frost reading his own poetry.) In addition, standard reference works such as encyclopedias and dictionaries are often available on CD-ROM, where they can be efficiently searched for background information or factual corroboration (names, dates, spelling) for your paper. Keep in mind that you may need to rely on your librarian to tell you about your library's holdings, because many CD-ROMs are not yet indexed in the same way as traditional books and magazines.

A wealth of information is available on the Internet as well, and, as with the information in the library, your goal is to find useful information efficiently, evaluate it carefully, and make effective use of it in your paper. Unfortunately, and unlike a library's sources, the information on the Internet is not indexed and organized to make it easily accessible to researchers. You will need to do a certain amount of "surfing" if you are to find appropriate materials for your project. A number of **search engines** (programs for finding information) are designed to help you track down documents on the Web, and if you are an old hand on the Internet, you can probably depend on search engines that have served you well in the past. Rather than searching for keywords, it is often more effective to use the feature of a search engine that allows you continually to narrow a topic until you arrive at the information desired.

For example, to find information on Kate Chopin, Rebecca launched the Web browser on her computer and went to *Yahoo!* From the menu of categories, she chose the following path, clicking on each entry successively: Arts/Humanities/Literature/Authors/Literary Fiction/Chopin, Kate. *Yahoo!* then provided her with several Web sites she could choose to visit, one of which contained the complete text of Chopin's novel *The Awakening* and several of her short stories. Other sites on the list provided a wealth of biographical and critical information about Chopin and her work as well as contextual information about southern literature, Chopin's contemporaries, and her culture. Had she entered Kate Chopin's name for a keyword search, these sources would also have turned up, but they would have been more difficult to find, as they would have been mixed with many other, less useful references to Chopin, from course syllabi to high-school term papers. (Similar information exists online for many of the other authors whose works appear in this book.)

Special care is needed to evaluate online sources, since anyone can put information on the Net. It will be up to you to determine if you are reading a piece of professional criticism or a middle-school term paper. When using online sources for serious research, look especially for work that has been signed by the author and is hosted by a respectable site, such as a university or a library.

Taking Notes: Summarizing, Paraphrasing, Quoting, and Avoiding Plagiarism

Once you have identified a number of sources for your paper and tracked down the books, periodicals, or other materials, it is time to begin reading, analyzing, and taking notes. At this point, it is especially important to keep yourself well organized and to write down *everything* that may be of use to you later. No matter how good your memory, do not count on remembering a few days (or even hours) later which notes or quotations come from which sources. Scrupulously write down page numbers and Web addresses, and double-check facts and spellings.

Many researchers find it easier to stay organized if they take notes on large note cards, with each card containing just one key point from one source. The notes you take from sources will fall into one of three basic categories: summaries, paraphrases, and quotations. (A fourth category is notes of your own ideas, prompted by your research. Write these down as well, keeping them separate and clearly labeled, as you would any other notes.)

Student researchers often rely too heavily on **quotations**, copying verbatim large sections from their research sources. Do not make this mistake. Instead, start your note taking with a **summary** of the source in question—just one or two sentences indicating in your own words the author's main point. Such summaries guarantee that you understand the gist of an author's argument and (since they are your own words) can readily be incorporated in your paper. You might think of a summary as a restatement of the author's principal claim, perhaps with a brief indication of the types of supporting evidence he or she marshals. You can also write summaries of supporting points—subsections of an author's argument—if they seem applicable to your paper. A summary should not, however, include quotations, exhaustive detail about subpoints, or a list of all the evidence in a given source. A summary is meant to provide a succinct overview—to demonstrate that you have grasped a point and can convey it to your readers.

Chances are you will want to take more specific notes as well, ones that **paraphrase** the most germane passages in a particular source. Unlike a summary, a paraphrase does not condense an argument or leave out supporting evidence; instead it puts the information into new words. A paraphrase is generally no shorter than the material being paraphrased, but it still has two advantages over a quotation. First, as with a summary, an accurate paraphrase proves that you understand the material you've read. Second, again as with a summary, a paraphrase is easier to integrate into your paper than a quotation, since it is already written in your own words and style. When you include a paraphrase in your notes, indicate on the note the page numbers in the original source.

The rule of thumb about summarizing or paraphrasing is that you must always clearly indicate which ideas are yours and which are those of others. It is **plagiarism**—a serious violation of academic standards—to accept credit for another's ideas, even if you put them in your own words. Ideas in your paper that are not attributed to a source will be assumed to be your own, so to avoid plagiarism it is important to leave no doubt in your reader's mind about when you are summarizing or paraphrasing. Always cite the source.

An exception to the rule is **common knowledge**—factual information that the average reader can be expected to know or is readily available in many easily accessible sources—which need not be referenced. For example, it is common knowledge that Kate Chopin was an American writer. It is also common knowledge that her original name was Katherine O'Flaherty and that she was born in St. Louis in 1851 and died there in 1904, even though most people would have to look that information up in an encyclopedia or biographical dictionary to verify it.

Sometimes, of course, you will want to copy quotations directly from a source. Do so sparingly, copying quotations only when the author's own words are especially succinct and pertinent. When you write down a quotation, enclose it in quotation marks, and record the *exact* wording, right down to the punctuation. As with a paraphrase, make note of the original page numbers for the quotation, as you will need to indicate this in your final paper.

Each time you take a note, be it summary, paraphrase, or quotation, take a moment to think about why you wrote it down. Why is this particular note from this source important? Write a brief commentary about the note's importance, maybe just a sentence or a few words, perhaps on the back of the note card (if you are using note cards). When the time comes to draft your paper, such commentaries will help you remember why you bothered to take the note and may restart your train of thought if it gets stuck.

And do not forget: If something you read in a source sparks an original idea, write it down and label it clearly as your own. Keep these notes with your notes from the primary and secondary sources. Without your own ideas, your paper will be little more than a report, a record of what others have said. Your ideas will provide the framework for an argument that is your own.

Writing the Paper: Integrating Sources

With your research completed (at least for the moment), it is time to get down to drafting the paper. At this point, many students find themselves overwhelmed with information and wonder if they are really in any better shape to begin writing than they were before starting their research. But having read and thought about a number of authors' ideas and arguments, you are almost certainly more prepared to construct an argument of your own. You can, of course, use any method that has worked for you in the past to devise a first draft of your paper. If you are having trouble getting started, though, you might look to Chapters 3 through 7 of this book, which discuss general strategies for exploring, planning, and drafting papers as well as more specific ideas for working with individual literary genres.

Start by revisiting your tentative claim. Refine it to take into account what you have learned during your research. Rebecca Stanley began with the claim that there was a connection between Chopin's imagery and the attitudes she expressed towards race relations in her society. Having done some research, Rebecca was now ready to claim that the patterns of imagery Chopin uses indicate not only the racial heritage of the main characters in the story but also how guilty or innocent they are of racism. While this is still not quite the thesis of Rebecca's final paper, it reflects the major focus of her research.

With your revised and refined claim at hand, examine your assembled notes, and try to subdivide them into groups of related ideas, each of which can form a single section of your paper or even a single piece of supporting evidence for your claim. You can then arrange the groups of notes according to a logical developmental pattern — for example, from cause to effect or from weakest to strongest evidence — which may provide a structure for the body of your essay. As you write, avoid using your own comments as a kind of glue to hold together other people's ideas. Instead, you are constructing an argument of your own, using secondary sources to support your own structure of claims and evidence.

Anytime you summarize, paraphrase, or quote another author, it should be clear how this author's ideas or words relate to your own argument. Keep in mind that, in your final paper, it is quite unlikely that every note you took deserves a place. Be prepared to discard any notes that do not, in some fashion, support your claim and strengthen your argument. Remember also that direct quotations should be used sparingly for greatest effect; papers that rely too heavily on them make for choppy reading. By contrast, summaries and paraphrases are in your own words and should be a clean and easy fit with your prose style.

Notice how Rebecca uses both summary and paraphrase in her essay (p. 211). For example, she summarizes two Supreme Court decisions on page 5 of her paper and paraphrases information from *The Jim Crow Guide* on pages 4 and 5. In both cases, her references clearly indicate that the information originated from a particular source. Notice also how smoothly she integrates these summaries and paraphrases into her own discussion of interracial relationships and shows how they connect to the Chopin story and to her claim. The following section on documenting sources (pp. 203–10) demonstrates the proper format for acknowledging authors whose work you summarize or paraphrase.

When you quote directly from either primary or secondary sources, you will need to follow special conventions of format and style. When quoting up to four lines of prose or three lines of poetry, integrate the quotation directly into your paragraph, enclosing the quoted material in double quotation marks and checking to make sure that the quotation accurately reflects the original. Longer quotations are set off from the text by starting a new line and indenting one inch on the left margin only; these are called **block quotations**. For these, quotation marks are omitted since the indention is enough to indicate that the material is a quotation. Examples of the correct format for both long and short quotations appear in Rebecca's paper.

When a short quotation is from a poem, line breaks in the poem are indicated by slash marks, with single spaces on either side. The example below demonstrates this using a short quotation from William Shakespeare's sonnet, "Let me not to the marriage of true minds." The number in parentheses is a page reference, and the format for these is explained in the next section, "Documenting Sources."

```
Shakespeare tells us that "Love is not love / Which
alters when it alteration finds, / Or bends with the
remover to remove" (345).
```

While it is essential to quote accurately, sometimes you may need to alter a quotation slightly, either by deleting text for brevity, or by adding or changing text to incorporate it grammatically. If you delete words from a quotation, indicate the deletion by inserting an ellipsis (three periods with spaces between them) as demonstrated below with another quotation from the Shakespeare sonnet.

```
Love, Shakespeare tells us, is "not Time's fool . . . But
bears it out even to the edge of doom" (345-46).
```

If you need to change or add words for clarity or grammatical correctness, indicate the changes with square brackets. If, for instance, you wanted to clarify the meaning of "It" in Shakespeare's line "It is the star to every wandering bark," you could do so like this:

```
Shakespeare claims that "[Love] is the star to every wan-
dering bark" (345).
```

In addition to these format considerations, remember a few general rules of thumb as you deploy primary and secondary sources in your paper. First, without stinting on necessary information, keep quotations as short as possible — your argument will flow more smoothly if you do. Quotations long enough to be blocked should be relatively rare. Second, never assume that a quotation is self-sufficient or its meaning self-evident. Every time you put a quotation in your paper, take the time to introduce it clearly and comment on it to demonstrate why you chose to include it in the first place. Finally, quote fairly and accurately, and stick to a consistent format (such as the MLA style explained below) when giving credit to your sources.

Documenting Sources: MLA Format

Documentation is the means by which you give credit to the authors of all primary and secondary sources cited within a research paper. It serves two principal purposes: (1) it allows your readers to find out more about the origin of the ideas you present; and (2) it protects you from charges of plagiarism. Every academic discipline follows slightly different conventions for documentation, but the method most commonly used for writing about literature is the format devised by the Modern Language Association (MLA). This documentation method encompasses **in-text citations**, which briefly identify within the body of your paper the source of a particular quotation, summary, or paraphrase, and a bibliography, called **Works Cited**, which gives more complete publication information.

While mastering the precise requirements of MLA punctuation and format can be time-consuming and even frustrating, getting it right adds immeasurably to the professionalism of a finished paper. More detailed information, including special circumstances and documentation styles for types of sources not covered here, will be found in the *MLA Handbook for Writers of Research Papers*, Sixth Edition, by Joseph Gibaldi (New York: Modern Language Association, 2003). Of course, if your instructor requests that you follow a different documentation method, you should follow his or her instructions instead.

MLA IN-TEXT CITATION

Each time you include information from any outside source — whether in the form of a summary, a paraphrase, or a quotation — you must provide your reader with a brief reference indicating the author and page number of the original. This reference directs the reader to the Works Cited list, where more complete information is available.

There are two basic methods for in-text citation. The first, and usually preferable, method is to include the author's name in the text of your essay and note the page number in parentheses at the end of the citation. The following paraphrase and quotation from James Joyce's "Araby" (p. 263) show the format to be followed for this method. Note that the page number (without the abbreviation "pg." or additional punctuation) is enclosed within the parentheses, and that the final punctuation for the sentence occurs after the parenthetical reference, effectively making the reference part of the preceding sentence. For a direct quotation, the closing quotation marks come before the page reference, but the final period is still saved until after the reference.

```
Joyce's narrator recounts how he thought of Mangan's sis-
ter constantly, even at the most inappropriate times
(264).

Joyce's narrator claims that he thought of Mangan's sis-
ter "even in places the most hostile to romance" (264).
```

The method is similar for long quotations (those set off from the main text of your essay). The only difference, as you can see on page 3 of Rebecca's essay, is that the final punctuation comes before the parenthetical page reference.

In those cases where citing the author's name in your text would be awkward or difficult, you may include both the author's last name and the page reference in the parenthetical citation. The example below draws a quotation from Victor Villanueva Jr.'s essay "Whose Voice Is It Anyway?", which comments on the ideas of Richard Rodriguez. (We juxtapose Villanueva's essay with Rodriguez's "Aria" in Chapter 12.)

```
According to one commentator, Rodriguez overlooks impor-
tant distinctions among America's immigrants, failing in
particular to acknowledge that "choice hardly entered
into most minorities' decisions to become Americans"
(Villanueva 525).
```

Knowing the last name of the author is enough to allow your reader to find out more about the reference in the Works Cited, and having the page number makes it easy to find the original of the quotation, summary, or paraphrase should your reader choose to. The only time more information is needed is if you cite more than one work by the same author. In this case, you will need to specify from which of the author's works a particular citation comes. Notice that since Rebecca includes more than one of Kate Chopin's works in her Works Cited list, she always makes clear, either in her lead-in to a citation or in the parenthetical reference, which story is the basis of a paraphrase or source of a quotation. Electronic sources, such as CD-ROMs and Internet sources, are generally not divided into numbered pages. If you cite from such a source, the parenthetical reference need only include the author's last name (or, if the work is anonymous, an identifying title).

MLA WORKS CITED

The second feature of the MLA format is the Works Cited list, or bibliography. This list should begin on a new page of your paper and should be double spaced throughout and use hanging indention, which means that all lines except the first are indented one half inch. The list is alphabetized by author's last name (or by the title in the case of anonymous works) and includes every primary and secondary source referred to in your paper. The format for the most common types of entries is given below. If any of the information called for is unavailable for a particular source, simply skip that element and keep the rest of the entry as close as possible to the given format. An anonymous work, for instance, skips the author's name and is alphabetized under the title. In addition to the explanations below, you can see examples of MLA bibliographic format in Rebecca's Works Cited.

Books

Entries in your Works Cited for books should contain as much of the following information as is available to you. Follow the order and format exactly as given, with a period after each numbered element below (between author and title, and so on). Not all of these elements will be needed for most books. Copy the information directly from the title and publication pages of the book, not from a library catalog or other reference, because these sources often leave out some information.

1. The name(s) of the author(s) (or editor, if no author is listed, or organization in the case of a corporate author), last name first.
2. The full title, underlined or in italics. If the book has a subtitle, put a colon between title and subtitle.
3. The name(s) of the editor(s), if the book has both an author and an editor, following the abbreviation "Ed."
4. The name(s) of the translator or compiler, following the abbreviation "Trans.," or "Comp," as appropriate.
5. The edition, if other than the first.
6. The volume(s) used, if the book is part of a multivolume set.
7. The name of any series to which the book belongs.
8. The city of publication (followed by a colon), name of the publisher (comma), and year.

The examples below cover the most common types of books you will encounter.

A book by a single author or editor.　　Simply follow the elements and format as listed above. The first example below is for a book by a single author; note also the abbreviation UP, for "University Press." The second example is a book by a single editor. The third is for a book with both author (Conrad) and an editor (Murfin); note also that it is a second edition and a book in a series, so these facts are listed as well.

Cima, Gay Gibson. <u>Performing Women: Female Characters, Male Playwrights, and the Modern Stage</u>.
Ithaca, NY: Cornell UP, 1993.

Tucker, Robert C., ed. <u>The Marx-Engels Reader</u>. New
York: Norton, 1972.

Conrad, Joseph. <u>Heart of Darkness</u>. Ed. Ross C Murfin.
2nd ed. Case Studies in Contemporary Criticism.
Boston: Bedford/St. Martin's, 1996.

A book with multiple authors or editors.　　If a book has two or three authors or editors , list all names, but note that only the first name is given last name first and the rest are in normal order. In cases where a book has four or more authors or editors, give only the first name listed on the title page, followed by a comma and the phrase *et al.* (Latin for "and others").

Leeming, David, and Jake Page. <u>God: Myths of the Male
Divine</u>. New York: Oxford UP, 1996.

Arrow, Kenneth Joseph, et al., eds. <u>Education in a
Research University</u>. Stanford: Stanford UP, 1996.

A book with a corporate author.　　When a book has a group, government agency, or other organization listed as its author, treat that organization in your Works Cited just as you would a single author.

```
National Conference on Undergraduate Research. Pro-
    ceedings of the National Conference on Under-
    graduate Research. Asheville: U of North Carolina,
    1995.
```

Short Works from Collections and Anthologies

Many scholarly books are collections of articles on a single topic by several different authors. When you cite an article from such a collection, include the information given below. The format is the same for works of literature that appear in an anthology, such as this one.

1. The name of the author(s) of the article or literary work.
2. The title of the short work, enclosed in quotation marks.
3. Name(s) of the editor(s) of the collection or anthology.
4. All relevant publication information, in the same order and format as it would appear in a book citation.
5. The inclusive page numbers for the shorter work.

A single work from a collection or anthology.   If you are citing only one article or literary work from any given collection or anthology, simply follow the format outlined above and demonstrated in the following examples.

```
Kirk, Russell. "Eliot's Christian Imagination." The
    Placing of T. S. Eliot. Ed. Jewel Spears Brooker.
    Columbia: U of Missouri P, 1991. 136-44.
Silko, Leslie Marmon. "Yellow Woman." Making
    Arguments about Literature: A Compact Guide and
    Anthology. Ed. John Schilb and John Clifford.
    Boston: Bedford/St. Martin's, 2005. 255-62.
```

Multiple works from the same collection or anthology.   If you are citing more than one short work from a single collection or anthology, it is often more efficient to set up a **cross-reference**. This means first writing a single general entry that provides full publication information for the collection or anthology as a whole. The entries for the shorter works then contain only the author and title of the shorter work, the names of the editors of the book, and the page numbers of the shorter work. The example below shows an entry for a short story cross-referenced with a general entry for this book; note that the entries remain in alphabetical order in your Works Cited, regardless of whether the general or specialized entry comes first.

```
Faulkner, William. "A Rose for Emily." Schilb and
    Clifford. 576-83.
Schilb, John, and John Clifford, eds. Making
    Arguments about Literature: A Compact Guide
```

`and Anthology`. Boston: Bedford/St. Martin's,

`2005`.

Works in Periodicals

The following information should be included, in the given order and format, when you cite articles and other short works from journals, magazines, or newspapers.

1. The name(s) of the author(s) of the short work.
2. The title of the short work, in quotation marks.
3. The title of the periodical, underlined or italicized.
4. All relevant publication information as explained in the examples below.
5. The inclusive page numbers for the shorter work.

A work in a scholarly journal.   Publication information for work from scholarly and professional journals should include the volume number (and also the issue number, if the journal paginates each issue separately), the year of publication in parentheses and followed by a colon, and the page numbers of the shorter work.

`Charles, Casey. "Gender Trouble in Twelfth Night."`

`   Theatre Journal 49 (1997): 121-41.`

An article in a magazine.   Publication information for articles in general-circulation magazines includes the month(s) of publication for a monthly (or bimonthly), and the date (day, month, then year) for a weekly or biweekly, followed by a colon and the page numbers of the article.

`Cowley, Malcolm. "It Took a Village." Utne Reader`

`   Nov.-Dec. 1997: 48-49.`

`Levy, Steven. "On the Net, Anything Goes." Newsweek 7`

`   July 1997: 28-30.`

An article in a newspaper.   When citing an article from a newspaper include the date (day, month, year) and the edition if one is listed on the masthead, followed by a colon and the page numbers (including the section number or letter, if applicable).

`Cobb, Nathan. "How to Dig Up a Family Tree." The`

`   Boston Globe 9 Mar. 1998: C7.`

CD-ROMs

CD-ROMs come in two basic types, those published in a single edition — including major reference works like dictionaries and encyclopedias — and those published serially on a regular basis. In a Works Cited list, the first type is treated like a book and the second like a periodical. Details of citation appear in the following examples.

Single-edition CD-ROMs. An entry for a single-edition CD-ROM is formatted like one for a book, but with the word *CD-ROM* preceding publication information. Most CD-ROMs are divided into smaller subsections, and these should be treated like short works from anthologies.

```
"Realism." The Oxford English Dictionary. 2nd ed.

     CD-ROM. Oxford: Oxford UP, 1992.
```

Serial CD-ROMs. Treat information published on periodically released CD-ROMs just as you would articles in print periodical, but also include the title of the CD-ROM, underlined or italicized, the word *CD-ROM*, the name of the vendor distributing the CD-ROM, and the date of electronic publication. Many such CD-ROMs contain reprints and abstracts of print works, and in these cases, the publisher and date for the print version should be listed as well, preceding the information for the electronic version.

```
Brodie, James Michael, and Barbara K. Curry. Sweet

     Words So Brave: The Story of African American

     Literature. Madison, WI: Knowledge Unlimited,

     1996. ERIC CD-ROM. SilverPlatter. 1997.
```

The Internet

Internet sources fall into several categories—World Wide Web documents and postings to newsgroups, listservs, and so on. Documentation for these sources should include as much of the following information as is available, in the order and format specified.

1. The name of the author(s), last name first (as for a print publication).
2. The title of the section of the work accessed (the subject line for e-mails and postings) in quotation marks.
3. The title of the full document or site, underlined or in italics.
4. Date the material was published or updated.
5. The protocol used for access (World Wide Web, FTP, USENET newsgroup, listserv, and so on).
6. The date you access a site, or the date specified on an e-mail or posting.
7. The electronic address or path followed for access, in angle brackets.

The examples below show entries for a Web site and a newsgroup citation, two of the most common sorts of Internet sources.

```
Brandes, Jay. "Maya Angelou: A Bibliography of

     Literary Criticism." 20 Aug. 1997. (10 Feb. 1998)

     <http://www.geocities.com/ResearchTriangle/1221/

     Angelou.htm>.

Broun, Mike. "Jane Austen Video Package Launched."

     1 Mar. 1998. (11 Mar. 1998) <rec.arts.prose>.
```

Personal Communication

In some cases you may get information directly from another person, either by conducting an interview or by receiving correspondence. In this case, include in your Works Cited the name of the person who gave you the information, the type of communication you had with that person, and the date of the communication.

```
McCorkle, Patrick. Personal [or Telephone] interview.
    12 Mar. 2004.
Aburrow, Clare. Letter [or E-mail] to the author. 15
    Apr. 2004.
```

Multiple Works by the Same Author

If you cite more than one work (in any medium) by a single author, the individual works are alphabetized by title. The author's full name is given only for the first citation in the Works Cited, after which it is replaced by three hyphens. The rest of the citation follows whatever format is appropriate for the medium of the source. The two entries below are for a work in an anthology and a book, both by the same author.

```
Faulkner, William. "A Rose for Emily." Making
    Arguments about Literature: A Compact Guide and
    Anthology. Ed. John Schilb and John Clifford.
    Boston: Bedford/St. Martin's, 2005. 576-83.
---. The Sound and the Fury. New York: Modern Li-
    brary, 1956.
```

Occasionally, you may have an idea or find a piece of information that seems important to your paper but that you just cannot work in smoothly without interrupting the flow of ideas. Such information can be included in the form of **endnotes**. A small superscript number in your text signals a note, and the notes themselves appear on a separate page at the end of your paper, before the Works Cited. Rebecca Stanley's paper includes an endnote, but for many research papers none will be needed.

Sample Student Research Paper

Of course, not all research follows exactly the pattern we have described; it varies from researcher to researcher and project to project. In working on your own research paper, you may find yourself taking more or less time on certain steps, doing the steps in a slightly different order, or looping back to further refine your claim or do more research. But if you take the time to think your project through, do the research right, and write and revise carefully, you should end up with a paper you can be proud of. Take a look at the paper Rebecca finally wrote, and note the annotations, which point out key features of her text and of the MLA format.

Stanley 1

Rebecca Stanley

Professor Gardner

English 102

15 April ----

Racial Disharmony and "Désirée's Baby"

The sensuous quality of Kate Chopin's works, as
well as the Creole and Cajun dialect that flavor
her diction, establish her as one of the nineteenth
century's foremost writers. Both her style and
themes have led to her being considered a precursor
to the "Southern Renaissance" of the 1920s (Evans).
In recent years, critics have especially focused on
the ground-breaking explorations of female autonomy
in her short novel The Awakening and in stories
like "The Story of an Hour." Another trait that
sets Chopin's writing ahead of her contemporaries'
is her advocacy of racial harmony, which is not
characteristic of early southern literature. The
racial issue is explored in "Désirée's Baby," in
which Chopin uses black and white imagery and an
ironic twist at the end to teach her audience a
profound truth about humanity. Rather than make
assumptions based upon appearance, individuals
should look beyond the exterior and notice the common humanity that binds all people together. Many
people in Chopin's audience had never learned this
lesson, and sadly enough, neither have many modern-
day Americans.

"Désirée's Baby" tells the tragic story of a
young woman's suffering in the face of her society's condemnation of mixed marriages. The reader
is introduced to the main character, Désirée, early
in her life, when she is a vulnerable infant, lacking any familial ties. Désirée has been abandoned
at the Valmondé gates, and a kindhearted Madame
Valmondé takes pity and adopts the child as her

*Separate title page
unnecessary. First page
gives student name,
teacher's name, course,
and due date in upper
left corner. Centered
below is paper's title.
Student's last name
and page number
appear in upper right
corner.*

*Information cited from
World Wide Web
source; no page
number in
parenthetical
reference.*

*Rebecca immediately
introduces issue of race
and makes two related
claims—one about
Chopin's imagery and
one about American
society.*

Stanley 2

own. Any doubts lurking in Madame Valmondé's mind regarding the baby's obscure origin are assuaged as the child blossoms into a "beautiful and gentle, affectionate and sincere" young adult--"the idol of Valmondé" (Chopin 570). This description is Chopin's first association of Désirée with good-ness, suggesting that the baby has been sent to Madame Valmondé "by a beneficent Providence" (570). Throughout the story, Chopin continually describes Désirée as innately good, and she supports this with imagery of light and undefiled whiteness.

Quotation cited with author's name and page number.

A character foil emerges when Armand Aubigny enters the scene on horseback. A dark and handsome knight of sorts, Armand's shadow falls across Désirée's whiteness as she stands at the gate of Valmondé. Eighteen years have passed since Désirée's initial arrival at the gate, and she has blossomed into an exquisite young woman. Their encounter ignites a fiery passion in Armand's soul, which "[sweeps] along like an avalanche, or like a prairie fire, or like anything that drives headlong over all obstacles" (570). The young girl's name-lessness does not concern Armand, for his Aubigny heritage--one of the oldest and proudest in Louisiana (570)--will compensate for her lack thereof. He hastily dismisses all differences, marrying Désirée as soon as the corbeille arrives from Paris.

Square brackets indicate alteration to quoted text. With the author's name already known, only the page number appears in parenthetical citation.

Désirée makes the symbolic transition from undefiled light to darkness when she takes up resi-dence in the Aubigny household, which, like the man of the house, is immediately characterized by its dark and somber presence:

Format for block quotation, indented one inch on left margin only. Ellipses indicate deletion from quota-tion. Note format for page reference.

> The roof came down steep and black like a cowl,
> reaching out beyond the wide galleries that
> encircled the yellow stuccoed house. Big,

> solemn oaks grew close to it, and their thick-
> leaved, far-reaching branches shadowed it like
> a pall. Young Aubigny's rule was a strict
> one . . . and under it his negroes had forgotten
> how to be gay. (570-71)

Désirée's presence brings sunshine to Armand's previously lonely world, and a new addition to the
Aubigny family further multiplies his joy as the
couple become the proud parents of a baby boy soon
after they are married. Chopin uses light imagery
in the description of Désirée's countenance, which
is "suffused with a glow that [is] happiness itself" (571), when she confides in Madame
Valmondé that Armand has undergone a total character change since the baby's arrival. Désirée
observes that the child's birth has indeed "softened Armand Aubigny's imperious and exacting nature
greatly" (571), marveling at the fact that none of
the blacks have been punished by him since the
baby's arrival. It is obvious that Désirée and
the baby bring an uncharacteristic happiness to
Armand, whose dark, handsome face, "[has] not
often been disfigured by frowns since the day he
fell in love" (571).

As Désirée reclines upon a couch, glowing in
her soft white muslins and laces, she is a vision
of perfect happiness and purity. Unfortunately,
this idyllic existence is short-lived. Something is
wrong with the child, something which will ultimately break many hearts and split the family asunder. Désirée slowly realizes that her child does
not appear to be of entirely white heritage. "Look
at our child," she pleads with Armand. "What does
it mean? tell me" (572). She clutches her husband's
arm in desperation yet he, with his heart of
stone, pushes her hand away in disgust. Finally,

Stanley 4

he replies that the child is not white because the
mother is not white. Eventually, bitter that
Désirée and the child are part black, he coldheart-
edly forces them both to leave.

Although Armand is guilty for harsh treatment
of someone whom he suspects is of mixed heritage,
the racism he demonstrates is common in the place
and time in which he lives. In New Orleans, where
"Désirée's Baby" takes place, personal relationships between the races were clearly forbidden by
society's rules of etiquette, as well as by state
law. Southern society abided by certain unspoken
rules that governed every type of interracial
encounter. Even the shaking of hands between members of different races, under any set of circumstances, was taboo (Kennedy 212). Racist groups,
most notably the Ku Klux Klan, were constantly on
the prowl for those who violated this code of etiquette. For those who dared to exceed the established limits of interracial contact, the social
ramifications were great. Oftentimes, death by
lynching was the punishment for such unacceptable
behavior.

In Armand's society, association with members
of another race was not merely a faux pas--it was a
flagrant violation of the law. Racism was enforced
by the state of Louisiana to the extent that both
races were forbidden to occupy space in the same
apartment building, even with the existence of
walls separating the races and segregated en-
trances. The only legal exception to this clause
existed where a member of one race was employed as
a servant of the other (Kennedy 74). The legal
system did its best to maintain a stratified class
structure that relegated blacks to the lowest position in society, dehumanizing them in the process.

*Connection
established between
original claims and the
specifics of the story.*

Since the legal system forbade even such casual physical contact as handshaking and was known to punish perpetrators with flogging (Kennedy 212), interracial sexual relations were clearly taboo. The language of Louisiana's legislation forbade "sexual intercourse, cohabitation, concubinage, and marriage between whites and all 'persons of color,'" who are "defined by the courts to include anyone having one-sixteenth or more Negro blood" (Kennedy 66). However, this racist legislation was not limited to the state of Louisiana or even to the deep South.

Quotation within a quotation: The phrase "persons of color" was in quotation marks in original source, and this is indicated by placing it in single quotation marks within the full quotation.

Legislation that restricted relations between the races were commonplace in state and federal laws across the nation. The United States' racial precedent was set early on when Article I, section 2, of the Constitution specified that each black was to be counted as three-fifths of a white person in the determination of the number of each state's representatives in Congress. However, legalized racism did not end with the addition of the Fourteenth Amendment to the Constitution, despite its guarantee of "life, liberty, and property" to every citizen. Before and after the Fourteenth Amendment was added, the U.S. Supreme Court repeatedly condoned the dehumanization of blacks in its rulings, as evidenced in such cases as the Dred Scott decision (1857) and Plessy v. Ferguson (1896). The earlier decision was an outright denial of the black race's humanity, in which the Court sought to bar the entire race from the benefits of citizenship and withhold the rights which are guaranteed to all through the Constitution (Scott v. Sandford). The subsequent decision sanctioned the forced segregation of the races (Plessy v. Ferguson). As long as the involved party rendered lip-service to the

Summaries of constitutional articles and court cases.

Constitution by stipulating that the facilities
provided were "separate but equal," the U.S. government turned a blind eye to blatant racial injustices (Kennedy 167-69) and relegated blacks to
their inferior position in society.

*Brief summary of
multiple pages in
original source.*

Succumbing to pressure from a social structure
and legal system so permeated with racism, Armand
forces his wife and their child to leave. Countless
happy homes, such as that of the Aubigny family,
have been torn apart by this demon of racism
throughout history. Some individuals in today's
society argue that the problem of race relations,
as well as the controversial issue of racial identity, are merely past conflicts that have been
overcome by a more enlightened people. However,
Louisiana--the very state in which the Aubigny family lived--was the location of a recent racial controversy, proving that the issue of race still
divides American society.

In 1983, an individual named Susie Guillory
Phipps requested that the Louisiana Bureau of Vital
Records change her racial classification from black
to white and attempted to sue the bureau after its
refusal to do so. Since Phipps is a descendent of
an eighteenth-century white planter and a black
slave, her birth certificate automatically classified her as black in accordance with a 1970 state
law that declared anyone with at least one-thirty-
second "Negro" blood to be black (Omi and Winant
13). Although Phipps's attorney argued that most
whites have at least one-twentieth "Negro" ancestry, the Court maintained its support of the
quantification of racial identity, and "in so
doing, affirmed the legality of assigning individuals to specific racial groupings" (13). Even as
late as 1986, Louisiana passed another racially

*Specific evidence
provided to support a
debatable claim.*

Stanley 7

divisive ruling in which a woman with "negligible
African heritage" was legally defined as black
(Cose 78).

These modern court rulings raise the specter of
racism which has haunted the South, and the entire
country to a lesser extent, since the country's
inception. It is the very same system that exists
in Chopin's world, where, according to Michele
Birnbaum:

> The "black," the "mulatto," the "quadroon,"
> and the "Griffe" are subtle indices to social
> status in the white community. Named according
> to the ratio of "Negro blood" in their veins,
> these representative figures function not as
> indictments of an arbitrary colorline, but as
> reminders and reinforcements of cultural tier-
> ing. (308)[1]

Superscript numeral refers reader to endnote.

The legal system's recent support of classification
based upon percentages of racial heritage only
maintains the rift that has divided the races by
stressing differences and has granted equality a
lesser significance. Countless potential relationships have been thwarted, and even terminated, by
the legal system and the social system's racial
codes. At times, the grounds for interracial
couples' painful separations have been entirely
false.

The agony of rejection undoubtedly breaks
Désirée's heart as she bids farewell to the
husband who has brought her much joy and the happy
home they once shared. The rays from the October
sunset illuminate the golden strands in her tresses
like a halo, and the thin white dress dances in the
breeze like an angel's robe. It is appropriate that
Chopin uses light imagery in her description of
Désirée, for the young woman is truly the only

218

Writing a Research Paper

sunshine that the miserable Armand has ever known.
Like the sun, the beautiful Désirée is as glorious
in her departure as she is in her arrival. However,
unlike the sun, there is no hope for her return
tomorrow.

A few weeks after Désirée's dramatic farewell,
the miserable Armand presides over a great bonfire
in the backyard of L'Abri. This scene conjures up
vivid images of the devil and is consistent with
the dark imagery that Chopin uses throughout
"Désirée's Baby" to describe Armand. As he sits
high above the spectacle, a half dozen blacks feed
the flames with every reminder of his love affair
and previously joyous existence. After the willow
cradle and the baby's layette as well as Désirée's
silk and velvet robes have been devoured by the
blaze, only the couple's love letters from their
days of espousal remain. Among them lingers a
curious scrap of paper scrawled in his own
mother's handwriting. In the note, she thanks God
for blessing her with the love of her husband. In
conclusion, she declares, "But, above all . . .
night and day, I thank the good God for having so
arranged our lives that our dear Armand will
never know that his mother, who adores him, belongs
to the race that is cursed with the brand of slavery" (574).

One may wish that Armand had only known in time
that it was he--not Désirée--who shared a common
heritage with the slaves! Chopin drops hints about
Armand's black ancestry throughout the story, fore-
shadowing the ending with dark and evil imagery
that mirrors common stereotypes of the black race.
However, the awareness of his own heritage eludes
Armand, who makes the mistake of a lifetime based

Stanley 9

upon societal prejudices. That knowledge would also save Désirée, and the blacks of L'Abri, from the misery that Armand has inflicted upon their lives by treating them as second-class citizens. Readers may wish he had only realized the "negro blood" coursing through his veins is no different than the "white," because the ending would have turned out so differently. The regrets will undoubtedly haunt Armand forever.

It is easy for the reader to judge Armand for rejecting someone he regards as an inferior, yet countless American citizens and the legal system are guilty of committing the same crime. American society has relegated an entire people to second-class status, while ignoring the fact that the only difference between the races is skin color. Most individuals regret America's dark past, if only due to the selfish realization that a countless number of Mozarts, Einsteins, and Shakespeares were branded with a stamp of inferiority and silenced by the legal and social systems. However, the daily paper reveals that acts of racism are still being committed, and the lesson of racial equality has yet to be learned. American society has done itself an immense disservice by making an issue of skin color in the past, and it continues to do so in the present. Until the world is perceived through color-blind eyes, barriers will divide the races and peace will remain an unattainable goal.

Endnote

[1] Birnbaum is referring here to racial classifications in Chopin's novel The Awakening, but clearly the same system applies in "Désirée's Baby."

Endnote provides information that could not be easily integrated into text of paper.

Stanley 10

Works Cited

Birnbaum, Michele A. "'Alien Hands': Kate Chopin
    and the Colonization of Race." American Litera-
    ture 66 (1994): 301-23.

Chopin, Kate. The Awakening. 1899. Ed. Nancy A.
    Walker. Boston: Bedford/St. Martin's, 1993.

---. "Désirée's Baby." Making Arguments about
    Literature: A Compact Guide and Anthology. Ed.
    John Schilb and John Clifford. Boston: Bedford/
    St. Martin's, 2005. 570-74.

---. "The Story of an Hour." Making Arguments about
    Literature: A Compact Guide and Anthology. Ed.
    John Schilb and John Clifford. Boston: Bed-
    ford/St. Martin's, 2005. 574-76.

Cose, Ellis. "One Drop of Bloody History." Newsweek
    13 Feb. 1995: 78+.

Evans, Patricia. "Southern Women Writers, An His-
    torical Overview." Literature of the South.
    World Wide Web. <http://falcon.jmu.edu/~ram-
    seyil/southwomen.htm> (8 Mar. 1998).

Kennedy, Stetson. The Jim Crow Guide: The Way It
    Was. N.p.: Lawrence & Wishart, 1959. Boca
    Raton: Florida Atlantic U, 1990.

Omi, Michael, and Harold Winant. "Racial Forma-
    tions." Race, Class, and Gender in the United
    States: An Integrated Study. Ed. Paula Rothen-
    berg. New York: St. Martin's, 1995. 13-22.

Plessy v. Ferguson. 163 US 537. US Supr. Ct. 1896.

Scott v. Sandford. 60 US 393. US Supr. Ct. 1856.

US Const. Amend. XIV, sec. 1.

*Citation for an article
in a scholarly journal.*

*Citation for a work in
an anthology. Note
style for multiple works
by the same author.*

*Citation for an ar-
ticle in a general-
circulation periodical.
Citation for a World
Wide Web source.*

Citation for a book.

*Citation for a chapter
in a book.*

*Citations for court
cases.*

*Citation for a
government document.*

Using a Literary Work as a Springboard for Examining Social Issues

Not every research paper that refers to a literary text is devoted mainly to analyzing it. Some research papers mention a work of literature but then focus on
examining a social issue raised by that work. An example of such a paper is the

following essay by student Jason Fisk. To prepare for writing his paper, Jason consulted numerous sources, and he turns to them during the course of his essay. The chief danger in a project like this is that it will become a mere "data dump" — that is, a paper in which the writer uncritically cites one source after another without really making an argument of his or her own. In writing an essay like Jason's, be sure to identify your main issue and claim clearly. Present youself as someone who is genuinely *testing* your sources, determining the specific ways in which they are relevant to your argument. Keep in mind that even if you are representing a source as useful, you can indicate how its ideas need to be further complicated. With at least some of your sources, analyze specific terms they employ, lingering over their language. Moreover, try to relate your sources to one another, orchestrating them into a well-organized conversation. We think Jason accomplishes all these objectives. Even if you disagree, aim to practice them yourself.

You will see that Jason begins by discussing Bharati Mukherjee's short story "The Management of Grief" (pp. 618–30 of this book). Soon, however, he goes beyond it. For most of his paper, he develops an argument concerning one of the story's subjects, the potential conflict between bureaucratic and individual ways of dealing with trauma. Basically, Jason identifies and addresses an issue of evaluation: How useful was the method of therapy practiced by teams of counselors who came to New York City after the destruction of the World Trade Center towers? In response to this issue, Jason argues that the counselors' favorite technique, psychological debriefing, was not necessarily helpful to people tormented by the disaster. As he develops his claim, Jason also works through an issue of definition related to Mukherjee's title. What, he wonders, can be meant by the phrase "the management of grief"? In one sense, it can refer to a corporate model of therapy. In another, it can refer to human beings' personal ways of coping with trauma. Jason ends by making clear that the first sense must take better account of the second.

Sample Student Research Paper

Jason Fisk

Professor Sorensen

English 104

15 March —

Effectively "Managing" Grief

Based on a real-life disaster, the terrorist bombing of an Air India plane in 1985, Bharati Mukherjee's short story "The Management of Grief" depicts the sorrow of several Indian immigrants to Canada who lost family members in this tragedy. One character who tries to help these immigrants, government counselor Judith Templeton, sees "the management of grief" as an administrative

procedure in which the beareaved follow certain rules of
behavior. Consulting "textbooks on grief management," she
expects the anguished immigrants to go through set stages
of mourning, and she despairs when not all of them stick
to this schedule. The mourning process of the narrator
and main character, Shaila, is in fact quite individualistic. When her husband and sons are killed in the bombing, Shaila realizes that the "terrible calm" she first
experiences is not typical of her native culture. She
even tells Judith that "By the standards of the people
you call hysterical, I am behaving very oddly and very
badly." Through much of the story, actually, Shaila is
haunted by the images and voices of her deceased family,
and only when she believes they have freed her does she
feel able to resume her life. Meanwhile, however, she
conceals her torment from Judith and others. Overall,
Shaila's style of mourning demonstrates the truth of a
statement that she makes to Judith: "We must all grieve
in our own way" (621). If Shaila achieves "the management
of grief," she does so in the sense that she is able to
overcome her sorrow in a manner that suits her own personality. By contrast, Judith's vision of "the management
of grief" is more institutional and impersonal, failing
to take adequate account of each mourner's particular
feelings and needs.

  Differences between personal and administrative ways
of managing grief can arise in other situations of disaster. For example, such differences emerged in the wake of
the September 11, 2001 destruction of New York City's
World Trade Towers. Government agencies and private companies in Manhattan assumed that many people who lost
family members or witnessed the terrorism would need psychological help. Therefore, several of these institutions
hired various counseling firms to provide such therapy.
Hundreds of so-called experts trained by the firms came
to Manhattan, ready to offer their assistance. In particular, they practiced and valued an approach known as psy-

chological debriefing. Yet the ability of these counselors to improve New Yorkers' mental health turned out
to be surprisingly limited. In general, the aftermath of
the World Trade Towers disaster shows that it can be pre-
sumptuous for people to believe that an administrative
"management of grief" will prove helpful. Organizations
that want to help victims of trauma must avoid a "one
therapy fits all" approach and recognize that these individuals may have their own particular ways of coping.

Grief is not the only human emotion that institutions are currently rushing to address. In her book The
Commercialization of Intimate Life, sociologist Arlie
Hochschild observes that people increasingly look to outside experts for help with personal relationships and
family matters that previously they might have tried to
handle within their private lives. She notes that these
experts now range from daycare workers to professional
party planners to TV and radio talk show hosts. In general, Hochschild points out, people are being "invited to
manage their needs more" (14), with "management" in this
case meaning the discipline provided by professional con-
sultants who may have their own agenda. Hochschild does
not refer to the experience of dealing with large-scale,
unforeseen trauma such as the World Trade Towers disaster. But included among the kinds of experts she refers
to are "professional therapists" (14), and the destruction of the Towers was yet another instance in which they
arrived on the scene to take charge of other human
beings' mental recovery. Because many of these counselors
were trained and employed by firms, the therapy they
sought to provide can even be seen as an extension of the
corporate "management" they encounter back at headquarters. Probably Hochschild would see their work as taking
her notion of needs management to a new bureaucratic
level.

Can these corporate theorists actually heal grief,
especially when it stems from mass tragedy? The question

becomes more and more important as increasing numbers of
these counselors swarm to sites of horror like Ground
Zero. As psychiatrist Martin Deahl points out, "The last
decade has witnessed the emergence of a 'disaster industry'" (931). Deahl is not the only writer who uses the
word "industry" to describe these service providers.
Physician Jerome Groopman entitled his magazine article
about them "The Grief Industry." As a term, "industry"
implies that these providers are very much a capitalist
enterprise, comparable to more blatantly profit-seeking
institutions such as stores, manufacturers, and banks.
There is, in fact, profit of various sorts to be gained
in offering the promise of psychological cure. In part,
Deahl suggests, teams of grief counselors are proliferat-
ing because they reap benefits from this work: "Indeed
research grants, as well as the livelihoods of individuals employed by companies contracted to provide debriefing services, might depend on it!" (931). Of course, the
industry may still be well-intentioned, desiring genuinely to help people. But the capitalist interests of
these firms, along with their sheer increase, should lead
us to evaluate carefully their effectiveness.

　　The Towers tragedy has turned out to be an important
test case, for researchers found that quite a few of the
grieving were able to recover without much assistance
from the armies of corporate-trained therapists. The number of such therapists who came to New York City was certainly large. In a journal article dealing with this
invasion, Richard M. McNally and his coauthors report
that one firm, Crisis Management International, filled a
Manhattan hotel with 350 of its employees (45). Psychologist Lauren Slater adds that "There were, by some esti-
mates, three shrinks for every victim" (48). Obviously
this statistic is rough, and surely it includes counselors already in New York as well as those sent to the
city by organizations that are purely charities. Still,
at least this figure reminds us that commercial firms
were a major force in the therapy offered, so the issue

of whether or not they proved effective is quite significant.

Ironically, there is no proof that their big presence
helped a lot of the bereaved recover. As McNally and his
coauthors report, actual use of these services was much
less than authorities had anticipated, one possible reason being that many New Yorkers traumatized by the disaster relied on their own inner resources and on the
assistance of friends as well as relatives (46). Perhaps,
like Shaila, they were able to "manage" their grief without depending on a corporate model of coping. Actually,
there is evidence that a lot of these sufferers succeeded
in regaining their mental stability not long after September 11. Groopman reports that even just a month or two
afterward, phone interviews with 988 adults found that
merely 7.5 percent were experiencing Post-Traumatic
Stress Disorder, and that a similar survey the following
March found just 1.7 percent of New Yorkers in this condition. To be sure, we must acknowledge that exact causes
of the wide-scale recovery have yet to be pinpointed.
Nevertheless, "the grief industry" seems to have played
little role in it.

Even if significant numbers of people tormented by
September 11 had used this industry's services, they may
not have benefitted much from its favorite kind of therapy. Usually referred to as psychological debriefing, the
treatment involves bringing victims of trauma together
in a group and asking each member to recall his or her
horrible experience in detail. Reviewing much of the
research done on this approach, McNally and his coauthors
report that while some studies indicate psychological
debriefing is good, other studies find its benefits less
clear-cut, and there are even studies that suggest it can
cause harm. Therefore, McNally's team concludes that this
method's effectiveness is highly questionable (64). In
addition, Deahl has arrived at the same judgment after
conducting his own research review (933). Indeed, he and
McNally's team undertook their reviews in the first place

because debriefing is a controversial approach in their field as a whole.

Of course, logically it seems possible for corporate-trained grief counselors to develop a variety of methods, deciding which suits a particular client best. Yet many institutions that buy a grief counseling service probably want it to use one approach, believing that this efficiency will keep the institution's costs down. As Deahl points out, "A single, stand-alone intervention is clearly popular with employers anxious to discharge their 'duty of care' as inexpensively as possible" (932). Furthermore, probably grief counselors are easier and less costly for their own employers to train if the model of therapy involved is standardized.

Whatever the economic issues, we should critically examine the work of therapists who participate in the corporate "management of grief," especially those who are fond of psychological debriefing. We need not assume they are evil people. Nor must we assume that their style of therapy has been completely discredited. Clearly much research remains to be done on the effectiveness of debriefing and other methods. But, as Bharati Mukherjee suggests in her story, it is important for us to keep in mind that victims of trauma may recover in ways unpredicted by manuals. The counselor who has a wide assortment of methods for dealing with grief will be in a better position to accommodate these victims' individuality.

Works Cited

Deahl, Martin. "Psychological Debriefing: Controversy and Challenge." Australian and New Zealand Journal of Psychiatry 34 (2000): 929-39.

Citation for an article in a scholarly journal.

Groopman, Jerome. "The Grief Industry." The New Yorker 26 Jan. 2004: 30+. Academic. LEXIS-NEXIS 27 Jan. 2004 <http://web.lexis-nexis.com/universe/>.

Citation for an article in a general-circulation periodical. Also citation for a World Wide Web source.

Hochschild, Arlie. The Commercialization of
   Intimate Life: Notes from Home and Work.
   Berkeley: U of California P, 1983.

McNally, Richard J., Richard A. Bryant, and
   Anke Ehlers. "Does Early Psychological
   Intervention Promote Recovery from Post-
   traumatic Stress?" Psychological Science
   in The Public Interest 4 (2003): 45-79.

Mukherjee, Bharati. "The Management of Grief."
   Making Arguments about Literature: A
   Compact Guide and Anthology. Ed. John
   Schilb and John Clifford. Boston: Bedford/
   St. Martin's, 2005. 618-30.

Slater, Lauren. "Repress Yourself." New York
   Times Magazine 23 Feb. 2003: 48+.

Citation for a book.

Citation for an article in a scholarly journal.

Citation for a work in an anthology.

Citation for an article in a general-circulation periodical. (Though the Times Magazine *can also be considered a newspaper.)*

SUMMING UP

- Writing a research paper draws mainly on the same kinds of knowledge and skills needed for writing other kinds of papers.

- Use a combination of *primary* and *secondary* sources. For a literary research paper, a *primary research source* is the literary work on which the paper will focus. *Secondary research sources* are historical, biographical, cultural, and critical documents used to support claims.

- In writing a research paper, first identify an issue that interests you, then a tentative main claim.

  Next, identify several secondary sources and construct a working bibliography. Start research by logging on to the school's computerized catalog or the *MLA International Bibliography*.

  Investigate electronic sources such as Internet Web sites *and* print sources as well.

  Take time to evaluate the materials you discover.

  Keep yourself well organized

  Record everything that may prove useful later — do not risk plagiarism by failing to distinguish between your own ideas and those of others.

(continued on next page)

SUMMING UP

* **Start composing by revisiting your tentative main claim, taking into account what you have learned through research.**

  Keep organized and sub-divide and arrange your notes in logical order.

  Focus on constructing an argument of your own, using secondary sources to support your claims and evidence.

  Follow MLA conventions for format and style.

* **Document your sources by following MLA guidelines.** (pp. 203–10)

* **For a research paper that refers to a literary work but focuses more on examining a social issue raised by that work:**

  As in any research paper, identify the main issue and claim clearly.

  Rather than citing one source after another — a "data dump" — keep focusing on making an argument of your own.

  Present yourself as someone who is genuinely *testing* your sources, determining the specific ways in which they are relevant to your argument. With at least some of your sources, analyze specific terms they employ.

  Even if you represent a source as useful, you can indicate how its ideas need to be further complicated.

  Relate your sources to one another, organizing them into a conversation.

Thematic Clusters
of Literature

9

Story Clusters

MOTHERS AND DAUGHTERS

TILLIE OLSEN, "I Stand Here Ironing"
AMY TAN, "Two Kinds"
ALICE WALKER, "Everyday Use"

We all know stories of parents who want to mold their children, mothers and fathers who push their reluctant children to be fashion models or beauty queens or little league stars. Some studies of adults playing musical instruments in orchestras say the biggest factor in their success was the commitment of their parents. But we also hear about tennis prodigies who burn out at sixteen because of parental pressure. Mothers and daughters have always struggled with each other over life goals and identity. How much guidance is enough? How much is too much? What is a reasonable balance between preparing a child for life's challenges and shaping a child to act out the mother's fantasy or her internal vision of what the good life is? And no matter where parents fall on this continuum, are there childhood events so powerful that we cannot get beyond them? The following three stories chart the difficulties mothers and daughters have with each other and with the social and cultural forces that influence our destiny.

BEFORE YOU READ

Are your parents responsible for your successes? Your failures? Do you wish that your parents had pushed you to succeed more insistently? Are you annoyed that your parents set unreasonable standards for you?

TILLIE OLSEN
I Stand Here Ironing

Born in Omaha, Nebraska, to Russian immigrants of Jewish descent and socialist views, Tillie Olsen (b. 1913) has been an activist in social and political causes all of her life, often choosing family, work, union, feminist, or other political causes over writing. Although her publishing record is short, its quality is greatly admired. In addition to critically respected short stories, Olsen has written a novel, Yonnondio *(1974), which paints a vivid picture of a coal-mining family during the Depression. Her essay collection,* Silences *(1978), stimulated debate about class and gender as factors in the creation of literature and led both directly and indirectly to the revived interest in works by women writers. The mother of four daughters, Olsen often writes about generational relationships within families. "I Stand Here Ironing" is from her 1961 collection of stories,* Tell Me a Riddle.

I stand here ironing, and what you asked me moves tormented back and forth with the iron.

"I wish you would manage the time to come in and talk with me about your daughter. I'm sure you can help me understand her. She's a youngster who needs help and whom I'm deeply interested in helping."

"Who needs help." . . . Even if I came, what good would it do? You think because I am her mother I have a key, or that in some way you could use me as a key? She has lived for nineteen years. There is all that life that has happened outside of me, beyond me.

And when is there time to remember, to sift, to weigh, to estimate, to total? I will start and there will be an interruption and I will have to gather it all together again. Or I will become engulfed with all I did or did not do, with what should have been and what cannot be helped.

She was a beautiful baby. The first and only one of our five that was beautiful   5
at birth. You do not guess how new and uneasy her tenancy in her now-loveliness. You did not know her all those years she was thought homely, or see her poring over her baby pictures, making me tell her over and over how beautiful she had been—and would be, I would tell her—and was now, to the seeing eye. But the seeing eyes were few or nonexistent. Including mine.

I nursed her. They feel that's important nowadays, I nursed all the children, but with her, with all the fierce rigidity of first motherhood, I did like the books then said. Though her cries battered me to trembling and my breasts ached with swollenness, I waited till the clock decreed.

Why do I put that first? I do not even know if it matters, or if it explains anything.

She was a beautiful baby. She blew shining bubbles of sound. She loved motion, loved light, loved color and music and textures. She would lie on the floor in her blue overalls patting the surface so hard in ecstasy her hands and feet would blur. She was a miracle to me, but when she was eight months old I had to leave her daytimes with the woman downstairs to whom she was no miracle at all, for I worked or looked for work and for Emily's father, who "could no longer endure" (he wrote in his good-bye note) "sharing want with us."

I was nineteen. It was the pre-relief, pre-WPA world of the depression. I would start running as soon as I got off the streetcar, running up the stairs, the place smelling sour, and awake or asleep to startle awake, when she saw me she would break into a clogged weeping that could not be comforted, a weeping I can hear yet.

After a while I found a job hashing at night so I could be with her days, and it 10 was better. But it came to where I had to bring her to his family and leave her.

It took a long time to raise the money for her fare back. Then she got chicken pox and I had to wait longer. When she finally came, I hardly knew her, walking quick and nervous like her father, looking like her father, thin, and dressed in a shoddy red that yellowed her skin and glared at the pockmarks. All the baby love-liness gone.

She was two. Old enough for nursery school they said, and I did not know then what I know now—the fatigue of the long day, and the lacerations of group life in the kinds of nurseries that are only parking places for children.

Except that it would have made no difference if I had known. It was the only place there was. It was the only way we could be together, the only way I could hold a job.

And even without knowing, I knew. I knew the teacher that was evil because all these years it has curdled into my memory, the little boy hunched in the cor-ner, her rasp, "why aren't you outside, because Alvin hits you? that's no reason, go out, scaredy." I knew Emily hated it even if she did not clutch and implore "don't go Mommy" like the other children, mornings.

She always had a reason why we should stay home. Momma, you look sick. 15 Momma, I feel sick. Momma, the teachers aren't there today, they're sick. Momma, we can't go, there was a fire there last night. Momma, it's a holiday today, no school, they told me.

But never a direct protest, never rebellion. I think of our others in their three-, four-year-oldness—the explosions, the tempers, the denunciations, the demands—and I feel suddenly ill. I put the iron down. What in me demanded that goodness in her? And what was the cost, the cost to her of such goodness?

The old man living in the back once said in his gentle way: "You should smile at Emily more when you look at her." What *was* in my face when I looked at her? I loved her. There were all the acts of love.

It was only with the others I remembered what he said, and it was the face of joy, and not of care or tightness or worry I turned to them—too late for Emily. She does not smile easily, let alone almost always as her brothers and sisters do. Her face is closed and sombre, but when she wants, how fluid. You must have seen it in her pantomimes, you spoke of her rare gift for comedy on the stage that rouses laughter out of the audience so dear they applaud and applaud and do not want to let her go.

Where does it come from, that comedy? There was none of it in her when she came back to me that second time, after I had to send her away again. She had a new daddy now to learn to love, and I think perhaps it was a better time.

Except when we left her alone nights, telling ourselves she was old enough.   20
"Can't you go some other time, Mommy, like tomorrow?" she would ask.
"Will it be just a little while you'll be gone? Do you promise?"

The time we came back, the front door open, the clock on the floor in the
hall. She rigid awake. "It wasn't just a little while. I didn't cry. Three times I called
you, just three times, and then I ran downstairs to open the door so you could
come faster. The clock talked loud. I threw it away, it scared me what it talked."

She said the clock talked loud again that night I went to the hospital to have
Susan. She was delirious with the fever that comes before red measles, but she
was fully conscious all the week I was gone and the week after we were home
when she could not come near the new baby or me.

She did not get well. She stayed skeleton thin, not wanting to eat, and night
after night she had nightmares. She would call for me, and I would rouse from
exhaustion to sleepily call back: "You're all right, darling, go to sleep, it's just a
dream," and if she still called, in a sterner voice, "now go to sleep, Emily, there's
nothing to hurt you." Twice, only twice, when I had to get up for Susan anyhow, I
went in to sit with her.

Now when it is too late (as if she would let me hold her and comfort her like   25
I do the others) I get up and go to her at once at her moan or restless stirring. "Are
you awake, Emily? Can I get you something?" And the answer is always the same:
"No, I'm all right, go back to sleep, Mother."

They persuaded me at the clinic to send her away to a convalescent home in
the country where "she can have the kind of food and care you can't manage for
her, and you'll be free to concentrate on the new baby." They still send children
to that place. I see pictures on the society page of sleek young women planning
affairs to raise money for it, or dancing at the affairs, or decorating Easter eggs or
filling Christmas stockings for the children.

They never have a picture of the children so I do not know if the girls still
wear those gigantic red bows and the ravaged looks on the every other Sunday
when parents can come to visit "unless otherwise notified" — as we were notified
the first six weeks.

Oh it is a handsome place, green lawns and tall trees and fluted flower beds.
High up on the balconies of each cottage the children stand, the girls in their red
bows and white dresses, the boys in white suits and giant red ties. The parents
stand below shrieking up to be heard and the children shriek down to be heard,
and between them the invisible wall "Not To Be Contaminated by Parental
Germs or Physical Affection."

There was a tiny girl who always stood hand in hand with Emily. Her parents
never came. One visit she was gone. "They moved her to Rose Cottage," Emily
shouted in explanation. "They don't like you to love anybody here."

She wrote once a week, the labored writing of a seven-year-old. "I am fine.·   30
How is the baby. If I write my leter nicly I will have a star. Love." There never was
a star. We wrote every other day, letters she could never hold or keep but only
hear read — once. "We simply do not have room for children to keep any personal
possessions," they patiently explained when we pieced one Sunday's shrieking

together to plead how much it would mean to Emily, who loved so to keep things, to be allowed to keep her letters and cards.

Each visit she looked frailer. "She isn't eating," they told us.

(They had runny eggs for breakfast or mush with lumps, Emily said later, I'd hold it in my mouth and not swallow. Nothing ever tasted good, just when they had chicken.)

It took us eight months to get her released home, and only the fact that she gained back so little of her seven lost pounds convinced the social worker.

I used to try to hold and love her after she came back, but her body would stay stiff, and after a while she'd push away. She ate little. Food sickened her, and I think much of life too. Oh she had physical lightness and brightness, twinkling by on skates, bouncing like a ball up and down up and down over the jump rope, skimming over the hill; but these were momentary.

She fretted about her appearance, thin and dark and foreign-looking at a   35
time when every little girl was supposed to look or thought she should look a chubby blonde replica of Shirley Temple. The doorbell sometimes rang for her, but no one seemed to come and play in the house or to be a best friend. Maybe because we moved so much.

There was a boy she loved painfully through two school semesters. Months later she told me how she had taken pennies from my purse to buy him candy. "Licorice was his favorite and I brought him some every day, but he still liked Jennifer better'n me. Why, Mommy?" The kind of question for which there is no answer.

School was a worry for her. She was not glib or quick in a world where glib-ness and quickness were easily confused with ability to learn. To her overworked and exasperated teachers she was an overconscientious "slow learner" who kept trying to catch up and was absent entirely too often.

I let her be absent, though sometimes the illness was imaginary. How differ-ent from my now-strictness about attendance with the others. I wasn't working. We had a new baby. I was home anyhow. Sometimes, after Susan grew old enough, I would keep her home from school, too, to have them all together.

Mostly Emily had asthma, and her breathing, harsh and labored, would fill the house with a curiously tranquil sound. I would bring the two old dresser mir-rors and her boxes of collections to her bed. She would select beads and single earrings, bottle tops and shells, dried flowers and pebbles, old postcards and scraps, all sorts of oddments; then she and Susan would play Kingdom, setting up landscapes and furniture, peopling them with action.

Those were the only times of peaceful companionship between her and   40
Susan. I have edged away from it, that poisonous feeling between them, that ter-rible balancing of hurts and needs I had to do between the two, and did so badly, those earlier years.

Oh there were conflicts between the others too, each one human, needing, demanding, hurting, taking—but only between Emily and Susan, no, Emily toward Susan that corroding resentment. It seems so obvious on the surface, yet it is not obvious; Susan, the second child, Susan, golden- and curly-haired and chubby, quick and articulate and assured, everything in appearance and manner

Emily was not; Susan, not able to resist Emily's precious things, losing or some-times clumsily breaking them; Susan telling jokes and riddles to company for applause while Emily sat silent (to say to me later: that was *my* riddle, Mother, I told it to Susan); Susan, who for all the five years' difference in age was just a year behind Emily in developing physically.

I am glad for that slow physical development that widened the difference between her and her contemporaries, though she suffered over it. She was too vul-nerable for that terrible world of youthful competition, of preening and parading, of constant measuring of yourself against every other, of envy, "If I had that copper hair," "If I had that skin. . . ." She tormented herself enough about not looking like the others, there was enough of unsureness, the having to be conscious of words before you speak, the constant caring—what are they thinking of me? without having it all magnified by the merciless physical drives.

Ronnie is calling. He is wet and I change him. It is rare there is such a cry now. That time of motherhood is almost behind me when the ear is not one's own but must always be racked and listening for the child cry, the child call. We sit for a while and I hold him, looking out over the city spread in charcoal with its soft aisles of light. "*Shoogily,*" he breathes and curls closer. I carry him back to bed, asleep. *Shoogily.* A funny word, a family word, inherited from Emily, invented by her to say: *comfort.*

In this and other ways she leaves her seal, I say aloud. And startle at my saying it. What do I mean? What did I start to gather together, to try and make coherent? I was at the terrible, growing years. War years. I do not remember them well. I was working, there were four smaller ones now, there was not time for her. She had to help be a mother, and housekeeper, and shopper. She had to get her seal. Mornings of crisis and near hysteria trying to get lunches packed, hair combed, coats and shoes found, everyone to school or Child Care on time, the baby ready for transportation. And always the paper scribbled on by a smaller one, the book looked at by Susan then mislaid, the homework not done. Running out to that huge school where she was one, she was lost, she was a drop; suffering over the unpreparedness, stammering and unsure in her classes.

There was so little time left at night after the kids were bedded down. She would struggle over books, always eating (it was in those years she developed her enormous appetite that is legendary in our family) and I would be ironing, or preparing food for the next day, or writing V-mail to Bill, or tending the baby. Sometimes, to make me laugh, or out of her despair, she would imitate happen-ings or types at school.

I think I said once: "Why don't you do something like this in the school ama-teur show?" One morning she phoned me at work, hardly understandable through the weeping: "Mother, I did it. I won, I won; they gave me first prize; they clapped and clapped and wouldn't let me go."

Now suddenly she was Somebody, and as imprisoned in her difference as she had been in anonymity.

She began to be asked to perform at other high schools, even in colleges, then at city and statewide affairs. The first one we went to, I only recognized her that first moment when thin, shy, she almost drowned herself into the curtains.

45

Then: Was this Emily? The control, the command, the convulsing and deadly clowning, the spell, then the roaring, stamping audience, unwilling to let this rare and precious laughter out of their lives.

Afterwards: You ought to do something about her with a gift like that—but without money or knowing how, what does one do? We have left it all to her, and the gift has so often eddied inside, clogged and clotted, as been used and growing.

She is coming. She runs up the stairs two at a time with her light graceful step, and I know she is happy tonight. Whatever it was that occasioned your call did not happen today.

"Aren't you ever going to finish the ironing, Mother? Whistler painted his mother in a rocker. I'd have to paint mine standing over an ironing board." This is one of her communicative nights and she tells me everything and nothing as she fixes herself a plate of food out of the icebox.

She is so lovely. Why did you want me to come in at all? Why were you concerned? She will find her way.

She starts up the stairs to bed. "Don't get me up with the rest in the morning." "But I thought you were having midterms." "Oh, those," she comes back in, kisses me, and says quite lightly, "in a couple of years when we'll all be atom-dead they won't matter a bit."

She has said it before. She *believes* it. But because I have been dredging the past, and all that compounds a human being is so heavy and meaningful in me, I cannot endure it tonight.

I will never total it all. I will never come in to say: She was a child seldom smiled at. Her father left me before she was a year old. I had to work her first six years when there was work, or I sent her home and to his relatives. There were years she had care she hated. She was dark and thin and foreign-looking in a world where the prestige went to blondeness and curly hair and dimples, she was slow where glibness was prized. She was a child of anxious, not proud, love. We were poor and could not afford for her the soil of easy growth. I was a young mother, I was a distracted mother. There were other children pushing up, demanding. Her younger sister seemed all that she was not. There were years she did not want me to touch her. She kept too much in herself, her life was such she had to keep too much in herself. My wisdom came too late. She has much to her and probably little will come of it. She is a child of her age, of depression, of war, of fear.

Let her be. So all that is in her will not bloom—but in how many does it? There is still enough left to live by. Only help her to know—help make it so there is cause for her to know—that she is more than this dress on the ironing board, helpless before the iron. [1961]

THINKING ABOUT THE TEXT

1. Is Olsen's last paragraph optimistic or pessimistic about personal destiny? Is there some support in the story for both perspectives?

2. There is an old expression: "To know all is to forgive all." Do you agree with this statement in regards to "I Stand Here Ironing"? Some critics

want to privilege personal responsibility; others, social conditions. Do you blame Emily's mother? Or is she just a victim?

3. How might this story be different if told from Emily's perspective? From Susan's? From Emily's teacher's? What are the advantages and disadvantages of writing a story from one character's point of view?

4. How would you describe the voice or voices we hear in the story? What qualities, dimensions, or emotions can you infer? Does one dominate? Are you sympathetic to this voice? Is that what Olsen wanted?

5. Do you agree with the mother's decision not to visit the school for a conference? What are her reasons? Are they sound? What do you think the teacher wants to discuss? How involved in a child's life should a teacher be?

AMY TAN
Two Kinds

Born to Chinese immigrants in Oakland, California, Amy Tan (b. 1952) weaves intricate stories about generational and intercultural relationships among women in families, basing much of her writing on her own family history. She earned a B.A. in English and an M.A. in linguistics at San Jose State University. Her novels dealing with mother-daughter relationships, The Joy Luck Club *(1989) and* The Kitchen God's Wife *(1991), have received awards and critical acclaim. The* Hundred Secret Senses *(1996) explores the relationship between sisters who grew up in different cultures. At the age of twenty-six, Tan herself learned that she had three half-sisters in China. Her latest novel is* The Bonesetter's Daughter *(2001) and her latest collection of essays is* The Opposite of Fate: A Book of Musings *(2003). "Two Kinds" is excerpted from* The Joy Luck Club.

My mother believed you could be anything you wanted to be in America. You could open a restaurant. You could work for the government and get good retirement. You could buy a house with almost no money down. You could become rich. You could become instantly famous.

"Of course you can be prodigy, too," my mother told me when I was nine. "You can be best anything. What does Auntie Lindo know? Her daughter, she is only best tricky."

America was where all my mother's hopes lay. She had come here in 1949 after losing everything in China: her mother and father, her family home, her first husband, and two daughters, twin baby girls. But she never looked back with regret. There were so many ways for things to get better.

We didn't immediately pick the right kind of prodigy. At first my mother thought I could be a Chinese Shirley Temple. We'd watch Shirley's old movies on TV as though they were training films. My mother would poke my arm and say,

"*Ni kan*"—You watch. And I would see Shirley tapping her feet, or singing a sailor song, or pursing her lips into a very round O while saying, "Oh my goodness."

"*Ni kan*," said my mother as Shirley's eyes flooded with tears. "You already know how. Don't need talent for crying!"   5

Soon after my mother got this idea about Shirley Temple, she took me to a beauty training school in the Mission district and put me in the hands of a student who could barely hold the scissors without shaking. Instead of getting big fat curls, I emerged with an uneven mass of crinkly black fuzz. My mother dragged me off to the bathroom and tried to wet down my hair.

"You look like Negro Chinese," she lamented, as if I had done this on purpose.

The instructor of the beauty training school had to lop off these soggy clumps to make my hair even again. "Peter Pan is very popular these days," the instructor assured my mother. I now had hair the length of a boy's, with straight-across bangs that hung at a slant two inches above my eyebrows. I liked the haircut and it made me actually look forward to my future fame.

In fact, in the beginning, I was just as excited as my mother, maybe even more so. I pictured this prodigy part of me as many different images, trying each one on for size. I was a dainty ballerina girl standing by the curtains, waiting to hear the right music that would send me floating on my tiptoes. I was like the Christ child lifted out of the straw manger, crying with holy indignity. I was Cinderella stepping from her pumpkin carriage with sparkly cartoon music filling the air.

In all of my imaginings, I was filled with a sense that I would soon become   10 *perfect*. My mother and father would adore me. I would be beyond reproach. I would never feel the need to sulk for anything.

But sometimes the prodigy in me became impatient. "If you don't hurry up and get me out of here, I'm disappearing for good," it warned. "And then you'll always be nothing."

Every night after dinner, my mother and I would sit at the Formica kitchen table. She would present new tests, taking her examples from stories of amazing children she had read in *Ripley's Believe It or Not*, or *Good Housekeeping*, *Reader's Digest*, and a dozen other magazines she kept in a pile in our bathroom. My mother got these magazines from people whose houses she cleaned. And since she cleaned many houses each week, we had a great assortment. She would look through them all, searching for stories about remarkable children.

The first night she brought out a story about a three-year-old boy who knew the capitals of all the states and even most of the European countries. A teacher was quoted as saying the little boy could also pronounce the names of the foreign cities correctly.

"What's the capital of Finland?" my mother asked me, looking at the magazine story.

All I knew was the capital of California, because Sacramento was the name   15 of the street we lived on in Chinatown. "Nairobi!" I guessed, saying the most foreign word I could think of. She checked to see if that was possibly one way to pronounce "Helsinki" before showing me the answer.

The tests got harder—multiplying numbers in my head, finding the queen of hearts in a deck of cards, trying to stand on my head without using my hands, predicting the daily temperatures in Los Angeles, New York, and London.

One night I had to look at a page from the Bible for three minutes and then report everything I could remember. "Now Jehoshaphat had riches and honor in abundance and . . . that's all I remember, Ma," I said.

And after seeing my mother's disappointed face once again, something inside of me began to die. I hated the tests, the raised hopes and failed expectations. Before going to bed that night, I looked in the mirror above the bathroom sink and when I saw only my face staring back—and that it would always be this ordinary face—I began to cry. Such a sad, ugly girl! I made high-pitched noises like a crazed animal, trying to scratch out the face in the mirror.

And then I saw what seemed to be the prodigy side of me—because I had never seen that face before. I looked at my reflection, blinking so I could see more clearly. The girl staring back at me was angry, powerful. This girl and I were the same. I had new thoughts, willful thoughts, or rather thoughts filled with lots of won'ts. I won't let her change me, I promised myself. I won't be what I'm not.

So now on nights when my mother presented her tests, I performed listlessly, my head propped on one arm. I pretended to be bored. And I was. I got so bored I started counting the bellows of the foghorns out on the bay while my mother drilled me in other areas. The sound was comforting and reminded me of the cow jumping over the moon. And the next day, I played a game with myself, seeing if my mother would give up on me before eight bellows. After a while I usually counted only one, maybe two bellows at most. At last she was beginning to give up hope. 20

Two or three months had gone by without any mention of my being a prodigy again. And then one day my mother was watching *The Ed Sullivan Show* on TV. The TV was old and the sound kept shorting out. Every time my mother got halfway up from the sofa to adjust the set, the sound would go back on and Ed would be talking. As soon as she sat down, Ed would go silent again. She got up, the TV broke into loud piano music. She sat down. Silence. Up and down, back and forth, quiet and loud. It was like a stiff embraceless dance between her and the TV set. Finally she stood by the set with her hand on the sound dial.

She seemed entranced by the music, a little frenzied piano piece with this mesmerizing quality, sort of quick passages and then teasing lilting ones before it returned to the quick playful parts.

"*Ni kan*," my mother said, calling me over with hurried hand gestures. "Look here."

I could see why my mother was fascinated by the music. It was being pounded out by a little Chinese girl, about nine years old, with a Peter Pan haircut. The girl had the sauciness of a Shirley Temple. She was proudly modest like a proper Chinese child. And she also did this fancy sweep of a curtsy, so that the fluffy skirt of her white dress cascaded slowly to the floor like the petals of a large carnation.

In spite of these warning signs, I wasn't worried. Our family had no piano 25 and we couldn't afford to buy one, let alone reams of sheet music and piano lessons. So I could be generous in my comments when my mother bad-mouthed the little girl on TV.

"Play note right, but doesn't sound good! No singing sound," complained my mother.

"What are you picking on her for?" I said carelessly. "She's pretty good. Maybe she's not the best, but she's trying hard." I knew almost immediately I would be sorry I said that.

"Just like you," she said. "Not the best. Because you not trying." She gave a little huff as she let go of the sound dial and sat down on the sofa.

The little Chinese girl sat down also to play an encore of "Anitra's Dance" by Grieg. I remember the song, because later on I had to learn how to play it.

Three days after watching *The Ed Sullivan Show*, my mother told me what my schedule would be for piano lessons and piano practice. She had talked to Mr. Chong, who lived on the first floor of our apartment building. Mr. Chong was a retired piano teacher and my mother had traded housecleaning services for weekly lessons and a piano for me to practice on every day, two hours a day, from four until six.

When my mother told me this, I felt as though I had been sent to hell. I whined and then kicked my foot a little when I couldn't stand it anymore.

"Why don't you like me the way I am? I'm *not* a genius! I can't play the piano. And even if I could, I wouldn't go on TV if you paid me a million dollars!" I cried.

My mother slapped me. "Who ask you be genius?" she shouted. "Only ask you be your best. For you sake. You think I want you be genius? Hnnh! What for! Who ask you!"

"So ungrateful," I heard her mutter in Chinese. "If she had as much talent as she has temper, she would be famous now."

Mr. Chong, whom I secretly nicknamed Old Chong, was very strange, always tapping his fingers to the silent music of an invisible orchestra. He looked ancient in my eyes. He had lost most of the hair on top of his head and he wore thick glasses and had eyes that always looked tired and sleepy. But he must have been younger than I thought, since he lived with his mother and was not yet married.

I met Old Lady Chong once and that was enough. She had this peculiar smell like a baby that had done something in its pants. And her fingers felt like a dead person's, like an old peach I once found in the back of the refrigerator; the skin just slid off the meat when I picked it up.

I soon found out why Old Chong had retired from teaching piano. He was deaf. "Like Beethoven!" he shouted to me. "We're both listening only in our head!" And he would start to conduct his frantic silent sonatas.

Our lessons went like this. He would open the book and point to different things, explaining their purpose: "Key! Treble! Bass! No sharps or flats! So this is C major! Listen now and play after me!"

And then he would play the C scale a few times, a simple chord, and then, as if inspired by an old, unreachable itch, he gradually added more notes and running trills and a pounding bass until the music was really something quite grand.

I would play after him, the simple scale, the simple chord, and then I just   40
played some nonsense that sounded like a cat running up and down on top of garbage cans. Old Chong smiled and applauded and then said, "Very good! But now you must learn to keep time!"

So that's how I discovered that Old Chong's eyes were too slow to keep up with the wrong notes I was playing. He went through the motions in half-time. To help me keep rhythm, he stood behind me, pushing down on my right shoulder for every beat. He balanced pennies on top of my wrists so I would keep them still as I slowly played scales and arpeggios. He had me curve my hand around an apple and keep that shape when playing chords. He marched stiffly to show me how to make each finger dance up and down, staccato like an obedient little soldier.

He taught me all these things, and that was how I also learned I could be lazy and get away with mistakes, lots of mistakes. If I hit the wrong notes because I hadn't practiced enough, I never corrected myself. I just kept playing in rhythm. And Old Chong kept conducting his own private reverie.

So maybe I never really gave myself a fair chance. I did pick up the basics pretty quickly, and I might have become a good pianist at that young age. But I was so determined not to try, not to be anybody different that I learned to play only the most ear-splitting preludes, the most discordant hymns.

Over the next year, I practiced like this, dutifully in my own way. And then one day I heard my mother and her friend Lindo Jong both talking in a loud bragging tone of voice so others could hear. It was after church, and I was leaning against the brick wall wearing a dress with stiff white petticoats. Auntie Lindo's daughter, Waverly, who was about my age, was standing farther down the wall about five feet away. We had grown up together and shared all the closeness of two sisters squabbling over crayons and dolls. In other words, for the most part, we hated each other. I thought she was snotty. Waverly Jong had gained a certain amount of fame as "Chinatown's Littlest Chinese Chess Champion."

"She bring home too many trophy," lamented Auntie Lindo that Sunday.   45
"All day she play chess. All day I have no time do nothing but dust off her winnings." She threw a scolding look at Waverly, who pretended not to see her.

"You lucky you don't have this problem," said Auntie Lindo with a sigh to my mother.

And my mother squared her shoulders and bragged: "Our problem worser than yours. If we ask Jing-mei wash dish, she hear nothing but music. It's like you can't stop this natural talent."

And right then, I was determined to put a stop to her foolish pride.

A few weeks later, Old Chong and my mother conspired to have me play in a talent show which would be held in the church hall. By then, my parents had saved up enough to buy me a secondhand piano, a black Wurlitzer spinet with a scarred bench. It was the showpiece of our living room.

For the talent show, I was to play a piece called "Pleading Child" from   50
Schumann's *Scenes from Childhood*. It was a simple, moody piece that sounded

more difficult than it was. I was supposed to memorize the whole thing, playing the repeat parts twice to make the piece sound longer. But I dawdled over it, playing a few bars and then cheating, looking up to see what notes followed. I never really listened to what I was playing. I daydreamed about being somewhere else, about being someone else.

The part I liked to practice best was the fancy curtsy: right foot out, touch the rose on the carpet with a pointed foot, sweep to the side, left leg bends, look up and smile.

My parents invited all the couples from the Joy Luck Club to witness my debut. Auntie Lindo and Uncle Tin were there. Waverly and her two older brothers had also come. The first two rows were filled with children both younger and older than I was. The littlest ones got to go first. They recited simple nursery rhymes, squawked out tunes on miniature violins, twirled Hula Hoops, pranced in pink ballet tutus, and when they bowed or curtsied, the audience would sigh in unison, "Awww," and then clap enthusiastically.

When my turn came, I was very confident. I remember my childish excitement. It was as if I knew, without a doubt, that the prodigy side of me really did exist. I had no fear whatsoever, no nervousness. I remember thinking to myself, This is it! This is it! I looked out over the audience, at my mother's blank face, my father's yawn, Auntie Lindo's stiff-lipped smile, Waverly's sulky expression. I had on a white dress layered with sheets of lace, and a pink bow in my Peter Pan haircut. As I sat down I envisioned people jumping to their feet and Ed Sullivan rushing up to introduce me to everyone on TV.

And I started to play. It was so beautiful. I was so caught up in how lovely I looked that at first I didn't worry how I would sound. So it was a surprise to me when I hit the first wrong note and I realized something didn't sound quite right. And then I hit another and another followed that. A chill started at the top of my head and began to trickle down. Yet I couldn't stop playing, as though my hands were bewitched. I kept thinking my fingers would adjust themselves back, like a train switching to the right track. I played this strange jumble through two repeats, the sour notes staying with me all the way to the end.

When I stood up, I discovered my legs were shaking. Maybe I had just been nervous and the audience, like Old Chong, had seen me go through the right motions and had not heard anything wrong at all. I swept my right foot out, went down on my knee, looked up and smiled. The room was quiet, except for Old Chong, who was beaming and shouting, "Bravo! Bravo! Well done!" But then I saw my mother's face, her stricken face. The audience clapped weakly, and as I walked back to my chair, with my whole face quivering as I tried not to cry, I heard a little boy whisper loudly to his mother, "That was awful," and the mother whispered back, "Well, she certainly tried."

And now I realized how many people were in the audience, the whole world it seemed. I was aware of eyes burning into my back. I felt the shame of my mother and father as they sat stiffly throughout the rest of the show.

We could have escaped during intermission. Pride and some strange sense of honor must have anchored my parents to their chairs. And so we watched it all: the eighteen-year-old boy with a fake mustache who did a magic show and

55

juggled flaming hoops while riding a unicycle. The breasted girl with white makeup who sang from *Madama Butterfly* and got honorable mention. And the eleven-year-old boy who won first prize playing a tricky violin song that sounded like a busy bee.

After the show, the Hsus, the Jongs, and the St. Clairs from the Joy Luck Club came up to my mother and father.

"Lots of talented kids," Auntie Lindo said vaguely, smiling broadly.

"That was somethin' else," said my father, and I wondered if he was referring   60
to me in a humorous way, or whether he even remembered what I had done.

Waverly looked at me and shrugged her shoulders. "You aren't a genius like me," she said matter-of-factly. And if I hadn't felt so bad, I would have pulled her braids and punched her stomach.

But my mother's expression was what devastated me: a quiet, blank look that said she had lost everything. I felt the same way, and it seemed as if everybody were now coming up, like gawkers at the scene of an accident, to see what parts were actually missing. When we got on the bus to go home, my father was humming the busy-bee tune and my mother was silent. I kept thinking she wanted to wait until we got home before shouting at me. But when my father unlocked the door to our apartment, my mother walked in and then went to the back, into the bedroom. No accusations. No blame. And in a way, I felt disappointed. I had been waiting for her to start shouting, so I could shout back and cry and blame her for all my misery.

I assumed my talent-show fiasco meant I never had to play the piano again. But two days later, after school, my mother came out of the kitchen and saw me watching TV.

"Four clock," she reminded me as if it were any other day. I was stunned, as though she were asking me to go through the talent-show torture again. I wedged myself more tightly in front of the TV.

"Turn off TV," she called from the kitchen five minutes later.   65

I didn't budge. And then I decided. I didn't have to do what my mother said anymore. I wasn't her slave. This wasn't China. I had listened to her before and look what happened. She was the stupid one.

She came out from the kitchen and stood in the arched entryway of the living room. "Four clock," she said once again, louder.

"I'm not going to play anymore," I said nonchalantly. "Why should I? I'm not a genius."

She walked over and stood in front of the TV. I saw her chest was heaving up and down in an angry way.

"No!" I said, and I now felt stronger, as if my true self had finally emerged. So   70
this was what had been inside me all along.

"No! I won't!" I screamed.

She yanked me by the arm, pulled me off the floor, snapped off the TV. She was frighteningly strong, half pulling, half carrying me toward the piano as I kicked the throw rugs under my feet. She lifted me up and onto the hard bench. I was sobbing by now, looking at her bitterly. Her chest was heaving even more and her mouth was open, smiling crazily as if she were pleased I was crying.

"You want me to be someone that I'm not!" I sobbed. "I'll never be the kind of daughter you want me to be!"

"Only two kinds of daughters," she shouted in Chinese. "Those who are obedient and those who follow their own mind! Only one kind of daughter can live in this house. Obedient daughter!"

"Then I wish I wasn't your daughter. I wish you weren't my mother," I   75
shouted. As I said these things I got scared. I felt like worms and toads and slimy things were crawling out of my chest, but it also felt good, as if this awful side of me had surfaced, at last.

"Too late change this," said my mother shrilly.

And I could sense her anger rising to its breaking point. I wanted to see it spill over. And that's when I remembered the babies she had lost in China, the ones we never talked about. "Then I wish I'd never been born!" I shouted. "I wish I were dead! Like them."

It was as if I had said the magic words, Alakazam! — and her face went blank, her mouth closed, her arms went slack, and she backed out of the room, stunned, as if she were blowing away like a small brown leaf, thin, brittle, lifeless.

It was not the only disappointment my mother felt in me. In the years that followed, I failed her so many times, each time asserting my own will, my right to fall short of expectations. I didn't get straight As. I didn't become class president. I didn't get into Stanford. I dropped out of college.

For unlike my mother, I did not believe I could be anything I wanted to be. I   80
could only be me.

And for all those years, we never talked about the disaster at the recital or my terrible accusations afterward at the piano bench. All that remained unchecked, like a betrayal that was now unspeakable. So I never found a way to ask her why she had hoped for something so large that failure was inevitable.

And even worse, I never asked her what frightened me the most: Why had she given up hope?

For after our struggle at the piano, she never mentioned my playing again. The lessons stopped, the lid to the piano was closed, shutting out the dust, my misery, and her dreams.

So she surprised me. A few years ago, she offered to give me the piano, for my thirtieth birthday. I had not played in all those years. I saw the offer as a sign of forgiveness, a tremendous burden removed.

"Are you sure?" I asked shyly. "I mean, won't you and Dad miss it?"   85

"No, this your piano," she said firmly. "Always your piano. You only one can play."

"Well, I probably can't play anymore," I said. "It's been years."

"You pick up fast," said my mother, as if she knew this was certain. "You have natural talent. You could been genius if you want to."

"No I couldn't."

"You just not trying," said my mother. And she was neither angry nor sad. She   90
said it as if to announce a fact that could never be disproved. "Take it," she said.

But I didn't at first. It was enough that she had offered it to me. And after that,
every time I saw it in my parents' living room, standing in front of the bay windows, it made me feel proud, as if it were a shiny trophy I had won back.

Last week I sent a tuner over to my parents' apartment and had the piano
reconditioned, for purely sentimental reasons. My mother had died a few months
before and I had been getting things in order for my father, a little bit at a time. I
put the jewelry in special silk pouches. The sweaters she had knitted in yellow,
pink, bright orange — all the colors I hated — I put those in moth-proof boxes.
I found some old Chinese silk dresses, the kind with little slits up the sides. I
rubbed the old silk against my skin, then wrapped them in tissue and decided to
take them home with me.

After I had the piano tuned, I opened the lid and touched the keys. It
sounded even richer than I remembered. Really, it was a very good piano. Inside
the bench were the same exercise notes with handwritten scales, the same secondhand music books with their covers held together with yellow tape.

I opened up the Schumann book to the dark little piece I had played at the
recital. It was on the left-hand side of the page, "Pleading Child." It looked more
difficult than I remembered. I played a few bars, surprised at how easily the notes
came back to me.

And for the first time, or so it seemed, I noticed the piece on the right-hand   95
side. It was called "Perfectly Contented." I tried to play this one as well. It had a
lighter melody but the same flowing rhythm and turned out to be quite easy.
"Pleading Child" was shorter but slower; "Perfectly Contented" was longer but
faster. And after I played them both a few times, I realized they were two halves of
the same song.   [1989]

THINKING ABOUT THE TEXT

1. Most sons and daughters struggle to establish their own identities. Does
   this seem true in "Two Kinds"? Does the cultural difference between the
   immigrant mother and Americanized daughter intensify their struggle?
   Do you think you have different goals in life than your parents do?

2. Do you agree with the mother's belief that "you could be anything you
   wanted to be in America" (para. 1)? Does race matter? Gender? Ethnicity? Religion? Sexual orientation?

3. What do you believe each character learned from the argument at the
   piano bench the day after the recital?

4. How does Tan establish the differing personalities of her characters?
   Through details? Dialogue? Anecdotes? Do the main characters change
   significantly? Does she tell us or show us?

5. Do you sympathize with the mother or the daughter? Should parents
   channel their children toward selected activities? Or should parents let

their children choose their own paths? Can parents push their children too much? Why would they do this?

MAKING COMPARISONS

1. Do you think Emily's mother in Olsen's story would want to be like the Chinese mother if given the opportunity? Which mother would you prefer to have? Why?

2. One mother seems to do too little, one too much. Is this your reading of the two stories? Is the lesson of Olsen's and Tan's stories that mothers can't win no matter what they do? Or do you have a more optimistic interpretation?

3. Which daughter's life seems more difficult? How possible is it to say from the outside looking in?

ALICE WALKER
Everyday Use

A native of Eatonton, Georgia, Alice Walker attended Spelman College and received her B.A. from Sarah Lawrence College in 1965. During the 1960s she was active in the civil rights movement, an experience reflected in her 1976 novel Meridian *and in her autobiographical 2000 book,* The Way Forward Is with a Broken Heart. *Walker is accomplished in many genres, and her essays, short stories, novels, and poems are widely read. She is perhaps best known for the novel* The Color Purple *(1976), which earned her both a Pulitzer Prize and an American Book Award and was made into a movie. Terming herself a "womanist" rather than a feminist in the essays of* In Search of Our Mothers' Gardens *(1983), Walker has confronted many issues concerning women, including abusive relationships, lesbian love, and the horrors of ritual genital mutilation in some African societies. Her daughter, Rebecca, has written her own memoir,* Black, White and Jewish, *dealing with her childhood and adolescence as the daughter of Alice Walker and activist lawyer Mel Leventhal, to whom Walker was married for nine years, after meeting him during voter registration drives in Mississippi in 1967. The short story "Everyday Use" from the collection* In Love and Trouble: Stories of Black Women *(1973) deals with definitions of history, heritage, and value in a changing world for African Americans in the midtwentieth century.*

I will wait for her in the yard that Maggie and I made so clean and wavy yesterday afternoon. A yard like this is more comfortable than most people know. It is not just a yard. It is like an extended living room. When the hard clay is swept clean as a floor and the fine sand around the edges lined with tiny, irregular grooves anyone can come and sit and look up into the elm tree and wait for the breezes that never come inside the house.

Maggie will be nervous until after her sister goes: she will stand hopelessly in corners homely and ashamed of the burn scars down her arms and legs, eyeing her sister with a mixture of envy and awe. She thinks her sister has held life always in the palm of one hand, that "no" is a word the world never learned to say to her.

You've no doubt seen those TV shows where the child who has "made it" is confronted, as a surprise, by her own mother and father, tottering in weakly from backstage. (A pleasant surprise, of course: What would they do if parent and child came on the show only to curse out and insult each other?) On TV mother and child embrace and smile into each other's faces. Sometimes the mother and father weep, the child wraps them in her arms and leans across the table to tell how she would not have made it without their help. I have seen these programs.

Sometimes I dream a dream in which Dee and I are suddenly brought together on a TV program of this sort. Out of a dark and soft-seated limousine I am ushered into a bright room filled with many people. There I meet a smiling, gray, sporty man like Johnny Carson who shakes my hand and tells me what a fine girl I have. Then we are on the stage and Dee is embracing me with tears in her eyes. She pins on my dress a large orchid, even though she has told me once that she thinks orchids are tacky flowers.

In real life I am a large, big-boned woman with rough, man-working hands.   5
In the winter I wear flannel nightgowns to bed and overalls during the day. I can kill and clean a hog as mercilessly as a man. My fat keeps me hot in zero weather. I can work outside all day, breaking ice to get water for washing; I can eat pork liver cooked over the open fire minutes after it comes steaming from the hog. One winter I knocked a bull calf straight in the brain between the eyes with a sledge hammer and had the meat hung up to chill before nightfall. But of course all this does not show on television. I am the way my daughter would want me to be: a hundred pounds lighter, my skin like an uncooked barley pancake. My hair glistens in the hot bright lights. Johnny Carson has much to do to keep up with my quick and witty tongue.

But that is a mistake. I know even before I wake up. Who ever knew a Johnson with a quick tongue? Who can even imagine me looking a strange white man in the eye? It seems to me I have talked to them always with one foot raised in flight, with my head turned in whichever way is farthest from them. Dee, though. She would always look anyone in the eye. Hesitation was no part of her nature.

"How do I look, Mama?" Maggie says, showing just enough of her thin body enveloped in pink skirt and red blouse for me to know she's there, almost hidden by the door.

"Come out into the yard," I say.

Have you ever seen a lame animal, perhaps a dog run over by some careless person rich enough to own a car, sidle up to someone who is ignorant enough to be kind to him? That is the way my Maggie walks. She has been like this, chin on chest, eyes on ground, feet in shuffle, ever since the fire that burned the other house to the ground.

Dee is lighter than Maggie, with nicer hair and a fuller figure. She's a   10
woman now, though sometimes I forget. How long ago was it that the other
house burned? Ten, twelve years? Sometimes I can still hear the flames and feel
Maggie's arms sticking to me, her hair smoking and her dress falling off her in
little black papery flakes. Her eyes seemed stretched open, blazed open by the
flames reflected in them. And Dee. I see her standing off under the sweet gum
tree she used to dig gum out of; a look of concentration on her face as she
watched the last dingy gray board of the house fall in toward the red-hot brick
chimney. Why don't you do a dance around the ashes? I'd wanted to ask her. She
had hated the house that much.

I used to think she hated Maggie, too. But that was before we raised the
money, the church and me, to send her to Augusta to school. She used to read to
us without pity; forcing words, lies, other folks' habits, whole lives upon us two,
sitting trapped and ignorant underneath her voice. She washed us in a river of
make-believe, burned us with a lot of knowledge we didn't necessarily need to
know. Pressed us to her with the serious way she read, to shove us away at just the
moment, like dimwits, we seemed about to understand.

Dee wanted nice things. A yellow organdy dress to wear to her graduation
from high school; black pumps to match a green suit she'd made from an old suit
somebody gave me. She was determined to stare down any disaster in her efforts.
Her eyelids would not flicker for minutes at a time. Often I fought off the temptation to shake her. At sixteen she had a style of her own: and knew what style was.

I never had an education myself. After second grade the school was closed
down. Don't ask me why: in 1927 colored asked fewer questions than they do
now. Sometimes Maggie reads to me. She stumbles along good-naturedly but
can't see well. She knows she is not bright. Like good looks and money, quickness passed her by. She will marry John Thomas (who has mossy teeth in an
earnest face) and then I'll be free to sit here and I guess just sing church songs
to myself. Although I never was a good singer. Never could carry a tune. I was
always better at a man's job. I used to love to milk till I was hooked in the side in
'49. Cows are soothing and slow and don't bother you, unless you try to milk them
the wrong way.

I have deliberately turned my back on the house. It is three rooms, just like
the one that burned, except the roof is tin; they don't make shingle roofs any
more. There are no real windows, just some holes cut in the sides, like the port-
holes in a ship, but not round and not square, with rawhide holding the shutters
up on the outside. This house is in a pasture, too, like the other one. No doubt
when Dee sees it she will want to tear it down. She wrote me once that no matter
where we "choose" to live, she will manage to come see us. But she will never
bring her friends. Maggie and I thought about this and Maggie asked me,
"Mama, when did Dee ever *have* any friends?"

She had a few. Furtive boys in pink shirts hanging about on washday after   15
school. Nervous girls who never laughed. Impressed with her they worshiped the
well-turned phrase, the cute shape, the scalding humor that erupted like bubbles
in lye. She read to them.

When she was courting Jimmy T she didn't have much time to pay to us, but turned all her faultfinding power on him. He *flew* to marry a cheap gal from a family of ignorant flashy people. She hardly had time to recompose herself.

When she comes I will meet — but there they are!

Maggie attempts to make a dash for the house, in her shuffling way, but I stay her with my hand. "Come back here," I say. And she stops and tries to dig a well in the sand with her toe.

It is hard to see them clearly through the strong sun. But even the first glimpse of leg out of the car tells me it is Dee. Her feet were always neat-looking, as if God himself had shaped them with a certain style. From the other side of the car comes a short, stocky man. Hair is all over his head a foot long and hanging from his chin like a kinky mule tail. I hear Maggie suck in her breath. "Uhnnnh," is what it sounds like. Like when you see the wriggling end of a snake just in front of your foot on the road. "Uhnnnh."

Dee next. A dress down to the ground, in this hot weather. A dress so loud it   20
hurts my eyes. There are yellows and oranges enough to throw back the light of the sun. I feel my whole face warming from the heat waves it throws out. Earrings gold, too, and hanging down to her shoulders. Bracelets dangling and making noises when she moves her arm up to shake the folds of the dress out of her armpits. The dress is loose and flows, and as she walks closer, I like it. I hear Maggie go "Uhnnnh" again. It is her sister's hair. It stands straight up like the wool on a sheep. It is black as night and around the edges are two long pigtails that rope about like small lizards disappearing behind her ears.

"Wa-su-zo-Tean-o!" she says, coming on in that gliding way the dress makes her move. The short stocky fellow with the hair to his navel is all grinning and he follows up with "Asalamalakim, my mother and sister!" He moves to hug Maggie but she falls back, right up against the back of my chair. I feel her trembling there and when I look up I see the perspiration falling off her chin.

"Don't get up," says Dee. Since I am stout it takes something of a push. You can see me trying to move a second or two before I make it. She turns, showing white heels through her sandals, and goes back to the car. Out she peeks next with a Polaroid. She stoops down quickly and lines up picture after picture of me sitting there in front of the house with Maggie cowering behind me. She never takes a shot without making sure the house is included. When a cow comes nibbling around the edge of the yard she snaps it and me and Maggie *and* the house. Then she puts the Polaroid in the back seat of the car, and comes up and kisses me on the forehead.

Meanwhile Asalamalakim is going through the motions with Maggie's hand. Maggie's hand is as limp as a fish, and probably as cold, despite the sweat, and she keeps trying to pull it back. It looks like Asalamalakim wants to shake hands but wants to do it fancy. Or maybe he don't know how people shake hands. Anyhow, he soon gives up on Maggie.

"Well," I say. "Dee."

"No, Mama," she says. "Not 'Dee,' Wangero Leewanika Kemanjo!"   25

"What happened to 'Dee'?" I wanted to know.

"She's dead," Wangero said. "I couldn't bear it any longer being named after the people who oppress me."

"You know as well as me you was named after your aunt Dicie," I said. Dicie is my sister. She named Dee. We called her "Big Dee" after Dee was born.

"But who was *she* named after?" asked Wangero.

"I guess after Grandma Dee," I said.   30

"And who was she named after?" asked Wangero.

"Her mother," I said, and saw Wangero was getting tired. "That's about as far back as I can trace it," I said. Though, in fact, I probably could have carried it back beyond the Civil War through the branches.

"Well," said Asalamalakim, "there you are."

"Uhnnnh," I heard Maggie say.

"There I was not," I said, "before 'Dicie' cropped up in our family, so why   35
should I try to trace it that far back?"

He just stood there grinning, looking down on me like somebody inspecting a Model A car. Every once in a while he and Wangero sent eye signals over my head.

"How do you pronounce this name?" I asked.

"You don't have to call me by it if you don't want to," said Wangero.

"Why shouldn't I?" I asked. "If that's what you want us to call you, we'll call you."

"I know it might sound awkward at first," said Wangero.   40

"I'll get used to it," I said. "Ream it out again."

Well, soon we got the name out of the way. Asalamalakim had a name twice as long and three times as hard. After I tripped over it two or three times he told me to just call him Hakim-a-barber. I wanted to ask him was he a barber, but I didn't really think he was, so I didn't ask.

"You must belong to those beef-cattle peoples down the road," I said. They said "Asalamalakim" when they met you, too, but they didn't shake hands. Always too busy: feeding the cattle, fixing the fences, putting up salt-lick shelters, throwing down hay. When the white folks poisoned some of the herd the men stayed up all night with rifles in their hands. I walked a mile and a half just to see the sight.

Hakim-a-barber said, "I accept some of their doctrines, but farming and raising cattle is not my style." (They didn't tell me, and I didn't ask, whether Wangero [Dee] had really gone and married him.)

We sat down to eat and right away he said he didn't eat collards and pork was   45
unclean. Wangero, though, went on through the chitlins and corn bread, the greens and everything else. She talked a blue streak over the sweet potatoes. Everything delighted her. Even the fact that we still used the benches her daddy made for the table when we couldn't afford to buy chairs.

"Oh, Mama!" she cried. Then turned to Hakim-a-barber. "I never knew how lovely these benches are. You can feel the rump prints," she said, running her hands underneath her and along the bench. Then she gave a sigh and her hand closed over Grandma Dee's butter dish. "That's it!" she said. "I knew there was something I wanted to ask you if I could have." She jumped up from the table and went over in the corner where the churn stood, the milk in it clabber by now. She looked at the churn and looked at it.

"This churn top is what I need," she said. "Didn't Uncle Buddy whittle it out of a tree you all used to have?"

"Yes," I said.

"Uh huh," she said happily. "And I want the dasher, too."

"Uncle Buddy whittle that, too?" asked the barber.   50

Dee (Wangero) looked up at me.

"Aunt Dee's first husband whittled the dash," said Maggie so low you almost couldn't hear her. "His name was Henry, but they called him Stash."

"Maggie's brain is like all elephant's," Wangero said, laughing. "I can use the churn top as a centerpiece for the alcove table," she said, sliding a plate over the churn, "and I'll think of something artistic to do with the dasher."

When she finished wrapping the dasher the handle stuck out. I took it for a moment in my hands. You didn't even have to look close to see where hands pushing the dasher up and down to make butter had left a kind of sink in the wood. In fact, there were a lot of small sinks; you could see where thumbs and fingers had sunk into the wood. It was beautiful light yellow wood, from a tree that grew in the yard where Big Dee and Stash had lived.

After dinner Dee (Wangero) went to the trunk at the foot of my bed and   55 started rifling through it. Maggie hung back in the kitchen over the dishpan. Out came Wangero with two quilts. They had been pieced by Grandma Dee and then Big Dee and me had hung them on the quilt frames on the front porch and quilted them. One was in the Lone Star pattern. The other was Walk Around the Mountain. In both of them were scraps of dresses Grandma Dee had worn fifty and more years ago. Bits and pieces of Grandpa Jarrell's paisley shirts. And one teeny faded blue piece, about the size of a penny matchbox, that was from Great Grandpa Ezra's uniform that he wore in the Civil War.

"Mama," Wangero said sweet as a bird. "Can I have these old quilts?"

I heard something fall in the kitchen, and a minute later the kitchen door slammed.

"Why don't you take one or two of the others?" I asked. "These old things was just done by me and Big Dee from some tops your grandma pieced before she died."

"No," said Wangero. "I don't want those. They are stitched around the borders by machine."

"That'll make them last better," I said.   60

"That's not the point," said Wangero. "These are all pieces of dresses Grandma used to wear. She did all this stitching by hand. Imagine!" She held the quilts securely in her arms, stroking them.

"Some of the pieces, like those lavender ones, come from old clothes her mother handed down to her," I said, moving up to touch the quilts. Dee (Wangero) moved back just enough so that I couldn't reach the quilts. They already belonged to her.

"Imagine!" she breathed again, clutching them closely to her bosom.

"The truth is," I said, "I promised to give them quilts to Maggie, for when she marries John Thomas."

She gasped like a bee had stung her.   65

"Maggie can't appreciate these quilts!" she said. "She'd probably be back-ward enough to put them to everyday use."

"I reckon she would," I said. "God knows I been saving 'em for long enough with nobody using 'em. I hope she will!" I didn't want to bring up how I had offered Dee (Wangero) a quilt when she went away to college. Then she had told me they were old-fashioned, out of style.

"But they're *priceless!*" she was saying now, furiously; for she has a temper. "Maggie would put them on the bed and in five years they'd be in rags. Less than that!"

"She can always make some more," I said. "Maggie knows how to quilt."

Dee (Wangero) looked at me with hatred. "You just will not understand. The   70 point is these quilts, *these* quilts!"

"Well," I said, stumped. "What would *you* do with them?"

"Hang them," she said. As if that was the only thing you *could* do with quilts.

Maggie by now was standing in the door. I could almost hear the sound her feet made as they scraped over each other.

"She can have them, Mama," she said, like somebody used to never winning anything, or having anything reserved for her. "I can 'member Grandma Dee without the quilts."

I looked at her hard. She had filled her bottom lip with checkerberry snuff   75 and it gave her face a kind of dopey, hangdog look. It was Grandma Dee and Big Dee who taught her how to quilt herself. She stood there with her scarred hands hidden in the folds of her skirt. She looked at her sister with something like fear but she wasn't mad at her. This was Maggie's portion. This was the way she knew God to work.

When I looked at her like that something hit me in the top of my head and ran down to the soles of my feet. Just like when I'm in church and the spirit of God touches me and I get happy and shout. I did something I never had done before: hugged Maggie to me, then dragged her on into the room, snatched the quilts out of Miss Wangero's hands and dumped them into Maggie's lap. Maggie just sat there on my bed with her mouth open.

"Take one or two of the others," I said to Dee.

But she turned without a word and went out to Hakim-a-barber.

"You just don't understand," she said, as Maggie and I came out to the car.

"What don't I understand?" I wanted to know.   80

"Your heritage," she said. And then she turned to Maggie, kissed her, and said, "You ought to try to make something of yourself, too, Maggie. It's really a new day for us. But from the way you and Mama still live you'd never know it."

She put on some sunglasses that hid everything above the tip of her nose and her chin.

Maggie smiled; maybe at the sunglasses. But a real smile, not scared. After we watched the car dust settle I asked Maggie to bring me a dip of snuff. And then the two of us sat there just enjoying, until it was time to go in the house and go to bed.   [1973]

THINKING ABOUT THE TEXT

1. Be specific in arguing that Mama is more sympathetic to Maggie than to Dee. Is Mama hostile to Dee? What values are involved in the tensions among Mama and Dee and Maggie?

2. Although many students seem to prefer Maggie to Dee, most would probably rather be Dee than Maggie. Is this true for you? Why?

3. Do you think Walker is against "getting back to one's roots"? Does she give a balanced characterization of Maggie? Of Dee? How might she portray Dee if she wanted to be more positive about her? Less positive?

4. Do you think it helps or hinders the social fabric to affirm ethnic differences? Do you think America is a melting pot? Is a quilt a better symbol to capture our diversity? Can you suggest another metaphor?

5. Do you think most mothers would side with daughters with whom they are more politically or culturally sympathetic? What might be the deciding factor? Are most mothers equally supportive of each of their children?

MAKING COMPARISONS

1. How do you think Maggie would fare if she were the first child in "I Stand Here Ironing"? In "Two Kinds"?

2. Might either Emily or the daughter in "Two Kinds" adopt attitudes similar to Dee?

3. Which one of the four daughters seems the kindest? The smartest? The most ambitious? The most troubled? The most likely to succeed? To find love? Do you think the mothers are responsible for how their daughters turn out?

WRITING ABOUT ISSUES

1. As Emily's teacher, write a letter to Emily's mother persuading her that she should still come in for a conference. Acknowledge her excuses and her side of the issue, but offer objections.

2. Write a brief essay arguing that each of the mothers presented in Olsen's, Tan's, and Walker's stories is either a good or bad model for parenting.

3. Write a personal experience narrative about a time when your parents pushed you too hard or too little or wanted you to be someone you thought you were not. Conclude with your present view of the consequences of their action.

4. Ask six males and six females if they feel their parents tried to shape their personalities, behavior, choice of friends, and so forth. Were the parents' efforts successful? Do the sons and daughters resent it now? Conclude your brief report with some generalizations, including how relevant gender is.

ROMANTIC DREAMS

LESLIE MARMON SILKO, "Yellow Woman"
JAMES JOYCE, "Araby"
JOHN UPDIKE, "A & P"

Although centuries old, the cliché that the human heart is a mystery still seems valid. We still wonder if falling in love is natural: Is love our inborn impulse to seek romance, or is it simply a physical attraction spurred on by our evolutionary need to procreate? Perhaps Western culture has socialized us to believe in the power of romantic love and the often irrational behavior that follows. Might it serve some deep psychological need to find a substitute for a beloved parent? Is it a giving emotion? A selfish one? Is it a psychological malady or the one thing worth giving everything up for? Do we need to believe in it whether or not it exists? Since we are often driven to irrational behavior, delusions, and heartbreak, might we be better off without romantic love? Or might life without it be intolerably flat?

In the following cluster, three fiction writers explore the ways romantic love can sometimes cloud judgment, encouraging us to act against our best interests.

Silko shows us a woman torn between myth and reality; Joyce shows us a boy in the throes of romantic idealism; and Updike gives us a memorable picture of how an indifferent world responds to romantic gestures.

BEFORE YOU READ

Can people be truly happy without being in love? Is there one person in the world who is your true love? Or are there only certain types of people you could love? If your love didn't make you "float on a cloud," would you be disappointed? Is true love unconditional? Have you ever been fooled by romantic dreams?

LESLIE MARMON SILKO

Yellow Woman

Leslie Marmon Silko (b. 1948) is a major figure in the American Indian Renaissance. Raised in "Old Laguna" on the Pueblo Reservation near Albuquerque, New Mexico, Silko weaves the mythology of her matrilineal society into stories that move freely through what she calls an "ocean of time." The Yellow Woman *character appears frequently in Silko's writing as both a traditional figure, closely connected with nature and heterosexuality, and as a female character awakening to her cultural and sexual identity. Silko writes both poetry and fiction, often synthesizing both genres into a single text. Her novels include* Storyteller *(1981), in which "Yellow Woman" appears;* Ceremony *(1977); and* Almanac of the Dead *(1991). Her latest novel is* Garden in the Dunes *(1999). She taught recently at the University of Arizona.*

1

My thigh clung to his with dampness, and I watched the sun rising up through the tamaracks and willows. The small brown water birds came to the river and hopped across the mud, leaving brown scratches in the alkali-white crust. They bathed in the river silently. I could hear the water, almost at our feet where the narrow fast channel bubbled and washed green ragged moss and fern leaves. I looked at him beside me, rolled in the red blanket on the white river sand. I cleaned the sand out of the cracks between my toes, squinting because the sun was above the willow trees. I looked at him for the last time, sleeping on the white river sand.

I felt hungry and followed the river south the way we had come the afternoon before, following our footprints that were already blurred by the lizard tracks and bug trails. The horses were still lying down, and the black one whinnied when he saw me but he did not get up—maybe it was because the corral was made out of thick cedar branches and the horses had not yet felt the sun like I had. I tried to look beyond the pale red mesas to the pueblo. I knew it was there, even if I could not see it, on the sand rock hill above the river, the same river that moved past me now and had reflected the moon last night.

The horse felt warm underneath me. He shook his head and pawed the sand. The bay whinnied and leaned against the gate trying to follow, and I remembered him asleep in the red blanket beside the river. I slid off the horse and tied him close to the other horse. I walked north with the river again, and the white sand broke loose in footprints over footprints.

"Wake up."

He moved in the blanket and turned his face to me with his eyes still closed.   5
I knelt down to touch him.

"I'm leaving."

He smiled now, eyes still closed. "You are coming with me, remember?" He sat up now with his bare dark chest and belly in the sun.

"Where?"

"To my place."

"And will I come back?"   10

He pulled his pants on. I walked away from him, feeling him behind me and smelling the willows.

"Yellow Woman," he said.

I turned to face him. "Who are you?" I asked.

He laughed and knelt on the low, sandy bank, washing his face in the river. "Last night you guessed my name, and you knew why I had come."

I stared past him at the shallow moving water and tried to remember the   15
night, but I could only see the moon in the water and remember his warmth around me.

"But I only said that you were him and that I was Yellow Woman—I'm not really her—I have my own name and I come from the pueblo on the other side of the mesa. Your name is Silva and you are a stranger I met by the river yesterday afternoon."

He laughed softly. "What happened yesterday has nothing to do with what you will do today, Yellow Woman."

"I know—that's what I'm saying—the old stories about the ka'tsina spirit° and Yellow Woman can't mean us."

My old grandpa liked to tell those stories best. There is one about Badger and Coyote who went hunting and were gone all day, and when the sun was going down they found a house. There was a girl living there alone, and she had light hair and eyes and she told them that they could sleep with her. Coyote wanted to be with her all night so he sent Badger into a prairie-dog hole, telling him he thought he saw something in it. As soon as Badger crawled in, Coyote blocked up the entrance with rocks and hurried back to Yellow Woman.

"Come here," he said gently.   20

He touched my neck and I moved close to him to feel his breathing and to hear his heart. I was wondering if Yellow Woman had known who she was—if she knew that she would become part of the stories. Maybe she'd had another name that her husband and relatives called her so that only the ka'tsina from the north and the storytellers would know her as Yellow Woman. But I didn't go on; I felt him all around me, pushing me down into the white river sand.

Yellow Woman went away with the spirit from the north and lived with him and his relatives. She was gone for a long time, but then one day she came back and she brought twin boys.

"Do you know the story?"

"What story?" He smiled and pulled me close to him as he said this. I was afraid lying there on the red blanket. All I could know was the way he felt, warm, damp, his body beside me. This is the way it happens in the stories, I was thinking, with no thought beyond the moment she meets the ka'tsina spirit and they go.

"I don't have to go. What they tell in stories was real only then, back in time   25
immemorial, like they say."

He stood up and pointed at my clothes tangled in the blanket. "Let's go," he said.

I walked beside him, breathing hard because he walked fast, his hand around my wrist. I had stopped trying to pull away from him, because his hand felt cool and the sun was high, drying the river bed into alkali. I will see someone, eventually I will see someone, and then I will be certain that he is only a man— some man from nearby—and I will be sure that I am not Yellow Woman. Because she is from out of time past and I live now and I've been to school and there are highways and pickup trucks that Yellow Woman never saw.

It was an easy ride north on horseback. I watched the change from the cottonwood trees along the river to the junipers that brushed past us in the foothills, and finally there were only piñons, and when I looked up at the rim of the mountain plateau I could see pine trees growing on the edge. Once I stopped to look down, but the pale sandstone had disappeared and the river was gone and the dark lava hills were all around. He touched my hand, not speaking, but always singing softly a mountain song and looking into my eyes.

ka'tsina spirit: A mountain spirit of the Laguna Pueblo Indians.

I felt hungry and wondered what they were doing at home now — my mother, my grandmother, my husband, and the baby. Cooking breakfast, saying, "Where did she go? — maybe kidnapped," and Al going to the tribal police with the details: "She went walking along the river."

The house was made with black lava rock and red mud. It was high above the spreading miles of arroyos and long mesas. I smelled a mountain smell of pitch and buck brush. I stood there beside the black horse, looking down on the small, dim country we had passed, and I shivered.

"Yellow Woman, come inside where it's warm."

2

He lit a fire in the stove. It was an old stove with a round belly and an enamel coffeepot on top. There was only the stove, some faded Navajo blankets, and a bedroll and cardboard box. The floor was made of smooth adobe plaster, and there was one small window facing east. He pointed at the box.

"There's some potatoes and the frying pan." He sat on the floor with his arms around his knees pulling them close to his chest and he watched me fry the potatoes. I didn't mind him watching me because he was always watching me — he had been watching me since I came upon him sitting on the river bank trimming leaves from a willow twig with his knife. We ate from the pan and he wiped the grease from his fingers on his Levis.

"Have you brought women here before?" He smiled and kept chewing, so I said, "Do you always use the same tricks?"

"What tricks?" He looked at me like he didn't understand.

"The story about being a ka'tsina from the mountains. The story about Yellow Woman."

Silva was silent; his face was calm.

"I don't believe it. Those stories couldn't happen now," I said.

He shook his head and said softly, "But someday they will talk about us, and they will say, 'Those two lived long ago when things like that happened.' "

He stood up and went out. I ate the rest of the potatoes and thought about things — about the noise the stove was making and the sound of the mountain wind outside. I remembered yesterday and the day before, and then I went outside.

I walked past the corral to the edge where the narrow trail cut through the black rim rock. I was standing in the sky with nothing around me but the wind that came down from the blue mountain peak behind me. I could see faint mountain images in the distance miles across the vast spread of mesas and valleys and plains. I wondered who was over there to feel the mountain wind on those sheer blue edges — who walks on the pine needles in those blue mountains.

"Can you see the pueblo?" Silva was standing behind me.

I shook my head. "We're too far away."

"From here I can see the world." He stepped out on the edge. "The Navajo reservation begins over there." He pointed to the east. "The Pueblo boundaries are over here." He looked below us to the south, where the narrow trail seemed to

30

35

40

come from. "The Texans have their ranches over there, starting with that valley, the Concho Valley. The Mexicans run some cattle over there too."

"Do you ever work for them?"   45

"I steal from them," Silva answered. The sun was dropping behind us and shadows were filling the land below. I turned away from the edge that dropped forever into the valleys below.

"I'm cold," I said; "I'm going inside." I started wondering about this man who could speak the Pueblo language so well but who lived on a mountain and rustled cattle. I decided that this man Silva must be Navajo, because Pueblo men didn't do things like that.

"You must be a Navajo."

Silva shook his head gently. "Little Yellow Woman," he said, "you never give up, do you? I have told you who I am. The Navajo people know me, too." He knelt down and unrolled the bedroll and spread the extra blankets out on a piece of canvas. The sun was down, and the only light in the house came from out-side — the dim orange light from sundown.

I stood there and waited for him to crawl under the blankets.   50

"What are you waiting for?" he said, and I lay down beside him. He undressed me slowly like the night before beside the river — kissing my face gen-tly and running his hands up and down my belly and legs. He took off my pants and then he laughed.

"Why are you laughing?"

"You are breathing so hard."

I pulled away from him and turned my back to him.

He pulled me around and pinned me down with his arms and chest. "You   55 don't understand, do you, little Yellow Woman? You will do what I want."

And again he was all around me with his skin slippery against mine, and I was afraid because I understood that his strength could hurt me. I lay underneath him and I knew that he could destroy me. But later, while he slept beside me, I touched his face and I had a feeling — the kind of feeling for him that overcame me that morning along the river. I kissed him on the forehead and he reached out for me.

When I woke up in the morning he was gone. It gave me a strange feeling because for a long time I sat there on the blankets and looked around the little house for some object of his — some proof that he had been there or maybe that he was coming back. Only the blankets and the cardboard box remained. The .30-30° that had been leaning in the corner was gone, and so was the knife I had used the night before. He was gone, and I had my chance to go now. But first I had to eat, because I knew it would be a long walk home.

I found some dried apricots in the cardboard box, and I sat down on a rock at the edge of the plateau rim. There was no wind and the sun warmed me. I was surrounded by silence. I drowsed with apricots in my mouth, and I didn't believe that there were highways or railroads or cattle to steal.

When I woke up, I stared down at my feet in the black mountain dirt. Little black ants were swarming over the pine needles around my foot. They must have

.30-30: A rifle.

smelled the apricots. I thought about my family far below me. They would be
wondering about me, because this had never happened to me before. The tribal
police would file a report. But if old Grandpa weren't dead he would tell them
what happened—he would laugh and say, "Stolen by a ka'tsina, a mountain
spirit. She'll come home—they usually do." There are enough of them to handle
things. My mother and grandmother will raise the baby like they raised me. Al
will find someone else, and they will go on like before, except that there will be a
story about the day I disappeared while I was walking along the river. Silva had
come for me; he said he had. I did not decide to go. I just went. Moonflowers
blossom in the sand hills before dawn, just as I followed him. That's what I was
thinking as I wandered along the trail through the pine trees.

It was noon when I got back. When I saw the stone house I remembered that I   60
had meant to go home. But that didn't seem important any more, maybe because
there were little blue flowers growing in the meadow behind the stone house and
the gray squirrels were playing in the pines next to the house. The horses were
standing in the corral, and there was a beef carcass hanging on the shady side of a
big pine in front of the house. Flies buzzed around the clotted blood that hung
from the carcass. Silva was washing his hands in a bucket full of water. He must
have heard me coming because he spoke to me without turning to face me.

"I've been waiting for you."

"I went walking in the big pine trees."

I looked into the bucket full of bloody water with brown-and-white animal
hairs floating in it. Silva stood there letting his hand drip, examining me intently.

"Are you coming with me?"

"Where?" I asked him.   65

"To sell the meat in Marquez."

"If you're sure it's O.K."

"I wouldn't ask you if it wasn't," he answered.

He sloshed the water around in the bucket before he dumped it out and set
the bucket upside down near the door. I followed him to the corral and watched
him saddle the horses. Even beside the horses he looked tall, and I asked him
again if he wasn't Navajo. He didn't say anything; he just shook his head and kept
cinching up the saddle.

"But Navajos are tall."   70

"Get on the horse," he said, "and let's go."

The last thing he did before we started down the steep trail was to grab the
.30–30 from the corner. He slid the rifle into the scabbard that hung from his saddle.

"Do they ever try to catch you?" I asked.

"They don't know who I am."

"Then why did you bring the rifle?"   75

"Because we are going to Marquez where the Mexicans live."

3

The trail leveled out on a narrow ridge that was steep on both sides like an
animal spine. On one side I could see where the trail went around the rocky gray
hills and disappeared into the southeast where the pale sandrock mesas stood in the

distance near my home. On the other side was a trail that went west, and as I looked far into the distance I thought I saw the little town. But Silva said no, that I was looking in the wrong place, that I just thought I saw houses. After that I quit looking off into the distance; it was hot and the wildflowers were closing up their deep-yellow petals. Only the waxy cactus flowers bloomed in the bright sun, and I saw every color that a cactus blossom can be; the white ones and the red ones were still buds, but the purple and the yellow were blossoms, open full and the most beautiful of all.

Silva saw him before I did. The white man was riding a big gray horse, coming up the trail toward us. He was traveling fast and the gray horse's feet sent rocks rolling off the trail into the dry tumbleweeds. Silva motioned for me to stop and we watched the white man. He didn't see us right away, but finally his horse whinnied at our horses and he stopped. He looked at us briefly before he loped the gray horse across the three hundred yards that separated us. He stopped his horse in front of Silva, and his young fat face was shadowed by the brim of his hat. He didn't look mad, but his small, pale eyes moved from the blood-soaked gunny sacks hanging from my saddle to Silva's face and then back to my face.

"Where did you get the fresh meat?" the white man asked.

"I've been hunting," Silva said, and when he shifted his weight in the saddle   80
the leather creaked.

"The hell you have, Indian. You've been rustling cattle. We've been looking for the thief for a long time."

The rancher was fat, and sweat began to soak through his white cowboy shirt and the wet cloth stuck to the thick rolls of belly fat. He almost seemed to be panting from the exertion of talking, and he smelled rancid, maybe because Silva scared him.

Silva turned to me and smiled. "Go back up the mountain, Yellow Woman."

The white man got angry when he heard Silva speak in a language he couldn't understand. "Don't try anything, Indian. Just keep riding to Marquez. We'll call the state police from there."

The rancher must have been unarmed because he was very frightened and if   85
he had a gun he would have pulled it out then. I turned my horse around and the rancher yelled, "Stop!" I looked at Silva for an instant and there was something ancient and dark — something I could feel in my stomach — in his eyes, and when I glanced at his hand I saw his finger on the trigger of the .30–30 that was still in the saddle scabbard. I slapped my horse across the flank and the sacks of raw meat swung against my knees as the horse leaped up the trail. It was hard to keep my balance, and once I thought I felt the saddle slipping backward; it was because of this that I could not look back.

I didn't stop until I reached the ridge where the trail forked. The horse was breathing deep gasps and there was a dark film of sweat on its neck. I looked down in the direction I had come from, but I couldn't see the place. I waited. The wind came up and pushed warm air past me. I looked up at the sky, pale blue and full of thin clouds and fading vapor trails left by jets.

I think four shots were fired — I remember hearing four hollow explosions that reminded me of deer hunting. There could have been more shots after that, but I couldn't have heard them because my horse was running again and the loose rocks were making too much noise as they scattered around his feet.

Horses have a hard time running downhill, but I went that way instead of uphill to the mountain because I thought it was safer. I felt better with the horse running southeast past the round gray hills that were covered with cedar trees and black lava rock. When I got to the plain in the distance I could see the dark green patches of tamaracks that grew along the river; and beyond the river I could see the beginning of the pale sandrock mesas. I stopped the horse and looked back to see if anyone was coming; then I got off the horse and turned the horse around, wondering if it would go back to its corral under the pines on the mountain. It looked back at me for a moment and then plucked a mouthful of green tumbleweeds before it trotted back up the trail with its ears pointed forward, carrying its head daintily to one side to avoid stepping on the dragging reins. When the horse disappeared over the last hill, the gunny sacks full of meat were still swinging and bouncing.

4

I walked toward the river on a wood-hauler's road that I knew would eventually lead to the paved road. I was thinking about waiting beside the road for someone to drive by, but by the time I got to the pavement I had decided it wasn't very far to walk if I followed the river back the way Silva and I had come.

The river water tasted good, and I sat in the shade under a cluster of silvery willows. I thought about Silva, and I felt sad at leaving him; still, there was something strange about him, and I tried to figure it out all the way back home.   90

I came back to the place on the river bank where he had been sitting the first time I saw him. The green willow leaves that he had trimmed from the branch were still lying there, wilted in the sand. I saw the leaves and I wanted to go back to him — to kiss him and to touch him — but the mountains were too far away now. And I told myself, because I believe it, he will come back sometime and be waiting again by the river.

I followed the path up from the river into the village. The sun was getting low, and I could smell supper cooking when I got to the screen door of my house. I could hear their voices inside — my mother was telling my grandmother how to fix the Jell-O and my husband, Al, was playing with the baby. I decided to tell them that some Navajo had kidnapped me, but I was sorry that old Grandpa wasn't alive to hear my story because it was the Yellow Woman stories he liked to tell best.   [1974]

THINKING ABOUT THE TEXT

1. Why does Yellow Woman run away with Silva? Does it have something to do with the coyote stories? What stories in your own culture have persuaded you to trust in romantic love?

2. How do myths and stories differ? Are either based on reality or fantasy? What are the social or cultural purposes of stories about love?

3. Do you trust the narrator's judgment? Sincerity? On what textual evidence are you basing this evaluation? What bearing does her cultural heritage have on your analysis of her?

4. What specific details of Silko's story do you remember? Is the narrator a careful observer? Explain. What effect does the narrator's "noticing little things" have on you as a reader?

5. Has Yellow Woman learned her lesson? Do societies change their views of romantic love? How?

JAMES JOYCE
Araby

James Joyce (1882–1941) is regarded as one of the most innovative and influential writers of the modernist movement of the early twentieth century. His use of interior monologue, wordplay, complex allusions, and other techniques variously delighted, offended, or puzzled readers. Joyce's work demanded attention and often received censorship during his lifetime. A Portrait of the Artist as a Young Man *(1916), set in Joyce's native Dublin, is largely autobiographical. Like his hero at the end of the novel, Joyce left Ireland at the age of twenty to spend the remainder of his life in Paris and other European cities. His long, complex novel* Ulysses *(1922), also set in Dublin, takes the reader through one day in the life of its protagonist and his city. In "Araby," published in* Dubliners *(1914), as in other stories in the collection, Joyce pictures the limited life of his character and leads him toward a sudden insight, or epiphany.*

North Richmond Street, being blind, was a quiet street except at the hour when the Christian Brothers' School set the boys free. An uninhabited house of two storeys stood at the blind end, detached from its neighbours in a square ground. The other houses of the street, conscious of decent lives within them, gazed at one another with brown imperturbable faces.

The former tenant of our house, a priest, had died in the back drawing-room. Air, musty from having been long enclosed, hung in all the rooms, and the waste room behind the kitchen was littered with old useless papers. Among these I found a few paper-covered books, the pages of which were curled and damp: *The Abbot*, by Walter Scott, *The Devout Communicant*, and *The Memoirs of Vidocq*. I liked the last best because its leaves were yellow. The wild garden behind the house contained a central apple-tree and a few straggling bushes under one of which I found the late tenant's rusty bicycle-pump. He had been a very charitable priest; in his will he had left all his money to institutions and the furniture of his house to his sister.

When the short days of winter came dusk fell before we had well eaten our dinners. When we met in the street the houses had grown sombre. The space of sky above us was the colour of ever-changing violet and towards it the lamps of the street lifted their feeble lanterns. The cold air stung us and we played till our bodies glowed. Our shouts echoed in the silent street. The career of our play brought us through the dark muddy lanes behind the houses where we ran the gauntlet of the rough tribes from the cottages, to the back doors of the dark dripping gardens where odours arose from the ashpits, to the dark odorous stables where a coach-man smoothed and combed the horse or shook music from the buckled harness. When we returned to the street light from the kitchen windows had filled the areas. If my uncle was seen turning the corner we hid in the shadow until we had seen him safely housed. Or if Mangan's sister came out on the doorstep to call her brother in to his tea we watched her from our shadow peer up and down the street. We waited to see whether she would remain or go in and, if she remained, we left our shadow and walked up to Mangan's steps resignedly. She was waiting for us, her figure defined by the light from the half-opened door. Her brother always teased her before he obeyed and I stood by the railings looking at her. Her dress swung as she moved her body and the soft rope of her hair tossed from side to side.

Every morning I lay on the floor in the front parlour watching her door. The blind was pulled down to within an inch of the sash so that I could not be seen. When she came out on the doorstep my heart leaped. I ran to the hall, seized my books, and followed her. I kept her brown figure always in my eye and, when we came near the point at which our ways diverged, I quickened my pace and passed her. This happened morning after morning. I had never spoken to her, except for a few casual words, and yet her name was like a summons to all my foolish blood.

Her image accompanied me even in places the most hostile to romance. On   5
Saturday evenings when my aunt went marketing I had to go to carry some of the parcels. We walked through the flaring streets, jostled by drunken men and bar-gaining women, amid the curses of labourers, the shrill litanies of shop-boys who stood on guard by the barrel of pigs' cheeks, the nasal chanting of street-singers, who sang a *come-all-you* about O'Donovan Rossa,° or a ballad about the troubles in our native land. These noises converged in a single sensation of life for me: I imagined that I bore my chalice safely through a throng of foes. Her name sprang to my lips at moments in strange prayers and praises which I myself did not understand. My eyes were often full of tears (I could not tell why) and at times a flood from my heart seemed to pour itself out into my bosom. I thought little of the future. I did not know whether I would ever speak to her or not or, if I spoke to her, how I could tell her of my confused adoration. But my body was like a harp and her words and gestures were like fingers running upon the wires.

One evening I went into the back drawing-room in which the priest had died. It was a dark rainy evening and there was no sound in the house. Through one of the broken panes I heard the rain impinge upon the earth, the fine inces-sant needles of water playing in the sodden beds. Some distant lamp or lighted window gleamed below me. I was thankful that I could see so little. All my senses seemed to desire to veil themselves and, feeling that I was about to slip from them, I pressed the palms of my hands together until they trembled, murmuring: *"O love! O love!"* many times.

At last she spoke to me. When she addressed the first words to me I was so confused that I did not know what to answer. She asked me was I going to *Araby*.

O'Donovan Rossa: Jeremiah O'Donovan (1831–1915) was nicknamed "Dynamite Rossa" for advocating violent means to achieve Irish independence.

I forgot whether I answered yes or no. It would be a splendid bazaar, she said she would love to go.

"And why can't you?" I asked.

While she spoke she turned a silver bracelet round and round her wrist. She could not go, she said, because there would be a retreat that week in her convent. Her brother and two other boys were fighting for their caps and I was alone at the railings. She held one of the spikes, bowing her head towards me. The light from the lamp opposite our door caught the white curve of her neck, lit up her hair that rested there and, falling, lit up the hand upon the railing. It fell over one side of her dress and caught the white border of a petticoat, just visible as she stood at ease.

"It's well for you," she said.

"If I go," I said, "I will bring you something."   10

What innumerable follies laid waste my waking and sleeping thoughts after that evening! I wished to annihilate the tedious intervening days. I chafed against the work of school. At night in my bedroom and by day in the classroom her image came between me and the page I strove to read. The syllables of the word *Araby* were called to me through the silence in which my soul luxuriated and cast an Eastern enchantment over me. I asked for leave to go to the bazaar on Saturday night. My aunt was surprised and hoped it was not some Freemason affair. I answered few questions in class. I watched my master's face pass from amiability to sternness; he hoped I was not beginning to idle. I could not call my wandering thoughts together. I had hardly any patience with the serious work of life which, now that it stood between me and my desire, seemed to me child's play, ugly monotonous child's play.

On Saturday morning I reminded my uncle that I wished to go to the bazaar in the evening. He was fussing at the hallstand, looking for the hat-brush, and answered me curtly:

"Yes, boy, I know."

As he was in the hall I could not go into the front parlour and lie at the win-   15
dow. I left the house in bad humour and walked slowly towards the school. The air was pitilessly raw and already my heart misgave me.

When I came home to dinner my uncle had not yet been home. Still it was early. I sat staring at the clock for some time and, when its ticking began to irritate me, I left the room. I mounted the staircase and gained the upper part of the house. The high cold empty gloomy rooms liberated me and I went from room to room singing. From the front window I saw my companions playing below in the street. Their cries reached me weakened and indistinct and, leaning my forehead against the cool glass, I looked over at the dark house where she lived. I may have stood there for an hour, seeing nothing but the brown-clad figure cast by my imagination, touched discreetly by the lamplight at the curved neck, at the hand upon the railings and at the border below the dress.

When I came downstairs again I found Mrs. Mercer sitting at the fire. She was an old garrulous woman, a pawnbroker's widow, who collected used stamps for some pious purpose. I had to endure the gossip of the tea-table. The meal was prolonged beyond an hour and still my uncle did not come. Mrs.

Mercer stood up to go: she was sorry she couldn't wait any longer, but it was after eight o'clock and she did not like to be out late, as the night air was bad for her. When she had gone I began to walk up and down the room, clenching my fists. My aunt said:

"I'm afraid you may put off your bazaar for this night of Our Lord."

At nine o'clock I heard my uncle's latchkey in the halldoor. I heard him talking to himself and heard the hallstand rocking when it had received the weight of his overcoat. I could interpret these signs. When he was midway through his dinner I asked him to give me the money to go to the bazaar. He had forgotten.

"The people are in bed and after their first sleep now," he said.   20

I did not smile. My aunt said to him energetically:

"Can't you give him the money and let him go? You've kept him late enough as it is."

My uncle said he was very sorry he had forgotten. He said he believed in the old saying: "All work and no play makes Jack a dull boy." He asked me where I was going and, when I had told him a second time he asked me did I know *The Arab's Farewell to his Steed.* When I left the kitchen he was about to recite the opening lines of the piece to my aunt.

I held a florin° tightly in my hand as I strode down Buckingham Street towards the station. The sight of the streets thronged with buyers and glaring with gas recalled to me the purpose of my journey. I took my seat in a third-class carriage of a deserted train. After an intolerable delay the train moved out of the station slowly. It crept onward among ruinous houses and over the twinkling river. At Westland Row Station a crowd of people pressed to the carriage doors; but the porters moved them back, saying that it was a special train for the bazaar. I remained alone in the bare carriage. In a few minutes the train drew up beside an improvised wooden platform. I passed out on to the road and saw by the lighted dial of a clock that it was ten minutes to ten. In front of me was a large building which displayed the magical name.

I could not find any sixpenny entrance and, fearing that the bazaar would   25 be closed, I passed in quickly through a turnstile, handing a shilling to a weary-looking man. I found myself in a big hall girdled at half its height by a gallery. Nearly all the stalls were closed and the greater part of the hall was in darkness. I recognised a silence like that which pervades a church after a service. I walked into the centre of the bazaar timidly. A few people were gathered about the stalls which were still open. Before a curtain, over which the words *Café Chantant* were written in coloured lamps, two men were counting money on a salver. I listened to the fall of the coins.

Remembering with difficulty why I had come I went over to one of the stalls and examined porcelain vases and flowered tea-sets. At the door of the stall a young lady was talking and laughing with two young gentlemen. I remarked their English accents and listened vaguely to their conversation.

"O, I never said such a thing!"

"O, but you did!"

florin: A silver coin worth two shillings.

"O, but I didn't!"

"Didn't she say that?"

"Yes. I heard her."

"O, there's a . . . fib!"

Observing me the young lady came over and asked me did I wish to buy anything. The tone of her voice was not encouraging; she seemed to have spoken to me out of a sense of duty. I looked humbly at the great jars that stood like eastern guards at either side of the dark entrance to the stall and murmured:

"No, thank you."

The young lady changed the position of one of the vases and went back to the two young men. They began to talk of the same subject. Once or twice the young lady glanced at me over her shoulder.

I lingered before her stall, though I knew my stay was useless, to make my interest in her wares seem the more real. Then I turned away slowly and walked down the middle of the bazaar. I allowed the two pennies to fall against the sixpence in my pocket. I heard a voice call from one end of the gallery that the light was out. The upper part of the hall was now completely dark.

Gazing up into the darkness I saw myself as a creature driven and derided by vanity; and my eyes burned with anguish and anger.   [1914]

THINKING ABOUT THE TEXT

1. Why do the boy's eyes burn with anguish and anger? Has he learned something about romantic love? Was he in love with Mangan's sister? Give evidence.

2. If this story is partly autobiographical, what is Joyce's attitude toward his younger self? Are you sympathetic or critical of your own initiations into the complexities of relationships?

3. Reread the first and last paragraph. In what ways might they be connected?

4. Find examples of religious imagery. What do you think is its purpose?

5. Do you think the boy's quest has symbolic meaning? Do you think cultures can also search for something?

MAKING COMPARISONS

1. Compare the growth of the boy with the wife in "Yellow Woman."

2. Make explicit the insight or epiphany the boy comes to at the end. What would be a comparable epiphany for the wife in "Yellow Woman"?

3. Is one ending more realistic than the other? Explain.

JOHN UPDIKE
A & P

John Updike was born in 1932 in Shillington, Pennsylvania, an only child of a father who taught high-school algebra and a mother who wrote short stories and novels. After graduating from Harvard, Updike studied art in England and later joined the staff of The New Yorker. *In 1959 he published his first novel,* The Poorhouse Fair, *and moved to Massachusetts, where he still lives. His many novels of contemporary American life are notable for their lyrical and accurate depiction of the details and concerns of modern America.* Rabbit Run *(1960) and the sequels* Rabbit Redux *(1971),* Rabbit Is Rich *(1981), and* Rabbit at Rest *(1990) are considered important and insightful records of American life. "A & P" comes from Updike's* Pigeon Feathers and Other Stories *(1962).*

In walks these three girls in nothing but bathing suits. I'm in the third checkout slot, with my back to the door, so I don't see them until they're over by the bread. The one that caught my eye first was the one in the plaid green two-piece. She was a chunky kid, with a good tan and a sweet broad soft-looking can with those two crescents of white just under it, where the sun never seems to hit, at the top of the backs of her legs. I stood there with my hand on a box of HiHo crackers trying to remember if I rang it up or not. I ring it up again and the customer starts giving me hell. She's one of these cash-register-watchers, a witch about fifty with rouge on her cheekbones and no eyebrows, and I know it made her day to trip me up. She'd been watching cash registers for fifty years and probably never seen a mistake before.

By the time I got her feathers smoothed and her goodies into a bag—she gives me a little snort in passing, if she'd been born at the right time they would have burned her over in Salem—by the time I get her on her way the girls had circled around the bread and were coming back, without a pushcart, back my way along the counters, in the aisle between the checkouts and the Special bins. They didn't even have shoes on. There was this chunky one, with the two-piece—it was bright green and the seams on the bra were still sharp and her belly was still pretty pale so I guessed she just got it (the suit)—there was this one, with one of those chubby berry-faces, the lips all bunched together under her nose, this one, and a tall one, with black hair that hadn't quite frizzed right, and one of these sunburns right across under the eyes, and a chin that was too long—you know, the kind of girl other girls think is very "striking" and "attractive" but never quite makes it, as they very well know, which is why they like her so much—and then the third one, that wasn't quite so tall. She was the queen. She kind of led them, the other two peeking around and making their shoulders round. She didn't look around, not this queen, she just walked straight on slowly, on these long white prima-donna legs. She came down a little hard on her heels, as if she didn't walk in her bare feet that much, putting down her heels and then letting the weight move along to her toes as if she was testing the floor with every step, putting a little deliberate extra action into it. You never know for sure how

girls' minds work (do you really think it's a mind in there or just a little buzz like a
bee in a glass jar?) but you got the idea she had talked the other two into coming
in here with her, and now she was showing them how to do it, walk slow and hold
yourself straight.

She had on a kind of dirty-pink — beige maybe, I don't know — bathing suit
with a little nubble all over it, and what got me, the straps were down. They were
off her shoulders looped loose around the cool tops of her arms, and I guess as a
result the suit had slipped a little on her, so all around the top of the cloth there
was this shining rim. If it hadn't been there you wouldn't have known there could
have been anything whiter than those shoulders. With the straps pushed off,
there was nothing between the top of the suit and the top of her head except just
her, this clean bare plane of the top of her chest down from the shoulder bones
like a dented sheet of metal tilted in the light. I mean, it was more than pretty.

She had sort of oaky hair that the sun and salt had bleached, done up in
a bun that was unravelling, and a kind of prim face. Walking into the A & P
with your straps down, I suppose it's the only kind of face you *can* have. She
held her head so high her neck, coming up out of those white shoulders, looked
kind of stretched, but I didn't mind. The longer her neck was, the more of her
there was.

She must have felt in the corner of her eye me and over my shoulder Stoke-   5
sie in the second slot watching, but she didn't tip. Not this queen. She kept her
eyes moving across the racks, and stopped, and turned so slow it made my
stomach rub the inside of my apron, and buzzed to the other two, who kind of
huddled against her for relief, and then they all three of them went up the cat-
and-dog-food-breakfast-cereal-macaroni-rice-raisins-seasonings-spreads-spaghetti-
soft-drinks-crackers-and-cookies aisle. From the third slot I look straight up this
aisle to the meat counter, and I watched them all the way. The fat one with the
tan sort of fumbled with the cookies, but on second thought she put the package
back. The sheep pushing their carts down the aisle — the girls were walking
against the usual traffic (not that we have one-way signs or anything) — were
pretty hilarious. You could see them, when Queenie's white shoulders dawned
on them, kind of jerk, or hop, or hiccup, but their eyes snapped back to their own
baskets and on they pushed. I bet you could set off dynamite in an A & P and the
people would by and large keep reaching and checking oatmeal off their lists and
muttering "Let me see, there was a third thing, began with A, asparagus, no, ah,
yes, applesauce!" or whatever it is they do mutter. But there was no doubt, this
jiggled them. A few houseslaves in pin curlers even looked around after pushing
their carts past to make sure what they had seen was correct.

You know, it's one thing to have a girl in a bathing suit down on the beach,
where what with the glare nobody can look at each other much anyway, and
another thing in the cool of the A & P, under the fluorescent lights, against all
those stacked packages, with her feet paddling along naked over our checkboard
green-and-cream rubber-tile floor.

"Oh Daddy," Stokesie said beside me. "I feel so faint."

"Darling," I said. "Hold me tight." Stokesie's married, with two babies
chalked up on his fuselage already, but as far as I can tell that's the only difference. He's twenty-two, and I was nineteen this April.

"Is it done?" he asks, the responsible married man finding his voice. I forgot to say he thinks he's going to be manager some sunny day, maybe in 1990 when it's called the Great Alexandrov and Petrooshki Tea Company or something.

What he meant was, our town is five miles from a beach, with a big summer   10 colony out on the Point, but we're right in the middle of town, and the women generally put on a shirt or shorts or something before they get out of the car into the street. And anyway these are usually women with six children and varicose veins mapping their legs and nobody, including them, could care less. As I say, we're right in the middle of town, and if you stand at our front doors you can see two banks and the Congregational church and the newspaper store and three real-estate offices and about twenty-seven old freeloaders tearing up Central Street because the sewer broke again. It's not as if we're on the Cape; we're north of Boston and there's people in this town haven't seen the ocean for twenty years.

The girls had reached the meat counter and were asking McMahon something. He pointed, they pointed, and they shuffled out of sight behind a pyramid of Diet Delight peaches. All that was left for us to see was old McMahon patting his mouth and looking after them sizing up their joints. Poor kids, I began to feel sorry for them, they couldn't help it.

Now here comes the sad part of the story, at least my family says it's sad, but I don't think it's so sad myself. The store's pretty empty, it being Thursday afternoon, so there was nothing much to do except lean on the register and wait for the girls to show up again. The whole store was like a pinball machine and I didn't know which tunnel they'd come out of. After a while they come around out of the far aisle, around the light bulbs, records at discount of the Caribbean Six or Tony Martin Sings or some such gunk you wonder they waste the wax on, sixpacks of candy bars, and plastic toys done up in cellophane that fall apart when a kid looks at them anyway. Around they come, Queenie still leading the way, and holding a little gray jar in her hand. Slots Three through Seven are unmanned and I could see her wondering between Stokes and me, but Stokesie with his usual luck draws an old party in baggy gray pants who stumbles up with four giant cans of pineapple juice (what do these bums *do* with all that pineapple juice? I've often asked myself) so the girls come to me. Queenie puts down the jar and I take it into my fingers icy cold. Kingfish Fancy Herring Snacks in Pure Sour Cream: 49¢. Now her hands are empty, not a ring or a bracelet, bare as God made them, and I wonder where the money's coming from. Still with that prim look she lifts a folded dollar bill out of the hollow at the center of her nubbled pink top. The jar went heavy in my hand. Really, I thought that was so cute.

Then everybody's luck begins to run out. Lengel comes in from haggling with a truck full of cabbages on the lot and is about to scuttle into that door marked MANAGER behind which he hides all day when the girls touch his eye. Lengel's pretty dreary, teaches Sunday school and the rest, but he doesn't miss that much. He comes over and says, "Girls, this isn't the beach."

Queenie blushes, though maybe it's just a brush of sunburn I was noticing for the first time, now that she was so close. "My mother asked me to pick up a jar of herring snacks." Her voice kind of startled me, the way voices do when you see the people first, coming out so flat and dumb yet kind of tony, too, the way it ticked over "pick up" and "snacks." All of a sudden I slid right down her voice into her living room. Her father and the other men were standing around in ice-cream coats and bow ties and the women were in sandals picking up herring snacks on toothpicks off a big glass plate and they were all holding drinks the color of water with olives and sprigs of mint in them. When my parents have somebody over they get lemonade and if it's a real racy affair Schlitz in tall glasses with "They'll Do It Every Time" cartoons stencilled on.

"That's all right," Lengel said. "But this isn't the beach." His repeating this   15
struck me as funny, as if it had just occurred to him, and he had been thinking all these years the A & P was a great big sand dune and he was the head lifeguard. He didn't like my smiling — as I say he doesn't miss much — but he concentrates on giving the girls that sad Sunday-school–superintendent stare.

Queenie's blush is no sunburn now, and the plump one in plaid, that I liked better from the back — a really sweet can — pipes up, "We weren't doing any shopping. We just came in for the one thing."

"That makes no difference," Lengel tells her, and I could see from the way his eyes went that he hadn't noticed she was wearing a two-piece before. "We want you decently dressed when you come in here."

"We *are* decent," Queenie says suddenly, her lower lip pushing, getting sore now that she remembers her place, a place from which the crowd that runs the A & P must look pretty crummy. Fancy Herring Snacks flashed in her very blue eyes.

"Girls, I don't want to argue with you. After this come in here with your shoulders covered. It's our policy." He turns his back. That's policy for you. Policy is what the kingpins want. What the others want is juvenile delinquency.

All this while, the customers had been showing up with their carts but, you   20
know, sheep, seeing a scene, they had all bunched up on Stokesie, who shook open a paper bag as gently as peeling a peach, not wanting to miss a word. I could feel in the silence everybody getting nervous, most of all Lengel, who asks me, "Sammy, have you rung up their purchase?"

I thought and said "No" but it wasn't about that I was thinking. I go through the punches, 4, 9, GROC, TOT — it's more complicated than you think, and after you do it often enough, it begins to make a little song, that you hear words to, in my case "Hello (*bing*) there, you (*gung*) hap-py *pee*-pul (*splat*)!" — the *splat* being the drawer flying out. I uncrease the bill, tenderly as you may imagine, it just having come from between the two smoothest scoops of vanilla I had ever known were there, and pass a half and a penny into her narrow pink palm, and nestle the herrings in a bag and twist its neck and hand it over, all the time thinking.

The girls, and who'd blame them, are in a hurry to get out, so I say "I quit" to Lengel enough for them to hear, hoping they'll stop and watch me, their unsuspected hero. They keep right on going, into the electric eye; the door flies open and they flicker across the lot to their car, Queenie and Plaid and Big Tall Goony-Goony (not that as raw material she was so bad), leaving me with Lengel and a kink in his eyebrow.

"Did you say something, Sammy?"

"I said I quit."

"I thought you did."   25

"You didn't have to embarrass them."

"It was they who were embarrassing us."

I started to say something that came out "Fiddle-de-doo." It's a saying of my grandmother's, and I know she would have been pleased.

"I don't think you know what you're saying," Lengel said.

"I know you don't," I said. "But I do." I pull the bow at the back of my apron   30
and start shrugging it off my shoulders. A couple customers that had been heading for my slot begin to knock against each other, like scared pigs in a chute.

Lengel sighs and begins to look very patient and old and gray. He's been a
friend of my parents for years. "Sammy, you don't want to do this to your Mom
and Dad," he tells me. It's true, I don't. But it seems to me that once you begin a
gesture it's fatal not to go through with it. I fold the apron, "Sammy" stitched in
red on the pocket, and put it on the counter, and drop the bow tie on top of it.
The bow tie is theirs, if you've ever wondered. "You'll feel this for the rest of your
life," Lengel says, and I know that's true, too, but remembering how he made that
pretty girl blush makes me so scrunchy inside I punch the No Sale tab and the
machine whirs "pee-pul" and the drawer splats out. One advantage to this scene
taking place in summer, I can follow this up with a clean exit, there's no fumbling around getting your coat and galoshes, I just saunter into the electric eye in
my white shirt that my mother ironed the night before, and the door heaves itself
open, and outside the sunshine is skating around on the asphalt.

I look around for my girls, but they're gone, of course. There wasn't anybody
but some young married screaming with her children about some candy they
didn't get by the door of a powder-blue Falcon station wagon. Looking back in
the big windows, over the bags of peat moss and aluminum lawn furniture
stacked on the pavement, I could see Lengel in my place in the slot, checking the
sheep through. His face was dark gray and his back stiff, as if he'd just had an
injection of iron, and my stomach kind of fell as I felt how hard the world was
going to be to me hereafter.   [1961]

THINKING ABOUT THE TEXT

1. Why do you think Sammy quits? Make a list of several plausible answers.

2. What would you do if you were in Sammy's position? What would your
   priorities be in this situation?

3. When Sammy hears Queenie's voice, he imagines an elegant cocktail
   party that he contrasts to his parents' "real racy affair" (para. 14) with
   lemonade and beer. What does this scene say about Sammy's attitude
   toward the girls? Toward his own social status?

4. Some critics have objected to Sammy's comment in the last sentence of
   paragraph 2 about "girls' minds." Is this a sexist observation? Does the
   time frame of the story figure in your opinion? Should it?

5. Comment on the last paragraph. What is the significance of the young
   married woman? Why does Sammy mention "sheep"? Why does Sammy

think the world will be hard on him? Do you agree? What does "hard" mean?

MAKING COMPARISONS

1. Are the three main characters in this cluster wiser at each story's end? Are they happier?
2. Which character's views about romance are most compatible with yours when you were, say, thirteen? With yours presently?
3. Compare the last paragraphs of "Araby" and "A & P." What attitudes do they express?

WRITING ABOUT ISSUES

1. Choose either Yellow Woman, the boy in "Araby," or Sammy, and argue that this character was or was not really in love. Support your argument with references to the text and your own cultural experience.
2. Write an essay that defends or denies the idea that romantic love is irrational. Use two of the stories from this cluster.
3. Would any of the characters in this cluster have been comfortable in the cultural context you were raised in? (Consider movies, books, TV, family narratives, and so forth in analyzing your culture.) Write a brief analysis of how well one or more of these characters would "fit in."
4. Look up information about Native American culture and the coyote stories referred to in "Yellow Woman." Do they help to explain her attitudes? Do the same for the culture of Joyce's Ireland, especially religion and romance. How about the 1950s in middle America? In a brief essay argue that each story is understood more fully when the cultural context is provided.

REVENGE

EDGAR ALLAN POE, "The Cask of Amontillado"
LOUISE ERDRICH, "Fleur"
ANDRE DUBUS, "Killings"

Many people consider revenge abhorrent. They hold that wrongdoers should be forgiven, left to the judgment of God ("Vengeance is mine, saith the Lord"), or dealt with through the supposed fair and rational processes of the judicial system. Yet others believe in getting even. They may tolerate or encourage revenge taken by others or retaliate themselves against perceived offenders, in effect following the ancient Babylonian principle of "an eye for an eye, a tooth for a tooth." In each of the following stories, a character expresses a judgment of one or more other characters by engaging in an act of revenge. As you read each story here, consider the logic, morality, context, and effects of the vengeance described.

BEFORE YOU READ

Do you believe it is ever justifiable for someone to avenge a crime or wrong-doing by going outside the law? What specific cases do you think about as you address this issue?

EDGAR ALLAN POE
The Cask of Amontillado

The life of Edgar Allan Poe (1809–1849) was relatively brief, its end tragically hastened by his alcohol and drug abuse, but his contributions to literature were unique. As a book reviewer, he produced pieces of literary criticism and theory that are still widely respected. As a poet, he wrote such classics as "The Raven" (1845), "The Bells" (1849), and "Annabel Lee" (1849). Moreover, his short fiction was groundbreaking and continues to be popular, a source for many films and television shows. With works such as "The Murders in the Rue Morgue" (1841), "The Gold Bug" (1843), and "The Purloined Letter" (1944), he pioneered the modern detective story. Others of Poe's tales are masterpieces of horror, including "The Fall of the House of Usher" (1842), "The Pit and the Pendulum" (1842), and the following story, which he wrote in 1846.

The thousand injuries of Fortunato I had borne as I best could; but when he ventured upon insult, I vowed revenge. You, who so well know the nature of my soul, will not suppose, however, that I gave utterance to a threat. *At length* I would be avenged; this was a point definitely settled — but the very definitiveness with which it was resolved precluded the idea of risk. I must not only punish, but punish with impunity. A wrong is unredressed when retribution overtakes its redresser. It is equally unredressed when the avenger fails to make himself felt as such to him who has done the wrong.

It must be understood, that neither by word nor deed had I given Fortunato cause to doubt my good-will. I continued, as was my wont, to smile in his face, and he did not perceive that my smile *now* was at the thought of his immolation.

He had a weak point — this Fortunato — although in other regards he was a man to be respected and even feared. He prided himself on his connoisseurship in wine. Few Italians have the true virtuoso spirit. For the most part their enthusiasm is adopted to suit the time and opportunity — to practise imposture upon the British and Austrian *millionnaires.* In painting and gemmary Fortunato, like his countrymen, was a quack — but in the matter of old wines he was sincere. In this respect I did not differ from him materially: I was skilful in the Italian vintages myself, and bought largely whenever I could.

It was about dusk, one evening during the supreme madness of the carnival season, that I encountered my friend. He accosted me with excessive warmth, for he had been drinking much. The man wore motley. He had on a tight-fitting parti-striped dress, and his head was surmounted by the conical cap and bells. I was so pleased to see him, that I thought I should never have done wringing his hand.

I said to him: "My dear Fortunato, you are luckily met. How remarkably well 5
you are looking to-day! But I have received a pipe° of what passes for Amontillado, and I have my doubts."

"How?" said he. "Amontillado? A pipe? Impossible! And in the middle of the carnival!"

"I have my doubts," I replied; "and I was silly enough to pay the full Amontillado price without consulting you in the matter. You were not to be found, and I was fearful of losing a bargain."

"Amontillado!"

"I have my doubts."

"Amontillado!"   10

"And I must satisfy them."

"Amontillado!"

"As you are engaged, I am on my way to Luchesi. If any one has a critical turn, it is he. He will tell me——"

"Luchesi cannot tell Amontillado from Sherry."

"And yet some fools will have it that his taste is a match for your own."   15

"Come, let us go."

"Whither?"

"To your vaults."

"My friend, no; I will not impose upon your good nature. I perceive you have an engagement. Luchesi——"

"I have no engagement;—come."   20

"My friend, no. It is not the engagement, but the severe cold with which I perceive you are afflicted. The vaults are insufferably damp. They are encrusted with nitre."

"Let us go, nevertheless. The cold is merely nothing. Amontillado! You have been imposed upon. And as for Luchesi, he cannot distinguish Sherry from Amontillado."

Thus speaking, Fortunato possessed himself of my arm. Putting on a mask of black silk, and drawing a *roquelaire*° closely about my person, I suffered him to hurry me to my palazzo.

There were no attendants at home; they had absconded to make merry in honor of the time. I had told them that I should not return until the morning, and had given them explicit orders not to stir from the house. These orders were sufficient, I well knew, to insure their immediate disappearance, one and all, as soon as my back was turned.

I took from their sconces two flambeaux, and giving one to Fortunato, bowed 25
him through several suites of rooms to the archway that led into the vaults. I

---

pipe: A large cask.   *roquelaire:* A short cloak.

passed down a long and winding staircase, requesting him to be cautious as he followed. We came at length to the foot of the descent, and stood together on the damp ground of the catacombs of the Montresors.

The gait of my friend was unsteady, and the bells upon his cap jingled as he strode.

"The pipe?" said he.

"It is farther on," said I; "but observe the white web-work which gleams from these cavern walls."

He turned toward me, and looked into my eyes with two filmy orbs that distilled the rheum of intoxication.

"Nitre?" he asked, at length. 30

"Nitre," I replied. "How long have you had that cough?"

"Ugh! ugh! ugh!—ugh! ugh! ugh!—ugh! ugh! ugh!—ugh! ugh! ugh!—ugh! ugh! ugh!"

My poor friend found it impossible to reply for many minutes.

"It is nothing," he said, at last.

"Come," I said, with decision, "we will go back; your health is precious. You 35 are rich, respected, admired, beloved; you are happy, as once I was. You are a man to be missed. For me it is no matter. We will go back; you will be ill, and I cannot be responsible. Besides, there is Luchesi——"

"Enough," he said; "the cough is a mere nothing; it will not kill me. I shall not die of a cough."

"True—true," I replied; "and, indeed, I had no intention of alarming you unnecessarily; but you should use all proper caution. A draught of this Medoc will defend us from the damps."

Here I knocked off the neck of a bottle which I drew from a long row of its fellows that lay upon the mould.

"Drink," I said, presenting him the wine.

He raised it to his lips with a leer. He paused and nodded to me familiarly, 40 while his bells jingled.

"I drink," he said, "to the buried that repose around us."

"And I to your long life."

He again took my arm, and we proceeded.

"These vaults," he said, "are extensive."

"The Montresors," I replied, "were a great and numerous family." 45

"I forget your arms."

"A huge human foot d'or,° in a field azure; the foot crushes a serpent rampant whose fangs are imbedded in the heel."

"And the motto?"

"*Nemo me impune lacessit.*"°

"Good!" he said. 50

The wine sparkled in his eyes and the bells jingled. My own fancy grew warm with the Medoc. We had passed through walls of piled bones, with casks and puncheons intermingling into the inmost recesses of the catacombs. I

d'or: Of gold.
Nemo me impune lacessit: "No one wounds with impunity" is the motto on the royal arms of Scotland.

paused again, and this time I made bold to seize Fortunato by an arm above the elbow.

"The nitre!" I said; "see, it increases. It hangs like moss upon the vaults. We are below the river's bed. The drops of moisture trickle among the bones. Come, we will go back ere it is too late. Your cough——"

"It is nothing," he said; "let us go on. But first, another draught of the Medoc."

I broke and reached him a flagon of De Grâve. He emptied it at a breath. His eyes flashed with a fierce light. He laughed and threw the bottle upward with a gesticulation I did not understand.

I looked at him in surprise. He repeated the movement—a grotesque one.   55

"You do not comprehend?" he said.

"Not I," I replied.

"Then you are not of the brotherhood."

"How?"

"You are not of the masons."   60

"Yes, yes," I said; "yes, yes."

"You? Impossible! A mason?"

"A mason," I replied.

"A sign," he said.

"It is this," I answered, producing a trowel from beneath the folds of my   65
roquelaire.

"You jest," he exclaimed, recoiling a few paces. "But let us proceed to the Amontillado."

"Be it so," I said, replacing the tool beneath the cloak, and again offering him my arm. He leaned upon it heavily. We continued our route in search of the Amontillado. We passed through a range of low arches, descended, passed on, and descending again, arrived at a deep crypt, in which the foulness of the air caused our flambeaux rather to glow than flame.

At the most remote end of the crypt there appeared another less spacious. Its walls had been lined with human remains, piled to the vault overhead, in the fashion of the great catacombs of Paris. Three sides of this interior crypt were still ornamented in this manner. From the fourth the bones had been thrown down, and lay promiscuously upon the earth, forming at one point a mound of some size. Within the wall thus exposed by the displacing of the bones, we perceived a still interior recess, in depth about four feet, in width three, in height six or seven. It seemed to have been constructed for no especial use within itself, but formed merely the interval between two of the colossal supports of the roof of the catacombs, and was backed by one of their circumscribing walls of solid granite.

It was in vain that Fortunato, uplifting his dull torch, endeavored to pry into the depth of the recess. Its termination the feeble light did not enable us to see.

"Proceed," I said; "herein is the Amontillado. As for Luchesi——"   70

"He is an ignoramus," interrupted my friend, as he stepped unsteadily forward, while I followed immediately at his heels. In an instant he had reached the extremity of the niche, and finding his progress arrested by the rock, stood stupidly bewildered. A moment more and I had fettered him to the granite. In its surface were two iron staples, distant from each other about two feet, horizontally.

From one of these depended a short chain, from the other a padlock. Throwing the links about his waist, it was but the work of a few seconds to secure it. He was too much astounded to resist. Withdrawing the key I stepped back from the recess.

"Pass your hand," I said, "over the wall; you cannot help feeling the nitre. Indeed it is *very* damp. Once more let me *implore* you to return. No? Then I must positively leave you. But I must first render you all the little attentions in my power."

"The Amontillado!" ejaculated my friend, not yet recovered from his astonishment.

"True," I replied; "the Amontillado."

As I said these words I busied myself among the pile of bones of which I have   75
before spoken. Throwing them aside, I soon uncovered a quantity of building stone and mortar. With these materials and with the aid of my trowel, I began vigorously to wall up the entrance of the niche.

I had scarcely laid the first tier of the masonry when I discovered that the intoxication of Fortunato had in a great measure worn off. The earliest indication I had of this was a low moaning cry from the depth of the recess. It was *not* the cry of a drunken man. There was then a long and obstinate silence. I laid the second tier, and the third, and the fourth; and then I heard the furious vibrations of the chain. The noise lasted for several minutes, during which, that I might hearken to it with the more satisfaction, I ceased my labors and sat down upon the bones. When at last the clanking subsided, I resumed the trowel, and finished without interruption the fifth, the sixth, and the seventh tier. The wall was now nearly upon a level with my breast. I again paused, and holding the flambeaux over the masonwork, threw a few feeble rays upon the figure within.

A succession of loud and shrill screams, bursting suddenly from the throat of the chained form, seemed to thrust me violently back. For a brief moment I hesitated—I trembled. Unsheathing my rapier, I began to grope with it about the recess; but the thought of an instant reassured me. I placed my hand upon the solid fabric of the catacombs, and felt satisfied. I reapproached the wall. I replied to the yells of him who clamored. I reechoed—I aided—I surpassed them in volume and in strength. I did this, and the clamorer grew still.

It was now midnight, and my task was drawing to a close. I had completed the eighth, the ninth, and the tenth tier. I had finished a portion of the last and the eleventh; there remained but a single stone to be fitted and plastered in. I struggled with its weight; I placed it partially in its destined position. But now there came from out the niche a low laugh that erected the hairs upon my head. It was succeeded by a sad voice, which I had difficulty in recognizing as that of the noble Fortunato. The voice said—

"Ha! ha! ha!—he! he!—a very good joke indeed—an excellent jest. We will have many a rich laugh about it at the palazzo—he! he! he!—over our wine—he! he! he!"

"The Amontillado!" I said.   80

"He! he! he!—he! he! he!—yes, the Amontillado. But is it not getting late? Will not they be awaiting us at the palazzo, the Lady Fortunato and the rest? Let us be gone."

"Yes," I said, "let us be gone."

"*For the love of God, Montresor!*"

"Yes," I said, "for the love of God!"

But to these words I hearkened in vain for a reply. I grew impatient. I called 　85
aloud:

"Fortunato!"

No answer. I called again:

"Fortunato!"

No answer still, I thrust a torch through the remaining aperture and let it fall within. There came forth in return only a jingling of the bells. My heart grew sick—on account of the dampness of the catacombs. I hastened to make an end of my labor. I forced the last stone into its position; I plastered it up. Against the new masonry I re-erected the old rampart of bones. For the half of a century no mortal has disturbed them. *In pace requiescat!°*　　　　[1846]

In pace requiescat:　In peace may he rest (Latin).

THINKING ABOUT THE TEXT

1. Evidently Montresor is recounting the story of his revenge fifty years after it took place. To whom might he be speaking? With what purposes?

2. Montresor does not describe in detail any of the offenses that Fortunato has supposedly committed against him. In considering how to judge Montresor, do you need such information? Why, or why not? State in your own words the principles of revenge he lays out in the first paragraph.

3. What, if anything, does Poe achieve by having this story take place during a carnival? By repeating the word *amontillado* so much?

4. What does Montresor mean when he echoes Fortunato's words "for the love of God" (para. 84)? What might Fortunato be attempting to communicate with his final "jingling of the bells" (para. 89)?

5. Do you sympathize with Montresor? With Fortunato? Explain. What emotion did you mainly feel as you read the story? Identify specific features of it that led to this emotion.

LOUISE ERDRICH
Fleur

Louise Erdrich (b. 1954) is of German American and Chippewa descent. She was raised in Wahpeton, North Dakota, where both of her parents worked for the Bureau of Indian Affairs. In 1976, she earned a degree in Native American Studies at Dartmouth College; a year later, she received a master's degree in creative writing from the Johns Hopkins University. Although she has published poetry, essays, and a nonfiction book entitled The Blue Jay's Dance: A Birth Year *(1995), Erdrich is chiefly known for her novels about Native American life. Several of these feature a continuing cast of characters, including* Love Medicine *(1984; revised and expanded edition 1993),* The Beet Queen *(1986),* Tracks *(1988),* The Bingo Palace *(1994),* Tales of Burning Love *(1996),* The Last Report on the Miracles at Little No Horse *(2002), and* The Master Butcher's Singing Club *(2004). She and her late husband Michael Dorris also collaborated on a novel entitled* The Crown of Columbus *(1991). "Fleur" was first published in a 1986 issue of* Esquire, *and later it became a chapter in* Tracks.

The first time she drowned in the cold and glassy waters of Lake Turcot, Fleur Pillager was only a girl. Two men saw the boat tip, saw her struggle in the waves. They rowed over to the place she went down, and jumped in. When they dragged her over the gunwales, she was cold to the touch and stiff, so they slapped her face, shook her by the heels, worked her arms back and forth, and pounded her back until she coughed up lake water. She shivered all over like a dog, then took a breath. But it wasn't long afterward that those two men disappeared. The first wandered off, and the other, Jean Hat, got himself run over by a cart.

It went to show, my grandma said. It figured to her, all right. By saving Fleur Pillager, those two men had lost themselves.

The next time she fell in the lake, Fleur Pillager was twenty years old and no one touched her. She washed onshore, her skin a dull dead gray, but when George Many Women bent to look closer, he saw her chest move. Then her eyes spun open, sharp black riprock, and she looked at him. "You'll take my place," she hissed. Everybody scattered and left her there, so no one knows how she dragged herself home. Soon after that we noticed Many Women changed, grew afraid, wouldn't leave his house, and would not be forced to go near water. For his caution, he lived until the day that his sons brought him a new tin bathtub. Then the first time he used the tub he slipped, got knocked out, and breathed water while his wife stood in the other room frying breakfast.

Men stayed clear of Fleur Pillager after the second drowning. Even though she was good-looking, nobody dared to court her because it was clear that Misshepeshu, the waterman, the monster, wanted her for himself. He's a devil, that one, love-hungry with desire and maddened for the touch of young girls, the strong and daring especially, the ones like Fleur.

Our mothers warn us that we'll think he's handsome, for he appears with   5
green eyes, copper skin, a mouth tender as a child's. But if you fall into his arms, he sprouts horns, fangs, claws, fins. His feet are joined as one and his skin, brass scales, rings to the touch. You're fascinated, cannot move. He casts a shell necklace at your feet, weeps gleaming chips that harden into mica on your breasts. He holds you under. Then he takes the body of a lion or a fat brown worm. He's made of gold. He's made of beach moss. He's a thing of dry foam, a thing of death by drowning, the death a Chippewa cannot survive.

Unless you are Fleur Pillager. We all knew she couldn't swim. After the first time, we thought she'd never go back to Lake Turcot. We thought she'd keep to herself, live quiet, stop killing men off by drowning in the lake. After the first time, we thought she'd keep the good ways. But then, after the second drowning, we knew that we were dealing with something much more serious. She was haywire, out of control. She messed with evil, laughed at the old women's advice, and dressed like a man. She got herself into some half-forgotten medicine, studied ways we shouldn't talk about. Some say she kept the finger of a child in her pocket and a powder of unborn rabbits in a leather thong around her neck. She laid the heart of an owl on her tongue so she could see at night, and went out, hunting, not even in her own body. We know for sure because the next morning, in the snow or dust, we followed the tracks of her bare feet and saw where they changed, where the claws sprang out, the pad broadened and pressed into the dirt. By night we heard her chuffing cough, the bear cough. By day her silence and the wide grin she threw to bring down our guard made us frightened. Some thought that Fleur Pillager should be driven off the reservation, but not a single person who spoke like this had the nerve. And finally, when people were just about to get together and throw her out, she left on her own and didn't come back all summer. That's what this story is about.

During that summer, when she lived a few miles south in Argus, things happened. She almost destroyed that town.

When she got down to Argus in the year of 1920, it was just a small grid of six streets on either side of the railroad depot. There were two elevators, one central, the other a few miles west. Two stores competed for the trade of the three hundred citizens, and three churches quarreled with one another for their souls. There was a frame building for Lutherans, a heavy brick one for Episcopalians, and a long narrow shingled Catholic church. This last had a tall slender steeple, twice as high as any building or tree.

No doubt, across the low, flat wheat, watching from the road as she came near Argus on foot, Fleur saw that steeple rise, a shadow thin as a needle. Maybe in that raw space it drew her the way a lone tree draws lightning. Maybe, in the end, the Catholics are to blame. For if she hadn't seen that sign of pride, that slim prayer, that marker, maybe she would have kept walking.

But Fleur Pillager turned, and the first place she went once she came into town was to the back door of the priest's residence attached to the landmark church. She didn't go there for a handout, although she got that, but to ask for work. She got that too, or the town got her. It's hard to tell which came out worse, her or the men or the town, although the upshot of it all was that Fleur lived.

The four men who worked at the butcher's had carved up about a thousand carcasses between them, maybe half of that steers and the other half pigs, sheep, and game animals like deer, elk, and bear. That's not even mentioning the chickens, which were beyond counting. Pete Kozka owned the place, and employed Lily Veddar, Tor Grunewald, and my stepfather, Dutch James, who had brought my mother down from the reservation the year before she disappointed him by dying. Dutch took me out of school to take her place. I kept house half the time and worked the other in the butcher shop, sweeping floors, putting sawdust down, running a hambone across the street to a customer's bean pot or a package of sausage to the corner. I was a good one to have around because until they

10

needed me, I was invisible. I blended into the stained brown walls, a skinny, big-nosed girl with staring eyes. Because I could fade into a corner or squeeze beneath a shelf, I knew everything, what the men said when no one was around, and what they did to Fleur.

Kozka's Meats served farmers for a fifty-mile area, both to slaughter, for it had a stock pen and chute, and to cure the meat by smoking it or spicing it in sausage. The storage locker was a marvel, made of many thicknesses of brick, earth insulation, and Minnesota timber, lined inside with sawdust and vast blocks of ice cut from Lake Turcot, hauled down from home each winter by horse and sledge.

A ramshackle board building, part slaughterhouse, part store, was fixed to the low, thick square of the lockers. That's where Fleur worked. Kozka hired her for her strength. She could lift a haunch or carry a pole of sausages without stumbling, and she soon learned cutting from Pete's wife, a string thin blonde who chain-smoked and handled the razor-sharp knives with nerveless precision, slicing close to her stained fingers. Fleur and Fritzie Kozka worked afternoons, wrapping their cuts in paper, and Fleur hauled the packages to the lockers. The meat was left outside the heavy oak doors that were only opened at 5:00 each afternoon, before the men ate supper.

Sometimes Dutch, Tor, and Lily ate at the lockers, and when they did I stayed too, cleaned floors, restoked the fires in the front smokehouses, while the men sat around the squat cast-iron stove spearing slats of herring onto hardtack bread. They played long games of poker or cribbage on a board made from the planed end of a salt crate. They talked and I listened, although there wasn't much to hear since almost nothing ever happened in Argus. Tor was married, Dutch had lost my mother, and Lily read circulars. They mainly discussed about the auctions to come, equipment, or women.

Every so often, Pete Kozka came out front to make a whist, leaving Fritzie to   15
smoke cigarettes and fry raised doughnuts in the back room. He sat and played a few rounds but kept his thoughts to himself. Fritzie did not tolerate him talking behind her back, and the one book he read was the New Testament. If he said something, it concerned weather or a surplus of sheep stomachs, a ham that smoked green or the markets for corn and wheat. He had a good-luck talisman, the opal-white lens of a cow's eye. Playing cards, he rubbed it between his fingers. That soft sound and the slap of cards was about the only conversation.

Fleur finally gave them a subject.

Her cheeks were wide and flat, her hands large, chapped, muscular. Fleur's shoulders were broad as beams, her hips fishlike, slippery, narrow. An old green dress clung to her waist, worn thin where she sat. Her braids were thick like the tails of animals, and swung against her when she moved, deliberately, slowly in her work, held in and half-tamed, but only half. I could tell, but the others never saw. They never looked into her sly brown eyes or noticed her teeth, strong and curved and very white. Her legs were bare, and since she padded around in beadwork moccasins they never saw that her fifth toes were missing. They never knew she'd drowned. They were blinded, they were stupid, they only saw her in the flesh.

And yet it wasn't just that she was a Chippewa, or even that she was a woman, it wasn't that she was good-looking or even that she was alone that made their brains hum. It was how she played cards.

Women didn't usually play with men, so the evening that Fleur drew a chair up to the men's table without being so much as asked, there was a shock of surprise.

"What's this," said Lily. He was fat, with a snake's cold pale eyes and precious skin, smooth and lily-white, which is how he got his name. Lily had a dog, a stumpy mean little bull of a thing with a belly drum-tight from eating pork rinds. The dog liked to play cards just like Lily, and straddled his barrel thighs through games of stud, rum poker, vingt-un. The dog snapped at Fleur's arm that first night, but cringed back, its snarl frozen, when she took her place.   20

"I thought," she said, her voice soft and stroking, "you might deal me in."

There was a space between the heavy bin of spiced flour and the wall where I just fit. I hunkered down there, kept my eyes open, saw her black hair swing over the chair, her feet solid on the wood floor. I couldn't see up on the table where the cards slapped down, so after they were deep in their game I raised myself up in the shadows, and crouched on a sill of wood.

I watched Fleur's hands stack and ruffle, divide the cards, spill them to each player in a blur, rake them up and shuffle again. Tor, short and scrappy, shut one eye and squinted the other at Fleur. Dutch screwed his lips around a wet cigar.

"Gotta see a man," he mumbled, getting up to go out back to the privy. The others broke, put their cards down, and Fleur sat alone in the lamplight that glowed in a sheen across the push of her breasts. I watched her closely, then she paid me a beam of notice for the first time. She turned, looked straight at me, and grinned the white wolf grin a Pillager turns on its victims, except that she wasn't after me.

"Pauline there," she said, "how much money you got?"   25

We'd all been paid for the week that day. Eight cents was in my pocket.

"Stake me," she said, holding out her long fingers. I put the coins in her palm and then I melted back to nothing, part of the walls and tables. It was a long time before I understood that the men would not have seen me no matter what I did, how I moved. I wasn't anything like Fleur. My dress hung loose and my back was already curved, an old woman's. Work had roughened me, reading made my eyes sore, caring for my mother before she died had hardened my face. I was not much to look at, so they never saw me.

When the men came back and sat around the table, they had drawn together. They shot each other small glances, stuck their tongues in their cheeks, burst out laughing at odd moments, to rattle Fleur. But she never minded. They played their vingt-un, staying even as Fleur slowly gained. Those pennies I had given her drew nickels and attracted dimes until there was a small pile in front of her.

Then she hooked them with five-card draw, nothing wild. She dealt, discarded, drew, and then she sighed and her cards gave a little shiver. Tor's eye gleamed, and Dutch straightened in his seat.

"I'll pay to see that hand," said Lily Veddar.   30

Fleur showed, and she had nothing there, nothing at all.

Tor's thin smile cracked open, and he threw his hand in too.

"Well, we know one thing," he said, leaning back in his chair, "the squaw can't bluff."

With that I lowered myself into a mound of swept sawdust and slept. I woke up during the night, but none of them had moved yet, so I couldn't either. Still later, the men must have gone out again, or Fritzie come out to break the game, because I was lifted, soothed, cradled in a woman's arms and rocked so quiet that I kept my eyes shut while Fleur rolled me into a closet of grimy ledgers, oiled paper, balls of string, and thick files that fit beneath me like a mattress.

The game went on after work the next evening. I got my eight cents back five times over, and Fleur kept the rest of the dollar she'd won for a stake. This time they didn't play so late, but they played regular, and then kept going at it night after night. They played poker now, or variations, for one week straight, and each time Fleur won exactly one dollar, no more and no less, too consistent for luck.

By this time, Lily and the other men were so lit with suspense that they got Pete to join the game with them. They concentrated, the fat dog sitting tense in Lily Veddar's lap, Tor suspicious, Dutch stroking his huge square brow, Pete steady. It wasn't that Fleur won that hooked them in so, because she lost hands too. It was rather that she never had a freak hand or even anything above a straight. She only took on her low cards, which didn't sit right. By chance, Fleur should have gotten a full or flush by now. The irritating thing was she beat with pairs and never bluffed, because she couldn't, and still she ended up each night with exactly one dollar. Lily couldn't believe, first of all, that a woman could be smart enough to play cards, but even if she was, that she would then be stupid enough to cheat for a dollar a night. By day I watched him turn the problem over, his hard white face dull, small fingers probing at his knuckles, until he finally thought he had Fleur figured out as a bit-time player, caution her game. Raising the stakes would throw her.

More than anything now, he wanted Fleur to come away with something but a dollar. Two bits less or ten more, the sum didn't matter, just so he broke her streak.

Night after night she played, won her dollar, and left to stay in a place that just Fritzie and I knew about. Fleur bathed in the slaughtering tub, then slept in the unused brick smokehouse behind the lockers, a windowless place tarred on the inside with scorched fats. When I brushed against her skin I noticed that she smelled of the walls, rich and woody, slightly burnt. Since that night she put me in the closet I was no longer afraid of her, but followed her close, stayed with her, became her moving shadow that the men never noticed, the shadow that could have saved her.

August, the month that bears fruit, closed around the shop, and Pete and Fritzie left for Minnesota to escape the heat. Night by night, running, Fleur had won thirty dollars, and only Pete's presence had kept Lily at bay. But Pete was gone now, and one payday, with the heat so bad no one could move but Fleur, the men sat and played and waited while she finished work. The cards sweat, limp in their

35

fingers, the table was slick with grease, and even the walls were warm to the touch. The air was motionless. Fleur was in the next room boiling heads.

Her green dress, drenched, wrapped her like a transparent sheet. A skin of   40
lakeweed. Black snarls of veining clung to her arms. Her braids were loose, half-unraveled, tied behind her neck in a thick loop. She stood in steam, turning skulls through a vat with a wooden paddle. When scraps boiled to the surface, she bent with a round tin sieve and scooped them out. She'd filled two dishpans.

"Ain't that enough now?" called Lily. "We're waiting." The stump of a dog trembled in his lap, alive with rage. It never smelled me or noticed me above Fleur's smoky skin. The air was heavy in my corner, and pressed me down. Fleur sat with them.

"Now what do you say?" Lily asked the dog. It barked. That was the signal for the real game to start.

"Let's up the ante," said Lily, who had been stalking this night all month. He had a roll of money in his pocket. Fleur had five bills in her dress. The men had each saved their full pay.

"Ante a dollar then," said Fleur, and pitched hers in. She lost, but they let her scrape along, cent by cent. And then she won some. She played unevenly, as if chance was all she had. She reeled them in. The game went on. The dog was stiff now, poised on Lily's knees, a ball of vicious muscle with its yellow eyes slit in concentration. It gave advice, seemed to sniff the lay of Fleur's cards, twitched and nudged. Fleur was up, then down, saved by a scratch. Tor dealt seven cards, three down. The pot grew, round by round, until it held all the money. Nobody folded. Then it all rode on one last card and they went silent. Fleur picked hers up and blew a long breath. The heat lowered like a bell. Her card shook, but she stayed in.

Lily smiled and took the dog's head tenderly between his palms.   45

"Say, Fatso," he said, crooning the words, "you reckon that girl's bluffing?"

The dog whined and Lily laughed. "Me too," he said, "let's show." He swept his bills and coins into the pot and then they turned their cards over.

Lily looked once, looked again, then he squeezed the dog up like a fist of dough and slammed it on the table.

Fleur threw her arms out and drew the money over, grinning that same wolf grin that she'd used on me, the grin that had them. She jammed the bills in her dress, scooped the coins up in waxed white paper that she tied with string.

"Let's go another round," said Lily, his voice choked with burrs. But Fleur   50
opened her mouth and yawned, then walked out back to gather slops for the one big hog that was waiting in the stock pen to be killed.

The men sat still as rocks, their hands spread on the oiled wood table. Dutch had chewed his cigar to damp shreds, Tor's eye was dull. Lily's gaze was the only one to follow Fleur. I didn't move. I felt them gathering, saw my stepfather's veins, the ones in his forehead that stood out in anger. The dog had rolled off the table and curled in a knot below the counter, where none of the men could touch it.

Lily rose and stepped out back to the closet of ledgers where Pete kept his private stock. He brought back a bottle, uncorked and tipped it between his fingers. The lump in his throat moved, then he passed it on. They drank, quickly felt the whiskey's fire, and planned with their eyes things they couldn't say out loud.

When they left, I followed. I hid out back in the clutter of broken boards and chicken crates beside the stock pen, where they waited. Fleur could not be seen at first, and then the moon broke and showed her, slipping cautiously along the rough board chute with a bucket in her hand. Her hair fell, wild and coarse, to her waist, and her dress was a floating patch in the dark. She made a pig-calling sound, rang the tin pail lightly against the wood, froze suspiciously. But too late. In the sound of the ring Lily moved, fat and nimble, stepped right behind Fleur and put out his creamy hands. At his first touch, she whirled and doused him with the bucket of sour slops. He pushed her against the big fence and the package of coins split, went clinking and jumping, winked against the wood. Fleur rolled over once and vanished in the yard.

The moon fell behind a curtain of ragged clouds, and Lily followed into the dark muck. But he tripped, pitched over the huge flank of the pig, who lay mired to the snout, heavily snoring. I sprang out of the weeds and climbed the side of the pen, stuck like glue. I saw the sow rise to her neat, knobby knees, gain her balance, and sway, curious, as Lily stumbled forward. Fleur had backed into the angle of rough wood just beyond, and when Lily tried to jostle past, the sow tipped up on her hind legs and struck, quick and hard as a snake. She plunged her head into Lily's thick side and snatched a mouthful of his shirt. She lunged again, caught him lower, so that he grunted in pained surprise. He seemed to ponder, breathing deep. Then he launched his huge body in a swimmer's dive.

The sow screamed as his body smacked over hers. She rolled, striking out   55
with her knife-sharp hooves, and Lily gathered himself upon her, took her foot-long face by the ears and scraped her snout and cheeks against the trestles of the pen. He hurled the sow's tight skull against an iron post, but instead of knocking her dead, he merely woke her from her dream.

She reared, shrieked, drew him with her so that they posed standing upright. They bowed jerkily to each other, as if to begin. Then his arms swung and flailed. She sank her black fangs into his shoulder, clasping him, dancing him forward and backward through the pen. Their steps picked up pace, went wild. The two dipped as one, box-stepped, tripped each other. She ran her split foot through his hair. He grabbed her kinked tail. They went down and came up, the same shape and then the same color, until the men couldn't tell one from the other in that light and Fleur was able to launch herself over the gates, swing down, hit gravel.

The men saw, yelled, and chased her at a dead run to the smokehouse. And Lily too, once the sow gave up in disgust and freed him. That is where I should have gone to Fleur, saved her, thrown myself on Dutch. But I went stiff with fear and couldn't unlatch myself from the trestles or move at all. I closed my eyes and put my head in my arms, tried to hide, so there is nothing to describe but what I couldn't block out, Fleur's hoarse breath, so loud it filled me, her cry in the old language, and my name repeated over and over among the words.

The heat was still dense the next morning when I came back to work. Fleur was gone but the men were there, slack-faced, hung over. Lily was paler and softer than ever, as if his flesh had steamed on his bones. They smoked, took pulls off a bottle. It wasn't noon yet. I worked awhile, waiting shop and sharpening steel. But I was sick, I was smothered, I was sweating so hard that my hands slipped on the knives, and I wiped my fingers clean of the greasy touch of the customers' coins. Lily opened his mouth and roared once, not in anger. There was no meaning to the sound. His boxer dog, sprawled limp beside his foot, never lifted its head. Nor did the other men.

They didn't notice when I stepped outside, hoping for a clear breath. And then I forgot them because I knew that we were all balanced, ready to tip, to fly, to be crushed as soon as the weather broke. The sky was so low that I felt the weight of it like a yoke. Clouds hung down, witch teats, a tornado's green-brown cones, and as I watched one flicked out and became a delicate probing thumb. Even as I picked up my heels and ran back inside, the wind blew suddenly, cold, and then came rain.

Inside, the men had disappeared already and the whole place was trembling as if a huge hand was pinched at the rafters, shaking it. I ran straight through, screaming for Dutch or for any of them, and then I stopped at the heavy doors of the lockers, where they had surely taken shelter. I stood there a moment. Everything went still. Then I heard a cry building in the wind, faint at first, a whistle and then a shrill scream that tore through the walls and gathered around me, spoke plain so I understood that I should move, put my arms out, and slam down the great iron bar that fit across the hasp and lock.

Outside, the wind was stronger, like a hand held against me. I struggled forward. The bushes tossed, the awnings flapped off storefronts, the rails of porches rattled. The odd cloud became a fat snout that nosed along the earth and sniffled, jabbed, picked at things, sucked them up, blew them apart, rooted around as if it was following a certain scent, then stopped behind me at the butcher shop and bored down like a drill.

I went flying, landed somewhere in a ball. When I opened my eyes and looked, stranger things were happening.

A herd of cattle flew through the air like giant birds, dropping dung, their mouths opened in stunned bellows. A candle, still lighted, blew past, and tables, napkins, garden tools, a whole school of drifting eyeglasses, jackets on hangers, hams, a checkerboard, a lampshade, and at last the sow from behind the lockers, on the run, her hooves a blur, set free, swooping, diving, screaming as everything in Argus fell apart and got turned upside down, smashed, and thoroughly wrecked.

Days passed before the town went looking for the men. They were bachelors, after all, except for Tor, whose wife had suffered a blow to the head that made her forgetful. Everyone was occupied with digging out, in high relief because even though the Catholic steeple had been torn off like a peaked cap and sent across five fields, those huddled in the cellar were unhurt. Walls had fallen, windows were demolished, but the stores were intact and so were the bankers and shop owners who had taken refuge in their safes or beneath their cash registers. It was a fair-minded disaster, no one could be said to have suffered much more than the next, at least not until Fritzie and Pete came home.

60

Of all the businesses in Argus, Kozka's Meats had suffered worst. The boards of the front building had been split to kindling, piled in a huge pyramid, and the shop equipment was blasted far and wide. Pete paced off the distance the iron bathtub had been flung—a hundred feet. The glass candy case went fifty, and landed without so much as a cracked pane. There were other surprises as well, for the back rooms where Fritzie and Pete lived were undisturbed. Fritzie said the dust still coated her china figures, and upon her kitchen table, in the ashtray, perched the last cigarette she'd put out in haste. She lit it up and finished it, looking through the window. From there, she could see that the old smokehouse Fleur had slept in was crushed to a reddish sand and the stockpens were completely torn apart, the rails stacked helter-skelter. Fritzie asked for Fleur. People shrugged. Then she asked about the others and, suddenly, the town understood that three men were missing.

There was a rally of help, a gathering of shovels and volunteers. We passed boards from hand to hand, stacked them, uncovered what lay beneath the pile of jagged splinters. The lockers, full of the meat that was Pete and Fritzie's investment, slowly came into sight, still intact. When enough room was made for a man to stand on the roof, there were calls, a general urge to hack through and see what lay below. But Fritzie shouted that she wouldn't allow it because the meat would spoil. And so the work continued, board by board, until at last the heavy oak doors of the freezer were revealed and people pressed to the entry. Everyone wanted to be the first, but since it was my stepfather lost, I was let go in when Pete and Fritzie wedged through into the sudden icy air.

Pete scraped a match on his boot, lit the lamp Fritzie held, and then the three of us stood still in its circle. Light glared off the skinned and hanging carcasses, the crates of wrapped sausages, the bright and cloudy blocks of lake ice, pure as winter. The cold bit into us, pleasant at first, then numbing. We must have stood there a couple of minutes before we saw the men, or more rightly, the humps of fur, the iced and shaggy hides they wore, the bearskins they had taken down and wrapped around themselves. We stepped closer and tilted the lantern beneath the flaps of fur into their faces. The dog was there, perched among them, heavy as a doorstop. The three had hunched around a barrel where the game was still laid out, and a dead lantern and an empty bottle, too. But they had thrown down their last hands and hunkered tight, clutching one another, knuckles raw from beating at the door they had also attacked with hooks. Frost stars gleamed off their eyelashes and the stubble of their beards. Their faces were set in concentration, mouths open as if to speak some careful thought, some agreement they'd come to in each other's arms.

Power travels in the bloodlines, handed out before birth. It comes down through the hands, which in the Pillagers were strong and knotted, big, spidery, and rough, with sensitive fingertips good at dealing cards. It comes through the eyes, too, belligerent, darkest brown, the eyes of those in the bear clan, impolite as they gaze directly at a person.

In my dreams, I look straight back at Fleur, at the men. I am no longer the watcher on the dark sill, the skinny girl.

The blood draws us back, as if it runs through a vein of earth. I've come   70
home and, except for talking to my cousins, live a quiet life. Fleur lives quiet too,
down on Lake Turcot with her boat. Some say she's married to the waterman,
Misshepeshu, or that she's living in shame with white men or windigos, or that
she's killed them all. I'm about the only one here who ever goes to visit her. Last
winter, I went to help out in her cabin when she bore the child, whose green eyes
and skin the color of an old penny made more talk, as no one could decide if the
child was mixed blood or what, fathered in a smokehouse, or by a man with brass
scales, or by the lake. The girl is bold, smiling in her sleep, as if she knows what
people wonder, as if she hears the old men talk, turning the story over. It comes
up different every time and has no ending, no beginning. They get the middle
wrong too. They only know that they don't know anything.   [1986]

THINKING ABOUT THE TEXT

1. Should this story be called "Pauline" since she is the narrator and commits the climactic act of revenge?

2. Repeatedly Pauline associates Fleur with supernatural forces. What is the
   effect of these associations on you? If Erdrich had omitted them, would
   the story's impact have been different? If so, how?

3. In the process of reading the story, did you expect that the men would violently turn on Fleur, or were you surprised when they did? Note specific
   things that affected your ability to predict what would happen.

4. How do racial differences figure in this story? What role do gender differences play? Are race and gender equally relevant here?

5. Before she closes the door on the men, Pauline evidently feels guilty
   because she didn't help Fleur fight them. Is Pauline right to feel this way?
   Why, or why not? Was Pauline justified in taking revenge? Identify some
   warrants or assumptions behind your answer.

MAKING COMPARISONS

1. In both Poe's and Erdrich's stories, the narrator takes revenge by entomb-
   ing someone. Compare how the stories describe this act. Does one story
   present it in a more horrifying way?

2. Both Poe's story and Erdrich's end by giving you brief glimpses of the
   avenger's thoughts some time after the act of revenge. Do these leaps forward have the same effect on you? Identify how each contributes to the
   overall meaning.

3. At the end of "Fleur," Pauline refers to the old men's talking about the origins of Fleur's child. Her last sentence is "They only know that they don't
   know anything." Would you apply the same statement to yourself as someone analyzing Erdrich's story? As someone attempting to understand
   Poe's? Explain your reasoning.

ANDRE DUBUS
Killings

Andre Dubus (1936–1999) served five years in the Marine Corps, attaining the rank of captain before becoming a full-time writer of short stories. Dubus lived in Haverhill, Massachusetts, and much of his fiction is set in the Merrimack Valley north of Boston. This is true of the following story, which appeared in his collection Finding a Girl in America *(1980) and was reprinted in his* Selected Stories *(1988). In 1991, Dubus also published a collection of essays,* Broken Vessels. *In part, the book deals with a 1986 accident that changed his life. Getting out of his car to aid stranded motorists, he was struck by another car; he eventually lost most of one leg and power over the other. Though confined to a wheelchair, Dubus continued to work actively. In 1996, he published his last collection of stories,* Dancing After Hours, *and in 1998, another volume of essays entitled* Meditations from a Moveable Chair. *Two years after he died came a much-acclaimed film adaptation of "Killings," entitled* In the Bedroom *(2001).*

On the August morning when Matt Fowler buried his youngest son, Frank, who had lived for twenty-one years, eight months, and four days, Matt's older son, Steve, turned to him as the family left the grave and walked between their friends, and said: "I should kill him." He was twenty-eight, his brown hair starting to thin in front where he used to have a cowlick. He bit his lower lip, wiped his eyes, then said it again. Ruth's arm, linked with Matt's, tightened; he looked at her. Beneath her eyes there was swelling from the three days she had suffered. At the limousine Matt stopped and looked back at the grave, the casket, and the Congregationalist minister who he thought had probably had a difficult job with the eulogy though he hadn't seemed to, and the old funeral director who was saying something to the six young pallbearers. The grave was on a hill and overlooked the Merrimack, which he could not see from where he stood; he looked at the opposite bank, at the apple orchard with its symmetrically planted trees going up a hill.

Next day Steve drove with his wife back to Baltimore where he managed the branch office of a bank, and Cathleen, the middle child, drove with her husband back to Syracuse. They had left the grandchildren with friends. A month after the funeral Matt played poker at Willis Trottier's because Ruth, who knew this was the second time he had been invited, told him to go, he couldn't sit home with her for the rest of her life, she was all right. After the game Willis went outside to tell everyone good night and, when the others had driven away, he walked with Matt to his car. Willis was a short, silver-haired man who had opened a diner after World War II, his trade then mostly very early breakfast, which he cooked, and then lunch for the men who worked at the leather and shoe factories. He now owned a large restaurant.

"He walks the Goddamn streets," Matt said.

"I know. He was in my place last night, at the bar. With a girl."

"I don't see him. I'm in the store all the time. Ruth sees him. She sees him   5
too much. She was at Sunnyhurst today getting cigarettes and aspirin, and there
he was. She can't even go out for cigarettes and aspirin. It's killing her."

"Come back in for a drink."

Matt looked at his watch. Ruth would be asleep. He walked with Willis back
into the house, pausing at the steps to look at the starlit sky. It was a cool summer
night; he thought vaguely of the Red Sox, did not even know if they were at home
tonight; since it happened he had not been able to think about any of the small
pleasures he believed he had earned, as he had earned also what was shattered
now forever: the quietly harried and quietly pleasurable days of fatherhood. They
went inside. Willis's wife, Martha, had gone to bed hours ago, in the rear of the
large house which was rigged with burglar and fire alarms. They went downstairs
to the game room: the television set suspended from the ceiling, the pool table,
the poker table with beer cans, cards, chips, filled ashtrays, and the six chairs
where Matt and his friends had sat, the friends picking up the old banter as
though he had only been away on vacation; but he could see the affection and
courtesy in their eyes. Willis went behind the bar and mixed them each a Scotch
and soda; he stayed behind the bar and looked at Matt sitting on the stool.

"How often have you thought about it?" Willis said.

"Every day since he got out. I didn't think about bail. I thought I wouldn't
have to worry about him for years. She sees him all the time. It makes her cry."

"He was in my place a long time last night. He'll be back."   10

"Maybe he won't."

"The band. He likes the band."

"What's he doing now?"

"He's tending bar up to Hampton Beach. For a friend. Ever notice even the
worst bastard always has friends? He couldn't get work in town. It's just tourists
and kids up to Hampton. Nobody knows him. If they do, they don't care. They
drink what he mixes."

"Nobody tells me about him."   15

"I hate him, Matt. My boys went to school with him. He was the same then.
Know what he'll do? Five at the most. Remember that woman about seven years
ago? Shot her husband and dropped him off the bridge in the Merrimack with a
hundred-pound sack of cement and said all the way through it that nobody
helped her. Know where she is now? She's in Lawrence now, a secretary. And
whoever helped her, where the hell is he?"

"I've got a .38 I've had for years, I take it to the store now. I tell Ruth it's for
the night deposits. I tell her things have changed: we got junkies here now too.
Lots of people without jobs. She knows though."

"What does she know?"

"She knows I started carrying it after the first time she saw him in town. She
knows it's in case I see him, and there's some kind of a situation —"

He stopped, looked at Willis, and finished his drink. Willis mixed him   20
another.

"What kind of situation?"

"Where he did something to me. Where I could get away with it."

"How does Ruth feel about that?"

"She doesn't know."

"You said she does, she's got it figured out."   25

He thought of her that afternoon: when she went into Sunnyhurst, Strout was waiting at the counter while the clerk bagged the things he had bought; she turned down an aisle and looked at soup cans until he left.

"Ruth would shoot him herself, if she thought she could hit him."

"You got a permit?"

"No."

"I do. You could get a year for that."   30

"Maybe I'll get one. Or maybe I won't. Maybe I'll just stop bringing it to the store."

Richard Strout was twenty-six years old, a high school athlete, football scholarship to the University of Massachusetts where he lasted for almost two semesters before quitting in advance of the final grades that would have forced him not to return. People then said: Dickie can do the work; he just doesn't want to. He came home and did construction work for his father but refused his father's offer to learn the business; his two older brothers had learned it, so that Strout and Sons trucks going about town, and signs on construction sites, now slashed wounds into Matt Fowler's life. Then Richard married a young girl and became a bartender, his salary and tips augmented and perhaps sometimes matched by his father, who also posted his bond. So his friends, his enemies (he had those: fist fights or, more often, boys and then young men who had not fought him when they thought they should have), and those who simply knew him by face and name, had a series of images of him which they recalled when they heard of the killing: the high school running back, the young drunk in bars, the oblivious hard-hatted young man eating lunch at a counter, the bartender who could perhaps be called courteous but not more than that: as he tended bar, his dark eyes and dark, wide-jawed face appeared less sullen, near blank.

One night he beat Frank. Frank was living at home and waiting for September, for graduate school in economics, and working as a lifeguard at Salisbury Beach, where he met Mary Ann Strout, in her first month of separation. She spent most days at the beach with her two sons. Before ten o'clock one night Frank came home; he had driven to the hospital first, and he walked into the living room with stitches over his right eye and both lips bright and swollen.

"I'm all right," he said, when Matt and Ruth stood up, and Matt turned off the television, letting Ruth get to him first: the tall, muscled but slender suntanned boy. Frank tried to smile at them but couldn't because of his lips.

"It was her husband, wasn't it?" Ruth said.   35

"Ex," Frank said. "He dropped in."

Matt gently held Frank's jaw and turned his face to the light, looked at the stitches, the blood under the white of the eye, the bruised flesh.

"Press charges," Matt said.

"No."

"What's to stop him from doing it again? Did you hit him at all? Enough so   40
he won't want to next time?"

"I don't think I touched him."

"So what are you going to do?"

"Take karate," Frank said, and tried again to smile.

"That's not the problem," Ruth said.

"You know you like her," Frank said.

"I like a lot of people. What about the boys? Did they see it?"

"They were asleep."

"Did you leave her alone with him?"

"He left first. She was yelling at him. I believe she had a skillet in her hand."

"Oh for God's sake," Ruth said.

Matt had been dealing with that too: at the dinner table on evenings when Frank wasn't home, was eating with Mary Ann; or, on the other nights—and Frank was with her every night—he talked with Ruth while they watched television, or lay in bed with the windows open and he smelled the night air and imagined, with both pride and muted sorrow, Frank in Mary Ann's arms. Ruth didn't like it because Mary Ann was in the process of divorce, because she had two children, because she was four years older than Frank, and finally—she told this in bed, where she had during all of their marriage told him of her deepest feelings: of love, of passion, of fears about one of the children, of pain Matt had caused her or she had caused him—she was against it because of what she had heard: that the marriage had gone bad early, and for most of it Richard and Mary Ann had both played around.

"That can't be true," Matt said. "Strout wouldn't have stood for it."

"Maybe he loves her."

"He's too hot-tempered. He couldn't have taken that."

But Matt knew Strout had taken it, for he had heard the stories too. He wondered who had told them to Ruth; and he felt vaguely annoyed and isolated: living with her for thirty-one years and still not knowing what she talked about with her friends. On these summer nights he did not so much argue with her as try to comfort her, but finally there was no difference between the two: she had concrete objections, which he tried to overcome. And in his attempt to do this, he neglected his own objections, which were the same as hers, so that as he spoke to her he felt as disembodied as he sometimes did in the store when he helped a man choose a blouse or dress or piece of costume jewelry for his wife.

"The divorce doesn't mean anything," he said. "She was young and maybe she liked his looks and then after a while she realized she was living with a bastard. I see it as a positive thing."

"She's not divorced yet."

"It's the same thing. Massachusetts has crazy laws, that's all. Her age is no problem. What's it matter when she was born? And that other business: even if it's true, which it probably isn't, it's got nothing to do with Frank, and it's in the past. And the kids are no problem. She's been married six years; she ought to have kids. Frank likes them. He plays with them. And he's not going to marry her anyway, so it's not a problem of money."

"Then what's he doing with her?"

"She probably loves him, Ruth. Girls always have. Why can't we just leave it at that?"

"He got home at six o'clock Tuesday morning."

"I didn't know you knew. I've already talked to him about it."

Which he had: since he believed almost nothing he told Ruth, he went to Frank with what he believed. The night before, he had followed Frank to the car after dinner.

"You wouldn't make much of a burglar," he said.

"How's that?"

Matt was looking up at him; Frank was six feet tall, an inch and a half taller than Matt, who had been proud when Frank at seventeen outgrew him; he had only felt uncomfortable when he had to reprimand or caution him. He touched Frank's bicep, thought of the young taut passionate body, believed he could sense the desire, and again he felt the pride and sorrow and envy too, not knowing whether he was envious of Frank or Mary Ann.

"When you came in yesterday morning, I woke up. One of these mornings your mother will. And I'm the one who'll have to talk to her. She won't interfere with you. Okay? I know it means—" But he stopped, thinking: I know it means getting up and leaving that suntanned girl and going sleepy to the car, I know—

"Okay," Frank said, and touched Matt's shoulder and got into the car.

There had been other talks, but the only long one was their first one: a night driving to Fenway Park, Matt having ordered the tickets so they could talk, and knowing when Frank said yes, he would go, that he knew the talk was coming too. It took them forty minutes to get to Boston, and they talked about Mary Ann until they joined the city traffic along the Charles River, blue in the late sun. Frank told him all the things that Matt would later pretend to believe when he told them to Ruth.

"It seems like a lot for a young guy to take on," Matt finally said.

"Sometimes it is. But she's worth it."

"Are you thinking about getting married?"

"We haven't talked about it. She can't for over a year. I've got school."

"I *do* like her," Matt said.

He did. Some evenings, when the long summer sun was still low in the sky, Frank brought her home; they came into the house smelling of suntan lotion and the sea, and Matt gave them gin and tonics and started the charcoal in the back- yard, and looked at Mary Ann in the lawn chair: long and very light brown hair (Matt thinking that twenty years ago she would have dyed it blonde), and the long brown legs he loved to look at; her face was pretty; she had probably never in her adult life gone unnoticed into a public place. It was in her wide brown eyes that she looked older than Frank; after a few drinks Matt thought what he saw in her eyes was something erotic, testament to the rumors about her; but he knew it wasn't that, or all that: she had, very young, been through a sort of pain that his children, and he and Ruth, had been spared. In the moments of his recognizing that pain, he wanted to tenderly touch her hair, wanted with some gesture to give her solace and hope. And he would glance at Frank, and hope they would love each other, hope Frank would soothe that pain in her heart, take it from her eyes; and her divorce, her age, and her children did not matter at all. On the first two evenings she did not bring her boys, and then Ruth asked her to bring them the next time. In bed that night Ruth said, "She hasn't brought them because she's embarrassed. She shouldn't feel embarrassed."

Richard Strout shot Frank in front of the boys. They were sitting on the living room floor watching television, Frank sitting on the couch, and Mary Ann just returning from the kitchen with a tray of sandwiches. Strout came in the front door and shot Frank twice in the chest and once in the face with a 9 mm automatic. Then he looked at the boys and Mary Ann, and went home to wait for the police.

It seemed to Matt that from the time Mary Ann called weeping to tell him until now, a Saturday night in September, sitting in the car with Willis, parked beside Strout's car, waiting for the bar to close, that he had not so much moved through his life as wandered through it, his spirits like a dazed body bumping into furniture and corners. He had always been a fearful father: when his children were young, at the start of each summer he thought of them drowning in a pond or the sea, and he was relieved when he came home in the evenings and they were there; usually that relief was his only acknowledgment of his fear, which he never spoke of, and which he controlled within his heart. As he had when they were very young and all of them in turn, Cathleen too, were drawn to the high oak in the backyard, and had to climb it. Smiling, he watched them, imagining the fall: and he was poised to catch the small body before it hit the earth. Or his legs were poised; his hands were in his pockets or his arms were folded and, for the child looking down, he appeared relaxed and confident while his heart beat with the two words he wanted to call out but did not: *Don't fall.* In winter he was less afraid: he made sure the ice would hold him before they skated, and he brought or sent them to places where they could sled without ending in the street. So he and his children had survived their childhood, and he only worried about them when he knew they were driving a long distance, and then he lost Frank in a way no father expected to lose his son, and he felt that all the fears he had borne while they were growing up, and all the grief he had been afraid of, had backed up like a huge wave and struck him on the beach and swept him out to sea. Each day he felt the same and when he was able to forget how he felt, when he was able to force himself not to feel that way, the eyes of his clerks and customers defeated him. He wished those eyes were oblivious, even cold; he felt he was withering in their tenderness. And beneath his listless wandering, every day in his soul he shot Richard Strout in the face; while Ruth, going about town on errands, kept seeing him. And at night in bed she would hold Matt and cry, or sometimes she was silent and Matt would touch her tightening arm, her clenched fist.

As his own right fist was now, squeezing the butt of the revolver, the last of the drinkers having left the bar, talking to each other, going to their separate cars which were in the lot in front of the bar, out of Matt's vision. He heard their voices, their cars, and then the ocean again, across the street. The tide was in and sometimes it smacked the sea wall. Through the windshield he looked at the dark red side wall of the bar, and then to his left, past Willis, at Strout's car, and through its windows he could see the now-emptied parking lot, the road, the sea wall. He could smell the sea.

The front door of the bar opened and closed again and Willis looked at Matt then at the corner of the building; when Strout came around it alone Matt got out of the car, giving up the hope he had kept all night (and for the past week) that Strout would come out with friends, and Willis would simply drive away; thinking: *All right then. All right*; and he went around the front of Willis's car, and at Strout's he stopped and aimed over the hood at Strout's blue shirt ten feet away. Willis was aiming too, crouched on Matt's left, his elbow resting on the hood.

"Mr. Fowler," Strout said. He looked at each of them, and at the guns. "Mr.   80
Trottier."

Then Matt, watching the parking lot and the road, walked quickly between the car and the building and stood behind Strout. He took one leather glove from his pocket and put it on his left hand.

"Don't talk. Unlock the front and back and get in."

Strout unlocked the front door, reached in and unlocked the back, then got in, and Matt slid into the back seat, closed the door with his gloved hand, and touched Strout's head once with the muzzle.

"It's cocked. Drive to your house."

When Strout looked over his shoulder to back the car, Matt aimed at his   85
temple and did not look at his eyes.

"Drive slowly," he said. "Don't try to get stopped."

They drove across the empty front lot and onto the road, Willis's headlights shining into the car; then back through town, the sea wall on the left hiding the beach, though far out Matt could see the ocean; he uncocked the revolver; on the right were the places, most with their neon signs off, that did so much business in summer: the lounges and cafés and pizza houses, the street itself empty of traffic, the way he and Willis had known it would be when they decided to take Strout at the bar rather than knock on his door at two o'clock one morning and risk that one insomniac neighbor. Matt had not told Willis he was afraid he could not be alone with Strout for very long, smell his smells, feel the presence of his flesh, hear his voice, and then shoot him. They left the beach town and then were on the high bridge over the channel: to the left the smacking curling white at the breakwater and beyond that the dark sea and the full moon, and down to his right the small fishing boats bobbing at anchor in the cove. When they left the bridge, the sea was blocked by abandoned beach cottages, and Matt's left hand was sweating in the glove. Out here in the dark in the car he believed Ruth knew. Willis had come to his house at eleven and asked if he wanted a nightcap; Matt went to the bedroom for his wallet, put the gloves in one trouser pocket and the .38 in the other and went back to the living room, his hand in his pocket covering the bulge of the cool cylinder pressed against his fingers, the butt against his palm. When Ruth said good night she looked at his face, and he felt she could see in his eyes the gun, and the night he was going to. But he knew he couldn't trust what he saw. Willis's wife had taken her sleeping pill, which gave her eight hours—the reason, Willis had told Matt, he had the alarms installed, for nights when he was late at the restaurant—and when it was all done and Willis got home he would leave ice and a trace of Scotch and soda in two glasses in the game room and tell Martha in the morning that he had left the restaurant early and brought Matt home for a drink.

"He was making it with my wife." Strout's voice was careful, not pleading.

Matt pressed the muzzle against Strout's head, pressed it harder than he wanted to, feeling through the gun Strout's head flinching and moving forward; then he lowered the gun to his lap.

"Don't talk," he said.   90

Strout did not speak again. They turned west, drove past the Dairy Queen closed until spring, and the two lobster restaurants that faced each other and were crowded all summer and were now also closed, onto the short bridge crossing the tidal stream, and over the engine Matt could hear through his open window the water rushing inland under the bridge; looking to his left he saw its swift moonlit current going back into the marsh which, leaving the bridge, they entered: the salt marsh stretching out on both sides, the grass tall in patches but mostly low and leaning earthward as though windblown, a large dark rock sitting as though it rested on nothing but itself, and shallow pools reflecting the bright moon.

Beyond the marsh they drove through woods, Matt thinking now of the hole he and Willis had dug last Sunday afternoon after telling their wives they were going to Fenway Park. They listened to the game on a transistor radio, but heard none of it as they dug into the soft earth on the knoll they had chosen because elms and maples sheltered it. Already some leaves had fallen. When the hole was deep enough they covered it and the piled earth with dead branches, then cleaned their shoes and pants and went to a restaurant farther up in New Hampshire where they ate sandwiches and drank beer and watched the rest of the game on television. Looking at the back of Strout's head he thought of Frank's grave; he had not been back to it; but he would go before winter, and its second burial of snow.

He thought of Frank sitting on the couch and perhaps talking to the children as they watched television, imagined him feeling young and strong, still warmed from the sun at the beach, and feeling loved, hearing Mary Ann moving about in the kitchen, hearing her walking into the living room; maybe he looked up at her and maybe she said something, looking at him over the tray of sandwiches, smiling at him, saying something the way women do when they offer food as a gift, then the front door opening and this son of a bitch coming in and Frank seeing that he meant the gun in his hand, this son of a bitch and his gun the last person and thing Frank saw on earth.

When they drove into town the streets were nearly empty: a few slow cars, a policeman walking his beat past the darkened fronts of stores. Strout and Matt both glanced at him as they drove by. They were on the main street, and all the stoplights were blinking yellow. Willis and Matt had talked about that too: the lights changed at midnight, so there would be no place Strout had to stop and where he might try to run. Strout turned down the block where he lived and Willis's headlights were no longer with Matt in the back seat. They had planned that too, had decided it was best for just the one car to go to the house, and again

Matt had said nothing about his fear of being alone with Strout, especially in his house: a duplex, dark as all the houses on the street were, the street itself lit at the corner of each block. As Strout turned into the driveway Matt thought of the one insomniac neighbor, thought of some man or woman sitting alone in the dark living room, watching the all-night channel from Boston. When Strout stopped the car near the front of the house, Matt said: "Drive it to the back."

He touched Strout's head with the muzzle.   95

"You wouldn't have it cocked, would you? For when I put on the brakes."
Matt cocked it, and said: "It is now."

Strout waited a moment; then he eased the car forward, the engine doing little more than idling, and as they approached the garage he gently braked. Matt opened the door, then took off the glove and put it in his pocket. He stepped out and shut the door with his hip and said: "All right."

Strout looked at the gun, then got out, and Matt followed him across the grass, and as Strout unlocked the door Matt looked quickly at the row of small backyards on either side, and scattered tall trees, some evergreens, others not, and he thought of the red and yellow leaves on the trees over the hole, saw them falling soon, probably in two weeks, dropping slowly, covering. Strout stepped into the kitchen.

"Turn on the light."   100

Strout reached to the wall switch, and in the light Matt looked at his wide back, the dark blue shirt, the white belt, the red plaid pants.

"Where's your suitcase?"

"My suitcase?"

"Where is it?"

"In the bedroom closet."   105

"That's where we're going then. When we get to a door you stop and turn on the light."

They crossed the kitchen, Matt glancing at the sink and stove and refrigerator: no dishes in the sink or even the dish rack beside it, no grease splashings on the stove, the refrigerator door clean and white. He did not want to look at any more but he looked quickly at all he could see: in the living room magazines and newspapers in a wicker basket, clean ashtrays, a record player, the records shelved next to it, then down the hall where, near the bedroom door, hung a color photograph of Mary Ann and the two boys sitting on a lawn—there was no house in the picture—Mary Ann smiling at the camera or Strout or whoever held the camera, smiling as she had on Matt's lawn this summer while he waited for the charcoal and they all talked and he looked at her brown legs and at Frank touching her arm, her shoulder, her hair; he moved down the hall with her smile in his mind, wondering: was that when they were both playing around and she was smiling like that at him and they were happy, even sometimes, making it worth it? He recalled her eyes, the pain in them, and he was conscious of the circles of love he was touching with the hand that held the revolver so tightly now as Strout stopped at the door at the end of the hall.

"There's no wall switch."

"Where's the light?"

"By the bed."   110

"Let's go."

Matt stayed a pace behind, then Strout leaned over and the room was lighted: the bed, a double one, was neatly made; the ashtray on the bedside table clean, the bureau top dustless, and no photographs; probably so the girl—who *was* she?— would not have to see Mary Ann in the bedroom she believed was theirs. But because Matt was a father and a husband, though never an ex-husband, he knew (and did not want to know) that this bedroom had never been theirs alone. Strout turned around; Matt looked at his lips, his wide jaw, and thought of Frank's doomed and fearful eyes looking up from the couch.

"Where's Mr. Trottier?"

"He's waiting. Pack clothes for warm weather."

"What's going on?"   115

"You're jumping bail."

"Mr. Fowler—"

He pointed the cocked revolver at Strout's face. The barrel trembled but not much, not as much as he had expected. Strout went to the closet and got the suit-case from the floor and opened it on the bed. As he went to the bureau, he said: "He was making it with my wife. I'd go pick up my kids and he'd be there. Sometimes he spent the night. My boys told me."

He did not look at Matt as he spoke. He opened the top drawer and Matt stepped closer so he could see Strout's hands: underwear and socks, the socks rolled, the underwear folded and stacked. He took them back to the bed, arranged them neatly in the suitcase, then from the closet he was taking shirts and trousers and a jacket; he laid them on the bed and Matt followed him to the bathroom and watched from the door while he packed those things a person accumulated and that became part of him so that at times in the store Matt felt he was selling more than clothes.

"I wanted to try to get together with her again." He was bent over the suit-   120 case. "I couldn't even talk to her. He was always with her. I'm going to jail for it; if I ever get out I'll be an old man. Isn't that enough?"

"You're not going to jail."

Strout closed the suitcase and faced Matt, looking at the gun. Matt went to his rear, so Strout was between him and the lighted hall; then using his handker-chief he turned off the lamp and said: "Let's go."

They went down the hall, Matt looking again at the photograph, and through the living room and kitchen, Matt turning off the lights and talking, frightened that he was talking, that he was telling this lie he had not planned: "It's the trial. We can't go through that, my wife and me. So you're leaving. We've got you a ticket, and a job. A friend of Mr. Trottier's. Out west. My wife keeps seeing you. We can't have that anymore."

Matt turned out the kitchen light and put the handkerchief in his pocket, and they went down the two brick steps and across the lawn. Strout put the suit-case on the floor of the back seat, then got into the front seat and Matt got in the back and put on his glove and shut the door.

"They'll catch me. They'll check passenger lists."   125

"We didn't use your name."

"They'll figure that out too. You think I wouldn't have done it myself if it was that easy?"

He backed into the street, Matt looking down the gun barrel but not at the profiled face beyond it.

"You were alone," Matt said. "We've got it worked out."

"There's no planes this time of night, Mr. Fowler."   130

"Go back through town. Then north on 125."

They came to the corner and turned, and now Willis's headlights were in the car with Matt.

"Why north, Mr. Fowler?"

"Somebody's going to keep you for a while. They'll take you to the airport." He uncocked the hammer and lowered the revolver to his lap and said wearily: "No more talking."

As they drove back through town, Matt's body sagged, going limp with his   135 spirit and its new and false bond with Strout, the hope his lie had given Strout. He had grown up in this town whose streets had become places of apprehension and pain for Ruth as she drove and walked, doing what she had to do; and for him too, if only in his mind as he worked and chatted six days a week in his store; he wondered now if his lie would have worked, if sending Strout away would have been enough; but then he knew that just thinking of Strout in Montana or whatever place lay at the end of the lie he had told, thinking of him walking the streets there, loving a girl there (who *was* she?) would be enough to slowly rot the rest of his days. And Ruth's. Again he was certain that she knew, that she was waiting for him.

They were in New Hampshire now, on the narrow highway, passing the shopping center at the state line, and then houses and small stores and sandwich shops. There were few cars on the road. After ten minutes he raised his trembling hand, touched Strout's neck with the gun, and said: "Turn in up here. At the dirt road."

Strout flicked on the indicator and slowed.

"Mr. Fowler?"

"They're waiting here."

Strout turned very slowly, easing his neck away from the gun. In the moon-   140 light the road was light brown, lighter and yellowed where the headlights shone; weeds and a few trees grew on either side of it, and ahead of them were the woods.

"There's nothing back here, Mr. Fowler."

"It's for your car. You don't think we'd leave it at the airport, do you?"

He watched Strout's large, big-knuckled hands tighten on the wheel, saw Frank's face that night: not the stitches and bruised eye and swollen lips, but his own hand gently touching Frank's jaw, turning his wounds to the light. They rounded a bend in the road and were out of sight of the highway: tall trees all around them now, hiding the moon. When they reached the abandoned gravel pit on the left, the bare flat earth and steep pale embankment behind it, and the black crowns of trees at its top, Matt said: "Stop here."

Strout stopped but did not turn off the engine. Matt pressed the gun hard against his neck, and he straightened in the seat and looked in the rearview mirror, Matt's eyes meeting his in the glass for an instant before looking at the hair at the end of the gun barrel.

"Turn it off."

145

Strout did, then held the wheel with two hands, and looked in the mirror.

"I'll do twenty years, Mr. Fowler; at least. I'll be forty-six years old."

"That's nine years younger than I am," Matt said, and got out and took off the glove and kicked the door shut. He aimed at Strout's ear and pulled back the hammer. Willis's headlights were off and Matt heard him walking on the soft thin layer of dust, the hard earth beneath it. Strout opened the door, sat for a moment in the interior light, then stepped out onto the road. Now his face was pleading. Matt did not look at his eyes, but he could see it in the lips.

"Just get the suitcase. They're right up the road."

Willis was beside him now, to his left. Strout looked at both guns. Then he 150 opened the back door, leaned in, and with a jerk brought the suitcase out. He was turning to face them when Matt said: "Just walk up the road. Just ahead."

Strout turned to walk, the suitcase in his right hand, and Matt and Willis followed; as Strout cleared the front of his car he dropped the suitcase and, ducking, took one step that was the beginning of a sprint to his right. The gun kicked in Matt's hand, and the explosion of the shot surrounded him, isolated him in a nimbus of sound that cut him off from all his time, all his history, isolated him standing absolutely still on the dirt road with the gun in his hand, looking down at Richard Strout squirming on his belly, kicking one leg behind him, pushing himself forward, toward the woods. Then Matt went to him and shot him once in the back of the head.

Driving south to Boston, wearing both gloves now, staying in the middle lane and looking often in the rearview mirror at Willis's headlights, he relived the suitcase dropping, the quick dip and turn of Strout's back, and the kick of the gun, the sound of the shot. When he walked to Strout, he still existed within the first shot, still trembled and breathed with it. The second shot and the burial seemed to be happening to someone else, someone he was watching. He and Willis each held an arm and pulled Strout face-down off the road and into the woods, his bouncing sliding belt white under the trees where it was so dark that when they stopped at the top of the knoll, panting and sweating, Matt could not see where Strout's blue shirt ended and the earth began. They pulled off the branches then dragged Strout to the edge of the hole and went behind him and lifted his legs and pushed him in. They stood still for a moment. The woods were quiet save for their breathing, and Matt remembered hearing the movements of birds and small animals after the first shot. Or maybe he had not heard them. Willis went down to the road. Matt could see him clearly out on the tan dirt, could see the glint of Strout's car and, beyond the road, the gravel pit. Willis came back up the knoll with the suitcase. He dropped it in the hole and took off his gloves and they went down to his car for the spades. They worked quietly. Sometimes they paused to listen to the woods. When they were finished Willis turned on his flashlight and they covered the earth with leaves and branches and then went down to the spot in front of the car, and while Matt held the light Willis crouched and sprinkled dust on the blood, backing up till he reached the grass and leaves, then he used leaves until they had worked up to the grave again. They did not stop. They walked around the grave and through the woods, using the light on the ground, looking up through the trees to where they ended at the lake. Neither of them spoke above the sounds of their heavy and clumsy strides through low brush and over fallen branches. Then they reached it: wide and dark, lapping softly at the bank, pine needles smooth under Matt's feet, moonlight on the lake, a small island near its middle, with black, tall evergreens. He took out the gun and threw for the island: taking two steps back on the pine needles, striding with the throw and going to one knee as he followed through, looking up to see the dark shapeless object arcing downward, splashing.

They left Strout's car in Boston, in front of an apartment building on Commonwealth Avenue. When they got back to town Willis drove slowly over the bridge and Matt threw the keys into the Merrimack. The sky was turning light. Willis let him out a block from his house, and walking home he listened for sounds from the houses he passed. They were quiet. A light was on in his living room. He turned it off and undressed in there, and went softly toward the bedroom; in the hall he smelled the smoke, and he stood in the bedroom doorway and looked at the orange of her cigarette in the dark. The curtains were closed. He went to the closet and put his shoes on the floor and felt for a hanger.

"Did you do it?" she said.

He went down the hall to the bathroom and in the dark he washed his hands   155
and face. Then he went to her, lay on his back, and pulled the sheet up to his throat.

"Are you all right?" she said.

"I think so."

Now she touched him, lying on her side, her hand on his belly, his thigh.

"Tell me," she said.

He started from the beginning, in the parking lot at the bar; but soon with his   160
eyes closed and Ruth petting him, he spoke of Strout's house: the order, the woman presence, the picture on the wall.

"The way she was smiling," he said.

"What about it?"

"I don't know. Did you ever see Strout's girl? When you saw him in town?"

"No."

"I wonder who she was."   165

Then he thought: *not was: is. Sleeping now she is his girl.* He opened his eyes, then closed them again. There was more light beyond the curtains. With Ruth now he left Strout's house and told again his lie to Strout, gave him again that hope that Strout must have for a while believed, else he would have to believe only the gun pointed at him for the last two hours of his life. And with Ruth he saw again the dropping suitcase, the darting move to the right: and he told of the first shot, feeling her hand on him but his heart isolated still, beating on the road still in that explosion like thunder. He told her the rest, but the words had no images for him, he did not see himself doing what the words said he had done; he only saw himself on that road.

"We can't tell the other kids," she said. "It'll hurt them, thinking he got away. But we mustn't."

"No."

She was holding him, wanting him, and he wished he could make love with her but he could not. He saw Frank and Mary Ann making love in her bed, their eyes closed, their bodies brown and smelling of the sea; the other girl was faceless, bodiless, but he felt her sleeping now; and he saw Frank and Strout, their faces alive; he saw red and yellow leaves falling on the earth, then snow: falling and freezing and falling; and holding Ruth, his cheek touching her breast, he shuddered with a sob that he kept silent in his heart.   [1979]

THINKING ABOUT THE TEXT

1. Here is an issue of cause and effect: Why, evidently, does Matt kill Richard Strout? Consider the possibility that he has more than one reason. Here is an issue of evaluation: To what extent should the reader sympathize with Matt? Identify some things that readers should especially consider in addressing this question.

2. Identify the argument that Richard Strout makes as he tries to keep Matt from killing him. What warrants or assumptions does Strout use? How common is his way of thinking?

3. Why does Willis help Matt take revenge? To what extent does Ruth's thinking resemble her husband's?

4. What is Matt's view of Mary Ann, his late son's girlfriend?

5. After beginning with Frank's funeral, the story features several flashbacks. Only gradually does Dubus provide certain seemingly important facts, such as exactly how Matt's son died. ("Richard Strout shot Frank in front of the boys.") What do you think might have been Dubus's purpose(s) in refusing to be more straightforward? In the last several pages, the story is pretty straightforward, moving step by step through the night of Matt's revenge. Why do you suppose Dubus changed his method of storytelling?

MAKING COMPARISONS

1. Montresor and Matt carefully plan their revenge. But Pauline appears to commit revenge spontaneously, not carefully planning it beforehand. Does this difference matter to you as you judge these three acts of revenge? Why, or why not?

2. How guilty does each of these three avengers feel? Compare their degrees of guilt by citing specific details from each text to support your impressions.

3. Do Poe, Erdrich, and Dubus seem equally committed to making you feel that the settings they describe really exist? Again, support your answer by referring to specific details from each text.

WRITING ABOUT ISSUES

1. Choose one of the three stories in this cluster and write an essay identifying the extent to which readers ought to feel sorry for the victim or victims of revenge. Argue for your position by citing details of the text.

2. In her book *Bird by Bird: Some Instructions on Writing and Life*, Anne Lamott advises would-be fiction writers that a story must culminate in "a killing or a healing or a domination." She goes on to explain:

> It can be a real killing, a murder, or it can be a killing of the spirit, or of something terrible inside one's soul, or it can be a killing of a deadness within, after which the person becomes alive again. The healing may be about union, reclamation, the rescue of a fragile prize. But whatever happens, we need to feel that it was inevitable, that even though we may be amazed, it feels absolutely right, that of course things would come to this, of course they would shake down in this way.

Choose two of the stories in this cluster and write an essay discussing the extent to which they obey Lamott's advice. Refer to specific words in the passage from her, as well as to specific details of the stories. If you wish, feel free to evaluate Lamott's advice. Do you think fiction writers ought to follow it?

3. Gerald Murphy, a famous socialite of the 1920s, once said that "living well is the best revenge." Murphy did not identify whom it was revenge against. Still, his statement is thought-provoking in its suggestion that revenge is not always recognizable as such. "Living well" may be revenge in disguise. Write an essay showing how a specific action you are familiar with can be seen as an act of revenge, even though many people wouldn't realize this. In your essay, also evaluate the action. Do you approve of this act of revenge? Why, or why not?

4. Write an essay examining a real-life legal case that involved one or more of the acts depicted in these stories: for example, rape, sexual relations between employer and employee, racial discrimination, reactions to perceived insults, acts of revenge. To learn important facts about the case, you may have to do research in the library. In your essay, point out at least one issue raised by the case, identify your position on the issue, and support your position. If you wish, refer to any of the stories in this cluster.

LOSING INNOCENCE: RE-VISIONS OF "LITTLE RED RIDING HOOD"

CHARLES PERRAULT, "Little Red Riding Hood"
JACOB AND WILHELM GRIMM, "Little Red Cap"
ANGELA CARTER, "The Company of Wolves"

The tale of Little Red Riding Hood is still told to children throughout the world. In a sense, her adventure is part of their education. What, though, do they learn from this narrative? Scholars have suggested various interpretations. Among the most well-known and provocative is that of psychoanalyst Bruno Bettelheim, who sees the tale as a symbolic treatment of a girl's effort to understand her sexual development. In this view, the story teaches girls to work through adolescent anxieties. But whatever decoding the tale receives, two aspects of it remain important. First, it depicts a child's move from innocence to experience, however these terms are defined. Little Red Riding Hood learns something, largely on her own. Second, more than one version of her story exists; by now, several do. Indeed, the story is worth analyzing because it serves as an instrument of children's education, focuses on a child's discovery, and yet circulates in various forms. Hence, we devote a re-vision cluster to this ever-popular tale, inviting you to compare three particular versions of it: Charles Perrault's from the seventeenth century, the Brothers Grimm's from the nineteenth century, and Angela Carter's modern variation.

BEFORE YOU READ

Write down what you remember about the story of Little Red Riding Hood, and then compare your version with those of your classmates. What elements of the story do your class's various renditions of it have in common? What differences, if any, emerge? Why do you think the story has been so popular?

CHARLES PERRAULT
Little Red Riding Hood

Along with the Brothers Grimm, Charles Perrault (1628–1703) was the most influential teller of the fairy tales many of us learned as children. Born in Paris to a fairly wealthy family, Perrault was trained as a lawyer. For his literary and philosophical achievements, however, Perrault was elected to the prestigious Academie Française in 1671. During his lifetime, he and others were involved in a major cultural dispute over the relative merits of ancient authors and modern ones, with Perrault favoring the more up-to-date group. Later generations remember him best, though, for his 1697 book, Stories or Tales from Times Past, with Morals: Tales of Mother Goose. *This collection included "Le Petit Chaperon Rouge," which English-speaking*

(Jacob and Wilhelm Grimm. Culver Pictures, Inc.)

(Charles Perrault. The Granger Collection, New York.)

(Angela Carter. Miriam Berkley.)

readers have come to know as "Little Red Riding Hood." This story did not completely originate with Perrault; probably he had heard folktales containing some of its narrative elements. Nevertheless, his version became popular on publication and has remained so ever since.

Once upon a time there lived in a certain village a little country girl, the prettiest creature who was ever seen. Her mother was excessively fond of her, and her grandmother doted on her still more. This good woman had a little red riding hood made for her. It suited the girl so extremely well that everybody called her Little Red Riding Hood.

One day her mother, having made some cakes, said to her, "Go, my dear, and see how your grandmother is doing, for I hear she has been very ill. Take her a cake, and this little pot of butter."

Little Red Riding Hood set out immediately to go to her grandmother, who lived in another village.

As she was going through the wood, she met with a wolf, who had a very great mind to eat her up, but he dared not, because of some woodcutters working nearby in the forest. He asked her where she was going. The poor child, who did not know that it was dangerous to stay and talk to a wolf, said to him, "I am going to see my grandmother and carry her a cake and a little pot of butter from my mother."

"Does she live far off?" said the wolf.   5

"Oh I say," answered Little Red Riding Hood. "It is beyond that mill you see there, at the first house in the village."

"Well," said the wolf, "and I'll go and see her too. I'll go this way and go you that, and we shall see who will be there first."

The wolf ran as fast as he could, taking the shortest path, and the little girl took a roundabout way, entertaining herself by gathering nuts, running after butterflies, and gathering bouquets of little flowers. It was not long before the wolf arrived at the old woman's house. He knocked at the door: tap, tap.

"Who's there?"

"Your grandchild, Little Red Riding Hood," replied the wolf, counterfeiting   10
her voice, "who has brought you a cake and a little pot of butter sent you by Mother."

The good grandmother, who was in bed because she was somewhat ill, cried out, "Pull the bobbin, and the latch will go up."

The wolf pulled the bobbin, and the door opened, and then he immediately fell upon the good woman and ate her up in a moment, for it had been more than three days since he had eaten. He then shut the door and got into the grandmother's bed, expecting Little Red Riding Hood, who came some time afterwards and knocked at the door: tap, tap.

"Who's there?"

Little Red Riding Hood, hearing the big voice of the wolf, was at first afraid but, believing her grandmother had a cold and was hoarse, answered, "It is your grandchild Little Red Riding Hood, who has brought you a cake and a little pot of butter Mother sends you."

The wolf cried out to her, softening his voice as much as he could, "Pull the   15
bobbin, and the latch will go up."

Little Red Riding Hood pulled the bobbin, and the door opened.

The wolf, seeing her come in, said to her, hiding himself under the bedclothes, "Put the cake and the little pot of butter upon the stool, and come get into bed with me."

Little Red Riding Hood took off her clothes and got into bed. She was greatly amazed to see how her grandmother looked in her nightclothes and said to her, "Grandmother, what big arms you have!"

"All the better to hug you with, my dear."

"Grandmother, what big legs you have!"   20

"All the better to run with, my child."

"Grandmother, what big ears you have!"

"All the better to hear with, my child."

"Grandmother, what big eyes you have!"

"All the better to see with, my child."   25

"Grandmother, what big teeth you have got!"

"All the better to eat you up with."

And saying these words, this wicked wolf fell upon Little Red Riding Hood, and ate her all up.

Moral: Children, especially attractive, well bred young ladies, should never talk to strangers, for if they should do so, they may well provide dinner for a wolf. I say "wolf," but there are various kinds of wolves. There are also those who are charming, quiet, polite, unassuming, complacent, and sweet, who pursue young women at home and in the streets. And unfortunately, it is these gentle wolves who are the most dangerous ones of all.   [1697]

THINKING ABOUT THE TEXT

1. To what extent does it matter to the story that Little Red Riding Hood is pretty? Would your reaction be the same if you learned she was homely or if you did not know how she looked? Explain.

2. The two main female characters are Little Red Riding Hood and her grandmother. Although the girl's mother appears briefly at the start, she then disappears from the narrative. What purposes are served by Perrault's leaving her out?

3. How would you describe Little Red Riding Hood as Perrault depicts her? Refer to specific details of the text.

4. In this version, Little Red Riding Hood dies. Would you draw different ideas from the text if she had lived? If so, what?

5. Does Perrault's moral seem well connected to the preceding story? Why, or why not? What metaphoric wolves might this moral apply to?

JACOB and WILHELM GRIMM
Little Red Cap

Jacob Grimm (1785–1863) and Wilhelm Grimm (1786–1859) were born in Hanau, Germany, and studied law at Marburg University. They served as linguistics professors at Gottingen University and made major contributions to the historical study of language. The Grimms began to collect folktales from various oral European traditions for their friends but later published their efforts for both children and adults. Their methods became a model for the scientific collection of folktales and folk songs. Today they are known best for their volume Children's and Household Tales, *which was first published in 1812 and went through six more editions, the last in 1857. Their book included their version of the Little Red Riding Hood story, although their title for it was (in English translation) "Little Red Cap."*

Once upon a time there was a sweet little girl. Everyone who saw her liked her, but most of all her grandmother, who did not know what to give the child next. Once she gave her a little cap made of red velvet. Because it suited her so well, and she wanted to wear it all the time, she came to be known as Little Red Cap.

One day her mother said to her, "Come Little Red Cap. Here is a piece of cake and a bottle of wine. Take them to your grandmother. She is sick and weak, and they will do her well. Mind your manners, and give her my greetings. Behave yourself on the way, and do not leave the path, or you might fall down and break the glass, and then there will be nothing for your grandmother. And when you enter her parlor, don't forget to say 'Good morning,' and don't peer into all the corners first."

"I'll do everything just right," said Little Red Cap, shaking her mother's hand.

The grandmother lived out in the woods, a half hour from the village. When Little Red Cap entered the woods, a wolf came up to her. She did not know what a wicked animal he was and was not afraid of him.

"Good day to you, Little Red Cap."   5

"Thank you, wolf."

"Where are you going so early, Little Red Cap?"

"To Grandmother's."

"And what are you carrying under your apron?"

"Grandmother is sick and weak, and I am taking her some cake and wine.   10
We baked yesterday, and they should be good for her and give her strength."

"Little Red Cap, just where does your grandmother live?"

"Her house is a good quarter hour from here in the woods, under the three large oak trees. There's a hedge of hazel bushes there. You must know the place," said Little Red Cap.

The wolf thought to himself, "Now that sweet young thing is a tasty bite for me. She will taste even better than the old woman. You must be sly, and you can catch them both."

He walked along a little while with Little Red Cap. Then he said, "Little Red Cap, just look at the beautiful flowers that are all around us. Why don't you go and take a look? And I don't believe you can hear how beautifully the birds are singing. You are walking along as though you were on your way to school. It is very beautiful in the woods."

Little Red Cap opened her eyes, and when she saw the sunbeams dancing to   15
and fro through the trees and how the ground was covered with beautiful flowers, she thought, "If I take a fresh bouquet to Grandmother, she will be very pleased. Anyway, it is still early, and I'll be home on time." And she ran off the path into the woods looking for flowers. Each time she picked one, she thought that she could see an even more beautiful one a little way off, and she ran after it, going farther and farther into the woods. But the wolf ran straight to the grandmother's house and knocked on the door.

"Who's there?"

"Little Red Cap. I'm bringing you some cake and wine. Open the door."

"Just press the latch," called out the grandmother. "I'm too weak to get up."

The wolf pressed the latch, and the door opened. He stepped inside, went straight to the grandmother's bed, and ate her up. Then he put on her clothes, put her cap on his head, got into her bed, and pulled the curtains shut.

Little Red Cap had run after the flowers. After she had gathered so many that   20
she could not carry any more, she remembered her grandmother and then continued on her way to her house. She found, to her surprise, that the door was open. She walked into the parlor, and everything looked so strange that she thought, "Oh, my God, why am I so afraid? I usually like it at Grandmother's."

She called out, "Good morning!" but received no answer.

Then she went to the bed and pulled back the curtains. Grandmother was lying there with her cap pulled down over her face and looking very strange.

"Oh, Grandmother, what big ears you have!"

"All the better to hear you with."

"Oh, Grandmother, what big eyes you have!"   25

"All the better to see you with."

"Oh, Grandmother, what big hands you have!"

"All the better to grab you with!"

"Oh, Grandmother, what a horribly big mouth you have!"

"All the better to eat you with!"   30

The wolf had scarcely finished speaking when he jumped from the bed with a single leap and ate up poor Little Red Cap. As soon as the wolf had satisfied his desires, he climbed back into bed, fell asleep, and began to snore very loudly.

A huntsman was just passing by. He thought, "The old woman is snoring so loudly. You had better see if something is wrong with her."

He stepped into the parlor, and when he approached the bed, he saw the wolf lying there. "So here I find you, you old sinner," he said. "I have been hunting for you a long time."

He was about to aim his rifle when it occurred to him that the wolf might have eaten the grandmother and that she still might be rescued. So instead of shooting, he took a pair of scissors and began to cut open the wolf's belly. After a few cuts he saw the red cap shining through, and after a few more cuts the girl jumped out, crying, "Oh, I was so frightened! It was so dark inside the wolf's body!"

And then the grandmother came out as well, alive but hardly able to breathe.   35
Then Little Red Cap fetched some large stones. She filled the wolf's body with them, and when he woke up and tried to run away, the stones were so heavy that he immediately fell down dead.

The three of them were happy. The huntsman skinned the wolf and went home with the pelt. The grandmother ate the cake and drank the wine that Little Red Cap had brought. And Little Red Cap thought, "As long as I live, I will never leave the path and run off into the woods by myself if Mother tells me not to."

They also tell how Little Red Cap was taking some baked things to her grandmother another time, when another wolf spoke to her and wanted her to leave the path. But Little Red Cap took care and went straight to Grandmother's.

She told her that she had seen the wolf and that he had wished her a good day but had stared at her in a wicked manner. "If we hadn't been on a public road, he would have eaten me up," she said.

"Come," said the grandmother. "Let's lock the door, so he can't get in."

Soon afterward the wolf knocked on the door and called out, "Open up, Grandmother. It's Little Red Cap, and I'm bringing you some baked things."

They remained silent and did not open the door. Gray-Head crept around 40 the house several times and finally jumped onto the roof. He wanted to wait until Little Red Cap went home that evening and then follow her and eat her up in the darkness. But the grandmother saw what he was up to. There was a large stone trough in front of the house.

"Fetch a bucket, Little Red Cap," she said to the child. "Yesterday I cooked some sausage. Carry the water that I boiled them with to the trough." Little Red Cap carried water until the large, large trough was clear full. The smell of sausage arose into the wolf's nose. He sniffed and looked down, stretching his neck so long that he could no longer hold himself, and he began to slide. He slid off the roof, fell into the trough, and drowned. And Little Red Cap returned home happily, and no one harmed her.   [1857]

THINKING ABOUT THE TEXT

1. Why do you think that, at the beginning of the tale, the Grimms emphasize how sweet and likable Little Red Cap is?

2. To what extent do you blame Little Red Cap for being distracted by the beauty of nature? Explain your reasoning.

3. The Grimms have Little Red Cap and her grandmother rescued by a hunter. What would you say to someone who sees the Grimms as implying that women always need help from a man?

4. The wolf dies because Little Red Cap has filled his body with stones. Why do you think the Grimms did not have the huntsman simply shoot the wolf after freeing Little Red Cap and her grandmother?

5. Why do you think the Grimms added the second story? What is its effect?

MAKING COMPARISONS

1. Does Red Riding Hood seem basically the same in both Perrault's version and the Grimms' version? Refer to specific details of both texts.

2. In Perrault's tale, the wolf persuades Red Riding Hood to take off her clothes and get into bed with him. In the Grimms' account, the wolf jumps up from the bed and eats her. How significant is this difference between the two versions?

3. In Perrault's version, Red Riding Hood and her grandmother die. The Grimms, on the other hand, have them rescued. Do you therefore see these two versions as putting forth different views of life? Explain.

ANGELA CARTER
The Company of Wolves

A native of Sussex, England, Angela Carter (1940–1991) worked in various genres, writing novels, short stories, screenplays, essays, and newspaper articles. Her fiction is most known for imaginatively refashioning classic tales of fantasy, including supernatural and Gothic thrillers as well as fairy tales. Often, Carter rewrote these narratives from a distinctly female point of view, challenging what she saw as their patriarchal values and using them to explore the psychology of both genders. "The Company of Wolves," her version of the Little Red Riding Hood tale, was first published in the journal Bananas *in 1977. It then appeared in Carter's short story volume* The Bloody Chamber *(1979) and was reprinted in* Burning Our Boats *(1995), a posthumous collection of all her stories. This tale also served as the basis for a 1984 film of the same title, which Carter wrote with director Neil Jordan.*

One beast and only one howls in the woods by night.

The wolf is carnivore incarnate, and he's as cunning as he is ferocious; once he's had a taste of flesh then nothing else will do.

At night, the eyes of wolves shine like candle flames, yellowish, reddish, but that is because the pupils of their eyes fatten on darkness and catch the light from your lantern to flash it back to you—red for danger; if a wolf's eyes reflect only moonlight, then they gleam a cold and unnatural green, a mineral, a piercing color. If the benighted traveler spies those luminous, terrible sequins stitched suddenly on the black thickets, then he knows he must run, if fear has not struck him stock-still.

But those eyes are all you will be able to glimpse of the forest assassins as they cluster invisibly round your smell of meat as you go through the wood unwisely late. They will be like shadows, they will be like wraiths, gray members of a congregation of nightmare; hark! his long, wavering howl . . . an aria of fear made audible.

The wolfsong is the sound of the rending you will suffer, in itself a murdering.   5

It is winter and cold weather. In this region of mountain and forest, there is now nothing for the wolves to eat. Goats and sheep are locked up in the byre,° the deer departed for the remaining pasturage on the southern slopes—wolves grow lean and famished. There is so little flesh on them that you could count the starveling ribs through their pelts, if they gave you time before they pounced. Those slavering jaws; the lolling tongue; the rime of saliva on the grizzled chops—of all the teeming perils of the night and the forest, ghosts, hobgoblins, ogres that grill babies upon gridirons, witches that fatten their captives in cages for cannibal tables, the wolf is worst for he cannot listen to reason.

You are always in danger in the forest, where no people are. Step between the portals of the great pines where the shaggy branches tangle about you, trapping

byre: Barn or shed.

the unwary traveler in nets as if the vegetation itself were in a plot with the wolves who live there, as though the wicked trees go fishing on behalf of their friends — step between the gateposts of the forest with the greatest trepidation and infinite precautions, for if you stray from the path for one instant, the wolves will eat you. They are gray as famine, they are as unkind as plague.

The grave-eyed children of the sparse villages always carry knives with them when they go out to tend the little flocks of goats that provide the homesteads with acrid milk and rank, maggoty cheeses. Their knives are half as big as they are, the blades are sharpened daily.

But the wolves have ways of arriving at your own hearthside. We try and try but sometimes we cannot keep them out. There is no winter's night the cottager does not fear to see a lean, gray, famished snout questing under the door, and there was a woman once bitten in her own kitchen as she was straining the macaroni.

Fear and flee the wolf; for, worst of all, the wolf may be more than he seems.   10

There was a hunter once, near here, that trapped a wolf in a pit. This wolf had massacred the sheep and goats; eaten up a mad old man who used to live by himself in a hut halfway up the mountain and sing to Jesus all day; pounced on a girl looking after the sheep, but she made such a commotion that men came with rifles and scared him away and tried to track him into the forest but he was cunning and easily gave them the slip. So this hunter dug a pit and put a duck in it, for bait, all alive-oh; and he covered the pit with straw smeared with wolf dung. Quack, quack! went the duck and a wolf came slinking out of the forest, a big one, a heavy one, he weighed as much as a grown man, and the straw gave way beneath him — into the pit he tumbled. The hunter jumped down after him, slit his throat, cut off all his paws for a trophy.

And then no wolf at all lay in front of the hunter but the bloody trunk of a man, headless, footless, dying, dead.

A witch from up the valley once turned an entire wedding party into wolves because the groom had settled on another girl. She used to order them to visit her, at night, from spite, and they would sit and howl around her cottage for her, serenading her with their misery.

Not so very long ago, a young woman in our village married a man who vanished clean away on her wedding night. The bed was made with new sheets and the bride lay down in it; the groom said, he was going out to relieve himself, insisted on it, for the sake of decency, and she drew the coverlet up to her chin and she lay there. And she waited and she waited and then she waited again — surely he's been gone a long time? Until she jumps up in bed and shrieks to hear a howling, coming on the wind from the forest.

That long-drawn, wavering howl has, for all its fearful resonance, some   15
inherent sadness in it, as if the beasts would love to be less beastly if only they knew how and never cease to mourn their own condition. There is a vast melancholy in the canticles° of the wolves, melancholy infinite as the forest, endless as these long nights of winter and yet that ghastly sadness, that mourning for their own, irremediable appetites, can never move the heart for not one phrase in it

canticles: Songs or chants.

hints at the possibility of redemption; grace could not come to the wolf from its own despair, only through some external mediator, so that, sometimes, the beast will look as if he half welcomes the knife that despatches him.

The young woman's brothers searched the outhouses and the haystacks but never found any remains, so the sensible girl dried her eyes and found herself another husband not too shy to piss into a pot who spent the nights indoors. She gave him a pair of bonny babies and all went right as a trivet until, one freezing night, the night of the solstice, the hinge of the year when things do not fit together as well as they should, the longest night, her first good man came home again.

A great thump on the door announced him as she was stirring the soup for the father of her children, and she knew him the moment she lifted the latch to him although it was years since she'd worn black for him and now he was in rags and his hair hung down his back and never saw a comb, alive with lice.

"Here I am again, missus," he said. "Get me my bowl of cabbage and be quick about it."

Then her second husband came in with wood for the fire and when the first one saw she'd slept with another man and, worse, clapped his red eyes on her little children who'd crept into the kitchen to see what all the din was about, he shouted: "I wish I were a wolf again, to teach this whore a lesson!" So a wolf he instantly became and tore off the eldest boy's left foot before he was chopped up with the hatchet they used for chopping logs. But when the wolf lay bleeding and gasping its last, the pelt peeled off again and he was just as he had been, years ago, when he ran away from his marriage bed, so that she wept and her second husband beat her.

They say there's an ointment the Devil gives you that turns you into a wolf   20
the minute you rub it on. Or that he was born feet first and had a wolf for his father and his torso is a man's but his legs and genitals are a wolf's. And he has a wolf's heart.

Seven years is a werewolf's natural span but if you burn his human clothing you condemn him to wolfishness for the rest of his life, so old wives hereabouts think it some protection to throw a hat or an apron at the werewolf, as if clothes made the man. Yet by the eyes, those phosphorescent eyes, you know him in all his shapes; the eyes alone unchanged by metamorphosis.

Before he can become a wolf, the lycanthrope° strips stark naked. If you spy a naked man among the pines, you must run as if the Devil were after you.

It is midwinter and the robin, the friend of man, sits on the handle of the gardener's spade and sings. It is the worst time in all the year for wolves, but this strong-minded child insists she will go off through the wood. She is quite sure the wild beasts cannot harm her although, well-warned, she lays a carving knife in the basket her mother has packed with cheeses. There is a bottle of harsh liquor distilled from brambles; a batch of flat oatcakes baked on the hearthstone; a pot or two of jam. The flaxen-haired girl will take these delicious gifts to a reclusive grandmother so old the burden of her years is crushing her to death. Granny lives

lycanthrope: Werewolf.

two hours' trudge through the winter woods; the child wraps herself up in her thick shawl, draws it over her head. She steps into her stout wooden shoes; she is dressed and ready and it is Christmas Eve. The malign door of the solstice still swings upon its hinges, but she has been too much loved ever to feel scared.

Children do not stay young for long in this savage country. There are no toys for them to play with, so they work hard and grow wise, but this one, so pretty and the youngest of her family, a little late-comer, had been indulged by her mother and the grandmother who'd knitted her the red shawl that, today, has the ominous if brilliant look of blood on snow. Her breasts have just begun to swell; her hair is like lint, so fair it hardly makes a shadow on her pale forehead; her cheeks are an emblematic scarlet and white and she has just started her woman's bleeding, the clock inside her that will strike, henceforward, once a month.

She stands and moves within the invisible pentacle° of her own virginity. She   25
is an unbroken egg; she is a sealed vessel; she has inside her a magic space the entrance to which is shut tight with a plug of membrane; she is a closed system; she does not know how to shiver. She has her knife and she is afraid of nothing.

Her father might forbid her, if he were home, but he is away in the forest, gathering wood, and her mother cannot deny her.

The forest closed upon her like a pair of jaws.

There is always something to look at in the forest, even in the middle of winter—the huddled mounds of birds, succumbed to the lethargy of the season, heaped on the creaking boughs and too forlorn to sing; the bright frills of the winter fungi on the blotched trunks of the trees; the cuneiform° slots of rabbits and deer, the herringbone tracks of the birds, a hare as lean as a rasher of bacon streaking across the path where the thin sunlight dapples the russet brakes of last year's bracken.

When she heard the freezing howl of a distant wolf, her practiced hand sprang to the handle of her knife, but she saw no sign of a wolf at all, nor of a naked man, neither, but then she heard a clattering among the brushwood and there sprang on to the path a fully clothed one, a very handsome young one, in the green coat and wide-awake hat of a hunter, laden with carcasses of game birds. She had her hand on her knife at the first rustle of twigs, but he laughed with a flash of white teeth when he saw her and made her a comic yet flattering little bow; she'd never seen such a fine fellow before, not among the rustic clowns of her native village. So on they went together, through the thickening light of the afternoon.

Soon they were laughing and joking like old friends. When he offered to   30
carry her basket, she gave it to him although her knife was in it because he told her his rifle would protect them. As the day darkened, it began to snow again; she felt the first flakes settle on her eyelashes, but now there was only half a mile to go and there would be a fire, and hot tea, and a welcome, a warm one, surely, for the dashing huntsman as well as for herself.

This young man had a remarkable object in his pocket. It was a compass. She looked at the little round glass face in the palm of his hand and watched the wavering needle with a vague wonder. He assured her this compass had taken him safely through the wood on his hunting trip because the needle always told

---

pentacle: Five-pointed star; also called a pentagram.   **cuneiform:** Wedge-shaped.

him with perfect accuracy where the north was. She did not believe it; she knew she should never leave the path on the way through the wood or else she would be lost instantly. He laughed at her again; gleaming trails of spittle clung to his teeth. He said, if he plunged off the path into the forest that surrounded them, he could guarantee to arrive at her grandmother's house a good quarter of an hour before she did, plotting his way through the undergrowth with his compass, while she trudged the long way, along the winding path.

I don't believe you. Besides, aren't you afraid of the wolves?

He only tapped the gleaming butt of his rifle and grinned.

Is it a bet? he asked her. Shall we make a game of it? What will you give me if I get to your grandmother's house before you?

What would you like? she asked disingenuously.   35

A kiss.

Commonplaces of a rustic seduction; she lowered her eyes and blushed.

He went through the undergrowth and took her basket with him but she forgot to be afraid of the beasts, although now the moon was rising, for she wanted to dawdle on her way to make sure the handsome gentleman would win his wager.

Grandmother's house stood by itself a little way out of the village. The freshly falling snow blew in eddies about the kitchen garden, and the young man stepped delicately up the snowy path to the door as if he were reluctant to get his feet wet, swinging his bundle of game and the girl's basket and humming a little tune to himself.

There is a faint trace of blood on his chin; he has been snacking on his catch.   40

He rapped upon the panels with his knuckles.

Aged and frail, granny is three-quarters succumbed to the mortality the ache in her bones promises her and almost ready to give in entirely. A boy came out from the village to build up her hearth for the night an hour ago and the kitchen crackles with busy firelight. She has her Bible for company, she is a pious old woman. She is propped up on several pillows in the bed set into the wall peasant-fashion, wrapped up in the patchwork quilt she made before she was married, more years ago than she cares to remember. Two china spaniels with liver-colored blotches on their coats and black noses sit on either side of the fireplace. There is a bright rug of woven rags on the pantiles. The grandfather clock ticks away her eroding time.

We keep the wolves outside by living well.

He rapped upon the panels with his hairy knuckles.

It is your granddaughter, he mimicked in a high soprano.   45

Lift up the latch and walk in, my darling.

You can tell them by their eyes, eyes of a beast of prey, nocturnal, devastating eyes as red as a wound; you can hurl your Bible at him and your apron after, granny, you thought that was a sure prophylactic against these infernal vermin . . . now call on Christ and his mother and all the angels in heaven to protect you but it won't do you any good.

His feral muzzle is sharp as a knife; he drops his golden burden of gnawed pheasant on the table and puts down your dear girl's basket, too. Oh, my God, what have you done with her?

Off with his disguise, that coat of forest-colored cloth, the hat with the feather tucked into the ribbon; his matted hair streams down his white shirt and she can see the lice moving in it. The sticks in the hearth shift and hiss; night and the forest has come into the kitchen with darkness tangled in its hair.

He strips off his shirt. His skin is the color and texture of vellum. A crisp   50
stripe of hair runs down his belly, his nipples are ripe and dark as poison fruit, but he's so thin you could count the ribs under his skin if only he gave you the time. He strips off his trousers and she can see how hairy his legs are. His genitals, huge. Ah! huge.

The last thing the old lady saw in all this world was a young man, eyes like cinders, naked as a stone, approaching her bed.

The wolf is carnivore incarnate.

When he had finished with her, he licked his chops and quickly dressed himself again, until he was just as he had been when he came through her door. He burned the inedible hair in the fireplace and wrapped the bones up in a napkin that he hid away under the bed in the wooden chest in which he found a clean pair of sheets. These he carefully put on the bed instead of the tell-tale stained ones he stowed away in the laundry basket. He plumped up the pillows and shook out the patchwork quilt, he picked up the Bible from the floor, closed it and laid it on the table. All was as it had been before except that grandmother was gone. The sticks twitched in the grate, the clock ticked and the young man sat patiently, deceitfully beside the bed in granny's nightcap.

Rat-a-tap-tap.

Who's there, he quavers in granny's antique falsetto.   55

Only your granddaughter.

So she came in, bringing with her a flurry of snow that melted in tears on the tiles, and perhaps she was a little disappointed to see only her grandmother sitting beside the fire. But then he flung off the blanket and sprang to the door, pressing his back against it so that she could not get out again.

The girl looked round the room and saw there was not even the indentation of a head on the smooth cheek of the pillow and how, for the first time she'd seen it so, the Bible lay closed on the table. The tick of the clock cracked like a whip. She wanted her knife from her basket, but she did not dare reach for it because his eyes were fixed upon her — huge eyes that now seemed to shine with a unique, interior light, eyes the size of saucers, saucers full of Greek fire, diabolic phosphorescence.

What big eyes you have.

All the better to see you with.   60

No trace at all of the old woman except for a tuft of white hair that had caught in the bark of an unburned log. When the girl saw that, she knew she was in danger of death.

Where is my grandmother?

There's nobody here but we two, my darling.

Now a great howling rose up all around them, near, very near, as close as the kitchen garden, the howling of a multitude of wolves; she knew the worst wolves are hairy on the inside and she shivered, in spite of the scarlet shawl she pulled more closely round herself as if it could protect her although it was as red as the blood she must spill.

Who has come to sing us carols, she said.   65

Those are the voices of my brothers, darling; I love the company of wolves. Look out of the window and you'll see them.

Snow half-caked the lattice and she opened it to look into the garden. It was a white night of moon and snow; the blizzard whirled round the gaunt, grey beasts who squatted on their haunches among the rows of winter cabbage, pointing their sharp snouts to the moon and howling as if their hearts would break. Ten wolves; twenty wolves—so many wolves she could not count them, howling in concert as if demented or deranged. Their eyes reflected the light from the kitchen and shone like a hundred candles.

It is very cold, poor things, she said; no wonder they howl so.

She closed the window on the wolves' threnody° and took off her scarlet shawl, the color of poppies, the color of sacrifices, the color of her menses, and, since her fear did her no good, she ceased to be afraid.

What shall I do with my shawl?   70

Throw it on the fire, dear one. You won't need it again.

She bundled up her shawl and threw it on the blaze, which instantly consumed it. Then she drew her blouse over her head; her small breasts gleamed as if the snow had invaded the room.

What shall I do with my blouse?

Into the fire with it, too, my pet.

The thin muslin went flaring up the chimney like a magic bird and now off   75
came her skirt, her woolen stockings, her shoes, and on to the fire they went, too, and were gone for good. The firelight shone through the edges of her skin; now she was clothed only in her untouched integument° of flesh. This dazzling, naked she combed out her hair with her fingers; her hair looked white as the snow outside. Then went directly to the man with red eyes in whose unkempt mane the lice moved; she stood up on tiptoe and unbuttoned the collar of his shirt.

What big arms you have.

All the better to hug you with.

Every wolf in the world now howled a prothalamion° outside the window as she freely gave the kiss she owed him.

What big teeth you have!

She saw how his jaw began to slaver and the room was full of the clamor of   80
the forest's Liebestod° but the wise child never flinched, even when he answered:

All the better to eat you with.

The girl burst out laughing; she knew she was nobody's meat. She laughed at him full in the face, she ripped off his shirt for him and flung it into the fire, in the fiery wake of her own discarded clothing. The flames danced like dead souls

---

threnody: Lament or dirge.   **integument:** Outer covering, such as animal skin or seed coat. **prothalamion:** Wedding song.   **Liebestod:** Final aria in Richard Wagner's opera *Tristan und Isolde*, in which Isolde sings over Tristan's dead body and ultimately dies herself.

on Walpurgisnacht,° and the old bones under the bed set up a terrible clattering, but she did not pay them any heed.

Carnivore incarnate, only immaculate flesh appeases him.

She will lay his fearful head on her lap and she will pick out the lice from his pelt and perhaps she will put the lice into her mouth and eat them, as he will bid her, as she would do in a savage marriage ceremony.

The blizzard will die down.   85

The blizzard died down, leaving the mountains as randomly covered with snow as if a blind woman had thrown a sheet over them, the upper branches of the forest pines limed, creaking, swollen with the fall.

Snowlight, moonlight, a confusion of paw-prints.

All silent, all still.

Midnight; and the clock strikes. It is Christmas Day, the werewolves' birthday, the door of the solstice stands wide open; let them all sink through.

See! sweet and sound she sleeps in granny's bed, between the paws of the   90
tender wolf.   [1977]

Walpurgisnacht: May Day eve, the medieval witches' sabbath.

THINKING ABOUT THE TEXT

1. The story begins with a section about wolves before it gets to the Red Riding Hood narrative. What image of wolves does this prologue convey? What in particular seems the purpose of the extended anecdote about the wife with two husbands?

2. Note places where Carter shifts tenses. Why do you suppose she does this?

3. Why does the girl not get to her grandmother's house before the wolf does? Be specific about her state of mind.

4. Bear in mind the story's title. What do you think is Carter's purpose in having the grandmother's house surrounded by a whole "company" of wolves? Note that Red Riding Hood is not mentioned in the title. Are wolves indeed more important than she is in Carter's story? Support your answer with details from the text.

5. What do you conclude about the girl from her behavior at the end of the story? To what extent is "savage marriage ceremony" (para. 84) indeed an apt term for what occurs?

MAKING COMPARISONS

1. To what extent is Carter's image of wolves different from Perrault's and the Grimms'? Refer to details of all three texts.

2. Several critics have described Carter's versions of fairy tales as feminist. To what extent can this term be applied to Perrault's and the Grimms' narratives as well as hers? Define what you mean by *feminist*.

3. Would you say Carter's writing style is more realistic than that of Perrault and the Grimms? Or is the term *realism* completely irrelevant in the case of fairy tales? Explain.

WRITING ABOUT ISSUES

1. Choose one of these versions of the Red Riding Hood story, and write an essay in which you elaborate a moral that modern *adults* might learn from it. Or write an essay in which you explain what a child might learn from Carter's version.

2. Does Carter's version radically depart from Perrault's and the Grimms', or does it basically resemble them? Write an essay that addresses this question by focusing on Carter's story and one of the other two.

3. Write an essay explaining what you think you learned from a fairy tale or other fictional story that you heard as a child. If you want to contrast your thinking about the story now with your thinking about it then, do so. Feel free to compare the story you focus on with any of the versions of Red Riding Hood in this cluster.

4. Write your own version of the story of Red Riding Hood, and on a separate piece of paper write the moral you think should be drawn from your text. Then give your version to a classmate, and see if he or she can guess your moral.

A WEB ASSIGNMENT

In the Web Assignments section of the *Making Arguments about Literature* Web site, you will find a link to The Red Riding Hood Project, developed by a class at the University of Southern Mississippi. The site contains sixteen versions of the Red Riding Hood tale, accompanied by visual images. Choose a version you have not read before, and write an essay comparing it to one of the three versions in this cluster. In particular, discuss the extent to which the version on the site significantly differs from the version you have selected from this cluster.

Visit www.bedfordstmartins.com/argumentsaboutlit

10

Poetry Clusters

RECONCILING WITH FATHERS

LUCILLE CLIFTON, "forgiving my father"
ROBERT HAYDEN, "Those Winter Sundays"
THEODORE ROETHKE, "My Papa's Waltz"
SHIRLEY GEOK-LIN LIM, "Father from Asia"

In childhood, our emotions are often intense. Fears about life arise because we feel so powerless. For some of us, our fathers held all the power. Fathers may use their power in various ways—some to control or abuse, others to comfort and protect. We form perceptions about our fathers from these early memories. Often we become judgmental about their failures in the world or their failures as parents. As we grow older, we sometimes come to terms with our fathers and see them simply as human beings with strengths and weaknesses. But it is not always so simple; some wounds may be too deep for us to reconcile. The four poets in this cluster approach memories of their fathers with different perspectives and purposes: some want to forgive, others will not.

BEFORE YOU READ

Make a list of four strong memories about your father from your childhood. Are the memories positive or not? Can you remember how you felt then? Is it different from how you feel now? How can you explain the difference?

LUCILLE CLIFTON
forgiving my father

Born in 1936 in a small town near Buffalo, New York, Lucille Clifton attended Howard University and Fredonia State Teacher's College and has taught poetry at a number of universities. Her numerous awards for writing include two creative writ-

ing fellowships from the National Endowment for the Arts (1970 and 1973), two Pulitzer Prize nominations (for Good Woman: Poems and a Memoir *and for* Next, *both in 1988), several major poetry awards, and an Emmy. She won the National Book Award for* Blessing the Boats: New and Selected Poems, 1988–2000. *The mother of six, Clifton's works include fifteen children's books. She is a former poet laureate of Maryland and has been the Distinguished Professor of Humanities at St. Mary's College since 1991. "Forgiving my father" is from her 1980 book,* Two-Headed Woman.

it is friday. we have come
to the paying of the bills.
all week you have stood in my dreams
like a ghost, asking for more time
but today is payday, payday old man,   5
my mother's hand opens in her early grave
and i hold it out like a good daughter.

there is no more time for you. there will
never be time enough daddy daddy old lecher
old liar. i wish you were rich so i could take it all   10
and give the lady what she was due
but you were the son of a needy father,
the father of a needy son,
you gave her all you had
which was nothing. you have already given her   15
all you had.

you are the pocket that was going to open
and come up empty any friday.
you were each other's bad bargain, not mine.
daddy old pauper   old prisoner,   old dead man   20
what am i doing here collecting?
you lie side by side in debtor's boxes
and no accounting will open them up.   [1980]

THINKING ABOUT THE TEXT

1. How might you answer the question in line 21? Are the last two lines of the poem a kind of answer? Is there some way we can "collect" from the dead?

2. Should we bury the dead—that is, should we let the past go and let bygones be bygones? Or is it necessary to settle old scores? What do you think Clifton's answer would be?

3. How consistently does Clifton use the payday analogy? Make a list of words that reinforce her overall scheme.

4. Would you think differently about the speaker's father if Clifton had written "elderly one" instead of "old man" (line 5) or "old playboy / old fibber" instead of "old lecher / old liar" (lines 9–10)?

5. Some readers look for tensions or contradictions early in a poem, hoping they will be resolved at the end. Does this poem end in a resolution of paying up and forgiving?

ROBERT HAYDEN
Those Winter Sundays

Born in Detroit, Michigan, African American poet Robert Hayden (1913–1980) grew up in a poor neighborhood where his natural parents left him with family friends. He grew up with the Hayden name, not discovering his original name until he was forty. Hayden attended Detroit City College (now Wayne State University) from 1932 to 1936, worked in the Federal Writer's Project, and later earned his M.A. at the University of Michigan in 1944. He taught at Fisk University from 1946 to 1968 and at the University of Michigan from 1968 to 1980 and published several collections of poetry. Although his poems sometimes contain autobiographical elements, Hayden is primarily a formalist poet who preferred that his poems not be limited to personal or ethnic interpretations. "Those Winter Sundays" is from Angle of Ascent *(1966).*

Sundays too my father got up early
and put his clothes on in the blueblack cold,
then with cracked hands that ached
from labor in the weekday weather made
banked fires blaze. No one ever thanked him.   5

I'd wake and hear the cold splintering, breaking.
When the rooms were warm, he'd call,
and slowly I would rise and dress,
fearing the chronic angers of that house,

Speaking indifferently to him,   10
who had driven out the cold
and polished my good shoes as well.
What did I know, what did I know
of love's austere and lonely offices?   [1962]

THINKING ABOUT THE TEXT

1. Is the concluding question meant rhetorically—that is, is the answer so obvious no real reply is expected? Write a response you think the son would give now.

2. Why did the children never thank their father? Is this common? What specific things might you thank your father (or mother) for? Do parents have basic responsibilities to their children that do not warrant thanks?

3. Is there evidence that the son loves his father now? Did he then? Why did he speak "indifferently" to his father? Is it clear what the "chronic angers" are? Should it be?

4. How might you fill in the gaps here? For example, how old do you think the boy is? How old is the father? What kind of a job might he have? What else can you infer?

5. What is the speaker's tone? Is he hoping for your understanding? Your sympathy? Are we responsible for the things we do in childhood? Is this speaker repentant or simply explaining?

MAKING COMPARISONS

1. What degrees of forgiveness do you see in Clifton's and Hayden's poems?

2. Writing a poem for one's father seems different from writing a poem about him. Explain this statement in reference to these poems.

3. Compare the purpose of the questions in each poem. How might each poet answer the other poet's questions?

THEODORE ROETHKE
My Papa's Waltz

Born in Saginaw, Michigan, Theodore Roethke (1908–1963) was strongly influenced by childhood experiences with his father, a usually stern man who sold plants and flowers and who kept a large greenhouse, the setting for many of Roethke's poems. Theodore Roethke was educated at the University of Michigan, took courses at Harvard, and taught at several universities before becoming poet-in-residence at the University of Washington in 1948. Roethke's books include The Lost Son and Other Poems *(1949), the source for "My Papa's Waltz";* The Waking *(1953), which won a Pulitzer Prize; and* Words for the Wind *(1958), which won the National Book Award. Roethke's intensely personal style insures his place among the most influential postmodern American poets.*

The whiskey on your breath
Could make a small boy dizzy;
But I hung on like death:
Such waltzing was not easy.

We romped until the pans   5
Slid from the kitchen shelf;

My mother's countenance
Could not unfrown itself.

The hand that held my wrist
Was battered on one knuckle;   10
At every step you missed
My right ear scraped a buckle.

You beat time on my head
With a palm caked hard by dirt,
Then waltzed me off to bed   15
Still clinging to your shirt.   [1948]

THINKING ABOUT THE TEXT

1. Is the narrator looking back at his father with fondness? Bitterness?

2. Would the poem make a different impression if we changed "romped" to "fought" and "waltzing" to "dancing"?

3. Why did the boy hang on and cling to his father? From fear? From affection?

4. What is the mother's role here? How would you characterize her frown?

5. Readers often have a negative view of the relationship represented here, but many change their minds, seeing some positive aspects to the father and son's waltz. How might you account for this revision?

MAKING COMPARISONS

1. Would you have read this poem differently if the poet had used Clifton's title "forgiving my father"?

2. How would you compare the tone of Roethke's poem with that of Hayden's? Do they miss their fathers?

3. Would you say that Roethke has more complex feelings about his father, whereas Clifton and Hayden seem clearer?

SHIRLEY GEOK-LIN LIM
Father from Asia

Born in 1944 in Malacca, Malaysia, Shirley Geok-lin Lim attended the University of Malaysia and came to study in the United States in the 1960s; she earned a Ph.D. from Brandeis University in 1971. Of her four published books of poetry, Crossing the Peninsula won the Commonwealth Poetry Prize in 1980, a first both for an Asian and for a woman. Her published works include two short-story collections and several editions of critical studies and anthologies focusing on gender and

Asian American issues, including The Forbidden Stitch: An Asian American
Women's Anthology *(1989), which won an American Book Award, and* Among
the White Moonfaces: Memoirs of a Nyonya Feminist *(1996). She recently published a novel,* Joss and Gold *(2001). She is a professor of English at the University of California at Santa Barbara. The poem that follows is from* Crossing the
Peninsula.

Father, you turn your hands toward me.
Large hollow bowls, they are empty
stigmata of poverty. Light pours
through them, and I back away,
for you are dangerous, father   5
of poverty, father of ten children,
father of nothing, from whose life
I have learned nothing for myself.
You are the father of childhood,
father from Asia, father of sacrifice.   10
I renounce you, keep you in my sleep,
keep you two oceans away, ghost
who eats his own children,
Asia who loved his children,
who didn't know abandonment,   15
father who lived at the center of the world,
whose life I dare not remember,
for memory is a wheel that crushes,
and Asia is dust, is dust.   [1980]

THINKING ABOUT THE TEXT

1. What does "I renounce you" (line 11) mean? If the speaker renounces
   her father, why does the line end with "keep you in my sleep"?

2. If you were to write a poem about your father, would it be for you? For
   him? For someone else? Do you think poets write for a specific audience
   or only for themselves? Which does Lim do?

3. "Father of nothing" (line 7) seems harsh. Does Lim mean it to be? Is
   "ghost / who eats his own children" (lines 12–13) hyperbolic — that is, a
   deliberate overstatement?

4. Why does Lim compare the father's hands to bowls? What other
   metaphors does she use? Rewrite the last line, being explicit about what
   you think she means.

5. Lim's speaker says she "learned nothing" (line 8) from her father's life.
   Is this possible? Is memory "a wheel that crushes" (line 18)? Is this poem a
   remembrance? Can we escape the past? Should we? Does the speaker?

MAKING COMPARISONS

1. Is Lim's speaker angrier than Clifton's, Hayden's, or Roethke's? Is there a resolution in Lim's poem? Is there in the other three poems?
2. Clifton's speaker seems to be forgiving her father for something. Is Lim's forgiving her father? Is Hayden's? Roethke's?
3. Which speaker's attitude seems the healthiest? Which the least?

WRITING ABOUT ISSUES

1. Choose one of the four preceding poems to argue that our feelings for our fathers are complex, not simple.
2. Jean-Paul Sartre writes in *Words* (1964) that "there is no good father, that is the rule." Use examples from the four poems to argue that this is, or is not, the case.
3. Do you think all children leave childhood or adolescence with unresolved tensions in their relationships with their fathers? Write a personal narrative that confronts this idea.
4. Locate at least six more poems that deal with memories of fathers. Write a brief report, noting the similarities to the four poems given here.

RESPONDING TO TEACHERS

LANGSTON HUGHES, "Theme for English B"
LINDA PASTAN, "Ethics"
HENRY REED, "Naming of Parts"
WALT WHITMAN, "When I Heard the Learn'd Astronomer"
ROSEMARY CATACALOS, "David Talamántez on the Last Day of Second Grade"

Each of the following poems features a student responding to someone given institutional authority to teach him or her. In the first poem, the speaker is an African American college student writing an essay assigned by his white instructor. The speaker in the second poem remembers ethics classes she took as a youth, recalling in particular how she treated a certain question the teacher liked to ask. The third poem seems to feature two speakers: while a military officer teaches recruits how to use a rifle, one student mentally plays with his instructor's words. In the fourth poem, the speaker chooses to observe the heavens by himself rather than hear a "learn'd astronomer" lecture about them. The final poem focuses on a boy whose exultation on the last day of second grade defies his teacher's criticisms of him.

By this point in your life, you have had many people officially designated as your teachers. Probably you have seen their lectures, questions, assignments, and overall behavior as reflecting their particular educational philosophy. At the same time, your reactions to them have said something about what you consider worth learning and how you think those subjects should be taught. In some cases, perhaps, your view of teaching and learning coincided with your teacher's. At other times, though, you may have suffered an unfortunate mismatch. With each poem here, identify the teacher's assumptions about teaching and learning. Also consider those expressed by the student in his or her response.

BEFORE YOU READ

Think of a past or present writing assignment that you have found especially challenging. What specifically was the assignment? What do you believe was the educational philosophy behind it? Why did you find it a challenge? Was it a worthwhile assignment? Why, or why not? In what ways, if any, would you have changed it?

LANGSTON HUGHES
Theme for English B

Langston Hughes (1902–1967) has long been regarded as a major African American writer. He is increasingly seen today as an important contributor to American literature in general. Hughes worked in a wide range of genres, including fiction, drama, and autobiography. Nevertheless, he is primarily known for his poems. He wrote "Theme for English B" in 1949, when he was twenty-five years older than the poem's speaker. He himself, though, had attended "a college on the hill above Harlem"—Columbia University.

The instructor said,
    Go home and write
    a page tonight.
    And let that page come out of you—
    Then, it will be true.   5

I wonder if it's that simple?
I am twenty-two, colored, born in Winston-Salem.
I went to school there, then Durham, then here
to this college on the hill above Harlem.
I am the only colored student in my class.   10
The steps from the hill lead down into Harlem,
through a park, then I cross St. Nicholas,
Eighth Avenue, Seventh, and I come to the Y,
the Harlem Branch Y, where I take the elevator
up to my room, sit down, and write this page: 15

◆　◆　◆

It's not easy to know what is true for you or me
at twenty-two, my age. But I guess I'm what
I feel and see and hear, Harlem, I hear you:
hear you, hear me — we two — you, me, talk on this page.
(I hear New York, too.) Me — who?   20
Well, I like to eat, sleep, drink, and be in love.
I like to work, read, learn, and understand life.
I like a pipe for a Christmas present,
or records — Bessie,° bop, or Bach.
I guess being colored doesn't make me *not* like   25
the same things other folks like who are other races.
So will my page be colored that I write?
Being me, it will not be white.
But it will be
a part of you, instructor.   30
You are white —
yet a part of me, as I am part of you.
That's American.
Sometimes perhaps you don't want to be a part of me.
Nor do I often want to be a part of you.   35
But we are, that's true!
As I learn from you,
I guess you learn from me —
although you're older — and white —
and somewhat more free.   40

This is my page for English B.   [1949]

24 Bessie: Bessie Smith (1898?–1937), the famous American blues singer.

THINKING ABOUT THE TEXT

1. Write a page in which you respond to the teacher's assignment. In what respects has your page "come out of you" (line 4)? In what respects is it "true" (line 5)? Do you find the assignment reasonable? Why, or why not?

2. What seems to be the speaker's evaluation of the assignment? To what extent does he critique or challenge the assignment rather than merely submit to it? Support your answer by referring to specific lines.

3. What does Hughes's speaker mean by "You are . . . a part of me, as I am part of you" (lines 31–32)? Do you think that in today's historical and cultural context any white teacher of a black student is "somewhat more free" (line 40) than that student? Why, or why not?

4. Identify where the poem rhymes. What is the effect of this rhyming?

5. What might be the teacher's reaction to the speaker's page? What would you like the teacher's reaction to be?

LINDA PASTAN
Ethics

Raised in New York City, Linda Pastan (b. 1932) now lives in Potomac, Maryland. She has published many books of poetry, including The Five Stages of Grief *(1981);* Waiting for My Life *(1981), where "Ethics" originally appeared; and* PM/AM: New and Selected Poems *(1982). Much of Pastan's poetry deals with her own family life. Increasingly, she has been concerned as well with issues of aging and mortality.*

In ethics class so many years ago
our teacher asked this question every fall:
if there were a fire in a museum
which would you save, a Rembrandt painting
or an old woman who hadn't many   5
years left anyhow? Restless on hard chairs
caring little for pictures or old age
we'd opt one year for life, the next for art
and always half-heartedly. Sometimes
the woman borrowed my grandmother's face   10
leaving her usual kitchen to wander
some drafty, half-imagined museum.
One year, feeling clever, I replied
why not let the woman decide herself?
Linda, the teacher would report, eschews   15
the burdens of responsibility.
This fall in a real museum I stand
before a real Rembrandt, old woman,
or nearly so, myself. The colors
within this frame are darker than autumn,   20
darker even than winter—the browns of earth,
though earth's most radiant elements burn
through the canvas. I know now that woman
and painting and season are almost one
and all beyond saving by children.   [1981]   25

THINKING ABOUT THE TEXT

1. What specific topics would you expect to see addressed in a college-level
   ethics class? Which do you think are appropriate for an ethics class at the
   high-school level? Should students be required to take such a class in earlier grades? Why, or why not? (You may want to consult a dictionary definition of the word *ethics*.)

2. How would you respond to the teacher's question? Do you think it an appropriate one to ask? Why, or why not? Judging by Linda's behavior in the poem, what do you think the teacher should have said about her?

3. What do you usually associate with fall and winter? Does Pastan seem to encourage these associations? Explain.

4. Note the speaker's description of the actual Rembrandt painting. Do you find it an objective description? Why, or why not?

5. State in your own words the lesson articulated in the poem's last sentence. Do you agree with the argument made there against the teacher's question? Why, or why not? Do you think the speaker is rejecting the whole subject of ethics? Why, or why not?

MAKING COMPARISONS

1. Compare the teacher's question in Pastan's poem to the assignment given Hughes's speaker. Do you prefer one to the other? Explain.

2. Unlike Hughes's poem, Pastan's explicitly leaps to a later stage in the speaker's life. Is this a significant difference? Why, or why not?

3. Is it fair to say that Pastan's poem is pessimistic, while Hughes's is optimistic? Elaborate your reasoning.

HENRY REED
Naming of Parts

The English writer Henry Reed (1914–1986) was primarily known as an author and translator of plays for radio. But he also wrote two volumes of poetry, A Map of Verona: Poems *(1946) and* Lessons of the War *(1970). The following poem, which appears in both volumes, is one in a series of poems collectively entitled "Naming of the Parts."*

Today we have naming of parts. Yesterday,
We had daily cleaning. And tomorrow morning,
We shall have what to do after firing. But today,
Today we have naming of parts. Japonica
Glistens like coral in all of the neighboring gardens,   5
       And today we have naming of parts.

This is the lower sling swivel. And this
Is the upper sling swivel, whose use you will see,
When you are given your slings. And this is the piling swivel,
Which in your case you have not got. The branches   10

Hold in the gardens their silent, eloquent gestures,
      Which in our case we have not got.

This is the safety-catch, which is always released
With an easy flick of the thumb. And please do not let me
See anyone using his finger. You can do it quite easy   15
If you have any strength in your thumb. The blossoms
Are fragile and motionless, never letting anyone see
      Any of them using their finger.

And this you can see is the bolt. The purpose of this
Is to open the breech, as you see. We can slide it   20
Rapidly backwards and forwards: we call this
Easing the spring. And rapidly backwards and forwards
The early bees are assaulting and fumbling the flowers:
      They call it easing the Spring.

They call it easing the Spring: it is perfectly easy   25
If you have any strength in your thumb: like the bolt,
And the breech, and the cocking-piece, and the point of balance,
Which in our case we have not got; and the almond-blossom
Silent in all of the gardens and the bees going backwards and forwards,
      For today we have naming of parts.   [1946]   30

THINKING ABOUT THE TEXT

1. Reed's poem features two voices. Identify the lines where each appears.
   What adjectives would you use to describe each?

2. Does this poem progress in any way, or does the situation it presents remain
   unchanged at the end? Refer to specific lines in supporting your response.

3. Do you take the poem to be antimilitary? Why, or why not?

4. The author visually isolates the last line of each stanza. Why do you think
   he does so?

5. The poem features a lot of repetition. What is its effect?

MAKING COMPARISONS

1. Does the scene of instruction that Reed presents seem very different from
   the classes evoked by Hughes and Pastan? From classes that you have
   taken? Explain.

2. The instructor in "Naming of Parts" speaks a lot more than the instructors
   in "Theme for English B" and "Ethics." Does this difference matter?
   Why, or why not?

3. Reed's poem seems very much concerned with language—specifically,
   the act of "naming" various things. Do the other two poems show similar

concerns, or do they deal with largely different topics? Refer to specific lines in each text.

WALT WHITMAN

When I Heard the Learn'd Astronomer

Walt Whitman (1819–1892) became one of the United States' most famous and influential poets. He was especially known for celebrating the human body and democracy. His most important volume of poetry was Leaves of Grass *(1855). Although it originally consisted of a dozen poems, Whitman added to it and revised its format as it went through several more editions, the final one appearing in 1892. Besides being a poet, Whitman worked as a printer, newspaper editor, journalist, and government clerk. During the Civil War, he tended wounded Union soldiers. He wrote the following poem in 1865.*

When I heard the learn'd astronomer,
When the proofs, the figures, were ranged in columns before me,
When I was shown the charts and diagrams, to add, divide, and measure them,
When I sitting heard the astronomer where he lectured with much applause in
      the lecture-room,
How soon unaccountable I became tired and sick,   5
Till rising and gliding out I wandered off by myself,
In the mystical moist night-air, and from time to time,
Looked up in perfect silence at the stars.   [1865]

THINKING ABOUT THE TEXT

1. How does Whitman's speaker seem to define *learn'd*? Do you think he would apply this term to himself? If so, what definition of it would he have in mind?

2. The first four lines all begin with the word *when*, a technique known as anaphora. What is its effect?

3. Describe how the lines change in length as the poem moves along. Do you think Whitman is justified in making the fourth line as long as it is? Explain your reasoning. Note that the poem is actually just one sentence; what does Whitman achieve by making it so?

4. What distinctions does the speaker make between his behavior in the first line and his behavior in the last? Do you see him as proposing another method of education than the astronomer's, or do you take him to be rejecting education altogether? Explain. How much do you think a person can learn by simply gazing at the stars?

5. The poem ends by apparently endorsing "perfect silence." Yet Whitman *is not* silent; after all, he wrote this poem. Do you think Whitman is contradicting himself? Why, or why not?

MAKING COMPARISONS

1. Of the poems in this cluster so far, only in Whitman's does a student walk out on a teacher. Does this action make you regard the student in Whitman's poem differently than you do the students in the other poems? Why, or why not?

2. In each of the first three poems, we see a teacher's words quoted. Whitman's poem, however, does not actually quote the astronomer. Is this a significant difference? Why, or why not?

3. In what ways, if any, does Whitman's word *unaccountable* apply to the first three poems?

ROSEMARY CATACALOS
David Talamántez on the Last Day of Second Grade

Rosemary Catacalos (b. 1944) grew up in San Antonio, Texas. Formerly a reporter and arts columnist, and executive director of San Francisco State University's Poetry Center and American Poetry Archives, she is currently the executive director of Gemini Ink, a literary center in San Antonio, Texas. Her own books of poetry, both published in 1984, are As Long As It Takes *and* Again for the First Time. *The following poem appeared in a 1996 issue of* The Texas Observer *and was subsequently included in the collection* Best American Poetry 1996.

San Antonio, Texas 1988

David Talamántez, whose mother is at work, leaves his mark,
    everywhere in the schoolyard,
tosses pages from a thick sheaf of lined paper high in the air one by
    one, watches them

catch on the teachers' car bumpers, drift into the chalky narrow shade   5
    of the water fountain.
One last batch, stapled together, he rolls tight into a makeshift horn
    through which he shouts

David! and *David, yes!* before hurling it away hard and darting across
    Barzos Street against   10
the light, the little sag of head and shoulders when, safe on the other
    side, he kicks a can

◆　◆　◆

in the gutter and wanders toward home. David Talamántez believes
    birds are warm blooded,
the way they are quick in the air and give out long strings of   15
    complicated music, different

all the time, not like cats and dogs. For this he was marked down in
    Science, and for putting
his name in the wrong place, on the right with the date instead on the
    left with Science   20

Questions, and for not skipping a line between his heading and
    answers. The X's for wrong
things are big, much bigger than Talamántez's tiny writing. *Write larger,*
    his teacher says

in red ink across the tops of many pages. *Messy!* she says on others   25
    where he has erased
and started over, erased and started over. Spelling, Language
    Expression, Sentences Using

the Following Words. *Neck. I have a neck name. No!* 20's, 30's. *Think*
    again! He's good   30
in Art, though, makes 70 on Reading Station Artist's Corner, where
    he's traced and colored

an illustration from *Henny Penny*. A goose with red-and-white striped
    shirt, a hen in a turquoise
dress. Points off for the birds, cloud and butterfly he's drawn in   35
    freehand. *Not in the original*

picture! Twenty-five points off for writing nothing in the blank after
    This is my favorite scene
in the book because . . . There's a page called Rules. *Listen! Always*
    working! Stay in your seat!   40

Raise your hand before you speak! No fighting! Be quiet! Rules copied from
    the board, no grade,
only a huge red checkmark. Later there is a test on Rules. *Listen! Alay*
    ercng! Sast in ao snet!

Rars aone bfo your spek! No finagn! Be cayt! He gets 70 on Rules, 10 on   45
    Spelling. An old man
stoops to pick up a crumpled drawing of a large family crowded
    around a table, an apartment

with bars on the windows in Alazán Courts, a huge sun in one corner
    saying, *To mush noys!*   50
After correcting the spelling, the grade is 90. *Nice details!* And there's
    another mark, on this paper

◆　◆　◆

and all the others, the one in the doorway of La Rosa Beauty Shop, the
    one that blew under
the pool table at La Tenampa, the ones older kids have wadded up like   55
    big spit balls, the ones run
over by cars. On every single page David Talamántez has crossed out
    the teacher's red numbers
and written in giant letters, blue ink, *Yes! David, yes!*   [1996]

THINKING ABOUT THE TEXT

1. In *Best American Poetry 1996,* Catacalos admits that "David Talamántez
   is a composite of many Chicano children in many times and places." As
   you read her poem, do you assume she based it on a real-life individual?
   Why, or why not? How conscious are you that the boy in this poem is Chicano? Do you think it could just as easily be about someone from a different ethnic background? Explain your reasoning.

2. Sum up and evaluate the teacher's judgments of David's writing and his
   other work. What are some of her values and assumptions?

3. What are some adjectives of your own for David? Note what he does with
   the papers he has gotten back. Is he engaging in significant acts of resistance? Explain your view.

4. Here is an issue of policy: What should be done about the kind of situation described in this poem? By whom?

5. Many sentences in this poem run from one line to the next—a technique
   called *enjambment.* What is the effect?

MAKING COMPARISONS

1. Of all the students in this cluster, David Talamántez is the only one
   shown merely as a child. Does he seem notably less mature than the other
   students you have encountered here? Why, or why not?

2. Whereas the students in the other four poems are also the speakers of the
   poems, David Talamántez is not. Does this difference produce a difference in effect? Explain.

3. David is tossing papers away. Is it fair, then, to say that he is more destructive than the students in the other poems? What details of the five texts do
   you have in mind as you answer this question?

WRITING ABOUT ISSUES

1. Choose any poem in this cluster, and write an essay describing and evaluating the relationship between student and teacher. Use specific lines to
   support your claims.

2. Choose two of the teachers in these poems, and write an essay comparing their educational philosophies. What do they think their students should know and do? What method of instruction might they think works best? What do you think of their approaches to teaching?

3. Think of a teacher whose style disturbed you at first. Did you eventually regard this person as a good teacher, or did you reach a different conclusion? Write an essay answering this question, making sure to define what you mean by *good*. Refer to specific interactions you had with the teacher and specific things that influenced your reactions to him or her. You may find it useful to refer to one or more poems in this cluster.

4. Ask five or more students not in this class the following questions: What basic goals should teachers have when they respond to their students' writing? What sorts of things should they comment on? How should they word their comments? How many comments should they make? Then write an essay presenting and arguing for your own answers to these questions, making reference to what your interviewees said.

GAYS AND LESBIANS IN FAMILIES

ESSEX HEMPHILL, "Commitments"
KITTY TSUI, "A Chinese Banquet"
MINNIE BRUCE PRATT, "Two Small-Sized Girls"

The late Essex Hemphill was gay; Kitty Tsui and Minnie Bruce Pratt are lesbian. All three writers in this cluster remind their audience that families may have gay or lesbian members. Usually the media give a different impression. The families depicted in most literature, films, television shows, and songs are heterosexual. Indeed, much of American society prefers this image. Families that do have gay or lesbian members may refuse to admit the fact, let alone accept it. Throughout history, of course, plenty of gays and lesbians have concealed their sexual identities from their families in the first place, fearing rejection.

Nowadays, though, increasing numbers of gays and lesbians are not only "coming out of the closet" but are also publicly claiming the term *family*. Many seek acceptance by the families they were raised in. Many also seek the right to form and raise families of their own. Recently Massachusetts legalized same-sex marriage (May 2004), although the governor and other officials are still trying to get the state supreme court ruling overturned. After a number of communities tried to follow Massachusetts's lead, President George W. Bush came out in favor of a constitutional amendment that would, in effect, ban same-sex marriage. The country is now and will for years debate this controversial issue. Note that in all these efforts, gays and lesbians have quite a few heterosexual allies, but they face heterosexual resistance too. As was demonstrated in the 1990s in the case of lesbian mother Sharon Bottoms, a parent who is not heterosexual can still lose custody of his or her children for that reason. Also, gays and lesbians are far from winning a universal right to adopt. When Hawaii seemed on the verge of permitting same-sex marriage, arguments about it raged throughout the United States, and the federal government sought to discourage it by passing the Defense of Marriage Act in 1996. Consider your own position on these matters as you read the following poems. Each refers to American society's widespread assumption that families are heterosexual; each also points out the suffering that can result from this belief.

BEFORE YOU READ

What, at present, is your attitude toward gays and lesbians? Try to identify specific people, experiences, and institutions that have shaped your view. If it has changed over the years, explain how. Finally, describe an occasion that made you quite conscious of the attitude you now hold.

ESSEX HEMPHILL
Commitments

Before his untimely death from AIDS-related complications, Essex Hemphill (1957–1995) explored through prose, poetry, and film what it meant to live as a black gay man. The following poem comes from his 1992 book Ceremonies: Prose and Poetry. *His other books include a collection he edited,* Brother to Brother: New Writings by Black Gay Men *(1991). Hemphill also appeared in the documentaries* Looking for Langston *and* Tongues Untied.

I will always be there.
When the silence is exhumed.
When the photographs are examined
I will be pictured smiling
among siblings, parents,					5
nieces and nephews.

In the background of the photographs
the hazy smoke of barbecue,
a checkered red-and-white tablecloth
laden with blackened chicken,					10
glistening ribs, paper plates,
bottles of beer, and pop.

In the photos
the smallest children
are held by their parents.					15

My arms are empty, or around
the shoulders of unsuspecting aunts
expecting to throw rice at me someday.

Or picture tinsel, candles,
ornamented, imitation trees,   20
or another table, this one
set for Thanksgiving,
a turkey steaming the lens.

My arms are empty
in those photos, too,   25
so empty they would break
around a lover.

I am always there
for critical emergencies,
graduations,   30
the middle of the night.

I am the invisible son.
In the family photos
nothing appears out of character.
I smile as I serve my duty.   [1992]   35

THINKING ABOUT THE TEXT

1. The speaker begins with the announcement "I will always be there," and yet later he says "I am the invisible son" (line 32). How can these two statements be reconciled? In the second line, he uses the word *exhumed.* Look up this word in a dictionary. What do you infer from the speaker's use of it?

2. Unlike the other stanzas, the second lacks verbs. Should Hemphill have included at least one verb there for the sake of consistency? Why, or why not? Is the scene described in the second stanza characteristic of your own family? Note similarities and differences.

3. What do you think the speaker means when he describes his arms in the photographs as "so empty they would break / around a lover" (lines 26–27)?

4. In line 34, the speaker refers to "character." How does he seem to define the term? He concludes the poem by noting, "I smile as I serve my duty." Should this line be taken as an indication of how he really feels about his family commitments? Why, or why not?

5. List some commitments that you think the speaker's family should be making toward him. What overall attitude of yours toward the family does your list suggest? What is your overall attitude toward the speaker?

KITTY TSUI
A Chinese Banquet

Born in Hong Kong in 1953, Kitty Tsui grew up there and in England before moving to the United States in 1969. Besides being a writer, she is an artist, an actor, and a bodybuilder. The following comes from her 1983 volume of poetry, The Words of a Woman Who Breathes Fire. *Her most recent book is* Sparks Fly (1997), *about San Francisco gay life.*

for the one who was not invited

it was not a very formal affair but
all the women over twelve
wore long gowns and a corsage,
except for me.

it was not a very formal affair, just   5
the family getting together,
poa poa,° *kuw fu*° without *kuw mow*°
(her excuse this year is a headache).

aunts and uncles and cousins,
the grandson who is a dentist,   10
the one who drives a mercedes benz,
sitting down for shark's fin soup.

they talk about buying a house and
taking a two week vacation in beijing.
i suck on shrimp and squab,   15
dreaming of the cloudscape in your eyes.

my mother, her voice beaded with sarcasm;
you're twenty six and not getting younger.
it's about time you got a decent job.
she no longer asks when i'm getting married.   20

you're twenty six and not getting younger.
what are you doing with your life?
you've got to make a living.
why don't you study computer programming?

she no longer asks when i'm getting married.   25
one day, wanting desperately to
bridge the boundaries that separate us,
wanting desperately to touch her,

◆　◆　◆

7 *poa poa:* Maternal grandmother.　*kuw fu:* Uncle.　*kuw mow:* Aunt.

tell her: mother, i'm gay,
mother i'm gay and so happy with her.   30
but she will not listen,
she shakes her head.

she sits across from me,
emotions invading her face.
her eyes are wet but   35
she will not let tears fall.

mother, i say,
you love a man.
i love a woman.
it is not what she wants to hear.   40

aunts and uncles and cousins,
very much a family affair.
but you are not invited,
being neither my husband nor my wife.

aunts and uncles and cousins   45
eating longevity noodles
fragrant with ham inquire:
sold that old car of yours yet?

i want to tell them: my back is healing,
i dream of dragons and water.   50
my home is in her arms,
our bedroom ceiling the wide open sky.   [1983]

THINKING ABOUT THE TEXT

1. How would you describe the speaker's relationship with her mother? Do you think the mother is wrong not to invite her daughter's lover? Identify specific values, principles, and experiences of yours that influence your answer.

2. How would you describe the conversations at the banquet? How familiar are such conversations to you? Where does the speaker contrast them with another kind of talk?

3. How helpful is the poem's title? Where specifically does the poem refer to Chinese culture? To what extent does ethnicity seem to matter in this text?

4. Note repetitions in the poem. What is their effect?

5. Tsui doesn't use capitalization. What is the effect of this move?

MAKING COMPARISONS

1. Do you sense that Hemphill's speaker, like Tsui's, is "wanting desperately to / bridge the boundaries that separate us" (lines 26–27)? Support your answer by referring to specific words in Hemphill's poem.

2. By focusing so much on photographs, Hemphill's poem emphasizes sight. Does Tsui's poem emphasize sight, or does it give at least as much attention to another sense? Support your answer by referring to details of the poem.

3. Tsui's poem addresses someone in particular; Hemphill's does not. Does this difference make for a significant difference in effect? Why, or why not?

MINNIE BRUCE PRATT
Two Small-Sized Girls

Minnie Bruce Pratt (b. 1946) has long been active in the women's movement. Her prose writings include Rebellion: Essays, 1980–1991 *(1991) and a 1995 volume of short pieces titled* S/HE. *As a poet, she has published* The Sound of One Fork *(1981);* Crime against Nature *(1990), which won the prestigious Lamont Prize of the American Academy of Poets; and* We Say We Love Each Other *(1992). Her latest book is* Walking Back Up Depot Street *(1999). In divorce proceedings, Pratt lost custody of her two sons because she is a lesbian. Many of the poems in* Crime against Nature, *including the following, refer to this experience.*

1.

Two small-sized girls, hunched in the corn crib,
skin prickly with heat and dust.   We rustle
in the corn husks and grab rough cobs gnawed
empty as bone.   We twist them with papery shreds.
Anyone passing would say we're making our dolls.   5

Almost sisters, like our mothers, we turn and shake
the shriveled beings.   We are not playing at babies.
We are doing, single-minded, what we've been watching
our grandmother do.   We are making someone.   We hunker
on splintered grey planks older than our mothers,   10
and ignore how the sun blazes across us, the straw husks,
the old door swung open for the new corn of the summer.

2.

Here's the cherry spool bed from her old room,
the white bedspread crocheted by Grandma,
rough straw baskets hanging on the blank wall,   15
snapshots from her last trip home, ramshackle
houses eaten up by kudzu.   The same past
haunts us.   We have ended up in the same present

♦   ♦   ♦

where I sit crosslegged with advice on how to keep
her children from being seized by their father
ten years after I lost my own.   The charge then:
crime against nature, going too far with women,
and not going back to men.   And hers?   Wanting
to have her small garden the way she wanted it,
and wanting to go her own way.   The memory:

> Her father's garden, immense rows of corn,
> cantaloupe and melon squiggling, us squatting,
> late afternoon, cool in the four o'clocks;
> waiting for them to open, making up stories,
> anything might happen, waiting in the garden.

20
25
30

3.

So much for the power of my ideas about oppression
and her disinterest in them.   In fact we've ended
in the same place.   Made wrong, knowing we've done
nothing wrong:

> Like the afternoon we burned up
> the backyard, wanting to see some fire.
> The match's seed opened into straw, paper,
> then bushes, like enormous red and orange
> lantana flowers.   We chased the abrupt power
> blooming around us down to charred straw,
> and Grandma bathed us, scorched and ashy,
> never saying a word.

> Despite our raw hearts,
guilt from men who used our going to take our children,
we know we've done nothing wrong, to twist and search
for the kernels of fire deep in the body's shaken husk.   [1990]

35
40
45

THINKING ABOUT THE TEXT

1. Do you think any behavior deserves to be called a "crime against nature" (line 22)? Explain your reasoning.
2. Ironically, one pattern in Pratt's poem is nature imagery. Do you consider some or all of this imagery to be symbolic, or do you accept the images simply as details of a physical scene? Refer to specific examples.
3. Compare the three sections of the poem. What are their common elements? How do they significantly differ from one another? Why does the speaker believe that she and her cousin have "ended / in the same place" (lines 32–33)?
4. How would you describe the two girls' relationship to their grandmother? Support your answer with specific details from the text.

5. Do you think this poem is an affirmation of family ties? A criticism of them? Both? Again, refer to specific details.

MAKING COMPARISONS

1. Both Tsui's speaker and Pratt's address another woman. In Tsui's poem, it is the "one who was not invited"; in Pratt's, it is the speaker's cousin. Are the speakers expressing pretty much the same message to these women? Support your answer with specific details from both poems.

2. Do you get the impression that all three speakers in this cluster are searching for Pratt's "kernels of fire deep in the body's shaken husk" (line 46)? Show how these words are or are not relevant in each case.

3. Do you sympathize with any of the three speakers more than the others? Why, or why not?

WRITING ABOUT ISSUES

1. Choose Hemphill's, Tsui's, or Pratt's poem, and write an essay arguing for or against a position held by someone in the poem. The person can be the speaker. Support your argument with specific details and examples.

2. Choose two of the poems in this cluster, and write an essay comparing how commitments figure in them. Be sure to cite specific words of each poem.

3. In the next week, observe and jot down things on your campus that you think might disturb a gay or lesbian student. (If you are a gay or lesbian student, you may have already thought about such matters.) Then write an essay addressing the issue of whether your campus is inviting to gay and lesbian students. In arguing for your position on this issue, refer to some of the observations you made. If you wish, refer as well to one or more of the poems in this cluster.

4. Increasingly, the United States is grappling with whether same-sex marriage should be legalized. Another debate is whether gays and lesbians should lose child custody rights because of their sexual orientation. Choose one of these issues, and read at least three articles about it. Then write an essay in which you not only put forth and support your own position on the issue but also state whether and how the articles affected your thinking. If you wish, you may refer as well to one or more of the poems in this cluster.

TRUE LOVE

WILLIAM SHAKESPEARE, "Let me not to the marriage of true minds"
ANNE BRADSTREET, "To My Dear and Loving Husband"
E. E. CUMMINGS, "somewhere i have never travelled"
EDNA ST. VINCENT MILLAY, "Love Is Not All"

Think about the term *true love*. Why *true*? Does *love* need this modification? Isn't love supposed to be true? Is there a *false* love? Or is something else implied that *love* doesn't convey by itself? Might it be something like *the one-and-only*? Some writers seem committed to the idea that true love lasts forever, for better or worse, regardless of circumstances. Is this just a fantasy, something we hope will be true? Or is it a reality, delivered to those who are lucky or who work hard to make it true? See if you agree with the five poets in this cluster.

BEFORE YOU READ

Do you believe there is one perfect person in the world for you? Is it possible to love someone forever, even if both of you change over the years from young adulthood to retirement and beyond?

WILLIAM SHAKESPEARE

Let me not to the marriage of true minds

William Shakespeare (1564–1616) is best known to modern readers as a dramatist; however, there is evidence that both he and his contemporaries valued his poetry above the plays. In 1598, for example, a writer praised Shakespeare's "sugared sonnets among his private friends." As with other aspects of his life and work, questions about how much autobiographical significance to attach to Shakespeare's subject matter continue to arise. Regardless of the discussion, there can be no doubt that the sonnets attributed to Shakespeare, at times directed to a man and at others directed to a woman, address the subject of love. Sonnet 116, which was written in 1609 and proposes a "marriage of true minds," is no exception.

Let me not to the marriage of true minds,
Admit impediments. Love is not love
Which alters when it alteration finds,
Or bends with the remover to remove:
Oh, no! it is an ever-fixèd mark,   5
That looks on tempests and is never shaken;
It is the star to every wandering bark,
Whose worth's unknown, although his height be taken.
Love's not Time's fool, though rosy lips and cheeks

Within his bending sickle's compass come;   10
Love alters not with his brief hours and weeks,
But bears it out even to the edge of doom.
If this be error and upon me proved,
I never writ, nor no man ever loved.   [1609]

THINKING ABOUT THE TEXT

1. Would you be pleased if your beloved wrote you this sonnet? Is he professing his love or giving a definition of true love as unchanging?

2. What if love didn't last "even to the edge of doom" (line 12)? Would it then be ordinary?

3. Shakespeare uses images to describe true love. Which one strikes you as apt? Can you suggest an image of your own?

4. The concluding couplet seems to be saying something like, "I'm absolutely right." Do you think Shakespeare is? Can you think of a situation in which love should bend or alter?

5. The world seems to demonstrate that true love seldom lasts forever. Why then do writers of all kinds profess the opposite? If you really believe that true love does not exist, would you still marry? If your beloved asked you if your love would last forever, would you truthfully answer, "Only time will tell"?

ANNE BRADSTREET
To My Dear and Loving Husband

Anne Bradstreet (1612?–1672), one of the earliest poets in the canon of American literature, was born in England and came to the Massachusetts Bay Colony as the daughter of a governor; later she married another of the colony's governors. Her writings include an autobiographical sketch, several religious works, and a collection of wise sayings written for her son's moral education. Her poems were published in The Tenth Muse Lately Sprang Up in America *(London, 1650; second edition 1678), which has the distinction of being the first book of original verse written in what would become the United States. True to her Puritan milieu, her poems have their share of piety, but they also speak of married love.*

If ever two were one, then surely we.
If ever man were loved by wife, then thee;
If ever wife was happy in a man,
Compare with me, ye women, if you can.
I prize thy love more than whole mines of gold   5
Or all the riches that the East doth hold.

My love is such that rivers cannot quench,
Nor ought but love from thee, give recompense.
Thy love is such I can no way repay,
The heavens reward thee manifold, I pray.   10
Then while we live, in love let's so persevere
That when we live no more, we may live ever.   [1678]

THINKING ABOUT THE TEXT

1. Do you believe that the speaker means what she says? Why?
2. Do you agree that the goal of true love is to be one? What does this mean? Is there a danger in such a relationship?
3. Do you like Bradstreet's rhymes? Are they sophisticated? Subtle? Simple?
4. Why might she feel she has to repay her husband's love? Is true love based on reciprocity?
5. Does Bradstreet's concluding couplet suggest a link between persevering in love on earth and living forever in heaven? Does this connection make sense to you?

MAKING COMPARISONS

1. Would Bradstreet agree with Shakespeare's sonnet?
2. Compare Shakespeare's images with Bradstreet's. Which do you find more original? More appropriate? More sincere?
3. Why are these two poets so concerned with loving "forever"?

E. E. CUMMINGS
somewhere i have never travelled

Edward Estlin Cummings (1894–1962), who for many years preferred the lower-case e. e. cummings, was a highly innovative writer, willing to experiment with language on every level. Born in Cambridge, Massachusetts, and educated at Harvard, he tried his hand at essays, plays, and other types of prose; in fact, it was a novel based on a World War I concentration camp experience in France, The Enormous Room *(1922), that first brought cummings attention. It is his poetry, however, that most readers immediately recognize for its eccentric use of typography and punctuation, its wordplay and slang usage, its jazz rhythms, and its childlike foregrounding of the concrete above the abstract. Cummings hated pretension and would only agree to deliver the prestigious Eliot lectures at Harvard in 1953 if they were called nonlectures. His two large volumes of* The Complete Poems 1913–1962, *published in 1972, include humor, understated satire, and celebrations of love and sex.*

somewhere i have never travelled,gladly beyond
any experience,your eyes have their silence:
in your most frail gesture are things which enclose me,
or which i cannot touch because they are too near

your slightest look easily will unclose me   5
though i have closed myself as fingers,
you open always petal by petal myself as Spring opens
(touching skilfully,mysteriously)her first rose

or if your wish be to close me,i and
my life will shut very beautifully,suddenly,   10
as when the heart of this flower imagines
the snow carefully everywhere descending;

nothing which we are to perceive in this world equals
the power of your intense fragility:whose texture
compels me with the colour of its countries,   15
rendering death and forever with each breathing

(i do not know what it is about you that closes
and opens;only something in me understands
the voice of your eyes is deeper than all roses)
nobody,not even the rain,has such small hands   [1931]   20

THINKING ABOUT THE TEXT

1. In your own words, what is cummings saying about the effect love has on him? Is this hyperbolic? Why?

2. Does love open us up? In what ways? Can you give a personal example of what a strong feeling did to you?

3. Is this a poem about love or obsession or romantic infatuation? What is the difference?

4. What do you think "the power of your intense fragility" (line 14) might mean? Is this a contradiction?

5. When cummings says "something in me understands" (line 18), what might he mean? Is love located inside us somewhere? In our hearts? Our brains?

MAKING COMPARISONS

1. Is cummings's flower imagery more effective than the images that Shakespeare and Bradstreet use?

2. All the poets here use *forever*. What do they intend?

3. What do you imagine Shakespeare and Bradstreet would think about cummings's sentence structure? His images?

EDNA ST. VINCENT MILLAY
Love Is Not All

Edna St. Vincent Millay (1892–1950) was born in Rockland, Maine. Her mother encouraged her to be ambitious and self-sufficient and taught her about literature at an early age. On the strength of her early poems Millay won a scholarship to Vassar where she became a romantic legend for breaking the "hearts of half the undergraduate class." She also soon became wildly famous for her love poetry, giving readings in large auditoriums across the country, much like a contemporary rock star. Openly bisexual, her fame, talent, beauty, and bohemian aura was said to drive her many admirers to distraction. A biography by Nancy Mitford, Savage Beauty *(2001), quotes from dozens of letters to Millay, whining, pleading, and groveling for her favors. Mitford writes that "she gave the Jazz Age its lyric voice." In fact, we still use a phrase that Salon.com says Millay "invented to describe a life of impudent abandon":*

> My candle burns at both ends;
>   It will not last the night;
> But oh, my foes, and oh, my friends —
>   It gives a lovely light!

Once called "the greatest female poet since Sappho," Millay's reputation in academic circles has fallen off somewhat. Perhaps compared to the cerebral and allusive free verse of poets like T. S. Eliot her work seems a bit obvious. But some critics still think of her as America's "most illustrious love poet." The title poem of Renascence and Other Poems *ranks as a landmark of modern literature, and the collection itself is ranked fifth on the New York Public Library's Books of the Century. The following poem is from* Fatal Interview *(1931).*

Love is not all: it is not meat nor drink
Nor slumber nor a roof against the rain;
Nor yet a floating spar to men that sink
And rise and sink and rise and sink again;
Love can not fill the thickened lung with breath,   5
Nor clean the blood, nor set the fractured bone;
Yet many a man is making friends with death
Even as I speak, for lack of love alone.
It well may be that in a difficult hour,
Pinned down by pain and moaning for release,   10
Or nagged by want past resolution's power,
I might be driven to sell your love for peace,
Or trade the memory of this night for food.
It well may be. I do not think I would.   [1931]

THINKING ABOUT THE TEXT

1. Would most people you know trade love for peace or the memory of a romantic night for food? Would you? What does it say about the narrator that she would not?

2. Do you think it is an exaggeration to say that "many a man is making friends with death / . . . for lack of love alone" (lines 7–8)?

3. When the narrator begins "Love is not all" followed by a colon, what expectations are raised? Are they satisfied?

4. What do you think of the rhyme scheme? Does it add to the poem's meaning? Would you rather read free verse than this sonnet form? Why, or why not?

5. Is this a poem about the tension between love and practicality? Explain.

MAKING COMPARISONS

1. What claims for love do all four poems make?

2. Compare the tone of each of the narrators. Which do you prefer? Is sincerity an issue or authenticity or passion?

WRITING ABOUT ISSUES

1. Translate the cummings poem into concrete prose. Try not to use images; just explain the individual lines as simply as you can.

2. Write a comparison of the effects Bradstreet's, cummings's, and Millay's poems had on you.

3. Write a position paper arguing for or against the reality of true love. Make reference to three of the poems given here.

4. Look at a couple of love poems written at the same time as Shakespeare's sonnet (1609). Are there similarities? Differences? Do you think Shakespeare (or any great poet) can transcend his or her attitudes toward true love? Write an essay that tries to answer this question, using the poems you found.

POETRY OF THE HOLOCAUST

MARTIN NIEMÖLLER, "First They Came for the Jews"
NELLY SACHS, "A Dead Child Speaks"
YEVGENY YEVTUSHENKO, "Babii Yar"
KAREN GERSHON, "Race"
ANNE SEXTON, "After Auschwitz"

Being shunned by neighbors because of religion, race, gender, or ethnicity creates painful psychological alienation for victims of such treatment. But what if your religion, cultural heritage, or sexual orientation were deemed dangerous to the well-being of your country? What if the powerful so dehumanized you that you were thought of as vermin to be disposed of? This would be more than alienation; this would be putting respect for human life beyond normal moral restraints. As in war, the different ones become the enemy who is less than human and who can be destroyed with impunity.

Of course, this describes exactly what happened during the Holocaust when the Nazis exterminated millions of Jews. Thousands of eyewitness accounts of this tragedy are written, but writers who were not there feel equally compelled to write about the events of the Holocaust. It is impossible to adequately represent such horrors: Some writers are furious; others are disciplined and controlled. It is one of a writer's challenges to express in words what is truly beyond description.

BEFORE YOU READ

Have you seen photographs of Holocaust survivors? Have you seem films, read books, or heard stories about these events? What are your feelings? Can you explain how systematic genocide is possible? Do such things still happen in the world?

MARTIN NIEMÖLLER
First They Came for the Jews

A German Protestant theologian and pastor, Martin Niemöller (1892–1984), who won the Iron Cross as a submarine commander in World War I, is best known as an outspoken critic of Adolf Hitler and Nazism during and preceding World War II. As the pastor of the Berlin congregation of the Evangelical Church from 1931, Niemöller led a group of clergy working to counter Nazism and earned Hitler's hatred. From 1937 to 1945, he was interned at the Dachau and Sachsenhausen concentration camps. After the war he concentrated his efforts on international disarmament and the recovery of the German church. He served as president of the World Council of Churches from 1961 to 1968.

First they came for the Jews
and I did not speak out
because I was not a Jew.
Then they came for the Communists
and I did not speak out   5
because I was not a Communist.
Then they came for the trade unionists
and I did not speak out
because I was not a trade unionist.
Then they came for me   10
and there was no one left
to speak out for me.   [1945]

THINKING ABOUT THE TEXT

1. The poem seems to merely narrate a sequence of events, but is there an implicit argument here? Should the writer have been more explicit?

2. As you read this poem do you think, "He's talking to me"? Do you think that might be Niemöller's intention?

3. Many poems are lyrical, filled with beautiful images and imaginative phrases. Would this poem be improved by moving in this direction?

4. Often in poetry, people and situations can be taken both literally and as symbols for something else. Do you think that is the case here with the Jews and Communists?

5. Most societies, even democracies, have insiders and outsiders, those with power and privilege and those with no influence. In your experience, does literature relate the feelings and experiences of both equally? Should this anthology balance the poems in this cluster with the experience of insiders?

NELLY SACHS
A Dead Child Speaks
Translated by Ruth and Matthew Mead

A poet and playwright born in Berlin of Jewish parents, Nelly Sachs (1891–1970) escaped from Nazi Germany in 1940 to Stockholm, where she became a Swedish citizen, and eventually won the Nobel Prize for literature in 1966. First published as a poet in Germany in 1921, she later used biblical forms and motifs and empathized with the millions who suffered in the Holocaust. Her best-known play, Eli: A Mystery Play of the Sufferings of Israel, *epitomizes this style, as does the following poem which uses pathos to evoke sympathy.*

My mother held me by my hand
Then someone raised the knife of parting:
So that it should not strike me,
My mother loosed her hand from mine,
But she lightly touched my thighs once more   5
And her hand was bleeding—

After that the knife of parting
Cut in two each bite I swallowed—
It rose before me with the sun at dawn
And began to sharpen itself in my eyes—   10
Wind and water ground in my ear
And every voice of comfort pierced my heart—

As I was led to death
I still felt in the last moment
The unsheathing of the great knife of parting.   [1971]   15

THINKING ABOUT THE TEXT

1. The Nazis often separated children from their parents on arrival at the concentration camps. How does Sachs represent the brutality of such a sorting?

2. Do you find it effective that Sachs's child narrator dies? What is gained by this point of view? Is anything lost?

3. Should Sachs have been more emotional? Less? When writing poetry about horrific events, is it better to underplay the horror or to be explicit?

4. What does the metaphor "the knife of parting" imply? Can you suggest another metaphor or simile that is less dramatic?

5. Do you think the poem suggests that parting is more painful than death? In what ways might this be true?

MAKING COMPARISONS

1. Even though both Niemöller's and Sachs's poems are about the Holocaust, are you able to relate to them from your own experiences?

2. With its central metaphor, Sachs's poem seems more typically poetic. Would Niemöller's poem have been improved with more poetic devices? Might Sachs's poem have been improved with less?

3. One might argue that these two poems are causally connected. Explain.

YEVGENY YEVTUSHENKO
Babii Yar

Translated by George Reavey

Born in Siberia near Lake Baikal in 1933, Yevgeny Yevtushenko is Russia's best-known living poet, attracting huge stadium audiences (30,000 at one reading). He has also written essays, directed films, and toured the world as a speaker. His most recent work is a novel, Don't Die Before You're Dead *(1991), which follows the Soviet Union from the end of World War II through the early 1990s. An honorary member of the American Academy of Arts and Letters, he divides his time between Russia and the United States, where he teaches poetry at the University of Tulsa and Queens College in New York. Although he was sometimes held in disfavor during the Soviet years (once labeled "the head of the intellectual juvenile delinquents" whose poems were "pygmy spittle"), Yevtushenko has been immensely popular from the early 1960s until the present. A poem from the early 1960s, "Babii Yar" responds to the refusal of anti-Semites in the Ukraine to place a monument on the spot of a Nazi massacre of the Jews.*

No monument stands over Babii Yar.
A drop sheer as a crude gravestone.
I am afraid.
   Today I am as old in years
as all the Jewish people.   5
Now I seem to be
    a Jew.
Here I plod through ancient Egypt.
Here I perish crucified, on the cross,
and to this day I bear the scars of nails.   10
I seem to be
    Dreyfus.°
The Philistine
    is both informer and judge.
I am behind bars.   15
    Beset on every side.
Hounded,
   spat on,
     slandered.
Squealing, dainty ladies in flounced Brussels lace   20
stick their parasols into my face.
I seem to be then

12 **Dreyfus:** A French army officer accused of spying for Germany around 1894. His trial caused a political crisis. Many feel that he was accused because he was Jewish.

a young boy in Byelostok.
Blood runs, spilling over the floors.
The barroom rabble-rousers   25
give off a stench of vodka and onion.
A boot kicks me aside, helpless.
In vain I plead with these pogrom bullies.
While they jeer and shout,
                              'Beat the Yids. Save Russia!'   30
Some grain-marketeer beats up my mother.
O my Russian people!
                    I know
                          you
are international to the core.   35
But those with unclean hands
have often made a jingle of your purest name.
I know the goodness of my land.
How vile these anti-Semites —
                              without a qualm   40
they pompously called themselves
the Union of the Russian People!

I seem to be
              Anne Frank°
transparent   45
              as a branch in April.
And I love.
              And have no need of phrases.
My need
              is that we gaze into each other.   50
How little we can see
                    or smell!
We are denied the leaves,
                        we are denied the sky.
Yet we can do so much —   55
                        tenderly
embrace each other in a darkened room.
They're coming here?
                    Be not afraid. Those are the booming
sounds of spring: 60
              spring is coming here.
Come then to me.
              Quick, give me your lips.
Are they smashing down the door?
                              No, it's the ice breaking . . .   65

44 Anne Frank: A fourteen-year-old Jewish girl captured by the Nazis after hiding in an attic for 22 months; she died in a concentration camp. Her diary was published posthumously.

The wild grasses rustle over Babii Yar.
The trees look ominous,
　　　　　　　　like judges.
Here all things scream silently,
　　　　　　　　　　　and, baring my head,　　　　　　　　70
slowly I feel myself
　　　　　　　　turning grey.
And I myself
　　　　　　am one massive, soundless scream
above the thousand thousand buried here.　　　　　　　　75
I am
　　　each old man
　　　　　　　　here shot dead.
I am
　　　every child　　　　　　　　　　　　　　　　　　80
　　　　　　　　here shot dead.
Nothing in me
　　　　　　　shall ever forget!
The 'Internationale,'° let it
　　　　　　　　　thunder　　　　　　　　　　　　85
when the last anti-Semite on earth
is buried for ever.
In my blood there is no Jewish blood.
In their callous rage, all anti-Semites
must hate me now as a Jew.　　　　　　　　　　　　90
For that reason
　　　　　　　I am a true Russian!　　　　　　　[c. 1960]

84 **The 'Internationale'**: The hymn of an international federation of workers influential in liberal causes.

THINKING ABOUT THE TEXT

1. Yevtushenko identifies with the Jews, claiming he is crucified, is Dreyfus, is Anne Frank. Why do you think he is so moved? Who is the target audience for this poem? Explain.

2. Do you think this is a poem of nationalist feelings? Are you proud of our American history? Are there episodes in our history that do not reflect our "real nature" as Americans?

3. What might "We are denied the leaves, / we are denied the sky" (lines 53–54) mean? Why would "The trees look ominous, / like judges" (lines 67–68)?

4. Make a list of the poetic devices used in the poem. How might you change some to convey a different feeling?

5. In line 88, Yevtushenko says he has "no Jewish blood." Does this contradict his earlier identification? What do you guess is his definition of "a true Russian" (line 92)? Could you extend his idea to "a true American"?

MAKING COMPARISONS

1. Sachs is a literal Jew; Yevtushenko is one metaphorically. Does this make sense to you?
2. Niemöller and Yevtushenko manage to speak specifically of the Holocaust, but their themes also seem more universal. How might you explain this?
3. Is it effective for Sachs and Yevtushenko to identify with the dead? Why, or why not?

KAREN GERSHON
Race

Later known by her married name, Karen Tripp, Gershon (1923–1993) escaped from Nazi Germany in 1939 as a teenager. Sent to England without her family, she wrote in her poetry of this experience and the loss of her parents, who died in the Holocaust. Gershon published eight books, contributed to numerous periodicals, and won much recognition, including the British Arts Council Award in 1967. Her poetry was widely read in the 1960s and later, perhaps influencing contemporaries Anne Sexton and Sylvia Plath, who borrowed the imagery of Holocaust survivors to describe family conflict and inner turmoil. "Race" is from Selected Poems *(1966).*

When I returned to my home town
believing that no one would care
who I was and what I thought
it was as if the people caught
an echo of me everywhere   5
they knew my story by my face
and I who am always alone
became a symbol of my race

Like every living Jew I have
in imagination seen   10
the gas-chamber the mass-grave
the unknown body which was mine
and found in every German face
behind the mask the mark of Cain
I will not make their thoughts my own   15
by hating people for their race.   [1966]

THINKING ABOUT THE TEXT

1. Is Gershon imagining or actually describing her reception? How can we tell?
2. Do you mind the poet speaking for "every living Jew" (line 9)? Do you think this is accurate? Can someone be a symbol of their race?

3. Does the title refer to Jews or Germans? Why is neither group mentioned in the title?

4. Gershon writes fairly straightforward poetry, letting her content speak for itself. What specific poetic devices does she employ? Should she use more?

5. Do you find the last four lines ambiguous? Does she see Germans as murderers, or does she reject such invidious generalizations? Should Germans be held accountable for the Holocaust? Should Americans be held accountable for slavery? Are only the people who specifically partake in evil deeds responsible, or is the whole culture that "allowed" it guilty as well?

MAKING COMPARISONS

1. Both Gershon and Yevtushenko revisit Holocaust sites. Describe their different perspectives.

2. Do you think Sachs could have written "Race"? Explain.

3. Which of the four poets finds something positive out of the horrors of the Holocaust?

ANNE SEXTON
After Auschwitz

Growing up in New England and attending elite boarding and finishing schools during the years of World War II, Anne Sexton (1928–1974) had an emotional connection with the Holocaust rather than a firsthand one: Her obsession with images of death and degradation and her "confessional" poetic stance blend seamlessly with such a theme. Additional biographical information appears on page 717. "After Auschwitz" is from The Awful Rowing Toward God *(1977).*

Anger,
as black as a hook,
overtakes me.
Each day,
each Nazi   5
took, at 8.00 a.m., a baby
and sautéed him for breakfast
in his frying pan.

And death looks on with a casual eye
and picks at the dirt under his fingernail.   10

Man is evil,
I say aloud.

Man is a flower
that should be burnt,
I say aloud.   15
Man
is a bird full of mud,
I say aloud.

And death looks on with a casual eye
and scratches his anus.   20

Man with his small pink toes,
with his miraculous fingers
is not a temple
but an outhouse,
I say aloud.   25
Let man never again raise his teacup.
Let man never again write a book.
Let man never again put on his shoe.
Let man never again raise his eyes,
on a soft July night.   30
Never. Never. Never. Never. Never.
I say these things aloud.

I beg the Lord not to hear.   [1977]

THINKING ABOUT THE TEXT

1. What is Sexton's purpose here if she really does not want God to listen?

2. What is your response to the image of Nazi cannibalism in lines 4–8? What about her inclusive accusation that "Man is evil" (line 11)?

3. As Sexton's editor, would you suggest that she change any specific words or phrases? Should she control the generally angry tone?

4. Sexton personifies death. Why? Why do you think she refers to man's "pink toes" and "miraculous fingers" in lines 21 and 22?

5. Sexton sees the Holocaust as an indictment of everyone. Do you agree with her?

MAKING COMPARISONS

1. Compare the ambivalence at the end of Sexton's poem to that of Gershon's poem.

2. Do you think Sachs's poem would be improved by Sexton's explicit anger? Would Sexton's poem be improved by Sachs's control?

3. Which of these five poets comes closest to expressing your feelings about the Holocaust?

WRITING ABOUT ISSUES

1. Argue that Sexton's indictment of humankind is either hyperbolic or accurate.
2. Make a case in a brief essay that "First They Came for the Jews" leads to "A Dead Child Speaks."
3. Write a brief personal response explaining your feelings about the Holocaust or suggesting what such an event tells us about human nature, if anything.
4. Rent Steven Spielberg's film about the Holocaust, *Schindler's List*. Write a review expressing your feelings and thoughts about its contents and its representation of the Holocaust. Include a comparison to the poems you read.

IMAGINING THE END: A COLLECTION OF WRITINGS BY EMILY DICKINSON

EMILY DICKINSON, "I like a look of Agony"
EMILY DICKINSON, "I've seen a Dying Eye"
EMILY DICKINSON, "I heard a Fly buzz—when I died—"
EMILY DICKINSON, "Because I could not stop for Death—"

Through the centuries, works of literature have depicted scenes of death, with all sorts of purposes, styles, and effects. Among the best-known death scenes in literature are those produced by Emily Dickinson (1830–1886), now regarded as one of the greatest American poets. Although Dickinson spent much of her adult life as a virtual recluse, rarely leaving the Amherst, Massachusetts, home where she was born, her poems constantly reveal a lively, passionate intelligence. Moreover, death was hardly her sole topic; she wrote hundreds of poems on other subjects. Her poems about death are wonderfully creative, even playful in their use of metaphor and detail and express a range of attitudes toward death, from sadness to curiosity to acceptance. They vary as well in the positions they accord the speaker: the "I" is sometimes the dying person, at other times a witness to someone else's death. The four poems included here illustrate just a few of the diverse approaches that Dickinson took to human mortality. They do have in common the large amount of room they leave for interpretation; see if you and your classmates agree on how to analyze them.

BEFORE YOU READ

Why do you think a poet might be interested in describing scenes of death? Do you assume there is something unhealthy about such a focus? Why, or why not?

(Amherst College
Archives and Special
Collections.)

EMILY DICKINSON
I like a look of Agony

Emily Dickinson was an avid reader and a prolific writer, producing almost two thousand poems. Only a few of them were published while she was alive, partly because male editors of her time had difficulty appreciating her sheer originality as a woman writer. Furthermore, posthumous editors of her work have not always reproduced her manuscripts faithfully. Often they have altered the spelling, punctuation, and overall form of her poems in an attempt to make them seem more conventional than they really are. Dickinson did not even give her poems titles. Following customary practice, we have identified the poems in this cluster by their first lines. The following poem was written around 1861.

I like a look of Agony,
Because I know it's true —
Men do not sham Convulsion,
Nor simulate, a Throe —

The Eyes glaze once — and that is Death —   5
Impossible to feign
The Beads upon the Forehead
By homely Anguish strung.   [c. 1861]

THINKING ABOUT THE TEXT

1. What would you say to someone who argues that the speaker is being
   sadistic in liking "a look of Agony," especially when many Americans were
   dying agonizing deaths in the Civil War? Do you share to any extent the
   speaker's values?
2. What is the effect of Dickinson's use of capitalization?
3. How does the second stanza of the poem relate to the first?
4. Look up the word *homely* in a dictionary. Is Dickinson using the word in
   any of the senses you find there? Should she?
5. Note the words *Beads* and *strung* at the end of the poem. What object do
   they normally suggest? How appropriate is this object as a concluding
   image for the poem?

EMILY DICKINSON
I've seen a Dying Eye

Dickinson wrote this poem around 1862.

I've seen a Dying Eye
Run round and round a Room —
In search of Something — as it seemed —
Then Cloudier become —
And then — obscure with Fog —   5
And then — be soldered down
Without disclosing what it be
'Twere blessed to have seen —   [c. 1862]

THINKING ABOUT THE TEXT

1. To what extent does this poem seem to be about the speaker rather than
   about the dying person? What adjectives would you use to describe each?
2. What would you say to someone who argues that the word *run* is too
   active a verb for someone who is dying?
3. Should readers try to guess what the dying person is searching for? Why, or
   why not? Do you get the impression that he or she was, in fact, "blessed"?
4. Trace the poem's pattern of *m* sounds. What is their effect?
5. What do you conclude from the fact that the word *seen* appears both at
   the beginning and at the end of the poem?

MAKING COMPARISONS

1. Do you get the impression that this poem depicts the "look of Agony" that the speaker in the first poem likes? Refer to specific lines in each text.
2. How vivid is the death scene in this poem compared to that in the first?
3. What words in this poem can be related to the word *glaze* in the first?

EMILY DICKINSON
I heard a Fly buzz—when I died—

Dickinson wrote the following poem, one of her most famous, around 1862.

I heard a Fly buzz—when I died—
The Stillness in the Room
Was like the Stillness in the Air—
Between the Heaves of Storm—

The Eyes around—had wrung them dry—   5
And Breaths were gathering firm
For that last Onset—when the King
Be witnessed—in the Room—

I willed my Keepsakes—Signed away
What portion of me be   10
Assignable—and then it was
There interposed a Fly—

With Blue—uncertain stumbling Buzz—
Between the light—and me—
And then the Windows failed—and then   15
I could not see to see—   [c. 1862]

THINKING ABOUT THE TEXT

1. Do you find this poem amusing? Horrifying? Both? Neither? Identify specific lines, as well as any experiences of yours, that influence your response.
2. Many might argue that the poem presents a logical impossibility: No one can recall when he or she died because death extinguishes thought. How would you respond to this charge?
3. Why do you think Dickinson repeats the word *Stillness* in the first stanza? Consult a dictionary definition of the word. Why do you think she repeats *see* in the last line?
4. Although Dickinson mentions the fly in the first line, she doesn't return to it until the last line of the third stanza. Why do you think she delays? What might she have been trying to achieve in the intervening lines?

5. Although Dickinson writes "And then the Windows failed," plainly it is the speaker's eyesight that is failing. Why do you think Dickinson states otherwise?

MAKING COMPARISONS

1. In the first two poems, the "I" is a witness to someone else's death. Here, the "I" dies. Do you therefore read this poem with different feelings? Why, or why not?

2. Note the reference to "the King" in the second stanza of this poem. Would someone be justified in concluding that "the King" is what the dying person is searching for in "I've seen a Dying Eye"? Why, or why not? Does the first poem have nothing to do with religion since it does not use expressions like "the King"?

3. The second stanza of this poem refers to "Eyes" and "Breaths" rather than whole people. Similarly, "I've seen a Dying Eye" refers just to an eye rather than explicitly mentioning a person. Moreover, the second stanza of "I like a look of Agony," focuses purely on the eyes and the forehead. What should readers conclude from Dickinson's emphasis on parts of bodies?

EMILY DICKINSON
Because I could not stop for Death—

This poem, also one of Dickinson's best known, was written about 1863.

Because I could not stop for Death—
He kindly stopped for me—
The Carriage held but just Ourselves—
And Immortality.

We slowly drove—He knew no haste   5
And I had put away
My labor and my leisure too,
For His Civility—

We passed the School, where Children strove
At Recess—in the Ring—   10
We passed the Fields of Gazing Grain—
We passed the Setting Sun—

Or rather—He passed Us—
The Dews drew quivering and chill—
For only Gossamer, my Gown—   15
My Tippet°—only Tulle—   *shawl*

♦ ♦ ♦

We paused before a House that seemed
A Swelling of the Ground —
The Roof was scarcely visible —
The Cornice — in the Ground —

Since then — 'tis Centuries — and yet
Feels shorter than the Day
I first surmised the Horses' Heads
Were toward Eternity —   [c. 1863]

20

THINKING ABOUT THE TEXT

1. Describe the speaker's tone. What do you think he or she means by "I could not stop for Death"? How, exactly, might "He kindly stopped for me" refer to something different? In what other lines, if any, do you sense the speaker expressing his or her feelings?

2. The first stanza ends by noting that immortality is a passenger in the carriage. Should readers conclude that the speaker is now immortal? Why, or why not?

3. What image of death do you get from this poem? List at least three adjectives of your own.

4. Note the things passed in the third stanza. Why do you think Dickinson chose to include these rather than other things? What is the effect of her making the ultimate destination a house?

5. Do you find this poem comforting? Remember that Dickinson wrote it when she was about thirty-three. If she had identified the speaker as being only that old, would you have reacted to the poem differently?

MAKING COMPARISONS

1. Do the first two lines of this poem seem applicable to the deaths in the other three poems? Explain your reasoning. In general, this poem develops the idea of dying as a journey. Is such a metaphor compatible with the death scenes of the other three poems? Refer to specific lines in them.

2. Is this poem sunnier than the other three? Explain.

3. Rank the four poems in this cluster from the one you like most to the one you like least. Identify the criteria you are using to make your evaluations.

WRITING ABOUT ISSUES

1. Each of the poems in this cluster refers to one or more efforts to see something. Choose one of the poems, and write an essay considering what is and isn't accomplished by whatever attempts at vision the poem discusses. Refer to specific lines.

2. Write an essay comparing two of the speakers in this cluster. Focus on identifying the extent to which they resemble each other in their feelings and thoughts. Refer to specific lines in each poem.

3. Choose one of the poems in this cluster and write an essay discussing how you would present the poem to a particular person you know. What about the poem would you emphasize to this person? What about the person's own life would you be thinking of? What kind of response would you hope for? If you wish, your essay can take the form of a letter to the person.

4. Obtain a contemporary sympathy card that features a poem. Then write an essay comparing the card's poem to a poem by Dickinson from this cluster. Focus on just one or two bases of comparison: for example, the poems' attitudes toward death, their language, their potential functions in society, their relative artistic quality. Be sure to quote from each of the two poems you discuss.

A WEB ASSIGNMENT

Emily Dickinson produced several handwritten manuscripts of her poem "I heard a Fly buzz—when I died—". The *Making Arguments about Literature* Web site will link you to an electronic reproduction of one such manuscript, at a site designed by Meredith Bishop and Brian Dillard for a class at the University of Texas, Austin. Looking at the manuscript, do you think a typeset version of it (such as the one in this book) can provide the same reading experience? Write an essay addressing this question. Consider in particular how slanted Dickinson's handwriting is. How relevant is this quality to your experience of the poem?

Visit www.bedfordstmartins.com/argumentsaboutlit

DISRESPECTING DEATH

JOHN DONNE, "Death Be Not Proud"
DYLAN THOMAS, "Do Not Go Gentle into That Good Night"
WISLAWA SZYMBORSKA, "On Death, without Exaggeration"

Through their works, writers of literature convey a wide range of attitudes toward death. Some take the opportunity to mourn the demise of a loved one, a friend, or a public figure. Others use the written word to stress that death is inevitable. Many literary works deal with death by expressing both sorrow and resignation. Each of the poems in this cluster expresses still another stance toward death: disrespect. Directly addressing death, John Donne's speaker virtually sneers at it. Addressing someone in danger of dying, Dylan Thomas's speaker portrays death as a force to resist. Finally, Wislawa Szymborska describes death in terms that considerably reduce its significance. As you read all three poems, think about whether disrespect toward death makes sense to you. Perhaps you feel that it is appropriate in certain circumstances but not others. If so, exactly when would you want death scorned? When would you call for acceptance of it, even reverence toward it?

BEFORE YOU READ

If you were to write a poem treating Death as a person and insulting him or her, what specific remarks might you make?

JOHN DONNE
Death Be Not Proud

Long regarded as a major English writer, John Donne (1572–1631) was also trained as a lawyer and clergyman. Around 1594, he converted from Catholicism to Anglicanism; in 1615, he was ordained; and in 1621, he was appointed to the prestigious position of dean of St. Paul's Cathedral in London. Today, his sermons continue to be studied as literature, yet he is more known for his poetry. When he was a young man, he often wrote about love, but later he focused on religious themes. The following poem, one of Donne's "holy sonnets," is from 1611.

Death be not proud, though some have callèd thee
Mighty and dreadful, for thou art not so;
For those whom thou think'st thou dost overthrow
Die not, poor Death, nor yet canst thou kill me.
From rest and sleep, which but thy pictures° be,   *images*   5
Much pleasure; then from thee much more must flow,
And soonest our best men with thee do go,
Rest of their bones, and soul's delivery.°   *deliverance*
Thou art slave to Fate, Chance, kings, and desperate men,
And dost with Poison, War, and Sickness dwell;   10
And poppy or charms can make us sleep as well,
And better than thy stroke; why swell'st° thou then?   *swell with pride*
One short sleep past, we wake eternally
And death shall be no more; Death, thou shalt die.   [1611]

THINKING ABOUT THE TEXT

1. In a sense, Death is the speaker's audience. But presumably Donne expected the living to read his poem. What reaction might he have wanted from this audience?
2. Is the speaker proud? Define what you mean by the term.

3. Evidently the speaker believes in an afterlife. What would you say to people who consider the speaker naive and the poem irrelevant because they don't believe that "we wake eternally"? How significant is this warrant or assumption? Do you share it?

4. Identify the rhyme patterns. How aware of them were you when you first read the poem?

5. Imagine Death writing a sonnet in response to the speaker. Perhaps it would be entitled "Life Be Not Proud." What might Death say in it?

DYLAN THOMAS
Do Not Go Gentle into That Good Night

Dylan Thomas (1914–1953) was a Welsh poet, short-story writer, and playwright. Among his most enduring works are his radio dramas Under Milk Wood *(1954) and* A Child's Christmas in Wales *(1955). A frequent visitor to the United States, Thomas built a devoted audience in this country through his electrifying public readings. Unfortunately, he was also well known for his alcoholism, which killed him at a relatively young age. He wrote the following poem in 1952, not long before his own death. It takes the form of a* villanelle, *which consists of nineteen lines: five tercets (three-line stanzas) followed by a quatrain (four-line stanza). The first and third lines of the opening tercet are used alternately to conclude each succeeding tercet, and they are joined to form a rhyme at the poem's end.*

Do not go gentle into that good night,
Old age should burn and rave at close of day;
Rage, rage against the dying of the light.

Though wise men at their end know dark is right,
Because their words had forked no lightning they   5
Do not go gentle into that good night.

Good men, the last wave by, crying how bright
Their frail deeds might have danced in a green bay,
Rage, rage against the dying of the light.

Wild men who caught and sang the sun in flight,   10
And learn, too late, they grieved it on its way,
Do not go gentle into that good night.

Grave men, near death, who see with blinding sight
Blind eyes could blaze like meteors and be gay,
Rage, rage against the dying of the light.   15

◆ ◆ ◆

And you, my father, there on the sad height,
Curse, bless, me now with your fierce tears, I pray.
Do not go gentle into that good night.
Rage, rage against the dying of the light.   [1952]

THINKING ABOUT THE TEXT

1. In what sense could the night possibly be "good," given that people are supposed to "rage" at it?

2. Why do you think Thomas has his speaker refer to "the dying of the light" instead of simply to "dying"? What other parts of the poem relate to the word *light*?

3. The speaker refers to four kinds of "men." Restate in your own words the description given of each. Should Thomas's language about them have been less abstract? Why, or why not?

4. What is the effect of climaxing the poem with a reference to "you, my father" (line 16)? If the father had been introduced in the first or second stanzas, would the effect have been quite different? If so, how?

5. What is the effect of the villanelle form? Judging by Thomas's poem, do you think it is worthwhile for a poet to write in this way, despite the technical challenges of the form? Should teachers of poetry writing push their students to write a villanelle? Explain your reasoning.

WISLAWA SZYMBORSKA
On Death, without Exaggeration

Translated by Stanislaw Baranczak and Clare Cavanagh

Although she has written several volumes of poetry, Wislawa Szymborska (b. 1923) was little known outside of her native Poland until she won the Nobel Prize for literature in 1996. Since then, readers in various countries have come to admire the blend of simplicity, wit, and wisdom in her writing. The Polish version of the following poem appeared in Szymborska's 1986 book The People on the Bridge. *Subsequently, Stanislaw Baranczak and Clare Cavanagh included it in their 1995 English collection of Szymborska's poems,* View with a Grain of Sand. *We present their translation of the text.*

It can't take a joke,
find a star, make a bridge.
It knows nothing about weaving, mining, farming,
building ships, or baking cakes.

* * *

In our planning for tomorrow,
it has the final word,
which is always beside the point.

It can't even get the things done
that are part of its trade:
dig a grave,   10
make a coffin,
clean up after itself.

Preoccupied with killing,
it does the job awkwardly,
without system or skill.   15
As though each of us were its first kill.

Oh, it has its triumphs,
but look at its countless defeats,
missed blows,
and repeat attempts!   20

Sometimes it isn't strong enough
to swat a fly from the air.
Many are the caterpillars
that have outcrawled it.

All those bulbs, pods,   25
tentacles, fins, tracheae,
nuptial plumage, and winter fur
show that it has fallen behind
with its halfhearted work.

Ill will won't help   30
and even our lending a hand with wars and coups d'état
is so far not enough.

Hearts beat inside eggs.
Babies' skeletons grow.
Seeds, hard at work, sprout their first tiny pair of leaves   35
and sometimes even tall trees fall away.

Whoever claims that it's omnipotent
is himself living proof
that it's not.

There's no life   40
that couldn't be immortal
if only for a moment.

Death
always arrives by that very moment too late.

◆   ◆   ◆

In vain it tugs at the knob   45
of the invisible door.
As far as you've come
can't be undone.   [1986]

THINKING ABOUT THE TEXT

1. Although the word *death* appears in the title, it doesn't appear in the text
   of the poem until the next-to-last stanza. Up till then, death is repeatedly
   referred to as "it." What is the effect of this pronoun? What might be the
   effect had Szymborska referred to death more explicitly throughout the text?

2. Evidently the speaker is trying not to exaggerate death. What sorts of
   remarks about death might the speaker see as an exaggeration of it?
   Define what you mean by *exaggeration*.

3. What images of death does the speaker create? Refer to specific lines.

4. In the eighth stanza, the speaker mentions that human beings are "lending a hand" to death. Do you take the speaker to be criticizing humanity
   at this point? Why, or why not?

5. Does the order of the stanzas matter? Could the speaker's observations
   about death appear in any order and have the same effect? Explain your
   reasoning.

MAKING COMPARISONS

1. Do all three poems in this cluster speak of death "without exaggeration"?
   Define what you mean by the term.

2. Does Szymborska's poem strike you as lighter, less serious than Donne's
   and Thomas's? Refer to specific lines in each text.

3. Suppose that you didn't know who wrote these three poems and were told
   that only one of the authors was female. What specific aspects of these
   poems, if any, would you consider as you tried to guess the one written by
   a woman?

WRITING ABOUT ISSUES

1. Choose Donne's, Thomas's, or Szymborska's poem, and write an essay
   analyzing the poem as an argument for a certain position on death. Specify the main claim and the evidence given in support of it. Feel free to
   evaluate the argument you discuss, although keep in mind that the artistic
   success of the poem may or may not depend on whether its argument is
   fully developed.

2. Write an essay comparing two of the poems in this cluster, focusing on
   the issue of whether they are basically similar or significantly different in
   the ideas and feelings they express. Refer to specific lines from each text.

3. Write an essay recalling a specific occasion when you had difficulty deciding whether to accept something as inevitable. In your essay, give details of the occasion, the difficulty, and your ultimate reasoning. Indicate as well what your final decision revealed about you. Perhaps you will want to distinguish between the self you were then and the self you are now. If you wish, refer to any of the poems in this cluster.

4. Imagine that you are on the staff of a nursing home. At a staff meeting, the chief administrator asks you and your colleagues to consider framing and hanging Donne's, Thomas's, or Szymborska's poem in the recreation room. Write a letter to the administrator in which you favor one of these poems or reject them all as inappropriate. Be sure to give reasons for your view.

11

A Drama Cluster

A FAMILY'S DREAMS: CULTURAL CONTEXTS FOR LORRAINE HANSBERRY'S *A RAISIN IN THE SUN*

LORRAINE HANSBERRY, A *Raisin in the Sun*

CULTURAL CONTEXTS:
THE CRISIS, "The Hansberrys of Chicago: They Join Business Acumen with Social Vision"
LORRAINE HANSBERRY, *April 23, 1964, Letter to the* New York Times
ALAN EHRENHALT, From *The Lost City: Discovering the Forgotten Virtues of Community in the Chicago of the 1950s*
SIDNEY POITIER, From *The Measure of a Man: A Spiritual Autobiography*

Hansberry's title comes from African American poet Langston Hughes's 1951 poem "Harlem," which begins by asking "What happens to a dream deferred? / Does it dry up / Like a raisin in the sun?" Hughes had in mind white America's continued thwarting of his own race's hopes for freedom, equality, and prosperity. This is a situation painfully familiar to the Youngers, the African American family of Hansberry's play, who live in a Chicago ghetto during the 1950s. Like other texts in Part One, the play deals with the topic of work. Most of the Youngers have survived by laboring for white people, though they have been stuck in near poverty all the same. Now, a large inheritance promises to fulfill their dreams at last—but these dreams conflict. Whereas Lena wants to buy a house, her son Walter Lee wants to invest in a liquor store to escape his degrading job as a chauffeur. Much of the play's drama occurs as these two characters clash.

BEFORE YOU READ

Think of your own family or another you know well. For outsiders to get a sense of this family, what do they have to know about its social and historical background? Do you think the phrase *a dream deferred* applies to this family? Why, or why not?

(AP/Wide World.)

LORRAINE HANSBERRY
A Raisin in the Sun

The life of Lorraine Hansberry (1930–1965) was brief. She died of cancer the day that her second play, The Sign in Sidney Brustein's Window *(1964), closed on Broadway. But even by then, she had been immensely productive as a writer and gained a considerable reputation for her work. In 1959, her first play,* A Raisin in the Sun, *was the first by an African American woman to be produced on Broadway. Later that year, it became the first play by an African American to win the New York Drama Critics Circle Award. In part, the play was based on an experience that Hansberry's own family endured while she was growing up in Chicago. Her father, Carl Hansberry, a prominent realtor and banker, made history in 1938 when he moved his family to an all-white section of Chicago's Hyde Park neighborhood. After encountering white resistance there, he fought a series of legal battles that went all the way to the Supreme Court. In 1940, the Court ruled in his favor, but its decision largely was not enforced; housing remained basically segregated in Chicago and in most of the* country. Embittered, Carl Hansberry considered moving his family permanently to Mexico, but before he could, he died of a cerebral hemorrhage there in 1946.

After attending the University of Wisconsin, Lorraine Hansberry moved to New York City. Besides plays, she wrote essays, articles, and pieces of journalism on a variety of subjects, including homophobia and racism. She also wrote the screenplay for the 1961 film version of A Raisin in the Sun, *which featured the original Broadway cast (including Sidney Poitier as Walter Lee Younger). In 1969, her husband Robert Nemiroff combined various writings of hers into a play called* To Be Young, Gifted, and Black. *In 1970, a book version of it was published, and that same year there was a Broadway production of Hansberry's final play,* Les Blancs. *In 2004,* Raisin *was revived on Broadway, with rap star Sean Combs as Walter Lee Younger and* The Cosby Show's *Phylicia Rashad as Mama.*

Harlem (A Dream Deferred)

What happens to a dream deferred?

Does it dry up
Like a raisin in the sun?
Or fester like a sore —
And then run?
Does it stink like rotten meat?
Or crust and sugar over —
Like a syrupy sweet?

Maybe it just sags
Like a heavy load.

Or does it explode?
— Langston Hughes

CHARACTERS (in order of appearance)

RUTH YOUNGER
TRAVIS YOUNGER
WALTER LEE YOUNGER, *brother*
BENEATHA YOUNGER
LENA YOUNGER, MAMA
JOSEPH ASAGAI
GEORGE MURCHISON
MRS. JOHNSON
KARL LINDNER
BOBO
MOVING MEN

The action of the play is set in Chicago's Southside, sometime between World War II *and the present.*

ACT 1, Scene 1

[*Friday morning.*]

The Younger living room would be a comfortable and well-ordered room if it were not for a number of indestructible contradictions to this state of being. Its furnishings are typical and undistinguished and their primary feature now is that they have clearly had to accommodate the living of too many people for too many years—and they are tired. Still, we can see that at some time, a time probably no longer remembered by the family (except perhaps for Mama), the furnishings of this room were actually selected with care and love and even hope—and brought to this apartment and arranged with taste and pride.

That was a long time ago. Now the once loved pattern of the couch upholstery has to fight to show itself from under acres of crocheted doilies and couch covers which have themselves finally come to be more important than the upholstery. And here a table or a chair has been moved to disguise the worn places in the carpet; but the carpet has fought back by showing its weariness, with depressing uniformity, elsewhere on its surface.

Weariness has, in fact, won in this room. Everything has been polished, washed, sat on, used, scrubbed too often. All pretenses but living itself have long since vanished from the very atmosphere of this room.

Moreover, a section of this room, for it is not really a room unto itself, though the landlord's lease would make it seem so, slopes backward to provide a small kitchen area, where the family prepares the meals that are eaten in the living room proper, which must also serve as dining room. The single window that has been provided for these "two" rooms is located in this kitchen area. The sole natural light the family may enjoy in the course of a day is only that which fights its way through this little window.

At left, a door leads to a bedroom which is shared by Mama and her daughter, Beneatha. At right, opposite, is a second room (which in the beginning of the life of this apartment was probably a breakfast room) which serves as a bedroom for Walter and his wife, Ruth.

Time: Sometime between World War II and the present.

Place: Chicago's Southside.

At Rise: It is morning dark in the living room. Travis is asleep on the make-down bed at center. An alarm clock sounds from within the bedroom at right, and presently Ruth enters from that room and closes the door behind her. She crosses sleepily toward the window. As she passes her sleeping son she reaches down and shakes him a little. At the window she raises the shade and a dusky Southside morning light comes in feebly. She fills a pot with water and puts it on to boil. She calls to the boy, between yawns, in a slightly muffled voice.

Ruth is about thirty. We can see that she was a pretty girl, even exceptionally so, but now it is apparent that life has been little that she expected, and disappointment has already begun to hang in her face. In a few years, before thirty-five even, she will be known among her people as a "settled woman."

She crosses to her son and gives him a good, final, rousing shake.

RUTH: Come on now, boy, it's seven thirty! *(Her son sits up at last, in a stupor of sleepiness.)* I say hurry up, Travis! You ain't the only person in the world got to use a bathroom! *(The child, a sturdy, handsome little boy of ten or eleven, drags himself out of the bed and almost blindly takes his towels and "today's clothes" from drawers and a closet and goes out to the bathroom, which is in an outside hall and which is shared by another family or families on the same floor. Ruth crosses to the bedroom door at right and opens it and calls in to her husband.)* Walter Lee! . . . It's after seven thirty! Lemme see you do some waking up in there now! *(She waits.)* You better get up from there, man! It's after seven thirty I tell you. *(She waits again.)* All right, you just go ahead and lay there and next thing you know Travis be finished and Mr. Johnson'll be in there and you'll be fussing and cussing round here like a madman! And be late too! *(She waits, at the end of patience.)* Walter Lee — it's time for you to GET UP!

She waits another second and then starts to go into the bedroom, but is apparently satisfied that her husband has begun to get up. She stops, pulls the door to, and returns to the kitchen area. She wipes her face with a moist cloth and runs her fingers through her sleep-disheveled hair in a vain effort and ties an apron around her housecoat. The bedroom door at right opens and her husband stands in the doorway in his pajamas, which are rumpled and mismated. He is a lean, intense young man in his middle thirties, inclined to quick nervous movements and erratic speech habits — and always in his voice there is a quality of indictment.

WALTER: Is he out yet?

RUTH: What you mean *out?* He ain't hardly got in there good yet.

WALTER *(wandering in, still more oriented to sleep than to a new day):*   Well, what was you doing all that yelling for if I can't even get in there yet? *(Stopping and thinking.)* Check coming today?

RUTH: They *said* Saturday and this is just Friday and I hopes to God you ain't going to get up here first thing this morning and start talking to me 'bout no money — 'cause I 'bout don't want to hear it.

WALTER: Something the matter with you this morning?

RUTH: No — I'm just sleepy as the devil. What kind of eggs you want?

WALTER: Not scrambled. *(Ruth starts to scramble eggs.)* Paper come? *(Ruth points impatiently to the rolled up* Tribune *on the table, and he gets it and spreads it out and vaguely reads the front page.)* Set off another bomb yesterday.

RUTH *(maximum indifference):*   Did they?

WALTER *(looking up):*   What's the matter with you?

RUTH: Ain't nothing the matter with me. And don't keep asking me that this morning.

WALTER: Ain't nobody bothering you. *(Reading the news of the day absently again.)* Say Colonel McCormick is sick.

RUTH *(affecting tea-party interest):*   Is he now? Poor thing.

WALTER *(sighing and looking at his watch):*   Oh, me. *(He waits.)* Now what is that boy doing in that bathroom all this time? He just going to have to start getting up earlier. I can't be being late to work on account of him fooling around in there.

RUTH *(turning on him)*:   Oh, no he ain't going to be getting up no earlier no such thing! It ain't his fault that he can't get to bed no earlier nights 'cause he got a bunch of crazy good-for-nothing clowns sitting up running their mouths in what is supposed to be his bedroom after ten o'clock at night . . .

WALTER: That's what you mad about, ain't it? The things I want to talk about with my friends just couldn't be important in your mind, could they?

He rises and finds a cigarette in her handbag on the table and crosses to the little window and looks out, smoking and deeply enjoying this first one.

RUTH *(almost matter of factly, a complaint too automatic to deserve emphasis)*:   Why you always got to smoke before you eat in the morning?

WALTER *(at the window)*:   Just look at 'em down there . . . Running and racing to work . . . *(He turns and faces his wife and watches her a moment at the stove, and then, suddenly.)* You look young this morning, baby.

RUTH *(indifferently)*:   Yeah?

WALTER: Just for a second—stirring them eggs. Just for a second it was—you looked real young again. *(He reaches for her; she crosses away. Then, drily.)* It's gone now—you look like yourself again!

RUTH: Man, if you don't shut up and leave me alone.

WALTER *(looking out to the street again)*:   First thing a man ought to learn in life is not to make love to no colored woman first thing in the morning. You all some eeeevil people at eight o'clock in the morning.

Travis appears in the hall doorway, almost fully dressed and quite wide awake now, his towels and pajamas across his shoulders. He opens the door and signals for his father to make the bathroom in a hurry.

TRAVIS *(watching the bathroom)*:   Daddy, come on!

Walter gets his bathroom utensils and flies out to the bathroom.

RUTH: Sit down and have your breakfast, Travis.

TRAVIS: Mama, this is Friday. *(Gleefully.)* Check coming tomorrow, huh?

RUTH: You get your mind off money and eat your breakfast.

TRAVIS *(eating)*:   This is the morning we supposed to bring the fifty cents to school.

RUTH: Well, I ain't got no fifty cents this morning.

TRAVIS: Teacher say we have to.

RUTH: I don't care what teacher say. I ain't got it. Eat your breakfast, Travis.

TRAVIS: I *am* eating.

RUTH: Hush up now and just eat!

The boy gives her an exasperated look for her lack of understanding, and eats grudgingly.

TRAVIS: You think Grandmama would have it?

RUTH: No! And I want you to stop asking your grandmother for money, you hear me?

TRAVIS *(outraged)*:   Gaaaleee! I don't ask her, she just gimme it sometimes!

RUTH: Travis Willard Younger—I got too much on me this morning to be—

TRAVIS: Maybe Daddy—

RUTH: *Travis!*

The boy hushes abruptly. They are both quiet and tense for several seconds.

TRAVIS *(presently):*   Could I maybe go carry some groceries in front of the super-market for a little while after school then?

RUTH: Just hush, I said. *(Travis jabs his spoon into his cereal bowl viciously, and rests his head in anger upon his fists.)* If you through eating, you can get over there and make up your bed.

The boy obeys stiffly and crosses the room, almost mechanically, to the bed and more or less folds the bedding into a heap, then angrily gets his books and cap.

TRAVIS *(sulking and standing apart from her unnaturally):*   I'm gone.

RUTH *(looking up from the stove to inspect him automatically):*   Come here. *(He crosses to her and she studies his head.)* If you don't take this comb and fix this here head, you better! *(Travis puts down his books with a great sigh of oppression, and crosses to the mirror. His mother mutters under her breath about his "slubbornness.")* 'Bout to march out of here with that head looking just like chickens slept in it! I just don't know where you get your slubborn ways . . . And get your jacket, too. Looks chilly out this morning.

TRAVIS *(with conspicuously brushed hair and jacket):*   I'm gone.

RUTH: Get carfare and milk money—*(Waving one finger.)*—and not a single penny for no caps, you hear me?

TRAVIS *(with sullen politeness):*   Yes'm.

He turns in outrage to leave. His mother watches after him as in his frustration he approaches the door almost comically. When she speaks to him, her voice has become a very gentle tease.

RUTH *(mocking; as she thinks he would say it):*   Oh, Mama makes me so mad sometimes, I don't know what to do! *(She waits and continues to his back as he stands stock-still in front of the door.)* I wouldn't kiss that woman good-bye for nothing in this world this morning! *(The boy finally turns around and rolls his eyes at her, knowing the mood has changed and he is vindicated; he does not, however, move toward her yet.)* Not for nothing in this world! *(She finally laughs aloud at him and holds out her arms to him and we see that it is a way between them, very old and practiced. He crosses to her and allows her to embrace him warmly but keeps his face fixed with masculine rigidity. She holds him back from her presently and looks at him and runs her fingers over the features of his face. With utter gentleness—.)* Now—whose little old angry man are you?

TRAVIS *(the masculinity and gruffness start to fade at last):*   Aw gaalee—Mama . . .

RUTH *(mimicking):*   Aw—gaaaaalleeeee, Mama! *(She pushes him, with rough playfulness and finality, toward the door.)* Get on out of here or you going to be late.

TRAVIS *(in the face of love, new aggressiveness):*   Mama, could I *please* go carry groceries?

RUTH: Honey, it's starting to get so cold evenings.

WALTER (*coming in from the bathroom and drawing a make-believe gun from a make-believe holster and shooting at his son*):   What is it he wants to do?

RUTH: Go carry groceries after school at the supermarket.

WALTER: Well, let him go . . .

TRAVIS (*quickly, to the ally*):   I *have* to—she won't gimme the fifty cents . . .

WALTER (*to his wife only*):   Why not?

RUTH (*simply, and with flavor*):   'Cause we don't have it.

WALTER (*to Ruth only*):   What you tell the boy things like that for? (*Reaching down into his pants with a rather important gesture.*) Here, son—

He hands the boy the coin, but his eyes are directed to his wife's. Travis takes the money happily.

TRAVIS: Thanks, Daddy.

He starts out. Ruth watches both of them with murder in her eyes. Walter stands and stares back at her with defiance, and suddenly reaches into his pocket again on an afterthought.

WALTER (*without even looking at his son, still staring hard at his wife*):   In fact, here's another fifty cents . . . Buy yourself some fruit today—or take a taxicab to school or something!

TRAVIS: Whoopee—

He leaps up and clasps his father around the middle with his legs, and they face each other in mutual appreciation; slowly Walter Lee peeks around the boy to catch the violent rays from his wife's eyes and draws his head back as if shot.

WALTER: You better get down now—and get to school, man.

TRAVIS (*at the door*):   O.K. Good-bye.

He exits.

WALTER (*after him, pointing with pride*):   That's my boy. (*She looks at him in disgust and turns back to her work.*) You know what I was thinking 'bout in the bathroom this morning?

RUTH: No.

WALTER: How come you always try to be so pleasant!

RUTH: What is there to be pleasant 'bout!

WALTER: You want to know what I was thinking 'bout in the bathroom or not!

RUTH: I know what you thinking 'bout.

WALTER (*ignoring her*):   'Bout what me and Willy Harris was talking about last night.

RUTH (*immediately—a refrain*):   Willy Harris is a good-for-nothing loudmouth.

WALTER: Anybody who talks to me has got to be a good-for-nothing loudmouth, ain't he? And what you know about who is just a good-for-nothing loudmouth? Charlie Atkins was just a "good-for-nothing loudmouth" too, wasn't he! When he wanted me to go in the dry-cleaning business with him. And now—he's grossing a hundred thousand a year. A hundred thousand dollars a year! You still call *him* a loudmouth!

RUTH (*bitterly*):   Oh, Walter Lee . . .

She folds her head on her arms over the table.

WALTER *(rising and coming to her and standing over her):*   You tired, ain't you? Tired of everything. Me, the boy, the way we live — this beat-up hole — everything. Ain't you? *(She doesn't look up, doesn't answer.)* So tired — moaning and groaning all the time, but you wouldn't do nothing to help, would you? You couldn't be on my side that long for nothing, could you?

RUTH: Walter, please leave me alone.

WALTER: A man needs for a woman to back him up . . .

RUTH: Walter —

WALTER: Mama would listen to you. You know she listen to you more than she do me and Bennie. She think more of you. All you have to do is just sit down with her when you drinking your coffee one morning and talking 'bout things like you do and — *(He sits down beside her and demonstrates graphically what he thinks her methods and tone should be.)* — you just sip your coffee, see, and say easy like that you been thinking 'bout that deal Walter Lee is so interested in, 'bout the store and all, and sip some more coffee, like what you saying ain't really that important to you — And the next thing you know, she be listening good and asking you questions and when I come home — I can tell her the details. This ain't no fly-by-night proposition, baby. I mean we figured it out, me and Willy and Bobo.

RUTH *(with a frown):*   Bobo?

WALTER: Yeah. You see, this little liquor store we got in mind cost seventy-five thousand and we figured the initial investment on the place be 'bout thirty thousand, see. That be ten thousand each. Course, there's a couple of hundred you got to pay so's you don't spend your life just waiting for them clowns to let your license get approved —

RUTH: You mean graft?

WALTER *(frowning impatiently):*   Don't call it that. See there, that just goes to show you what women understand about the world. Baby, don't *nothing* happen for you in the world 'less you pay *somebody* off!

RUTH: Walter, leave me alone! *(She raises her head and stares at him vigorously — then says, more quietly.)* Eat your eggs, they gonna be cold.

WALTER *(straightening up from her and looking off):*   That's it. There you are. Man say to his woman: I got me a dream. His woman say: Eat your eggs. *(Sadly, but gaining in power.)* Man say: I got to take hold of this here world, baby! And a woman will say: Eat your eggs and go to work. *(Passionately now.)* Man say: I got to change my life, I'm choking to death, baby! And his woman say — *(In utter anguish as he brings his fists down on his thighs.)* — Your eggs is getting cold!

RUTH *(softly):*   Walter, that ain't none of our money.

WALTER *(not listening at all or even looking at her):*   This morning, I was lookin' in the mirror and thinking about it . . . I'm thirty-five years old; I been married eleven years and I got a boy who sleeps in the living room — *(Very, very quietly.)* — and all I got to give him is stories about how rich white people live . . .

RUTH: Eat your eggs, Walter.

WALTER *(slams the table and jumps up)*:   —DAMN MY EGGS—DAMN ALL THE EGGS THAT EVER WAS!

RUTH: Then go to work.

WALTER *(looking up at her)*:   See—I'm trying to talk to you 'bout myself— *(Shaking his head with the repetition.)*—and all you can say is eat them eggs and go to work.

RUTH *(wearily)*:   Honey, you never say nothing new. I listen to you every day, every night and every morning, and you never say nothing new. *(Shrugging.)* So you would rather *be* Mr. Arnold than be his chauffeur. So—I would *rather* be living in Buckingham Palace.

WALTER: That is just what is wrong with the colored woman in this world . . . Don't understand about building their men up and making 'em feel like they somebody. Like they can do something.

RUTH *(drily, but to hurt)*:   There *are* colored men who do things.

WALTER: No thanks to the colored woman.

RUTH: Well, being a colored woman, I guess I can't help myself none.

She rises and gets the ironing board and sets it up and attacks a huge pile of rough-dried clothes, sprinkling them in preparation for the ironing and then rolling them into tight fat balls.

WALTER *(mumbling)*:   We one group of men tied to a race of women with small minds!

His sister Beneatha enters. She is about twenty, as slim and intense as her brother. She is not as pretty as her sister-in-law, but her lean, almost intellectual face has a handsomeness of its own. She wears a bright-red flannel nightie, and her thick hair stands wildly about her head. Her speech is a mixture of many things; it is different from the rest of the family's insofar as education has permeated her sense of English—and perhaps the Midwest rather than the South has finally—at last—won out in her inflection; but not altogether, because over all of it is a soft slurring and transformed use of vowels which is the decided influence of the Southside. She passes through the room without looking at either Ruth or Walter and goes to the outside door and looks, a little blindly, out to the bathroom. She sees that it has been lost to the Johnsons. She closes the door with a sleepy vengeance and crosses to the table and sits down a little defeated.

BENEATHA: I am going to start timing those people.

WALTER: You should get up earlier.

BENEATHA *(her face in her hands. She is still fighting the urge to go back to bed)*:   Really—would you suggest dawn? Where's the paper?

WALTER *(pushing the paper across the table to her as he studies her almost clinically, as though he has never seen her before)*:   You a horrible-looking chick at this hour.

BENEATHA *(drily)*:   Good morning, everybody.

WALTER *(senselessly)*:   How is school coming?

BENEATHA *(in the same spirit)*:   Lovely. Lovely. And you know, biology is the greatest. *(Looking up at him.)* I dissected something that looked just like you yesterday.

WALTER: I just wondered if you've made up your mind and everything.

BENEATHA *(gaining in sharpness and impatience):*   And what did I answer yesterday morning — and the day before that?

RUTH *(from the ironing board, like someone disinterested and old):*   Don't be so nasty, Bennie.

BENEATHA *(still to her brother):*   And the day before that and the day before that!

WALTER *(defensively):*   I'm interested in you. Something wrong with that? Ain't many girls who decide —

WALTER AND BENEATHA *(in unison):*   — "to be a doctor."

Silence.

WALTER: Have we figured out yet just exactly how much medical school is going to cost?

RUTH: Walter Lee, why don't you leave that girl alone and get out of here to work?

BENEATHA *(exits to the bathroom and bangs on the door):*   Come on out of there, please!

She comes back into the room.

WALTER *(looking at his sister intently):*   You know the check is coming tomorrow.

BENEATHA *(turning on him with a sharpness all her own):*   That money belongs to Mama, Walter, and it's for her to decide how she wants to use it. I don't care if she wants to buy a house or a rocket ship or just nail it up somewhere and look at it. It's hers. Not ours — *hers.*

WALTER *(bitterly):*   Now ain't that fine! You just got your mother's interest at heart, ain't you, girl? You such a nice girl — but if Mama got that money she can always take a few thousand and help you through school too — can't she?

BENEATHA: I have never asked anyone around here to do anything for me!

WALTER: No! And the line between asking and just accepting when the time comes is big and wide — ain't it!

BENEATHA *(with fury):*   What do you want from me, Brother — that I quit school or just drop dead, which!

WALTER: I don't want nothing but for you to stop acting holy 'round here. Me and Ruth done made some sacrifices for you — why can't you do something for the family?

RUTH: Walter, don't be dragging me in it.

WALTER: You are in it — Don't you get up and go work in somebody's kitchen for the last three years to help put clothes on her back?

RUTH: Oh, Walter — that's not fair . . .

WALTER: It ain't that nobody expects you to get on your knees and say thank you, Brother; thank you, Ruth; thank you, Mama — and thank you, Travis, for wearing the same pair of shoes for two semesters —

BENEATHA *(dropping to her knees):*   Well — I *do* — all right? — thank everybody! And forgive me for ever wanting to be anything at all! *(Pursuing him on her knees across the floor.)* FORGIVE ME, FORGIVE ME, FORGIVE ME!

RUTH: Please stop it! Your mama'll hear you.

WALTER: Who the hell told you you had to be a doctor? If you so crazy 'bout messing 'round with sick people — then go be a nurse like other women — or just get married and be quiet . . .

BENEATHA: Well—you finally got it said . . . It took you three years but you finally got it said. Walter, give up; leave me alone—it's Mama's money.

WALTER: *He was my father, too!*

BENEATHA: So what? He was mine, too—and Travis' grandfather—but the insurance money belongs to Mama. Picking on me is not going to make her give it to you to invest in any liquor stores—*(Under breath, dropping into a chair.)*—and I for one say, God bless Mama for that!

WALTER *(to Ruth):*   See—did you hear? Did you hear!

RUTH: Honey, please go to work.

WALTER: Nobody in this house is ever going to understand me.

BENEATHA: Because you're a nut.

WALTER: Who's a nut?

BENEATHA: You—you are a nut. Thee is mad, boy.

WALTER *(looking at his wife and his sister from the door, very sadly):*   The world's most backward race of people, and that's a fact.

BENEATHA *(turning slowly in her chair):*   And then there are all those prophets who would lead us out of the wilderness—*(Walter slams out of the house.)*—into the swamps!

RUTH: Bennie, why you always gotta be pickin' on your brother? Can't you be a little sweeter sometimes? *(Door opens. Walter walks in. He fumbles with his cap, starts to speak, clears throat, looks everywhere but at Ruth. Finally:)*

WALTER *(to Ruth):*   I need some money for carfare.

RUTH *(looks at him, then warms; teasing, but tenderly):*   Fifty cents? *(She goes to her bag and gets money.)* Here—take a taxi!

Walter exits. Mama enters. She is a woman in her early sixties, full-bodied and strong. She is one of those women of a certain grace and beauty who wear it so unobtrusively that it takes a while to notice. Her dark-brown face is surrounded by the total whiteness of her hair, and, being a woman who has adjusted to many things in life and overcome many more, her face is full of strength. She has, we can see, wit and faith of a kind that keep her eyes lit and full of interest and expectancy. She is, in a word, a beautiful woman. Her bearing is perhaps most like the noble bearing of the women of the Hereros of Southwest Africa—rather as if she imagines that as she walks she still bears a basket or a vessel upon her head. Her speech, on the other hand, is as careless as her carriage is precise—she is inclined to slur everything—but her voice is perhaps not so much quiet as simply soft.

MAMA: Who that 'round here slamming doors at this hour?

She crosses through the room, goes to the window, opens it, and brings in a feeble little plant growing doggedly in a small pot on the window sill. She feels the dirt and puts it back out.

RUTH: That was Walter Lee. He and Bennie was at it again.

MAMA: My children and they tempers. Lord, if this little old plant don't get more sun than it's been getting it ain't never going to see spring again. *(She turns from the window.)* What's the matter with you this morning, Ruth? You looks right peaked. You aiming to iron all them things? Leave some for me. I'll get to 'em this afternoon. Bennie honey, it's too drafty for you to be sitting 'round half dressed. Where's your robe?

BENEATHA: In the cleaners.

MAMA: Well, go get mine and put it on.

BENEATHA: I'm not cold, Mama, honest.

MAMA: I know—but you so thin . . .

BENEATHA *(irritably)*:   Mama, I'm not cold.

MAMA *(seeing the make-down bed as Travis has left it)*:   Lord have mercy, look at that poor bed. Bless his heart—he tries, don't he?

She moves to the bed Travis has sloppily made up.

RUTH: No—he don't half try at all 'cause he knows you going to come along behind him and fix everything. That's just how come he don't know how to do nothing right now—you done spoiled that boy so.

MAMA *(folding bedding)*:   Well—he's a little boy. Ain't supposed to know 'bout housekeeping. My baby, that's what he is. What you fix for his breakfast this morning?

RUTH *(angrily)*:   I feed my son, Lena!

MAMA: I ain't meddling—*(Under breath; busy-bodyish.)* I just noticed all last week he had cold cereal, and when it starts getting this chilly in the fall a child ought to have some hot grits or something when he goes out in the cold—

RUTH *(furious)*:   I gave him hot oats—is that all right!

MAMA: I ain't meddling. *(Pause.)* Put a lot of nice butter on it? *(Ruth shoots her an angry look and does not reply.)* He likes lots of butter.

RUTH *(exasperated)*:   Lena—

MAMA *(to Beneatha. Mama is inclined to wander conversationally sometimes)*:   What was you and your brother fussing 'bout this morning?

BENEATHA: It's not important, Mama.

She gets up and goes to look out at the bathroom, which is apparently free, and she picks up her towels and rushes out.

MAMA: What was they fighting about?

RUTH: Now you know as well as I do.

MAMA *(shaking her head)*:   Brother still worrying hisself sick about that money?

RUTH: You know he is.

MAMA: You had breakfast?

RUTH: Some coffee.

MAMA: Girl, you better start eating and looking after yourself better. You almost thin as Travis.

RUTH: Lena—

MAMA: Un-hunh?

RUTH: What are you going to do with it?

MAMA: Now don't you start, child. It's too early in the morning to be talking about money. It ain't Christian.

RUTH: It's just that he got his heart set on that store—

MAMA: You mean that liquor store that Willy Harris want him to invest in?

RUTH: Yes—

MAMA: We ain't no business people, Ruth. We just plain working folks.

RUTH: Ain't nobody business people till they go into business. Walter Lee say colored people ain't never going to start getting ahead till they start gambling on some different kinds of things in the world—investments and things.

MAMA: What done got into you, girl? Walter Lee done finally sold you on investing.

RUTH: No. Mama, something is happening between Walter and me. I don't know what it is—but he needs something—something I can't give him any more. He needs this chance, Lena.

MAMA *(frowning deeply):* But liquor, honey—

RUTH: Well—like Walter say—I spec people going to always be drinking themselves some liquor.

MAMA: Well—whether they drinks it or not ain't none of my business. But whether I go into business selling it to 'em *is*, and I don't want that on my ledger this late in life. *(Stopping suddenly and studying her daughter-in-law.)* Ruth Younger, what's the matter with you today? You look like you could fall over right there.

RUTH: I'm tired.

MAMA: Then you better stay home from work today.

RUTH: I can't stay home. She'd be calling up the agency and screaming at them, "My girl didn't come in today—send me somebody! My girl didn't come in!" Oh, she just have a fit . . .

MAMA: Well, let her have it. I'll just call her up and say you got the flu—

RUTH *(laughing):* Why the flu?

MAMA: 'Cause it sounds respectable to 'em. Something white people get, too. They know 'bout the flu. Otherwise they think you been cut up or something when you tell 'em you sick.

RUTH: I got to go in. We need the money.

MAMA: Somebody would of thought my children done all but starved to death the way they talk about money here late. Child, we got a great big old check coming tomorrow.

RUTH *(sincerely, but also self-righteously):* Now that's your money. It ain't got nothing to do with me. We all feel like that—Walter and Bennie and me—even Travis.

MAMA *(thoughtfully, and suddenly very far away):* Ten thousand dollars—

RUTH: Sure is wonderful.

MAMA: Ten thousand dollars.

RUTH: You know what you should do, Miss Lena? You should take yourself a trip somewhere. To Europe or South America or someplace—

MAMA *(throwing up her hands at the thought):* Oh, child!

RUTH: I'm serious. Just pack up and leave! Go on away and enjoy yourself some. Forget about the family and have yourself a ball for once in your life—

MAMA *(drily):* You sound like I'm just about ready to die. Who'd go with me? What I look like wandering 'round Europe by myself?

RUTH: Shoot—these here rich white women do it all the time. They don't think nothing of packing up they suitcases and piling on one of them big steamships and—swoosh!—they gone, child.

MAMA: Something always told me I wasn't no rich white woman.

RUTH: Well—what are you going to do with it then?

MAMA: I ain't rightly decided. *(Thinking. She speaks now with emphasis.)* Some of it got to be put away for Beneatha and her schoolin'—and ain't nothing going to touch that part of it. Nothing. *(She waits several seconds, trying to make up her mind about something, and looks at Ruth a little tentatively before going on.)* Been thinking that we maybe could meet the notes on a little old two-story somewhere, with a yard where Travis could play in the summertime, if we use part of the insurance for a down payment and everybody kind of pitch in. I could maybe take on a little day work again, few days a week—

RUTH *(studying her mother-in-law furtively and concentrating on her ironing, anxious to encourage without seeming to):*   Well, Lord knows, we've put enough rent into this here rat trap to pay for four houses by now . . .

MAMA *(looking up at the words "rat trap" and then looking around and leaning back and sighing—in a suddenly reflective mood—):*   "Rat trap"—yes, that's all it is. *(Smiling.)* I remember just as well the day me and Big Walter moved in here. Hadn't been married but two weeks and wasn't planning on living here no more than a year. *(She shakes her head at the dissolved dream.)* We was going to set away, little by little, don't you know, and buy a little place out in Morgan Park. We had even picked out the house. *(Chuckling a little.)* Looks right dumpy today. But Lord, child, you should know all the dreams I had 'bout buying that house and fixing it up and making me a little garden in the back—*(She waits and stops smiling.)* And didn't none of it happen.

Dropping her hands in a futile gesture.

RUTH *(keeps her head down, ironing):*   Yes, life can be a barrel of disappointments, sometimes.

MAMA: Honey, Big Walter would come in here some nights back then and slump down on that couch there and just look at the rug, and look at me and look at the rug and then back at me—and I'd know he was down then . . . really down. *(After a second very long and thoughtful pause; she is seeing back to times that only she can see.)* And then, Lord, when I lost that baby—little Claude—I almost thought I was going to lose Big Walter too. Oh, that man grieved hisself! He was one man to love his children.

RUTH: Ain't nothin' can tear at you like losin' your baby.

MAMA: I guess that's how come that man finally worked hisself to death like he done. Like he was fighting his own war with this here world that took his baby from him.

RUTH: He sure was a fine man, all right. I always liked Mr. Younger.

MAMA: Crazy 'bout his children! God knows there was plenty wrong with Walter Younger—hard-headed, mean, kind of wild with women—plenty wrong with him. But he sure loved his children. Always wanted them to have something—be something. That's where Brother gets all these notions, I reckon. Big Walter used to say, he'd get right wet in the eyes sometimes, lean his head back with the water standing in his eyes and say, "Seem like God didn't see fit to give the black man nothing but dreams—but He did give us children to make them dreams seem worthwhile." *(She smiles.)* He could talk like that, don't you know.

RUTH: Yes, he sure could. He was a good man, Mr. Younger.

MAMA: Yes, a fine man — just couldn't never catch up with his dreams, that's all.

Beneatha comes in, brushing her hair and looking up to the ceiling, where the sound of a vacuum cleaner has started up.

BENEATHA: What could be so dirty on that woman's rugs that she has to vacuum them every single day?

RUTH: I wish certain young women 'round here who I could name would take inspiration about certain rugs in a certain apartment I could also mention.

BENEATHA *(shrugging)*:   How much cleaning can a house need, for Christ's sakes.

MAMA *(not liking the Lord's name used thus)*:   Bennie!

RUTH: Just listen to her — just listen!

BENEATHA: Oh, God!

MAMA: If you use the Lord's name just one more time —

BENEATHA *(a bit of a whine)*:   Oh, Mama —

RUTH: Fresh — just fresh as salt, this girl!

BENEATHA *(drily)*:   Well — if the salt loses its savor —

MAMA: Now that will do. I just ain't going to have you 'round here reciting the scriptures in vain — you hear me?

BENEATHA: How did I manage to get on everybody's wrong side by just walking into a room?

RUTH: If you weren't so fresh —

BENEATHA: Ruth, I'm twenty years old.

MAMA: What time you be home from school today?

BENEATHA: Kind of late. *(With enthusiasm.)* Madeline is going to start my guitar lessons today.

Mama and Ruth look up with the same expression.

MAMA: Your *what* kind of lessons?

BENEATHA: Guitar.

RUTH: Oh, Father!

MAMA: How come you done taken it in your mind to learn to play the guitar?

BENEATHA: I just want to, that's all.

MAMA *(smiling)*:   Lord, child, don't you know what to do with yourself? How long it going to be before you get tired of this now — like you got tired of that little play-acting group you joined last year? *(Looking at Ruth.)* And what was it the year before that?

RUTH: The horseback-riding club for which she bought that fifty-five-dollar riding habit that's been hanging in the closet ever since!

MAMA *(to Beneatha)*:   Why you got to flit so from one thing to another, baby?

BENEATHA *(sharply)*:   I just want to learn to play the guitar. Is there anything wrong with that?

MAMA: Ain't nobody trying to stop you. I just wonders sometimes why you has to flit so from one thing to another all the time. You ain't never done nothing with all that camera equipment you brought home —

BENEATHA: I don't flit! I — I experiment with different forms of expression —

RUTH: Like riding a horse?

BENEATHA: — People have to express themselves one way or another.

MAMA: What is it you want to express?

BENEATHA *(angrily)*:   Me! *(Mama and Ruth look at each other and burst into raucous laughter.)* Don't worry—I don't expect you to understand.

MAMA *(to change the subject)*:   Who you going out with tomorrow night?

BENEATHA *(with displeasure)*:   George Murchison again.

MAMA *(pleased)*:   Oh—you getting a little sweet on him?

RUTH: You ask me, this child ain't sweet on nobody but herself—*(Under breath.)* Express herself!

They laugh.

BENEATHA: Oh—I like George all right, Mama. I mean I like him enough to go out with him and stuff, but—

RUTH *(for devilment)*:   What does *and stuff* mean?

BENEATHA: Mind your own business.

MAMA: Stop picking at her now, Ruth. *(She chuckles—then a suspicious sudden look at her daughter as she turns in her chair for emphasis.)* What DOES it mean?

BENEATHA *(wearily)*:   Oh, I just mean I couldn't ever really be serious about George. He's—he's so shallow.

RUTH: Shallow—what do you mean he's shallow? He's *rich!*

MAMA: Hush, Ruth.

BENEATHA: I know he's rich. He knows he's rich, too.

RUTH: Well—what other qualities a man got to have to satisfy you, little girl?

BENEATHA: You wouldn't even begin to understand. Anybody who married Walter could not possibly understand.

MAMA *(outraged)*:   What kind of way is that to talk about your brother?

BENEATHA: Brother is a flip—let's face it.

MAMA *(to Ruth, helplessly)*:   What's a flip?

RUTH *(glad to add kindling)*:   She's saying he's crazy.

BENEATHA: Not crazy. Brother isn't really crazy yet—he—he's an elaborate neurotic.

MAMA: Hush your mouth!

BENEATHA: As for George. Well. George looks good—he's got a beautiful car and he takes me to nice places and, as my sister-in-law says, he is probably the richest boy I will ever get to know and I even like him sometimes—but if the Youngers are sitting around waiting to see if their little Bennie is going to tie up the family with the Murchisons, they are wasting their time.

RUTH: You mean you wouldn't marry George Murchison if he asked you some-day? That pretty, rich thing? Honey, I knew you was odd—

BENEATHA: No I would not marry him if all I felt for him was what I feel now. Besides, George's family wouldn't really like it.

MAMA: Why not?

BENEATHA: Oh, Mama—The Murchisons are honest-to-God-real-*live*-rich colored people, and the only people in the world who are more snobbish than rich white people are rich colored people. I thought everybody knew that. I've met Mrs. Murchison. She's a scene!

MAMA: You must not dislike people 'cause they well off, honey.

BENEATHA: Why not? It makes just as much sense as disliking people 'cause they are poor, and lots of people do that.

RUTH *(a wisdom-of-the-ages manner. To Mama)*:   Well, she'll get over some of this —

BENEATHA: Get over it? What are you talking about, Ruth? Listen, I'm going to be a doctor. I'm not worried about who I'm going to marry yet — if I ever get married.

MAMA and RUTH: *If!*

MAMA: Now, Bennie —

BENEATHA: Oh, I probably will . . . but first I'm going to be a doctor, and George, for one, still thinks that's pretty funny. I couldn't be bothered with that. I am going to be a doctor and everybody around here better understand that!

MAMA *(kindly)*:   'Course you going to be a doctor, honey, God willing.

BENEATHA *(drily)*:   God hasn't got a thing to do with it.

MAMA: Beneatha — that just wasn't necessary.

BENEATHA: Well — neither is God. I get sick of hearing about God.

MAMA: Beneatha!

BENEATHA: I mean it! I'm just tired of hearing about God all the time. What has He got to do with anything? Does He pay tuition?

MAMA: You 'bout to get your fresh little jaw slapped!

RUTH: That's just what she needs, all right!

BENEATHA: Why? Why can't I say what I want to around here, like everybody else?

MAMA: It don't sound nice for a young girl to say things like that — you wasn't brought up that way. Me and your father went to trouble to get you and Brother to church every Sunday.

BENEATHA: Mama, you don't understand. It's all a matter of ideas, and God is just one idea I don't accept. It's not important. I am not going out and be immoral or commit crimes because I don't believe in God. I don't even think about it. It's just that I get tired of Him getting credit for all the things the human race achieves through its own stubborn effort. There simply is no blasted God — there is only man and it is *He* who makes miracles!

Mama absorbs this speech, studies her daughter, and rises slowly and crosses to Beneatha and slaps her powerfully across the face. After, there is only silence and the daughter drops her eyes from her mother's face, and Mama is very tall before her.

MAMA: Now — you say after me, in my mother's house there is still God. *(There is a long pause and Beneatha stares at the floor wordlessly. Mama repeats the phrase with precision and cool emotion.)* In my mother's house there is still God.

BENEATHA: In my mother's house there is still God.

A long pause.

MAMA *(walking away from Beneatha, too disturbed for triumphant posture. Stopping and turning back to her daughter)*:   There are some ideas we ain't going to have in this house. Not long as I am at the head of this family.

BENEATHA: Yes, ma'am.

Mama walks out of the room.

RUTH *(almost gently, with profound understanding):*   You think you a woman, Bennie—but you still a little girl. What you did was childish—so you got treated like a child.

BENEATHA: I see. *(Quietly.)* I also see that everybody thinks it's all right for Mama to be a tyrant. But all the tyranny in the world will never put a God in the heavens!

She picks up her books and goes out. Pause.

RUTH *(goes to Mama's door):*   She said she was sorry.

MAMA *(coming out, going to her plant):*   They frightens me, Ruth. My children.

RUTH: You got good children, Lena. They just a little off sometimes—but they're good.

MAMA: No—there's something come down between me and them that don't let us understand each other and I don't know what it is. One done almost lost his mind thinking 'bout money all the time and the other done commence to talk about things I can't seem to understand in no form or fashion. What is it that's changing, Ruth.

RUTH *(soothingly, older than her years):*   Now . . . you taking it all too seriously. You just got strong-willed children and it takes a strong woman like you to keep 'em in hand.

MAMA *(looking at her plant and sprinkling a little water on it):*   They spirited all right, my children. Got to admit they got spirit—Bennie and Walter. Like this little old plant that ain't never had enough sunshine or nothing—and look at it . . .

She has her back to Ruth, who has had to stop ironing and lean against something and put the back of her hand to her forehead.

RUTH *(trying to keep Mama from noticing):*   You . . . sure . . . loves that little old thing, don't you? . . .

MAMA: Well, I always wanted me a garden like I used to see sometimes at the back of the houses down home. This plant is close as I ever got to having one. *(She looks out of the window as she replaces the plant.)* Lord, ain't nothing as dreary as the view from this window on a dreary day, is there? Why ain't you singing this morning, Ruth? Sing that "No Ways Tired." That song always lifts me up so—*(She turns at last to see that Ruth has slipped quietly to the floor, in a state of semiconsciousness.)* Ruth! Ruth honey—what's the matter with you . . . Ruth!

Curtain.

Scene 2

It is the following morning; a Saturday morning, and house cleaning is in progress at the Youngers'. Furniture has been shoved hither and yon and Mama is giving the kitchen-area walls a washing down. Beneatha, in dungarees, with a handkerchief tied around her face, is spraying insecticide into the cracks in the walls. As they work, the radio is on and a Southside disk-jockey program is inappropriately filling the house with a rather exotic saxophone blues. Travis, the sole idle one, is leaning on his arms, looking out of the window.

TRAVIS: Grandmama, that stuff Bennie is using smells awful. Can I go downstairs, please?

MAMA: Did you get all them chores done already? I ain't seen you doing much.

TRAVIS: Yes'm—finished early. Where did Mama go this morning?

MAMA *(looking at Beneatha)*:   She had to go on a little errand.

The phone rings. Beneatha runs to answer it and reaches it before Walter, who has entered from bedroom.

TRAVIS: Where?

MAMA: To tend to her business.

BENEATHA: Haylo . . . *(Disappointed.)* Yes, he is. *(She tosses the phone to Walter, who barely catches it.)* It's Willie Harris again.

WALTER *(as privately as possible under Mama's gaze)*:   Hello, Willie. Did you get the papers from the lawyer? . . . No, not yet. I told you the mailman doesn't get here till ten-thirty . . . No, I'll come there . . . Yeah! Right away. *(He hangs up and goes for his coat.)*

BENEATHA: Brother, where did Ruth go?

WALTER *(as he exits)*:   How should I know!

TRAVIS: Aw come on, Grandma. Can I go outside?

MAMA: Oh, I guess so. You stay right in front of the house, though, and keep a good lookout for the postman.

TRAVIS: Yes'm. *(He darts into bedroom for stickball and bat, reenters, and sees Beneatha on her knees spraying under sofa with behind upraised. He edges closer to the target, takes aim, and lets her have it. She screams.)* Leave them poor little cockroaches alone, they ain't bothering you none! *(He runs as she swings the spraygun at him viciously and playfully.)* Grandma! Grandma!

MAMA: Look out there, girl, before you be spilling some of that stuff on that child!

TRAVIS *(safely behind the bastion of Mama)*:   That's right—look out, now! *(He exits.)*

BENEATHA *(drily)*:   I can't imagine that it would hurt him—it has never hurt the roaches.

MAMA: Well, little boys' hides ain't as tough as Southside roaches. You better get over there behind the bureau. I seen one marching out of there like Napoleon yesterday.

BENEATHA: There's really only one way to get rid of them, Mama—

MAMA: How?

BENEATHA: Set fire to this building! Mama, where did Ruth go?

MAMA *(looking at her with meaning)*:   To the doctor, I think.

BENEATHA: The doctor? What's the matter? *(They exchange glances.)* You don't think—

MAMA *(with her sense of drama)*:   Now I ain't saying what I think. But I ain't never been wrong 'bout a woman neither.

The phone rings.

BENEATHA *(at the phone)*:   Hay-lo . . . *(Pause, and a moment of recognition.)* Well—when did you get back! . . . And how was it? . . . Of course I've missed you—in my way . . . This morning? No . . . house cleaning and all that and Mama hates it if I let people come over when the house is like this . . . You *have?* Well, that's different . . . What is it—Oh, what the hell, come on over . . . Right, see you then. *Arrividerci.*

She hangs up.

MAMA *(who has listened vigorously, as is her habit)*:   Who is that you inviting over here with this house looking like this? You ain't got the pride you was born with!

BENEATHA: Asagai doesn't care how houses look, Mama—he's an intellectual.

MAMA: *Who?*

BENEATHA: Asagai—Joseph Asagai. He's an African boy I met on campus. He's been studying in Canada all summer.

MAMA: What's his name?

BENEATHA: Asagai, Joseph. Ah-sah-guy . . . He's from Nigeria.

MAMA: Oh, that's the little country that was founded by slaves way back . . .

BENEATHA: No, Mama—that's Liberia.

MAMA: I don't think I never met no African before.

BENEATHA: Well, do me a favor and don't ask him a whole lot of ignorant questions about Africans. I mean, do they wear clothes and all that—

MAMA: Well, now, I guess if you think we so ignorant 'round here maybe you shouldn't bring your friends here—

BENEATHA: It's just that people ask such crazy things. All anyone seems to know about when it comes to Africa is Tarzan—

MAMA *(indignantly)*:   Why should I know anything about Africa?

BENEATHA: Why do you give money at church for the missionary work?

MAMA: Well, that's to help save people.

BENEATHA: You mean save them from *heathenism*—

MAMA *(innocently)*:   Yes.

BENEATHA: I'm afraid they need more salvation from the British and the French.

Ruth comes in forlornly and pulls off her coat with dejection. They both turn to look at her.

RUTH *(dispiritedly)*:   Well, I guess from all the happy faces—everybody knows.

BENEATHA: You pregnant?

MAMA: Lord have mercy, I sure hope it's a little old girl. Travis ought to have a sister.

Beneatha and Ruth give her a hopeless look for this grandmotherly enthusiasm.

BENEATHA: How far along are you?

RUTH: Two months.

BENEATHA: Did you mean to? I mean did you plan it or was it an accident?

MAMA: What do you know about planning or not planning?

BENEATHA: Oh, Mama.

RUTH *(wearily)*:   She's twenty years old, Lena.

BENEATHA: Did you plan it, Ruth?

RUTH: Mind your own business.

BENEATHA: It is my business—where is he going to live, on the *roof? (There is silence following the remark as the three women react to the sense of it.)* Gee—I didn't mean that, Ruth, honest. Gee, I don't feel like that at all. I—I think it is wonderful.

RUTH *(dully)*:   Wonderful.

BENEATHA: Yes—really.

MAMA *(looking at Ruth, worried)*:   Doctor say everything going to be all right?

RUTH *(far away)*:   Yes—she says everything is going to be fine . . .

MAMA *(immediately suspicious)*:   "She"—What doctor you went to?

Ruth folds over, near hysteria.

MAMA *(worriedly hovering over Ruth)*:   Ruth honey—what's the matter with you—you sick?

Ruth has her fists clenched on her thighs and is fighting hard to suppress a scream that seems to be rising in her.

BENEATHA: What's the matter with her, Mama?

MAMA *(working her fingers in Ruth's shoulders to relax her)*:   She be all right. Women gets right depressed sometimes when they get her way. *(Speaking softly, expertly, rapidly.)* Now you just relax. That's right . . . just lean back, don't think 'bout nothing at all . . . nothing at all—

RUTH: I'm all right . . .

The glassy-eyed look melts and then she collapses into a fit of heavy sobbing. The bell rings.

BENEATHA: Oh, my God—that must be Asagai.

MAMA *(to Ruth)*:   Come on now, honey. You need to lie down and rest awhile . . . then have some nice hot food.

They exit, Ruth's weight on her mother-in-law. Beneatha, herself profoundly disturbed, opens the door to admit a rather dramatic-looking young man with a large package.

ASAGAI: Hello, Alaiyo—

BENEATHA *(holding the door open and regarding him with pleasure)*:   Hello . . . *(Long pause.)* Well—come in. And please excuse everything. My mother was very upset about my letting anyone come here with the place like this.

ASAGAI *(coming into the room)*:   You look disturbed too . . . Is something wrong?

BENEATHA *(still at the door, absently)*:   Yes . . . we've all got acute ghetto-itus. *(She smiles and comes toward him, finding a cigarette and sitting.)* So—sit down! No! Wait! *(She whips the spraygun off sofa where she had left it and puts the cushions back. At last perches on arm of sofa. He sits.)* So, how was Canada?

ASAGAI *(a sophisticate)*:   Canadian.

BENEATHA *(looking at him)*:   Asagai, I'm very glad you are back.

ASAGAI *(looking back at her in turn)*:   Are you really?

BENEATHA: Yes—very.

ASAGAI: Why?—you were quite glad when I went away. What happened?

BENEATHA: You went away.

ASAGAI: Ahhhhhhhh.

BENEATHA: Before—you wanted to be so serious before there was time.

ASAGAI: How much time must there be before one knows what one feels?

BENEATHA (*stalling this particular conversation. Her hands pressed together, in a deliberately childish gesture*):   What did you bring me?

ASAGAI (*handing her the package*):   Open it and see.

BENEATHA (*eagerly opening the package and drawing out some records and the colorful robes of a Nigerian woman*):   Oh Asagai! . . . You got them for me! . . . How beautiful . . . and the records too! (*She lifts out the robes and runs to the mirror with them and holds the drapery up in front of herself.*)

ASAGAI (*coming to her at the mirror*):   I shall have to teach you how to drape it properly. (*He flings the material about her for the moment and stands back to look at her.*) Ah—Oh-pay-gay-day, oh-gbah-mu-shay. (*A Yoruba exclamation for admiration.*) You wear it well . . . very well . . . mutilated hair and all.

BENEATHA (*turning suddenly*):   My hair—what's wrong with my hair?

ASAGAI (*shrugging*):   Were you born with it like that?

BENEATHA (*reaching up to touch it*):   No . . . of course not.

She looks back to the mirror, disturbed.

ASAGAI (*smiling*):   How then?

BENEATHA: You know perfectly well how . . . as crinkly as yours . . . that's how.

ASAGAI: And it is ugly to you that way?

BENEATHA (*quickly*):   Oh, no—not ugly . . . (*More slowly, apologetically.*) But it's so hard to manage when it's, well—raw.

ASAGAI: And so to accommodate that—you mutilate it every week?

BENEATHA: It's not mutilation!

ASAGAI (*laughing aloud at her seriousness*):   Oh . . . please! I am only teasing you because you are so very serious about these things. (*He stands back from her and folds his arms across his chest as he watches her pulling at her hair and frowning in the mirror.*) Do you remember the first time you met me at school? . . . (*He laughs.*) You came up to me and you said—and I thought you were the most serious little thing I had ever seen—you said: (*He imitates her.*) "Mr. Asagai—I want very much to talk with you. About Africa. You see, Mr. Asagai, I am looking for my *identity!*"

He laughs.

BENEATHA (*turning to him, not laughing*):   Yes—

Her face is quizzical, profoundly disturbed.

ASAGAI (*still teasing and reaching out and taking her face in his hands and turning her profile to him*):   Well . . . it is true that this is not so much a profile of a Hollywood queen as perhaps a queen of the Nile—(*A mock dismissal of the importance of the question.*) But what does it matter? Assimilationism is so popular in your country.

BENEATHA (*wheeling, passionately, sharply*):   I am not an assimilationist!

ASAGAI (*the protest hangs in the room for a moment and Asagai studies her, his laughter fading*):   Such a serious one. (*There is a pause.*) So — you like the robes? You must take excellent care of them — they are from my sister's personal wardrobe.

BENEATHA (*with incredulity*):   You — you sent all the way home — for me?

ASAGAI (*with charm*):   For you — I would do much more . . . Well, that is what I came for. I must go.

BENEATHA: Will you call me Monday?

ASAGAI: Yes . . . We have a great deal to talk about. I mean about identity and time and all that.

BENEATHA: Time?

ASAGAI: Yes. About how much time one needs to know what one feels.

BENEATHA: You see! You never understood that there is more than one kind of feeling which can exist between a man and a woman — or, at least, there should be.

ASAGAI (*shaking his head negatively but gently*):   No. Between a man and a woman there need be only one kind of feeling. I have that for you . . . Now even . . . right this moment . . .

BENEATHA: I know — and by itself — it won't do. I can find that anywhere.

ASAGAI: For a woman it should be enough.

BENEATHA: I know — because that's what it says in all the novels that men write. But it isn't. Go ahead and laugh — but I'm not interested in being someone's little episode in America or — (*With feminine vengeance.*) — one of them! (*Asagai has burst into laughter again.*) That's funny as hell, huh!

ASAGAI: It's just that every American girl I have known has said that to me. White — black — in this you are all the same. And the same speech, too!

BENEATHA (*angrily*):   Yuk, yuk, yuk!

ASAGAI: It's how you can be sure that the world's most liberated women are not liberated at all. You all talk about it too much!

Mama enters and is immediately all social charm because of the presence of a guest.

BENEATHA: Oh — Mama — this is Mr. Asagai.

MAMA: How do you do?

ASAGAI (*total politeness to an elder*):   How do you do, Mrs. Younger. Please forgive me for coming at such an outrageous hour on a Saturday.

MAMA: Well, you are quite welcome. I just hope you understand that our house don't always look like this. (*Chatterish.*) You must come again. I would love to hear all about — (*Not sure of the name.*) — your country. I think it's so sad the way our American Negroes don't know nothing about Africa 'cept Tarzan and all that. And all that money they pour into these churches when they ought to be helping you people over there drive out them French and Englishmen done taken away your land.

The mother flashes a slightly superior look at her daughter upon completion of the recitation.

ASAGAI (*taken aback by this sudden and acutely unrelated expression of sympathy*):   Yes . . . yes . . .

MAMA (*smiling at him suddenly and relaxing and looking him over*):   How many miles is it from here to where you come from?

ASAGAI: Many thousands.

MAMA (*looking at him as she would Walter*):   I bet you don't half look after yourself, being away from your mama either. I spec you better come 'round here from time to time to get yourself some decent homecooked meals . . .

ASAGAI (*moved*):   Thank you. Thank you very much. (*They are all quiet, then—*) Well . . . I must go. I will call you Monday, Alaiyo.

MAMA: What's that he call you?

ASAGAI: Oh—"Alaiyo." I hope you don't mind. It is what you would call a nickname, I think. It is a Yoruba word. I am a Yoruba.

MAMA (*looking at Beneatha*):   I—I thought he was from—(*Uncertain.*)

ASAGAI (*understanding*):   Nigeria is my country. Yoruba is my tribal origin—

BENEATHA: You didn't tell us what Alaiyo means . . . for all I know, you might be calling me Little Idiot or something . . .

ASAGAI: Well . . . let me see . . . I do not know how just to explain it . . . The sense of a thing can be so different when it changes languages.

BENEATHA: You're evading.

ASAGAI: No—really it is difficult . . . (*Thinking.*) It means . . . it means One for Whom Bread—Food—Is Not Enough. (*He looks at her.*) Is that all right?

BENEATHA (*understanding, softly*):   Thank you.

MAMA (*looking from one to the other and not understanding any of it*):   Well . . . that's nice . . . You must come see us again—Mr.—

ASAGAI: Ah-sah-guy . . .

MAMA: Yes . . . Do come again.

ASAGAI: Good-bye.

He exits.

MAMA (*after him*):   Lord, that's a pretty thing just went out here! (*Insinuatingly, to her daughter.*) Yes, I guess I see why we done commence to get so interested in Africa 'round here. Missionaries my aunt Jenny!

She exits.

BENEATHA: Oh, Mama! . . .

She picks up the Nigerian dress and holds it up to her in front of the mirror again. She sets the headdress on haphazardly and then notices her hair again and clutches at it and then replaces the headdress and frowns at herself. Then she starts to wriggle in front of the mirror as she thinks a Nigerian woman might. Travis enters and stands regarding her.

TRAVIS: What's the matter, girl, you cracking up?

BENEATHA: Shut up.

She pulls the headdress off and looks at herself in the mirror and clutches at her hair again and squinches her eyes as if trying to imagine something. Then, suddenly, she gets her raincoat and kerchief and hurriedly prepares for going out.

MAMA (*coming back into the room*):   She's resting now. Travis, baby, run next door and ask Miss Johnson to please let me have a little kitchen cleanser. This here can is empty as Jacob's kettle.

TRAVIS: I just came in.

MAMA: Do as you told. *(He exits and she looks at her daughter.)* Where you going?

BENEATHA *(halting at the door)*: To become a queen of the Nile!

She exits in a breathless blaze of glory. Ruth appears in the bedroom doorway.

MAMA: Who told you to get up?

RUTH: Ain't nothing wrong with me to be lying in no bed for. Where did Bennie go?

MAMA *(drumming her fingers)*: Far as I could make out — to Egypt. *(Ruth just looks at her.)* What time is it getting to?

RUTH: Ten twenty. And the mailman going to ring that bell this morning just like he done every morning for the last umpteen years.

Travis comes in with the cleanser can.

TRAVIS: She say to tell you that she don't have much.

MAMA *(angrily)*: Lord, some people I could name sure is tight-fisted! *(Directing her grandson.)* Mark two cans of cleanser on the list there. If she that hard up for kitchen cleanser, I sure don't want to forget to get her none!

RUTH: Lena — maybe the woman is just short on cleanser —

MAMA *(not listening)*: — Much baking powder as she done borrowed from me all these years, she could of done gone into the baking business!

The bell sounds suddenly and sharply and all three are stunned — serious and silent — midspeech. In spite of all the other conversations and distractions of the morning, this is what they have been waiting for, even Travis, who looks helplessly from his mother to his grandmother. Ruth is the first to come to life again.

RUTH *(to Travis)*: Get down them steps, boy!

Travis snaps to life and flies out to get the mail.

MAMA *(her eyes wide, her hand to her breast)*: You mean it done really come?

RUTH *(excited)*: Oh, Miss Lena!

MAMA *(collecting herself)*: Well . . . I don't know what we all so excited about 'round here for. We known it was coming for months.

RUTH: That's a whole lot different from having it come and being able to hold it in your hands . . . a piece of paper worth ten thousand dollars . . . *(Travis bursts back into the room. He holds the envelope high above his head, like a little dancer, his face is radiant and he is breathless. He moves to his grandmother with sudden slow ceremony and puts the envelope into her hands. She accepts it, and then merely holds it and looks at it.)* Come on! Open it . . . Lord have mercy, I wish Walter Lee was here!

TRAVIS: Open it, Grandmama!

MAMA *(staring at it)*: Now you all be quiet. It's just a check.

RUTH: Open it . . .

MAMA *(still staring at it)*: Now don't act silly . . . We ain't never been no people to act silly 'bout no money —

RUTH *(swiftly)*: We ain't never had none before — OPEN IT!

Mama finally makes a good strong tear and pulls out the thin blue slice of paper and inspects it closely. The boy and his mother study it raptly over Mama's shoulders.

MAMA: Travis! *(She is counting off with doubt.)* Is that the right number of zeros?

TRAVIS: Yes'm . . . ten thousand dollars. Gaalee, grandmama, you rich.

MAMA *(She holds the check away from her, still looking at it. Slowly her face sobers into a mask of unhappiness):*   Ten thousand dollars. *(She hands it to Ruth.)* Put it away somewhere, Ruth. *(She does not look at Ruth; her eyes seem to be seeing something somewhere very far off.)* Ten thousand dollars they give you. Ten thousand dollars.

TRAVIS *(to his mother, sincerely):*   What's the matter with Grandmama—don't she want to be rich?

RUTH *(distractedly):*   You go on out and play now, baby. *(Travis exits. Mama starts wiping dishes absently, humming intently to herself. Ruth turns to her, with kind exasperation.)* You've gone and got yourself upset.

MAMA *(not looking at her):*   I spec if it wasn't for you all . . . I would just put that money away or give it to the church or something.

RUTH: Now what kind of talk is that. Mr. Younger would just be plain mad if he could hear you talking foolish like that.

MAMA *(stopping and staring off):*   Yes . . . he sure would. *(Sighing.)* We got enough to do with that money, all right. *(She halts then, and turns and looks at her daughter-in-law hard; Ruth avoids her eyes and Mama wipes her hands with finality and starts to speak firmly to Ruth.)* Where did you go today, girl?

RUTH: To the doctor.

MAMA *(impatiently):*   Now, Ruth . . . you know better than that. Old Doctor Jones is strange enough in his way but there ain't nothing 'bout him make somebody slip and call him "she"—like you done this morning.

RUTH: Well, that's what happened—my tongue slipped.

MAMA: You went to see that woman, didn't you?

RUTH *(defensively, giving herself away):*   What woman you talking about?

MAMA *(angrily):*   That woman who—

Walter enters in great excitement.

WALTER: Did it come?

MAMA *(quietly):*   Can't you give people a Christian greeting before you start asking about money?

WALTER *(to Ruth):*   Did it come? *(Ruth unfolds the check and lays it quietly before him, watching him intently with thoughts of her own. Walter sits down and grasps it close and counts off the zeros.)* Ten thousand dollars—*(He turns suddenly, frantically to his mother and draws some papers out of his breast pocket.)* Mama—look. Old Willy Harris put everything on paper—

MAMA: Son—I think you ought to talk to your wife . . . I'll go on out and leave you alone if you want—

WALTER: I can talk to her later—Mama, look—

MAMA: Son—

WALTER: WILL SOMEBODY PLEASE LISTEN TO ME TODAY!

MAMA *(quietly):*   I don't 'low no yellin' in this house, Walter Lee, and you know it—*(Walter stares at them in frustration and starts to speak several times.)* And there ain't going to be no investing in no liquor stores.

WALTER: But, Mama, you ain't even looked at it.

MAMA: I don't aim to have to speak on that again.

A long pause.

WALTER: You ain't looked at it and you don't aim to have to speak on that again? You ain't even looked at it and *you* have decided—*(Crumpling his papers.)* Well, *you* tell that to my boy tonight when you put him to sleep on the living-room couch . . . *(Turning to Mama and speaking directly to her.)* Yeah—and tell it to my wife, Mama, tomorrow when she has to go out of here to look after somebody else's kids. And tell it to *me*, Mama, every time we need a new pair of curtains and I have to watch *you* go out and work in somebody's kitchen. Yeah, you tell me then!

Walter starts out.

RUTH: Where you going?

WALTER: I'm going out!

RUTH: Where?

WALTER: Just out of this house somewhere—

RUTH *(getting her coat):*   I'll come too.

WALTER: I don't want you to come!

RUTH: I got something to talk to you about, Walter.

WALTER: That's too bad.

MAMA *(still quietly):*   Walter Lee—*(She waits and he finally turns and looks at her.)* Sit down.

WALTER: I'm a grown man, Mama.

MAMA: Ain't nobody said you wasn't grown. But you still in my house and my presence. And as long as you are—you'll talk to your wife civil. Now sit down.

RUTH *(suddenly):*   Oh, let him go on out and drink himself to death! He makes me sick to my stomach! *(She flings her coat against him and exits to bedroom.)*

WALTER *(violently flinging the coat after her):*   And you turn mine too, baby! *(The door slams behind her.)* That was my biggest mistake—

MAMA *(still quietly):*   Walter, what is the matter with you?

WALTER: Matter with me? Ain't nothing the matter with *me!*

MAMA: Yes there is. Something eating you up like a crazy man. Something more than me not giving you this money. The past few years I been watching it happen to you. You get all nervous acting and kind of wild in the eyes—*(Walter jumps up impatiently at her words.)* I said sit there now, I'm talking to you!

WALTER: Mama—I don't need no nagging at me today.

MAMA: Seem like you getting to a place where you always tied up in some kind of knot about something. But if anybody ask you 'bout it you just yell at 'em and bust out the house and go out and drink somewheres. Walter Lee, people can't live with that. Ruth's a good, patient girl in her way—but you getting to be too much. Boy, don't make the mistake of driving that girl away from you.

WALTER: Why—what she do for me?

MAMA: She loves you.

WALTER: Mama—I'm going out. I want to go off somewhere and be by myself for a while.

MAMA: I'm sorry 'bout your liquor store, son. It just wasn't the thing for us to do. That's what I want to tell you about—

WALTER: I got to go out, Mama—

He rises.

MAMA: It's dangerous, son.

WALTER: What's dangerous?

MAMA: When a man goes outside his home to look for peace.

WALTER *(beseechingly)*:   Then why can't there never be no peace in this house then?

MAMA: You done found it in some other house?

WALTER: No—there ain't no woman! Why do women always think there's a woman somewhere when a man gets restless. *(Picks up the check.)* Do you know what this money means to me? Do you know what this money can do for us? *(Puts it back.)* Mama—Mama—I want so many things . . .

MAMA: Yes, son—

WALTER: I want so many things that they are driving me kind of crazy . . . Mama—look at me.

MAMA: I'm looking at you. You a good-looking boy. You got a job, a nice wife, a fine boy, and—

WALTER: A job. *(Looks at her.)* Mama, a job? I open and close car doors all day long. I drive a man around in his limousine and I say, "Yes, sir; no, sir; very good, sir; shall I take the Drive, sir?" Mama, that ain't no kind of job . . . that ain't nothing at all. *(Very quietly.)* Mama, I don't know if I can make you understand.

MAMA: Understand what, baby?

WALTER *(quietly)*:   Sometimes it's like I can see the future stretched out in front of me—just plain as day. The future, Mama. Hanging over there at the edge of my days. Just waiting for me—a big, looming blank space—full of *nothing*. Just waiting for *me*. But it don't have to be. *(Pause. Kneeling beside her chair.)* Mama—sometimes when I'm downtown and I pass them cool, quiet-looking restaurants where them white boys are sitting back and talking 'bout things . . . sitting there turning deals worth millions of dollars . . . sometimes I see guys don't look much older than me—

MAMA: Son—how come you talk so much 'bout money?

WALTER *(with immense passion)*:   Because it is life, Mama!

MAMA *(quietly)*:   Oh—*(Very quietly.)* So now it's life. Money is life. Once upon a time freedom used to be life—now it's money. I guess the world really do change . . .

WALTER: No—it was always money, Mama. We just didn't know about it.

MAMA: No . . . something has changed. *(She looks at him.)* You something new, boy. In my time we was worried about not being lynched and getting to the

North if we could and how to stay alive and still have a pinch of dignity too . . . Now here come you and Beneatha—talking 'bout things we ain't never even thought about hardly, me and your daddy. You ain't satisfied or proud of nothing we done. I mean that you had a home; that we kept you out of trouble till you was grown; that you don't have to ride to work on the back of nobody's streetcar—You my children—but how different we done become.

WALTER *(a long beat. He pats her hand and gets up)*:   You just don't understand, Mama, you just don't understand.

MAMA: Son—do you know your wife is expecting another baby? *(Walter stands, stunned, and absorbs what his mother has said.)* That's what she wanted to talk to you about. *(Walter sinks down into a chair.)* This ain't for me to be telling—but you ought to know. *(She waits.)* I think Ruth is thinking 'bout getting rid of that child.

WALTER *(slowly understanding)*:   —No—no—Ruth wouldn't do that.

MAMA: When the world gets ugly enough—a woman will do anything for her family. *The part that's already living.*

WALTER: You don't know Ruth, Mama, if you think she would do that.

Ruth opens the bedroom door and stands there a little limp.

RUTH *(beaten)*:   Yes I would too, Walter. *(Pause.)* I gave her a five-dollar down payment.

There is total silence as the man stares at his wife and the mother stares at her son.

MAMA *(presently)*:   Well—*(Tightly.)* Well—son, I'm waiting to hear you say something . . . *(She waits.)* I'm waiting to hear how you be your father's son. Be the man he was . . . *(Pause. The silence shouts.)* Your wife say she going to destroy your child. And I'm waiting to hear you talk like him and say we a people who give children life, not who destroys them—*(She rises.)* I'm waiting to see you stand up and look like your daddy and say we done give up one baby to poverty and that we ain't going to give up nary another one . . . I'm waiting.

WALTER: Ruth—*(He can say nothing.)*

MAMA: If you a son of mine, tell her! *(Walter picks up his keys and his coat and walks out. She continues, bitterly.)* You . . . you are a disgrace to your father's memory. Somebody get me my hat!

Curtain.

ACT 2, Scene 1

Time: Later the same day.

At rise: Ruth is ironing again. She has the radio going. Presently Beneatha's bedroom door opens and Ruth's mouth falls and she puts down the iron in fascination.

RUTH: What have we got on tonight!

BENEATHA *(emerging grandly from the doorway so that we can see her thoroughly robed in the costume Asagai brought)*:   You are looking at what a well-dressed Nigerian woman wears—*(She parades for Ruth, her hair completely hidden by the headdress; she is coquettishly fanning herself with an ornate oriental fan, mistakenly more like Butterfly than any Nigerian that ever was.)* Isn't it beautiful? *(She promenades to the radio and, with an arrogant flourish, turns off the good loud blues that is playing.)* Enough of this assimilationist junk! *(Ruth follows her with her eyes as she goes to the phonograph and puts on a record and turns and waits ceremoniously for the music to come up. Then, with a shout—)* OCOMOGOSIAY!

Ruth jumps. The music comes up, a lovely Nigerian melody. Beneatha listens, enraptured, her eyes far way—"back to the past." She begins to dance. Ruth is dumfounded.

RUTH: What kind of dance is that?

BENEATHA: A folk dance.

RUTH *(Pearl Bailey):*   What kind of folks do that, honey?

BENEATHA: It's from Nigeria. It's a dance of welcome.

RUTH: Who you welcoming?

BENEATHA: The men back to the village.

RUTH: Where they been?

BENEATHA: How should I know—out hunting or something. Anyway, they are coming back now . . .

RUTH: Well, that's good.

BENEATHA *(with the record):*

Alundi, alundi

Alundi alunya

Jop pu a jeepua

Ang gu soooooooooo

Ai yai yae . . .

Ayehaye—alundi . . .

Walter comes in during this performance; he has obviously been drinking. He leans against the door heavily and watches his sister, at first with distaste. Then his eyes look off—"back to the past"—as he lifts both his fists to the roof, screaming.

WALTER: YEAH . . . AND ETHIOPIA STRETCH FORTH HER HANDS AGAIN! . . .

RUTH *(drily, looking at him):*   Yes—and Africa sure is claiming her own tonight. *(She gives them both up and starts ironing again.)*

WALTER *(all in a drunken, dramatic shout):*   Shut up! . . . I'm diggin them drums . . . them drums move me! . . . *(He makes his weaving way to his wife's face and leans in close to her.)* In my *heart of hearts*—*(He thumps his chest.)*—I am much warrior!

RUTH *(without even looking up):*   In your heart of hearts you are much drunkard.

WALTER *(coming away from her and starting to wander around the room, shouting):* Me and Jomo . . . *(Intently, in his sister's face. She has stopped dancing to watch him in this unknown mood.)* That's my man, Kenyatta. *(Shouting and thumping his chest.)* FLAMING SPEAR! HOT DAMN! *(He is suddenly in possession of an imaginary spear and actively spearing enemies all over the room.)* OCOMOGOSIAY . . .

BENEATHA *(to encourage Walter, thoroughly caught up with this side of him):* OCOMOGOSIAY, FLAMING SPEAR!

WALTER: THE LION IS WAKING . . . OWIMOWEH!

He pulls his shirt open and leaps up on the table and gestures with his spear.

BENEATHA: OWIMOWEH!

WALTER (on the table, very far gone, his eyes pure glass sheets. He sees what we cannot, that he is a leader of his people, a great chief, a descendant of Chaka, and that the hour to march has come):   Listen, my black brothers —

BENEATHA: OCOMOGOSIAY!

WALTER: — Do you hear the waters rushing against the shores of the coastlands —

BENEATHA: OCOMOGOSIAY!

WALTER: — Do you hear the screeching of the cocks in yonder hills beyond where the chiefs meet in council for the coming of the mighty war —

BENEATHA: OCOMOGOSIAY!

And now the lighting shifts subtly to suggest the world of Walter's imagination, and the mood shifts from pure comedy. It is the inner Walter speaking: the South-side chauffeur has assumed an unexpected majesty.

WALTER: — Do you hear the beating of the wings of the birds flying low over the mountains and the low places of our land —

BENEATHA: OCOMOGOSIAY!

WALTER: — Do you hear the singing of the women, singing the war songs of our fathers to the babies in the great houses? Singing the sweet war songs! *(The doorbell rings.)* OH, DO YOU HEAR, MY *BLACK* BROTHERS!

BENEATHA *(completely gone):*   We hear you, Flaming Spear —

Ruth shuts off the phonograph and opens the door. George Murchison enters.

WALTER: Telling us to prepare for the GREATNESS OF THE TIME! *(Lights back to normal. He turns and sees George.)* Black Brother!

He extends his hand for the fraternal clasp.

GEORGE: Black Brother, hell!

RUTH *(having had enough, and embarrassed for the family):*   Beneatha, you got company — what's the matter with you? Walter Lee Younger, get down off that table and stop acting like a fool . . .

Walter comes down off the table suddenly and makes a quick exit to the bathroom.

RUTH: He's had a little to drink . . . I don't know what her excuse is.

GEORGE *(to Beneatha):*   Look honey, we're going to the theater — we're not going to be *in* it . . . so go change, huh?

Beneatha looks at him and slowly, ceremoniously, lifts her hands and pulls off the headdress. Her hair is close-cropped and unstraightened. George freezes mid-sentence and Ruth's eyes all but fall out of her head.

GEORGE: What in the name of —

RUTH *(touching Beneatha's hair):*   Girl, you done lost your natural mind? Look at your head!

GEORGE: What have you done to your head — I mean your hair!

BENEATHA: Nothing — except cut it off.

RUTH: Now that's the truth—it's what ain't been done to it! You expect this boy to go out with you with your head all nappy like that?

BENEATHA *(looking at George):*   That's up to George. If he's ashamed of his heritage—

GEORGE: Oh, don't be so proud of yourself, Bennie—just because you look eccentric.

BENEATHA: How can something that's natural be eccentric?

GEORGE: That's what being eccentric means—being natural. Get dressed.

BENEATHA: I don't like that, George.

RUTH: Why must you and your brother make an argument out of everything people say?

BENEATHA: Because I hate assimilationist Negroes!

RUTH: Will somebody please tell me what assimila-whoever means!

GEORGE: Oh, it's just a college girl's way of calling people Uncle Toms—but that isn't what it means at all.

RUTH: Well, what does it mean?

BENEATHA *(cutting George off and staring at him as she replies to Ruth):*   It means someone who is willing to give up his own culture and submerge himself completely in the dominant, and in this case *oppressive* culture!

GEORGE: Oh, dear, dear, dear! Here we go! A lecture on the African past! On our Great West African Heritage! In one second we will hear all about the great Ashanti empires; the great Songhay civilizations; and the great sculpture of Bénin—and then some poetry in the Bantu—and the whole monologue will end with the word *heritage!* *(Nastily.)* Let's face it, baby, your heritage is nothing but a bunch of raggedy-assed spirituals and some grass huts!

BENEATHA: GRASS HUTS! *(Ruth crosses to her and forcibly pushes her toward the bedroom.)* See there . . . you are standing there in your splendid ignorance talking about people who were the first to smelt iron on the face of the earth! *(Ruth is pushing her through the door.)* The Ashanti were performing surgical operations when the English—*(Ruth pulls the door to, with Beneatha on the other side, and smiles graciously at George. Beneatha opens the door and shouts the end of the sentence defiantly at George.)*—were still tatooing themselves with blue dragons! *(She goes back inside.)*

RUTH: Have a seat, George. *(They both sit. Ruth folds her hands rather primly on her lap, determined to demonstrate the civilization of the family.)* Warm, ain't it? I mean for September. *(Pause.)* Just like they always say about Chicago weather: if it's too hot or cold for you, just wait a minute and it'll change. *(She smiles happily at this cliché of clichés.)* Everybody say it's got to do with them bombs and things they keep setting off. *(Pause.)* Would you like a nice cold beer?

GEORGE: No, thank you. I don't care for beer. *(He looks at his watch.)* I hope she hurries up.

RUTH: What time is the show?

GEORGE: It's an eight-thirty curtain. That's just Chicago, though. In New York standard curtain time is eight forty.

He is rather proud of this knowledge.

RUTH *(properly appreciating it)*:   You get to New York a lot?

GEORGE *(offhand)*:   Few times a year.

RUTH: Oh — that's nice. I've never been to New York.

Walter enters. We feel he has relieved himself, but the edge of unreality is still with him.

WALTER: New York ain't got nothing Chicago ain't. Just a bunch of hustling people all squeezed up together — being "Eastern."

He turns his face into a screw of displeasure.

GEORGE: Oh — you've been?

WALTER: *Plenty* of times.

RUTH *(shocked at the lie)*:   Walter Lee Younger!

WALTER *(staring her down)*:   Plenty! *(Pause.)* What we got to drink in this house? Why don't you offer this man some refreshment. *(To George.)* They don't know how to entertain people in this house, man.

GEORGE: Thank you — I don't really care for anything.

WALTER *(feeling his head; sobriety coming)*:   Where's Mama?

RUTH: She ain't come back yet.

WALTER *(looking Murchison over from head to toe, scrutinizing his carefully casual tweed sports jacket over cashmere V-neck sweater over soft eyelet shirt and tie, and soft slacks, finished off with white buckskin shoes)*:   Why all you college boys wear them faggoty-looking white shoes?

RUTH: Walter Lee!

George Murchison ignores the remark.

WALTER *(to Ruth)*:   Well, they look crazy as hell — white shoes, cold as it is.

RUTH *(crushed)*:   You have to excuse him —

WALTER: No he don't! Excuse me for what? What you always excusing me for! I'll excuse myself when I needs to be excused! *(A pause.)* They look as funny as them black knee socks Beneatha wears out of here all the time.

RUTH: It's the college *style*, Walter.

WALTER: Style, hell. She looks like she got burnt legs or something!

RUTH: Oh, Walter —

WALTER *(an irritable mimic)*:   Oh, Walter! Oh, Walter! *(To Murchison.)* How's your old man making out? I understand you all going to buy that big hotel on the Drive? *(He finds a beer in the refrigerator, wanders over to Murchison, sipping and wiping his lips with the back of his hand, and straddling a chair backwards to talk to the other man.)* Shrewd move. Your old man is all right, man. *(Tapping his head and half winking for emphasis.)* I mean he knows how to operate. I mean he thinks *big*, you know what I mean, I mean for a *home*, you know? But I think he's kind of running out of ideas now. I'd like to talk to him. Listen, man, I got some plans that could turn this city upside down. I mean think like he does. *Big*. Invest big, gamble big, hell, lose *big* if you have to, you know what I mean. It's hard to find a man on this whole Southside who understands my kind of thinking — you dig? *(He scrutinizes Murchison again, drinks his beer, squints his eyes and leans in close, confidential, man to man.*) Me and you ought to sit down and talk sometimes, man. Man, I got me some ideas . . .

MURCHISON *(with boredom)*: Yeah—sometimes we'll have to do that, Walter.

WALTER *(understanding the indifference, and offended)*: Yeah—well, when you get the time, man. I know you a busy little boy.

RUTH: Walter, please—

WALTER *(bitterly, hurt)*: I know ain't nothing in this world as busy as you colored college boys with your fraternity pins and white shoes . . .

RUTH *(covering her face with humiliation)*: Oh, Walter Lee—

WALTER: I see you all all the time—with the books tucked under your arms—going to your *(British A—a mimic.)* "clahsses." And for what! What the hell you learning over there? Filling up your heads—*(Counting off on his fingers.)*—with the sociology and the psychology—but they teaching you how to be a man? How to take over and run the world? They teaching you how to run a rubber plantation or a steel mill? Naw—just to talk proper and read books and wear them faggoty-looking white shoes . . .

GEORGE *(looking at him with distaste, a little above it all)*: You're all wacked up with bitterness, man.

WALTER *(intently, almost quietly, between the teeth, glaring at the boy)*: And you—ain't you bitter, man? Ain't you just about had it yet? Don't you see no stars gleaming that you can't reach out and grab? You happy?—You contented son-of-a-bitch—you happy? You got it made? Bitter? Man, I'm a volcano. Bitter? Here I am a giant—surrounded by ants! Ants who can't even understand what it is the giant is talking about.

RUTH *(passionately and suddenly)*: Oh, Walter—ain't you with nobody!

WALTER *(violently)*: No! 'Cause ain't nobody with me! Not even my own mother!

RUTH: Walter, that's a terrible thing to say!

Beneatha enters, dressed for the evening in a cocktail dress and earrings, hair natural.

GEORGE: Well—hey—*(Crosses to Beneatha; thoughtful, with emphasis, since this is a reversal.)* You look great!

WALTER *(seeing his sister's hair for the first time)*: What's the matter with your head?

BENEATHA *(tired of the jokes now)*: I cut it off, Brother.

WALTER *(coming close to inspect it and walking around her)*: Well, I'll be damned. So that's what they mean by the African bush . . .

BENEATHA: Ha ha. Let's go, George.

GEORGE *(looking at her)*: You know something? I like it. It's sharp. I mean it really is. *(Helps her into her wrap.)*

RUTH: Yes—I think so, too. *(She goes to the mirror and starts to clutch at her hair.)*

WALTER: Oh no! You leave yours alone, baby. You might turn out to have a pin-shaped head or something!

BENEATHA: See you all later.

RUTH: Have a nice time.

GEORGE: Thanks. Good night. *(Half out the door, he reopens it. To Walter.)* Good night, Prometheus!

Beneatha and George exit.

WALTER *(to Ruth):*   Who is Prometheus?

RUTH: I don't know. Don't worry about it.

WALTER *(in fury, pointing after George):*   See there—they get to a point where they can't insult you man to man—they got to go talk about something ain't nobody never heard of!

RUTH: How do you know it was an insult? *(To humor him.)* Maybe Prometheus is a nice fellow.

WALTER: Prometheus! I bet there ain't even no such thing! I bet that simple-minded clown—

RUTH: Walter—

She stops what she is doing and looks at him.

WALTER *(yelling):*   Don't start!

RUTH: Start what?

WALTER: Your nagging! Where was I? Who was I with? How much money did I spend?

RUTH *(plaintively):*   Walter Lee—why don't we just try to talk about it . . .

WALTER *(not listening):*   I been out talking with people who understand me. People who care about the things I got on my mind.

RUTH *(wearily):*   I guess that means people like Willy Harris.

WALTER: Yes, people like Willy Harris.

RUTH *(with a sudden flash of impatience):*   Why don't you all just hurry up and go into the banking business and stop talking about it!

WALTER: Why? You want to know why? 'Cause we all tied up in a race of people that don't know how to do nothing but moan, pray and have babies!

The line is too bitter even for him and he looks at her and sits down.

RUTH: Oh, Walter . . . *(Softly.)* Honey, why can't you stop fighting me?

WALTER *(without thinking):*   Who's fighting you? Who even cares about you?

This line begins the retardation of his mood.

RUTH: Well—*(She waits a long time, and then with resignation starts to put away her things.)* I guess I might as well go on to bed . . . *(More or less to herself.)* I don't know where we lost it . . . but we have . . . *(Then, to him.)* I—I'm sorry about this new baby, Walter. I guess maybe I better go on and do what I started . . . I guess I just didn't realize how bad things was with us . . . I guess I just didn't really realize—*(She starts out to the bedroom and stops.)* You want some hot milk?

WALTER: Hot milk?

RUTH: Yes—hot milk.

WALTER: Why hot milk?

RUTH: 'Cause after all that liquor you come home with you ought to have something hot in your stomach.

WALTER: I don't want no milk.

RUTH: You want some coffee then?

WALTER: No, I don't want no coffee. I don't want nothing hot to drink. *(Almost plaintively.)* Why you always trying to give me something to eat?

RUTH *(standing and looking at him helplessly)*:   What *else* can I give you, Walter Lee Younger?

She stands and looks at him and presently turns to go out again. He lifts his head and watches her going away from him in a new mood which began to emerge when he asked her "Who cares about you?"

WALTER: It's been rough, ain't it, baby? *(She hears and stops but does not turn around and he continues to her back.)* I guess between two people there ain't never as much understood as folks generally thinks there is. I mean like between me and you — *(She turns to face him.)* How we gets to the place where we scared to talk softness to each other. *(He waits, thinking hard himself.)* Why you think it got to be like that? *(He is thoughtful, almost as a child would be.)* Ruth, what is it gets into people ought to be close?

RUTH: I don't know, honey. I think about it a lot.

WALTER: On account of you and me, you mean? The way things are with us. The way something done come down between us.

RUTH: There ain't so much between us, Walter . . . Not when you come to me and try to talk to me. Try to be with me . . . a little even.

WALTER *(total honesty)*:   Sometimes . . . sometimes . . . I don't even know how to try.

RUTH: Walter —

WALTER: Yes?

RUTH *(coming to him, gently and with misgiving, but coming to him)*:   Honey . . . life don't have to be like this. I mean sometimes people can do things so that things are better . . . You remember how we used to talk when Travis was born . . . about the way we were going to live . . . the kind of house . . . *(She is stroking his head.)* Well, it's all starting to slip away from us . . .

He turns her to him and they look at each other and kiss, tenderly and hungrily. The door opens and Mama enters — Walter breaks away and jumps up. A beat.

WALTER: Mama, where have you been?

MAMA: My — them steps is longer than they used to be. Whew! *(She sits down and ignores him.)* How you feeling this evening, Ruth?

Ruth shrugs, disturbed at having been interrupted and watching her husband knowingly.

WALTER: Mama, where have you been all day?

MAMA *(still ignoring him and leaning on the table and changing to more comfortable shoes)*:   Where's Travis?

RUTH: I let him go out earlier and he ain't come back yet. Boy, is he going to get it!

WALTER: Mama!

MAMA *(as if she has heard him for the first time)*:   Yes, son?

WALTER: Where did you go this afternoon?

MAMA: I went downtown to tend to some business that I had to tend to.

WALTER: What kind of business?

MAMA: You know better than to question me like a child, Brother.

WALTER *(rising and bending over the table):*   Where were you, Mama? *(Bringing his fists down and shouting.)* Mama, you didn't go do something with that insurance money, something crazy?

The front door opens slowly, interrupting him, and Travis peeks his head in, less than hopefully.

TRAVIS *(to his mother):*   Mama, I —

RUTH: "Mama I" nothing! You're going to get it, boy! Get on in that bedroom and get yourself ready!

TRAVIS: But I —

MAMA: Why don't you all never let the child explain hisself.

RUTH: Keep out of it now, Lena.

Mama clamps her lips together, and Ruth advances toward her son menacingly.

RUTH: A thousand times I have told you not to go off like that —

MAMA *(holding out her arms to her grandson):*   Well — at least let me tell him something. I want him to be the first one to hear . . . Come here, Travis. *(The boy obeys, gladly.)* Travis — *(She takes him by the shoulder and looks into his face.)* — you know that money we got in the mail this morning?

TRAVIS: Yes'm —

MAMA: Well — what you think your grandmama gone and done with that money?

TRAVIS: I don't know, Grandmama.

MAMA *(putting her finger on his nose for emphasis):*   She went out and she bought you a house! *(The explosion comes from Walter at the end of the revelation and he jumps up and turns away from all of them in a fury. Mama continues, to Travis.)* You glad about the house? It's going to be yours when you get to be a man.

TRAVIS: Yeah — I always wanted to live in a house.

MAMA: All right, gimme some sugar then — *(Travis puts his arms around her neck as she watches her son over the boy's shoulder. Then, to Travis, after the embrace.)* Now when you say your prayers tonight, you thank God and your grandfather — 'cause it was him who give you the house — in his way.

RUTH *(taking the boy from Mama and pushing him toward the bedroom):*   Now you get out of here and get ready for your beating.

TRAVIS: Aw, Mama —

RUTH: Get on in there — *(Closing the door behind him and turning radiantly to her mother-in-law.)* So you went and did it!

MAMA *(quietly, looking at her son with pain):*   Yes, I did.

RUTH *(raising both arms classically):*   PRAISE GOD! *(Looks at Walter a moment, who says nothing. She crosses rapidly to her husband.)* Please, honey — let me be glad . . . you be glad too. *(She has laid her hands on his shoulders, but he shakes himself free of her roughly, without turning to face her.)* Oh, Walter . . . a home . . . a home. *(She comes back to Mama.)* Well — where is it? How big is it? How much it going to cost?

MAMA: Well —

RUTH: When we moving?

MAMA (*smiling at her*):   First of the month.

RUTH (*throwing back her head with jubilance*):   Praise God!

MAMA (*tentatively, still looking at her son's back turned against her and Ruth*): It's — it's a nice house too . . . (*She cannot help speaking directly to him. An imploring quality in her voice, her manner, makes her almost like a girl now.*) Three bedrooms — nice big one for you and Ruth . . . Me and Beneatha still have to share our room, but Travis have one of his own — and (*With difficulty.*) I figure if the — new baby — is a boy, we could get one of them double-decker outfits . . . And there's a yard with a little patch of dirt where I could maybe get to grow me a few flowers . . . And a nice big basement . . .

RUTH: Walter honey, be glad —

MAMA (*still to his back, fingering things on the table*):   'Course I don't want to make it sound fancier than it is . . . It's just a plain little old house — but it's made good and solid — and it will be *ours*. Walter Lee — it makes a difference in a man when he can walk on floors that belong to *him* . . .

RUTH: Where is it?

MAMA (*frightened at this telling*):   Well — well — it's out there in Clybourne Park —

Ruth's radiance fades abruptly, and Walter finally turns slowly to face his mother with incredulity and hostility.

RUTH: Where?

MAMA (*matter-of-factly*):   Four o six Clybourne Street, Clybourne Park.

RUTH: Clybourne Park? Mama, there ain't no colored people living in Clybourne Park.

MAMA (*almost idiotically*):   Well, I guess there's going to be some now.

WALTER (*bitterly*):   So that's the peace and comfort you went out and bought for us today!

MAMA (*raising her eyes to meet his finally*):   Son — I just tried to find the nicest place for the least amount of money for my family.

RUTH (*trying to recover from the shock*):   Well — well — 'course I ain't one never been 'fraid of no crackers, mind you — but — well, wasn't there no other houses nowhere?

MAMA: Them houses they put up for colored in them areas way out all seem to cost twice as much as other houses. I did the best I could.

RUTH (*struck senseless with the news, in its various degrees of goodness and trouble, she sits a moment, her fists propping her chin in thought, and then she starts to rise, bringing her fists down with vigor, the radiance spreading from cheek to cheek again*):   Well — well — All I can say is — if this is my time in life — MY TIME — to say good-bye — (*And she builds with momentum as she starts to circle the room with an exuberant, almost tearfully happy release.*) — to these Goddamned cracking walls! — (*She pounds the walls.*) — and these marching roaches! — (*She wipes at an imaginary army of marching roaches.*) — and this cramped little closet which ain't now or never was no kitchen! . . . then I say it loud and good, HALLELUJAH! AND GOOD-BYE MISERY . . . I DON'T NEVER WANT TO SEE YOUR UGLY FACE AGAIN! (*She laughs joyously, having practically destroyed the apartment, and flings her arms up and lets them come down happily, slowly, reflectively, over her abdomen, aware for the first time perhaps that the life therein pulses with happiness and not despair.)* Lena?

MAMA *(moved, watching her happiness):*   Yes, honey?

RUTH *(looking off):*   Is there — is there a whole lot of sunlight?

MAMA *(understanding):*   Yes, child, there's a whole lot of sunlight.

Long pause.

Ruth *(collecting herself and going to the door of the room Travis is in):*   Well — I guess I better see 'bout Travis. *(To Mama.)* Lord, I sure don't feel like whipping nobody today!

She exits.

Mama *(the mother and son are left alone now and the mother waits a long time, considering deeply, before she speaks):*   Son — you — you understand what I done, don't you? *(Walter is silent and sullen.)* I — I just seen my family falling apart today . . . just falling to pieces in front of my eyes . . . We couldn't of gone on like we was today. We was going backwards 'stead of forwards — talking 'bout killing babies and wishing each other was dead . . . When it gets like that in life — you just got to do something different, push on out and do something bigger . . . *(She waits.)* I wish you say something, son . . . I wish you'd say how deep inside you you think I done the right thing —

WALTER *(crossing slowly to his bedroom door and finally turning there and speaking measuredly):*   What you need me to say you done right for? You the head of this family. You run our lives like you want to. It was your money and you did what you wanted with it. So what you need for me to say it was all right for? *(Bitterly, to hurt her as deeply as he knows is possible.)* So you butchered up a dream of mine — you — who always talking 'bout your children's dreams . . .

MAMA: Walter Lee —

He just closes the door behind him. Mama sits alone, thinking heavily.

Curtain.

Scene 2

Time: Friday night, a few weeks later.

    At rise: Packing crates mark the intention of the family to move. Beneatha and George come in, presumably from an evening out again.

GEORGE: O.K. . . . O.K., whatever you say . . . *(They both sit on the couch. He tries to kiss her. She moves away.)* Look, we've had a nice evening; let's not spoil it, huh? . . .

He again turns her head and tries to nuzzle in and she turns away from him, not with distaste but with momentary lack of interest; in a mood to pursue what they were talking about.

BENEATHA: I'm *trying* to talk to you.

GEORGE: We always talk.

BENEATHA: Yes—and I love to talk.

GEORGE *(exasperated; rising):*   I know it and I don't mind it sometimes . . . I want you to cut it out, see—The moody stuff, I mean. I don't like it. You're a nice-looking girl . . . all over. That's all you need, honey, forget the atmosphere. Guys aren't going to go for the atmosphere—they're going to go for what they see. Be glad for that. Drop the Garbo routine. It doesn't go with you. As for myself, I want a nice—*(Groping.)*—simple *(Thoughtfully.)*—sophisticated girl . . . not a poet—O.K.?

He starts to kiss her, she rebuffs him again and he jumps up.

BENEATHA: Why are you angry, George?

GEORGE: Because this is stupid! I don't go out with you to discuss the nature of "quiet desperation" or to hear all about your thoughts—because the world will go on thinking what it thinks regardless—

BENEATHA: Then why read books? Why go to school?

GEORGE *(with artificial patience, counting on his fingers):*   It's simple. You read books—to learn facts—to get grades—to pass the course—to get a degree. That's all—it has nothing to do with thoughts.

A long pause.

BENEATHA: I see. *(He starts to sit.)* Good night, George.

George looks at her a little oddly, and starts to exit. He meets Mama coming in.

GEORGE: Oh—hello, Mrs. Younger.

MAMA: Hello, George, how you feeling?

GEORGE: Fine—fine, how are you?

MAMA: Oh, a little tired. You know them steps can get you after a day's work. You all have a nice time tonight?

GEORGE: Yes—a fine time. A fine time.

MAMA: Well, good night.

GEORGE: Good night. *(He exits. Mama closes the door behind her.)* Hello, honey. What you sitting like that for?

BENEATHA: I'm just sitting.

MAMA: Didn't you have a nice time?

BENEATHA: No.

MAMA: No? What's the matter?

BENEATHA: Mama, George is a fool—honest. *(She rises.)*

MAMA *(hustling around unloading the packages she has entered with. She stops):* Is he, baby?

BENEATHA: Yes.

Beneatha makes up Travis's bed as she talks.

MAMA: You sure?

BENEATHA: Yes.

MAMA: Well—I guess you better not waste your time with no fools.

Beneatha looks up at her mother, watching her put groceries in the refrigerator. Finally she gathers up her things and starts into the bedroom. At the door she stops and looks back at her mother.

BENEATHA: Mama—
MAMA: Yes, baby—
BENEATHA: Thank you.
MAMA: For what?
BENEATHA: For understanding me this time.

She exits quickly and the mother stands, smiling a little, looking at the place where Beneatha just stood. Ruth enters.

RUTH: Now don't you fool with any of this stuff, Lena—
MAMA: Oh, I just thought I'd sort a few things out. Is Brother here?
RUTH: Yes.
MAMA *(with concern)*:   Is he—
RUTH *(reading her eyes)*:   Yes.

Mama is silent and someone knocks on the door. Mama and Ruth exchange weary and knowing glances and Ruth opens it to admit the neighbor, Mrs. Johnson,° who is a rather squeaky wide-eyed lady of no particular age, with a newspaper under her arm.

Mama (changing her expression to acute delight and a ringing cheerful greeting):   Oh—hello there, Johnson.
JOHNSON *(this is a woman who decided long ago to be enthusiastic about EVERY-THING in life and she is inclined to wave her wrist vigorously at the height of her exclamatory comments)*:   Hello there, yourself! H'you this evening, Ruth?
RUTH *(not much of a deceptive type)*:   Fine, Mis' Johnson, h'you?
JOHNSON: Fine. *(Reaching out quickly, playfully, and patting Ruth's stomach.)* Ain't you starting to poke out none yet! *(She mugs with delight at the over familiar remark and her eyes dart around looking at the crates and packing preparation; Mama's face is a cold sheet of endurance.)* Oh, ain't we getting ready round here, though! Yessir! Lookathere! I'm telling you the Youngers is really getting ready to "move on up a little higher!"—Bless God!
MAMA *(a little drily, doubting the total sincerity of the Blesser)*:   Bless God.
JOHNSON: He's good, ain't He?
MAMA: Oh yes, He's good.
JOHNSON: I mean sometimes He works in mysterious ways . . . but He works, don't He!
MAMA *(the same)*:   Yes, he does.
JOHNSON: I'm just soooooo happy for y'all. And this here child—*(About Ruth.)* looks like she could just pop open with happiness, don't she. Where's all the rest of the family?
MAMA: Bennie's gone to bed—

Mrs. Johnson: This character and the scene of her visit were cut from the original production and early editions of the play.

JOHNSON: Ain't no . . . *(The implication is pregnancy.)* sickness done hit you—I hope . . . ?

MAMA: No—she just tired. She was out this evening.

JOHNSON *(all is a coo, an emphatic coo)*:   Aw—ain't that lovely. She still going out with the little Murchison boy?

MAMA *(drily)*:   Ummmm huh.

JOHNSON: That's lovely. You sure got lovely children, Younger. Me and Isaiah talks all the time 'bout what fine children you was blessed with. We sure do.

MAMA: Ruth, give Mis' Johnson a piece of sweet potato pie and some milk.

JOHNSON: Oh honey, I can't stay hardly a minute—I just dropped in to see if there was anything I could do. *(Accepting the food easily.)* I guess y'all seen the news what's all over the colored paper this week . . .

MAMA: No—didn't get mine yet this week.

JOHNSON *(lifting her head and blinking with the spirit of catastrophe)*:   You mean you ain't read 'bout them colored people that was bombed out their place out there?

Ruth straightens with concern and takes the paper and reads it. Johnson notices her and feeds commentary.

JOHNSON: Ain't it something how bad these here white folks is getting here in Chicago! Lord, getting so you think you right down in Mississippi! *(With a tremendous and rather insincere sense of melodrama.)* 'Course I thinks it's wonderful how our folk keeps on pushing out. You hear some of these Negroes round here talking 'bout how they don't go where they ain't wanted and all that—but not me, honey! *(This is a lie.)* Wilhemenia Othella Johnson goes anywhere, any time she feels like it! *(With head movement for emphasis.)* Yes I do! Why if we left it up to these here crackers, the poor niggers wouldn't have nothing—*(She clasps her hand over her mouth.)* Oh, I always forgets you don't 'low that word in your house.

MAMA *(quietly, looking at her)*:   No—I don't 'low it.

JOHNSON *(vigorously again)*:   Me neither! I was just telling Isaiah yesterday when he come using it in front of me—I said, "Isaiah, it's just like Mis' Younger says all the time—"

MAMA: Don't you want some more pie?

JOHNSON: No—no thank you; this was lovely. I got to get on over home and have my midnight coffee. I hear some people say it don't let them sleep but I finds I can't close my eyes right lessen I done had that laaaast cup of coffee . . . *(She waits. A beat. Undaunted.)* My Goodnight coffee, I calls it!

MAMA *(with much eye-rolling and communication between herself and Ruth)*:   Ruth, why don't you give Mis' Johnson some coffee.

Ruth gives Mama an unpleasant look for her kindness.

JOHNSON *(accepting the coffee)*:   Where's Brother tonight?

MAMA: He's lying down.

JOHNSON: MMmmmmm, he sure gets his beauty rest, don't he? Good-looking man. Sure is a good-looking man! *(Reaching out to pat Ruth's stomach again.)* I guess that's how come we keep on having babies around here. *(She winks at*

Mama.) One thing 'bout Brother, he always know how to have a *good* time. And soooooo ambitious! I bet it was his idea y'all moving out to Clybourne Park. Lord—I bet this time next month y'all's names will have been in the papers plenty—*(Holding up her hands to mark off each word of the headline she can see in front of her.)* "NEGROES INVADE CLYBOURNE PARK— BOMBED!"

MAMA *(she and Ruth look at the woman in amazement):*   We ain't exactly moving out there to get bombed.

JOHNSON: Oh honey—you know I'm praying to God every day that don't noth- ing like that happen! But you have to think of life like it is—and these here Chicago peckerwoods is some baaaad peckerwoods.

MAMA *(wearily):*   We done thought about all that Mis' Johnson.

Beneatha comes out of the bedroom in her robe and passes through to the bath- room. Mrs. Johnson turns.

JOHNSON: Hello there, Bennie!

BENEATHA *(crisply):*   Hello, Mrs. Johnson.

JOHNSON: How is school?

BENEATHA *(crisply):*   Fine, thank you. *(She goes out.)*

JOHNSON *(insulted):*   Getting so she don't have much to say to nobody.

MAMA: The child was on her way to the bathroom.

JOHNSON: I know—but sometimes she act like ain't got time to pass the time of day with nobody ain't been to college. Oh—I ain't criticizing her none. It's just—you know how some of our young people gets when they get a little education. *(Mama and Ruth say nothing, just look at her.)* Yes—well. Well, I guess I better get on home. *(Unmoving.)* 'Course I can understand how she must be proud and everything—being the only one in the family to make something of herself. I know just being a chauffeur ain't never satisfied Brother none. He shouldn't feel like that, though. Ain't nothing wrong with being a chauffeur.

MAMA: There's plenty wrong with it.

JOHNSON: What?

MAMA: Plenty. My husband always said being any kind of a servant wasn't a fit thing for a man to have to be. He always said a man's hands was made to make things, or to turn the earth with—not to drive nobody's car for 'em— or—*(She looks at her own hands.)* carry they slop jars. And my boy is just like him—he wasn't meant to wait on nobody.

JOHNSON *(rising, somewhat offended):*   Mmmmmmmmmm. The Youngers is too much for me! *(She looks around.)* You sure one proud-acting bunch of col- ored folks. Well—I always thinks like Booker T. Washington said that time— "Education has spoiled many a good plow hand"—

MAMA: Is that what old Booker T. said?

JOHNSON: He sure did.

MAMA: Well, it sounds just like him. The fool.

JOHNSON *(indignantly):*   Well—he was one of our great men.

MAMA: Who said so?

JOHNSON *(nonplussed)*:　You know, me and you ain't never agreed about some things, Lena Younger. I guess I better be going—

RUTH *(quickly)*:　Good night.

JOHNSON:　Good night. Oh—*(Thrusting it at her.)* You can keep the paper! *(With a trill.)* 'Night.

MAMA:　Good night, Mis' Johnson.

Mrs. Johnson exits.

RUTH:　If ignorance was gold . . .

MAMA:　Shush. Don't talk about folks behind their backs.

RUTH:　You do.

MAMA:　I'm old and corrupted. *(Beneatha enters.)* You was rude to Mis' Johnson, Beneatha, and I don't like it at all.

BENEATHA *(at her door)*:　Mama, if there are two things we, as a people, have got to overcome, one is the Klu Klux Klan—and the other is Mrs. Johnson. *(She exits.)*

MAMA:　Smart aleck.

The phone rings.

RUTH:　I'll get it.

MAMA:　Lord, ain't this a popular place tonight.

RUTH *(at the phone)*:　Hello—Just a minute. *(Goes to door.)* Walter, it's Mrs. Arnold. *(Waits. Goes back to the phone. Tense.)* Hello. Yes, this is his wife speaking . . . He's lying down now. Yes . . . well, he'll be in tomorrow. He's been very sick. Yes—I know we should have called, but we were so sure he'd be able to come in today. Yes—yes, I'm very sorry. Yes . . . Thank you very much. *(She hangs up. Walter is standing in the doorway of the bedroom behind her.)* That was Mrs. Arnold.

WALTER *(indifferently)*:　Was it?

RUTH:　She said if you don't come in tomorrow that they are getting a new man . . .

WALTER:　Ain't that sad—ain't that crying sad.

RUTH:　She said Mr. Arnold has had to take a cab for three days . . . Walter, you ain't been to work for three days! *(This is a revelation to her.)* Where you been, Walter Lee Younger? *(Walter looks at her and starts to laugh.)* You're going to lose your job.

WALTER:　That's right . . . *(He turns on the radio.)*

RUTH:　Oh, Walter, and with your mother working like a dog every day—

A steamy, deep blues pours into the room.

WALTER:　That's sad too—Everything is sad.

MAMA:　What you been doing for these three days, son?

WALTER:　Mama—you don't know all the things a man what got leisure can find to do in this city . . . What's this—Friday night? Well—Wednesday I borrowed Willy Harris' car and I went for a drive . . . just me and myself and I drove and drove . . . Way out . . . way past South Chicago, and I parked the car and I sat and looked at the steel mills all day long. I just sat in the car and looked at them big black chimneys for hours. Then I drove back and I went to the

Green Hat. *(Pause.)* And Thursday—Thursday I borrowed the car again and I got in it and I pointed it the other way and I drove the other way— for hours—way, way up to Wisconsin, and I looked at the farms. I just drove and looked at the farms. Then I drove back and I went to the Green Hat. *(Pause.)* And today—today I didn't get the car. Today I just walked. All over the Southside. And I looked at the Negroes and they looked at me and finally I just sat down on the curb at Thirty-ninth and South Parkway and I just sat there and watched the Negroes go by. And then I went to the Green Hat. You all sad? You all depressed? And you know where I am going right now—

Ruth goes out quietly.

MAMA: Oh, Big Walter, is this the harvest of our days?

WALTER: You know what I like about the Green Hat? I like this little cat they got there who blows a sax . . . He blows. He talks to me. He ain't but 'bout five feet tall and he's got a conked head and his eyes is always closed and he's all music—

MAMA *(rising and getting some papers out of her handbag):*   Walter—

WALTER: And there's this other guy who plays the piano . . . and they got a sound. I mean they can work on some music . . . They got the best little combo in the world in the Green Hat . . . You can just sit there and drink and listen to them three men play and you realize that don't nothing matter worth a damn, but just being there—

MAMA: I've helped do it to you, haven't I, son? Walter, I been wrong.

WALTER: Naw—you ain't never been wrong about nothing, Mama.

MAMA: Listen to me, now. I say I been wrong, son. That I been doing to you what the rest of the world been doing to you. *(She turns off the radio.)* Walter— *(She stops and he looks up slowly at her and she meets his eyes pleadingly.)* What you ain't never understood is that I ain't got nothing, don't own nothing, ain't never really wanted nothing that wasn't for you. There ain't nothing as precious to me . . . There ain't nothing worth holding on to, money, dreams, nothing else—if it means—if it means it's going to destroy my boy. *(She takes an envelope out of her handbag and puts it in front of him and he watches her without speaking or moving.)* I paid the man thirty-five hundred dollars down on the house. That leaves sixty-five hundred dollars. Monday morning I want you to take this money and take three thousand dollars and put it in a savings account for Beneatha's medical schooling. The rest you put in a checking account—with your name on it. And from now on any penny that come out of it or that go in it is for you to look after. For you to decide. *(She drops her hands a little helplessly.)* It ain't much, but it's all I got in the world and I'm putting it in your hands. I'm telling you to be the head of this family from now on like you supposed to be.

WALTER *(stares at the money):*   You trust me like that, Mama?

MAMA: I ain't never stop trusting you. Like I ain't never stop loving you.

She goes out, and Walter sits looking at the money on the table. Finally, in a decisive gesture, he gets up, and, in mingled joy and desperation, picks up the money. At the same moment, Travis enters for bed.

TRAVIS: What's the matter, Daddy? You drunk?

WALTER *(sweetly, more sweetly than we have ever known him)*: No, Daddy ain't drunk. Daddy ain't going to never be drunk again . . .

TRAVIS: Well, good night, Daddy.

The father has come from behind the couch and leans over, embracing his son.

WALTER: Son, I feel like talking to you tonight.

TRAVIS: About what?

WALTER: Oh, about a lot of things. About you and what kind of man you going to be when you grow up . . . Son — son, what do you want to be when you grow up?

TRAVIS: A bus driver.

WALTER *(laughing a little)*: A what? Man, that ain't nothing to want to be!

TRAVIS: Why not?

WALTER: 'Cause, man — it ain't big enough — you know what I mean.

TRAVIS: I don't know then. I can't make up my mind. Sometimes Mama asks me that too. And sometimes when I tell her I just want to be like you — she says she don't want me to be like that and sometimes she says she does. . . .

WALTER *(gathering him up in his arms)*: You know what, Travis? In seven years you going to be seventeen years old. And things is going to be very different with us in seven years, Travis. . . . One day when you are seventeen I'll come home — home from my office downtown somewhere —

TRAVIS: You don't work in no office, Daddy.

WALTER: No — but after tonight. After what your daddy gonna do tonight, there's going to be offices — a whole lot of offices. . . .

TRAVIS: What you gonna do tonight, Daddy?

WALTER: You wouldn't understand yet, son, but your daddy's gonna make a transaction . . . a business transaction that's going to change our lives. . . . That's how come one day when you 'bout seventeen years old I'll come home and I'll be pretty tired, you know what I mean, after a day of conferences and secretaries getting things wrong the way they do . . .'cause an executive's life is hell, man — *(The more he talks the farther away he gets.)* And I'll pull the car up on the driveway . . . just a plain black Chrysler, I think, with white walls — no — black tires. More elegant. Rich people don't have to be flashy . . . though I'll have to get something a little sportier for Ruth — maybe a Cadillac convertible to do her shopping in. . . . And I'll come up the steps to the house and the gardener will be clipping away at the hedges and he'll say, "Good evening, Mr. Younger." And I'll say, "Hello, Jefferson, how are you this evening?" And I'll go inside and Ruth will come downstairs and meet me at the door and we'll kiss each other and she'll take my arm and we'll go up to your room to see you sitting on the floor with the catalogues of all the great schools in America around you. . . . All the great schools in the world! And — and I'll say, all right son — it's your seventeenth birthday, what is it you've decided? . . . Just tell me where you want to go to school and you'll *go*. Just tell me, what it is you want to be — and you'll *be* it. . . . Whatever you want to be — Yessir! *(He holds his arms open for Travis.)* You just name it, son . . . *(Travis leaps into them.)* and I hand you the world!

*Walter's voice has risen in pitch and hysterical promise and on the last line he lifts
Travis high.*

    Blackout.

Scene 3

Time: Saturday, moving day, one week later.

    *Before the curtain rises, Ruth's voice, a strident, dramatic church alto, cuts
through the silence.*

    *It is, in the darkness, a triumphant surge, a penetrating statement of expecta-
tion: "Oh, Lord, I don't feel no ways tired! Children, oh, glory hallelujah!"*

    *As the curtain rises we see that Ruth is alone in the living room, finishing up
the family's packing. It is moving day. She is nailing crates and tying cartons.
Beneatha enters, carrying a guitar case, and watches her exuberant sister-in-law.*

RUTH: Hey!

BENEATHA *(putting away the case)*: Hi.

RUTH *(pointing at a package)*: Honey—look in that package there and see what
    I found on sale this morning at the South Center. *(Ruth gets up and moves to
    the package and draws out some curtains.)* Lookahere—hand-turned hems!

BENEATHA: How do you know the window size out there?

RUTH *(who hadn't thought of that)*: Oh—Well, they bound to fit something in
    the whole house. Anyhow, they was too good a bargain to pass up. *(Ruth
    slaps her head, suddenly remembering something.)* Oh, Bennie—I meant to
    put a special note on that carton over there. That's your mama's good china
    and she wants 'em to be very careful with it.

BENEATHA: I'll do it.

Beneatha finds a piece of paper and starts to draw large letters on it.

RUTH: You know what I'm going to do soon as I get in that new house?

BENEATHA: What?

RUTH: Honey—I'm going to run me a tub of water up to here . . . *(With her fin-
    gers practically up to her nostrils.)* And I'm going to get in it—and I am going
    to sit . . . and sit . . . and sit in that hot water and the first person who knocks
    to tell *me* to hurry up and come out—

BENEATHA: Gets shot at sunrise.

RUTH *(laughing happily)*: You said it, sister! *(Noticing how large Beneatha is
    absent-mindedly making the note)*: Honey, they ain't going to read that from
    no airplane.

BENEATHA *(laughing herself)*: I guess I always think things have more emphasis
    if they are big, somehow.

RUTH *(looking up at her and smiling)*: You and your brother seem to have that as
    a philosophy of life. Lord, that man—done changed so 'round here. You
    know—you know what we did last night? Me and Walter Lee?

BENEATHA: What?

RUTH *(smiling to herself)*: We went to the movies. *(Looking at Beneatha to see if
    she understands.)* We went to the movies. You know the last time me and
    Walter went to the movies together?

BENEATHA: No.

RUTH: Me neither. That's how long it been. (*Smiling again.*) But we went last night. The picture wasn't much good, but that didn't seem to matter. We went — and we held hands.

BENEATHA: Oh, Lord!

RUTH: We held hands — and you know what?

BENEATHA: What?

RUTH: When we come out of the show it was late and dark and all the stores and things was closed up . . . and it was kind of chilly and there wasn't many people on the streets . . . and we was still holding hands, me and Walter.

BENEATHA: You're killing me.

Walter enters with a large package. His happiness is deep in him; he cannot keep still with his newfound exuberance. He is singing and wiggling and snapping his fingers. He puts his package in a corner and puts a phonograph record, which he has brought in with him, on the record player. As the music, soulful and sensuous, comes up he dances over to Ruth and tries to get her to dance with him. She gives in at last to his raunchiness and in a fit of giggling allows herself to be drawn into his mood. They dip and she melts into his arms in a classic, body-melting "slow drag."

BENEATHA (*regarding them a long time as they dance, then drawing in her breath for a deeply exaggerated comment which she does not particularly mean*): Talk about — olddddddddddd-fashionedddddddd — Negroes!

WALTER (*stopping momentarily*):   What kind of Negroes?

He says this in fun. He is not angry with her today, nor with anyone. He starts to dance with his wife again.

BENEATHA: Old-fashioned.

WALTER (*as he dances with Ruth*):   You know, when these *New Negroes* have their convention — (*Pointing at his sister.*) — that is going to be the chairman of the Committee on Unending Agitation. (*He goes on dancing, then stops.*) Race, race, race! . . . Girl, I do believe you are the first person in the history of the entire human race to successfully brainwash yourself. (*Beneatha breaks up and he goes on dancing. He stops again, enjoying his tease.*) Damn, even the N double A C P takes a holiday sometimes! (*Beneatha and Ruth laugh. He dances with Ruth some more and starts to laugh and stops and pantomimes someone over an operating table.*) I can just see that chick someday looking down at some poor cat on an operating table and before she starts to slice him, she says . . . (*Pulling his sleeves back maliciously.*) "By the way, what are your views on civil rights down there? . . ."

He laughs at her again and starts to dance happily. The bell sounds.

BENEATHA: Sticks and stones may break my bones but . . . words will never hurt me!

Beneatha goes to the door and opens it as Walter and Ruth go on with the clowning. Beneatha is somewhat surprised to see a quiet-looking middle-aged white man in a business suit holding his hat and a briefcase in his hand and consulting a small piece of paper.

MAN: Uh—how do you do, miss. I am looking for a Mrs.—*(He looks at the slip of paper.)* Mrs. Lena Younger? *(He stops short, struck dumb at the sight of the oblivious Walter and Ruth.)*

BENEATHA *(smoothing her hair with slight embarrassment):*   Oh—yes, that's my mother. Excuse me. *(She closes the door and turns to quiet the other two.)* Ruth! Brother! *(Enunciating precisely but soundlessly: "There's a white man at the door!" They stop dancing, Ruth cuts off the phonograph, Beneatha opens the door. The man casts a curious quick glance at all of them.)* Uh—come in please.

MAN *(coming in):*   Thank you.

BENEATHA: My mother isn't here just now. Is it business?

MAN: Yes . . . well, of a sort.

WALTER *(freely, the Man of the House):*   Have a seat. I'm Mrs. Younger's son. I look after most of her business matters.

Ruth and Beneatha exchange amused glances.

MAN *(regarding Walter, and sitting):*   Well—My name is Karl Lindner . . .

WALTER *(stretching out his hand):*   Walter Younger. This is my wife—*(Ruth nods politely.)*—and my sister.

LINDNER: How do you do.

WALTER *(amiably, as he sits himself easily on a chair, leaning forward on his knees with interest and looking expectantly into the newcomer's face):*   What can we do for you, Mr. Lindner!

LINDNER *(some minor shuffling of the hat and briefcase on his knees):*   Well—I am a representative of the Clybourne Park Improvement Association—

WALTER *(pointing):*   Why don't you sit your things on the floor?

LINDNER: Oh—yes. Thank you. *(He slides the briefcase and hat under the chair.)* And as I was saying—I am from the Clybourne Park Improvement Association and we have had it brought to our attention at the last meeting that you people—or at least your mother—has bought a piece of residential property at—*(He digs for the slip of paper again.)*—four o six Clybourne Street . . .

WALTER: That's right. Care for something to drink? Ruth, get Mr. Lindner a beer.

LINDNER *(upset for some reason):*   Oh—no, really. I mean thank you very much, but no thank you.

RUTH *(innocently):*   Some coffee?

LINDNER: Thank you, nothing at all.

Beneatha is watching the man carefully.

LINDNER: Well, I don't know how much you folks know about our organization. *(He is a gentle man; thoughtful and somewhat labored in his manner.)* It is one of these community organizations set up to look after—oh, you know, things like block upkeep and special projects and we also have what we call our New Neighbors Orientation Committee . . .

BENEATHA *(drily):*   Yes—and what do they do?

LINDNER *(turning a little to her and then returning the main force to Walter):*   Well—it's what you might call a sort of welcoming committee, I guess. I mean they, we — I'm the chairman of the committee — go around and see the new people who move into the neighborhood and sort of give them the low-down on the way we do things out in Clybourne Park.

BENEATHA (*with appreciation of the two meanings, which escape Ruth and Walter*):   Un-huh.

LINDNER: And we also have the category of what the association calls — (*He looks elsewhere.*) — uh — special community problems . . .

BENEATHA: Yes — and what are some of those?

WALTER: Girl, let the man talk.

LINDNER (*with understated relief*):   Thank you. I would sort of like to explain this thing in my own way. I mean I want to explain to you in a certain way.

WALTER: Go ahead.

LINDNER: Yes. Well. I'm going to try to get right to the point. I'm sure we'll all appreciate that in the long run.

BENEATHA: Yes.

WALTER: Be still now!

LINDNER: Well —

RUTH (*still innocently*):   Would you like another chair — you don't look comfortable.

LINDNER (*more frustrated than annoyed*):   No, thank you very much. Please. Well — to get right to the point, I — (*A great breath, and he is off at last.*) I am sure you people must be aware of some of the incidents which have happened in various parts of the city when colored people have moved into certain areas — (*Beneatha exhales heavily and starts tossing a piece of fruit up and down in the air.*) Well — because we have what I think is going to be a unique type of organization in American community life — not only do we deplore that kind of thing — but we are trying to do something about it. (*Beneatha stops tossing and turns with a new and quizzical interest to the man.*) We feel — (*gaining confidence in his mission because of the interest in the faces of the people he is talking to.*) — we feel that most of the trouble in this world, when you come right down to it — (*He hits his knee for emphasis.*) — most of the trouble exists because people just don't sit down and talk to each other.

RUTH (*nodding as she might in church, pleased with the remark*):   You can say that again, mister.

LINDNER (*more encouraged by such affirmation*):   That we don't try hard enough in this world to understand the other fellow's problem. The other guy's point of view.

RUTH: Now that's right.

Beneatha and Walter merely watch and listen with genuine interest.

LINDNER: Yes — that's the way we feel out in Clybourne Park. And that's why I was elected to come here this afternoon and talk to you people. Friendly like, you know, the way people should talk to each other and see if we couldn't find some way to work this thing out. As I say, the whole business is a matter of *caring* about the other fellow. Anybody can see that you are a nice family of folks, hard working and honest I'm sure. (*Beneatha frowns slightly, quizzically, her head tilted regarding him.)* Today everybody knows what it means to be on the outside of *something*. And of course, there is always somebody who is out to take advantage of people who don't always understand.

WALTER: What do you mean?

LINDNER: Well—you see our community is made up of people who've worked hard as the dickens for years to build up that little community. They're not rich and fancy people; just hard-working, honest people who don't really have much but those little homes and a dream of the kind of community they want to raise their children in. Now, I don't say we are perfect and there is a lot wrong in some of the things they want. But you've got to admit that a man, right or wrong, has the right to want to have the neighborhood he lives in a certain kind of way. And at the moment the overwhelming majority of our people out there feel that people get along better, take more of a common interest in the life of the community, when they share a common background. I want you to believe me when I tell you that race prejudice simply doesn't enter into it. It is a matter of the people of Clybourne Park believing, rightly or wrongly, as I say, that for the happiness of all concerned that our Negro families are happier when they live in their *own* communities.

BENEATHA *(with a grand and bitter gesture)*:   This, friends, is the Welcoming Committee!

WALTER *(dumfounded, looking at Lindner)*:   Is this what you came marching all the way over here to tell us?

LINDNER: Well, now we've been having a fine conversation. I hope you'll hear me all the way through.

WALTER *(tightly)*:   Go ahead, man.

LINDNER: You see—in the face of all the things I have said, we are prepared to make your family a very generous offer . . .

BENEATHA: Thirty pieces and not a coin less!

WALTER: Yeah?

LINDNER *(putting on his glasses drawing a form out of the briefcase)*:   Our association is prepared, through the collective effort of our people, to buy the house from you at a financial gain to your family.

RUTH: Lord have mercy, ain't this the living gall!

WALTER: All right, you through?

LINDNER: Well, I want to give you the exact terms of the financial arrangement—

WALTER: We don't want to hear no exact terms of no arrangements. I want to know if you got any more to tell us 'bout getting together?

LINDNER *(taking off his glasses)*:   Well—I don't suppose that you feel . . .

WALTER: Never mind how I feel—you got any more to say 'bout how people ought to sit down and talk to each other? . . . Get out of my house, man.

He turns his back and walks to the door.

LINDNER *(looking around at the hostile faces and reaching and assembling his hat and briefcase)*:   Well—I don't understand why you people are reacting this way. What do you think you are going to gain by moving into a neighborhood where you just aren't wanted and where some elements—

well—people can get awful worked up when they feel that their whole way of life and everything they've ever worked for is threatened.

WALTER: Get out.

LINDNER (*at the door, holding a small card*):   Well—I'm sorry it went like this.

WALTER: Get out.

LINDNER (*almost sadly regarding Walter*):   You just can't force people to change their hearts, son.

He turns and puts his card on a table and exits. Walter pushes the door to with stinging hatred, and stands looking at it. Ruth just sits and Beneatha just stands. They say nothing. Mama and Travis enter.

MAMA: Well—this all the packing got done since I left out of here this morning. I testify before God that my children got all the energy of the *dead!* What time the moving men due?

BENEATHA: Four o'clock. You had a caller, Mama.

She is smiling, teasingly.

MAMA: Sure enough—who?

BENEATHA (*her arms folded saucily*):   The Welcoming Committee.

Walter and Ruth giggle.

MAMA (*innocently*):   Who?

BENEATHA: The Welcoming Committee. They said they're sure going to be glad to see you when you get there.

WALTER (*devilishly*):   Yeah, they said they can't hardly wait to see your face.

Laughter.

MAMA (*sensing their facetiousness*):   What's the matter with you all?

WALTER: Ain't nothing the matter with us. We just telling you 'bout the gentleman who came to see you this afternoon. From the Clybourne Park Improvement Association.

MAMA: What he want?

RUTH (*in the same mood as Beneatha and Walter*):   To welcome you, honey.

WALTER: He said they can't hardly wait. He said the one thing they don't have, that they just *dying* to have out there is a fine family of fine colored people! (*To Ruth and Beneatha.*) Ain't that right!

RUTH (*mockingly*):   Yeah! He left his card—

BENEATHA (*handing card to Mama*):   In case.

Mama reads and throws it on the floor—understanding and looking off as she draws her chair up to the table on which she has put her plant and some sticks and some cord.

MAMA: Father, give us strength. (*Knowingly—and without fun.*) Did he threaten us?

BENEATHA: Oh—Mama—they don't do it like that any more. He talked Brotherhood. He said everybody ought to learn how to sit down and hate each other with good Christian fellowship.

She and Walter shake hands to ridicule the remark.

MAMA (*sadly*):   Lord, protect us . . .

RUTH: You should hear the money those folks raised to buy the house from us. All we paid and then some.

BENEATHA: What they think we going to do — eat 'em?

RUTH: No, honey, marry 'em.

MAMA (*shaking her head*):   Lord, Lord, Lord . . .

RUTH: Well — that's the way the crackers crumble. (*A beat.*) Joke.

BENEATHA (*laughingly noticing what her mother is doing*):   Mama, what are you doing?

MAMA: Fixing my plant so it won't get hurt none on the way . . .

BENEATHA: Mama, you going to take *that* to the new house?

MAMA: Un-huh —

BENEATHA: That raggedy-looking old thing?

MAMA (*stopping and looking at her*):   It expresses ME!

RUTH (*with delight, to Beneatha*):   So there, Miss Thing!

Walter comes to Mama suddenly and bends down behind her and squeezes her in his arms with all his strength. She is overwhelmed by the suddenness of it and, though delighted, her manner is like that of Ruth and Travis.

MAMA: Look out now, boy! You make me mess up my thing here!

WALTER (*his face lit, he slips down on his knees beside her, his arms still about her*):   Mama . . . you know what it means to climb up in the chariot?

MAMA (*gruffly, very happy*):   Get on away from me now . . .

RUTH (*near the gift-wrapped package, trying to catch Walter's eye*):   Psst —

WALTER: What the old song say, Mama . . .

RUTH: Walter — Now?

She is pointing at the package.

WALTER (*speaking the lines, sweetly, playfully, in his mother's face*):
    I got wings . . . you got wings . . .
    All God's children got wings . . .

MAMA: Boy — get out of my face and do some work . . .

WALTER:
    When I get to heaven gonna put on my wings,
    Gonna fly all over God's heaven . . .

BENEATHA (*teasingly, from across the room*):   Everybody talking 'bout heaven ain't going there!

WALTER (*to Ruth, who is carrying the box across to them*):   I don't know, you think we ought to give her that . . . Seems to me she ain't been very appreciative around here.

MAMA (*eying the box, which is obviously a gift*):   What is that?

WALTER (*taking it from Ruth and putting it on the table in front of Mama*):   Well — what you all think? Should we give it to her?

RUTH: Oh — she was pretty good today.

MAMA: I'll good you —

She turns her eyes to the box again.

BENEATHA: Open it, Mama.

She stands up, looks at it, turns and looks at all of them, and then presses her hands together and does not open the package.

WALTER *(sweetly):*   Open it, Mama. It's for you. *(Mama looks in his eyes. It is the first present in her life without its being Christmas. Slowly she opens her package and lifts out, one by one, a brand-new sparkling set of gardening tools. Walter continues, prodding.)* Ruth made up the note—read it . . .

MAMA *(picking up the card and adjusting her glasses):*   "To our own Mrs. Miniver—Love from Brother, Ruth, and Beneatha." Ain't that lovely . . .

TRAVIS *(tugging at his father's sleeve):*   Daddy, can I give her mine now?

WALTER: All right, son. *(Travis flies to get his gift.)*

MAMA: Now I don't have to use my knives and forks no more . . .

WALTER: Travis didn't want to go in with the rest of us, Mama. He got his own. *(Somewhat amused.)* We don't know what it is . . .

TRAVIS *(racing back in the room with a large hatbox and putting it in front of his grandmother):*   Here!

MAMA: Lord have mercy, baby. You done gone and bought your grandmother a hat?

TRAVIS *(very proud):*   Open it!

She does and lifts out an elaborate, but very elaborate, wide gardening hat, and all the adults break up at the sight of it.

RUTH: Travis, honey, what is that?

TRAVIS *(who thinks it is beautiful and appropriate):*   It's a gardening hat! Like the ladies always have on in the magazines when they work in their gardens.

BENEATHA *(giggling fiercely):*   Travis—we were trying to make Mama Mrs. Miniver—not Scarlett O'Hara!

MAMA *(indignantly):*   What's the matter with you all! This here is a beautiful hat! *(Absurdly.)* I always wanted me one just like it!

She pops it on her head to prove it to her grandson, and the hat is ludicrous and considerably oversized.

RUTH: Hot dog! Go, Mama!

WALTER *(doubled over with laughter):*   I'm sorry, Mama—but you look like you ready to go out and chop you some cotton sure enough!

They all laugh except Mama, out of deference to Travis's feelings.

MAMA *(gathering the boy up to her):*   Bless your heart—this is the prettiest hat I ever owned—*(Walter, Ruth, and Beneatha chime in—noisily, festively, and insincerely congratulating Travis on his gift.)* What are we all standing around here for? We ain't finished packin' yet. Bennie, you ain't packed one book.

The bell rings.

BENEATHA: That couldn't be the movers . . . it's not hardly two good yet—

Beneatha goes into her room. Mama starts for door.

WALTER (*turning, stiffening*):   Wait—wait—I'll get it.

He stands and looks at the door.

MAMA: You expecting company, son?

WALTER (*just looking at the door*):   Yeah—yeah . . .

Mama looks at Ruth, and they exchange innocent and unfrightened glances.

MAMA (*not understanding*):   Well, let them in, son.

BENEATHA (*from her room*):   We need some more string.

MAMA: Travis—you run to the hardware and get me some string cord.

Mama goes out and Walter turns and looks at Ruth. Travis goes to a dish for money.

RUTH: Why don't you answer the door, man?

WALTER (*suddenly bounding across the floor to embrace her*):   'Cause sometimes
    it hard to let the future begin! (*Stooping down in her face.*)
    I got wings! You got wings!
    All God's children got wings!

*He crosses to the door and throws it open. Standing there is a very slight little man
in a not-too-prosperous business suit and with haunted frightened eyes and a hat
pulled down tightly, brim up, around his forehead. Travis passes between the men
and exits. Walter leans deep in the man's face, still in his jubilance.*

    When I get to heaven gonna put on my wings,
    Gonna fly all over God's heaven . . .

The little man just stares at him.

    Heaven—

Suddenly he stops and looks past the little man into the empty hallway.

    Where's Willy, man?

BOBO: He ain't with me.

WALTER (*not disturbed*):   Oh—come on in. You know my wife.

BOBO (*dumbly, taking off his hat*):   Yes—h'you, Miss Ruth.

RUTH (*quietly, a mood apart from her husband already, seeing Bobo*):   Hello,
    Bobo.

WALTER: You right on time today . . . Right on time. That's the way! (*He slaps
    Bobo on his back.*) Sit down . . . lemme hear.

*Ruth stands stiffly and quietly in back of them, as though somehow she senses
death, her eyes fixed on her husband.*

BOBO (*his frightened eyes on the floor, his hat in his hands*):   Could I please get a
    drink of water, before I tell you about it, Walter Lee?

*Walter does not take his eyes off the man. Ruth goes blindly to the tap and gets a
glass of water and brings it to Bobo.*

WALTER: There ain't nothing wrong, is there?

BOBO: Lemme tell you—

WALTER: Man—didn't nothing go wrong?

BOBO: Lemme tell you—Walter Lee. (*Looking at Ruth and talking to her more
    than to Walter.*) You know how it was. I got to tell you how it was. I mean first

I got to tell you how it was all the way . . . I mean about the money I put in,
Walter Lee . . .

WALTER *(with taut agitation now):*   What about the money you put in?

BOBO: Well — it wasn't much as we told you — me and Willy — *(He stops.)* I'm
sorry, Walter. I got a bad feeling about it. I got a real bad feeling about it . . .

WALTER: Man, what you telling me about all this for? . . . Tell me what happened in Springfield . . .

BOBO: Springfield.

RUTH *(like a dead woman):*   What was supposed to happen in Springfield?

BOBO *(to her):*   This deal that me and Walter went into with Willy — Me and
Willy was going to go down to Springfield and spread some money 'round
so's we wouldn't have to wait so long for the liquor license . . . That's what we
were going to do. Everybody said that was the way you had to do, you understand, Miss Ruth?

WALTER: Man — what happened down there?

BOBO *(a pitiful man, near tears):*   I'm trying to tell you, Walter.

WALTER *(screaming at him suddenly):*   THEN TELL ME, GODDAMMIT . . .
WHAT'S THE MATTER WITH YOU?

BOBO: Man . . . I didn't go to no Springfield, yesterday.

WALTER *(halted, life hanging in the moment):*   Why not?

BOBO *(the long way, the hard way to tell):*   'Cause I didn't have no reasons to . . .

WALTER: Man, what are you talking about!

BOBO: I'm talking about the fact that when I got to the train station yesterday morning — eight o'clock like we planned . . . Man — *Willy didn't never show up.*

WALTER: Why . . . where was he . . . where is he?

BOBO: That's what I'm trying to tell you . . . I don't know . . . I waited six
hours . . . I called his house . . . and I waited . . . six hours . . . I waited in
that train station six hours . . . *(Breaking into tears.)* That was all the extra
money I had in the world . . . *(Looking up at Walter with the tears running
down his face.)* Man, *Willy is gone.*

WALTER: Gone, what you mean Willy is gone? Gone where? You mean he went
by himself. You mean he went off to Springfield by himself — to take care of
getting the license — *(Turns and looks anxiously at Ruth.)* You mean maybe he
didn't want too many people in on the business down there? *(Looks to Ruth
again, as before.)* You know Willy got his own ways. *(Looks back to Bobo.)*
Maybe you was late yesterday and he just went on down there without you.
Maybe — maybe — he's been callin' you at home tryin' to tell you what happened or something. Maybe — maybe — he just got sick. He's somewhere —
he's got to be somewhere. We just got to find him — me and you got to find
him. *(Grabs Bobo senselessly by the collar and starts to shake him.)* We got to!

BOBO *(in sudden angry, frightened agony):*   What's the matter with you, Walter!
When a cat take off with your money he don't leave you no road maps!

WALTER *(turning madly, as though he is looking for Willy in the very room):*
Willy! . . . Willy . . . don't do it . . . Please don't do it . . . Man, not with that
money . . . Man, please, not with that money . . . Oh, God . . . Don't let it be
true . . . *(He is wandering around, crying out for Willy and looking for him or*

perhaps for help from God.) Man . . . I trusted you . . . Man, I put my life in your hands . . . *(He starts to crumple down on the floor as Ruth just covers her face in horror. Mama opens the door and comes into the room, with Beneatha behind her.)* Man . . . *(He starts to pound the floor with his fists, sobbing wildly.)* THAT MONEY IS MADE OUT OF MY FATHER'S FLESH—

BOBO *(standing over him helplessly):* I'm sorry, Walter . . . *(only Walter's sobs reply. Bobo puts on his hat.)* I had my life staked on this deal, too . . .

He exits.

MAMA *(to Walter):* Son—*(She goes to him, bends down to him, talks to his bent head.)* Son . . . Is it gone? Son, I gave you sixty-five hundred dollars. Is it gone? All of it? Beneatha's money too?

WALTER *(lifting his head slowly):* Mama . . . I never . . . went to the bank at all . . .

MAMA *(not wanting to believe him):* You mean . . . your sister's school money . . . you used that too . . . Walter? . . .

WALTER: Yessss! All of it . . . It's all gone . . .

There is total silence. Ruth stands with her face covered with her hands; Beneatha leans forlornly against a wall, fingering a piece of red ribbon from the mother's gift. Mama stops and looks at her son without recognition and then, quite without thinking about it, starts to beat him senselessly in the face. Beneatha goes to them and stops it.

BENEATHA: Mama!

Mama stops and looks at both of her children and rises slowly and wanders vaguely, aimlessly away from them.

MAMA: I seen . . . him . . . night after night . . . come in . . . and look at that rug . . . and then look at me . . . the red showing in his eyes . . . the veins moving in his head . . . I seen him grow thin and old before he was forty . . . working and working and working like somebody's old horse . . . killing himself . . . and you—you give it all away in a day—*(She raises her arms to strike him again.)*

BENEATHA: Mama—

MAMA: Oh, God . . . *(She looks up to Him.)* Look down here—and show me the strength.

BENEATHA: Mama—

MAMA *(folding over):* Strength . . .

BENEATHA *(plaintively):* Mama . . .

MAMA: Strength!

Curtain.

ACT 3

Time: An hour later.

　　At curtain, there is a sullen light of gloom in the living room, gray light not unlike that which began the first scene of Act 1. At left we can see Walter within his room, alone with himself. He is stretched out on the bed, his shirt out and open, his *arms under his head. He does not smoke, he does not cry out, he merely lies there, looking up at the ceiling, much as if he were alone in the world.*

In the living room Beneatha sits at the table, still surrounded by the now almost ominous packing crates. She sits looking off. We feel that this is a mood struck perhaps an hour before, and it lingers now, full of the empty sound of profound disappointment. We see on a line from her brother's bedroom the sameness of their attitudes. Presently the bell rings and Beneatha rises without ambition or interest in answering. It is Asagai, smiling broadly, striding into the room with energy and happy expectation and conversation.

ASAGAI: I came over . . . I had some free time. I thought I might help with the packing. Ah, I like the look of packing crates! A household in preparation for a journey! It depresses some people . . . but for me . . . it is another feeling. Something full of the flow of life, do you understand? Movement, progress . . . It makes me think of Africa.

BENEATHA: Africa!

ASAGAI: What kind of a mood is this? Have I told you how deeply you move me?

BENEATHA: He gave away the money, Asagai . . .

ASAGAI: Who gave away what money?

BENEATHA: The insurance money. My brother gave it away.

ASAGAI: Gave it away?

BENEATHA: He made an investment! With a man even Travis wouldn't have trusted with his most worn-out marbles.

ASAGAI: And it's gone?

BENEATHA: Gone!

ASAGAI: I'm very sorry . . . And you, now?

BENEATHA: Me? . . . Me? . . . Me, I'm nothing . . . Me. When I was very small . . . we used to take our sleds out in the wintertime and the only hills we had were the ice-covered stone steps of some houses down the street. And we used to fill them in with snow and make them smooth and slide down them all day . . . and it was very dangerous, you know . . . far too steep . . . and sure enough one day a kid named Rufus came down too fast and hit the sidewalk and we saw his face just split open right there in front of us . . . And I remember standing there looking at his bloody open face thinking that was the end of Rufus. But the ambulance came and they took him to the hospital and they fixed the broken bones and they sewed it all up . . . and the next time I saw Rufus he just had a little line down the middle of his face . . . I never got over that . . .

ASAGAI: What?

BENEATHA: That that was what one person could do for another, fix him up — sew up the problem, make him all right again. That was the most marvelous thing in the world . . . I wanted to do that. I always thought it was the one concrete thing in the world that a human being could do. Fix up the sick, you know — and make them whole again. This was truly being God . . .

ASAGAI: You wanted to be God?

BENEATHA: No—I wanted to cure. It used to be so important to me. I wanted to cure. It used to matter. I used to care. I mean about people and how their bodies hurt . . .

ASAGAI: And you've stopped caring?

BENEATHA: Yes—I think so.

ASAGAI: Why?

BENEATHA *(bitterly)*:   Because it doesn't seem deep enough, close enough to what ails mankind! It was a child's way of seeing things—or an idealist's.

ASAGAI: Children see things very well sometimes—and idealists even better.

BENEATHA: I know that's what you think. Because you are still where I left off. You with all your talk and dreams about Africa! You still think you can patch up the world. Cure the Great Sore of Colonialism—*(Loftily, mocking it.)* with the Penicillin of Independence—!

ASAGAI: Yes!

BENEATHA: Independence *and then what?* What about all the crooks and thieves and just plain idiots who will come into power and steal and plunder the same as before—only now they will be black and do it in the name of the new Independence—WHAT ABOUT THEM?!

ASAGAI: That will be the problem for another time. First we must get there.

BENEATHA: And where does it end?

ASAGAI: End? Who even spoke of an end? To life? To living?

BENEATHA: An end to misery! To stupidity! Don't you see there isn't any real progress, Asagai, there is only one large circle that we march in, around and around, each of us with our own little picture in front of us—our own little mirage that we think is the future.

ASAGAI: That is the mistake.

BENEATHA: What?

ASAGAI: What you just said—about the circle. It isn't a circle—it is simply a long line—as in geometry, you know, one that reaches into infinity. And because we cannot see the end—we also cannot see how it changes. And it is very odd but those who see the changes—who dream, who will not give up—are called idealists . . . and those who see only the circle—we call *them* the "realists"!

BENEATHA: Asagai, while I was sleeping in that bed in there, people went out and took the future right out of my hands! And nobody asked me, nobody consulted me—they just went out and changed my life!

ASAGAI: Was it your money?

BENEATHA: What?

ASAGAI: Was it your money he gave away?

BENEATHA: It belonged to all of us.

ASAGAI: But did you earn it? Would you have had it at all if your father had not died?

BENEATHA: No.

ASAGAI: Then isn't there something wrong in a house—in a world—where all dreams, good or bad, must depend on the death of a man? I never thought to see *you* like this, Alaiyo. You! Your brother made a mistake and you are grateful to him so that now you can give up the ailing human race on account of it! You talk about what good is struggle, what good is anything! Where are we all going and why are we bothering!

BENEATHA: AND YOU CANNOT ANSWER IT!

ASAGAI *(shouting over her)*:   *I LIVE THE ANSWER! (Pause.)* In my village at home it is the exceptional man who can even read a newspaper . . . or who ever sees a book at all. I will go home and much of what I will have to say will seem strange to the people of my village. But I will teach and work and things will happen, slowly and swiftly. At times it will seem that nothing changes at all . . . and then again the sudden dramatic events which make history leap into the future. And then quiet again. Retrogression even. Guns, murder, revolution. And I even will have moments when I wonder if the quiet was not better than all that death and hatred. But I will look about my village at the illiteracy and disease and ignorance and I will not wonder long. And perhaps . . . perhaps I will be a great man . . . I mean perhaps I will hold on to the substance of truth and find my way always with the right course . . . and perhaps for it I will be butchered in my bed some night by the servants of empire . . .

BENEATHA: *The martyr!*

ASAGAI *(he smiles)*:   . . . or perhaps I shall live to be a very old man, respected and esteemed in my new nation . . . And perhaps I shall hold office and this is what I'm trying to tell you, Alaiyo: perhaps the things I believe now for my country will be wrong and outmoded, and I will not understand and do terrible things to have things my way or merely to keep my power. Don't you see that there will be young men and women — not British soldiers then, but my own black countrymen — to step out of the shadows some evening and slit my then useless throat? Don't you see they have always been there . . . that they always will be. And that such a thing as my own death will be an advance? They who might kill me even . . . actually replenish all that I was.

BENEATHA: Oh, Asagai, I know all that.

ASAGAI: Good! Then stop moaning and groaning and tell me what you plan to do.

BENEATHA: Do?

ASAGAI: I have a bit of a suggestion.

BENEATHA: What?

ASAGAI *(rather quietly for him)*:   That when it is all over — that you come home with me —

BENEATHA *(staring at him and crossing away with exasperation)*:   Oh — Asagai — at this moment you decide to be romantic!

ASAGAI *(quickly understanding the misunderstanding)*:   My dear, young creature of the New World — I do not mean across the city — I mean across the ocean: home — to Africa.

BENEATHA *(slowly understanding and turning to him with murmured amazement)*: To Africa?

ASAGAI: Yes! . . . *(smiling and lifting his arms playfully.)* Three hundred years later the African Prince rose up out of the seas and swept the maiden back across the middle passage over which her ancestors had come —

BENEATHA *(unable to play)*:   To — to Nigeria?

ASAGAI: Nigeria. Home. *(Coming to her with genuine romantic flippancy.)* I will show you our mountains and our stars; and give you cool drinks from gourds and teach you the old songs and the ways of our people — and, in time, we will pretend that — *(Very softly.)* — you have only been away for a day. Say that you'll come — *(He swings her around and takes her full in his arms in a kiss which proceeds to passion.)*

BENEATHA *(pulling away suddenly)*:   You're getting me all mixed up —

ASAGAI: Why?

BENEATHA: Too many things — too many things have happened today. I must sit down and think. I don't know what I feel about anything right this minute.

She promptly sits down and props her chin on her fist.

ASAGAI *(charmed)*:   All right, I shall leave you. No — don't get up. *(Touching her, gently, sweetly.)* Just sit awhile and think . . . Never be afraid to sit awhile and think. *(He goes to door and looks at her.)* How often I have looked at you and said, "Ah — so this is what the New World hath finally wrought . . ."

He exits. Beneatha sits on alone. Presently Walter enters from his room and starts to rummage through things, feverishly looking for something. She looks up and turns in her seat.

BENEATHA *(hissingly)*:   Yes — just look at what the New World hath wrought! . . . Just look! *(She gestures with bitter disgust.)* There he is! *Monsieur le petit bourgeois noir*° — himself! There he is — Symbol of a Rising Class! Entrepreneur! Titan of the system! *(Walter ignores her completely and continues frantically and destructively looking for something and hurling things to floor and tearing things out of their place in his search. Beneatha ignores the eccentricity of his actions and goes on with the monologue of insult.)* Did you dream of yachts on Lake Michigan, Brother? Did you see yourself on that Great Day sitting down at the Conference Table, surrounded by all the mighty bald-headed men in America? All halted, waiting, breathless, waiting for your pronouncements on industry? Waiting for you — Chairman of the Board! *(Walter finds what he is looking for — a small piece of white paper — and pushes it in his pocket and puts on his coat and rushes out without ever having looked at her. She shouts after him.)* I look at you and I see the final triumph of stupidity in the world!

The door slams and she returns to just sitting again. Ruth comes quickly out of Mama's room.

RUTH: Who was that?

BENEATHA: Your husband.

RUTH: Where did he go?

BENEATHA: Who knows — maybe he has an appointment at U.S. Steel.

RUTH *(anxiously, with frightened eyes)*:   You didn't say nothing bad to him, did you?

Monsieur le petit bourgeois noir: Mr. Black Bourgoisie (French).

BENEATHA: Bad? Say anything bad to him? No—I told him he was a sweet boy and full of dreams and everything is strictly peachy keen, as the ofay kids say!

Mama enters from her bedroom. She is lost, vague, trying to catch hold, to make some sense of her former command of the world, but it still eludes her. A sense of waste overwhelms her gait; a measure of apology rides on her shoulders. She goes to her plant, which has remained on the table, looks at it, picks it up and takes it to the window sill and sits it outside, and she stands and looks at it a long moment. Then she closes the window, straightens her body with effort and turns around to her children.

MAMA: Well—ain't it a mess in here, though? (A *false cheerfulness, a beginning of something.*) I guess we all better stop moping around and get some work done. All this unpacking and everything we got to do. *(Ruth raises her head slowly in response to the sense of the line; and Beneatha in similar manner turns very slowly to look at her mother.)* One of you all better call the moving people and tell 'em not to come.

RUTH: Tell 'em not to come?

MAMA: Of course, baby. Ain't no need in 'em coming all the way here and having to go back. They charges for that too. *(She sits down, fingers to her brow, thinking.)* Lord, ever since I was a little girl, I always remembers people saying, "Lena—Lena Eggleston, you aims too high all the time. You needs to slow down and see life a little more like it is. Just slow down some." That's what they always used to say down home—"Lord, that Lena Eggleston is a high-minded thing. She'll get her due one day!"

RUTH: No, Lena . . .

MAMA: Me and Big Walter just didn't never learn right.

RUTH: Lena, no! We gotta go. Bennie—tell her . . .

She rises and crosses to Beneatha with her arms outstretched. Beneatha doesn't respond.

Tell her we can still move . . . the notes ain't but a hundred and twenty-five a month. We got four grown people in this house—we can work . . .

MAMA *(to herself)*:   Just aimed too high all the time—

RUTH *(turning and going to Mama fast—the words pouring out with urgency and desperation)*:   Lena—I'll work . . . I'll work twenty hours a day in all the kitchens in Chicago . . . I'll strap my baby on my back if I have to and scrub all the floors in America and wash all the sheets in America if I have to—but we got to MOVE! We got to get OUT OF HERE!!

Mama reaches out absently and pats Ruth's hand.

MAMA: No—I sees things differently now. Been thinking 'bout some of the things we could do to fix this place up some. I seen a second-hand bureau over on Maxwell Street just the other day that could fit right there. *(She points to where the new furniture might go. Ruth wanders away from her.)* Would need some new handles on it and then a little varnish and it look like something brand-new. And—we can put up them new curtains in the kitchen . . . Why this place be looking fine. Cheer us all up so that we forget trouble ever come . . . *(To Ruth.)* And you could get some nice screens to put up in your room round the baby's bassinet . . . *(She looks at both of them pleadingly.)* Sometimes you just got to know when to give up some things . . . and hold on to what you got . . .

Walter enters from the outside, looking spent and leaning against the door, his coat hanging from him.

MAMA: Where you been, son?

WALTER *(breathing hard)*:   Made a call.

MAMA: To who, son?

WALTER: To The Man. *(He heads for his room.)*

MAMA: What man, baby?

WALTER *(stops in the door)*:   The Man, Mama. Don't you know who The Man is?

RUTH: Walter Lee?

WALTER: *The Man.* Like the guys in the streets say — The Man. Captain Boss — Mistuh Charley . . . Old Cap'n Please Mr. Bossman . . .

BENEATHA *(suddenly)*:   Lindner!

WALTER: That's right! That's good. I told him to come right over.

BENEATHA *(fiercely, understanding)*:   For what? What do you want to see him for!

WALTER *(looking at his sister)*:   We going to do business with him.

MAMA: What you talking 'bout, son?

WALTER: Talking 'bout life, Mama. You all always telling me to see life like it is. Well — I laid in there on my back today . . . and I figured it out. Life just like it is. Who gets and who don't get. *(He sits down with his coat on and laughs.)* Mama, you know it's all divided up. Life is. Sure enough. Between the takers and the "tooken." *(He laughs.)* I've figured it out finally. *(He looks around at them.)* Yeah. Some of us always getting "tooken." *(He laughs.)* People like Willy Harris, they don't never get "tooken." And you know why the rest of us do? 'Cause we all mixed up. Mixed up bad. We get to looking 'round for the right and the wrong; and we worry about it and cry about it and stay up nights trying to figure out 'bout the wrong and the right of things all the time . . . And all the time, man, them takers is out there operating, just taking and taking. Willy Harris? Shoot — Willy Harris don't even count. He don't even count in the big scheme of things. But I'll say one thing for old Willy Harris . . . he's taught me something. He's taught me to keep my eye on what counts in this world. Yeah — *(Shouting out a little.)* Thanks, Willy!

RUTH: What did you call that man for, Walter Lee?

WALTER: Called him to tell him to come on over to the show. Gonna put on a show for the man. Just what he wants to see. You see, Mama, the man came here today and he told us that them people out there where you want us to move — well they so upset they willing to pay us *not* to move! *(He laughs again.)* And — and oh, Mama — you would of been proud of the way me and Ruth and Bennie acted. We told him to get out . . . Lord have mercy! We told the man to get out! Oh, we was some proud folks this afternoon, yeah. *(He lights a cigarette.)* We were still full of that old-time stuff . . .

RUTH *(coming toward him slowly)*: You talking 'bout taking them people's money to keep us from moving in that house?

WALTER: I ain't just talking 'bout it, baby — I'm telling you that's what's going to happen!

BENEATHA: Oh, God! Where is the bottom! Where is the real honest-to-God bottom so he can't go any farther!

WALTER: See — that's the old stuff. You and that boy that was here today. You all want everybody to carry a flag and a spear and sing some marching songs, huh? You wanna spend your life looking into things and trying to find the right and the wrong part, huh? Yeah. You know what's going to happen to that boy someday — he'll find himself sitting in a dungeon, locked in forever — and the takers will have the key! Forget it, baby! There ain't no causes — there ain't nothing but taking in this world, and he who takes most is smartest — and it don't make a damn bit of difference *how*.

MAMA: You making something inside me cry, son. Some awful pain inside me.

WALTER: Don't cry, Mama. Understand. That white man is going to walk in that door able to write checks for more money than we ever had. It's important to him and I'm going to help him . . . I'm going to put on the show, Mama.

MAMA: Son — I come from five generations of people who was slaves and share-croppers — but ain't nobody in my family never let nobody pay 'em no money that was a way of telling us we wasn't fit to walk the earth. We ain't never been that poor. *(Raising her eyes and looking at him.)* We ain't never been that — dead inside.

BENEATHA: Well — we are dead now. All the talk about dreams and sunlight that goes on in this house. It's all dead now.

WALTER: What's the matter with you all! I didn't make this world! It was give to me this way! Hell, yes, I want me some yachts someday! Yes, I want to hang some real pearls 'round my wife's neck. Ain't she supposed to wear no pearls? Somebody tell me — tell me, who decides which women is suppose to wear pearls in this world. I tell you I am a *man* — and I think my wife should wear some pearls in this world!

This last line hangs a good while and Walter begins to move about the room. The word "Man" has penetrated his consciousness; he mumbles it to himself repeatedly between strange agitated pauses as he moves about.

MAMA: Baby, how you going to feel on the inside?

WALTER: Fine! . . . Going to feel fine . . . a man . . .

MAMA: You won't have nothing left then, Walter Lee.

WALTER *(coming to her)*: I'm going to feel fine, Mama. I'm going to look that son-of-a-bitch in the eyes and say — *(He falters.)* — and say, "All right, Mr. Lindner — *(He falters even more.)* — that's *your* neighborhood out there! You got the right to keep it like you want! You got the right to have it like you want! Just write the check and — the house is yours." And — and I am going to say — *(His voice almost breaks.)* "And you — you people just put the money in my hand and you won't have to live next to this bunch of stinking niggers! . . ." (*He straightens up and moves away from his mother, walking around the room.*) And maybe—maybe I'll just get down on my black knees . . . (*He does so; Ruth and Bennie and Mama watch him in frozen horror.*) "Captain, Mistuh, Bossman—(*Groveling and grinning and wringing his hands in profoundly anguished imitation of the slow-witted movie stereotype.*) A-hee-hee-hee! Oh, yassuh boss! Yasssssuh! Great white—(*Voice breaking, he forces himself to go on.*)—Father, just gi' ussen de money, fo' God's sake, and we's—we's ain't gwine come out deh and dirty up yo' white folks neighborhood . . ." (*He breaks down completely.*) And I'll feel fine! Fine! FINE! (*He gets up and goes into the bedroom.*)

BENEATHA: That is not a man. That is nothing but a toothless rat.

MAMA: Yes—death done come in this here house. (*She is nodding, slowly, reflectively.*) Done come walking in my house on the lips of my children. You what supposed to be my beginning again. You—what supposed to be my harvest. (*To Beneatha.*) You—you mourning your brother?

BENEATHA: He's no brother of mine.

MAMA: What you say?

BENEATHA: I said that that individual in that room is no brother of mine.

MAMA: That's what I thought you said. You feeling like you better than he is today? (*Beneatha does not answer.*) Yes? What you tell him a minute ago? That he wasn't a man? Yes? You give him up for me? You done wrote his epitaph too—like the rest of the world? Well, who give you the privilege?

BENEATHA: Be on my side for once! You saw what he just did, Mama! You saw him—down on his knees. Wasn't it you who taught me to despise any man who would do that? Do what he's going to do?

MAMA: Yes—I taught you that. Me and your daddy. But I thought I taught you something else too . . . . I thought I taught you to love him.

BENEATHA: Love him? There is nothing left to love.

MAMA: There is *always* something left to love. And if you ain't learned that, you ain't learned nothing. (*Looking at her.*) Have you cried for that boy today? I don't mean for yourself and for the family 'cause we lost the money. I mean for him: what he been through and what it done to him. Child, when do you think is the time to love somebody the most? When they done good and made things easy for everybody? Well then, you ain't through learning—because that ain't the time at all. It's when he's at his lowest and can't believe in hisself 'cause the world done whipped him so! When you starts measuring somebody, measure him right, child, measure him right. Make sure you done taken into account what hills and valleys he come through before he got to wherever he is.

Travis bursts into the room at the end of the speech, leaving the door open.

TRAVIS: Grandmama—the moving men are downstairs! The truck just pulled up.

MAMA (*turning and looking at him*):   Are they, baby? They downstairs?

She sighs and sits. Lindner appears in the doorway. He peers in and knocks lightly, to gain attention, and comes in. All turn to look at him.

LINDNER *(hat and briefcase in hand)*:   Uh — hello . . .

Ruth crosses mechanically to the bedroom door and opens it and lets it swing open freely and slowly as the lights come up on Walter within, still in his coat, sitting at the far corner of the room. He looks up and out through the room to Lindner.

RUTH: He's here.

A long minute passes and Walter slowly gets up.

LINDNER *(coming to the table with efficiency, putting his briefcase on the table and starting to unfold papers and unscrew fountain pens)*:   Well, I certainly was glad to hear from you people. *(Walter has begun the trek out of the room, slowly and awkwardly, rather like a small boy, passing the back of his sleeve across his mouth from time to time.)* Life can really be so much simpler than people let it be most of the time. Well — with whom do I negotiate? You, Mrs. Younger, or your son here? *(Mama sits with her hands folded on her lap and her eyes closed as Walter advances. Travis goes closer to Lindner and looks at the papers curiously.)* Just some official papers, sonny.

RUTH: Travis, you go downstairs —

MAMA *(opening her eyes and looking into Walter's)*:   No. Travis, you stay right here. And you make him understand what you doing, Walter Lee. You teach him good. Like Willy Harris taught you. You show where our five generations done come to. *(Walter looks from her to the boy, who grins at him innocently.)* Go ahead, son — *(She folds her hands and closes her eyes.)* Go ahead.

WALTER *(at last crosses to Lindner, who is reviewing the contract)*:   Well, Mr. Lindner. *(Beneatha turns away.)* We called you — *(There is a profound, simple groping quality in his speech.)* — because, well, me and my family *(He looks around and shifts from one foot to the other.)* Well — we are very plain people . . .

LINDNER: Yes —

WALTER: I mean — I have worked as a chauffeur most of my life — and my wife here, she does domestic work in people's kitchens. So does my mother. I mean — we are plain people . . .

LINDNER: Yes, Mr. Younger —

WALTER *(really like a small boy, looking down at his shoes and then up at the man)*:   And — uh — well, my father, well, he was a laborer most of his life. . . .

LINDNER *(absolutely confused)*:   Uh, yes — yes, I understand. *(He turns back to the contract.)*

WALTER *(a beat; staring at him)*:   And my father — *(With sudden intensity.)* My father almost *beat a man to death* once because this man called him a bad name or something, you know what I mean?

LINDNER *(looking up, frozen)*:   No, no, I'm afraid I don't —

WALTER *(a beat. The tension hangs; then Walter steps back from it)*:   Yeah. Well — what I mean is that we come from people who had a lot of *pride*. I mean — we are very proud people. And that's my sister over there and she's going to be a doctor — and we are very proud —

LINDNER: Well—I am sure that is very nice, but—

WALTER: What I am telling you is that we called you over here to tell you that we are very proud and that this—*(Signaling to Travis.)* Travis, come here. *(Travis crosses and Walter draws him before him facing the man.)* This is my son, and he makes the sixth generation our family in this country. And we have all thought about your offer—

LINDNER: Well, good . . . good—

WALTER: And we have decided to move into our house because my father—my father—he earned it for us brick by brick. *(Mama has her eyes closed and is rocking back and forth as though she were in church, with her head nodding the Amen yes.)* We don't want to make no trouble for nobody or fight no causes, and we will try to be good neighbors. And that's *all* we got to say about that. *(He looks the man absolutely in the eyes.)* We don't want your money. *(He turns and walks away.)*

LINDNER *(looking around at all of them)*:   I take it then—that you have decided to occupy . . .

BENEATHA: That's what the man said.

LINDNER *(to Mama in her reverie)*:   Then I would like to appeal to you, Mrs. Younger. You are older and wiser and understand things better I am sure . . .

MAMA: I am afraid you don't understand. My son said we was going to move and there ain't nothing left for me to say. *(Briskly.)* You know how these young folks is nowadays, mister. Can't do a thing with 'em! *(As he opens his mouth, she rises.)* Good-bye.

LINDNER *(folding up his materials)*:   Well—if you are that final about it . . . there is nothing left for me to say. *(He finishes, almost ignored by the family, who are concentrating on Walter Lee. At the door Lindner halts and looks around.)* I sure hope you people know what you're getting into.

He shakes his head and exits.

RUTH *(looking around and coming to life)*:   Well, for God's sake—if the moving men are here—LET'S GET THE HELL OUT OF HERE!

MAMA *(into action)*:   Ain't it the truth! Look at all this here mess. Ruth, put Travis' good jacket on him . . . Walter Lee, fix your tie and tuck your shirt in, you look like somebody's hoodlum! Lord have mercy, where is my plant? *(She flies to get it amid the general bustling of the family, who are deliberately trying to ignore the nobility of the past moment.)* You all start on down . . . Travis child, don't go empty-handed . . . Ruth, where did I put that box with my skillets in it? I want to be in charge of it myself . . . I'm going to make us the biggest dinner we ever ate tonight . . . Beneatha, what's the matter with them stockings? Pull them things up, girl . . .

The family starts to file out as two moving men appear and begin to carry out the heavier pieces of furniture, bumping into the family as they move about.

BENEATHA: Mama, Asagai asked me to marry him today and go to Africa—

MAMA *(in the middle of her getting-ready activity)*:   He did? You ain't old enough to marry nobody—*(Seeing the moving men lifting one of her chairs precari-*

ously.) Darling, that ain't no bale of cotton, please handle it so we can sit in it again! I had that chair twenty-five years . . .

The movers sigh with exasperation and go on with their work.

BENEATHA *(girlishly and unreasonably trying to pursue the conversation):*   To go to Africa, Mama — be a doctor in Africa . . .

MAMA *(distracted):*   Yes, baby —

WALTER: Africa! What he want you to go to Africa for?

BENEATHA: To practice there . . .

WALTER: Girl, if you don't get all them silly ideas out your head! You better marry yourself a man with some loot . . .

BENEATHA *(angrily, precisely as in the first scene of the play):*   What have you got to do with who I marry!

WALTER: Plenty. Now I think George Murchison —

BENEATHA: *George Murchison!* I wouldn't marry him if he was Adam and I was Eve!

Walter and Beneatha go out yelling at each other vigorously and the anger is loud and real till their voices diminish. Ruth stands at the door and turns to Mama and smiles knowingly.

MAMA *(fixing her hat at last):*   Yeah — they something all right, my children . . .

RUTH: Yeah — they're something. Let's go, Lena.

MAMA *(stalling, starting to look around at the house):*   Yes — I'm coming. Ruth —

RUTH: Yes?

MAMA *(quietly, woman to woman):*   He finally come into his manhood today, didn't he? Kind of like a rainbow after the rain . . .

RUTH *(biting her lip lest her own pride explode in front of Mama):*   Yes, Lena.

Walter's voice calls for them raucously.

WALTER *(offstage):*   Y'all come on! These people charges by the hour, you know!

MAMA *(waving Ruth out vaguely):*   All right, honey — go on down. I be down directly.

Ruth hesitates, then exits. Mama stands, at last alone in the living room, her plant on the table before her as the lights start to come down. She looks around at all the walls and ceilings and suddenly, despite herself, while the children call below, a great heaving thing rises in her and she puts her fist to her mouth to stifle it, takes a final desperate look, pulls her coat about her, pats her hat, and goes out. The lights dim down. The door opens and she comes back in, grabs her plant, and goes out for the last time.

Curtain.   [1959]

THINKING ABOUT THE TEXT

1. The play's main characters are Walter Lee, Mama, Ruth, and Beneatha. List three or more adjectives to describe each of these characters. What basic values does each character seem to express during the arguments

that occur in their family? Do you sympathize with them equally? Why, or why not? What, evidently, was Walter Lee's father like?

2. At the end of the play, speaking to Ruth about Walter Lee, Mama says "He finally come into his manhood today, didn't he"? How does Mama appear to be defining *manhood*? What other possible definitions of *manhood* come up directly or indirectly in the play? Identify places where characteristics of *womanhood* are brought up. In general, would you say that gender is at least as important in this play as race is? Why, or why not?

3. Analyze Asagai's conversations with Beneatha and the rest of her family. What does Hansberry suggest about the relations of Africans and African Americans in the late 1950s?

4. Although there is a white character, he makes only two relatively brief appearances, and no other white characters are shown. Why do you suppose Hansberry keeps the presence of whites minimal?

5. Do you think this play is universal in its truths and concerns, or are you more inclined to see it as specifically about African Americans? Explain. In what ways is this 1959 play relevant to life in the United States today?

THE CRISIS

The Hansberrys of Chicago:
They Join Business Acumen
with Social Vision

The following article appeared in the April 1941 issue of The Crisis, *the journal of the National Association for the Advancement of Colored People (NAACP). The photographs to which the article refers are omitted. The NAACP was established in 1909 and* The Crisis *a year later, its founder and first editor being the noted African American intellectual W. E. B. Du Bois. This article pays tribute to Lorraine Hansberry's parents; it notes their successful real estate business, the foundation they established to get civil rights laws enforced, and their 1940 Supreme Court victory. The Court's decision was meant to erode at least some racial covenants, policies by which white neighborhoods kept out blacks. However, the decision lacked enforcement and very little changed.*

Mr. and Mrs. Carl A. Hansberry of Chicago, Ill., have the distinction not only of conducting one of the largest real estate enterprises in the country operated by Negroes but they are unique business people because they are spending much of their wealth to safeguard the civil rights of colored citizens in their city, state, and nation.

The properties shown on these pages are a part of the $250,000.00 worth of Chicago real estate from which The Hansberry Enterprises and The Hansberry Foundation receive a gross annual income of $100,000.00. The real estate firm makes available to Negroes with limited income apartments within their economic reach, while the profits from this enterprise are used to safeguard the Negro's civil rights and to make additional housing available to him. The Hansberrys played a very significant role in the recent Chicago restrictive covenant case before the United States Supreme Court whose decision opened blocks of houses and apartment buildings from which Negroes formerly had been excluded.

THE HANSBERRY ENTERPRISES

The Hansberry Enterprises is a real estate syndicate founded by Mr. Hansberry in 1929. From a very modest beginning, the business has grown to be one of the largest in the Mid-West. The property owned and controlled by the company is in excess of $250,000 in value and accommodates four hundred families. During the past ten years the payroll and commissions have aggregated more than $350,000.00.

The offices of the Hansberry Enterprises are located at 4247 Indiana Avenue, Chicago, Ill.

THE HANSBERRY FOUNDATION

The Hansberry Foundation was established in 1936 by Mrs. N. Louise Hansberry, and her husband, Carl A. Hansberry, with substantial grants of the interest from the Hansberry Enterprises. Mr. Hansberry is the Director. The Foundation was set up as a Trust Fund and only the members of the immediate Hansberry family may contribute to this Fund. A provision of the Trust provides "That during the first ten (10) years only 60 percent of the income of the trust may be used, thereafter, both the income and the principal may be used, but at no time shall the principal be reduced to less than Ten Thousand ($10,000.00) dollars."

The purpose of the Foundation is to encourage and promote respect for all laws, and especially those laws as related to the Civil Rights of American citizens. The following paragraph taken from a letter to the Cook County Bar Association under date of April 27, 1937, gives a precise statement of the purpose and scope of the Hansberry Foundation:

> The Creators of the Hansberry Foundation believe that the Illinois Civil Rights Law represents the crystallized views of the best citizens of Illinois and were made in the best interest of the whole people of Illinois. They therefore believed, that the Civil Rights Code should be enforced; that the passiveness of any citizen should cease. Because of and in view of the foregoing premises, the Hansberry Foundation was created and now therefore announces its desire to cooperate with sympathetic public officials, associations, or organizations, likewise interested in the active enforcement of the Civil Rights Laws of Illinois and throughout the Nation. The Foundation will assume (at its discretion) a part, or all of the costs of prosecuting violations of the law

wherever, and/or whenever, the authorities willfully neglect or refuse to act; and where the victims are financially unable to protect themselves.

[1941]

THINKING ABOUT THE TEXT

1. What do you sense is the main rhetorical purpose of *The Crisis* in publishing this article? Does anyone in *A Raisin in the Sun* share the values expressed by the article? To what extent do you aim to "join business acumen with social vision"?

2. Much of the article consists of quotations from legal documents associated with the Hansberry Foundation. What do you think of this rhetorical strategy?

3. The article makes clear that when Lorraine Hansberry's family sought to live in an all-white part of Chicago, they were wealthier than the Youngers. What would you say to someone who argued that it would have been more honest of Hansberry to focus her play on a family as well-off as hers?

LORRAINE HANSBERRY
April 23, 1964, Letter to the New York Times

Here is part of a letter by Lorraine Hansberry written five years after A Raisin in the Sun. *Once again, she quotes the poem by Langston Hughes containing her play's title. Now, however, she is expressing approval of civil rights activists' aggressive tactics, including attempts by the Congress of Racial Equality (CORE) to block traffic. In her letter, Hansberry also recalls her family's fight against racial covenants and her father's subsequent death in Mexico. Although the* New York Times *never published Hansberry's letter, some of it was included by her husband Robert Nemiroff in his 1969 compilation of her writings,* To Be Young, Gifted, and Black.

April 23, 1964

To the Editor,
The New York Times:
    . . . My father was typical of a generation of Negroes who believed that the "American way" could successfully be made to work to democratize the United States. Thus, twenty-five years ago, he spent a small personal fortune, his considerable talents, and many years of his life fighting, in association with NAACP attorneys, Chicago's "restrictive covenants" in one of this nation's ugliest ghettoes.

    That fight also required that our family occupy the disputed property in a hellishly hostile "white neighborhood" in which, literally, howling mobs surrounded our house. One of their missiles almost took the life of the then eight-year-old signer of this letter. My memories of this "correct" way of fighting white supremacy in America include being spat at, cursed and pummeled in the daily trek to and from school. And I also remember my desperate and courageous mother, patrolling our house all night with a loaded German luger, doggedly guarding her four children, while my father fought the respectable part of the battle in the Washington court.

The fact that my father and the NAACP "won" a Supreme Court decision, in a now famous case which bears his name in the lawbooks, is—ironically— the sort of "progress" our satisfied friends allude to when they presume to deride the more radical means of struggle. The cost, in emotional turmoil, time and money, which led to my father's early death as a permanently embittered exile in a foreign country when he saw that after such sacrificial efforts the Negroes of Chicago were as ghetto-locked as ever, does not seem to figure in their calculations.

That is the reality that I am faced with when I now read that some Negroes my own age and younger say that we must now lie down in the streets, tie up traffic, do whatever we can—take to the hills with guns if necessary—and fight back. Fatuous people remark these days on our "bitterness." Why, of course we are bitter. The entire situation suggests that the nation be reminded of the too little noted final lines of Langston Hughes' mighty poem:

What happens to a dream deferred?

Does it dry up
Like a raisin in the sun?
Or fester like a sore —
And then run?
Does it stink like rotten meat?
Or crust and sugar over—
Like a syrupy sweet?

Maybe it just sags
Like a heavy load.

Or does it explode?

Sincerely,
Lorraine Hansberry
[1964]

THINKING ABOUT THE TEXT

1. Hansberry indicates that she is "bitter." Is *bitter* a word that you associate with the author of *A Raisin in the Sun*? Why, or why not? Do you get the sense that the bitterness she refers to in her letter is justified? Why, or why not?

2. Does Hansberry's play give you the impression that the family in it will suffer the same kinds of things described in the second paragraph of Hansberry's letter? Support your answer with details from the play.

3. In the letter, Hansberry seems to condone acts of civil disobedience. In what kinds of cases, if any, do you think people are justified in breaking the law?

ALAN EHRENHALT

From *The Lost City: Discovering the Forgotten Virtues of Community in the Chicago of the 1950s*

Alan Ehrenhalt (b. 1947) is the executive editor of Governing *magazine and was formerly political editor of* Congressional Quarterly. *In much of his writing, he argues that Americans will achieve true democracy only if they regain the sense of community they once had. This is the basic claim of Ehrenhalt's first book,* The United States of Ambition: Politicians, Power, and the Pursuit of Office *(1991). In his second,* The Lost City: Discovering the Forgotten Virtues of Community in the Chicago of the 1950s *(1995), he extends his concern with community spirit by focusing on the role it played in Chicago during the 1950s. The following excerpts deal with Bronzeville, the South Side ghetto where Lorraine Hansberry grew up and where her 1959 play* A Raisin in the Sun *takes place.*

If St. Nick's parish° was a world of limited choices, a far more limited world existed five miles further east, where the bulk of Chicago's black community — hundreds of thousands of people — lived together in Bronzeville, a neighborhood they were all but prohibited from escaping.

Any discussion of the city we have lost during the past generation must eventually confront the issue of Bronzeville, and the question that may be most troublesome of all: Have we lost something important that existed even in the worst place that the Chicago of the 1950s had to offer?

Anybody who did not live in a black ghetto is bound to be leery of asking the question, with its implied assumption that segregation hid its good points. But the fact remains, long after Bronzeville's disappearance from the map, that a remarkable number of people who did live there find themselves asking it.

"Fifty-first and Dearborn was a bunch of shacks," Alice Blair wrote thirty years later, after she had become Chicago's deputy superintendent of education. "We didn't have hot water — and the houses were torn down for slum clearance to build Robert Taylor Homes. But in those shacks, there was something different from what is there now."

What was it, exactly? Several things. "People took a great deal of pride in just   5
being where they were," says John Stroger, the first black president of the Cook County Board of Commissioners. "It was economically poor, but spiritually and socially rich. People had hope that things would be better." Stroger echoes what Vernon Jarrett, the longtime Chicago newspaper columnist, said rather hauntingly a few years ago. "The ghetto used to have something going for it. It had a beat, it had a certain rhythm, and it was all hope. I don't care how rough things were."

St. Nick's parish: St. Nicholas of Tolentine parish, a postimmigrant, working-class neighborhood of Chicago.

Then there is the bluntness of Timuel Black, a lifelong civil rights activist, looking back at age seventy-five on the South Side as it used to be and as it has become: "I would say," he declares at the end of a long conversation, "at this point in my life and experience, that we made a mistake leaving the ghetto."

These fragments prove nothing. To many who read them, they will suggest merely that nostalgia is not only powerful but dangerous, that late in life it can generate a fondness for times and places that should be properly remembered with nothing more than relief that they are gone. And yet something valuable did die with Bronzeville, and we can learn something about community and authority, faith and hope, by tracing their presence even in what was, by common agreement, an unjust and constricted corner of the world.

What Bronzeville had, and so many of its graduates continue to mourn, was a sense of posterity—a feeling that, however difficult the present might be, the future was worth thinking about and planning for in some detail. Most of the inhabitants of Bronzeville were farsighted people, able to focus on events and ideas whose outlines were hazy and whose arrival might still be very far away. They were looking forward to a time in which it would be possible to break free of the constrictions and indignities of the moment.

Forty years later, in a time-shortened world hooked on fax machines, microwave popcorn, and MTV, the word *posterity* carries far less meaning than it once did. Its gradual disappearance is one of the genuine losses of modern life. To find the concept so vibrant and well entrenched in a place as deprived as Bronzeville in the 1950s seems to mock the freer but far less anchored world that most of us inhabit today.

The indignities of life for a black person on the South Side in the 1950s are unlikely to come as news to very many readers of any race, but some details are worth dredging up. They reveal the triumphs and comforts of Bronzeville society to have been that much more impressive. 10

It was, for example, uncommonly dangerous for a black Chicagoan to get sick. Of the seventy-seven hospitals in the metropolitan area, only six would accept black patients at all, and five of those had quotas, so that once a certain small number of beds were occupied by blacks, the next black patient would be turned away, no matter how ill he or she was. It was not unusual for blacks who could perfectly well afford private hospital care to be taken to Cook County Hospital, the spartan and overcrowded charity institution on the West Side.

Most of the time, though, even in an emergency, they would be rushed to Provident, the city's only "black" hospital, sometimes speeding past one white facility after another to get to the Provident emergency room. In 1956, Provident saw an emergency patient every nineteen minutes, five times the average for the city's other hospitals. And it was, of course, the only place where a black doctor could aspire to practice; the other hospitals did their hiring on a strict Jim Crow basis.

Getting stopped for a traffic ticket on the South Side was not the same experience for blacks that it was for whites. Until 1958, all traffic tickets in Chicago mentioned the race of the driver. The police maintained a special task force, known to just about everybody as the "flying squad," which was supposed to zero in on high-crime neighborhoods but in fact spent a good deal of its time harassing black citizens, middle-class as well as poor. It was standard practice for flying squad officers to stop black motorists for traffic violations, frisk them, and search their cars before writing the ticket, often abusing them verbally and physically in the process. The abuses nearly always took place when someone was driving alone, so there were rarely any witnesses.

The force that patrolled these neighborhoods was still mostly white, and the supervisors were essentially all white. There were 1,200 black police officers in Chicago in 1957, but only one black captain, and no lieutenants. In the Englewood district, where many of the new recruits were sent, black patrolmen were nearly always given the most tedious assignments: guard duty night after night, or a motorcycle beat in the depths of winter. The two-man teams were all segregated; blacks and whites were not allowed to work together.

Meanwhile, the public schools were not only segregated but demonstrably unequal. Most of the white elementary schools on the South Side were underused, while the black ones were jammed far beyond capacity. Some black schools in Bronzeville were handling more than 2,000 pupils a day on a double-shift basis, with one set of children in attendance from 8 A.M. to noon and another from noon to 4 P.M. At the same time, there were nearly 300 vacant classrooms elsewhere in the city and more than 1,000 classrooms being used for nonessential activities of one sort or another. But the school board did not want to adjust the district lines to permit black kids to take advantage of the space that existed beyond the racial borders.

The incidents of hospital bias, police harassment, and school inequity pointed up just how indifferent Jim Crow was to class distinctions in the 1950s: having money was simply no help in these situations. There was a fourth indignity that somehow makes this point even clearer, and it had to do with travel and vacations.

For $20 a year in 1957, a black family could join an organization called the Tourist Motor Club. What they received in return was a list of hotels and restaurants where blacks would be allowed inside the door, and a guarantee of $500 in bond money in case they found themselves being arrested for making the wrong choice. "Are you ready for any traveling emergency—even in a hostile town?" the Tourist Motor Club asked in its ads, and not unreasonably. "What would you do if you were involved in a highway accident in a hostile town—far away from home. You could lose your life savings—you could be kept in jail without adequate reason. You could lose your entire vacation fighting unjust prejudice."

Vacations were for those who could afford them. The problem that united everyone in the black community—wealthy, working class, and poor—was housing. Unlike St. Nick's or any other white community in Chicago, the ghetto was almost impossible to move out of. The rules of segregation simply made it difficult for a black family to live anywhere else, whether it could afford to or not.

By 1957, that had begun to change. Chicago's South Side black population was expanding, block by block, into what had been white working-class territory on its southern and western borders, and a new, separate black enclave had

15

emerged a few miles west of downtown. But as a practical matter, the number of decent housing opportunities opening up for blacks was far smaller than the number needed. Thus, most of the city's black community remained where it had been since the 1920s: in a narrow strip south of Twenty-third Street, roughly eight miles long and still no more than two or three miles wide.

This ghetto had been badly overcrowded by the time of World War II, and in the years since then it had grown more crowded still. The number of black people in Chicago had increased nearly 40 percent between 1950 and 1956, while the white population was declining. And the newcomers were simply stacking up on top of one another. The Kenwood-Oakland neighborhood, centered around Forty-seventh Street, had gone from 13,000 white residents to 80,000 blacks in a matter of a few years. "A new Negro reaches this sprawling city every fifteen minutes," the young black journalist Carl Rowan wrote in 1957, seeming a little overwhelmed himself. Parts of the South Side that had once been relatively spacious and comfortable now held more people than anyone had imagined possible.

The physical world that those migrants confronted was the world of the infamous "kitchenette"—a one-room flat with an icebox, a bed, and a hotplate, typically in an ancient building that once held a few spacious apartments but had been cut up into the tiniest possible pieces to bring the landlord more money. The bathroom and stove were shared with neighbors, a dozen or more people taking turns with the same meager facilities. . . .

In Bronzeville, hope and authority tended to come out of the same package. If the ultimate authority figures were wealthy white people somewhere far away, the most familiar and important ones were right there, inside the community. They were people who had maneuvered their way through the currents of segregated life, made careers and often fortunes for themselves, and remained in the neighborhood, hammering home the message that there were victories to strive for. They were employers and entrepreneurs of all sorts: businessmen, politicians, and entertainers, gambling czars and preachers of the Gospel. They were people whose moral flaws and weaknesses were no secret to those around them, and those weaknesses were a frequent topic of discussion in the community. But they were leaders nevertheless. They led by command, sometimes rather crudely, and they also led by example.

It is easy to forget, forty years later, just how many successful black-owned businesses there were in Chicago. There were black entrepreneurs all up and down the commercial streets in the 1950s, able to stay afloat because they were guaranteed a clientele. They provided services that white businesses simply did not want to provide to blacks. They ran barber shops and beauty parlors, restaurants and taverns, photography studios and small hotels. Many of them were mom-and-pop operations but quite a few evolved into sizable corporations. "Business," as Dempsey Travis says, "was the pillar of optimism."

The nation's largest black-owned bank was at Forty-seventh Street and Cottage Grove Avenue. Parker House Sausage Company, at Forty-sixth and State, called itself the "Jackie Robinson of meat-packing." At Twenty-seventh and Wabash, S. B. Fuller operated a giant cosmetics business that touted three hundred different products, maintained thirty-one branches all over the country, and

20

employed five thousand salesmen. "Anyone can succeed," Fuller used to say, "if he has the desire."

But the great symbols of the entrepreneurial spirit in Bronzeville were the   25
funeral parlors and the insurance companies. In many cases they were related businesses, a legacy of the burial insurance associations that had existed among black sharecroppers in Mississippi and Arkansas early in the century. Undertakers were the largest single source of advertising in the *Defender*; they were also, like their white counterparts elsewhere in the city, mainstays of every community organization: lodges, churches, social clubs.

The opening of a new funeral parlor was a community event in itself. In the spring of 1957, the Jackson funeral home opened a state-of-the art facility on Cottage Grove Avenue, complete, with three large chapels, slumber rooms, a powder room, and a smoking lounge. On the first day, three thousand people came to see it. The Jackson family also owned Jackson Mutual, the fifth largest insurance company in Bronzeville, employing one hundred and twenty people and writing nearly $2 million worth of policies every year.

Insurance actually was a service that white corporations were willing to provide to black customers. Thousands of Bronzeville residents had policies with Metropolitan Life, paying a dollar or two every month to an agent who came by door-to-door to collect. But this was one case where black firms could compete fairly easily. Met Life charged black families more than it charged whites for the same policies, its agents didn't like to come at night when customers were home, and they often seemed to resent having to be there at all. There were billboards all over the neighborhood urging people to buy their insurance from a Negro company.

The result was that by the mid-1950s, the five largest black-owned insurance companies in Chicago had nearly $50 million in assets and more than two thousand employees among them. "Negro life insurance companies," said Walter Lowe, one of the leading agents, "represent the core of Negro economic life. It is the axis upon which are revolved the basic financial activities of a world constricted by the overpowering forces of discrimination."

But it was more than that. It was the underwriter of the extended time horizons that made life in Bronzeville tolerable in the first place. It was the primary symbol of hope for people burdened with a difficult present but unwilling to abandon their focus on the future. In 1954, *Ebony* magazine, published in Chicago, took a survey of its black readership and found that 42 percent owned washing machines, 44 percent owned cars, and 60 percent owned television sets. But 86 percent said they carried life insurance.

The *Defender's* tribute to the life insurance companies was reprinted every   30
year to coincide with National Negro Insurance Week: "I am the destroyer of poverty and the enemy of crime," it said. "I bring sunshine and happiness wherever I am given half the welcome I deserve. I do not live for the day nor for the morrow but for the unfathomable future. I am your best friend — I am life insurance." . . .

Overcoming evil was a job at which most of Bronzeville worked very hard every Sunday, in congregations that ranged in size from tiny to immense. There were five churches whose sanctuary had a seating capacity of two thousand or more, and at least two churches had more than ten thousand people on their membership rolls. But a majority of the churches in the community, even in the late 1950s, were basically storefront operations — often a couple of dozen worshipers or even fewer than that.

In the bigger churches, Sunday worship was an all-day affair: Sunday school at nine in the morning and the main service at eleven; an evening musicale later on, with the full choir and Gospel chorus; and then, for many of the faithful, a radio sermon from one of the big-name Bronzeville preachers before retiring for the night. Music was at the heart of the experience. Most churches had choirs that accompanied the pastor when he preached as a guest in another pulpit, which all of them did. Some choirs spent considerable time traveling outside the city.

Between Sundays, the odds were that a larger congregation would be busy with some social activity every single night. All these churches had a wide variety of auxiliary organizations — youth groups, missionary societies, sewing circles — and some had as many as two dozen different ones in existence at the same time. Of all the Bronzeville social institutions of the 1950s, the churches were the most uniformly successful and self-reliant. "In their own churches in their own denominational structures," the historian C. Eric Lincoln was to write in retrospect, "black Christians had become accustomed to a sense of dignity and self-fulfillment impossible even to contemplate in the white church in America. . . . To be able to say that 'I belong to Mount Nebo Baptist' or 'We go to Mason's Chapel Methodist' was the accepted way of establishing identity and status."

The storefront churches had to make do without the elaborate network of groups and social involvement. But the key distinction was not the size of the facility; it was the style of worship and particularly the level of emotion. Many of the storefronts, perhaps most, were Holiness or Pentecostal churches — Holy Rollers, as the outside world had already come to know them. The service combined shouting, faith healing, and speaking in tongues; as much as three hours of singing, accompanied by guitar, drum, and tambourine; and vivid story-telling sermons about such things as the fiery furnace or the prodigal son. Some churches employed attendants in white uniforms to calm the shouting worshipers when they became too excited. In a liturgy that devoted a great deal of its time to discussing the nature and consequences of sin — and the specific sins of alcohol, tobacco, profanity, gambling, and adultery — there was intense joy as well. "I have known the sisters and the brothers to become so happy," one woman told Horace Cayton and St. Clair Drake in *Black Metropolis*, "that persons around them are in actual danger of getting knocked in the face."

The popularity of these storefronts was something of a problem for the mainline Baptist and African Methodist Episcopal (AME) congregations that aimed for what they saw as a higher level of decorum and dignity. Some ministers used to upbraid their worshipers for becoming too emotional during the service. By the mid-1950s, however, the liturgical distinction between the storefronts and the mainline institutions was blurring. Dozens of preachers who had begun with nothing had built their churches into successful operations, all without departing significantly from the Holiness or Pentecostal script.

The mid-1950s were an exciting time for Bronzeville churches of all varieties. Congregations were growing, debts were being paid, and churches everywhere seemed to be moving into larger, more elaborate facilities: the shouters as well as the elite. . . .

Bronzeville no longer exists. That is not merely because no one would use such a name anymore, but because most of the buildings that comprised the neighborhood have long since been leveled. With the completion in 1962 of Robert Taylor Homes, the nation's largest public housing project and quite possibly its most squalid, the area once called Bronzeville ceased to run the gamut from worn-out but respectable apartment buildings to gruesome kitchenettes. It became a much more uniform high-rise slum, punctuated every half-mile or so by decrepit commercial strips, hosting intermittent taverns, barbecues, and convenience stores and suggesting only a remnant of the much more thriving business streets that once existed.

Bronzeville is long gone not only physically but socially; it passed out of existence as a community as soon as the middle class left, which was as soon as it was permitted to leave with the lifting of segregation. By 1960, the middle-class exodus had already begun, and by 1970, it was virtually complete. Thousands of families who had been the pillars of Bronzeville society returned at most once a week, for church on Sunday.

So much his been written about the impact of middle-class departure on the life of the ghetto that it seems unnecessary to belabor the point. Perhaps it is sufficient to say that Bronzeville was a community unique in America, that its uniqueness depended on the presence of people from all classes and with all sorts of values, living and struggling together, and that with the disappearance of that diversity, the community could not have continued to exist, even if there had been no physical changes at all.

In thinking about what has disappeared, however, there is no shortage of ironies to ponder. The policy racket is legal now, run neither by local black gamblers nor by the Mafia but by the state of Illinois, which calls it a lottery. The game that was once considered an emblem of sin by much of white Chicago is now depended upon as a contributor to the financing of public education. Policy is merely a business now, managed by a colorless bureaucracy far away — it is no longer a cult or a neighborhood institution. There is no demand for dream books anymore on the South Side, no circus-like drawings in crowded basements with a light over the entrance. People play the legal numbers game with a humorless compulsiveness that has little in common with the old-fashioned emotional experience.

Legal businesses have fared almost as badly as illegal ones. Notwithstanding Earl Dickerson's prediction that Supreme Liberty Life would thrive under integration to become a billion-dollar insurance business by the end of the century, the company was simply absorbed into United of America, becoming a piece of a gigantic white institution, and a rather small and inconspicuous piece at that. Not that there was anything racist about such a consolidation; plenty of smaller white-owned insurance companies suffered the same fate. But the cumulative effect on black economic life was powerful: the old life insurance companies were the one significant engine of capital in Chicago's black community, and by 1990, not a single firm was left.

The *Chicago Defender* remains in business at the same location it occupied in the 1950s, published by the same man, John Sengstacke. But it never really found a coherent role to play as a voice of its people in an integrated city. Once the white newspapers began printing news about blacks on the South Side, the paper lost its franchise as virtually the sole source of information within the community. It played a surprisingly passive role in the civil rights confrontations of the 1960s, serving neither as a conspicuous engine of militant activism nor as a persistent critic. By the 1970s, the *Defender* had essentially been superseded as a forum for political debate by the plethora of black radio stations that had sprung up on the South Side. The Bud Billiken parade is still held each summer in Washington Park, attracting a huge contingent of Chicago politicians, white as well as black, but it is no longer the signature event of a powerful black journalistic institution: it is a reminder of the influence that institution once had.

Of all the fixtures of Bronzeville life, the churches come the closest to having survived in recognizable form. Olivet Baptist stands as an impressive edifice at Thirty-first Street and King Drive, its front lawn dominated by a statue of the Reverend J. H. Jackson, pugnacious in stone as he was in life, along with quotations from some of his sermons and praise for him from around the world. Olivet, South Park Baptist, and some of the other Bronzeville churches still turn out crowds at services on Sunday morning, attracting families who return from the far South Side and the suburbs, senior citizens who have remained in the neighborhood, and a sprinkling of children and adults from the projects nearby.

Some of the churches still maintain choirs, Sunday schools, Bible study groups, and social outreach programs, struggling rather heroically against the social disorganization that is all around them. But they have ceased to be voices of clear authority. No preacher can deliver instruction and expect compliance in the way that J. H. Jackson could in his prime. And while sin remains a familiar topic in the South Side black churches on Sundays—a more important topic than at St. Nick's or Elmhurst Presbyterian—the subject no longer has the hold over its listeners that it had a generation ago.

Only in politics can one really argue that Bronzeville has gained more than it has lost. William L. Dawson was a power broker and even a role model of sorts, but he was a leader whose rewards from the white machine were disappointingly meager, somehow not commensurate with the job he did in guaranteeing the election of Richard J. Daley and other white politicians. Dawson's machine yielded in the 1980s to something truly remarkable—a citywide coalition that made possible the election of Harold Washington as the city's first black mayor. Washington's victory in 1983, in a campaign with "Our Turn" as its most conspicuous slogan, was a psychological triumph far beyond anything the old Dawson organization could possibly accomplish, perhaps beyond anything blacks had experienced in any American city. And while the extent of Washington's tangible achievements in office can be debated, the fact that he died in 1987 with his heroic status in the black community intact, and his respect growing even among whites, represented a victory comparable in its way to the first one.

Black political power in Chicago, however, seemed to disappear almost as suddenly as it emerged. Ten years after Washington's first election, Chicago was

45

again being governed by a white mayor, Richard M. Daley, son of the old boss, and by a majority coalition in which Hispanics, not blacks, were the significant minority partner. Meanwhile, the black community was deeply divided over whom to follow and how to proceed, seemingly years away from the level of influence it had had in city politics in the mid-1980s.

In the black community, unlike the white working-class neighborhoods or white suburbia, it may seem perverse — or at least misleading — to dwell on the losses of the past generation. At the individual level, there have been so many gains — in personal freedom, in job opportunities, in income. Today's black middle class is far larger in proportional terms than the one that existed in Bronzeville in the 1950s, much of it living comfortably in neighborhoods scattered all across the Chicago metropolitan area.

When it comes to community institutions, however, the losses are no less real for Chicago's blacks than for white ethnics or for the split-level suburbanites of the 1950s generation. If anything, they are more real. Nearly all of the things that gave texture and coherence to life in Bronzeville, demeaning as that life often was, are simply not reproducible in the freer, more individualistic, more bewildering world of the 1990s.   [1995]

THINKING ABOUT THE TEXT

1. Does reading these passages from Ehrenhalt's book make you think differently about any of the events and characters in A Raisin in the Sun? Why, or why not?

2. To what extent does the neighborhood described by Ehrenhalt resemble where you grew up? Identify specific similarities and differences.

3. Note Ehrenhalt's last sentence. While he recognizes that Bronzeville was segregated, evidently he feels some regret over its passing, mourning in particular what he sees as the death of its community spirit. Does his attitude make sense to you? Explain your reasoning. What do you think he might say about the Younger family's decision to leave the neighborhood? How much does it matter to you that this historian of Bronzeville is white?

SIDNEY POITIER
From The Measure of a Man:
A Spiritual Autobiography

Raised in the Bahamas, Sidney Poitier (b. 1927) became the leading African American film star of his generation. For his 1963 movie Lilies of the Field, *he won the Academy Award for best actor, the first African American to do so. He has also acted in such important films as* The Blackboard Jungle *(1955),* The Defiant Ones *(1958),* A Patch of Blue *(1965),* Guess Who's Coming to Dinner *(1967),* In the Heat of the Night *(1967),* To Sir, With Love *(1967), and* A Raisin in the Sun

(1961), where he again portrayed Walter Lee Younger, his role in the play's original production. In the following excerpt from his memoir The Measure of a Man: A Spiritual Autobiography *(2000), Poitier recalls that first staging, especially his struggle in getting other members of the company to accept his view of the play.*

I finished a six-month run, but by the time I left the production the actress who played the mother wasn't speaking to me. She hated me. Need I tell you that this is a difficult position to find yourself in as the member of an ensemble of actors?

Claudia McNeil, a fine performer, was in complete dominance over most of the other members of the cast. Naturally enough, she perceived the play as being best when it unfolded from the mother's point of view. I perceived the play as being best when it unfolded from the son's point of view, however, and I argued that position. In fact, we argued constantly.

I prevailed, I guess because I was considered the principal player who was responsible for getting the piece mounted. I suppose there might have been some who didn't agree with me but simply acquiesced to my position. But I wasn't just throwing my weight around. I was not, and am not, in the habit of doing that. I genuinely felt that when tragedy fell on the family in *Raisin*, the most devastating effects were visited upon the son, because the mother was such a towering figure.

In my opinion, it was the son who carried the theatrical obligation as the force between the audience and the play. The eyes of those watching were on the son to see if the tragedy would destroy him, would blow him apart beyond recovery. And it was also my opinion that there was no such feeling between the audience and the mother. The audience witnessed the sadness that was visited on her. They saw that her family was in disarray, but they also saw her as a force beyond that kind of vulnerability. If they were to vote, they would say, "Oh, but she's going to be okay."

So where's the drama in the piece?

The drama asks an audience to *care*. This was my argument to the playwright and the director and the producer, all of whom were my friends. If you're going to ask that audience to care, you're going to have to take them to the place where the most damage is possible so they can feel that pain.

If you keep them focused on the mother, they're going to say, "Oh, that's too bad that happened—but listen, that family's going to be okay."

Well, I had learned in my experience as an actor and as a theater participant that wherever there's threatened destruction of a human being, that's where the focus is; and the only existence that was threatened in *Raisin* was the son's. There was simply no guarantee that he would survive. It was fifty-fifty that this boy couldn't do it, wouldn't be able to bounce back. It was highly probable that he wouldn't have the resilience, the guts, the stamina, or the determination. Or, looked at another way, it was possible that he wouldn't be able to experience the catharsis as fully as necessary for him to be reborn. That's what the audience had to see to be fully engaged: the rebirth of this person.

Now, there was no ego in that. I mean, I was a theater person. I had spent most of my early years in theater—not on Broadway necessarily, but I had done

5

many, many off-Broadway shows. I'd seen dozens and dozens of plays, I'd *worked* in dozens of plays, so I felt comfortable in my sense of what drama is made of, both in theatrical terms and in life terms.

So that was my position, and I was fought tooth and nail on it by the director and the writer and the producer. Ruby Dee and I saw more eye to eye than did either of us with the others, so it was my intent, and she concurred, that I would play the drama on opening night the way I believed it *should* be played. That didn't require changing the words, only making a fundamental change in the attitude of the individual.

Now, this gets to the very core of what acting is. How do you shift the emphasis of a play when, as is the case in *A Raisin in the Sun*, there are two characters who are very forceful and quite strong? Here's how: if you see the son's need as not just personal but a need on behalf of his family, then the emotional center shifts, and it becomes a different play.

The action of the play turns on the death of the father, and the fact that the mother receives ten thousand dollars in insurance money because her husband was killed in an accident on the job. The son wants to use the money in the most constructive way he can think of, which is to start a business, to move the family in some structural way up from where they are.

The mother, on the other hand, wants to use the money to buy a house. But the son says to her, in effect. "The money used to buy a house wouldn't affect the family circumstances in that I'd still chauffeur for somebody else, my wife still works as a maid, and you'd still work as a maid. There'd be no shifting of dynamics here. But there could be, with some sweat and tears, there could be some shifting of dynamics if that money were used as down payment for a business that we could all work at. Then in two years or five years, what we'd have done would be substantial enough for us to be thinking about getting a house and, hopefully, then the business would grow and we could have two such businesses or three such businesses in ten years by the time my son is ready for college."

That's his argument, and the mother's argument runs something like, "You want to spend that money to open a liquor store?" She insists, "My husband's memory is not going to be tied in with the selling of liquor. I'm going to use that money to buy a house, to put a roof over our heads."

He says to his mother, "Isn't it better that my father's death advances the family? You have a daughter who's going off to college, hopefully, but where is the money coming from? I have a son who is going to be soon a young man. What are the lessons in this for him? I am a chauffeur. Where are we going to be down the line? Am I going to be a chauffeur at the age of sixty, and is my son going to take over chauffeuring?"

So that's the heart of it. Therefore, the playing of this man has to be such that the audience believes that his need for his family is absolutely elemental, and that this is the last chance, *his* last chance. If he fails now, he'll never be able to gather the steam, gather the courage and the determination to spend himself again in a losing effort. He just won't be able to.

It's this sense of possible destruction that prepares the audience for tragedy when the mother *does* give him the money, after he really fights and struggles for it, and the money is lost. All of it.

The audience is primed to see either total destruction of this man or his resurrection, you follow? But there's no resurrection for the mother, regardless. She gives the money to her son because she finally decides to let him have his shot at being a man, his own man—and then he fucks it up. Well, sad as it might be for her as a mother, there's no great tragedy in that for her as an individual. She loses ten grand that she didn't really have in the first place.

But this young man—he's destroyed. That's what the audience assumes. But in the third act he comes out of the ashes, and that's where the real drama is, because he looks at that boy of his, and he talks to him. In fact, he's talking to the audience *through* the boy; and when he speaks, the audience just goes nuts. I mean, it's so *dramatic*.

Well, that was my position—the position I acted from. The other position, as I said, was held very strongly by the actress who played the mother, as well as by the producer, the director, and the playwright—my friends. When I left the fold to go make movies and they had to replace me, the several men who, over time, took the part had to play it the other way, the mother's way, because the continued success of the play depended on having Claudia McNeil.

Well, the audiences didn't seem to mind one bit. The play continued to work well because it had garnered such recognition by then. And the guys who took over the part were all very fine actors, all extremely fine actors, one of whom was Ruby Dee's husband, Ossie Davis.

So what was the lesson in all this?

I would say that sometimes convictions firmly held can cost more than we're willing to pay. And irrevocable change occurs when we're not up to paying, and irrevocable change occurs when we *are* up to paying. Either way, we have to live with the consequences. If I'm up to paying the price in a certain situation, I walk away from the experience with some kind of self-respect because I took the heat. And if I go the other way, feeling that the cost is too high, then however bright the situation turns out, I feel that something is missing.

For an actor to go onstage every night with the sort of hostile undercurrent we experienced with *A Raisin in the Sun*—it can only be described as being like a bad marriage. I felt that Claudia McNeil wasn't giving me what I needed. She knew where my big moments were, and she knew when to hold back and take the air out—and I lived through that opposition for months.

It was very painful for me to know the effect our disagreement was having on my colleagues. If you're a producer, certainly you're irritated by dissension that threatens to interrupt the life of a hit play. Now, my friend Philip Rose, the producer, disagreed with me completely, and I believe that his disagreement was genuine, because I've known the man all these years, and today he's still one of my closest friends. But at the time, I was leaving his play. He had a play that would run, if he could hold it together and keep Claudia McNeil happy, for years and years. So he wasn't especially sympathetic to my concerns.

The playwright's sympathies were completely against me. She saw the play as weighted toward the mother; that's how she'd *written* it. She was a very intelligent young black woman, and she came from a family of achievers. Her whole family were achievers, especially the women, and she had a certain mindset about women and their potential, especially black women in America. So she wrote a play about a matriarch faced with this dilemma. But in that formulation the son is just a ne'er-do-well. He's a fuckup, not a tragic figure, not a man whose life is on the line. I simply couldn't do it that way, because in my mind the dramatic possibilities were so much greater the other way.

Then, of course, there was the director, Lloyd Richards. Again, a very close friend with whom I had very little quarrel on the question, because his first responsibility was to the work by the playwright. He had gone inside the play with her; she had taken him on an excursion into the inner selves of these characters. So he saw the play as she conceived it, and when he put it together, he put it together that way. He didn't have any conflict with it. But I did—because I had to face an audience, you know?—and I just couldn't face an audience playing it with less than the attitude I thought was necessary for this drama.

Out of town in New Haven I played it their way, but I was looking for answers. I wasn't altogether comfortable. We went on to Philadelphia. Same thing. The play was working fine, but there was something missing. It was working overall, but I wasn't really there. We went to Chicago. Same thing. So Ruby Dee and I started exploring, and in Chicago magic started to happen. Wham! And I started to play differently.

Then we went to New York, and on opening night the energy was at its apex. The director saw it, but he wouldn't characterize the added excitement he sensed as coming from the way I had played the role. The producer saw it too, but he said it was just a great night. The playwright was in the audience, and I went out and helped her up on the stage so that all the world could see this magnificent young woman, this gifted person. She assumed that the incredible night of theater we'd all just experienced was as she wrote it.

Well, I say it played well because there was something special in the conviction I held, and I carried it from Chicago to New York.   30

There's a special moment in the third act, just before the end. They had put a down payment on a house before they lost the money, but a man comes to tell them that they're not wanted in that neighborhood. My character, the son, has to stand up and talk to this man. He's talking to this man about his family. After a given point in the speech, he says, "This is my mother." Then he says, "This is my sister." And then he says. "This is my wife,—and she is"—pride, pain, and love overpower him and he's not able to get her name out. And by the time he turns to his son, his emotions are more than any words could express. The tears roll down his cheeks and he begins to cry. He gestures to the boy, but the words won't come out, and finally he forces out the words. He says, "This is my son," and the house goes nuts, you hear me?

I know from my own experience that when a guy is just afraid, and he wishes to succeed *because he's afraid of failure*, that's not much of a commitment. But there's another kind of drive to succeed. I think of my father, going from bar to bar selling his cigars, probing my arm because he's worried that I'm not getting enough to eat. Then sitting down to write a letter to his eldest son, telling him that he's no longer able to control and guide his youngest, that he needs help. You find a man like that, with a need to do something that's over and above his own ego-requirement—a need that's for his *family*, as he sees it—and you get every ounce of his energy. When a man says, "This is for my *child*," you get over and above that which he thinks he's capable of.

My father was with me every moment as I performed in *A Raisin in the Sun*. The themes, too, seemed like so many threads from my own life. The days in Nassau and Miami and New York when I seemed to be in such a downward spiral and there was no promise of resurrection. All the risks I took, all the brushes with destruction. I know how much it pained my family, but there was nothing they could do. It was this art form that saved me. Ultimately, by taking even greater risks — by going to New York and then by choosing a life in the theater — I came through. And it wasn't just for myself. It was for Reggie too.

THINKING ABOUT THE TEXT

1. Poitier's experience with the play was very much that of an actor involved in performing it. Does his account make you aware of anything that you did not realize when you simply *read* the play? If so, what?

2. Poitier reports that even author Hansberry disagreed with his view of the play. In such cases, do you think the performer should usually defer to the playwright? Why or why not?

3. Does Poitier succeed in persuading you that his view of the play made more sense than its rival? Specify things that affect your response to his argument.

WRITING ABOUT ISSUES

1. Choose a particular moment in *A Raisin in the Sun* when characters disagree. Then write an essay analyzing their disagreement. More specifically, identify the different positions they take, the warrants or assumptions that seem to underlie their positions, the outcome of their disagreement, your own evaluation of their views, and the relationship of this moment to the rest of the play. Be sure to quote from the text.

2. Imagine that Hansberry's play is being republished and that you are asked to edit it. Imagine further that the publisher asks you to introduce the play with one of the four background documents in this cluster. Write an essay stating which document you would choose and why.

3. Choose a family you know well, and write an essay comparing it with the Younger family. Above all, consider whether your chosen family, too, has conflicting dreams.

4. Spend time in the library examining newspapers and magazines from 1959, the year *A Raisin in the Sun* opened on Broadway. In particular, try to identify a variety of events and trends that might have affected an American family that year. Next, imagine a specific American family living in 1959. Finally, write an essay describing a play that might be written about your imagined family's reaction to a specific event or trend back then. Give details of the plot, the family's social background, and its members' personalities. If you wish, present some dialogue.

──────────── **A WEB ASSIGNMENT** ────────────

Visit the Web Assignments section of the *Making Arguments about Literature* Web site, where you will find a link to a site entitled "Racial Restrictive Covenants in the United States." At this site, historian Wendy Plotkin has assembled various documents related to community agreements ("covenants") that kept African Americans out of white neighborhoods. Many of Plotkin's documents deal with legal efforts to get these agreements invalidated. One such struggle she chronicles is the case of *Hansberry v. Lee, et al.*, which went all the way to the Supreme Court. The "Hansberry" of the case was Lorraine Hansberry's father Carl, who had moved his family to a white neighborhood that was now trying to evict him. The playwright had this case in mind when she later wrote *A Raisin in the Sun.* Choose at least two of the documents that Plotkin has gathered for this case, and write an essay relating them to specific conversations in the play. You may be especially interested in the articles that Plotkin has transcribed from the *Chicago Defender,* the city's leading black-owned newspaper at the time.

──────────── Visit **www.bedfordstmartins.com/argumentsaboutlit** ────────────

|12|

Essay Clusters

Community Justice

SCOTT RUSSELL SANDERS, "Doing Time in the Thirteenth Chair"
JOYCE CAROL OATES, "I, the Juror"
MAXINE HONG KINGSTON, "No Name Woman"

Decisions about justice are often made in the name of an entire community. Even when rulers issue a policy that reflects merely their own mind, they may claim that it enacts their whole society's will. In the American legal system, people act as representatives of their community when they serve on a jury. Of course, jurors may disagree as they try to decide a case, revealing individual values in the process. Moreover, any particular version of community justice is subject to further debate. When the white police officers who were videotaped beating African American motorist Rodney King were initially acquitted by a jury from a predominantly white Los Angeles suburb, many people accused the jurors of racial prejudice. The verdicts delivered by juries in the criminal and civil trials of O. J. Simpson also produced divided opinions about how fair his two juries were.

The first two essays here encourage you to consider the relationship between jurors' social backgrounds and their ultimate decisions. Scott Russell Sanders and Joyce Carol Oates recall their own experiences as alternate juror and juror, respectively. Sanders evidently feels that the white middle-class people he served with fairly decided the fate of a working-class man. Oates, on the other hand, believes that race seriously influenced her jury's thinking.

Juries are not the only means through which communities express their sense of justice. Throughout the centuries, collective judgments have taken plenty of other forms. In the third essay here, the "no name woman" of the title is author Maxine Hong Kingston's aunt, who killed herself in her village in China after neighbors attacked her farm because of her adulterous pregnancy. Kingston's American family continued to punish the aunt by being silent about her life and death. Why and how do communities punish individuals? What criteria should we use in evaluating both formal and informal styles of justice?

BEFORE YOU READ

Have you ever served on a jury? If so, what was the experience like? If not, would you like to be on a jury? Why, or why not? In general, do you have faith in the jury system? What specifically comes to mind as you consider this question?

SCOTT RUSSELL SANDERS
Doing Time in the Thirteenth Chair

Scott Russell Sanders (b. 1945) spent much of his youth at a military munitions base, where his father worked. He describes this experience in the title essay of his 1987 book The Paradise of Bombs, *which also includes the following piece. Today, Sanders is a professor of English at Indiana University. Besides essays, he has published fiction, a study of the writer D. H. Lawrence, and book-length nonfictional works including* Staying Put: Making a Home in a Restless World *(1993) and* Hunting for Hope: A Father's Journeys *(1998). His latest books are* The Country of Language *(1999) and* The Force of Spirit *(2001).*

The courtroom is filled with the ticking of a clock and the smell of mold. Listening to the minutes click away, I imagine bombs or mechanical hearts sealed behind the limestone walls. Forty of us have been yanked out of our usual orbits and called to appear for jury duty in this ominous room, beneath the stained-glass dome of the county courthouse. We sit in rows like strangers in a theater, coats rumpled in our laps, crossing and uncrossing our legs, waiting for the show to start.

I feel sulky and rebellious, the way I used to feel when a grade-school teacher made me stay inside during recess. This was supposed to have been the first day of my Christmas vacation, and the plain, uncitizenly fact is that I don't want to be here. I want to be home hammering together some bookshelves for my wife. I want to be out tromping the shores of Lake Monroe with my eye cocked skyward for bald eagles and sharp-shinned hawks.

But the computer-printed letter said to report today for jury duty, and so here I sit. The judge beams down at us from his bench. Tortoise-shell glasses, twenty-dollar haircut, square boyish face: although probably in his early forties, he could pass for a student-body president. He reminds me of an owlish television know-it-all named Mr. Wizard who used to conduct scientific experiments (Magnetism! Litmus tests! Sulphur dioxide!) on a kids' show in the 1950s. Like Mr. Wizard, he lectures us in slow, pedantic speech: trial by one's peers, tradition stretching back centuries to England, defendant innocent until proven guilty beyond a reasonable doubt, and so abundantly on. I spy around for the clock. It must be overhead, I figure, up in the cupola above the dome, raining its ticktocks down on us.

When the lecture is finished, the judge orders us to rise, lift our hands, and swear to uphold the truth. There is a cracking of winter-stiff knees as we stand

and again as we sit down. Then he introduces the principal actors: the sleek young prosecutor, who peacocks around like a politician on the hustings; the married pair of brooding, elegantly dressed defense lawyers; and the defendant. I don't want to look at this man who is charged with crimes against the "peace and dignity" of the State of Indiana. I don't want anything to do with his troubles. But I grab an image anyway, of a squat, slit-eyed man about my age, mid-thirties, stringy black hair parted in the middle and dangling like curtains across his face, sparse black beard. The chin whiskers and squinted-up eyes make him look faintly Chinese, and faintly grimacing.

Next the judge reads a list of twelve names, none of them mine, and twelve   5
sworn citizens shuffle into the jury box. The lawyers have at them, darting questions. How do you feel about drugs? Would you say the defendant there looks guilty because he has a beard? Are you related to any police officers? Are you pregnant? When these twelve have finished answering, the attorneys scribble names on sheets of paper which they hand to the judge, and eight of the first bunch are sent packing. The judge reads eight more names, the jury box fills up with fresh bodies, the questioning resumes. Six of these get the heave-ho. And so the lawyers cull through the potential jurors, testing and chucking them like two men picking over apples in the supermarket. At length they agree on a dozen, and still my name has not been called. Hooray, I think. I can build those bookshelves after all, can watch those hawks.

Before setting the rest of us free, however, the judge consults his list. "I am calling alternate juror number one," he says, and then he pronounces my name.

Groans echo down my inmost corridors. For the first time I notice a thirteenth chair beside the jury box, and that is where the judge orders me to go.

"Yours is the most frustrating job," the judge advises me soothingly. "Unless someone else falls ill or gets called away, you will have to listen to all the proceedings without taking part in the jury's final deliberations or decisions."

I feel as though I have been invited to watch the first four acts of a five-act play. Never mind, I console myself: the lawyers will throw me out. I'm the only one in the courtroom besides the defendant who sports a beard or long hair. A backpack decorated with NO NUKES and PEACE NOW and SAVE THE WHALES buttons leans against my boots. How can they expect me, a fiction writer, to confine myself to facts? I am unreliable, a confessed fabulist, a marginal Quaker and Wobbly socialist, a man so out of phase with my community that I am thrown into fits of rage by the local newspaper. The lawyers will take a good look at me and race one another to the bench for the privilege of having the judge boot me out.

But neither Mr. Defense nor Mr. Prosecution quite brings himself to focus   10
on my shady features. Each asks me a perfunctory question, the way vacationers will press a casual thumb against the spare tire before hopping into the car for a trip. If there's air in the tire, you don't bother about blemishes. And that is all I am, a spare juror stashed away in the trunk of the court, in case one of the twelve originals gives out during the trial.

Ticktock. The judge assures us that we should be finished in five days, just in time for Christmas. The real jurors exchange forlorn glances. Here I sit, number thirteen, and nobody looks my way. Knowing I am stuck here for the duration, I perk up, blink my eyes. Like the bear going over the mountain, I might as well see what I can see.

What I see is a parade of mangled souls. Some of them sit on the witness stand and reveal their wounds; some of them remain offstage, summoned up only by the words of those who testify. The case has to do with the alleged sale, earlier this year, of hashish and cocaine to a confidential informer. First the prosecutor stands at a podium in front of the jury and tells us how it all happened, detail by criminal detail, and promises to prove every fact to our utter satisfaction. Next, one of the defense attorneys has a fling at us. It is the husband of the Mr.-and-Mrs. team, a melancholy-looking man with bald pate and mutton-chop sideburns, deep creases in the chocolate skin of his forehead. Leaning on the podium, he vows that he will raise a flock of doubts in our minds — grave doubts, reasonable doubts — particularly regarding the seedy character of the confidential informer. They both speak well, without hemming and hawing, without stumbling over syntactic cliffs, better than senators at a press conference. Thus, like rival suitors, they begin to woo the jury.

At mid-morning, before hearing from the first witness, we take a recess. (It sounds more and more like school.) Thirteen of us with peel-away JUROR tags stuck to our shirts and sweaters retreat to the jury room. We drink coffee and make polite chat. Since the only thing we have in common is this trial, and since the judge has just forbidden us to talk about that, we grind our gears trying to get a conversation started. I find out what everybody does in the way of work: a bar waitress, a TV repairman (losing customers while he sits here), a department store security guard, a dentist's assistant, an accountant, a nursing home nurse, a cleaning woman, a caterer, a mason, a boisterous old lady retired from rearing children (and married, she tells us, to a school-crossing guard), a meek college student with the demeanor of a groundhog, a teacher. Three of them right now are unemployed. Six men, six women, with ages ranging from twenty-one to somewhere above seventy. Chaucer could gather this bunch together for a literary pilgrimage, and he would not have a bad sampling of smalltown America.

Presently the bailiff looks in to see what we're up to. She is a jowly woman, fiftyish, with short hair the color and texture of buffed aluminum. She wears silvery half-glasses of the sort favored by librarians; in the courtroom she peers at us above the frames with a librarian's skeptical glance, as if to make sure we are awake. To each of us she now gives a small yellow pad and a ballpoint pen. We are to write our names on the back, take notes on them during the trial, and surrender them to her whenever we leave the courtroom. (School again.) Without saying so directly, she lets us know that we are her flock and she is our shepherd. Anything we need, any yen we get for traveling, we should let her know.

I ask her whether I can go downstairs for a breath of air, and the bailiff answers "sure." On the stairway I pass a teenage boy who is listlessly polishing with a rag the wrought-iron filigree that supports the banister. Old men sheltering from December slouch on benches just inside the ground-floor entrance of the courthouse. Their faces have been caved in by disappointment and the loss of

15

teeth. Two-dollar cotton work gloves, the cheapest winter hand-covers, stick out of their back pockets. They are veterans of this place; so when they see me coming with the blue JUROR label pasted on my chest, they look away. Don't tamper with jurors, especially under the very nose of the law. I want to tell them I'm not a real juror, only a spare, number thirteen. I want to pry old stories out of them, gossip about hunting and dogs, about their favorite pickup trucks, their worst jobs. I want to ask them when and how it all started to go wrong for them. Did they hear a snap when the seams of their life began to come apart? But they will not be fooled into looking at me, not these wily old men with the crumpled faces. They believe the label on my chest and stare down at their unlaced shoes.

I stick my head out the door and swallow some air. The lighted thermometer on the bank reads twenty-eight degrees. Schmaltzy Christmas organ music rebounds from the brick-and-limestone shopfronts of the town square. The Salvation Army bell rings and rings. Delivery trucks hustling through yellow lights blare their horns at jaywalkers.

The bailiff must finally come fetch me, and I feel like a wayward sheep. On my way back upstairs, I notice the boy dusting the same square foot of iron filigree, and realize that he is doing this as a penance. Some judge ordered him to clean the metalwork. I'd like to ask the kid what mischief he's done, but the bailiff, looking very dour, is at my heels.

In the hallway she lines us up in our proper order, me last. Everybody stands up when we enter the courtroom, and then, as if we have rehearsed these routines, we all sit down at once. Now come the facts.

The facts are a mess. They are full of gaps, chuckholes, switchbacks, and dead ends — just like life.

At the outset we are shown three small plastic bags. Inside the first is a wad of 20 aluminum foil about the size of an earlobe; the second contains two white pills; the third holds a pair of stamp-sized, squarish packets of folded brown paper. A chemist from the state police lab testifies that he examined these items and found cocaine inside the brown packets, hashish inside the wad of aluminum foil. As for the white pills, they are counterfeits of a popular barbiturate, one favored by politicians and movie stars. They're depressants — downers — but they contain no "controlled substances."

There follows half a day's worth of testimony about how the bags were sealed, who locked them in the narcotics safe at the Bloomington police station, which officer drove them up to the lab in Indianapolis and which drove them back again, who carried them in his coat pocket and who carried them in his briefcase. Even the judge grows bored during this tedious business. He yawns, tips back in his chair, sips coffee from a mug, folds and unfolds with deft thumbs a square of paper about the size of the cocaine packets. The wheels of justice grind slowly. We hear from police officers in uniform, their handcuffs clanking, and from mustachioed officers in civvies, revolvers bulging under their suitcoats. From across the courtroom, the bailiff glares at us above her librarian's glasses, alert to catch us napping. She must be an expert at judging the degrees of tedium.

◆ ◆ ◆

"Do you have to go back and be in the jail again tomorrow?" my little boy asks me at supper.

"Not jail," I correct him. "*Jury.* I'm in the jury."

"With real police?"

"Yes."

"And guns?"

"Yes, real guns."

25

On the second day there is much shifting of limbs in the jury box when the confidential informer, whom the police call I90, takes the stand. Curly-haired, thirty-three years old, bear-built and muscular like a middle-range wrestler, slow of eye, calm under the crossfire of questions, I90 works—when he works—as a drywall finisher. (In other words, he gets plasterboard ready for painting. It's a dusty, blinding job; you go home powdered white as a ghost, and you taste the joint-filler all night.) Like roughly one-quarter of the construction workers in the county, right now he's unemployed.

The story he tells is essentially this: Just under a year ago, two cops showed up at his house. They'd been tipped off that he had a mess of stolen goods in his basement, stuff he'd swiped from over in a neighboring county. "Now look here," the cops said to him, "you help us out with some cases we've got going, and we'll see what we can do to help you when this here burglary business comes to court." "Like how?" he said. "Like tell us what you know about hot property, and maybe finger a drug dealer or so." He said yes to that, with the two cops sitting at his kitchen table, and—zap!—he was transformed into I90. (Hearing of this miraculous conversion, I am reminded of Saul on the road to Damascus, the devil's agent suddenly seeing the light and joining the angels.) In this new guise he gave information that led to several arrests and some prison terms, including one for his cousin and two or three for other buddies.

In this particular case, his story goes on, he asked a good friend of his where a guy could buy some, you know, drugs. The friend's brother led him to Bennie's trailer, where Bennie offered to sell I90 about any kind of drug a man's heart could desire. "All I want's some hash," I90 told him, "but I got to go get some money off my old lady first." "Then go get it," said Bennie.

Where I90 went was to the police station. There they fixed him up to make a "controlled buy": searched him, searched his car; strapped a radio transmitter around his waist; took his money and gave him twenty police dollars to make the deal. Back I90 drove to Bennie's place, and on his tail in an unmarked police car drove Officer B., listening over the radio to every burp and glitch sent out by I90's secret transmitter. On the way, I90 picked up a six-pack of Budweiser. ("If you walk into a suspect's house drinking a can of beer," Officer B. later tells us, "usually nobody'll guess you're working for the police.") Inside the trailer, the woman Bennie lives with was now fixing supper, and her three young daughters were playing cards on the linoleum floor. I90 bought a gram of blond Lebanese hashish from Bennie for six dollars. Then I90 said that his old lady was on him bad to get her some downers, and Bennie obliged by selling him a couple of 714's (the white pills favored by movie stars and politicians) at seven dollars for the pair.

30

They shot the bull awhile, Bennie bragging about how big a dealer he used to be (ten pounds of hash and five hundred hits of acid a week), I90 jawing along like an old customer. After about twenty minutes in the trailer, I90 drove to a secluded spot near the L & N railroad depot, and there he handed over the hash and pills to Officer B., who milked the details out of him.

Four days later, I90 went through the same routine, this time buying two packets of cocaine — two "dimes' " worth — from Bennie for twenty dollars. Inside the trailer were half a dozen or so of Bennie's friends, drinking whiskey and smoking pot and watching TV and playing backgammon and generally getting the most out of a Friday night. Again Officer B. tailed I90, listened to the secret radio transmission, and took it all down in a debriefing afterwards behind the Colonial Bakery.

The lawyers burn up a full day leading I90 through this story, dropping questions like breadcrumbs to lure him on, Mr. Prosecutor trying to guide him out of the labyrinth of memory and Mr. Defense trying to get him lost. I90 refuses to get lost. He tells and retells his story without stumbling, intent as a wrestler on a dangerous hold.

On the radio news I hear that U.S. ships have intercepted freighters bound out from Beirut carrying tons and tons of Lebanese hashish, the very same prize strain of hash that I90 claims he bought from Bennie. Not wanting to irk the Lebanese government, the radio says, our ships let the freighters through. Tons and tons sailing across the Mediterranean — into how many one-gram slugs could that cargo be divided?

Out of jail the defense lawyers subpoena one of I90's brothers, who is awaiting his own trial on felony charges. He has a rabbity look about him, face pinched with fear, ready to bolt for the nearest exit. His canary yellow T-shirt is emblazoned with a scarlet silhouette of the Golden Gate Bridge. The shirt and the fear make looking at him painful. He is one of seven brothers and four sisters. Hearing that total of eleven children — the same number as in my father's family — I wonder if the parents were ever booked for burglary or other gestures of despair.

This skittish gent tells us that he always buys his drugs from his brother, good old I90. And good old I90, he tells us further, has a special fondness for snorting cocaine. Glowing there on the witness stand in his yellow shirt, dear brother gives the lie to one after another of I90's claims. But just when I'm about ready, hearing all of this fraternal gossip, to consign I90 to the level of hell reserved by Dante for liars, the prosecutor takes over the questioning. He soon draws out a confession that there has been a bitter feud recently between the two brothers. "And haven't you been found on three occasions to be mentally incompetent to stand trial?" the prosecutor demands.

"Yessir," mutters the brother.

"And haven't you spent most of the past year in and out of mental institutions?"

"Yessir."

This second admission is so faint, like a wheeze, that I must lean forward to   40
hear it, even though I am less than two yards away. While the prosecutor lets this
damning confession sink into the jury, the rabbity brother just sits there, as if
exposed on a rock while the hawks dive, his eyes pinched closed.

By day three of the trial, we jurors are no longer strangers to one another.
Awaiting our entry into court, we exhibit wallet photos of our children, of nieces
and nephews. We moan in chorus about our Christmas shopping lists. The
caterer tells about serving 3,000 people at a basketball banquet. The boisterous
old lady, to whom we have all taken a liking, explains how the long hairs on her
white cats used to get on her husband's black suit pants until she put the cats out
in the garage with heating pads in their boxes.

"Where do you leave your car?" the accountant asks.

"On the street," explains the lady. "I don't want to crowd those cats. They're
particular as all get-out."

People compare their bowling scores, their insurance rates, their diets. The
mason, who now weighs about 300 pounds, recounts how he once lost 129
pounds in nine months. His blood pressure got so bad he had to give up dieting,
and inside of a year he'd gained all his weight back and then some. The nurse,
who wrestles the bloated or shriveled bodies of elderly paupers at the city's old
folks' home, complains about her leg joints, and we all sympathize. The security
guard entertains us with sagas about shoplifters. We compare notes on car wrecks,
on where to get a transmission overhauled, on the outgoing college football
coach and the incoming city mayor. We talk, in fact, about everything under the
sun except the trial.

In the hall, where we line up for our reentry into the courtroom, a sullen boy   45
sits at a table scrawling on a legal pad. Line after line he copies the same sentence: "I never will steal anything ever again." More penance. He's balancing on
the first rung of a ladder that leads up—or down—to the electric chair. Somewhere in the middle of the ladder is a good long prison sentence, and that, I calculate, is what is at stake in our little drug-dealing case.

On the third day of testimony, we learn that I90 has been hidden away
overnight by police. After he stepped down from the witness stand yesterday,
Bennie's mate, Rebecca, greeted the informant outside in the lobby and threatened to pull a bread knife out of her purse and carve him into mincemeat. I look
with new interest at the stolid, bulky, black-haired woman who has been sitting
since the beginning of the trial right behind the defendant. From time to time
she has leaned forward, touched Bennie on the shoulder, and bent close to whisper something in his good ear. She reminds me of the Amish farm wives of my
Ohio childhood—stern, unpainted, built stoutly for heavy chores, her face a
fortress against outsiders.

When Rebecca takes the stand, just half a dozen feet from where I sit in
chair thirteen, I sense a tigerish fierceness beneath her numb surface. She plods
along behind the prosecutor's questions until he asks her, rhetorically, whether
she would like to see Bennie X put in jail; then she lashes out. God no, she

doesn't want him locked away. Didn't he take her in when she had two kids already and a third in the oven, and her first husband run off, and the cupboards empty? And haven't they been living together just as good as married for eight years, except while he was in jail, and don't her three little girls call him Daddy? And hasn't he been working on the city garbage trucks, getting up at four in the morning, coming home smelling like other people's trash, and hasn't she been bagging groceries at the supermarket, her hands slashed with paper cuts, and her mother looking after the girls, all so they can keep off the welfare? Damn right she doesn't want him going to any prison.

What's more, Rebecca declares, Bennie don't deserve prison because he's clean. Ever since he got out of the slammer a year ago, he's quit dealing. He's done his time and he's mended his ways and he's gone straight. What about that sale of cocaine? the prosecutor wants to know. It never happened, Rebecca vows. She was there in the trailer the whole blessed night, and she never saw Bennie sell nobody nothing, least of all cocaine, which he never used because it's too expensive — it'll run you seventy-five dollars a day — and which he never sold even when he was dealing. The prosecutor needles her: How can she remember that particular night so confidently? She can remember, she flares at him, because early that evening she got a call saying her sister's ten-year-old crippled boy was fixing to die, and all the family was going to the children's hospital in Indianapolis to watch him pass away. That was a night she'll never forget as long as she lives.

When I was a boy, my friends and I believed that if you killed a snake, the mate would hunt you out in your very bed and strangle or gnaw or smother you. We held a similar belief regarding bears, wolves, and mountain lions, although we were much less likely to run into any of those particular beasts. I have gone years without remembering that bit of child's lore, until today, when Rebecca's tigerish turn on the witness stand revives it. I can well imagine her stashing a bread knife in her purse. And if she loses her man for years and stony years, and has to rear those three girls alone, the cupboards empty again, she might well jerk that knife out of her purse one night and use it on something other than bread.

During recess, we thirteen sit in the jury room and pointedly avoid talking about the bread knife. The mason tells how a neighbor kid's Ford Pinto skidded across his lawn and onto his front porch, blocking the door and nosing against the picture window. "I took the wheels off and chained the bumper to my maple tree until his daddy paid for fixing my porch." 50

Everyone, it seems, has been assaulted by a car or truck. Our vehicular yarns wind closer and closer about the courthouse. Finally, two of the women jurors — the cigarillo-smoking caterer and the elderly cat lady — laugh nervously. The two of them were standing just inside the plate-glass door of the courthouse last night, the caterer says, when along came a pickup truck, out poked an arm from the window, up flew a smoking beer can, and then BAM! the can exploded. "We jumped a yard in the air!" cries the old woman. "We thought it was some of Bennie's mean-looking friends," the caterer admits. Everybody laughs at the tableau of speeding truck, smoking can, exploding cherry bomb, leaping jurors. Then we choke into sudden silence, as if someone has grabbed each of us by the throat.

◆ ◆ ◆

Four of Bennie's friends—looking not so much mean as broken, like shell-shocked refugees—testify on his behalf during the afternoon of day three. Two of them are out-of-work men in their twenties, with greasy hair to their shoulders, fatigue jackets, and clodhopper boots: their outfits and world-weary expressions are borrowed from record jackets. They are younger versions of the old men with caved-in faces who crouch on benches downstairs, sheltering from December. The other two witnesses are young women with reputations to keep up, neater than the scruffy men; gold crosses dangle over their sweaters, and gum cracks between crooked teeth. All four speak in muttered monosyllables and orphaned phrases, as if they are breaking a long vow of silence and must fetch bits and pieces of language from the archives of memory. They were all at Bennie's place on the night of the alleged cocaine sale, and they swear in unison that no such sale took place.

Officer B., the puppetmaster who pulled the strings on I90, swears just as adamantly that both the sales, of cocaine and of hash, *did* take place, for he listened to the proceedings over the radio in his unmarked blue Buick. He is a sleepy-eyed man in his mid-thirties, about the age of the informant and the defendant, a law-upholding alter ego for those skewed souls.

Double-chinned, padded with the considerable paunch that seems to be issued along with the police badge, Officer B. answers Mr. Prosecutor and Mr. Defense in a flat, walkie-talkie drawl, consulting a sheaf of notes in his lap, never contradicting himself. Yes, he neglected to tape the opening few minutes of the first buy, the minutes when the exchange of hashish and money actually took place. Why? "I had a suspicion my batteries were weak, and I wanted to hold off." And, yes, he did erase the tape of the debriefing that followed buy number one. Why? "It's policy to reuse the old cassettes. Saves the taxpayers' money." And, yes, the tape of the second buy is raw, indecipherable noise, because a blaring TV in the background drowns out all human voices. (Listening to the tape, we can understand nothing in the scrawking except an ad for the American Express Card.) The tapes, in other words, don't prove a thing. What it all boils down to is the word of the law and of the unsavory informer versus the word of the many-times-convicted defendant, his mate, and his friends.

Toward the end of Officer B.'s testimony, there is a resounding clunk, like a   55
muffled explosion, at the base of the witness stand. We all jump—witness, judge, jury, onlookers—and only relax when the prosecutor squats down and discovers that a pair of handcuffs has fallen out of Officer B.'s belt. Just a little reminder of the law's muscle. All of us were envisioning bombs. When Officer B. steps down, the tail of his sportcoat is hitched up over the butt of his gun.

The arrest: A squad car pulls up to the front of the trailer, and out the trailer's back door jumps Bennie, barefooted, wearing T-shirt and cut-off jeans. He dashes away between tarpaper shacks, through dog yards, over a stubbled field (his bare feet bleeding), through a patch of woods to a railroad cut. Behind him puffs a skinny cop (who recounts this scene in court), shouting, "Halt! Police!" But Bennie never slows down until he reaches that railroad cut, where he stumbles, falls, rolls down to the tracks like the sorriest hobo. The officer draws his gun.

Bennie lifts his hands for the familiar steel cuffs. The two of them trudge back to the squad car, where Officer B. reads the arrest warrant and Bennie blisters everybody with curses.

The judge later instructs us that flight from arrest may be regarded as evidence, not of guilt but of *consciousness* of guilt. Oh ho! A fine distinction! Guilt for what! Selling drugs? Playing hooky? Original sin? Losing his job at Coca-Cola? I think of those bleeding feet, the sad chase. I remember a drunken uncle who stumbled down a railroad cut, fell asleep between the tracks, and died of fear when a train passed over.

On day four of the trial, Bennie himself takes the stand. He is shorter than I thought, and fatter — too many months of starchy jail food and no exercise. With exceedingly long thumbnails he scratches his jaw. When asked a question, he rolls his eyes, stares at the ceiling, then answers in a gravelly country voice, the voice of a late-night disk jockey. At first he is gruffly polite, brief in his replies, but soon he gets cranked up and rants in a grating monologue about his painful history.

He graduated from high school in 1968, worked eight months at RCA and Coca-Cola, had a good start, had a sweetheart, then the Army got him, made him a cook, shipped him to Vietnam. After a few weeks in the kitchen, he was transferred to the infantry because the fodder-machine was short of foot soldiers. "Hey, listen, man, I ain't nothing but a cook," he told them. "I ain't been trained for combat." And they said, "Don't you worry; you'll get on-the-job training. Learn or die." The artillery ruined his hearing. (Throughout the trial he has held a hand cupped behind one ear, and has followed the proceedings like a grandfather.) Some of his buddies got shot up. He learned to kill people. "We didn't even know what we was there for." To relieve his constant terror, he started doing drugs: marijuana, opium, just about anything that would ease a man's mind. Came home from Vietnam in 1971 a wreck, got treated like dirt, like a babykiller, like a murdering scumbag, and found no jobs. His sweetheart married an insurance salesman.

Within a year after his return he was convicted of shoplifting and burglary. He was framed on the second charge by a friend, but couldn't use his only alibi because he had spent the day of the robbery in bed with a sixteen-year-old girl, whose father would have put him away for statutory rape. As it was, he paid out two years in the pen, where he sank deeper into drugs than ever before. "If you got anything to buy or trade with, you can score more stuff in the state prisons than on the streets of Indianapolis." After prison, he still couldn't find work, couldn't get any help for his drug-thing from the Veterans' Administration, moved in with Rebecca and her three girls, eventually started selling marijuana and LSD. "Everytime I went to somebody for drugs, I got ripped off. That's how I got into dealing. If you're a user, you're always looking for a better deal."

In 1979 he was busted for selling hash, in 1980 for possessing acid, betrayed in both cases by the man from whom he had bought his stock. "He's a snitch, just a filthy snitch. You can't trust nobody." Back to prison for a year, back out again in December 1981. No jobs, no jobs, no damn jobs; then part-time on the city garbage truck, up at four in the morning, minus five degrees and the wind blowing

60

and the streets so cold his gloves stuck to the trash cans. Then March came, and this I90 guy showed up, wanted to buy some drugs, and "I told him I wasn't dealing any more. I done my time and gone straight. I told him he didn't have enough money to pay me for no thirty years in the can." (The prosecutor bristles, the judge leans meaningfully forward: we jurors are not supposed to have any notion of the sentence that might follow a conviction on this drug charge.)

In his disk-jockey voice, Bennie denies ever selling anything to this I90 snitch. (He keeps using the word "snitch": I think of tattle-tales, not this adult betrayal.) It was I90, he swears, who tried to sell *him* the hash. Now the pills, why, those he had lying around for a friend who never picked them up, and so he just gave them to I90. "They was give to me, and so I couldn't charge him nothing. They wasn't for me anyway. Downers I do not use. To me, life is a downer. Just to cope with every day, that is way down low enough for me." And as for the cocaine, he never laid eyes on it until the man produced that little plastic bag in court. "I don't use coke. It's too expensive. That's for the bigwigs and the upstanding citizens, as got the money."

Sure, he admits, he ran when the police showed up at his trailer. "I'm flat scared of cops. I don't like talking to them about anything. Since I got back from Vietnam, every time they cross my path they put bracelets on me." (He holds up his wrists. They are bare now, but earlier this morning, when I saw a deputy escorting him into the courthouse, they were handcuffed.) He refuses to concede that he is a drug addict, but agrees he has a terrible habit, "a gift from my country in exchange for me going overseas and killing a bunch of strangers."

After the arrest, forced to go cold turkey on his dope, he begged the jail doctor—"He's no kind of doctor, just one of them that fixes babies"—to zonk him out on something. And so, until the trial, he has spent eight months drowsing under Valium and Thorazine. "You can look down your nose at me for that if you want, but last month another vet hung himself two cells down from me." (The other guy was a scoutmaster, awaiting trial for sexually molesting one of his boys. He had a record of severe depression dating from the war, and used his belt for the suicide.)

"The problem with my life," says Bennie, "is Vietnam." For awhile after coming home, he slept with a knife under his pillow. Once, wakened suddenly, thinking he was still in Vietnam, he nearly killed his best friend. During the week of our trial, another Vietnam vet up in Indianapolis shot his wife in the head, imagining she was a gook. Neighbors got to him before he could pull out her teeth, as he used to pull out the teeth of the enemies he bagged over in Vietnam.

When I look at Bennie, I see a double image. He was drafted during the same month in which I, studying in England, gave Uncle Sam the slip. I hated that war, and feared it, for exactly the reasons he describes—because it was foul slaughter, shameful, sinful, pointless butchery. While he was over there killing and dodging, sinking into the quicksand of drugs, losing his hearing, storing up a lifetime's worth of nightmares, I was snug in England, filling my head with words. We both came home to America in the same year, I to job and family, he to nothing. Ten years after that homecoming, we stare across the courtroom at one another as into a funhouse mirror.

65

♦   ♦   ♦

As the twelve jurors file past me into the room where they will decide on Bennie's guilt or innocence, three of them pat my arm in a comradely way. They withdraw beyond a brass-barred gate; I sit down to wait on a deacon's bench in the hallway outside the courtroom. I feel stymied, as if I have rocketed to the moon only to be left riding the ship round and round in idle orbit while my fellow astronauts descend to the moon's surface. At the same time I feel profoundly relieved, because, after the four days of testimony, I still cannot decide whether Bennie truly sold those drugs, or whether I90, to cut down on his own prison time, set up this ill-starred Bennie for yet another fall. Time, time — it always comes down to time: in jail, job, and jury box we are spending and hoarding our only wealth, the currency of days.

Even through the closed door of the courtroom, I still hear the ticking of the clock. The sound reminds me of listening to my daughter's pulse through a stethoscope when she was still riding, curled up like a stowaway, in my wife's womb. Ask not for whom this heart ticks, whispered my unborn daughter through the stethoscope: it ticks for thee. So does the courtroom clock. It grabs me by the ear and makes me fret about time — about how little there is of it, about how we are forever bumming it from one another as if it were cups of sugar or pints of blood ("You got a minute?" "Sorry, have to run, not a second to spare"). Seize the day, we shout, to cheer ourselves; but the day has seized us and flings us forward pell-mell toward the end of all days.

Now and again there is a burst of laughter from the jury room, but it is always squelched in a hurry. They are tense, and laugh to relieve the tension, and then feel ashamed of their giddiness. Lawyers traipse past me — the men smoking, striking poses, their faces like lollipops atop their ties; the women teetering on high heels. The bailiff walks into our judge's office carrying a bread knife. To slice her lunch? As evidence against Rebecca? A moment later she emerges bearing a piece of cake and licking her fingers. Christmas parties are breaking out all over the courthouse.

Rebecca herself paces back and forth at the far end of my hallway, her steps as regular as the clock's tick, killing time. Her bearded and cross-wearing friends sidle up to comfort her, but she shrugs them away. Once she paces down my way, glances at the barred door of the jury room, hears muffled shouts. This she must take for good news, because she throws me a rueful smile before turning back.   70

Evidently the other twelve are as muddled by the blurred and contradictory "facts" of the case as I am, for they spend from noon until five reaching their decision. They ask for lunch. They ask for a dictionary. They listen again to the tapes. Sullen teenagers, following in the footsteps of Bennie and I90, slouch into the misdemeanor office across the hall from me; by and by they slouch back out again, looking unrepentant. At length the 300-pound mason lumbers up to the gate of the jury room and calls the bailiff. "We're ready as we're going to be." He looks bone-weary, unhappy, and dignified. Raising his eyebrows at me, he shrugs. Comrades in uncertainty.

The cast reassembles in the courtroom, the judge asks the jury for its decision, and the mason stands up to pronounce Bennie guilty. I stare at my boots. Finally I glance up, not at Bennie or Rebecca or the lawyers, but at my fellow jurors. They look distraught, wrung-out and despairing, as if they have just crawled out of a mine after an explosion and have left some of their buddies behind. Before quitting the jury room, they composed and signed a letter to the judge pleading with him to get some help—drug help, mind help, any help—for Bennie.

The ticking of the clock sounds louder in my ears than the judge's closing recital. But I do, with astonishment, hear him say that we must all come back tomorrow for one last piece of business. He is sorry, he knows we are worn out, but the law has prevented him from warning us ahead of time that we might have to decide on one more question of guilt.

The legal question posed for us on the morning of day five is simple: Has Bennie been convicted, prior to this case, of two or more unrelated felonies? If so, then he is defined by Indiana state law as a "habitual offender," and we must declare him to be such. We are shown affidavits for those earlier convictions—burglary, sale of marijuana, possession of LSD—and so the answer to the legal question is clear.

But the moral and psychological questions are tangled, and they occupy the jury for nearly five more hours on this last day of the trial. Is it fair to sentence a person again, after he has already served time for his earlier offenses? How does the prosecutor decide when to apply the habitual offender statute, and does its use in this case have anything to do with the political ambitions of the sleek young attorney? Did Bennie really steal that $150 stereo, for which he was convicted a decade ago, or did he really spend the day in bed with his sixteen-year-old girlfriend? Did Vietnam poison his mind and blight his life?

Two sheriff's deputies guard the jury today; another guards me in my own little cell. The bailiff would not let me stay out on the deacon's bench in the hall, and so, while a plainclothes detective occupies my old seat, I sit in a room lined with file cabinets and stare out like a prisoner through the glass door. "I have concluded," wrote Pascal, "that the whole misfortune of men comes from a single thing, and that is their inability to remain at rest in a room." I agree with him; nothing but that cruising deputy would keep me here.

This time, when the verdict is announced, Rebecca has her daughters with her, three little girls frightened into unchildlike stillness by the courtroom. Their lank hair and washed-out eyes remind me of my childhood playmates, the children of dead-end, used-up West Virginia coalminers who'd moved to Ohio in search of work. The mother and daughter are surrounded by half a dozen rough customers, guys my age with hair down over their shoulders and rings in their ears, with flannel shirts, unfocused eyes. Doubtless they are the reason so many holstered deputies and upholstered detectives are patrolling the courthouse, and the reason I was locked safely away in a cell while the jury deliberated.

When the mason stands to pronounce another verdict of guilty, I glimpse what I do not want to glimpse: Bennie flinging his head back, Rebecca snapping hers forward into her palms, the girls wailing.

The judge accompanies all thirteen of us into the jury room, where he keeps us for an hour while the deputies clear the rough customers from the courthouse. We are not to be alarmed, he reassures us; he is simply being cautious, since so much was at stake for the defendant. "How much?" the mason asks. "Up to twenty-four years for the drug convictions, plus a mandatory thirty years for the habitual offender charges," the judge replies. The cleaning woman, the nurse, and the TV repairman begin crying. I swallow carefully. For whatever it's worth, the judge declares comfortingly, he agrees with our decisions. If we knew as much about this Bennie as he knows, we would not be troubled. And that is just the splinter in the brain, the fact that we know so little — about Bennie, about Vietnam, about drugs, about ourselves — and yet we must grope along in our ignorance, pronouncing people guilty or innocent, squeezing out of one another that precious fluid, time.

And so I do my five days in the thirteenth chair. Bennie may do as many as   80
fifty-four years in prison, buying his drugs from meaner dealers, dreaming of land mines and of his adopted girls, checking the date on his watch, wondering at what precise moment the hinges of his future slammed shut.   [1987]

THINKING ABOUT THE TEXT

1. Trace the references to time in this essay. In what ways does Sanders make it a central subject? Note his references to bombs. What is the effect of his emphasis on them?

2. On the whole, is your impression of the jury positive? Negative? Somewhere in between? Identify some things that influence your opinion. Is there any other information about the jury that you wish Sanders had provided? If so, what sort of information?

3. Rather than being a full-fledged juror, Sanders was an alternate, occupying the thirteenth chair. What, if any, were the advantages of his position for him as an observer? What, if any, were the disadvantages?

4. At one point in his essay, Sanders compares himself to Bennie. Does this comparison make sense to you? Why, or why not? Throughout the essay, Sanders emphasizes the sense of community that developed among the jurors. To what extent does he call attention to Bennie's community — that is, Bennie's friends and family? Does he treat this community in a way you think appropriate? Explain.

5. Are you inclined to believe that justice was served in Bennie's case? Why, or why not? What additional sort of information, if any, would you need to be sure?

JOYCE CAROL OATES
I, the Juror

Since the early 1960s, Joyce Carol Oates (b. 1938) has published prolifically in all the genres represented in this book. In the 1990s alone, she wrote several well-regarded novels, including Because It Is Bitter, and Because It Is My Heart *(1990),* Black Water *(1992),* Foxfire *(1993),* What I Lived For *(1994), and* We Were the Mulvaneys *(1996). She has also written a book of essays,* The Faith of a Writer:

Life, Craft, Art (2003), *about writing. Her most recent book is a collection of stories,* I Am No One You Know (2004). *At present, Oates teaches at Princeton University. The following essay was first published in a 1995 issue of the literary journal* Witness.

In pursuit of an abstract principle of Justice. In pursuit of that sense of community of which Justice is both the consequence and the catalyst. In pursuit of some wavering, insubstantial, indefinable expression of one's heart's desire — that, as citizens of a country, and not mere "individuals," we participate in an action that is unbiased, fair, equitable, *right.*

Yet — "Judge not, lest ye be judged." As if the very action through which Justice might be realized brings with it mortal risk.

When the pink, smudgily computer-printed summons from the Sheriff's Office, County of Mercer, Trenton, New Jersey, arrived in the mail for SMITH, JOYCE C., notifying that I was scheduled to serve as a petit juror for no less than five days in late August, in the Mercer County Courthouse, my feelings were ambivalent. Throughout adulthood I had always hoped to be called for jury duty — while living in Detroit, and more recently in Princeton — but I had never been selected; I did not think of it as a "duty" so much as a privilege, very likely an adventure. To live out one's life as an American citizen without having once served as a juror, no matter how minor the trial, would be a pity — wouldn't it? Like not being caught up, at least once, in the romance of a Presidential campaign; indeed, like never having voted. We who oscillate between idealism and skepticism, with the quicksilver instability of those sub-atomic particles that are now one thing and now its opposite, begin after all as idealists.

The very *impersonality* of the summons had an air of romance for me — for it was "Joyce C. Smith" and not "Joyce Carol Oates" who had been called. Rare for me now, thus the more precious, any public experience in which I can be invisible, as if bodiless: that fundamental necessity for the writer.

Strictly speaking, "Joyce C. Smith" has no existence except as a legal entity: a husband's wife in a patriarchal society. (One day, will the acquisition of a husband's name, and the eradication of one's maiden name, come to seem as curious a custom as its reverse would seem now?) This legal entity is duly registered as a property (co-)owner and voter. There are no publications indexed under "Joyce C. Smith" in any library, and there is no one on the faculty of Princeton University, where I teach, bearing that name. Since there was no provision in the questionnaire accompanying the summons for the explanation of a "career" name, and I feared a punitive misfiring in the unimaginative computer brain in Trenton, I thought it most pragmatic to identify "Joyce C. Smith" as a housewife and teacher. (Some years ago, in Detroit and Windsor, Ontario, "Joyce C. Smith" had in fact taught college.) This seemed to me to conform to the letter of the law, and to give me a fair chance to get onto a jury.

(I should explain that the local consensus is that Princeton residents are routinely dismissed from juries in Trenton, no matter our hope to serve. Prosecutors don't want us because we are collectively perceived as "liberals" likely to interpret

5

crime in terms of societal pressures; defense attorneys don't want us because we are perceived as "intellectuals" likely to resist rhetorical manipulation.)

Any relationship with the law, as with any governmental bureaucracy, is qualified by a certain air of menace and threat; and so I did, for all my theoretical enthusiasm, feel ambivalent about the summons. To serve as a juror is not a volitional option: names are randomly selected from a merged list of registered voters and licensed drivers, and once your name is on such a list, stored in the computer, it is virtually impossible to get it off. And there is, in the New Jersey Statute, this inhospitable warning: *Every person summoned as a Grand or Petit Juror who shall either fail to appear or refuse, without reasonable excuse, to serve or be sworn, shall be fined by the Court and may be punished as for Contempt of Court.* (Meaning, bluntly, that you can be sent to jail for declining to participate in an action that may send another person to jail.)

Though, as a novelist, I have done extensive research into criminal law and into courtroom procedure, I had attended only a single trial in my life, and that not on a daily basis, long ago, in the 1950s, when I was a junior high school student in Lockport, New York. Two young men were being tried on charges of first-degree murder in a robbery slaying. Vivid as certain memories of that experience are—the old courthouse, the airlessness, the stiff, resigned postures of the accused men seated at the defense table, the elderly judge on his raised platform, in his somber judicial gown—I seem not to remember the verdict. (Probably I was not there for the verdict.) My general sense of the trial was its deliberate snail's pace, its lethargy. Its public display of an adult, and therefore an impenetrable ritual of which I had no clearer comprehension than an observer, say, of a gigantic grinding machine would have of its inner workings, seen from without. Your instinct is to know that you don't ever want to get caught in it.

One afternoon, during an interlude of fatiguing, seemingly pointless repetition, I must have surreptitiously opened a book to read, and a sheriff's deputy leaned toward me, to say in an undertone, "Better close that book. The judge will kick you out of the courtroom if he sees you reading." How startled I was, and how struck by the fact that in a courtroom, this highest expression of adult ritual, the judge, the emblem of all patriarchy, has the authority to determine where an individual's eyes might rest!

Fortunately, they can't see into our skulls.   10

The Mercer County Courthouse, built in 1903 in the generic American courthouse style, still exudes, from the street, a weatherworn dignity; its dank, antiquated interior exudes what might be called "atmosphere." We prospective jurors descended in a rambling herd into the basement, promptly at 8:30 A.M. on August 26, 1991, where we were crowded together in two low-ceilinged rooms, where we would sit on folding chairs while we waited to be called up to a courtroom on the fifth floor.

A prophetic sign was posted on a wall: *They also serve who only stand and wait.—John Milton.* The sign was yellowed with age.

And so we waited. Some of us tried to read or work, until the blaring television sets (game shows, soap operas) became too distracting; a few of us, the more restless, began to pace in the corridor immediately outside the jury assembly room, which was allowed by our overseers so long as it appeared, or could be made to appear, that we were really going to or coming from the restrooms. Other areas of the courthouse were forbidden to us (we were wearing white jurors' badges), and doors at the far end of two long corridors, opening to the outside, were conspicuously posted EMERGENCY ONLY — ALARM SET OFF IF OPENED. Already, by 11:00 A.M., I was tracing elongated figure eights in the corridors, with a hope of forestalling early glimmerings of panic.

I learned that, of the 599 citizens of Mercer County who had been summoned for jury duty that week, 500 had managed to exempt themselves. This in itself was certainly deflating; yet more deflating was it to be warned, by one of the assembly room overseers (they were all women, with a look of being prison matrons in disguise as office workers), that, should any of us leave the courthouse without authorization, an officer from the Mercer County Sheriff's Department was empowered to follow after us and arrest us — "This has been known to happen." Indeed, the bulletin boards in the assembly room were festooned with clippings celebrating the power of the state to arrest, fine, and confine: accounts of citizens who, having failed to comply with the summons to jury duty, were surprised and arrested in their homes or in their places of work, fined hundreds of dollars, jailed for three days and/or sentenced to one hundred hours of "community service."

I asked one of the administrators how long we might wait to be called up to a courtroom, and the woman answered, curtly, "Until you're called." Was it possible, I asked, that we would not be called at all that day? "Yes, it's possible," she said. I approached another administrator, a woman of my approximate age, to ask why the system was so punitive, and so inefficient; and the woman stared at me with a hurt, swimming look, and said, "I'm sorry you find it so!" "But don't *you* find it so?" I asked reasonably, indicating the dreary room of glassy-eyed men and women, and the woman said angrily, "The way it used to be done, two hundred people were here for two solid weeks — and that was that." When I expressed dismay, she repeated, with an air of threat, "The way it used to be done, two hundred people were here for two solid weeks — *and that was that.*"

"I see," I said.

At last, shortly before noon, a panel of fifty men and women, including "Joyce C. Smith, Juror 552," was summoned to a courtroom on the fifth floor. Though I'd been warned that this part of the jury selection can be deadly — no reading material is allowed in the courtroom, and, of course, no pacing is permitted — it was impossible not to feel a hopeful anticipation.

We were welcomed to her courtroom by Judge Judith A. Yaskin, an attractive, highly articulate woman in her mid- or late forties, who presented the case to be tried and explained the jury selection process. The case was aggravated assault; the defendant, a thirty-year-old black man, and his attorney, and the prosecuting attorney, were in the room. Selecting the jury begins with sheer chance: pellets with numbers corresponding to jurors' numbers are shuffled and drawn by an officer of the court, as in a bingo game. In theory, the jury of fourteen (including two alternates) could be drawn from the first fourteen pellets, but during the voir

15

dire jurors are exempted for various reasons (admitted prejudices, prior knowledge of the case to be tried, connections with the defendant, law enforcement officials, etc., as well as the peremptory challenge dismissals by the prosecuting and defense attorneys) and new jurors have to be selected and questioned. The procedure involves numberless repetitions and can be protracted for weeks in a trial of major proportions; the case to be tried, here, fortunately, was a minor one, and a jury was constituted by early afternoon.

To my surprise, number 552 was drawn from the lottery, and I took my seat in the jury box as Juror Number Eleven. When Judge Yaskin questioned me I identified myself as a housewife and teacher, with the intention of explaining my professional career in more detail if required; but the judge had no further questions. (As it would turn out at the trial's end, Judge Yaskin had recognized me as a writer, but seemed to have thought that my writing career was not relevant to the procedure. Neither the defense counsel nor the prosecuting attorney took the slightest interest in me, except perhaps as a malleable presence on the jury. What good fortune: I'd had a nightmare fantasy of being forced to explain to a gathering of quizzical, bemused strangers that I was a "writer," of whom no one would have heard — like the tragic Dorothy Richardson, in a nursing home at the end of her life, believed delusional because she insisted she'd been a novelist.) The focus of the voir dire was on jurors who had been victims of crimes: could they be impartial in judging a criminal case? How sobering to learn that so many jurors, most of them residents of Trenton, were victims of multiple crimes. Burglary, vandalism, assault. One woman had been burglarized five times in recent years, but insisted she would be impartial as a juror. In each case Judge Yaskin asked if the criminals had been apprehended, and in each case, remarkably, the answer was "No." A message rippled through our midst: *Crime goes largely unpunished in Trenton;* and, a variant, *Criminals lead charmed lives in certain regions of America.*

But here we were gathered, in a solemn ritual, to isolate, contemplate, and pass judgment on a crime. One had to conclude that the defendant was sheerly unlucky to have been caught.

Of course most of the crime victims were summarily rejected by the defense counsel, as if their insistences upon being impartial were handily recognized as lies. The defense counsel also rejected the only juror in the box to have acknowledged living in Princeton (I had not been asked where I lived), and the single man, of the approximately fifty male prospective jurors in the courthouse that day, to be wearing a suit.

(What of courtroom attire? To my surprise, the majority of my fellow jurors were dressed extremely casually. Here and there a man conspicuous in sport coat and tie, a few women in high heels and stockings, but, overall, the tide of prospective jurors looked as if they'd wandered off from a tour bus, in quintessentially American play clothes for adults. Blue jeans, slacks, T-shirts, shorts were in colorful abundance, contrasting with the more formal, subdued attire of the officers of the court. One youngish man made a comical sight as, in brief nylon-blue running shorts and T-shirt cut high on the shoulders, he came from the rear of the courtroom when his number was called to enter the jury box, passing close below the judge in her black robe. The death penalty is still on the statute in New

20

Jersey: I couldn't help but wonder if jurors in Mickey Mouse sweatshirts vote to send defendants to their deaths.)

Another startling development, for those of us new to courtroom procedure, was the mechanical rejection of certain jurors on the basis of skin pigmentation. Overt racial prejudice has become so anachronistic, we like to think, or, in any case, associated with marginal renegade behavior, it is both shocking and puzzling to encounter it in a public place; still more, in the churchy atmosphere of a courtroom. Since the defendant to be tried was black, however, the prosecuting attorney exercised his right of peremptory challenge to reject as many persons of color as possible. Here was the most crude, the most brainless, racial discrimination in action, entirely countenanced by law: "Your Honor, please thank and excuse Juror Number Two," the attorney said, and a light-skinned black, startled, was urged to leave the box. Another juror was called, a young Chinese-American woman, and again the attorney said, "Your Honor, please thank and excuse Juror Number Two," and she too left the box. Another lottery draw, another juror, everyone stared as another black man came forward, and again — "Your Honor, please thank and excuse Juror Number Two." And he too left. Was this a comic routine? The next juror, as an oddity of luck would have it (by far the majority of the prospective jurors were Caucasian), was also a black man — an undergraduate, as it would turn out, at Middlebury College; hardly was he seated when the prosecuting attorney said, in a flat, inflectionless voice, "Your Honor, please thank and excuse Juror Number Two." And the young man too was ushered out, with a look of surprise, disappointment, hurt, embarrassment. Perhaps he had never before experienced such crude racial discrimination so personally? so publicly? in a gathering of elders?

Finally, and ironically, Juror Number Two was in fact a black man. The prosecuting attorney must have run out of options.

There is a mystique, homey and comforting as Norman Rockwell paintings, 25 of trial-by-jury in America. Trial-by-jury-of-one's-peers.

A mystique predicated upon not having contemplated one's peers very closely in a while.

There is a mystique, too, accruing to the dignity, the sanctity of the court, which is meant to resemble a church. Were we not all obliged to swear, on the Holy Bible, to truthfulness? (In fact, there were not enough Bibles for fourteen jurors, so we had to share them, awkwardly. I wondered at my integrity as, an atheist, I murmured with the others, "I do swear." Perhaps my fingers were not exactly touching the simulated-leather hide of the Holy Book?) Somewhere in our judicial tradition the separation of church and state, surely one of the great principles of American society, seems to have been overlooked.

The trial was not a complex one, though with interruptions and delays it stretched out over several days. There were only five witnesses, four for the prosecution, and the defendant himself, who testified last. The charge of aggravated assault had been brought against a thirty-year-old black man apparently involved in the drug trade who had beaten a young black woman who he believed had informed on him to the police after a drug raid in January 1990; one had the sense (as a juror, denied virtually any contextual information, and made, from time to time, to leave the courtroom, one is absorbed in trying to figure out what *really* happened, what the *real* story is) that the defendant was someone the Trenton police and the prosecutor's office hoped to send to prison since, perhaps, they had not succeeded in sending him away on other charges. Otherwise the case, in crime-afflicted Trenton, seemed an anomaly.

"I am the judge of the law," Judge Yaskin told the jury several times, with the patience of a grade school teacher, "— and you are the judge of the facts." Hearing witnesses' testimonies that often conflicted, forced to sift through such "facts" as are proffered by such testimony, and having to remember everything (jurors may not take notes in the courtroom), one quickly becomes bedazzled, confused. Why take the word of one witness over another, when all sound sincere and plausible? Is there a singular truth that *must* exist, and can be brought to bear against the exactitude of the New Jersey criminal statute? (We jurors were to decide whether aggravated assault had been committed — whether the defendant "knowingly, purposefully, and recklessly intended to inflict serious physical injury, or did inflict serious physical injury." As if there were no significant difference between act and intention.) The witnesses' testimonies gave us, all but one of us Caucasian, a painfully intimate look at the black Trenton underclass; I found myself close to tears during the victim's testimony, hearing of her life, her activities as a crack addict, forced to examine, with the other jurors, her slightly disfigured left eyelid — the claim of the prosecution being that the woman had suffered permanent damage as a result of the beating. And what irony — the woman had her right arm in a sling, and a badly bruised face, from what was apparently a very recent beating, unrelated to the case being tried. (Of course, the woman's present condition was never explained.)

There was much sorrow here, and sordidness; and hopelessness; yet an air now and then of the farcical as well. As in a ghetto version of "Rashomon," witnesses supplied wildly varying details, each convinced he or she was remembering correctly. Did the alleged assault take place at noon of January 21, 1990? at 4:30 P.M.? at 7:30 P.M.? Was the defendant, charged with kicking the victim in the head, wearing yellow steel-toed boots, as the victim swore, or black leather boots, as his cousin swore, or, as the defendant swore, black sneakers? One eyewitness saw only kicks, not punches; another saw punches, but no kicks. All of the prosecution witnesses, it developed through cross-examination, had criminal records; yet, because of legal protocol, we were never told if the defendant had a criminal record. (Later, during the jury's deliberation, some of the jurors seemed actually to have thought that the defendant was "clean.") How frustrating the testimonies were, how tediously protracted by the defense counsel's cross-examination, how repetitive, stupefyingly dull — as we traced and retraced the same narrow terrain, like a snail with a motor imbalance. I wondered if, my eyes open, I might begin to hallucinate.

And then, of course, as in fictionalized trials, the attorneys quickly called out, "Your Honor, I object!" when questioning got interesting; when crucial matters arose, as often they did, the judge and the attorneys conferred out of earshot, while we jurors looked on deaf and mute; at any time court might be recessed,

30

and we would be sent out to the jury room, forbidden to discuss the case, and with no knowledge of when we might be summoned back, or if we would be summoned back at all. (Trials often end abruptly, and jurors, to that moment flattered into believing themselves essential to the execution of justice, are summarily dismissed and sent home.) To experience the legal system as a layman is to discover yourself on a playing field in the midst of a bizarre, intricately structured game with unknown rules and a private language; the jury itself, though the fabled glory of our American criminal justice system, resembles nothing so much as a large, ungainly, anachronistic beast with one eye patched over, a gag in its mouth, cotton stuffed in an ear, a leg shackled. Yet the delusion persists, the jury judges "facts."

"She was fidgeting all the time, she was nervous."

"She said she was going *down* the stairs, not *up.*"

"How can you believe her—she's a crack addict."

"People like that, Walnut Street, Trenton—that's how they live."   35

"Her eye didn't look like it was hurt that bad."

"I'd almost believe the defendant, over her."

"They're all a pack of liars."

So often, in recent years, has the reflex of blaming the victim been exposed by the media, some of us have been led to think it no longer presents much of a danger to impartial judgment in cases of assault and rape, especially cases of male defendant and female victims. Certainly, feminists would like to think that this is so, that some progress has been made. Yet, clearly, human instinct is conservative, even primitive: if you are a female victim pleading your case, and others can discover a way to blame you for your misfortune, they will do so. (After the St. John's University trial, in which white defendants were found not guilty of sexual assault against a young black woman, a commentator asked, "When have white men ever been found guilty of raping black women?") As if the victim, and not the defendant, were on trial. And especially, as in our case, if the victim is of another class and race, a self-confessed, if former, drug addict . . . The unvoiced judgment is: *She got what she deserved.*

The jury on which I served was very likely a representative cross-section of   40
area citizens, equally divided in gender, middle to lower-middle class incomes, eleven Caucasians and one black; and my experience in their midst left me shaken and depressed for days. So this is what a jury thinks, says, does! So this is the mystique in action! Certainly these men and women were not evil, nor even malicious. I am not suggesting that. I believe that most of them were well-intentioned and not racist, at least not consciously racist. But they were not thoughtful people; they were not, in a way, serious people. Among them, I was the only one to take notes during our recesses from the court; I was the only one, as it would turn out, who seemed to have considered the black witnesses, and especially the victim, as human beings like myself. (How vain this sounds! I wish there were some other way to express it.) When we were sequestered in our jury room and might have used the time to think quietly about the case (discussions

are forbidden until a trial is over), most of the jurors chatted and laughed as if there were nothing of much import going on. Testimony that seemed to me self-evidently painful, heartrending in what it suggested of the profound distance between our worlds and theirs, slid off them as if uttered in a foreign language: a language that had nothing to do with them. (What of the single black juror? He was an older man, and probably said about five words during the discussion. Younger and possibly more assertive blacks had been bumped from the jury.) White jurors, reflecting the bias of their society, are notorious for not taking very seriously crimes by blacks committed against blacks, and this bias was borne out by our jury; if the victim had been, not black, but a young white woman, they would surely have seen the charge differently.

As it was, I was astonished by the ferocity of my fellow jurors' attack on the victim's testimony, which was not only pitiless but derisive, contemptuous. Men led the attack immediately, before we were even seated around the table—the most vociferous was, in fact, the man who had showed up on the first day in running shorts—but women joined in, too. Hours of earnest testimony were discounted by a wave of the hand, a "gut-level" opinion; inconsistencies in testimony were interpreted as evidence of falsehood even as the jurors themselves misremembered facts. There was no effort on the part of the jury foreman to assure an orderly discussion, and very likely this would not have made much of a difference in the quality of the discourse, which was on about the level of a group of people discussing where to go to eat.

Perhaps human beings have only a measure of sympathy for others, and little to spare. Perhaps there is a human instinct, a gene for survival, that shuts down identification with men and women in distress who are different from ourselves, and without power. I am trying to separate my own biases from those of my fellow jurors, who of course have a right to bias, and, as sworn jurors, the privilege of voting as intuition urged: they reacted swiftly, and they reacted without subtlety or ambiguity, and they reacted in near-unanimity in rejecting the prosecution's charge against the defendant. They simply did not take it, nor the world from which it sprang, seriously.

After deliberation, the twelve of us agreed upon a verdict of "guilty" for the lesser charge of simple assault. (Even the defense counsel acknowledged that something had been done to the victim to account for her injuries.) How many hours we jurors spent together, how many hours the protracted ceremony of the trial consumed, like an antique machine clanking and grinding and laboring to bring forth a verdict any Trenton judge might have handed down after a few hours' review of the case—multiply this by thousands, hundreds of thousands, adding in such cases as the child molestation trial in Los Angeles a few years ago that took two years—two years!—and you have a criminal justice system that not only fails to guarantee "justice" but is cumbersome, inefficient, outmoded. If jurors were really possessed of unique qualities of divination conferred upon them when they are sworn in, the archaic system might justify itself; but, as my personal experience suggests, this is not the case.

Moreover, verdicts of "guilty" handed down by petit juries are frequently of little real consequence. Judges do the actual sentencing, which might be a fine, or probation, or community service, or months in prison, or years; if years, the prison parole board determines the sentence. This is as it should be, since the idea of juries also determining sentences would be a nightmare.

In retrospect, I am grateful for my experience as a juror in Trenton, New Jersey, though it is not one I am eager to repeat. I came into contact with an estimable, indeed judicious judge; I experienced the procedure of a small, circumscribed criminal case; I was disabused, by my fellow jurors, of certain romantic illusions. And I was paid $5 a day by the State of New Jersey—which, considering the contribution we made, seems about right.

45

Afterword

I wrote this essay immediately after the conclusion of the trial. Months later, I am still haunted by the experience. What most distressed me was the assumption, so unexamined as to be chilling, on the part of the white jurors, that they belonged to a world, if not to a species, wholly distinct from the blacks of Trenton's underclass whom they were empowered to judge. There is *we*, and there is *they*—and an unbridgeable distance between.

In Richard Wright's classic novel *Native Son* (1940), the tragic argument is made that white racist America has so dehumanized Negro Americans that, like Bigger Thomas, the eponymous hero of the novel, some of the more aggressive are in danger of becoming primitive, brutalized, unfeeling killers (of Negroes as well as Caucasians: Bigger Thomas murders a young black woman as viciously and as gratuitously as he murders the white millionaire's daughter); these very Negroes are then loathed, repudiated, and sentenced to death, for being dehumanized. Bigger Thomas can have no "feeling" for his victims because he has been made incapable of human feeling.

Yet, as Wright says in his memoir *Black Boy* (1944):

> After I had learned other ways of life I used to brood upon the unconscious irony of those who felt that Negroes led so passional an existence! I saw that what had been taken as our emotional strength was our negative confusions, our flights, our frenzy under pressure.

In judging others, the burden is ours to transcend the limits of self; in terms of race, the limits, and blindnesses, of race. How is this possible? Who is qualified? Is the concept of human Justice a commonly held delusion, as readily served by, say, a lottery, as by human effort and collaboration? After so many weeks, I am still preoccupied with the experience of having been a juror, serving on that particular jury, in a representative American city of the present time. I hear again the smug assertions of certain of my fellow jurors; I see several faces with unwanted oneiric clarity; obsessively, I see the purse-lipped white-haired retiree who had denounced the blacks in the trial as a "pack of liars" sitting reading the New Testament, as he had done somewhat conspicuously during some of our sequestered time together. Though I am Caucasian, thus one of their own, the proposition unnerved me: *What if these people were entrusted with my life? What sympathy would they have for me?—or for one another?*

The shadow that falls upon us at such sobering moments is nothing less than   50 our estrangement from humanity, and surely there is no estrangement more profound and more corrosive. For juries too should submit to judgment. But in what court—and who to preside?   [1995]

THINKING ABOUT THE TEXT

1. What images do you get of Oates as you read her essay? Refer to details of the text that influence your impression of her. Overall, to what extent do you trust and respect her as a reporter?

2. In the second half of her essay, Oates focuses on the trial itself and the jury's subsequent deliberations. What do you sense her basically doing in the first half?

3. Oates seems to have been surprised by the behavior of the other jurors. Does the conduct she describes surprise you? Identify aspects of your past experiences that affect your answer. After Oates published her essay, the U.S. Supreme Court ruled that attorneys cannot exclude a potential juror on racial grounds. Evidently Oates believes that her jury would have behaved more responsibly if it had, in fact, included more African Americans. Do you agree? Why, or why not?

4. How do you think the jurors should have acted? Identify things you wish they had done.

5. Oates suggests that her experience as a juror reveals problems with the American criminal justice system as a whole. Do you think it is reasonable of her to generalize in this way? Explain.

MAKING COMPARISONS

1. Evidently Sanders believes that his jury behaved well, even though its members' social class apparently differed from the defendant's. Oates, on the other hand, suggests that her jurors were guilty of racism toward people involved in the case they judged. Are you convinced that the Indiana jury was, in fact, much better than the New Jersey one? Does Sanders lead you to think that the American criminal justice system is better than Oates suggests? Identify some of the warrants or assumptions behind your answers.

2. For the most part, Sanders and Oates use different tenses. He recounts his trial in present tense, while she uses the past. Do you like one of these rhetorical strategies more than the other? Why, or why not?

3. Is time as important a subject in Oates's essay as it is in Sanders's? Refer to specific details of both.

MAXINE HONG KINGSTON
No Name Woman

Born in Stockton, California, to Chinese immigrants, Maxine Hong Kingston's (b. 1940) first language was Say Yup, a dialect of Cantonese. As a member of a close-knit community, many of whose members came from the same village in China, she was immersed in the storytelling tradition of her particular Chinese culture and soon became a gifted writer in her second language, English. Winning eleven scholarships, Kingston began her education at the University of California at Berkeley as an engineering major but soon moved into English literature, receiving her B.A. in 1962 and her teaching certificate in 1965. After teaching in Hawaii for ten years, Kingston published her first book in 1976. The Woman Warrior: Memoirs of a Girlhood among Ghosts, the book from which our selection comes, won the National Book Critics Circle Award for nonfiction. This reinterpretation of oral traditions is continued in Kingston's later books, including Tripmaster Monkey: His Fake Book (1989). Her most recent work is To Be a Poet (2003), a memoir written in verse, and The Fifth Book of Peace (2003), a combination of memoir, history, and fantasy.

"You must not tell anyone," my mother said, "what I am about to tell you. In China your father had a sister who killed herself. She jumped into the family well. We say that your father has all brothers because it is as if she had never been born.

"In 1924 just a few days after our village celebrated seventeen hurry-up weddings — to make sure that every young man who went 'out on the road' would responsibly come home — your father and his brothers and your grandfather and his brothers and your aunt's new husband sailed for America, the Gold Mountain. It was your grandfather's last trip. Those lucky enough to get contracts waved good-bye from the decks. They fed and guarded the stowaways and helped them off in Cuba, New York, Bali, Hawaii. 'We'll meet in California next year,' they said. All of them sent money home.

"I remember looking at your aunt one day when she and I were dressing; I had not noticed before that she had such a protruding melon of a stomach. But I did not think, 'She's pregnant,' until she began to look like other pregnant women, her shirt pulling and the white tops of her black pants showing. She could not have been pregnant, you see, because her husband had been gone for years. No one said anything. We did not discuss it. In early summer she was ready to have the child, long after the time when it could have been possible.

"The village had also been counting. On the night the baby was to be born the villagers raided our house. Some were crying. Like a great saw, teeth strung with lights, files of people walked zigzag across our land, tearing the rice. Their lanterns doubled in the disturbed black water, which drained away through the broken bunds. As the villagers closed in, we could see that some of them, probably men and women we knew well, wore white masks. The people with long hair hung it over their faces. Women with short hair made it stand up on end. Some had tied white bands around their foreheads, arms, and legs.

"At first they threw mud and rocks at the house. Then they threw eggs and   5
began slaughtering our stock. We could hear the animals scream their deaths — the roosters, the pigs, a last great roar from the ox. Familiar wild heads flared in our night windows; the villagers encircled us. Some of the faces stopped to peer at us, their eyes rushing like searchlights. The hands flattened against the panes, framed heads, and left red prints.

"The villagers broke in the front and the back doors at the same time, even though we had not locked the doors against them. Their knives dripped with the blood of our animals. They smeared blood on the doors and walls. One woman swung a chicken, whose throat she had slit, splattering blood in red arcs about her. We stood together in the middle of our house, in the family hall with the pictures and tables of the ancestors around us, and looked straight ahead.

"At that time the house had only two wings. When the men came back, we would build two more to enclose our courtyard and a third one to begin a second courtyard. The villagers pushed through both wings, even your grandparents' rooms, to find your aunt's, which was also mine until the men returned. From this room a new wing for one of the younger families would grow. They ripped up her clothes and shoes and broke her combs, grinding them underfoot. They tore her work from the loom. They scattered the cooking fire and rolled the new weaving in it. We could hear them in the kitchen breaking our bowls and banging the pots. They overturned the great waist-high earthenware jugs; duck eggs, pickled fruits, vegetables burst out and mixed in acrid torrents. The old woman from the next field swept a broom through the air and loosed the spirits-of-the-broom over our heads. 'Pig.' 'Ghost.' 'Pig,' they sobbed and scolded while they ruined our house.

"When they left, they took sugar and oranges to bless themselves. They cut pieces from the dead animals. Some of them took bowls that were not broken and clothes that were not torn. Afterward we swept up the rice and sewed it back up into sacks. But the smells from the spilled preserves lasted. Your aunt gave birth in the pigsty that night. The next morning when I went for the water, I found her and the baby plugging up the family well.

"Don't let your father know that I told you. He denies her. Now that you have started to menstruate, what happened to her could happen to you. Don't humiliate us. You wouldn't like to be forgotten as if you had never been born. The villagers are watchful."

Whenever she had to warn us about life, my mother told stories that ran like   10
this one, a story to grow up on. She tested our strength to establish realities. Those in the emigrant generations who could not reassert brute survival died young and far from home. Those of us in the first American generations have had to figure out how the invisible world the emigrants built around our childhoods fits in solid America.

The emigrants confused the gods by diverting their curses, misleading them with crooked streets and false names. They must try to confuse their offspring as well, who, I suppose, threaten them in similar ways — always trying to get things straight, always trying to name the unspeakable. The Chinese I know hide their names; sojourners take new names when their lives change and guard their real names with silence.

Chinese-Americans, when you try to understand what things in you are Chinese, how do you separate what is peculiar to childhood, to poverty, insanities, one family, your mother who marked your growing with stories, from what is Chinese? What is Chinese tradition and what is the movies?

If I want to learn what clothes my aunt wore, whether flashy or ordinary, I would have to begin, "Remember Father's drowned-in-the-well sister?" I cannot ask that. My mother has told me once and for all the useful parts. She will add nothing unless powered by Necessity, a riverbank that guides her life. She plants vegetable gardens rather than lawns; she carries the odd-shaped tomatoes home from the fields and eats food left for the gods.

Whenever we did frivolous things, we used up energy; we flew high kites. We children came up off the ground over the melting cones our parents brought home from work and the American movie on New Year's Day — *Oh, You Beautiful Doll* with Betty Grable one year, and *She Wore a Yellow Ribbon* with John Wayne another year. After the one carnival ride each, we paid in guilt; our tired father counted his change on the dark walk home.

Adultery is extravagance. Could people who hatch their own chicks and eat   15
the embryos and the heads for delicacies and boil the feet in vinegar for party food, leaving only the gravel, eating even the gizzard lining — could such people engender a prodigal aunt? To be a woman, to have a daughter in starvation time was a waste enough. My aunt could not have been the lone romantic who gave up everything for sex. Women in the old China did not choose. Some man had commanded her to lie with him and be his secret evil. I wonder whether he masked himself when he joined the raid on her family.

Perhaps she had encountered him in the fields or on the mountain where the daughters-in-law collected fuel. Or perhaps he first noticed her in the marketplace. He was not a stranger because the village housed no strangers. She had to have dealings with him other than sex. Perhaps he worked an adjoining field, or he sold her the cloth for the dress she sewed and wore. His demand must have surprised, then terrified her. She obeyed him; she always did as she was told.

When the family found a young man in the next village to be her husband, she had stood tractably beside the best rooster, his proxy, and promised before they met that she would be his forever. She was lucky that he was her age and she would be the first wife, an advantage secure now. The night she first saw him, he had sex with her. Then he left for America. She had almost forgotten what he looked like. When she tried to envision him, she only saw the black and white face in the group photograph the men had had taken before leaving.

The other man was not, after all, much different from her husband. They both gave orders: she followed. "If you tell your family, I'll beat you. I'll kill you. Be here again next week." No one talked sex, ever. And she might have separated the rapes from the rest of living if only she did not have to buy her oil from him or gather wood in the same forest. I want her fear to have lasted just as long as rape lasted so that the fear could have been contained. No drawn-out fear. But women at sex hazarded birth and hence lifetimes. The fear did not stop but permeated everywhere. She told the man, "I think I'm pregnant." He organized the raid against her.

On nights when my mother and father talked about their life back home, sometimes they mentioned an "outcast table" whose business they still seemed to be settling, their voices tight. In a commensal tradition, where food is precious, the powerful older people made wrongdoers eat alone. Instead of letting them start separate new lives like the Japanese, who could become samurais and geishas, the Chinese family, faces averted but eyes glowering sideways, hung on to the offenders and fed them leftovers. My aunt must have lived in the same house as my parents and eaten at an outcast table. My mother spoke about the raid as if she had seen it, when she and my aunt, a daughter-in-law to a different household, should not have been living together at all. Daughters-in-law lived with their husbands' parents, not their own; a synonym for marriage in Chinese is "taking a daughter-in-law." Her husband's parents could have sold her, mortgaged her, stoned her. But they had sent her back to her own mother and father, a mysterious act hinting at disgraces not told me. Perhaps they had thrown her out to deflect the avengers.

She was the only daughter; her four brothers went with her father, husband, and uncles "out on the road" and for some years became western men. When the goods were divided among the family, three of the brothers took land, and the youngest, my father, chose an education. After my grandparents gave their daughter away to her husband's family, they had dispensed all the adventure and all the property. They expected her alone to keep the traditional ways, which her brothers, now among the barbarians, could fumble without detection. The heavy, deep-rooted women were to maintain the past against the flood, safe for returning. But the rare urge west had fixed upon our family, and so my aunt crossed boundaries not delineated in space. 20

The work of preservation demands that the feelings playing about in one's guts not be turned into action. Just watch their passing like cherry blossoms. But perhaps my aunt, my forerunner, caught in a slow life, let dreams grow and fade and after some months or years went toward what persisted. Fear at the enormities of the forbidden kept her desires delicate, wire and bone. She looked at a man because she liked the way the hair was tucked behind his ears, or she liked the question-mark line of a long torso curving at the shoulder and straight at the hip. For warm eyes or a soft voice or a slow walk—that's all—a few hairs, a line, a brightness, a sound, a pace, she gave up family. She offered us up for a charm that vanished with tiredness, a pigtail that didn't toss when the wind died. Why, the wrong lighting could erase the dearest thing about him.

It could very well have been, however, that my aunt did not take subtle enjoyment of her friend, but, a wild woman, kept rollicking company. Imagining her free with sex doesn't fit, though. I don't know any women like that, or men either. Unless I see her life branching into mine, she gives me no ancestral help.

To sustain her being in love, she often worked at herself in the mirror, guessing at the colors and shapes that would interest him, changing them frequently in order to hit on the right combination. She wanted him to look back.

On a farm near the sea, a woman who tended her appearance reaped a reputation for eccentricity. All the married women blunt-cut their hair in flaps about their ears or pulled it back in tight buns. No nonsense. Neither style blew easily into heart-catching tangles. And at their weddings they displayed themselves in their long hair for the last time. "It brushed the backs of my knees," my mother tells me. "It was braided, and even so, it brushed the backs of my knees."

At the mirror my aunt combined individuality into her bob. A bun could   25
have been contrived to escape into black streamers blowing in the wind or in quiet wisps about her face, but only the older women in our picture album wear buns. She brushed her hair back from her forehead, tucking the flaps behind her ears. She looped a piece of thread, knotted into a circle between her index fingers and thumbs, and ran the double strand across her forehead. When she closed her fingers as if she were making a pair of shadow geese bite, the string twisted together catching the little hairs. Then she pulled the thread away from her skin, ripping the hairs out neatly, her eyes watering from the needles of pain. Opening her fingers, she cleaned the thread, then rolled it along her hairline and the tops of her eyebrows. My mother did the same to me and my sisters and herself. I used to believe that the expression "caught by the short hairs" meant a captive held with a depilatory string. It especially hurt at the temples, but my mother said we were lucky we didn't have to have our feet bound when we were seven. Sisters used to sit on their beds and cry together, she said, as their mothers or their slave removed the bandages for a few minutes each night and let the blood gush back into their veins. I hope that the man my aunt loved appreciated a smooth brow, that he wasn't just a tits-and-ass man.

Once my aunt found a freckle on her chin, at a spot that the almanac said predestined her for unhappiness. She dug it out with a hot needle and washed the wound with peroxide.

More attention to her looks than these pullings of hairs and pickings at spots would have caused gossip among the villagers. They owned work clothes and good clothes, and they wore good clothes for feasting the new seasons. But since a woman combing her hair hexes beginnings, my aunt rarely found an occasion to look her best. Women looked like great sea snails — the corded wood, babies, and laundry they carried were the whorls on their backs. The Chinese did not admire a bent back; goddesses and warriors stood straight. Still there must have been a marvelous freeing of beauty when a worker laid down her burden and stretched and arched.

Such commonplace loveliness, however, was not enough for my aunt. She dreamed of a lover for the fifteen days of New Year's, the time for families to exchange visits, money, and food. She plied her secret comb. And sure enough she cursed the year, the family, the village, and herself.

Even as her hair lured her imminent lover, many other men looked at her. Uncles, cousins, nephews, brothers would have looked, too, had they been home between journeys. Perhaps they had already been restraining their curiosity, and they left, fearful that their glances, like a field of nesting birds, might be startled and caught. Poverty hurt, and that was their first reason for leaving. But another, final reason for leaving the crowded house was the never-said.

She may have been unusually beloved, the precious only daughter, spoiled and mirror gazing because of the affection the family lavished on her. When her husband left, they welcomed the chance to take her back from the in-laws; she could live like the little daughter for just a while longer. There are stories that my grandfather was different from other people, "crazy ever since the little Jap bayoneted him in the head." He used to put his naked penis on the dinner table, laughing. And one day he brought home a baby girl, wrapped up inside his brown western-style greatcoat. He had traded one of his sons, probably my father, the youngest, for her. My grandmother made him trade back. When he finally got a daughter of his own, he doted on her. They must have all loved her, except perhaps my father, the only brother who never went back to China, having once been traded for a girl.

Brothers and sisters, newly men and women, had to efface their sexual color and present plain miens. Disturbing hair and eyes, a smile like no other, threatened the ideal of five generations living under one roof. To focus blurs, people shouted face to face and yelled from room to room. The immigrants I know have loud voices, unmodulated to American tones even after years away from the village where they called their friendships out across the fields. I have not been able to stop my mother's screams in public libraries or over telephones. Walking erect (knees straight, toes pointed forward, not pigeon-toed, which is Chinese-feminine) and speaking in an inaudible voice, I have tried to turn myself American-feminine. Chinese communication was loud, public. Only sick people had to whisper. But at the dinner table, where the family members came nearest one another, no one could talk, not the outcasts nor any eaters. Every word that falls from the mouth is a coin lost. Silently they gave and accepted food with both hands. A preoccupied child who took his bowl with one hand got a sideways glare. A complete moment of total attention is due everyone alike. Children and lovers have no singularity here, but my aunt used a secret voice, a separate attentiveness.

She kept the man's name to herself throughout her labor and dying; she did not accuse him that he be punished with her. To save her inseminator's name she gave silent birth.

He may have been somebody in her own household, but intercourse with a man outside the family would have been no less abhorrent. All the village were kinsmen, and the titles shouted in loud country voices never let kinship be forgotten. Any man within visiting distance would have been neutralized as a lover — "brother," "younger brother," "older brother" — one hundred and fifteen relationship titles. Parents researched birth charts probably not so much to assure good fortune as to circumvent incest in a population that has but one hundred surnames. Everybody has eight million relatives. How useless then sexual mannerisms, how dangerous.

As if it came from an atavism deeper than fear, I used to add "brother" silently to boys' names. It hexed the boys, who would or would not ask me to dance, and made them less scary and as familiar and deserving of benevolence as girls.

But, of course, I hexed myself also — no dates. I should have stood up, both arms waving, and shouted out across libraries, "Hey, you! Love me back." I had no idea, though, how to make attraction selective, how to control its direction and magnitude. If I made myself American-pretty so that the five or six Chinese boys in the class fell in love with me, everyone else — the Caucasian, Negro, and Japanese boys — would too. Sisterliness, dignified and honorable, made much more sense.

Attraction eludes control so stubbornly that whole societies designed to organize relationships among people cannot keep order, not even when they bind people to one another from childhood and raise them together. Among the very poor and the wealthy, brothers married their adopted sisters, like doves. Our family allowed some romance, paying adult brides' prices and providing dowries so that their sons and daughters could marry strangers. Marriage promises to turn strangers into friendly relatives — a nation of siblings.

In the village structure, spirits shimmered among the live creatures, balanced and held in equilibrium by time and land. But one human being flaring up into violence could open up a black hole, a maelstrom that pulled in the sky. The frightened villagers, who depended on one another to maintain the real, went to my aunt to show her a personal, physical representation of the break she had made in the "roundness." Misallying couples snapped off the future, which was to be embodied in true offspring. The villagers punished her for acting as if she could have a private life, secret and apart from them.

If my aunt had betrayed the family at a time of large grain yields and peace, when many boys were born, and wings were being built on many houses, perhaps, she might have escaped such severe punishment. But the men — hungry, greedy, tired of planting in dry soil — had been forced to leave the village in order to send food-money home. There were ghost plagues, bandit plagues, wars with the Japanese, floods. My Chinese brother and sister had died of an unknown sickness. Adultery, perhaps only a mistake during good times, became a crime when the village needed food.

The round moon cakes and round doorways, the round tables of graduated size that fit one roundness inside another, round windows and rice bowls — these talismans had lost their power to warn this family of the law: a family must be whole, faithfully keeping the descent line by having sons to feed the old and the dead, who in turn look after the family. The villagers came to show my aunt and her lover-in-hiding a broken house. The villagers were speeding up the circling of events because she was too shortsighted to see that her infidelity had already harmed the village, that waves of consequences would return unpredictably, sometimes in disguise, as now, to hurt her. This roundness had to be made coin-sized so that she would see its circumference: punish her at the birth of her baby. Awaken her to the inexorable. People who refused fatalism because they could invent small resources insisted on culpability. Deny accidents and wrest fault from the stars.

35

After the villagers left, their lanterns now scattering in various directions 40
toward home, the family broke their silence and cursed her. "Aiaa, we're going to
die. Death is coming. Death is coming. Look what you've done. You've killed us.
Ghost! Dead ghost! Ghost! You've never been born." She ran out into the fields,
far enough from the house so that she could no longer hear their voices, and
pressed herself against the earth, her own land no more. When she felt the birth
coming, she thought that she had been hurt. Her body seized together. "They've
hurt me too much," she thought. "This is gall, and it will kill me." With forehead
and knees against the earth, her body convulsed and then relaxed. She turned on
her back, lay on the ground. The black well of sky and stars went out and out and
out forever; her body and her complexity seemed to disappear. She was one of the
stars, a bright dot in blackness, without home, without a companion, in eternal
cold and silence. An agoraphobia rose in her, speeding higher and higher, bigger
and bigger; she would not be able to contain it; there would be no end to fear.

Flayed, unprotected against space, she felt pain return, focusing her body.
This pain chilled her — a cold, steady kind of surface pain. Inside, spasmodically,
the other pain, the pain of the child, heated her. For hours she lay on the ground,
alternately body and space. Sometimes a vision of normal comfort obliterated
reality: she saw the family in the evening gambling at the dinner table, the young
people massaging their elders' backs. She saw them congratulating one another,
high joy on the mornings the rice shoots came up. When these pictures burst, the
stars drew yet further apart. Black space opened.

She got to her feet to fight better and remembered that old-fashioned women
gave birth in their pigsties to fool the jealous, pain-dealing gods, who do not
snatch piglets. Before the next spasms could stop her, she ran to the pigsty, each
step a rushing out into emptiness. She climbed over the fence and knelt in the
dirt. It was good to have a fence enclosing her, a tribal person alone.

Laboring, this woman who had carried her child as a foreign growth that
sickened her every day, expelled it at last. She reached down to touch the hot,
wet, moving mass, surely smaller than anything human, and could feel that it was
human after all — fingers, toes, nails, nose. She pulled it up on to her belly, and it
lay curled there, butt in the air, feet precisely tucked one under the other. She
opened her loose shirt and buttoned the child inside. After resting, it squirmed
and thrashed and she pushed it up to her breast. It turned its head this way and
that until it found her nipple. There, it made little snuffling noises. She clenched
her teeth at its preciousness, lovely as a young calf, a piglet, a little dog.

She may have gone to the pigsty as a last act of responsibility: she would protect this child as she had protected its father. It would look after her soul, leaving
supplies on her grave. But how would this tiny child without family find her grave
when there would be no marker for her anywhere, neither in the earth nor the
family hall? No one would give her a family hall name. She had taken the child
with her into the wastes. At its birth the two of them had felt the same raw pain of
separation, a wound that only the family pressing tight could close. A child with
no descent line would not soften her life but only trail after her, ghostlike, begging her to give it purpose. At dawn the villagers on their way to the fields would
stand around the fence and look.

Full of milk, the little ghost slept. When it awoke, she hardened her breasts   45
against the milk that crying loosens. Toward morning she picked up the baby and
walked to the well.

Carrying the baby to the well shows loving. Otherwise abandon it. Turn its
face into the mud. Mothers who love their children take them along. It was probably a girl; there is some hope of forgiveness for boys.

"Don't tell anyone you had an aunt. Your father does not want to hear her
name. She has never been born." I have believed that sex was unspeakable and
words so strong and fathers so frail that "aunt" would do my father mysterious
harm. I have thought that my family, having settled among immigrants who had
also been their neighbors in the ancestral land, needed to clean their name, and a
wrong word would incite the kinspeople even here. But there is more to this
silence: they want me to participate in her punishment. And I have.

In the twenty years since I heard this story I have not asked for details nor said
my aunt's name; I do not know it. People who can comfort the dead can also
chase after them to hurt them further—a reverse ancestor worship. The real punishment was not the raid swiftly inflicted by the villagers, but the family's deliberately forgetting her. Her betrayal so maddened them, they saw to it that she would
suffer forever, even after death. Always hungry, always needing, she would have to
beg food from other ghosts, snatch and steal it from those whose living descendants give them gifts. She would have to fight the ghosts massed at crossroads for
the buns a few thoughtful citizens leave to decoy her away from village and home
so that the ancestral spirits could feast unharassed. At peace, they could act like
gods, not ghosts, their descent lines providing them with paper suits and dresses,
spirit money, paper houses, paper automobiles, chicken, meat, and rice into eternity—essences delivered up in smoke and flames, steam and incense rising from
each rice bowl. In an attempt to make the Chinese care for people outside the
family, Chairman Mao encourages us now to give our paper replicas to the spirits
of outstanding soldiers and workers, no matter whose ancestors they may be. My
aunt remains forever hungry. Goods are not distributed evenly among the dead.

My aunt haunts me—her ghost drawn to me because now, after fifty years of
neglect, I alone devote pages of paper to her, though not origamied into houses
and clothes. I do not think she always means me well. I am telling on her, and she
was a spite suicide, drowning herself in the drinking water. The Chinese are
always very frightened of the drowned one, whose weeping ghost, wet hair hanging and skin bloated, waits silently by the water to pull down a substitute. [1976]

THINKING ABOUT THE TEXT

1. This cautionary tale is meant to persuade Kingston to conform to her parents' values. What is the argument behind the narrative the mother tells?
   Does it make sense to you? What might be a contemporary argument in a
   middle-class American family?

2. Were you ever put at an "outcast table" (para. 19) or anything comparable
   in your house or school? Did you ever hear of such a ritual? What did

happen when you were punished? What kinds of things were you punished for? Why do you think these specific things were chosen?

3. Is this also a tale about gender inequality? How does Kingston suggest this? How are relations between men and women portrayed here?

4. How do ghosts and spirits function in this essay? Which parts of this piece seem true to you, and which seem fictional? Why do you suppose Kingston blends these elements?

5. Sexual mores change over time and from country to country. What specifically about the aunt's context made her transgression so severe? How would her "crime" be viewed in contemporary America? Why? What do you think an ideal response would be?

MAKING COMPARISONS

1. Whereas Sanders and Oates were involved in the cases they report, Kingston was only told a story about her aunt's death and heard it many years after the event. In what ways, if any, is this difference relevant?

2. Does the community that judged Kingston's aunt seem less rational than the juries discussed by Sanders and Oates? Define what you mean by *rational*.

3. To what extent do the judging groups in all three essays concern themselves with behavior that you consider private rather than public? Again, define what you mean by these terms.

WRITING ABOUT ISSUES

1. In effect, Sanders, Oates, and Kingston invite you to judge the community justice they describe. Choose one of the essays, and think of the questions you would ask to guide your evaluation of the community behavior that the author describes. Then write an essay in which you state whether and how the author addresses these questions.

2. Sanders, Oates, and Kingston tell you things about themselves. Choose two of these authors, and write an essay in which you compare their self-disclosures. Do you get pretty much the same impression of both authors, or do the images they project of themselves strike you as significantly different? Refer to specific details of their texts.

3. In 1991, four white police officers went on trial for various offenses related to their videotaped beating of an African American man, Rodney King, who was resisting arrest. The judge felt that the officers could not receive a fair trial in southeast Los Angeles, where the beating occurred. Therefore, the trial was moved to a suburb, Simi Valley. The jury's ten whites, one Hispanic, and one Asian reflected the predominantly white middle-class makeup of the town. Critics argued that a Los Angeles jury probably would have been partially or even predominantly black. The

Simi Valley jurors proceeded to acquit the officers of almost every charge. Many Americans protested the outcome, believing that a more racially diverse jury would have reached more responsible verdicts and that the trial should have taken place where the complaint was filed. In the *Washington Post*, however, a letter writer disagreed: "As for the change of venue, the Constitution guarantees us a jury of our peers. The Simi Valley jury was surely more representative of the officers' peers than a southeast Los Angeles jury would have been." Write an essay in which you identify and defend what you think should be meant by the phrase "a jury of one's peers." In arguing for your definition, refer to at least one actual case. Possibilities include the King case; the cases described by Sanders, Oates, or Kingston; the two O. J. Simpson trials; and cases in your local community.

4. Write an essay analyzing and evaluating the behavior of a particular jury. It might be a jury that you sat on or observed. Then again, it might be a jury that someone told you about or that you read about. Feel free to compare your chosen jury with any of the judging groups in this cluster's essays.

REFLECTING ON KILLING ANIMALS

GEORGE ORWELL, "Shooting an Elephant"
ANNIE DILLARD, "The Deer at Providencia"
BRUCE WEIGL, "Spike"

When you think about death, probably you think about your own fate or that of other people. But occasions may arise when you have to ponder the death of an animal. At such times, you may agonize, especially if you have witnessed the death or felt somehow responsible for it. Perhaps you have had to consider ending a sick pet's life. Or perhaps you have wondered whether to protest social practices deadly to animals, such as hunting, laboratory experiments with monkeys, and the slaughter of cattle for human consumption. Of course, your social context may greatly influence your attitude toward the killing of animals, as the following three essays show. George Orwell's essay, written in the mid-1930s, is an account of his service as a British colonial policeman in Burma. He recalls a day when he shot an elephant merely to preserve his status in the village he patrolled. In effect, Orwell reminds his readers that the killing of animals can occur within and be influenced by human power struggles. Annie Dillard's essay, which dates from the early 1980s, is about an expedition she made with other Americans to a village in Ecuador. While there, she and the rest of her group came face to face with the mortal suffering of a deer captured by their hosts. Like Orwell's account, Dillard's suggests that cultural differences can significantly affect people's responses when an animal is slain. Finally, Bruce Weigl recalls his boyhood in a 1950s Ohio mill town, particularly the time when his dog got rabies and had to be shot.

Even now, Weigl seems pained by the death, for his pet had brightened the difficult life of Weigl's working-class family. This third piece, then, joins the other two in suggesting that social circumstances can influence human beings' attitudes toward an animal's demise.

GEORGE ORWELL
Shooting an Elephant

George Orwell was the pen name of Eric Arthur Blair (1903–1950). Although born in India, he traveled widely. After his schooling in England, he joined the Indian Imperial Police in Burma, where he served from 1922 to 1927. Later, Orwell lived in Paris and London, studied the lives of coal miners in the north of England, and fought on the Republican side in the Spanish Civil War against the fascist forces of General Francisco Franco. Probably Orwell is best known today for two novels he wrote as warnings against totalitarianism, Animal Farm *(1945) and* Nineteen Eighty-Four *(1949). But he also wrote much journalism and many essays, often exploring through these writings how political ideologies influence human thinking, language, and behavior. The following essay, which tells of an event during his service in Burma, was first published in 1936.*

In Moulmein, in Lower Burma, I was hated by large numbers of people — the only time in my life that I have been important enough for this to happen to me. I was sub-divisional police officer of the town, and in an aimless, petty kind of way anti-European feeling was very bitter. No one had the guts to raise a riot, but if a European woman went through the bazaars alone somebody would probably spit betel juice over her dress. As a police officer I was an obvious target and was baited whenever it seemed safe to do so. When a nimble Burman tripped me up on the football field and the referee (another Burman) looked the other way, the crowd yelled with hideous laughter. This happened more than once. In the end the sneering yellow faces of young men that met me everywhere, the insults hooted after me when I was at a safe distance, got badly on my nerves. The young Buddhist priests were the worst of all. There were several thousands of them in the town and none of them seemed to have anything to do except stand on street corners and jeer at Europeans.

All this was perplexing and upsetting. For at that time I had already made up my mind that imperialism was an evil thing and the sooner I chucked up my job and got out of it the better. Theoretically — and secretly, of course — I was all for the Burmese and all against their oppressors, the British. As for the job I was doing, I hated it more bitterly than I can perhaps make clear. In a job like that you see the dirty work of Empire at close quarters. The wretched prisoners huddling in the stinking cages of the lockups, the grey, cowed faces of the long-term convicts, the scarred buttocks of the men who had been flogged with bamboos — all these oppressed me with an intolerable sense of guilt. But I could get nothing into perspective. I was young and ill-educated and I had had to think out my problems in the utter silence that is imposed on every Englishman in the East. I did not even know that the British Empire is dying, still less did I know that it is a great deal better than the younger empires that are going to supplant it.° All I knew was that I was stuck between my hatred of the empire I served and my rage against the evil-spirited little beasts who tried to make my job impossible. With one part of my mind I thought of the British Raj° as an unbreakable tyranny, as something clamped down, in *saecula saeculorum,*° upon the will of prostrate peoples; with another part I thought that the greatest joy in the world would be to drive a bayonet into a Buddhist priest's guts. Feelings like these are the normal by-products of imperialism; ask any Anglo-Indian official, if you can catch him off duty.

One day something happened which in a roundabout way was enlightening. It was a tiny incident in itself, but it gave me a better glimpse than I had had before of the real nature of imperialism—the real motives for which despotic governments act. Early one morning the sub-inspector at a police station the other end of the town rang me up on the phone and said that an elephant was ravaging the bazaar. Would I please come and do something about it? I did not know what I could do, but I wanted to see what was happening and I got on to a pony and started out. I took my rifle, an old .44 Winchester and much too small to kill an elephant, but I thought the noise might be useful *in terrorem.*° Various Burmans stopped me on the way and told me about the elephant's doings. It was not, of course, a wild elephant, but a tame one which had gone "must."° It had been chained up, as tame elephants always are when their attack of "must" is due, but on the previous night it had broken its chain and escaped. Its mahout,° the only person who could manage it when it was in that state, had set out in pursuit, but had taken the wrong direction and was now twelve hours' journey away, and in the morning the elephant had suddenly reappeared in the town. The Burmese population had no weapons and were quite helpless against it. It had already destroyed somebody's bamboo hut, killed a cow, and raided some fruit-stalls and devoured the stock; also it had met the municipal rubbish van and, when the driver jumped out and took to his heels, had turned the van over and inflicted violences upon it.

The Burmese sub-inspector and some Indian constables were waiting for me in the quarter where the elephant had been seen. It was a very poor quarter, a labyrinth of squalid bamboo huts, thatched with palm-leaf, winding all over a steep hillside. I remember that it was a cloudy, stuffy morning at the beginning of the rains. We began questioning people as to where the elephant had gone, and, as usual, failed to get any definite information. That is invariably the case in the East; a story always sounds clear enough at a distance, but the nearer you get to the scene of events the vaguer it becomes. Some of the people said that the elephant had gone in one direction, some said that he had gone in another, some

---

younger empires . . . supplant it: In 1936, Hitler and Stalin were in power and World War II was only three years away.   **Raj:** Sovereignty.   *saecula saeculorum:* From time immemorial. *in terrorem:* In terrorizing him.   **must:** That is, gone into a state of frenzy.   **mahout:** A keeper and driver of an elephant.

professed not even to have heard of an elephant. I had almost made up my mind that the whole story was a pack of lies, when we heard yells a little distance away. There was a loud, scandalized cry of "Go away, child! Go away this instant!" and an old woman with a switch in her hand came round the corner of a hut, violently shooing away a crowd of naked children. Some more women followed, clicking their tongues and exclaiming; evidently there was something that the children ought not to have seen. I rounded the hut and saw a man's dead body sprawling in the mud. He was an Indian, a black Dravidian coolie, almost naked, and he could not have been dead many minutes. The people said that the elephant had come suddenly upon him round the corner of the hut, caught him with its trunk, put its foot on his back, and ground him into the earth. This was the rainy season and the ground was soft, and his face had scored a trench a foot deep and a couple of yards long. He was lying on his belly with arms crucified and head sharply twisted to one side. His face was coated with mud, the eyes wide open, the teeth bared and grinning with an expression of unendurable agony. (Never tell me, by the way, that the dead look peaceful. Most of the corpses I have seen looked devilish.) The friction of the great beast's foot had stripped the skin from his back as neatly as one skins a rabbit. As soon as I saw the dead man I sent an orderly to a friend's house nearby to borrow an elephant rifle. I had already sent back the pony, not wanting it to go mad with fright and throw me if it smelled the elephant.

The orderly came back in a few minutes with a rifle and five cartridges, and meanwhile some Burmans had arrived and told us that the elephant was in the paddy fields below, only a few hundred yards away. As I started forward practically the whole population of the quarter flocked out of the houses and followed me. They had seen the rifle and were all shouting excitedly that I was going to shoot the elephant. They had not shown much interest in the elephant when he was merely ravaging their homes, but it was different now that he was going to be shot. It was a bit of fun to them, as it would be to an English crowd; besides they wanted the meat. It made me vaguely uneasy. I had no intention of shooting the elephant—I had merely sent for the rifle to defend myself if necessary—and it is always unnerving to have a crowd following you. I marched down the hill, looking and feeling a fool, with the rifle over my shoulder and an ever-growing army of people jostling at my heels. At the bottom, when you got away from the huts, there was a metalled road and beyond that a miry waste of paddy fields a thousand yards across, not yet ploughed but soggy from the first rains and dotted with coarse grass. The elephant was standing eight yards from the road, his left side towards us. He took not the slightest notice of the crowd's approach. He was tearing up bunches of grass, beating them against his knees to clean them and stuffing them into his mouth.

I had halted on the road. As soon as I saw the elephant I knew with perfect certainty that I ought not to shoot him. It is a serious matter to shoot a working elephant—it is comparable to destroying a huge and costly piece of machinery—and obviously one ought not to do it if it can possibly be avoided. And at that distance, peacefully eating, the elephant looked no more dangerous than a cow. I thought then and I think now that his attack of "must" was already passing off; in

5

which case he would merely wander harmlessly about until the mahout came back and caught him. Moreover, I did not in the least want to shoot him. I decided that I would watch him for a little while to make sure that he did not turn savage again, and then go home.

But at that moment I glanced round at the crowd that had followed me. It was an immense crowd, two thousand at the least and growing every minute. It blocked the road for a long distance on either side. I looked at the sea of yellow faces above the garish clothes—faces all happy and excited over this bit of fun, all certain that the elephant was going to be shot. They were watching me as they would watch a conjurer about to perform a trick. They did not like me, but with the magical rifle in my hands I was momentarily worth watching. And suddenly I realized that I should have to shoot the elephant after all. The people expected it of me and I had got to do it; I could feel their two thousand wills pressing me forward, irresistibly. And it was at this moment, as I stood there with the rifle in my hands, that I first grasped the hollowness, the futility of the white man's dominion in the East. Here was I, the white man with his gun, standing in front of the unarmed native crowd—seemingly the leading actor of the piece; but in reality I was only an absurd puppet pushed to and fro by the will of those yellow faces behind. I perceived in this moment that when the white man turns tyrant it is his own freedom that he destroys. He becomes a sort of hollow, posing dummy, the conventionalized figure of a sahib.° For it is the condition of his rule that he shall spend his life in trying to impress the "natives," and so in every crisis he has got to do what the "natives" expect of him. He wears a mask, and his face grows to fit it. I had got to shoot the elephant. I had committed myself to doing it when I sent for the rifle. A sahib has got to act like a sahib; he has got to appear resolute, to know his own mind and do definite things. To come all that way, rifle in hand, with two thousand people marching at my heels, and then to trail feebly away, having done nothing—no, that was impossible. The crowd would laugh at me. And my whole life, every white man's life in the East, was one long struggle not to be laughed at.

But I did not want to shoot the elephant. I watched him beating his bunch of grass against his knees, with the preoccupied grandmotherly air that elephants have. It seemed to me that it would be murder to shoot him. At that age I was not squeamish about killing animals, but I had never shot an elephant and never wanted to. (Somehow it always seems worse to kill a *large* animal.) Besides, there was the beast's owner to be considered. Alive, the elephant was worth at least a hundred pounds; dead, he would only be worth the value of his tusks, five pounds, possibly. But I had got to act quickly. I turned to some experienced-looking Burmans who had been there when we arrived, and asked them how the elephant had been behaving. They all said the same thing: he took no notice of you if you left him alone, but he might charge if you went too close to him.

It was perfectly clear to me what I ought to do. I ought to walk up to within, say, twenty-five yards of the elephant and test his behavior. If he charged I could shoot, if he took no notice of me it would be safe to leave him until the mahout

sahib: Term used among Hindus and Muslims in Colonial India when speaking of an official.

came back. But also I knew that I was going to do no such thing. I was a poor shot with a rifle and the ground was soft mud into which one would sink at every step. If the elephant charged and I missed him, I should have about as much chance as a toad under a steamroller. But even then I was not thinking particularly of my own skin, only of the watchful yellow faces behind. For at that moment, with the crowd watching me, I was not afraid in the ordinary sense, as I would have been if I had been alone. A white man mustn't be frightened in front of "natives"; and so, in general, he isn't frightened. The sole thought in my mind was that if anything went wrong those two thousand Burmans would see me pursued, caught, trampled on, and reduced to a grinning corpse like that Indian up the hill. And if that happened it was quite probable that some of them would laugh. That would never do. There was only one alternative. I shoved the cartridges into the magazine and lay down on the road to get a better aim.

The crowd grew very still, and a deep, low, happy sigh, as of people who see the theater curtain go up at last, breathed from innumerable throats. They were going to have their bit of fun after all. The rifle was a beautiful German thing with cross-hair sights. I did not then know that in shooting an elephant one would shoot to cut an imaginary bar running from ear-hole to ear-hole. I ought, therefore, as the elephant was sideways on, to have aimed straight at his ear-hole; actually I aimed several inches in front of this, thinking the brain would be further forward.

10

When I pulled the trigger I did not hear the bang or feel the kick — one never does when a shot goes home — but I heard the devilish roar of glee that went up from the crowd. In that instant, in too short a time, one would have thought, even for the bullet to get there, a mysterious, terrible change had come over the elephant. He neither stirred nor fell, but every line on his body had altered. He looked suddenly stricken, shrunken, immensely old, as though the frightful impact of the bullet had paralyzed him without knocking him down. At last, after what seemed a long time — it might have been five seconds, I dare say — he sagged flabbily to his knees. His mouth slobbered. An enormous senility seemed to have settled upon him. One could have imagined him thousands of years old. I fired again into the same spot. At the second shot he did not collapse but climbed with desperate slowness to his feet and stood weakly upright, with legs sagging and head drooping. I fired a third time. That was the shot that did for him. You could see the agony of it jolt his whole body and knock the last remnant of strength from his legs. But in falling he seemed for a moment to rise, for as his hind legs collapsed beneath him he seemed to tower upwards like a huge rock toppling, his trunk reaching skywards like a tree. He trumpeted, for the first and only time. And then down he came, his belly towards me, with a crash that seemed to shake the ground even where I lay.

I got up. The Burmans were already racing past me across the mud. It was obvious that the elephant would never rise again, but he was not dead. He was breathing very rhythmically with long rattling gasps, his great mound of a side painfully rising and falling. His mouth was wide open — I could see far down into the caverns of pale pink throat. I waited a long time for him to die, but his breathing did not weaken. Finally, I fired my two remaining shots into the spot where I thought his heart must be. The thick blood welled out of him like red velvet, but still he did not die. His body did not even jerk when the shots hit him, the tortured breathing continued without a pause. He was dying, very slowly and in great agony, but in some world remote from me where not even a bullet could damage him further. I felt that I had got to put an end to that dreadful noise. It seemed dreadful to see the great beast lying there, powerless to move and yet powerless to die, and not even to be able to finish him. I sent back for my small rifle and poured shot after shot into his heart and down his throat. They seemed to make no impression. The tortured gasps continued as steadily as the ticking of a clock.

In the end I could not stand it any longer and went away. I heard later that it took him half an hour to die. Burmans were bringing dahs° and baskets even before I left, and I was told they had stripped his body almost to the bones by the afternoon.

Afterwards, of course, there were endless discussions about the shooting of the elephant. The owner was furious, but he was only an Indian and could do nothing. Besides, legally I had done the right thing, for a mad elephant has to be killed, like a mad dog, if its owner fails to control it. Among the Europeans opinion was divided. The older men said I was right, the younger men said it was a damn shame to shoot an elephant for killing a coolie, because an elephant was worth more than any damn Coringhee coolie. And afterwards I was very glad that the coolie had been killed; it put me legally in the right and it gave me a sufficient pretext for shooting the elephant. I often wondered whether any of the others grasped that I had done it solely to avoid looking a fool.   [1936]

THINKING ABOUT THE TEXT

1. Why is the writer focusing on this particular day in his past? What is he using it to illustrate? What other kinds of significance might one find in this episode?

2. On the basis of this essay, how would you describe the younger Orwell's attitude toward the Burmese villagers? Cite specific statements that you find especially helpful in answering this question. Does the older Orwell who is writing the essay seem much different from his younger self? Again, identify specific statements that affect your thinking on this issue.

3. According to the essay, at what points might the shooting of the elephant have been avoided? Why at these points did the younger Orwell nevertheless find himself heading toward the act of killing?

4. Reread the description of the elephant's suffering after he is shot. How does the writer's language encourage you to compare the elephant's physical decline with the eventual decline of the British Empire?

5. "Shooting an Elephant" has appeared in many essay anthologies, especially those intended for composition classes. Why is it anthologized so much, do you think? Should it be? Identify some of your warrants or assumptions in addressing this issue of evaluation.

---

dahs: Large heavy knives.

ANNIE DILLARD
The Deer at Providencia

Annie Dillard (b. 1945) teaches creative writing at Wesleyan University in Middle-town, Connecticut. She first came to national attention with her 1975 Pulitzer Prize–winning book Pilgrim at Tinker Creek, *which chronicled her nature walks in Virginia's Roanoke Valley. Since then, she has published several full-length books, including* Holy the Firm *(1978),* Living by Fiction *(1982), For the Time Being (1999), an autobiography entitled* An American Childhood *(1987), and a novel called* The Living *(1982). She is also a poet, having produced the collections* Tick-ets for a Prayer Wheel *(1974) and* Mornings Like This *(1995). But many of her readers are most familiar with Dillard's essays, which often deal with her travels to various places, her explorations of nature, and her spiritual quests. The following piece appears in her 1982 volume of essays* Teaching a Stone to Talk.

There were four of us North Americans in the jungle, in the Ecuadorian jungle on the banks of the Napo River in the Amazon watershed. The other three North Americans were metropolitan men. We stayed in tents in one riverside vil-lage, and visited others. At the village called Providencia we saw a sight which moved us, and which shocked the men.

The first thing we saw when we climbed the riverbank to the village of Provi-dencia was the deer. It was roped to a tree on the grass clearing near the thatch shelter where we would eat lunch.

The deer was small, about the size of a whitetail fawn, but apparently full-grown. It had a rope around its neck and three feet caught in the rope. Someone said that the dogs had caught it that morning and the villagers were going to cook and eat it that night.

This clearing lay at the edge of the little thatched-hut village. We could see the villagers going about their business, scattering feed corn for hens about their houses, and wandering down paths to the river to bathe. The village headman was our host; he stood beside us as we watched the deer struggle. Several village boys were interested in the deer; they formed part of the circle we made around it in the clearing. So also did four businessmen from Quito who were attempting to guide us around the jungle. Few of the very different people standing in this circle had a common language. We watched the deer, and no one said much.

The deer lay on its side at the rope's very end, so the rope lacked slack to let it   5
rest its head in the dust. It was "pretty," delicate of bone like all deer, and thin-skinned for the tropics. Its skin looked virtually hairless, in fact, and almost translucent, like a membrane. Its neck was no thicker than my wrist; it was rubbed open on the rope, and gashed. Trying to paw itself free of the rope, the deer had scratched its own neck with its hooves. The raw underside of its neck showed red stripes and some bruises bleeding inside the muscles. Now three of its feet were hooked in the rope under its jaw. It could not stand, of course, on one

leg, so it could not move to slacken the rope and ease the pull on its throat and enable it to rest its head.

Repeatedly the deer paused, motionless, its eyes veiled, with only its rib cage in motion, and its breaths the only sound. Then, after I would think, "It has given up; now it will die," it would heave. The rope twanged; the tree leaves clattered; the deer's free foot beat the ground. We stepped back and held our breaths. It thrashed, kicking, but only one leg moved; the other three legs tightened inside the rope's loop. Its hip jerked; its spine shook. Its eyes rolled; its tongue, thick with spittle, pushed in and out. Then it would rest again. We watched this for fifteen minutes.

Once three young native boys charged in, released its trapped legs, and jumped back to the circle of people. But instantly the deer scratched up its neck with its hooves and snared its forelegs in the rope again. It was easy to imagine a third and then a fourth leg soon stuck, like Brer Rabbit and the Tar Baby.

We watched the deer from the circle, and then we drifted on to lunch. Our palm-roofed shelter stood on a grassy promontory from which we could see the deer tied to the tree, pigs and hens walking under village houses, and black-and-white cattle standing in the river. There was even a breeze.

Lunch, which was the second and better lunch we had that day, was hot and fried. There was a big fish called *doncella*, a kind of catfish, dipped whole in corn flour and beaten egg, then deep fried. With our fingers we pulled soft fragments of it from its sides to our plates, and ate; it was delicate fish-flesh, fresh and mild. Someone found the roe, and I ate of that too — it was fat and stronger, like egg yolk, naturally enough, and warm.

There was also a stew of meat in shreds with rice and pale brown gravy. I had asked what kind of deer it was tied to the tree; Pepe had answered in Spanish, "*Gama*." Now they told us this was *gama* too, stewed. I suspect the word means merely game or venison. At any rate, I heard that the village dogs had cornered another deer just yesterday, and it was this deer which we were now eating in full sight of the whole article. It was good. I was surprised at its tenderness. But it is a fact that high levels of lactic acid, which builds up in muscle tissues during exertion, tenderizes.

After the fish and meat we ate bananas fried in chunks and served on a tray; they were sweet and full of flavor. I felt terrific. My shirt was wet and cool from swimming; I had had a night's sleep, two decent walks, three meals, and a swim — everything tasted good. From time to time each one of us, separately, would look beyond our shaded roof to the sunny spot where the deer was still convulsing in the dust. Our meal completed, we walked around the deer and back to the boats.

That night I learned that while we were watching the deer, the others were watching me.

We four North Americans grew close in the jungle in a way that was not the usual artificial intimacy of travelers. We liked each other. We stayed up all that night talking, murmuring, as though we rocked on hammocks slung above time. The others were from big cities: New York, Washington, Boston. They all said

10

that I had no expression on my face when I was watching the deer — or at any rate, not the expression they expected.

They had looked to see how I, the only woman, and the youngest, was taking the sight of the deer's struggles. I looked detached, apparently, or hard, or calm, or focused, still. I don't know. I was thinking. I remember feeling very old and energetic. I could say like Thoreau that I have traveled widely in Roanoke, Virginia. I have thought a great deal about carnivorousness; I eat meat. These things are not issues; they are mysteries.

Gentlemen of the city, what surprises you? That there is suffering here, or that I know it?   15

We lay in the tent and talked. "If it had been my wife," one man said with special vigor, amazed, "she wouldn't have cared *what* was going on; she would have dropped *everything* right at that moment and gone in the village from here to there to there, she would not have *stopped* until that animal was out of its suffering one way or another. She couldn't *bear* to see a creature in agony like that."

I nodded.

Now I am home. When I wake I comb my hair before the mirror above my dresser. Every morning for the past two years I have seen in that mirror, beside my sleep-softened face, the blackened face of a burnt man. It is a wire-service photograph clipped from a newspaper and taped to my mirror. The caption reads: "Alan McDonald in Miami hospital bed." All you can see in the photograph is a smudged triangle of face from his eyelids to his lower lip; the rest is bandages. You cannot see the expression in his eyes; the bandages shade them.

The story, headed MAN BURNED FOR SECOND TIME, begins:

"Why does God hate me?" Alan McDonald asked from his hospital bed.
    "When the gunpowder went off, I couldn't believe it," he said. "I just couldn't believe it. I said, 'No, God couldn't do this to me again.'"

He was in a burn ward in Miami, in serious condition. I do not even know if he lived. I wrote him a letter at the time, cringing.

He had been burned before, thirteen years previously, by flaming gasoline.   20
For years he had been having his body restored and his face remade in dozens of operations. He had been a boy, and then a burnt boy. He had already been stunned by what could happen, by how life could veer.

Once I read that people who survive bad burns tend to go crazy; they have a very high suicide rate. Medicine cannot ease their pain; drugs just leak away, soaking the sheets, because there is no skin to hold them in. The people just lie there and weep. Later they kill themselves. They had not known, before they were burned, that the world included such suffering, that life could permit them personally such pain.

This time a bowl of gunpowder had exploded on McDonald.

"I didn't realize what had happened at first," he recounted. "And then I heard that sound from 13 years ago. I was burning. I rolled to put the fire out and I thought, 'Oh God, not again.'"

"If my friend hadn't been there, I would have jumped into a canal with a rock around my neck."

His wife concludes the piece, "Man, it just isn't fair."

I read the whole clipping again every morning. This is the Big Time here, every minute of it. Will someone please explain to Alan McDonald in his dignity, to the deer at Providencia in his dignity, what is going on? And mail me the carbon.

When we walked by the deer at Providencia for the last time, I said to Pepe, with a pitying glance at the deer, *"Pobrecito"* — "poor little thing." But I was trying out Spanish. I knew at the time it was a ridiculous thing to say.   [1982]

THINKING ABOUT THE TEXT

1. Why did the men with whom Dillard was traveling expect her to act differently than she did? How do you think she should have behaved when she saw the villagers tormenting the deer? How do you feel about the satisfaction she derived from the deer-meat stew? Identify some of the warrants or assumptions behind your answers.

2. What do you make of Dillard's obsession with Alan McDonald? Do you believe his case belongs in this essay? Why, or why not?

3. Dillard declares, "These things are not issues; they are mysteries" (para. 14). What distinction does she make between *issues* and *mysteries*? How does she define these terms? Do you agree that the things she reports are better viewed as mysteries than as issues? Explain your reasoning.

4. At the end of the essay, Dillard returns to a moment back in Ecuador; she could have described this moment in the first section of the essay. Why do you think she chooses to conclude with it?

5. What does the word *Providencia* signify? (You may need to consult a classmate or a Spanish-English dictionary.) Why do you suppose Dillard included the word in her title?

MAKING COMPARISONS

1. Does Dillard seem less narrow-minded than Orwell? Identify details of both texts that you think especially important for you to consider as you answer this question.

2. Orwell's essay is pretty much one continuous story, whereas Dillard begins with the story of the deer and then jumps to her ongoing obsession with Alan McDonald. Does Dillard's essay seem less dramatic or intense than Orwell's because it is less continuous? Why, or why not?

3. Obviously gender is relevant to Dillard's essay. Is it as relevant to Orwell's essay? Explain.

BRUCE WEIGL

Spike

The son of a mill worker, Bruce Weigl (b. 1949) grew up in Lima, Ohio. After graduating from high school in 1967, he joined the United States Army and was sent to Vietnam. Today, Weigl is chiefly known as a poet, the latest collections of his own verse being The Unraveling Strangeness: Poems *(2002). He has also edited and translated Vietnamese and Romanian poetry. Originally, "Spike" appeared in a 1995 issue of* Ohio Review, *but we present the slightly revised version featured in Weigl's memoir* The Circle of Hanh *(2000).*

When my father brought Spike home in a box, I was sitting near the coal stove with my sister. We came together there with our different lives and sat near the stove to keep warm. He put the box down on the kitchen table. I saw it move and shake.

I want to say that my sister cried, that she ran behind our mother at the sink and pulled at her skirts, but it was me who cried when the box moved. I cried because even then I had seen the veil lifted a time or two. Even then I knew to fear things that moved inside of boxes your father brought home from the mill.

Spike was my dog when I was five. A ratty rattailed terrier with bent ears and a crazy dog grin. Some old man couldn't handle him anymore, so he gave him to my father. We had a small apartment then next to St. Peter's church with its outdoor rock altar and its blue bottomed holy pond, a grim four-family building where you had to share the bathroom with the drunk who sometimes would piss on the radiator in winter, a smell you could not wash away. When the old drunk would piss there in his drunkenness, my mother would wake to scrub it with a rough brush and lye soap. Even in winter she would open the window to let out the smell of human acids.

Three rooms and a bathroom you shared with strangers. Not a bad life, though I have always known a longing there, an emptiness I dwelled in even then.

When Spike hit the light of our kitchen where the coal stove sang and the family came together, it was as if a whirlwind had been released, a water spout or perhaps a small tornado. He spun his small tight muscle of a body all through the three rooms with such speed he was a blur. He ran so fast he seemed at times to run up the very walls, and he flew through the rooms so wildly that his running made them bigger, made us pause in our lives that had been headed somewhere else that night, somewhere not as bright or easy. We had already seen an empty table in that house, already we had felt the cold through cracks in the wall, but Spike somehow raised us above that grim life, above the mill noise and the slag dust. He caused us to look away from the sorrow and from the not having.

For a long time that night we could only stare, amazed. I had never seen a dog behave this way before. Nor had my father, who twice almost rose, I think to knock him down. Twice he almost rose. But after supper, after the mill noise lowered like a voice is quieted in the evening, Spike began to slow down, and as if to calm himself, he came to each of us and put his head in our hands, and like that he was inside of us.

Spike was my dog, but this is not the boy-and-dog story we're wont to tell. Not the noble dog who's taken from the boy in the city by evil men and delivered to hard labor in the cold. Not the dog who saves the boy from the fire, or from the well, or from the wild animal, or from the abandoned cave, or from the escaped con. Not that boy, and not that dog.

In the bedroom I shared with my sister, one window faced the street. Light from the church streaked in too. Two small beds only inches apart. A small dresser. Some shelves. One small light on a table between us. One small box for some toys. Autumn dusk, some yellow slag air on the rise. I'm busy at the toy box with a broken thing I'm trying to fix, sitting down facing the door, when dust suddenly shimmers in the light through the window, suddenly fills the light, and I see Spike between me and the door in a knot of shadows becoming something else. He begins to quiver and to jerk his head. He takes a wide stance and struts in the twelve-by-six-foot space between me and the door.

(I went back there once and troubled the poor people of those rooms to let me in. I stood in that room and felt it get smaller and smaller. They watched me shyly from the doorway. On the wall of the room where Spike had entered that other realm, they had a picture of Jesus Christ, glossy blood on his feet and hands; blood dripped from the crown of thorns, but no spirit of Spike, no boy, no residue of terror.)

Spike struts that wide stance and growls in a way I'd never heard him growl   10
before, almost a human word comes out, almost a begging for release, and he whines high and painfully, and he makes a strange yelp too from time to time, and he jumps with all four feet in the air. But I am not afraid. Spike has never hurt me. He would never bite or scratch or snap at me. Not his boy, not even when I'd smacked him. Not even when I'd bitten him and shook his neck in my own mouth. I am not afraid. I only wonder why he moves in this strange way, and why that movement freezes me in place, my brain shutting things down on its own. Only when I see my father's face at the door, looking down at Spike, and then at me, do I know to be afraid.

"Don't move," he shouts, and Spike yelps like a spirit and jumps with all four feet so he makes me laugh. "Don't move and don't say nothing," my father shouts, and he shakes his fist at me, or at Spike.

I can't tell if he's mad at me in my dumb fear, unmoving, or at the dog, whose body is shaking and twitchy and making ugly yelps that must be wrong and bad. I can't tell until I see my father move towards me through the threshold with a grace I didn't know he possessed. He wants to lift me away, he says with his eyes, but Spike is at him like the spinning wild dog he had been the night my father brought him home, with that wild uncontrollable need.

My father jerks back when Spike does this, which makes me know a different terror: the one where the father is mortal. The one where the floodgates open to the world's bright debris. My father can only stand back in the hall, Spike stopped in the doorway, almost stilled in a slow rocking into himself, making quiet, low whines I think sound a lot like crying; they sound a lot like crying to me.

I entered another world then. A world of two small and terrible continents. Two small islands. On one I float in strange light with Spike. Distempered. Rabid, they said in those days. 1953, where Spike will not come towards me when I call him in all the voices that would usually make him come to me or hop and dance, or whine in song for scraps. He only wags his tail a bit when he hears his name, an act that must take unfathomable dog courage to call up from the spinning tunnel of his sickness.

On the other island is my father, and the whole rest of the world as I know it 15 and care for it and want so badly to be among again. But Spike will not have it. I am his, and whenever my father tries to move towards me, Spike leaps, spit and snarl and yelp, from all fours like a toy dog, or like a dog in a cartoon, at my father's throat and drives him back into the hall. A ferocity like beauty.

"Don't move," my father says, and goes away.

Sometimes I feel free and light and brave as that boy I was by my toy box on that island of my sweet life, kept and claimed by the rabid dog who would not let anyone near, who even in his frenzy thought to keep them all away from me, his brain gone wrong except for that. Sometimes I want only to lie down and let it all go.

The time it took for my father to leave and return with a policeman close behind, I can measure only with the weight of need. Mine to simply sit there in my dullness and be the boy I was. Spike's to guard me hard and to the end.

The policeman has a steel bar. I think he'll hit the dog and make him stop, but instead he jabs the bar from the doorway at Spike's head as if to tease. In the policeman's eyes I see his fearful wonder, like in my father's eyes, and this makes me choke and gag. The policeman jabs the bar again until Spike snaps and the policeman pulls the bar away, dragging Spike by his clamped jaw.

I don't remember making words come. I don't remember caring for words, 20 but I remember screaming *Stop* until Spike wags his tail again and almost turns around as if to drag up one more speck of memoried light, before he clenches down hard one last time on the bar and holds it in his rat dog's jaw.

Things move quickly now. I don't search for resolution anymore. What's done is done. I don't know why we long so for the dead who can do us no good.

The policeman drags Spike down the flight of dark stairs. My father follows. I'm left in the room, alone. I can't seem to stand or move until I hear a ruckus on the stairs. Even now, even tonight, with snow like a blanket over the broken day lilies, all of these lives and lives later, even now, I hear that snarling, snapping spit of a dog fighting for his life, and I hear the voices of the men too high in their panic. I run from the room towards the stairs and find my father behind the policeman who has Spike in a noose at the end of a long pole. He pushes Spike down. I grab my father's startled arm and hang on tight. He doesn't even hold me.

"Stay back," is all he says, and he pushes me away.

Outside the policeman holds Spike at bay at the end of the long pole. *That's what kind of trouble you can get into,* I think. He drags Spike towards the back where the garbage is heaped and the broken cars commune. My father stands beside him when he takes his pistol out. No one looks to me on the porch. I watch the policeman take his pistol out, that lovely practiced move. No one looks to me on the porch. I am five years old, and I know enough. My father half turns his head away when the policeman draws the hammer back and squeezes off a round into the rat dog's brain.

This is the end of things, I think. Nothing can go on from this. No light would   25
ever find us again. No peace could fill our hearts. No laughter near the coal stove with the wild dog who danced on his hind legs and turned a dancer's turn and fell and flew around the rooms for us. The end near the garbage heap. My ears ringing, I stand on the porch and let wash over me all the grief and fear and love that keeps blossoming, even now, inside me. World of hurt. Deepest, what remains.

                                                                        [2000]

THINKING ABOUT THE TEXT

1. Where in the text does Weigl seem to express the perspective of his younger self? Where does he seem to express the perspective of the adult writer? Refer to specific passages.

2. What was Spike like before he turned rabid? Describe him in your own words. Why, apparently, did the young Weigl value him? Would you have enjoyed having him as a pet? Why, or why not?

3. Why do you think Weigl included the parenthetical paragraph about his returning to the apartment as an adult?

4. What is the effect when Weigl uses the present tense? Why do you suppose he begins with the past tense instead of using the present tense throughout?

5. What do you take Weigl's last sentence to mean?

MAKING COMPARISONS

1. Unlike Orwell and Dillard, Weigl owned the animal that is killed. How significant is this difference? Also unlike Orwell and Dillard, Weigl was a child when the animal was killed. Again, how significant is this difference?

2. Both Orwell and Dillard recall people watching them during the episodes they write about. Is someone else's gaze just as important in Weigl's essay? Explain.

3. Do all three writers strike you as remembering things objectively? Refer to specific passages that influence your answer.

WRITING ABOUT ISSUES

1. Choose Orwell's, Dillard's, or Weigl's piece, and write an essay explaining how appropriately you think the writer behaved when the animal was killed. Take into account the specific circumstances the writer was in. Also provide reasons for your judgment.

2. Choose Orwell's or Weigl's piece. Then write an essay determining how applicable to your chosen text is Dillard's statement "these things are not issues; they are mysteries." Make clear how Dillard seems to define *issues* and *mysteries*.

3. Write an essay analyzing your behavior at a time when you had to decide how much to endorse the killing of a certain animal or of a certain group of animals. What thoughts ran through your mind? What specific pressures did you face? How did you believe your conduct would be viewed by others? Indicate any significant differences between your younger self and the kind of person you are now.

4. Research a group that is against hunting, against the killing of animals in lab experiments, or against the killing of animals for human consumption. Find out especially about the rhetorical strategies this group uses to advance its cause. Then write an essay identifying and evaluating some of these methods of persuasion.

COMPARING SCHOOL CULTURE WITH THE CULTURE OF HOME: CRITICAL COMMENTARIES ON RICHARD RODRIGUEZ'S "ARIA"

RICHARD RODRIGUEZ, "Aria"

CRITICAL COMMENTARIES:
RAMÓN SALDÍVAR, From *Chicano Narrative*
TOMÁS RIVERA, From "Richard Rodriguez's *Hunger of Memory* as Humanistic Antithesis"
VICTOR VILLANUEVA JR., From "Whose Voice Is It Anyway?"

For many American children, the culture of school differs greatly from the one they know at home. Children of immigrants to America may sense such a cultural divide, especially if their teachers speak English in the classroom while their parents speak another language at home. In his 1982 memoir *Hunger of Memory*, Richard Rodriguez recalls how he faced exactly this situation as the child of Mexican immigrants. Rodriguez uses his own experiences to argue that if the children of immigrants are to succeed in the United States, they must separate themselves from their home culture and immerse themselves in the English-oriented atmosphere of the American school. In making this argument, Rodriguez comes out against bilingual education and affirmative action. When it was first published, many people praised his book for its eloquence, honesty, and realism. Subsequently, however, the book received strong criticism, especially from Hispanic American educators. Several of them disagree with the positions it takes; moreover, they worry that Rodriguez will be seen as the authoritative guide to Hispanic American life. Here we include an excerpt from Rodriguez's book along with comments by three of his Hispanic critics. Although three of these texts are from the 1980s, the issues they examine are still very much alive. In the twenty-first century, people continue to debate how American immigrants and their children should be educated, arguing over such things as California's Proposition 209 (which outlawed racial preferences) and the English Only movement (which wants laws requiring government business to be conducted entirely in English).

BEFORE YOU READ

The following excerpt from Richard Rodriguez's *Hunger of Memory* ends with his claim that "the day I raised my hand in class and spoke loudly to an entire roomful of faces, my childhood started to end." When do you think your childhood started to end? Think of a particular moment or set of experiences.

RICHARD RODRIGUEZ
Aria

A native of San Francisco, California, Richard Rodriguez (b. 1944), is the son of Mexican immigrants. Until he entered school at the age of six, he spoke primarily Spanish. His 1982 memoir Hunger of Memory *describes how English language instruction distanced him from his parents' native culture. Rodriguez went on to attend Stanford University and the University of California at Berkeley, where he earned a doctorate in English Renaissance literature. He is also the author of* Days of Obligation: An Argument with My Mexican Father *(1992) and* Brown: The Last Discovery of America *(2003). Currently Rodriguez is a contributing editor for* Harper's *magazine and a commentator on public television's NewsHour.*

1

I remember to start with that day in Sacramento—a California now nearly thirty years past—when I first entered a classroom, able to understand some fifty stray English words.

The third of four children, I had been preceded to a neighborhood Roman Catholic school by an older brother and sister. But neither of them had revealed very much about their classroom experiences. Each afternoon they returned, as they left in the morning, always together, speaking in Spanish as they climbed the five steps of the porch. And their mysterious books, wrapped in shopping-bag paper, remained on the table next to the door, closed firmly behind them.

An accident of geography sent me to a school where all my classmates were white, many the children of doctors and lawyers and business executives. All my classmates certainly must have been uneasy on that first day of school—as most children are uneasy—to find themselves apart from their families in the first institution of their lives. But I was astonished.

(Photograph by Robert
Messick, Courtesy of
David R. Godine Pub-
lishers Incorporated.)

The nun said, in a friendly but oddly impersonal voice, "Boys and girls, this is Richard Rodriguez." (I heard her sound out: *Rich-heard Road-ree-guess.*) It was the first time I had heard anyone name me in English. "Richard," the nun repeated more slowly, writing my name down in her black leather book. Quickly I turned to see my mother's face dissolve in a watery blur behind the pebbled glass door.

Many years later there is something called bilingual education—a scheme   5
proposed in the late 1960s by Hispanic-American social activists, later endorsed by a congressional vote. It is a program that seeks to permit non-English-speaking children, many from lower-class homes, to use their family language as the language of school. (Such is the goal its supporters announce.) I hear them and am forced to say no: It is not possible for a child—any child—ever to use his family's language in school. Not to understand this is to misunderstand the public uses of schooling and to trivialize the nature of intimate life—a family's "language."

Memory teaches me what I know of these matters; the boy reminds the adult. I was a bilingual child, a certain kind — socially disadvantaged — the son of working-class parents, both Mexican immigrants.

In the early years of my boyhood, my parents coped very well in America. My father had steady work. My mother managed at home. They were nobody's victims. Optimism and ambition led them to a house (our home) many blocks from the Mexican south side of town. We lived among *gringos* and only a block from the biggest, whitest houses. It never occurred to my parents that they couldn't live wherever they chose. Nor was the Sacramento of the fifties bent on teaching them a contrary lesson. My mother and father were more annoyed than intimidated by those two or three neighbors who tried initially to make us unwelcome. ("Keep your brats away from my sidewalk!") But despite all they achieved, perhaps because they had so much to achieve, any deep feeling of ease, the confidence of "belonging" in public was withheld from them both. They regarded the people at work, the faces in crowds, as very distant from us. They were the others, *los gringos*. That term was interchangeable in their speech with another, even more telling, *los americanos*.

I grew up in a house where the only regular guests were my relations. For one day, enormous families of relatives would visit and there would be so many people that the noise and the bodies would spill out to the backyard and front porch. Then, for weeks, no one came by. (It was usually a salesman who rang the doorbell.) Our house stood apart. A gaudy yellow in a row of white bungalows. We were the people with the noisy dog. The people who raised pigeons and chickens. We were the foreigners on the block. A few neighbors smiled and waved. We waved back. But no one in the family knew the names of the old couple who lived next door; until I was seven years old, I did not know the names of the kids who lived across the street.

In public, my father and mother spoke a hesitant, accented, not always grammatical English. And they would have to strain — their bodies tense — to catch the sense of what was rapidly said by *los gringos*. At home they spoke Spanish. The language of their Mexican past sounded in counterpoint to the English of public society. The words would come quickly, with ease. Conveyed through those sounds was the pleasing, soothing, consoling reminder of being at home.

During those years when I was first conscious of hearing, my mother and   10
father addressed me only in Spanish; in Spanish I learned to reply. By contrast, English (*inglés*), rarely heard in the house, was the language I came to associate with *gringos*. I learned my first words of English overhearing my parents speak to strangers. At five years of age, I knew just enough English for my mother to trust me on errands to stores one block away. No more.

I was a listening child, careful to hear the very different sounds of Spanish and English. Wide-eyed with hearing, I'd listen to sounds more than words. First, there were English (*gringo*) sounds. So many words were still unknown that when the butcher or the lady at the drugstore said something to me, exotic polysyllabic sounds would bloom in the midst of their sentences. Often, the speech of people in public seemed to me very loud, booming with confidence. The man behind the counter would literally ask, "What can I do for you?" But by being so firm and so clear, the sound of his voice said that he was a *gringo;* he belonged in public society.

I would also hear then the high nasal notes of middle-class American speech. The air stirred with sound. Sometimes, even now, when I have been traveling abroad for several weeks, I will hear what I heard as a boy. In hotel lobbies or airports, in Turkey or Brazil, some Americans will pass, and suddenly I will hear it again — the high sound of American voices. For a few seconds I will hear it with pleasure, for it is now the sound of *my* society — a reminder of home. But inevitably — already on the flight headed for home — the sound fades with repetition. I will be unable to hear it anymore.

When I was a boy, things were different. The accent of *los gringos* was never pleasing nor was it hard to hear. Crowds at Safeway or at bus stops would be noisy with sound. And I would be forced to edge away from the chirping chatter above me.

I was unable to hear my own sounds, but I knew very well that I spoke English poorly. My words could not stretch far enough to form complete thoughts. And the words I did speak I didn't know well enough to make into distinct sounds. (Listeners would usually lower their heads, better to hear what I was trying to say.) But it was one thing for *me* to speak English with difficulty. It was more troubling for me to hear my parents speak in public: their high-whining vowels and guttural consonants; their sentences that got stuck with "eh" and "ah" sounds; the confused syntax; the hesitant rhythm of sounds so different from the way *gringos* spoke. I'd notice, moreover, that my parents' voices were softer than those of *gringos* we'd meet.

I am tempted now to say that none of this mattered. In adulthood I am embarrassed by childhood fears. And in a way, it didn't matter very much that my parents could not speak English with ease. Their linguistic difficulties had no serious consequences. My mother and father made themselves understood at the county hospital clinic and at government offices. And yet, in another way, it mattered very much — it was unsettling to hear my parents struggle with English. Hearing them, I'd grow nervous, my clutching trust in their protection and power weakened.

There were many times like the night at a brightly lit gasoline station (a blaring white memory) when I stood uneasily, hearing my father. He was talking to a teenaged attendant. I do not recall what they were saying, but I cannot forget the sounds my father made as he spoke. At one point his words slid together to form one word — sounds as confused as the threads of blue and green oil in the puddle next to my shoes. His voice rushed through what he had left to say. And, toward the end, reached falsetto notes, appealing to his listener's understanding. I looked away to the lights of passing automobiles. I tried not to hear anymore. But I heard only too well the calm, easy tones in the attendant's reply. Shortly afterward, walking toward home with my father, I shivered when he put his hand on my shoulder. The very first chance that I got, I evaded his grasp and ran on ahead into the dark, skipping with feigned boyish exuberance.

But then there was Spanish. *Español:* my family's language. *Español:* the language that seemed to me a private language. I'd hear strangers on the radio and in the Mexican Catholic church across town speaking in Spanish, but I

15

couldn't really believe that Spanish was a public language, like English. Spanish speakers, rather, seemed related to me, for I sensed that we shared — through our language — the experience of feeling apart from *los gringos.* It was thus a ghetto Spanish that I heard and I spoke. Like those whose lives are bound by a barrio, I was reminded by Spanish of my separateness from *los otros, los gringos* in power. But more intensely than for most barrio children — because I did not live in a barrio — Spanish seemed to me the language of home. (Most days it was only at home that I'd hear it.) It became the language of joyful return.

A family member would say something to me and I would feel myself specially recognized. My parents would say something to me and I would feel embraced by the sounds of their words. Those sounds said: *I am speaking with ease in Spanish. I am addressing you in words I never use with* los gringos. *I recognize you as someone special, close, like no one outside. You belong with us. In the family.*

(*Ricardo.*)

At the age of five, six, well past the time when most other children no longer easily notice the difference between sounds uttered at home and words spoken in public, I had a different experience. I lived in a world magically compounded of sounds. I remained a child longer than most; I lingered too long, poised at the edge of language — often frightened by the sounds of *los gringos,* delighted by the sounds of Spanish at home. I shared with my family a language that was startlingly different from that used in the great city around us.   20

For me there were none of the gradations between public and private society so normal to a maturing child. Outside the house was public society; inside the house was private. Just opening or closing the screen door behind me was an important experience. I'd rarely leave home all alone or without reluctance. Walking down the sidewalk, under the canopy of tall trees, I'd warily notice the — suddenly — silent neighborhood kids who stood warily watching me. Nervously, I'd arrive at the grocery store to hear there the sounds of the *gringo* — foreign to me — reminding me that in this world so big, I was a foreigner. But then I'd return. Walking back toward our house, climbing the steps from the sidewalk, when the front door was open in summer, I'd hear voices beyond the screen door talking in Spanish. For a second or two, I'd stay, linger there, listening. Smiling, I'd hear my mother call out, saying in Spanish (words): "Is that you, Richard?" All the while her sounds would assure me: *You are home now; come closer; inside. With us.*

"*Sí,*" I'd reply.

Once more inside the house I would resume (assume) my place in the family. The sounds would dim, grow harder to hear. Once more at home, I would grow less aware of that fact. It required, however, no more than the blurt of the doorbell to alert me to listen to sounds all over again. The house would turn instantly still while my mother went to the door. I'd hear her hard English sounds. I'd wait to hear her voice return to soft-sounding Spanish, which assured me, as surely as did the clicking tongue of the lock on the door, that the stranger was gone.

Plainly, it is not healthy to hear such sounds so often. It is not healthy to distinguish public words from private sounds so easily. I remained cloistered by sounds, timid and shy in public, too dependent on voices at home. And yet it needs to be emphasized: I was an extremely happy child at home. I remember many nights when my father would come back from work, and I'd hear him call out to my mother in Spanish, sounding relieved. In Spanish, he'd sound light and free notes he never could manage in English. Some nights I'd jump up just at hearing his voice. With *mis hermanos* I would come running into the room where he was with my mother. Our laughing (so deep was the pleasure!) became screaming. Like others who know the pain of public alienation, we transformed the knowledge of our public separateness and made it consoling — the reminder of intimacy. Excited, we joined our voices in a celebration of sounds. *We are speaking now the way we never speak out in public. We are alone — together,* voices sounded, surrounded to tell me. Some nights, no one seemed willing to loosen the hold sounds had on us. At dinner, we invented new words. (Ours sounded Spanish, but made sense only to us.) We pieced together new words by taking, say, an English verb and giving it Spanish endings. My mother's instructions at bedtime would be lacquered with mock-urgent tones. Or a word like *sí* would become, in several notes, able to convey added measures of feeling. Tongues explored the edges of words, especially the fat vowels. And we happily sounded that military drum roll, the twirling roar of the Spanish *r*. Family language: my family's sounds. The voices of my parents and sisters and brother. Their voices insisting: *You belong here. We are family members. Related. Special to one another. Listen!* Voices singing and sighing, rising, straining, then surging, teeming with pleasure that burst syllables into fragments of laughter. At times it seemed there was steady quiet only when, from another room, the rustling whispers of my parents faded and I moved closer to sleep.

2

Supporters of bilingual education today imply that students like me miss a   25
great deal by not being taught in their family's language. What they seem not to recognize is that, as a socially disadvantaged child, I considered Spanish to be a private language. What I needed to learn in school was that I had the right — and the obligation — to speak the public language of *los gringos*. The odd truth is that my first-grade classmates could have become bilingual, in the conventional sense of that word, more easily than I. Had they been taught (as upper-middle-class children are often taught early) a second language like Spanish or French, they could have regarded it simply as that: another public language. In my case such bilingualism could not have been so quickly achieved. What I did not believe was that I could speak a single public language.

Without question, it would have pleased me to hear my teachers address me in Spanish when I entered the classroom. I would have felt much less afraid. I would have trusted them and responded with ease. But I would have delayed — for how long postponed? — having to learn the language of public society. I would have evaded—and for how long could I have afforded to delay?—learning the great lesson of school, that I had a public identity.

Fortunately, my teachers were unsentimental about their responsibility. What they understood was that I needed to speak a public language. So their voices would search me out, asking me questions. Each time I'd hear them, I'd look up in surprise to see a nun's face frowning at me. I'd mumble, not really meaning to answer. The nun would persist, "Richard, stand up. Don't look at the floor. Speak up. Speak to the entire class, not just to me!" But I couldn't believe that the English language was mine to use. (In part, I did not want to believe it.) I continued to mumble. I resisted the teacher's demands. (Did I somehow suspect that once I learned public language my pleasing family life would be changed?) Silent, waiting for the bell to sound, I remained dazed, diffident, afraid.

Because I wrongly imagined that English was intrinsically a public language and Spanish an intrinsically private one, I easily noted the difference between class-room language and the language of home. At school, words were directed to a general audience of listeners. ("Boys and girls.") Words were meaningfully ordered. And the point was not self-expression alone but to make oneself understood by many others. The teacher quizzed: "Boys and girls, why do we use that word in this sentence? Could we think of a better word to use there? Would the sentence change its meaning if the words were differently arranged? And wasn't there a better way of saying much the same thing?" (I couldn't say. I wouldn't try to say.)

Three months, Five. Half a year passed. Unsmiling, ever watchful, my teachers noted my silence. They began to connect my behavior with the difficult progress my older sister and brother were making. Until one Saturday morning three nuns arrived at the house to talk to our parents. Stiffly, they sat on the blue living room sofa. From the doorway of another room, spying the visitors, I noted the incongruity—the clash of two worlds, the faces and voices of school intruding upon the familiar setting of home. I overheard one voice gently wondering, "Do your children speak only Spanish at home, Mrs. Rodriguez?" While another voice added, "That Richard especially seems so timid and shy."

That Rich-heard!   30

With great tact the visitors continued, "Is it possible for you and your husband to encourage your children to practice their English when they are home?" Of course, my parents complied. What would they not do for their children's well-being? And how could they have questioned the Church's authority which those women represented? In an instant, they agreed to give up the language (the sounds) that had revealed and accentuated our family's closeness. The moment after the visitors left, the change was observed. "*Ahora*, speak to us *en inglés*," my father and mother united to tell us.

At first, it seemed a kind of game. After dinner each night, the family gathered to practice "our" English. (It was still then *inglés*, a language foreign to us, so we felt drawn as strangers to it.) Laughing, we would try to define words we could not pronounce. We played with strange English sounds, often overanglicizing our pronunciations. And we filled the smiling gaps of our sentences with familiar Spanish sounds. But that was cheating, somebody shouted. Everyone laughed. In school, meanwhile, like my brother and sister, I was required to attend a daily tutoring session. I needed a full year of special attention. I also needed my teachers to keep my attention from straying in class by calling out, *Rich-heard*—their English voices slowly prying loose my ties to my other name, its three notes, *Ri-car-do*. Most of all I needed to hear my mother and father speak to me in a moment of seriousness in broken—suddenly heartbreaking—English. The scene was inevitable: One Saturday morning I entered the kitchen where my parents were talking in Spanish. I did not realize that they were talking in Spanish however until, at the moment they saw me, I heard their voices change to speak English. Those *gringo* sounds they uttered startled me. Pushed me away. In that moment of trivial misunderstanding and profound insight, I felt my throat twisted by unsounded grief. I turned quickly and left the room. But I had no place to escape to with Spanish. (The spell was broken.) My brother and sisters were speaking English in another part of the house.

Again and again in the days following, increasingly angry, I was obliged to hear my mother and father: "Speak to us *en inglés.*" (*Speak.*) Only then did I determine to learn classroom English. Weeks after, it happened: One day in school I raised my hand to volunteer an answer. I spoke out in a loud voice. And I did not think it remarkable when the entire class understood. That day, I moved very far from the disadvantaged child I had been only days earlier. The belief, the calming assurance that I belonged in public, had at last taken hold.

Shortly after, I stopped hearing the high and loud sounds of *los gringos*. A more and more confident speaker of English, I didn't trouble to listen to *how* strangers sounded, speaking to me. And there simply were too many English-speaking people in my day for me to hear American accents anymore. Conversations quickened. Listening to persons who sounded eccentrically pitched voices, I usually noted their sounds for an initial few seconds before I concentrated on *what* they were saying. Conversations became content-full. Transparent. Hearing someone's *tone* of voice—angry or questioning or sarcastic or happy or sad—I didn't distinguish it from the words it expressed. Sound and word were thus tightly wedded. At the end of a day, I was often bemused, always relieved, to realize how "silent," though crowded with words, my day in public had been. (This public silence measured and quickened the change in my life.)

At last, seven years old, I came to believe what had been technically true   35
since my birth: I was an American citizen.

But the special feeling of closeness at home was diminished by then. Gone was the desperate, urgent, intense feeling of being at home; rare was the experience of feeling myself individualized by family intimates. We remained a loving family, but one greatly changed. No longer so close; no longer bound tight by the pleasing and troubling knowledge of our public separateness. Neither my older brother nor sister rushed home after school anymore. Nor did I. When I arrived home there would often be neighborhood kids in the house. Or the house would be empty of sounds.

Following the dramatic Americanization of their children, even my parents grew more publicly confident. Especially my mother. She learned the names of all the people on our block. And she decided we needed to have a telephone installed in the house. My father continued to use the word *gringo*. But it was no longer charged with the old bitterness or distrust. (Stripped of any emotional content, the word simply became a name for those Americans not of Hispanic descent.) Hearing him, sometimes, I wasn't sure if he was pronouncing the Spanish word *gringo* or saying gringo in English.

Matching the silence I started hearing in public was a new quiet at home. The family's quiet was partly due to the fact that, as we children learned more and more English, we shared fewer and fewer words with our parents. Sentences needed to be spoken slowly when a child addressed his mother or father. (Often the parent wouldn't understand.) The child would need to repeat himself. (Still the parent misunderstood.) The young voice, frustrated, would end up saying, "Never mind"—the subject was closed. Dinners would be noisy with the clinking of knives and forks against dishes. My mother would smile softly between her remarks; my father at the other end of the table would chew and chew at his food, while he stared over the heads of his children.

My *mother!* My *father!* After English became my primary language, I no longer knew what words to use in addressing my parents. The old Spanish words (those tender accents of sound) I had used earlier—*mamá* and *papá*—I couldn't use anymore. They would have been too painful reminders of how much had changed in my life. On the other hand, the words I heard neighborhood kids call *their* parents seemed equally unsatisfactory. *Mother* and *Father*; *Ma, Papa, Pa, Dad, Pop* (how I hated the all-American sound of that last word especially)—all these terms I felt were unsuitable, not really terms of address for *my* parents. As a result, I never used them at home. Whenever I'd speak to my parents, I would try to get their attention with eye contact alone. In public conversations, I'd refer to "my parents" or "my mother and father."

My mother and father, for their part, responded differently, as their children spoke to them less. She grew restless, seemed troubled and anxious at the scarcity of words exchanged in the house. It was she who would question me about my day when I came home from school. She smiled at small talk. She pried at the edges of my sentences to get me to say something more. (What?) She'd join conversations she overheard, but her intrusions often stopped her children's talking. By contrast, my father seemed reconciled to the new quiet. Though his English improved somewhat, he retired into silence. At dinner he spoke very little. One night his children and even his wife helplessly giggled at his garbled English pronunciation of the Catholic Grace before Meals. Thereafter he made his wife recite the prayer at the start of each meal, even on formal occasions, when there were guests in the house. Hers became the public voice of the family. On official business, it was she, not my father, one would usually hear on the phone or in stores, talking to strangers. His children grew so accustomed to his silence that, years later, they would speak routinely of his shyness. (My mother would often try to explain: Both his parents died when he was eight. He was raised by an uncle who treated him like little more than a menial servant. He was never encouraged to speak. He grew up alone. A man of few words.) But my father was not shy, I realized, when I'd watch him speaking Spanish with relatives. Using Spanish, he was quickly effusive. Especially when talking with other men, his voice would spark, flicker, flare alive with sounds. In Spanish, he expressed ideas and feelings he rarely revealed in English. With firm Spanish sounds, he conveyed confidence and authority English would never allow him.

The silence at home, however, was finally more than a literal silence. Fewer words passed between parent and child, but more profound was the silence that resulted from my inattention to sounds. At about the time I no longer bothered to listen with care to the sounds of English in public, I grew careless about listening to the sounds family members made when they spoke. Most of the time I heard someone speaking at home and didn't distinguish his sounds from the words people uttered in public. I didn't even pay much attention to my parents' accented and ungrammatical speech. At least not at home. Only when I was with them in public would I grow alert to their accents. Though, even then, their sounds caused me less and less concern. For I was increasingly confident of my own public identity.

I would have been happier about my public success had I not sometimes recalled what it had been like earlier, when my family had conveyed its intimacy through a set of conveniently private sounds. Sometimes in public, hearing a stranger, I'd hark back to my past. A Mexican farmworker approached me downtown to ask directions to somewhere. "*¿Hijito . . . ?*" he said. And his voice summoned deep longing. Another time, standing beside my mother in the visiting room of a Carmelite convent, before the dense screen which rendered the nuns shadowy figures, I heard several Spanish-speaking nuns — their busy, singsong overlapping voices — assure us that yes, yes, we were remembered, all our family was remembered in their prayers. (Their voices echoed faraway family sounds.) Another day, a dark-faced old woman — her hand light on my shoulder — steadied herself against me as she boarded a bus. She murmured something I couldn't quite comprehend. Her Spanish voice came near, like the face of a never-before-seen relative in the instant before I was kissed. Her voice, like so many of the Spanish voices I'd hear in public, recalled the golden age of my youth. Hearing Spanish then, I continued to be a careful, if sad, listener to sounds. Hearing a Spanish-speaking family walking behind me, I turned to look. I smiled for an instant, before my glance found the Hispanic-looking faces of strangers in the crowd going by.

Today I hear bilingual educators say that children lose a degree of "individuality" by becoming assimilated into public society. (Bilingual schooling was popularized in the seventies, that decade when middle-class ethnics began to resist the process of assimilation — the American melting pot.) But the bilingualists simplistically scorn the value and necessity of assimilation. They do not seem to realize that there are *two* ways a person is individualized. So they do not realize that while one suffers a diminished sense of *private* individuality by becoming assimilated into public society, such assimilation makes possible the achievement of *public* individuality.

The bilingualists insist that a student should be reminded of his difference from others in mass society, his heritage. But they equate mere separateness with individuality. The fact is that only in private — with intimates — is separateness from the crowd a prerequisite for individuality. (An intimate draws me apart, tells me that I am unique, unlike all others.) In public, by contrast, full individuality is achieved, paradoxically, by those who are able to consider themselves members of the crowd. Thus it happened for me: Only when I was able to think of myself as an American, no longer an alien in *gringo* society, could I seek the rights and opportunities necessary for full public individuality. The social and political advantages I enjoy as a man result from the day that I came to believe that my name, indeed, is *Rich-heard Road-ree-guess*. It is true that my public society today is often impersonal. (My public society is usually mass society.) Yet despite the anonymity of the crowd and despite the fact that the individuality I achieve in public is often tenuous — because it depends on my being one in a crowd — I celebrate the day I acquired my new name. Those middle-class ethnics who scorn assimilation seem to me filled with decadent self-pity, obsessed by the burden of public life. Dangerously, they romanticize public separateness and they trivialize the dilemma of the socially disadvantaged.

My awkward childhood does not prove the necessity of bilingual education.   45
My story discloses instead an essential myth of childhood — inevitable pain. If I rehearse here the changes in my private life after my Americanization, it is finally to emphasize the public gain. The loss implies the gain: The house I returned to each afternoon was quiet. Intimate sounds no longer rushed to the door to greet me. There were other noises inside. The telephone rang. Neighborhood kids ran past the door of the bedroom where I was reading my schoolbooks — covered with shopping-bag paper. Once I learned public language, it would never again be easy for me to hear intimate family voices. More and more of my day was spent hearing words. But that may only be a way of saying that the day I raised my hand in class and spoke loudly to an entire roomful of faces, my childhood started to end.   [1982]

THINKING ABOUT THE TEXT

1. What distinctions does Rodriguez make between the "private" and "public" worlds of his childhood? Ultimately, he brings up the possibility of "*public* individuality" (para. 43). What does he mean by this? Does this concept make sense to you?

2. What, according to Rodriguez, were the changes he experienced? With what tone does he recall these changes? Consider in particular the way he describes his changing relationship to his parents.

3. Do you agree with Rodriguez that the changes he went through were necessary? To what extent is your answer influenced by your own social position?

4. Rodriguez declares, "Those middle-class ethnics who scorn assimilation seem to me filled with decadent self-pity, obsessed by the burden of public life. Dangerously, they romanticize public separateness and they trivialize the dilemma of the socially disadvantaged" (para. 44). Evaluate this claim. Would you say that you are a "middle-class ethnic"? Why, or why not?

5. Rodriguez suggests that a student must speak up in class to succeed in school. Do you agree? Rodriguez indicates that matters of language play a crucial role in a child's education. Have you found this true? Be specific.

RAMÓN SALDÍVAR
From *Chicano Narrative*

Ramón Saldívar (b. 1949) is the Hoagland Family Professor of English and Comparative Literature at Stanford University. There he is also associate dean in the School of Humanities and Sciences as well as vice provost for undergraduate education. The following remarks about Hunger of Memory *come from Saldívar's 1990 book* Chicano Narrative.

Once Rodriguez learns a public language, he acquires a public identity. But he realizes that in his transformation from the private person of the home-centered Mexican culture to the public assimilated man of the Anglo society he has lost something. Each world's language brought out different emotions. Spanish radiated family intimacy but also provoked shame and embarrassment. English opened doors to society's networks, rewards, and recognitions, but also subverted the family's sense of intimacy. His life then becomes a tenuous attempt to hold off these contradictions, to accept the benefits of his Mexican-ness while rejecting its demands, until he must irrevocably choose between them.

And choose he does. He chooses with great anxiety and precious sadness to reject the duality of his working-class origins and his middle-class manners; he chooses to market his existential anguish to the most receptive audience imaginable: the right-wing establishment and the liberal academic intelligentsia. His writings against bilingual education [because it is a hindrance to the access to a "public" language] and against affirmative action [because it denigrates the achievements of those who have made it on their own merits] involve him, whether he admits it or not, in a political service to the Right. Rodriguez chooses to assimilate without ever considering whether he acted by will or merely submitted to an unquestioned grander scheme of political ideology.   [1990]

TOMÁS RIVERA
From *"Richard Rodriguez's* Hunger of Memory *as Humanistic Antithesis"*

Tomás Rivera (1935–1984) was chancellor of the University of California at the time he wrote the following comments. They appear in his article "Richard Rodriguez's Hunger of Memory *as Humanistic Antithesis," which was published posthumously in a 1984 issue of the journal* Melus.

[Rodriguez's] search for life and form in the literary form of autobiography has as a premise the basic core of family life. But then Richard Rodriguez struggles with the sense of dissociation from that basic culture. Clearly, he opts to dissociate, and, as a scholar, attempts to rationalize that only through dissociation from a native culture was he to gain and thus has gained the "other," that is, the "public" world. Without wisdom he almost forgets the original passions of human life. Is he well educated in literature? For literature above all gives and inculcates in the student and scholar the fundamental original elements of humanistic endeavor without regard to race or language, much less with regards to a public voice. The most important ideas that the study of the humanities relates are the fundamental values and elements of human beings, regardless of race and nationality. Ultimately, the study of the humanities teaches the idea that life is a relationship with the totality of people within its circumstance.

Then we come to the question of place and being. In Spanish there are two verbs meaning "to be," *ser* and *estar*. This is quite important to *Hunger of Memory*. Being born into a family is equal to being, *ser*. Education and instruction teaches us to be, *estar*. Both are fundamental verbs. *Ser* is an interior stage, and *estar* is an exterior one. To leave the *ser* only for the *estar* is a grievous error. Richard Rodriguez implies, at times explicitly, that the authentic being is and can be only in the *estar* (public voice) and only there is he/she complete. And further, he states that authenticity can only come by being an exterior being in English in the English speaking world. In the Hispanic world, the interior world of *ser* is ultimately more important than the world of *estar*. *Honra*, honesty, emanates from and is important to the *ser*. Richard Rodriguez opts for the *estar* world as the more important and does not give due importance to the world of *ser*. He has problems, in short, with the world from which he came. Surely this is an antithesis to a humanistic development

As with memory, the centrality of language is a constant pattern in the book. For the Hispanic reader the struggle quickly becomes English versus Spanish. His parents do not know the grand development of the Spanish language and its importance beyond their immediate family. However, Richard Rodriguez should, as an educated person, recognize this grand development. Surely, he could have given credit to the development of a language that has existed over six hundred years, which has elaborated a world literature, which has mixed with the many languages of the American continents, which is perhaps the most analytical of the romance languages, and which will be of such importance in the twenty-first century. Instead Richard Rodriguez flees, as a young man, from this previous human achievement. This fleeing is understandable as a symbol of the pressures of the Americanization process. Yet, as a formally educated scholar, reflecting upon that flight, he does not dare to signal the importance that the language has. Instead he sees it as an activity that has no redeeming value. He gives no value to the Hispanic language, its culture, its arts. It is difficult to believe that as an educated humanist he doesn't recognize the most important element of Hispanic culture — the context of the development of the distinct religions in the Spanish peninsula — the Judaic, the Christian, and the Moorish. These distinct cultures reached their apogees and clearly influenced Spanish. As a humanist, surely he must know this. The Hispanic world has elaborated and developed much in the history of ideas. Richard Rodriguez seems to indicate that the personal Spanish voice lacks the intelligence and ability to communicate beyond the sensibilities of the personal interactions of personal family life. This is intolerable. Hispanic culture has a historical tradition of great intellectual development.

[1984]

VICTOR VILLANUEVA JR.
From *"Whose Voice Is It Anyway?"*

Of Puerto Rican descent, Victor Villanueva Jr. (b. 1948) grew up in New York City. Currently he is Professor and Chair of English at Washington State University in Pullman, Washington. In 1993 he published an autobiography entitled Bootstraps: The Autobiography of an Academic of Color. *The following remarks come from his article "Whose Voice Is It Anyway? Rodriguez's Speech in Retrospect," which appeared in a 1987 issue of* English Journal. *As its title implies, Villanueva's article concerns not only* Hunger of Memory *but also a speech that Richard Rodriguez gave at a convention of English teachers.*

[Rodriguez] is a fine writer; of that there can be no doubt. But it is his message that has brought him fame, a message that states that the minority is no different than any other immigrant who came to this country not knowing its culture or its language, leaving much of the old country behind to become part of this new one, and in becoming part of America subtly changing what it means to be American. . . .

But choice hardly entered into most minorities' decisions to become American. Most of us recognize this when it comes to Blacks or American Indians. Slavery, forcible displacement, and genocide are fairly clear-cut. Yet the circumstances by which most minorities became Americans are no less clear-cut. The minority became an American almost by default, as part of the goods in big-time real-estate deals or as some of the spoils of war. What is true for the Native American applies to the Alaska Native, the Pacific Islander (including the Asian), Mexican Americans, Puerto Ricans. Puerto Rico was part of Christopher Columbus's great discovery, Arawaks and Boriquens among his "Indians," a real-estate coup for the Queen of Spain. Then one day in 1898, the Puerto Ricans who had for nearly four hundred years been made proud to be the offspring of Spain, so much so that their native Arawak and Boricua languages and ways were virtually gone, found themselves the property of the United States, property without the rights and privileges of citizenship until — conveniently — World War I. But citizenship notwithstanding, Puerto Rico remains essentially a colony today.

One day in 1845 and in 1848 other descendants of Spain who had all but lost their Indian identities found themselves Americans. These were the longtime residents and landowners of the Republic of Texas and the California Republic: the area from Texas to New Mexico, Arizona, Utah, and California. Residents in the newly established U.S. territories were given the option to relocate to Mexico or to remain on their native lands, with the understanding that should they remain they would be guaranteed American Constitutional rights. Those who stayed home saw their rights not very scrupulously guarded, falling victim over time to displacement, dislocation, and forced expatriation. There is something tragic in losing a long-established birthright, tragic but not heroic — especially not heroic to those whose ancestors had fled their homelands rather than acknowledge external rule.

The immigrant gave up much in the name of freedom — and for the sake of dignity. For the Spanish-speaking minority in particular, the freedom to be American without once again relinquishing one's ancestry is also a matter of dignity. . . .

Today I sport a doctorate in English from a major university, study and teach   5
rhetoric at another university, do research in and teach composition, continue to enjoy and teach English literature. I live in an all-American city in the heart of America. And I know I am not quite assimilated. In one weekend I was asked if I was Iranian one day and East Indian the next. "No," I said. "You have an accent," I was told. Yet tape recordings and passing comments throughout the years have told me that though there is a "Back East" quality to my voice, there isn't much of New York to it anymore, never mind the Black English of my younger years or the Spanish of my youngest. My "accent" was in my not sounding midwestern, which does have a discernible, though not usually a pronounced, regional quality. And my "accent," I would guess, was in my "foreign" features (which pale alongside the brown skin of Richard Rodriguez).

Friends think I make too much of such incidents. Minority hypersensitivity, they say. They desensitize me (and display their liberal attitudes) with playful jabs at Puerto Ricans: greasy-hair jokes, knife-in-pocket jokes, spicy-food jokes (and Puerto Ricans don't even eat hot foods, unless we're eating Mexican or East Indian foods). If language alone were the secret to assimilation, the rate of Puerto Rican and Mexican success would be greater, I think. So many Mexican Americans and Puerto Ricans remain in the barrios — even those who are monolingual, who have never known Spanish. If language alone were the secret, wouldn't the secret have gotten out long before Richard Rodriguez recorded his memoirs?

[1987]

MAKING COMPARISONS

1. Do you agree with Saldívar that Rodriguez's narrative serves the interests of political conservatives? Why, or why not?

2. To Rivera, Rodriguez fails to appreciate the rich cultural heritage behind Spanish as a language. Is it possible to value this heritage and yet still feel that the nuns were right to insist that his parents speak English at home? Explain.

3. How does Villanueva see minorities as different from immigrants? Does this distinction make sense to you? He argues that minorities need more than mastery of English if other Americans are to accept them. What do you think is required for such acceptance?

WRITING ABOUT ISSUES

1. Write an essay arguing for a particular characterization of the older Rodriguez, focusing on particular words that he uses as he recalls his childhood.

2. Should the young Rodriguez's school have been more respectful toward his home language and culture? Write an essay stating and arguing for your answer to this question. Refer to at least one of the critics quoted here. (Keep in mind that you don't have to agree with any of them.)

3. Write an essay recalling an experience that made you aware of the extent to which school had distanced you from the values and habits you knew at home. Perhaps you came to see the distance as vast; then again, perhaps you decided that it was minimal or nonexistent. Describe the experience with specific details and identify the conclusions it led you to. Also indicate whether you feel the same way as you look back on the experience now.

4. Write an essay arguing for your position on bilingual education or the English Only movement. Refer to at least two articles on your chosen topic. If you wish, refer to one or more of the selections in this cluster.

A WEB ASSIGNMENT

In the Web Assignments section of the *Making Arguments about Literature* Web site, you will find a link to the oral and visual "essays" that Richard Rodriguez has presented on PBS's *NewsHour*. Choose one of these pieces, and write an essay in which you relate it to "Aria." You may be especially interested in Rodriguez's essay for September 15, 1998, entitled "Language or Silence." (You can reach it by clicking the "Additional Essays" sign at the bottom of the original screen.) In this selection, Rodriguez examines issues surrounding the word *gay*. Furthermore, he states that he himself is gay and that he considers it important to acknowledge publicly his sexual orientation. In "Aria," however, and in the book *Hunger of Memory* from which it comes, Rodriguez did not reveal his homosexuality. In fact, many gays and lesbians have criticized him for this omission. If you wish, use your essay to explore how "Aria" nevertheless anticipates ideas he raises in "Language or Silence."

Visit www.bedfordstmartins.com/argumentsaboutlit

A Gallery
of Literature

13

A Gallery of Stories

JAMES BALDWIN
Sonny's Blues

James Baldwin (1924–1987) wanted to be a writer since he was a boy growing up in Harlem. He continued his writing through high school while also following in his foster father's footsteps by doing some preaching. On his own since he was eighteen, Baldwin left Greenwich Village in 1948 and moved to Paris. He lived in France for eight years before returning to New York, where he wrote widely about the civil rights movement. Indeed, passionate and eloquent essays like those in Notes of a Native Son *(1955) and* The Fire Next Time *(1963) exploring the place of African Americans in contemporary society are considered among the best nonfiction of Baldwin's generation.*

Being an artist and an African American were lifelong central issues for Baldwin. His fiction confronts the psychological challenges that were inevitable for black writers searching for identity in America. Themes of responsibility, pain, identity, frustration, and bitterness are woven into his fiction along with understanding, equanimity, love, and tolerance. "Sonny's Blues," from Going to Meet the Man *(1965), is one of his strongest dramatizations of the struggles and achievements of black artists.*

I read about it in the paper, in the subway, on my way to work. I read it, and I couldn't believe it, and I read it again. Then perhaps I just stared at it, at the newsprint spelling out his name, spelling out the story. I stared at it in the swinging lights of the subway car, and in the faces and bodies of the people, and in my own face, trapped in the darkness which roared outside.

It was not to be believed and I kept telling myself that, as I walked from the subway station to the high school. And at the same time I couldn't doubt it. I was scared, scared for Sonny. He became real to me again. A great block of ice got settled in my belly and kept melting there slowly all day long, while I taught my classes algebra. It was a special kind of ice. It kept melting, sending trickles of ice water all up and down my veins, but it never got less. Sometimes it hardened and seemed to expand until I felt my guts were going to come spilling out or that I was going to choke or scream. This would always be at a moment when I was remembering some specific thing Sonny had once said or done.

When he was about as old as the boys in my classes his face had been bright and open, there was a lot of copper in it; and he'd had wonderfully direct brown eyes, and great gentleness and privacy. I wondered what he looked like now. He had been picked up, the evening before, in a raid on an apartment downtown, for peddling and using heroin.

I couldn't believe it: but what I mean by that is that I couldn't find any room for it anywhere inside me. I had kept it outside me for a long time. I hadn't wanted to know. I had had suspicions, but I didn't name them, I kept putting them away. I told myself that Sonny was wild, but he wasn't crazy. And he'd always been a good boy, he hadn't ever turned hard or evil or disrespectful, the way kids can, so quick, so quick, especially in Harlem. I didn't want to believe that I'd ever see my brother going down, coming to nothing, all that light in his face gone out, in the condition I'd already seen so many others. Yet it had happened and here I was, talking about algebra to a lot of boys who might, every one of them for all I knew, be popping off needles every time they went to the head. Maybe it did more for them than algebra could.

I was sure that the first time Sonny had ever had horse, he couldn't have been much older than these boys were now. These boys, now, were living as we'd been living then, they were growing up with a rush and their heads bumped abruptly against the low ceiling of their actual possibilities. They were filled with rage. All they really knew were two darknesses, the darkness of their lives, which was now closing in on them, and the darkness of the movies, which had blinded them to that other darkness, and in which they now, vindictively, dreamed, at once more together than they were at any other time, and more alone.   5

When the last bell rang, the last class ended, I let out my breath. It seemed I'd been holding it for all that time. My clothes were wet—I may have looked as though I'd been sitting in a steam bath, all dressed up, all afternoon. I sat alone in the classroom a long time. I listened to the boys outside, downstairs, shouting and cursing and laughing. Their laughter struck me for perhaps the first time. It was not the joyous laughter which—God knows why—one associates with children. It was mocking and insular, its intent to denigrate. It was disenchanted, and in this, also, lay the authority of their curses. Perhaps I was listening to them because I was thinking about my brother and in them I heard my brother. And myself.

One boy was whistling a tune, at once very complicated and very simple, it seemed to be pouring out of him as though he were a bird, and it sounded very cool and moving through all that harsh, bright air, only just holding its own through all those other sounds.

I stood up and walked over to the window and looked down into the courtyard. It was the beginning of the spring and the sap was rising in the boys. A teacher passed through them every now and again, quickly, as though he or she couldn't wait to get out of that courtyard, to get those boys out of their sight and off their minds. I started collecting my stuff. I thought I'd better get home and talk to Isabel.

The courtyard was almost deserted by the time I got downstairs. I saw this boy standing in the shadow of a doorway, looking just like Sonny. I almost called his name. Then I saw that it wasn't Sonny, but somebody we used to know, a boy from around our block. He'd been Sonny's friend. He'd never been mine, having been too young for me, and, anyway, I'd never liked him. And now, even though he was a grown-up man, he still hung around that block, still spent hours on the street corners, was always high and raggy. I used to run into him from time to time and he'd often work around to asking me for a quarter or fifty cents. He always had some real good excuse, too, and I always gave it to him, I don't know why.

But now, abruptly, I hated him. I couldn't stand the way he looked at me, partly like a dog, partly like a cunning child. I wanted to ask him what the hell he was doing in the school courtyard.   10

He sort of shuffled over to me, and he said, "I see you got the papers. So you already know about it."

"You mean about Sonny? Yes, I already know about it. How come they didn't get you?"

He grinned. It made him repulsive and it also brought to mind what he'd looked like as a kid. "I wasn't there. I stay away from them people."

"Good for you." I offered him a cigarette and I watched him through the smoke. "You come all the way down here just to tell me about Sonny?"

"That's right." He was sort of shaking his head and his eyes looked strange, as   15
though they were about to cross. The bright sun deadened his damp dark brown skin and it made his eyes look yellow and showed up the dirt in his kinked hair. He smelled funky. I moved a little away from him and I said, "Well, thanks. But I already know about it and I got to get home."

"I'll walk you a little ways," he said. We started walking. There were a couple of kids still loitering in the courtyard and one of them said goodnight to me and looked strangely at the boy beside me.

"What're you going to do?" he asked me. "I mean, about Sonny?"

"Look. I haven't seen Sonny for over a year. I'm not sure I'm going to do anything. Anyway, what the hell *can* I do?"

"That's right," he said quickly, "ain't nothing you can do. Can't much help old Sonny no more, I guess."

It was what I was thinking and so it seemed to me he had no right to say it.   20

"I'm surprised at Sonny, though," he went on—he had a funny way of talking, he looked straight ahead as though he were talking to himself—"I thought Sonny was a smart boy, I thought he was too smart to get hung."

"I guess he thought so too," I said sharply, "and that's how he got hung. And now about you? You're pretty goddamn smart, I bet."

Then he looked directly at me, just for a minute. "I ain't smart," he said. "If I was smart, I'd have reached for a pistol a long time ago."

"Look. Don't tell *me* your sad story, if it was up to me, I'd give you one." Then I felt guilty—guilty, probably, for never having supposed that the poor bastard *had* a story of his own, much less a sad one, and I asked, quickly, "What's going to happen to him now?"

He didn't answer this. He was off by himself some place. "Funny thing," he   25
said, and from his tone we might have been discussing the quickest way to get to
Brooklyn, "when I saw the papers this morning, the first thing I asked myself was
if I had anything to do with it. I felt sort of responsible."

I began to listen more carefully. The subway station was on the corner, just
before us, and I stopped. He stopped, too. We were in front of a bar and he
ducked slightly, peering in, but whoever he was looking for didn't seem to be
there. The juke box was blasting away with something black and bouncy and I
half watched the barmaid as she danced her way from the juke box to her place
behind the bar. And I watched her face as she laughingly responded to something
someone said to her, still keeping time to the music. When she smiled one saw
the little girl, one sensed the doomed, still-struggling woman beneath the battered face of the semi-whore.

"I never *give* Sonny nothing," the boy said finally, "but a long time ago I come
to school high and Sonny asked me how it felt." He paused, I couldn't bear to watch
him, I watched the barmaid, and I listened to the music which seemed to be causing the pavement to shake. "I told him it felt great." The music stopped, the barmaid paused and watched the juke box until the music began again. "It did."

All this was carrying me some place I didn't want to go. I certainly didn't
want to know how it felt. It filled everything, the people, the houses, the music,
the dark, quicksilver barmaid, with menace; and this menace was their reality.

"What's going to happen to him now?" I asked again.

"They'll send him away some place and they'll try to cure him." He shook his   30
head. "Maybe he'll even think he's kicked the habit. Then they'll let him
loose" — he gestured, throwing his cigarette into the gutter. "That's all."

"What do you mean, that's *all*?"

But I knew what he meant.

"I *mean*, that's *all*." He turned his head and looked at me, pulling down the
corners of his mouth. "Don't you know what I mean?" he asked, softly.

"How the hell *would* I know what you mean?" I almost whispered it, I don't
know why.

"That's right," he said to the air, "how would *he* know what I mean?" He   35
turned toward me again, patient and calm, and yet I somehow felt him shaking,
shaking as though he were going to fall apart. I felt that ice in my guts again, the
dread I'd felt all afternoon; and again I watched the barmaid, moving about the
bar, washing glasses, and singing. "Listen. They'll let him out and then it'll just
start all over again. That's what I mean."

"You mean — they'll let him out. And then he'll just start working his way
back in again. You mean he'll never kick the habit. Is that what you mean?"

"That's right," he said, cheerfully. "*You* see what I mean."

"Tell me," I said at last, "why does he want to die? He must want to die, he's
killing himself, why does he want to die?"

He looked at me in surprise. He licked his lips. "He don't want to die. He
wants to live. Don't nobody want to die, ever."

Then I wanted to ask him — too many things. He could not have answered,   40
or if he had, I could not have borne the answers. I started walking. "Well, I guess
it's none of my business."

"It's going to be rough on old Sonny," he said. We reached the subway station. "This is your station?" he asked. I nodded. I took one step down. "Damn!" he said, suddenly. I looked up at him. He grinned again. "Damn it if I didn't leave all my money home. You ain't got a dollar on you, have you? Just for a couple of days, is all."

All at once something inside gave and threatened to come pouring out of me. I didn't hate him any more. I felt that in another moment I'd start crying like a child.

"Sure," I said. "Don't sweat." I looked in my wallet and didn't have a dollar, I only had a five. "Here," I said. "That hold you?"

He didn't look at it—he didn't want to look at it. A terrible closed look came over his face, as though he were keeping the number on the bill a secret from him and me. "Thanks," he said, and now he was dying to see me go. "Don't worry about Sonny. Maybe I'll write him or something."

"Sure," I said. "You do that. So long."   45

"Be seeing you," he said. I went on down the steps.

And I didn't write Sonny or send him anything for a long time. When I finally did, it was just after my little girl died, he wrote me back a letter which made me feel like a bastard.

Here's what he said:

> Dear brother,
> You don't know how much I needed to hear from you. I wanted to write you many a time but I dug how much I must have hurt you and so I didn't write. But now I feel like a man who's been trying to climb up out of some deep, real deep and funky hole and just saw the sun up there, outside. I got to get outside.
> I can't tell you much about how I got here. I mean I don't know how to tell you. I guess I was afraid of something or I was trying to escape from something and you know I have never been very strong in the head (smile). I'm glad Mama and Daddy are dead and can't see what's happened to their son and I swear if I'd known what I was doing I would never have hurt you so, you and a lot of other fine people who were nice to me and who believed in me.
> I don't want you to think it had anything to do with me being a musician. It's more than that. Or maybe less than that. I can't get anything straight in my head down here and I try not to think about what's going to happen to me when I get outside again. Sometime I think I'm going to flip and *never* get outside and sometime I think I'll come straight back. I tell you one thing, though, I'd rather blow my brains out than go through this again. But that's what they all say, so they tell me. If I tell you when I'm coming to New York and if you could meet me, I sure would appreciate it. Give my love to Isabel and the kids and I was sure sorry to hear about little Gracie. I wish I could be like Mama and say the Lord's will be done, but I don't know it seems to me that trouble is the one thing that never does get stopped and I don't know what good it does to blame it on the Lord. But maybe it does some good if you believe it.
>
> Your brother,
> Sonny

Then I kept in constant touch with him and I sent him whatever I could and I went to meet him when he came back to New York. When I saw him many things I thought I had forgotten came flooding back to me. This was because I had begun, finally, to wonder about Sonny, about the life that Sonny lived inside. This life, whatever it was, had made him older and thinner and it had deepened the distant stillness in which he had always moved. He looked very unlike my baby brother. Yet, when he smiled, when we shook hands, the baby brother I'd never known looked out from the depths of his private life, like an animal waiting to be coaxed into the light.

"How you been keeping?" he asked me.   50

"All right. And you?"

"Just fine." He was smiling all over his face. "It's good to see you again."

"It's good to see you."

The seven years' difference in our ages lay between us like a chasm: I wondered if these years would ever operate between us as a bridge. I was remembering, and it made it hard to catch my breath, that I had been there when he was born; and I had heard the first words he had ever spoken. When he started to walk, he walked from our mother straight to me. I caught him just before he fell when he took the first steps he ever took in this world.

"How's Isabel?"   55

"Just fine. She's dying to see you."

"And the boys?"

"They're fine, too. They're anxious to see their uncle."

"Oh, come on. You know they don't remember me."

"Are you kidding? Of course they remember you."   60

He grinned again. We got into a taxi. We had a lot to say to each other, far too much to know how to begin.

As the taxi began to move, I asked, "You still want to go to India?"

He laughed. "You still remember that. Hell, no. This place is Indian enough for me."

"It used to belong to them," I said.

And he laughed again. "They damn sure knew what they were doing when   65
they got rid of it."

Years ago, when he was around fourteen, he'd been all hipped on the idea of going to India. He read books about people sitting on rocks, naked, in all kinds of weather, but mostly bad, naturally, and walking barefoot through hot coals and arriving at wisdom. I used to say that it sounded to me as though they were getting away from wisdom as fast as they could. I think he sort of looked down on me for that.

"Do you mind," he asked, "if we have the driver drive alongside the park? On the west side—I haven't seen the city in so long."

"Of course not," I said. I was afraid that I might sound as though I were humoring him, but I hoped he wouldn't take it that way.

So we drove along, between the green of the park and the stony, lifeless elegance of hotels and apartment buildings, toward the vivid, killing streets of our childhood. These streets hadn't changed, though housing projects jutted up out

of them now like rocks in the middle of a boiling sea. Most of the houses in which
we had grown up had vanished, as had the stores from which we had stolen, the
basements in which we had first tried sex, the rooftops from which we had hurled
tin cans and bricks. But houses exactly like the houses of our past yet dominated
the landscape, boys exactly like the boys we once had been found themselves
smothering in these houses, came down into the streets for light and air and
found themselves encircled by disaster. Some escaped the trap, most didn't.
Those who got out always left something of themselves behind, as some animals
amputate a leg and leave it in the trap. It might be said, perhaps, that I had
escaped, after all, I was a school teacher; or that Sonny had, he hadn't lived in
Harlem for years. Yet, as the cab moved uptown through streets which seemed,
with a rush, to darken with dark people, and as I covertly studied Sonny's face, it
came to me that what we both were seeking through our separate cab windows
was that part of ourselves which had been left behind. It's always at the hour of
trouble and confrontation that the missing member aches.

We hit 110th Street and started rolling up Lenox Avenue. And I'd known this   70
avenue all my life, but it seemed to me again, as it had seemed on the day I'd first
heard about Sonny's trouble, filled with a hidden menace which was its very
breath of life.

"We almost there," said Sonny.

"Almost." We were both too nervous to say anything more.

We live in a housing project. It hasn't been up long. A few days after it was up
it seemed uninhabitably new, now, of course, it's already rundown. It looks like a
parody of the good, clean, faceless life—God knows the people who live in it do
their best to make it a parody. The beat-looking grass lying around isn't enough to
make their lives green, the hedges will never hold out the streets, and they know
it. The big windows fool no one, they aren't big enough to make space out of no
space. They don't bother with the windows, they watch the TV screen instead.
The playground is most popular with the children who don't play at jacks, or skip
rope, or roller skate, or swing, and they can be found in it after dark. We moved in
partly because it's not too far from where I teach, and partly for the kids; but it's
really just like the houses in which Sonny and I grew up. The same things happen, they'll have the same things to remember. The moment Sonny and I started
into the house I had the feeling that I was simply bringing him back into the danger he had almost died trying to escape.

Sonny has never been talkative. So I don't know why I was sure he'd be dying
to talk to me when supper was over the first night. Everything went fine, the oldest boy remembered him, and the youngest boy liked him, and Sonny had
remembered to bring something for each of them; and Isabel, who is really much
nicer than I am, more open and giving, had gone to a lot of trouble about dinner
and was genuinely glad to see him. And she's always been able to tease Sonny in a
way that I haven't. It was nice to see her face so vivid again and to hear her laugh
and watch her make Sonny laugh. She wasn't, or, anyway, she didn't seem to be,
at all uneasy or embarrassed. She chatted as though there were no subject which
had to be avoided and she got Sonny past his first, faint stiffness. And thank God
she was there, for I was filled with that icy dread again. Everything I did seemed

awkward to me, and everything I said sounded freighted with hidden meaning. I was trying to remember everything I'd heard about dope addiction and I couldn't help watching Sonny for signs. I wasn't doing it out of malice. I was trying to find out something about my brother. I was dying to hear him tell me he was safe.

"Safe!" my father grunted, whenever Mama suggested trying to move to a   75 neighborhood which might be safer for children. "Safe, hell! Ain't no place safe for kids, nor nobody."

He always went on like this, but he wasn't, ever, really as bad as he sounded, not even on weekends, when he got drunk. As a matter of fact, he was always on the lookout for "something a little better," but he died before he found it. He died suddenly, during a drunken weekend in the middle of the war, when Sonny was fifteen. He and Sonny hadn't ever got on too well. And this was partly because Sonny was the apple of his father's eye. It was because he loved Sonny so much and was frightened for him, that he was always fighting with him. It doesn't do any good to fight with Sonny. Sonny just moves back, inside himself, where he can't be reached. But the principal reason that they never hit it off is that they were so much alike. Daddy was big and rough and loud-talking, just the opposite of Sonny, but they both had—that same privacy.

Mama tried to tell me something about this, just after Daddy died. I was home on leave from the army.

This was the last time I ever saw my mother alive. Just the same, this picture gets all mixed up in my mind with pictures I had of her when she was younger. The way I always see her is the way she used to be on a Sunday afternoon, say, when the old folks were talking after the big Sunday dinner. I always see her wearing pale blue. She'd be sitting on the sofa. And my father would be sitting in the easy chair, not far from her. And the living room would be full of church folks and relatives. There they sit, in chairs all around the living room, and the night is creeping up outside, but nobody knows it yet. You can see the darkness growing against the windowpanes and you hear the street noises every now and again, or maybe the jangling beat of a tambourine from one of the churches close by, but it's real quiet in the room. For a moment nobody's talking, but every face looks darkening, like the sky outside. And my mother rocks a little from the waist, and my father's eyes are closed. Everyone is looking at something a child can't see. For a minute they've forgotten the children. Maybe a kid is lying on the rug, half asleep. Maybe somebody's got a kid in his lap and is absent-mindedly stroking the kid's head. Maybe there's a kid, quiet and big-eyed, curled up in a big chair in the corner. The silence, the darkness coming, and the darkness in the faces frightens the child obscurely. He hopes that the hand which strokes his forehead will never stop—will never die. He hopes that there will never come a time when the old folks won't be sitting around the living room, talking about where they've come from, and what they've seen, and what's happened to them and their kinfolk.

But something deep and watchful in the child knows that this is bound to end, is already ending. In a moment someone will get up and turn on the light. Then the old folks will remember the children and they won't talk any more that day. And when light fills the room, the child is filled with darkness. He knows that every time this happens he's moved just a little closer to that darkness outside.

The darkness outside is what the old folks have been talking about. It's what they've come from. It's what they endure. The child knows that they won't talk any more because if he knows too much about what's happened to *them,* he'll know too much too soon, about what's going to happen to *him.*

The last time I talked to my mother, I remember I was restless. I wanted to get out and see Isabel. We weren't married then and we had a lot to straighten out between us.

There Mama sat, in black, by the window. She was humming an old church song, *Lord, you brought me from a long ways off.* Sonny was out somewhere. Mama kept watching the streets.

"I don't know," she said, "if I'll ever see you again, after you go off from here. But I hope you'll remember the things I tried to teach you."

"Don't talk like that," I said, and smiled. "You'll be here a long time yet."

She smiled, too, but she said nothing. She was quiet for a long time. And I said, "Mama, don't you worry about nothing. I'll be writing all the time, and you be getting the checks. . . ."

"I want to talk to you about your brother," she said, suddenly. "If anything happens to me he ain't going to have nobody to look out for him."

"Mama," I said, "ain't nothing going to happen to you *or* Sonny. Sonny's all right. He's a good boy and he's got good sense."

"It ain't a question of his being a good boy," Mama said, "nor of his having good sense. It ain't only the bad ones, nor yet the dumb ones that gets sucked under." She stopped, looking at me. "Your Daddy once had a brother," she said, and she smiled in a way that made me feel she was in pain. "You didn't never know that, did you?"

"No," I said, "I never knew that," and I watched her face.

"Oh, yes," she said, "your Daddy had a brother." She looked out of the window again. "I know you never saw your Daddy cry. But *I* did—many a time, through all these years."

I asked her, "What happened to his brother? How come nobody's ever talked about him?"

This was the first time I ever saw my mother look old.

"His brother got killed," she said, "when he was just a little younger than you are now. I knew him. He was a fine boy. He was maybe a little full of the devil, but he didn't mean nobody no harm."

Then she stopped and the room was silent, exactly as it had sometimes been on those Sunday afternoons. Mama kept looking out into the streets.

"He used to have a job in the mill," she said, "and, like all young folks, he just liked to perform on Saturday nights. Saturday nights, him and your father would drift around to different places, go to dances and things like that, or just sit around with people they knew, and your father's brother would sing, he had a fine voice, and play along with himself on his guitar. Well, this particular Saturday night, him and your father was coming home from some place, and they were both a little drunk and there was a moon that night, it was bright like day. Your father's brother was feeling kind of good, and he was whistling to himself, and he had his guitar slung over his shoulder. They was coming down a hill and beneath them

80

85

90

was a road that turned off from the highway. Well, your father's brother, being always kind of frisky, decided to run down this hill, and he did, with that guitar banging and clanging behind him, and he ran across the road, and he was making water behind a tree. And your father was sort of amused at him and he was still coming down the hill, kind of slow. Then he heard a car motor and that same minute his brother stepped from behind the tree, into the road, in the moonlight. And he started to cross the road. And your father started to run down the hill, he says he don't know why. This car was full of white men. They was all drunk, and when they seen your father's brother they let out a great whoop and holler and they aimed the car straight at him. They was having fun, they just wanted to scare him, the way they do sometimes, you know. But they was drunk. And I guess the boy, being drunk, too, and scared, kind of lost his head. By the time he jumped it was too late. Your father says he heard his brother scream when the car rolled over him, and he heard the wood of that guitar when it give, and he heard them strings go flying, and he heard them white men shouting, and the car kept on a-going and it ain't stopped till this day. And, time your father got down the hill, his brother weren't nothing but blood and pulp."

Tears were gleaming on my mother's face. There wasn't anything I could say.   95

"He never mentioned it," she said, "because I never let him mention it before you children. Your Daddy was like a crazy man that night and for many a night thereafter. He says he never in his life seen anything as dark as that road after the lights of that car had gone away. Weren't nothing, weren't nobody on that road, just your Daddy and his brother and that busted guitar. Oh, yes. Your Daddy never did really get right again. Till the day he died he weren't sure but that every white man he saw was the man that killed his brother."

She stopped and took out her handkerchief and dried her eyes and looked at me.

"I ain't telling you all this," she said, "to make you scared or bitter or to make you hate nobody. I'm telling you this because you got a brother. And the world ain't changed."

I guess I didn't want to believe this. I guess she saw this in my face. She turned away from me, toward the window again, searching those streets.

"But I praise my Redeemer," she said at last, "that He called your Daddy   100 home before me. I ain't saying it to throw no flowers at myself, but, I declare, it keeps me from feeling too cast down to know I helped your father get safely through this world. Your father always acted like he was the roughest, strongest man on earth. And everybody took him to be like that. But if he hadn't had *me* there—to see his tears!"

She was crying again. Still, I couldn't move. I said, "Lord, Lord, Mama, I didn't know it was like that."

"Oh, honey," she said, "there's a lot that you don't know. But you are going to find it out." She stood up from the window and came over to me. "You got to hold on to your brother," she said, "and don't let him fall, no matter what it looks like is happening to him and no matter how evil you gets with him. You going to be evil with him many a time. But don't you forget what I told you, you hear?"

"I won't forget," I said. "Don't you worry, I won't forget. I won't let nothing happen to Sonny."

My mother smiled as though she were amused at something she saw in my face. Then, "You may not be able to stop nothing from happening. But you got to let him know you's *there*."

Two days later I was married, and then I was gone. And I had a lot of things   105
on my mind and I pretty well forgot my promise to Mama until I got shipped home on a special furlough for her funeral.

And, after the funeral, with just Sonny and me alone in the empty kitchen, I tried to find out something about him.

"What do you want to do?" I asked him.

"I'm going to be a musician," he said.

For he had graduated, in the time I had been away, from dancing to the juke box to finding out who was playing what, and what they were doing with it, and he had bought himself a set of drums.

"You mean, you want to be a drummer?" I somehow had the feeling that   110
being a drummer might be all right for other people but not for my brother Sonny.

"I don't think," he said, looking at me very gravely, "that I'll ever be a good drummer. But I think I can play a piano."

I frowned. I'd never played the role of the older brother quite so seriously before, had scarcely ever, in fact, *asked* Sonny a damn thing. I sensed myself in the presence of something I didn't really know how to handle, didn't understand. So I made my frown a little deeper as I asked: "What kind of musician do you want to be?"

He grinned. "How many kinds do you think there are?"

"Be *serious*," I said.

He laughed, throwing his head back, and then looked at me. "I *am* serious."   115

"Well, then, for Christ's sake, stop kidding around and answer a serious question. I mean, do you want to be a concert pianist, you want to play classical music and all that, or—or what?" Long before I finished he was laughing again. "For Christ's *sake*, Sonny!"

He sobered, but with difficulty. "I'm sorry. But you sound so—*scared!*" and he was off again.

"Well, you may think it's funny now, baby, but it's not going to be so funny when you have to make your living at it, let me tell you *that*." I was furious because I knew he was laughing at me and I didn't know why.

"No," he said, very sober now, and afraid, perhaps, that he'd hurt me, "I don't want to be a classical pianist. That isn't what interests me. I mean"—he paused, looking hard at me, as though his eyes would help me to understand, and then gestured helplessly, as though perhaps his hand would help—"I mean, I'll have a lot of studying to do, and I'll have to study *everything*, but, I mean, I want to play *with*—jazz musicians." He stopped. "I want to play jazz," he said.

Well, the word had never before sounded as heavy, as real, as it sounded that   120
afternoon in Sonny's mouth. I just looked at him and I was probably frowning a real frown by this time. I simply couldn't see why on earth he'd want to spend his time hanging around nightclubs, clowning around on bandstands, while people pushed each other around a dance floor. It seemed—beneath him, somehow. I had never thought about it before, had never been forced to, but I suppose

I had always put jazz musicians in a class with what Daddy called "good-time people."

"Are you *serious?*"

"Hell, *yes,* I'm serious."

He looked more helpless than ever, and annoyed, and deeply hurt.

I suggested, helpfully: "You mean — like Louis Armstrong?"

His face closed as though I'd struck him. "No. I'm not talking about none of   125
that old-time, down home crap."

"Well, look, Sonny, I'm sorry, don't get mad. I just don't altogether get it,
that's all. Name somebody — you know, a jazz musician you admire."

"Bird."

"Who?"

"Bird! Charlie Parker! Don't they teach you nothing in the goddamn army?"

I lit a cigarette. I was surprised and then a little amused to discover that I was   130
trembling. "I've been out of touch," I said. "You'll have to be patient with me.
Now. Who's this Parker character?"

"He's just one of the greatest jazz musicians alive," said Sonny, sullenly, his
hands in his pockets, his back to me. "Maybe *the* greatest," he added, bitterly,
"that's probably why *you* never heard of him."

"All right," I said, "I'm ignorant. I'm sorry. I'll go out and buy all the cat's
records right away, all right?"

"It don't," said Sonny, with dignity, "make any difference to me. I don't care
what you listen to. Don't do me no favors."

I was beginning to realize that I'd never seen him so upset before. With
another part of my mind I was thinking that this would probably turn out to be
one of those things kids go through and that I shouldn't make it seem important
by pushing it too hard. Still, I didn't think it would do any harm to ask: "Doesn't
all this take a lot of time? Can you make a living at it?"

He turned back to me and half leaned, half sat, on the kitchen table. "Every-   135
thing takes time," he said, "and — well, yes, sure, I can make a living at it. But
what I don't seem to be able to make you understand is that it's the only thing I
want to do."

"Well, Sonny," I said, gently, "you know people can't always do exactly what
they *want* to do —"

"*No,* I don't know that," said Sonny, surprising me. "I think people *ought* to
do what they want to do, what else are they alive for?"

"You getting to be a big boy," I said desperately, "it's time you started thinking
about your future."

"I'm thinking about my future," said Sonny, grimly. "I think about it all the
time."

I gave up. I decided, if he didn't change his mind, that we could always talk   140
about it later. "In the meantime," I said, "you got to finish school." We had
already decided that he'd have to move in with Isabel and her folks. I knew this
wasn't the ideal arrangement because Isabel's folks are inclined to be dicty and
they hadn't especially wanted Isabel to marry me. But I didn't know what else to
do. "And we have to get you fixed up at Isabel's."

There was a long silence. He moved from the kitchen table to the window. "That's a terrible idea. You know it yourself."

"Do you have a *better* idea?"

He just walked up and down the kitchen for a minute. He was as tall as I was. He had started to shave. I suddenly had the feeling that I didn't know him at all.

He stopped at the kitchen table and picked up my cigarettes. Looking at me with a kind of mocking, amused defiance, he put one between his lips. "You mind?"

"You smoking already?"   145

He lit the cigarette and nodded, watching me through the smoke. "I just wanted to see if I'd have the courage to smoke in front of you." He grinned and blew a great cloud of smoke to the ceiling. "It was easy." He looked at my face. "Come on, now. I bet you was smoking at my age, tell the truth."

I didn't say anything but the truth was on my face, and he laughed. But now there was something very strained in his laugh. "Sure. And I bet that ain't all you was doing."

He was frightening me a little. "Cut the crap," I said. "We already decided that you was going to go and live at Isabel's. Now what's got into you all of a sudden?"

"*You* decided it," he pointed out. "*I* didn't decide nothing." He stopped in front of me, leaning against the stove, arms loosely folded. "Look, brother. I don't want to stay in Harlem no more, I really don't." He was very earnest. He looked at me, then over toward the kitchen window. There was something in his eyes I'd never seen before, some thoughtfulness, some worry all his own. He rubbed the muscle of one arm. "It's time I was getting out of here."

"Where do you want to *go*, Sonny?"   150

"I want to join the army. Or the navy, I don't care. If I say I'm old enough, they'll believe me."

Then I got mad. It was because I was so scared. "You must be crazy. You goddamn fool, what the hell do you want to go and join the *army* for?"

"I just told you. To get out of Harlem."

"Sonny, you haven't even finished *school*. And if you really want to be a musician, how do you expect to study if you're in the *army*?"

He looked at me, trapped, and in anguish. "There's ways. I might be able to   155 work out some kind of deal. Anyway, I'll have the G.I. Bill when I come out."

"*If* you come out." We stared at each other. "Sonny, please. Be reasonable. I know the setup is far from perfect. But we got to do the best we can."

"I ain't learning nothing in school," he said. "Even when I go." He turned away from me and opened the window and threw his cigarette out into the narrow alley. I watched his back. "At least, I ain't learning nothing you'd want me to learn." He slammed the window so hard I thought the glass would fly out, and turned back to me. "And I'm sick of the stink of these garbage cans!"

"Sonny," I said, "I know how you feel. But if you don't finish school now, you're going to be sorry later that you didn't." I grabbed him by the shoulders. "And you only got another year. It ain't so bad. And I'll come back and I swear I'll help you do *whatever* you want to do. Just try to put up with it till I come back. Will you please do that? For me?"

He didn't answer and he wouldn't look at me.

"Sonny. You hear me?"

160

He pulled away. "I hear you. But you never hear anything *I* say."

I didn't know what to say to that. He looked out of the window and then back at me. "OK," he said, and sighed. "I'll try."

Then I said, trying to cheer him up a little, "They got a piano at Isabel's. You can practice on it."

And as a matter of fact, it did cheer him up for a minute. "That's right," he said to himself. "I forgot that." His face relaxed a little. But the worry, the thoughtfulness, played on it still, the way shadows play on a face which is staring into the fire.

But I thought I'd never hear the end of that piano. At first, Isabel would write

165

me, saying how nice it was that Sonny was so serious about his music and how, as soon as he came in from school, or wherever he had been when he was supposed to be at school, he went straight to that piano and stayed there until suppertime. And, after supper, he went back to that piano and stayed there until everybody went to bed. He was at the piano all day Saturday and all day Sunday. Then he bought a record player and started playing records. He'd play one record over and over again, all day long sometimes, and he'd improvise along with it on the piano. Or he'd play one section of the record, one chord, one change, one progression, then he'd do it on the piano. Then back to the record. Then back to the piano.

Well, I really don't know how they stood it. Isabel finally confessed that it wasn't like living with a person at all, it was like living with sound. And the sound didn't make any sense to her, didn't make any sense to any of them — naturally. They began, in a way, to be afflicted by this presence that was living in their home. It was as though Sonny were some sort of god, or monster. He moved in an atmosphere which wasn't like theirs at all. They fed him and he ate, he washed himself, he walked in and out of their door; he certainly wasn't nasty or unpleasant or rude, Sonny isn't any of those things; but it was as though he were all wrapped up in some cloud, some fire, some vision all his own; and there wasn't any way to reach him.

At the same time, he wasn't really a man yet, he was still a child, and they had to watch out for him in all kinds of ways. They certainly couldn't throw him out. Neither did they dare to make a great scene about that piano because even they dimly sensed, as I sensed, from so many thousands of miles away, that Sonny was at that piano playing for his life.

But he hadn't been going to school. One day a letter came from the school board and Isabel's mother got it — there had, apparently, been other letters but Sonny had torn them up. This day, when Sonny came in, Isabel's mother showed him the letter and asked where he'd been spending his time. And she finally got it out of him that he'd been down in Greenwich Village, with musicians and other characters, in a white girl's apartment. And this scared her and she started to scream at him and what came up, once she began — though she denies it to this day — was what sacrifices they were making to give Sonny a decent home and how little he appreciated it.

Sonny didn't play the piano that day. By evening, Isabel's mother had calmed down but then there was the old man to deal with, and Isabel herself. Isabel says she did her best to be calm but she broke down and started crying. She says she just watched Sonny's face. She could tell, by watching him, what was happening with him. And what was happening was that they penetrated his cloud, they had reached him. Even if their fingers had been a thousand times more gentle than human fingers ever are, he could hardly help feeling that they had stripped him naked and were spitting on that nakedness. For he also had to see that his presence, that music, which was life or death to him, had been torture for them and that they had endured it, not at all for his sake, but only for mine. And Sonny couldn't take that. He can take it a little better today than he could then but he's still not very good at it and, frankly, I don't know anybody who is.

The silence of the next few days must have been louder than the sound of all the music ever played since time began. One morning, before she went to work, Isabel was in his room for something and she suddenly realized that all of his records were gone. And she knew for certain that he was gone. And he was. He went as far as the navy would carry him. He finally sent me a postcard from some place in Greece and that was the first I knew that Sonny was still alive. I didn't see him any more until we were both back in New York and the war had long been over.

He was a man by then, of course, but I wasn't willing to see it. He came by the house from time to time, but we fought almost every time we met. I didn't like the way he carried himself, loose and dreamlike all the time, and I didn't like his friends, and his music seemed to be merely an excuse for the life he led. It sounded just that weird and disordered.

Then we had a fight, a pretty awful fight, and I didn't see him for months. By and by I looked him up, where he was living, in a furnished room in the Village, and I tried to make it up. But there were lots of people in the room and Sonny just lay on his bed, and he wouldn't come downstairs with me, and he treated these other people as though they were his family and I weren't. So I got mad and then he got mad, and then I told him that he might just as well be dead as live the way he was living. Then he stood up and he told me not to worry about him any more in life, that he *was* dead as far as I was concerned. Then he pushed me to the door and the other people looked on as though nothing were happening, and he slammed the door behind me. I stood in the hallway, staring at the door. I heard somebody laugh in the room and then the tears came to my eyes. I started down the steps, whistling to keep from crying, I kept whistling to myself, *You going to need me, baby, one of these cold, rainy days.*

I read about Sonny's trouble in the spring. Little Grace died in the fall. She was a beautiful little girl. But she only lived a little over two years. She died of polio and she suffered. She had a slight fever for a couple of days, but it didn't seem like anything and we just kept her in bed. And we would certainly have called the doctor, but the fever dropped, she seemed to be all right. So we thought it had just been a cold. Then, one day, she was up, playing, Isabel was in the kitchen fixing lunch for the two boys when they'd come in from school, and she heard Grace fall down in the living room. When you have a lot of children you don't always start running when one of them falls, unless they start screaming

170

or something. And, this time, Grace was quiet. Yet, Isabel says that when she heard that *thump* and then that silence, something happened in her to make her afraid. And she ran to the living room and there was little Grace on the floor, all twisted up, and the reason she hadn't screamed was that she couldn't get her breath. And when she did scream, it was the worst sound, Isabel says, that she'd ever heard in all her life, and she still hears it sometimes in her dreams. Isabel will sometimes wake me up with a low, moaning, strangled sound and I have to be quick to awaken her and hold her to me and where Isabel is weeping against me seems a mortal wound.

I think I may have written Sonny the very day that little Grace was buried. I was sitting in the living room in the dark, by myself, and I suddenly thought of Sonny. My trouble made his real.

One Saturday afternoon, when Sonny had been living with us, or, anyway, been in our house, for nearly two weeks, I found myself wandering aimlessly about the living room, drinking from a can of beer, and trying to work up the courage to search Sonny's room. He was out, he was usually out whenever I was home, and Isabel had taken the children to see their grandparents. Suddenly I was standing still in front of the living room window, watching Seventh Avenue. The idea of searching Sonny's room made me still. I scarcely dared to admit to myself what I'd be searching for. I didn't know what I'd do if I found it. Or if I didn't. 175

On the sidewalk across from me, near the entrance to a barbecue joint, some people were holding an old-fashioned revival meeting. The barbecue cook, wearing a dirty white apron, his conked hair reddish and metallic in the pale sun, and a cigarette between his lips, stood in the doorway, watching them. Kids and older people paused in their errands and stood there, along with some older men and a couple of very tough-looking women who watched everything that happened on the avenue, as though they owned it, or were maybe owned by it. Well, they were watching this, too. The revival was being carried on by three sisters in black, and a brother. All they had were their voices and their Bibles and a tambourine. The brother was testifying and while he testified two of the sisters stood together, seeming to say, amen, and the third sister walked around with the tambourine outstretched and a couple of people dropped coins into it. Then the brother's testimony ended and the sister who had been taking up the collection dumped the coins into her palm and transferred them to the pocket of her long black robe. Then she raised both hands, striking the tambourine against the air, and then against one hand, and she started to sing. And the two other sisters and the brother joined in.

It was strange, suddenly, to watch, though I had been seeing these street meetings all my life. So, of course, had everybody else down there. Yet, they paused and watched and listened and I stood still at the window. *"Tis the old ship of Zion,"* they sang, and the sister with the tambourine kept a steady, jangling beat, *"it has rescued many a thousand!"* Not a soul under the sound of their voices was hearing this song for the first time, not one of them had been rescued. Nor had they seen much in the way of rescue work being done around them. Neither did they especially believe in the holiness of the three sisters and the brother, they knew too much about them, knew where they lived, and how. The woman with the tambourine, whose voice dominated the air, whose face was bright with joy, was divided by very little from the woman who stood watching her, a cigarette between her heavy, chapped lips, her hair a cuckoo's nest, her face scarred and swollen from many beatings, and her black eyes glittering like coal. Perhaps they both knew this, which was why, when, as rarely, they addressed each other, they addressed each other as Sister. As the singing filled the air the watching, listening faces underwent a change, the eyes focusing on something within; the music seemed to soothe a poison out of them; and time seemed, nearly, to fall away from the sullen, belligerent, battered faces, as though they were fleeing back to their first condition, while dreaming of their last. The barbecue cook half shook his head and smiled, and dropped his cigarette and disappeared into his joint. A man fumbled in his pockets for change and stood holding it in his hand impatiently, as though he had just remembered a pressing appointment further up the avenue. He looked furious. Then I saw Sonny, standing on the edge of the crowd. He was carrying a wide, flat notebook with a green cover, and it made him look, from where I was standing, almost like a schoolboy. The coppery sun brought out the copper in his skin, he was very faintly smiling, standing very still. Then the singing stopped, the tambourine turned into a collection plate again. The furious man dropped in his coins and vanished, so did a couple of the women, and Sonny dropped some change in the plate, looking directly at the woman with a little smile. He started across the avenue, toward the house. He has a slow, loping walk, something like the way Harlem hipsters walk, only he's imposed on this his own half-beat. I had never really noticed it before.

I stayed at the window, both relieved and apprehensive. As Sonny disappeared from my sight, they began singing again. And they were still singing when his key turned in the lock.

"Hey," he said.

"Hey, yourself. You want some beer?"   180

"No. Well, maybe." But he came up to the window and stood beside me, looking out. "What a warm voice," he said.

They were singing *If I could only hear my mother pray again!*

"Yes," I said, "and she can sure beat that tambourine."

"But what a terrible song," he said, and laughed. He dropped his notebook on the sofa and disappeared into the kitchen. "Where's Isabel and the kids?"

"I think they went to see their grandparents. You hungry?"   185

"No." He came back into the living room with his can of beer. "You want to come some place with me tonight?"

I sensed, I don't know how, that I couldn't possibly say no. "Sure. Where?"

He sat down on the sofa and picked up his notebook and started leafing through it. "I'm going to sit in with some fellows in a joint in the Village."

"You mean, you're going to play, tonight?"

"That's right." He took a swallow of his beer and moved back to the window.   190
He gave me a sidelong look. "If you can stand it."

"I'll try," I said.

He smiled to himself and we both watched as the meeting across the way broke up. The three sisters and the brother, heads bowed, were singing *God be with you till we meet again.* The faces around them were very quiet. Then the song ended. The small crowd dispersed. We watched the three women and the lone man walk slowly up the avenue.

"When she was singing before," said Sonny, abruptly, "her voice reminded me for a minute of what heroin feels like sometimes—when it's in your veins. It makes you feel sort of warm and cool at the same time. And distant. And—and sure." He sipped his beer, very deliberately not looking at me. I watched his face. "It makes you feel—in control. Sometimes you've got to have that feeling."

"Do you?" I sat down slowly in the easy chair.

"Sometimes." He went to the sofa and picked up his notebook again. "Some people do."   195

"In order," I asked, "to play?" And my voice was very ugly, full of contempt and anger.

"Well"—he looked at me with great, troubled eyes, as though, in fact, he hoped his eyes would tell me things he could never otherwise say—"they *think* so. And *if* they think so—!"

"And what do *you* think?" I asked.

He sat on the sofa and put his can of beer on the floor. "I don't know," he said, and I couldn't be sure if he were answering my question or pursuing his thoughts. His face didn't tell me. "It's not so much to *play*. It's to *stand* it, to be able to make it at all. On any level." He frowned and smiled: "In order to keep from shaking to pieces."

"But these friends of yours," I said, "they seem to shake themselves to pieces   200 pretty goddamn fast."

"Maybe." He played with the notebook. And something told me that I should curb my tongue, that Sonny was doing his best to talk, that I should listen. "But of course you only know the ones that've gone to pieces. Some don't—or at least they haven't *yet* and that's just about all *any* of us can say." He paused. "And then there are some who just live, really, in hell, and they know it and they see what's happening and they go right on. I don't know." He sighed, dropped the notebook, folded his arms. "Some guys, you can tell from the way they play, they on something *all* the time. And you can see that, well, it makes something real for them. But of course," he picked up his beer from the floor and sipped it and put the can down again, "they *want* to, too, you've got to see that. Even some of them that say they don't—*some*, not all."

"And what about you?" I asked—I couldn't help it. "What about you? Do *you* want to?"

He stood up and walked to the window and remained silent for a long time. Then he sighed. "Me," he said. Then: "While I was downstairs before, on my way here, listening to that woman sing, it struck me all of a sudden how much suffering she must have had to go through—to sing like that. It's *repulsive* to think you have to suffer that much."

I said: "But there's no way not to suffer—is there, Sonny?"

"I believe not," he said and smiled, "but that's never stopped anyone from   205 trying." He looked at me. "Has it?" I realized, with this mocking look, that there stood between us, forever, beyond the power of time or forgiveness, the fact that I had held silence—so long!—when he had needed human speech to help him. He turned back to the window. "No, there's no way not to suffer. But you try all kinds of ways to keep from drowning in it, to keep on top of it, and to make it seem—well, like *you*. Like you did something, all right, and now you're suffering for it. You know?" I said nothing. "Well you know," he said, impatiently, "why *do* people suffer? Maybe it's better to do something to give it a reason, *any* reason."

"But we just agreed," I said, "that there's no way not to suffer. Isn't it better, then, just to—take it?"

"But nobody just takes it," Sonny cried, "that's what I'm telling you! *Every-body* tries not to. You're just hung up on the *way* some people try—it's not *your* way!"

The hair on my face began to itch, my face felt wet. "That's not true," I said, "that's not true. I don't give a damn what other people do, I don't even care how they suffer. I just care how *you* suffer." And he looked at me. "Please believe me," I said, "I don't want to see you—die—trying not to suffer."

"I won't," he said, flatly, "die trying not to suffer. At least, not any faster than anybody else."

"But there's no need," I said, trying to laugh, "is there? in killing yourself." 210

I wanted to say more, but I couldn't. I wanted to talk about will power and how life could be—well, beautiful. I wanted to say that it was all within; but was it? or, rather, wasn't that exactly the trouble? And I wanted to promise that I would never fail him again. But it would all have sounded—empty words and lies.

So I made the promise to myself and prayed that I would keep it.

"It's terrible sometimes, inside," he said, "that's what's the trouble. You walk these streets, black and funky and cold, and there's not really a living ass to talk to, and there's nothing shaking, and there's no way of getting it out—that storm inside. You can't talk it and you can't make love with it, and when you finally try to get with it and play it, you realize *nobody's* listening. So *you've* got to listen. You got to find a way to listen."

And then he walked away from the window and sat on the sofa again, as though all the wind had suddenly been knocked out of him. "Sometimes you'll do *anything* to play, even cut your mother's throat." He laughed and looked at me. "Or your brother's." Then he sobered. "Or your own." Then: "Don't worry. I'm all right now and I think I'll *be* all right. But I can't forget—where I've been. I don't mean just the physical place I've been, I mean where I've *been*. And *what* I've been."

"What have you been, Sonny?" I asked. 215

He smiled—but sat sideways on the sofa, his elbow resting on the back, his fingers playing with his mouth and chin, not looking at me. "I've been something I didn't recognize, didn't know I could be. Didn't know anybody could be." He stopped, looking inward, looking helplessly young, looking old. "I'm not talking about it now because I feel *guilty* or anything like that—maybe it would be better if I did, I don't know. Anyway, I can't really talk about it. Not to you, not to anybody," and now he turned and faced me. "Sometimes, you know, and it was actually when

I was most *out* of the world, I felt that I was in it, that I was *with* it, really, and I could play or I didn't really have to *play*, it just came out of me, it was there. And I don't know how I played, thinking about it now, but I know I did awful things, those times, sometimes, to people. Or it wasn't that I *did* anything to them—it was that they weren't real." He picked up the beer can; it was empty; he rolled it between his palms: "And other times—well, I needed a fix, I needed to find a place to lean, I needed to clear a space to *listen*—and I couldn't find it, and I—went crazy, I did terrible things to *me*, I was terrible *for* me." He began pressing the beer can between his hands, I watched the metal begin to give. It glittered, as he played with it, like a knife, and I was afraid he would cut himself, but I said nothing. "Oh well. I can never tell you. I was all by myself at the bottom of something, stinking and sweating and crying and shaking, and I smelled it, you know? *my* stink, and I thought I'd die if I couldn't get away from it and yet, all the same, I knew that everything I was doing was just locking me in with it. And I didn't know," he paused, still flattening the beer can, "I didn't know, I still *don't* know, something kept telling me that maybe it was good to smell your own stink, but I didn't think that *that* was what I'd been trying to do—and—who can stand it?" and he abruptly dropped the ruined beer can, looking at me with a small, still smile, and then rose, walking to the window as though it were the lodestone rock. I watched his face, he watched the avenue. "I couldn't tell you when Mama died—but the reason I wanted to leave Harlem so bad was to get away from drugs. And then, when I ran away, that's what I was running from—really. When I came back, nothing had changed, *I* hadn't changed, I was just—older." And he stopped, drumming with his fingers on the windowpane. The sun had vanished, soon darkness would fall. I watched his face. "It can come again," he said, almost as though speaking to himself. Then he turned to me. "It can come again," he repeated. "I just want you to know that."

"All right," I said, at last. "So it can come again, All right."

He smiled, but the smile was sorrowful. "I had to try to tell you," he said.

"Yes," I said. "I understand that."

"You're my brother," he said, looking straight at me, and not smiling at all.   220

"Yes," I repeated, "yes. I understand that."

He turned back to the window, looking out. "All that hatred down there," he said, "all that hatred and misery and love. It's a wonder it doesn't blow the avenue apart."

We went to the only nightclub on a short, dark street, downtown. We squeezed through the narrow, chattering, jam-packed bar to the entrance of the big room, where the bandstand was. And we stood there for a moment, for the lights were very dim in this room and we couldn't see. Then, "Hello, boy," said a voice and an enormous black man, much older than Sonny or myself, erupted out of all that atmospheric lighting and put an arm around Sonny's shoulder. "I been sitting right here," he said, "waiting for you."

He had a big voice, too, and heads in the darkness turned toward us.

Sonny grinned and pulled a little away, and said, "Creole, this is my brother.   225
I told you about him."

Creole shook my hand. "I'm glad to meet you, son," he said, and it was clear that he was glad to meet me *there*, for Sonny's sake. And he smiled, "You got a real musician in *your* family," and he took his arm from Sonny's shoulder and slapped him, lightly, affectionately, with the back of his hand.

"Well. Now I've heard it all," said a voice behind us. This was another musician, and a friend of Sonny's, a coal-black, cheerful-looking man, built close to the ground. He immediately began confiding to me, at the top of his lungs, the most terrible things about Sonny, his teeth gleaming like a lighthouse and his laugh coming up out of him like the beginning of an earthquake. And it turned out that everyone at the bar knew Sonny, or almost everyone; some were musicians, working there, or nearby, or not working, some were simply hangers-on, and some were there to hear Sonny play. I was introduced to all of them and they were all very polite to me. Yet, it was clear that, for them, I was only Sonny's brother. Here, I was in Sonny's world. Or, rather: his kingdom. Here, it was not even a question that his veins bore royal blood.

They were going to play soon and Creole installed me, by myself, at a table in a dark corner. Then I watched them, Creole, and the little black man, and Sonny, and the others, while they horsed around, standing just below the bandstand. The light from the bandstand spilled just a little short of them and, watching them laughing and gesturing and moving about, I had the feeling that they, nevertheless, were being most careful not to step into that circle of light too suddenly: that if they moved into the light too suddenly, without thinking, they would perish in flame. Then, while I watched, one of them, the small, black man, moved into the light and crossed the bandstand and started fooling around with his drums. Then—being funny and being, also, extremely ceremonious—Creole took Sonny by the arm and led him to the piano. A woman's voice called Sonny's name and a few hands started clapping. And Sonny, also being funny and being ceremonious, and so touched, I think, that he could have cried, but neither hiding it nor showing it, riding it like a man, grinned, and put both hands to his heart and bowed from the waist.

Creole then went to the bass fiddle and a lean, very bright-skinned brown man jumped up on the bandstand and picked up his horn. So there they were, and the atmosphere on the bandstand and in the room began to change and tighten. Someone stepped up to the microphone and announced them. Then there were all kinds of murmurs. Some people at the bar shushed others. The waitress ran around, frantically getting in the last orders, guys and chicks got closer to each other, and the lights on the bandstand, on the quartet, turned to a kind of indigo. Then they all looked different there. Creole looked about him for the last time, as though he were making certain that all his chickens were in the coop, and then he—jumped and struck the fiddle. And there they were.

All I know about music is that not many people ever really hear it. And even then, on the rare occasions when something opens within, and the music enters, what we mainly hear, or hear corroborated, are personal, private, vanishing evocations. But the man who creates the music is hearing something else, is dealing with the roar rising from the void and imposing order on it as it hits the air. What is evoked in him, then, is of another order, more terrible because it has no words, and triumphant, too, for that same reason. And his triumph, when he triumphs, is ours. I just watched Sonny's face. His face was troubled, he was working hard, but he wasn't with it. And I had the feeling that, in a way, everyone on

230

the bandstand was waiting for him, both waiting for him and pushing him along. But as I began to watch Creole, I realized that it was Creole who held them all back. He had them on a short rein. Up there, keeping the beat with his whole body, wailing on the fiddle, with his eyes half closed, he was listening to everything, but he was listening to Sonny. He was having a dialogue with Sonny. He wanted Sonny to leave the shoreline and strike out for the deep water. He was Sonny's witness that deep water and drowning were not the same thing—he had been there, and he knew. And he wanted Sonny to know. He was waiting for Sonny to do the things on the keys which would let Creole know that Sonny was in the water.

And, while Creole listened, Sonny moved, deep within, exactly like someone in torment. I had never before thought of how awful the relationship must be between the musician and his instrument. He has to fill it, this instrument, with the breath of life, his own. He has to make it do what he wants it to do. And a piano is just a piano. It's made out of so much wood and wires and little hammers and big ones, and ivory. While there's only so much you can do with it, the only way to find this out is to try; to try and make it do everything.

And Sonny hadn't been near a piano for over a year. And he wasn't on much better terms with his life, not the life that stretched before him now. He and the piano stammered, started one way, got scared, stopped; started another way, panicked, marked time, started again; then seemed to have found a direction, panicked again, got stuck. And the face I saw on Sonny I'd never seen before. Everything had been burned out of it, and, at the same time, things usually hidden were being burned in, by the fire and fury of the battle which was occurring in him up there.

Yet, watching Creole's face as they neared the end of the first set, I had the feeling that something had happened, something I hadn't heard. Then they finished, there was scattered applause, and then, without an instant's warning, Creole started into something else, it was almost sardonic, it was *Am I Blue*. And, as though he commanded, Sonny began to play. Something began to happen. And Creole let out the reins. The dry, low, black man said something awful on the drums, Creole answered, and the drums talked back. Then the horn insisted, sweet and high, slightly detached perhaps, and Creole listened, commenting now and then, dry, and driving, beautiful and calm and old. Then they all came together again, and Sonny was part of the family again. I could tell this from his face. He seemed to have found, right there beneath his fingers, a damn brand-new piano. It seemed that he couldn't get over it. Then, for awhile, just being happy with Sonny, they seemed to be agreeing with him that brand-new pianos certainly were a gas.

Then Creole stepped forward to remind them that what they were playing was the blues. He hit something in all of them, he hit something in me, myself, and the music tightened and deepened, apprehension began to beat the air. Creole began to tell us what the blues were all about. They were not about anything very new. He and his boys up there were keeping it new, at the risk of ruin, destruction, madness, and death, in order to find new ways to make us listen. For, while the tale of how we suffer, and how we are delighted, and how we may triumph is never new, it always must be heard. There isn't any other tale to tell, it's the only light we've got in all this darkness.

And this tale, according to that face, that body, those strong hands on those   235
strings, has another aspect in every country, and a new depth in every generation.
Listen, Creole seemed to be saying, listen. Now these are Sonny's blues. He
made the little black man on the drums know it, and the bright, brown man on
the horn. Creole wasn't trying any longer to get Sonny in the water. He was wishing him Godspeed. Then he stepped back, very slowly, filling the air with the
immense suggestion that Sonny speak for himself.

Then they all gathered around Sonny and Sonny played. Every now and
again one of them seemed to say, amen. Sonny's fingers filled the air with life, his
life. But that life contained so many others. And Sonny went all the way back, he
really began with the spare, flat statement of the opening phrase of the song. Then
he began to make it his. It was very beautiful because it wasn't hurried and it was
no longer a lament. I seemed to hear with what burning he had made it his, with
what burning we had yet to make it ours, how we could cease lamenting. Freedom
lurked around us and I understood, at last, that he could help us to be free if we
would listen, that he would never be free until we did. Yet, there was no battle in
his face now. I heard what he had gone through, and would continue to go
through until he came to rest in earth. He had made it his: that long line, of which
we knew only Mama and Daddy. And he was giving it back, as everything must be
given back, so that, passing through death, it can live forever. I saw my mother's
face again, and felt, for the first time, how the stones of the road she had walked on
must have bruised her feet. I saw the moonlit road where my father's brother died.
And it brought something else back to me, and carried me past it. I saw my little
girl again and felt Isabel's tears again, and I felt my own tears begin to rise. And I
was yet aware that this was only a moment, that the world waited outside, as hungry as a tiger, and that trouble stretched above us, longer than the sky.

Then it was over. Creole and Sonny let out their breath, both soaking wet,
and grinning. There was a lot of applause and some of it was real. In the dark, the
girl came by and I asked her to take drinks to the bandstand. There was a long
pause, while they talked up there in the indigo light and after awhile I saw the girl
put a Scotch and milk on top of the piano for Sonny. He didn't seem to notice it,
but just before they started playing again, he sipped from it and looked toward
me, and nodded. Then he put it back on top of the piano. For me, then, as they
began to play again, it glowed and shook above my brother's head like the very
cup of trembling.   [1957]

FOR THINKING AND WRITING

1. Were you sympathetic to the older brother in the beginning of the story?
   Did this become more so or less so as the story progressed? Is Sonny a
   sympathetic character in the beginning? At the end?

2. In real life, what do you believe is the role of an older brother? Do you
   have a responsibility to the members of your family regardless of their
   behavior? Explain. What is Sonny's mother's view of this?

3. Baldwin refers to the "darkness outside" several times. What do you think
   this means for Sonny? For Sonny's mother and father? For the older brother?

4. Listening seems to play an important function for Sonny and his brother. Cite specific examples of how they do or do not listen to each other. What might be some definitions of *listening* in this context?

5. One might think that brothers would understand each other better than outsiders. But is that the case here? In your experience? In other stories or movies? How might you account for this difficulty?

TONI CADE BAMBARA
The Lesson

Toni Cade Bambara (1939–1995) taught at various colleges and worked as a community activist. She edited The Black Woman *(1970), a collection of essays that became a landmark of contemporary black feminism. Also a fiction writer, she received the American Book Award for her 1980 novel* The Salt Eaters *and has produced several collections of short stories. "The Lesson" comes from her first short-story collection,* Gorilla, My Love *(1972).*

Back in the days when everyone was old and stupid or young and foolish and me and Sugar were the only ones just right, this lady moved on our block with nappy hair and proper speech and no makeup. And quite naturally we laughed at her, laughed the way we did at the junk man who went about his business like he was some big-time president and his sorry-ass horse his secretary. And we kinda hated her too, hated the way we did the winos who cluttered up our parks and pissed on our handball walls and stank up our hallways and stairs so you couldn't halfway play hide-and-seek without a goddamn gas mask. Miss Moore was her name. The only woman on the block with no first name. And she was black as hell, cept for her feet, which were fish-white and spooky. And she was always planning these boring-ass things for us to do, us being my cousin, mostly, who lived on the block cause we all moved North the same time and to the same apartment then spread out gradual to breathe. And our parents would yank our heads into some kinda shape and crisp up our clothes so we'd be presentable for travel with Miss Moore, who always looked like she was going to church, though she never did. Which is just one of the things the grownups talked about when they talked behind her back like a dog. But when she came calling with some sachet she'd sewed up or some gingerbread she'd made or some book, why then they'd all be too embarrassed to turn her down and we'd get handed over all spruced up. She'd been to college and said it was only right that she should take responsibility for the young ones' education, and she not even related by marriage or blood. So they'd go for it. Specially Aunt Gretchen. She was the main gofer in the family. You got some ole dumb shit foolishness you want somebody to go for, you send for Aunt Gretchen. She been screwed into the go-along for so long, it's a blood-deep natural thing with her. Which is how she got saddled with me and Sugar and Junior in the first place while our mothers were in a la-de-da apartment up the block having a good ole time.

So this one day, Miss Moore rounds us all up at the mailbox and it's puredee hot and she's knockin herself out about arithmetic. And school suppose to let up in summer I heard, but she don't never let up. And the starch in my pinafore scratching the shit outta me and I'm really hating this nappy-head bitch and her goddamn college degree. I'd much rather go to the pool or to the show where it's cool. So me and Sugar leaning on the mailbox being surly, which is a Miss Moore word. And Flyboy checking out what everybody brought for lunch. And Fat Butt already wasting his peanut-butter-and-jelly sandwich like the pig he is. And Junebug punchin on Q.T.'s arm for potato chips. And Rosie Giraffe shifting from one hip to the other waiting for somebody to step on her foot or ask her if she from Georgia so she can kick ass, preferably Mercedes'. And Miss Moore asking us do we know what money is, like we a bunch of retards. I mean real money, she say, like it's only poker chips or monopoly papers we lay on the grocer. So right away I'm tired of this and say so. And would much rather snatch Sugar and go to the Sunset and terrorize the West Indian kids and take their hair ribbons and their money too. And Miss Moore files that remark away for next week's lesson on brotherhood, I can tell. And finally I say we oughta get to the subway cause it's cooler and besides we might meet some cute boys. Sugar done swiped her mama's lipstick, so we ready.

So we heading down the street and she's boring us silly about what things cost and what our parents make and how much goes for rent and how money ain't divided up right in this country. And then she gets to the part about we all poor and live in the slums, which I don't feature. And I'm ready to speak on that, but she steps out in the street and hails two cabs just like that. Then she hustles half the crew in with her and hands me a five-dollar bill and tells me to calculate 10 percent tip for the driver. And we're off. Me and Sugar and Junebug and Flyboy hangin out the window and hollering to everybody, putting lipstick on each other cause Flyboy a faggot anyway, and making farts with our sweaty armpits. But I'm mostly trying to figure how to spend this money. But they all fascinated with the meter ticking and Junebug starts laying bets as to how much it'll read when Flyboy can't hold his breath no more. Then Sugar lays bets as to how much it'll be when we get there. So I'm stuck. Don't nobody want to go for my plan, which is to jump out at the next light and run off to the first bar-b-que we can find. Then the driver tells us to get the hell out cause we there already. And the meter reads eighty-five cents. And I'm stalling to figure out the tip and Sugar say give him a dime. And I decide he don't need it bad as I do, so later for him. But then he tries to take off with Junebug foot still in the door so we talk about his mama something ferocious. Then we check out that we on Fifth Avenue and everybody dressed up in stockings. One lady in a fur coat, hot as it is. White folks crazy.

"This is the place," Miss Moore say, presenting it to us in the voice she uses at the museum. "Let's look in the windows before we go in."

"Can we steal?" Sugar asks very serious like she's getting the ground rules squared away before she plays. "I beg your pardon," say Miss Moore, and we fall out. So she leads us around the windows of the toy store and me and Sugar screamin, "This is mine, that's mine, I gotta have that, that was made for me, I was born for that," till Big Butt drowns us out.

5

"Hey, I'm goin to buy that there."

"That there? You don't even know what it is, stupid."

"I do so," he say punchin on Rosie Giraffe. "It's a microscope."

"Whatcha gonna do with a microscope, fool?"

"Look at things."   10

"Like what, Ronald?" ask Miss Moore. And Big Butt ain't got the first notion. So here go Miss Moore gabbing about the thousands of bacteria in a drop of water and the somethinorother in a speck of blood and the million and one living things in the air around us is invisible to the naked eye. And what she say that for? Junebug go to town on that "naked" and we rolling. Then Miss Moore ask what it cost. So we all jam into the window smudgin it up and the price tag say $300. So then she ask how long'd take for Big Butt and Junebug to save up their allowances. "Too long," I say. "Yeh," adds Sugar, "outgrown it by that time." And Miss Moore say no, you never outgrow learning instruments. "Why, even medical students and interns and," blah, blah, blah. And we ready to choke Big Butt for bringing it up in the first damn place.

"This here costs four hundred eighty dollars," says Rosie Giraffe. So we pile up all over her to see what she pointin out. My eyes tell me it's a chunk of glass cracked with something heavy, and different-color inks dripped into the splits, then the whole thing put into a oven or something. But for $480 it don't make sense.

"That's a paperweight made of semi-precious stones fused together under tremendous pressure," she explains slowly, with her hands doing the mining and all the factory work.

"So what's a paperweight?" asks Rosie Giraffe.

"To weigh paper with, dumbbell," say Flyboy, the wise man from the East.   15

"Not exactly," say Miss Moore, which is what she say when you warm or way off too. "It's to weigh paper down so it won't scatter and make your desk untidy." So right away me and Sugar curtsy to each other and then to Mercedes who is more the tidy type.

"We don't keep paper on top of the desk in my class," say Junebug, figuring Miss Moore crazy or lyin one.

"At home, then," she say. "Don't you have a calendar and pencil case and a blotter and a letter-opener on your desk at home where you do your homework?" And she know damn well what our homes look like cause she nosys around in them every chance she gets.

"I don't even have a desk," say Junebug. "Do we?"

"No. And I don't get no homework neither," says Big Butt.   20

"And I don't even have a home," say Flyboy like he do at school to keep the white folks off his back and sorry for him. Send this poor kid to camp posters, is his specialty.

"I do," says Mercedes. "I have a box of stationery on my desk and a picture of my cat. My godmother bought the stationery and the desk. There's a big rose on each sheet and the envelopes smell like roses."

"Who wants to know about your smelly-ass stationery," say Rosie Giraffe fore I can get my two cents in.

"It's important to have a work area all your own so that . . ."

"Will you look at this sailboat, please," say Flyboy, cuttin her off and pointin   25
to the thing like it was his. So once again we tumble all over each other to gaze at
this magnificent thing in the toy store which is just big enough to maybe sail two
kittens across the pond if you strap them to the posts tight. We all start reciting the
price tag like we in assembly. "Handcrafted sailboat of fiberglass at one thousand
one hundred ninety-five dollars."

"Unbelievable," I hear myself say and am really stunned. I read it again for
myself just in case the group recitation put me in a trance. Same thing. For some
reason this pisses me off. We look at Miss Moore and she lookin at us, waiting for
I dunno what.

"Who'd pay all that when you can buy a sailboat set for a quarter at Pop's, a
tube of glue for a dime, and a ball of string for eight cents? It must have a motor
and a whole lot else besides," I say. "My sailboat cost me about fifty cents."

"But will it take water?" say Mercedes with her smart ass.

"Took mine to Alley Pond Park once," say Flyboy. "String broke. Lost it. Pity."

"Sailed mine in Central Park and it keeled over and sank. Had to ask my   30
father for another dollar."

"And you got the strap," laugh Big Butt. "The jerk didn't even have a string
on it. My old man wailed on his behind."

Little Q.T. was staring hard at the sailboat and you could see he wanted it
bad. But he too little and somebody'd just take it from him. So what the hell.
"This boat for kids, Miss Moore?"

"Parents silly to buy something like that just to get all broke up," say Rosie
Giraffe.

"That much money it should last forever," I figure.

"My father'd buy it for me if I wanted it."   35

"Your father, my ass," say Rosie Giraffe getting a chance to finally push Mercedes.

"Must be rich people shop here," say Q.T.

"You are a very bright boy," say Flyboy. "What was your first clue?" And he
rap him on the head with the back of his knuckles, since Q.T. the only one he
could get away with. Though Q.T. liable to come up behind you years later and
get his licks in when you half expect it.

"What I want to know is," I says to Miss Moore though I never talk to her, I
wouldn't give the bitch that satisfaction, "is how much a real boat costs? I figure a
thousand'd get you a yacht any day."

"Why don't you check that out," she says, "and report back to the group?"   40
Which really pains my ass. If you gonna mess up a perfectly good swim day least
you could do is have some answers. "Let's go in," she say like she got something
up her sleeve. Only she don't lead the way. So me and Sugar turn the corner to
where the entrance is, but when we get there I kinda hang back. Not that I'm
scared, what's there to be afraid of, just a toy store. But I feel funny, shame. But
what I got to be shamed about? Got as much right to go in as anybody. But somehow I can't seem to get hold of the door, so I step away from Sugar to lead. But
she hangs back too. And I look at her and she looks at me and this is ridiculous. I

mean, damn, I have never ever been shy about doing nothing or going nowhere. But then Mercedes steps up and then Rosie Giraffe and Big Butt crowd in behind and shove, and next thing we all stuffed into the doorway with only Mercedes squeezing past us, smoothing out her jumper and walking right down the aisle. Then the rest of us tumble in like a glued-together jigsaw done all wrong. And people lookin at us. And it's like the time me and Sugar crashed into the Catholic church on a dare. But once we got in there and everything so hushed and holy and the candles and the bowin and the handkerchiefs on all the drooping heads, I just couldn't go through with the plan. Which was for me to run up to the altar and do a tap dance while Sugar played the nose flute and messed around in the holy water. And Sugar kept givin me the elbow. Then later teased me so bad I tied her up in the shower and turned it on and locked her in. And she'd be there till this day if Aunt Gretchen hadn't finally figured I was lying about the boarder takin a shower.

Same thing in the store. We all walkin on tiptoe and hardly touchin the games and puzzles and things. And I watched Miss Moore who is steady watchin us like she waitin for a sign. Like Mama Drewery watches the sky and sniffs the air and takes note of just how much slant is in the bird formation. Then me and Sugar bump smack into each other, so busy gazing at the toys, 'specially the sail-boat. But we don't laugh and go into our fat-lady bump-stomach routine. We just stare at that price tag. Then Sugar run a finger over the whole boat. And I'm jeal-ous and want to hit her. Maybe not her, but I sure want to punch somebody in the mouth.

"Watcha bring us here for, Miss Moore?"

"You sound angry, Sylvia. Are you mad about something?" Givin me one of them grins like she tellin a grown-up joke that never turns out to be funny. And she's lookin very closely at me like maybe she plannin to do my portrait from memory. I'm mad, but I won't give her that satisfaction. So I slouch around the store bein very bored and say, "Let's go."

Me and Sugar at the back of the train watchin the tracks whizzin by large then small then getting gobbled up in the dark. I'm thinkin about this tricky toy I saw in the store. A clown that somersaults on a bar then does chin-ups just cause you yank lightly at his leg. Cost $35. I could see me askin my mother for a $35 birthday clown. "You wanna who that costs what?" she'd say, cocking her head to the side to get a better view of the hole in my head. Thirty-five dollars could buy new bunk beds for Junior and Gretchen's boy. Thirty-five dollars and the whole household could go visit Grand-daddy Nelson in the country. Thirty-five dollars would pay for the rent and the piano bill too. Who are these people that spend that much for performing clowns and $1000 for toy sailboats? What kinda work they do and how they live and how come we ain't in on it? Where we are is who we are, Miss Moore always pointin out. But it don't necessarily have to be that way, she always adds then waits for somebody to say that poor people have to wake up and demand their share of the pie and don't none of us know what kind of pie she talking about in the first damn place. But she ain't so smart cause I still got her four dollars from the taxi and she sure ain't gettin it. Messin up my day with this shit. Sugar nudges me in my pocket and winks.

Miss Moore lines us up in front of the mailbox where we started from, seem   45
like years ago, and I got a headache for thinkin so hard. And we lean all over each
other so we can hold up under the draggy-ass lecture she always finishes us off with
at the end before we thank her for borin us to tears. But she just looks at us like she
readin tea leaves. Finally she say, "Well, what did you think of F. A. O. Schwarz?"

Rosie Giraffe mumbles, "White folks crazy."

"I'd like to go there again when I get my birthday money," says Mercedes,
and we shove her out the pack so she has to lean on the mailbox by herself.

"I'd like a shower. Tiring day," say Flyboy.

Then Sugar surprises me by sayin, "You know, Miss Moore, I don't think all
of us here put together eat in a year what that sailboat costs." And Miss Moore
lights up like somebody goosed her. "And?" she say, urging Sugar on. Only I'm
standin on her foot so she don't continue.

"Imagine for a minute what kind of society it is in which some people can   50
spend on a toy what it would cost to feed a family of six or seven. What do you
think?"

"I think," say Sugar pushing me off her feet like she never done before, cause
I whip her ass in a minute, "that this is not much of a democracy if you ask me.
Equal chance to pursue happiness means an equal crack at the dough, don't it?"
Miss Moore is beside herself and I am disgusted with Sugar's treachery. So I stand
on her foot one more time to see if she'll shove me. She shuts up, and Miss
Moore looks at me, sorrowfully I'm thinkin. And somethin weird is goin on, I can
feel it in my chest.

"Anybody else learn anything today?" lookin dead at me. I walk away and
Sugar has to run to catch up and don't even seem to notice when I shrug her arm
off my shoulder.

"Well, we got four dollars anyway," she says.

"Uh hunh."

"We could go to Hascombs and get half a chocolate layer and then go to the   55
Sunset and still have plenty money for potato chips and ice cream sodas."

"Un hunh."

"Race you to Hascombs," she say.

We start down the block and she gets ahead which is O.K. by me cause I'm
going to the West End and then over to the Drive to think this day through. She
can run if she want to and even run faster. But ain't nobody gonna beat me at
nuthin.   [1972]

FOR THINKING AND WRITING

1. Bambara's story begins with "Back in the days," which suggests that Sylvia
   is significantly older now than she was then. How much time do you
   think has passed since the events she recalls? Does it matter to you how
   old she is now? Why, or why not?

2. Miss Moore is not officially a teacher. Nor is she a relative of the children
   she instructs. Is it right, then, for her to "take responsibility for the young
   ones' education" (para. 1)? Make arguments for and against her doing so.

3. Consider Miss Moore herself as making an argument. What are her claims? Which of her strategies, if any, seem effective in persuading her audience? Which, if any, seem ineffective?

4. What statements by the children articulate the lesson that Miss Moore teaches? Are all these statements saying pretty much the same thing? At the end of the story is Sylvia ready to agree with all of them? Explain.

5. Do class and race seem equally important in this story, or does one seem more important than the other? Elaborate your reasoning.

RAYMOND CARVER
What We Talk about
When We Talk about Love

Raymond Carver (1938–1988) re-creates in what has been called a "stripped-down and muscular prose style" the minutiae of everyday life in mid-twentieth-century America. Brought up in the Pacific Northwest in a working-class family, Carver began writing in high school and married early. While both he and his young wife worked at low-paying jobs, Carver took college courses and struggled to find time to write. In 1958, he studied fiction writing with John Gardner and graduated in 1963 from what is now the California State University at Humboldt. He received national recognition in 1967 when a story was included in The Best American Short Stories *annual anthology. Although Carver was a National Endowment for the Arts fellow in poetry in 1971, fiction has remained his primary genre, earning him numerous awards and fellowships, including O. Henry awards in 1974, 1975, and 1980. Despite his success as a writer, alcoholism plagued Carver for most of his life until, with the help of Alcoholics Anonymous, he stopped drinking in 1982, soon after his divorce. "What We Talk about When We Talk about Love" was the title story in his 1981 collection.*

My friend Mel McGinnis was talking. Mel McGinnis is a cardiologist, and sometimes that gives him the right.

The four of us were sitting around his kitchen table drinking gin. Sunlight filled the kitchen from the big window behind the sink. There were Mel and me and his second wife, Teresa—Terri, we called her—and my wife, Laura. We lived in Albuquerque then. But we were all from somewhere else.

There was an ice bucket on the table. The gin and the tonic water kept going around, and we somehow got on the subject of love. Mel thought real love was nothing less than spiritual love. He said he'd spent five years in a seminary before quitting to go to medical school. He said he still looked back on those years in the seminary as the most important years in his life.

Terri said the man she lived with before she lived with Mel loved her so much he tried to kill her. Then Terri said, "He beat me up one night. He dragged me around the living room by my ankles. He kept saying, 'I love you, I love you,

you bitch.' He went on dragging me around the living room. My head kept knocking on things." Terri looked around the table. "What do you do with love like that?"

She was a bone-thin woman with a pretty face, dark eyes, and brown hair that hung down her back. She liked necklaces made of turquoise, and long pendant earrings.

"My God, don't be silly. That's not love, and you know it," Mel said. "I don't know what you'd call it, but I sure know you wouldn't call it love."

"Say what you want to, but I know it was," Terri said. "It may sound crazy to you, but it's true just the same. People are different, Mel. Sure, sometimes he may have acted crazy. Okay. But he loved me. In his own way maybe, but he loved me. There was love there, Mel. Don't say there wasn't."

Mel let out his breath. He held his glass and turned to Laura and me. "The man threatened to kill me," Mel said. He finished his drink and reached for the gin bottle. "Terri's a romantic. Terri's of the kick-me-so-I'll-know-you-love-me school. Terri, hon, don't look that way." Mel reached across the table and touched Terri's cheek with his fingers. He grinned at her.

"Now he wants to make up," Terri said.

"Make up what?" Mel said. "What is there to make up? I know what I know. That's all."

"How'd we get started on this subject, anyway?" Terri said. She raised her glass and drank from it. "Mel always has love on his mind," she said. "Don't you, honey?" She smiled, and I thought that was the last of it.

"I just wouldn't call Ed's behavior love. That's all I'm saying, honey," Mel said. "What about you guys?" Mel said to Laura and me. "Does that sound like love to you?"

"I'm the wrong person to ask," I said. "I didn't even know the man. I've only heard his name mentioned in passing. I wouldn't know. You'd have to know the particulars. But I think what you're saying is that love is an absolute."

Mel said, "The kind of love I'm talking about is. The kind of love I'm talking about, you don't try to kill people."

Laura said, "I don't know anything about Ed, or anything about the situation. But who can judge anyone else's situation?"

I touched the back of Laura's hand. She gave me a quick smile. I picked up Laura's hand. It was warm, the nails polished, perfectly manicured. I encircled the broad wrist with my fingers, and I held her.

"When I left, he drank rat poison," Terri said. She clasped her arms with her hands. "They took him to the hospital in Sante Fe. That's where we lived then, about ten miles out. They saved his life. But his gums went crazy from it. I mean they pulled away from his teeth. After that, his teeth stood out like fangs. My God," Terri said. She waited a minute, then let go of her arms and picked up her glass.

"What people won't do!" Laura said.

"He's out of the action now," Mel said. "He's dead."

Mel handed me the saucer of limes. I took a section, squeezed it over my drink, and stirred the ice cubes with my finger.

"It gets worse," Terri said. "He shot himself in the mouth. But he bungled that too. Poor Ed," she said. Terri shook her head.

"Poor Ed nothing," Mel said. "He was dangerous."

Mel was forty-five years old. He was tall and rangy with curly soft hair. His face and arms were brown from the tennis he played. When he was sober, his gestures, all his movements, were precise, very careful.

"He did love me though, Mel. Grant me that," Terri said. "That's all I'm asking. He didn't love me the way you love me. I'm not saying that. But he loved me. You can grant me that, can't you?"

"What do you mean, he bungled it?" I said.   25

Laura leaned forward with her glass. She put her elbows on the table and held her glass in both hands. She glanced from Mel to Terri and waited with a look of bewilderment on her open face, as if amazed that such things happened to people you were friendly with.

"How'd he bungle it when he killed himself?" I said.

"I'll tell you what happened," Mel said. "He took this twenty-two pistol he'd bought to threaten Terri and me with. Oh, I'm serious, the man was always threatening. You should have seen the way we lived in those days. Like fugitives. I even bought a gun myself. Can you believe it? A guy like me? But I did. I bought one for self-defense and carried it in the glove compartment. Sometimes I'd have to leave the apartment in the middle of the night. To go to the hospital, you know? Terri and I weren't married then, and my first wife had the house and kids, the dog, everything, and Terri and I were living in this apartment here. Sometimes, as I say, I'd get a call in the middle of the night and have to go in to the hospital at two or three in the morning. It'd be dark out there in the parking lot, and I'd break into a sweat before I could even get to my car. I never knew if he was going to come up out of the shrubbery or from behind a car and start shooting. I mean, the man was crazy. He was capable of wiring a bomb, anything. He used to call my service at all hours and say he needed to talk to the doctor, and when I'd return the call, he'd say, 'Son of a bitch, your days are numbered.' Little things like that. It was scary, I'm telling you."

"I still feel sorry for him," Terri said.

"It sounds like a nightmare," Laura said. "But what exactly happened after he   30
shot himself?"

Laura is a legal secretary. We'd met in a professional capacity. Before we knew it, it was a courtship. She's thirty-five, three years younger than I am. In addition to being in love, we like each other and enjoy one another's company. She's easy to be with.

"What happened?" Laura said.

Mel said, "He shot himself in the mouth in his room. Someone heard the shot and told the manager. They came in with a passkey, saw what had happened, and called an ambulance. I happened to be there when they brought him in, alive but past recall. The man lived for three days. His head swelled up to twice the size of a normal head. I'd never seen anything like it, and I hope I never do again. Terri wanted to go in and sit with him when she found out about it. We had a fight over it. I didn't think she should see him like that. I didn't think she should see him, and I still don't."

"Who won the fight?" Laura said.

"I was in the room with him when he died," Terri said. "He never came up out of it. But I sat with him. He didn't have anyone else."

"He was dangerous," Mel said. "If you call that love, you can have it."

"It was love," Terri said. "Sure, it's abnormal in most people's eyes. But he was willing to die for it. He did die for it."

"I sure as hell wouldn't call it love," Mel said. "I mean, no one knows what he did it for. I've seen a lot of suicides, and I couldn't say anyone ever knew what they did it for."

Mel put his hands behind his neck and tilted his chair back. "I'm not interested in that kind of love," he said. "If that's love, you can have it."

Terri said, "We were afraid. Mel even made a will out and wrote to his brother in California who used to be a Green Beret. Mel told him who to look for if something happened to him."

Terri drank from her glass. She said, "But Mel's right—we lived like fugitives. We were afraid. Mel was, weren't you, honey? I even called the police at one point, but they were no help. They said they couldn't do anything until Ed actually did something. Isn't that a laugh?" Terri said.

She poured the last of the gin into her glass and waggled the bottle. Mel got up from the table and went to the cupboard. He took down another bottle.

"Well, Nick and I know what love is," Laura said. "For us, I mean," Laura said. She bumped my knee with her knee. "You're supposed to say something now," Laura said, and turned her smile on me.

For an answer, I took Laura's hand and raised it to my lips. I made a big production out of kissing her hand. Everyone was amused.

"We're lucky," I said.

"You guys," Terri said. "Stop that now. You're making me sick. You're still on the honeymoon, for God's sake. You're still gaga, for crying out loud. Just wait. How long have you been together now? How long has it been? A year? Longer than a year?"

"Going on a year and a half," Laura said, flushed and smiling.

"Oh, now," Terri said. "Wait awhile."

She held her drink and gazed at Laura.

"I'm only kidding," Terri said.

Mel opened the gin and went around the table with the bottle.

"Here, you guys," he said. "Let's have a toast. I want to propose a toast. A toast to love. To true love," Mel said.

We touched glasses.

"To love," we said.

Outside in the backyard, one of the dogs began to bark. The leaves of the aspen that leaned past the window ticked against the glass. The afternoon sun was like a presence in this room, the spacious light of ease and generosity. We could

35

40

45

50

55

have been anywhere, somewhere enchanted. We raised our glasses again and grinned at each other like children who had agreed on something forbidden.

"I'll tell you what real love is," Mel said. "I mean, I'll give you a good example. And then you can draw your own conclusions." He poured more gin into his glass. He added an ice cube and a sliver of lime. We waited and sipped our drinks. Laura and I touched knees again. I put a hand on her warm thigh and left it there.

"What do any of us really know about love?" Mel said. "It seems to me we're just beginners at love. We say we love each other and we do, I don't doubt it. I love Terri and Terri loves me, and you guys love each other too. You know the kind of love I'm talking about now. Physical love, that impulse that drives you to someone special, as well as love of the other person's being, his or her essence, as it were. Carnal love and, well, call it sentimental love, the day-to-day caring about the other person. But sometimes I have a hard time accounting for the fact that I must have loved my first wife too. But I did, I know I did. So I suppose I am like Terri in that regard. Terri and Ed." He thought about it and then he went on. "There was a time when I thought I loved my first wife more than life itself. But now I hate her guts. I do. How do you explain that? What happened to that love? What happened to it, is what I'd like to know. I wish someone could tell me. Then there's Ed. Okay, we're back to Ed. He loves Terri so much he tries to kill her and he winds up killing himself." Mel stopped talking and swallowed from his glass. "You guys have been together eighteen months and you love each other. It shows all over you. You glow with it. But you both loved other people before you met each other. You've both been married before, just like us. And you probably loved other people before that too, even. Terri and I have been together five years, been married for four. And the terrible thing, the terrible thing is, but the good thing too, the saving grace, you might say, is that if something happened to one of us—excuse me for saying this—but if something happened to one of us tomorrow I think the other one, the other person, would grieve for a while, you know, but then the surviving party would go out and love again, have someone else soon enough. All this, all of this love we're talking about, it would just be a memory. Maybe not even a memory. Am I wrong? Am I way off base? Because I want you to set me straight if you think I'm wrong. I want to know. I mean, I don't know anything, and I'm the first one to admit it."

"Mel, for God's sake," Terri said. She reached out and took hold of his wrist. "Are you getting drunk? Honey? Are you drunk?"

"Honey, I'm just talking," Mel said. "All right? I don't have to be drunk to say what I think. I mean, we're all just talking, right?" Mel said. He fixed his eyes on her.

"Sweetie, I'm not criticizing," Terri said.

She picked up her glass.

"I'm not on call today," Mel said. "Let me remind you of that. I am not on call," he said.

"Mel, we love you," Laura said.

Mel looked at Laura. He looked at her as if he could not place her, as if she was not the woman she was.

60

"Love you too, Laura," Mel said. "And you, Nick, love you too. You know   65
something?" Mel said. "You guys are our pals," Mel said.

He picked up his glass.

Mel said, "I was going to tell you about something. I mean, I was going to
prove a point. You see, this happened a few months ago, but it's still going on
right now, and it ought to make us feel ashamed when we talk like we know what
we're talking about when we talk about love."

"Come on now," Terri said. "Don't talk like you're drunk if you're not drunk."

"Just shut up for once in your life," Mel said very quietly. "Will you do me a
favor and do that for a minute? So as I was saying, there's this old couple who had
this car wreck out on the interstate. A kid hit them and they were all torn to shit
and nobody was giving them much chance to pull through."

Terri looked at us and then back at Mel. She seemed anxious, or maybe that's   70
too strong a word.

Mel was handing the bottle around the table.

"I was on call that night," Mel said. "It was May or maybe it was June. Terri
and I had just sat down to dinner when the hospital called. There'd been this thing
out on the interstate. Drunk kid, teenager, plowed his dad's pickup into this
camper with this old couple in it. They were up in their mid-seventies, that
couple. The kid — eighteen, nineteen, something — he was DOA. Taken the steering wheel through his sternum. The old couple, they were alive, you understand. I
mean, just barely. But they had everything. Multiple fractures, internal injuries,
hemorrhaging, contusions, lacerations, the works, and they each of them had
themselves concussions. They were in a bad way, believe me. And, of course, their
age was two strikes against them. I'd say she was worse off than he was. Ruptured
spleen along with everything else. Both kneecaps broken. But they'd been wearing
their seatbelts and, God knows, that's what saved them for the time being."

"Folks, this is an advertisement for the National Safety Council," Terri said.
"This is your spokesman, Dr. Melvin R. McGinnis, talking." Terri laughed.
"Mel," she said, "sometimes you're just too much. But I love you, hon," she said.

"Honey, I love you," Mel said.

He leaned across the table. Terri met him halfway. They kissed.   75

"Terri's right," Mel said as he settled himself again. "Get those seatbelts on.
But seriously, they were in some shape, those oldsters. By the time I got down
there, the kid was dead, as I said. He was off in a corner, laid out on a gurney. I
took one look at the old couple and told the ER nurse to get me a neurologist and
an orthopedic man and a couple of surgeons down there right away."

He drank from his glass. "I'll try to keep this short," he said. "So we took the
two of them up to the OR and worked like fuck on them most of the night. They
had these incredible reserves, those two. You see that once in a while. So we did
everything that could be done, and toward morning we're giving them a fifty-fifty
chance, maybe less than that for her. So here they are, still alive the next morning. So, okay, we move them into the ICU, which is where they both kept plugging away at it for two weeks, hitting it better and better on all the scopes. So we
transfer them out to their own room."

Mel stopped talking. "Here," he said, "let's drink this cheapo gin the hell up. Then we're going to dinner, right? Terri and I know a new place. That's where we'll go, to this new place we know about. But we're not going until we finish up this cut-rate, lousy gin."

Terri said, "We haven't actually eaten there yet. But it looks good. From the outside, you know."

"I like food," Mel said. "If I had it to do all over again, I'd be a chef, you   80
know? Right, Terri?" Mel said.

He laughed. He fingered the ice in his glass.

"Terri knows," he said. "Terri can tell you. But let me say this. If I could come back again in a different life, a different time and all, you know what? I'd like to come back as a knight. You were pretty safe wearing all that armor. It was all right being a knight until gunpowder and muskets and pistols came along."

"Mel would like to ride a horse and carry a lance," Terri said.

"Carry a woman's scarf with you everywhere," Laura said.

"Or just a woman," Mel said.   85

"Shame on you," Laura said.

Terri said, "Suppose you came back as a serf. The serfs didn't have it so good in those days," Terri said.

"The serfs never had it good," Mel said. "But I guess even the knights were vessels to someone. Isn't that the way it worked? But then everyone is always a vessel to someone. Isn't that right? Terri? But what I liked about knights, besides their ladies, was that they had that suit of armor, you know, and they couldn't get hurt very easy. No cars in those days, you know? No drunk teenagers to tear into your ass."

"Vassals," Terri said.

"What?" Mel said.   90

"Vassals," Terri said. "They were called vassals, not vessels."

"Vassals, vessels," Mel said, "what the fuck's the difference? You knew what I meant anyway. All right," Mel said. "So I'm not educated. I learned my stuff. I'm a heart surgeon, sure, but I'm just a mechanic. I go in and I fuck around and I fix things. Shit," Mel said.

"Modesty doesn't become you," Terri said.

"He's just a humble sawbones," I said. "But sometimes they suffocated in all that armor, Mel. They'd even have heart attacks if it got too hot and they were too tired and worn out. I read somewhere that they'd fall off their horses and not be able to get up because they were too tired to stand with all that armor on them. They got trampled by their own horses sometimes."

"That's terrible," Mel said. "That's a terrible thing, Nicky. I guess they'd just   95
lay there and wait until somebody came along and made a shish kebab out of them."

"Some other vessel," Terri said.

"That's right," Mel said. "Some vassal would come along and spear the bastard in the name of love. Or whatever the fuck it was they fought over in those days."

"Same things we fight over these days," Terri said.

Laura said, "Nothing's changed."

The color was still high in Laura's cheeks. Her eyes were bright. She brought   100
her glass to her lips.

Mel poured himself another drink. He looked at the label closely as if studying a long row of numbers. Then he slowly put the bottle down on the table and
slowly reached for the tonic water.

"What about the old couple?" Laura said. "You didn't finish that story you
started."

Laura was having a hard time lighting her cigarette. Her matches kept going
out.

The sunshine inside the room was different now, changing, getting thinner.
But the leaves outside the window were still shimmering, and I stared at the pattern they made on the panes and on the Formica counter. They weren't the same
patterns, of course.

"What about the old couple?" I said.   105

"Older but wiser," Terri said.

Mel stared at her.

Terri said, "Go on with your story, hon. I was only kidding. Then what happened?"

"Terri, sometimes," Mel said.

"Please, Mel," Terri said. "Don't always be so serious, sweetie. Can't you take   110
a joke?"

"Where's the joke?" Mel said.

He held his glass and gazed steadily at his wife.

"What happened?" Laura said.

Mel fastened his eyes on Laura. He said, "Laura, if I didn't have Terri and if I
didn't love her so much, and if Nick wasn't my best friend, I'd fall in love with
you, I'd carry you off, honey," he said.

"Tell your story," Terri said. "Then we'll go to that new place, okay?"   115

"Okay," Mel said. "Where was I?" he said. He stared at the table and then he
began again.

"I dropped in to see each of them every day, sometimes twice a day if I was
up doing other calls anyway. Casts and bandages, head to foot, the both of them.
You know, you've seen it in the movies. That's just the way they looked, just like
in the movies. Little eye-holes and nose-holes and mouth-holes. And she had to
have her legs slung up on top of it. Well, the husband was very depressed for the
longest while. Even after he found out that his wife was going to pull through, he
was still very depressed. Not about the accident, though. I mean, the accident was
one thing, but it wasn't everything. I'd get up to his mouth-hole, you know, and
he'd say no, it wasn't the accident exactly but it was because he couldn't see her
through his eye-holes. He said that was what was making him feel so bad. Can
you imagine? I'm telling you, the man's heart was breaking because he couldn't
turn his goddamn head and *see* his goddamn wife."

Mel looked around the table and shook his head at what he was going to say.

"I mean, it was killing the old fart just because he couldn't *look* at the fucking woman."

We all looked at Mel.   120

"Do you see what I'm saying?" he said.

Maybe we were a little drunk by then. I know it was hard keeping things in focus. The light was draining out of the room, going back through the window where it had come from. Yet nobody made a move to get up from the table to turn on the overhead light.

"Listen," Mel said. "Let's finish this fucking gin. There's about enough left here for one shooter all around. Then let's go eat. Let's go to the new place."

"He's depressed," Terri said. "Mel, why don't you take a pill?"

Mel shook his head. "I've taken everything there is."   125

"We all need a pill now and then," I said.

"Some people are born needing them," Terri said.

She was using her finger to rub at something on the table. Then she stopped rubbing.

"I think I want to call my kids," Mel said. "Is that all right with everybody? I'll call my kids," he said.

Terri said, "What if Marjorie answers the phone? You guys, you've heard us   130
on the subject of Marjorie? Honey, you know you don't want to talk to Marjorie. It'll make you feel even worse."

"I don't want to talk to Marjorie," Mel said. "But I want to talk to my kids."

"There isn't a day goes by that Mel doesn't say he wishes she'd get married again. Or else die," Terri said. "For one thing," Terri said, "she's bankrupting us. Mel says it's just to spite him that she won't get married again. She has a boy-friend who lives with her and the kids, so Mel is supporting the boyfriend too."

"She's allergic to bees," Mel said. "If I'm not praying she'll get married again, I'm praying she'll get herself stung to death by a swarm of fucking bees."

"Shame on you," Laura said.

"Bzzzzzzz," Mel said, turning his fingers into bees and buzzing them at   135
Terri's throat. Then he let his hands drop all the way to his sides.

"She's vicious," Mel said. "Sometimes I think I'll go up there dressed like a beekeeper. You know, that hat that's like a helmet with the plate that comes down over your face, the big gloves, and the padded coat? I'll knock on the door and let loose a hive of bees in the house. But first I'd make sure the kids were out, of course."

He crossed one leg over the other. It seemed to take him a lot of time to do it. Then he put both feet on the floor and leaned forward, elbows on the table, his chin cupped in his hands.

"Maybe I won't call the kids, after all. Maybe it isn't such a hot idea. Maybe we'll just go eat. How does that sound?"

"Sounds fine to me," I said. "Eat or not eat. Or keep drinking. I could head right on out into the sunset."

"What does that mean, honey?" Laura said.   140

"It just means what I said," I said. "It means I could just keep going. That's all it means."

"I could eat something myself," Laura said. "I don't think I've ever been so hungry in my life. Is there something to nibble on?"

"I'll put out some cheese and crackers," Terri said.

But Terri just sat there. She did not get up to get anything.

Mel turned his glass over. He spilled it out on the table.   145

"Gin's gone," Mel said.

Terri said, "Now what?"

I could hear my heart beating. I could hear everyone's heart. I could hear the human noise we sat there making, not one of us moving, not even when the room went dark.   [1981]

FOR THINKING AND WRITING

1. The argument between the couples seems to be about the nature of love. Which character's ideas make the most sense to you? What kinds of love are discussed? Are these demonstrated in the story? Do you think true love is an illusion?

2. Do you see similarities between Mel and Ed? Do any of the characters seem aware of any similarities? Is Mel a perceptive person? What are his problems? Is he in love with Terri? How do you interpret his fantasy with the bees and Marjorie?

3. Why does Mel seem so interested in knights? Is this symbolic? Are there other symbols here (light? dark? cardiologist?)? What do you make of the last paragraph? Why does it end with beating hearts and silence?

4. Is this story optimistic or pessimistic about true love? Is the old couple a positive or a negative example of true love? What about Nick and Laura? What about Ed? Could you argue that he was in love?

5. What does the title mean? Be specific, especially about the first word. Do you tell stories about love? Have you heard some recently? What lessons or information do they give about love?

KATE CHOPIN
Désirée's Baby

Kate Chopin (1851–1904) is known for her evocations of the unique, multiethnic Creole and Cajun societies of late-nineteenth-century Louisiana; however, her characters transcend the limitation of regional genre writing, striking a particularly resonant note among feminist readers. Born Katherine O'Flaherty in St. Louis, Missouri, she married Oscar Chopin in 1870 and went to live with him in New Orleans and on his Mississippi River plantation. Her short stories were collected in Bayou Folk *(1894) and* A Night in Acadie *(1897). Chopin's last novel,* The Awakening, *scandalized readers at the time of its publication in 1899 because of its frank portrayal of female sexuality in the context of an extramarital affair. Long ignored by readers and critics, her work was revived in the 1960s and continues to provoke heated discussion of her female characters: Are they women who seek freedom in the only ways available to them, or are they willing participants in their own victimhood?*

"Désirée's Baby" was written in 1892 and published in Bayou Folk *(1894). The story reflects Chopin's experience among the French Creoles in Louisiana.*

As the day was pleasant, Madame Valmondé drove over to L'Abri to see Désirée and the baby.

It made her laugh to think of Désirée with a baby. Why, it seemed but yesterday that Désirée was little more than a baby herself; when Monsieur in riding through the gateway of Valmondé had found her lying asleep in the shadow of the big stone pillar.

The little one awoke in his arms and began to cry for "Dada." That was as much as she could do or say. Some people thought she might have strayed there of her own accord, for she was of the toddling age. The prevailing belief was that she had been purposely left by a party of Texans, whose canvas-covered wagon, late in the day, had crossed the ferry that Coton Maïs kept, just below the plantation. In time Madame Valmondé abandoned every speculation but the one that Désirée had been sent to her by a beneficent Providence to be the child of her affection, seeing that she was without child of the flesh. For the girl grew to be beautiful and gentle, affectionate and sincere, — the idol of Valmondé.

It was no wonder, when she stood one day against the stone pillar in whose shadow she had lain asleep, eighteen years before, that Armand Aubigny riding by and seeing her there, had fallen in love with her. That was the way all the Aubignys fell in love, as if struck by a pistol shot. The wonder was that he had not loved her before; for he had known her since his father brought him home from Paris, a boy of eight, after his mother died there. The passion that awoke in him that day, when he saw her at the gate, swept along like an avalanche, or like a prairie fire, or like anything that drives headlong over all obstacles.

Monsieur Valmondé grew practical and wanted things well considered: that is, the girl's obscure origin. Armand looked into her eyes and did not care. He was reminded that she was nameless. What did it matter about a name when he could give her one of the oldest and proudest in Louisiana? He ordered the *corbeille* from Paris, and contained himself with what patience he could until it arrived; then they were married.

Madame Valmondé had not seen Désirée and the baby for four weeks. When she reached L'Abri she shuddered at the first sight of it, as she always did. It was a sad looking place, which for many years had not known the gentle presence of a mistress, old Monsieur Aubigny having married and buried his wife in France, and she having loved her own land too well ever to leave it. The roof

5

came down steep and black like a cowl, reaching out beyond the wide galleries that encircled the yellow stuccoed house. Big, solemn oaks grew close to it, and their thick-leaved, far-reaching branches shadowed it like a pall. Young Aubigny's rule was a strict one, too, and under it his negroes had forgotten how to be gay, as they had been during the old master's easy-going and indulgent lifetime.

The young mother was recovering slowly, and lay full length, in her soft white muslins and laces, upon a couch. The baby was beside her, upon her arm, where he had fallen sleep, at her breast. The yellow nurse woman sat beside a window fanning herself.

Madame Valmondé bent her portly figure over Désirée and kissed her, holding her an instant tenderly in her arms. Then she turned to the child.

"This is not the baby!" she exclaimed, in startled tones. French was the language spoken at Valmondé in those days.

"I knew you would be astonished," laughed Désirée, "at the way he has grown. The little *cochon de lait!*° Look at his legs, mamma, and his hands and fingernails,—real fingernails. Zandrine had to cut them this morning. Isn't it true, Zandrine?" 10

The woman bowed her turbaned head majestically, "Mais si, Madame."

"And the way he cries," went on Désirée, "is deafening. Armand heard him the other day as far away as La Blanche's cabin."

Madame Valmondé had never removed her eyes from the child. She lifted it and walked with it over to the window that was lightest. She scanned the baby narrowly, then looked as searchingly at Zandrine, whose face was turned to gaze across the fields.

"Yes, the child has grown, has changed," said Madame Valmondé, slowly, as she replaced it beside its mother. "What does Armand say?"

Désirée's face became suffused with a glow that was happiness itself. 15

"Oh, Armand is the proudest father in the parish, I believe, chiefly because it is a boy, to bear his name; though he says not,—that he would have loved a girl as well. But I know it isn't true. I know he says that to please me. And mamma," she added, drawing Madame Valmondé's head down to her and speaking in a whisper, "he hasn't punished one of them—not one of them—since baby is born. Even Négrillon, who pretended to have burnt his leg that he might rest from work—he only laughed, and said Négrillon was a great scamp. Oh, mamma, I'm so happy; it frightens me."

What Désirée said was true. Marriage, and later the birth of his son had softened Armand Aubigny's imperious and exacting nature greatly. This was what made the gentle Désirée so happy, for she loved him desperately. When he frowned she trembled, but loved him. When he smiled, she asked no greater blessing of God. But Armand's dark, handsome face had not often been disfigured by frowns since the day he fell in love with her.

When the baby was about three months old, Désirée awoke one day to the conviction that there was something in the air menacing her peace. It was at first

cochon de lait: French for "suckling pig"; an endearment.

too subtle to grasp. It had only been a disquieting suggestion; an air of mystery among the blacks; unexpected visits from far-off neighbors who could hardly account for their coming. Then a strange, an awful change in her husband's manner, which she dared not ask him to explain. When he spoke to her, it was with averted eyes, from which the old love-light seemed to have gone out. He absented himself from home; and when there, avoided her presence and that of her child, without excuse. And the very spirit of Satan seemed suddenly to take hold of him in his dealings with the slaves. Désirée was miserable enough to die.

She sat in her room, one hot afternoon, in her *peignoir*, listlessly drawing through her fingers the strands of her long, silky brown hair that hung about her shoulders. The baby, half naked, lay asleep upon her own great mahogany bed, that was like a sumptuous throne, with its satin-lined half-canopy. One of La Blanche's little quadroon boys — half naked too — stood fanning the child slowly with a fan of peacock feathers. Désirée's eyes had been fixed absently and sadly upon the baby, while she was striving to penetrate the threatening mist that she felt closing about her. She looked from her child to the boy who stood beside him, and back again; over and over. "Ah!" It was a cry that she could not help; which she was not conscious of having uttered. The blood turned like ice in her veins, and a clammy moisture gathered upon her face.

She tried to speak to the little quadroon boy; but no sound would come, at   20
first. When he heard his name uttered, he looked up, and his mistress was pointing to the door. He laid aside the great, soft fan, and obediently stole away, over the polished floor, on his bare tiptoes.

She stayed motionless, with gaze riveted upon her child, and her face the picture of fright.

Presently her husband entered the room, and without noticing her, went to a table and began to search among some papers which covered it.

"Armand," she called to him, in a voice which must have stabbed him, if he was human. But he did not notice. "Armand," she said again. Then she rose and tottered towards him. "Armand," she panted once more, clutching his arm, "look at our child. What does it mean? tell me."

He coldly but gently loosened her fingers from about his arm and thrust the hand away from him. "Tell me what it means!" she cried despairingly.

"It means," he answered lightly, "that the child is not white; it means that   25
you are not white."

A quick conception of all that this accusation meant for her nerved her with unwonted courage to deny it. "It is a lie; it is not true, I am white! Look at my hair, it is brown; and my eyes are gray, Armand, you know they are gray. And my skin is fair," seizing his wrist. "Look at my hand; whiter than yours, Armand," she laughed hysterically.

"As white as La Blanche's," he returned cruelly; and went away leaving her alone with their child.

When she could hold a pen in her hand, she sent a despairing letter to Madame Valmondé.

"My mother, they tell me I am not white. Armand has told me I am not white. For God's sake tell them it is not true. You must know it is not true. I shall die. I must die. I cannot be so unhappy, and live."

The answer that came was as brief: 30

"My own Désirée: Come home to Valmondé; back to your mother who loves you. Come with your child."

When the letter reached Désirée she went with it to her husband's study, and laid it open upon the desk before which he sat. She was like a stone image: silent, white, motionless after she placed it there.

In silence he ran his cold eyes over the written words. He said nothing. "Shall I go, Armand?" she asked in tones sharp with agonized suspense.

"Yes, go."

"Do you want me to go?"   35

"Yes, I want you to go."

He thought Almighty God had dealt cruelly and unjustly with him; and felt, somehow, that he was paying Him back in kind when he stabbed thus into his wife's soul. Moreover he no longer loved her, because of the unconscious injury she had brought upon his home and his name.

She turned away like one stunned by a blow, and walked slowly towards the door, hoping he would call her back.

"Good-by, Armand," she moaned.

He did not answer her. That was his last blow at fate.   40

Désirée went in search of her child. Zandrine was pacing the sombre gallery with it. She took the little one from the nurse's arms with no word of explanation, and descending the steps, walked away, under the live-oak branches.

It was an October afternoon; the sun was just sinking. Out in the still fields the negroes were picking cotton.

Désirée had not changed the thin white garment nor the slippers which she wore. Her hair was uncovered and the sun's rays brought a golden gleam from its brown meshes. She did not take the broad, beaten road which led to the far-off plantation of Valmondé. She walked across a deserted field, where the stubble bruised her tender feet, so delicately shod, and tore her thin gown to shreds.

She disappeared among the reeds and willows that grew thick along the banks of the deep, sluggish bayou; and she did not come back again.

Some weeks later there was a curious scene enacted at L'Abri. In the centre   45
of the smoothly swept back yard was a great bonfire. Armand Aubigny sat in the wide hallway that commanded a view of the spectacle; and it was he who dealt out to a half dozen negroes the material which kept this fire ablaze.

A graceful cradle of willow, with all its dainty furbishings, was laid upon the pyre, which had already been fed with the richness of a priceless *layette*. Then there were silk gowns, and velvet and satin ones added to these; laces, too, and embroideries; bonnets and gloves; for the *corbeille* had been of rare quality.

The last thing to go was a tiny bundle of letters; innocent little scribblings that Désirée had sent to him during the days of their espousal. There was the remnant of one back in the drawer from which he took them. But it was not Désirée's; it was part of an old letter from his mother to his father. He read it. She was thanking God for the blessing of her husband's love: —

"But, above all," she wrote, "night and day, I thank the good God for having so arranged our lives that our dear Armand will never know that his mother, who adores him, belongs to the race that is cursed with the brand of slavery."   [1892]

FOR THINKING AND WRITING

1. Does Armand really love Désirée? Explain.

2. Armand seems to have fallen in love "at first sight." Is this possible? Can love conquer all, even racial bias? Is Chopin skeptical?

3. What would you have done if you were Désirée? What will Armand do now that he knows?

4. Are we able to break free of our cultural heritage? What are the ways society tries to keep us in line? How do some people break free? Is there a danger in disregarding societal norms? Are there benefits?

5. Could this story happen this way today?

KATE CHOPIN
The Story of an Hour

"The Story of an Hour" was first published in Bayou Folk *(1894). It is typical of Chopin's controversial works and caused a sensation among the reading public.*

Knowing that Mrs. Mallard was afflicted with a heart trouble, great care was taken to break to her as gently as possible the news of her husband's death.

It was her sister Josephine who told her, in broken sentences; veiled hints that revealed in half concealing. Her husband's friend Richards was there, too, near her. It was he who had been in the newspaper office when intelligence of the railroad disaster was received, with Brently Mallard's name leading the list of "killed." He had only taken the time to assure himself of its truth by a second telegram, and had hastened to forestall any less careful, less tender friend in bearing the sad message.

She did not hear the story as many women have heard the same, with a paralyzed inability to accept its significance. She wept at once, with sudden, wild abandonment, in her sister's arms. When the storm of grief had spent itself she went away to her room alone. She would have no one follow her.

There stood, facing the open window, a comfortable, roomy armchair. Into this she sank, pressed down by a physical exhaustion that haunted her body and seemed to reach into her soul.

She could see in the open square before her house the tops of trees that were all aquiver with the new spring life. The delicious breath of rain was in the air. In   5 the street below a peddler was crying his wares. The notes of a distant song which some one was singing reached her faintly, and countless sparrows were twittering in the eaves.

There were patches of blue sky showing here and there through the clouds that had met and piled one above the other in the west facing her window.

She sat with her head thrown back upon the cushion of the chair, quite motionless, except when a sob came up into her throat and shook her, as a child who had cried itself to sleep continues to sob in its dreams.

She was young, with a fair, calm face, whose lines bespoke repression and even a certain strength. But now there was a dull stare in her eyes, whose gaze was fixed away off yonder on one of those patches of blue sky. It was not a glance of reflection, but rather indicated a suspension of intelligent thought.

There was something coming to her and she was waiting for it, fearfully. What was it? She did not know; it was too subtle and elusive to name. But she felt it, creeping out of the sky, reaching toward her through the sounds, the scents, the color that filled the air.

Now her bosom rose and fell tumultuously. She was beginning to recognize   10 this thing that was approaching to possess her, and she was striving to beat it back with her will — as powerless as her two white slender hands would have been.

When she abandoned herself a little whispered word escaped her slightly parted lips. She said it over and over under her breath: "free, free, free!" The vacant stare and the look of terror that had followed it went from her eyes. They stayed keen and bright. Her pulses beat fast, and the coursing blood warmed and relaxed every inch of her body.

She did not stop to ask if it were or were not a monstrous joy that held her. A clear and exalted perception enabled her to dismiss the suggestion as trivial.

She knew that she would weep again when she saw the kind, tender hands folded in death; the face that had never looked save with love upon her, fixed and gray and dead. But she saw beyond that bitter moment a long procession of years to come that would belong to her absolutely. And she opened and spread her arms out to them in welcome.

There would be no one to live for her during those coming years: she would live for herself. There would be no powerful will bending hers in that blind persistence with which men and women believe they have a right to impose a private will upon a fellow-creature. A kind intention or a cruel intention made the act seem no less a crime as she looked upon it in that brief moment of illumination.

And yet she had loved him — sometimes. Often she had not. What did it mat-   15 ter! What could love, the unsolved mystery, count for in face of this possession of self-assertion which she suddenly recognized as the strongest impulse of her being!

"Free! Body and soul free!" she kept whispering.

Josephine was kneeling before the closed door with her lips to the keyhole, imploring for admission. "Louise, open the door! I beg; open the door — you will make yourself ill. What are you doing, Louise? For heaven's sake open the door."

"Go away. I am not making myself ill." No; she was drinking in a very elixir of life through that open window.

Her fancy was running riot along those days ahead of her. Spring days, and summer days, and all sorts of days that would be her own. She breathed a quick prayer that life might be long. It was only yesterday she had thought with a shudder that life might be long.

She arose at length and opened the door to her sister's importunities. There [20] was a feverish triumph in her eyes, and she carried herself unwittingly like a goddess of Victory. She clasped her sister's waist, and together they descended the stairs. Richards stood waiting for them at the bottom.

Some one was opening the front door with a latchkey. It was Brently Mallard who entered, a little travel-stained, composedly carrying his gripsack and umbrella. He had been far from the scene of accident, and did not even know there had been one. He stood amazed at Josephine's piercing cry; at Richards' quick motion to screen him from the view of his wife.

But Richards was too late.

When the doctors came they said she had died of heart disease—of joy that kills.   [1894]

FOR THINKING AND WRITING

1. Is Louise Mallard really in love with her husband? Regardless of your answer, would she ever leave him? Is it possible to confuse love with duty?

2. Is it possible to assign blame for this tragedy? To Mr. Mallard? Mrs. Mallard? The culture?

3. Why did Chopin keep the story so brief? What would you like to know more about?

4. What specifically do you think Mrs. Mallard was thinking about in the room?

5. Do you think this situation was common during Chopin's time? Today?

WILLIAM FAULKNER
A Rose for Emily

William Faulkner (1897–1962) is recognized not only as one of the greatest American novelists and storytellers but as one of the major figures of world literature, having won the Nobel Prize in 1949. This acclaim failed to impress the people of his hometown, however, where his genteel poverty and peculiar ways earned him the title "Count No Count." Born in New Albany, Mississippi, and raised in Oxford, the home of the University of Mississippi, Faulkner briefly attended college there after World War I but was reduced to working odd jobs while continuing his writing. His fiction is most often set in Yoknapatawpha County, a created world whose history, geography, and complex genealogies parallel those of the American South. His many novels and stories blend the grotesquely comic with the appallingly tragic.

The Sound and the Fury (1929) *is often considered his finest work. In later years, Faulkner's "odd jobs" included scriptwriting for Hollywood movies, speaking at universities, and writing magazine articles. "A Rose for Emily," first published in* Forum, *presents a story of love as told by citizens of Yoknapatawpha County.*

1

When Miss Emily Grierson died, our whole town went to her funeral: the men through a sort of respectful affection for a fallen monument, the women mostly out of curiosity to see the inside of her house, which no one save an old manservant—a combined gardener and cook—had seen in at least ten years.

It was a big, squarish frame house that had once been white, decorated with cupolas and spires and scrolled balconies in the heavily lightsome style of the seventies, set on what had once been our most select street. But garages and cotton gins had encroached and obliterated even the august names of that neighborhood; only Miss Emily's house was left, lifting its stubborn and coquettish decay above the cotton wagons and the gasoline pumps—an eyesore among eyesores. And now Miss Emily had gone to join the representatives of those august names where they lay in the cedar-bemused cemetery among the ranked and anonymous graves of Union and Confederate soldiers who fell at the battle of Jefferson.

Alive, Miss Emily had been a tradition, a duty, and a care; a sort of hereditary obligation upon the town, dating from that day in 1894 when Colonel Sartoris, the mayor—he who fathered the edict that no Negro woman should appear on the streets without an apron—remitted her taxes, the dispensation dating from the death of her father on into perpetuity. Not that Miss Emily would have accepted charity. Colonel Sartoris invented an involved tale to the effect that Miss Emily's father had loaned money to the town, which the town, as a matter of business, preferred this way of repaying. Only a man of Colonel Sartoris' generation and thought could have invented it, and only a woman could have believed it.

When the next generation, with its more modern ideas, became mayors and aldermen, this arrangement created some little dissatisfaction. On the first of the year they mailed her a tax notice. February came, and there was no reply. They wrote her a formal letter, asking her to call at the sheriff's office at her convenience. A week later the mayor wrote her himself, offering to call or to send his car for her, and received in reply a note on paper of an archaic shape, in a thin, flowing calligraphy in faded ink, to the effect that she no longer went out at all. The tax notice was also enclosed, without comment.

They called a special meeting of the Board of Aldermen. A deputation waited upon her, knocked at the door through which no visitor had passed since she ceased giving china-painting lessons eight or ten years earlier. They were admitted by the old Negro into a dim hall from which a stairway mounted into still more shadow. It smelled of dust and disuse—a close, dank smell. The Negro led them into the parlor. It was furnished in heavy, leather-covered furniture. When the Negro opened the blinds of one window, they could see that the

5

leather was cracked; and when they sat down, a faint dust rose sluggishly about their thighs, spinning with slow motes in the single sun-ray. On a tarnished gilt easel before the fireplace stood a crayon portrait of Miss Emily's father.

They rose when she entered—a small, fat woman in black, with a thin gold chain descending to her waist and vanishing into her belt, leaning on an ebony cane with a tarnished gold head. Her skeleton was small and spare; perhaps that was why what would have been merely plumpness in another was obesity in her. She looked bloated, like a body long submerged in motionless water, and of that pallid hue. Her eyes, lost in the fatty ridges of her face, looked like two small pieces of coal pressed into a lump of dough as they moved from one face to another while the visitors stated their errand.

She did not ask them to sit. She just stood in the door and listened quietly until the spokesman came to a stumbling halt. Then they could hear the invisible watch ticking at the end of the gold chain.

Her voice was dry and cold. "I have no taxes in Jefferson. Colonel Sartoris explained it to me. Perhaps one of you can gain access to the city records and satisfy yourselves."

"But we have. We are the city authorities, Miss Emily. Didn't you get a notice from the sheriff, signed by him?"

"I received a paper, yes," Miss Emily said. "Perhaps he considers himself the   10
sheriff. . . . I have no taxes in Jefferson."

"But there is nothing on the books to show that, you see. We must go by the—"

"See Colonel Sartoris. I have no taxes in Jefferson."

"But, Miss Emily—"

"See Colonel Sartoris." (Colonel Sartoris had been dead almost ten years.) "I have no taxes in Jefferson. Tobe!" The Negro appeared. "Show these gentlemen out."

2

So she vanquished them, horse and foot, just as she had vanquished their   15
fathers thirty years before about the smell. That was two years after her father's death and a short time after her sweetheart—the one we believed would marry her—had deserted her. After her father's death she went out very little; after her sweetheart went away, people hardly saw her at all. A few of the ladies had the temerity to call, but were not received, and the only sign of life about the place was the Negro man—a young man then—going in and out with a market basket.

"Just as if a man—any man—could keep a kitchen properly," the ladies said; so they were not surprised when the smell developed. It was another link between the gross, teeming world and the high and mighty Griersons.

A neighbor, a woman, complained to the mayor, Judge Stevens, eighty years old.

"But what will you have me do about it, madam?" he said.

"Why, send her word to stop it," the woman said. "Isn't there a law?"

"I'm sure that won't be necessary," Judge Stevens said. "It's probably just a   20
snake or a rat that nigger of hers killed in the yard. I'll speak to him about it."

The next day he received two more complaints, one from a man who came
in diffident deprecation. "We really must do something about it, Judge. I'd be the
last one in the world to bother Miss Emily, but we've got to do something." That
night the Board of Aldermen met—three graybeards and one younger man, a
member of the rising generation.

"It's simple enough," he said. "Send her word to have her place cleaned up.
Give her a certain time to do it in, and if she don't. . . ."

"Dammit, sir," Judge Stevens said, "will you accuse a lady to her face of
smelling bad?"

So the next night, after midnight, four men crossed Miss Emily's lawn and
slunk about the house like burglars, sniffing along the base of the brickwork and
at the cellar openings while one of them performed a regular sowing motion with
his hand out of a sack slung from his shoulder. They broke open the cellar door
and sprinkled lime there, and in all the outbuildings. As they recrossed the lawn,
a window that had been dark was lighted and Miss Emily sat in it, the light
behind her, and her upright torso motionless as that of an idol. They crept quietly
across the lawn and into the shadow of the locusts that lined the street. After a
week or two the smell went away.

That was when people had begun to feel really sorry for her. People in our   25
town, remembering how old lady Wyatt, her great-aunt, had gone completely
crazy at last, believed that the Griersons held themselves a little too high for what
they really were. None of the young men were quite good enough for Miss Emily
and such. We had long thought of them as a tableau, Miss Emily a slender figure
in white in the background, her father a spraddled silhouette in the foreground,
his back to her and clutching a horsewhip, the two of them framed by the back-
flung front door. So when she got to be thirty and was still single, we were not
pleased exactly, but vindicated; even with insanity in the family she wouldn't
have turned down all of her chances if they had really materialized.

When her father died, it got about that the house was all that was left to her;
and in a way, people were glad. At last they could pity Miss Emily. Being left
alone, and a pauper, she had become humanized. Now she too would know the
old thrill and the old despair of a penny more or less.

The day after his death all the ladies prepared to call at the house and offer
condolence and aid, as is our custom. Miss Emily met them at the door, dressed
as usual and with no trace of grief on her face. She told them that her father was
not dead. She did that for three days, with the ministers calling on her, and the
doctors, trying to persuade her to let them dispose of the body. Just as they were
about to resort to law and force, she broke down, and they buried her father
quickly.

We did not say she was crazy then. We believed she had to do that. We
remembered all the young men her father had driven away, and we knew that
with nothing left, she would have to cling to that which had robbed her, as
people will.

3

She was sick for a long time. When we saw her again, her hair was cut short, making her look like a girl, with a vague resemblance to those angels in colored church windows — sort of tragic and serene.

The town had just let the contracts for paving the sidewalks, and in the sum- 30
mer after her father's death they began the work. The construction company came with niggers and mules and machinery, and a foreman named Homer Barron, a Yankee — a big, dark, ready man, with a big voice and eyes lighter than his face. The little boys would follow in groups to hear him cuss the niggers, and the niggers singing in time to the rise and fall of picks. Pretty soon he knew everybody in town. Whenever you heard a lot of laughing anywhere about the square, Homer Barron would be in the center of the group. Presently, we began to see him and Miss Emily on Sunday afternoons driving in the yellow-wheeled buggy and the matched team of bays from the livery stable.

At first we were glad that Miss Emily would have an interest, because the ladies all said, "Of course a Grierson would not think seriously of a Northerner, a day laborer." But there were still others, older people, who said that even grief could not cause a real lady to forget *noblesse oblige* — without calling it *noblesse oblige*. They just said, "Poor Emily. Her kinsfolk should come to her." She had some kin in Alabama; but years ago her father had fallen out with them over the estate of old lady Wyatt, the crazy woman, and there was no communication between the two families. They had not even been represented at the funeral.

And as soon as the old people said, "Poor Emily," the whispering began. "Do you suppose it's really so?" they said to one another. "Of course it is. What else could. . . ." This behind their hands; rustling of craned silk and satin behind jalousies closed upon the sun of Sunday afternoon as the thin, swift clop-clop-clop of the matched team passed: "Poor Emily."

She carried her head high enough — even when we believed that she was fallen. It was as if she demanded more than ever the recognition of her dignity as the last Grierson; as if it had wanted that touch of earthiness to reaffirm her imperviousness. Like when she bought the rat poison, the arsenic. That was over a year after they had begun to say "Poor Emily," and while the two female cousins were visiting her.

"I want some poison," she said to the druggist. She was over thirty then, still a slight woman, though thinner than usual, with cold, haughty black eyes in a face the flesh of which was strained across the temples and about the eyesockets as you imagine a lighthouse-keeper's face ought to look. "I want some poison," she said.

"Yes, Miss Emily. What kind? For rats and such? I'd recom——" 35
"I want the best you have. I don't care what kind."

The druggist named several. "They'll kill anything up to an elephant. But what you want is——"

"Arsenic," Miss Emily said. "Is that a good one?"

"Is . . . arsenic? Yes, ma'am. But what you want——"

"I want arsenic." 40

The druggist looked down at her. She looked back at him, erect, her face like a strained flag. "Why, of course," the druggist said. "If that's what you want. But the law requires you to tell what you are going to use it for."

Miss Emily just stared at him, her head tilted back in order to look him eye for eye, until he looked away and went and got the arsenic and wrapped it up. The Negro delivery boy brought her the package; the druggist didn't come back. When she opened the package at home there was written on the box, under the skull and bones: "For rats."

4

So the next day we all said, "She will kill herself"; and we said it would be the best thing. When she had first begun to be seen with Homer Barron, we had said, "She will marry him." Then we said, "She will persuade him yet," because Homer himself had remarked—he liked men, and it was known that he drank with the younger men in the Elks' Club—that he was not a marrying man. Later we said, "Poor Emily" behind the jalousies as they passed on Sunday afternoon in the glittering buggy, Miss Emily with her head high and Homer Barron with his hat cocked and a cigar in his teeth, reins and whip in a yellow glove.

Then some of the ladies began to say that it was a disgrace to the town and a bad example to the young people. The men did not want to interfere, but at last the ladies forced the Baptist minister—Miss Emily's people were Episcopal—to call upon her. He would never divulge what happened during that interview, but he refused to go back again. The next Sunday they again drove about the streets, and the following day the minister's wife wrote to Miss Emily's relations in Alabama.

So she had blood-kin under her roof again and we sat back to watch develop- 45
ments. At first nothing happened. Then we were sure that they were to be married. We learned that Miss Emily had been to the jeweler's and ordered a man's toilet set in silver, with the letters H.B. on each piece. Two days later we learned that she had bought a complete outfit of men's clothing, including a nightshirt, and we said, "They are married." We were really glad. We were glad because the two female cousins were even more Grierson than Miss Emily had ever been.

So we were not surprised when Homer Barron—the streets had been finished some time since—was gone. We were a little disappointed that there was not a public blowing-off, but we believed that he had gone on to prepare for Miss Emily's coming, or to give her a chance to get rid of the cousins. (By that time it was a cabal, and we were all Miss Emily's allies to help circumvent the cousins.) Sure enough, after another week they departed. And, as we had expected all along, within three days Homer Barron was back in town. A neighbor saw the Negro man admit him at the kitchen door at dusk one evening.

And that was the last we saw of Homer Barron. And of Miss Emily for some time. The Negro man went in and out with the market basket, but the front door remained closed. Now and then we would see her at the window for a moment, as the men did that night when they sprinkled the lime, but for almost six months she did not appear on the streets. Then we knew that this was to be expected too;

as if that quality of her father which had thwarted her woman's life so many times
had been too virulent and too furious to die.

When we next saw Miss Emily, she had grown fat and her hair was turning
gray. During the next few years it grew grayer and grayer until it attained an even
pepper-and-salt iron-gray, when it ceased turning. Up to the day of her death at
seventy-four it was still that vigorous iron-gray, like the hair of an active man.

From that time on her front door remained closed, save during a period of six
or seven years, when she was about forty, during which she gave lessons in china-
painting. She fitted up a studio in one of the downstairs rooms, where the daughters and granddaughters of Colonel Sartoris' contemporaries were sent to her
with the same regularity and in the same spirit that they were sent to church on
Sundays with a twenty-five-cent piece for the collection plate. Meanwhile her
taxes had been remitted.

Then the newer generation became the backbone and the spirit of the town,   50
and the painting pupils grew up and fell away and did not send their children to
her with boxes of color and tedious brushes and pictures cut from the ladies' magazines. The front door closed upon the last one and remained closed for good.
When the town got free postal delivery, Miss Emily alone refused to let them fas-
ten the metal numbers above her door and attach a mailbox to it. She would not
listen to them.

Daily, monthly, yearly we watched the Negro grow grayer and more stooped,
going in and out with the market basket. Each December we sent her a tax
notice, which would be returned by the post office a week later, unclaimed. Now
and then we would see her in one of the downstairs windows — she had evidently
shut up the top floor of the house — like the carven torso of an idol in a niche,
looking or not looking at us, we could never tell which. Thus she passed from
generation to generation — dear, inescapable, impervious, tranquil, and perverse.

And so she died. Fell ill in the house filled with dust and shadows, with only
a doddering Negro man to wait on her. We did not even know she was sick; we
had long since given up trying to get any information from the Negro. He talked
to no one, probably not even to her, for his voice had grown harsh and rusty, as if
from disuse.

She died in one of the downstairs rooms, in a heavy walnut bed with a curtain, her gray head propped on a pillow yellow and moldy with age and lack of
sunlight.

5

The Negro met the first of the ladies at the front door and let them in, with their
hushed, sibilant voices and their quick, curious glances, and then he disappeared.
He walked right through the house and out the back and was not seen again.

The two female cousins came at once. They held the funeral on the second   55
day, with the town coming to look at Miss Emily beneath a mass of bought flowers, with the crayon face of her father musing profoundly above the bier and the
ladies sibilant and macabre; and the very old men — some in their brushed Confederate uniforms — on the porch and the lawn, talking of Miss Emily as if she

had been a contemporary of theirs, believing that they had danced with her and courted her perhaps, confusing time with its mathematical progression, as the old do, to whom all the past is not a diminishing road but, instead, a huge meadow which no winter ever quite touches, divided from them now by the narrow bottle-neck of the most recent decade of years.

Already we knew that there was one room in that region above stairs which no one had seen in forty years, and which would have to be forced. They waited until Miss Emily was decently in the ground before they opened it.

The violence of breaking down the door seemed to fill this room with per-vading dust. A thin, acrid pall as of the tomb seemed to lie everywhere upon this room decked and furnished as for a bridal: upon the valance curtains of faded rose color, upon the rose-shaded lights, upon the dressing table, upon the deli-cate array of crystal and the man's toilet things backed with tarnished silver, silver so tarnished that the monogram was obscured. Among them lay a collar and tie, as if they had just been removed, which, lifted, left upon the surface a pale cres-cent in the dust. Upon a chair hung the suit, carefully folded; beneath it the two mute shoes and the discarded socks.

The man himself lay in the bed.

For a long while we just stood there, looking down at the profound and flesh-less grin. The body had apparently once lain in the attitude of an embrace, but now the long sleep that outlasts love, that conquers even the grimace of love, had cuckolded him. What was left of him, rotted beneath what was left of the night-shirt, had become inextricable from the bed in which he lay; and upon him and upon the pillow beside him lay that even coating of the patient and biding dust.

Then we noticed that in the second pillow was the indentation of a head. 60 One of us lifted something from it, and leaning forward, that faint and invisible dust dry and acrid in the nostrils, we saw a long strand of iron-gray hair.   [1931]

FOR THINKING AND WRITING

1. Do you think someone can love another so much they simply cannot bear for them to leave? Is it possible Emily was like this?

2. Can a disturbed person be in love? Does love have to be healthy? Is sanity culturally defined? Can you imagine a society that would accept Emily's behavior?

3. Who do you think the narrator of "A Rose for Emily" is? Why would Faulkner tell the story from this perspective? Why not from Emily's?

4. Look at the last sentence of paragraph 51. What do you make of the five adjectives used? Are they understandable in terms of the story?

5. Some critics think this story is not a love story but a political allegory about the South. Does this make sense to you? What else does the story suggest to you?

6. Comment on the various kinds of repression — social and psychological — that occur throughout the story. What connections can you draw, and what generalizations might you make about them?

7. Reread "A Rose for Emily." How does your knowledge of the ending of the story affect your second reading? What details of the narrative tend to stand out the second time around?

GABRIEL GARCÍA MÁRQUEZ
The Handsomest Drowned Man in the World

A TALE FOR CHILDREN

Translated by Gregory Rabassa

Gabriel García Márquez (b. 1928) has achieved international renown, certified by his 1982 Nobel Prize for literature. For several years, though, he lived in exile from his native Colombia because he opposed its dictatorship. García Márquez's fiction is often described as "magic realism" because it mixes everyday life and fantastic events. His several novels include the frequently taught One Hundred Years of Solitude *(1967). The following piece is from a 1973 book by García Márquez entitled* Leaf Storm and Other Stories.

The first children who saw the dark and slinky bulge approaching through the sea let themselves think it was an enemy ship. Then they saw it had no flags or masts and they thought it was a whale. But when it washed up on the beach, they removed the clumps of seaweed, the jellyfish tentacles, and the remains of fish and flotsam, and only then did they see that it was a drowned man.

They had been playing with him all afternoon, burying him in the sand and digging him up again, when someone chanced to see them and spread the alarm in the village. The men who carried him to the nearest house noticed that he weighed more than any dead man they had ever known, almost as much as a horse, and they said to each other that maybe he'd been floating too long and the water had got into his bones. When they laid him on the floor they said he'd been taller than all other men because there was barely enough room for him in the house, but they thought that maybe the ability to keep on growing after death was part of the nature of certain drowned men. He had the smell of the sea about him and only his shape gave one to suppose that it was the corpse of a human being, because the skin was covered with a crust of mud and scales.

They did not even have to clean off his face to know that the dead man was a stranger. The village was made up of only twenty-odd wooden houses that had stone courtyards with no flowers and which were spread about on the end of a desertlike cape. There was so little land that mothers always went about with the fear that the wind would carry off their children and the few dead that the years had caused among them had to be thrown off the cliffs. But the sea was calm and bountiful and all the men fit into seven boats. So when they found the drowned man they simply had to look at one another to see that they were all there.

That night they did not go out to work at sea. While the men went to find out if anyone was missing in neighboring villages, the women stayed behind to care for the drowned man. They took the mud off with grass swabs, they removed the underwater stones entangled in his hair, and they scraped the crust off with tools used for scaling fish. As they were doing that they noticed that the vegetation on him came from faraway oceans and deep water and that his clothes were in tatters, as if he had sailed through labyrinths of coral. They noticed too that he bore his death with pride, for he did not have the lonely look of other drowned men who came out of the sea or that haggard, needy look of men who drowned in rivers. But only when they finished cleaning him off did they become aware of the kind of man he was and it left them breathless. Not only was he the tallest, strongest, most virile, and best built man they had ever seen, but even though they were looking at him there was no room for him in their imagination.

They could not find a bed in the village large enough to lay him on nor was   5 there a table solid enough to use for his wake. The tallest men's holiday pants would not fit him, nor the fattest ones' Sunday shirts, nor the shoes of the one with the biggest feet. Fascinated by his huge size and his beauty, the women then decided to make him some pants from a large piece of sail and a shirt from some bridal Brabant linen so that he could continue through his death with dignity. As they sewed, sitting in a circle and gazing at the corpse between stitches, it seemed to them that the wind had never been so steady nor the sea so restless as on that night and they supposed that the change had something to do with the dead man. They thought that if that magnificent man had lived in the village, his house would have had the widest doors, the highest ceiling, and the strongest floor; his bedstead would have been made from a midship frame held together by iron bolts, and his wife would have been the happiest woman. They thought that he would have had so much authority that he could have drawn fish out of the sea simply by calling their names and that he would have put so much work into his land that springs would have burst forth from among the rocks so that he would have been able to plant flowers on the cliffs. They secretly compared him to their own men, thinking that for all their lives theirs were incapable of doing what he could do in one night, and they ended up dismissing them deep in their hearts as the weakest, meanest, and most useless creatures on earth. They were wandering through that maze of fantasy when the oldest woman, who as the oldest had looked upon the drowned man with more compassion than passion, sighed:

"He has the face of someone called Esteban."

It was true. Most of them had only to take another look at him to see that he could not have any other name. The more stubborn among them, who were the youngest, still lived for a few hours with the illusion that when they put his clothes on and he lay among the flowers in patent leather shoes his name might be Lautaro. But it was a vain illusion. There had not been enough canvas, the poorly cut and worse sewn pants were too tight, and the hidden strength of his heart popped the buttons on his shirt. After midnight the whistling of the wind died down and the sea fell into its Wednesday drowsiness. The silence put an end to any last doubts: he was Esteban. The women who had dressed him, who had combed his hair, had cut his nails and shaved him were unable to hold back a shudder of pity when they had to resign themselves to his being dragged along the ground. It was then that they understood how unhappy he must have been with that huge body since it bothered him even after death. They could see him in life, condemned to going through doors sideways, cracking his head on cross-beams, remaining on his feet during visits, not knowing what to do with his soft pink, sealion hands while the lady of the house looked for her most resistant chair and begged him, frightened to death, sit here, Esteban, please, and he, leaning against the wall, smiling, don't bother, ma'am, I'm fine where I am, his heels raw and his back roasted from having done the same thing so many times whenever he paid a visit, don't bother, ma'am, I'm fine where I am, just to avoid the embarrassment of breaking up the chair, and never knowing perhaps that the ones who said don't go, Esteban, at least wait till the coffee's ready, were the ones who later on would whisper the big boob finally left, how nice, the handsome fool has gone. That was what the women were thinking beside the body a little before dawn. Later, when they covered his face with a handkerchief so that the light would not bother him, he looked so forever dead, so defenseless, so much like their men that the first furrows of tears opened in their hearts. It was one of the younger ones who began the weeping. The others, coming to, went from sighs to wails, and the more they sobbed the more they felt like weeping, because the drowned man was becoming all the more Esteban for them, and so they wept so much, for he was the most destitute, most peaceful, and most obliging man on earth, poor Esteban. So when the men returned with the news that the drowned man was not from the neighboring villages either, the women felt an opening of jubilation in the midst of their tears.

"Praise the Lord," they sighed, "he's ours!"

The men thought the fuss was only womanish frivolity. Fatigued because of the difficult nighttime inquiries, all they wanted was to get rid of the bother of the newcomer once and for all before the sun grew strong on that arid, windless day. They improvised a litter with the remains of foremasts and gaffs, tying it together with rigging so that it would bear the weight of the body until they reached the cliffs. They wanted to tie the anchor from a cargo ship to him so that he would sink easily into the deepest waves, where fish are blind and divers die of nostalgia, and bad currents would not bring him back to shore, as had happened with other bodies. But the more they hurried, the more the women thought of ways to waste time. They walked about like startled hens, pecking with the sea charms on their breasts, some interfering on one side to put a scapular of the good wind on the drowned man, some on the other side to put a wrist compass on him, and after a great deal of *get away from there, woman, stay out of the way, look, you almost made me fall on top of the dead man*, the men began to feel mistrust in their livers and started grumbling about why so many main-altar decorations for a stranger, because no matter how many nails and holy-water jars he had on him, the sharks would chew him all the same, but the women kept on piling on their junk relics, running back and forth, stumbling, while they released in sighs what they did not in tears, so that the men finally exploded with *since when has there ever been such a fuss over a drifting corpse, a drowned nobody, a piece of cold Wednesday meat*. One of the women, mortified by so much lack of care, then removed the handkerchief from the dead man's face and the men were left breathless too.

He was Esteban. It was not necessary to repeat it for them to recognize him. If they had been told Sir Walter Raleigh, even they might have been impressed with his gringo accent, the macaw on his shoulder, his cannibal-killing blunderbuss, but there could be only one Esteban in the world and there he was, stretched out like a sperm whale, shoeless, wearing the pants of an undersized child, and with those stony nails that had to be cut with a knife. They had only to take the handkerchief off his face to see that he was ashamed, that it was not his fault that he was so big or so heavy or so handsome, and if he had known that this was going to happen, he would have looked for a more discreet place to drown in; seriously, I even would have tied the anchor off a galleon around my neck and staggered off a cliff like someone who doesn't like things in order not to be upsetting people now with this Wednesday dead body, as you people say, in order not to be bothering anyone with this filthy piece of cold meat that doesn't have anything to do with me. There was so much truth in his manner that even the most mistrustful men, the ones who felt the bitterness of endless nights at sea fearing that their women would tire of dreaming about them and begin to dream of drowned men, even they and others who were harder still shuddered in the marrow of their bones at Esteban's sincerity.

That was how they came to hold the most splendid funeral they could conceive of for an abandoned drowned man. Some women who had gone to get flowers in the neighboring villages returned with other women who could not believe what they had been told, and those women went back for more flowers when they saw the dead man, and they brought more and more until there were so many flowers and so many people that it was hard to walk about. At the final moment it pained them to return him to the waters as an orphan and they chose a father and mother from among the best people, and aunts and uncles and cousins, so that through him all the inhabitants of the village became kinsmen. Some sailors who heard the weeping from a distance went off course, and people heard of one who had himself tied to the mainmast, remembering ancient fables about sirens. While they fought for the privilege of carrying him on their shoulders along the steep escarpment by the cliffs, men and women became aware for the first time of the desolation of their streets, the dryness of their courtyards, the narrowness of their dreams as they faced the splendor and beauty of their drowned man. They let him go without an anchor so that he could come back if he wished and whenever he wished, and they all held their breath for the fraction of centuries the body took to fall into the abyss. They did not need to look at one another to realize that they were no longer all present, that they would never be. But they also knew that everything would be different from then on, that their houses would have wider doors, higher ceilings, and stronger floors so that Esteban's memory could go everywhere without bumping into beams and so that no one in the future would dare whisper the big boob finally died, too bad, the handsome fool has finally died, because they were going to paint their house fronts gay colors to make Esteban's memory eternal and they were going to break their backs digging for springs among the stones and planting flowers on the cliffs so that in future years at dawn the passengers on great liners would awaken, suffocated by the smell of gardens on the high seas, and the captain would have to come down from the bridge in his dress uniform, with his astrolabe, his pole star, and his row of war medals and, pointing to the promontory of roses on the horizon, he would say in fourteen languages, look there, where the wind is so peaceful now that it's gone to sleep beneath the beds, over there, where the sun's so bright that the sunflowers don't know which way to turn, yes, over there, that's Esteban's village.   [1973]

FOR THINKING AND WRITING

1. The subtitle of this story is "A Tale for Children." Is García Márquez being ironic, or does his story indeed fit that genre? How do you think an audience of children might react to it?

2. Identify the villagers' various conceptions of the dead man. What gender differences emerge? What should a reader conclude from the fact that these conceptions change? What would you say to someone who argues that the villagers are being foolish in giving the dead man a name and making so much of him?

3. Do you find humor in this story? If so, in what specific passages?

4. What, if anything, seems realistic about this story? Where, if anywhere, does García Márquez strike you as departing from realism? Elaborate how you are defining *realism*.

5. Identify the various sentence lengths in this story, using specific examples. Note in particular where García Márquez's sentences get quite long. Are these long sentences effective, or should he have broken them into shorter ones? Explain your reasoning.

CHARLOTTE PERKINS GILMAN
The Yellow Wallpaper

Charlotte Perkins Gilman (1860–1935) was a major activist and theorist in America's first wave of feminism. During her lifetime, she was chiefly known for her 1898 book Women and Economics. *In it she argued that women should not be confined to the household and made economically dependent on men. Gilman also advanced such ideas through her many public speaking appearances and her magazine* The Forerunner, *which she edited from 1909 to 1916. Gilman wrote many articles and works of fiction for* The Forerunner, *including a tale called* Herland *(1915) in which she envisioned an all-female utopia. Today, however, Gilman is best known for her short story "The Yellow Wallpaper," which she published first in an 1892 issue of the* New England Magazine. *The story is based on Gilman's struggle with depression after the birth of her daughter Katharine in 1885. Seeking help for emotional turmoil, Gilman consulted the eminent neurologist Silas Weir Mitchell, who prescribed his famous "rest cure." This treatment, which forbade Gilman to work, actually worsened her distress. She improved only after she moved to California, divorced her husband, let him raise Katharine with his new wife,* married someone else, and plunged fully into a literary and political career. As Gilman noted in her posthumously published autobiography, The Living of Charlotte Perkins Gilman (1935), she never fully recovered from the debilitation that had led her to Dr. Mitchell, but she ultimately managed to be enormously productive. Although "The Yellow Wallpaper" is a work of fiction rather than a factual account of her experience with Mitchell, Gilman used the story to criticize the doctor's patriarchal approach as well as society's efforts to keep women passive.

It is very seldom that mere ordinary people like John and myself secure ancestral halls for the summer.

A colonial mansion, a hereditary estate, I would say a haunted house and reach the height of romantic felicity—but that would be asking too much of fate!

Still I will proudly declare that there is something queer about it.

Else, why should it be let so cheaply? And why have stood so long untenanted?

John laughs at me, of course, but one expects that in marriage.   5

John is practical in the extreme. He has no patience with faith, an intense horror of superstition, and he scoffs openly at any talk of things not to be felt and seen and put down in figures.

John is a physician, and *perhaps*—(I would not say it to a living soul, of course, but this is dead paper and a great relief to my mind)—*perhaps* that is one reason I do not get well faster.

You see, he does not believe I am sick!

And what can one do?

If a physician of high standing, and one's own husband, assures friends and   10 relatives that there is really nothing the matter with one but temporary nervous depression—a slight hysterical tendency—what is one to do?

My brother is also a physician, and also of high standing, and he says the same thing.

So I take phosphates or phosphites—whichever it is, and tonics, and journeys, and air, and exercise, and am absolutely forbidden to "work" until I am well again.

Personally, I disagree with their ideas.

Personally, I believe that congenial work, with excitement and change, would do me good.

But what is one to do?   15

I did write for a while in spite of them; but it *does* exhaust me a good deal— having to be so sly about it, or else meet with heavy opposition.

I sometimes fancy that in my condition if I had less opposition and more society and stimulus—but John says the very worst thing I can do is to think about my condition, and I confess it always makes me feel bad.

So I will let it alone and talk about the house.

The most beautiful place! It is quite alone, standing well back from the road, quite three miles from the village. It makes me think of English places that you read about, for there are hedges and walls and gates that lock, and lots of separate little houses for the gardeners and people.

There is a *delicious* garden! I never saw such a garden—large and shady, full   20
of box-bordered paths, and lined with long grape-covered arbors with seats under
them.

There were greenhouses, too, but they are all broken now.

There was some legal trouble, I believe, something about the heirs and co-
heirs; anyhow, the place has been empty for years.

That spoils my ghostliness, I am afraid, but I don't care—there is something
strange about the house—I can feel it.

I even said so to John one moonlight evening, but he said what I felt was a
draught, and shut the window.

I get unreasonably angry with John sometimes. I'm sure I never used to be so   25
sensitive. I think it is due to this nervous condition.

But John says if I feel so, I shall neglect proper self-control; so I take pains to
control myself—before him, at least, and that makes me very tired.

I don't like our room a bit. I wanted one downstairs that opened on the
piazza and had roses all over the window, and such pretty old-fashioned chintz
hangings! but John would not hear of it.

He said there was only one window and not room for two beds, and no near
room for him if he took another.

He is very careful and loving, and hardly lets me stir without special direction.

I have a schedule prescription for each hour in the day; he takes all care from   30
me, and so I feel basely ungrateful not to value it more.

He said we came here solely on my account, that I was to have perfect rest
and all the air I could get. "Your exercise depends on your strength, my dear,"
said he, "and your food somewhat on your appetite; but air you can absorb all the
time." So we took the nursery at the top of the house.

It is a big, airy room, the whole floor nearly, with windows that look all ways,
and air and sunshine galore. It was nursery first and then playroom and gymna-
sium, I should judge; for the windows are barred for little children, and there are
rings and things in the walls.

The paint and paper look as if a boys' school had used it. It is stripped off—
the paper—in great patches all around the head of my bed, about as far as I can
reach, and in a great place on the other side of the room low down. I never saw a
worse paper in my life.

One of those sprawling flamboyant patterns committing every artistic sin.

It is dull enough to confuse the eye in following, pronounced enough to con-   35
stantly irritate and provoke study, and when you follow the lame uncertain curves
for a little distance they suddenly commit suicide—plunge off at outrageous
angles, destroy themselves in unheard of contradictions.

The color is repellant, almost revolting; a smouldering unclean yellow,
strangely faded by the slow-turning sunlight.

It is a dull yet lurid orange in some places, a sickly sulphur tint in others.

No wonder the children hated it! I should hate it myself if I had to live in this
room long.

There comes John, and I must put this away,—he hates to have me write a
word.

◆   ◆   ◆

We have been here two weeks, and I haven't felt like writing before, since 40
that first day.

I am sitting by the window now, up in this atrocious nursery, and there is
nothing to hinder my writing as much as I please, save lack of strength.

John is away all day, and even some nights when his cases are serious.

I am glad my case is not serious!

But these nervous troubles are dreadfully depressing.

John does not know how much I really suffer. He knows there is no *reason* to 45
suffer, and that satisfies him.

Of course it is only nervousness. It does weigh on me so not to do my duty in
any way!

I meant to be such a help to John, such a real rest and comfort, and here I am
a comparative burden already!

Nobody would believe what an effort it is to do what little I am able, — to
dress and entertain, and order things.

It is fortunate Mary is so good with the baby. Such a dear baby!

And yet I *cannot* be with him, it makes me so nervous. 50

I suppose John never was nervous in his life. He laughs at me so about this
wall-paper!

At first he meant to repaper the room, but afterward he said that I was letting
it get the better of me, and that nothing was worse for a nervous patient than to
give way to such fancies.

He said that after the wall-paper was changed it would be the heavy bedstead,
and then the barred windows, and then that gate at the head of the stairs, and so on.

"You know the place is doing you good," he said, "and really, dear, I don't
care to renovate the house just for a three months' rental."

"Then do let us go downstairs," I said, "there are such pretty rooms there." 55

Then he took me in his arms and called me a blessed little goose, and said
he would go down cellar, if I wished, and have it whitewashed into the bargain.

But he is right enough about the beds and windows and things.

It is an airy and comfortable room as anyone need wish, and, of course, I
would not be so silly as to make him uncomfortable just for a whim.

I'm really getting quite fond of the big room, all but that horrid paper.

Out of one window I can see the garden, those mysterious deep-shaded 60
arbors, the riotous old-fashioned flowers, and bushes and gnarly trees.

Out of another I get a lovely view of the bay and a little private wharf belonging to the estate. There is a beautiful shaded lane that runs down there from the
house. I always fancy I see people walking in these numerous paths and arbors,
but John has cautioned me not to give way to fancy in the least. He says that with
my imaginative power and habit of story-making, a nervous weakness like mine is
sure to lead to all manner of excited fancies, and that I ought to use my will and
good sense to check the tendency. So I try.

I think sometimes that if I were only well enough to write a little it would
relieve the press of ideas and rest me.

But I find I get pretty tired when I try.

It is so discouraging not to have any advice and companionship about my
work. When I get really well, John says we will ask Cousin Henry and Julia down

for a long visit; but he says he would as soon put fireworks in my pillow-case as to let me have those stimulating people about now.

I wish I could get well faster.   65

But I must not think about that. This paper looks to me as if it *knew* what a vicious influence it had!

There is a recurrent spot where the pattern lolls like a broken neck and two bulbous eyes stare at you upside down.

I get positively angry with the impertinence of it and the everlastingness. Up and down and sideways they crawl, and those absurd, unblinking eyes are everywhere. There is one place where two breadths didn't match, and the eyes go all up and down the line, one a little higher than the other.

I never saw so much expression in an inanimate thing before, and we all know how much expression they have! I used to lie awake as a child and get more entertainment and terror out of blank walls and plain furniture than most children could find in a toy-store.

I remember what a kindly wink the knobs of our big, old bureau used to   70 have, and there was one chair that always seemed like a strong friend.

I used to feel that if any of the other things looked too fierce I could always hop into that chair and be safe.

The furniture in this room is no worse than inharmonious, however, for we had to bring it all from downstairs. I suppose when this was used as a playroom they had to take the nursery things out, and no wonder! I never saw such ravages as the children have made here.

The wall-paper, as I said before, is torn off in spots, and it sticketh closer than a brother—they must have had perseverance as well as hatred.

Then the floor is scratched and gouged and splintered, the plaster itself is dug out here and there, and this great heavy bed, which is all we found in the room, looks as if it had been through the wars.

But I don't mind it a bit—only the paper.   75

There comes John's sister. Such a dear girl as she is, and so careful of me! I must not let her find me writing.

She is a perfect and enthusiastic housekeeper, and hopes for no better profession. I verily believe she thinks it is the writing which made me sick!

But I can write when she is out, and see her a long way off from these windows.

There is one that commands the road, a lovely shaded winding road, and one that just looks off over the country. A lovely country, too, full of great elms and velvet meadows.

This wallpaper has a kind of sub-pattern in a different shade, a particularly   80 irritating one, for you can only see it in certain lights, and not clearly then.

But in the places where it isn't faded and where the sun is just so—I can see a strange, provoking, formless sort of figure, that seems to skulk about behind that silly and conspicuous front design.

There's sister on the stairs!

Well, the Fourth of July is over! The people are all gone and I am tired out. John thought it might do me good to see a little company, so we just had mother and Nellie and the children down for a week.

Of course I didn't do a thing. Jennie sees to everything now.

But it tired me all the same.   85

John says if I don't pick up faster he shall send me to Weir Mitchell° in the fall.

But I don't want to go there at all. I had a friend who was in his hands once, and she says he is just like John and my brother, only more so!

Besides, it is such an undertaking to go so far.

I don't feel as if it was worthwhile to turn my hand over for anything, and I'm getting dreadfully fretful and querulous.

I cry at nothing, and cry most of the time.   90

Of course I don't when John is here, or anybody else, but when I am alone.

And I am alone a good deal just now. John is kept in town very often by serious cases, and Jennie is good and lets me alone when I want her to.

So I walk a little in the garden or down that lovely lane, sit on the porch under the roses, and lie down up here a good deal.

I'm getting really fond of the room in spite of the wallpaper. Perhaps *because* of the wallpaper.

It dwells in my mind so!   95

I lie here on this great immovable bed—it is nailed down, I believe—and follow that pattern about by the hour. It is as good as gymnastics, I assure you. I start, we'll say, at the bottom, down in the corner over there where it has not been touched, and I determine for the thousandth time that I *will* follow that pointless pattern to some sort of a conclusion.

I know a little of the principle of design, and I know this thing was not arranged on any laws of radiation, or alternation, or repetition, or symmetry, or anything else that I ever heard of.

It is repeated, of course, by the breadths, but not otherwise.

Looked at in one way each breadth stands alone, the bloated curves and flourishes—a kind of "debased Romanesque" with *delirium tremens*—go waddling up and down in isolated columns of fatuity.

But, on the other hand, they connect diagonally, and the sprawling outlines   100
run off in great slanting waves of optic horror, like a lot of wallowing seaweeds in full chase.

The whole thing goes horizontally, too, at least it seems so, and I exhaust myself in trying to distinguish the order of its going in that direction.

They have used a horizontal breadth for a frieze, and that adds wonderfully to the confusion.

There is one end of the room where it is almost intact, and there, when the crosslights fade and the low sun shines directly upon it, I can almost fancy radiation after all,—the interminable grotesques seem to form around a common centre and rush off in headlong plunges of equal distraction.

It makes me tired to follow it. I will take a nap I guess.

◆   ◆   ◆

Weir Mitchell: Dr. S. Weir Mitchell (1829–1914) was an eminent Philadelphia neurologist who advocated "rest cures" for nervous disorders. He was the author of *Diseases of the Nervous System, Especially of Women* (1881).

I don't know why I should write this. 105

I don't want to.

I don't feel able.

And I know John would think it absurd. But I *must* say what I feel and think in some way — it is such a relief!

But the effort is getting to be greater than the relief.

Half the time now I am awfully lazy, and lie down ever so much. 110

John says I mustn't lose my strength, and has me take cod liver oil and lots of tonics and things, to say nothing of ale and wine and rare meat.

Dear John! He loves me very dearly, and hates to have me sick. I tried to have a real earnest reasonable talk with him the other day, and tell him how I wish he would let me go and make a visit to Cousin Henry and Julia.

But he said I wasn't able to go, nor able to stand it after I got there; and I did not make out a very good case for myself, for I was crying before I had finished.

It is getting to be a great effort for me to think straight. Just this nervous weakness I suppose.

And dear John gathered me up in his arms, and just carried me upstairs and 115 laid me on the bed, and sat by me and read to me till it tired my head.

He said I was his darling and his comfort and all he had, and that I must take care of myself for his sake, and keep well.

He says no one but myself can help me out of it, that I must use my will and self-control and not let any silly fancies run away with me.

There's one comfort, the baby is well and happy, and does not have to occupy this nursery with the horrid wallpaper.

If we had not used it, that blessed child would have! What a fortunate escape! Why, I wouldn't have a child of mine, an impressionable little thing, live in such a room for worlds.

I never thought of it before, but it is lucky that John kept me here after all, I 120 can stand it so much easier than a baby, you see.

Of course I never mention it to them any more — I am too wise, but I keep watch of it all the same.

There are things in the wallpaper that nobody knows but me, or ever will.

Behind that outside pattern the dim shapes get clearer every day.

It is always the same shape, only very numerous.

And it is like a woman stooping down and creeping about behind that pat- 125 tern. I don't like it a bit. I wonder — I begin to think — I wish John would take me away from here!

It is so hard to talk with John about my case, because he is so wise, and because he loves me so.

But I tried it last night.

It was moonlight. The moon shines in all around just as the sun does.

I hate to see it sometimes, it creeps so slowly, and always comes in by one window or another.

John was asleep and I hated to waken him, so I kept still and watched the 130 moonlight on that undulating wallpaper till I felt creepy.

The faint figure behind seemed to shake the pattern, just as if she wanted to get out.

I got up softly and went to feel and see if the paper *did* move, and when I came back John was awake.

"What is it, little girl?" he said. "Don't go walking about like that—you'll get cold."

I thought it was a good time to talk, so I told him that I really was not gaining here, and that I wished he would take me away.

"Why, darling!" said he, "our lease will be up in three weeks, and I can't see   135
how to leave before.

"The repairs are not done at home, and I cannot possibly leave town just now. Of course if you were in any danger, I could and would, but you really are better, dear, whether you can see it or not. I am a doctor, dear, and I know. You are gaining flesh and color, your appetite is better, I feel really much easier about you."

"I don't weigh a bit more," said I, "nor as much; and my appetite may be better in the evening when you are here but it is worse in the morning when you are away!"

"Bless her little heart!" said he with a big hug, "she shall be as sick as she pleases! But now let's improve the shining hours by going to sleep, and talk about it in the morning!"

"And you won't go away?" I asked gloomily.

"Why, how can I, dear? It is only three weeks more and then we will take a   140
nice little trip of a few days while Jennie is getting the house ready. Really dear you are better!"

"Better in body perhaps—" I began, and stopped short, for he sat up straight and looked at me with such a stern, reproachful look that I could not say another word.

"My darling," said he, "I beg you, for my sake and for our child's sake, as well as for your own, that you will never for one instant let that idea enter your mind! There is nothing so dangerous, so fascinating, to a temperament like yours. It is a false and foolish fancy. Can you trust me as a physician when I tell you so?"

So of course I said no more on that score, and we went to sleep before long. He thought I was asleep first, but I wasn't, and lay there for hours trying to decide whether that front pattern and the back pattern really did move together or separately.

On a pattern like this, by daylight, there is a lack of sequence, a defiance of law, that is a constant irritant to a normal mind.

The color is hideous enough, and unreliable enough, and infuriating   145
enough, but the pattern is torturing.

You think you have mastered it, but just as you get well underway in following, it turns a back-somersault and there you are. It slaps you in the face, knocks you down, and tramples upon you. It is like a bad dream.

The outside pattern is a florid arabesque, reminding one of a fungus. If you can imagine a toadstool in joints, an interminable string of toadstools, budding and sprouting in endless convolutions—why, that is something like it.

That is, sometimes!

There is one marked peculiarity about this paper, a thing nobody seems to notice but myself, and that is that it changes as the light changes.

When the sun shoots in through the east window—I always watch for that 150 first long, straight ray—it changes so quickly that I never can quite believe it.

That is why I watch it always.

By moonlight—the moon shines in all night when there is a moon—I wouldn't know it was the same paper.

At night in any kind of light, in twilight, candlelight, lamplight, and worst of all by moonlight, it becomes bars! The outside pattern I mean, and the woman behind it is as plain as can be.

I didn't realize for a long time what the thing was that showed behind, that dim sub-pattern, but now I am quite sure it is a woman.

By daylight she is subdued, quiet. I fancy it is the pattern that keeps her so 155 still. It is so puzzling. It keeps me quiet by the hour.

I lie down ever so much now. John says it is good for me, and to sleep all I can.

Indeed he started the habit by making me lie down for an hour after each meal.

It is a very bad habit I am convinced, for you see I don't sleep.

And that cultivates deceit, for I don't tell them I'm awake—O, no!

The fact is I am getting a little afraid of John. 160

He seems very queer sometimes, and even Jennie has an inexplicable look.

It strikes me occasionally, just as a scientific hypothesis,—that perhaps it is the paper!

I have watched John when he did not know I was looking, and come into the room suddenly on the most innocent excuses, and I've caught him several times *looking at the paper!* And Jennie too. I caught Jennie with her hand on it once.

She didn't know I was in the room, and when I asked her in a quiet, a very quiet voice, with the most restrained manner possible, what she was doing with the paper—she turned around as if she had been caught stealing, and looked quite angry—asked me why I should frighten her so!

Then she said that the paper stained everything it touched, that she had 165 found yellow smooches on all my clothes and John's, and she wished we would be more careful!

Did not that sound innocent? But I know she was studying that pattern, and I am determined that nobody shall find it out but myself!

Life is very much more exciting now than it used to be. You see I have something more to expect, to look forward to, to watch. I really do eat better, and am more quiet than I was.

John is so pleased to see me improve! He laughed a little the other day, and said I seemed to be flourishing in spite of my wall-paper.

I turned it off with a laugh. I had no intention of telling him it was *because* of the wall-paper—he would make fun of me. He might even want to take me away.

I don't want to leave now until I have found it out. There is a week more, and   170
I think that will be enough.

I'm feeling ever so much better! I don't sleep much at night, for it is so interesting to watch developments; but I sleep a good deal in the daytime.

In the daytime it is tiresome and perplexing.

There are always new shoots on the fungus, and new shades of yellow all over it. I cannot keep count of them, though I have tried conscientiously.

It is the strangest yellow, that wall-paper! It makes me think of all the yellow things I ever saw — not beautiful ones like buttercups, but old foul, bad yellow things.

But there is something else about that paper — the smell! I noticed it the   175
moment we came into the room, but with so much air and sun it was not bad. Now we have had a week of fog and rain, and whether the windows are open or not, the smell is here.

It creeps all over the house.

I find it hovering in the dining-room, skulking in the parlor, hiding in the hall, lying in wait for me on the stairs.

It gets into my hair.

Even when I go to ride, if I turn my head suddenly and surprise it — there is that smell!

Such a peculiar odor, too! I have spent hours in trying to analyze it, to find   180
what it smelled like.

It is not bad — at first, and very gentle, but quite the subtlest, most enduring odor I ever met.

In this damp weather it is awful, I wake up in the night and find it hanging over me.

It used to disturb me at first. I thought seriously of burning the house — to reach the smell.

But now I am used to it. The only thing I can think of that it is like is the *color* of the paper! A yellow smell.

There is a very funny mark on this wall, low down, near the mopboard. A   185
streak that runs round the room. It goes behind every piece of furniture, except the bed, a long, straight, even *smooch*, as if it had been rubbed over and over.

I wonder how it was done and who did it, and what they did it for. Round and round and round — round and round and round — it makes me dizzy!

I really have discovered something at last.

Through watching so much at night, when it changes so, I have finally found out.

The front pattern *does* move — and no wonder! The woman behind shakes it!

Sometimes I think there are a great many women behind, and sometimes   190
only one, and she crawls around fast, and her crawling shakes it all over.

Then in the very bright spots she keeps still, and in the very shady spots she just takes hold of the bars and shakes them hard.

And she is all the time trying to climb through. But nobody could climb through that pattern — it strangles so; I think that is why it has so many heads.

They get through, and then the pattern strangles them off and turns them upside down, and makes their eyes white!

If those heads were covered or taken off it would not be half so bad.

I think that woman gets out in the daytime!   195
And I'll tell you why — privately — I've seen her!

I can see her out of every one of my windows!

It is the same woman, I know, for she is always creeping, and most women do not creep by daylight.

I see her in that long shaded lane, creeping up and down. I see her in those dark grape arbors, creeping all around the garden.

I see her on that long road under the trees, creeping along, and when a car-   200
riage comes she hides under the blackberry vines.

I don't blame her a bit. It must be very humiliating to be caught creeping by daylight!

I always lock the door when I creep by daylight. I can't do it at night, for I know John would suspect something at once.

And John is so queer now, that I don't want to irritate him. I wish he would take another room! Besides, I don't want anybody to get that woman out at night but myself.

I often wonder if I could see her out of all the windows at once.

But, turn as fast as I can, I can only see out of one at one time.   205

And though I always see her, she *may* be able to creep faster than I can turn!

I have watched her sometimes away off in the open country, creeping as fast as a cloud shadow in a high wind.

If only that top pattern could be gotten off from the under one! I mean to try it, little by little.

I have found out another funny thing, but I shan't tell it this time! It does not do to trust people too much.

There are only two more days to get this paper off, and I believe John is   210
beginning to notice. I don't like the look in his eyes.

And I heard him ask Jennie a lot of professional questions, about me. She had a very good report to give.

She said I slept a good deal in the daytime.

John knows I don't sleep very well at night, for all I'm so quiet!

He asked me all sorts of questions too, and pretended to be very loving and kind.

As if I couldn't see through him!   215

Still, I don't wonder he acts so, sleeping under this paper for three months.

It only interests me, but I feel sure John and Jennie are secretly affected by it.

Hurrah! This is the last day, but it is enough. John to stay in town over night, and won't be out until this evening.

Jennie wanted to sleep with me — the sly thing! But I told her I should undoubtedly rest better for a night all alone.

That was clever, for really I wasn't alone a bit! As soon as it was moonlight   220
and that poor thing began to crawl and shake the pattern, I got up and ran to
help her.

I pulled and she shook, I shook and she pulled, and before morning we had
peeled off yards of that paper.

A strip about as high as my head and half around the room.

And then when the sun came and that awful pattern began to laugh at me, I
declared I would finish it to-day!

We go away to-morrow, and they are moving all my furniture down again to
leave things as they were before.

Jennie looked at the wall in amazement, but I told her merrily that I did it   225
out of pure spite at the vicious thing.

She laughed and said she wouldn't mind doing it herself, but I must not get
tired.

How she betrayed herself that time!

But I am here, and no person touches this paper but me,—not *alive!*

She tried to get me out of the room—it was too patent! But I said it was so
quiet and empty and clean now that I believed I would lie down again and sleep
all I could, and not to wake me even for dinner—I would call when I woke.

So now she is gone, and the servants are gone, and the things are gone, and   230
there is nothing left but that great bedstead nailed down, with the canvas mattress
we found on it.

We shall sleep downstairs to-night, and take the boat home to-morrow.

I quite enjoy the room, now it is bare again.

How those children did tear about here!

This bedstead is fairly gnawed!

But I must get to work.   235

I have locked the door and thrown the key down into the front path.

I don't want to go out, and I don't want to have anybody come in, till John
comes.

I want to astonish him.

I've got a rope up here that even Jennie did not find. If that woman does get
out, and tries to get away, I can tie her!

But I forgot I could not reach far without anything to stand on!   240

This bed will *not* move!

I tried to lift and push it until I was lame, and then I got so angry I bit off a
little piece at one corner—but it hurt my teeth.

Then I peeled off all the paper I could reach standing on the floor. It sticks
horribly and the pattern just enjoys it! All those strangled heads and bulbous eyes
and waddling fungus growths just shriek with derision!

I am getting angry enough to do something desperate. To jump out of the
window would be admirable exercise, but the bars are too strong even to try.

Besides I wouldn't do it. Of course not. I know well enough that a step like   245
that is improper and might be misconstrued.

I don't like to *look* out of the windows even—there are so many of those
creeping women, and they creep so fast.

I wonder if they all come out of that wall-paper as I did?

But I am securely fastened now by my well-hidden rope—you don't get *me* out in the road there!

I suppose I shall have to get back behind the pattern when it comes night, and that is hard!

It is so pleasant to be out in this great room and creep around as I please!	250

I don't want to go outside. I won't, even if Jennie asks me to.

For outside you have to creep on the ground, and everything is green instead of yellow.

But here I can creep smoothly on the floor, and my shoulder just fits in that long smooch around the wall, so I cannot lose my way.

Why, there's John at the door!

It is no use, young man, you can't open it!	255

How he does call and pound!

Now he's crying for an axe.

It would be a shame to break down that beautiful door!

"John dear!" said I in the gentlest voice, "the key is down by the front steps, under a plantain leaf!"

That silenced him for a few moments.	260

Then he said—very quietly indeed, "Open the door, my darling!"

"I can't," said I. "The key is down by the front door under a plantain leaf!"

And then I said it again, several times, very gently and slowly, and said it so often that he had to go and see, and he got it of course, and came in. He stopped short by the door.

"What is the matter?" he cried. "For God's sake, what are you doing!"

I kept on creeping just the same, but I looked at him over my shoulder.	265

"I've got out at last," said I, "in spite of you and Jane. And I've pulled off most of the paper, so you can't put me back!"

Now why should that man have fainted? But he did, and right across my path by the wall, so that I had to creep over him every time!	[1892]

FOR THINKING AND WRITING

1. What psychological stages does the narrator go through as the story progresses?

2. How does the wallpaper function as a symbol in this story? What do you conclude about the narrator when she becomes increasingly interested in the woman she finds there?

3. Explain your ultimate view of the narrator, by using specific details of the story and by identifying some of the warrants or assumptions behind your opinion. Do you admire her? Sympathize with her? Recoil from her? What would you say to someone who simply dismisses her as crazy?

4. The story is narrated in the present tense. Would its effect be different if it were narrated in the past? Why, or why not?

5. In real life, Gilman's husband and her doctor were two separate people. In the story, the narrator's husband is her doctor as well. Why do you think Gilman made this change? What is the effect of her combining husband and doctor?

NATHANIEL HAWTHORNE
Young Goodman Brown

Nathaniel Hawthorne (1804–1864) was born in Salem, Massachusetts, into a family that was founded by New England's Puritan colonists. This lineage troubled Hawthorne, especially because his ancestor John Hathorne was involved as a judge in the Salem witch trials. After graduating from Maine's Bowdoin College in 1825, Hawthorne returned to Salem and began his career as a writer. In 1832, he self-published his first novel, Fanshawe, *but considered it an artistic as well as commercial failure and tried to destroy all unsold copies of it. He was more successful with his 1832 short-story collection* Twice-Told Tales *(reprinted and enlarged in 1842). In the early 1840s, Hawthorne worked as a surveyor in the Boston Custom House, briefly joined the Utopian community of Brook Farm, and then moved to Concord. There he published several children's books and lived with his wife, Sophia, in writer Ralph Waldo Emerson's former home, the Old Manse. In 1846, he produced a second collection of short stories,* Mosses from an Old Manse. *For the next three years, Hawthorne worked in a custom house in his home town of Salem before publishing his most famous analysis of Puritan culture,* The Scarlet Letter *(1850). Later novels included* The House of the Seven Gables *(1851),* The Blithedale Romance *(an 1852 satire on Brook Farm), and* The Marble Faun *(1860). When his friend Franklin Pierce became president of the United States, Hawthorne served as American consul in Liverpool, England, for four years, and then traveled in Italy for two more. At his death in 1864, he was already highly respected as a writer. Much of his fiction deals with conflicted characters whose hearts and souls are torn by sin, guilt, pride, and isolation. Indeed, his good friend Herman Melville, author of* Moby-Dick, *praised "the power of blackness" he found in Hawthorne's works. The allegorical story "Young Goodman Brown" is an especially memorable example of this power. Hawthorne wrote the tale in 1835 and later included it in* Mosses from an Old Manse.

Young Goodman Brown came forth at sunset into the street at Salem village; but put his head back, after crossing the threshold, to exchange a parting kiss with his young wife. And Faith, as the wife was aptly named, thrust her own pretty head into the street, letting the wind play with the pink ribbons of her cap while she called to Goodman Brown.

"Dearest heart," whispered she, softly and rather sadly, when her lips were close to his ear, "prithee put off your journey until sunrise and sleep in your own bed to-night. A lone woman is troubled with such dreams and such thoughts that she's afeared of herself sometimes. Pray tarry with me this night, dear husband, of all nights in the year."

"My love and my Faith," replied young Goodman Brown, "of all nights in the year, this one night must I tarry away from thee. My journey, as thou callest it, forth and back again, must needs be done 'twixt now and sunrise. What, my sweet, pretty wife, dost thou doubt me already, and we but three months married?"

"Then God bless you!" said Faith, with the pink ribbons; "and may you find all well when you come back."

"Amen!" cried Goodman Brown. "Say thy prayers, dear Faith, and go to bed at dusk, and no harm will come to thee." 5

So they parted; and the young man pursued his way until, being about to turn the corner by the meeting-house, he looked back and saw the head of Faith still peeping after him with a melancholy air, in spite of her pink ribbons.

"Poor little Faith!" thought he, for his heart smote him. "What a wretch am I to leave her on such an errand! She talks of dreams, too. Methought as she spoke there was trouble in her face, as if a dream had warned her what work is to be done to-night. But no, no; 't would kill her to think it. Well, she's a blessed angel on earth, and after this one night I'll cling to her skirts and follow her to heaven."

With this excellent resolve for the future, Goodman Brown felt himself justified in making more haste on his present evil purpose. He had taken a dreary road, darkened by all the gloomiest trees of the forest, which barely stood aside to let the narrow path creep through, and closed immediately behind. It was all as lonely as could be; and there is this peculiarity in such a solitude, that the traveller knows not who may be concealed by the innumerable trunks and the thick boughs overhead; so that with lonely footsteps he may yet be passing through an unseen multitude.

"There may be a devilish Indian behind every tree," said Goodman Brown to himself; and he glanced fearfully behind him as he added, "What if the devil himself should be at my very elbow!"

His head being turned back, he passed a crook of the road, and, looking forward again, beheld the figure of a man, in grave and decent attire, seated at the foot of an old tree. He arose at Goodman Brown's approach and walked onward side by side with him. 10

"You are late, Goodman Brown," said he. "The clock of the Old South was striking as I came through Boston, and that is full fifteen minutes agone."

"Faith kept me back a while," replied the young man, with a tremor in his voice, caused by the sudden appearance of his companion, though not wholly unexpected.

It was now deep dusk in the forest, and deepest in that part of it where these two were journeying. As nearly as could be discerned, the second traveller was about fifty years old, apparently in the same rank of life as Goodman Brown, and bearing a considerable resemblance to him, though perhaps more in expression than features. Still they might have been taken for father and son. And yet, though the elder person was as simply clad as the younger, and as simple in manner too, he had an indescribable air of one who knew the world, and who would not have felt abashed at the governor's dinner table or in King William's court, were it possible that his affairs should call him thither. But the only thing about him that could be fixed upon as remarkable was his staff, which bore the likeness of a great black snake, so curiously wrought that it might almost be seen to twist and wriggle itself like a living serpent. This, of course, must have been an ocular deception, assisted by the uncertain light.

"Come, Goodman Brown," cried his fellow-traveller, "this is a dull pace for the beginning of a journey. Take my staff, if you are so soon weary."

"Friend," said the other, exchanging his slow pace for a full stop, "having   15
kept covenant by meeting thee here, it is my purpose now to return whence I came. I have scruples touching the matter thou wot'st of."

"Sayest thou so?" replied he of the serpent, smiling apart. "Let us walk on, nevertheless, reasoning as we go; and if I convince thee not thou shalt turn back. We are but a little way in the forest yet."

"Too far! too far!" exclaimed the goodman, unconsciously resuming his walk. "My father never went into the woods on such an errand, nor his father before him. We have been a race of honest men and good Christians since the days of the martyrs; and shall I be the first of the name of Brown that ever took this path and kept" —

"Such company, thou wouldst say," observed the elder person, interpreting his pause. "Well said, Goodman Brown! I have been as well acquainted with your family as with ever a one among the Puritans; and that's no trifle to say. I helped your grandfather, the constable, when he lashed the Quaker woman so smartly through the streets of Salem; and it was I that brought your father a pitch-pine knot, kindled at my own hearth, to set fire to an Indian village, in King Philip's war.° They were my good friends, both; and many a pleasant walk have we had along this path, and returned merrily after midnight. I would fain be friends with you for their sake."

"If it be as thou sayest," replied Goodman Brown, "I marvel they never spoke of these matters; or, verily, I marvel not, seeing that the least rumor of the sort would have driven them from New England. We are a people of prayer, and good works to boot, and abide no such wickedness."

"Wickedness or not," said the traveller with the twisted staff, "I have a very   20
general acquaintance here in New England. The deacons of many a church have drunk the communion wine with me; the selectmen of divers towns make me their chairman; and a majority of the Great and General Court are firm supporters of my interest. The governor and I, too — But these are state secrets."

"Can this be so?" cried Goodman Brown, with a stare of amazement at his undisturbed companion. "Howbeit, I have nothing to do with the governor and council; they have their own ways, and are no rule for a simple husbandman like me. But, were I to go on with thee, how should I meet the eye of that good old

King Philip's war: King Philip, a Wampanoag chief, waged a bloody war against the New England colonists from 1675 to 1676.

man, our minister, at Salem village? Oh, his voice would make me tremble both Sabbath day and lecture day."

Thus far the elder traveller had listened with due gravity; but now burst into a fit of irrepressible mirth, shaking himself so violently that his snake-like staff actually seemed to wriggle in sympathy.

"Ha! ha! ha!" shouted he again and again; then composing himself, "Well, go on, Goodman Brown, go on; but, prithee, don't kill me with laughing."

"Well, then, to end the matter at once," said Goodman Brown, considerably nettled, "there is my wife, Faith. It would break her dear little heart; and I'd rather break my own."

"Nay, if that be the case," answered the other, "e'en go thy ways, Goodman   25
Brown. I would not for twenty old women like the one hobbling before us that Faith should come to any harm."

As he spoke he pointed his staff at a female figure on the path, in whom Goodman Brown recognized a very pious and exemplary dame, who had taught him his catechism in youth, and was still his moral and spiritual adviser, jointly with the minister and Deacon Gookin.

"A marvel, truly that Goody Cloyse should be so far in the wilderness at nightfall," said he. "But with your leave, friend, I shall take a cut through the woods until we have left this Christian woman behind. Being a stranger to you, she might ask whom I was consorting with and whither I was going."

"Be it so," said his fellow-traveller. "Betake you to the woods, and let me keep the path."

Accordingly the young man turned aside, but took care to watch his companion, who advanced softly along the road until he had come within a staff's length of the old dame. She, meanwhile, was making the best of her way, with singular speed for so aged a woman, and mumbling some indistinct words—a prayer, doubtless—as she went. The traveller put forth his staff and touched her withered neck with what seemed the serpent's tail.

"The devil!" screamed the pious old lady.   30

"Then Goody Cloyse knows her old friend?" observed the traveller, confronting her and leaning on his writhing stick.

"Ah, forsooth, and is it your worship indeed?" cried the good dame. "Yea, truly is it, and in the very image of my old gossip, Goodman Brown, the grandfather of the silly fellow that now is. But—would your worship believe it?—my broomstick hath strangely disappeared, stolen, as I suspect, by that unhanged witch, Goody Cory, and that, too, when I was all anointed with the juice of smallage, and cinquefoil, and wolf's bane"—

"Mingled with fine wheat and the fat of a new-born babe," said the shape of old Goodman Brown.

"Ah, your worship knows the recipe," cried the old lady, cackling aloud. "So, as I was saying, being all ready for the meeting, and no horse to ride on, I made up my mind to foot it; for they tell me there is a nice young man to be taken into communion to-night. But now your good worship will lend me your arm, and we shall be there in a twinkling."

"That can hardly be," answered her friend. "I may not spare you my arm,   35
Goody Cloyse; but here is my staff, if you will."

So saying, he threw it down at her feet, where, perhaps, it assumed life, being one of the rods which its owner had formerly lent to the Egyptian magi. Of this fact, however, Goodman Brown could not take cognizance. He had cast up his eyes in astonishment, and, looking down again, beheld neither Goody Cloyse nor the serpentine staff, but his fellow-traveller alone, who waited for him as calmly as if nothing had happened.

"That old woman taught me my catechism," said the young man; and there was a world of meaning in this simple comment.

They continued to walk onward, while the elder traveller exhorted his companion to make good speed and persevere in the path, discoursing so aptly that his arguments seemed rather to spring up in the bosom of his auditor than to be suggested by himself. As they went, he plucked a branch of maple to serve for a walking stick, and began to strip it of the twigs and little boughs, which were wet with evening dew. The moment his fingers touched them they became strangely withered and dried up as with a week's sunshine. Thus the pair proceeded, at a good free pace, until suddenly, in a gloomy hollow of the road, Goodman Brown sat himself down on the stump of a tree and refused to go any farther.

"Friend," he said, stubbornly, "my mind is made up. Not another step will I budge on this errand. What if a wretched old woman do choose to go to the devil when I thought she was going to heaven: is that any reason why I should quit my dear Faith and go after her?"

"You will think better of this by and by," said his acquaintance, composedly. 40 "Sit here and rest yourself a while; and when you feel like moving again, there is my staff to help you along."

Without more words, he threw his companion the maple stick, and was as speedily out of sight as if he had vanished into the deepening gloom. The young man sat a few moments by the roadside, applauding himself greatly, and thinking with how clear a conscience he should meet the minister in his morning walk, nor shrink from the eye of good old Deacon Gookin. And what calm sleep would be his that very night, which was to have been spent so wickedly, but so purely and sweetly now, in the arms of Faith! Amidst these pleasant and praiseworthy meditations, Goodman Brown heard the tramp of horses along the road, and deemed it advisable to conceal himself within the verge of the forest, conscious of the guilty purpose that had brought him thither, though now so happily turned from it.

On came the hoof tramps and the voices of the riders, two grave old voices, conversing soberly as they drew near. These mingled sounds appeared to pass along the road, within a few yards of the young man's hiding-place; but, owing doubtless to the depth of the gloom at that particular spot, neither the travellers nor their steeds were visible. Though their figures brushed the small boughs by the wayside, it could not be seen that they intercepted, even for a moment, the faint gleam from the strip of bright sky athwart which they must have passed. Goodman Brown alternately crouched and stood on tiptoe, pulling aside the branches and thrusting forth his head as far as he durst without discerning so much as a shadow. It vexed him the more, because he could have sworn, were such a thing possible, that he recognized the voices of the minister and Deacon Gookin, jogging along quietly, as they were wont to do, when bound to some ordination or ecclesiastical council. While yet within hearing, one of the riders stopped to pluck a switch.

"Of the two, reverend sir," said the voice like the deacon's, "I had rather miss an ordination dinner than to-night's meeting. They tell me that some of our community are to be here from Falmouth and beyond, and others from Connecticut and Rhode Island, besides several of the Indian powwows, who, after their fashion, know almost as much deviltry as the best of us. Moreover, there is a goodly young woman to be taken into communion."

"Mighty well, Deacon Gookin!" replied the solemn old tones of the minister. "Spur up, or we shall be late. Nothing can be done, you know, until I get on the ground."

The hoofs clattered again; and the voices, talking so strangely in the empty air, passed on through the forest, where no church had ever been gathered or solitary Christian prayed. Whither, then, could these holy men be journeying so deep into the heathen wilderness? Young Goodman Brown caught hold of a tree for support, being ready to sink down on the ground, faint and overburdened with the heavy sickness of his heart. He looked up to the sky, doubting whether there really was a heaven above him. Yet there was the blue arch, and the stars brightening in it.

"With heaven above and Faith below, I will yet stand firm against the devil!" cried Goodman Brown.

While he still gazed upward into the deep arch of the firmament and had lifted his hands to pray, a cloud, though no wind was stirring, hurried across the zenith and hid the brightening stars. The blue sky was still visible, except directly overhead, where this black mass of cloud was sweeping swiftly northward. Aloft in the air, as if from the depths of the cloud, came a confused and doubtful sound of voices. Once the listener fancied that he could distinguish the accents of towns-people of his own, men and women, both pious and ungodly, many of whom he had met at the communion table, and had seen others rioting at the tavern. The next moment, so indistinct were the sounds, he doubted whether he had heard aught but the murmur of the old forest, whispering without a wind. Then came a stronger swell of those familiar tones, heard daily in the sunshine at Salem village, but never until now from a cloud of night. There was one voice, of a young woman, uttering lamentations, yet with an uncertain sorrow, and entreating for some favor, which, perhaps, it would grieve her to obtain; and all the unseen multitude, both saints and sinners, seemed to encourage her onward.

"Faith!" shouted Goodman Brown, in a voice of agony and desperation; and the echoes of the forest mocked him, crying, "Faith! Faith!" as if bewildered wretches were seeking her all through the wilderness.

The cry of grief, rage, and terror was yet piercing the night, when the unhappy husband held his breath for a response. There was a scream, drowned immediately in a louder murmur of voices, fading into far-off laughter, as the dark cloud swept away, leaving the clear and silent sky above Goodman Brown. But something fluttered lightly down through the air and caught on the branch of a tree. The young man seized it, and beheld a pink ribbon.

"My Faith is gone!" cried he after one stupefied moment. "There is no good   50
on earth; and sin is but a name. Come, devil; for to thee is this world given."

And, maddened with despair, so that he laughed loud and long, did Goodman Brown grasp his staff and set forth again, at such a rate that he seemed to fly
along the forest path rather than to walk or run. The road grew wilder and drea-
rier and more faintly traced, and vanished at length, leaving him in the heart of
the dark wilderness, still rushing onward with the instinct that guides mortal man
to evil. The whole forest was peopled with frightful sounds—the creaking of the
trees, the howling of wild beasts, and the yell of Indians; while sometimes the
wind tolled like a distant church bell, and sometimes gave a broad roar around
the traveller, as if all Nature were laughing him to scorn. But he was himself the
chief horror of the scene, and shrank not from its other horrors.

"Ha! ha! ha!" roared Goodman Brown when the wind laughed at him. "Let
us hear which will laugh loudest. Think not to frighten me with your deviltry.
Come witch, come wizard, come Indian powwow, come devil himself, and here
comes Goodman Brown. You may as well fear him as he fear you."

In truth, all through the haunted forest there could be nothing more frightful than the figure of Goodman Brown. On he flew among the black pines, bran-
dishing his staff with frenzied gestures, now giving vent to an inspiration of horrid
blasphemy, and now shouting forth such laughter as set all the echoes of the forest laughing like demons around him. The fiend in his own shape is less hideous
than when he rages in the breast of man. Thus sped the demoniac on his course,
until, quivering among the trees, he saw a red light before him, as when the felled
trunks and branches of a clearing have been set on fire, and throw up their lurid
blaze against the sky, at the hour of midnight. He paused, in a lull of the tempest
that had driven him onward, and heard the swell of what seemed a hymn, rolling
solemnly from a distance with the weight of many voices. He knew the tune; it
was a familiar one in the choir of the village meeting-house. The verse died heavily away, and was lengthened by a chorus, not of human voices, but of all the
sounds of the benighted wilderness pealing in awful harmony together. Goodman Brown cried out, and his cry was lost to his own ear by its unison with the cry
of the desert.

In the interval of silence he stole forward until the light glared full upon his
eyes. At one extremity of an open space, hemmed in by the dark wall of the forest,
arose a rock, bearing some rude, natural resemblance either to an altar or a
pulpit, and surrounded by four blazing pines, their tops aflame, their stems untouched, like candles at an evening meeting. The mass of foliage that had over-
grown the summit of the rock was all on fire, blazing high into the night and
fitfully illuminating the whole field. Each pendent twig and leafy festoon was in a
blaze. As the red light arose and fell, a numerous congregation alternately shone
forth, then disappeared in shadow, and again grew, as it were, out of the darkness,
peopling the heart of the solitary woods at once.

"A grave and dark-clad company," quoth Goodman Brown.   55

In truth they were such. Among them, quivering to and fro between gloom
and splendor, appeared faces that would be seen next day at the council board
of the province, and others which, Sabbath after Sabbath, looked devoutly

heavenward, and benignantly over the crowded pews, from the holiest pulpits in the land. Some affirm that the lady of the governor was there. At least there were high dames well known to her, and wives of honored husbands, and widows, a great multitude, and ancient maidens, all of excellent repute, and fair young girls, who trembled lest their mothers should espy them. Either the sudden gleams of light flashing over the obscure field bedazzled Goodman Brown, or he recognized a score of the church members of Salem village famous for their especial sanctity. Good old Deacon Gookin had arrived, and waited at the skirts of that venerable saint, his revered pastor. But, irreverently consorting with these grave, reputable, and pious people, these elders of the church, these chaste dames and dewy virgins, there were men of dissolute lives and women of spotted fame, wretches given over to all mean and filthy vice, and suspected even of horrid crimes. It was strange to see that the good shrank not from the wicked, nor were the sinners abashed by the saints. Scattered also among their pale-faced enemies were the Indian priests, or powwows, who had often scared their native forest with more hideous incantations than any known to English witchcraft.

"But where is Faith?" thought Goodman Brown; and, as hope came into his heart, he trembled.

Another verse of the hymn arose, a slow and mournful strain, such as the pious love, but joined to words which expressed all that our nature can conceive of sin, and darkly hinted at far more. Unfathomable to mere mortals is the lore of fiends. Verse after verse was sung; and still the chorus of the desert swelled between like the deepest tone of a mighty organ; and with the final peal of that dreadful anthem there came a sound, as if the roaring wind, the rushing streams, the howling beasts, and every other voice of the unconcerted wilderness were mingling and according with the voice of guilty man in homage to the prince of all. The four blazing pines threw up a loftier flame, and obscurely discovered shapes and visages of horror on the smoke wreaths above the impious assembly. At the same moment the fire on the rock shot redly forth and formed a flowing arch above its base, where now appeared a figure. With reverence be it spoken, the figure bore no slight similitude, both in garb and manner, to some grave divine of the New England churches.

"Bring forth the converts!" cried a voice that echoed through the field and rolled into the forest.

At the word, Goodman Brown stepped forth from the shadow of the trees and approached the congregation, with whom he felt a loathful brotherhood by the sympathy of all that was wicked in his heart. He could have well-nigh sworn that the shape of his own dead father beckoned him to advance, looking downward from a smoke wreath, while a woman, with dim features of despair, threw out her hand to warn him back. Was it his mother? But he had no power to retreat one step, nor to resist, even in thought, when the minister and good old Deacon Gookin seized his arms and led him to the blazing rock. Thither came also the slender form of a veiled female, led between Goody Cloyse, that pious teacher of the catechism, and Martha Carrier, who had received the devil's promise to be queen of hell. A rampant hag was she. And there stood the proselytes beneath the canopy of fire.

60

"Welcome, my children," said the dark figure, "to the communion of your race. Ye have found thus young your nature and your destiny. My children, look behind you!"

They turned; and flashing forth, as it were, in a sheet of flame, the fiend worshippers were seen; the smile of welcome gleamed darkly on every visage.

"There," resumed the sable form, "are all whom ye have reverenced from youth. Ye deemed them holier than yourselves and shrank from your own sin, contrasting it with their lives of righteousness and prayerful aspirations heavenward. Yet here are they all in my worshipping assembly. This night it shall be granted you to know their secret deeds: how hoary-bearded elders of the church have whispered wanton words to the young maids of their households; how many a woman, eager for widows' weeds, has given her husband a drink at bedtime and let him sleep his last sleep in her bosom; how beardless youths have made haste to inherit their fathers' wealth; and how fair damsels—blush not, sweet ones—have dug little graves in the garden, and bidden me, the sole guest, to an infant's funeral. By the sympathy of your human hearts for sin ye shall scent out all the places—whether in church, bedchamber, street, field, or forest—where crime has been committed, and shall exult to behold the whole earth one stain of guilt, one mighty blood spot. Far more than this. It shall be yours to penetrate, in every bosom, the deep mystery of sin, the fountain of all wicked arts, and which inexhaustibly supplies more evil impulses than human power—than my power at its utmost—can make manifest in deeds. And now, my children, look upon each other."

They did so; and, by the blaze of the hell-kindled torches, the wretched man beheld his Faith, and the wife her husband, trembling before that unhallowed altar.

"Lo, there ye stand, my children," said the figure, in a deep and solemn tone, almost sad with its despairing awfulness, as if his once angelic nature could yet mourn for our miserable race. "Depending upon one another's hearts, ye had still hoped that virtue were not all a dream. Now are ye undeceived. Evil is the nature of mankind. Evil must be your only happiness. Welcome again, my children, to the communion of your race."

"Welcome," repeated the fiend worshippers, in one cry of despair and triumph.

And there they stood, the only pair, as it seemed, who were yet hesitating on the verge of wickedness in this dark world. A basin was hallowed, naturally, in the rock. Did it contain water, reddened by the lurid light? or was it blood? or, perchance, a liquid flame? Herein did the shape of evil dip his hand and prepare to lay the mark of baptism upon their foreheads, that they might be partakers of the mystery of sin, more conscious of the secret guilt of others, both in deed and thought, than they could now be of their own. The husband cast one look at his pale wife, and Faith at him. What polluted wretches would the next glance show them to each other, shuddering alike at what they disclosed and what they saw!

"Faith! Faith!" cried the husband, "look up to heaven, and resist the wicked one."

65

Whether Faith obeyed he knew not. Hardly had he spoken when he found himself amid calm night and solitude, listening to a roar of the wind which died heavily away through the forest. He staggered against the rock, and felt it chill and damp; while a hanging twig, that had been all on fire, besprinkled his cheek with the coldest dew.

The next morning young Goodman Brown came slowly into the street of   70
Salem village, staring around him like a bewildered man. The good old minister was taking a walk along the graveyard to get an appetite for breakfast and medi-tate his sermon, and bestowed a blessing, as he passed, on Goodman Brown. He shrank from the venerable saint as if to avoid an anathema. Old Deacon Gookin was at domestic worship, and the holy words of his prayer were heard through the open window. "What God doth the wizard pray to?" quoth Goodman Brown. Goody Cloyse, that excellent old Christian, stood in the early sunshine at her own lattice, catechizing a little girl who had brought her a pint of morning's milk. Goodman Brown snatched away the child as from the grasp of the fiend himself. Turning the corner by the meeting-house, he spied the head of Faith, with the pink ribbons, gazing anxiously forth, and bursting into such joy at sight of him that she skipped along the street and almost kissed her husband before the whole village. But Goodman Brown looked sternly and sadly into her face, and passed on without a greeting.

Had Goodman Brown fallen asleep in the forest and only dreamed a wild dream of a witch-meeting?

Be it so if you will; but, alas! it was a dream of evil omen for young Goodman Brown. A stern, a sad, a darkly meditative, a distrustful, if not a desperate man did he become from the night of that fearful dream. On the Sabbath day, when the congregation were singing a holy psalm, he could not listen because an anthem of sin rushed loudly upon his ear and drowned all the blessed strain. When the minister spoke from the pulpit with power and fervid eloquence, and, with his hand on the open Bible, of the sacred truths of our religion, and of saint-like lives and triumphant deaths, and of future bliss or misery unutterable, then did Good-man Brown turn pale, dreading lest the roof should thunder down upon the gray blasphemer and his hearers. Often, awaking suddenly at midnight, he shrank from the bosom of Faith; and at morning or eventide, when the family knelt down at prayer, he scowled and muttered to himself, and gazed sternly at his wife, and turned away. And when he had lived long, and was borne to his grave a hoary corpse, followed by Faith, an aged woman, and children and grandchildren, a goodly procession, besides neighbors not a few, they carved no hopeful verse upon his tombstone, for his dying hour was gloom.   [1835]

FOR THINKING AND WRITING

1. "Young Goodman Brown" seems quite allegorical with journeys in the night woods and statements like "my Faith is gone" (para. 50). How would you explain this allegorical story? What is Brown looking for? What does he find out? How does he deal with his discoveries?

2. If you were a good friend of Brown's, what might you tell him to try to save him from a life of gloom?

3. The devil suggests that there is more evil in the human heart "than my power at its utmost" (para. 63). Do you agree? If so, is this a message to despair about?

4. The devil says he is well acquainted with Brown's family. What has his family done? Is Brown innocent and naive, or perhaps stubborn and arrogant, in his refusal to admit that evil exists all around us?

5. Do you suspect that Brown merely dreamed or imagined his experience in the woods? Or do you think it really took place? Refer to specific details of the text.

PAM HOUSTON

How to Talk to a Hunter

Pam Houston (b. 1962) is the director of Creative Writing at the University of California, Davis. She is not a hunter, though she is a hunting guide and has edited the book Women on Hunting *(1994). The following story was published in a 1989 issue of the journal* Quarterly West. *It was then included in* The Best American Short Stories *(1990), in the paperback edition of* The Best American Short Stories of the Century *(2000), and in a 1992 volume of her own stories entitled* Cowboys Are My Weakness. *Houston's most recent books are another collection of her stories,* Waltzing the Cat *(1998), and a collection of essays,* A Little More about Me *(1999). Her first novel,* Sightbound, *is forthcoming.*

When he says "Skins or blankets?" it will take you a moment to realize that he's asking which you want to sleep under. And in your hesitation he'll decide that he wants to see your skin wrapped in the big black moose hide. He carried it, he'll say, soaking wet and heavier than a dead man, across the tundra for two — was it hours or days or weeks? But the payoff, now, will be to see it fall across one of your white breasts. It's December, and your skin is never really warm, so you will pull the bulk of it around you and pose for him, pose for his camera, without having to narrate this moose's death.

You will spend every night in this man's bed without asking yourself why he listens to top-forty country. Why he donated money to the Republican Party. Why he won't play back his messages while you are in the room. You are there so often the messages pile up. Once you noticed the bright green counter reading as high as fifteen.

He will have lured you here out of a careful independence that you spent months cultivating; though it will finally be winter, the dwindling daylight and the threat of Christmas, that makes you give in. Spending nights with this man means suffering the long face of your sheepdog, who likes to sleep on your bed, who worries when you don't come home. But the hunter's house is so much warmer than yours, and he'll give you a key, and just like a woman, you'll think that means something. It will snow hard for thirteen straight days. Then it will really get cold. When it is sixty below there will be no wind and no clouds, just still air and cold sunshine. The sun on the windows will lure you out of bed, but he'll pull you back under. The next two hours he'll devote to your body. With his hands, with his tongue, he'll express what will seem to you like the most eternal of loves. Like the house key, this is just another kind of lie. Even in bed; especially in bed, you and he cannot speak the same language. The machine will answer the incoming calls. From under an ocean of passion and hide and hair you'll hear a woman's muffled voice between the beeps.

Your best female friend will say, "So what did you think? That a man who sleeps under a dead moose is capable of commitment?"

This is what you learned in college: A man desires the satisfaction of his   5
desire; a woman desires the condition of desiring.

The hunter will talk about spring in Hawaii, summer in Alaska. The man who says he was always better at math will form the sentences so carefully it will be impossible to tell if you are included in these plans. When he asks you if you would like to open a small guest ranch way out in the country, understand that this is a rhetorical question. Label these conversations future perfect, but don't expect the present to catch up with them. Spring is an inconceivable distance from the December days that just keep getting shorter and gray.

He'll ask you if you've ever shot anything, if you'd like to, if you ever thought about teaching your dog to retrieve. Your dog will like him too much, will drop the stick at his feet every time, will roll over and let the hunter scratch his belly.

One day he'll leave you sleeping to go split wood or get the mail and his phone will ring again. You'll sit very still while a woman who calls herself something like Janie Coyote leaves a message on his machine: She's leaving work, she'll say, and the last thing she wanted to hear was the sound of his beautiful voice. Maybe she'll talk only in rhyme. Maybe the counter will change to sixteen. You'll look a question at the mule deer on the wall, and the dark spots on either side of his mouth will tell you he shares more with this hunter than you ever will. One night, drunk, the hunter told you he was sorry for taking that deer, that every now and then there's an animal that isn't meant to be taken, and he should have known that deer was one.

Your best male friend will say, "No one who needs to call herself Janie Coyote can hold a candle to you, but why not let him sleep alone a few nights, just to make sure?"

The hunter will fill your freezer with elk burger, venison sausage, organic   10
potatoes, fresh pecans. He'll tell you to wear your seat belt, to dress warmly, to

drive safely. He'll say you are always on his mind, that you're the best thing that's ever happened to him, that you make him glad that he's a man.

Tell him it don't come easy, tell him freedom's just another word for nothing left to lose.

These are the things you'll know without asking: The coyote woman wears her hair in braids. She uses words like "howdy." She's man enough to shoot a deer.

A week before Christmas you'll rent *It's a Wonderful Life* and watch it together, curled on your couch, faces touching. Then you'll bring up the word "monogamy." He'll tell you how badly he was hurt by your predecessor. He'll tell you he couldn't be happier spending every night with you. He'll say there's just a few questions he doesn't have the answers for. He'll say he's just scared and confused. Of course this isn't exactly what he means. Tell him you understand. Tell him you are scared too. Tell him to take all the time he needs. Know that you could never shoot an animal; and be glad of it.

Your best female friend will say, "You didn't tell him you loved him, did you?" Don't even tell her the truth. If you do you'll have to tell her that he said this: "I feel exactly the same way."

Your best male friend will say, "Didn't you know what would happen when you said the word 'commitment'?"   15
But that isn't the word that you said.
He'll say, "Commitment, monogamy, it all means just one thing."

The coyote woman will come from Montana with the heavier snows. The hunter will call you on the day of the solstice to say he has a friend in town and can't see you. He'll leave you hanging your Christmas lights; he'll give new meaning to the phrase "longest night of the year." The man who has said he's not so good with words will manage to say eight things about his friend without using a gender-determining pronoun. Get out of the house quickly. Call the most understanding person you know who will let you sleep in his bed.

Your best female friend will say, "So what did you think? That he was capable of living outside his gender?"

When you get home in the morning there's a candy tin on your pillow.   20
Santa, obese and grotesque, fondles two small children on the lid. The card will say something like "From your not-so-secret admirer." Open it. Examine each carefully made truffle. Feed them, one at a time, to the dog. Call the hunter's machine. Tell him you don't speak chocolate.

Your best female friend will say, "At this point, what is it about him that you could possibly find appealing?"

◆   ◆   ◆

Your best male friend will say, "Can't you understand that this is a good sign? Can't you understand that this proves how deep he's in with you?" Hug your best male friend. Give him the truffles the dog wouldn't eat.

Of course the weather will cooperate with the coyote woman. The highways will close, she will stay another night. He'll tell her he's going to work so he can come and see you. He'll even leave her your number and write "Me at Work" on the yellow pad of paper by his phone. Although you shouldn't, you'll have to be there. It will be you and your nauseous dog and your half-trimmed tree all waiting for him like a series of questions.

This is what you learned in graduate school: In every assumption is contained the possibility of its opposite.

In your kitchen he'll hug you like you might both die there. Sniff him for coyote. Don't hug him back.

He will say whatever he needs to to win. He'll say it's just an old friend. He'll say the visit was all the friend's idea. He'll say the night away from you has given him time to think about how much you mean to him. Realize that nothing short of sleeping alone will ever make him realize how much you mean to him. He'll say that if you can just be a little patient, some good will come out of this for the two of you after all. He still won't use a gender-specific pronoun.

Put your head in your hands. Think about what it means to be patient. Think about the beautiful, smart, strong, clever woman you thought he saw when he looked at you. Pull on your hair. Rock your body back and forth. Don't cry.

He'll say that after holding you it doesn't feel right holding anyone else. For "holding," substitute "fucking." Then take it as a compliment.

He will get frustrated and rise to leave. He may, or may not be bluffing. Stall for time. Ask a question he can't immediately answer. Tell him you want to make love on the floor. When he tells you your body is beautiful say, "I feel exactly the same way." Don't, under any circumstances, stand in front of the door.

Your best female friend will say, "They lie to us, they cheat on us, and we love them more for it." She'll say, "It's our fault; we raise them to be like that."

Tell her it can't be your fault. You've never raised anything but dogs.

The hunter will say it's late and he has to go home to sleep. He'll emphasize the last word in the sentence. Give him one kiss that he'll remember while he's fucking the coyote woman. Give him one kiss that ought to make him cry if he's capable of it, but don't notice when he does. Tell him to have a good night.

Your best male friend will say, "We all do it. We can't help it. We're self-destructive. It's the old bad-boy routine. You have a male dog, don't you?"

The next day the sun will be out and the coyote woman will leave. Think about how easy it must be for a coyote woman and a man who listens to top-forty

25

30

country. The coyote woman would never use a word like "monogamy"; the coyote woman will stay gentle on his mind.

If you can, let him sleep alone for at least one night. If you can't, invite him over to finish trimming your Christmas tree. When he asks how you are, tell him you think it's a good idea to keep your sense of humor during the holidays.

Plan to be breezy and aloof and full of interesting anecdotes about all the other men you've ever known. Plan to be hotter than ever before in bed, and a little cold out of it. Remember that necessity is the mother of invention. Be flexible.

First, he will find the faulty bulb that's been keeping all the others from lighting. He will explain, in great detail, the most elementary electrical principles. You will take turns placing the ornaments you and other men, he and other women, have spent years carefully choosing. Under the circumstances, try to let this be a comforting thought.

He will thin the clusters of tinsel you put on the tree. He'll say something ambiguous like "Next year you should string popcorn and cranberries." Finally, his arm will stretch just high enough to place the angel on the top of the tree.

Your best female friend will say, "Why can't you ever fall in love with a man who will be your friend?"

Your best male friend will say, "You ought to know this by now: Men always cheat on the best women."

This is what you learned in the pop psychology book: Love means letting go of fear.

Play Willie Nelson's "Pretty Paper." He'll ask you to dance, and before you can answer he'll be spinning you around your wood stove, he'll be humming in your ear. Before the song ends he'll be taking off your clothes, setting you lightly under the tree, hovering above you with tinsel in his hair. Through the spread of the branches the all-white lights you insisted on will shudder and blur, outlining the ornaments he brought: a pheasant, a snow goose, a deer.

The record will end. Above the crackle of the wood stove and the rasp of the hunter's breathing you'll hear one long low howl break the quiet of the frozen night: your dog, chained and lonely and cold. You'll wonder if he knows enough to stay in his doghouse. You'll wonder if he knows that the nights are getting shorter now.   [1989]

FOR THINKING AND WRITING

1. Describe the narrator, listing at least three adjectives. What do you think of her? On what do you base your evaluation?

2. What would you say to someone who argued that this story engages in gender stereotypes? To someone who argued that it stereotypes hunters?

3. Do you think the "you" is the narrator herself? Why or why not? At any rate, Houston could have had the narrator dispense with references to "you" and

just describe her own life. What are the possible purposes and effects of having the story be in the form of instructions? In what places does the narrator predict what the "you" will do rather than telling the "you" how to act?

4. Note the word *talk* in the title. In what ways does the story emphasize talking? What amount and kind of talk do you think should occur between the couple?

5. Would you say that the story has a happy ending? Why, or why not?

JAMAICA KINCAID
Girl

Originally named Elaine Potter Richardson, Jamaica Kincaid was born on the island of Antigua in the West Indies in 1949. At the time, Antigua was a British colony. Kincaid lived there until she was seventeen, when she emigrated to the United States. Soon after she arrived in this country, she became a nanny for the family of Michael Arlen, television critic of The New Yorker. *Eventually, her own short stories were published in that magazine, and during the early 1990s she wrote gardening columns for it as well. Although she continues to live in the United States, residing for the last several years in Vermont, almost all of her writing deals with her native land. In particular, she has written about Antiguan women growing up under British domination. "Girl" appeared in* The New Yorker *in 1978 and was later reprinted in Kincaid's first book, a 1984 collection of short stories entitled* At the Bottom of the River. *Subsequently, she has published the novels* Annie John *(1985),* Lucy *(1990), and* Autobiography of My Mother *(1996). Her books of nonfiction include* A Small Place, *an analysis of Antigua (1988); a memoir,* My Brother *(1997);* My Garden (Book) *(1999); and* Talk Stories *(2001), a collection of brief observations that she originally wrote for* The New Yorker.

Wash the white clothes on Monday and put them on the stone heap; wash the color clothes on Tuesday and put them on the clothesline to dry; don't walk barehead in the hot sun; cook pumpkin fritters in very hot sweet oil; soak your little cloths right after you take them off; when buying cotton to make yourself a nice blouse, be sure that it doesn't have gum on it, because that way it won't hold up well after a wash; soak salt fish overnight before you cook it; is it true that you sing benna° in Sunday school?; always eat your food in such a way that it won't turn someone else's stomach; on Sundays try to walk like a lady and not like the slut you are so bent on becoming; don't sing benna in Sunday school; you mustn't speak to wharf-rat boys, not even to give directions; don't eat fruits on the street—flies will follow you; *but I don't sing benna on Sundays at all and never in Sunday school*; this is how to sew on a button; this is how to make a button-hole for the but-

benna: Calypso music.

ton you have just sewed on; this is how to hem a dress when you see the hem coming down and so to prevent yourself from looking like the slut I know you are so bent on becoming; this is how you iron your father's khaki shirt so that it doesn't have a crease; this is how you iron your father's khaki pants so that they don't have a crease; this is how you grow okra — far from the house, because okra tree harbors red ants; when you are growing dasheen, make sure it gets plenty of water or else it makes your throat itch when you are eating it; this is how you sweep a corner; this is how you sweep a whole house; this is how you sweep a yard; this is how you smile to someone you don't like too much; this is how you smile to someone you don't like at all; this is how you smile to someone you like completely; this is how you set a table for tea; this is how you set a table for dinner; this is how you set a table for dinner with an important guest; this is how you set a table for lunch; this is how you set a table for breakfast; this is how to behave in the presence of men who don't know you very well, and this way they won't recognize immediately the slut I have warned you against becoming; be sure to wash every day, even if it is with your own spit; don't squat down to play marbles — you are not a boy, you know; don't pick people's flowers — you might catch something; don't throw stones at blackbirds, because it might not be a blackbird at all; this is how to make a bread pudding; this is how to make doukona;° this is how to make pepper pot; this is how to make a good medicine for a cold; this is how to make a good medicine to throw away a child before it even becomes a child; this is how to catch a fish; this is how to throw back a fish you don't like, and that way something bad won't fall on you; this is how to bully a man; this is how a man bullies you; this is how to love a man, and if this doesn't work there are other ways, and if they don't work don't feel too bad about giving up; this is how to spit up in the air if you feel like it, and this is how to move quick so that it doesn't fall on you; this is how to make ends meet; always squeeze bread to make sure it's fresh; *but what if the baker won't let me feel the bread?*; you mean to say that after all you are really going to be the kind of woman who the baker won't let near the bread?   [1978]

doukona: A spicy plantain pudding.

FOR THINKING AND WRITING

1. Is "Girl" really a story? What characteristics of a story come to mind as you consider this issue?

2. Describe the culture depicted in "Girl" as well as the role of females in that culture. Is either the culture or the role of females in it different from what you are familiar with? Explain.

3. Do you think that the instructions to this girl are all given on the same occasion? Why, or why not? Who do you suppose is giving the instructions? Would you say that the instructor is oppressive or domineering? Identify some of the assumptions or warrants behind your position.

4. What effect does Kincaid achieve by making this text a single long sentence? By having the girl speak at only two brief moments?

5. At one point, the girl is shown "how to make a good medicine to throw away a child before it even becomes a child." What do you think of the instructor's willingness to give such advice? What do you conclude from its position in the text between "how to make a good medicine for a cold" and "how to catch a fish"? Does the order of the various pieces of advice matter? Could Kincaid have presented them in a different order without changing their effects?

BHARATI MUKHERJEE
The Management of Grief

A native of Calcutta, Bharati Mukherjee (b. 1942) grew up in India. She attended the universities of Calcutta and Boroda, earning a master's degree in English and ancient Indian culture. In 1961, she moved to the United States. There, she attended the University of Iowa's renowned Writers Workshop, where she earned a master of fine arts as well as a doctorate in English. From 1966 to 1980, Mukherjee taught at McGill University in Canada; currently, she is a professor of English at the University of California in Berkeley. Her novels include The Tiger's Daughter *(1971),* Wife *(1972),* Jasmine *(1989),* The Holder of the World *(1993), and* Desirable Daughters *(2002). In addition, she has published two volumes of short stories,* Darkness *(1985) and* The Middleman and Other Stories *(1988). "The Management of Grief" appears in the latter volume, which won the National Book Critics Circle Award for fiction. The story was also selected for* The Best American Short Stories 1987. *With her husband Clark Blaise, Mukherjee has written two nonfiction books. In the first,* Days and Nights in Calcutta *(1979), they each give an account of a trip they made to India. In the second,* The Sorrow and the Terror: The Haunting Legacy of the Air India Tragedy *(1987), they examine the real-life disaster on which the following story is based.*

A woman I don't know is boiling tea the Indian way in my kitchen. There are a lot of women I don't know in my kitchen, whispering and moving tactfully. They open doors, rummage through the pantry, and try not to ask me where things are kept. They remind me of when my sons were small, on Mother's Day or when Vikram and I were tired, and they would make big, sloppy omelets. I would lie in bed pretending I didn't hear them.

Dr. Sharma, the treasurer of the Indo-Canada Society, pulls me into the hallway. He wants to know if I am worried about money. His wife, who has just come up from the basement with a tray of empty cups and glasses, scolds him. "Don't bother Mrs. Bhave with mundane details." She looks so monstrously pregnant her baby must be days overdue. I tell her she shouldn't be carrying heavy things. "Shaila," she says, smiling, "this is the fifth." Then she grabs a teenager by his shirttails. He slips his Walkman off his head. He has to be one of her four children; they have the same domed and dented foreheads. "What's the official word now?" she demands. The boy slips the headphones back on. "They're acting evasive, Ma. They're saying it could be an accident or a terrorist bomb."

All morning, the boys have been muttering, Sikh bomb, Sikh bomb. The men, not using the word, bow their heads in agreement. Mrs. Sharma touches her forehead at such a word. At least they've stopped talking about space debris and Russian lasers.

Two radios are going in the dining room. They are tuned to different stations. Someone must have brought the radios down from my boys' bedrooms. I haven't gone into their rooms since Kusum came running across the front lawn in her bathrobe. She looked so funny, I was laughing when I opened the door.

The big TV in the den is being whizzed through American networks and   5 cable channels.

"Damn!" some man swears bitterly. "How can these preachers carry on like nothing's happened?" I want to tell him we're not that important. You look at the audience, and at the preacher in his blue robe with his beautiful white hair, the potted palm trees under a blue sky, and you know they care about nothing.

The phone rings and rings. Dr. Sharma's taken charge. "We're with her," he keeps saying. "Yes, yes, the doctor has given calming pills. Yes, yes, pills are having necessary effect." I wonder if pills alone explain this calm. Not peace, just a deadening quiet. I was always controlled, but never repressed. Sound can reach me, but my body is tensed, ready to scream. I hear their voices all around me. I hear my boys and Vikram cry, "Mommy, Shaila!" and their screams insulate me, like headphones.

The woman boiling water tells her story again and again. "I got the news first. My cousin called from Halifax before six A.M., can you imagine? He'd gotten up for prayers and his son was studying for medical exams and heard on a rock channel that something had happened to a plane. They said first it had disappeared from the radar, like a giant eraser just reached out. His father called me, so I said to him, what do you mean, 'something bad'? You mean a hijacking? And he said, *Behn,* there is no confirmation of anything yet, but check with your neighbors because a lot of them must be on that plane. So I called poor Kusum straightaway. I knew Kusum's husband and daughter were booked to go yesterday."

Kusum lives across the street from me. She and Satish had moved in less than a month ago. They said they needed a bigger place. All these people, the Sharmas and friends from the Indo-Canada Society, had been there for the housewarming. Satish and Kusum made tandoori on their big gas grill and even the white neighbors piled their plates high with that luridly red, charred, juicy chicken. Their younger daughter had danced, and even our boys had broken away from the Stanley Cup telecast to put in a reluctant appearance. Everyone took pictures for their albums and for the community newspapers—another of our families had made it big in Toronto—and now I wonder how many of those happy faces are gone. "Why does God give us so much if all along He intends to take it away?" Kusum asks me.

I nod. We sit on carpeted stairs, holding hands like children. "I never once   10 told him that I loved him," I say. I was too much the well-brought-up woman. I was so well brought up I never felt comfortable calling my husband by his first name.

"It's all right," Kusum says. "He knew. My husband knew. They felt it. Modern young girls have to say it because what they feel is fake."

Kusum's daughter Pam runs in with an overnight case. Pam's in her McDonald's uniform. "Mummy! You have to get dressed!" Panic makes her cranky. "A reporter's on his way here."

"Why?"

"You want to talk to him in your bathrobe?" She starts to brush her mother's long hair. She's the daughter who's always in trouble. She dates Canadian boys and hangs out in the mall, shopping for tight sweaters. The younger one, the goody-goody one according to Pam, the one with a voice so sweet that when she sang *bhajans* for Ethiopian relief even a frugal man like my husband wrote out a hundred-dollar check, *she* was on that plane. *She* was going to spend July and August with grandparents because Pam wouldn't go. Pam said she'd rather waitress at McDonald's. "If it's a choice between Bombay and Wonderland, I'm picking Wonderland," she'd said.

"Leave me alone," Kusum yells. "You know what I want to do? If I didn't   15
have to look after you now, I'd hang myself."

Pam's young face goes blotchy with pain. "Thanks," she says, "don't let me stop you."

"Hush," pregnant Mrs. Sharma scolds Pam. "Leave your mother alone. Mr. Sharma will tackle the reporters and fill out the forms. He'll say what has to be said."

Pam stands her ground. "You think I don't know what Mummy's thinking? *Why her?* That's what. That's sick! Mummy wishes my little sister were alive and I were dead."

Kusum's hand in mine is trembly hot. We continue to sit on the stairs.

She calls before she arrives, wondering if there's anything I need. Her name   20
is Judith Templeton and she's an appointee of the provincial government. "Multiculturalism?" I ask, and she says "partially," but that her mandate is bigger. "I've been told you knew many of the people on the flight," she says. "Perhaps if you'd agree to help us reach the others . . . ?"

She gives me time at least to put on tea water and pick up the mess in the front room. I have a few *samosas* from Kusum's housewarming that I could fry up, but then I think, why prolong this visit?

Judith Templeton is much younger than she sounded. She wears a blue suit with a white blouse and a polka-dot tie. Her blond hair is cut short, her only jewelry is pearl-drop earrings. Her briefcase is new and expensive looking, a gleaming cordovan leather. She sits with it across her lap. When she looks out the front windows onto the street, her contact lenses seem to float in front of her light blue eyes.

"What sort of help do you want from me?" I ask. She has refused the tea, out of politeness, but I insist, along with some slightly stale biscuits.

"I have no experience," she admits. "That is, I have an M.S.W. and I've worked in liaison with accident victims, but I mean I have no experience with a tragedy of this scale —"

"Who could?" I ask.   25

"— and with the complications of culture, language, and customs. Someone mentioned that Mrs. Bhave is a pillar—because you've taken it more calmly."

At this, perhaps, I frown, for she reaches forward, almost to take my hand. "I hope you understand my meaning, Mrs. Bhave. There are hundreds of people in Metro directly affected, like you, and some of them speak no English. There are some widows who've never handled money or gone on a bus, and there are old parents who still haven't eaten or gone outside their bedrooms. Some houses and apartments have been looted. Some wives are still hysterical. Some husbands are in shock and profound depression. We want to help, but our hands are tied in so many ways. We have to distribute money to some people, and there are legal documents—these things can be done. We have interpreters, but we don't always have the human touch, or maybe the right human touch. We don't want to make mistakes, Mrs. Bhave, and that's why we'd like to ask you to help us."

"More mistakes, you mean," I say.

"Police matters are not in my hands," she answers.

"Nothing I can do will make any difference," I say. "We must all grieve in our   30
own way."

"But you are coping very well. All the people said, Mrs. Bhave is the strongest person of all. Perhaps if the others could see you, talk with you, it would help them."

"By the standards of the people you call hysterical, I am behaving very oddly and very badly, Miss Templeton." I want to say to her, *I wish I could scream, starve, walk into Lake Ontario, jump from a bridge.* "They would not see me as a model. I do not see myself as a model."

I am a freak. No one who has ever known me would think of me reacting this way. This terrible calm will not go away.

She asks me if she may call again, after I get back from a long trip that we all must make. "Of course," I say. "Feel free to call, anytime."

Four days later, I find Kusum squatting on a rock overlooking a bay in Ire-   35
land. It isn't a big rock, but it juts sharply out over water. This is as close as we'll ever get to them. June breezes balloon out her sari and unpin her knee-length hair. She has the bewildered look of a sea creature whom the tides have stranded.

It's been one hundred hours since Kusum came stumbling and screaming across my lawn. Waiting around the hospital, we've heard many stories. The police, the diplomats, they tell us things thinking that we're strong, that knowledge is helpful to the grieving, and maybe it is. Some, I know, prefer ignorance, or their own versions. The plane broke into two, they say. Unconsciousness was instantaneous. No one suffered. My boys must have just finished their breakfasts. They loved eating on planes, they loved the smallness of plates, knives, and forks. Last year they saved the airline salt and pepper shakers. Half an hour more and they would have made it to Heathrow.

Kusum says that we can't escape our fate. She says that all those people — our husbands, my boys, her girl with the nightingale voice, all those Hindus, Christians, Sikhs, Muslims, Parsis, and atheists on that plane—were fated to die together off this beautiful bay. She learned this from a swami in Toronto.

I have my Valium.

Six of us "relatives" — two widows and four widowers — chose to spend the day today by the waters instead of sitting in a hospital room and scanning photographs of the dead. That's what they call us now: relatives. I've looked through twenty-seven photos in two days. They're very kind to us, the Irish are very understanding. Sometimes understanding means freeing a tourist bus for this trip to the bay, so we can pretend to spy our loved ones through the glassiness of waves or in sun-speckled cloud shapes.

I could die here, too, and be content.

"What is that, out there?" She's standing and flapping her hands, and for a moment I see a head shape bobbing in the waves. She's standing in the water, I on the boulder. The tide is low, and a round, black, head-sized rock has just risen from the waves. She returns, her sari end dripping and ruined, and her face is a twisted remnant of hope, the way mine was a hundred hours ago, still laughing but inwardly knowing that nothing but the ultimate tragedy could bring two women together at six o'clock on a Sunday morning. I watch her face sag into blankness.

"That water felt warm, Shaila," she says at length.

"You can't," I say. "We have to wait for our turn to come."

I haven't eaten in four days, haven't brushed my teeth.

"I know," she says. "I tell myself I have no right to grieve. They are in a better place than we are. My swami says depression is a sign of our selfishness."

Maybe I'm selfish. Selfishly I break away from Kusum and run, sandals slapping against stones, to the water's edge. What if my boys aren't lying pinned under the debris? What if they aren't stuck a mile below that innocent blue chop? What if, given the strong currents. . . .

Now I've ruined my sari, one of my best. Kusum has joined me, knee deep in water that feels to me like a swimming pool. I could settle in the water, and my husband would take my hand and the boys would slap water in my face just to see me scream.

"Do you remember what good swimmers my boys were, Kusum?"

"I saw the medals," she says.

One of the widowers, Dr. Ranganathan from Montreal, walks out to us, carrying his shoes in one hand. He's an electrical engineer. Someone at the hotel mentioned his work is famous around the world, something about the place where physics and electricity come together. He has lost a huge family, something indescribable. "With some good luck," Dr. Ranganathan suggests to me, "a good swimmer could make it safely to some island. It is quite possible that there may be many, many microscopic islets scattered around."

"You're not just saying that?" I tell Dr. Ranganathan about Vinod, my elder son. Last year he took diving as well.

"It's a parent's duty to hope," he says. "It is foolish to rule out possibilities that have not been tested. I myself have not surrendered hope."

Kusum is sobbing once again. "Dear lady," he says, laying his free hand on her arm, and she calms down.

"Vinod is how old?" he asks me. He's very careful, as we all are. *Is*, not was.

"Fourteen. Yesterday he was fourteen. His father and uncle were going to   55
take him down to the Taj and give him a big birthday party. I couldn't go with
them because I couldn't get two weeks off from my stupid job in June." I process
bills for a travel agent. June is a big travel month.

Dr. Ranganathan whips the pockets of his suit jacket inside out. Squashed
roses, in darkening shades of pink, float on the water. He tore the roses off creep-
ers in somebody's garden. He didn't ask anyone if he could pluck the roses, but
now there's been an article about it in the local papers. When you see an Indian
person, it says, please give them flowers.

"A strong youth of fourteen," he says, "can very likely pull to safety a younger
one."

My sons, though four years apart, were very close. Vinod wouldn't let Mithun
drown. *Electrical engineering,* I think, foolishly perhaps: this man knows important secrets of the universe, things closed to me. Relief spins me lightheaded. No
wonder my boys' photographs haven't turned up in the gallery of photos of the
recovered dead. "Such pretty roses," I say.

"My wife loved pink roses. Every Friday I had to bring a bunch home. I used
to say, Why? After twenty-odd years of marriage you're still needing proof positive
of my love?" He has identified his wife and three of his children. Then others
from Montreal, the lucky ones, intact families with no survivors. He chuckles as
he wades back to shore. Then he swings around to ask me a question. "Mrs.
Bhave, you are wanting to throw in some roses for your loved ones? I have two big
ones left."

But I have other things to float: Vinod's pocket calculator; a half-painted   60
model B-52 for my Mithun. They'd want them on their island. And for my husband? For him I let fall into the calm, glassy waters a poem I wrote in the hospital
yesterday. Finally he'll know my feelings for him.

"Don't tumble, the rocks are slippery," Dr. Ranganathan cautions. He holds
out a hand for me to grab.

Then it's time to get back on the bus, time to rush back to our waiting posts
on hospital benches.

Kusum is one of the lucky ones. The lucky ones flew here, identified in multi-
plicate their loved ones, then will fly to India with the bodies for proper ceremonies.
Satish is one of the few males who surfaced. The photos of faces we saw on the walls
in an office at Heathrow and here in the hospital are mostly of women. Women
have more body fat, a nun said to me matter-of-factly. They float better.

Today I was stopped by a young sailor on the street. He had loaded bodies,
he'd gone into the water when—he checks my face for signs of strength—when
the sharks were first spotted. I don't blush, and he breaks down. "It's all right," I
say. "Thank you." I heard about the sharks from Dr. Ranganathan. In his orderly
mind, science brings understanding, it holds no terror. It is the shark's duty. For
every deer there is a hunter, for every fish a fisherman.

The Irish are not shy; they rush to me and give me hugs and some are crying.   65
I cannot imagine reactions like that on the streets of Toronto. Just strangers, and I
am touched. Some carry flowers with them and give them to any Indian they see.

After lunch, a policeman I have gotten to know quite well catches hold of me. He says he thinks he has a match for Vinod. I explain what a good swimmer Vinod is.

"You want me with you when you look at photos?" Dr. Ranganathan walks ahead of me into the picture gallery. In these matters, he is a scientist, and I am grateful. It is a new perspective. "They have performed miracles," he says. "We are indebted to them."

The first day or two the policemen showed us relatives only one picture at a time; now they're in a hurry, they're eager to lay out the possibles, and even the probables.

The face on the photo is of a boy much like Vinod; the same intelligent eyes, the same thick brows dipping into a V. But this boy's features, even his cheeks, are puffier, wider, mushier.

"No." My gaze is pulled by other pictures. There are five other boys who look   70
like Vinod.

The nun assigned to console me rubs the first picture with a fingertip. "When they've been in the water for a while, love, they look a little heavier." The bones under the skin are broken, they said on the first day—try to adjust your memories. It's important.

"It's not him. I'm his mother. I'd know."

"I know this one!" Dr. Ranganathan cries out, and suddenly from the back of the gallery. "And this one!" I think he senses that I don't want to find my boys. "They are the Kutty brothers. They were also from Montreal." I don't mean to be crying. On the contrary, I am ecstatic. My suitcase in the hotel is packed heavy with dry clothes for my boys.

The policeman starts to cry. "I am so sorry. I am so sorry, ma'am. I really thought we had a match."

With the nun ahead of us and the policeman behind, we, the unlucky ones   75
without our children's bodies, file out of the makeshift gallery.

From Ireland most of us go on to India. Kusum and I take the same direct flight to Bombay, so I can help her clear customs quickly. But we have to argue with a man in uniform. He has large boils on his face. The boils swell and glow with sweat as we argue with him. He wants Kusum to wait in line and he refuses to take authority because his boss is on a tea break. But Kusum won't let her coffins out of sight, and I shan't desert her though I know that my parents, elderly and diabetic, must be waiting in a stuffy car in a scorching lot.

"You bastard!" I scream at the man with the popping boils. Other passengers press closer. "You think we're smuggling contraband in those coffins!"

Once upon a time we were well-brought-up women; we were dutiful wives who kept our heads veiled, our voices shy and sweet.

In India, I become, once again, an only child of rich, ailing parents. Old friends of the family come to pay their respects. Some are Sikh, and inwardly, involuntarily, I cringe. My parents are progressive people; they do not blame communities for a few individuals.

In Canada it is a different story now.   80

"Stay longer," my mother pleads. "Canada is a cold place. Why would you want to be by yourself?" I stay.

Three months pass. Then another.

"Vikram wouldn't have wanted you to give up things!" they protest. They call my husband by the name he was born with. In Toronto he'd changed to Vik so the men he worked with at his office would find his name as easy as Rod or Chris. "You know, the dead aren't cut off from us!"

My grandmother, the spoiled daughter of a rich zamindar,° shaved her head with rusty razor blades when she was widowed at sixteen. My grandfather died of childhood diabetes when he was nineteen, and she saw herself as the harbinger of bad luck. My mother grew up without parents, raised indifferently by an uncle, while her true mother slept in a hut behind the main estate house and took her food with the servants. She grew up a rationalist. My parents abhor mindless mortification.

The zamindar's daughter kept stubborn faith in Vedic rituals; my parents   85
rebelled. I am trapped between two modes of knowledge. At thirty-six, I am too old to start over and too young to give up. Like my husband's spirit, I flutter between worlds.

Courting aphasia, we travel. We travel with our phalanx of servants and poor relatives. To hill stations and to beach resorts. We play contract bridge in dusty gymkhana clubs. We ride stubby ponies up crumbly mountain trails. At tea dances, we let ourselves be twirled twice round the ballroom. We hit the holy spots we hadn't made time for before. In Varanasi, Kalighat, Rishikesh, Hardwar, astrologers and palmists seek me out and for a fee offer me cosmic consolations.

Already the widowers among us are being shown new bride candidates. They cannot resist the call of custom, the authority of their parents and older brothers. They must marry; it is the duty of a man to look after a wife. The new wives will be young widows with children, destitute but of good family. They will make loving wives, but the men will shun them. I've had calls from the men over crackling Indian telephone lines. "Save me," they say, these substantial, educated, successful men of forty. "My parents are arranging a marriage for me." In a month they will have buried one family and returned to Canada with a new bride and partial family.

I am comparatively lucky. No one here thinks of arranging a husband for an unlucky widow.

Then, on the third day of the sixth month into this odyssey, in an abandoned temple in a tiny Himalayan village, as I make my offering of flowers and sweetmeats to the god of a tribe of animists, my husband descends to me. He is squatting next to a scrawny sadhu° in moth-eaten robes. Vikram wears the vanilla suit he wore the last time I hugged him. The sadhu tosses petals on a butter-fed flame, reciting Sanskrit mantras, and sweeps his face of flies. My husband takes my hands in his.

You're beautiful, he starts. Then, *What are you doing here?*   90

zamindar: Feudal landlord in British India.   sadhu: Ascetic or holy man.

Shall I stay? I ask. He only smiles, but already the image is fading. *You must finish alone what we started together.* No seaweed wreathes his mouth. He speaks too fast, just as he used to when we were an envied family in our pink split-level. He is gone.

In the windowless altar room, smoky with joss sticks and clarified butter lamps, a sweaty hand gropes for my blouse. I do not shriek. The sadhu arranges his robe. The lamps hiss and sputter out.

When we come out of the temple, my mother says, "Did you feel something weird in there?"

My mother has no patience with ghosts, prophetic dreams, holy men, and cults.

"No," I lie. "Nothing."   95

But she knows that she's lost me. She knows that in days I shall be leaving.

Kusum's put up her house for sale. She wants to live in an ashram in Hardwar. Moving to Hardwar was her swami's idea. Her swami runs two ashrams, the one in Hardwar and another here in Toronto.

"Don't run away," I tell her.

"I'm not running away," she says. "I'm pursuing inner peace. You think you or that Ranganathan fellow are better off?"

Pam's left for California. She wants to do some modeling, she says. She says   100
when she comes into her share of the insurance money she'll open a yoga-cum-aerobics studio in Hollywood. She sends me postcards so naughty I daren't leave them on the coffee table. Her mother has withdrawn from her and the world.

The rest of us don't lose touch, that's the point. Talk is all we have, says Dr. Ranganathan, who has also resisted his relatives and returned to Montreal and to his job, alone. He says, Whom better to talk with than other relatives? We've been melted down and recast as a new tribe.

He calls me twice a week from Montreal. Every Wednesday night and every Saturday afternoon. He is changing jobs, going to Ottawa. But Ottawa is over a hundred miles away, and he is forced to drive two hundred and twenty miles a day from his home in Montreal. He can't bring himself to sell his house. The house is a temple, he says; the king-sized bed in the master bedroom is a shrine. He sleeps on a folding cot. A devotee.

There are still some hysterical relatives. Judith Templeton's list of those needing help and those who've "accepted" is in nearly perfect balance. Acceptance means you speak of your family in the past tense and you make active plans for moving ahead with your life. There are courses at Seneca and Ryerson we could be taking. Her gleaming leather briefcase is full of college catalogues and lists of cultural societies that need our help. She has done impressive work, I tell her.

"In the textbooks on grief management," she replies — I am her confidante, I realize, one of the few whose grief has not sprung bizarre obsessions — "there are stages to pass through: rejection, depression, acceptance, reconstruction." She has compiled a chart and finds that six months after the tragedy, none of us still rejects reality, but only a handful are reconstructing. "Depressed acceptance" is the plateau we've reached. Remarriage is a major step in reconstruction (though she's a little surprised, even shocked, over *how* quickly some of the men have taken on new families). Selling one's house and changing jobs and cities is healthy.

How to tell Judith Templeton that my family surrounds me, and that like   105
creatures in epics, they've changed shapes? She sees me as calm and accepting but worries that I have no job, no career. My closest friends are worse off than I. I cannot tell her my days, even my nights, are thrilling.

She asks me to help with families she can't reach at all. An elderly couple in Agincourt whose sons were killed just weeks after they had brought their parents over from a village in Punjab. From their names, I know they are Sikh. Judith Templeton and a translator have visited them twice with offers of money for airfare to Ireland, with bank forms, power-of-attorney forms, but they have refused to sign, or to leave their tiny apartment. Their sons' money is frozen in the bank. Their sons' investment apartments have been trashed by tenants, the furnishings sold off. The parents fear that anything they sign or any money they receive will end the company's or the country's obligations to them. They fear they are selling their sons for two airline tickets to a place they've never seen.

The high-rise apartment is a tower of Indians and West Indians, with a sprinkling of Orientals. The nearest bus-stop kiosk is lined with women in saris. Boys practice cricket in the parking lot. Inside the building, even I wince a bit from the ferocity of onion fumes, the distinctive and immediate Indianness of frying ghee, but Judith Templeton maintains a steady flow of information. These poor old people are in imminent danger of losing their place and all their services.

I say to her, "They are Sikh. They will not open up to a Hindu woman." And what I want to add is, as much as I try not to, I stiffen now at the sight of beards and turbans. I remember a time when we all trusted each other in this new country, it was only the new country we worried about.

The two rooms are dark and stuffy. The lights are off, and an oil lamp sputters on the coffee table. The bent old lady has let us in, and her husband is wrapping a white turban over his oiled, hip-length hair. She immediately goes to the kitchen, and I hear the most familiar sound of an Indian home, tap water hitting and filling a teapot.

They have not paid their utility bills, out of fear and inability to write a   110
check. The telephone is gone, electricity and gas and water are soon to follow. They have told Judith their sons will provide. They are good boys, and they have always earned and looked after their parents.

We converse a bit in Hindi. They do not ask about the crash and I wonder if I should bring it up. If they think I am here merely as a translator, then they may feel insulted. There are thousands of Punjabi speakers, Sikhs, in Toronto to do a better job. And so I say to the old lady, "I too have lost my sons, and my husband, in the crash."

Her eyes immediately fill with tears. The man mutters a few words which sound like a blessing. "God provides and God takes away," he says.

I want to say, But only men destroy and give back nothing. "My boys and my husband are not coming back," I say. "We have to understand that."

Now the old woman responds. "But who is to say? Man alone does not decide these things." To this her husband adds his agreement.

Judith asks about the bank papers, the release forms. With a stroke of the   115
pen, they will have a provincial trustee to pay their bills, invest their money, send them a monthly pension.

"Do you know this woman?" I ask them.

The man raises his hand from the table, turns it over, and seems to regard each finger separately before he answers. "This young lady is always coming here, we make tea for her, and she leaves papers for us to sign." His eyes scan a pile of papers in the corner of the room. "Soon we will be out of tea, then will she go away?"

The old lady adds, "I have asked my neighbors and no one else gets *angrezi*° visitors. What have we done?"

"It's her job," I try to explain. "The government is worried. Soon you will have no place to stay, no lights, no gas, no water."

"Government will get its money. Tell her not to worry, we are honorable   120
people."

I try to explain the government wishes to give money, not take. He raises his hand. "Let them take," he says. "We are accustomed to that. That is no problem."

"We are strong people," says the wife. "Tell her that."

"Who needs all this machinery?" demands the husband. "It is unhealthy, the bright lights, the cold air on a hot day, the cold food, the four gas rings. God will provide, not government."

"When our boys return," the mother says.

Her husband sucks his teeth. "Enough talk," he says.   125

Judith breaks in. "Have you convinced them?" The snaps on her cordovan briefcase go off like firecrackers in that quiet apartment. She lays the sheaf of legal papers on the coffee table. "If they can't write their names, an X will do—I've told them that."

Now the old lady has shuffled to the kitchen and soon emerges with a pot of tea and two cups. "I think my bladder will go first on a job like this," Judith says to me, smiling. "If only there was some way of reaching them. Please thank her for the tea. Tell her she's very kind."

I nod in Judith's direction and tell them in Hindi, "She thanks you for the tea. She thinks you are being very hospitable but she doesn't have the slightest idea what it means."

I want to say, Humor her. I want to say, My boys and my husband are with me too, more than ever. I look in the old man's eyes and I can read his stubborn, peasant's message: *I have protected this woman as best I can. She is the only person I have left. Give to me or take from me what you will, but I will not sign for it. I will not pretend that I accept.*

In the car, Judith says, "You see what I'm up against? I'm sure they're lovely   130
people, but their stubbornness and ignorance are driving me crazy. They think signing a paper is signing their sons' death warrants, don't they?"

angrezi: English or Anglo.

I am looking out the window. I want to say, *In our culture, it is a parent's duty to hope.*

"Now Shaila, this next woman is a real mess. She cries day and night, and she refuses all medical help. We may have to —"

"Let me out at the subway," I say.

"I beg your pardon?" I can feel those blue eyes staring at me.

It would not be like her to disobey. She merely disapproves, and slows at   135
a corner to let me out. Her voice is plaintive. "Is there anything I said? Anything I did?"

I could answer her suddenly in a dozen ways, but I choose not to. "Shaila? Let's talk about it," I hear, then slam the door.

A wife and mother begins her life in a new country, and that life is cut short. Yet her husband tells her: Complete what we have started. We, who stayed out of politics and came half way around the world to avoid religious and political feuding, have been the first in the New World to die from it. I no longer know what we started, nor how to complete it. I write letters to the editors of local papers and to members of Parliament. Now at least they admit it was a bomb. One MP answers back, with sympathy, but with a challenge. You want to make a difference? Work on a campaign. Work on mine. Politicize the Indian voter.

My husband's old lawyer helps me set up a trust. Vikram was a saver and a careful investor. He had saved the boys' boarding school and college fees. I sell the pink house at four times what we paid for it and take a small apartment downtown. I am looking for a charity to support.

We are deep in the Toronto winter, gray skies, icy pavements. I stay indoors, watching television. I have tried to assess my situation, how best to live my life, to complete what we began so many years ago. Kusum has written me from Hardwar that her life is now serene. She has seen Satish and has heard her daughter sing again. Kusum was on a pilgrimage, passing through a village, when she heard a young girl's voice, singing one of her daughter's favorite *bhajans*. She followed the music through the squalor of a Himalayan village, to a hut where a young girl, an exact replica of her daughter, was fanning coals under the kitchen fire. When she appeared, the girl cried out, "Ma!" and ran away. What did I think of that?

I think I can only envy her.   140

Pam didn't make it to California, but writes me from Vancouver. She works in a department store, giving makeup hints to Indian and Oriental girls. Dr. Ranganathan has given up his commute, given up his house and job, and accepted an academic position in Texas, where no one knows his story and he has vowed not to tell it. He calls me now once a week.

I wait, I listen and I pray, but Vikram has not returned to me. The voices and the shapes and the nights filled with visions ended abruptly several weeks ago.

I take it as a sign.

One rare, beautiful, sunny day last week, returning from a small errand on Yonge Street, I was walking through the park from the subway to my apartment. I

live equidistant from the Ontario Houses of Parliament and the University of
Toronto. The day was not cold, but something in the bare trees caught my attention. I looked up from the gravel, into the branches and the clear blue sky
beyond. I thought I heard the rustling of larger forms, and I waited a moment for
voices. Nothing.

"What?" I asked.   145

Then as I stood in the path looking north to Queen's Park and west to the
university, I heard the voices of my family one last time. *Your time has come,* they
said. *Go, be brave.*

I do not know where this voyage I have begun will end. I do not know which
direction I will take. I dropped the package on a park bench and started walking.

[1988]

FOR THINKING AND READING

1. In what sense does this story involve culture? Define the term.

2. In what ways does Shaila develop during the story? Does she go through
   the stages of grief that Judith Templeton mentions?

3. Consider the title. Can grief be managed? Define the term *manage*. What
   characters in the story, if any, attempt to manage grief? In what ways?

4. Evaluate Judith Templeton's words and actions. Does she deserve any
   sympathy?

5. Identify the role of gender in the story. If Shaila had been male, what
   other elements of the story, if any, might have been different?

TIM O'BRIEN
The Things They Carried

*A native of Minnesota, Tim O'Brien (b. 1946) was drafted after he graduated from
Macalester College. Subsequently, he served in the Vietnam War, during which he
received a Purple Heart. In one way or another, practically all of his fiction deals
with the war, although he has been repeatedly ambiguous about how and when his
work incorporates his own Vietnam experiences. O'Brien's novels include* If I Die
in a Combat Zone *(1973),* Going After Cacciato *(which won the National
Book Award in 1978),* In the Lake of the Woods *(a 1994 book that touches on the
massacre at My Lai),* Tomcat in Love *(1998), and* July, July *(2002). Originally
published in* Esquire *magazine, the following story was reprinted in* The Best
American Short Stories 1987. *It then appeared along with related stories by
O'Brien in a 1990 book also entitled* The Things They Carried.

First Lieutenant Jimmy Cross carried letters from a girl named Martha, a
junior at Mount Sebastian College in New Jersey. They were not love letters, but
Lieutenant Cross was hoping, so he kept them folded in plastic at the bottom of

his rucksack. In the late afternoon, after a day's march, he would dig his foxhole, wash his hands under a canteen, unwrap the letters, hold them with the tips of his fingers, and spend the last hour of light pretending. He would imagine romantic camping trips into the White Mountains in New Hampshire. He would sometimes taste the envelope flaps, knowing her tongue had been there. More than anything, he wanted Martha to love him as he loved her, but the letters were mostly chatty, elusive on the matter of love. She was a virgin, he was almost sure. She was an English major at Mount Sebastian, and she wrote beautifully about her professors and roommates and midterm exams, about her respect for Chaucer and her great affection for Virginia Woolf. She often quoted lines of poetry; she never mentioned the war, except to say, Jimmy, take care of yourself. The letters weighed ten ounces. They were signed "Love, Martha," but Lieutenant Cross understood that "Love" was only a way of signing and did not mean what he sometimes pretended it meant. At dusk, he would carefully return the letters to his rucksack. Slowly, a bit distracted, he would get up and move among his men, checking the perimeter, then at full dark he would return to his hole and watch the night and wonder if Martha was a virgin.

The things they carried were largely determined by necessity. Among the necessities or near necessities were P-38 can openers, pocket knives, heat tabs, wrist watches, dog tags, mosquito repellant, chewing gum, candy, cigarettes, salt tablets, packets of Kool-Aid, lighters, matches, sewing kits, Military Payment Certificates, C rations, and two or three canteens of water. Together, these items weighed between fifteen and twenty pounds, depending upon a man's habits or rate of metabolism. Henry Dobbins, who was a big man, carried extra rations; he was especially fond of canned peaches in heavy syrup over pound cake. Dave Jensen, who practiced field hygiene, carried a toothbrush, dental floss, and several hotel-size bars of soap he'd stolen on R&R in Sydney, Australia. Ted Lavender, who was scared, carried tranquilizers until he was shot in the head outside the village of Than Khe in mid-April. By necessity, and because it was SOP,° they all carried steel helmets that weighed five pounds including the liner and camouflage cover. They carried the standard fatigue jackets and trousers. Very few carried underwear. On their feet they carried jungle boots — 2.1 pounds — and Dave Jensen carried three pairs of socks and a can of Dr. Scholl's foot powder as a precaution against trench foot. Until he was shot, Ted Lavender carried six or seven ounces of premium dope, which for him was a necessity. Mitchell Sanders, the RTO,° carried condoms. Norman Bowker carried a diary. Rat Kiley carried comic books. Kiowa, a devout Baptist, carried an illustrated New Testament that had been presented to him by his father, who taught Sunday school in Oklahoma City, Oklahoma. As a hedge against bad times, however, Kiowa also carried his grandmother's distrust of the white man, his grandfather's old hunting hatchet. Necessity dictated. Because the land was mined and booby-trapped, it was SOP for each man to carry a steel-centered, nylon-covered flak jacket, which weighed 6.7 pounds, but which on hot days seemed much heavier. Because you could die so quickly, each man carried at least one large compress bandage, usually in the helmet band for easy access. Because the nights were cold, and because the

SOP: Standard operating procedure. **RTO:** Radiotelephone operator.

monsoons were wet, each carried a green plastic poncho that could be used as a raincoat or ground sheet or makeshift tent. With its quilted liner, the poncho weighed almost two pounds, but it was worth every ounce. In April, for instance, when Ted Lavender was shot, they used his poncho to wrap him up, then to carry him across the paddy, then to lift him into the chopper that took him away.

They were called legs or grunts.

To carry something was to "hump" it, as when Lieutenant Jimmy Cross humped his love for Martha up the hills and through the swamps. In its intransitive form, "to hump" meant "to walk," or "to march," but it implied burdens far beyond the intransitive.

Almost everyone humped photographs. In his wallet, Lieutenant Cross carried two photographs of Martha. The first was a Kodachrome snapshot signed "Love," though he knew better. She stood against a brick wall. Her eyes were gray and neutral, her lips slightly open as she stared straight-on at the camera. At night, sometimes, Lieutenant Cross wondered who had taken the picture, because he knew she had boyfriends, because he loved her so much, and because he could see the shadow of the picture taker spreading out against the brick wall. The second photograph had been clipped from the 1968 Mount Sebastian yearbook. It was an action shot — women's volleyball — and Martha was bent horizontal to the floor, reaching, the palms of her hands in sharp focus, the tongue taut, the expression frank and competitive. There was no visible sweat. She wore white gym shorts. Her legs, he thought, were almost certainly the legs of a virgin, dry and without hair, the left knee cocked and carrying her entire weight, which was just over one hundred pounds. Lieutenant Cross remembered touching that left knee. A dark theater, he remembered, and the movie was *Bonnie and Clyde,* and Martha wore a tweed skirt, and during the final scene, when he touched her knee, she turned and looked at him in a sad, sober way that made him pull his hand back, but he would always remember the feel of the tweed skirt and the knee beneath it and the sound of the gunfire that killed Bonnie and Clyde, how embarrassing it was, how slow and oppressive. He remembered kissing her good night at the dorm door. Right then, he thought, he should've done something brave. He should've carried her up the stairs to her room and tied her to the bed and touched that left knee all night long. He should've risked it. Whenever he looked at the photographs, he thought of new things he should've done.

What they carried was partly a function of rank, partly of field specialty.

As a first lieutenant and platoon leader, Jimmy Cross carried a compass, maps, code books, binoculars, and a .45-caliber pistol that weighed 2.9 pounds fully loaded. He carried a strobe light and the responsibility for the lives of his men.

As an RTO, Mitchell Sanders carried the PRC-25 radio, a killer, twenty-six pounds with its battery.

As a medic, Rat Kiley carried a canvas satchel filled with morphine and plasma and malaria tablets and surgical tape and comic books and all the things a medic must carry, including M&M's for especially bad wounds, for a total weight of nearly twenty pounds.

As a big man, therefore a machine gunner, Henry Dobbins carried the M-60,   10
which weighed twenty-three pounds unloaded, but which was almost always
loaded. In addition, Dobbins carried between ten and fifteen pounds of ammunition draped in belts across his chest and shoulders.

As PFCs or Spec 4s, most of them were common grunts and carried the standard M-16 gas-operated assault rifle. The weapon weighed 7.5 pounds unloaded,
8.2 pounds with its full twenty-round magazine. Depending on numerous factors, such as topography and psychology, the riflemen carried anywhere from
twelve to twenty magazines, usually in cloth bandoliers, adding on another 8.4
pounds at minimum, fourteen pounds at maximum. When it was available, they
also carried M-16 maintenance gear—rods and steel brushes and swabs and
tubes of LSA on—all of which weighed about a pound. Among the grunts, some
carried the M-79 grenade launcher, 5.9 pounds unloaded, a reasonably light
weapon except for the ammunition, which was heavy. A single round weighed
ten ounces. The typical load was twenty-five rounds. But Ted Lavender, who was
scared, carried thirty-four rounds when he was shot and killed outside Than Khe,
and he went down under an exceptional burden, more than twenty pounds of
ammunition, plus the flak jacket and helmet and rations and water and toilet
paper and tranquilizers and all the rest, plus the unweighed fear. He was dead
weight. There was no twitching or flopping. Kiowa, who saw it happen, said it was
like watching a rock fall, or a big sandbag or something—just boom, then
down—not like the movies where the dead guy rolls around and does fancy spins
and goes ass over teakettle—not like that, Kiowa said, the poor bastard just flat-
fuck fell. Boom. Down. Nothing else. It was a bright morning in mid-April. Lieutenant Cross felt the pain. He blamed himself. They stripped off Lavender's
canteens and ammo, all the heavy things, and Rat Kiley said the obvious, the
guy's dead, and Mitchell Sanders used his radio to report one U.S. KIA° and to
request a chopper. Then they wrapped Lavender in his poncho. They carried
him out to a dry paddy, established security, and sat smoking the dead man's dope
until the chopper came. Lieutenant Cross kept to himself. He pictured Martha's
smooth young face, thinking he loved her more than anything, more than his
men, and now Ted Lavender was dead because he loved her so much and could
not stop thinking about her. When the dust-off arrived, they carried Lavender
aboard. Afterward they burned Than Khe. They marched until dusk, then dug
their holes, and that night Kiowa kept explaining how you had to be there, how
fast it was, how the poor guy just dropped like so much concrete. Boom-down, he
said. Like cement.

In addition to the three standard weapons—the M-60, M-16, and M-79—
they carried whatever presented itself, or whatever seemed appropriate as a
means of killing or staying alive. They carried catch-as-catch-can. At various
times, in various situations, they carried M-14s and CAR-15s and Swedish Ks
and grease guns and captured AK-47s and Chi-Coms and RPGs and Simonov
carbines and black-market Uzis and .38-caliber Smith & Wesson handguns and
66 mm LAWs and shotguns and silencers and blackjacks and bayonets and

KIA: Killed in action.

C-4 plastic explosives. Lee Strunk carried a slingshot; a weapon of last resort, he called it. Mitchell Sanders carried brass knuckles. Kiowa carried his grandfather's feathered hatchet. Every third or fourth man carried a Claymore antipersonnel mine—3.5 pounds with its firing device. They all carried fragmentation grenades—fourteen ounces each. They all carried at least one M-18 colored smoke grenade—twenty-four ounces. Some carried CS or tear-gas grenades. Some carried white-phosphorus grenades. They carried all they could bear, and then some, including a silent awe for the terrible power of the things they carried.

In the first week of April, before Lavender died, Lieutenant Jimmy Cross received a good-luck charm from Martha. It was a simple pebble, an ounce at most. Smooth to the touch, it was a milky-white color with flecks of orange and violet, oval-shaped, like a miniature egg. In the accompanying letter, Martha wrote that she had found the pebble on the Jersey shoreline, precisely where the land touched water at high tide, where things came together but also separated. It was this separate-but-together quality, she wrote, that had inspired her to pick up the pebble and to carry it in her breast pocket for several days, where it seemed weightless, and then to send it through the mail, by air, as a token of her truest feelings for him. Lieutenant Cross found this romantic. But he wondered what her truest feelings were, exactly, and what she meant by separate-but-together. He wondered how the tides and waves had come into play on that afternoon along the Jersey shoreline when Martha saw the pebble and bent down to rescue it from geology. He imagined bare feet. Martha was a poet, with the poet's sensibilities, and her feet would be brown and bare, the toenails unpainted, the eyes chilly and somber like the ocean in March, and though it was painful, he wondered who had been with her that afternoon. He imagined a pair of shadows moving along the strip of sand where things came together but also separated. It was phantom jealousy, he knew, but he couldn't help himself. He loved her so much. On the march, through the hot days of early April, he carried the pebble in his mouth, turning it with his tongue, tasting sea salts and moisture. His mind wandered. He had difficulty keeping his attention on the war. On occasion he would yell at his men to spread out the column, to keep their eyes open, but then he would slip away into daydreams, just pretending, walking barefoot along the Jersey shore, with Martha, carrying nothing. He would feel himself rising. Sun and waves and gentle winds, all love and lightness.

What they carried varied by mission.

When a mission took them to the mountains, they carried mosquito netting, machetes, canvas tarps, and extra bug juice.   15

If a mission seemed especially hazardous, or if it involved a place they knew to be bad, they carried everything they could. In certain heavily mined AOs,° where the land was dense with Toe Poppers and Bouncing Betties, they took turns humping a twenty-eight-pound mine detector. With its headphones and big sensing plate, the equipment was a stress on the lower back and shoulders, awk-

---

AOs: Areas of operations.

ward to handle, often useless because of the shrapnel in the earth, but they carried it anyway, partly for safety, partly for the illusion of safety.

On ambush, or other night missions, they carried peculiar little odds and ends. Kiowa always took along his New Testament and a pair of moccasins for silence. Dave Jensen carried night-sight vitamins high in carotin. Lee Strunk carried his slingshot; ammo, he claimed, would never be a problem. Rat Kiley carried brandy and M&M's. Until he was shot, Ted Lavender carried the starlight scope, which weighed 6.3 pounds with its aluminum carrying case. Henry Dobbins carried his girlfriend's pantyhose wrapped around his neck as a comforter. They all carried ghosts. When dark came, they would move out single file across the meadows and paddies to their ambush coordinates, where they would quietly set up the Claymores and lie down and spend the night waiting.

Other missions were more complicated and required special equipment. In mid-April, it was their mission to search out and destroy the elaborate tunnel complexes in the Than Khe area south of Chu Lai. To blow the tunnels, they carried one-pound blocks of pentrite high explosives, four blocks to a man, sixty-eight pounds in all. They carried wiring, detonators, and battery-powered clackers. Dave Jensen carried earplugs. Most often, before blowing the tunnels, they were ordered by higher command to search them, which was considered bad news, but by and large they just shrugged and carried out orders. Because he was a big man, Henry Dobbins was excused from tunnel duty. The others would draw numbers. Before Lavender died there were seventeen men in the platoon, and whoever drew the number seventeen would strip off his gear and crawl in head first with a flashlight and Lieutenant Cross's .45-caliber pistol. The rest of them would fan out as security. They would sit down or kneel, not facing the hole, listening to the ground beneath them, imagining cobwebs and ghosts, whatever was down there—the tunnel walls squeezing in—how the flashlight seemed impossibly heavy in the hand and how it was tunnel vision in the very strictest sense, compression in all ways, even time, and how you had to wiggle in—ass and elbows—a swallowed-up feeling—and how you found yourself worrying about odd things—will your flashlight go dead? Do rats carry rabies? If you screamed, how far would the sound carry? Would your buddies hear it? Would they have the courage to drag you out? In some respects, though not many, the waiting was worse than the tunnel itself. Imagination was a killer.

On April 16, when Lee Strunk drew the number seventeen, he laughed and muttered something and went down quickly. The morning was hot and very still. Not good, Kiowa said. He looked at the tunnel opening, then out across a dry paddy toward the village of Than Khe. Nothing moved. No clouds or birds or people. As they waited, the men smoked and drank Kool-Aid, not talking much, feeling sympathy for Lee Strunk but also feeling the luck of the draw. You win some, you lose some, said Mitchell Sanders, and sometimes you settle for a rain check. It was a tired line and no one laughed.

Henry Dobbins ate a tropical chocolate bar. Ted Lavender popped a tranquilizer and went off to pee.

After five minutes, Lieutenant Jimmy Cross moved to the tunnel, leaned down, and examined the darkness. Trouble, he thought—a cave-in maybe. And

20

then suddenly, without willing it, he was thinking about Martha. The stresses and fractures, the quick collapse, the two of them buried alive under all that weight. Dense, crushing love. Kneeling, watching the hole, he tried to concentrate on Lee Strunk and the war, all the dangers, but his love was too much for him, he felt paralyzed, he wanted to sleep inside her lungs and breathe her blood and be smothered. He wanted her to be a virgin and not a virgin, all at once. He wanted to know her. Intimate secrets — why poetry? Why so sad? Why the grayness in her eyes? Why so alone? Not lonely, just alone — riding her bike across campus or sitting off by herself in the cafeteria. Even dancing, she danced alone — and it was the aloneness that filled him with love. He remembered telling her that one evening. How she nodded and looked away. And how, later, when he kissed her, she received the kiss without returning it, her eyes wide open, not afraid, not a virgin's eyes, just flat and uninvolved.

Lieutenant Cross gazed at the tunnel. But he was not there. He was buried with Martha under the white sand at the Jersey shore. They were pressed together, and the pebble in his mouth was her tongue. He was smiling. Vaguely, he was aware of how quiet the day was, the sullen paddies, yet he could not bring himself to worry about matters of security. He was beyond that. He was just a kid at war, in love. He was twenty-two years old. He couldn't help it.

A few moments later Lee Strunk crawled out of the tunnel. He came up grinning, filthy but alive. Lieutenant Cross nodded and closed his eyes while the others clapped Strunk on the back and made jokes about rising from the dead.

Worms, Rat Kiley said. Right out of the grave. Fuckin' zombie.

The men laughed. They all felt great relief.   25

Spook City, said Mitchell Sanders.

Lee Strunk made a funny ghost sound, a kind of moaning, yet very happy, and right then, when Strunk made that high happy moaning sound, when he went *Ahhooooo*, right then Ted Lavender was shot in the head on his way back from peeing. He lay with his mouth open. The teeth were broken. There was a swollen black bruise under his left eye. The cheekbone was gone. Oh shit, Rat Kiley said, the guy's dead. The guy's dead, he kept saying, which seemed profound — the guy's dead. I mean really.

The things they carried were determined to some extent by superstition. Lieutenant Cross carried his good-luck pebble. Dave Jensen carried a rabbit's foot. Norman Bowker, otherwise a very gentle person, carried a thumb that had been presented to him as a gift by Mitchell Sanders. The thumb was dark brown, rubbery to the touch, and weighed four ounces at most. It had been cut from a VC corpse, a boy of fifteen or sixteen. They'd found him at the bottom of an irrigation ditch, badly burned, flies in his mouth and eyes. The boy wore black shorts and sandals. At the time of his death he had been carrying a pouch of rice, a rifle, and three magazines of ammunition.

You want my opinion, Mitchell Sanders said, there's a definite moral here.

He put his hand on the dead boy's wrist. He was quiet for a time, as if counting a pulse, then he patted the stomach, almost affectionately, and used Kiowa's hunting hatchet to remove the thumb.   30

Henry Dobbins asked what the moral was.

Moral?

You know. *Moral.*

Sanders wrapped the thumb in toilet paper and handed it across to Norman Bowker. There was no blood. Smiling, he kicked the boy's head, watched the flies scatter, and said, It's like with that old TV show—Paladin. Have gun, will travel.

Henry Dobbins thought about it.   35

Yeah, well, he finally said. I don't see no moral.

There it *is*, man.

Fuck off.

They carried USO stationery and pencils and pens. They carried Sterno, safety pins, trip flares, signal flares, spools of wire, razor blades, chewing tobacco, liberated joss sticks and statuettes of the smiling Buddha, candles, grease pencils, *The Stars and Stripes*, fingernail clippers, Psy Ops° leaflets, bush hats, bolos, and much more. Twice a week, when the resupply choppers came in, they carried hot chow in green Mermite cans and large canvas bags filled with iced beer and soda pop. They carried plastic water containers, each with a two-gallon capacity. Mitchell Sanders carried a set of starched tiger fatigues for special occasions. Henry Dobbins carried Black Flag insecticide. Dave Jensen carried empty sandbags that could be filled at night for added protection. Lee Strunk carried tanning lotion. Some things they carried in common. Taking turns, they carried the big PRC-77 scrambler radio, which weighed thirty pounds with its battery. They shared the weight of memory. They took up what others could no longer bear. Often, they carried each other, the wounded or weak. They carried infections. They carried chess sets, basketballs, Vietnamese-English dictionaries, insignia of rank, Bronze Stars and Purple Hearts, plastic cards imprinted with the Code of Conduct. They carried diseases, among them malaria and dysentery. They carried lice and ringworm and leeches and paddy algae and various rots and molds. They carried the land itself—Vietnam, the place, the soil—a powdery orange-red dust that covered their boots and fatigues and faces. They carried the sky. The whole atmosphere, they carried it, the humidity, the monsoons, the stink of fungus and decay, all of it, they carried gravity. They moved like mules. By daylight they took sniper fire, at night they were mortared, but it was not battle, it was just the endless march, village to village, without purpose, nothing won or lost. They marched for the sake of the march. They plodded along slowly, dumbly, leaning forward against the heat, unthinking, all blood and bone, simple grunts, soldiering with their legs, toiling up the hills and down into the paddies and across the rivers and up again and down, just humping, one step and then the next and then another, but no volition, no will, because it was automatic, it was anatomy, and the war was entirely a matter of posture and carriage, the hump was everything, a kind of inertia, a kind of emptiness, a dullness of desire and intellect and conscience and hope and human sensibility. Their principles were in their feet. Their calculations were biological. They had no sense of strategy or mission.

Psy Ops: Psychological operations.

They searched the villages without knowing what to look for, not caring, kicking over jars of rice, frisking children and old men, blowing tunnels, sometimes setting fires and sometimes not, then forming up and moving on to the next village, then other villages, where it would always be the same. They carried their own lives. The pressures were enormous. In the heat of early afternoon, they would remove their helmets and flak jackets, walking bare, which was dangerous but which helped ease the strain. They would often discard things along the route of march. Purely for comfort, they would throw away rations, blow their Claymores and grenades, no matter, because by nightfall the resupply choppers would arrive with more of the same, then a day or two later still more, fresh watermelons and crates of ammunition and sunglasses and woolen sweaters—the resources were stunning—sparklers for the Fourth of July, colored eggs for Easter. It was the great American war chest—the fruits of science, the smokestacks, the canneries, the arsenals at Hartford, the Minnesota forests, the machine shops, the vast fields of corn and wheat—they carried like freight trains; they carried it on their backs and shoulders—and for all the ambiguities of Vietnam, all the mysteries and unknowns, there was at least the single abiding certainty that they would never be at a loss for things to carry.

After the chopper took Lavender away, Lieutenant Jimmy Cross led his men   40
into the village of Than Khe. They burned everything. They shot chickens and dogs, they trashed the village well, they called in artillery and watched the wreckage, then they marched for several hours through the hot afternoon, and then at dusk, while Kiowa explained how Lavender died, Lieutenant Cross found himself trembling.

He tried not to cry. With his entrenching tool, which weighed five pounds, he began digging a hole in the earth.

He felt shame. He hated himself. He had loved Martha more than his men, and as a consequence Lavender was now dead, and this was something he would have to carry like a stone in his stomach for the rest of the war.

All he could do was dig. He used his entrenching tool like an ax, slashing, feeling both love and hate, and then later, when it was full dark, he sat at the bottom of his foxhole and wept. It went on for a long while. In part, he was grieving for Ted Lavender, but mostly it was for Martha, and for himself, because she belonged to another world, which was not quite real, and because she was a junior at Mount Sebastian College in New Jersey, a poet and a virgin and uninvolved, and because he realized she did not love him and never would.

Like cement, Kiowa whispered in the dark. I swear to God—boom-down. Not a word.

I've heard this, said Norman Bowker.   45

A pisser, you know? Still zipping himself up. Zapped while zipping.

All right, fine. That's enough.

Yeah, but you had to see it, the guy just—

I *heard*, man. Cement. So why not shut the fuck *up?*

Kiowa shook his head sadly and glanced over at the hole where Lieutenant   50
Jimmy Cross sat watching the night. The air was thick and wet. A warm, dense
fog had settled over the paddies and there was the stillness that precedes rain.

After a time Kiowa sighed.

One thing for sure, he said. The Lieutenant's in some deep hurt. I mean that
crying jag—the way he was carrying on—it wasn't fake or anything, it was real
heavy-duty hurt. The man cares.

Sure, Norman Bowker said.

Say what you want, the man does care.

We all got problems.   55

Not Lavender.

No, I guess not, Bowker said. Do me a favor, though.

Shut up?

That's a smart Indian. Shut up.

Shrugging, Kiowa pulled off his boots. He wanted to say more, just to lighten   60
up his sleep, but instead he opened his New Testament and arranged it beneath
his head as a pillow. The fog made things seem hollow and unattached. He tried
not to think about Ted Lavender, but then he was thinking how fast it was, no
drama, down and dead, and how it was hard to feel anything except surprise. It
seemed un-Christian. He wished he could find some great sadness, or even
anger, but the emotion wasn't there and he couldn't make it happen. Mostly he
felt pleased to be alive. He liked the smell of the New Testament under his
cheek, the leather and ink and paper and glue, whatever the chemicals were. He
liked hearing the sounds of night. Even his fatigue, it felt fine, the stiff muscles
and the prickly awareness of his own body, a floating feeling. He enjoyed not
being dead. Lying there, Kiowa admired Lieutenant Jimmy Cross's capacity for
grief. He wanted to share the man's pain, he wanted to care as Jimmy Cross
cared. And yet when he closed his eyes, all he could think was Boom-down, and
all he could feel was the pleasure of having his boots off and the fog curling in
around him and the damp soil and the Bible smells and the plush comfort of
night.

After a moment Norman Bowker sat up in the dark.

What the hell, he said. You want to talk, *talk*. Tell it to me.

Forget it.

No, man, go on. One thing I hate, it's a silent Indian.

For the most part they carried themselves with poise, a kind of dignity. Now   65
and then, however, there were times of panic, when they squealed or wanted to
squeal but couldn't, when they twitched and made moaning sounds and covered their heads and said Dear Jesus and flopped around on the earth and fired
their weapons blindly and cringed and sobbed and begged for the noise to stop
and went wild and made stupid promises to themselves and to God and to their
mothers and fathers, hoping not to die. In different ways, it happened to all of
them. Afterward, when the firing ended, they would blink and peek up. They
would touch their bodies, feeling shame, then quickly hiding it. They would

force themselves to stand. As if in slow motion, frame by frame, the world would take on the old logic — absolute silence, then the wind, then sunlight, then voices. It was the burden of being alive. Awkwardly, the men would reassemble themselves, first in private, then in groups, becoming soldiers again. They would repair the leaks in their eyes. They would check for casualties, call in dust-offs, light cigarettes, try to smile, clear their throats and spit and begin cleaning their weapons. After a time someone would shake his head and say, No lie, I almost shit my pants, and someone else would laugh, which meant it was bad, yes, but the guy had obviously not shit his pants, it wasn't that bad, and in any case nobody would ever do such a thing and then go ahead and talk about it. They would squint into the dense, oppressive sunlight. For a few moments, perhaps, they would fall silent, lighting a joint and tracking its passage from man to man, inhaling, holding in the humiliation. Scary stuff, one of them might say. But then someone else would grin or flick his eyebrows and say, Roger-dodger, almost cut me a new asshole, *almost.*

There were numerous such poses. Some carried themselves with a sort of wistful resignation, others with pride or stiff soldierly discipline or good humor or macho zeal. They were afraid of dying but they were even more afraid to show it.

They found jokes to tell.

They used a hard vocabulary to contain the terrible softness. *Greased,* they'd say. *Offed, lit up, zapped while zipping.* It wasn't cruelty, just stage presence. They were actors and the war came at them in 3-D. When someone died, it wasn't quite dying, because in a curious way it seemed scripted, and because they had their lines mostly memorized, irony mixed with tragedy, and because they called it by other names, as if to encyst and destroy the reality of death itself. They kicked corpses. They cut off thumbs. They talked grunt lingo. They told stories about Ted Lavender's supply of tranquilizers, how the poor guy didn't feel a thing, how incredibly tranquil he was.

There's a moral here, said Mitchell Sanders.

They were waiting for Lavender's chopper, smoking the dead man's dope. 70

The moral's pretty obvious, Sanders said, and winked. Stay away from drugs. No joke, they'll ruin your day every time.

Cute, said Henry Dobbins.

Mind-blower, get it? Talk about wiggy — nothing left, just blood and brains.

They made themselves laugh.

There it is, they'd say, over and over, as if the repetition itself were an act of 75 poise, a balance between crazy and almost crazy, knowing without going. There it is, which meant be cool, let it ride, because oh yeah, man, you can't change what can't be changed, there it is, there it is, there it absolutely and positively and fucking well *is.*

They were tough.

They carried all the emotional baggage of men who might die. Grief, terror, love, longing — these were intangibles, but the intangibles had their own mass and specific gravity, they had tangible weight. They carried shameful memories. They carried the common secret of cowardice barely restrained, the instinct to run or freeze or hide, and in many respects this was the heaviest burden of all, for it could never be put down, it required perfect balance and perfect posture. They carried their reputations. They carried the soldier's greatest fear, which was the fear of blushing. Men killed, and died, because they were embarrassed not to. It was what had brought them to the war in the first place, nothing positive, no dreams of glory or honor, just to avoid the blush of dishonor. They died so as not to die of embarrassment. They crawled into tunnels and walked point and advanced under fire. Each morning, despite the unknowns, they made their legs move. They endured. They kept humping. They did not submit to the obvious alternative, which was simply to close the eyes and fall. So easy, really. Go limp and tumble to the ground and let the muscles unwind and not speak and not budge until your buddies picked you up and lifted you into the chopper that would roar and dip its nose and carry you off to the world. A mere matter of falling, yet no one ever fell. It was not courage, exactly; the object was not valor. Rather, they were too frightened to be cowards.

By and large they carried these things inside, maintaining the masks of composure. They sneered at sick call. They spoke bitterly about guys who had found release by shooting off their own toes or fingers. Pussies, they'd say. Candyasses. It was fierce, mocking talk, with only a trace of envy or awe, but even so, the image played itself out behind their eyes.

They imagined the muzzle against flesh. They imagined the quick, sweet pain, then the evacuation to Japan, then a hospital with warm beds and cute geisha nurses.

They dreamed of freedom birds.

80

At night, on guard, staring into the dark, they were carried away by jumbo jets. They felt the rush of takeoff. *Gone!* they yelled. And then velocity, wings and engines, a smiling stewardess — but it was more than a plane, it was a real bird, a big sleek silver bird with feathers and talons and high screeching. They were flying. The weights fell off, there was nothing to bear. They laughed and held on tight, feeling the cold slap of wind and altitude, soaring, thinking *It's over, I'm gone!* — they were naked, they were light and free — it was all lightness, bright and fast and buoyant, light as light, a helium buzz in the brain, a giddy bubbling in the lungs as they were taken up over the clouds and the war, beyond duty, beyond gravity and mortification and global entanglements — *Sin loi!*° they yelled, *I'm sorry, motherfuckers, but I'm out of it, I'm goofed, I'm on a space cruise, I'm gone!* — and it was a restful, disencumbered sensation, just riding the light waves, sailing that big silver freedom bird over the mountains and oceans, over America, over the farms and great sleeping cities and cemeteries and highways and the golden arches of McDonald's. It was flight, a kind of fleeing, a kind of falling, falling higher and higher, spinning off the edge of the earth and beyond the sun and through the vast, silent vacuum where there were no burdens and where everything weighed exactly nothing. *Gone!* they screamed, *I'm sorry but I'm gone!* And so at night, not quite dreaming, they gave themselves over to lightness, they were carried, they were purely borne.

♦　♦　♦

Sin loi: "Sorry about that!"

On the morning after Ted Lavender died, First Lieutenant Jimmy Cross crouched at the bottom of his foxhole and burned Martha's letters. Then he burned the two photographs. There was a steady rain falling, which made it difficult, but he used heat tabs and Sterno to build a small fire, screening it with his body, holding the photographs over the tight blue flame with the tips of his fingers.

He realized it was only a gesture. Stupid, he thought. Sentimental, too, but mostly just stupid.

Lavender was dead. You couldn't burn the blame.

Besides, the letters were in his head. And even now, without photographs,   85
Lieutenant Cross could see Martha playing volleyball in her white gym shorts and yellow T-shirt. He could see her moving in the rain.

When the fire died out, Lieutenant Cross pulled his poncho over his shoulders and ate breakfast from a can.

There was no great mystery, he decided.

In those burned letters Martha had never mentioned the war, except to say, Jimmy, take care of yourself. She wasn't involved. She signed the letters "Love," but it wasn't love, and all the fine lines and technicalities did not matter.

The morning came up wet and blurry. Everything seemed part of everything else, the fog and Martha and the deepening rain.

It was a war, after all.   90

Half smiling, Lieutenant Jimmy Cross took out his maps. He shook his head hard, as if to clear it, then bent forward and began planning the day's march. In ten minutes, or maybe twenty, he would rouse the men and they would pack up and head west, where the maps showed the country to be green and inviting. They would do what they had always done. The rain might add some weight, but otherwise it would be one more day layered upon all the other days.

He was realistic about it. There was that new hardness in his stomach.

No more fantasies, he told himself.

Henceforth, when he thought about Martha, it would be only to think that she belonged elsewhere. He would shut down the daydreams. This was not Mount Sebastian, it was another world, where there were no pretty poems or midterm exams, a place where men died because of carelessness and gross stupidity. Kiowa was right. Boom-down, and you were dead, never partly dead.

Briefly, in the rain, Lieutenant Cross saw Martha's gray eyes gazing back   95
at him.

He understood.

It was very sad, he thought. The things men carried inside. The things men did or felt they had to do.

He almost nodded at her, but didn't.

Instead he went back to his maps. He was now determined to perform his duties firmly and without negligence. It wouldn't help Lavender, he knew that, but from this point on he would comport himself as a soldier. He would dispose of his good-luck pebble. Swallow it, maybe, or use Lee Strunk's slingshot, or just drop it along the trail. On the march he would impose strict field discipline. He would be careful to send out flank security, to prevent straggling or bunching up, to keep his troops moving at the proper pace and at the proper interval. He would insist on clean weapons. He would confiscate the remainder of Lavender's dope. Later in the day, perhaps, he would call the men together and speak to them plainly. He would accept the blame for what had happened to Ted Lavender. He would be a man about it. He would look them in the eyes, keeping his chin level, and he would issue the new SOPs in a calm, impersonal tone of voice, an officer's voice, leaving no room for argument or discussion. Commencing immediately, he'd tell them, they would no longer abandon equipment along the route of march. They would police up their acts. They would get their shit together, and keep it together, and maintain it neatly and in good working order.

He would not tolerate laxity. He would show strength, distancing himself.   100

Among the men there would be grumbling, of course, and maybe worse, because their days would seem longer and their loads heavier, but Lieutenant Cross reminded himself that his obligation was not to be loved but to lead. He would dispense with love; it was not now a factor. And if anyone quarreled or complained, he would simply tighten his lips and arrange his shoulders in the correct command posture. He might give a curt little nod. Or he might not. He might just shrug and say Carry on, then they would saddle up and form into a column and move out toward the villages of Than Khe.   [1986]

FOR THINKING AND WRITING

1. A significant pattern in this story is the repeated references to "the things they carried." How does this pattern affect you? What might O'Brien have hoped to accomplish with it? At what points in the story are there variations on this pattern—changes in the kinds of things that the narrator reports being carried?

2. Describe the structure of this story. Is there a central event? If so, what is it, and why do you consider it central?

3. Evaluate Lieutenant Cross's fascination with Martha, including his preoccupation with the issue of whether she is a virgin. How sympathetic are you to him? At the end of the story, Cross blames himself for Ted Lavender's death. Is this a fair self-evaluation, or is he too hard on himself? Identify some of the warrants or assumptions behind your answer.

4. Do the other members of the company seem mostly alike, or are there significant differences among them? Explain. What is your evaluation of the company as a whole? List some adjectives for it.

5. Does the war depicted in this story appear significantly different from other wars, such as World War II? If so, in what ways? Is this an antiwar story? Identify characteristics you associate with the genre.

FLANNERY O'CONNOR
A Good Man Is Hard to Find

Flannery O'Connor (1925–1964) spent most of her life in Millidgeville, Georgia, where she raised peacocks on a farm with her mother. She died of lupus at the age of thirty-nine, when she was at the peak of her creative powers. All of her fiction reflects her Roman Catholic faith and Southern heritage, as do her nonfiction writings, which were collected after her death in Mystery and Manners *(1969). Critics have often seen in her work Christian parables of grace and redemption in the face of random violence. Like other Southern writers such as William Faulkner and Carson McCullers, she uses grotesque characters to suggest our own morally flawed humanity. O'Connor's early stories won her a scholarship to the University of Iowa, where she received her M.F.A. She went on to produce two novels,* Wise Blood *(1952) and* The Violent Bear It Away *(1960), but she is known and admired mostly for her short fiction. The following story was first published in the volume* Modern Writing 1 *in 1953. O'Connor then included it in her 1955 collection entitled* A Good Man Is Hard to Find and Other Stories. *The book won her national acclaim, as did a later collection, the posthumously published* Everything That Rises Must Converge *(1965). These two volumes were combined in 1979 as* The Complete Stories of Flannery O'Connor, *which won the National Book Award for fiction.*

> The dragon is by the side of the road, watching those who pass. Beware lest he devour you. We go to the Father of Souls, but it is necessary to pass by the dragon.
>
> — St. Cyril of Jerusalem

The grandmother didn't want to go to Florida. She wanted to visit some of her connections in east Tennessee and she was seizing at every chance to change Bailey's mind. Bailey was the son she lived with, her only boy. He was sitting on the edge of his chair at the table, bent over the orange sports section of the *Journal*. "Now look here, Bailey," she said, "see here, read this," and she stood with one hand on her thin hip and the other rattling the newspaper at his bald head. "Here this fellow that calls himself The Misfit is aloose from the Federal Pen and headed toward Florida and you read here what it says he did to these people. Just you read it. I wouldn't take my children in any direction with a criminal like that aloose in it. I couldn't answer to my conscience if I did."

Bailey didn't look up from his reading so she wheeled around then and faced the children's mother, a young woman in slacks, whose face was as broad and innocent as a cabbage and was tied around with a green head-kerchief that had two points on the top like rabbit's ears. She was sitting on the sofa, feeding the baby his apricots out of a jar. "The children have been to Florida before," the old lady said. "You all ought to take them somewhere else for a change so they would see different parts of the world and be broad. They never have been to east Tennessee."

The children's mother didn't seem to hear her but the eight-year-old boy, John Wesley, a stocky child with glasses, said, "If you don't want to go to Florida, why dontcha stay at home?" He and the little girl, June Star, were reading the funny papers on the floor.

"She wouldn't stay at home to be queen for a day," June Star said without raising her yellow head.

"Yes and what would you do if this fellow, The Misfit, caught you?" the grandmother asked.   5

"I'd smack his face," John Wesley said.

"She wouldn't stay at home for a million bucks," June Star said. "Afraid she'd miss something. She has to go everywhere we go."

"All right, Miss," the grandmother said. "Just remember that the next time you want me to curl your hair."

June Star said her hair was naturally curly.

The next morning the grandmother was the first one in the car, ready to go.   10
She had her big black valise that looked like the head of a hippopotamus in one corner, and underneath it she was hiding a basket with Pitty Sing, the cat, in it. She didn't intend for the cat to be left alone in the house for three days because he would miss her too much and she was afraid he might brush against one of the gas burners and accidentally asphyxiate himself. Her son, Bailey, didn't like to arrive at a motel with a cat.

She sat in the middle of the back seat with John Wesley and June Star on either side of her. Bailey and the children's mother and the baby sat in front and they left Atlanta at eight forty-five with the mileage on the car at 55890. The grandmother wrote this down because she thought it would be interesting to say how many miles they had been when they got back. It took them twenty minutes to reach the outskirts of the city.

The old lady settled herself comfortably, removing her white cotton gloves and putting them up with her purse on the shelf in front of the back window. The children's mother still had on slacks and still had her head tied up in a green kerchief, but the grandmother had on a navy blue straw sailor hat with a bunch of white violets on the brim and a navy blue dress with a small white dot in the print. Her collars and cuffs were white organdy trimmed with lace and at her neckline she had pinned a purple spray of cloth violets containing a sachet. In case of an accident, anyone seeing her dead on the highway would know at once that she was a lady.

She said she thought it was going to be a good day for driving, neither too hot nor too cold, and she cautioned Bailey that the speed limit was fifty-five miles an hour and that the patrolmen hid themselves behind billboards and small clumps of trees and sped out after you before you had a chance to slow down. She pointed out interesting details of the scenery: Stone Mountain; the blue granite that in some places came up to both sides of the highway; the brilliant red clay banks slightly streaked with purple; and the various crops that made rows of green lace-work on the ground. The trees were full of silver-white sunlight and the meanest of them sparkled. The children were reading comic magazines and their mother had gone back to sleep.

"Let's go through Georgia fast so we won't have to look at it much," John
Wesley said.

"If I were a little boy," said the grandmother, "I wouldn't talk about my native   15
state that way. Tennessee has the mountains and Georgia has the hills."

"Tennessee is just a hillbilly dumping ground," John Wesley said, "and Georgia is a lousy state too."

"You said it," June Star said.

"In my time," said the grandmother, folding her thin veined fingers, "children were more respectful of their native states and their parents and everything
else. People did right then. Oh look at the cute little pickaninny!" she said and
pointed to a Negro child standing in the door of a shack. "Wouldn't that make a
picture, now?" she asked and they all turned and looked at the little Negro out of
the back window. He waved.

"He didn't have any britches on," June Star said.

"He probably didn't have any," the grandmother explained. "Little niggers in   20
the country don't have things like we do. If I could paint, I'd paint that picture,"
she said.

The children exchanged comic books.

The grandmother offered to hold the baby and the children's mother passed
him over the front seat to her. She set him on her knee and bounced him and
told him about the things they were passing. She rolled her eyes and screwed up
her mouth and stuck her leathery thin face into his smooth bland one. Occasionally he gave her a faraway smile. They passed a large cotton field with five or six
graves fenced in the middle of it, like a small island. "Look at the graveyard!" the
grandmother said, pointing it out. "That was the old family burying ground. That
belonged to the plantation."

"Where's the plantation?" John Wesley asked.

"Gone with the Wind," said the grandmother. "Ha. Ha."

When the children finished all the comic books they had brought, they   25
opened the lunch and ate it. The grandmother ate a peanut butter sandwich and
an olive and would not let the children throw the box and the paper napkins out
the window. When there was nothing else to do they played a game by choosing a
cloud and making the other two guess what shape it suggested. John Wesley took
one the shape of a cow and June Star guessed a cow and John Wesley said, no, an
automobile, and June Star said he didn't play fair, and they began to slap each
other over the grandmother.

The grandmother said she would tell them a story if they would keep quiet.
When she told a story, she rolled her eyes and waved her head and was very
dramatic. She said once when she was a maiden lady she had been courted by a
Mr. Edgar Atkins Teagarden from Jasper, Georgia. She said he was a very good-
looking man and a gentleman and that he brought her a watermelon every Saturday afternoon with his initials cut in it, E. A. T. Well, one Saturday, she said, Mr.
Teagarden brought the watermelon and there was nobody at home and he left it
on the front porch and returned in his buggy to Jasper, but she never got the
watermelon, she said, because a nigger boy ate it when he saw the initials, E. A.
T.! This story tickled John Wesley's funny bone and he giggled and giggled but
June Star didn't think it was any good. She said she wouldn't marry a man that

just brought her a watermelon on Saturday. The grandmother said she would have done well to marry Mr. Teagarden because he was a gentleman and had bought Coca-Cola stock when it first came out and that he had died only a few years ago, a very wealthy man.

They stopped at The Tower for barbecued sandwiches. The Tower was a part stucco and part wood filling station and dance hall set in a clearing outside of Timothy. A fat man named Red Sammy Butts ran it and there were signs stuck here and there on the building and for miles up and down the highway saying, TRY RED SAMMY'S FAMOUS BARBECUE. NONE LIKE FAMOUS RED SAMMY'S! RED SAM! THE FAT BOY WITH THE HAPPY LAUGH. A VETERAN! RED SAMMY'S YOUR MAN!

Red Sammy was lying on the bare ground outside The Tower with his head under a truck while a gray monkey about a foot high, chained to a small china-berry tree, chattered nearby. The monkey sprang back into the tree and got on the highest limb as soon as he saw the children jump out of the car and run toward him.

Inside, The Tower was a long dark room with a counter at one end and tables at the other and dancing space in the middle. They all sat down at a board table next to the nickelodeon and Red Sam's wife, a tall burnt-brown woman with hair and eyes lighter than her skin, came and took their order. The children's mother put a dime in the machine and played "The Tennessee Waltz," and the grand-mother said that tune always made her want to dance. She asked Bailey if he would like to dance but he only glared at her. He didn't have a naturally sunny disposition like she did and trips made him nervous. The grandmother's brown eyes were very bright. She swayed her head from side to side and pretended she was dancing in her chair. June Star said play something she could tap to so the children's mother put in another dime and played a fast number and June Star stepped out onto the dance floor and did her tap routine.

"Ain't she cute?" Red Sam's wife said, leaning over the counter. "Would you like to come be my little girl?" 30

"No I certainly wouldn't," June Star said. "I wouldn't live in a broken-down place like this for a million bucks!" and she ran back to the table.

"Ain't she cute?" the woman repeated, stretching her mouth politely.

"Aren't you ashamed?" hissed the grandmother.

Red Sam came in and told his wife to quit lounging on the counter and hurry up with these people's order. His khaki trousers reached just to his hip bones and his stomach hung over them like a sack of meal swaying under his shirt. He came over and sat down at a table nearby and let out a combination sigh and yodel. "You can't win," he said. "You can't win," and he wiped his sweating red face off with a gray handkerchief. "These days you don't know who to trust," he said. "Ain't that the truth?"

"People are certainly not nice like they used to be," said the grandmother. 35

"Two fellers come in here last week," Red Sammy said, "driving a Chrysler. It was a old beat-up car but it was a good one and these boys looked all right to me. Said they worked at the mill and you know I let them fellers charge the gas they bought? Now why did I do that?"

"Because you're a good man!" the grandmother said at once.

"Yes'm, I suppose so," Red Sam said as if he were struck with this answer.

His wife brought the orders, carrying the five plates all at once without a tray, two in each hand and one balanced on her arm. "It isn't a soul in this green world of God's that you can trust," she said. "And I don't count nobody out of that, not nobody," she repeated, looking at Red Sammy.

"Did you read about that criminal, The Misfit, that's escaped?" asked the   40
grandmother.

"I wouldn't be a bit surprised if he didn't attact this place right here," said the woman. "If he hears about it being here, I wouldn't be none surprised to see him. If he hears it's two cent in the cash register, I wouldn't be a tall surprised if he . . ."

"That'll do," Red Sam said. "Go bring these people their Co'-Colas," and the woman went off to get the rest of the order.

"A good man is hard to find," Red Sammy said. "Everything is getting terrible. I remember the day you could go off and leave your screen door unlatched. Not no more."

He and the grandmother discussed better times. The old lady said that in her opinion Europe was entirely to blame for the way things were now. She said the way Europe acted you would think we were made of money and Red Sam said it was no use talking about it, she was exactly right. The children ran outside into the white sunlight and looked at the monkey in the lacy chinaberry tree. He was busy catching fleas on himself and biting each one carefully between his teeth as if it were a delicacy.

They drove off again into the hot afternoon. The grandmother took cat naps   45
and woke up every few minutes with her own snoring. Outside of Toombsboro she woke up and recalled an old plantation that she had visited in this neighborhood once when she was a young lady. She said the house had six white columns across the front and that there was an avenue of oaks leading up to it and two little wooden trellis arbors on either side in front where you sat down with your suitor after a stroll in the garden. She recalled exactly which road to turn off to get to it. She knew that Bailey would not be willing to lose any time looking at an old house, but the more she talked about it, the more she wanted to see it once again and find out if the little twin arbors were still standing. "There was a secret panel in this house," she said craftily, not telling the truth but wishing that she were, "and the story went that all the family silver was hidden in it when Sherman came through but it was never found . . ."

"Hey!" John Wesley said. "Let's go see it! We'll find it! We'll poke all the woodwork and find it! Who lives there? Where do you turn off at? Hey Pop, can't we turn off there?"

"We never have seen a house with a secret panel!" June Star shrieked. "Let's go to the house with the secret panel! Hey Pop, can't we go see the house with the secret panel!"

"It's not far from here, I know," the grandmother said. "It wouldn't take over twenty minutes."

Bailey was looking straight ahead. His jaw was as rigid as a horseshoe. "No," he said.

The children began to yell and scream that they wanted to see the house   50
with the secret panel. John Wesley kicked the back of the front seat and June Star

hung over her mother's shoulder and whined desperately into her ear that they never had any fun even on their vacation, that they could never do what THEY wanted to do. The baby began to scream and John Wesley kicked the back of the seat so hard that his father could feel the blows in his kidney.

"All right!" he shouted and drew the car to a stop at the side of the road. "Will you all shut up? Will you all just shut up for one second? If you don't shut up, we won't go anywhere."

"It would be very educational for them," the grandmother murmured.

"All right," Bailey said, "but get this: this is the only time we're going to stop for anything like this. This is the one and only time."

"The dirt road that you have to turn down is about a mile back," the grandmother directed. "I marked it when we passed."

"A dirt road," Bailey groaned.   55

After they had turned around and were headed toward the dirt road, the grandmother recalled other points about the house, the beautiful glass over the front doorway and the candle-lamp in the hall. John Wesley said that the secret panel was probably in the fireplace.

"You can't go inside this house," Bailey said. "You don't know who lives there."

"While you all talk to the people in front, I'll run around behind and get in a window," John Wesley suggested.

"We'll all stay in the car," his mother said.

They turned onto the dirt road and the car raced roughly along in a swirl of   60
pink dust. The grandmother recalled the times when there were no paved roads and thirty miles was a day's journey. The dirt road was hilly and there were sudden washes in it and sharp curves on dangerous embankments. All at once they would be on a hill, looking down over the blue tops of trees for miles around, then the next minute, they would be in a red depression with the dust-coated trees looking down on them.

"This place had better turn up in a minute," Bailey said, "or I'm going to turn around."

The road looked as if no one had traveled on it in months.

"It's not much farther," the grandmother said and just as she said it, a horrible thought came to her. The thought was so embarrassing that she turned red in the face and her eyes dilated and her feet jumped up, upsetting her valise in the corner. The instant the valise moved, the newspaper top she had over the basket under it rose with a snarl and Pitty Sing, the cat, sprang onto Bailey's shoulder.

The children were thrown to the floor and their mother, clutching the baby, was thrown out the door onto the ground; the old lady was thrown into the front seat. The car turned over once and landed right-side-up in a gulch off the side of the road. Bailey remained in the driver's seat with the cat—gray-striped with a broad white face and an orange nose—clinging to his neck like a caterpillar.

As soon as the children saw they could move their arms and legs, they   65
scrambled out of the car, shouting, "We've had an ACCIDENT!" The grandmother was curled up under the dashboard, hoping she was injured so that Bailey's wrath would not come down on her all at once. The horrible thought she had had before the accident was that the house she had remembered so vividly was not in Georgia but in Tennessee.

Bailey removed the cat from his neck with both hands and flung it out the window against the side of a pine tree. Then he got out of the car and started looking for the children's mother. She was sitting against the side of the red gutted ditch, holding the screaming baby, but she only had a cut down her face and a broken shoulder. "We've had an ACCIDENT!" the children screamed in a frenzy of delight.

"But nobody's killed," June Star said with disappointment as the grandmother limped out of the car, her hat still pinned to her head but the broken front brim standing up at a jaunty angle and the violet spray hanging off the side. They all sat down in the ditch, except the children, to recover from the shock. They were all shaking.

"Maybe a car will come along," said the children's mother hoarsely.

"I believe I have injured an organ," said the grandmother, pressing her side, but no one answered her. Bailey's teeth were clattering. He had on a yellow sport shirt with bright blue parrots designed in it and his face was as yellow as the shirt. The grandmother decided that she would not mention that the house was in Tennessee.

The road was about ten feet above and they could only see the tops of the   70 trees on the other side of it. Behind the ditch they were sitting in there were more woods, tall and dark and deep. In a few minutes they saw a car some distance away on top of a hill, coming slowly as if the occupants were watching them. The grandmother stood up and waved both arms dramatically to attract their attention. The car continued to come on slowly, disappeared around a bend and appeared again, moving even slower, on top of the hill they had gone over. It was a big black battered hearse-like automobile. There were three men in it.

It came to a stop just over them and for some minutes, the driver looked down with a steady expressionless gaze to where they were sitting, and didn't speak. Then he turned his head and muttered something to the other two and they got out. One was a fat boy in black trousers and a red sweat shirt with a silver stallion embossed on the front of it. He moved around on the right side of them and stood staring, his mouth partly open in a kind of loose grin. The other had on khaki pants and a blue striped coat and a gray hat pulled very low, hiding most of his face. He came around slowly on the left side. Neither spoke.

The driver got out of the car and stood by the side of it, looking down at them. He was an older man than the other two. His hair was just beginning to gray and he wore silver-rimmed spectacles that gave him a scholarly look. He had a long creased face and didn't have on any shirt or undershirt. He had on blue jeans that were too tight for him and was holding a black hat and a gun. The two boys also had guns.

"We've had an ACCIDENT!" the children screamed.

The grandmother had the peculiar feeling that the bespectacled man was someone she knew. His face was as familiar to her as if she had known him all her life but she could not recall who he was. He moved away from the car and began to come down the embankment, placing his feet carefully so that he wouldn't slip. He had on tan and white shoes and no socks, and his ankles were red and thin. "Good afternoon," he said. "I see you all had you a little spill."

"We turned over twice!" said the grandmother.   75

"Oncet," he corrected. "We seen it happen. Try their car and see will it run, Hiram," he said quietly to the boy with the gray hat.

"What you got that gun for?" John Wesley asked. "Whatcha gonna do with that gun?"

"Lady," the man said to the children's mother, "would you mind calling them children to sit down by you? Children make me nervous. I want all you all to sit down right together there where you're at."

"What are you telling US what to do for?" June Star asked.

Behind them the line of woods gaped like a dark open mouth. "Come here,"   80
said the mother.

"Look here now," Bailey began suddenly, "we're in a predicament! We're in . . ."

The grandmother shrieked. She scrambled to her feet and stood staring. "You're The Misfit!" she said. "I recognized you at once!"

"Yes'm," the man said, smiling slightly as if he were pleased in spite of himself to be known, "but it would have been better for all of you, lady, if you hadn't of reckernized me."

Bailey turned his head sharply and said something to his mother that shocked even the children. The old lady began to cry and The Misfit reddened.

"Lady," he said, "don't you get upset. Sometimes a man says things he don't   85
mean. I don't reckon he meant to talk to you thataway."

"You wouldn't shoot a lady, would you?" the grandmother said and removed a clean handkerchief from her cuff and began to slap at her eyes with it.

The Misfit pointed the toe of his shoe into the ground and made a little hole and then covered it up again. "I would hate to have to," he said.

"Listen," the grandmother almost screamed, "I know you're a good man. You don't look a bit like you have common blood. I know you must come from nice people!"

"Yes mam," he said, "finest people in the world." When he smiled he showed a row of strong white teeth. "God never made a finer woman than my mother and my daddy's heart was pure gold," he said. The boy with the red sweat shirt had come around behind them and was standing with his gun at his hip. The Misfit squatted down on the ground. "Watch them children, Bobby Lee," he said. "You know they make me nervous." He looked at the six of them huddled together in front of him and he seemed to be embarrassed as if he couldn't think of anything to say. "Ain't a cloud in the sky," he remarked, looking up at it. "Don't see no sun but don't see no cloud neither."

"Yes, it's a beautiful day," said the grandmother. "Listen," she said, "you   90
shouldn't call yourself The Misfit because I know you're a good man at heart. I can just look at you and tell."

"Hush!" Bailey yelled. "Hush! Everybody shut up and let me handle this!" He was squatting in the position of a runner about to sprint forward but he didn't move.

"I pre-chate that, lady," The Misfit said and drew a little circle in the ground with the butt of his gun.

"It'll take a half a hour to fix this here car," Hiram called, looking over the raised hood of it.

"Well, first you and Bobby Lee get him and that little boy to step over yonder with you," The Misfit said, pointing to Bailey and John Wesley. "The boys want to ast you something," he said to Bailey. "Would you mind stepping back in them woods there with them?"

"Listen," Bailey began, "we're in a terrible predicament! Nobody realizes   95 what this is," and his voice cracked. His eyes were as blue and intense as the parrots in his shirt and he remained perfectly still.

The grandmother reached up to adjust her hat brim as if she were going to the woods with him but it came off in her hand. She stood staring at it and after a second she let it fall on the ground. Hiram pulled Bailey up by the arm as if he were assisting an old man. John Wesley caught hold of his father's hand and Bobby Lee followed. They went off toward the woods and just as they reached the dark edge, Bailey turned and supporting himself against a gray naked pine trunk, he shouted, "I'll be back in a minute, Mamma, wait on me!"

"Come back this instant!" his mother shrilled but they all disappeared into the woods.

"Bailey Boy!" the grandmother called in a tragic voice but she found she was looking at The Misfit squatting on the ground in front of her. "I just know you're a good man," she said desperately. "You're not a bit common!"

"Nome, I ain't a good man," The Misfit said after a second as if he had considered her statement carefully, "but I ain't the worst in the world neither. My daddy said I was a different breed of dog from my brothers and sisters. 'You know,' Daddy said, 'it's some that can live their whole life out without asking about it and it's others has to know why it is, and this boy is one of the latters. He's going to be into everything!' " He put on his black hat and looked up suddenly and then away deep into the woods as if he were embarrassed again. "I'm sorry I don't have on a shirt before you ladies," he said, hunching his shoulders slightly. "We buried our clothes that we had on when we escaped and we're just making do until we can get better. We borrowed these from some folks we met," he explained.

"That's perfectly all right," the grandmother said. "Maybe Bailey has an extra   100 shirt in his suitcase."

"I'll look and see terrectly," The Misfit said.

"Where are they taking him?" the children's mother screamed.

"Daddy was a card himself," The Misfit said. "You couldn't put anything over on him. He never got in trouble with the Authorities though. Just had the knack of handling them."

"You could be honest too if you'd only try," said the grandmother. "Think how wonderful it would be to settle down and live a comfortable life and not have to think about somebody chasing you all the time."

The Misfit kept scratching in the ground with the butt of his gun as if he   105 were thinking about it. "Yes'm, somebody is always after you," he murmured.

The grandmother noticed how thin his shoulder blades were just behind his hat because she was standing up looking down at him. "Do you ever pray?" she asked.

He shook his head. All she saw was the black hat wiggle between his shoulder blades. "Nome," he said.

There was a pistol shot from the woods, followed closely by another. Then silence. The old lady's head jerked around. She could hear the wind move through the tree tops like a long satisfied insuck of breath. "Bailey Boy!" she called.

"I was a gospel singer for a while," The Misfit said. "I been most everything. Been in the arm service, both land and sea, at home and abroad, been twict married, been an undertaker, been with the railroads, plowed Mother Earth, been in a tornado, seen a man burnt alive oncet," and he looked up at the children's mother and the little girl who were sitting close together, their faces white and their eyes glassy; "I even seen a woman flogged," he said.

"Pray, pray," the grandmother began, "pray, pray . . ."   110

"I never was a bad boy that I remember of," The Misfit said in an almost dreamy voice, "but somewheres along the line I done something wrong and got sent to the penitentiary. I was buried alive," and he looked up and held her attention to him by a steady stare.

"That's when you should have started to pray," she said. "What did you do to get sent to the penitentiary, that first time?"

"Turn to the right, it was a wall," The Misfit said, looking up again at the cloudless sky. "Turn to the left, it was a wall. Look up it was a ceiling, look down it was a floor. I forgot what I done, lady. I set there and set there, trying to remember what it was I done and I ain't recalled it to this day. Oncet in a while, I would think it was coming to me, but it never come."

"Maybe they put you in by mistake," the old lady said vaguely.

"Nome," he said. "It wasn't no mistake. They had the papers on me."   115

"You must have stolen something," she said.

The Misfit sneered slightly. "Nobody had nothing I wanted," he said. "It was a head-doctor at the penitentiary said what I had done was kill my daddy but I known that for a lie. My daddy died in nineteen ought nineteen of the epidemic flu and I never had a thing to do with it. He was buried in the Mount Hopewell Baptist churchyard and you can go there and see for yourself."

"If you would pray," the old lady said, "Jesus would help you."

"That's right," The Misfit said.

"Well then, why don't you pray?" she asked trembling with delight suddenly.   120

"I don't want no hep," he said. "I'm doing all right by myself."

Bobby Lee and Hiram came ambling back from the woods. Bobby Lee was dragging a yellow shirt with bright blue parrots in it.

"Thow me that shirt, Bobby Lee," The Misfit said. The shirt came flying at him and landed on his shoulder and he put it on. The grandmother couldn't name what the shirt reminded her of. "No, lady," The Misfit said while he was buttoning it up, "I found out the crime don't matter. You can do one thing or you can do another, kill a man or take a tire off his car, because sooner or later you're going to forget what it was you done and just be punished for it."

The children's mother had begun to make heaving noises as if she couldn't get her breath. "Lady," he asked, "would you and that little girl like to step off yonder with Bobby Lee and Hiram and join your husband?"

"Yes, thank you," the mother said faintly. Her left arm dangled helplessly and   125
she was holding the baby, who had gone to sleep, in the other. "Hep that lady up,
Hiram," The Misfit said as she struggled to climb out of the ditch, "and Bobby
Lee, you hold onto that little girl's hand."

"I don't want to hold hands with him," June Star said. "He reminds me of
a pig."

The fat boy blushed and laughed and caught her by the arm and pulled her
off into the woods after Hiram and her mother.

Alone with The Misfit, the grandmother found that she had lost her voice.
There was not a cloud in the sky nor any sun. There was nothing around her but
woods. She wanted to tell him that he must pray. She opened and closed her
mouth several times before anything came out. Finally she found herself saying,
"Jesus. Jesus," meaning, Jesus will help you, but the way she was saying it, it
sounded as if she might be cursing.

"Yes'm," The Misfit said as if he agreed. "Jesus thown everything off balance.
It was the same case with Him as with me except He hadn't committed any crime
and they could prove I had committed one because they had the papers on me.
Of course," he said, "they never shown me my papers. That's why I sign myself
now. I said long ago, you get you a signature and sign everything you do and keep
a copy of it. Then you'll know what you done and you can hold up the crime to
the punishment and see do they match and in the end you'll have something to
prove you ain't been treated right. I call myself The Misfit," he said, "because I
can't make what all I done wrong fit what all I gone through in punishment."

There was a piercing scream from the woods, followed closely by a pistol   130
report. "Does it seem right to you, lady, that one is punished a heap and another
ain't punished at all?"

"Jesus!" the old lady cried. "You've got good blood! I know you wouldn't
shoot a lady! I know you come from nice people! Pray! Jesus, you ought not to
shoot a lady. I'll give you all the money I've got!"

"Lady," The Misfit said, looking beyond her far into the woods, "there never
was a body that give the undertaker a tip."

There were two more pistol reports and the grandmother raised her head like
a parched old turkey hen crying for water and called, "Bailey Boy, Bailey Boy!" as
if her heart would break.

"Jesus was the only One that ever raised the dead," The Misfit continued,
"and He shouldn't have done it. He thown everything off balance. If He did what
He said, then it's nothing for you to do but thow away everything and follow Him,
and if He didn't, then it's nothing for you to do but enjoy the few minutes you got
left the best you can — by killing somebody or burning down his house or doing
some other meanness to him. No pleasure but meanness," he said and his voice
had become almost a snarl.

"Maybe He didn't raise the dead," the old lady mumbled, not knowing what   135
she was saying and feeling so dizzy that she sank down in the ditch with her legs
twisted under her.

"I wasn't there so I can't say He didn't," The Misfit said. "I wisht I had of been
there," he said, hitting the ground with his fist. "It ain't right I wasn't there because

if I had of been there I would of known. Listen lady," he said in a high voice, "if I had of been there I would of known and I wouldn't be like I am now." His voice seemed about to crack and the grandmother's head cleared for an instant. She saw the man's face twisted close to her own as if he were going to cry and she murmured, "Why you're one of my babies. You're one of my own children!" She reached out and touched him on the shoulder. The Misfit sprang back as if a snake had bitten him and shot her three times through the chest. Then he put his gun down on the ground and took off his glasses and began to clean them.

Hiram and Bobby Lee returned from the woods and stood over the ditch, looking down at the grandmother who half sat and half lay in a puddle of blood with her legs crossed under her like a child's and her face smiling up at the cloudless sky.

Without his glasses, The Misfit's eyes were red-rimmed and pale and defenseless-looking. "Take her off and thow her where you thown the others," he said, picking up the cat that was rubbing itself against his leg.

"She was a talker, wasn't she?" Bobby Lee said, sliding down the ditch with a yodel.

"She would of been a good woman," The Misfit said, "if it had been some- 140 body there to shoot her every minute of her life."

"Some fun!" Bobby Lee said.

"Shut up, Bobby Lee," The Misfit said. "It's no real pleasure in life."　　[1955]

FOR THINKING AND WRITING

1. Although this story begins with comedy, ultimately it shocks many readers. Did it shock you? Why, or why not? What would you say to someone who argues that the shift in tone is a flaw in the story?

2. Note places where the word *good* comes up in this story. How is it defined? Do the definitions change? Do you think the author has in mind a definition that does not occur to the characters? If so, what might that definition be?

3. What in his life history is The Misfit unsure about? Why do you think he is hazy about these matters? Should O'Connor have resolved for us all the issues of fact that bother him? Why, or why not?

4. Does The Misfit have any redeeming qualities? Does the grandmother? Explain. What do you think the grandmother means when she murmurs, "Why you're one of my babies. You're one of my own children!" (para. 136)? Why do you think The Misfit responds as he does?

5. There is much talk about Jesus and Christianity in this story. Should O'Connor have done more to help non-Christian readers see the story as relevant to them? Explain your reasoning.

14

A Gallery of Poems

SHERMAN ALEXIE
Capital Punishment

Born in Spokane, Washington, Sherman Alexie (b. 1966) is a member of the Spokane/Coeur d'Alene tribe. His fiction includes two novels, Reservation Blues *(1996) and* Indian Killer *(1997). He has also produced three collections of short stories,* Ten Little Indians *(2003),* The Toughest Indian in the World *(2001), and* The Lone Ranger and Tonto Fistfight in Heaven *(1994), which he adapted for the acclaimed 1998 film* Smoke Signals. *Alexie is a poet, too, with his collections of verse including* The Business of Fancy Dancing *(1992),* Old Shirts and New Skins *(1993),* First Indian on the Moon *(1993),* Drums Like This *(1996), and* One Stick Song *(2000). "Capital Punishment" appeared in a 1996 issue of* Indiana Review *and, that same year, in Alexie's collection* The Summer of Black Widows. *It was also selected for the 1996 edition of* The Best American Poetry. *Alexie wrote the poem after reading media coverage of an actual execution in the state of Washington.*

I prepare the last meal
for the Indian man to be executed

but this killer doesn't want much:
baked potato, salad, tall glass of ice water.

(I am not a witness)   5

It's mostly the dark ones
who are forced to sit in the chair

especially when white people die.
It's true, you can look it up

◆   ◆   ◆

and this Indian killer pushed   10
his fists all the way down

a white man's throat, just to win a bet
about the size of his heart.

Those Indians are always gambling.
Still, I season this last meal   15

with all I have. I don't have much
but I send it down the line

with the handsome guard
who has fallen in love

with the Indian killer.   20
I don't care who loves whom.

(I am not a witness)

I don't care if I add too much
salt or pepper to the warden's stew.

He can eat what I put in front of him.   25
I just cook for the boss

but I cook just right
for the Indian man to be executed.

The temperature is the thing.
I once heard a story   30

about a black man who was electrocuted
in that chair and lived to tell about it

before the court decided to sit him back down
an hour later and kill him all over again.

I have an extra sandwich hidden away   35
in the back of the refrigerator

in case this Indian killer survives
that first slow flip of the switch

and gets hungry while he waits
for the engineers to debate the flaws.   40

(I am not a witness)

I prepare the last meal for free
just like I signed up for the last war.

I learned how to cook
by lasting longer than any of the others.   45

◆　◆　◆

Tonight, I'm just the last one left
after the handsome guard takes the meal away.

I turn off the kitchen lights
and sit alone in the dark

because the whole damn prison dims   50
when the chair is switched on.

You can watch a light bulb flicker
on a night like this

and remember it too clearly
like it was your first kiss   55

or the first hard kick to your groin.
It's all the same

when I am huddled down here
trying not to look at the clock

look at the clock, no, don't   60
look at the clock, when all of it stops

making sense: a salad, a potato
a drink of water all taste like heat.

(I am not a witness)

I want you to know I tasted a little   65
of that last meal before I sent it away.

It's the cook's job, to make sure
and I was sure I ate from the same plate

and ate with the same fork and spoon
that the Indian killer used later   70

in his cell. Maybe a little bit of me
lodged in his stomach, wedged between

his front teeth, his incisors, his molars
when he chewed down on the bit

and his body arced like modern art   75
curving organically, smoke rising

from his joints, wispy flames decorating
the crown of his head, the balls of his feet.

(I am not a witness)

I sit here in the dark kitchen   80
when they do it, meaning

◆   ◆   ◆

when they kill him, kill
and add another definition of the word

to the dictionary. America fills
its dictionary. We write down *kill* and everybody   85

in the audience shouts out exactly how
they spell it, what it means to them

and all of the answers are taken down
by the pollsters and secretaries

who take care of the small details: 90
time of death, pulse rate, press release.

I heard a story once about some reporters
at a hanging who wanted the hood removed

from the condemned's head, so they could look
into his eyes and tell their readers   95

what they saw there. What did they expect?
All of the stories should be simple.

1 death + 1 death = 2 deaths.
But we throw the killers in one grave

and victims in another. We form sides   100
and have two separate feasts.

(I am a witness)

I prepared the last meal
for the Indian man who was executed

and have learned this: If any of us   105
stood for days on top of a barren hill

during an electrical storm
then lightning would eventually strike us

and we'd have no idea for which of our sins
we were reduced to headlines and ash.   [1996]   110

FOR THINKING AND WRITING

1. Alexie reports that in writing this poem, he aimed "to call for the abolition of the death penalty." In reading the poem, do you sense that this is his aim? Why, or why not? In what respects might the poem be seen as arguing against the death penalty? State how you viewed capital punishment before and after you read it. Did Alexie affect your attitude? If so, how?

2. Why do you think Alexie cast the speaker as the condemned man's cook? How do you explain the speaker's shift from denying that he is a witness to acknowledging that he is one? Identify how he seems to define the term

witness. What would you say to someone who argues that the speaker is unreasonably stretching the meaning of this word, because apparently he didn't directly observe the execution?

3. How does race figure in this poem? Should people consider race when discussing capital punishment? If so, what about race should they especially ponder? In examining Alexie's poem, should readers bear in mind that the author is Native American? Why, or why not?

4. The film *Dead Man Walking* (1995), which deals with arguments about capital punishment, shows in chilling detail an execution by injection. Yet at the moment the condemned man dies, the film also shows the faces of his two victims. By contrast, Alexie doesn't dwell on the victims of the executed men he writes about. Should he have mentioned them more? Identify some of the values reflected in your answer.

5. Summarize and evaluate the lesson delivered by the speaker at the end of the poem. What do you think headlines might say about you if you were killed in the manner he describes?

JULIA ALVAREZ
How I Learned to Sweep

Although born in New York City, Julia Alvarez (b. 1950) was raised in the Dominican Republic until she was ten. Her first novel, How the Garcia Girls Lost Their Accents *(1991), concerns Dominican immigrants living in Manhattan. Her second,* In the Time of the Butterflies *(1994), is based on real-life women who were murdered by the regime of the Dominican dictator Rafael Leonidas Trujillo. Her third novel,* Yo! *(1996), centers on a writer much like Alvarez herself. Alvarez has also published volumes of poetry, including* Homecoming *(1984; revised edition, 1996),* The Other Side/El Otro Lado *(1995), and* The Woman I Kept to Myself *(2004). The following poem appears in* Homecoming *as one of a series of thirteen poems collectively entitled "Housekeeping."*

My mother never taught me sweeping. . . .
One afternoon she found me watching
t.v. She eyed the dusty floor
boldly, and put a broom before
me, and said she'd like to be able   5
to eat her dinner off that table,
and nodded at my feet, then left.
I knew right off what she expected
and went at it. I stepped and swept;
the t.v. blared the news; I kept   10
my mind on what I had to do,

until in minutes, I was through.
Her floor was as immaculate
as a just-washed dinner plate.
I waited for her to return   15
and turned to watch the President,
live from the White House, talk of war:
in the Far East our soldiers were
landing in their helicopters
into jungles their propellers   20
swept like weeds seen underwater
while perplexing shots were fired
from those beautiful green gardens
into which these dragonflies
filled with little men descended.   25
I got up and swept again
as they fell out of the sky.
I swept all the harder when
I watched a dozen of them die . . .
as if their dust fell through the screen   30
upon the floor I had just cleaned.
She came back and turned the dial;
the screen went dark. *That's beautiful,*
she said, and ran her clean hand through
my hair, and on, over the window-   35
sill, coffee table, rocker, desk,
and held it up — I held my breath —
That's beautiful, she said, impressed,
she hadn't found a speck of death.   [1984]

FOR THINKING AND WRITING

1. In line 1, the speaker begins by announcing "My mother never taught me sweeping. . . ." How is it, then, that the speaker "knew right off what she expected" (line 8)?

2. Identify rhyming patterns in this poem. What is their effect? Identify sections where there is no rhyme. What is their effect?

3. How old do you think the speaker was when she learned how to sweep? Why do you think the sight of dying soldiers made her sweep "all the harder" (line 28)? What response to the war might reasonably have been expected of her?

4. What do you conclude about the speaker's mother from the last two lines?

5. What other things do children or parents like to sweep away?

MATTHEW ARNOLD
Dover Beach

Victorian poet Matthew Arnold (1822–1889) was the eldest son of Thomas Arnold, an influential clergyman and historian and headmaster of one of England's most prestigious college preparatory schools, Rugby. He grew up in an educational milieu in which religious, political, and social issues were discussed in depth. He went on to Oxford, where he eventually achieved success despite his irreverence and eccentricity. In 1851, he became an inspector of schools and served in this capacity for thirty-five years. He drew on his experiences with people of diverse social classes to become a keen critic of British education and culture, and he expressed his views of society in critical essays on literary, social, and religious issues as well as in poems. Living during an age in which Charles Darwin published The Origin of Species *(1871) and religious dogma was being questioned in many ways, Arnold suggests in "Dover Beach" that human love becomes especially important in such a world. The poem may have been written during the months just before or just after Arnold's marriage and honeymoon, which included a ferry ride from Dover, England, to Calais, France.*

The sea is calm tonight.
The tide is full, the moon lies fair
Upon the straits; — on the French coast the light
Gleams and is gone; the cliffs of England stand,
Glimmering and vast, out in the tranquil bay.   5
Come to the window, sweet is the night-air!
Only, from the long line of spray
Where the sea meets the moon-blanched land,
Listen! you hear the grating roar
Of pebbles which the waves draw back, and fling,   10
At their return, up the high strand,
Begin, and cease, and then again begin,
With tremulous cadence slow, and bring
The eternal note of sadness in.

Sophocles long ago   15
Heard it on the Aegean, and it brought
Into his mind the turbid ebb and flow
Of human misery;° we
Find also in the sound a thought,
Hearing it by this distant northern sea.   20

◆   ◆   ◆

15–18 Sophocles . . . misery: In *Antigone,* Sophocles compares the disasters that beset the house of Oedipus to a mounting tide.

The Sea of Faith
Was once, too, at the full, and round earth's shore
Lay like the folds of a bright girdle furled.
But now I only hear
Its melancholy, long, withdrawing roar,   25
Retreating, to the breath
Of the night-wind, down the vast edges drear
And naked shingles° of the world.

Ah, love, let us be true
To one another! for the world, which seems   30
To lie before us like a land of dreams,
So various, so beautiful, so new,
Hath really neither joy, nor love, nor light,
Nor certitude, nor peace, nor help for pain;
And we are here as on a darkling plain   35
Swept with confused alarms of struggle and flight,
Where ignorant armies clash by night.   [1867]

28 **shingles:** Pebble beach.

FOR THINKING AND WRITING

1. In trying to re-create this scene—say, for a movie script—what would you have the lovers look like? Where would the couple be positioned? If you were the director, how would you explain the scene to the actors—that is, what is the speaker saying? Put another way, what argument is being made?

2. What does Arnold seem to be using the sea as a metaphor for? What other metaphors and similes are used? Are they effective in making his point?

3. Some feminist readers see this poem as yet another example of a man who hopes to escape temporarily from the troubles of the world by finding comfort and support from a woman. Is there some validity to this point? Why, for example, doesn't the woman speak?

4. In the recent film *The Anniversary Party*, Kevin Kline's character reads the last stanza of this poem to a couple celebrating their sixth wedding anniversary. Some critics saw it as an ironic joke, others as a parody of a "sweet" love poem. What is it about the poem that seems to make it inappropriate for such an occasion? Would you send it to your beloved? Why?

5. What specific reasons are given by the speaker for the lovers to be true to one another, beginning with "for the world" (line 30)? Is this an attitude you share? Do you know others who agree? Is this an extreme position? What would the opposite view be? Is this extreme, as well?

ELIZABETH BISHOP
One Art

Although she also wrote short stories, Elizabeth Bishop (1911–1979) became known primarily for her poetry, winning both a Pulitzer Prize and a National Book Award for it. Born in Worcester, Massachusetts, she spent much of her youth in Nova Scotia. As an adult, she lived in various places, including New York City, Florida, Mexico, and Brazil. Much of her poetry observes and reflects on a particular object or figure. "One Art" appeared in Geography III *(1976), the last book that Bishop published during her lifetime. The poem is a* villanelle, *a centuries-old French form that is technically challenging for a writer. A villanelle is a nineteen-line poem consisting of five tercets (three-line stanzas) followed by a quatrain (four-line stanza); the first and third lines of the first tercet are used alternately to conclude each succeeding tercet, and they are joined to form a rhyme at the poem's end.*

The art of losing isn't hard to master;
so many things seem filled with the intent
to be lost that their loss is no disaster.

Lose something every day. Accept the fluster
of lost door keys, the hour badly spent.   5
The art of losing isn't hard to master.

Then practice losing farther, losing faster:
places, and names, and where it was you meant
to travel. None of these will bring disaster.

I lost my mother's watch. And look! my last, or   10
next-to-last, of three loved houses went.
The art of losing isn't hard to master.

I lost two cities, lovely ones. And, vaster,
some realms I owned, two rivers, a continent.
I miss them, but it wasn't a disaster.   15

— Even losing you (the joking voice, a gesture
I love) I shan't have lied. It's evident
the art of losing's not too hard to master
though it may look like (*Write* it!) like disaster.   [1976]

FOR THINKING AND WRITING

1. What effects does Bishop achieve by writing this poem as a villanelle?
2. Describe the speaker's tone. Is it consistent? What do you conclude about the speaker's attitude toward "The art of losing" (lines 6, 12, 18)?

3. Look at the advice given in the third stanza. In what ways can it be considered useful? Would you argue that this advice shouldn't be heeded? Why, or why not?

4. In line 16, the word *you* is suddenly introduced. What is the effect?

5. The parenthetical expression "(*Write* it!)" in line 19 is a departure from the sheer repetition of lines characteristic of a villanelle. What do you make of this break? Do you think it appropriate, or do you find it merely jarring?

ELIZABETH BISHOP
The Fish

Elizabeth Bishop wrote "The Fish" in 1940 and then included it in her 1946 book
North and South.

I caught a tremendous fish
and held him beside the boat
half out of water, with my hook
fast in a corner of his mouth.
He didn't fight.   5
He hadn't fought at all.
He hung a grunting weight,
battered and venerable
and homely. Here and there
his brown skin hung in strips   10
like ancient wall-paper,
and its pattern of darker brown
was like wall-paper:
shapes like full-blown roses
stained and lost through age.   15
He was speckled with barnacles,
fine rosettes of lime,
and infested
with tiny white sea-lice,
and underneath two or three   20
rags of green weed hung down.
While his gills were breathing in
the terrible oxygen
—the frightening gills,
fresh and crisp with blood,   25
that can cut so badly—
I thought of the coarse white flesh
packed in like feathers,

the big bones and the little bones,
the dramatic reds and blacks   30
of his shiny entrails,
and the pink swim-bladder
like a big peony.
I looked into his eyes
which were far larger than mine   35
but shallower, and yellowed,
the irises backed and packed
with tarnished tinfoil
seen through the lenses
of old scratched isinglass.   40
They shifted a little, but not
to return my stare.
— It was more like the tipping
of an object toward the light.
I admired his sullen face,   45
the mechanism of his jaw,
and then I saw
that from his lower lip
— if you could call it a lip —
grim, wet, and weapon-like,   50
hung five old pieces of fish-line,
or four and a wire leader
with the swivel still attached,
with all their five big hooks
grown firmly in his mouth.   55
A green line, frayed at the end
where he broke it, two heavier lines,
and a fine black thread
still crimped from the strain and snap
when it broke and he got away.   60
Like medals with their ribbons
frayed and wavering,
a five-haired beard of wisdom
trailing from his aching jaw.
I stared and stared   65
and victory filled up
the little rented boat,
from the pool of bilge
where oil had spread a rainbow
around the rusted engine   70
to the bailer rusted orange,
the sun-cracked thwarts,
the oarlocks on their strings,

the gunnels — until everything
was rainbow, rainbow, rainbow!   75
And I let the fish go.   [1946]

FOR THINKING AND WRITING

1. Does the speaker change her attitude toward the fish, or does it stay pretty much the same? Support your reasoning by referring to specific lines. Are you surprised that the speaker lets the fish go? Why, or why not? How effective a conclusion is her release of the fish?

2. To what extent is the speaker describing the fish objectively? In what ways, if any, does her description of him seem to reflect her own particular values? Refer to specific lines.

3. The speaker reports that "victory filled up / the little rented boat" (lines 66–67). Whose victory might she have in mind? Why might she use this word? Often, a victory for one is a defeat for another. Is that the case here?

4. Where does the poem refer to acts and instruments of seeing? What conclusions might be drawn from these references?

5. How significant is it that the fish is male?

GWENDOLYN BROOKS
The Mother

Gwendolyn Brooks (1917–2000) became the first African American to win the Pulitzer Prize, receiving it in 1950 for a book of poems entitled Annie Allen. *She garnered many other awards for her poetry, besides serving as poet laureate of Illinois and poetry consultant to the Library of Congress. In most of her work, Brooks was concerned with the lives of African Americans, including issues of civil rights. "The Mother" appeared in her first book of poetry,* A Street in Bronzeville *(1945). Other collections of her verse include* Selected Poems *(1963, 1999),* Blacks *(1987), and* Children Coming Home *(1992). Brooks also published a novel,* Maud Martha *(1953), and an autobiography,* Report from Part One *(1972).*

Abortions will not let you forget.
You remember the children you got that you did not get,
The damp small pulps with a little or with no hair,
The singers and workers that never handled the air.
You will never neglect or beat   5
Them, or silence or buy with a sweet.
You will never wind up the sucking-thumb
Or scuttle off ghosts that come.

You will never leave them, controlling your luscious sigh,
Return for a snack of them, with gobbling mother-eye. 　　　　10

I have heard in the voices of the wind the voices of my dim killed children
I have contracted. I have eased
My dim dears at the breasts they could never suck.
I have said, Sweets, if I sinned, if I seized
Your luck 　　　　15
And your lives from your unfinished reach,
If I stole your births and your names,
Your straight baby tears and your games,
Your stilted or lovely loves, your tumults, your marriages, aches, and your deaths,
If I poisoned the beginnings of your breaths, 　　　　20
Believe that even in my deliberateness I was not deliberate.
Though why should I whine,
Whine that the crime was other than mine? —
Since anyhow you are dead.
Or rather, or instead, 　　　　25
You were never made.
But that too, I am afraid,
Is faulty: oh, what shall I say, how is the truth to be said?
You were born, you had body, you died.
It is just that you never giggled or planned or cried. 　　　　30

Believe me, I loved you all.
Believe me, I knew you, though faintly, and I loved, I loved you
All. 　　　　　　　　　　　　　　　　　　　　　　[1945]

FOR THINKING AND WRITING

1. What in the poem helps you (or doesn't help you) understand the narrator's decision? Are there specific questions you would still want to ask?

2. Why does the narrator use "you" instead of "me" throughout the poem?

3. What are the points at which the speaker seems to waver? Why does she?

4. Since the "children" were never born, how can she talk to them? How can she love them?

5. Is this a defense of abortion? An attack on abortion? A plea for understanding? An emotional snapshot of a regretful woman? How do you read the poem?

ROBERT BROWNING
My Last Duchess

Today, Robert Browning (1812–1889) is regarded as one of the greatest poets of nineteenth-century England, but in his own time he was not nearly as celebrated as

his wife, the poet Elizabeth Barrett Browning. He is chiefly known for his achieve-
ments with the dramatic monologue, a genre of poetry that emphasizes the
speaker's own distinct personality. Often Browning's speakers are his imaginative
re-creations of people who once existed in real life. He was especially interested in
religious, political, and artistic figures from the Renaissance. The following poem,
perhaps Browning's most famous, was written in 1842, and its speaker, Duke of
Ferrara, was an actual man.

    Ferrara°

That's my last Duchess painted on the wall,
Looking as if she were alive. I call
That piece a wonder, now: Frà Pandolf's° hands
Worked busily a day, and there she stands.
Will't please you sit and look at her? I said   5
"Frà Pandolf" by design, for never read
Strangers like you that pictured countenance,
The depth and passion of its earnest glance,
But to myself they turned (since none puts by
The curtain I have drawn for you, but I)   10
And seemed as they would ask me, if they durst,
How such a glance came there; so, not the first
Are you to turn and ask thus. Sir, 'twas not
Her husband's presence only, called that spot
Of joy into the Duchess' cheek: perhaps   15
Frà Pandolf chanced to say "Her mantle laps
Over my lady's wrist too much," or "Paint
Must never hope to reproduce the faint
Half-flush that dies along her throat": such stuff
Was courtesy, she thought, and cause enough   20
For calling up that spot of joy. She had
A heart—how shall I say?—too soon made glad,
Too easily impressed; she liked whate'er
She looked on, and her looks went everywhere.
Sir, 'twas all one! My favor at her breast,   25
The dropping of the daylight in the West,
The bough of cherries some officious fool
Broke in the orchard for her, the white mule
She rode with round the terrace—all and each
Would draw from her alike the approving speech,   30
Or blush, at least. She thanked men,—good! but thanked
Somehow—I know not how—as if she ranked

EPIGRAPH: Ferrara: In the sixteenth century, the duke of this Italian city arranged to marry a
second time after the mysterious death of his very young first wife.   **3 Frà Pandolf:** A fictitious
artist.

My gift of a nine-hundred-years-old name
With anybody's gift. Who'd stoop to blame
This sort of trifling? Even had you skill   35
In speech — which I have not — to make your will
Quite clear to such an one, and say, "Just this
Or that in you disgusts me; here you miss,
Or there exceed the mark" — and if she let
Herself be lessoned so, nor plainly set   40
Her wits to yours, forsooth, and made excuse,
— E'en then would be some stooping; and I choose
Never to stoop. Oh sir, she smiled, no doubt,
Whene'er I passed her; but who passed without
Much the same smile? This grew; I gave commands;   45
Then all smiles stopped together. There she stands
As if alive. Will't please you rise? We'll meet
The company below, then. I repeat,
The Count your master's known munificence
Is ample warrant that no just pretense   50
Of mine for dowry will be disallowed;
Though his fair daughter's self, as I avowed
At starting, is my object. Nay, we'll go
Together down, sir. Notice Neptune, though,
Taming a sea-horse, thought a rarity,   55
Which Claus of Innsbruck° cast in bronze for me!   [1842]

56 Claus of Innsbruck: A fictitious artist.

FOR THINKING AND WRITING

1. The duke offers a history of his first marriage. Summarize his story in your
   own words, including the reasons he gives for his behavior. How would
   you describe him? Do you admire anything about him? If so, what?

2. Try to reconstruct the rhetorical situation in which the duke is making his
   remarks. Who might be his audience? What might be his goals? What
   strategies is he using to accomplish them? Cite details that support your
   conjectures.

3. When you read the poem aloud, how conscious are you of its rhymes?
   What is its rhyme scheme? What is the effect of Browning's using just one
   stanza rather than breaking the poem into several?

4. Going by this example of the genre, what are the advantages of writing a
   poem as a dramatic monologue? What are the disadvantages?

5. Browning suggests that the setting of this poem is Renaissance Italy. What
   relevance might his poem have had for readers in mid-nineteenth-
   century England? What relevance might it have for audiences in the
   United States today?

COUNTEE CULLEN
Incident

Countee Cullen (1903–1946) was one of the leading writers of the Harlem Renaissance, a New York–based movement of African American authors, artists, and intellectuals that flourished from World War I to the Great Depression. Cullen's place of birth may have been Baltimore, Louisville, or New York, but by 1918 he was living in New York as the adopted son of a Methodist minister. Cullen wrote poetry and received prizes for it even as he attended New York University. In 1925, while pursuing a master's degree from Harvard, he published his first book of poems, Color, *which contained "Incident." His later books included* Copper Sun *(1927),* The Black Christ and Other Poems *(1929), a translation of Euripides' play* Medea *(1935), and a children's book,* The Lost Zoo *(1940). Cullen gained much attention when, in 1928, he wed the daughter of famed African American writer and scholar W. E. B. DuBois, but their marriage ended just two years later. During the 1930s, Cullen's writing did not earn him enough to live on, so he taught English and French at Frederick Douglass High School. At the time of his death in 1946, he was collaborating on the Broadway musical* St. Louis Woman. *In part because he died relatively young, Cullen's reputation faded. Langston Hughes became much better known as a Harlem Renaissance figure. "Incident," however, has been consistently anthologized, and today Cullen is being rediscovered along with other contributors to African American literature.*

Once riding in old Baltimore
    Heart-filled, head-filled with glee,
I saw a Baltimorean
    Keep looking straight at me.

Now I was eight and very small,   5
    And he was no whit bigger,
And so I smiled, but he poked out
    His tongue and called me, "Nigger."

I saw the whole of Baltimore
    From May until December: 10
Of all the things that happened there
    That's all that I remember.

                           [1925]

FOR THINKING AND WRITING

1. Why do you think the speaker calls attention to his heart *and* his head in the second line? Might referring to just one of these things have been enough?

2. "Baltimorean" (line 3) seems a rather unusual and abstract term for the boy that the speaker encountered. How do you explain its presence in the

poem? How important is it that the speaker name the city where the incident occurred?

3. Although the incident that the speaker recalls must have been painful for him, why do you think he does not state his feelings about it more explicitly? What is the effect of his relative reticence about it?

4. The rhythm of this poem is rather sing-songy. Why do you think Cullen made it so?

5. The speaker states that he was eight at the time of the incident. How old might he be now? How important is his age?

TOI DERRICOTTE
Fears of the Eighth Grade

Toi Derricotte (b. 1941) is professor of English at the University of Pittsburgh. She has published poetry in several journals and written four books of it. The following poem appears in her 1989 volume Captivity.

When I ask what things they fear,
their arms raise like soldiers volunteering for battle:
Fear of going into a dark room, my murderer is waiting.
Fear of taking a shower, someone will stab me.
Fear of being kidnapped, raped.   5
Fear of dying in war.
When I ask how many fear this,
all the children raise their hands.

I think of this little box of consecrated land,
the bombs somewhere else,   10
the dead children in their mothers' arms,
women crying at the gates of the bamboo palace.

How thin the veneer!
The paper towels, napkins, toilet paper — everything
burned up in a day.   15

These children see the city after Armageddon°
The demons stand visible in the air
between their friends talking.
They see fire in a spring day
the instant before conflagration.   20
They feel blood through closed faucets,
the dead rising from boiling seas.   [1989]

16 **Armageddon:** In the Bible (Rev. 16:16), Armageddon is associated with the end of the world; specifically, it is the place where the forces of good and evil fight their final battle.

FOR THINKING AND WRITING

1. Evidently the speaker is referring to a particular group of eighth graders whom she has interviewed. Do you think many other eighth graders would have the same fears? What else might the speaker have asked these children to learn how they view the world?

2. Does Derricotte's speaker seem to express a particular attitude toward the children's statements? Or do you see her as leaving you free to make your own judgment of them? Refer to specific lines.

3. Where, specifically, might the "somewhere else" in line 10 be? Think of particular countries.

4. Does the reference to Armageddon in line 16 make sense? Do you assume that the last stanza truly conveys what "These children see"? Again, support your answers by referring to specific lines.

5. What would you say to these children? In what ways would you address their fears if you were their teacher? In your view, to what extent does the typical eighth-grade curriculum address their concerns?

MARK DOTY
Night Ferry

Mark Doty (b. 1953) was born in Tennessee, but his father, who was a builder working for the Army Corps of Engineers, was a man who could not get along with supervisors and often moved the family. In the autobiographical Firebird *(1999), Doty describes growing up as "a sissy" in a Southern Gothic family. He attended high school in Tucson, Arizona, where he first developed an interest in writing, then briefly attended the University of Tucson, but dropped out and married when he was eighteen. He attended Drake University in Iowa in the 1970s, where he and his wife published chapbooks of poetry together. In 1981, he dissolved his marriage when he acknowledged his homosexuality. He received his M.F.A. at Goddard College in Vermont and taught there, eventually moving with his partner to Provincetown, Massachusetts. After his partner died from complications of AIDS in 1984, Doty's poetry took on a new intensity and significance. Doty has taught at several universities and now teaches at the University of Houston. He has published six poetry collections and two memoirs. His awards and fellowships include the National Book Critics Award and the T. S. Eliot Prize in 1993 for* My Alexandria.

We're launched into the darkness,
half a load of late passengers
   gliding onto the indefinite
      black surface, a few lights vague

          ◆   ◆   ◆

and shimmering on the island shore.   5
Behind us, between the landing's twin flanks
      (wooden pylons strapped with old tires),
            the docklights shatter in our twin,

      folding wakes, their colors
on the roughened surface combed   10
      like the patterns of Italian bookpaper,
            lustrous and promising. The narrative

      of the ferry begins and ends brilliantly,
and its text is this moving out
      into what is soon before us   15
            and behind: the night going forward,

      sentence by sentence, as if on faith,
into whatever takes place.
      It's strange how we say things *take place*,
            as if occurrence were a location —   20

      the dark between two shores,
for instance, where for a little while
      we're on no solid ground. Twelve minutes,
            precisely, the night ferry hurries

      across the lake. And what happens   25
is always the body of water,
      its skin like the wrong side of satin.
            I love to stand like this,

      where the prow pushes blunt into the future,
knowing, more than seeing, how   30
      the surface rushes and doesn't even break
            but simply slides under us.

      Lake melds into shoreline,
one continuous black moiré;
      the boatmen follow the one course they know   35
            toward a dock nearly the mirror

      of the first, mercury lamps vaporing
over the few late birds
      attending the pier. Even the bored men
            at the landing, who wave   40

      their flashlights for the last travelers,
steering us toward the road, will seem
      the engineers of our welcome,
            their red-sheathed lights marking

◆ ◆ ◆

the completion of our, or anyone's, crossing. 45
Twelve dark minutes. Love,
    we are between worlds, between
        unfathomed water and I don't know how much

    light-flecked black sky, the fogged circles
of island lamps. I am almost not afraid 50
    on this good boat, breathing its good smell
        of grease and kerosene,

    warm wind rising up the stairwell
from the engine's serious study.
    There's no beautiful binding 55
        for this story, only the temporary,

    liquid endpapers of the hurried water,
shot with random color. But in the gliding forward's
    a scent so quick and startling
        it might as well be blowing 60

off the stars. Now, just before we arrive,
the wind carries a signal and a comfort,
    lovely, though not really meant for us:
        woodsmoke risen from the chilly shore. [1993]

FOR THINKING AND WRITING

1. The poem seems to be a sustained metaphor for life's journey. In what ways does this comparison make sense? What other significant metaphor is developed?

2. As symbols, what do the following images suggest: "a few lights vague / and shimmering" (lines 4–5), "like the patterns of Italian bookpaper, / lustrous and promising" (lines 11–12), "no beautiful binding / for this story, only the temporary, / liquid endpapers of the hurried water, / shot with random color" (lines 55–58)?

3. How did you evaluate the speaker's attitude when he says, "I am almost not afraid / on this good boat, breathing its good smell" (lines 50–51)?

4. Does the image of "a scent . . . / . . . blowing / off the stars" in lines 59 to 61 seem more mysterious than Doty's other images? What idea might the poet be after with such imagery?

5. Can we sustain the journey-of-life metaphor into the last stanza? Where might the passengers be arriving? What is the signal "not really meant for us" (line 63)? Why woodsmoke? Why "the chilly shore" (line 64)?

CORNELIUS EADY
Who Am I?

Cornelius Eady (b. 1954) has published several books of poetry, including Victims
of the Latest Dance Craze *(1986),* The Gathering of My Name *(1991),* You
Don't Miss Your Water *(1995), and* The Autobiography of a Jukebox *(1997). He
has also taught creative writing at several colleges, including the State University
of New York at Stony Brook, City College of New York, and the New School. The
following poem first appeared in a 1996 issue of the literary journal* Ploughshares
and was also included in Eady's most recent book, Brutal Imagination *(2001). It
deals with the 1994 case of Susan Smith, a Southern white woman who claimed
that an African American man had kidnapped her two sons but was discovered to
have drowned them herself, a crime for which she is now serving a life sentence.
Throughout Eady's sequence, the speaker is the imaginary African American whom
Smith blamed for her children's disappearance.*

Who are you, mister?
One of the boys asks
From the eternal backseat
And here is the one good thing:
If I am alive, then so, briefly, are they,   5
Two boys returned, three and one,
Quiet and scared, bunched together
Breathing like small beasts.
They can't place me, yet there's
Something familiar.   10
Though my skin and sex are different, maybe
It's the way I drive
Or occasionally glance back
With concern,
Maybe it's the mixed blessing   15
Someone, perhaps circumstance,
Has given us,
The secret thrill of hiding,
Childish, in plain sight,
Seen, but not seen,   20
As if suddenly given the power
To move through walls,
To know every secret without permission.
We roll sleepless through the dark streets, but inside
The cab is lit with brutal imagination.   [2001]   25

FOR THINKING AND WRITING

1. Why do you suppose Susan Smith claimed that her children's kidnapper was an African American man?

2. The title of this poem is a question. Does the poem answer it? If so, how?

3. Describe the speaker's relationship with the two boys. What, conceivably, does he have in mind when he says that they sense "Something familiar" (line 10) about him?

4. The word *secret* is repeated. What is its role in the poem?

5. What does the speaker apparently have in mind with his final phrase, "brutal imagination"? (This is also the title of the book where the poem appears.)

T. S. ELIOT
The Love Song of J. Alfred Prufrock

One of the most respected intellectuals of his time, Thomas Stearns Eliot (1888–1965) was a poet, playwright (Murder in the Cathedral), and critic (The Sacred Wood). His poem "The Waste Land" (1922), considered a modernist masterpiece, is perhaps this century's most influential poem. The long-running Broadway play Cats is based on some of Eliot's lighter poems. Born in America and educated at Harvard, Eliot lived his mature life in England. He was awarded the Nobel Prize for literature in 1948.

> *S'io credesse che mia risposta fosse*
> *A persona che mai tornasse al mondo,*
> *Questa fiamma staria senza più scosse.*
> *Ma perciocchè giammai di questo fondo*
> *Non tornò vivo alcun, s'i'odo il vero,*
> *Senza tema d'infamia ti rispondo.*°

Let us go then, you and I,
When the evening is spread out against the sky
Like a patient etherized upon a table;
Let us go, through certain half-deserted streets,
The muttering retreats   5
Of restless nights in one-night cheap hotels
And sawdust restaurants with oyster-shells:
Streets that follow like a tedious argument
Of insidious intent
To lead you to an overwhelming question . . .   10
                          ◆　◆　◆

EPIGRAPH: *S'io . . . rispondo:* In Dante's *Inferno*, a sufferer in hell says, "If I thought I was talking to someone who might return to earth, this flame would cease; but if what I have heard is true, no one does return; therefore, I can speak to you without fear of infamy."

Oh, do not ask, "What is it?"
Let us go and make our visit.

In the room the women come and go
Talking of Michelangelo.

The yellow fog that rubs its back upon the window panes,   15
The yellow smoke that rubs its muzzle on the window panes
Licked its tongue into the corners of the evening,
Lingered upon the pools that stand in drains,
Let fall upon its back the soot that falls from chimneys,
Slipped by the terrace, made a sudden leap,   20
And seeing that it was a soft October night,
Curled once about the house, and fell asleep.

And indeed there will be time°
For the yellow smoke that slides along the street,
Rubbing its back upon the window panes;   25
There will be time, there will be time
To prepare a face to meet the faces that you meet;
There will be time to murder and create,
And time for all the works and days° of hands
That lift and drop a question on your plate: 30
Time for you and time for me,
And time yet for a hundred indecisions,
And for a hundred visions and revisions,
Before the taking of a toast and tea.

In the room the women come and go   35
Talking of Michelangelo.

And indeed there will be time
To wonder, "Do I dare?" and, "Do I dare?" —
Time to turn back and descend the stair,
With a bald spot in the middle of my hair —   40
(They will say: "How his hair is growing thin!")
My morning coat, my collar mounting firmly to the chin,
My necktie rich and modest, but asserted by a simple pin —
(They will say: "But how his arms and legs are thin!")
Do I dare   45
Disturb the universe?
In a minute there is time
For decisions and revisions which a minute will reverse.

For I have known them all already, known them all:
Have known the evenings, mornings, afternoons,   50
I have measured out my life with coffee spoons;

23 there will be time: An allusion to Ecclesiastes 3:1–8: "To everything there is a season, and a time to every purpose under heaven."   **29 works and days:** Hesiod's eighth century B.C.E. poem gave practical advice.

I know the voices dying with a dying fall
Beneath the music from a farther room.
        So how should I presume?

        And I have known the eyes already, known them all —   55
The eyes that fix you in a formulated phrase.
And when I am formulated, sprawling on a pin,
When I am pinned and wriggling on the wall,
Then how should I begin
To spit out all the butt-ends of my days and ways?   60
        And how should I presume?

        And I have known the arms already, known them all —
Arms that are braceleted and white and bare
(But in the lamplight, downed with light brown hair!)
        Is it perfume from a dress   65
        That makes me so digress?
Arms that lie along a table, or wrap about a shawl.
        And should I then presume?
        And how should I begin?

        Shall I say, I have gone at dusk through narrow streets,   70
And watched the smoke that rises from the pipes
Of lonely men in shirtsleeves, leaning out of windows? . . .

I should have been a pair of ragged claws
Scuttling across the floors of silent seas.

        And the afternoon, the evening, sleeps so peacefully!   75
Smoothed by long fingers,
Asleep . . . tired . . . or it malingers,
Stretched on the floor, here beside you and me.
Should I, after tea and cakes and ices,
Have the strength to force the moment to its crisis?   80
But though I have wept and fasted, wept and prayed,
Though I have seen my head (grown slightly bald) brought in upon a platter,°
I am no prophet — and here's no great matter;
I have seen the moment of my greatness flicker,
And I have seen the eternal Footman hold my coat, and snicker,   85
        And in short, I was afraid.

        And would it have been worth it, after all,
After the cups, the marmalade, the tea,
Among the porcelain, among some talk of you and me,
Would it have been worth while   90
To have bitten off the matter with a smile,
To have squeezed the universe into a ball°

---

82 head . . . platter: Like John the Baptist (Matt. 14:1–12).   **92 squeezed . . . ball:** See lines
41–42 of Marvell's "To His Coy Mistress" (p. 707).

To roll it toward some overwhelming question,
To say: "I am Lazarus,° come from the dead,
Come back to tell you all, I shall tell you all" —   95
If one, settling a pillow by her head,
    Should say: "That is not what I meant at all;
    That is not it, at all."

    And would it have been worth it, after all,
Would it have been worth while,   100
After the sunsets and the dooryards and the sprinkled streets,
After the novels, after the teacups, after the skirts that trail along the floor —
And this, and so much more? —
It is impossible to say just what I mean!
But as if a magic lantern threw the nerves in patterns on a screen: 105
Would it have been worth while
If one, settling a pillow or throwing off a shawl,
And turning toward the window, should say:
    "That is not it at all,
    That is not what I meant, at all."   110

No! I am not Prince Hamlet, nor was meant to be;
Am an attendant lord,° one that will do
To swell a progress,° start a scene or two
Advise the prince: withal, an easy tool,
Deferential, glad to be of use,   115
Politic, cautious, and meticulous;
Full of high sentence, but a bit obtuse;
At times, indeed, almost ridiculous —
Almost, at times, the Fool.

I grow old . . . I grow old . . .   120
I shall wear the bottoms of my trowsers rolled.

    Shall I part my hair behind?° Do I dare to eat a peach?
I shall wear white flannel trowsers, and walk upon the beach.
I have heard the mermaids singing, each to each.

I do not think that they will sing to me.   125

I have seen them riding seaward on the waves,
Combing the white hair of the waves blown back
When the wind blows the water white and black.

We have lingered in the chambers of the sea
By seagirls wreathed with seaweed red and brown,   130
Till human voices wake us, and we drown.   [1917]

---

94 I am Lazarus: Raised from the dead by Jesus.   **112 attendant lord:** Like Polonius in Shakespeare's *Hamlet*.   **113 progress:** state procession.   **121–122 trowsers rolled . . . part my hair behind:** The latest fashion.

FOR THINKING AND WRITING

1. To what is Prufrock referring when he says, "Do I dare?" (line 38)? How about "that is not it, at all" (lines 98, 109)? What is Prufrock so anxious about?

2. Prufrock seems to characterize himself quite severely in lines 111 to 119. How would you describe him? Do you know people like him?

3. Do you think the imagery of the opening stanza sets the right tone for Prufrock's journey? How would you describe the tone—ironic, self-mocking, depressed, overly cautious, too self-conscious?

4. Is Prufrock making an argument against getting involved in a romance? What evidence does he use to support his argument?

5. Critics have given widely different interpretations of the two couplets, "In the room the women come and go / Talking of Michelangelo" (lines 13–14) and "I should have been a pair of ragged claws / Scuttling across the floors of silent seas" (lines 73–74). What do you think these lines mean?

CAROLYN FORCHÉ
The Colonel

In her poetry, Carolyn Forché (b. 1950) often addresses contemporary abuses of power. Her first book of poems, Gathering the Tribes *(1976), won the Yale Series of Younger Poets competition. The following poem is from her second,* The Country between Us *(1981), which won the Lamont Award from the Academy of American Poets. Much of this book is based on Forché's experiences during her stay in El Salvador, which at the time was beset by civil war. Forché's latest book of poetry is* The Blue Hour *(2003), and she has also edited a collection entitled* Against Forgetting: Twentieth-Century Poetry of Witness *(1993). She lives in Rockville, Maryland, and teaches creative writing at George Mason University in Fairfax, Virginia.*

What you have heard is true. I was in his house. His wife carried a tray of coffee and sugar. His daughter filed her nails, his son went out for the night. There were daily papers, pet dogs, a pistol on the cushion beside him. The moon swung bare on its black cord over the house. On the television was a cop show. It was in English. Broken bottles were embedded in the walls around the house to scoop   5
the kneecaps from a man's legs or cut his hands to lace. On the windows there were gratings like those in liquor stores. We had dinner, rack of lamb, good wine, a gold bell was on the table for calling the maid. The maid brought green mangoes, salt, a type of bread. I was asked how I enjoyed the country. There was a brief commercial in Spanish. His wife took everything away. There was some talk   10
then of how difficult it had become to govern. The parrot said hello on the terrace. The colonel told it to shut up, and pushed himself from the table. My

friend said to me with his eyes: say nothing. The colonel returned with a sack
used to bring groceries home. He spilled many human ears on the table. They
were like dried peach halves. There is no other way to say this. He took one of   15
them in his hands, shook it in our faces, dropped it into a water glass. It came
alive there. I am tired of fooling around he said. As for the rights of anyone, tell
your people they can go fuck themselves. He swept the ears to the floor with his
arm and held the last of his wine in the air. Something for your poetry, no? he
said. Some of the ears on the floor caught this scrap of his voice. Some of the ears   20
on the floor were pressed to the ground.   [1978]

FOR THINKING AND WRITING

1. How do you characterize the colonel? List a number of specific adjectives
   and supporting details. Does your impression of him change as you read,
   or does it stay pretty much the same? Explain.

2. Forché calls this text a poem, and yet it seems to consist of one long prose
   paragraph. Here is an issue of genre: Is it *really* a poem? Support your
   answer by identifying what you think are characteristics of poetry. What is
   the effect of Forché's presenting the text as a poem? Note what the colonel
   says about poetry. How might this text be considered a response to him?

3. Forché uses many short sentences here. What is the effect of this strategy?
   Even though she quotes the colonel, she does not use quotation marks.
   What is the effect of this choice?

4. The poem begins, "What you have heard is true." Do you think the situation it describes really occurred? Identify some warrants or assumptions
   that influence your answer. Where else does the poem refer to hearing?
   How might it be seen as being about audiences and their responses?

5. Forché wrote "The Colonel" after a stay in El Salvador, and so it is rea-
   sonable for her audience to conclude that the poem is set in that country.
   Yet she does not actually specify the setting. Should she have done so?
   Why, or why not?

ROBERT FROST
After Apple-Picking

*Robert Frost (1874–1963) became one of the United States's best-known and
beloved poets. During his lifetime, he was such a public figure that he was asked to
read his poetry at the 1961 inauguration of President John F. Kennedy. In particular, Frost has been celebrated for his poems about New England farm life. Clearly,
"After Apple-Picking" reflects work that Frost himself did in that setting. When he
wrote the poem in 1913, however, he was living temporarily in England, so the
poem reflects his memories of farm work more than his current experience of it.
Indeed, Frost hardly spent all his life on farms. He was born in the city of San Fran-*

cisco, and as an adult he taught at numerous colleges, including Amherst College and the University of Michigan. Nor was he immediately acclaimed as a poet. He was thirty-eight years old when his first book of verse, A Boy's Will, *appeared in 1912, and it came out in England rather than the United States. His American reputation soared only with the 1914 publication of his second volume,* North of Boston, *which included "After Apple-Picking" as well as "Mending Wall."*

My long two-pointed ladder's sticking through a tree
Toward heaven still,
And there's a barrel that I didn't fill
Beside it, and there may be two or three
Apples I didn't pick upon some bough.   5
But I am done with apple-picking now.
Essence of winter sleep is on the night,
The scent of apples: I am drowsing off.
I cannot rub the strangeness from my sight
I got from looking through a pane of glass   10
I skimmed this morning from the drinking trough
And held against the world of hoary grass.
It melted, and I let it fall and break.
But I was well
Upon my way to sleep before it fell,   15
And I could tell
What form my dreaming was about to take.
Magnified apples appear and disappear,
Stem end and blossom end,
And every fleck of russet showing clear.   20
My instep arch not only keeps the ache,
It keeps the pressure of a ladder-round.
I feel the ladder sway as the boughs bend.
And I keep hearing from the cellar bin
The rumbling sound   25
Of load on load of apples coming in.
For I have had too much
Of apple-picking: I am overtired
Of the great harvest I myself desired.
There were ten thousand thousand fruit to touch,   30
Cherish in hand, lift down, and not let fall.
For all
That struck the earth,
No matter if not bruised or spiked with stubble,
Went surely to the cider-apple heap   35
As of no worth.
One can see what will trouble
This sleep of mine, whatever sleep it is.

Were he not gone,
The woodchuck could say whether it's like his   40
Long sleep, as I describe its coming on,
Or just some human sleep.   [1914]

FOR THINKING AND WRITING

1. What details in this poem can be taken to indicate that it deals with matters of religion and the afterlife? In your own view, to what extent *does* it concern such matters? In what ways, if any, might it refer to the writing of poetry? Are there other subjects that the poem seems to address? If so, what?

2. If you find the verb tenses in this poem a bit confusing, you are not alone. Frost seems deliberately to make past, present, and future hard to distinguish here. Why, do you think? Try, at any rate, to figure out the chronological order of the speaker's day. What happened in the morning, what happened later on, and what may occur when the speaker falls asleep?

3. In lines 28 and 29, the speaker declares that "I am overtired / Of the great harvest I myself desired." What do you think the speaker really wanted? What do you think he really wants now?

4. Which of his physical senses does the speaker refer to? Identify specific lines where these come up. How realistic is his description of his physical experience? Do any of his sensory details seem exaggerated or distorted? If so, which?

5. At the end, the speaker wonders if "human sleep" resembles that of a woodchuck. More generally, he encourages us to compare human beings with animals. What other details of the poem seem relevant to this comparison? How close a connection between humans and animals are you inclined to make after reading Frost's poem?

ROBERT FROST
Mending Wall

Something there is that doesn't love a wall,
That sends the frozen-ground-swell under it,
And spills the upper boulders in the sun;
And makes gaps even two can pass abreast.
The work of hunters is another thing: 5
I have come after them and made repair
Where they have left not one stone on a stone,
But they would have the rabbit out of hiding,
To please the yelping dogs. The gaps I mean,
No one has seen them made or heard them made,   10

But at spring mending-time we find them there.
I let my neighbor know beyond the hill;
And on a day we meet to walk the line
And set the wall between us once again.
We keep the wall between us as we go.   15
To each the boulders that have fallen to each.
And some are loaves and some so nearly balls
We have to use a spell to make them balance:
"Stay where you are until our backs are turned!"
We wear our fingers rough with handling them.   20
Oh, just another kind of outdoor game,
One on a side. It comes to little more:
There where it is we do not need the wall:
He is all pine and I am apple orchard.
My apple trees will never get across   25
And eat the cones under his pines, I tell him.
He only says, "Good fences make good neighbors."
Spring is the mischief in me, and I wonder
If I could put a notion in his head:
"*Why* do they make good neighbors? Isn't it   30
Where there are cows? But here there are no cows.
Before I built a wall I'd ask to know
What I was walling in or walling out,
And to whom I was like to give offense.
Something there is that doesn't love a wall,   35
That wants it down." I could say "Elves" to him,
But it's not elves exactly, and I'd rather
He said it for himself. I see him there
Bringing a stone grasped firmly by the top
In each hand, like an old-stone savage armed.   40
He moves in darkness as it seems to me,
Not of woods only and the shade of trees.
He will not go behind his father's saying,
And he likes having thought of it so well
He says again, "Good fences make good neighbors."   [1914]   45

FOR THINKING AND WRITING

1. How do you interpret the first word of the poem? What are the "things" the
   narrator cites that don't "love a wall"? Is he suggesting walls are unnatural?

2. What is the narrator's rebuttal to his neighbor's assertion that "Good
   fences make good neighbors" (lines 27 and 45)? Do you agree with him?

3. Even though they often make an important point, titles of poems are
   often overlooked by readers. Is *mending* used here as an adjective or a
   verb? Could the meaning of *mending* change the theme of the poem?

4. Some readers see contradictions in the speaker's attitudes and his behavior; for example, if he does not like walls, why does he "let [his] neighbor know" (line 12) that the wall needs repair?

5. Although it appears at first that the narrator doesn't love walls or conformists like his neighbor, his actual behavior does seem somewhat ambivalent. Write an essay in which you argue that walls do (or do not) make good neighbors. You might first want to decide to view "walls" as metaphorical or literal.

NIKKI GIOVANNI
Legacies

Raised near Cincinnati, Ohio, Nikki Giovanni (b. 1943) returned as a teenager to her birthplace and "spiritual" home in Knoxville, Tennessee, where she experienced the strong influence of her grandmother, Louvenia Watson. She studied at the University of Cincinnati from 1961–1963 and earned a B.A. at Fisk University in 1967. She also attended the University of Pennsylvania School of Social Work (1967) and Columbia University School of the Arts (1968). She has taught at a number of universities, since 1987 at Virginia Polytechnic Institute, where she is a professor of English. Her poetry, essays, and works for children reflect her commitment to African American community, family, and womanhood. Her latest book is The Collected Poetry of Nikki Giovanni: 1968–1998 *(2003). "Legacies" is from Giovanni's 1972 book,* My House.

her grandmother called her from the playground
    "yes, ma'am"
    "i want chu to learn how to make rolls," said the old
woman proudly
but the little girl didn't want   5
to learn how because she knew
even if she couldn't say it that
that would mean when the old one died she would be less
dependent on her spirit so
she said   10
    "i don't want to know how to make no rolls"
with her lips poked out
and the old woman wiped her hands on
her apron saying "lord
    these children"   15
and neither of them ever
said what they meant
and i guess nobody ever does   [1972]

FOR THINKING AND WRITING

1. Does the dialogue in Giovanni's poem reveal the true feelings of the grandmother and the girl? Be explicit about what is really going on in their minds. Is the girl superstitious?

2. Is it true that "nobody" (line 18) says what she really means? Do you? Is this an indication of honesty or something else — say, tact or convention? Are poets more likely to tell the truth?

3. What makes this piece a poem? Would you prefer more metaphors or similes, allusions, or flowery language? Is "proudly" (line 4) an important word here?

4. Change the grandmother's words to those that reflect more of what is in her heart. Might the girl respond differently if the grandmother were more forthright?

5. The title is only referred to obliquely. Why? What does it refer to? Is contemporary society concerned with legacies? Are you? Are they important or irrelevant?

LOUISE GLÜCK
The School Children

For many years, Louise Glück (b. 1943) has taught creative writing at Goddard College in Vermont. She has also published several volumes of poetry, winning the Pulitzer Prize for The Wild Iris *(1992). Recently she was appointed Poet Laureate of the United States. In her poetry, Glück often deals with domestic life, though with mythic references that make it seem more mysterious than familiar. The following poem comes from her 1975 book,* The House on Marshland.

The children go forward with their little satchels.
And all morning the mothers have labored
to gather the late apples, red and gold,
like words of another language.

And on the other shore   5
are those who wait behind great desks
to receive these offerings.

How orderly they are — the nails
on which the children hang
their overcoats of blue or yellow wool.   10

And the teachers shall instruct them in silence
and the mothers shall scour the orchards for a way out,
drawing to themselves the gray limbs of the fruit trees
bearing so little ammunition.

[1975]

FOR THINKING AND WRITING

1. Do you think Glück is commenting on a very particular group of school-children or on schoolchildren in general? Explain your reasoning.

2. The words "How orderly they are" (line 8) appear before Glück identifies the "they." Only afterward does she indicate that "they" refers to "the nails." Why do you think she delays? What is the effect?

3. Although the poem's title suggests that it will focus on the schoolchildren, the poem also refers to mothers and teachers. After reading it, do you think the schoolchildren are indeed its focus? Support your claim by referring to specific lines.

4. What roles do colors play in this poem? Identify each color mentioned and some things that a reader might associate with each.

5. What are some specific ways in which a teacher might instruct children "in silence" (line 11)? Has a teacher of yours ever done so? In what sense might the mothers of schoolchildren need "a way out" (line 12) and "ammunition" (line 14)?

SEAMUS HEANEY
Punishment

For his distinguished career as a poet, Seamus Heaney (b. 1939) won the Nobel Prize for literature in 1995. He was raised as a Catholic in Northern Ireland, where Protestants remained in the majority and frequently conflicted with Catholics. Until the Peace Accord of 1997, the region was controlled by the British govern-ment, whereas now it is ruled by a mixed body representing both religions. Several of Heaney's poems deal with Catholic resistance to the longtime British domina-tion of his native land. Heaney moved to Dublin in the Republic of Ireland in the early 1970s, but he has often visited the United States, even holding an appoint-ment as Boylston Professor of Rhetoric at Harvard University. The following poem appears in Heaney's 1975 book North. *It is part of a whole sequence of poems based on P. V. Glob's 1969 book* The Bog People. *Heaney was drawn to Glob's photographs of Iron Age people whose preserved bodies were discovered in bogs of Denmark and other European countries.*

I can feel the tug
of the halter at the nape
of her neck, the wind
on her naked front.

It blows her nipples   5
to amber beads,

it shakes the frail rigging
of her ribs.

I can see her drowned
body in the bog,   10
the weighing stone,
the floating rods and boughs.

Under which at first
she was a barked sapling
that is dug up   15
oak-bone, brain-firkin:

her shaved head
like a stubble of black corn,
her blindfold a soiled bandage,
her noose a ring   20

to store
the memories of love.
Little adulteress,
before they punished you

you were flaxen-haired,   25
undernourished, and your
tar-black face was beautiful.
My poor scapegoat,

I almost love you
but would have cast, I know,   30
the stones of silence.°
I am the artful voyeur

of your brain's exposed
and darkened combs,
your muscles' webbing   35
and all your numbered bones:

I who have stood dumb
when your betraying sisters,
cauled in tar,
wept by the railings,°   40

◆ ◆ ◆

30–31 would have cast . . . of silence: In John 8:7–9, Jesus confronts a mob about to stone an adulterous woman and makes the famous statement "He that is without sin among you, let him first cast a stone at her." The crowd retreats, "being convicted by their own conscience." **37–40 I who . . . by the railings:** In 1969, the British army became highly visible occupiers of Northern Ireland. In Heaney's native city of Belfast, the Irish Republican Army retaliated against Irish Catholic women who dated British soldiers. Punishments included shaving the women's heads, stripping and tarring them, and handcuffing them to the city's railings.

who would connive
in civilized outrage
yet understand the exact
and tribal, intimate revenge.   [1975]

FOR THINKING AND WRITING

1. Summarize your impression of the bog woman. Where does the speaker
   begin directly addressing her? Why do you suppose Heaney has him
   refrain from addressing her right away?

2. Who is the main subject of this poem? The bog woman? The "betraying
   sisters" (line 38)? The speaker? Some combination of these people?

3. The speaker refers to himself as a "voyeur" (line 32). Consult a dictionary
   definition of this word. How might it apply to the speaker? Do you think it
   is ultimately the best label for him? Explain. Do you feel like a voyeur
   reading this poem? Why, or why not?

4. What are the speaker's thoughts in the last stanza? What connotation do
   you attach to the word *connive*? (You might want to consult a dictionary
   definition of it.) What is the speaker's attitude toward "the exact /
   and tribal, intimate revenge"? Do you see him as tolerating violence?

5. What words in this poem, if any, are unfamiliar to you? What is their effect
   on you? Each stanza has four lines. Does this pattern create steady rhythm
   or one more fragmented than harmonious? Try reading it aloud.

LINDA HOGAN

Heritage

*Born in 1947 in Denver, Colorado, Linda Hogan is a contemporary Native Ameri-
can poet who calls on her Chickasaw heritage to interpret environmental, anti-
nuclear, and other spiritual and societal issues. Her published works include poems,
stories, screenplays, essays, and novels. Her novel* Power *(1998) has been praised
for its beauty of language, mythical structure, and allegorical power. Her many
honors include an American Book Award for* Seeing Through the Sun *(1985), a
Colorado Book Award and a Pulitzer nomination for* The Book of Medicines
*(1993), fellowships from the Guggenheim Foundation and the National Endow-
ment for the Arts, and a Lannan Award. Hogan received her M.A. from the University of Colorado at Boulder, where she currently teaches creative writing.
"Heritage" is from her 1978 book titled* Calling Myself Home.

From my mother, the antique mirror
where I watch my face take on her lines.
She left me the smell of baking bread

to warm fine hairs in my nostrils,
she left the large white breasts that weigh down 5
my body.

From my father I take his brown eyes,
the plague of locusts that leveled our crops,
they flew in formation like buzzards.

From my uncle the whittled wood 10
that rattles like bones
and is white
and smells like all our old houses
that are no longer there. He was the man
who sang old chants to me, the words 15
my father was told not to remember.

From my grandfather who never spoke
I learned to fear silence.
I learned to kill a snake
when you're begging for rain. 20

And Grandmother, blue-eyed woman
whose skin was brown,
she used snuff.
When her coffee can full of black saliva
spilled on me 25
it was like the brown cloud of grasshoppers
that leveled her fields.
It was the brown stain
that covered my white shirt,
my whiteness a shame. 30
That sweet black liquid like the food
she chewed up and spit into my father's mouth
when he was an infant.
It was the brown earth of Oklahoma
stained with oil. 35
She said tobacco would purge your body of poisons.
It has more medicine than stones and knives
against your enemies.
That tobacco is the dark night that covers me.

She said it is wise to eat the flesh of deer 40
so you will be swift and travel over many miles.
She told me how our tribe has always followed a stick
that pointed west
that pointed east.
From my family I have learned the secrets 45
of never having a home.   [1978]

FOR THINKING AND WRITING

1. The last sentence seems to contain a contradiction. "From my family I have learned the secrets" might lead you to expect something positive. But maybe the last phrase is not meant to be positive. What is your reading of Hogan's conclusion?

2. What does the narrator learn from her mother? Her father? Her uncle? Her grandfather? Her grandmother? What kinds of things did you learn from your family members? Use concrete images.

3. Why does she say "my whiteness a shame" (line 30)? Is this a racial comment?

4. Examine the "black saliva" section in lines 21–39. Does it start off negatively? Does it change? Explain.

5. We all learn things from our families, both positive and negative. Is Hogan giving a balanced account? Should she? Would you? Do poets have any responsibility to the larger culture? Or should they just follow their own inner vision?

GERARD MANLEY HOPKINS
Spring and Fall

Gerard Manley Hopkins (1844–1889) was a Jesuit priest who published few of his poems during his lifetime; they became widely known only after the second collected edition of them appeared in 1930. Hopkins is now especially famous for his development of a technique he called sprung rhythm. *As "Spring and Fall" demonstrates, a poem that uses it may include several stressed syllables in each line, and the number of stresses per line may vary. Sprung rhythm allows a poet to emphasize words as he or she sees fit, without following a regular pattern. The following poem was written in 1880.*

To a Young Child

Márgarét áre you gríeving
Over Goldengrove unleaving?
Leáves, like the things of man, you
With your fresh thoughts care for, can you?
Áh! ás the heart grows older   5
It will come to such sights colder
By and by, nor spare a sigh
Though worlds of wanwood leafmeal lie;°

8 **Though worlds of wanwood leafmeal lie:** The trees have shed leaves that now lie in piecemeal fashion on the ground. Probably Hopkins is describing these trees as pale, the most common modern meaning of *wan.* He may, however, be seeking to create the opposite impression, for *wan* resembles an Old English word that means "dark."

And yet you wíll weep and know why.
Now no matter, child, the name: 10
Sórrow's springs áre the same.
Nor mouth had, no nor mind, expressed
What heart heard of, ghost° guessed:
It ís the blight man was born for,
it is Margaret you mourn for.   [1880]   15

13 ghost: Soul.

FOR THINKING AND WRITING

1. In what respects does the poem relate to its title, "Spring and Fall"? Refer to specific lines.

2. What do you take to be the reasoning behind the speaker's ultimate claim — "it is Margaret you mourn for" (line 15)? Why do you suppose the speaker addresses Margaret this way? Could a child actually benefit from hearing such a message? If so, how?

3. Suppose the poem had been about Margaret rather than addressed to Margaret. Might its effect on you have been different? If so, how?

4. As we pointed out in the headnote, Hopkins was a priest. Does the poem seem to have been written by a religious person? What words of the text should someone especially consider in answering this question? How do you define *religious*?

5. Identify places where Hopkins uses alliteration, rhyming, and unusual words. How effective is each of these devices?

A. E. HOUSMAN
Loveliest of trees, the cherry now

A native of Fockbury, England, Alfred Edward Housman (1859–1936) became an accomplished scholar of classics, teaching Latin at University College in London and at Cambridge University. Today, though, he is known primarily as a poet. The following poem appeared in his first book of verse, A Shropshire Lad *(1896), which grew increasingly popular during the twentieth century. Housman published another volume,* Last Poems, *in 1922, and in 1936 his* More Poems *appeared shortly after his death. Interest in his life was renewed with Tom Stoppard's 1997 play* The Invention of Love, *which imagines conversations between Housman's younger and older selves. The relationship between youth and age is, in fact, a central concern of Housman's poetry, as you will see in this poem.*

Loveliest of trees, the cherry now
Is hung with bloom along the bough,

And stands about the woodland ride
Wearing white for Eastertide.

Now, of my threescore years and ten,   5
Twenty will not come again,
And take from seventy springs a score,
It only leaves me fifty more.

And since to look at things in bloom
Fifty springs are little room,   10
About the woodlands I will go
To see the cherry hung with snow.   [1896]

FOR THINKING AND WRITING

1. The word "now" appears in the first line of the first two stanzas. Why do you think Housman makes it so prominent?

2. According to the second stanza, how old is the speaker? What is the effect of showing him engaged in calculations?

3. The last word of the poem could have been "white," which is evidently the present color of the cherry trees. Yet Housman concludes the poem with "snow," a word not usually associated with "Eastertide." Why do you think he chose this particular word to end with?

4. Does the reference to "Eastertide" lead you to assume that this poem is meant to have religious implications? Why, or why not?

5. What is the tone of this poem? How does the rhyme scheme contribute to the tone?

JOHN KEATS
Ode on a Grecian Urn

Despite his early death from tuberculosis, John Keats (1795–1821) produced several poems still regarded as masterpieces of British Romanticism. The following poem is from a series of odes that Keats composed in 1819; others include "Ode to a Nightingale" and "Ode on Melancholy." At this period in his life, Keats was experiencing emotional turmoil. Already he was suffering from the disease that would kill him, while he also felt growing passion for a woman named Fanny Brawne. In turning to the genre of the ode, Keats was perpetuating a kind of poem that dates back to ancient Greece, where it adhered to a fixed structure involving three stanzas. By Keats's time, the ode's form had become more flexible. Often it featured more than three stanzas, which could vary in rhythm and length. In subject matter, the modern ode often dealt with topics that Keats addresses here: on the one hand, the speaker's desire for enduring beauty; on the other, the reality of a changing world.

1

Thou still unravished bride of quietness,
   Thou foster-child of silence and slow time,
Sylvan° historian, who canst thus express
   A flowery tale more sweetly than our rhyme:
What leaf-fringed legend haunts about thy shape   5
   Of deities or mortals, or of both,
      In Tempe or the dales of Arcady?°
What men or gods are these? What maidens loath?
   What mad pursuit? What struggle to escape?
      What pipes and timbrels? What wild ecstasy?   10

2

Heard melodies are sweet, but those unheard
   Are sweeter; therefore, ye soft pipes, play on;
Not to the sensual ear, but, more endeared,
   Pipe to the spirit ditties of no tone:
Fair youth, beneath the trees, thou canst not leave   15
   Thy song, nor ever can those trees be bare;
      Bold Lover, never, never canst thou kiss,
Though winning near the goal — yet, do not grieve;
   She cannot fade, though thou hast not thy bliss,
      For ever wilt thou love, and she be fair!   20

3

Ah, happy, happy boughs! that cannot shed
   Your leaves, nor ever bid the Spring adieu;
And, happy melodist, unwearièd,
   For ever piping songs for ever new;
More happy love! more happy, happy love!   25
   For ever warm and still to be enjoyed,
      For ever panting, and for ever young;
All breathing human passion far above,
   That leaves a heart high-sorrowful and cloyed,
      A burning forehead, and a parching tongue.   30

4

Who are these coming to the sacrifice?
   To what green altar, O mysterious priest,

---

3 Sylvan: Rustic; the urn is decorated with a forest scene.   **7 Tempe . . . Arcady:** Beautiful rural valleys in Greece.

Lead'st thou that heifer lowing at the skies,
    And all her silken flanks with garlands drest?
What little town by river or sea shore,   35
    Or mountain-built with peaceful citadel,
        Is emptied of this folk, this pious morn?
And, little town, thy streets for evermore
    Will silent be; and not a soul to tell
        Why thou art desolate, can e'er return.   40

5

O Attic° shape! Fair attitude! with brede°
    Of marble men and maidens overwrought,
With forest branches and the trodden weed;
    Thou, silent form, dost tease us out of thought
As doth eternity: Cold Pastoral!   45
    When old age shall this generation waste,
        Thou shalt remain, in midst of other woe
Than ours, a friend to man, to whom thou say'st,
    Beauty is truth, truth beauty—that is all
        Ye know on earth, and all ye need to know.   [1819]   50

41 Attic: Possessing classic Athenian simplicity.   **brede:** Design.

FOR THINKING AND WRITING

1. Visualize the urn based on Keats's lines about it. (You might draw a picture of it and compare your drawing with a classmate's.) How objective does the speaker's description of this object seem?

2. Two of the poem's stanzas are packed with questions. In general, what are these questions about?

3. What image of love does the speaker describe the urn as presenting? To what extent is it an image that you believe should be treasured?

4. What is the effect of the speaker's reference to the deserted town in the fourth stanza? Why do you think the speaker focuses on such an image at this point?

5. Why do you think the speaker calls the urn "cold" in line 45? Critics have long debated how to interpret the poem's last two lines. Do you agree with the speaker's statement that "Beauty is truth, truth beauty" is "all ye need to know"? Explain your reasoning.

MAXINE KUMIN
Woodchucks

Maxine Kumin (b. 1925) is a Pulitzer Prize–winning poet. She writes in a range of genres, however; her work includes four novels, a short-story collection, two volumes of essays, several children's books, and a memoir. "Woodchucks" comes from her 1971 collection of poems Our Ground Time Here Will Be Brief. *Like much of Kumin's writing, this poem deals with the world of nature. Kumin lives on a farm in New Hampshire, where she raises horses.*

Gassing the woodchucks didn't turn out right.
The knockout bomb from the Feed and Grain Exchange
was featured as merciful, quick at the bone
and the case we had against them was airtight,
both exits shoehorned shut with puddingstone,°   5
but they had a sub-sub-basement out of range.

Next morning they turned up again, no worse
for the cyanide than we for our cigarettes
and state-store Scotch, all of us up to scratch.
They brought down the marigolds as a matter of course   10
and then took over the vegetable patch
nipping the broccoli shoots, beheading the carrots.

The food from our mouths, I said, righteously thrilling
to the feel of the .22, the bullets' neat noses.
I, a lapsed pacifist fallen from grace   15
puffed with Darwinian° pieties for killing,
now drew a bead on the littlest woodchuck's face.
He died down in the everbearing roses.

Ten minutes later I dropped the mother. She
flipflopped in the air and fell, her needle teeth   20
still hooked in a leaf of early Swiss chard.
Another baby next. O one-two-three
the murderer inside me rose up hard,
the hawkeye killer came on stage forthwith.

There's one chuck left. Old wily fellow, he keeps   25
me cocked and ready day after day after day.
All night I hunt his humped-up form. I dream
I sight along the barrel in my sleep.
If only they'd all consented to die unseen
gassed underground the quiet Nazi way.   [1972]   30

5 puddingstone: Cement mixed with pebbles.   **16 Darwinian:** Charles Darwin (1809–1882), an English naturalist who first theorized about evolution and natural selection.

FOR THINKING AND WRITING

1. In line 4, the word *case* evidently refers to a method of entrapping the woodchucks, but probably it refers as well to the speaker's reasons for hunting them. Does the speaker have a good "case" for going after them? What is important to consider in evaluating her behavior? In what ways does your experience with farms and gardens affect your view of her?

2. Identify the stages in the speaker's campaign to get rid of the woodchucks. What psychological changes does she go through? In particular, what attitude toward her behavior does she express in the third and fourth stanzas? Support your answer by referring to specific words of hers.

3. Rewrite stanzas 3, 4, or 5 using the third person rather than the first. What is the effect of such a change? What advantages, if any, does the poet gain by resorting to the first person?

4. Trace the poem's rhyme pattern. Where does Kumin use alliteration as well? What effect do her technical choices have?

5. Presumably the last line alludes to the mass exterminations of the Holocaust. What would you say to someone who argues that this is an inappropriate, even tasteless, way to end a poem about woodchucks?

D. H. LAWRENCE
Snake

David Herbert Lawrence (1885–1930) was a leading novelist and short-story writer in the first half of the twentieth century. The son of a coal miner and a former schoolteacher, he describes his English working-class upbringing in his autobiographical novel Sons and Lovers *(1913). Probably he remains best known for his 1928 novel* Lady Chatterley's Lover. *For many years, it was banned in England and the United States because it explicitly described the sexual relationship between an aristocratic woman and her husband's gamekeeper. In most of his work, Lawrence endorses human passion, although he argued that people needed to exist in harmony with nature as well as with one another. Besides writing fiction, he painted and wrote poetry. "Snake," published in 1913, is based on Lawrence's stay in Sicily, one of the many places he went as he searched for a land friendly to his ideals.*

A snake came to my water-trough
On a hot, hot day, and I in pyjamas for the heat,
To drink there.

In the deep, strange-scented shade of the great dark carob-tree
I came down the steps with my pitcher
And must wait, must stand and wait, for there he was at the trough before me.

♦   ♦   ♦

5

He reached down from a fissure in the earth-wall in the gloom
And trailed his yellow-brown slackness soft-bellied down, over the edge of the
        stone trough
And rested his throat upon the stone bottom,
And where the water had dripped from the tap, in a small clearness,   10
He sipped with his straight mouth,
Softly drank through his straight gums, into his slack long body,
Silently.

Someone was before me at my water-trough,
And I, like a second comer, waiting.   15

He lifted his head from his drinking, as cattle do,
And looked at me vaguely, as drinking cattle do,
And flickered his two-forked tongue from his lips, and mused a moment,
And stooped and drank a little more,
Being earth-brown, earth-golden from the burning bowels of the earth   20
On the day of Sicilian July, with Etna smoking.

The voice of my education said to me
He must be killed,
For in Sicily the black, black snakes are innocent, the gold are venomous.

And voices in me said, If you were a man   25
You would take a stick and break him now, and finish him off.

But must I confess how I liked him,
How glad I was he had come like a guest in quiet, to drink at my water-trough
And depart peaceful, pacified, and thankless,
Into the burning bowels of this earth?   30

Was it cowardice, that I dared not kill him?
Was it perversity, that I longed to talk to him?
Was it humility, to feel so honoured?
I felt so honoured.

And yet those voices: 35
If you were not afraid, you would kill him!

And truly I was afraid, I was most afraid,
But even so, honoured still more
That he should seek my hospitality
From out the dark door of the secret earth.   40

He drank enough
And lifted his head, dreamily, as one who has drunken,
And flickered his tongue like a forked night on the air, so black;
Seeming to lick his lips,
And looked around like a god, unseeing, into the air,   45
And slowly turned his head,

And slowly, very slowly, as if thrice adream,
Proceeded to draw his slow length curving round
And climb again the broken bank of my wall-face.

And as he put his head into that dreadful hole,   50
And as he slowly drew up, snake-easing his shoulders, and entered farther,
A sort of horror, a sort of protest against his withdrawing into that horrid black
        hole,
Deliberately going into the blackness, and slowly drawing himself after,
Overcame me now his back was turned.

I looked round, I put down my pitcher,   55
I picked up a clumsy log
And threw it at the water-trough with a clatter.

I think it did not hit him,
But suddenly that part of him that was left behind convulsed in undignified haste,
Writhed like lightning, and was gone   60
Into the black hole, the earth-lipped fissure in the wall-front,
At which, in the intense still noon, I stared with fascination.

And immediately I regretted it.
I thought how paltry, how vulgar, what a mean act!
I despised myself and the voices of my accursed human education.   65

And I thought of the albatross,°
And I wished he would come back, my snake.

For he seemed to me again like a king,
Like a king in exile, uncrowned in the underworld,
Now due to be crowned again.   70

And so, I missed my chance with one of the lords
Of life.
And I have something to expiate;
A pettiness.   [1913]

66 albatross: In Samuel Taylor Coleridge's "Rime of the Ancient Mariner," a seaman brings
misfortune to the crew of his ship by killing an albatross, an ocean bird.

FOR THINKING AND WRITING

1. What did you associate with snakes before reading this poem? Does
   Lawrence push you to look at snakes differently, or does his poem endorse
   the view you already had? Develop your answer by referring to specific
   lines.

2. Discuss the poem as an argument involving various "voices." How do you
   think you would have reacted to the snake if you had been the speaker?
   What "voices" might you have heard inside your own mind? What people
   or institutions would these "voices" have come from?

3. Why does the speaker throw the log just as the snake is leaving? Note the explanation the speaker gives as well as the judgment he then makes about his act. Do both make sense to you? Why, or why not?

4. Lawrence begins many lines with the word *and*. What is the effect of his doing so?

5. In "Snake," Lawrence writes positively about an animal that is often feared. Think of a similar poem that you might write. What often-feared animal would you choose? What positive qualities would you point out or suggest in describing this animal? If you wish, try actually writing such a poem.

DENISE LEVERTOV
The Ache of Marriage

Denise Levertov (1923–1997) was born in England and educated entirely at home by literary parents. She claims to have decided to become a writer at age five, waiting until seventeen, however, to publish her first poem. She moved to the United States and became a citizen in 1956. Influenced by William Carlos Williams, she was associated with the Black Mountain poets of North Carolina. She later developed an open, experimental style, and her Here and Now *(1956) was considered an important avant-garde work. She published over twenty volumes of poetry and won a number of important awards. She spent the last decade of her life in Seattle. Her posthumous collection* This Great Unknowing: Last Poems *was published by New Directions in 1999. "The Ache of Marriage" is from* Poems, 1960–1967.

The ache of marriage:

thigh and tongue, beloved,
are heavy with it,
it throbs in the teeth

We look for communion   5
and are turned away, beloved,
each and each

It is leviathan and we
in its belly
looking for joy, some joy   10
not to be known outside it

two by two in the ark of
the ache of it.   [1967]

FOR THINKING AND WRITING

1. What does comparing marriage to a leviathan suggest to you (line 8)? Why didn't she compare marriage to a whale? Is this comparison consistent with contemporary representations in films, novels, and TV?

2. What would you say is a good definition for *ache* (line 1)? What if she had used *pain*? How about *itch*?

3. If the narrator were more explicit and detailed, how might she amplify the phrase "We look for communion / and are turned away" (lines 5–6)?

4. One critic says the poet doesn't romanticize or lament. What do you think this means? Do you agree?

5. How would you explain the following phrases used by critics in discussing this poem: "inexorable separateness of lovers," "intentionally desperate and clumsy," "paradoxes of separateness-in-togetherness."

PHILIP LEVINE
Among Children

Philip Levine (b. 1928) is a leading contemporary American poet. Much of his writing deals with his youth in the industrial city of Detroit, especially his work in various factories there. He won the National Book Award for his 1991 volume What Work Is. *We feature its title poem in Chapter 5, and the following poem comes from the same book.*

I walk among the rows of bowed heads—
the children are sleeping through fourth grade
so as to be ready for what is ahead,
the monumental boredom of junior high
and the rush forward tearing their wings   5
loose and turning their eyes forever inward.
These are the children of Flint, their fathers
work at the spark plug factory or truck
bottled water in 5 gallon sea-blue jugs
to the widows of the suburbs. You can see   10
already how their backs have thickened,
how their small hands, soiled by pig iron,
leap and stutter even in dreams. I would like
to sit down among them and read slowly
from *The Book of Job*° until the windows   15
pale and the teacher rises out of a milky sea

15 *The Book of Job*: In the Old Testament, Job is a virtuous man whose faith in God is tested when God allows horrible suffering to be inflicted on him. In Chapter 39, God speaks to Job about the vast differences in their knowledge and power. A particular passage from this speech seems especially pertinent to Levine's poem (Job 39:19–25, King James Version):

of industrial scum, her gowns streaming
with light, her foolish words transformed
into song, I would like to arm each one
with a quiver of arrows so that they might   20
rush like wind there where no battle rages
shouting among the trumpets, Ha! Ha!
How dear the gift of laughter in the face
of the 8 hour day, the cold winter mornings
without coffee and oranges, the long lines   25
of mothers in old coats waiting silently
where the gates have closed. Ten years ago
I went among these same children, just born,
in the bright ward of the Sacred Heart and leaned
down to hear their breaths delivered that day,   30
burning with joy. There was such wonder
in their sleep, such purpose in their eyes
closed against autumn, in their damp heads
blurred with the hair of ponds, and not one
turned against me or the light, not one   35
said, I am sick, I am tired, I will go home,
not one complained or drifted alone,
unloved, on the hardest day of their lives.
Eleven years from now they will become
the men and women of Flint or Paradise,   40
the majors of a minor town, and I
will be gone into smoke or memory,
so I bow to them here and whisper
all I know, all I will never know.   [1991]

FOR THINKING AND WRITING

1. Characterize the poem's speaker, using at least three adjectives of your own. What specific lines support your characterization?

2. The speaker describes these children at various stages in their lives. Besides discussing their present situation, he refers back to their births and forward to their adulthoods "Eleven years from now" (line 39). Do you find his comments about each stage plausible? Why, or why not?

Hast thou given the horse strength? Hast thou clothed his neck with thunder? Canst thou make him afraid as a grasshopper? The glory of his nostrils *is* terrible.

He paweth in the valley, and rejoiceth in *his* strength; he goeth on to meet the armed men.

He mocketh at fear, and is not affrighted; neither turneth he back from the sword. The quiver rattleth against him, the glittering spear and the shield.

He swalloweth the ground with fierceness and rage; neither believeth he that *it* is the sound of the trumpet.

He saith among the trumpets, Ha, ha; and he smelleth the battle afar off, the thunder of the captains, and the shouting.

3. In line 7, the speaker specifically identifies his subjects as "the children of Flint," an industrial city in Michigan. In what ways does their situation resemble that of schoolchildren in other places?

4. Do you find Levine's reference to the Book of Job (line 15) effective, or does it reduce your ability to understand and appreciate the poem? Explain.

5. At the end of the poem, the speaker reports that "I bow to them here and whisper / all I know, all I will never know" (lines 43–44). What would you say to someone who doubts that the speaker actually bows to these children and whispers such things to them? What would you say to someone who argues that the speaker should have taken more active steps to improve the children's lot?

ROBERT LOWELL
To Speak of the Woe That Is in Marriage

Robert Lowell (1917–1977) spent much of his life as a poet reacting to cultural and historical influences that threatened to define him and to define American literature as well. As the descendant of Mayflower New Englanders and the relative of poets James Russell Lowell and Amy Lowell, he struggled toward an individualistic vision and voice that greatly influenced his contemporaries in the 1950s and 1960s. Beginning at Harvard as a student of English literature, he moved to Kenyon College and later to Louisiana State University to study with various New Critics, thus placing himself in the midst of intellectual debates about literature. Lowell also found himself in conflict with tradition when he protested both World War II and the Vietnam War and as he wrestled with the place of religion in poetry, with the morality of capitalism, and with the vicissitudes of three marriages. Although the more formal verse of Lord Weary's Castle *(1946) won the Pulitzer Prize, he is best known for the confessional tone of* Life Studies *(1959), from which "To Speak of the Woe That Is in Marriage" is taken. Lowell's* Collected Poems *appeared in 2003.*

It is the future generation that presses into being by means of these exuberant feelings and supersensible soap bubbles of ours.
— Schopenhauer

"The hot night makes us keep our bedroom windows open.
Our magnolia blossoms. Life begins to happen.
My hopped up husband drops his home disputes,
and hits the streets to cruise for prostitutes,
free-lancing out along the razor's edge.   5
This screwball might kill his wife, then take the pledge.
Oh the monotonous meanness of his lust. . . .

It's the injustice . . . he is so unjust—
whiskey-blind, swaggering home at five.
My only thought is how to keep alive.   10
What makes him tick? Each night now I tie
ten dollars and his car key to my thigh. . . .
Gored by the climacteric of his want,
he stalls above me like an elephant."   [1959]

FOR THINKING AND WRITING

1. What do you think the "home disputes" in line 3 are about? Why does he go to look for paid sex? Is the husband at fault here? Could he be the victim instead of the wife?

2. The ten dollars tied to the wife's thigh seems symbolic and confusing. Is the money meant to provide him with an escape? Her with an escape? Is it meant to entice him? Is it possible to know?

3. The poem and its language are conversational in tone. What effect does this wife's monologue have on you? Is this intentional?

4. *Climacteric* (line 13) has a specific meaning. Look it up in a dictionary. Does this definition change your attitude toward the husband?

5. Since this poem was written in 1959, divorce has become quite common in America. Would Lowell be pleased? Are you?

CHRISTOPHER MARLOWE
The Passionate Shepherd to His Love

Best known for turning dramatic blank verse into high art in his play Doctor Faustus, *Marlowe (1564–1593) was also a major poet and one of the most learned and controversial writers of his time. He led a tempestuous and dangerous life and was often accused of being an atheist, a serious charge at the time. He was killed in a bar fight at the age of twenty-nine, the circumstances of which are still being debated. The official story that he was stabbed over the tavern bill is dubious given the informers, spies, and conspirators involved in the fight. Nevertheless, Marlowe's reputation as an Elizabethan dramatist is second only to Shakespeare's. The following poem, published posthumously, is his only surviving lyric and suggests his impulsive attitude to live for the moment.*

Come live with me and be my love,
And we will all the pleasure prove
That valleys, groves, hills, and fields,
Woods, or steepy mountain yields.

♦ ♦ ♦

And we will sit upon the rocks,   5
Seeing the shepherds feed their flocks,
By shallow rivers to whose falls
Melodious birds sing madrigals.

And I will make thee beds of roses
And a thousand fragrant posies,   10
A cap of flowers, and a kirtle°
Embroidered all with leaves of myrtle;

A gown made of the finest wool
Which from our pretty lambs we pull;
Fair lined slippers for the cold,   15
With buckles of the purest gold;

A belt of straw and ivy buds,
With coral clasps and amber studs:
And if these pleasures may thee move,
Come live with me, and be my love.   20

The shepherd swains shall dance and sing
For thy delight each May morning:
If these delights thy mind may move,
Then live with me and be my love.   [c. 1599]

11 **kirtle:** Dress or skirt.

FOR THINKING AND WRITING

1. As an argument, how persuasive do you think the shepherd's case is? Might his argument charm his listener? Might the speaker be more sophisticated than one would expect?

2. Marlowe is writing in the pastoral tradition, which highlights youth, optimism, and eternal love. Might Marlowe be dealing with a serious topic behind these idealized fancies?

3. What elements of reality or human nature does the speaker omit from his plea?

4. Carpe diem ("seize the day") was a popular attitude in Marlowe's day, as this poem suggests. Is it today? Can you give examples from popular culture? What are the advantages of adopting such an attitude? The disadvantages?

5. Do you think that love conquers all? Is sex a necessary prelude to love? Do you think love is more, or less, possible in certain settings—for example, at the beach, in the country, or perhaps in prison or a hospital? Does being in love depend on one's economic or psychological well-being?

ANDREW MARVELL
To His Coy Mistress

Andrew Marvell (1621–1678) was famous in his own time as an adroit politician and a writer of satire, but modern readers admire him for the style and content of his lyric, metaphysical poetry. Born into a Protestant family, Marvell was tolerant of Catholicism from a young age, and his willingness to somehow circumvent the religious prejudices of seventeenth-century England allowed his continued success. He traveled to Holland, France, Italy, and Spain—possibly to avoid the English civil war as a young man and undoubtedly to spy for England in later years. He tutored Cromwell's ward and later served on his Council of State, but was influential enough during the Restoration to get his fellow poet and mentor, John Milton, released from prison. Although admired by the Romantic poets of the early nineteenth century, Andrew Marvell's poetry (much of it published after his death) was revived in the twentieth century by T. S. Eliot and has been widely read for its ironic approach to the conventions of love.

Had we but world enough, and time,
This coyness, lady, were no crime.
We would sit down, and think which way
To walk, and pass our long love's day.
Thou by the Indian Ganges'° side   5
Shouldst rubies find; I by the tide
Of Humber° would complain.° I would
Love you ten years before the Flood,
And you should, if you please, refuse
Till the conversion of the Jews.   10
My vegetable love should grow°
Vaster than empires, and more slow;
An hundred years should go to praise
Thine eyes and on thy forehead gaze,
Two hundred to adore each breast,   15
But thirty thousand to the rest:
An age at least to every part,
And the last age should show your heart.
For, lady, you deserve this state,
Nor would I love at lower rate.   20
　　　But at my back I always hear
Time's wingèd chariot hurrying near;
And yonder all before us lie

---

5 **Ganges:** A river in India sacred to the Hindus.　7 **Humber:** An estuary that flows through Marvell's native town, Hull.　**complain:** Sing love songs.　11 **My vegetable love . . . grow:** A slow, insensible growth, like that of a vegetable.

Deserts of vast eternity.
Thy beauty shall no more be found,   25
Nor in thy marble vault shall sound
My echoing song; then worms shall try
That long preserved virginity,
And your quaint honor turn to dust,
And into ashes all my lust.   30
The grave's a fine and private place,
But none, I think, do there embrace.
        Now, therefore, while the youthful hue
Sits on thy skin like morning dew,
And while thy willing soul transpires°   35
At every pore with instant fires,
Now let us sport us while we may,
And now, like amorous birds of prey,
Rather at once our time devour
Than languish in his slow-chapped° power.   40
Let us roll all our strength and all
Our sweetness up into one ball,
And tear our pleasures with rough strife
Thorough° the iron gates of life.
Thus, though we cannot make our sun   45
Stand still, yet we will make him run.   [1681]

35 transpires: Breathes forth.   **40 slow-chapped:** Slow-jawed.   **44 Thorough:** Through.

FOR THINKING AND WRITING

1. Considered as both an intellectual and an emotional argument, what is
   the narrator's goal and what specific claims does he make? Are they convincing? Do you think they were in 1681? Do you think women three
   hundred years ago worried about virginity? Why?

2. What does this poem say about the needs of Marvell's audience? What
   assumptions about women does the poem make?

3. How many sections does this poem have? What is the purpose of each?
   How is the concluding couplet in each related to that section? Is the
   rhyme scheme related to the meaning of these couplets?

4. Is the speaker passionate? Sincere? How do you make such a decision?
   Do you look at his language or his message?

5. Some feminist readers see in the last ten lines a kind of indirect threat, a
   suggestion of force through the use of violent images. Is this a plausible
   reading? If this is the case, what do you now think of the narrator's pleading?

MARGE PIERCY
To Be of Use

Born in 1936, Marge Piercy was a child of the Great Depression, and her roots are thoroughly working class. She grew up Jewish in Detroit, Michigan, a city that was "black and white by blocks." When she won a scholarship to the University of Michigan, Piercy became the first member of her family to go to college. She went on to earn a master of arts degree from Northwestern University. Piercy has worked as a secretary, a switchboard operator, a department store clerk, an artist's model, and a low-paid part-time instructor. She has also been actively involved in political work, participating in the civil rights, antiwar, feminist, and environmentalist movements. In both her poems and her fiction, her goal is to portray ordinary working people who are also thinking people. She has published fourteen books of poetry, fifteen novels, and a book of essays about the work of writing poetry. Her recent work includes the poetry collection, What Are Big Girls Made Of? *(1997), the novels* Storm Tide *(1998; with Ira Wood) and* Three Women *(1999), and a memoir,* Sleeping with Cats *(2001).*

The people I love the best
jump into work head first
without dallying in the shallows
and swim off with sure strokes almost out of sight.
They seem to become natives of that element,   5
the black sleek heads of seals
bouncing like half-submerged balls.

I love people who harness themselves, an ox to a heavy cart,
who pull like water buffalo, with massive patience,
who strain in the mud and the muck to move things forward,   10
who do what has to be done, again and again.

I want to be with people who submerge
in the task, who go into the fields to harvest
and work in a row and pass the bags along,
who are not parlor generals and field deserters   15
but move in a common rhythm
when the food must come in or the fire be put out.

The work of the world is common as mud.
Botched, it smears the hands, crumbles to dust.
But the thing worth doing well done   20
has a shape that satisfies, clean and evident.
Greek amphoras for wine or oil,
Hopi vases that held corn, are put in museums

but you know they were made to be used.
The pitcher cries for water to carry   25
and a person for work that is real.   [1974]

FOR THINKING AND WRITING

1. Do you think Piercy is talking only about people who do physical work? What is your idea of the "the thing worth doing well done"?

2. Is the swimming analogy effective? What other analogies, similes, and metaphors does she use?

3. Is the key idea here one's attitude, the kind of work available in a society, or something else?

4. What do you think she is referring to in the phrase "parlor generals and field deserters"?

5. What is your reading of "real" in the last line? What are some examples of such work in our society?

SYLVIA PLATH
Daddy

Born to middle-class parents in suburban Boston, Sylvia Plath (1932–1963) became known as an intensely emotional "confessional" poet whose work is primarily auto-biographical. Her father, a professor of biology and German, died when she was eight, the year her first poem was published. She graduated with honors from Smith College in 1950, after an internship at Mademoiselle *and a suicide attempt in her junior year, experiences described in her novel* The Bell Jar *(1963). She won a Ful-bright Scholarship to study at Cambridge, England, where she met and married poet Ted Hughes. The couple had two children; the marriage ended the year before her suicide in 1963. "Daddy" is from* Ariel, *published posthumously in 1965.*

You do not do, you do not do
Any more, black shoe
In which I have lived like a foot
For thirty years, poor and white,
Barely daring to breathe or Achoo.   5

Daddy, I have had to kill you.
You died before I had time—
Marble-heavy, a bag full of God,
Ghastly statue with one gray toe
Big as a Frisco seal   10

◆ ◆ ◆

And a head in the freakish Atlantic
Where it pours bean green over blue
In the waters off beautiful Nauset.°   *Cape Cod inlet*
I used to pray to recover you.
Ach, du.°   *Oh, you*   15

In the German tongue, in the Polish Town°
Scraped flat by the roller
Of wars, wars, wars.
But the name of the town is common.
My Polack friend   20

Says there are a dozen or two.
So I never could tell where you
Put your foot, your root,
I never could talk to you.
The tongue stuck in my jaw.   25

It stuck in a barb wire snare.
Ich, ich, ich, ich,°   *I, I, I, I*
I could hardly speak.
I thought every German was you.
And the language obscene   30

An engine, an engine
Chuffing me off like a Jew.
A Jew to Dachau, Auschwitz, Belsen.°
I began to talk like a Jew.
I think I may well be a Jew.   35

The snows of the Tyrol, the clear beer of Vienna
Are not very pure or true.
With my gypsy-ancestress and my weird luck
And my Taroc° pack and my Taroc pack
I may be a bit of a Jew.   40

I have always been scared of *you*,
With your Luftwaffe,° your gobbledygoo.
And your neat mustache
And your Aryan eye, bright blue.
Panzer-man, panzer-man,° O You —   45

Not God but a swastika
So black no sky could squeak through.

16 Polish town: Plath's father was born in Granbow, Poland.   **33 Dachau . . . Belsen:** Nazi
death camps in World War II.   **39 Taroc:** Tarot cards used to tell fortunes. The practice may
have originated among the early Jewish Cabalists and was then widely adopted by European
Gypsies during the Middle Ages.   **42 Luftwaffe:** World War II German air force.   **45 panzer-
man:** A member of the German armored vehicle division.

Every woman adores a Fascist,
The boot in the face, the brute
Brute heart of a brute like you.   50

You stand at the blackboard, daddy,
In the picture I have of you,
A cleft in your chin instead of your foot
But no less a devil for that, no not
Any less the black man who   55

Bit my pretty red heart in two.
I was ten when they buried you.
At twenty I tried to die
And get back, back, back to you.
I thought even the bones would do   60

But they pulled me out of the sack,
And they stuck me together with glue.
And then I knew what to do.
I made a model of you,
A man in black with a Meinkampf° look   65

And a love of the rack and the screw.
And I said I do, I do.
So daddy, I'm finally through.
The black telephone's off at the root,
The voices just can't worm through.   70

If I've killed one man, I've killed two —
The vampire who said he was you
And drank my blood for a year,
Seven years, if you want to know.
Daddy, you can lie back now.   75

There's a stake in your fat black heart
And the villagers never liked you.
They are dancing and stamping on you.
They always *knew* it was you.
Daddy, daddy, you bastard, I'm through.   [1962]   80

65 Meinkampf: Hitler's autobiography (*My Struggle*).

FOR THINKING AND WRITING

1. Can this poem be seen as a series of arguments for why Plath has to forget
   her father? What complaints does the speaker seem to have against her
   father?

2. Some psychologists claim that we all have a love-hate relationship with
   our parents. Do you agree? Would Plath's speaker agree?

3. How effective is it for the speaker to compare herself to a Jew in Hitler's Germany? What other similes and metaphors are used to refer to her father? Do they work, or are they too extreme? Perhaps Plath wants them to be outrageous. Why might she?

4. Plath combines childhood rhymes and words with brutal images. What effect does this have on you? Why do you think Plath does this? What odd stylistic features can you point to here?

5. Why do you think it is necessary for the speaker to be finally "through" with her father? Is it normal young adult rebelliousness? What else might it be?

SIR WALTER RALEIGH
The Nymph's Reply to the Shepherd

Sir Walter Raleigh (1554–1618) was an English soldier and explorer as well as a writer. He was a favorite of Elizabeth I, even though his outspokenness and interest in skeptical philosophy made him many enemies at court. In 1585, Raleigh sent the first of two groups of settlers to Roanoke Island, the second of which vanished without a trace by 1591. After he led an unsuccessful expedition to Guyana in search of gold, he was imprisoned in the Tower of London and eventually executed for trying to overthrow James I. The following poem exhibits his practical and skeptical bent.

If all the world and love were young,
And truth in every shepherd's tongue,
These pretty pleasures might me move
To live with thee and be thy love.

Time drives the flocks from field to fold   5
When rivers rage and rocks grow cold,
And Philomel° becometh dumb;
The rest complains of cares to come.

The flowers do fade, and wanton fields
To wayward winter reckoning yields;   10
A honey tongue, a heart of gall,
Is fancy's spring, but sorrow's fall.

Thy gowns, thy shoes, thy beds of roses,
Thy cap, thy kirtle, and thy posies
Soon break, soon wither, soon forgotten —   15
In folly ripe, in reason rotten.

◆ ◆ ◆

7 **Philomel:** The nightingale.

Thy belt of straw and ivy buds,
Thy coral clasps and amber studs,
All these in me no means can move
To come to thee and be thy love. 20

But could youth last and love still breed,
Had joys no date° nor age no need,
Then these delights my mind might move
To live with thee and be thy love. [1600]

22 date: End.

FOR THINKING AND WRITING

1. How might you consider this poem a refusal for a sexual affair? What arguments are put forth as a refutation?
2. Read between the lines. What might convince the speaker to be the shepherd's love? Or is that impossible?
3. What is the speaker's tone? Do you hear hostility or contempt?
4. What does Raleigh mean in line 16 by "In folly ripe, in reason rotten"?
5. What part does gender play in this poem? Is the speaker being stereotyped?

ALBERTO RÍOS
Mi Abuelo°

Alberto Ríos (b. 1952) has said that being bilingual in English and Spanish is like going through life with a pair of binoculars; having at least two words for everything opens one's eyes to the world. Ríos is a person of the border in several ways: his father was from Chiapas, Mexico, and his mother from Lancashire, England. He grew up in the city of Nogales, Arizona, where he could stand with one foot in the United States and another in Mexico; and as a writer, he crosses the line between poetry and prose, having written seven books of poetry, three collections of short stories, and a memoir. He is an instructor of creative writing, since 1994 the Regents Professor of English at Arizona State University, where he has taught since 1982. He received his B.A. (1974) and his M.F.A. in creative writing (1979) from the University of Arizona. His work appears in ninety anthologies, including the Norton Anthology of Modern Poetry, *and his awards include fellowships from the Guggenheim Foundation and the National Endowment for the Arts and the 1982 Walt Whitman Award for* Whispering to Fool the Wind.

Mi Abuelo: My grandfather (Spanish).

Where my grandfather is is in the ground
where you can hear the future
like an Indian with his ear at the tracks.
A pipe leads down to him so that sometimes
he whispers what will happen to a man 5
in town or how he will meet the best
dressed woman tomorrow and how the best
man at her wedding will chew the ground
next to her. Mi abuelo is the man
who speaks through all the mouths in my house. 10
An echo of me hitting the pipe sometimes
to stop him from saying *my hair is a*
sieve is the only other sound. It is a phrase
that among all others is the best,
he says, and *my hair is a sieve* is sometimes 15
repeated for hours out of the ground
when I let him, which is not often.
An abuelo should be much more than a man
like you! He stops then, and speaks: *I am a man*
who has served ants with the attitude 20
of a waiter, who has made each smile as only
an ant who is fat can, and they liked me best,
but there is nothing left. Yet I know he ground
green coffee beans as a child, and sometimes
he will talk about his wife, and sometimes 25
about when he was deaf and a man
cured him by mail and he heard groundhogs
talking, or about how he walked with a cane
he chewed on when he got hungry.
At best, mi abuelo is a liar. 30
I see an old picture of him at nani's with an
off-white yellow center mustache and sometimes
that's all I know for sure. He talks best
about these hills, *slowest waves,* and where this man
is going, and I'm convinced his hair is a sieve, 35
that his fever is cooled now underground.
Mi abuelo is an ordinary man.
I look down the pipe, sometimes, and see a
ripple-topped stream in its best suit, in the ground. [1990]

FOR THINKING AND WRITING

1. The narrator seems ambivalent about his abuelo. What specific things
   does he know about him? Can you tell his attitude toward him? How do
   you read the line, "At best, mi abuelo is a liar" (line 30)? What might the
   worst be?

2. When the grandfather speaks from the grave ("*I am a man . . .*") (lines 19–23), he seems odd indeed. Is he a bit crazy, or do you see meaning in his ant speech?

3. What does Ríos mean when he writes that his abuelo "speaks through all the mouths in my house" (line 10)? Could this be a positive notion?

4. Ríos seems convinced his grandfather's "fever is cooled now" (line 36). Should we take this literally?

5. Do you agree that Ríos wants to continue conversing with his dead abuelo? Why? Can we see this as a metaphor?

EDWIN ARLINGTON ROBINSON
Richard Cory

Edwin Arlington Robinson (1869–1935) eventually gained fame through poems such as the following, but he spent much of his life in relative obscurity. Robinson was born in Head Tide, Maine, and educated at Harvard University, though he had to give up his college studies when his family went bankrupt and his mother grew ill. Living in the Maine town of Gardner, he began writing poems based on his community, which he fictionally renamed Tilbury Town. These works included "Richard Cory," which evidently was inspired by the shotgun suicide of a Gardner man. The poem appeared in Robinson's 1897 book The Children of the Night. *That same year, depressed when the woman he loved married his brother, Robinson moved to New York City. Far from being able to live as a poet, he wound up working as a checker of shale in the subway system then under construction. Fortunately, Robinson's poems came to the attention of President Theodore Roosevelt, who got him a job at the New York Customs House. Later, Robinson moved back to Gardner and in his remaining years saw his national reputation increase. He won the Pulitzer Prize for poetry three times.*

Whenever Richard Cory went down town,
We people on the pavement looked at him:
He was a gentleman from sole to crown,
Clean favored, and imperially slim.

And he was always quietly arrayed,   5
And he was always human when he talked;
But still he fluttered pulses when he said,
"Good-morning," and he glittered when he walked.

And he was rich—yes, richer than a king—
And admirably schooled in every grace: 10
In fine, we thought that he was everything
To make us wish that we were in his place.

◆   ◆   ◆

So on we worked, and waited for the light,
And went without the meat, and cursed the bread;
And Richard Cory, one calm summer night,   15
Went home and put a bullet through his head.   [1897]

FOR THINKING AND WRITING

1. Were you surprised by the ending? Why, or why not? On reading the poem again, do you get any sense of why Richard Cory killed himself? If so, what?

2. What is the speaker's tone toward Richard Cory? Toward the townspeople? Toward himself?

3. Why do you think the speaker feels obliged to add "yes, richer than a king" (line 9) instead of simply saying "he was rich"?

4. What is the rhyme scheme of this poem? What role, if any, does the rhyme scheme play in the poem's overall effect?

5. What would you say to someone who argued that this poem's theme is simply "Money can't buy happiness"?

ANNE SEXTON
The Farmer's Wife

Anne Sexton (1928–1974) began writing poetry as therapy for repeated mental breakdowns and suicide attempts following the birth of her first child in 1951. Among the writers Robert Lowell, Sylvia Plath, Maxine Kumin, W. D. Snodgrass, and others often grouped as confessional poets, Sexton learned to use the intense, intimate materials of personal life in her poetry, maintaining little distance between herself and her readers. Her first collection of poetry, To Bedlam and Part Way Back *(1960), reflects this intensely confessional, female perspective, as do the later collections* All My Pretty Ones *(1962) and* Live or Die *(1966), which won the Pulitzer Prize. In the poems of* Transformations *(1971) Sexton retells Grimm fairy tales with a wry, bitter, feminist twist. Anne Sexton committed suicide in 1974. "The Farmer's Wife" is from* To Bedlam and Part Way Back.

From the hodge porridge
of their country lust,
their local life in Illinois,
where all their acres look
like a sprouting broom factory,   5
they name just ten years now
that she has been his habit;
as again tonight he'll say
honey bunch let's go

and she will not say how there   10
must be more to living
than this brief bright bridge
of the raucous bed or even
the slow braille touch of him
like a heavy god grown light,   15
that old pantomime of love
that she wants although
it leaves her still alone,
built back again at last,
minds apart from him, living   20
her own self in her own words
and hating the sweat of the house
they keep when they finally lie
each in separate dreams
and then how she watches him,   25
still strong in the blowzy bag
of his usual sleep while
her young years bungle past
their same marriage bed
and she wishes him cripple, or poet,   30
or even lonely, or sometimes,
better, my lover, dead.   [1960]

FOR THINKING AND WRITING

1. The last line seems to move in two directions. She calls him "my lover"
   but then says she sometimes wishes him dead. Does this make sense?

2. How can making love with her husband leave the farmer's wife "still
   alone" (line 18)? Is this her fault? His? Their fault? No one's fault?

3. Is the wife dissatisfied with sex? With her husband? With marriage itself?
   What do you think of her solution? What would you do?

4. Describe what you think the connotation of "his habit" is in line 7. How
   about "honey bunch" (line 9) and the "old pantomime of love" (line 16)?

5. Does Sexton's poem reflect marriages in general or only those in rural
   areas? Only ten-year-old marriages? Just this particular relationship?

PERCY BYSSHE SHELLEY
Ozymandias

*Before his untimely death by drowning, Percy Bysshe Shelley (1792–1822) com-
posed many poems that are now regarded as masterpieces of British Romanticism.
Shelley published the following poem in 1818 after a visit to the British Museum.
On exhibit there were artifacts from the tomb of the ancient Egyptian pharaoh*

*Rameses II, called Ozymandias by many of Shelley's contemporaries. These objects
included a broken statue of the pharaoh.*

I met a traveler from an antique land
Who said: Two vast and trunkless legs of stone
Stand in the desert. . . . Near them, on the sand,
Half sunk, a shattered visage lies, whose frown,
And wrinkled lip, and sneer of cold command,   5
Tell that its sculptor well those passions read
Which yet survive, stamped on these lifeless things,
The hand that mocked them, and the heart that fed:
And on the pedestal these words appear:
"My name is Ozymandias, King of Kings: 10
Look on my works, ye Mighty, and despair!"
Nothing beside remains. Round the decay
Of that colossal wreck, boundless and bare
The lone and level sands stretch far away.   [1818]

FOR THINKING AND WRITING

1. "Ozymandias" is a sonnet, a poem consisting of fourteen lines. Often
   there is a significant division in content between a sonnet's first eight lines
   and its last six. Is there such a division in Shelley's poem? Explain.

2. How is the poem a comment on the epitaph it quotes from the statue's
   pedestal? Describe Ozymandias by listing at least three adjectives for him,
   and identify the specific lines that make you think of them.

3. Although the poem begins by referring to "I," this is not the main speaker
   of the poem; soon we are presented with the report of the "traveler." Shelley could have had the traveler narrate the whole poem. Why might he
   have begun with the "I"?

4. Both Shelley and the sculptor are artists. To what extent do they resemble
   each other? Note that the poem describes the sculptor as someone who
   "well those passions read" (line 6). Why does Shelley associate him with
   the act of reading?

5. According to this poem, what survives? What does not?

STEVIE SMITH
Not Waving but Drowning

*Stevie Smith was the pen name of Florence Martin Smith (1902–1971). For much
of her adult life, she was anything but a public figure; rather, she spent much time
taking care of her aunt in a London suburb. During the 1960s, however, Smith
became increasingly known in England for her poetry; she even read from it aloud*

on numerous radio broadcasts. Her Collected Poems *was published posthumously in 1975. The following poem, Smith's best known, appeared in a 1957 book that was also entitled* Not Waving but Drowning.

Nobody heard him, the dead man,
But still he lay moaning:
I was much further out than you thought
And not waving but drowning.

Poor chap, he always loved larking   5
And now he's dead
It must have been too cold for him his heart gave way,
They said.

Oh, no, no, no, it was too cold always
(Still the dead one lay moaning)   10
I was much too far out all my life
And not waving but drowning.   [1957]

FOR THINKING AND WRITING

1. In what senses might the dead man have been drowning? In what senses might he have been "too cold" and "much too far out"?
2. How do you think it was possible for "They" to misunderstand the dead man's real situation?
3. Smith might have ended the poem with the first stanza. What do the second and third stanzas contribute?
4. What, if anything, does the dead man hope to achieve through his moaning?
5. Is it unrealistic for Smith to have a dead man speak?

CATHY SONG
The Grammar of Silk

Cathy Song (b. 1955) was born and raised in Honolulu, Hawaii, and currently teaches at the University of Hawaii at Manoa. Her first volume of poetry, Picture Bride, *won the 1982 Yale Series of Younger Poets Award and was nominated for the National Book Critics Circle Award. She has published three others:* Frameless Windows, Available Light *(1988);* School Figures *(1994), which includes the following poem; and* The Land of Bliss *(2001).*

On Saturdays in the morning
my mother sent me to Mrs. Umemoto's sewing school.
It was cool and airy in her basement,
pleasant—a word I choose

to use years later to describe   5
the long tables where we sat
and cut, pinned, and stitched,
the Singer's companionable whirr,
the crisp, clever bite of scissors
parting like silver fish a river of calico.   10

The school was in walking distance
to Kaimuki Dry Goods
where my mother purchased my supplies—
small cards of buttons,
zippers and rickrack packaged like licorice,   15
lifesaver rolls of thread
in fifty-yard lengths,
spun from spools, tough as tackle.
Seamstresses waited at the counters
like librarians to be consulted.   20
Pens and scissors dangled like awkward pendants
across flat chests,
a scarf of measuring tape flung across a shoulder,
time as a pincushion bristled at the wrist.
They deciphered a dress's blueprints   25
with an architect's keen eye.

This evidently was a sanctuary,
a place where women confined with children
conferred, consulted the oracle,
the stone tablets of the latest pattern books.   30
Here mothers and daughters paused in symmetry,
offered the proper reverence—
hushed murmurings for the shantung silk
which required a certain sigh,
as if it were a piece from the Ming Dynasty.   35

My mother knew there would be no shortcuts
and headed for the remnants,
the leftover bundles with yardage
enough for a heart-shaped pillow,
a child's dirndl, a blouse without darts.   40
Along the aisles
my fingertips touched the titles—
satin, tulle, velvet,
peach, lavender, pistachio,
sherbet-colored linings—   45
and settled for the plain brown-and-white composition
of polka dots on kettle cloth
my mother held up in triumph.

◆   ◆   ◆

She was determined that I should sew
as if she knew what she herself was missing,   50
a moment when she could have come up for air—
the children asleep,
the dishes drying on the rack—
and turned on the lamp
and pulled back the curtain of sleep.   55
To inhabit the night,
the night as a black cloth, white paper,
a sheet of music in which she might find herself singing.

On Saturdays at Mrs. Umemoto's sewing school,
when I took my place beside the other girls,   60
bent my head and went to work,
my foot keeping time on the pedal,
it was to learn the charitable oblivion
of hand and mind as one—
a refuge such music affords the maker—   65
the pleasure of notes in perfectly measured time.   [1994]

FOR THINKING AND WRITING

1. How do you think Song defines the word *grammar*? Note that the word
   appears only in the poem's title and is not usually applied to silk. Why,
   then, do you think Song calls her poem "The Grammar of Silk"? Which
   lines seem related to this title?

2. Even as she uses the word *pleasant* to describe Mrs. Umemoto's basement, the speaker admits that it is "a word I choose / to use years later"
   (lines 4–5). What other lines seem to reflect the adult's perspective more
   than the child's?

3. Only the first and last stanzas describe the sewing school itself. What
   might Song's purpose be in including the four middle stanzas? How
   important do they seem compared with the first and last stanzas?

4. Describe the speaker's mother with three adjectives of your own. What, in
   your own words, does she seem to have been "missing" (line 50)? Do you
   mainly think of her as missing something, or are you more conscious of
   what she had?

5. Does the culture evoked in this poem seem different from your own?
   What specific aspects of the poem's culture and your own come to mind
   as you try to answer this question?

GARY SOTO
Behind Grandma's House

Born in 1952 in Fresno, California, Gary Soto gives voice to San Joaquín Valley agricultural workers whose deprivations have been part of his experience and social awareness from an early age. After graduating with honors from California State University in 1974, Soto went on to earn an M.F.A. in creative writing from the University of California at Irvine in 1976 and to teach in the university system. He has received numerous writing awards, including the distinction of being the first writer identifying himself as Chicano to be nominated for a Pulitzer Prize. His most recent book is New and Selected Poems *(1995). His Mexican American heritage continues to be central to his work. The poem reprinted here is from Soto's 1985 book,* Black Hair.

At ten I wanted fame. I had a comb
And two Coke bottles, a tube of Bryl-creem.
I borrowed a dog, one with
Mismatched eyes and a happy tongue,
And wanted to prove I was tough   5
In the alley, kicking over trash cans,
A dull chime of tuna cans falling.
I hurled light bulbs like grenades
And men teachers held their heads,
Fingers of blood lengthening   10
On the ground. I flicked rocks at cats,
Their goofy faces spurred with foxtails.
I kicked fences. I shooed pigeons.
I broke a branch from a flowering peach
And frightened ants with a stream of spit.   15
I said "Shit," "Fuck you," and "No way
Daddy-O" to an imaginary priest
Until grandma came into the alley,
Her apron flapping in a breeze,
Her hair mussed, and said, "Let me help you,"   20
And punched me between the eyes.   [1985]

FOR THINKING AND WRITING

1. Were you glad or disturbed when the narrator's grandmother hit him? Does he deserve it? Are you angry or sympathetic to his attempts to be tough? Do you understand why he wants to appear older? Is this normal?

2. What did you want at ten? Did your grandparents know your desires? Did they support you? Did they ever set you straight? Are our grandparents' values too dated to matter?

3. Are the concrete details meaningful to you? Does the profanity help Soto achieve authenticity, or is it unnecessary?

4. Does the speaker learn something here, or is this just a snapshot of an event?

5. How would you describe our culture's ideas of the different roles of parents and grandparents? Do grandparents in today's culture have less influence than in the past? Is this a good thing or not?

WILLIAM STAFFORD
Traveling through the Dark

Besides being a poet himself, William Stafford (1914–1995) was a mentor to many others. During World War II, he was a conscientious objector. Later, he wrote and taught poetry at a variety of places in the United States, eventually settling in Oregon. The following poem was written in 1960 and subsequently appeared in a 1962 collection of Stafford's poems, also entitled Traveling through the Dark.

Traveling through the dark I found a deer
dead on the edge of the Wilson River road.
It is usually best to roll them into the canyon:
that road is narrow; to swerve might make more dead.

By glow of the tail-light I stumbled back of the car   5
and stood by the heap, a doe, a recent killing;
she had stiffened already, almost cold.
I dragged her off; she was large in the belly.

My fingers touching her side brought me the reason —
her side was warm; her fawn lay there waiting,   10
alive, still, never to be born.
Beside that mountain road I hesitated.

The car aimed ahead its lowered parking lights;
under the hood purred the steady engine.
I stood in the glare of the warm exhaust turning red;   15
around our group I could hear the wilderness listen.

I thought hard for us all — my only swerving —
then pushed her over the edge into the river.   [1962]

FOR THINKING AND WRITING

1. At the end of the poem, the speaker says "I thought hard for us all." Who does "us" refer to? What might the speaker have said to defend what he

did? What might be an argument against his act? What would you have done, and why?

2. "To swerve" appears in the first stanza, "swerving" in the last. How would you define these words as they appear in the poem? What does Stafford achieve by using them to frame it?

3. Note in the fourth stanza what verbs the speaker associates with the car and the engine. What is the effect of these verbs on you?

4. Note, too, the last line of the fourth stanza. What would you say to someone who criticized this line because it is impossible for someone to "hear" someone else "listen"?

5. Though Stafford begins his poem with the phrase "Traveling through the dark," the rest of the poem deals with what happened when the speaker stopped traveling for a moment. How appropriate, then, is the poem's title?

WISLAWA SZYMBORSKA
True Love

Translated by Stanislaw Baránczak and Clare Cavanagh

Wislawa Szymborska (b. 1923) was born in Poland and has lived in Krakow since 1931, studying literature at Jagiellonian University. She worked as a poetry editor for almost twenty years for a well-known literary journal in Krakow. She has published sixteen collections of poetry, many of which have been widely translated, and has won many prizes, including, most notably, the Nobel Prize for literature in 1996 "for poetry that with ironic precision allows the historical and biological context to come to light in fragments of human reality." The following poem is from View with a Grain of Sand *(1995).*

True love. Is it normal,
is it serious, is it practical?
What does the world get from two people
who exist in a world of their own?

Placed on the same pedestal for no good reason,   5
drawn randomly from millions, but convinced
it had to happen this way — in reward for what?
        For nothing.
The light descends from nowhere.
Why on these two and not on others?   10
Doesn't this outrage justice? Yes it does.
Doesn't it disrupt our painstakingly erected principles,
and cast the moral from the peak? Yes on both accounts.

◆   ◆   ◆

Look at the happy couple.
Couldn't they at least try to hide it,   15
fake a little depression for their friends' sake!
Listen to them laughing—it's an insult.
The language they use—deceptively clear.
And their little celebrations, rituals,
the elaborate mutual routines—   20
it's obviously a plot behind the human race's back!

It's hard even to guess how far things might go
if people start to follow their example.
What could religion and poetry count on?
What would be remembered? What renounced?   25
Who'd want to stay within bounds?

True love. Is it really necessary?
Tact and common sense tell us to pass over it in silence,
like a scandal in Life's highest circles.
Perfectly good children are born without its help.   30
It couldn't populate the planet in a million years,
it comes along so rarely.

Let the people who never find true love
keep saying that there's no such thing.

Their faith will make it easier for them to live and die.   [1972] 35

FOR THINKING AND WRITING

1. The tone of the poem seems to be crucial. Is Szymborska being ironic?
   Does it really matter to her if true love is practical?

2. Why does the poet ask a series of questions and then answer them? Would
   you have answered them in the same way she does?

3. Reading between the lines, what kind of behavior do those in "true love"
   exhibit? Is this true in your experience?

4. Can people just "follow their example" (line 23)? Is falling in love an act
   of will? Is it an accident? Does she really worry about "how far things
   might go" (line 22)?

5. How could this poem be seen as an argument against true love? As an
   argument for true love? Does the last line make you think the poet really
   does believe in true love? How would you explain the meaning of the last
   line?

WILLIAM CARLOS WILLIAMS
The Last Words of My English Grandmother

For most of his eighty years, William Carlos Williams (1883–1963) lived and prac-
ticed medicine in Rutherford, New Jersey, his birthplace, and in the nearby city of
Paterson, the setting for his influential poetry sequence. He earned his medical
degree at the University of Pennsylvania in 1906 and studied pediatrics in Ger-
many. An important voice among modernist poets of the early twentieth century,
Williams focused his theoretical prose on ideas and experiences that he saw as dis-
tinctly American and incorporated the rhythms and color of American speech into
his poetry. Deceptively simple, his poems are crafted with deliberate precision. This
poem appears in The Collected Poems of William Carlos Williams, 1909–1939.

There were some dirty plates
and a glass of milk
beside her on a small table
near the rank, disheveled bed—

Wrinkled and nearly blind   5
she lay and snored
rousing with anger in her tones
to cry for food,

Gimme something to eat—
They're starving me—   10
I'm all right I won't go
to the hospital. No, no, no

Give me something to eat
Let me take you
to the hospital, I said   15
and after you are well

you can do as you please.
She smiled, Yes
you do what you please first
then I can do what I please—   20

Oh, oh, oh! she cried
as the ambulance men lifted
her to the stretcher—
Is this what you call

making me comfortable?   25
By now her mind was clear—
Oh you think you're smart
you young people,

◆   ◆   ◆

she said, but I'll tell you
you don't know anything.   30
Then we started.
On the way

we passed a long row
of elms. She looked at them
awhile out of   35
the ambulance window and said,

What are all those
fuzzy-looking things out there?
Trees? Well, I'm tired
of them and rolled her head away.   [1924]   40

FOR THINKING AND WRITING

1. What is the speaker's attitude toward his grandmother? What is yours?
   Could you argue that the grandmother is brave and independent? Frightened and bitter?

2. What does the grandmother mean by saying young people "don't know
   anything" (line 30)? Do children "know anything" in your view?

3. Poets sometimes like to present concrete images that carry emotional
   weight instead of telling the reader what they intend. How do you
   respond to some of Williams's specific images? What do they suggest?

4. Rewrite "Well, I'm tired / of them" (lines 39–40) to something else, and
   explain how your change alters the meaning of the poem.

5. Should the grandmother's requests be honored? Is the speaker right to
   intervene? Are we responsible for how our grandparents want to act?

JAMES WRIGHT

Lying in a Hammock at William Duffy's Farm in Pine Island, Minnesota

*James Wright (1927–1980) was born and raised in the industrial town of Martin's
Ferry, Ohio. In his lifetime he published nine books of poetry, and two more were
published after his death, including* Above the River: The Complete Poems
*(1992). Many of Wright's poems deal with the working-class life he experienced
growing up. Early in his career as a poet, he wrote in conventional forms, but later
he became much more experimental. The following poem, perhaps Wright's most
famous, is a case in point.*

Over my head, I see the bronze butterfly,
Asleep on the black trunk,
Blowing like a leaf in green shadow.
Down the ravine behind the empty house,
The cowbells follow one another   5
Into the distances of the afternoon.
To my right,
In a field of sunlight between two pines,
The droppings of last year's horses
Blaze up into golden stones.   10
I lean back, as the evening darkens and comes on.
A chicken hawk floats over, looking for home.
I have wasted my life.   [1963]

FOR THINKING AND WRITING

1. Does the last line surprise you? Why, or why not? Looking back over the poem, does the last line fit well with the previous ones? Why, or why not?

2. How objective does the speaker seem in each of his observations?

3. Would the poem's meaning and effect be different if the speaker's observations about nature were put in a different order? Explain. What would have been the effect had the speaker begun with the statement that now concludes the poem?

4. The title is quite specific about the poem's setting. Why evidently does Wright point out whose farm it is and exactly where it is located?

5. Despite the specificity of the title, the speaker isn't specific about how he has wasted his life. Why evidently does Wright refuse to provide such detail? What things do you plan to do so that you do not feel that you have wasted your life?

WILLIAM BUTLER YEATS
The Second Coming

William Butler Yeats (1865–1939) was one of the most revered and influential modern poets, winning the Nobel Prize for literature in 1923. He was born in Dublin, Ireland, and although he spent part of his childhood in London, he is closely associated with his native country. Besides writing poetry, he cofounded Dublin's Abbey Theatre and wrote books of literary criticism along with treatises on mystical philosophy. Yeats was also strongly involved in Irish politics. Both in his literary works and in his civic life, he was dedicated to resurrecting Irish folklore traditions and overthrowing British rule. In 1922, he was even elected as a senator for the newly established Irish Free Republic.

Some of Yeats's writing was more personal than political. Several of his poems mourn his troubled romantic relationship with the Irish rebel Maud Gonne, who eventually married another man. But certainly "The Second Coming" shows Yeats's interest in using poetry to comment on national and even international events. This particular poem, included in Yeats's 1921 book Michael Robartes and the Dancer, reflects his concern over recent political violence, including World War I, the Russian Revolution of 1917, and of course Great Britain's efforts to keep Ireland under its control. To express his anguish, Yeats draws on Christian narratives of Jesus and the Apocalypse. But he borrows, too, from Eastern religions that see the history of the universe as cyclical, and he also refers to the Egyptian legend of the Sphinx. In the years since the poem's publication, several lines from it have become famous, serving as titles of literary works and as quotations appropriate for disastrous occasions. For many readers, the poem foreshadowed the rise of fascism in Europe during the 1920s and 1930s. With the September 11, 2001, attacks, "The Second Coming" struck many as relevant again.

Turning and turning in the widening gyre°
The falcon cannot hear the falconer;
Things fall apart; the center cannot hold;
Mere anarchy is loosed upon the world,
The blood-dimmed tide is loosed, and everywhere   5
The ceremony of innocence is drowned;
The best lack all conviction, while the worst
Are full of passionate intensity.

Surely some revelation is at hand;
Surely the Second Coming is at hand;   10
The Second Coming! Hardly are those words out
When a vast image out of Spiritus Mundi°
Troubles my sight: somewhere in sands of the desert
A shape with lion body and the head of a man,
A gaze blank and pitiless as the sun,   15
Is moving its slow thighs, while all about it
Reel shadows of the indignant desert birds.
The darkness drops again; but now I know
That twenty centuries of stony sleep
Were vexed to nightmare by a rocking cradle,   20
And what rough beast, its hour come round at last,
Slouches towards Bethlehem to be born?   [1921]

gyre: Circle or spiral.   Spiritus Mundi: Spirit of the universe.

FOR THINKING AND WRITING

1. Many people associate the phrase "the second coming" with the return of Jesus, whom they see as the Messiah. In what ways, if any, does the poem reinforce this definition? In what ways, if any, does the poem complicate it?

2. The poem consists of just two stanzas. What are the key differences between them?

3. What does the speaker seem certain about? Uncertain about? What questions do *you* have after reading the poem? Do you think the poem would be more effective if it answered these questions? Explain.

4. One of the most quoted statements from the poem is "The best lack all conviction, while the worst / Are full of passionate intensity" (lines 7–8). What current situations could this statement be applied to?

5. Look up the word *apocalypse* in a dictionary or encyclopedia. To what extent, and in what ways, does it apply to the scenes described in this poem?

ADAM ZAGAJEWSKI
Try to Praise the Mutilated World
Translated by Clare Cavanaugh

Soon after the September 11, 2001, attacks, this poem drew much attention. When The New Yorker *poetry editor Alice Quinn put it on the last page of the magazine's issue about the disaster, it was widely read, and then it was broadly circulated on the Internet. Ironically, Zagajewski had written the poem two years before. "I was born into a mutilated world, right after World War II," he said in a* USA Today *interview, "and the feeling that we tread on a frail ground has never left me." Born in the Ukraine, Adam Zagajewski (b. 1945) grew up in Poland and became one of that country's dissident writers during the last years of its Communist regime. Although he has kept a home in France since 1982 and has taught at the University of Houston since 1988, his writing continues to reflect his sensitivity to Polish history. Prose by Zagajewski available in English translation includes a memoir,* Another Beauty (2000), *along with two collections of essays,* Solitude and Solidarity (1990) *and* Two Cities (1995). *English versions of his poetry volumes include* Tremor (1985), Canvas (1991), Mysticism for Beginners (1997), *and* Without End: New and Selected Poems (2002), *which features "Try to Praise the Mutilated World."*

Try to praise the mutilated world.
Remember June's long days,
and wild strawberries, drops of wine, the dew.
The nettles that methodically overgrow

the abandoned homesteads of exiles.   5
You must praise the mutilated world.
You watched the stylish yachts and ships;
one of them had a long trip ahead of it,
while salty oblivion awaited others.
You've seen the refugees heading nowhere,   10
you've heard the executioners sing joyfully.
You should praise the mutilated world.
Remember the moments when we were together
in a white room and the curtain fluttered.
Return in thought to the concert where music flared.   15
You gathered acorns in the park in autumn
and leaves eddied over the earth's scars.
Praise the mutilated world
and the gray feather a thrush lost,
and the gentle light that strays and vanishes   20
and returns.   [2001]

FOR THINKING AND WRITING

1. What is the effect of addressing the poem to a "you"? Can you identify
   with this "you"? Why, or why not?

2. What specific things does the poem identify as worthy of praise? What, if
   anything, do they have in common?

3. Where does Zagajewski repeat, and yet vary, the first line? How significant are the changes he makes in it?

4. The speaker declares, "You've seen the refugees heading nowhere, /
   you've heard the executioners sing joyfully" (lines 10–11). What would
   you say to readers who insist that they haven't seen or heard such people?

5. Near the start, the poem refers to June. Near the end, it refers to autumn.
   Why this shift of seasons, do you think?

15

A Gallery of Plays

SOPHOCLES
Antigone

Translated by Robert Fagles

Antigone *was first produced in 441* B.C.E., *more than a decade before* Oedipus the King *was first produced. Just before the action of* Antigone *begins, the heroine's two brothers have killed each other in battle. One, Eteocles, was defending Thebes; the other, Polynices, was leading an army against it. The current ruler of Thebes, Antigone's uncle Creon, now forbids burial of Polynices — a command that Antigone will defy.*

CHARACTERS

ANTIGONE, *daughter of Oedipus and Jocasta*
ISMENE, *sister of Antigone*
A CHORUS *of old Theban citizens and their* LEADER
CREON, *king of Thebes, uncle of Antigone and Ismene*
A SENTRY
HAEMON, *son of Creon and Eurydice*
TIRESIAS, *a blind prophet*
A MESSENGER
EURYDICE, *wife of Creon*
GUARDS, ATTENDANTS, AND A BOY

TIME AND SCENE: *The royal house of Thebes. It is still night, and the invading armies of Argos have just been driven from the city. Fighting on opposite sides, the sons of Oedipus, Eteocles and Polynices, have killed each other in combat. Their uncle, Creon, is now king of Thebes.*

  Enter Antigone, slipping through the central doors of the palace. She motions to her sister, Ismene, who follows her cautiously toward an altar at the center of the stage.

ANTIGONE: My own flesh and blood — dear sister, dear Ismene,
    how many griefs our father Oedipus handed down!
    Do you know one, I ask you, one grief
    that Zeus° will not perfect for the two of us
    while we still live and breathe? There's nothing,   5
    no pain — our lives are pain — no private shame,
    no public disgrace, nothing I haven't seen
    in your griefs and mine. And now this:
    an emergency decree, they say, the Commander
    has just declared for all of Thebes.   10
    What, haven't you heard? Don't you see?
    The doom reserved for enemies
    marches on the ones we love the most.
ISMENE: Not I, I haven't heard a word, Antigone.
    Nothing of loved ones,   15
    no joy or pain has come my way, not since
    the two of us were robbed of our two brothers,
    both gone in a day, a double blow —
    not since the armies of Argos vanished,
    just this very night. I know nothing more,   20
    whether our luck's improved or ruin's still to come.
ANTIGONE: I thought so. That's why I brought you out here,
    past the gates, so you could hear in private.
ISMENE: What's the matter? Trouble, clearly . . .
    you sound so dark, so grim.   25
ANTIGONE: Why not? Our own brothers' burial!
    Hasn't Creon graced one with all the rites,
    disgraced the other? Eteocles, they say,
    has been given full military honors,
    rightly so — Creon's laid him in the earth   30
    and he goes with glory down among the dead.
    But the body of Polynices, who died miserably —
    why, a city-wide proclamation, rumor has it,
    forbids anyone to bury him, even mourn him.
    He's to be left unwept, unburied, a lovely treasure   35
    for birds that scan the field and feast to their heart's content.

    Such, I hear, is the martial law our good Creon
    lays down for you and me — yes, me, I tell you —
    and he's coming here to alert the uninformed
    in no uncertain terms,   40
    and he won't treat the matter lightly. Whoever
    disobeys in the least will die, his doom is sealed:
    stoning to death inside the city walls!

4 Zeus: The highest Olympian deity.

There you have it. You'll soon show what you are,
worth your breeding, Ismene, or a coward—   45
for all your royal blood.
ISMENE: My poor sister, if things have come to this,
who am I to make or mend them, tell me,
what good am I to you?
ANTIGONE: Decide.
Will you share the labor, share the work?   50
ISMENE: What work, what's the risk? What do you mean?
ANTIGONE:

Raising her hands.

Will you lift up his body with these bare hands
and lower it with me?
ISMENE: What? You'd bury him—
when a law forbids the city?
ANTIGONE: Yes!
He is my brother and—deny it as you will—   55
your brother too.
No one will ever convict me for a traitor.
ISMENE: So desperate, and Creon has expressly—
ANTIGONE: No,
he has no right to keep me from my own.
ISMENE: Oh my sister, think—   60
think how our own father died, hated,
his reputation in ruins, driven on
by the crimes he brought to light himself
to gouge out his eyes with his own hands—
then mother . . . his mother and wife, both in one,   65
mutilating her life in the twisted noose—
and last, our two brothers dead in a single day,
both shedding their own blood, poor suffering boys,
battling out their common destiny hand-to-hand.

Now look at the two of us, left so alone . . .   70
think what a death we'll die, the worst of all
if we violate the laws and override
the fixed decree of the throne, its power—
we must be sensible. Remember we are women,
we're not born to contend with men. Then too,   75
we're underlings, ruled by much stronger hands,
so we must submit in this, and things still worse.

I, for one, I'll beg the dead to forgive me—
I'm forced, I have no choice—I must obey
the ones who stand in power. Why rush to extremes?   80

It's madness, madness.
                    I won't insist,
ANTIGONE:
    no, even if you should have a change of heart,
    I'd never welcome you in the labor, not with me.
    So, do as you like, whatever suits you best —
    I'll bury him myself.   85
    And even if I die in the act, that death will be a glory.
    I'll lie with the one I love and loved by him —
    an outrage sacred to the gods! I have longer
    to please the dead than please the living here:
    in the kingdom down below I'll lie forever.   90
    Do as you like, dishonor the laws
    the gods hold in honor.
ISMENE: I'd do them no dishonor . . .
    but defy the city? I have no strength for that.
ANTIGONE: You have your excuses. I am on my way,
    I'll raise a mound for him, for my dear brother.   95
ISMENE: Oh Antigone, you're so rash — I'm so afraid for you!
ANTIGONE: Don't fear for me. Set your own life in order.
ISMENE: Then don't, at least, blurt this out to anyone.
    Keep it a secret. I'll join you in that, I promise.
ANTIGONE: Dear god, shout it from the rooftops. I'll hate you   100
    all the more for silence — tell the world!
ISMENE: So fiery — and it ought to chill your heart.
ANTIGONE: I know I please where I must please the most.
ISMENE: Yes, if you can, but you're in love with impossibility.
ANTIGONE: Very well then, once my strength gives out   105
    I will be done at last.
ISMENE: You're wrong from the start,
    you're off on a hopeless quest.
ANTIGONE: If you say so, you will make me hate you,
    and the hatred of the dead, by all rights,
    will haunt you night and day.   110
    But leave me to my own absurdity, leave me
    to suffer this — dreadful thing. I'll suffer
    nothing as great as death without glory.

Exit to the side.

ISMENE: Then go if you must, but rest assured,
    wild, irrational as you are, my sister,   115
    you are truly dear to the ones who love you.

*Withdrawing to the palace. Enter a Chorus, the old citizens of Thebes, chanting as
the sun begins to rise.*

CHORUS: Glory! — great beam of sun, brightest of all
    that ever rose on the seven gates of Thebes,

you burn through night at last!
           Great eye of the golden day,   120
mounting the Dirce's° banks you throw him back—
the enemy out of Argos, the white shield, the man of bronze—
he's flying headlong now
         the bridle of fate stampeding him with pain!

     And he had driven against our borders,   125
     launched by the warring claims of Polynices—
     like an eagle screaming, winging havoc
     over the land, wings of armor
     shielded white as snow,
     a huge army massing,   130
     crested helmets bristling for assault.

He hovered above our roofs, his vast maw gaping
closing down around our seven gates,
     his spears thirsting for the kill
         but now he's gone, look,   135
before he could glut his jaws with Theban blood
or the god of fire put our crown of towers to the torch.
He grappled the Dragon none can master—Thebes—
     the clang of our arms like thunder at his back!

     Zeus hates with a vengeance all bravado,   140
     the mighty boasts of men. He watched them
     coming on in a rising flood, the pride
     of their golden armor ringing shrill—
     and brandishing his lightning
     blasted the fighter just at the goal,   145
     rushing to shout his triumph from our walls.

Down from the heights he crashed, pounding down on the earth!
And a moment ago, blazing torch in hand—
     mad for attack, ecstatic
he breathed his rage, the storm   150
     of his fury hurling at our heads!
But now his high hopes have laid him low
and down the enemy ranks the iron god of war
     deals his rewards, his stunning blows—Ares°
     rapture of battle, our right arm in the crisis.   155

     Seven captains marshaled at seven gates
     seven against their equals, gave
     their brazen trophies up to Zeus,
     god of the breaking rout of battle,

---

121 the Dirce: A river near Thebes.   **154 Ares:** God of war.

all but two: those blood brothers,   160
one father, one mother—matched in rage,
spears matched for the twin conquest—
clashed and won the common prize of death.

But now for Victory! Glorious in the morning,
joy in her eyes to meet our joy   165
    she is winging down to Thebes,
our fleets of chariots wheeling in her wake—
    Now let us win oblivion from the wars,
thronging the temples of the gods
in singing, dancing choirs through the night!   170
    Lord Dionysus,° god of the dance
    that shakes the land of Thebes, now lead the way!

Enter Creon from the palace, attended by his guard.

    But look, the king of the realm is coming,
    Creon, the new man for the new day,
    whatever the gods are sending now . . .   175
    what new plan will he launch?
    Why this, this special session?
    Why this sudden call to the old men
    summoned at one command?

CREON: My countrymen,
the ship of state is safe. The gods who rocked her,   180
after a long, merciless pounding in the storm,
have righted her once more.
                            Out of the whole city
I have called you here alone. Well I know,
first, your undeviating respect
for the throne and royal power of King Laius.   185
Next, while Oedipus steered the land of Thebes,
and even after he died, your loyalty was unshakable,
you still stood by their children. Now then,
since the two sons are dead—two blows of fate
in the same day, cut down by each other's hands,   190
both killers, both brothers stained with blood—
as I am next in kin to the dead,
I now possess the throne and all its powers.

Of course you cannot know a man completely,
his character, his principles, sense of judgment,   195
not till he's shown his colors, ruling the people,
making laws. Experience, there's the test.
As I see it, whoever assumes the task,

---

171 Dionysus: God of fertility and wine.

the awesome task of setting the city's course,
and refuses to adopt the soundest policies   200
but fearing someone, keeps his lips locked tight,
he's utterly worthless. So I rate him now,
I always have. And whoever places a friend
above the good of his own country, he is nothing:
I have no use for him. Zeus my witness,   205
Zeus who sees all things, always—
I could never stand by silent, watching destruction
march against our city, putting safety to rout,
nor could I ever make that man a friend of mine
who menaces our country. Remember this: 210
our country *is* our safety.
Only while she voyages true on course
can we establish friendships, truer than blood itself.
Such are my standards. They make our city great.

Closely akin to them I have proclaimed,   215
just now, the following decree to our people
concerning the two sons of Oedipus.
Eteocles, who died fighting for Thebes,
excelling all in arms: he shall be buried,
crowned with a hero's honors, the cups we pour   220
to soak the earth and reach the famous dead.

But as for his blood brother, Polynices,
who returned from exile, home to his father-city
and the gods of his race, consumed with one desire—
to burn them roof to roots—who thirsted to drink   225
his kinsmen's blood and sell the rest to slavery:
that man—a proclamation has forbidden the city
to dignify him with burial, mourn him at all.
No, he must be left unburied, his corpse
carrion for the birds and dogs to tear,   230
an obscenity for the citizens to behold!

These are my principles. Never at my hands
will the traitor be honored above the patriot.
But whoever proves his loyalty to the state:
I'll prize that man in death as well as life.   235
LEADER: If this is your pleasure, Creon, treating
our city's enemy and our friend this way . . .
The power is yours, I suppose, to enforce it
with the laws, both for the dead and all of us,
the living.
CREON: Follow my orders closely then,   240
be on your guard.
              We're too old.

LEADER:
    Lay that burden on younger shoulders.
CREON: No, no,
    I don't mean the body—I've posted guards already.
LEADER: What commands for us then? What other service?
CREON: See that you never side with those who break my orders.   245
LEADER: Never. Only a fool could be in love with death.
CREON: Death is the price—you're right. But all too often
    the mere hope of money has ruined many men.

A Sentry enters from the side.

SENTRY: My lord,
    I can't say I'm winded from running, or set out
    with any spring in my legs either—no sir,   250
    I was lost in thought, and it made me stop, often,
    dead in my tracks, wheeling, turning back,
    and all the time a voice inside me muttering,
    "Idiot, why? You're going straight to your death."
    Then muttering, "Stopped again, poor fool?   255
    If somebody gets the news to Creon first,
    what's to save your neck?"
                And so,
    mulling it over, on I trudged, dragging my feet,
    you can make a short road take forever . . .
    but at last, look, common sense won out,   260
    I'm here, and I'm all yours,
    and even though I come empty-handed
    I'll tell my story just the same, because
    I've come with a good grip on one hope,
    what will come will come, whatever fate—   265
CREON: Come to the point!
    What's wrong—why so afraid?
SENTRY: First, myself, I've got to tell you,
    I didn't do it, didn't see who did—
    Be fair, don't take it out on me.   270
CREON: You're playing it safe, soldier,
    barricading yourself from any trouble.
    It's obvious, you've something strange to tell.
SENTRY: Dangerous too, and danger makes you delay
    for all you're worth.   275
CREON: Out with it—then dismiss!
SENTRY: All right, here it comes. The body—
    someone's just buried it, then run off . . .
    sprinkled some dry dust on the flesh,
    given it proper rites.
CREON: What?   280
    What man alive would dare—

SENTRY: I've no idea, I swear it.
   There was no mark of a spade, no pickaxe there,
   no earth turned up, the ground packed hard and dry,
   unbroken, no tracks, no wheelruts, nothing,
   the workman left no trace. Just at sunup   285
   the first watch of the day points it out—
   it was a wonder! We were stunned . . .
   a terrific burden too, for all of us, listen:
   you can't see the corpse, not that it's buried,
   really, just a light cover of road-dust on it,   290
   as if someone meant to lay the dead to rest
   and keep from getting cursed.
   Not a sign in sight that dogs or wild beasts
   had worried the body, even torn the skin.

   But what came next! Rough talk flew thick and fast,   295
   guard grilling guard—we'd have come to blows
   at last, nothing to stop it; each man for himself
   and each the culprit, no one caught red-handed,
   all of us pleading ignorance, dodging the charges,
   ready to take up red-hot iron in our fists,   300
   go through fire, swear oaths to the gods—
   "I didn't do it, I had no hand in it either,
   not in the plotting, not in the work itself!"

   Finally, after all this wrangling came to nothing,
   one man spoke out and made us stare at the ground,   305
   hanging our heads in fear. No way to counter him,
   no way to take his advice and come through
   safe and sound. Here's what he said:
   "Look, we've got to report the facts to Creon,
   we can't keep this hidden." Well, that won out,   310
   and the lot fell on me, condemned me,
   unlucky as ever, I got the prize. So here I am,
   against my will and yours too, well I know—
   no one wants the man who brings bad news.
LEADER: My king,
   ever since he began I've been debating in my mind,   315
   could this possibly be the work of the gods?
CREON: Stop—
   before you make me choke with anger—the gods!
   You, you're senile, must you be insane?
   You say—why it's intolerable—say the gods
   could have the slightest concern for that corpse?   320
   Tell me, was it for meritorious service
   they proceeded to bury him, prized him so? The hero
   who came to burn their temples ringed with pillars,
   their golden treasures—scorch their hallowed earth

and fling their laws to the winds.   325
Exactly when did you last see the gods
celebrating traitors? Inconceivable!

No, from the first there were certain citizens
who could hardly stand the spirit of my regime,
grumbling against me in the dark, heads together,   330
tossing wildly, never keeping their necks beneath
the yoke, loyally submitting to their king.
These are the instigators, I'm convinced —
they've perverted my own guard, bribed them
to do their work.
               Money! Nothing worse   335
in our lives, so current, rampant, so corrupting.
Money — you demolish cities, root men from their homes,
you train and twist good minds and set them on
to the most atrocious schemes. No limit,
you make them adept at every kind of outrage,   340
every godless crime — money!
                    Everyone —
the whole crew bribed to commit this crime,
they've made one thing sure at least:
sooner or later they will pay the price.

Wheeling on the Sentry.

You —   345
I swear to Zeus as I still believe in Zeus,
if you don't find the man who buried that corpse,
the very man, and produce him before my eyes,
simple death won't be enough for you,
not till we string you up alive   350
and wring the immorality out of you.
Then you can steal the rest of your days,
better informed about where to make a killing.
You'll have learned, at last, it doesn't pay
to itch for rewards from every hand that beckons.   355
Filthy profits wreck most men, you'll see —
they'll never save your life.

SENTRY: Please,
    may I say a word or two, or just turn and go?
CREON: Can't you tell? Everything you say offends me.
SENTRY: Where does it hurt you, in the ears or in the heart?   360
CREON: And who are you to pinpoint my displeasure?
SENTRY: The culprit grates on your feelings,
    I just annoy your ears.
CREON: Still talking?
    You talk too much! A born nuisance —

SENTRY: Maybe so,
but I never did this thing, so help me!
CREON: Yes you did — 365
what's more, you squandered your life for silver!
SENTRY: Oh it's terrible when the one who does the judging
judges things all wrong.
CREON: Well now,
you just be clever about your judgments —
if you fail to produce the criminals for me, 370
you'll swear your dirty money brought you pain.

Turning sharply, reentering the palace.

SENTRY: I hope he's found. Best thing by far.
But caught or not, that's in the lap of fortune;
I'll never come back, you've seen the last of me.
I'm saved, even now, and I never thought, 375
I never hoped —
dear gods, I owe you all my thanks!

Rushing out.

CHORUS: Numberless wonders
terrible wonders walk the world but none the match for man —
that great wonder crossing the heaving gray sea,
driven on by the blasts of winter 380
on through breakers crashing left and right,
holds his steady course
and the oldest of the gods he wears away —
the Earth, the immortal, the inexhaustible —
as his plows go back and forth, year in, year out 385
with the breed of stallions turning up the furrows.

And the blithe, lightheaded race of birds he snares,
the tribes of savage beasts, the life that swarms the depths —
with one fling of his nets
woven and coiled tight, he takes them all, 390
man the skilled, the brilliant!
He conquers all, taming with his techniques
the prey that roams the cliffs and wild lairs,
training the stallion, clamping the yoke across
his shaggy neck, and the tireless mountain bull. 395

And speech and thought, quick as the wind
and the mood and mind for law that rules the city —
all these he has taught himself
and shelter from the arrows of the frost
when there's rough lodging under the cold clear sky 400
and the shafts of lashing rain —
ready, resourceful man!

Never without resources
never an impasse as he marches on the future —
only Death, from Death alone he will find no rescue   405
but from desperate plagues he has plotted his escapes.

Man the master, ingenious past all measure
past all dreams, the skills within his grasp —
   he forges on, now to destruction
now again to greatness. When he weaves in   410
the laws of the land, and the justice of the gods
that binds his oaths together
      he and his city rise high —
        but the city casts out
that man who weds himself to inhumanity   415
thanks to reckless daring. Never share my hearth
never think my thoughts, whoever does such things.

Enter Antigone from the side, accompanied by the Sentry.

Here is a dark sign from the gods —
what to make of this? I know her,
how can I deny it? That young girl's Antigone!   420
Wretched, child of a wretched father,
Oedipus. Look, is it possible?
They bring you in like a prisoner —
why? did you break the king's laws?
Did they take you in some act of mad defiance?   425

SENTRY: She's the one, she did it single-handed —
we caught her burying the body. Where's Creon?

Enter Creon from the palace.

LEADER: Back again, just in time when you need him.
CREON: In time for what? What is it?
SENTRY: My king,
there's nothing you can swear you'll never do —   430
second thoughts make liars of us all.
I could have sworn I wouldn't hurry back
(what with your threats, the buffeting I just took),
but a stroke of luck beyond our wildest hopes,
what a joy, there's nothing like it. So,   435
back I've come, breaking my oath, who cares?
I'm bringing in our prisoner — this young girl —
we took her giving the dead the last rites.
But no casting lots this time; this is *my* luck,
my prize, no one else's.
               Now, my lord,   440
here she is. Take her, question her,

cross-examine her to your heart's content.
But set me free, it's only right—
I'm rid of this dreadful business once for all.

CREON: Prisoner! Her? You took her—where, doing what?   445
SENTRY: Burying the man. That's the whole story.
CREON: What?
You mean what you say, you're telling me the truth?
SENTRY: She's the one. With my own eyes I saw her
bury the body, just what you've forbidden.
There. Is that plain and clear?   450
CREON: What did you see? Did you catch her in the act?
SENTRY: Here's what happened. We went back to our post,
those threats of yours breathing down our necks—
we brushed the corpse clean of the dust that covered it,
stripped it bare . . . it was slimy, going soft,   455
and we took to high ground, backs to the wind
so the stink of him couldn't hit us;
jostling, baiting each other to keep awake,
shouting back and forth—no napping on the job,
not this time. And so the hours dragged by   460
until the sun stood dead above our heads,
a huge white ball in the noon sky, beating,
blazing down, and then it happened—
suddenly, a whirlwind!
Twisting a great dust-storm up from the earth,   465
a black plague of the heavens, filling the plain,
ripping the leaves off every tree in sight,
choking the air and sky. We squinted hard
and took our whipping from the gods.

And after the storm passed—it seemed endless—   470
there, we saw the girl!
And she cried out a sharp, piercing cry,
like a bird come back to an empty nest,
peering into its bed, and all the babies gone . . .
Just so, when she sees the corpse bare   475
she bursts into a long, shattering wail
and calls down withering curses on the heads
of all who did the work. And she scoops up dry dust,
handfuls, quickly, and lifting a fine bronze urn,
lifting it high and pouring, she crowns the dead   480
with three full libations.
                    Soon as we saw
we rushed her, closed on the kill like hunters,
and she, she didn't flinch. We interrogated her,
charging her with offenses past and present—

she stood up to it all, denied nothing. I tell you, 485
it made me ache and laugh in the same breath.
It's pure joy to escape the worst yourself,
it hurts a man to bring down his friends.
But all that, I'm afraid, means less to me
than my own skin. That's the way I'm made.

CREON:

Wheeling on Antigone.

You, 490
with your eyes fixed on the ground—speak up.
Do you deny you did this, yes or no?

ANTIGONE: I did it. I don't deny a thing.

CREON:

To the Sentry.

You, get out, wherever you please—
you're clear of a very heavy charge. 495

He leaves; Creon turns back to Antigone.

You, tell me briefly, no long speeches—
were you aware a decree had forbidden this?

ANTIGONE: Well aware. How could I avoid it? It was public.

CREON: And still you had the gall to break this law?

ANTIGONE: Of course I did. It wasn't Zeus, not in the least, 500
who made this proclamation—not to me.
Nor did that Justice, dwelling with the gods
beneath the earth, ordain such laws for men.
Nor did I think your edict had such force
that you, a mere mortal, could override the gods, 505
the great unwritten, unshakable traditions.
They are alive, not just today or yesterday:
they live forever, from the first of time,
and no one knows when they first saw the light.

These laws—I was not about to break them, 510
not out of fear of some man's wounded pride,
and face the retribution of the gods.
Die I must, I've known it all my life—
how could I keep from knowing?—even without
your death-sentence ringing in my ears. 515
And if I am to die before my time
I consider that a gain. Who on earth,
alive in the midst of so much grief as I,
could fail to find his death a rich reward?
So for me, at least, to meet this doom of yours 520
is precious little pain. But if I had allowed
my own mother's son to rot, an unburied corpse—

that would have been an agony! This is nothing.
And if my present actions strike you as foolish,
let's just say I've been accused of folly   525
by a fool.

LEADER: Like father like daughter,
      passionate, wild . . .
      she hasn't learned to bend before adversity.

CREON: No? Believe me, the stiffest stubborn wills
      fall the hardest; the toughest iron,   530
      tempered strong in the white-hot fire,
      you'll see it crack and shatter first of all.
      And I've known spirited horses you can break
      with a light bit—proud, rebellious horses.
      There's no room for pride, not in a slave,   535
      not with the lord and master standing by.

      This girl was an old hand at insolence
      when she overrode the edicts we made public.
      But once she'd done it—the insolence,
      twice over—to glory in it, laughing,   540
      mocking us to our face with what she'd done.
      I'm not the man, not now: she is the man
      if this victory goes to her and she goes free.

      Never! Sister's child or closer in blood
      than all my family clustered at my altar   545
      worshiping Guardian Zeus—she'll never escape,
      she and her blood sister, the most barbaric death.
      Yes, I accuse her sister of an equal part
      in scheming this, this burial.

To his attendants.

                          Bring her here!
      I just saw her inside, hysterical, gone to pieces.   550
      It never fails: the mind convicts itself
      in advance, when scoundrels are up to no good,
      plotting in the dark. Oh but I hate it more
      when a traitor, caught red-handed,
      tries to glorify his crimes.   555

ANTIGONE: Creon, what more do you want
      than my arrest and execution?

CREON: Nothing. Then I have it all.

ANTIGONE: Then why delay? Your moralizing repels me,
      every word you say—pray god it always will.   560
      So naturally all I say repels you too.
                          Enough.
      Give me glory! What greater glory could I win

than to give my own brother decent burial?
These citizens here would all agree,

To the Chorus.

they'd praise me too   565
if their lips weren't locked in fear.

Pointing to Creon.

Lucky tyrants — the perquisites of power!
Ruthless power to do and say whatever pleases *them.*
CREON: You alone, of all the people in Thebes,
see things that way.
ANTIGONE: They see it just that way   570
but defer to you and keep their tongues in leash.
CREON: And you, aren't you ashamed to differ so from them?
So disloyal!
ANTIGONE: Not ashamed for a moment,
not to honor my brother, my own flesh and blood.
CREON: Wasn't Eteocles a brother too — cut down, facing him?   575
ANTIGONE: Brother, yes, by the same mother, the same father.
CREON: Then how can you render his enemy such honors,
such impieties in his eyes?
ANTIGONE: He'll never testify to that,
Eteocles dead and buried.
CREON: He will —   580
if you honor the traitor just as much as him.
ANTIGONE: But it was his brother, not some slave that died —
CREON: Ravaging our country! —
but Eteocles died fighting in our behalf.
ANTIGONE: No matter — Death longs for the same rites for all.   585
CREON: Never the same for the patriot and the traitor.
ANTIGONE: Who, Creon, who on earth can say the ones below
don't find this pure and uncorrupt?
CREON: Never. Once an enemy, never a friend,
not even after death.   590
ANTIGONE: I was born to join in love, not hate —
that is my nature.
CREON: Go down below and love,
if love you must — love the dead! While I'm alive,
no woman is going to lord it over me.

Enter Ismene from the palace, under guard.

CHORUS: Look,
Ismene's coming, weeping a sister's tears,   595
loving sister, under a cloud . . .
her face is flushed, her cheeks streaming.
Sorrow puts her lovely radiance in the dark.

CREON: You—
    in my house, you viper, slinking undetected,
    sucking my life-blood! I never knew 600
    I was breeding twin disasters, the two of you
    rising up against my throne. Come, tell me,
    will you confess your part in the crime or not?
    Answer me. Swear to me.
ISMENE: I did it, yes—
    if only she consents—I share the guilt, 605
    the consequences too.
ANTIGONE: No,
    Justice will never suffer that—not you,
    you were unwilling. I never brought you in.
ISMENE: But now you face such dangers . . . I'm not ashamed
    to sail through trouble with you, 610
    make your troubles mine.
ANTIGONE: Who did the work?
    Let the dead and the god of death bear witness!
    I've no love for a friend who loves in words alone.
ISMENE: Oh no, my sister, don't reject me, please,
    let me die beside you, consecrating 615
    the dead together.
ANTIGONE: Never share my dying,
    don't lay claim to what you never touched.
    My death will be enough.
ISMENE: What do I care for life, cut off from you?
ANTIGONE: Ask Creon. Your concern is all for him. 620
ISMENE: Why abuse me so? It doesn't help you now.
ANTIGONE: You're right—
    if I mock you, I get no pleasure from it,
    only pain.
ISMENE: Tell me, dear one,
    what can I do to help you, even now?
ANTIGONE: Save yourself. I don't grudge you your survival. 625
ISMENE: Oh no, no, denied my portion in your death?
ANTIGONE: You chose to live, I chose to die.
ISMENE: Not, at least,
    without every kind of caution I could voice.
ANTIGONE: Your wisdom appealed to one world—mine, another.
ISMENE: But look, we're both guilty, both condemned to death. 630
ANTIGONE: Courage! Live your life. I gave myself to death,
    long ago, so I might serve the dead.
CREON: They're both mad, I tell you, the two of them.
    One's just shown it, the other's been that way
    since she was born.
ISMENE: True, my king, 635
    the sense we were born with cannot last forever . . .

commit cruelty on a person long enough
and the mind begins to go.
CREON: Yours did,
when you chose to commit your crimes with her.
ISMENE: How can I live alone, without her?
CREON: Her?   640
Don't even mention her—she no longer exists.
ISMENE: What? You'd kill your own son's bride?
CREON: Absolutely:
there are other fields for him to plow.
ISMENE: Perhaps,
but never as true, as close a bond as theirs.
CREON: A worthless woman for my son? It repels me.   645
ISMENE: Dearest Haemon, your father wrongs you so!
CREON: Enough, enough—you and your talk of marriage!
ISMENE: Creon—you're really going to rob your son of Antigone?
CREON: Death will do it for me—break their marriage off.
LEADER: So, it's settled then? Antigone must die?   650
CREON: Settled, yes—we both know that.

To the guards.

Stop wasting time. Take them in.
From now on they'll act like women.
Tie them up, no more running loose;
even the bravest will cut and run,   655
once they see Death coming for their lives.

The guards escort Antigone and Ismene into the palace. Creon remains while the old citizens form their chorus.

CHORUS: Blest, they are the truly blest who all their lives
have never tasted devastation. For others, once
the gods have rocked a house to its foundations
      the ruin will never cease, cresting on and on   660
from one generation on throughout the race—
like a great mounting tide
driven on by savage northern gales,
      surging over the dead black depths
roiling up from the bottom dark heaves of sand   665
and the headlands, taking the storm's onslaught full-force,
roar, and the low moaning
                  echoes on and on
                        and now
as in ancient times I see the sorrows of the house,
the living heirs of the old ancestral kings,
piling on the sorrows of the dead   670
      and one generation cannot free the next—
some god will bring them crashing down,
the race finds no release.

And now the light, the hope
    springing up from the late last root   675
in the house of Oedipus, that hope's cut down in turn
by the long, bloody knife swung by the gods of death
by a senseless word
                     by fury at the heart.
                                 Zeus,
yours is the power, Zeus, what man on earth
can override it, who can hold it back?   680
Power that neither Sleep, the all-ensnaring
    no, nor the tireless months of heaven
can ever overmaster — young through all time,
mighty lord of power, you hold fast
    the dazzling crystal mansions of Olympus.   685
And throughout the future, late and soon
as through the past, your law prevails:
no towering form of greatness
          enters into the lives of mortals
                  free and clear of ruin.
                               True,   690
our dreams, our high hopes voyaging far and wide
bring sheer delight to many, to many others
    delusion, blithe, mindless lusts
and the fraud steals on one slowly . . . unaware
till he trips and puts his foot into the fire.   695
    He was a wise old man who coined
the famous saying: "Sooner or later
foul is fair, fair is foul
to the man the gods will ruin" —
    He goes his way for a moment only   700
                 free of blinding ruin.

Enter Haemon from the palace.

    Here's Haemon now, the last of all your sons.
    Does he come in tears for his bride,
    his doomed bride, Antigone —
    bitter at being cheated of their marriage?   705
CREON: We'll soon know, better than seers could tell us.

Turning to Haemon.

    Son, you've heard the final verdict on your bride?
    Are you coming now, raving against your father?
    Or do you love me, no matter what I do?
HAEMON: Father, I'm your *son* . . . you in your wisdom   710
    set my bearings for me — I obey you.
    No marriage could ever mean more to me than you,
    whatever good direction you may offer.
CREON: Fine, Haemon.

That's how you ought to feel within your heart,
subordinate to your father's will in every way.   715
That's what a man prays for: to produce good sons—
households full of them, dutiful and attentive,
so they can pay his enemy back with interest
and match the respect their father shows his friend.
But the man who rears a brood of useless children,   720
what has he brought into the world, I ask you?
Nothing but trouble for himself, and mockery
from his enemies laughing in his face.
                              Oh Haemon,
never lose your sense of judgment over a woman.
The warmth, the rush of pleasure, it all goes cold   725
in your arms, I warn you . . . a worthless woman
in your house, a misery in your bed.
What wound cuts deeper than a loved one
turned against you? Spit her out,
like a mortal enemy—let the girl go.   730
Let her find a husband down among the dead.

Imagine it: I caught her in naked rebellion,
the traitor, the only one in the whole city.
I'm not about to prove myself a liar,
not to my people, no, I'm going to kill her!   735
That's right—so let her cry for mercy, sing her hymns
to Zeus who defends all bonds of kindred blood.
Why, if I bring up my own kin to be rebels,
think what I'd suffer from the world at large.
Show me the man who rules his household well: 740
I'll show you someone fit to rule the state.
That good man, my son,
I have every confidence he and he alone
can give commands and take them too. Staunch
in the storm of spears he'll stand his ground,   745
a loyal, unflinching comrade at your side.

But whoever steps out of line, violates the laws
or presumes to hand out orders to his superiors,
he'll win no praise from me. But that man
the city places in authority, his orders   750
must be obeyed, large and small,
right and wrong.
                    Anarchy—
show me a greater crime in all the earth!
She, she destroys cities, rips up houses,
breaks the ranks of spearmen into headlong rout.   755
But the ones who last it out, the great mass of them

owe their lives to discipline. Therefore
we must defend the men who live by law,
never let some woman triumph over us.
Better to fall from power, if fall we must,   760
at the hands of a man—never be rated
inferior to a woman, never.
LEADER: To us,
   unless old age has robbed us of our wits,
   you seem to say what you have to say with sense.
HAEMON: Father, only the gods endow a man with reason,   765
   the finest of all their gifts, a treasure.
   Far be it from me—I haven't the skill,
   and certainly no desire, to tell you when,
   if ever, you make a slip in speech . . . though
   someone else might have a good suggestion.   770

   Of course it's not for you,
   in the normal run of things, to watch
   whatever men say or do, or find to criticize.
   The man in the street, you know, dreads your glance,
   he'd never say anything displeasing to your face.   775
   But it's for me to catch the murmurs in the dark,
   the way the city mourns for this young girl.
   "No woman," they say, "ever deserved death less,
   and such a brutal death for such a glorious action.
   She, with her own dear brother lying in his blood—   780
   she couldn't bear to leave him dead, unburied,
   food for the wild dogs or wheeling vultures.
   Death? She deserves a glowing crown of gold!"
   So they say, and the rumor spreads in secret,
   darkly . . .
                 I rejoice in your success, father—   785
   nothing more precious to me in the world.
   What medal of honor brighter to his children
   than a father's growing glory? Or a child's
   to his proud father? Now don't, please,
   be quite so single-minded, self-involved,   790
   or assume the world is wrong and you are right.
   Whoever thinks that he alone possesses intelligence,
   the gift of eloquence, he and no one else,
   and character too . . . such men, I tell you,
   spread them open—you will find them empty.
                                          No,   795
   it's no disgrace for a man, even a wise man,
   to learn many things and not to be too rigid.
   You've seen trees by a raging winter torrent,

how many sway with the flood and salvage every twig,
but not the stubborn — they're ripped out, roots and all.   800
Bend or break. The same when a man is sailing:
haul your sheets too taut, never give an inch,
you'll capsize, go the rest of the voyage
keel up and the rowing-benches under.

Oh give way. Relax your anger — change!   805
I'm young, I know, but let me offer this:
it would be best by far, I admit,
if a man were born infallible, right by nature.
If not — and things don't often go that way,
it's best to learn from those with good advice.   810
LEADER: You'd do well, my lord, if he's speaking to the point,
    to learn from him,

Turning to Haemon.

                    and you, my boy, from him.
    You both are talking sense.
CREON: So,
    men our age, we're to be lectured, are we? —
    schooled by a boy his age?   815
HAEMON: Only in what is right. But if I seem young,
    look less to my years and more to what I do.
CREON: Do? Is admiring rebels an achievement?
HAEMON: I'd never suggest that you admire treason.
CREON: Oh? —
    isn't that just the sickness that's attacked her?   820
HAEMON: The whole city of Thebes denies it, to a man.
CREON: And is Thebes about to tell me how to rule?
HAEMON: Now, you see? Who's talking like a child?
CREON: Am I to rule this land for others — or myself?
HAEMON: It's no city at all, owned by one man alone.   825
CREON: What? The city *is* the king's — that's the law!
HAEMON: What a splendid king you'd make of a desert island —
    you and you alone.
CREON:

To the Chorus.

                    This boy, I do believe,
    is fighting on her side, the woman's side.
HAEMON: If you are a woman, yes;   830
    my concern is all for you.
CREON: Why, you degenerate — bandying accusations,
    threatening me with justice, your own father!
HAEMON: I see my father offending justice — wrong.
CREON: Wrong?
    To protect my royal rights?

HAEMON: Protect your rights?   835
   When you trample down the honors of the gods?
CREON: You, you soul of corruption, rotten through—
   woman's accomplice!
HAEMON: That may be,
   but you'll never find me accomplice to a criminal.
CREON: That's what *she* is,   840
   and every word you say is a blatant appeal for her—
HAEMON: And you, and me, and the gods beneath the earth.
CREON: You'll never marry her, not while she's alive.
HAEMON: Then she'll die . . . but her death will kill another.
CREON: What, brazen threats? You go too far!
HAEMON: What threat?   845
   Combating your empty, mindless judgments with a word?
CREON: You'll suffer for your sermons, you and your empty wisdom!
HAEMON: If you weren't my father, I'd say you were insane.
CREON: Don't flatter me with Father—you woman's slave!
HAEMON: You really expect to fling abuse at me   850
   and not receive the same?
CREON: Is that so!
   Now, by heaven, I promise you, you'll pay—
   taunting, insulting me! Bring her out,
   that hateful—she'll die now, here,
   in front of his eyes, beside her groom!   855
HAEMON: No, no, she will never die beside me—
   don't delude yourself. And you will never
   see me, never set eyes on my face again.
   Rage your heart out, rage with friends
   who can stand the sight of you.   860

Rushing out.

LEADER: Gone, my king, in a burst of anger.
   A temper young as his . . . hurt him once,
   he may do something violent.
CREON: Let him do—
   dream up something desperate, past all human limit!
   Good riddance. Rest assured,   865
   he'll never save those two young girls from death.
LEADER: Both of them, you really intend to kill them both?
CREON: No, not her, the one whose hands are clean;
   you're quite right.
LEADER: But Antigone—
   what sort of death do you have in mind for her?   870
CREON: I'll take her down some wild, desolate path
   never trod by men, and wall her up alive
   in a rocky vault, and set out short rations,
   just a gesture of piety

to keep the entire city free of defilement.   875
There let her pray to the one god she worships:
Death—who knows?—may just reprieve her from death.
Or she may learn at last, better late than never,
what a waste of breath it is to worship Death.

Exit to the palace.

CHORUS: Love, never conquered in battle   880
Love the plunderer laying waste the rich!
Love standing the night-watch
                    guarding a girl's soft cheek,
you range the seas, the shepherds' steadings off in the wilds—
not even the deathless gods can flee your onset,   885
nothing human born for a day—
whoever feels your grip is driven mad.
                                              Love
you wrench the minds of the righteous into outrage,
swerve them to their ruin—you have ignited this,
this kindred strife, father and son at war   890
                    and Love alone the victor—
warm glance of the bride triumphant, burning with desire!
Throned in power, side-by-side with the mighty laws!
Irresistible Aphrodite,° never conquered—
Love, you mock us for your sport.   895

Antigone is brought from the palace under guard.

            But now, even I'd rebel against the king,
            I'd break all bounds when I see this—
            I fill with tears, can't hold them back,
            not any more . . . I see Antigone make her way
            to the bridal vault where all are laid to rest.   900
ANTIGONE: Look at me, men of my fatherland,
                setting out on the last road
            looking into the last light of day
            the last I'll ever see . . .
            the god of death who puts us all to bed   905
            takes me down to the banks of Acheron° alive—
                denied my part in the wedding-songs,
            no wedding-song in the dusk has crowned my marriage—
            I go to wed the lord of the dark waters.
CHORUS: Not crowned with glory, crowned with a dirge,   910
                you leave for the deep pit of the dead.
                No withering illness laid you low,
                no strokes of the sword—a law to yourself,

---

894 **Aphrodite:** Goddess of love.   906 **Acheron:** A river in the underworld, to which the
dead go.

alone, no mortal like you, ever, you go down
    to the halls of Death alive and breathing.   915
ANTIGONE: But think of Niobe° — well I know her story —
    think what a living death she died,
Tantalus' daughter, stranger queen from the east:
there on the mountain heights, growing stone
binding as ivy, slowly walled her round   920
and the rains will never cease, the legends say
the snows will never leave her . . .
    wasting away, under her brows the tears
showering down her breasting ridge and slopes —
a rocky death like hers puts me to sleep.   925
CHORUS: But she was a god, born of gods,
    and we are only mortals born to die.
    And yet, of course, it's a great thing
    for a dying girl to hear, just hear
    she shares a destiny equal to the gods,   930
    during life and later, once she's dead.
ANTIGONE: O you mock me!
Why, in the name of all my fathers' gods
why can't you wait till I am gone —
    must you abuse me to my face?
O my city, all your fine rich sons!   935
And you, you springs of the Dirce,
holy grove of Thebes where the chariots gather,
    you at least, you'll bear me witness, look,
unmourned by friends and forced by such crude laws
I go to my rockbound prison, strange new tomb —   940
    always a stranger, O dear god,
    I have no home on earth and none below,
    not with the living, not with the breathless dead.
CHORUS: You went too far, the last limits of daring —
    smashing against the high throne of Justice!   945
        Your life's in ruins, child — I wonder . . .
    do you pay for your father's terrible ordeal?
ANTIGONE: There — at last you've touched it, the worst pain
the worst anguish! Raking up the grief for father
    three times over, for all the doom   950
that's struck us down, the brilliant house of Laius.
O mother, your marriage-bed
the coiling horrors, the coupling there —
    you with your own son, my father — doomstruck mother!
Such, such were my parents, and I their wretched child.   955

---

916 Niobe: A queen of Thebes who was punished by the gods for her pride and was turned into stone.

I go to them now, cursed, unwed, to share their home —
    I am a stranger! O dear brother, doomed
    in your marriage — your marriage murders mine,
        your dying drags me down to death alive!

Enter Creon.

CHORUS: Reverence asks some reverence in return —   960
    but attacks on power never go unchecked,
        not by the man who holds the reins of power.
    Your own blind will, your passion has destroyed you.

ANTIGONE: No one to weep for me, my friends,
    no wedding-song — they take me away   965
    in all my pain . . . the road lies open, waiting.
    Never again, the law forbids me to see
    the sacred eye of day. I am agony!
    No tears for the destiny that's mine,
    no loved one mourns my death.

CREON: Can't you see?   970
    If a man could wail his own dirge *before* he dies,
    he'd never finish.

To the guards.

                Take her away, quickly!
    Wall her up in the tomb, you have your orders.
    Abandon her there, alone, and let her choose —
    death or a buried life with a good roof for shelter.   975
    As for myself, my hands are clean. This young girl —
    dead or alive, she will be stripped of her rights,
    her stranger's rights, here in the world above.

ANTIGONE: O tomb, my bridal-bed — my house, my prison
    cut in the hollow rock, my everlasting watch!   980
    I'll soon be there, soon embrace my own,
    the great growing family of our dead
    Persephone° has received among her ghosts.
                         I,
    the last of them all, the most reviled by far,
    go down before my destined time's run out.   985
    But still I go, cherishing one good hope:
    my arrival may be dear to father,
    dear to you, my mother,
    dear to you, my loving brother, Eteocles —
    When you died I washed you with my hands,   990
    I dressed you all, I poured the cups
    across your tombs. But now, Polynices,
    because I laid your body out as well,
    this, this is my reward. Nevertheless

983 Persephone: Queen of the underworld.

I honored you—the decent will admit it—   995
well and wisely too.
                    Never, I tell you,
if I had been the mother of children
or if my husband died, exposed and rotting—
I'd never have taken this ordeal upon myself,
never defied our people's will. What law,   1000
you ask, do I satisfy with what I say?
A husband dead, there might have been another.
A child by another too, if I had lost the first.
But mother and father both lost in the halls of Death,
no brother could ever spring to light again.   1005

For this law alone I held you first in honor.
For this, Creon, the king, judges me a criminal
guilty of dreadful outrage, my dear brother!
And now he leads me off, a captive in his hands,
with no part in the bridal-song, the bridal-bed,   1010
denied all joy of marriage, raising children—
deserted so by loved ones, struck by fate,
I descend alive to the caverns of the dead.

What law of the mighty gods have I transgressed?
Why look to the heavens any more, tormented as I am?   1015
Whom to call, what comrades now? Just think,
my reverence only brands me for irreverence!
Very well: if this is the pleasure of the gods,
once I suffer I will know that I was wrong.
But if these men are wrong, let them suffer   1020
nothing worse than they mete out to me—
these masters of injustice!

LEADER: Still the same rough winds, the wild passion
raging through the girl.

CREON:

To the guards.

                Take her away.
You're wasting time—you'll pay for it too.   1025

ANTIGONE: Oh god, the voice of death. It's come, it's here.

CREON: True. Not a word of hope—your doom is sealed.

ANTIGONE: Land of Thebes, city of all my fathers—
       O you gods, the first gods of the race!
       They drag me away, now, no more delay.   1030
       Look on me, you noble sons of Thebes—
       the last of a great line of kings,
       I alone, see what I suffer now
       at the hands of what breed of men—
       all for reverence, my reverence for the gods!   1035

She leaves under guard; the Chorus gathers.

CHORUS: Danaë, Danaë°—
    even she endured a fate like yours,
        in all her lovely strength she traded
    the light of day for the bolted brazen vault—
    buried within her tomb, her bridal-chamber,   1040
    wed to the yoke and broken.
        But she was of glorious birth
                my child, my child
    and treasured the seed of Zeus within her womb,
    the cloudburst streaming gold!   1045
        The power of fate is a wonder,
        dark, terrible wonder—
        neither wealth nor armies
        towered walls nor ships
        black hulls lashed by the salt   1050
        can save us from that force.

The yoke tamed him too
    young Lycurgus° flaming in anger
king of Edonia, all for his mad taunts
Dionysus clamped him down, encased   1055
in the chain-mail of rock
    and there his rage
              his terrible flowering rage burst—
sobbing, dying away . . . at last that madman
came to know his god—   1060
    the power he mocked, the power
    he taunted in all his frenzy
    trying to stamp out
    the women strong with the god—
    the torch, the raving sacred cries—   1065
    enraging the Muses° who adore the flute.

And far north where the Black Rocks
    cut the sea in half
and murderous straits
split the coast of Thrace   1070
    a forbidding city stands
where once, hard by the walls
the savage Ares thrilled to watch
a king's new queen, a Fury rearing in rage
    against his two royal sons—   1075
        her bloody hands, her dagger-shuttle

1036 Danaë: Locked in a cell by her father because it was prophesied that her son would kill him, but visited by Zeus in the form of a shower of gold. Their son was Perseus.   **1053 Lycurgus:** Punished by Dionysus because he would not worship him.   **1066 Muses:** Goddesses of the arts.

stabbing out their eyes — cursed, blinding wounds —
their eyes blind sockets screaming for revenge!

They wailed in agony, cries echoing cries
　　　　the princes doomed at birth . . .　　　　　　　　　　1080
and their mother doomed to chains,
walled off in a tomb of stone —
　　　but she traced her own birth back
to a proud Athenian line and the high gods
and off in caverns half the world away,　　　　　　　　　1085
born of the wild North Wind
　　　she sprang on her father's gales,
　　　　　racing stallions up the leaping cliffs —
child of the heavens. But even on her the Fates
the gray everlasting Fates rode hard　　　　　　　　　　1090
my child, my child.

Enter Tiresias, the blind prophet, led by a boy.

TIRESIAS:　　　　　　　Lords of Thebes,
　I and the boy have come together,
　hand in hand. Two see with the eyes of one . . .
　so the blind must go, with a guide to lead the way.
CREON:　What is it, old Tiresias? What news now?　　　　　1095
TIRESIAS:　I will teach you. And you obey the seer.
CREON:　　　　　　　　　　　　　　　　　I will,
　I've never wavered from your advice before.
TIRESIAS:　And so you kept the city straight on course.
CREON:　I owe you a great deal, I swear to that.
TIRESIAS:　Then reflect, my son: you are poised,　　　　　　1100
　once more, on the razor-edge of fate.
CREON:　What is it? I shudder to hear you.
TIRESIAS:　　　　　　　　　　　　　　　You will learn
　when you listen to the warnings of my craft.
　As I sat on the ancient seat of augury,°
　in the sanctuary where every bird I know　　　　　　　1105
　will hover at my hands — suddenly I heard it,
　a strange voice in the wingbeats, unintelligible,
　barbaric, a mad scream! Talons flashing, ripping,
　they were killing each other — that much I knew —
　the murderous fury whirring in those wings　　　　　　1110
　made that much clear!
　　　　　　　　　　　I was afraid,
　I turned quickly, tested the burnt-sacrifice,
　ignited the altar at all points — but no fire,
　the god in the fire never blazed.
　Not from those offerings . . . over the embers　　　　　1115

1104 **seat of augury:** Where Tiresias looked for omens among birds.

slid a heavy ooze from the long thighbones,
smoking, sputtering out, and the bladder
puffed and burst—spraying gall into the air—
and the fat wrapping the bones slithered off
and left them glistening white. No fire!   1120
The rites failed that might have blazed the future
with a sign. So I learned from the boy here;
he is my guide, as I am guide to others.
                                             And it's you—
your high resolve that sets this plague on Thebes.
The public altars and sacred hearths are fouled,   1125
one and all, by the birds and dogs with carrion
torn from the corpse, the doomstruck son of Oedipus!
And so the gods are deaf to our prayers, they spurn
the offerings in our hands, the flame of holy flesh.
No birds cry out an omen clear and true—   1130
they're gorged with the murdered victim's blood and fat.
Take these things to heart, my son, I warn you.
All men make mistakes, it is only human.
But once the wrong is done, a man
can turn his back on folly, misfortune too,   1135
if he tries to make amends, however low he's fallen,
and stops his bullnecked ways. Stubbornness
brands you for stupidity—pride is a crime.
No, yield to the dead!
Never stab the fighter when he's down.   1140
Where's the glory, killing the dead twice over?

I mean you well. I give you sound advice.
It's best to learn from a good adviser
when he speaks for your own good:
it's pure gain.
CREON: Old man—all of you! So,   1145
you shoot your arrows at my head like archers at the target—
I even have *him* loosed on me, this fortune-teller.
Oh his ilk has tried to sell me short
and ship me off for years. Well,
drive your bargains, traffic—much as you like—   1150
in the gold of India, silver-gold of Sardis.
You'll never bury that body in the grave,
not even if Zeus's eagles rip the corpse
and wing their rotten pickings off to the throne of god!
Never, not even in fear of such defilement   1155
will I tolerate his burial, that traitor.
Well I know, we can't defile the gods—
no mortal has the power.
                     No,

reverend old Tiresias, all men fall,
it's only human, but the wisest fall obscenely   1160
when they glorify obscene advice with rhetoric —
all for their own gain.
TIRESIAS: Oh god, is there a man alive
who knows, who actually believes . . .
CREON: What now?
What earth-shattering truth are you about to utter?   1165
TIRESIAS: . . . just how much a sense of judgment, wisdom
is the greatest gift we have?
CREON: Just as much, I'd say,
as a twisted mind is the worst affliction going.
TIRESIAS: You are the one who's sick, Creon, sick to death.
CREON: I am in no mood to trade insults with a seer.   1170
TIRESIAS: You have already, calling my prophecies a lie.
CREON: Why not?
You and the whole breed of seers are mad for money!
TIRESIAS: And the whole race of tyrants lusts to rake it in.
CREON: This slander of yours —
are you aware you're speaking to the king?   1175
TIRESIAS: Well aware. Who helped you save the city?
CREON: You —
you have your skills, old seer, but you lust for injustice!
TIRESIAS: You will drive me to utter the dreadful secret in my heart.
CREON: Spit it out! Just don't speak it out for profit.
TIRESIAS: Profit? No, not a bit of profit, not for you.   1180
CREON: Know full well, you'll never buy off my resolve.
TIRESIAS: Then know this too, learn this by heart!
The chariot of the sun will not race through
so many circuits more, before you have surrendered
one born of your own loins, your own flesh and blood,   1185
a corpse for corpses given in return, since you have thrust
to the world below a child sprung for the world above,
ruthlessly lodged a living soul within the grave —
then you've robbed the gods below the earth,
keeping a dead body here in the bright air,   1190
unburied, unsung, unhallowed by the rites.

You, you have no business with the dead,
nor do the gods above — this is violence
you have forced upon the heavens.
And so the avengers, the dark destroyers late   1195
but true to the mark, now lie in wait for you,
the Furies sent by the gods and the god of death
to strike you down with the pains that you perfected!

There. Reflect on that, tell me I've been bribed.
The day comes soon, no long test of time, not now,   1200

that wakes the wails for men and women in your halls.
Great hatred rises against you—
cities in tumult, all whose mutilated sons
the dogs have graced with burial, or the wild beasts,
some wheeling crow that wings the ungodly stench of carrion   1205
back to each city, each warrior's hearth and home.

These arrows for your heart! Since you've raked me
I loose them like an archer in my anger,
arrows deadly true. You'll never escape
their burning, searing force.   1210

Motioning to his escort.

Come, boy, take me home.
So he can vent his rage on younger men,
and learn to keep a gentler tongue in his head
and better sense than what he carries now.

Exit to the side.

LEADER: The old man's gone, my king—   1215
terrible prophecies. Well I know,
since the hair on this old head went gray,
he's never lied to Thebes.

CREON: I know it myself—I'm shaken, torn.
It's a dreadful thing to yield . . . but resist now?   1220
Lay my pride bare to the blows of ruin?
That's dreadful too.

LEADER: But good advice,
Creon, take it now, you must.

CREON: What should I do? Tell me . . . I'll obey.

LEADER: Go! Free the girl from the rocky vault   1225
and raise a mound for the body you exposed.

CREON: That's your advice? You think I should give in?

LEADER: Yes, my king, quickly. Disasters sent by the gods
cut short our follies in a flash.

CREON: Oh it's hard.
giving up the heart's desire . . . but I will do it—   1230
no more fighting a losing battle with necessity.

LEADER: Do it now, go, don't leave it to others.

CREON: Now—I'm on my way! Come, each of you,
take up axes, make for the high ground,
over there, quickly! I and my better judgment   1235
have come round to this—I shackled her,
I'll set her free myself. I am afraid . . .
it's best to keep the established laws
to the very day we die.

Rushing out, followed by his entourage. The Chorus clusters around the altar.

CHORUS: God of a hundred names!
                                          Great Dionysus—   1240
                        Son and glory of Semele! Pride of Thebes—
Child of Zeus whose thunder rocks the clouds—
Lord of the famous lands of evening—
King of the Mysteries!
                                          King of Eleusis, Demeter's plain°
her breasting hills that welcome in the world—   1245
Great Dionysus!
                        Bacchus,° living in Thebes
the mother-city of all your frenzied women—
                                                              Bacchus
                        living along the Ismenus'° rippling waters
standing over the field sown with the Dragon's teeth!

You—we have seen you through the flaring smoky fires,   1250
        your torches blazing over the twin peaks
where nymphs of the hallowed cave climb onward
                        fired with you, your sacred rage—
we have seen you at Castalia's running spring°
and down from the heights of Nysa° crowned with ivy   1255
the greening shore rioting vines and grapes
                down you come in your storm of wild women
                        ecstatic, mystic cries—
                                          Dionysus—
down to watch and ward the roads of Thebes!

First of all cities, Thebes you honor first   1260
you and your mother, bride of the lightning—
come, Dionysus! now your people lie
in the iron grip of plague,
come in your racing, healing stride
                        down Parnassus'° slopes   1265
or across the moaning straits.
                                          Lord of the dancing—
dance, dance the constellations breathing fire!
Great master of the voices of the night!
Child of Zeus, God's offspring, come, come forth!
Lord, king, dance with your nymphs, swirling, raving   1270
arm-in-arm in frenzy through the night
                they dance you, Iacchus°—

1244 Demeter's plain: The goddess of grain was worshiped at Eleusis, near Athens.
1246 Bacchus: Another name for Dionysus.   **1248 Ismenus:** A river near Thebes where the
founders of the city were said to have sprung from a dragon's teeth.   **1254 Castalia's running
spring:** The sacred spring of Apollo's oracle at Delphi.   **1255 Nysa:** A mountain where Dionysus was worshiped.   **1265 Parnassus:** A mountain in Greece that was sacred to Dionysus as
well as other gods and goddesses.   **1272 Iacchus:** Dionysus.

Dance, Dionysus
    giver of all good things!

Enter a Messenger from the side.

MESSENGER: Neighbors,
    friends of the house of Cadmus° and the kings,
    there's not a thing in this life of ours   1275
    I'd praise or blame as settled once for all.
    Fortune lifts and Fortune fells the lucky
    and unlucky every day. No prophet on earth
    can tell a man his fate. Take Creon:
    there was a man to rouse your envy once,   1280
    as I see it. He saved the realm from enemies;
    taking power, he alone, the lord of the fatherland,
    he set us true on course—flourished like a tree
    with the noble line of sons he bred and reared . . .
    and now it's lost, all gone.
                      Believe me,   1285
    when a man has squandered his true joys,
    he's good as dead, I tell you, a living corpse.
    Pile up riches in your house, as much as you like—
    live like a king with a huge show of pomp,
    but if real delight is missing from the lot,   1290
    I wouldn't give you a wisp of smoke for it,
    not compared with joy.
LEADER: What now?
    What new grief do you bring the house of kings?
MESSENGER: Dead, dead—and the living are guilty of their death!
LEADER: Who's the murderer? Who is dead? Tell us.   1295
MESSENGER: Haemon's gone, his blood spilled by the very hand—
LEADER: His father's or his own?
MESSENGER: His own . . .
    raging mad with his father for the death—
LEADER: Oh great seer,
    you saw it all, you brought your word to birth!
MESSENGER: Those are the facts. Deal with them as you will.   1300

As he turns to go, Eurydice enters from the palace.

LEADER: Look, Eurydice. Poor woman, Creon's wife,
    so close at hand. By chance perhaps,
    unless she's heard the news about her son.
EURYDICE: My countrymen,
    all of you—I caught the sound of your words
    as I was leaving to do my part,   1305
    to appeal to queen Athena° with my prayers.

1274 Cadmus: The legendary founder of Thebes.   **1306 Athena:** Goddess of wisdom and protector of Greek cities.

I was just loosing the bolts, opening the doors,
when a voice filled with sorrow, family sorrow,
struck my ears, and I fell back, terrified,
into the women's arms—everything went black.   1310
Tell me the news, again, whatever it is . . .
sorrow and I are hardly strangers;
I can bear the worst.

MESSENGER: I—dear lady,
I'll speak as an eye-witness. I was there.
And I won't pass over one word of the truth.   1315
Why should I try to soothe you with a story,
only to prove a liar in a moment?
Truth is always best.
                    So,
I escorted your lord, I guided him
to the edge of the plain where the body lay,   1320
Polynices, torn by the dogs and still unmourned.
And saying a prayer to Hecate of the Crossroads,
Pluto° too, to hold their anger and be kind,
we washed the dead in a bath of holy water
and plucking some fresh branches, gathering . . .   1325
what was left of him, we burned them all together
and raised a high mound of native earth, and then
we turned and made for that rocky vault of hers,
the hollow, empty bed of the bride of Death.
And far off, one of us heard a voice,   1330
a long wail rising, echoing
out of that unhallowed wedding-chamber;
he ran to alert the master and Creon pressed on,
closer—the strange, inscrutable cry came sharper,
throbbing around him now, and he let loose   1335
a cry of his own, enough to wrench the heart,
"Oh god, am I the prophet now? going down
the darkest road I've ever gone? My son—
it's *his* dear voice, he greets me! Go, men,
closer, quickly! Go through the gap,   1340
the rocks are dragged back—
right to the tomb's very mouth—and look,
see if it's Haemon's voice I think I hear,
or the gods have robbed me of my senses."

The king was shattered. We took his orders,   1345
went and searched, and there in the deepest,
dark recesses of the tomb we found her . . .
hanged by the neck in a fine linen noose,
strangled in her veils—and the boy,

1322–1323 **Hecate, Pluto:** Gods of the underworld.

his arms flung around her waist,   1350
clinging to her, wailing for his bride,
dead and down below, for his father's crimes
and the bed of his marriage blighted by misfortune.
When Creon saw him, he gave a deep sob,
he ran in, shouting, crying out to him,   1355
"Oh my child—what have you done? what seized you,
what insanity? what disaster drove you mad?
Come out, my son! I beg you on my knees!"
But the boy gave him a wild burning glance,
spat in his face, not a word in reply,   1360
he drew his sword—his father rushed out,
running as Haemon lunged and missed!—
and then, doomed, desperate with himself,
suddenly leaning his full weight on the blade,
he buried it in his body, halfway to the hilt.   1365
And still in his senses, pouring his arms around her,
he embraced the girl and breathing hard,
released a quick rush of blood,
bright red on her cheek glistening white.
And there he lies, body enfolding body . . .   1370
he has won his bride at last, poor boy,
not here but in the houses of the dead.

Creon shows the world that of all the ills
afflicting men the worst is lack of judgment.

Eurydice turns and reenters the palace.

LEADER: What do you make of that? The lady's gone,   1375
    without a word, good or bad.
MESSENGER: I'm alarmed too
    but here's my hope—faced with her son's death,
    she finds it unbecoming to mourn in public.
    Inside, under her roof, she'll set her women
    to the task and wail the sorrow of the house.   1380
    She's too discreet. She won't do something rash.
LEADER: I'm not so sure. To me, at least,
    a long heavy silence promises danger,
    just as much as a lot of empty outcries.
MESSENGER: We'll see if she's holding something back,   1385
    hiding some passion in her heart.
    I'm going in. You may be right—who knows?
    Even too much silence has its dangers.

*Exit to the palace. Enter Creon from the side, escorted by attendants carrying
Haemon's body on a bier.*

LEADER: The king himself! Coming toward us,
    look, holding the boy's head in his hands.   1390

Clear, damning proof, if it's right to say so —
proof of his own madness, no one else's,
    no, his own blind wrongs.

CREON: Ohhh,
so senseless, so insane . . . my crimes,
my stubborn, deadly —   1395
Look at us, the killer, the killed,
father and son, the same blood — the misery!
My plans, my mad fanatic heart,
my son, cut off so young!
Ai, dead, lost to the world,   1400
not through your stupidity, no, my own.

LEADER: Too late,
too late, you see what justice means.

CREON: Oh I've learned
through blood and tears! Then, it was then,
when the god came down and struck me — a great weight
shattering, driving me down that wild savage path,   1405
ruining, trampling down my joy. Oh the agony,
    the heartbreaking agonies of our lives.

Enter the Messenger from the palace.

MESSENGER: Master,
what a hoard of grief you have, and you'll have more.
The grief that lies to hand you've brought yourself —

Pointing to Haemon's body.

the rest, in the house, you'll see it all too soon.   1410

CREON: What now? What's worse than this?

MESSENGER: The queen is dead.
The mother of this dead boy . . . mother to the end —
poor thing, her wounds are fresh.

CREON: No, no,
harbor of Death, so choked, so hard to cleanse! —
why me? why are you killing me?   1415
Herald of pain, more words, more grief?
I died once, you kill me again and again!
What's the report, boy . . . some news for me?
My wife dead? O dear god!
Slaughter heaped on slaughter?

The doors open; the body of Eurydice is brought out on her bier.

MESSENGER: See for yourself: 1420
now they bring her body from the palace.

CREON: Oh no,
another, a second loss to break the heart.
What next, what fate still waits for me?
I just held my son in my arms and now,

look, a new corpse rising before my eyes—   1425
    wretched, helpless mother—O my son!

MESSENGER: She stabbed herself at the altar,
    then her eyes went dark, after she'd raised
    a cry for the noble fate of Megareus,° the hero
    killed in the first assault, then for Haemon,   1430
    then with her dying breath she called down
    torments on your head—you killed her sons.

CREON: Oh the dread,
    I shudder with dread! Why not kill me too?—
    run me through with a good sharp sword?
    Oh god, the misery, anguish—   1435
    I, I'm churning with it, going under.

MESSENGER: Yes, and the dead, the woman lying there,
    piles the guilt of all their deaths on you.

CREON: How did she end her life, what bloody stroke?

MESSENGER: She drove home to the heart with her own hand,   1440
    once she learned her son was dead . . . that agony.

CREON: And the guilt is all mine—
    can never be fixed on another man,
    no escape for me. I killed you,
    I, god help me, I admit it all!   1445

To his attendants.

    Take me away, quickly, out of sight.
    I don't even exist—I'm no one. Nothing.

LEADER: Good advice, if there's any good in suffering.
    Quickest is best when troubles block the way.

CREON:

Kneeling in prayer.

    Come, let it come!—that best of fates for me   1450
    that brings the final day, best fate of all.
    Oh quickly, now—
    so I never have to see another sunrise.

LEADER: That will come when it comes;
    we must deal with all that lies before us.   1455
    The future rests with the ones who tend the future.

CREON: That prayer—I poured my heart into that prayer!

LEADER: No more prayers now. For mortal men
    there is no escape from the doom we must endure.

CREON: Take me away, I beg you, out of sight.   1460
    A rash, indiscriminate fool!
    I murdered you, my son, against my will—

1429 Megareus: A son of Creon and Eurydice; he died when Thebes was attacked.

you too, my wife . . .
> Wailing wreck of a man,
whom to look to? where to lean for support?

Desperately turning from Haemon to Eurydice on their biers.

Whatever I touch goes wrong—once more   1465
a crushing fate's come down upon my head.

The Messenger and attendants lead Creon into the palace.

CHORUS: Wisdom is by far the greatest part of joy,
and reverence toward the gods must be safeguarded.
The mighty words of the proud are paid in full
with mighty blows of fate, and at long last   1470
those blows will teach us wisdom.

The old citizens exit to the side.   [c. 441 B.C.E.]

FOR THINKING AND WRITING

1. Is Antigone admirable in her steadfastness or just too stubborn? Are there
   principles worth dying for? Is Antigone a rebel fighting against injustice or
   a social misfit? Is there a middle ground?

2. Describe the argument between Antigone and Ismene. What point is
   Ismene making? Do you agree with her or with Antigone?

3. Some critics argue that Creon is the play's main character because he
   changes and Antigone doesn't. Does this argument have some credibility?
   What specifically does Creon learn?

4. How might you respond to this play if you were the mayor of a city? A religious leader of an orthodox faith with strict burial rituals? A feminist leader?
   A rebel? A conformist? How might your present context affect your reading?

5. Creon does not want to appear to be a weak leader, so he stays firm. Should
   he have bent the rules for his family? How would you have responded
   if he did so? Should contemporary leaders be strong, flexible, safe, and
   innovative?

WILLIAM SHAKESPEARE
Hamlet, Prince of Denmark

*William Shakespeare's reputation as the greatest dramatist in the English lan-
guage is built on his five major tragedies:* Romeo and Juliet *(1594),* Hamlet
(1600), Othello *(1604),* Macbeth *(1605), and* King Lear *(1605). But he was also a
master in other genres, including comedies (*As You Like It *in 1599), histories
(*Henry IV *in 1597), and romances (*The Tempest *in 1611). And his collection of
sonnets is considered art of the highest order.*

Very little is known about Shakespeare's personal life. He attended the grammar school at Stratford-upon-Avon, where he was born in 1564. He married Anne Hathaway in 1582 and had three children. Around 1590 he moved to London, where he became an actor and began writing plays. He was an astute businessperson, becoming a shareholder in London's famous Globe Theatre. After writing thirty-seven plays, he retired to Stratford in 1611. When he died in 1616, he left behind the most respected body of work in literature. Shakespeare's ability to use artistic language to convey a wide range of humor and emotion is perhaps unsurpassed.

[DRAMATIS PERSONAE

CLAUDIUS, *King of Denmark*
HAMLET, *son to the late and nephew to the present king*
POLONIUS, *lord chamberlain*
HORATIO, *friend to Hamlet*
LAERTES, *son to Polonius*
VOLTIMAND
CORNELIUS
ROSENCRANTZ   } *courtiers*
GUILDENSTERN
OSRIC
A GENTLEMAN
A PRIEST
MARCELLUS   } *officers*
BERNARDO
FRANCISCO, *a soldier*
REYNALDO, *servant to Polonius*
PLAYERS
TWO CLOWNS, *grave-diggers*
FORTINBRAS, *Prince of Norway*
A CAPTAIN
ENGLISH AMBASSADORS
GERTRUDE, *Queen of Denmark, and mother to Hamlet*
OPHELIA, *daughter to Polonius*
LORDS, LADIES, OFFICERS, SOLDIERS, SAILORS, MESSENGERS, AND OTHER
     ATTENDANTS
GHOST *of Hamlet's Father*

SCENE: *Denmark.*]

[ACT 1, Scene 1]

Elsinore. A platform° before the castle.]
     Enter Bernardo and Francisco, two sentinels.

ACT 1, SCENE 1. **platform:** A level space on the battlements of the royal castle at Elsinore, a Danish seaport; now Helsingör.

BERNARDO: Who's there?

FRANCISCO: Nay, answer me:° stand, and unfold yourself.

BERNARDO: Long live the king!°

FRANCISCO: Bernardo?

BERNARDO: He.   5

FRANCISCO: You come most carefully upon your hour.

BERNARDO: 'Tis now struck twelve; get thee to bed, Francisco.

FRANCISCO: For this relief much thanks: 'tis bitter cold,
    And I am sick at heart.

BERNARDO: Have you had quiet guard?

FRANCISCO: Not a mouse stirring.   10

BERNARDO: Well, good night.
    If you do meet Horatio and Marcellus,
    The rivals° of my watch, bid them make haste.

Enter Horatio and Marcellus.

FRANCISCO: I think I hear them. Stand, ho! Who is there?

HORATIO: Friends to this ground.

MARCELLUS: And liegemen to the Dane.   15

FRANCISCO: Give you° good night.

MARCELLUS: O, farewell, honest soldier:
    Who hath reliev'd you?

FRANCISCO: Bernardo hath my place.
    Give you good night.   *Exit Francisco.*

MARCELLUS: Holla! Bernardo!

BERNARDO: Say,
    What, is Horatio there?

HORATIO: A piece of him.

BERNARDO: Welcome, Horatio: welcome, good Marcellus.   20

MARCELLUS: What, has this thing appear'd again to-night?

BERNARDO: I have seen nothing.

MARCELLUS: Horatio says 'tis but our fantasy,
    And will not let belief take hold of him
    Touching this dreaded sight, twice seen of us: 25
    Therefore I have entreated him along
    With us to watch the minutes of this night;
    That if again this apparition come,
    He may approve° our eyes and speak to it.

HORATIO: Tush, tush, 'twill not appear.

BERNARDO: Sit down awhile;   30
    And let us once again assail your ears,
    That are so fortified against our story
    What we have two nights seen.

---

2 **me:** This is emphatic, since Francisco is the sentry.   3 **Long live the king:** Either a password or greeting; Horatio and Marcellus use a different one in line 15.   13 **rivals:** Partners.   16 **Give you:** God give you.   29 **approve:** Corroborate.

HORATIO: Well, sit we down,
    And let us hear Bernardo speak of this.
BERNARDO: Last night of all,   35
    When yond same star that's westward from the pole°
    Had made his course t' illume that part of heaven
    Where now it burns, Marcellus and myself,
    The bell then beating one, —

Enter Ghost.

MARCELLUS: Peace, break thee off; look, where it comes again!   40
BERNARDO: In the same figure, like the king that's dead.
MARCELLUS: Thou art a scholar;° speak to it, Horatio.
BERNARDO: Looks 'a not like the king? mark it, Horatio.
HORATIO: Most like: it harrows° me with fear and wonder.
BERNARDO: It would be spoke to.°
MARCELLUS: Speak to it, Horatio.   45
HORATIO: What art thou that usurp'st this time of night,
    Together with that fair and warlike form
    In which the majesty of buried Denmark°
    Did sometimes march? by heaven I charge thee, speak!
MARCELLUS: It is offended.
BERNARDO: See it stalks away!   50
HORATIO: Stay! speak, speak! I charge thee, speak!   *Exit Ghost.*
MARCELLUS: 'Tis gone, and will not answer.
BERNARDO: How now, Horatio! you tremble and look pale:
    Is not this something more than fantasy?
    What think you on 't?   55
HORATIO: Before my God, I might not this believe
    Without the sensible and true avouch
    Of mine own eyes.
MARCELLUS: Is it not like the king?
HORATIO: As thou art to thyself:
    Such was the very armour he had on   60
    When he the ambitious Norway combated;
    So frown'd he once, when, in an angry parle,
    He smote° the sledded Polacks° on the ice.
    'Tis strange.
MARCELLUS: Thus twice before, and jump° at this dead hour,   65
    With martial stalk hath he gone by our watch.
HORATIO: In what particular thought to work I know not;
    But in the gross and scope° of my opinion,
    This bodes some strange eruption to our state.

36 pole: Polestar.   **42 scholar:** Exorcisms were performed in Latin, which Horatio as an educated man would be able to speak.   **44 harrows:** Lacerates the feelings.   **45 It . . . to:** A ghost could not speak until spoken to.   **48 buried Denmark:** The buried king of Denmark.   **63 smote:** Defeated;   **sledded Polacks:** Polanders using sledges.   **65 jump:** Exactly.   **68 gross and scope:** General drift.

MARCELLUS: Good now,° sit down, and tell me, he that knows,   70
    Why this same strict and most observant watch
    So nightly toils° the subject° of the land,
    And why such daily cast° of brazen cannon,
    And foreign mart° for implements of war;
    Why such impress° of shipwrights, whose sore task   75
    Does not divide the Sunday from the week;
    What might be toward, that this sweaty haste
    Doth make the night joint-labourer with the day:
    Who is't that can inform me?
HORATIO: That can I;
    At least, the whisper goes so. Our last king,   80
    Whose image even but now appear'd to us,
    Was, as you know, by Fortinbras of Norway,
    Thereto prick'd on° by a most emulate° pride,
    Dar'd to the combat; in which our valiant Hamlet—
    For so this side of our known world esteem'd him—   85
    Did slay this Fortinbras; who, by a seal'd compact,
    Well ratified by law and heraldry,°
    Did forfeit, with his life, all those his lands
    Which he stood seiz'd° of, to the conqueror:
    Against the which, a moiety competent°   90
    Was gaged by our king; which had return'd
    To the inheritance of Fortinbras,
    Had he been vanquisher; as, by the same comart,°
    And carriage° of the article design'd,
    His fell to Hamlet. Now, sir, young Fortinbras,   95
    Of unimproved° mettle hot and full,°
    Hath in the skirts of Norway here and there
    Shark'd up° a list of lawless resolutes,°
    For food and diet,° to some enterprise
    That hath a stomach in't; which is no other—   100
    As it doth well appear unto our state—
    But to recover of us, by strong hand
    And terms compulsatory, those foresaid lands
    So by his father lost: and this, I take it,
    Is the main motive of our preparations,   105
    The source of this our watch and the chief head
    Of this post-haste and romage° in the land.

---

70 **Good now:** An expression denoting entreaty or expostulation.   72 **toils:** Causes or makes to toil;   **subject:** People, subjects.   73 **cast:** Casting, founding.   74 **mart:** Buying and selling, traffic.   75 **impress:** Impressment.   83 **prick'd on:** Incited;   **emulate:** Rivaling.   87 **law and heraldry:** Heraldic law, governing combat.   89 **seiz'd:** Possessed.   90 **moiety competent:** Adequate or sufficient portion.   93 **comart:** Joint bargain.   94 **carriage:** Import, bearing.   96 **unimproved:** Not turned to account;   **hot and full:** Full of fight.   98 **Shark'd up:** Got together in haphazard fashion;   **resolutes:** Desperadoes.   99 **food and diet:** No pay but their keep.   107 **romage:** Bustle, commotion.

BERNARDO: I think it be no other but e'en so:
    Well may it sort° that this portentous figure
    Comes armed through our watch; so like the king 110
    That was and is the question of these wars.
HORATIO: A mote° it is to trouble the mind's eye.
    In the most high and palmy state° of Rome,
    A little ere the mightiest Julius fell,
    The graves stood tenantless and the sheeted dead 115
    Did squeak and gibber in the Roman streets:
    As stars with trains of fire° and dews of blood,
    Disasters° in the sun; and the moist star°
    Upon whose influence Neptune's empire° stands
    Was sick almost to doomsday with eclipse: 120
    And even the like precurse° of fear'd events,
    As harbingers preceding still the fates
    And prologue to the omen coming on,
    Have heaven and earth together demonstrated
    Unto our climatures and countrymen. — 125

Enter Ghost.

    But soft, behold! lo, where it comes again!
    I'll cross° it, though it blast me. Stay, illusion!
    If thou hast any sound, or use of voice,
    Speak to me!   *It° spreads his arms.*
    If there be any good thing to be done, 130
    That may to thee do ease and grace to me,
    Speak to me!
    If thou art privy to thy country's fate,
    Which, happily, foreknowing may avoid,
    O, speak! 135
    Or if thou hast uphoarded in thy life
    Extorted treasure in the womb of earth,
    For which, they say, you spirits oft walk in death,   *The cock crows.*
    Speak of it:° stay, and speak! Stop it, Marcellus.
MARCELLUS: Shall I strike at it with my partisan?° 140
HORATIO: Do, if it will not stand.
BERNARDO: 'Tis here!
HORATIO: 'Tis here!
MARCELLUS: 'Tis gone!   *[Exit Ghost.]*
    We do it wrong, being so majestical,

---

109 **sort**: Suit. 112 **mote**: Speck of dust. 113 **palmy state**: Triumphant sovereignty. 117 **stars . . . fire**: I.e., comets. 118 **Disasters**: Unfavorable aspects; **moist star**: The moon, governing tides. 119 **Neptune's empire**: The sea. 121 **precurse**: Heralding. 127 **cross**: Meet, face, thus bringing down the evil influence on the person who crosses it. 129 **It**: The Ghost, or perhaps Horatio. 133–139 **If . . . it**: Horatio recites the traditional reasons why ghosts might walk. 140 **partisan**: Long-handled spear with a blade having lateral projections.

To offer it the show of violence;
For it is, as the air, invulnerable,   145
And our vain blows malicious mockery.

BERNARDO: It was about to speak, when the cock crew.°
HORATIO: And then it started like a guilty thing
Upon a fearful summons. I have heard,
The cock, that is the trumpet to the morn,   150
Doth with his lofty and shrill-sounding throat
Awake the god of day; and, at his warning,
Whether in sea or fire, in earth or air,
Th' extravagant and erring° spirit hies
To his confine:° and of the truth herein   155
This present object made probation.°

MARCELLUS: It faded on the crowing of the cock.
Some say that ever 'gainst° that season comes
Wherein our Saviour's birth is celebrated,
The bird of dawning singeth all night long: 160
And then, they say, no spirit dare stir abroad;
The nights are wholesome; then no planets strike,°
No fairy takes, nor witch hath power to charm,
So hallow'd and so gracious° is that time.

HORATIO: So have I heard and do in part believe it.   165
But, look, the morn, in russet mantle clad,
Walks o'er the dew of yon high eastward hill:
Break we our watch up; and by my advice,
Let us impart what we have seen to-night
Unto young Hamlet; for, upon my life,   170
This spirit, dumb to us, will speak to him.
Do you consent we shall acquaint him with it,
As needful in our loves, fitting our duty?

MARCELLUS: Let's do 't, I pray; and I this morning know
Where we shall find him most conveniently.   *Exeunt.*   175

[Scene 2]

[A room of state in the castle.]

Flourish. Enter Claudius, King of Denmark, Gertrude the Queen, Coun-
cilors, Polonius and his son Laertes, Hamlet, cum aliis° [including Voltimand and
Cornelius].

KING: Though yet of Hamlet our dear brother's death
The memory be green, and that it us befitted

---

147 cock crew: According to traditional ghost lore, spirits returned to their confines at cock-
crow.   **154 extravagant and erring:** Wandering. Both words mean the same thing.
155 confine: Place of confinement.   **156 probation:** Proof, trial.   **158 'gainst:** Just before.
162 planets strike: It was thought that planets were malignant and might strike travelers by
night.   **164 gracious:** Full of goodness.   SCENE 2.   **cum aliis:** With others.

To bear our hearts in grief and our whole kingdom
To be contracted in one brow of woe,
Yet so far hath discretion fought with nature   5
That we with wisest sorrow think on him,
Together with remembrance of ourselves.
Therefore our sometime sister, now our queen,
Th' imperial jointress° to this warlike state,
Have we, as 'twere with a defeated joy, —   10
With an auspicious and a dropping eye,
With mirth in funeral and with dirge in marriage,
In equal scale weighing delight and dole, —
Taken to wife: nor have we herein barr'd
Your better wisdoms, which have freely gone   15
With this affair along. For all, our thanks.
Now follows, that° you know, young Fortinbras,
Holding a weak supposal° of our worth,
Or thinking by our late dear brother's death
Our state to be disjoint° and out of frame,°   20
Colleagued° with this dream of his advantage,°
He hath not fail'd to pester us with message,
Importing° the surrender of those lands
Lost by his father, with all bands of law,
To our most valiant brother. So much for him.   25
Now for ourself and for this time of meeting:
Thus much the business is: we have here writ
To Norway, uncle of young Fortinbras, —
Who, impotent and bed-rid, scarcely hears
Of this his nephew's purpose, — to suppress   30
His further gait° herein; in that the levies,
The lists and full proportions, are all made
Out of his subject:° and we here dispatch
You, good Cornelius, and you, Voltimand,
For bearers of this greeting to old Norway;   35
Giving to you no further personal power
To business with the king, more than the scope
Of these delated° articles allow.
Farewell, and let your haste commend your duty.

CORNELIUS: ⎫
VOLTIMAND: ⎬ In that and all things will we show our duty.   40
KING: We doubt it nothing: heartily farewell.

[Exeunt Voltimand and Cornelius.]

---

9 jointress: Woman possessed of a jointure, or, joint tenancy of an estate.   **17 that:** That which.   **18 weak supposal:** Low estimate.   **20 disjoint:** Distracted, out of joint;   **frame:** Order.   **21 Colleagued:** Added to;   **dream ... advantage:** Visionary hope of success.   **23 Importing:** Purporting, pertaining to.   **31 gait:** Proceeding.   **33 Out of his subject:** At the expense of Norway's subjects (collectively).   **38 delated:** Expressly stated.

And now, Laertes, what's the news with you?
You told us of some suit; what is 't, Laertes?
You cannot speak of reason to the Dane,°
And lose your voice:° what wouldst thou beg, Laertes,   45
That shall not be my offer, not thy asking?
The head is not more native° to the heart,
The hand more instrumental° to the mouth,
Than is the throne of Denmark to thy father.
What wouldst thou have, Laertes?

LAERTES: My dread lord,   50
Your leave and favour to return to France;
From whence though willingly I came to Denmark,
To show my duty in your coronation,
Yet now, I must confess, that duty done,
My thoughts and wishes bend again toward France   55
And bow them to your gracious leave and pardon.°

KING: Have you your father's leave? What says Polonius?

POLONIUS: He hath, my lord, wrung from me my slow leave
By laboursome petition, and at last
Upon his will I seal'd my hard consent: 60
I do beseech you, give him leave to go.

KING: Take thy fair hour, Laertes; time be thine,
And thy best graces spend it at thy will!
But now, my cousin° Hamlet, and my son, —

HAMLET *[aside]*:   A little more than kin, and less than kind!°   65

KING: How is it that the clouds still hang on you?

HAMLET: Not so, my lord; I am too much in the sun.°

QUEEN: Good Hamlet, cast thy nighted colour off,
And let thine eye look like a friend on Denmark.
Do not for ever with thy vailed lids   70
Seek for thy noble father in the dust:
Thou know'st 'tis common; all that lives must die,
Passing through nature to eternity.

HAMLET: Ay, madam, it is common.°

QUEEN: If it be,
Why seems it so particular with thee?   75

---

44 the Dane: Danish king.   **45 lose your voice:** Speak in vain.   **47 native:** Closely connected, related.   **48 instrumental:** Serviceable.   **56 leave and pardon:** Permission to depart.   **64 cousin:** Any kin not of the immediate family.   **65 A little . . . kind:** My relation to you has become more than kinship warrants; it has also become unnatural.   **67 I am . . . sun:** (1) I am too much out of doors, (2) I am too much in the sun of your grace (ironical), (3) I am too much of a son to you. Possibly an allusion to the proverb "Out of heaven's blessing into the warm sun"; i.e., Hamlet is out of house and home in being deprived of the kingship. **74 Ay . . . common:** It is common, but it hurts nevertheless; possibly a reference to the commonplace quality of the queen's remark.

HAMLET: Seems, madam! nay, it is; I know not "seems."
　　　'Tis not alone my inky cloak, good mother,
　　　Nor customary suits° of solemn black,
　　　Nor windy suspiration° of forc'd breath,
　　　No, nor the fruitful river in the eye,　　　　　　　　　　　80
　　　Nor the dejected 'haviour of the visage,
　　　Together with all forms, moods, shapes of grief,
　　　That can denote me truly: these indeed seem,
　　　For they are actions that a man might play:
　　　But I have that within which passeth show;　　　　　　　85
　　　These but the trappings and the suits of woe.
KING: 'Tis sweet and commendable in your nature, Hamlet,
　　　To give these mourning duties to your father:
　　　But, you must know, your father lost a father;
　　　That father lost, lost his, and the survivor bound　　　　90
　　　In filial obligation for some term
　　　To do obsequious° sorrow: but to persever
　　　In obstinate condolement° is a course
　　　Of impious stubbornness; 'tis unmanly grief;
　　　It shows a will most incorrect° to heaven,　　　　　　　95
　　　A heart unfortified, a mind impatient,
　　　An understanding simple and unschool'd:
　　　For what we know must be and is as common
　　　As any the most vulgar thing° to sense,
　　　Why should we in our peevish opposition　　　　　　　100
　　　Take it to heart? Fie! 'tis a fault to heaven,
　　　A fault against the dead, a fault to nature,
　　　To reason most absurd; whose common theme
　　　Is death of fathers, and who still hath cried,
　　　From the first corse till he that died to-day,　　　　　　105
　　　"This must be so." We pray you, throw to earth
　　　This unprevailing° woe, and think of us
　　　As of a father: for let the world take note,
　　　You are the most immediate° to our throne;
　　　And with no less nobility° of love　　　　　　　　　110
　　　Than that which dearest father bears his son,
　　　Do I impart° toward you. For your intent
　　　In going back to school in Wittenberg,°
　　　It is most retrograde° to our desire:
　　　And we beseech you, bend you° to remain　　　　　　115

---

78 **customary suits:** Suits prescribed by custom for mourning.　79 **windy suspiration:** Heavy sighing.　92 **obsequious:** Dutiful.　93 **condolement:** Sorrowing.　95 **incorrect:** Untrained, uncorrected.　99 **vulgar thing:** Common experience.　107 **unprevailing:** Unavailing. 109 **most immediate:** Next in succession.　110 **nobility:** High degree.　112 **impart:** The object is apparently *love* (line 110).　113 **Wittenberg:** Famous German university founded in 1502.　114 **retrograde:** Contrary.　115 **bend you:** Incline yourself; imperative.

Here, in the cheer and comfort of our eye,
Our chiefest courtier, cousin, and our son.
QUEEN: Let not thy mother lose her prayers, Hamlet:
I pray thee, stay with us; go not to Wittenberg.
HAMLET: I shall in all my best obey you, madam.   120
KING: Why, 'tis a loving and a fair reply:
Be as ourself in Denmark. Madam, come;
This gentle and unforc'd accord of Hamlet
Sits smiling to my heart: in grace whereof,
No jocund health that Denmark drinks to-day,   125
But the great cannon to the clouds shall tell,
And the king's rouse° the heaven shall bruit again,°
Re-speaking earthly thunder. Come away.

               Flourish. Exeunt all but Hamlet.

HAMLET: O, that this too too sullied flesh would melt,
Thaw and resolve itself into a dew!   130
Or that the Everlasting had not fix'd
His canon 'gainst self-slaughter! O God! God!
How weary, stale, flat and unprofitable,
Seem to me all the uses of this world!
Fie on't! ah fie! 'tis an unweeded garden,   135
That grows to seed; things rank and gross in nature
Possess it merely.° That it should come to this!
But two months dead: nay, not so much, not two:
So excellent a king; that was, to this,
Hyperion° to a satyr; so loving to my mother   140
That he might not beteem° the winds of heaven
Visit her face too roughly. Heaven and earth!
Must I remember? why, she would hang on him,
As if increase of appetite had grown
By what it fed on: and yet, within a month —   145
Let me not think on't — Frailty, thy name is woman! —
A little month, or ere those shoes were old
With which she followed my poor father's body,
Like Niobe,° all tears: — why she, even she —
O God! a beast, that wants discourse of reason,°   150
Would have mourn'd longer — married with my uncle,
My father's brother, but no more like my father
Than I to Hercules: within a month:

---

127 rouse: Draft of liquor; **bruit again:** Echo. **137 merely:** Completely, entirely.
140 Hyperion: God of the sun in the older regime of ancient gods. **141 beteem:** Allow.
149 Niobe: Tantalus's daughter, who boasted that she had more sons and daughters than Leto;
for this Apollo and Artemis slew her children. She was turned into stone by Zeus on Mount
Sipylus. **150 discourse of reason:** Process or faculty of reason.

Ere yet the salt of most unrighteous tears
Had left the flushing in her galled° eyes,   155
She married. O, most wicked speed, to post
With such dexterity° to incestuous sheets!
It is not nor it cannot come to good:
But break, my heart; for I must hold my tongue.

Enter Horatio, Marcellus, and Bernardo.

HORATIO: Hail to your lordship!
HAMLET: I am glad to see you well: 160
    Horatio! — or I do forget myself.
HORATIO: The same, my lord, and your poor servant ever.
HAMLET: Sir, my good friend; I'll change that name with you:°
    And what make you from Wittenberg, Horatio?
    Marcellus?   165
MARCELLUS: My good lord—
HAMLET: I am very glad to see you. Good even, sir.
    But what, in faith, make you from Wittenberg?
HORATIO: A truant disposition, good my lord.
HAMLET: I would not hear your enemy say so,   170
    Nor shall you do my ear that violence,
    To make it truster of your own report
    Against yourself: I know you are no truant.
    But what is your affair in Elsinore?
    We'll teach you to drink deep ere you depart.   175
HORATIO: My lord, I came to see your father's funeral.
HAMLET: I prithee, do not mock me, fellow-student;
    I think it was to see my mother's wedding.
HORATIO: Indeed, my lord, it follow'd hard° upon.
HAMLET: Thrift, thrift, Horatio! the funeral bak'd meats°   180
    Did coldly furnish forth the marriage tables.
    Would I had met my dearest° foe in heaven
    Or ever I had seen that day, Horatio!
    My father! — methinks I see my father.
HORATIO: Where, my lord!
HAMLET: In my mind's eye, Horatio.   185
HORATIO: I saw him once; 'a° was a goodly king.
HAMLET: 'A was a man, take him for all in all,
    I shall not look upon his like again.
HORATIO: My lord, I think I saw him yesternight.
HAMLET: Saw? who?   190

---

155 galled: Irritated.   **157 dexterity:** Facility.   **163 I'll . . . you:** I'll be your servant, you shall be my friend; also explained as "I'll exchange the name of friend with you."   **179 hard:** Close.   **180 bak'd meats:** Meat pies.   **182 dearest:** Direst. The adjective *dear* in Shakespeare has two different origins: O.E. *deore*, "beloved," and O.E. *deor*, "fierce." *Dearest* is the superlative of the second.   **186 'a:** He.

HORATIO: My lord, the king your father.
HAMLET: The king my father!
HORATIO: Season your admiration° for a while
    With an attent ear, till I may deliver,
    Upon the witness of these gentlemen,
    This marvel to you.
HAMLET: For God's love, let me hear.   195
HORATIO: Two nights together had these gentlemen,
    Marcellus and Bernardo, on their watch,
    In the dead waste and middle of the night,
    Been thus encount'red. A figure like your father,
    Armed at point exactly, cap-a-pe,°   200
    Appears before them, and with solemn march
    Goes slow and stately by them: thrice he walk'd
    By their oppress'd° and fear-surprised eyes,
    Within his truncheon's° length; whilst they, distill'd°
    Almost to jelly with the act° of fear,   205
    Stand dumb and speak not to him. This to me
    In dreadful secrecy impart they did;
    And I with them the third night kept the watch:
    Where, as they had deliver'd, both in time,
    Form of the thing, each word made true and good,   210
    The apparition comes: I knew your father;
    These hands are not more like.
HAMLET: But where was this?
MARCELLUS: My lord, upon the platform where we watch'd.
HAMLET: Did you not speak to it?
HORATIO: My lord, I did;
    But answer made it none: yet once methought   215
    It lifted up it° head and did address
    Itself to motion, like as it would speak;
    But even then the morning cock crew loud,
    And at the sound it shrunk in haste away,
    And vanish'd from our sight.
HAMLET: 'Tis very strange.   220
HORATIO: As I do live, my honour'd lord, 'tis true;
    And we did think it writ down in our duty
    To let you know of it.
HAMLET: Indeed, indeed, sirs, but this troubles me.
    Hold you the watch to-night?
MARCELLUS: ⎫
                      We do, my lord.   225
BERNARDO: ⎭

---

192 **Season your admiration:** Restrain your astonishment.   200 **cap-a-pe:** From head to foot.
203 **oppress'd:** Distressed.   204 **truncheon:** Officer's staff;   **distill'd:** Softened, weakened.
205 **act:** Action.   216 **it:** Its.

HAMLET: Arm'd, say you?

MARCELLUS: ⎫
                              Arm'd, my lord.
BERNARDO: ⎭

HAMLET: From top to toe?

MARCELLUS: ⎫
                              My lord, from head to foot.
BERNARDO: ⎭

HAMLET: Then saw you not his face?

HORATIO: O, yes, my lord; he wore his beaver° up.

HAMLET: What, look'd he frowningly?

HORATIO: A countenance more   230
    In sorrow than in anger.

HAMLET: Pale or red?

HORATIO: Nay, very pale.

HAMLET: And fix'd his eyes upon you?

HORATIO: Most constantly.

HAMLET: I would I had been there.

HORATIO: It would have much amaz'd you.

HAMLET: Very like, very like. Stay'd it long?   235

HORATIO: While one with moderate haste might tell a hundred.

MARCELLUS: ⎫
                              Longer, longer.
BERNARDO: ⎭

HORATIO: Not when I saw't.

HAMLET: His beard was grizzled,—no?

HORATIO: It was, as I have seen it in his life,
    A sable° silver'd.

HAMLET: I will watch to-night;   240
    Perchance 'twill walk again.

HORATIO: I warr'nt it will.

HAMLET: If it assume my noble father's person,
    I'll speak to it, though hell itself should gape
    And bid me hold my peace. I pray you all,
    If you have hitherto conceal'd this sight,   245
    Let it be tenable in your silence still;
    And whatsoever else shall hap to-night,
    Give it an understanding, but no tongue:
    I will requite your loves. So, fare you well:
    Upon the platform, 'twixt eleven and twelve,   250
    I'll visit you.

ALL: Our duty to your honour.

HAMLET: Your loves, as mine to you: farewell.   *Exeunt [all but Hamlet].*
    My father's spirit in arms! all is not well;
    I doubt° some foul play: would the night were come!
    Till then sit still, my soul: foul deeds will rise,   255
    Though all the earth o'erwhelm them, to men's eyes.   *Exit.*

---

229 beaver: Visor on the helmet.   **240 sable:** Black color.   **254 doubt:** Fear.

[Scene 3]

[A room in Polonius's house.]
> *Enter Laertes and Ophelia, his Sister.*

LAERTES: My necessaries are embark'd: farewell:
    And, sister, as the winds give benefit
    And convoy is assistant,° do not sleep,
    But let me hear from you.
OPHELIA: Do you doubt that?
LAERTES: For Hamlet and the trifling of his favour,   5
    Hold it a fashion° and a toy in blood,°
    A violet in the youth of primy° nature,
    Forward,° not permanent, sweet, not lasting,
    The perfume and suppliance of a minute;°
    No more.
OPHELIA: No more but so?
LAERTES: Think it no more: 10
    For nature, crescent,° does not grow alone
    In thews° and bulk, but, as this temple° waxes,
    The inward service of the mind and soul
    Grows wide withal. Perhaps he loves you now,
    And now no soil° nor cautel° doth besmirch   15
    The virtue of his will: but you must fear,
    His greatness weigh'd,° his will is not his own;
    For he himself is subject to his birth:
    He may not, as unvalued persons do,
    Carve for himself; for on his choice depends   20
    The safety and health of this whole state;
    And therefore must his choice be circumscrib'd
    Unto the voice and yielding° of that body
    Whereof he is the head. Then if he says he loves you,
    It fits your wisdom so far to believe it   25
    As he in his particular act and place
    May give his saying deed;° which is no further
    Than the main voice of Denmark goes withal.
    Then weigh what loss your honour may sustain,
    If with too credent° ear you list his songs,   30
    Or lose your heart, or your chaste treasure open
    To his unmast'red° importunity.

SCENE 3.   3 **convoy is assistant:** Means of conveyance are available.   6 **fashion:** Custom, prevailing usage;   **toy in blood:** Passing amorous fancy.   7 **primy:** In its prime.   8 **Forward:** Precocious.   9 **suppliance of a minute:** Diversion to fill up a minute.   11 **crescent:** Growing, waxing.   12 **thews:** Bodily strength;   **temple:** Body.   15 **soil:** Blemish;   **cautel:** Crafty device.   17 **greatness weigh'd:** High position considered.   23 **voice and yielding:** Assent, approval.   27 **deed:** Effect.   30 **credent:** Credulous.   32 **unmast'red:** Unrestrained.

Fear it, Ophelia, fear it, my dear sister,
And keep you in the rear of your affection,
Out of the shot and danger of desire.   35
The chariest° maid is prodigal enough,
If she unmask her beauty to the moon:
Virtue itself 'scapes not calumnious strokes:
The canker galls the infants of the spring,°
Too oft before their buttons° be disclos'd,°   40
And in the morn and liquid dew° of youth
Contagious blastments° are most imminent.
Be wary then; best safety lies in fear:
Youth to itself rebels, though none else near.

OPHELIA: I shall the effect of this good lesson keep,   45
As watchman to my heart. But, good my brother,
Do not, as some ungracious° pastors do,
Show me the steep and thorny way to heaven;
Whiles, like a puff'd° and reckless libertine,
Himself the primrose path of dalliance treads,   50
And recks° not his own rede.°

Enter Polonius.

LAERTES: O, fear me not.
I stay too long: but here my father comes.
A double° blessing is a double grace;
Occasion° smiles upon a second leave.

POLONIUS: Yet here, Laertes? aboard, aboard, for shame!   55
The wind sits in the shoulder of your sail,
And you are stay'd for. There; my blessing with thee!
And these few precepts° in thy memory
Look thou character.° Give thy thoughts no tongue,
Nor any unproportion'd° thought his act.   60
Be thou familiar, but by no means vulgar.°
Those friends thou hast, and their adoption tried,
Grapple them to thy soul with hoops of steel;
But do not dull thy palm with entertainment
Of each new-hatch'd, unfledg'd° comrade. Beware   65
Of entrance to a quarrel, but being in,
Bear't that th' opposed may beware of thee.
Give every man thy ear, but few thy voice;

---

36 **chariest:** Most scrupulously modest.   39 **The canker . . . spring:** The cankerworm destroys
the young plants of spring.   40 **buttons:** Buds;   **disclos'd:** Opened.   41 **liquid dew:** I.e., time
when dew is fresh.   42 **blastments:** Blights.   47 **ungracious:** Graceless.   49 **puff'd:** Bloated.
51 **recks:** Heeds;   **rede:** Counsel.   53 **double:** I.e., Laertes has already bade his father good-by.
54 **Occasion:** Opportunity.   58 **precepts:** Many parallels have been found to the series of
maxims which follows, one of the closer being that in Lyly's *Euphues.*   59 **character:** Inscribe.
60 **unproportion'd:** Inordinate.   61 **vulgar:** Common.   65 **unfledg'd:** Immature.

Take each man's censure, but reserve thy judgement.
Costly thy habit as thy purse can buy,   70
But not express'd in fancy;° rich, not gaudy;
For the apparel oft proclaims the man,
And they in France of the best rank and station
Are of a most select and generous chief in that.°
Neither a borrower nor a lender be;   75
For loan oft loses both itself and friend,
And borrowing dulleth edge of husbandry.°
This above all: to thine own self be true,
And it must follow, as the night the day,
Thou canst not then be false to any man.   80
Farewell: my blessing season° this in thee!

LAERTES: Most humbly do I take my leave, my lord.

POLONIUS: The time invites you; go; your servants tend.

LAERTES: Farewell, Ophelia; and remember well
What I have said to you.

OPHELIA: 'Tis in my memory lock'd,   85
And you yourself shall keep the key of it.

LAERTES: Farewell.   *Exit Laertes.*

POLONIUS: What is 't, Ophelia, he hath said to you?

OPHELIA: So please you, something touching the Lord Hamlet.

POLONIUS: Marry, well bethought: 90
'Tis told me, he hath very oft of late
Given private time to you; and you yourself
Have of your audience been most free and bounteous:
If it be so, as so 'tis put on° me,
And that in way of caution, I must tell you,   95
You do not understand yourself so clearly
As it behooves my daughter and your honour.
What is between you? give me up the truth.

OPHELIA: He hath, my lord, of late made many tenders°
Of his affection to me.   100

POLONIUS: Affection! pooh! you speak like a green girl,
Unsifted° in such perilous circumstance.
Do you believe his tenders, as you call them?

OPHELIA: I do not know, my lord, what I should think.

POLONIUS: Marry, I will teach you: think yourself a baby;   105
That you have ta'en these tenders° for true pay,
Which are not sterling.° Tender° yourself more dearly;

---

71 express'd in fancy: Fantastical in design.   **74 Are . . . that:** *Chief* is usually taken as a substantive meaning "head," "eminence."   **77 husbandry:** Thrift.   **81 season:** Mature. **94 put on:** Impressed on.   **99, 103 tenders:** Offers.   **102 Unsifted:** Untried.   **106 tenders:** Promises to pay.   **107 sterling:** Legal currency;   **Tender:** Hold.

Or — not to crack the wind° of the poor phrase,
Running it thus — you'll tender me a fool.°

OPHELIA: My lord, he hath importun'd me with love   110
In honourable fashion.

POLONIUS: Ay, fashion° you may call it; go to, go to.

OPHELIA: And hath given countenance° to his speech, my lord,
With almost all the holy vows of heaven.

POLONIUS: Ay, springes° to catch woodcocks.° I do know,   115
When the blood burns, how prodigal the soul
Lends the tongue vows: these blazes, daughter,
Giving more light than heat, extinct in both,
Even in their promise, as it is a-making,
You must not take for fire. From this time   120
Be somewhat scanter of your maiden presence;
Set your entreatments° at a higher rate
Than a command to parley.° For Lord Hamlet,
Believe so much in him,° that he is young,
And with a larger tether may he walk   125
Than may be given you: in few,° Ophelia,
Do not believe his vows; for they are brokers;°
Not of that dye° which their investments° show,
But mere implorators of° unholy suits,
Breathing° like sanctified and pious bawds,   130
The better to beguile. This is for all:
I would not, in plain terms, from this time forth,
Have you so slander° any moment leisure,
As to give words or talk with the Lord Hamlet.
Look to 't, I charge you: come your ways.   135

OPHELIA: I shall obey, my lord.   *Exeunt.*

[Scene 4]

[The platform.]
Enter Hamlet, Horatio, and Marcellus.

HAMLET: The air bites shrewdly; it is very cold.

HORATIO: It is a nipping and an eager air.

HAMLET: What hour now?

HORATIO: I think it lacks of twelve.

MARCELLUS: No, it is struck.

---

108 **crack the wind:** I.e., run it until it is broken-winded.   109 **tender . . . fool:** Show me a fool
(for a daughter).   112 **fashion:** Mere form, pretense.   113 **countenance:** Credit, support.
115 **springes:** Snares;   **woodcocks:** Birds easily caught, type of stupidity.   122 **entreatments:**
Conversations, interviews.   123 **command to parley:** Mere invitation to talk.   124 **so . . .
him:** This much concerning him.   126 **in few:** Briefly.   127 **brokers:** Go-betweens, pro-
curers.   128 **dye:** Color or sort;   **investments:** Clothes.   129 **implorators of:** Solicitors of.
130 **Breathing:** Speaking.   133 **slander:** Bring disgrace or reproach upon.

HORATIO: Indeed? I heard it not: then it draws near the season   5
    Wherein the spirit held his wont to walk.

A flourish of trumpets, and two pieces go off.

    What does this mean, my lord?

HAMLET: The king doth wake° to-night and takes his rouse,°
    Keeps wassail,° and the swagg'ring up-spring° reels;°
    And, as he drains his draughts of Rhenish° down,   10
    The kettle-drum and trumpet thus bray out
    The triumph of his pledge.°

HORATIO: Is it a custom?

HAMLET: Ay, marry, is 't:
    But to my mind, though I am native here
    And to the manner born,° it is a custom   15
    More honour'd in the breach than the observance.
    This heavy-headed revel east and west
    Makes us traduc'd and tax'd of other nations:
    They clepe° us drunkards, and with swinish phrase°
    Soil our addition;° and indeed it takes   20
    From our achievements, though perform'd at height,
    The pith and marrow of our attribute.°
    So, oft it chances in particular men,
    That for some vicious mole of nature° in them,
    As, in their birth — wherein they are not guilty,   25
    Since nature cannot choose his origin —
    By the o'ergrowth of some complexion,
    Oft breaking down the pales° and forts of reason,
    Or by some habit that too much o'er-leavens°
    The form of plausive° manners, that these men,   30
    Carrying, I say, the stamp of one defect,
    Being nature's livery,° or fortune's star,° —
    Their virtues else — be they as pure as grace,
    As infinite as man may undergo —
    Shall in the general censure take corruption   35
    From that particular fault: the dram of eale°

SCENE 4. 8 wake: Stay awake, hold revel;   **rouse:** Carouse, drinking bout.   **9 wassail:** Carousal;
up-spring: Last and wildest dance at German merry-makings;   **reels:** Reels through.   **10 Rhen-**
ish: Rhine wine.   **12 triumph . . . pledge:** His glorious achievement as a drinker.   **15 to . . .**
born: Destined by birth to be subject to the custom in question.   **19 clepe:** Call;   **with swinish**
phrase: By calling us swine.   **20 addition:** Reputation.   **22 attribute:** Reputation.   **24 mole**
of nature: Natural blemish in one's constitution.   **28 pales:** Palings (as of a fortification).
29 o'er-leavens: Induces a change throughout (as yeast works in bread).   **30 plausive:** Pleasing.
32 nature's livery: Endowment from nature;   **fortune's star:** The position in which one is
placed by fortune, a reference to astrology. The two phrases are aspects of the same thing.
36–38 the dram . . . scandal: A famous crux: *dram of eale* has had various interpretations, the
preferred one being probably, "a dram of evil."

Doth all the noble substance of a doubt
To his own scandal.°

Enter Ghost.

HORATIO: Look, my lord, it comes!
HAMLET: Angels and ministers of grace° defend us!
    Be thou a spirit of health or goblin damn'd,   40
    Bring with thee airs from heaven or blasts from hell,
    Be thy intents wicked or charitable,
    Thou com'st in such a questionable° shape
    That I will speak to thee: I'll call thee Hamlet,
    King, father, royal Dane: O, answer me!   45
    Let me not burst in ignorance; but tell
    Why thy canoniz'd° bones, hearsed° in death,
    Have burst their cerements;° why the sepulchre,
    Wherein we saw thee quietly interr'd,
    Hath op'd his ponderous and marble jaws,   50
    To cast thee up again. What may this mean,
    That thou, dead corse, again in complete steel
    Revisits thus the glimpses of the moon,°
    Making night hideous; and we fools of nature°
    So horridly to shake our disposition   55
    With thoughts beyond the reaches of our souls?
    Say, why is this? wherefore? what should we do?

[Ghost] beckons [Hamlet].

HORATIO: It beckons you to go away with it,
    As if it some impartment° did desire
    To you alone.
MARCELLUS: Look, with what courteous action   60
    It waves you to a more removed° ground:
    But do not go with it.
HORATIO: No, by no means.
HAMLET: It will not speak; then I will follow it.
HORATIO: Do not, my lord!
HAMLET: Why, what should be the fear?
    I do not set my life at a pin's fee;   65
    And for my soul, what can it do to that,
    Being a thing immortal as itself?
    It waves me forth again: I'll follow it.
HORATIO: What if it tempt you toward the flood, my lord,
    Or to the dreadful summit of the cliff   70

---

39 **ministers of grace:** Messengers of God.   43 **questionable:** Inviting question or conversation.   47 **canoniz'd:** Buried according to the canons of the church;   **hearsed:** Coffined.
48 **cerements:** Grave-clothes.   53 **glimpses of the moon:** The earth by night.   54 **fools of nature:** Mere men, limited to natural knowledge.   59 **impartment:** Communication.
61 **removed:** Remote.

That beetles o'er° his base into the sea,
And there assume some other horrible form,
Which might deprive your sovereignty of reason°
And draw you into madness? think of it:
The very place puts toys of desperation,°   75
Without more motive, into every brain
That looks so many fathoms to the sea
And hears it roar beneath.

HAMLET: It waves me still.
Go on; I'll follow thee.

MARCELLUS: You shall not go, my lord.

HAMLET: Hold off your hands!   80

HORATIO: Be rul'd; you shall not go.

HAMLET: My fate cries out,
And makes each petty artere° in this body
As hardy as the Nemean lion's° nerve.°
Still am I call'd. Unhand me, gentlemen.
By heaven, I'll make a ghost of him that lets° me!   85
I say, away! Go on; I'll follow thee.   *Exeunt Ghost and Hamlet.*

HORATIO: He waxes desperate with imagination.

MARCELLUS: Let's follow; 'tis not fit thus to obey him.

HORATIO: Have after. To what issue° will this come?

MARCELLUS: Something is rotten in the state of Denmark.   90

HORATIO: Heaven will direct it.°

MARCELLUS: Nay, let's follow him.   *Exeunt.*

[Scene 5]

[Another part of the platform.]
    Enter Ghost and Hamlet.

HAMLET: Whither wilt thou lead me? speak; I'll go no further.

GHOST: Mark me.

HAMLET: I will.

GHOST: My hour is almost come,
When I to sulphurous and tormenting flames
Must render up myself.

HAMLET: Alas, poor ghost!

---

71 beetles o'er: Overhangs threateningly.   **73 deprive . . . reason:** Take away the sovereignty of your reason. It was thought that evil spirits would sometimes assume the form of departed spirits in order to work madness in a human creature.   **75 toys of desperation:** Freakish notions of suicide.   **82 artere:** Artery.   **83 Nemean lion's:** The Nemean lion was one of the monsters slain by Hercules;   **nerve:** Sinew, tendon. The point is that the arteries which were carrying the spirits out into the body were functioning and were as stiff and hard as the sinews of the lion.   **85 lets:** Hinders.   **89 issue:** Outcome.   **91 it:** I.e., the outcome.

GHOST: Pity me not, but lend thy serious hearing   5
    To what I shall unfold.
HAMLET: Speak; I am bound to hear.
GHOST: So art thou to revenge, when thou shalt hear.
HAMLET: What?
GHOST: I am thy father's spirit,
    Doom'd for a certain term to walk the night,   10
    And for the day confin'd to fast° in fires,
    Till the foul crimes done in my days of nature
    Are burnt and purg'd away. But that I am forbid
    To tell the secrets of my prison-house,
    I could a tale unfold whose lightest word   15
    Would harrow up thy soul, freeze thy young blood,
    Make thy two eyes, like stars, start from their spheres,°
    Thy knotted° and combined° locks to part
    And each particular hair to stand an end,
    Like quills upon the fretful porpentine:°   20
    But this eternal blazon° must not be
    To ears of flesh and blood. List, list, O, list!
    If thou didst ever thy dear father love—
HAMLET: O God!
GHOST: Revenge his foul and most unnatural° murder.   25
HAMLET: Murder!
GHOST: Murder most foul, as in the best it is;
    But this most foul, strange and unnatural.
HAMLET: Haste me to know't, that I, with wings as swift
    As meditation or the thoughts of love,   30
    May sweep to my revenge.
GHOST: I find thee apt;
    And duller shouldst thou be than the fat weed°
    That roots itself in ease on Lethe wharf,°
    Wouldst thou not stir in this. Now, Hamlet, hear:
    'Tis given out that, sleeping in my orchard,   35
    A serpent stung me; so the whole ear of Denmark
    Is by a forged process of my death
    Rankly abus'd: but know, thou noble youth,
    The serpent that did sting thy father's life
    Now wears his crown.

SCENE 5. 11 **fast:** Probably, do without food. It has been sometimes taken in the sense of doing general penance. 17 **spheres:** Orbits. 18 **knotted:** Perhaps intricately arranged; **combined:** Tied, bound. 20 **porpentine:** Porcupine. 21 **eternal blazon:** Promulgation or proclamation of eternity, revelation of the hereafter. 25 **unnatural:** I.e., pertaining to fratricide. 32 **fat weed:** Many suggestions have been offered as to the particular plant intended, including asphodel; probably a general figure for plants growing along rotting wharves and piles. 33 **Lethe wharf:** Bank of the river of forgetfulness in Hades.

HAMLET: O my prophetic soul!   40
    My uncle!
GHOST: Ay, that incestuous, that adulterate° beast,
    With witchcraft of his wit, with traitorous gifts,—
    O wicked wit and gifts, that have the power
    So to seduce!—won to his shameful lust   45
    The will of my most seeming-virtuous queen:
    O Hamlet, what a falling-off was there!
    From me, whose love was of that dignity
    That it went hand in hand even with the vow
    I made to her in marriage, and to decline   50
    Upon a wretch whose natural gifts were poor
    To those of mine!
    But virtue, as it never will be moved,
    Though lewdness court it in a shape of heaven,
    So lust, though to a radiant angel link'd,   55
    Will sate itself in a celestial bed,
    And prey on garbage.
    But, soft! methinks I scent the morning air;
    Brief let me be. Sleeping within my orchard,
    My custom always of the afternoon,   60
    Upon my secure° hour thy uncle stole,
    With juice of cursed hebona° in a vial,
    And in the porches of my ears did pour
    The leperous° distilment; whose effect
    Holds such an enmity with blood of man   65
    That swift as quicksilver it courses through
    The natural gates and alleys of the body,
    And with a sudden vigour it doth posset°
    And curd, like eager° droppings into milk,
    The thin and wholesome blood: so did it mine;   70
    And a most instant tetter bark'd about,
    Most lazar-like,° with vile and loathsome crust,
    All my smooth body.
    Thus was I, sleeping, by a brother's hand
    Of life, of crown, of queen, at once dispatch'd:°   75
    Cut off even in the blossoms of my sin,
    Unhous'led,° disappointed,° unanel'd,°
    No reck'ning made, but sent to my account
    With all my imperfections on my head:

42 **adulterate:** Adulterous.   61 **secure:** Confident, unsuspicious.   62 **hebona:** Generally supposed to mean henbane, conjectured *hemlock*; *ebenus*, meaning "yew."   64 **leperous:** Causing leprosy.   68 **posset:** Coagulate, curdle.   69 **eager:** Sour, acid.   72 **lazar-like:** Leperlike.   75 **dispatch'd:** Suddenly bereft.   77 **Unhous'led:** Without having received the sacrament;   **disappointed:** Unready, without equipment for the last journey;   **unanel'd:** Without having received extreme unction.

O, horrible! O, horrible! most horrible!°   80
If thou hast nature in thee, bear it not;
Let not the royal bed of Denmark be
A couch for luxury° and damned incest.
But, howsomever thou pursues this act,
Taint not thy mind,° nor let thy soul contrive   85
Against thy mother aught: leave her to heaven
And to those thorns that in her bosom lodge,
To prick and sting her. Fare thee well at once!
The glow-worm shows the matin° to be near,
And 'gins to pale his uneffectual fire:°   90
Adieu, adieu, adieu! remember me.   *[Exit.]*
HAMLET: O all you host of heaven! O earth! what else?
And shall I couple° hell? O, fie! Hold, hold, my heart;
And you, my sinews, grow not instant old,
But bear me stiffly up. Remember thee!   95
Ay, thou poor ghost, whiles memory holds a seat
In this distracted globe.° Remember thee!
Yea, from the table of my memory
I'll wipe away all trivial fond records,
All saws° of books, all forms, all pressures° past,   100
That youth and observation copied there;
And thy commandment all alone shall live
Within the book and volume of my brain,
Unmix'd with baser matter: yes, by heaven!
O most pernicious woman!   105
O villain, villain, smiling, damned villain!
My tables,°—meet it is I set it down,
That one may smile, and smile, and be a villain;
At least I am sure it may be so in Denmark: *[Writing.]*
So, uncle, there you are. Now to my word;°   110
It is "Adieu, adieu! remember me,"
I have sworn't.

Enter Horatio and Marcellus.

HORATIO: My lord, my lord—
MARCELLUS: Lord Hamlet,—
HORATIO: Heavens secure him!
HAMLET: So be it!
MARCELLUS: Hillo, ho, ho,° my lord!   115

---

80 **O . . . horrible:** Many editors give this line to Hamlet; Garrick and Sir Henry Irving spoke it in
that part.   83 **luxury:** Lechery.   85 **Taint . . . mind:** Probably, deprave not thy character, do
nothing except in the pursuit of a natural revenge.   89 **matin:** Morning.   90 **uneffectual fire:**
Cold light.   93 **couple:** Add.   97 **distracted globe:** Confused head.   100 **saws:** Wise sayings;
pressures: Impressions stamped.   107 **tables:** Probably a small portable writing-tablet carried at
the belt.   110 **word:** Watchword.   115 **Hillo, ho, ho:** A falconer's call to a hawk in air.

HAMLET: Hillo, ho, ho, boy! come, bird, come.
MARCELLUS: How is't, my noble lord?
HORATIO: What news, my lord?
HAMLET: O, wonderful!
HORATIO: Good my lord, tell it.
HAMLET: No; you will reveal it.
HORATIO: Not I, my lord, by heaven.
MARCELLUS: Nor I, my lord.   120
HAMLET: How say you, then; would heart of man once think it?
    But you'll be secret?
HORATIO: ⎫
              ⎬   Ay, by heaven, my lord.
MARCELLUS: ⎭
HAMLET: There's ne'er a villain dwelling in all Denmark
    But he's an arrant° knave.
HORATIO: There needs no ghost, my lord, come from the grave   125
    To tell us this.
HAMLET: Why, right; you are in the right;
    And so, without more circumstance at all,
    I hold it fit that we shake hands and part:
    You, as your business and desire shall point you;
    For every man has business and desire,   130
    Such as it is; and for my own poor part,
    Look you, I'll go pray.
HORATIO: These are but wild and whirling words, my lord.
HAMLET: I am sorry they offend you, heartily;
    Yes, 'faith, heartily.
HORATIO: There's no offence, my lord.   135
HAMLET: Yes, by Saint Patrick,° but there is, Horatio,
    And much offence too. Touching this vision here,
    It is an honest° ghost, that let me tell you:
    For your desire to know what is between us,
    O'ermaster 't as you may. And now, good friends,   140
    As you are friends, scholars and soldiers,
    Give me one poor request.
HORATIO: What is 't, my lord? we will.
HAMLET: Never make known what you have seen to-night.
HORATIO: ⎫
              ⎬   My lord, we will not.
MARCELLUS: ⎭
HAMLET: Nay, but swear 't.
HORATIO: In faith,   145
    My lord, not I.
MARCELLUS: Nor I, my lord, in faith.

---

124 arrant: Thoroughgoing.   **136 Saint Patrick:** St. Patrick was keeper of Purgatory and patron saint of all blunders and confusion.   **138 honest:** I.e., a real ghost and not an evil spirit.

HAMLET: Upon my sword.°
MARCELLUS: We have sworn, my lord, already.
HAMLET: Indeed, upon my sword, indeed.   *Ghost cries under the stage.*
GHOST: Swear.
HAMLET: Ah, ha, boy! say'st thou so? art thou there, truepenny?°   150
      Come on — you hear this fellow in the cellarage —
      Consent to swear.
HORATIO: Propose the oath, my lord.
HAMLET: Never to speak of this that you have seen,
      Swear by my sword.
GHOST *[beneath]*:   Swear.   155
HAMLET: Hic et ubique?° then we'll shift our ground.
      Come hither, gentlemen,
      And lay your hands again upon my sword:
      Swear by my sword,
      Never to speak of this that you have heard.   160
GHOST *[beneath]*:   Swear by his sword.
HAMLET: Well said, old mole! canst work i' th' earth so fast?
      A worthy pioner!° Once more remove, good friends.
HORATIO: O day and night, but this is wondrous strange!
HAMLET: And therefore as a stranger give it welcome.   165
      There are more things in heaven and earth, Horatio,
      Than are dreamt of in your philosophy.
      But come;
      Here, as before, never, so help you mercy,
      How strange or odd soe'er I bear myself,   170
      As I perchance hereafter shall think meet
      To put an antic° disposition on,
      That you, at such times seeing me, never shall,
      With arms encumb'red° thus, or this head-shake,
      Or by pronouncing of some doubtful phrase,   175
      As "Well, well, we know," or "We could, an if we would,"
      Or "If we list to speak," or "There be, an if they might,"
      Or such ambiguous giving out,° to note°
      That you know aught of me: this not to do,
      So grace and mercy at your most need help you,   180
      Swear.
GHOST *[beneath]*:   Swear.
HAMLET: Rest, rest, perturbed spirit! *[They swear.]* So, gentlemen,
      With all my love I do commend me to you:
      And what so poor a man as Hamlet is   185
      May do, t' express his love and friending° to you,

---

147 **sword**: I.e., the hilt in the form of a cross.   150 **truepenny**: Good old boy, or the like.
156 **Hic et ubique?**: Here and everywhere?   163 **pioner**: Digger, miner.   172 **antic**: Fantastic.   174 **encumb'red**: Folded or entwined.   178 **giving out**: Profession of knowledge;
to note: To give a sign.   186 **friending**: Friendliness.

God willing, shall not lack. Let us go in together;
And still your fingers on your lips, I pray.
The time is out of joint: O cursed spite,
That ever I was born to set it right!   190
Nay, come, let's go together.   *Exeunt.*

[ACT 2, Scene 1]

[A room in Polonius's house.]
    Enter old Polonius with his man [Reynaldo].

POLONIUS: Give him this money and these notes, Reynaldo.
REYNALDO: I will, my lord.
POLONIUS: You shall do marvellous wisely, good Reynaldo,
      Before you visit him, to make inquire
      Of his behaviour.
REYNALDO: My lord, I did intend it.   5
POLONIUS: Marry, well said; very well said. Look you, sir,
      Inquire me first what Danskers° are in Paris;
      And how, and who, what means, and where they keep,°
      What company, at what expense; and finding
      By this encompassment° and drift° of question   10
      That they do know my son, come you more nearer
      Than your particular demands will touch it:°
      Take° you as 'twere, some distant knowledge of him;
      As thus, "I know his father and his friends,
      And in part him": do you mark this, Reynaldo?   15
REYNALDO: Ay, very well, my lord.
POLONIUS: "And in part him; but" you may say "not well:
      But, if 't be he I mean, he's very wild;
      Addicted so and so": and there put on° him
      What forgeries° you please; marry, none so rank   20
      As may dishonour him; take heed of that;
      But, sir, such wanton,° wild and usual slips
      As are companions noted and most known
      To youth and liberty.
REYNALDO: As gaming, my lord.
POLONIUS: Ay, or drinking, fencing,° swearing, quarrelling,   25
      Drabbing;° you may go so far.
REYNALDO: My lord, that would dishonour him.

ACT 2, SCENE 1.   7 **Danskers:** Danke was a common variant for "Denmark"; hence "Dane."
8 **keep:** Dwell.   10 **encompassment:** Roundabout talking;   **drift:** Gradual approach or course.
11–12 **come . . . it:** I.e., you will find out more this way than by asking pointed questions.
13 **Take:** Assume, pretend.   19 **put on:** Impute to.   20 **forgeries:** Invented tales.   22 **wanton:** Sportive, unrestrained.   25 **fencing:** Indicative of the ill repute of professional fencers and
fencing schools in Elizabethan times.   26 **Drabbing:** Associating with immoral women.

POLONIUS: 'Faith, no; as you may season it in the charge.
    You must not put another scandal on him,
    That he is open to incontinency;°   30
    That's not my meaning: but breathe his faults so quaintly°
    That they may seem the taints of liberty,°
    The flash and outbreak of a fiery mind,
    A savageness in unreclaimed° blood,
    Of general assault.°
REYNALDO: But, my good lord,—   35
POLONIUS: Wherefore should you do this?
REYNALDO: Ay, my lord,
    I would know that.
POLONIUS: Marry, sir, here's my drift;
    And, I believe, it is a fetch of wit:°
    You laying these slight sullies on my son,
    As 'twere a thing a little soil'd i' th' working,   40
    Mark you,
    Your party in converse, him you would sound,
    Having ever° seen in the prenominate° crimes
    The youth you breathe of guilty, be assur'd
    He closes with you in this consequence;°   45
    "Good sir," or so, or "friend," or "gentleman,"
    According to the phrase or the addition
    Of man and country.
REYNALDO: Very good, my lord.
POLONIUS: And then, sir, does 'a this—'a does—what was I about to say? By the
    mass, I was about to say something: where did I leave?   50
REYNALDO: At "closes in the consequence," at "friend or so," and "gentle-
    man."
POLONIUS: At "closes in the consequence," ay, marry;
    He closes thus: "I know the gentleman;
    I saw him yesterday, or t' other day,   55
    Or then, or then; with such, or such; and, as you say,
    There was 'a gaming; there o'ertook in 's rouse;°
    There falling out at tennis": or perchance,
    "I saw him enter such a house of sale,"
    Videlicet,° a brothel, or so forth.   60
    See you now;
    Your bait of falsehood takes this carp of truth:
    And thus do we of wisdom and of reach,°

---

30 incontinency: Habitual loose behavior. **31 quaintly:** Delicately, ingeniously.
32 taints of liberty: Blemishes due to freedom. **34 unreclaimed:** Untamed. **35 general
assault:** Tendency that assails all untrained youth. **38 fetch of wit:** Clever trick. **43 ever:** At
any time; **prenominate:** Before-mentioned. **45 closes . . . consequence:** Agrees with you
in this conclusion. **57 o'ertook in 's rouse:** Overcome by drink. **60 Videlicet:** Namely.
63 reach: Capacity, ability.

With windlasses° and with assays of bias,°
By indirections° find directions° out: 65
So by my former lecture° and advice,
Shall you my son. You have me, have you not?
REYNALDO: My lord, I have.
POLONIUS: God bye ye;° fare ye well.
REYNALDO: Good my lord!
POLONIUS: Observe his inclination in yourself.°   70
REYNALDO: I shall, my lord.
POLONIUS: And let him ply his music.°
REYNALDO: Well, my lord.
POLONIUS: Farewell!   *Exit Reynaldo.*

Enter Ophelia.

                    How now, Ophelia! what's the matter?
OPHELIA: O, my lord, my lord, I have been so affrighted!
POLONIUS: With what, i' th' name of God?   75
OPHELIA: My lord, as I was sewing in my closet,°
    Lord Hamlet, with his doublet° all unbrac'd;°
    No hat upon his head; his stockings foul'd,
    Ungart'red, and down-gyved° to his ankle;
    Pale as his shirt; his knees knocking each other;   80
    And with a look so piteous in purport
    As if he had been loosed out of hell
    To speak of horrors, — he comes before me.
POLONIUS: Mad for thy love?
OPHELIA: My lord, I do not know;
    But truly, I do fear it.
POLONIUS: What said he?   85
OPHELIA: He took me by the wrist and held me hard;
    Then goes he to the length of all his arm;
    And, with his other hand thus o'er his brow,
    He falls to such perusal of my face
    As 'a would draw it. Long stay'd he so;   90
    At last, a little shaking of mine arm
    And thrice his head thus waving up and down,
    He rais'd a sigh so piteous and profound
    As it did seem to shatter all his bulk°
    And end his being: that done, he lets me go: 95

64 **windlasses**: I.e., circuitous paths;   **assays of bias**: Attempts that resemble the course of the
bowl, which, being weighted on one side, has a curving motion.   65 **indirections**: Devious
courses;   **directions**: Straight courses, i.e., the truth.   66 **lecture**: Admonition.   68 **bye ye**:
Be with you.   70 **Observe . . . yourself**: In your own person, not by spies; or conform your
own conduct to his inclination; or test him by studying yourself.   72 **ply his music**: Probably
to be taken literally.   76 **closet**: Private chamber.   77 **doublet**: Close-fitting coat;   **unbrac'd**:
Unfastened.   79 **down-gyved**: Fallen to the ankles (like gyves or fetters).   94 **bulk**: Body.

And, with his head over his shoulder turn'd,
He seem'd to find his way without his eyes;
For out o' doors he went without their helps,
And, to the last, bended their light on me.

POLONIUS: Come, go with me: I will go seek the king.   100
This is the very ecstasy of love,
Whose violent property° fordoes° itself
And leads the will to desperate undertakings
As oft as any passion under heaven
That does afflict our natures. I am sorry.   105
What, have you given him any hard words of late?

OPHELIA: No, my good lord, but, as you did command,
I did repel his letters and denied
His access to me.

POLONIUS: That hath made him mad.
I am sorry that with better heed and judgement   110
I had not quoted° him: I fear'd he did but trifle,
And meant to wrack thee; but, beshrew my jealousy!°
By heaven, it is as proper to our age
To cast beyond° ourselves in our opinions
As it is common for the younger sort   115
To lack discretion. Come, go we to the king:
This must be known; which, being kept close, might move
More grief to hide than hate to utter love.°
Come.   *Exeunt.*

[Scene 2]

[A room in the castle.]
Flourish. Enter King and Queen, Rosencrantz, and Guildenstern [with others].

KING: Welcome, dear Rosencrantz and Guildenstern!
Moreover that° we much did long to see you,
The need we have to use you did provoke
Our hasty sending. Something have you heard
Of Hamlet's transformation; so call it,   5
Sith° nor th' exterior nor the inward man
Resembles that it was. What it should be,
More than his father's death, that thus hath put him
So much from th' understanding of himself,
I cannot dream of: I entreat you both,   10

102 property: Nature; **fordoes:** Destroys.   **111 quoted:** Observed.   **112 beshrew my jealousy:** Curse my suspicions.   **114 cast beyond:** Overshoot, miscalculate.   **117–118 might . . .
love:** I.e., I might cause more grief to others by hiding the knowledge of Hamlet's love to Ophelia than hatred to me and mine by telling of it.   SCENE 2.   **2 Moreover that:** Besides the fact
that.   **6 Sith:** Since.

That, being of so young days° brought up with him,
And sith so neighbour'd to his youth and haviour,
That you vouchsafe your rest° here in our court
Some little time: so by your companies
To draw him on to pleasures, and to gather,   15
So much as from occasion you may glean,
Whether aught, to us unknown, afflicts him thus,
That, open'd, lies within our remedy.
QUEEN: Good gentlemen, he hath much talk'd of you;
And sure I am two men there are not living   20
To whom he more adheres. If it will please you
To show us so much gentry° and good will
As to expend your time with us awhile,
For the supply and profit° of our hope,
Your visitation shall receive such thanks   25
As fits a king's remembrance.
ROSENCRANTZ: Both your majesties
Might, by the sovereign power you have of us,
Put your dread pleasures more into command
Than to entreaty.
GUILDENSTERN: But we both obey,
And here give up ourselves, in the full bent°   30
To lay our service freely at your feet,
To be commanded.
KING: Thanks, Rosencrantz and gentle Guildenstern.
QUEEN: Thanks, Guildenstern and gentle Rosencrantz:
And I beseech you instantly to visit   35
My too much changed son. Go, some of you,
And bring these gentlemen where Hamlet is.
GUILDENSTERN: Heavens make our presence and our practices
Pleasant and helpful to him!
QUEEN: Ay, amen!
            Exeunt Rosencrantz and Guildenstern [with some Attendants].

Enter Polonius.

POLONIUS: Th' ambassadors from Norway, my good lord,   40
Are joyfully return'd.
KING: Thou still hast been the father of good news.
POLONIUS: Have I, my lord? I assure my good liege,
I hold my duty, as I hold my soul,
Both to my God and to my gracious king: 45
And I do think, or else this brain of mine

---

11 **of . . . days:** From such early youth.   13 **vouchsafe your rest:** Please to stay.   22 **gentry:**
Courtesy.   24 **supply and profit:** Aid and successful outcome.   30 **in . . . bent:** To the
utmost degree of our mental capacity.

Hunts not the trail of policy so sure
As it hath us'd to do, that I have found
The very cause of Hamlet's lunacy.
KING: O, speak of that; that do I long to hear.   50
POLONIUS: Give first admittance to th' ambassadors;
My news shall be the fruit to that great feast.
KING: Thyself do grace to them, and bring them in.   *[Exit Polonius.]*
He tells me, my dear Gertrude, he hath found
The head and source of all your son's distemper.   55
QUEEN: I doubt° it is no other but the main;°
His father's death, and our o'erhasty marriage.
KING: Well, we shall sift him.

Enter Ambassadors [Voltimand and Cornelius, with Polonius.]
                              Welcome, my good friends!
Say, Voltimand, what from our brother Norway?
VOLTIMAND: Most fair return of greetings and desires.   60
Upon our first, he sent out to suppress
His nephew's levies; which to him appear'd
To be a preparation 'gainst the Polack;
But, better look'd into, he truly found
It was against your highness: whereat griev'd,   65
That so his sickness, age and impotence
Was falsely borne in hand,° sends out arrests
On Fortinbras; which he, in brief, obeys;
Receives rebuke from Norway, and in fine°
Makes vow before his uncle never more   70
To give th' assay° of arms against your majesty.
Whereon old Norway, overcome with joy,
Gives him three score thousand crowns in annual fee,
And his commission to employ those soldiers,
So levied as before, against the Polack: 75
With an entreaty, herein further shown,   *[Giving a paper.]*
That it might please you to give quiet pass
Through your dominions for this enterprise,
On such regards of safety and allowance°
As therein are set down.
KING: It likes° us well;   80
And at our more consider'd° time we'll read,
Answer, and think upon this business.
Meantime we thank you for your well-took labour:
Go to your rest; at night we'll feast together:

---

56 doubt: Fear; **main:** Chief point, principal concern. **67 borne in hand:** Deluded.
69 in fine: In the end. **71 assay:** Assault, trial (of arms). **79 safety and allowance:** Pledges
of safety to the country and terms of permission for the troops to pass. **80 likes:** Pleases.
81 consider'd: Suitable for deliberation.

Most welcome home!   *Exeunt Ambassadors.*
POLONIUS: This business is well ended.   85
   My liege, and madam, to expostulate
   What majesty should be, what duty is,
   Why day is day, night night, and time is time,
   Were nothing but to waste night, day and time.
   Therefore, since brevity is the soul of wit,°   90
   And tediousness the limbs and outward flourishes,°
   I will be brief: your noble son is mad:
   Mad call I it; for, to define true madness
   What is 't but to be nothing else but mad?
   But let that go.
QUEEN: More matter, with less art.   95
POLONIUS: Madam, I swear I use no art at all.
   That he is mad, 'tis true: 'tis true 'tis pity;
   And pity 'tis 'tis true: a foolish figure;°
   But farewell it, for I will use no art.
   Mad let us grant him, then: and now remains   100
   That we find out the cause of this effect,
   Or rather say, the cause of this defect,
   For this effect defective comes by cause:
   Thus it remains, and the remainder thus.
   Perpend.°   105
   I have a daughter — have while she is mine —
   Who, in her duty and obedience, mark,
   Hath given me this: now gather, and surmise.
   [Reads the letter.] "To the celestial and my soul's idol, the most beautified
   Ophelia," —   110
   That's an ill phrase, a vile phrase; "beautified" is a vile phrase: but you shall
   hear. Thus: *[Reads.]*
   "In her excellent white bosom, these, & c."
QUEEN: Came this from Hamlet to her?
POLONIUS: Good madam, stay awhile; I will be faithful.   *[Reads.]*   115
      "Doubt thou the stars are fire;
        Doubt that the sun doth move;
      "Doubt truth to be a liar;
        But never doubt I love.
   "O dear Ophelia, I am ill at these numbers;° I have not art to reckon°   120
   my groans: but that I love thee best, O most best, believe it. Adieu.
     "Thine evermore, most dear lady, whilst this machine° is to him,
                                 HAMLET."

---

90 **wit**: Sound sense or judgment.   91 **flourishes**: Ostentation, embellishments.   98 **figure**:
Figure of speech.   105 **Perpend**: Consider.   120 **ill . . . numbers**: Unskilled at writing
verses;   **reckon**: Number metrically, scan.   122 **machine**: Bodily frame.

This, in obedience, hath my daughter shown me,
And more above,° hath his solicitings,   125
As they fell out° by time, by means° and place,
All given to mine ear.

KING: But how hath she
Receiv'd his love?

POLONIUS: What do you think of me?

KING: As of a man faithful and honourable.

POLONIUS: I would fain prove so. But what might you think,   130
When I had seen this hot love on the wing—
As I perceiv'd it, I must tell you that,
Before my daughter told me—what might you,
Or my dear majesty your queen here, think,
If I had play'd the desk or table-book,°   135
Or given my heart a winking,° mute and dumb,
Or look'd upon this love with idle sight;
What might you think? No, I went round to work,
And my young mistress thus I did bespeak:°
"Lord Hamlet is a prince, out of thy star;°   140
This must not be": and then I prescripts gave her,
That she should lock herself from his resort,
Admit no messengers, receive no tokens.
Which done, she took the fruits of my advice;
And he, repelled—a short tale to make—   145
Fell into a sadness, then into a fast,
Thence to a watch,° thence into a weakness,
Thence to a lightness,° and, by this declension,°
Into the madness wherein now he raves,
And all we mourn for.

KING: Do you think 'tis this?   150

QUEEN: It may be, very like.

POLONIUS: Hath there been such a time—I would fain know that—
That I have positively said " 'Tis so,"
When it prov'd otherwise?

KING: Not that I know.

POLONIUS [pointing to his head and shoulder]:   Take this from this, if this be
     otherwise: 155
If circumstances lead me, I will find
Where truth is hid, though it were hid indeed
Within the centre.°

KING: How may we try it further?

125 more above: Moreover.   126 fell out: Occurred;   means: Opportunities (of access).
135 play'd . . . table-book: I.e., remained shut up, concealed this information.   136 given . . .
winking: Given my heart a signal to keep silent.   139 bespeak: Address.   140 out . . . star:
Above thee in position.   147 watch: State of sleeplessness.   148 lightness: Lightheadedness;
declension: Decline, deterioration.   158 centre: Middle point of the earth.

POLONIUS: You know, sometimes he walks four hours together
Here in the lobby.
QUEEN: So he does indeed.   160
POLONIUS: At such a time I'll loose my daughter to him:
Be you and I behind an arras° then;
Mark the encounter: if he love her not
And be not from his reason fall'n thereon,°
Let me be no assistant for a state,   165
But keep a farm and carters.
KING: We will try it.

Enter Hamlet [reading on a book].

QUEEN: But, look, where sadly the poor wretch comes reading.
POLONIUS: Away, I do beseech you both, away:
                              Exeunt King and Queen [with Attendants].
I'll board° him presently. O, give me leave.
How does my good Lord Hamlet?   170
HAMLET: Well, God-a-mercy.
POLONIUS: Do you know me, my lord?
HAMLET: Excellent well; you are a fishmonger.°
POLONIUS: Not I, my lord.
HAMLET: Then I would you were so honest a man.   175
POLONIUS: Honest, my lord!
HAMLET: Ay, sir; to be honest, as this world goes, is to be one man picked out of
ten thousand.
POLONIUS: That's very true, my lord.
HAMLET: For if the sun breed maggots in a dead dog, being a good kissing   180
carrion,° — Have you a daughter?
POLONIUS: I have, my lord.
HAMLET: Let her not walk i' the sun:° conception° is a blessing: but as your
daughter may conceive — Friend, look to 't.
POLONIUS *[aside]*:   How say you by° that? Still harping on my daughter: yet he   185
knew me not at first; 'a said I was a fishmonger: 'a is far gone, far gone: and
truly in my youth I suffered much extremity for love; very near this. I'll speak
to him again. What do you read, my lord?
HAMLET: Words, words, words.
POLONIUS: What is the matter,° my lord?   190
HAMLET: Between who?°
POLONIUS: I mean, the matter that you read, my lord.

---

162 arras: Hanging, tapestry.   **164 thereon:** On that account.   **169 board:** Accost.   **173 fishmonger:** An opprobrious expression meaning "bawd," "procurer."   **180–181 good kissing carrion:** I.e., a good piece of flesh for kissing (?).   **183 i' the sun:** In the sunshine of princely
favors;   **conception:** Quibble on "understanding" and "pregnancy."   **185 by:** Concerning.
190 matter: Substance.   **191 Between who:** Hamlet deliberately takes *matter* as meaning
"basis of dispute."

HAMLET: Slanders, sir: for the satirical rogue says here that old men have grey beards, that their faces are wrinkled, their eyes purging° thick amber and plum-tree gum and that they have a plentiful lack of wit, together with most 195 weak hams: all which, sir, though I most powerfully and potently believe, yet I hold it not honesty° to have it thus set down, for yourself, sir, should be old as I am, if like a crab you could go backward.

POLONIUS [*aside*]: Though this be madness, yet there is method in 't. — Will you walk out of the air, my lord? 200

HAMLET: Into my grave.

POLONIUS: Indeed, that's out of the air. (*Aside.*) How pregnant sometimes his replies are! a happiness° that often madness hits on, which reason and sanity could not so prosperously° be delivered of. I will leave him, and suddenly contrive the means of meeting between him and my daughter. — My hon- 205 ourable lord, I will most humbly take my leave of you.

HAMLET: You cannot, sir, take from me any thing that I will more willingly part withal: except my life, except my life, except my life.

Enter Guildenstern and Rosencrantz.

POLONIUS: Fare you well, my lord.

HAMLET: These tedious old fools! 210

POLONIUS: You go to seek the Lord Hamlet; there he is.

ROSENCRANTZ [*to Polonius*]: God save you, sir! [*Exit Polonius.*]

GUILDENSTERN: My honoured lord!

ROSENCRANTZ: My most dear lord!

HAMLET: My excellent good friends! How dost thou, Guildenstern? Ah, Rosen- 215 crantz! Good lads, how do ye both?

ROSENCRANTZ: As the indifferent° children of the earth.

GUILDENSTERN: Happy, in that we are not over-happy;
On Fortune's cap we are not the very button.

HAMLET: Nor the soles of her shoe? 220

ROSENCRANTZ: Neither, my lord.

HAMLET: Then you live about her waist, or in the middle of her favours?

GUILDENSTERN: 'Faith, her privates° we.

HAMLET: In the secret parts of Fortune? O, most true; she is a strumpet. What's the news? 225

ROSENCRANTZ: None, my lord, but that the world's grown honest.

HAMLET: Then is doomsday near: but your news is not true. Let me question more in particular: what have you, my good friends, deserved at the hands of Fortune, that she sends you to prison hither?

GUILDENSTERN: Prison, my lord! 230

HAMLET: Denmark's a prison.

ROSENCRANTZ: Then is the world one.

---

194 purging: discharging. **197 honesty:** Decency. **203 happiness:** Felicity of expression. **204 prosperously:** Successfully. **217 indifferent:** Ordinary. **223 privates:** I.e., ordinary men (sexual pun on *private parts*).

HAMLET: A goodly one; in which there are many confines,° wards and dungeons, Denmark being one o' the worst.

ROSENCRANTZ: We think not so, my lord.   235

HAMLET: Why, then, 'tis none to you; for there is nothing either good or bad,
but thinking makes it so: to me it is a prison.

ROSENCRANTZ: Why then, your ambition makes it one; 'tis too narrow for your
mind.

HAMLET: O God, I could be bounded in a nutshell and count myself a king of   240
infinite space, were it not that I have bad dreams.

GUILDENSTERN: Which dreams indeed are ambition, for the very substance of
the ambitious° is merely the shadow of a dream.

HAMLET: A dream itself is but a shadow.

ROSENCRANTZ: Truly, and I hold ambition of so airy and light a quality that it is   245
but a shadow's shadow.

HAMLET: Then are our beggars bodies, and our monarchs and outstretched
heroes the beggars' shadows. Shall we to the court? for, by my fay,° I cannot
reason.°

ROSENCRANTZ: ⎫
              ⎬ We'll wait upon° you.   250
GUILDENSTERN: ⎭

HAMLET: No such matter: I will not sort° you with the rest of my servants, for, to
speak to you like an honest man, I am most dreadfully attended.° But, in the
beaten way of friendship,° what make you at Elsinore?

ROSENCRANTZ: To visit you, my lord: no other occasion.

HAMLET: Beggar that I am, I am ever poor in thanks; but I thank you: and sure,   255
dear friends, my thanks are too dear a° halfpenny. Were you not sent for? Is it
your own inclining? Is it a free visitation? Come, come, deal justly with me:
come, come; nay, speak.

GUILDENSTERN: What should we say, my lord?

HAMLET: Why, any thing, but to the purpose. You were sent for; and there is a   260
kind of confession in your looks which your modesties have not craft enough
to colour: I know the good king and queen have sent for you.

ROSENCRANTZ: To what end, my lord?

HAMLET: That you must teach me. But let me conjure° you, by the rights of our
fellowship, by the consonancy of our youth,° by the obligation of our ever-   265
preserved love, and by what more dear a better proposer° could charge you
withal, be even and direct with me, whether you were sent for, or no?

ROSENCRANTZ *[aside to Guildenstern]:*   What say you?

HAMLET *[aside]:*   Nay, then, I have an eye of you. — If you love me, hold not off.

GUILDENSTERN: My lord, we were sent for.   270

---

233 confines: Places of confinement.   **242–243 very . . . ambitious:** That seemingly most
substantial thing which the ambitious pursue.   **248 fay:** Faith.   **249 reason:** Argue.   **250 wait
upon:** Accompany.   **251 sort:** Class.   **252 dreadfully attended:** Poorly provided with servants.   **252–253 in the . . . friendship:** As a matter of course among friends.   **256 a:** I.e., at a.
264 conjure: Adjure, entreat.   **265 consonancy of our youth:** The fact that we are of the
same age.   **266 better proposer:** One more skillful in finding proposals.

HAMLET: I will tell you why; so shall my anticipation prevent your discovery,°
and your secrecy to the king and queen moult no feather. I have of late — but
wherefore I know not — lost all my mirth, forgone all custom of exercises;
and indeed it goes so heavily with my disposition that this goodly frame, the
earth, seems to me a sterile promontory, this most excellent canopy, the air,   275
look you, this brave o'erhanging firmament, this majestical roof fretted° with
golden fire, why, it appeareth nothing to me but a foul and pestilent congregation of vapours. What a piece of work is a man! how noble in reason! how
infinite in faculties!° in form and moving how express° and admirable! in
action how like an angel! in apprehension° how like a god! the beauty of the   280
world! the paragon of animals! And yet, to me, what is this quintessence° of
dust? man delights not me: no, nor woman neither, though by your smiling
you seem to say so.

ROSENCRANTZ: My lord, there was no such stuff in my thoughts.

HAMLET: Why did you laugh then, when I said "man delights not me"?   285

ROSENCRANTZ: To think, my lord, if you delight not in man, what lenten° entertainment the players shall receive from you: we coted° them on the way; and
hither are they coming, to offer you service.

HAMLET: He that plays the king shall be welcome; his majesty shall have tribute
of me; the adventurous knight shall use his foil and target;° the lover shall   290
not sigh gratis; the humorous man° shall end his part in peace; the clown
shall make those laugh whose lungs are tickle o' the sere;° and the lady shall
say her mind freely, or the blank verse shall halt for 't.° What players are
they?

ROSENCRANTZ: Even those you were wont to take delight in, the tragedians of   295
the city.

HAMLET: How chances it they travel? their residence,° both in reputation and
profit, was better both ways.

ROSENCRANTZ: I think their inhibition° comes by the means of the late innovation.°   300

HAMLET: Do they hold the same estimation they did when I was in the city? are
they so followed?

ROSENCRANTZ: No, indeed, are they not.

HAMLET: How° comes it? do they grow rusty?

---

271 prevent your discovery: Forestall your disclosure.   **276 fretted:** Adorned.   **279 faculties:** Capacity;   **express:** Well-framed (?), exact (?).   **280 apprehension:** Understanding.
281 quintessence: The fifth essence of ancient philosophy, supposed to be the substance of
the heavenly bodies and to be latent in all things.   **286 lenten:** Meager.   **287 coted:** Overtook and passed beyond.   **290 foil and target:** Sword and shield.   **291 humorous man:**
Actor who takes the part of the humor characters.   **292 tickle o' the sere:** Easy on the trigger.
292–293 the lady . . . for 't: The lady (fond of talking) shall have opportunity to talk, blank
verse or no blank verse.   **297 residence:** Remaining in one place.   **299 inhibition:** Formal
prohibition (from acting plays in the city or, possibly, at court).   **299–300 innovation:** The
new fashion in satirical plays performed by boy actors in the "private" theaters.   **304–322
How . . . load:** The passage is the famous one dealing with the War of the Theatres (1599–1602);
namely, the rivalry between the children's companies and the adult actors.

ROSENCRANTZ: Nay, their endeavour keeps in the wonted pace: but there is,   305
sir, an aery° of children, little eyases,° that cry out on the top of question,°
and are most tyrannically° clapped for 't: these are now the fashion, and so
berattle° the common stages°—so they call them—that many wearing
rapiers° are afraid of goose-quills° and dare scarce come thither.

HAMLET: What, are they children? who maintains 'em? how are they escoted?°   310
Will they pursue the quality° no longer than they can sing?° will they not say
afterwards, if they should grow themselves to common° players—as it is most
like, if their means are no better—their writers do them wrong, to make
them exclaim against their own succession?°

ROSENCRANTZ: 'Faith, there has been much to do on both sides; and the nation   315
holds it no sin to tarre° them to controversy: there was, for a while, no money
bid for argument,° unless the poet and the player went to cuffs° in the
question.°

HAMLET: Is 't possible?

GUILDENSTERN: O, there has been much throwing about of brains.   320

HAMLET: Do the boys carry it away?°

ROSENCRANTZ: Ay, that they do, my lord; Hercules and his load° too.

HAMLET: It is not very strange; for my uncle is king of Denmark, and those that
would make mows° at him while my father lived, give twenty, forty, fifty, a
hundred ducats° a-piece for his picture in little.° 'Sblood, there is something   325
in this more than natural, if philosophy could find it out.

A flourish [of trumpets within].

GUILDENSTERN: There are the players.

HAMLET: Gentlemen, you are welcome to Elsinore. Your hands, come then:
the appurtenance of welcome is fashion and ceremony: let me comply° with
you in this garb,° lest my extent° to the players, which, I tell you, must show   330
fairly outwards, should more appear like entertainment than yours. You are
welcome: but my uncle-father and aunt-mother are deceived.

GUILDENSTERN: In what, my dear lord?

HAMLET: I am but mad north-north-west:° when the wind is southerly I know a
hawk from a handsaw.°   335

306 **aery:** Nest;   **eyases:** Young hawks;   **cry . . . question:** Speak in a high key dominating conversation; clamor forth the height of controversy; probably "excel"; perhaps intended to decry leaders of
the dramatic profession.   307 **tyrannically:** Outrageously.   308 **berattle:** Berate;   **common
stages:** Public theaters.   308–309 **many wearing rapiers:** Many men of fashion, who were afraid
to patronize the common players for fear of being satirized by the poets who wrote for the children.
309 **goose-quills:** I.e., pens of satirists.   310 **escoted:** Maintained.   311 **quality:** Acting profession;   **no longer . . . sing:** I.e., until their voices change.   312 **common:** Regular, adult.
314 **succession:** Future careers.   316 **tarre:** Set on (as dogs).   317 **argument:** Probably, plot for
a play;   **went to cuffs:** Came to blows.   318 **question:** Controversy.   321 **carry it away:** Win the
day.   322 **Hercules . . . load:** Regarded as an allusion to the sign of the Globe Theatre, which was
Hercules bearing the world on his shoulder.   324 **mows:** Grimaces.   325 **ducats:** Gold coins
worth 9s. 4d;   **in little:** In miniature.   329 **comply:** Observe the formalities of courtesy.
330 **garb:** Manner;   **extent:** Showing of kindness.   334 **I am . . . north-north-west:** I am only
partly mad, i.e., in only one point of the compass.   335 **handsaw:** A proposed reading of *hernshaw*
would mean "heron"; *handsaw* may be an early corruption of *hernshaw*. Another view regards *hawk*
as the variant of *hack*, a tool of the pickax type, and *handsaw* as a saw operated by hand.

Enter Polonius.

POLONIUS: Well be with you, gentlemen!

HAMLET: Hark you, Guildenstern; and you too: at each ear a hearer: that great
baby you see there is not yet out of his swaddling-clouts.°

ROSENCRANTZ: Happily he is the second time come to them; for they say an old
man is twice a child.   340

HAMLET: I will prophesy he comes to tell me of the players; mark it. — You say
right, sir: o' Monday morning;° 'twas then indeed.

POLONIUS: My lord, I have news to tell you.

HAMLET: My lord, I have news to tell you. When Roscius° was an actor in
Rome, —   345

POLONIUS: The actors are come hither, my lord.

HAMLET: Buz, buz!°

POLONIUS: Upon my honour, —

HAMLET: Then came each actor on his ass, —

POLONIUS: The best actors in the world, either for tragedy, comedy, history,   350
pastoral, pastoral-comical, historical-pastoral, tragical-historical, tragical-
comical-historical-pastoral, scene individable,° or poem unlimited:° Seneca°
cannot be too heavy, nor Plautus° too light. For the law of writ and the
liberty,° these are the only men.

HAMLET: O Jephthah, judge of Israel,° what a treasure hadst thou!   355

POLONIUS: What a treasure had he, my lord?

HAMLET: Why,
"One fair daughter, and no more,
    The which he loved passing well."

POLONIUS [*aside*]:   Still on my daughter.   360

HAMLET: Am I not i' the right, old Jephthah?

POLONIUS: If you call me Jephthah, my lord, I have a daughter that I love
passing° well.

HAMLET: Nay, that follows not.

POLONIUS: What follows, then, my lord?   365

HAMLET: Why,
"As by lot, God wot,"
and then, you know,
"It came to pass, as most like° it was," —
the first row° of the pious chanson° will show you more; for look, where my   370
abridgement comes.°

---

338 swaddling-clouts: Cloths in which to wrap a newborn baby.   **342 o' Monday morning:**
Said to mislead Polonius.   **344 Roscius:** A famous Roman actor.   **347 Buz, buz:** An interjec-
tion used at Oxford to denote stale news.   **352 scene individable:** A play observing the unity of
place;   **poem unlimited:** A play disregarding the unities of time and place;   **Seneca:** Writer of
Latin tragedies, model of early Elizabethan writers of tragedy.   **353 Plautus:** Writer of Latin comedy.   **353–354 law . . . liberty:** Pieces written according to rules and without rules, i.e., "classical"
and "romantic" dramas.   **355 Jephthah . . . Israel:** Jephthah had to sacrifice his daughter; see
Judges 11.   **363 passing:** Surpassingly.   **369 like:** Probable.   **370 row:** Stanza;   **chanson:**
Ballad.   **371 abridgement comes:** Opportunity comes for cutting short the conversation.

Enter the Players.

You are welcome, masters; welcome, all. I am glad to see thee well. Welcome,
good friends. O, old friend! why, thy face is valanced° since I saw thee last:
comest thou to beard me in Denmark? What, my young lady and mistress!
By'r lady, your ladyship is nearer to heaven than when I saw you last, by the   375
altitude of a chopine.° Pray God, your voice, like a piece of uncurrent° gold,
be not cracked within the ring.° Masters, you are all welcome. We'll e'en to 't
like French falconers, fly at any thing we see: we'll have a speech straight:
come, give us a taste of your quality; come, a passionate speech.

FIRST PLAYER: What speech, my good lord?   380

HAMLET: I heard thee speak me a speech once, but it was never acted; or, if it
was, not above once; for the play, I remember, pleased not the million; 'twas
caviary to the general:° but it was — as I received it, and others, whose judgements in such matters cried in the top of° mine — an excellent play, well
digested in the scenes, set down with as much modesty as cunning.° I remem-   385
ber, one said there were no sallets° in the lines to make the matter savoury,
nor no matter in the phrase that might indict° the author of affectation; but
called it an honest method, as wholesome as sweet, and by very much more
handsome than fine.° One speech in 't I chiefly loved: 'twas Æneas' tale to
Dido;° and thereabout of it especially, where he speaks of Priam's slaughter: if 390
it live in your memory, begin at this line: let me see, let me see —
"The rugged Pyrrhus,° like th' Hyrcanian beast,"° —
'tis not so: — it begins with Pyrrhus: —
"The rugged Pyrrhus, he whose sable arms,
Black as his purpose, did the night resemble   395
When he lay couched in the ominous horse,°
Hath now this dread and black complexion smear'd
With heraldry more dismal; head to foot
Now is he total gules;° horridly trick'd°
With blood of fathers, mothers, daughters, sons,   400
Bak'd and impasted° with the parching streets,
That lend a tyrannous and a damned light
To their lord's murder: roasted in wrath and fire,

---

373 **valanced:** Fringed (with a beard).   376 **chopine:** Kind of shoe raised by the thickness of
the heel; worn in Italy, particularly at Venice;   **uncurrent:** Not passable as lawful coinage.
377 **cracked within the ring:** In the center of coins were rings enclosing the sovereign's head;
if the coin was cracked within this ring, it was unfit for currency.   383 **caviary to the general:**
Not relished by the multitude.   384 **cried in the top of:** Spoke with greater authority than.
385 **cunning:** Skill.   386 **sallets:** Salads: here, spicy improprieties.   387 **indict:** Convict.
388–389 **as wholesome . . . fine:** Its beauty was not that of elaborate ornament, but that of
order and proportion.   389–390 **Æneas' tale to Dido:** The lines recited by the player are imitated from Marlowe and Nashe's *Dido Queen of Carthage* (2.1.214 ff.). They are written in such
a way that the conventionality of the play within a play is raised above that of ordinary drama.
392 **Pyrrhus:** A Greek hero in the Trojan War;   **Hyrcanian beast:** The tiger; see Virgil,
Aeneid, 4.266.   396 **ominous horse:** Trojan horse.   399 **gules:** Red, a heraldic term;
trick'd: Spotted, smeared.   401 **impasted:** Made into a paste.

And thus o'er-sized° with coagulate gore,
With eyes like carbuncles, the hellish Pyrrhus   405
Old grandsire Priam seeks."
So, proceed you.

POLONIUS: 'Fore God, my lord, well spoken, with good accent and good discretion.

FIRST PLAYER: "Anon he finds him   410
Striking too short at Greeks; his antique sword,
Rebellious to his arm, lies where it falls,
Repugnant° to command: unequal match'd,
Pyrrhus at Priam drives; in rage strikes wide;
But with the whiff and wind of his fell sword   415
Th' unnerved father falls. Then senseless Ilium,°
Seeming to feel this blow, with flaming top
Stoops to his base, and with a hideous crash
Takes prisoner Pyrrhus' ear: for, lo! his sword
Which was declining on the milky head   420
Of reverend Priam, seem'd i' th' air to stick:
So, as a painted tyrant,° Pyrrhus stood,
And like a neutral to his will and matter,°
Did nothing.
But, as we often see, against° some storm,   425
A silence in the heavens, the rack° stand still,
The bold winds speechless and the orb below
As hush as death, anon the dreadful thunder
Doth rend the region,° so, after Pyrrhus' pause,
Aroused vengeance sets him new a-work;   430
And never did the Cyclops' hammers fall
On Mars's armour forg'd for proof eterne°
With less remorse than Pyrrhus' bleeding sword
Now falls on Priam.
Out, out, thou strumpet, Fortune! All you gods,   435
In general synod,° take away her power;
Break all the spokes and fellies° from her wheel,
And bowl the round nave° down the hill of heaven,
As low as to the fiends!"

POLONIUS: This is too long.   440

HAMLET: It shall to the barber's, with your beard. Prithee, say on: he's for a jig°
or a tale of bawdry,° or he sleeps: say on: come to Hecuba.°

FIRST PLAYER: "But who, ah woe! had seen the mobled° queen—"

---

404 o'er-sized: Covered as with size or glue.   **413 Repugnant:** Disobedient.   **416 Then senseless Ilium:** Insensate Troy.   **422 painted tyrant:** Tyrant in a picture.   **423 matter:** Task.   **425
against:** Before.   **426 rack:** Mass of clouds.   **429 region:** Assembly.   **432 proof eterne:** External resistance to assault.   **436 synod:** Assembly.   **437 fellies:** Pieces of wood forming the rim of
a wheel.   **438 nave:** Hub.   **441 jig:** Comic performance given at the end or in an interval of a
play.   **442 bawdry:** Indecency;   **Hecuba:** Wife of Priam, king of Troy.   **443 mobled:** Muffled.

HAMLET: "The mobled queen?"

POLONIUS: That's good; "mobled queen" is good.   445

FIRST PLAYER: "Run barefoot up and down, threat'ning the flames
    With bisson rheum;° a clout° upon that head
    Where late the diadem stood, and for a robe,
    About her lank and all o'er-teemed° loins,
    A blanket, in the alarm of fear caught up;   450
    Who this had seen, with tongue in venom steep'd,
    'Gainst Fortune's state would treason have pronounc'd:°
    But if the gods themselves did see her then
    When she saw Pyrrhus make malicious sport
    In mincing with his sword her husband's limbs,   455
    The instant burst of clamour that she made,
    Unless things mortal move them not at all,
    Would have made milch° the burning eyes of heaven,
    And passion in the gods."

POLONIUS: Look, whe'r he has not turned° his colour and has tears in 's eyes.   460
    Prithee, no more.

HAMLET: 'Tis well; I'll have thee speak out the rest soon. Good my lord, will you
see the players well bestowed? Do you hear, let them be well used; for they
are the abstract° and brief chronicles of the time: after your death you were
better have a bad epitaph than their ill report while you live.   465

POLONIUS: My lord, I will use them according to their desert.

HAMLET: God's bodykins,° man, much better: use every man after his desert,
and who shall 'scape whipping? Use them after your own honour and dignity: the less they deserve, the more merit is in your bounty. Take them in.

POLONIUS: Come, sirs.   470

HAMLET: Follow him, friends: we'll hear a play tomorrow. *[Aside to First Player.]*
    Dost thou hear me, old friend; can you play the Murder of Gonzago?

FIRST PLAYER: Ay, my lord.

HAMLET: We'll ha 't to-morrow night. You could, for a need, study a speech of
some dozen or sixteen lines,° which I would set down and insert in 't, could   475
you not?

FIRST PLAYER: Ay, my lord.

HAMLET: Very well. Follow that lord; and look you mock him not. — My good
    friends, I'll leave you till night: you are welcome to Elsinore.
                                     Exeunt Polonius and Players.

ROSENCRANTZ: Good my lord!   *Exeunt [Rosencrantz and Guildenstern.]*   480

HAMLET: Ay, so, God bye to you. — Now I am alone.
    O, what a rogue and peasant° slave am I!

---

447 bisson rheum: Blinding tears; **clout:** Piece of cloth. **449 o'er-teemed:** Worn out with
bearing children. **452 pronounc'd:** Proclaimed. **458 milch:** Moist with tears. **460 turned:**
Changed. **464 abstract:** Summary account. **467 bodykins:** Diminutive form of the oath
"by God's body." **475 dozen or sixteen lines:** Critics have amused themselves by trying to
locate Hamlet's lines. Lucianus's speech 3.2.222–227 is the best guess. **482 peasant:** Base.

Is it not monstrous that this player here,
But in a fiction, in a dream of passion,
Could force his soul so to his own conceit   485
That from her working all his visage wann'd,°
Tears in his eyes, distraction in 's aspect,
A broken voice, and his whole function suiting
With forms to his conceit?° and all for nothing!
For Hecuba!   490
What's Hecuba to him, or he to Hecuba,
That he should weep for her? What would he do,
Had he the motive and the cue for passion
That I have? He would drown the stage with tears
And cleave the general ear with horrid speech,   495
Make mad the guilty and appall the free,
Confound the ignorant, and amaze indeed
The very faculties of eyes and ears.
Yet I,
A dull and muddy-mettled° rascal, peak,°   500
Like John-a-dreams,° unpregnant of° my cause,
And can say nothing; no, not for a king.
Upon whose property° and most dear life
A damn'd defeat was made. Am I a coward?
Who calls me villain? breaks my pate across?   505
Plucks off my beard, and blows it in my face?
Tweaks me by the nose? gives me the lie i' th' throat,
As deep as to the lungs? who does me this?
Ha!
'Swounds, I should take it: for it cannot be   510
But I am pigeon-liver'd° and lack gall
To make oppression bitter, or ere this
I should have fatted all the region kites°
With this slave's offal: bloody, bawdy villain!
Remorseless, treacherous, lecherous, kindless° villain!   515
O, vengeance!
Why, what an ass am I! This is most brave,
That I, the son of a dear father murder'd,
Prompted to my revenge by heaven and hell,
Must, like a whore, unpack my heart with words,   520

---

486 wann'd: Grew pale. **488–489 his whole ... conceit:** His whole being responded
with forms to suit his thought. **500 muddy-mettled:** Dull-spirited; **peak:** Mope, pine.
501 John-a-dreams: An expression occurring elsewhere in Elizabethan literature to indicate a
dreamer; **unpregnant of:** Not quickened by. **503 property:** Proprietorship (of crown and
life). **511 pigeon-liver'd:** The pigeon was supposed to secrete no gall; if Hamlet, so he says,
had had gall, he would have felt the bitterness of oppression, and avenged it. **513 region
kites:** Kites of the air. **515 kindless:** Unnatural.

And fall a-cursing, like a very drab,°
A stallion!°
Fie upon 't! foh! About,° my brains! Hum, I have heard
That guilty creatures sitting at a play
Have by the very cunning of the scene   525
Been struck so to the soul that presently
They have proclaim'd their malefactions;
For murder, though it have no tongue, will speak
With most miraculous organ. I'll have these players
Play something like the murder of my father   530
Before mine uncle: I'll observe his looks:
I'll tent° him to the quick: if 'a do blench,°
I know my course. The spirit that I have seen
May be the devil:° and the devil hath power
T' assume a pleasing shape; yea, and perhaps   535
Out of my weakness and my melancholy,
As he is very potent with such spirits,°
Abuses me to damn me: I'll have grounds
More relative° than this:° the play's the thing
Wherein I'll catch the conscience of the king.   *Exit.*   540

[ACT 3, Scene 1]

[A room in the castle.]
Enter King, Queen, Polonius, Ophelia, Rosencrantz, Guildenstern, Lords.

KING: And can you, by no drift of conference,°
Get from him why he puts on this confusion,
Grating so harshly all his days of quiet
With turbulent and dangerous lunacy?
ROSENCRANTZ: He does confess he feels himself distracted;   5
But from what cause 'a will by no means speak.
GUILDENSTERN: Nor do we find him forward° to be sounded,
But, with a crafty madness, keeps aloof,
When we would bring him on to some confession
Of his true state.
QUEEN: Did he receive you well?   10
ROSENCRANTZ: Most like a gentleman.
GUILDENSTERN: But with much forcing of his disposition.°

---

521 **drab:** Prostitute.   522 **stallion:** Prostitute (male or female).   523 **About:** About it,
or turn thou right about.   532 **tent:** Probe;   **blench:** Quail, flinch.   534 **May be the
devil:** Hamlet's suspicion is properly grounded in the belief of the time.   537 **spirits:** Humors.
539 **relative:** Closely related, definite;   **this:** I.e., the ghost's story.   ACT 3, SCENE 1.   1 **drift
of conference:** Device of conversation.   7 **forward:** Willing.   12 **forcing of his disposition:**
I.e., against his will.

ROSENCRANTZ: Niggard of question;° but, of our demands,
    Most free in his reply.
QUEEN: Did you assay° him
    To any pastime?   15
ROSENCRANTZ: Madam, it so fell out, that certain players
    We o'er-raught° on the way: of these we told him;
    And there did seem in him a kind of joy
    To hear of it: they are here about the court,
    And, as I think, they have already order   20
    This night to play before him.
POLONIUS: 'Tis most true:
    And he beseech'd me to entreat your majesties
    To hear and see the matter.
KING: With all my heart; and it doth much content me
    To hear him so inclin'd.   25
    Good gentlemen, give him a further edge,°
    And drive his purpose into these delights.
ROSENCRANTZ: We shall, my lord.   *Exeunt Rosencrantz and Guildenstern.*
KING: Sweet Gertrude, leave us too;
    For we have closely° sent for Hamlet hither,
    That he, as 'twere by accident, may here   30
    Affront° Ophelia:
    Her father and myself, lawful espials,°
    Will so bestow ourselves that, seeing, unseen,
    We may of their encounter frankly judge,
    And gather by him, as he is behav'd,   35
    If 't be th' affliction of his love or no
    That thus he suffers for.
QUEEN: I shall obey you.
    And for your part, Ophelia, I do wish
    That your good beauties be the happy cause
    Of Hamlet's wildness:° so shall I hope your virtues   40
    Will bring him to his wonted way again,
    To both your honours.
OPHELIA: Madam, I wish it may.   *[Exit Queen.]*
POLONIUS: Ophelia, walk you here. Gracious,° so please you,
    We will bestow ourselves. *[To Ophelia.]* Read on this book;
    That show of such an exercise° may colour°   45
    Your loneliness. We are oft to blame in this,—
    'Tis too much prov'd—that with devotion's visage

---

13 Niggard of question: Sparing of conversation.   **14 assay:** Try to win.   **17 o'er-raught:** Overtook.   **26 edge:** Incitement.   **29 closely:** Secretly.   **31 Affront:** Confront.   **32 lawful espials:** Legitimate spies.   **40 wildness:** Madness.   **43 Gracious:** Your grace (addressed to the king).   **45 exercise:** Act of devotion (the book she reads is one of devotion); **colour:** Give a plausible appearance to.

And pious action we do sugar o'er
The devil himself.

KING: *[aside]* O, 'tis too true!
How smart a lash that speech doth give my conscience!   50
The harlot's cheek, beautied with plast'ring art,
Is not more ugly to° the thing° that helps it
Than is my deed to my most painted word:
O heavy burthen!

POLONIUS: I hear him coming: let's withdraw, my lord.   55

[Exeunt King and Polonius.]

Enter Hamlet.

HAMLET: To be, or not to be: that is the question:
Whether 'tis nobler in the mind to suffer
The slings and arrows of outrageous fortune,
Or to take arms against a sea° of troubles,
And by opposing end them? To die: to sleep;   60
No more; and by a sleep to say we end
The heart-ache and the thousand natural shocks
That flesh is heir to, 'tis a consummation
Devoutly to be wish'd. To die, to sleep;
To sleep: perchance to dream: ay, there's the rub;   65
For in that sleep of death what dreams may come
When we have shuffled° off this mortal coil,°
Must give us pause: there's the respect°
That makes calamity of so long life;°
For who would bear the whips and scorns of time,°   70
Th' oppressor's wrong, the proud man's contumely,
The pangs of despis'd° love, the law's delay,
The insolence of office° and the spurns°
That patient merit of th' unworthy takes,
When he himself might his quietus° make   75
With a bare bodkin?° who would fardels° bear,
To grunt and sweat under a weary life,
But that the dread of something after death,
The undiscover'd country from whose bourn°
No traveller returns, puzzles the will   80
And makes us rather bear those ills we have

---

52 to: Compared to; **thing:** I.e., the cosmetic. **59 sea:** The mixed metaphor of this speech has often been commented on; a later emendation *siege* has sometimes been spoken on the stage. **67 shuffled:** Sloughed, cast; **coil:** Usually means "turmoil"; here, possibly "body" (conceived of as wound about the soul like rope); *clay, soil, veil,* have been suggested as emendations. **68 respect:** Consideration. **69 of . . . life:** So long-lived. **70 time:** The world. **72 despis'd:** Rejected. **73 office:** Office-holders; **spurns:** Insults. **75 quietus:** Acquittance; here, death. **76 bare bodkin:** Mere dagger; *bare* is sometimes understood as "unsheathed"; **fardels:** Burdens. **79 bourn:** Boundary.

Than fly to others that we know not of?
Thus conscience° does make cowards of us all;
And thus the native hue° of resolution
Is sicklied o'er° with the pale cast° of thought,   85
And enterprises of great pitch° and moment°
With this regard° their currents° turn awry,
And lose the name of action—Soft you now!
The fair Ophelia! Nymph, in thy orisons°
Be all my sins rememb'red.

OPHELIA: Good my lord,   90
How does your honour for this many a day?

HAMLET: I humbly thank you; well, well, well.

OPHELIA: My lord, I have remembrances of yours,
That I have longed long to re-deliver;
I pray you, now receive them.

HAMLET: No, not I;   95
I never gave you aught.

OPHELIA: My honour'd lord, you know right well you did;
And, with them, words of so sweet breath compos'd
As made the things more rich: their perfume lost,
Take these again; for to the noble mind   100
Rich gifts wax poor when givers prove unkind.
There, my lord.

HAMLET: Ha, ha! are you honest?°

OPHELIA: My lord?

HAMLET: Are you fair?   105

OPHELIA: What means your lordship?

HAMLET: That if you be honest and fair, your honesty° should admit no discourse to° your beauty.

OPHELIA: Could beauty, my lord, have better commerce° than with honesty?

HAMLET: Ay, truly; for the power of beauty will sooner transform honesty from   110
what it is to a bawd than the force of honesty can translate beauty into his
likeness: this was sometime a paradox, but now the time° gives it proof. I did
love you once.

OPHELIA: Indeed, my lord, you made me believe so.

HAMLET: You should not have believed me; for virtue cannot so inoculate° our   115
old stock but we shall relish of it:° I loved you not.

---

83 **conscience:** Probably, inhibition by the faculty of reason restraining the will from doing
wrong.   84 **native hue:** Natural color; metaphor derived from the color of the face.   85 **sicklied o'er:** Given a sickly tinge;   **cast:** Shade of color.   86 **pitch:** Height (as of a falcon's flight);
moment: Importance.   87 **regard:** Respect, consideration;   **currents:** Courses.   89 **orisons:**
Prayers.   103–108 **are you honest . . . beauty:** *Honest* meaning "truthful" and "chaste" and
fair meaning "just, honorable" (line 105) and "beautiful" (line 107) are not mere quibbles; the
speech has the irony of a *double entendre.*   107 **your honesty:** Your chastity.   107–108 **discourse to:** Familiar intercourse with.   109 **commerce:** Intercourse.   112 **the time:** The present age.   115 **inoculate:** Graft (metaphorical).   116 **but . . . it:** I.e., that we do not still
have about us a taste of the old stock; i.e., retain our sinfulness.

OPHELIA: I was the more deceived.

HAMLET: Get thee to a nunnery: why wouldst thou be a breeder of sinners? I am myself indifferent honest;° but yet I could accuse me of such things that it were better my mother had not borne me: I am very proud, revengeful, ambitious, with more offences at my beck° than I have thoughts to put them in, imagination to give them shape, or time to act them in. What should such fellows as I do crawling between earth and heaven? We are arrant knaves, all; believe none of us. Go thy ways to a nunnery. Where's your father? 120

125

OPHELIA: At home, my lord.

HAMLET: Let the doors be shut upon him, that he may play the fool no where but in 's own house. Farewell.

OPHELIA: O, help him, you sweet heavens!

HAMLET: If thou dost marry, I'll give thee this plague for thy dowry: be thou as chaste as ice, as pure as snow, thou shalt not escape calumny. Get thee to a nunnery, go: farewell. Or, if thou wilt needs marry, marry a fool; for wise men know well enough what monsters° you make of them. To a nunnery, go, and quickly too. Farewell. 130

OPHELIA: O heavenly powers, restore him! 135

HAMLET: I have heard of your° paintings too, well enough; God hath given you one face, and you make yourselves another: you jig,° you amble, and you lisp; you nick-name God's creatures, and make your wantonness your ignorance.° Go to, I'll no more on 't; it hath made me mad. I say, we will have no moe marriage: those that are married already, all but one,° shall live; the rest shall keep as they are. To a nunnery, go.   *Exit.* 140

OPHELIA: O, what a noble mind is here o'er-thrown!
The courtier's, soldier's, scholar's, eye, tongue, sword;
Th' expectancy and rose° of the fair state,
The glass of fashion and the mould of form,°
Th' observ'd of all observers,° quite, quite down!
And I, of ladies most deject and wretched,
That suck'd the honey of his music vows,
Now see that noble and most sovereign reason,
Like sweet bells jangled, out of time and harsh;
That unmatch'd form and feature of blown° youth
Blasted with ecstasy:° O, woe is me,
T' have seen what I have seen, see what I see! 145

150

---

119 **indifferent honest:** Moderately virtuous.   121 **beck:** Command.   133 **monsters:** An allusion to the horns of a cuckold.   136 **your:** Indefinite use.   137 **jig:** Move with jerky motion; probably allusion to the *jig*, or song and dance, of the current stage.   138–139 **make . . . ignorance:** I.e., excuse your wantonness on the ground of your ignorance.   140 **one:** I.e., the king.   144 **expectancy and rose:** Source of hope.   145 **The glass . . . form:** The mirror of fashion and the pattern of courtly behavior.   146 **observ'd . . . observers:** I.e., the center of attention in the court.   151 **blown:** Blooming.   152 **ecstasy:** Madness.

Enter King and Polonius.

KING: Love! his affections do not that way tend;
Nor what he spake, though it lack'd form a little,   155
Was not like madness. There's something in his soul,
O'er which his melancholy sits on brood;
And I do doubt° the hatch and the disclose°
Will be some danger: which for to prevent,
I have in quick determination   160
Thus set it down: he shall with speed to England,
For the demand of our neglected tribute:
Haply the seas and countries different
With variable° objects shall expel
This something-settled° matter in his heart,   165
Whereon his brains still beating puts him thus
From fashion of himself.° What think you on 't?

POLONIUS: It shall do well: but yet do I believe
The origin and commencement of his grief
Sprung from neglected love. How now, Ophelia!   170
You need not tell us what Lord Hamlet said;
We heard it all. My lord, do as you please;
But, if you hold it fit, after the play
Let his queen mother all alone entreat him
To show his grief: let her be round° with him;   175
And I'll be plac'd, so please you, in the ear
Of all their conference. If she find him not,
To England send him, or confine him where
Your wisdom best shall think.

KING: It shall be so: 180
Madness in great ones must not unwatch'd go.   *Exeunt.*

[Scene 2]

[A hall in the castle.]
Enter Hamlet and three of the Players.

HAMLET: Speak the speech, I pray you, as I pronounced it to you, trippingly on the tongue: but if you mouth it, as many of your° players do, I had as lief the town-crier spoke my lines. Nor do not saw the air too much with your hand, thus, but use all gently; for in the very torrent, tempest, and, as I may say, whirlwind of your passion, you must acquire and beget a temperance that   5
may give it smoothness. O, it offends me to the soul to hear a robustious° periwig-pated° fellow tear a passion to tatters, to very rags, to split the ears of

158 **doubt:** Fear;   **disclose:** Disclosure or revelation (by chipping of the shell).   **164 variable:** Various.   **165 something-settled:** Somewhat settled.   **167 From . . . himself:** Out of his natural manner.   **175 round:** Blunt.   SCENE 2. **2 your:** Indefinite use.   **6 robustious:** Violent, boisterous.   **7 periwig-pated:** Wearing a wig.

the groundlings,° who for the most part are capable of° nothing but inexplic-
able° dumb-shows and noise: I would have such a fellow whipped for o'er-
doing Termagant;° it out-herods Herod:° pray you, avoid it.   10

FIRST PLAYER: I warrant your honour.

HAMLET: Be not too tame neither, but let your own discretion be your tutor: suit
the action to the word, the word to the action; with this special observance,
that you o'er-step not the modesty of nature: for any thing so overdone is
from the purpose of playing, whose end, both at the first and now, was and is,   15
to hold, as 't were, the mirror up to nature; to show virtue her own feature,
scorn her own image, and the very age and body of the time his form and
pressure.° Now this overdone, or come tardy off,° though it make the unskil-
ful laugh, cannot but make the judicious grieve; the censure of the which
one° must in your allowance o'erweigh a whole theatre of others. O, there be   20
players that I have seen play, and heard others praise, and that highly, not to
speak it profanely, that, neither having the accent of Christians nor the gait
of Christian, pagan, nor man, have so strutted and bellowed that I have
thought some of nature's journeymen° had made men and not made them
well, they imitated humanity so abominably.   25

FIRST PLAYER: I hope we have reformed that indifferently° with us, sir.

HAMLET: O, reform it altogether. And let those that play your clowns speak no
more than is set down for them; for there be of° them that will themselves
laugh, to set on some quantity of barren° spectators to laugh too; though, in
the mean time, some necessary question of the play be then to be consid-   30
ered: that's villanous, and shows a most pitiful ambition in the fool that uses
it. Go, make you ready.   *[Exeunt Players.]*

Enter Polonius, Guildenstern, and Rosencrantz.

How now, my lord! will the king hear this piece of work?

POLONIUS: And the queen too, and that presently.

HAMLET: Bid the players make haste.   *[Exit Polonius.]*   35
Will you two help to hasten them?

ROSENCRANTZ: ⎫
                    ⎬ We will, my lord.   *Exeunt they two.*
GUILDENSTERN: ⎭

HAMLET: What ho! Horatio!

Enter Horatio.

HORATIO: Here, sweet lord, at your service.

---

8 **groundlings:** Those who stood in the yard of the theater;   **capable of:** Susceptible of being
influenced by.   8–9 **inexplicable:** Of no significance worth explaining.   10 **Termagant:** A
god of the Saracens; a character in the St. Nicholas play, where one of his worshipers, leaving
him in charge of goods, returns to find them stolen; whereupon he beats the god (or idol), which
howls vociferously;   **Herod:** Herod of Jewry; a character in *The Slaughter of the Innocents* and
other cycle plays. The part was played with great noise and fury.   18 **pressure:** Stamp,
impressed character;   **come tardy off:** Inadequately done.   19–20 **the censure . . . one:** The
judgment of even one of whom.   24 **journeymen:** Laborers not yet masters in their trade.
26 **indifferently:** Fairly, tolerably.   28 **of:** I.e., some among them.   29 **barren:** I.e., of wit.

HAMLET: Horatio, thou art e'en as just° a man
    As e'er my conversation cop'd withal.   40
HORATIO: O, my dear lord, —
HAMLET: Nay, do not think I flatter;
    For what advancement may I hope from thee
    That no revenue hast but thy good spirits,
    To feed and clothe thee? Why should the poor be flatter'd?
    No, let the candied tongue lick absurd pomp,   45
    And crook the pregnant° hinges of the knee
    Where thrift° may follow fawning. Dost thou hear?
    Since my dear soul was mistress of her choice
    And could of men distinguish her election,
    S' hath seal'd thee for herself; for thou hast been   50
    As one, in suff'ring all, that suffers nothing,
    A man that fortune's buffets and rewards
    Hast ta'en with equal thanks: and blest are those
    Whose blood and judgement are so well commeddled,
    That they are not a pipe for fortune's finger   55
    To sound what stop° she please. Give me that man
    That is not passion's slave, and I will wear him
    In my heart's core, ay, in my heart of heart,
    As I do thee. — Something too much of this. —
    There is a play to-night before the king;   60
    One scene of it comes near the circumstance
    Which I have told thee of my father's death:
    I prithee, when thou seest that act afoot,
    Even with the very comment of thy soul°
    Observe my uncle: if his occulted° guilt   65
    Do not itself unkennel in one speech,
    It is a damned° ghost that we have seen,
    And my imaginations are as foul
    As Vulcan's stithy.° Give him heedful note;
    For I mine eyes will rivet to his face,   70
    And after we will both our judgements join
    In censure of his seeming.°
HORATIO: Well, my lord:
    If 'a steal aught the whilst this play is playing,
    And 'scape detecting, I will pay the theft.

Enter trumpets and kettledrums, King, Queen, Polonius, Ophelia, [Rosencrantz, Guildenstern, and others].

---

39 just: Honest, honorable.   **46 pregnant:** Pliant.   **47 thrift:** Profit.   **56 stop:** Hole in a wind instrument for controlling the sound.   **64 very . . . soul:** Inward and sagacious criticism. **65 occulted:** Hidden.   **67 damned:** In league with Satan.   **69 stithy:** Smithy, place of *stiths* (anvils).   **72 censure . . . seeming:** Judgment of his appearance or behavior.

HAMLET: They are coming to the play; I must be idle:° Get you a place. 75
KING: How fares our cousin Hamlet?
HAMLET: Excellent, i' faith; of the chameleon's dish:° I eat the air, promise-crammed: you cannot feed capons so.
KING: I have nothing with° this answer, Hamlet; these words are not mine.°
HAMLET: No, nor mine now. *[To Polonius.]* My lord, you played once i' the uni- 80
versity, you say?
POLONIUS: That did I, my lord; and was accounted a good actor.
HAMLET: What did you enact?
POLONIUS: I did enact Julius Cæsar: I was killed i' the Capitol; Brutus killed me.
HAMLET: It was a brute part of him to kill so capital a calf there. Be the players 85
ready?
ROSENCRANTZ: Ay, my lord; they stay upon your patience.
QUEEN: Come hither, my dear Hamlet, sit by me.
HAMLET: No, good mother, here's metal more attractive.
POLONIUS *[to the king]*: O, ho! do you mark that? 90
HAMLET: Lady, shall I lie in your lap?   *[Lying down at Ophelia's feet.]*
OPHELIA: No, my lord.
HAMLET: I mean, my head upon your lap?
OPHELIA: Ay, my lord.
HAMLET: Do you think I meant country° matters? 95
OPHELIA: I think nothing, my lord.
HAMLET: That's a fair thought to lie between maids' legs.
OPHELIA: What is, my lord?
HAMLET: Nothing.
OPHELIA: You are merry, my lord. 100
HAMLET: Who, I?
OPHELIA: Ay, my lord.
HAMLET: O God, your only° jig-maker.° What should a man do but be merry?
for, look you, how cheerfully my mother looks, and my father died within's
two hours. 105
OPHELIA: Nay, 'tis twice two months, my lord.
HAMLET: So long? Nay then, let the devil wear black, for I'll have a suit of
sables.° O heavens! die two months ago, and not forgotten yet? Then there's
hope a great man's memory may outlive his life half a year: but, by 'r lady, 'a
must build churches, then; or else shall 'a suffer not thinking on,° with the 110
hobbyhorse, whose epitaph is "For, O, for, O, the hobbyhorse is forgot."°

The trumpets sound. Dumb show follows.

---

75 idle: Crazy, or not attending to anything serious. **77 chameleon's dish:** Chameleons
were supposed to feed on air. (Hamlet deliberately misinterprets the king's "fares" as "feeds.")
79 have . . . with: Make nothing of; **are not mine:** Do not respond to what I ask. **95 country:** With a bawdy pun. **103 your only:** Only your; **jig-maker:** Composer of jigs (song and
dance). **107–108 suit of sables:** Garments trimmed with the fur of the sable, with a quibble
on *sable* meaning "black." **110 suffer . . . on:** Undergo oblivion. **111 "For . . . forgot":**
Verse of a song occurring also in *Love's Labour's Lost*, 3.1.30. The hobbyhorse was a character
in the Morris Dance.

Enter a King and a Queen [very lovingly]; the Queen embracing him, and he her. [She kneels, and makes show of protestation unto him.] He takes her up, and declines his head upon her neck: he lies him down upon a bank of flowers: she, seeing him asleep, leaves him. Anon comes in another man, takes off his crown, kisses it, pours poison in the sleeper's ears, and leaves him. The Queen returns; finds the King dead, makes passionate action. The Poisoner, with some three or four come in again, seem to condole with her. The dead body is carried away. The Poisoner woos the Queen with gifts: she seems harsh awhile, but in the end accepts love. [Exeunt.]

OPHELIA: What means this, my lord?

HAMLET: Marry, this is miching mallecho;° it means mischief.

OPHELIA: Belike this show imports the argument of the play.

Enter Prologue.

HAMLET: We shall know by this fellow: the players cannot keep counsel; they'll   115
tell all.

OPHELIA: Will 'a tell us what this show meant?

HAMLET: Ay, or any show that you'll show him: be not you ashamed to show,
he'll not shame to tell you what it means.

OPHELIA: You are naught, you are naught:° I'll mark the play.   120

PROLOGUE: For us, and for our tragedy,
Here stooping° to your clemency,
We beg your hearing patiently.   *[Exit.]*

HAMLET: Is this a prologue, or the posy° of a ring?

OPHELIA: 'Tis brief, my lord.   125

HAMLET: As woman's love.

Enter [two Players as] King and Queen.

PLAYER KING: Full thirty times hath Phoebus' cart gone round
Neptune's salt wash° and Tellus'° orbed ground,
And thirty dozen moons with borrowed° sheen
About the world have times twelve thirties been,   130
Since love our hearts and Hymen° did our hands
Unite commutual° in most sacred bands.

PLAYER QUEEN: So many journeys may the sun and moon
Make us again count o'er ere love be done!
But, woe is me, you are so sick of late,   135
So far from cheer and from your former state,
That I distrust° you. Yet, though I distrust,
Discomfort you, my lord, it nothing must:
For women's fear and love holds quantity;°

---

113 miching mallecho: Sneaking mischief.   **120 naught:** Indecent.   **122 stooping:** Bowing.   **124 posy:** Motto.   **128 salt wash:** The sea; **Tellus:** Goddess of the earth (*orbed ground*).   **129 borrowed:** I.e., reflected.   **131 Hymen:** God of matrimony.   **132 commutual:** Mutually.   **137 distrust:** Am anxious about.   **139 holds quantity:** Keeps proportion between.

In neither aught, or in extremity.   140
Now, what my love is, proof hath made you know;
And as my love is siz'd, my fear is so:
Where love is great, the littlest doubts are fear;
Where little fears grow great, great love grows there.
PLAYER KING: 'Faith, I must leave thee, love, and shortly too;   145
My operant° powers their functions leave° to do:
And thou shalt live in this fair world behind,
Honour'd, belov'd; and haply one as kind
For husband shalt thou—
PLAYER QUEEN: O, confound the rest!
Such love must needs be treason in my breast: 150
In second husband let me be accurst!
None wed the second but who kill'd the first.
HAMLET (*aside*):   Wormwood, wormwood.
PLAYER QUEEN: The instances that second marriage move
Are base respects of thrift, but none of love: 155
A second time I kill my husband dead,
When second husband kisses me in bed.
PLAYER KING: I do believe you think what now you speak;
But what we do determine oft we break.
Purpose is but the slave to memory,   160
Of violent birth, but poor validity:
Which now, like fruit unripe, sticks on the tree;
But fall, unshaken, when they mellow be.
Most necessary 'tis that we forget
To pay ourselves what to ourselves is debt: 165
What to ourselves in passion we propose,
The passion ending, doth the purpose lose.
The violence of either grief or joy
Their own enactures° with themselves destroy:
Where joy most revels, grief doth most lament;   170
Grief joys, joy grieves, on slender accident.
This world is not for aye,° nor 'tis not strange
That even our loves should with our fortunes change;
For 'tis a question left us yet to prove,
Whether love lead fortune, or else fortune love.   175
The great man down, you mark his favourite flies;
The poor advanc'd makes friends of enemies.
And hitherto doth love on fortune tend;
For who° not needs shall never lack a friend,
And who in want a hollow friend doth try,   180

146 **operant:** Active;   **leave:** Cease.   169 **enactures:** Fulfillments.   172 **aye:** Ever.   179 **who:** Whoever.

Directly seasons° him his enemy.
But, orderly to end where I begun,
Our wills and fates do so contrary run
That our devices still are overthrown;
Our thoughts are ours, their ends° none of our own: 185
So think thou wilt no second husband wed;
But die thy thoughts when thy first lord is dead.

PLAYER QUEEN: Nor earth to me give food, nor heaven light!
Sport and repose lock from me day and night!
To desperation turn my trust and hope!   190
An anchor's° cheer° in prison be my scope!
Each opposite° that blanks° the face of joy
Meet what I would have well and it destroy!
Both here and hence pursue me lasting strife,
If, once a widow, ever I be wife!   195

HAMLET: If she should break it now!

PLAYER KING: 'Tis deeply sworn. Sweet, leave me here awhile;
My spirits grow dull, and fain I would beguile
The tedious day with sleep.   *[Sleeps.]*

PLAYER QUEEN: Sleep rock thy brain;
And never come mischance between us twain!   *Exit.*   200

HAMLET: Madam, how like you this play?

QUEEN: The lady doth protest too much, methinks.

HAMLET: O, but she'll keep her word.

KING: Have you heard the argument? Is there no offence in 't?

HAMLET: No, no, they do but jest, poison in jest; no offence i' the world.   205

KING: What do you call the play?

HAMLET: The Mouse-trap. Marry, how? Tropically.° This play is the image of a
murder done in Vienna: Gonzago° is the duke's name; his wife, Baptista:
you shall see anon; 't is a knavish piece of work: but what o' that? your
majesty and we that have free souls, it touches us not: let the galled jade°   210
winch,° our withers° are unwrung.°

Enter Lucianus.

This is one Lucianus, nephew to the king.

OPHELIA: You are as good as a chorus,° my lord.

---

181 seasons: Matures, ripens.   **185 ends:** Results.   **191 An anchor's:** An anchorite's;
cheer: Fare; sometimes printed as *chair*.   **192 opposite:** Adverse thing;   **blanks:** Causes to
blanch or grow pale.   **207 Tropically:** Figuratively, *tropically* suggests a pun on *trap* in *Mouse-trap* (line 207).   **208 Gonzago:** In 1538 Luigi Gonzago murdered the Duke of Urbano by
pouring poisoned lotion in his ears.   **210 galled jade:** Horse whose hide is rubbed by saddle
or harness.   **211 winch:** Wince;   **withers:** The part between the horse's shoulder blades;
unwrung: Not wrung or twisted.   **213 chorus:** In many Elizabethan plays the action was
explained by an actor known as the "chorus"; at a puppet show the actor who explained the
action was known as an "interpreter," as indicated by the lines following.

HAMLET: I could interpret between you and your love, if I could see the puppets
       dallying.°   215

OPHELIA: You are keen, my lord, you are keen.

HAMLET: It would cost you a groaning to take off my edge.

OPHELIA: Still better, and worse.°

HAMLET: So you mistake° your husbands. Begin, murderer; pox,° leave thy
       damnable faces, and begin. Come: the croaking raven doth bellow for   220
       revenge.

LUCIANUS: Thoughts black, hands apt, drugs fit, and time agreeing;
       Confederate° season, else no creature seeing;
       Thou mixture rank, of midnight weeds collected,
       With Hecate's° ban° thrice blasted, thrice infected,   225
       Thy natural magic and dire property,
       On wholesome life usurp immediately.

                                           [Pours the poison into the sleeper's ears.]

HAMLET: 'A poisons him i' the garden for his estate. His name's Gonzago: the
       story is extant, and written in very choice Italian: you shall see anon how the
       murderer gets the love of Gonzago's wife.   230

OPHELIA: The king rises.

HAMLET: What, frighted with false fire!°

QUEEN: How fares my lord?

POLONIUS: Give o'er the play.

KING: Give me some light: away!   235

POLONIUS: Lights, lights, lights!   *Exeunt all but Hamlet and Horatio.*

HAMLET: Why, let the strucken deer go weep,
       The hart ungalled play;
       For some must watch, while some must sleep:
       Thus runs the world away.°   240
       Would not this,° sir, and a forest of feathers° — if the rest of my fortunes turn
       Turk with° me — with two Provincial roses° on my razed° shoes, get me a
       fellowship in a cry° of players,° sir?

HORATIO: Half a share.°

HAMLET: A whole one, I.   245

---

215 dallying: With sexual suggestion, continued in *keen* (sexually aroused), *groaning* (i.e., in pregnancy), and *edge* (i.e., sexual desire or impetuosity).   **218 Still . . . worse:** More keen, less decorous.   **219 mistake:** Err in taking;   **pox:** An imprecation.   **223 Confederate:** Conspiring (to assist the murderer).   **225 Hecate:** The goddess of witchcraft;   **ban:** Curse.   **232 false fire:** Fireworks, or a blank discharge.   **237–240 Why . . . away:** Probably from an old ballad, with allusion to the popular belief that a wounded deer retires to weep and die. Cf. *As You Like It*, 2.1.66.   **241 this:** I.e., the play;   **feathers:** Allusion to the plumes which Elizabethan actors were fond of wearing.   **241–242 turn Turk with:** Go back on.   **242 two Provincial roses:** Rosettes of ribbon like the roses of Provins near Paris, or else the roses of Provence;   **razed:** Cut, slashed (by way of ornament).   **243 cry:** Pack (as of hounds);   **fellowship . . . players:** Partnership in a theatrical company.   **244 Half a share:** Allusion to the custom in dramatic companies of dividing the ownership into a number of shares among the householders.

For thou dost know, O Damon dear,
   This realm dismantled° was
Of Jove himself; and now reigns here
   A very, very° — pajock.°

HORATIO: You might have rhymed.   250

HAMLET: O good Horatio, I'll take the ghost's word for a thousand pound. Didst perceive?

HORATIO: Very well, my lord.

HAMLET: Upon the talk of the poisoning?

HORATIO: I did very well note him.   255

HAMLET: Ah, ha! Come, some music! come, the recorders!°
For if the king like not the comedy,
Why then, belike, he likes it not, perdy.°
Come, some music!

Enter Rosencrantz and Guildenstern.

GUILDENSTERN: Good my lord, vouchsafe me a word with you.   260

HAMLET: Sir, a whole history.

GUILDENSTERN: The king, sir, —

HAMLET: Ay, sir, what of him?

GUILDENSTERN: Is in his retirement marvellous distempered.

HAMLET: With drink, sir?   265

GUILDENSTERN: No, my lord, rather with choler.°

HAMLET: Your wisdom should show itself more richer to signify this to his doctor; for, for me to put him to his purgation would perhaps plunge him into far more choler.

GUILDENSTERN: Good my lord, put your discourse into some frame° and start   270
not so wildly from my affair.

HAMLET: I am tame, sir: pronounce.

GUILDENSTERN: The queen, your mother, in most great affliction of spirit, hath sent me to you.

HAMLET: You are welcome.   275

GUILDENSTERN: Nay, good my lord, this courtesy is not of the right breed. If it shall please you to make me a wholesome° answer, I will do your mother's commandment; if not, your pardon and my return shall be the end of my business.

HAMLET: Sir, I cannot.   280

GUILDENSTERN: What, my lord?

HAMLET: Make you a wholesome answer; my wit's diseased: but, sir, such answer as I can make, you shall command; or, rather, as you say, my mother: therefore no more, but to the matter:° my mother, you say, —

---

247 **dismantled:** Stripped, divested.   246–249 **For . . . very:** Probably from an old ballad having to do with Damon and Pythias.   249 **pajock:** Peacock (a bird with a bad reputation). Possibly the word was *patchock*, diminutive of *patch*, clown.   256 **recorders:** Wind instruments of the flute kind.   258 **perdy:** Corruption of *par dieu*.   266 **choler:** Bilious disorder, with quibble on the sense "anger."   270 **frame:** Order.   277 **wholesome:** Sensible.   284 **matter:** Matter in hand.

ROSENCRANTZ: Then thus she says; your behaviour hath struck her into amaze-   285
ment and admiration.

HAMLET: O wonderful son, that can so 'stonish a mother! But is there no sequel
at the heels of this mother's admiration? Impart.

ROSENCRANTZ: She desires to speak with you in her closet, ere you go to bed.

HAMLET: We shall obey, were she ten times our mother. Have you any further   290
trade with us?

ROSENCRANTZ: My lord, you once did love me.

HAMLET: And do still, by these pickers and stealers.°

ROSENCRANTZ: Good my lord, what is your cause of distemper? you do, surely,
bar the door upon your own liberty, if you deny your griefs to your friend.   295

HAMLET: Sir, I lack advancement.

ROSENCRANTZ: How can that be, when you have the voice° of the king himself
for your succession in Denmark?

HAMLET: Ay, sir, but "While the grass grows,"°—the proverb is something
musty.   300

Enter the Players with recorders.

O, the recorders! let me see one. To withdraw° with you:—why do you go
about to recover the wind° of me, as if you would drive me into a toil?°

GUILDENSTERN: O, my lord, if my duty be too bold, my love is too unmannerly.°

HAMLET: I do not well understand that. Will you play upon this pipe?   305

GUILDENSTERN: My lord, I cannot.

HAMLET: I pray you.

GUILDENSTERN: Believe me, I cannot.

HAMLET: I beseech you.

GUILDENSTERN: I know no touch of it, my lord.   310

HAMLET: 'Tis as easy as lying: govern these ventages° with your fingers and
thumb, give it breath with your mouth, and it will discourse most eloquent
music. Look you, these are the stops.

GUILDENSTERN: But these cannot I command to any utterance of harmony; I
have not the skill.   315

HAMLET: Why, look you now, how unworthy a thing you make of me! You
would play upon me; you would seem to know my stops; you would pluck
out the heart of my mystery; you would sound me from my lowest note to the
top of my compass:° and there is much music, excellent voice, in this little
organ;° yet cannot you make it speak. 'Sblood, do you think I am easier to be   320

---

293 **pickers and stealers:** Hands, so called from the catechism "to keep my hands from picking
and stealing."   297 **voice:** Support.   299 **"While . . . grows":** The rest of the proverb is "the
silly horse starves." Hamlet may be destroyed while he is waiting for the succession to the kingdom.   301 **withdraw:** Speak in private.   302 **recover the wind:** Get to the windward side;
toil: Snare.   303–304 **if . . . unmannerly:** If I am using an unmannerly boldness, it is my love
which occasions it.   311 **ventages:** Stops of the recorders.   319 **compass:** Range of voice.
320 **organ:** Musical instrument, i.e., the pipe.

played on than a pipe? Call me what instrument you will, though you can
fret° me, you cannot play upon me.

Enter Polonius.

God bless you, sir!

POLONIUS: My lord, the queen would speak with you, and presently.

HAMLET: Do you see yonder cloud that's almost in shape of a camel?   325

POLONIUS: By the mass, and 'tis like a camel, indeed.

HAMLET: Methinks it is like a weasel.

POLONIUS: It is backed like a weasel.

HAMLET: Or like a whale?

POLONIUS: Very like a whale.   330

HAMLET: Then I will come to my mother by and by. *[Aside.]* They fool me to
the top of my bent.° — I will come by and by.°

POLONIUS: I will say so.   *[Exit.]*

HAMLET: By and by is easily said.

Leave me, friends.   *[Exeunt all but Hamlet.]*   335

'Tis now the very witching time° of night,
When churchyards yawn and hell itself breathes out
Contagion to this world: now could I drink hot blood,
And do such bitter business as the day
Would quake to look on. Soft! now to my mother.   340
O heart, lose not thy nature; let not ever
The soul of Nero° enter this firm bosom:
Let me be cruel, not unnatural:
I will speak daggers to her, but use none;
My tongue and soul in this be hypocrites;   345
How in my words somever she be shent,°
To give them seals° never, my soul, consent!   *Exit.*

[Scene 3]

[A room in the castle.]
Enter King, Rosencrantz, and Guildenstern.

KING: I like him not, nor stands it safe with us
To let his madness range. Therefore prepare you;
I your commission will forthwith dispatch,°
And he to England shall along with you:
The terms° of our estate° may not endure   5
Hazard so near us as doth hourly grow

---

322 fret: Quibble on meaning "irritate" and the piece of wood, gut, or metal which regulates
the fingering.   **332 top of my bent:** Limit of endurance, i.e., extent to which a bow may be
bent;   **by and by:** Immediately.   **336 witching time:** I.e., time when spells are cast.
342 Nero: Murderer of his mother, Agrippina.   **346 shent:** Rebuked.   **347 give them seals:**
Confirm with deeds.   SCENE 3. **3 dispatch:** Prepare.   **5 terms:** Condition, circumstances;
estate: State.

Out of his brows.°

GUILDENSTERN: We will ourselves provide:
    Most holy and religious fear it is
    To keep those many many bodies safe
    That live and feed upon your majesty.   10
ROSENCRANTZ: The single and peculiar° life is bound,
    With all the strength and armour of the mind,
    To keep itself from noyance;° but much more
    That spirit upon whose weal depend and rest
    The lives of many. The cess° of majesty   15
    Dies not alone; but, like a gulf,° doth draw
    What's near it with it: it is a massy wheel,
    Fix'd on the summit of the highest mount,
    To whose huge spokes ten thousand lesser things
    Are mortis'd and adjoin'd; which, when it falls,   20
    Each small annexment, petty consequence,
    Attends° the boist'rous ruin. Never alone
    Did the king sigh, but with a general groan.
KING: Arm° you, I pray you, to this speedy voyage;
    For we will fetters put about this fear,   25
    Which now goes too free-footed.
ROSENCRANTZ: We will haste us.
             Exeunt Gentlemen [Rosencrantz and Guildenstern].

Enter Polonius.

POLONIUS: My lord, he's going to his mother's closet:
    Behind the arras° I'll convey° myself,
    To hear the process;° I'll warrant she'll tax him home:°
    And, as you said, and wisely was it said,   30
    'Tis meet that some more audience than a mother,
    Since nature makes them partial, should o'erhear
    The speech, of vantage.° Fare you well, my liege:
    I'll call upon you ere you go to bed,
    And tell you what I know.
KING: Thanks, dear my lord.   *Exit [Polonius].*   35
    O, my offence is rank, it smells to heaven;
    It hath the primal eldest curse° upon't,
    A brother's murder. Pray can I not,
    Though inclination be as sharp as will:°

---

7 **brows:** Effronteries.   11 **single and peculiar:** Individual and private.   13 **noyance:** Harm.
15 **cess:** Decease.   16 **gulf:** Whirlpool.   22 **Attends:** Participates in.   24 **Arm:** Prepare.
28 **arras:** Screen of tapestry placed around the walls of household apartments;   **convey:** Implication of secrecy, *convey* was often used to mean "steal."   29 **process:** Proceedings;   **tax him
home:** Reprove him severely.   33 **of vantage:** From an advantageous place.   37 **primal
eldest curse:** The curse of Cain, the first to kill his brother.   39 **sharp as will:** I.e., his desire is
as strong as his determination.

My stronger guilt defeats my strong intent;   40
And, like a man to double business bound,
I stand in pause where I shall first begin,
And both neglect. What if this cursed hand
Were thicker than itself with brother's blood,
Is there not rain enough in the sweet heavens   45
To wash it white as snow? Whereto serves mercy
But to confront° the visage of offence?
And what's in prayer but this two-fold force,
To be forestalled° ere we come to fall,
Or pardon'd being down? Then I'll look up;   50
My fault is past. But, O, what form of prayer
Can serve my turn? "Forgive me my foul murder"?
That cannot be: since I am still possess'd
Of those effects for which I did the murder,
My crown, mine own ambition° and my queen.   55
May one be pardon'd and retain th' offence?°
In the corrupted currents° of this world
Offence's gilded hand° may shove by justice,
And oft 'tis seen the wicked prize° itself
Buys out the law: but 'tis not so above;   60
There is no shuffling,° there the action lies°
In his true nature; and we ourselves compell'd,
Even to the teeth and forehead° of our faults,
To give in evidence. What then? what rests?°
Try what repentance can: what can it not?   65
Yet what can it when one can not repent?
O wretched state! O bosom black as death!
O limed° soul, that, struggling to be free,
Art more engag'd!° Help, angels! Make assay!°
Bow, stubborn knees; and, heart with strings of steel,   70
Be soft as sinews of the new-born babe!
All may be well.   *[He kneels.]*

Enter Hamlet.

HAMLET: Now might I do it pat,° now he is praying;
And now I'll do't. And so 'a goes to heaven;
And so am I reveng'd. That would be scann'd:°   75
A villain kills my father; and for that,

---

47 confront: Oppose directly.   **49 forestalled:** Prevented.   **55 ambition:** I.e., realization of
ambition.   **56 offence:** Benefit accruing from offense.   **57 currents:** Courses.   **58 gilded
hand:** Hand offering gold as a bribe.   **59 wicked prize:** Prize won by wickedness.   **61 shuffling:** Escape by trickery;   **lies:** Is sustainable.   **63 teeth and forehead:** Very face.   **64 rests:**
Remains.   **68 limed:** Caught as with birdlime.   **69 engag'd:** Embedded;   **assay:** Trial.
73 pat: Opportunely.   **75 would be scann'd:** Needs to be looked into.

I, his sole son, do this same villain send
To heaven.
Why, this is hire and salary, not revenge.
'A took my father grossly, full of bread;°   80
With all his crimes broad blown,° as flush° as May;
And how his audit stands who knows save heaven?
But in our circumstance and course° of thought,
'Tis heavy with him: and am I then reveng'd,
To take him in the purging of his soul,   85
When he is fit and season'd for his passage?°
No!
Up, sword; and know thou a more horrid hent:°
When he is drunk asleep,° or in his rage,
Or in th' incestuous pleasure of his bed;   90
At game, a-swearing, or about some act
That has no relish of salvation in 't;
Then trip him, that his heels may kick at heaven,
And that his soul may be as damn'd and black
As hell, whereto it goes. My mother stays: 95
This physic° but prolongs thy sickly days.   *Exit.*
KING: *[Rising]* My words fly up, my thoughts remain below:
Words without thoughts never to heaven go.   *Exit.*

[Scene 4]

[The Queen's closet.]
Enter [Queen] Gertrude and Polonius.

POLONIUS: 'A will come straight. Look you lay° home to him:
Tell him his pranks have been too broad° to bear with,
And that your grace hath screen'd and stood between
Much heat° and him. I'll sconce° me even here.
Pray you, be round° with him.   5
HAMLET *(within):*   Mother, mother, mother!
QUEEN: I'll warrant you,
Fear me not: withdraw, I hear him coming.

                             [Polonius hides behind the arras.]
Enter Hamlet.

HAMLET: Now, mother, what's the matter?
QUEEN: Hamlet, thou hast thy father° much offended.

---

80 **full of bread:** Enjoying his worldly pleasures (see Ezekiel 16:49).   81 **broad blown:** In full
bloom;   **flush:** Lusty.   83 **in . . . course:** As we see it in our mortal situation.   86 **fit . . . passage:** I.e., reconciled to heaven by forgiveness of his sins.   88 **hent:** Seizing; or more probably,
occasion of seizure.   89 **drunk asleep:** In a drunken sleep.   96 **physic:** Purging (by prayer).
SCENE 4. 1 **lay:** Thrust.   2 **broad:** Unrestrained.   4 **Much heat:** I.e., the king's anger;
sconce: Hide.   5 **round:** Blunt.   9–10 **thy father, my father:** I.e., Claudius, the elder Hamlet.

HAMLET: Mother, you have my father much offended.   10
QUEEN: Come, come, you answer with an idle tongue.
HAMLET: Go, go, you question with a wicked tongue.
QUEEN: Why, how now, Hamlet!
HAMLET: What's the matter now?
QUEEN: Have you forgot me?
HAMLET: No, by the rood,° not so:
    You are the queen, your husband's brother's wife;   15
    And—would it were not so!—you are my mother.
QUEEN: Nay, then, I'll set those to you that can speak.
HAMLET: Come, come, and sit you down; you shall not budge;
    You go not till I set you up a glass
    Where you may see the inmost part of you.   20
QUEEN: What wilt thou do? thou wilt not murder me?
    Help, help, ho!
POLONIUS *[behind]*:   What, ho! help, help; help!
HAMLET *[drawing]*:   How now! a rat? Dead, for a ducat, dead!
                                          [Makes a pass through the arras.]
POLONIUS *[behind]*:   O, I am slain!   *[Falls and dies.]*   25
QUEEN: O me, what hast thou done?
HAMLET: Nay, I know not:
    Is it the king?
QUEEN: O, what a rash and bloody deed is this!
HAMLET: A bloody deed! almost as bad, good mother,
    As kill a king, and marry with his brother.   30
QUEEN: As kill a king!
HAMLET: Ay, lady, it was my word.
                            [Lifts up the arras and discovers Polonius.]
    Thou wretched, rash, intruding fool, farewell!
    I took thee for thy better: take thy fortune;
    Thou find'st to be too busy is some danger.
    Leave wringing of your hands: peace! sit you down,   35
    And let me wring your heart; for so I shall,
    If it be made of penetrable stuff,
    If damned custom have not braz'd° it so
    That it be proof and bulwark against sense.
QUEEN: What have I done, that thou dar'st wag thy tongue   40
    In noise so rude against me?
HAMLET: Such an act
    That blurs the grace and blush of modesty,
    Calls virtue hypocrite, takes off the rose
    From the fair forehead of an innocent love
    And sets a blister° there, makes marriage-vows   45

---

14 **rood:** Cross.   38 **braz'd:** Brazened, hardened.   45 **sets a blister:** Brands as a harlot.

As false as dicers' oaths: O, such a deed
As from the body of contraction° plucks
The very soul, and sweet religion° makes
A rhapsody° of words: heaven's face does glow
O'er this solidity and compound mass   50
With heated visage, as against the doom
Is thought-sick at the act.°

QUEEN: Ay me, what act,
That roars so loud, and thunders in the index?°

HAMLET: Look here, upon this picture, and on this.
The counterfeit presentment° of two brothers.   55
See, what a grace was seated on this brow;
Hyperion's° curls; the front° of Jove himself;
An eye like Mars, to threaten and command;
A station° like the herald Mercury
New-lighted on a heaven-kissing hill;   60
A combination and a form indeed,
Where every god did seem to set his seal,
To give the world assurance° of a man:
This was your husband. Look you now, what follows:
Here is your husband; like a mildew'd ear,°   65
Blasting his wholesome brother. Have you eyes?
Could you on this fair mountain leave to feed,
And batten° on this moor?° Ha! have you eyes?
You cannot call it love; for at your age
The hey-day° in the blood is tame, it's humble,   70
And waits upon the judgement: and what judgement
Would step from this to this? Sense, sure, you have,
Else could you not have motion;° but sure, that sense
Is apoplex'd;° for madness would not err,
Nor sense to ecstasy was ne'er so thrall'd°   75
But it reserv'd some quantity of choice,°
To serve in such a difference. What devil was't
That thus hath cozen'd° you at hoodman-blind?°
Eyes without feeling, feeling without sight,
Ears without hands or eyes, smelling sans° all,   80

---

47 **contraction:** The marriage contract.   48 **religion:** Religious vows.   49 **rhapsody:** Sense-less string.   **49–52 heaven's . . . act:** Heaven's face blushes to look down on this world, and Gertrude's marriage makes heaven feel as sick as though the day of doom were near.   53 **index:** Prelude or preface.   55 **counterfeit presentment:** Portrayed representation.   57 **Hyperion's:** The sun god's;   **front:** Brow.   59 **station:** Manner of standing.   63 **assurance:** Pledge, guarantee.   65 **mildew'd ear:** See Genesis 41:5–7.   68 **batten:** Grow fat;   **moor:** Barren upland.   70 **hey-day:** State of excitement.   72–73 **Sense . . . motion:** Sense and motion are functions of the middle or sensible soul, the possession of sense being the basis of motion.   74 **apoplex'd:** Paralyzed. Mental derangement was thus of three sorts: apoplexy, ecstasy, and diabolic possession.   75 **thrall'd:** Enslaved.   76 **quantity of choice:** Fragment of the power to choose.   78 **cozen'd:** Tricked, cheated;   **hoodman-blind:** Blindman's buff.   80 **sans:** Without.

Or but a sickly part of one true sense
Could not so mope.°
O shame! where is thy blush? Rebellious hell,
If thou canst mutine° in a matron's bones,
To flaming youth let virtue be as wax,   85
And melt in her own fire: proclaim no shame
When the compulsive ardour gives the charge,°
Since frost itself as actively doth burn
And reason pandars will.°

QUEEN: O Hamlet, speak no more:
Thou turn'st mine eyes into my very soul;   90
And there I see such black and grained° spots
As will not leave their tinct.

HAMLET: Nay, but to live
In the rank sweat of an enseamed° bed,
Stew'd in corruption, honeying and making love
Over the nasty sty, —

QUEEN: O, speak to me no more;   95
These words, like daggers, enter in mine ears;
No more, sweet Hamlet!

HAMLET: A murderer and a villain;
A slave that is not twentieth part the tithe
Of your precedent lord;° a vice of kings;°
A cutpurse of the empire and the rule,   100
That from a shelf the precious diadem stole,
And put it in his pocket!

QUEEN: No more!

Enter Ghost.

HAMLET: A king of shreds and patches,° —
Save me, and hover o'er me with your wings,
You heavenly guards! What would your gracious figure?   105

QUEEN: Alas, he's mad!

HAMLET: Do you not come your tardy son to chide,
That, laps'd in time and passion,° lets go by
Th' important° acting of your dread command?
O, say!   110

---

82 mope: Be in a depressed, spiritless state, act aimlessly.   **84 mutine:** Mutiny, rebel.
87 gives the charge: Delivers the attack.   **89 reason pandars will:** The normal and proper situation was one in which reason guided the will in the direction of good; here, reason is perverted and leads in the direction of evil.   **91 grained:** Dyed in grain.   **93 enseamed:** Loaded
with grease, greased.   **99 precedent lord:** I.e., the elder Hamlet;   **vice of kings:** Buffoon of
kings; a reference to the Vice, or clown, of the morality plays and interludes.   **103 shreds and
patches:** I.e., motley, the traditional costume of the Vice.   **108 laps'd . . . passion:** Having
suffered time to slip and passion to cool; also explained as "engrossed in casual events and
lapsed into mere fruitless passion, so that he no longer entertains a rational purpose."
109 important: Urgent.

GHOST: Do not forget: this visitation
    Is but to whet thy almost blunted purpose.
    But, look, amazement° on thy mother sits:
    O, step between her and her fighting soul:
    Conceit in weakest bodies strongest works: 115
    Speak to her, Hamlet.
HAMLET: How is it with you, lady?
QUEEN: Alas, how is 't with you,
    That you do bend your eye on vacancy
    And with th' incorporal° air do hold discourse?
    Forth at your eyes your spirits wildly peep;   120
    And, as the sleeping soldiers in th' alarm,
    Your bedded° hair, like life in excrements,°
    Start up, and stand an° end. O gentle son,
    Upon the heat and flame of thy distemper
    Sprinkle cool patience. Whereon do you look?   125
HAMLET: On him, on him! Look you, how pale he glares!
    His form and cause conjoin'd,° preaching to stones,
    Would make them capable. — Do not look upon me;
    Lest with this piteous action you convert
    My stern effects:° then what I have to do   130
    Will want true colour;° tears perchance for blood.
QUEEN: To whom do you speak this?
HAMLET: Do you see nothing there?
QUEEN: Nothing at all; yet all that is I see.
HAMLET: Nor did you nothing hear?
QUEEN: No, nothing but ourselves.
HAMLET: Why, look you there! look, how it steals away!   135
    My father, in his habit as he liv'd!
    Look, where he goes, even now, out at the portal!   *Exit Ghost.*
QUEEN: This is the very coinage of your brain:
    This bodiless creation ecstasy
    Is very cunning in.
HAMLET: Ecstasy!   140
    My pulse, as yours, doth temperately keep time,
    And makes as healthful music: it is not madness
    That I have utt'red: bring me to the test,
    And I the matter will re-word,° which madness
    Would gambol° from. Mother, for love of grace,   145

---

113 amazement: Frenzy, distraction.   **119 incorporal:** Immaterial.   **122 bedded:** Laid in smooth layers;   **excrements:** The hair was considered an excrement or voided part of the body.   **123 an:** On.   **127 conjoin'd:** United.   **129–130 convert . . . effects:** Divert me from my stern duty. For *effects*, possibly *affects* (affections of the mind).   **131 want true colour:** Lack good reason so that (with a play on the normal sense of *colour*) I shall shed tears instead of blood.   **144 re-word:** Repeat in words.   **145 gambol:** Skip away.

Lay not that flattering unction° to your soul,
That not your trespass, but my madness speaks:
It will but skin and film the ulcerous place,
Whiles rank corruption, mining° all within,
Infects unseen. Confess yourself to heaven;   150
Repent what's past; avoid what is to come;°
And do not spread the compost° on the weeds,
To make them ranker. Forgive me this my virtue;°
For in the fatness° of these pursy° times
Virtue itself of vice must pardon beg,   155
Yea, curb° and woo for leave to do him good.

QUEEN: O Hamlet, thou hast cleft my heart in twain.

HAMLET: O, throw away the worser part of it,
And live the purer with the other half.
Good night: but go not to my uncle's bed;   160
Assume a virtue, if you have it not.
That monster, custom, who all sense doth eat,
Of habits devil, is angel yet in this,
That to the use of actions fair and good
He likewise gives a frock or livery,   165
That aptly is put on. Refrain to-night,
And that shall lend a kind of easiness
To the next abstinence: the next more easy;
For use almost can change the stamp of nature,
And either . . . the devil, or throw him out°   170
With wondrous potency. Once more, good night:
And when you are desirous to be bless'd,°
I'll blessing beg of you. For this same lord,   *[Pointing to Polonius.]*
I do repent: but heaven hath pleas'd it so,
To punish me with this and this with me,   175
That I must be their scourge and minister.
I will bestow him, and will answer well
The death I gave him. So, again, good night.
I must be cruel, only to be kind:
Thus bad begins and worse remains behind.   180
One word more, good lady.

QUEEN: What shall I do?

HAMLET: Not this, by no means, that I bid you do:
Let the bloat° king tempt you again to bed;
Pinch wanton on your cheek; call you his mouse;

---

146 unction: Ointment used medicinally or as a rite; suggestion that forgiveness for sin may
not be so easily achieved.   **149 mining:** Working under the surface.   **151 what is to come:**
I.e., the sins of the future.   **152 compost:** Manure.   **153 this my virtue:** My virtuous talk in
reproving you.   **154 fatness:** Grossness;   **pursy:** Short-winded, corpulent.   **156 curb:** Bow,
bend the knee.   **170** Defective line usually emended by inserting *master* after *either*.   **172 be
bless'd:** Become blessed, i.e., repentant.   **183 bloat:** Bloated.

And let him, for a pair of reechy° kisses,   185
Or paddling in your neck with his damn'd fingers,
Make you to ravel all this matter out,
That I essentially° am not in madness,
But mad in craft. 'Twere good you let him know;
For who, that's but a queen, fair, sober, wise,   190
Would from a paddock,° from a bat, a gib,°
Such dear concernings° hide? who would do so?
No, in despite of sense and secrecy,
Unpeg the basket on the house's top,
Let the birds fly, and, like the famous ape,°   195
To try conclusions,° in the basket creep,
And break your own neck down.
QUEEN: Be thou assur'd, if words be made of breath,
And breath of life, I have no life to breathe
What thou hast said to me.   200
HAMLET: I must to England; you know that?
QUEEN: Alack,
I had forgot: 'tis so concluded on.
HAMLET: There's letters seal'd: and my two schoolfellows,
Whom I will trust as I will adders fang'd,
They bear the mandate; they must sweep my way,°   205
And marshal me to knavery. Let it work;
For 'tis the sport to have the enginer°
Hoist° with his own petar:° and 't shall go hard
But I will delve one yard below their mines,
And blow them at the moon: O, 'tis most sweet,   210
When in one line two crafts° directly meet.
This man shall set me packing:°
I'll lug the guts into the neighbour room.
Mother, good night. Indeed this counsellor
Is now most still, most secret and most grave,   215
Who was in life a foolish prating knave.
Come, sir, to draw° toward an end with you.
Good night, mother.   *Exeunt [severally; Hamlet dragging in Polonius.]*

---

185 **reechy:** Dirty, filthy.   188 **essentially:** In my essential nature.   191 **paddock:** Toad;
gib: Tomcat.   192 **dear concernings:** Important affairs.   195 **the famous ape:** A letter from
Sir John Suckling seems to supply other details of the story, otherwise not identified: "It is the
story of the jackanapes and the partridges; thou starest after a beauty till it be lost to thee, then
let'st out another, and starest after that till it is gone too."   196 **conclusions:** Experiments.
205 **sweep my way:** Clear my path.   207 **enginer:** Constructor of military works, or possibly,
artilleryman.   208 **Hoist:** Blown up;   **petar:** Defined as a small engine of war used to blow in
a door or make a breach, and as a case filled with explosive materials.   211 **two crafts:** Two
acts of guile, with quibble on the sense of "two ships."   212 **set me packing:** Set me to making
schemes, and set me to lugging (him), and, also, send me off in a hurry.   217 **draw:** Come,
with quibble on literal sense.

[ACT 4, Scene 1]

[A room in the castle.]
    Enter King and Queen, with Rosencrantz and Guildenstern.

KING: There's matter in these sighs, these profound heaves:
    You must translate: 'tis fit we understand them.
    Where is your son?
QUEEN: Bestow this place on us a little while.
                      [Exeunt Rosencrantz and Guildenstern.]
    Ah, mine own lord, what have I seen to-night!   5
KING: What, Gertrude? How does Hamlet?
QUEEN: Mad as the sea and wind, when both contend
    Which is the mightier: in his lawless fit,
    Behind the arras hearing something stir,
    Whips out his rapier, cries, "A rat, a rat!"   10
    And, in this brainish° apprehension,° kills
    The unseen good old man.
KING: O heavy deed!
    It had been so with us, had we been there:
    His liberty is full of threats to all;
    To you yourself, to us, to every one.   15
    Alas, how shall this bloody deed be answer'd?
    It will be laid to us, whose providence°
    Should have kept short,° restrain'd and out of haunt,°
    This mad young man: but so much was our love,
    We would not understand what was most fit;   20
    But, like the owner of a foul disease,
    To keep it from divulging,° let it feed
    Even on the pith of life. Where is he gone?
QUEEN: To draw apart the body he hath kill'd:
    O'er whom his very madness, like some ore   25
    Among a mineral° of metals base,
    Shows itself pure; 'a weeps for what is done.
KING: O Gertrude, come away!
    The sun no sooner shall the mountains touch,
    But we will ship him hence: and this vile deed   30
    We must, with all our majesty and skill,
    Both countenance and excuse. Ho, Guildenstern!

Enter Rosencrantz and Guildenstern.

    Friends both, go join you with some further aid:
    Hamlet in madness hath Polonius slain,

ACT 4, SCENE 1. **11 brainish:** Headstrong, passionate; **apprehension:** Conception, imagination. **17 providence:** Foresight. **18 short:** I.e., on a short tether; **out of haunt:** Secluded. **22 divulging:** Becoming evident. **26 mineral:** Mine.

And from his mother's closet hath he dragg'd him: 35
Go seek him out; speak fair, and bring the body
Into the chapel. I pray you, haste in this.
                              [Exeunt Rosencrantz and Guildenstern.]
Come, Gertrude, we'll call up our wisest friends;
And let them know, both what we mean to do,
And what's untimely done . . .°   40
Whose whisper o'er the world's diameter,°
As level° as the cannon to his blank,°
Transports his pois'ned shot, may miss our name,
And hit the woundless° air. O, come away!
My soul is full of discord and dismay.   *Exeunt.*   45

[Scene 2]

[Another room in the castle.]
   Enter Hamlet.

HAMLET: Safely stowed.

ROSENCRANTZ:
                    (within) Hamlet! Lord Hamlet!
GUILDENSTERN:

HAMLET: But soft, what noise? who calls on Hamlet? O, here they come.

Enter Rosencrantz and Guildenstern.

ROSENCRANTZ: What have you done, my lord, with the dead body?

HAMLET: Compounded it with dust, whereto 'tis kin.

ROSENCRANTZ: Tell us where 'tis, that we may take it thence   5
   And bear it to the chapel.

HAMLET: Do not believe it.

ROSENCRANTZ: Believe what?

HAMLET: That I can keep your counsel° and not mine own. Besides, to be
   demanded of a sponge! what replication° should be made by the son of a king?   10

ROSENCRANTZ: Take you me for a sponge, my lord?

HAMLET: Ay, sir, that soaks up the king's countenance, his rewards, his authorities.° But such officers do the king best service in the end: he keeps them,
   like an ape an apple, in the corner of his jaw; first mouthed, to be last swallowed: when he needs what you have gleaned, it is but squeezing you, and,   15
   sponge, you shall be dry again.

ROSENCRANTZ: I understand you not, my lord.

HAMLET: I am glad of it: a knavish speech sleeps in a foolish ear.

ROSENCRANTZ: My lord, you must tell us where the body is, and go with us to
   the king.   20

---

40 Defective line; some editors add: *so, haply, slander;* others add: *for, haply, slander;* other
conjectures.   **41 diameter:** Extent from side to side.   **42 level:** Straight;   **blank:** White spot
in the center of a target.   **44 woundless:** Invulnerable.   **SCENE 2. 9 keep your counsel:**
Hamlet is aware of their treachery but says nothing about it.   **10 replication:** Reply.
12–13 authorities: Authoritative backing.

HAMLET: The body is with the king, but the king is not with the body.° The king
    is a thing—
GUILDENSTERN: A thing, my lord!
HAMLET: Of nothing: bring me to him. Hide fox, and all after.°   *Exeunt.*

[Scene 3]

[Another room in the castle.]
    Enter King, and two or three.

KING: I have sent to seek him, and to find the body.
    How dangerous is it that this man goes loose!
    Yet must not we put the strong law on him:
    He's lov'd of the distracted° multitude,
    Who like not in their judgement, but their eyes;   5
    And where 'tis so, th' offender's scourge° is weigh'd,°
    But never the offence. To bear all smooth and even,
    This sudden sending him away must seem
    Deliberate pause:° diseases desperate grown
    By desperate appliance are reliev'd,   10
    Or not at all.

Enter Rosencrantz, [Guildenstern,] and all the rest.

              How now! what hath befall'n?
ROSENCRANTZ: Where the dead body is bestow'd, my lord,
    We cannot get from him.
KING: But where is he?
ROSENCRANTZ: Without, my lord; guarded, to know your pleasure.
KING: Bring him before us.   15
ROSENCRANTZ: Ho! bring in the lord.

They enter [with Hamlet].

KING: Now, Hamlet, where's Polonius?
HAMLET: At supper.
KING: At supper! where?
HAMLET: Not where he eats, but where 'a is eaten: a certain convocation of   20
    politic° worms° are e'en at him. Your worm is your only emperor for diet: we
    fat all creatures else to fat us, and we fat ourselves for maggots: your fat king
    and your lean beggar is but variable service,° two dishes, but to one table:
    that's the end.
KING: Alas, alas!   25

---

21 The body . . . body: There are many interpretations; possibly, "The body lies in death with
the king, my father; but my father walks disembodied"; or "Claudius has the bodily possession of
kingship, but kingliness, or justice of inheritance, is not with him."   **24 Hide . . . after:** An old
signal cry in the game of hide-and-seek.   **SCENE 3. 4 distracted:** I.e., without power of forming logical judgments.   **6 scourge:** Punishment;   **weigh'd:** Taken into consideration.
9 Deliberate pause: Considered action.   **20–21 convocation . . . worms:** Allusion to the
Diet of Worms (1521).   **21 politic:** Crafty.   **23 variable service:** A variety of dishes.

HAMLET: A man may fish with the worm that hath eat of a king, and eat of the
    fish that hath fed of that worm.

KING: What dost thou mean by this?

HAMLET: Nothing but to show you how a king may go a progress° through the
    guts of a beggar.   30

KING: Where is Polonius?

HAMLET: In heaven; send thither to see: if your messenger find him not there,
    seek him i' the other place yourself. But if indeed you find him not within
    this month, you shall nose him as you go up the stairs into the lobby.

KING *[to some Attendants]:*   Go seek him there.   35

HAMLET: 'A will stay till you come.   *[Exeunt Attendants.]*

KING: Hamlet, this deed, for thine especial safety, —
    Which we do tender,° as we dearly grieve
    For that which thou hast done, — must send thee hence
    With fiery quickness: therefore prepare thyself;   40
    The bark is ready, and the wind at help,
    Th' associates tend, and everything is bent
    For England.

HAMLET: For England!

KING: Ay, Hamlet.

HAMLET: Good.

KING: So is it, if thou knew'st our purposes.

HAMLET: I see a cherub° that sees them. But, come; for England! Farewell, dear   45
    mother.

KING: Thy loving father, Hamlet.

HAMLET: My mother: father and mother is man and wife; man and wife is one
    flesh; and so, my mother. Come, for England!   *Exit.*

KING: Follow him at foot;° tempt him with speed aboard;   50
    Delay it not; I'll have him hence to-night:
    Away! for every thing is seal'd and done
    That else leans on th' affair: pray you, make haste.

                                                                [Exeunt all but the King.]

    And, England, if my love thou hold'st at aught—
    As my great power thereof may give thee sense,   55
    Since yet thy cicatrice° looks raw and red
    After the Danish sword, and thy free awe°
    Pays homage to us—thou mayst not coldly set
    Our sovereign process; which imports at full,
    By letters congruing to that effect,   60
    The present death of Hamlet. Do it, England;
    For like the hectic° in my blood he rages,
    And thou must cure me: till I know 'tis done,
    Howe'er my haps,° my joys were ne'er begun.   *Exit.*

---

29 **progress:** Royal journey of state.   38 **tender:** Regard, hold dear.   45 **cherub:** Cherubim
are angels of knowledge.   50 **at foot:** Close behind, at heel.   56 **cicatrice:** Scar.   57 **free
awe:** Voluntary show of respect.   62 **hectic:** Fever.   64 **haps:** Fortunes.

[Scene 4]

[A plain in Denmark.]
    Enter Fortinbras with his Army over the stage.

FORTINBRAS: Go, captain, from me greet the Danish king;
    Tell him that, by his license,° Fortinbras
    Craves the conveyance° of a promis'd march
    Over his kingdom. You know the rendezvous.
    If that his majesty would aught with us,   5
    We shall express our duty in his eye;°
    And let him know so.
CAPTAIN: I will do't, my lord.
FORTINBRAS: Go softly° on.   *[Exeunt all but Captain.]*

Enter Hamlet, Rosencrantz, [Guildenstern,] &c.

HAMLET: Good sir, whose powers are these?
CAPTAIN: They are of Norway, sir.   10
HAMLET: How purpos'd, sir, I pray you?
CAPTAIN: Against some part of Poland.
HAMLET: Who commands them, sir?
CAPTAIN: The nephew to old Norway, Fortinbras.
HAMLET: Goes it against the main° of Poland, sir,   15
    Or for some frontier?
CAPTAIN: Truly to speak, and with no addition,
    We go to gain a little patch of ground
    That hath in it no profit but the name.
    To pay five ducats, five, I would not farm it;°   20
    Nor will it yield to Norway or the Pole
    A ranker rate, should it be sold in fee.°
HAMLET: Why, then the Polack never will defend it.
CAPTAIN: Yes, it is already garrison'd.
HAMLET: Two thousand souls and twenty thousand ducats   25
    Will not debate the question of this straw:°
    This is th' imposthume° of much wealth and peace,
    That inward breaks, and shows no cause without
    Why the man dies. I humbly thank you, sir.
CAPTAIN: God be wi' you, sir.   *[Exit.]*
ROSENCRANTZ: Will 't please you go, my lord?   30
HAMLET: I'll be with you straight. Go a little before.

                    [Exeunt all except Hamlet.]

    How all occasions° do inform against° me,
    And spur my dull revenge! What is a man,

SCENE 4. **2 license:** Leave. **3 conveyance:** Escort, convoy. **6 in his eye:** In his presence. **8 softly:** Slowly. **15 main:** Country itself. **20 farm it:** Take a lease of it. **22 fee:** Fee simple. **26 debate . . . straw:** Settle this trifling matter. **27 imposthume:** Purulent abscess or swelling. **32 occasions:** Incidents, events; **inform against:** Generally defined as "show," "betray" (i.e., his tardiness); more probably *inform* means "take shape," as in *Macbeth*, 2.1.48.

If his chief good and market of his time°
Be but to sleep and feed? a beast, no more.   35
Sure, he that made us with such large discourse,
Looking before and after, gave us not
That capability and god-like reason
To fust° in us unus'd. Now, whether it be
Bestial oblivion, or some craven scruple   40
Of thinking too precisely on th' event,
A thought which, quarter'd, hath but one part wisdom
And ever three parts coward, I do not know
Why yet I live to say "This thing 's to do";
Sith I have cause and will and strength and means   45
To do 't. Examples gross as earth exhort me:
Witness this army of such mass and charge
Led by a delicate and tender prince,
Whose spirit with divine ambition puff'd
Makes mouths at the invisible event,   50
Exposing what is mortal and unsure
To all that fortune, death and danger dare,
Even for an egg-shell. Rightly to be great
Is not to stir without great argument,
But greatly to find quarrel in a straw   55
When honour's at the stake. How stand I then,
That have a father kill'd, a mother stain'd,
Excitements of° my reason and my blood,
And let all sleep? while, to my shame, I see
The imminent death of twenty thousand men,   60
That, for a fantasy and trick° of fame,
Go to their graves like beds, fight for a plot°
Whereon the numbers cannot try the cause,
Which is not tomb enough and continent
To hide the slain? O, from this time forth,   65
My thoughts be bloody, or be nothing worth!   *Exit.*

[Scene 5]

[Elsinore. A room in the castle.]
   Enter Horatio, [Queen] Gertrude, and a Gentleman.
QUEEN: I will not speak with her.
GENTLEMAN: She is importunate, indeed distract:
   Her mood will needs be pitied.
QUEEN: What would she have?

---

34 **market of his time:** The best use he makes of his time, or, that for which he sells his time.
39 **fust:** Grow moldy.   58 **Excitements of:** Incentives to.   61 **trick:** Toy, trifle.   62 **plot:**
Piece of ground.

GENTLEMAN: She speaks much of her father; says she hears
    There's tricks° i' th' world; and hems, and beats her heart;°   5
    Spurns enviously at straws;° speaks things in doubt,
    That carry but half sense: her speech is nothing,
    Yet the unshaped° use of it doth move
    The hearers to collection;° they yawn° at it,
    And botch° the words up fit to their own thoughts;   10
    Which, as her winks, and nods, and gestures yield° them,
    Indeed would make one think there might be thought,
    Though nothing sure, yet much unhappily.°
HORATIO: 'Twere good she were spoken with: for she may strew
    Dangerous conjectures in ill-breeding minds.°   15
QUEEN: Let her come in.   *[Exit Gentleman.]*
    [Aside.] To my sick soul, as sin's true nature is,
    Each toy seems prologue to some great amiss:°
    So full of artless jealousy is guilt,
    It spills itself in fearing to be spilt.°   20

Enter Ophelia [distracted].

OPHELIA: Where is the beauteous majesty of Denmark?
QUEEN: How now, Ophelia!
OPHELIA *(she sings)*:   How should I your true love know
    From another one?
    By his cockle hat° and staff,   25
    And his sandal shoon.°
QUEEN: Alas, sweet lady, what imports this song?
OPHELIA: Say you? nay, pray you mark.
    (Song) He is dead and gone, lady,
    He is dead and gone;   30
    At his head a grass-green turf,
    At his heels a stone.
    O, ho!
QUEEN: Nay, but, Ophelia—
OPHELIA: Pray you, mark   35
    [Sings.] White his shroud as the mountain snow,—

Enter King.

QUEEN: Alas, look here, my lord.

SCENE 5. **5 tricks:** Deceptions;   **heart:** I.e., breast.   **6 Spurns . . . straws:** Kicks spitefully at
small objects in her path.   **8 unshaped:** Unformed, artless.   **9 collection:** Inference, a guess
at some sort of meaning;   **yawn:** Wonder.   **10 botch:** Patch.   **11 yield:** Deliver, bring forth
(her words).   **13 much unhappily:** Expressive of much unhappiness.   **15 ill-breeding
minds:** Minds bent on mischief.   **18 great amiss:** Calamity, disaster.   **19–20 So . . . spilt:**
Guilt is so full of suspicion that it unskillfully betrays itself in fearing to be betrayed.
25 cockle hat: Hat with cockleshell stuck in it as a sign that the wearer has been a pilgrim to
the shrine of St. James of Compostella. The pilgrim's garb was a conventional disguise for
lovers.   **26 shoon:** Shoes.

OPHELIA *(Song):*   Larded° all with flowers;
   Which bewept to the grave did not go
     With true-love showers.   40
KING: How do you, pretty lady?
OPHELIA: Well, God 'ild° you! They say the owl° was a baker's daughter.
   Lord, we know what we are, but know not what we may be. God be at your
   table!
KING: Conceit upon her father.   45
OPHELIA: Pray let's have no words of this; but when they ask you what it means,
   say you this:
   (Song) To-morrow is Saint Valentine's day,
     All in the morning betime,
   And I a maid at your window,   50
     To be your Valentine.°
   Then up he rose, and donn'd his clothes,
     And dupp'd° the chamber-door;
   Let in the maid, that out a maid
     Never departed more.   55
KING: Pretty Ophelia!
OPHELIA: Indeed, la, without an oath, I'll make an end on 't:
   [Sings.] By Gis° and by Saint Charity,
     Alack, and fie for shame!
   Young men will do 't, if they come to 't;   60
     By cock,° they are to blame.
   Quoth she, before you tumbled me,
     You promis'd me to wed.
   So would I ha' done, by yonder sun,
     An thou hadst not come to my bed.   65
KING: How long hath she been thus?
OPHELIA: I hope all will be well. We must be patient: but I cannot choose
   but weep, to think they would lay him i' the cold ground. My brother
   shall know of it: and so I thank you for your good counsel. Come, my
   coach! Good night, ladies; good night, sweet ladies; good night, good   70
   night.   *[Exit.]*
KING: Follow her close; give her good watch, I pray you.   *[Exit Horatio.]*
   O, this is the poison of deep grief; it springs
   All from her father's death. O Gertrude, Gertrude,
   When sorrows come, they come not single spies,   75
   But in battalions. First, her father slain:
   Next your son gone; and he most violent author
   Of his own just remove: the people muddied,

---

38 Larded: Decorated.   **42 God 'ild:** God yield or reward;   **owl:** Reference to a monkish
legend that a baker's daughter was turned into an owl for refusing bread to the Savior.
51 Valentine: This song alludes to the belief that the first girl seen by a man on the morning of
this day was his valentine or true love.   **53 dupp'd:** Opened.   **58 Gis:** Jesus.   **61 cock:** Per-
version of "God" in oaths.

Thick and unwholesome in their thoughts and whispers,
For good Polonius' death; and we have done but greenly,°   80
In hugger-mugger° to inter him: poor Ophelia
Divided from herself and her fair judgement,
Without the which we are pictures, or mere beasts:
Last, and as much containing as all these,
Her brother is in secret come from France;   85
Feeds on his wonder, keeps himself in clouds,°
And wants not buzzers° to infect his ear
With pestilent speeches of his father's death;
Wherein necessity, of matter beggar'd,°
Will nothing stick° our person to arraign   90
In ear and ear.° O my dear Gertrude, this,
Like to a murd'ring-piece,° in many places
Gives me superfluous death.   *A noise within.*
QUEEN: Alack, what noise is this?
KING: Where are my Switzers?° Let them guard the door.

Enter a Messenger.

What is the matter?
MESSENGER: Save yourself, my lord: 95
The ocean, overpeering° of his list,°
Eats not the flats with more impiteous haste
Than young Laertes, in a riotous head,
O'erbears your officers. The rabble call him lord;
And, as the world were now but to begin,   100
Antiquity forgot, custom not known,
The ratifiers and props of every word,°
They cry "Choose we: Laertes shall be king":
Caps, hands, and tongues, applaud it to the clouds:
"Laertes shall be king, Laertes king!"   *A noise within.* 105
QUEEN: How cheerfully on the false trail they cry!
O, this is counter,° you false Danish dogs!
KING: The doors are broke.

Enter Laertes with others.

LAERTES: Where is this king? Sirs, stand you all without.
DANES: No, let's come in.
LAERTES: I pray you, give me leave.   110
DANES: We will, we will.   *[They retire without the door.]*
LAERTES: I thank you: keep the door. O thou vile king,

---

80 **greenly:** Foolishly. 81 **hugger-mugger:** Secret haste. 86 **in clouds:** Invisible.
87 **buzzers:** Gossipers. 89 **of matter beggar'd:** Unprovided with facts. 90 **nothing stick:**
Not hesitate. 91 **In ear and ear:** In everybody's ears. 92 **murd'ring-piece:** Small cannon or
mortar; suggestion of numerous missiles fired. 94 **Switzers:** Swiss guards, mercenaries.
96 **overpeering:** Overflowing; **list:** Shore. 102 **word:** Promise. 107 **counter:** A hunting
term meaning to follow the trail in a direction opposite to that which the game has taken.

Give me my father!

QUEEN: Calmly, good Laertes.

LAERTES: That drop of blood that's calm proclaims me bastard,
Cries cuckold to my father, brands the harlot   115
Even here, between the chaste unsmirched brow
Of my true mother.

KING: What is the cause, Laertes,
That thy rebellion looks so giant-like?
Let him go, Gertrude; do not fear our person:
There's such divinity doth hedge a king,   120
That treason can but peep to° what it would,°
Acts little of his will. Tell me, Laertes,
Why thou art thus incens'd. Let him go, Gertrude.
Speak, man.

LAERTES: Where is my father?

KING: Dead.

QUEEN: But not by him.   125

KING: Let him demand his fill.

LAERTES: How came he dead? I'll not be juggled with:
To hell, allegiance! vows, to the blackest devil!
Conscience and grace, to the profoundest pit!
I dare damnation. To this point I stand,   130
That both the worlds I give to negligence,°
Let come what comes; only I'll be reveng'd
Most throughly° for my father.

KING: Who shall stay you?

LAERTES: My will,° not all the world's:
And for my means, I'll husband them so well,   135
They shall go far with little.

KING: Good Laertes,
If you desire to know the certainty
Of your dear father, is 't writ in your revenge,
That, swoopstake,° you will draw both friend and foe,
Winner and loser?   140

LAERTES: None but his enemies.

KING: Will you know them then?

LAERTES: To his good friends thus wide I'll ope my arms;
And like the kind life-rend'ring pelican,°
Repast° them with my blood.

KING: Why, now you speak
Like a good child and a true gentleman.   145

---

121 **peep to:** I.e., look at from afar off; **would:** Wishes to do. **131 give to negligence:** He
despises both the here and the hereafter. **133 throughly:** thoroughly. **134 My will:** He will
not be stopped except by his own will. **139 swoopstake:** Literally, drawing the whole stake at
once, i.e., indiscriminately. **143 pelican:** Reference to the belief that the pelican feeds its
young with its own blood. **144 Repast:** Feed.

That I am guiltless of your father's death,
And am most sensibly in grief for it,
It shall as level to your judgement 'pear
As day does to your eye.   *A noise within: "Let her come in."*
LAERTES: How now! what noise is that?   150

Enter Ophelia.

O heat,° dry up my brains! tears seven times salt,
Burn out the sense and virtue of mine eye!
By heaven, thy madness shall be paid with weight,
Till our scale turn the beam. O rose of May!
Dear maid, kind sister, sweet Ophelia!   155
O heavens! is 't possible, a young maid's wits
Should be as mortal as an old man's life?
Nature is fine in love, and where 'tis fine,
It sends some precious instance of itself
After the thing it loves.   160

OPHELIA *(Song):*   They bore him barefac'd on the bier;
     Hey non nonny, nonny, hey nonny;
     And in his grave rain'd many a tear: —
     Fare you well, my dove!

LAERTES: Hadst thou thy wits, and didst persuade revenge,   165
It could not move thus.

OPHELIA *[sings]:*   You must sing a-down a-down,
     An you call him a-down-a.
O, how the wheel° becomes it! It is the false steward,° that stole his master's
daughter.   170

LAERTES: This nothing's more than matter.

OPHELIA: There's rosemary,° that's for remembrance; pray you, love, remember: and there is pansies,° that's for thoughts.

LAERTES: A document° in madness, thoughts and remembrance fitted.

OPHELIA: There's fennel° for you, and columbines:° there's rue° for you; and   175
here's some for me: we may call it herb of grace o' Sundays: O, you must
wear your rue with a difference. There's a daisy:° I would give you some
violets,° but they withered all when my father died: they say 'a made a
good end, —
[Sings.] For bonny sweet Robin is all my joy.°   180

---

151 **heat:** Probably the heat generated by the passion of grief.   169 **wheel:** Spinning wheel as
accompaniment to the song refrain;   **false steward:** The story is unknown.   172 **rosemary:**
Used as a symbol of remembrance both at weddings and at funerals.   173 **pansies:** Emblems
of love and courtship (from the French *pensée*).   174 **document:** Piece of instruction or lesson.   175 **fennel:** Emblem of flattery;   **columbines:** Emblem of unchastity (?) or ingratitude
(?);   **rue:** Emblem of repentance. It was usually mingled with holy water and then known as
herb of grace. Ophelia is probably playing on the two meanings of *rue,* "repentant" and "even
for ruth (pity)"; the former signification is for the queen, the latter for herself.   177 **daisy:**
Emblem of dissembling, faithlessness.   178 **violets:** Emblems of faithfulness.   180 **For . . .
joy:** Probably a line from a Robin Hood ballad.

LAERTES: Thought° and affliction, passion, hell itself,
   She turns to favour and to prettiness.
OPHELIA *(Song):*   And will 'a not come again?°
   And will 'a not come again?
      No, no, he is dead: 185
      Go to thy death-bed:
   He never will come again.

   His beard was as white as snow,
   All flaxen was his poll:°
      He is gone, he is gone,   190
      And we cast away° moan:
   God ha' mercy on his soul!
   And of all Christian souls, I pray God. God be wi' you.   *[Exit.]*
LAERTES: Do you see this, O God?
KING: Laertes, I must commune with your grief,   195
   Or you deny me right.° Go but apart,
   Make choice of whom your wisest friends you will,
   And they shall hear and judge 'twixt you and me:
   If by direct or by collateral° hand
   They find us touch'd,° we will our kingdom give,   200
   Our crown, our life, and all that we call ours,
   To you in satisfaction; but if not,
   Be you content to lend your patience to us,
   And we shall jointly labour with your soul
   To give it due content.
LAERTES: Let this be so;   205
   His means of death, his obscure funeral —
   No trophy, sword, nor hatchment° o'er his bones,
   No noble rite nor formal ostentation —
   Cry to be heard, as 'twere from heaven to earth,
   That I must call 't in question.
KING: So you shall;   210
   And where th' offence is let the great axe fall.
   I pray you, go with me.   *Exeunt.*

[Scene 6]

[Another room in the castle.]
   Enter Horatio and others.

HORATIO: What are they that would speak with me?
GENTLEMAN: Sea-faring men, sir: they say they have letters for you.

---

181 Thought: Melancholy thought.   **183 And . . . again:** This song appeared in the song-books as "The Merry Milkmaids' Dumps."   **189 poll:** Head.   **191 cast away:** Shipwrecked.   **196 right:** My rights.   **199 collateral:** Indirect.   **200 touch'd:** Implicated.   **207 hatchment:** Tablet displaying the armorial bearings of a deceased person.

HORATIO: Let them come in.   *[Exit Gentleman.]*
    I do not know from what part of the world
    I should be greeted, if not from lord Hamlet.   5

Enter Sailors.

FIRST SAILOR: God bless you, sir.
HORATIO: Let him bless thee too.
FIRST SAILOR: 'A shall sir, an 't please him. There's a letter for you, sir; it comes
    from the ambassador that was bound for England; if your name be Horatio,
    as I am let to know it is.   10
HORATIO *[reads]*:   "Horatio, when thou shalt have overlooked this, give these fel-
    lows some means° to the king: they have letters for him. Ere we were two
    days old at sea, a pirate of very warlike appointment gave us chase. Finding
    ourselves too slow of sail, we put on a compelled valour, and in the grapple I
    boarded them: on the instant they got clear of our ship; so I alone became   15
    their prisoner. They have dealt with me like thieves of mercy:° but they knew
    what they did; I am to do a good turn for them. Let the king have the letters I
    have sent; and repair thou to me with as much speed as thou wouldest fly
    death. I have words to speak in thine ear will make thee dumb; yet are they
    much too light for the bore° of the matter. These good fellows will bring thee   20
    where I am. Rosencrantz and Guildenstern hold their course for England: of
    them I have much to tell thee. Farewell.
                                   "He that thou knowest thine, HAMLET."
    Come, I will give you way for these your letters;
    And do 't the speedier, that you may direct me
    To him from whom you brought them.   *Exeunt.*   25

[Scene 7]

[Another room in the castle.]
    Enter King and Laertes.

KING: Now must your conscience° my acquittance seal,
    And you must put me in your heart for friend,
    Sith you have heard, and with a knowing ear,
    That he which hath your noble father slain
    Pursued my life.
LAERTES: It well appears: but tell me   5
    Why you proceeded not against these feats,
    So criminal and so capital° in nature,
    As by your safety, wisdom, all things else,
    You mainly° were stirr'd up.
KING: O, for two special reasons;
    Which may to you, perhaps, seem much unsinew'd,°   10

SCENE 6.   **12 means:** Means of access.   **16 thieves of mercy:** Merciful thieves.   **20 bore:**
Caliber, importance.   SCENE 7.   **1 conscience:** Knowledge that this is true.   **7 capital:** Punishable by death.   **9 mainly:** Greatly.   **10 unsinew'd:** Weak.

But yet to me th' are strong. The queen his mother
Lives almost by his looks; and for myself—
My virtue or my plague, be it either which—
She's so conjunctive° to my life and soul,
That, as the star moves not but in his sphere,°   15
I could not but by her. The other motive,
Why to a public count° I might not go,
Is the great love the general gender° bear him;
Who, dipping all his faults in their affection,
Would, like the spring° that turneth wood to stone,   20
Convert his gyves° to graces; so that my arrows,
Too slightly timber'd° for so loud° a wind,
Would have reverted to my bow again,
And not where I had aim'd them.
LAERTES: And so have I a noble father lost;   25
A sister driven into desp'rate terms,°
Whose worth, if praises may go back° again,
Stood challenger on mount° of all the age°
For her perfections: but my revenge will come.
KING: Break not your sleeps for that: you must not think   30
That we are made of stuff so flat and dull
That we can let our beard be shook with danger
And think it pastime. You shortly shall hear more:
I lov'd your father, and we love ourself;
And that, I hope, will teach you to imagine—   35

Enter a Messenger with letters.

How now! what news?
MESSENGER: Letters, my lord, from Hamlet:
These to your majesty; this to the queen.°
KING: From Hamlet! who brought them?
MESSENGER: Sailors, my lord, they say; I saw them not:
They were given me by Claudio;° he receiv'd them   40
Of him that brought them.
KING: Laertes, you shall hear them.
Leave us.   *[Exit Messenger.]*
[Reads.] "High and mighty, You shall know I am set naked° on your king-
dom. Tomorrow shall I beg leave to see your kingly eyes: when I shall, first

---

14 **conjunctive:** Conformable (the next line suggesting planetary conjunction). 15 **sphere:**
The hollow sphere in which, according to Ptolemaic astronomy, the planets were supposed to
move. 17 **count:** Account, reckoning. 18 **general gender:** Common people. 20 **spring:**
I.e., one heavily charged with lime. 21 **gyves:** Fetters; here, faults, or possibly, punishments
inflicted (on him). 22 **slightly timber'd:** Light; **loud:** Strong. 26 **terms:** State, condition.
27 **go back:** Return to Ophelia's former virtues. 28 **on mount:** Set up on high; mounted
(on horseback); **of all the age:** Qualifies *challenger* and not *mount*. 37 **to the queen:** One
hears no more of the letter to the queen. 40 **Claudio:** This character does not appear in the
play. 43 **naked:** Unprovided (with retinue).

asking your pardon thereunto, recount the occasion of my sudden and   45
more strange return.   "HAMLET."
What should this mean? Are all the rest come back?
Or is it some abuse, and no such thing?

LAERTES: Know you the hand?

KING: 'Tis Hamlet's character. "Naked!"
And in a postscript here, he says "alone."   50
Can you devise° me?

LAERTES: I'm lost in it, my lord. But let him come;
It warms the very sickness in my heart,
That I shall live and tell him to his teeth,
"Thus didst thou."

KING: If it be so, Laertes—   55
As how should it be so? how otherwise?°—
Will you be rul'd by me?

LAERTES: Ay, my lord;
So you will not o'errule me to a peace.

KING: To thine own peace. If he be now return'd,
As checking at° his voyage, and that he means   60
No more to undertake it, I will work him
To an exploit, now ripe in my device,
Under the which he shall not choose but fall:
And for his death no wind of blame shall breathe,
But even his mother shall uncharge the practice°   65
And call it accident.

LAERTES: My lord, I will be rul'd;
The rather, if you could devise it so
That I might be the organ.°

KING: It falls right.
You have been talk'd of since your travel much,
And that in Hamlet's hearing, for a quality   70
Wherein, they say, you shine: your sum of parts
Did not together pluck such envy from him
As did that one, and that, in my regard,
Of the unworthiest siege.°

LAERTES: What part is that, my lord?

KING: A very riband in the cap of youth,   75
Yet needful too; for youth no less becomes
The light and careless livery that it wears
Than settled age his sables° and his weeds,

---

51 devise: Explain to.   **56 As . . . otherwise?** How can this (Hamlet's return) be true? (yet)
how otherwise than true (since we have the evidence of his letter)? Some editors read *How
should it not be so*, etc., making the words refer to Laertes's desire to meet with Hamlet.
60 checking at: Used in falconry of a hawk's leaving the quarry to fly at a chance bird; turn
aside.   **65 uncharge the practice:** Acquit the stratagem of being a plot.   **68 organ:** Agent,
instrument.   **74 siege:** Rank.   **78 sables:** Rich garments.

Importing health and graveness. Two months since,
Here was a gentleman of Normandy: —   80
I have seen myself, and serv'd against, the French,
And they can well° on horseback: but this gallant
Had witchcraft in 't; he grew unto his seat;
And to such wondrous doing brought his horse,
As had he been incorps'd and demi-natur'd°   85
With the brave beast: so far he topp'd° my thought,
That I, in forgery° of shapes and tricks,
Come short of what he did.

LAERTES: A Norman was 't?

KING: A Norman.

LAERTES: Upon my life, Lamord.°

KING: The very same.   90

LAERTES: I know him well: he is the brooch indeed
And gem of all the nation.

KING: He made confession° of you,
And gave you such a masterly report
For art and exercise° in your defence°   95
And for your rapier most especial,
That he cried out, 'twould be a sight indeed,
If one could match you: the scrimers° of their nation,
He swore, had neither motion, guard, nor eye,
If you oppos'd them. Sir, this report of his   100
Did Hamlet so envenom with his envy
That he could nothing do but wish and beg
Your sudden coming o'er, to play° with you.
Now, out of this, —

LAERTES: What out of this, my lord?

KING: Laertes, was your father dear to you?   105
Or are you like the painting of a sorrow,
A face without a heart?

LAERTES: Why ask you this?

KING: Not that I think you did not love your father;
But that I know love is begun by time;
And that I see, in passages of proof,°   110
Time qualifies the spark and fire of it.
There lives within the very flame of love
A kind of wick or snuff that will abate it;
And nothing is at a like goodness still;

---

82 can well: Are skilled.   **85 incorps'd and demi-natur'd:** Of one body and nearly of one nature (like the centaur).   **86 topp'd:** Surpassed.   **87 forgery:** Invention.   **90 Lamord:** This refers possibly to Pietro Monte, instructor to Louis XII's master of the horse.   **93 confession:** Grudging admission of superiority.   **95 art and exercise:** Skillful exercise;   **defence:** Science of defense in sword practice.   **98 scrimers:** Fencers.   **103 play:** Fence.   **110 passages of proof:** Proved instances.

For goodness, growing to a plurisy,°   115
Dies in his own too much:° that we would do,
We should do when we would; for this "would" changes
And hath abatements° and delays as many
As there are tongues, are hands, are accidents;°
And then this "should" is like a spendthrift° sigh,   120
That hurts by easing. But, to the quick o' th' ulcer:° —
Hamlet comes back: what would you undertake,
To show yourself your father's son in deed
More than in words?
LAERTES: To cut his throat i' th' church.
KING: No place, indeed, should murder sanctuarize;°   125
Revenge should have no bounds. But, good Laertes,
Will you do this, keep close within your chamber.
Hamlet return'd shall know you are come home:
We'll put on those shall praise your excellence
And set a double varnish on the fame   130
The Frenchman gave you, bring you in fine together
And wager on your heads: he, being remiss,
Most generous and free from all contriving,
Will not peruse the foils; so that, with ease,
Or with a little shuffling, you may choose   135
A sword unbated,° and in a pass of practice°
Requite him for your father.
LAERTES: I will do 't:
And, for that purpose, I'll anoint my sword.
I bought an unction of a mountebank,°
So mortal that, but dip a knife in it,   140
Where it draws blood no cataplasm° so rare,
Collected from all simples° that have virtue
Under the moon,° can save the thing from death
That is but scratch'd withal: I'll touch my point
With this contagion, that, if I gall° him slightly,   145
It may be death.
KING: Let's further think of this;
Weigh what convenience both of time and means
May fit us to our shape:° if this should fail,

115 **plurisy:** Excess, plethora.   116 **in his own too much:** Of its own excess.   118 **abatements:** Diminutions.   119 **accidents:** Occurrences, incidents.   120 **spendthrift:** An allusion to the belief that each sigh cost the heart a drop of blood.   121 **quick o' th' ulcer:** Heart of the difficulty.   125 **sanctuarize:** Protect from punishment; allusion to the right of sanctuary with which certain religious places were invested.   136 **unbated:** Not blunted, having no button;   **pass of practice:** Treacherous thrust.   139 **mountebank:** Quack doctor.   141 **cataplasm:** Plaster or poultice.   142 **simples:** Herbs.   143 **Under the moon:** I.e., when collected by moonlight to add to their medicinal value.   145 **gall:** Graze, wound.   148 **shape:** Part we propose to act.

And that our drift look through our bad performance,°
'Twere better not assay'd: therefore this project   150
Should have a back or second, that might hold,
If this should blast in proof.° Soft! let me see:
We'll make a solemn wager on your cunnings:°
I ha 't:
When in your motion you are hot and dry—   155
As make your bouts more violent to that end —
And that he calls for drink, I'll have prepar'd him
A chalice° for the nonce, whereon but sipping,
If he by chance escape your venom'd stuck,°
Our purpose may hold there. But stay, what noise?   160

Enter Queen.

QUEEN: One woe doth tread upon another's heel,
So fast they follow: your sister's drown'd, Laertes.
LAERTES: Drown'd! O, where?
QUEEN: There is a willow° grows askant° the brook,
That shows his hoar° leaves in the glassy stream;   165
There with fantastic garlands did she make
Of crow-flowers,° nettles, daisies, and long purples°
That liberal° shepherds give a grosser name,
But our cold maids do dead men's fingers call them:
There, on the pendent boughs her crownet° weeds   170
Clamb'ring to hang, an envious sliver° broke;
When down her weedy° trophies and herself
Fell in the weeping brook. Her clothes spread wide;
And, mermaid-like, awhile they bore her up:
Which time she chanted snatches of old lauds;°   175
As one incapable° of her own distress,
Or like a creature native and indued°
Upon that element: but long it could not be
Till that her garments, heavy with their drink,
Pull'd the poor wretch from her melodious lay   180
To muddy death.
LAERTES: Alas, then, she is drown'd?
QUEEN: Drown'd, drown'd.
LAERTES: Too much of water hast thou, poor Ophelia,

---

149 **drift . . . performance:** Intention be disclosed by our bungling.   152 **blast in proof:**
Burst in the test (like a cannon).   153 **cunnings:** Skills.   158 **chalice:** Cup.   159 **stuck:**
Thrust (from *stoccado*).   164 **willow:** For its significance of forsaken love; **askant:** Aslant.
165 **hoar:** White (i.e., on the underside).   167 **crow-flowers:** Buttercups; **long purples:**
Early purple orchids.   168 **liberal:** Probably, free-spoken.   170 **crownet:** Coronet; made
into a chaplet.   171 **sliver:** Branch.   172 **weedy:** I.e., of plants.   175 **lauds:** Hymns.
176 **incapable:** Lacking capacity to apprehend.   177 **indued:** Endowed with qualities fitting
her for living in water.

And therefore I forbid my tears: but yet
It is our trick;° nature her custom holds,   185
Let shame say what it will: when these are gone,
The woman will be out.° Adieu, my lord:
I have a speech of fire, that fain would blaze,
But that this folly drowns it.   *Exit.*

KING: Let's follow, Gertrude:
How much I had to do to calm his rage!   190
Now fear I this will give it start again;
Therefore let 's follow.   *Exeunt.*

[ACT 5, Scene 1]

[A churchyard.]
Enter two Clowns° [with spades, &c.].

FIRST CLOWN: Is she to be buried in Christian burial when she wilfully seeks
her own salvation?

SECOND CLOWN: I tell thee she is; therefore make her grave straight:° the
crowner° hath sat on her, and finds it Christian burial.

FIRST CLOWN: How can that be, unless she drowned herself in her own   5
defence?

SECOND CLOWN: Why, 'tis found so.

FIRST CLOWN: It must be "se offendendo";° it cannot be else. For here lies the
point: if I drown myself wittingly,° it argues an act: and an act hath three
branches;° it is, to act, to do, and to perform: argal,° she drowned herself   10
wittingly.

SECOND CLOWN: Nay, but hear you, goodman delver,° —

FIRST CLOWN: Give me leave. Here lies the water; good: here stands the man;
good: if the man go to this water, and drown himself, it is, will he, nill he, he
goes, — mark you that; but if the water come to him and drown him, he   15
drowns not himself: argal, he that is not guilty of his own death shortens not
his own life.

SECOND CLOWN: But is this law?

FIRST CLOWN: Ay, marry, is 't; crowner's quest° law.

SECOND CLOWN: Will you ha' the truth on 't? If this had not been a gentle-   20
woman, she should have been buried out o' Christian burial.

---

185 **trick:** Way.   186–187 **when . . . out:** When my tears are all shed, the woman in me will
be satisfied.   ACT 5, SCENE 1. **Clowns:** The word *clown* was used to denote peasants as well as
humorous characters; here applied to the rustic type of clown.   3 **straight:** Straightway, immediately; some interpret "from east to west in a direct line, parallel with the church."
4 **crowner:** Coroner.   8 **"se offendendo":** For *se defendendo,* term used in verdicts of justifiable homicide.   9 **wittingly:** Intentionally.   9–10 **three branches:** Parody of legal phraseol-
ogy.   10 **argal:** Corruption of *ergo,* therefore.   12 **delver:** Digger.   19 **quest:** Inquest.

FIRST CLOWN: Why, there thou say'st:° and the more pity that great folk should have countenance° in this world to drown or hang themselves, more than their even° Christian. Come, my spade. There is no ancient gentlemen but gardeners, ditchers, and grave-makers: they hold up° Adam's profession.   25

SECOND CLOWN: Was he a gentleman?

FIRST CLOWN: 'A was the first that ever bore arms.

SECOND CLOWN: Why, he had none.

FIRST CLOWN: What, art a heathen? How dost thou understand the Scripture?   30
The Scripture says "Adam digged": could he dig without arms? I'll put another question to thee: if thou answerest me not to the purpose, confess thyself° —

SECOND CLOWN: Go to.°

FIRST CLOWN: What is he that builds stronger than either the mason, the ship-   35
wright, or the carpenter?

SECOND CLOWN: The gallows-maker; for that frame outlives a thousand tenants.

FIRST CLOWN: I like thy wit well, in good faith: the gallows does well; but how does it well? it does well to those that do ill: now thou dost ill to say the gal-   40
lows is built stronger than the church: argal, the gallows may do well to thee. To 't again, come.

SECOND CLOWN: "Who builds stronger than a mason, a shipwright, or a carpenter?"

FIRST CLOWN: Ay, tell me that, and unyoke.°   45

SECOND CLOWN: Marry, now I can tell.

FIRST CLOWN: To 't.

SECOND CLOWN: Mass,° I cannot tell.

Enter Hamlet and Horatio [at a distance].

FIRST CLOWN: Cudgel thy brains no more about it, for your dull ass will not mend his pace with beating; and, when you are asked this question next, say   50
"a grave-maker": the houses he makes lasts till doomsday. Go, get thee in, and fetch me a stoup° of liquor.   *[Exit Second Clown.] Song. [He digs.]*

In youth, when I did love, did love,
    Methought it was very sweet,
To contract — O — the time, for — a — my behove,°   55
    O, methought, there — a — was nothing — a — meet.

HAMLET: Has this fellow no feeling of his business, that 'a sings at grave-making?

HORATIO: Custom hath made it in him a property of easiness.°

---

22 **there thou say'st:** That's right.   23 **countenance:** Privilege.   24 **even:** Fellow.   25 **hold up:** Maintain, continue.   32–33 **confess thyself:** "And be hanged" completes the proverb. 34 **Go to:** Perhaps, "begin," or some other form of concession.   45 **unyoke:** After this great effort you may unharness the team of your wits.   48 **Mass:** By the Mass.   52 **stoup:** Two-quart measure.   55 **behove:** Benefit.   59 **property of easiness:** A peculiarity that now is easy.

HAMLET: 'Tis e'en so: the hand of little employment hath the daintier sense.   60
FIRST CLOWN: *(Song.)* But age, with his stealing steps,
    Hath claw'd me in his clutch,
And hath shipped me into the land
    As if I had never been such.   *[Throws up a skull.]*
HAMLET: That skull had a tongue in it, and could sing once: how the knave   65
jowls° it to the ground, as if 'twere Cain's jaw-bone,° that did the first murder!
This might be the pate of a politician,° which this ass now o'er-reaches;° one
that would circumvent God, might it not?
HORATIO: It might, my lord.
HAMLET: Or of a courtier; which could say "Good morrow, sweet lord! How   70
dost thou, sweet lord?" This might be my lord such-a-one, that praised my
lord such-a-one's horse, when he meant to beg it; might it not?
HORATIO: Ay, my lord.
HAMLET: Why, e'en so: and now my Lady Worm's; chapless,° and knocked
about the mazzard° with a sexton's spade: here's fine revolution, an we had   75
the trick to see 't. Did these bones cost no more the breeding, but to play at
loggats° with 'em? mine ache to think on 't.
FIRST CLOWN: *(Song.)* A pick-axe, and a spade, a spade,
    For and° a shrouding sheet:
O, a pit of clay for to be made   80
    For such a guest is meet.   *[Throws up another skull.]*
HAMLET: There's another: why may not that be the skull of a lawyer? Where be
his quiddities° now, his quillities,° his cases, his tenures,° and his tricks? why
does he suffer this mad knave now to knock him about the sconce° with a
dirty shovel, and will not tell him of his action of battery? Hum! This fellow   85
might be in 's time a great buyer of land, with his statutes, his recognizances,° his fines, his double vouchers,° his recoveries:° is this the fine° of
his fines, and the recovery of his recoveries, to have his fine pate full of fine
dirt? will his vouchers vouch him no more of his purchases, and double ones
too, than the length and breadth of a pair of indentures?° The very con-   90
veyances of his lands will scarcely lie in this box; and must the inheritor°
himself have no more, ha?
HORATIO: Not a jot more, my lord.
HAMLET: Is not parchment made of sheep-skins?
HORATIO: Ay, my lord, and of calf-skins° too.   95

---

66 jowls: Dashes;   **Cain's jaw-bone:** Allusion to the old tradition that Cain slew Abel with the
jawbone of an ass.   **67 politician:** Schemer, plotter;   **o'er-reaches:** Quibble on the literal sense
and the sense "circumvent."   **74 chapless:** Having no lower jaw.   **75 mazzard:** Head.   **77 log-**
gats: A game in which six sticks are thrown to lie as near as possible to a stake fixed in the ground, or
block of wood on a floor.   **79 For and:** And moreover.   **83 quiddities:** Subtleties, quibbles;
quillities: Verbal niceties, subtle distinctions;   **tenures:** The holding of a piece of property or office
or the conditions or period of such holding.   **84 sconce:** Head.   **86–87 statutes, recognizances:**
Legal terms connected with the transfer of land.   **87 vouchers:** Persons called on to warrant a tenant's title;   **recoveries:** Process for transfer of entailed estate;   **fine:** The four uses of this word are
as follows: (1) end, (2) legal process, (3) elegant, (4) small.   **90 indentures:** Conveyances or contracts.   **91 inheritor:** Possessor, owner.   **95 calf-skins:** Parchments.

HAMLET: They are sheep and calves which seek out assurance in that.° I will speak to this fellow. Whose grave's this, sirrah?

FIRST CLOWN: Mine, sir.

[*Sings.*] O, a pit of clay for to be made
For such a guest is meet.   100

HAMLET: I think it be thine, indeed; for thou liest in 't.

FIRST CLOWN: You lie out on 't, sir, and therefore 't is not yours: for my part, I do not lie in 't, yet it is mine.

HAMLET: Thou dost lie in 't, to be in 't and say it is thine: 'tis for the dead, not for the quick; therefore thou liest.   105

FIRST CLOWN: 'Tis a quick lie, sir; 'twill away again, from me to you.

HAMLET: What man dost thou dig it for?

FIRST CLOWN: For no man, sir.

HAMLET: What woman, then?

FIRST CLOWN: For none, neither.   110

HAMLET: Who is to be buried in 't?

FIRST CLOWN: One that was a woman, sir; but, rest her soul, she's dead.

HAMLET: How absolute° the knave is! we must speak by the card,° or equivocation° will undo us. By the Lord, Horatio, these three years I have taken note of it; the age is grown so picked° that the toe of the peasant comes so near the   115
heel of the courtier, he galls° his kibe.° How long hast thou been a grave-maker?

FIRST CLOWN: Of all the day i' the year, I came to 't that day that our last king Hamlet overcame Fortinbras.

HAMLET: How long is that since?   120

FIRST CLOWN: Cannot you tell that? every fool can tell that: it was the very day that young Hamlet was born; he that is mad, and sent into England.

HAMLET: Ay, marry, why was he sent into England?

FIRST CLOWN: Why, because 'a was mad: 'a shall recover his wits there; or, if 'a do not, 'tis no great matter there.   125

HAMLET: Why?

FIRST CLOWN: 'Twill not be seen in him there; there the men are as mad as he.

HAMLET: How came he mad?

FIRST CLOWN: Very strangely, they say.

HAMLET: How strangely?   130

FIRST CLOWN: Faith, e'en with losing his wits.

HAMLET: Upon what ground?

FIRST CLOWN: Why, here in Denmark: I have been sexton here, man and boy, thirty years.°

HAMLET: How long will a man lie i' the earth ere he rot?   135

---

96 assurance in that: Safety in legal parchments.   **113 absolute:** Positive, decided;   **by the card:** With precision, i.e., by the mariner's card on which the points of the compass were marked.   **113–114 equivocation:** Ambiguity in the use of terms.   **115 picked:** Refined, fastidious.   **116 galls:** Chafes;   **kibe:** Chilblain.   **134 thirty years:** This statement with that in line 122 shows Hamlet's age to be thirty years.

FIRST CLOWN: Faith, if 'a be not rotten before 'a die — as we have many pocky°
corses now-a-days, that will scarce hold the laying in — 'a will last you some
eight year or nine year: a tanner will last you nine year.

HAMLET: Why he more than another?

FIRST CLOWN: Why, sir, his hide is so tanned with his trade, that 'a will keep out   140
water a great while; and your water is a sore decayer of your whoreson dead
body. Here's a skull now hath lain you i' th' earth three and twenty years.

HAMLET: Whose was it?

FIRST CLOWN: A whoreson mad fellow's it was: whose do you think it was?

HAMLET: Nay, I know not.   145

FIRST CLOWN: A pestilence on him for a mad rogue! 'a poured a flagon of Rhen-
ish on my head once. This same skull, sir, was Yorick's skull, the king's jester.

HAMLET: This?

FIRST CLOWN: E'en that.

HAMLET: Let me see. *[Takes the skull.]* Alas, poor Yorick! I knew him, Horatio: a   150
fellow of infinite jest, of most excellent fancy: he hath borne me on his back
a thousand times; and now, how abhorred in my imagination it is! my gorge
rises at it. Here hung those lips that I have kissed I know not how oft. Where
be your gibes now? your gambols? your songs? your flashes of merriment,
that were wont to set the table on a roar? Not one now, to mock your own   155
grinning? quite chap-fallen? Now get you to my lady's chamber, and tell her,
let her paint an inch thick, to this favour she must come; make her laugh at
that. Prithee, Horatio, tell me one thing.

HORATIO: What's that, my lord?

HAMLET: Dost thou think Alexander looked o' this fashion i' the earth?   160

HORATIO: E'en so.

HAMLET: And smelt so? pah!   *[Puts down the skull.]*

HORATIO: E'en so, my lord.

HAMLET: To what base uses we may return, Horatio! Why may not imagination
trace the noble dust of Alexander, till 'a find it stopping a bung-hole?   165

HORATIO: 'Twere to consider too curiously,° to consider so.

HAMLET: No, faith, not a jot; but to follow him thither with modesty enough,
and likelihood to lead it: as thus: Alexander died, Alexander was buried,
Alexander returneth into dust; the dust is earth; of earth we make loam;° and
why of that loam, whereto he was converted, might they not stop a beer-   170
barrel?
Imperious° Cæsar, dead and turn'd to clay,
Might stop a hole to keep the wind away:
O, that that earth, which kept the world in awe,
Should patch a wall t'expel the winter's flaw!°   175
But soft! but soft awhile! here comes the king,

*Enter King, Queen, Laertes, and the Corse of [Ophelia, in procession, with Priest,
Lords, etc.].*

---

136 pocky: Rotten, diseased. **166 curiously:** Minutely. **169 loam:** Clay paste for brick-
making. **172 Imperious:** Imperial. **175 flaw:** Gust of wind.

The queen, the courtiers: who is this they follow?
And with such maimed rites? This doth betoken
The corse they follow did with desp'rate hand
Fordo° it° own life: 'twas of some estate.   180
Couch° we awhile, and mark.   *[Retiring with Horatio.]*
LAERTES: What ceremony else?
HAMLET: That is Laertes,
A very noble youth: mark.
LAERTES: What ceremony else?
FIRST PRIEST: Her obsequies have been as far enlarg'd°   185
As we have warranty: her death was doubtful;
And, but that great command o'ersways the order,
She should in ground unsanctified have lodg'd
Till the last trumpet; for charitable prayers,
Shards,° flints and pebbles should be thrown on her: 190
Yet here she is allow'd her virgin crants,°
Her maiden strewments° and the bringing home
Of bell and burial.°
LAERTES: Must there no more be done?
FIRST PRIEST: No more be done:
We should profane the service of the dead   195
To sing a requiem and such rest to her
As to peace-parted° souls.
LAERTES: Lay her i' th' earth:
And from her fair and unpolluted flesh
May violets spring! I tell thee, churlish priest,
A minist'ring angel shall my sister be,   200
When thou liest howling.°
HAMLET: What, the fair Ophelia!
QUEEN: Sweets to the sweet: farewell!   *[Scattering flowers.]*
I hop'd thou shouldst have been my Hamlet's wife;
I thought thy bride-bed to have deck'd, sweet maid,
And not have strew'd thy grave.
LAERTES: O, treble woe   205
Fall ten times treble on that cursed head,
Whose wicked deed thy most ingenious sense°
Depriv'd thee of! Hold off the earth awhile,
Till I have caught her once more in mine arms: *[Leaps into the grave.]*
Now pile your dust upon the quick and dead,   210
Till of this flat a mountain you have made,

---

180 **Fordo:** Destroy; **it:** Its.   181 **Couch:** Hide, lurk.   185 **enlarg'd:** Extended, referring to the fact that suicides are not given full burial rites.   190 **Shards:** Broken bits of pottery.   191 **crants:** Garlands customarily hung upon the biers of unmarried women.   192 **strewments:** Traditional strewing of flowers.   192–193 **bringing . . . burial:** The laying to rest of the body, to the sound of the bell.   197 **peace-parted:** Allusion to the text "Lord, now lettest thou thy servant depart in peace."   201 **howling:** I.e., in hell.   207 **ingenious sense:** Mind endowed with finest qualities.

T' o'ertop old Pelion,° or the skyish head
Of blue Olympus.
HAMLET: *[Advancing]* What is he whose grief
Bears such an emphasis? whose phrase of sorrow
Conjures the wand'ring stars,° and makes them stand   215
Like wonder-wounded hearers? This is I,
Hamlet the Dane.   *[Leaps into the grave.]*
LAERTES: The devil take thy soul!   *[Grappling with him.]*
HAMLET: Thou pray'st not well.
I prithee, take thy fingers from my throat;
For, though I am not splenitive° and rash,   220
Yet have I in me something dangerous,
Which let thy wisdom fear: hold off thy hand.
KING: Pluck them asunder.
QUEEN: Hamlet, Hamlet!
ALL: Gentlemen, —
HORATIO: Good my lord, be quiet.

[The Attendants part them, and they come out of the grave.]

HAMLET: Why, I will fight with him upon this theme   225
Until my eyelids will no longer wag.°
QUEEN: O my son, what theme?
HAMLET: I lov'd Ophelia: forty thousand brothers
Could not, with all their quantity° of love,
Make up my sum. What wilt thou do for her?   230
KING: O, he is mad, Laertes.
QUEEN: For love of God, forbear° him.
HAMLET: 'Swounds,° show me what thou 'lt do:
Woo 't° weep? woo 't fight? woo 't fast? woo 't tear thyself?
Woo 't drink up eisel?° eat a crocodile?   235
I'll do 't. Dost thou come here to whine?
To outface me with leaping in her grave?
Be buried quick with her, and so will I:
And, if thou prate of mountains, let them throw
Millions of acres on us, till our ground,   240
Singeing his pate against the burning zone,°
Make Ossa like a wart! Nay, an thou 'lt mouth,
I'll rant as well as thou.
QUEEN: This is mere madness:
And thus awhile the fit will work on him;

212 **Pelion:** Olympus, Pelion, and Ossa are mountains in the north of Thessaly.   215 **wand'ring stars:** Planets.   220 **splenitive:** Quick-tempered.   226 **wag:** Move (not used ludicrously).
229 **quantity:** Some suggest that the word is used in a deprecatory sense (little bits, fragments).
232 **forbear:** Leave alone.   233 **'Swounds:** Oath, "God's wounds."   234 **Woo 't:** Wilt thou.
235 **eisel:** Vinegar. Some editors have taken this to be the name of a river, such as the Yssel, the Weissel, and the Nile.   241 **burning zone:** Sun's orbit.

Anon, as patient as the female dove.   245
When that her golden couplets° are disclos'd,
His silence will sit drooping.

HAMLET: Hear you, sir;
What is the reason that you use me thus?
I lov'd you ever: but it is no matter;
Let Hercules himself do what he may,   250
The cat will mew and dog will have his day.

KING: I pray thee, good Horatio, wait upon him.   *Exit Hamlet and Horatio.*
[*To Laertes.*] Strengthen your patience in° our last night's speech;
We'll put the matter to the present push.°
Good Gertrude, set some watch over your son.   255
This grave shall have a living° monument:
An hour of quiet shortly shall we see;
Till then, in patience our proceeding be.   *Exeunt.*

[Scene 2]

[*A hall in the castle.*]
Enter Hamlet and Horatio.

HAMLET: So much for this, sir: now shall you see the other;
You do remember all the circumstance?

HORATIO: Remember it, my lord!

HAMLET: Sir, in my heart there was a kind of fighting,
That would not let me sleep: methought I lay   5
Worse than the mutines in the bilboes.° Rashly,°
And prais'd be rashness for it, let us know,
Our indiscretion sometime serves us well,
When our deep plots do pall:° and that should learn us
There's a divinity that shapes our ends,   10
Rough-hew° them how we will, —

HORATIO: That is most certain.

HAMLET: Up from my cabin,
My sea-gown° scarf'd about me, in the dark
Grop'd I to find out them; had my desire,
Finger'd° their packet, and in fine° withdrew   15
To mine own room again; making so bold,
My fears forgetting manners, to unseal
Their grand commission; where I found, Horatio, —

246 golden couplets: The pigeon lays two eggs; the young when hatched are covered with golden down.   **253 in:** By recalling.   **254 present push:** Immediate test.   **256 living:** Lasting; also refers (for Laertes's benefit) to the plot against Hamlet.   **SCENE 2. 6 mutines in the bilboes:** Mutineers in shackles; **Rashly:** Goes with line 12.   **9 pall:** Fail.   **11 Rough-hew:** Shape roughly; it may mean "bungle."   **13 sea-gown:** "A sea-gown, or a coarse, high-collered, and short-sleeved gowne, reaching down to the mid-leg, and used most by seamen and saylors" (Cotgrave, quoted by Singer).   **15 Finger'd:** Pilfered, filched;   **in fine:** Finally.

O royal knavery! — an exact command,
Larded° with many several sorts of reasons   20
Importing Denmark's health and England's too,
With, ho! such bugs° and goblins in my life,°
That, on the supervise,° no leisure bated,°
No, not to stay the grinding of the axe,
My head should be struck off.
HORATIO: Is 't possible?   25
HAMLET: Here's the commission: read it at more leisure.
      But wilt thou hear me how I did proceed?
HORATIO: I beseech you.
HAMLET: Being thus be-netted round with villanies, —
      Ere I could make a prologue to my brains,   30
      They had begun the play°— I sat me down,
      Devis'd a new commission, wrote it fair:
      I once did hold it, as our statists° do,
      A baseness to write fair° and labour'd much
      How to forget that learning, but, sir, now   35
      It did me yeoman's° service: wilt thou know
      Th' effect of what I wrote?
HORATIO: Ay, good my lord.
HAMLET: An earnest conjuration from the king,
      As England was his faithful tributary,
      As love between them like the palm might flourish,   40
      As peace should still her wheaten garland° wear
      And stand a comma° 'tween their amities,
      And many such-like 'As'es° of great charge,°
      That, on the view and knowing of these contents,
      Without debatement further, more or less,   45
      He should the bearers put to sudden death,
      Not shriving-time° allow'd.
HORATIO: How was this seal'd?
HAMLET: Why, even in that was heaven ordinant.°
      I had my father's signet in my purse,
      Which was the model of that Danish seal;   50
      Folded the writ up in the form of th' other,
      Subscrib'd it, gave 't th' impression, plac'd it safely,
      The changeling never known. Now, the next day

---

20 Larded: Enriched.   **22 bugs:** Bugbears;   **such . . . life:** Such imaginary dangers if I were
allowed to live.   **23 supervise:** Perusal;   **leisure bated:** Delay allowed.   **30–31 prologue . . .
play:** I.e., before I could begin to think, my mind had made its decision.   **33 statists:** States-
men.   **34 fair:** In a clear hand.   **36 yeoman's:** I.e., faithful.   **41 wheaten garland:** Symbol
of peace.   **42 comma:** Smallest break or separation. Here *amity* begins and *amity* ends the
period, and *peace* stands between like a dependent clause. The comma indicates continuity,
link.   **43 'As'es:** The "whereases" of a formal document, with play on the word *ass*;   **charge:**
Import, and burden.   **47 shriving-time:** Time for absolution.   **48 ordinant:** Directing.

Was our sea-fight; and what to this was sequent°
Thou know'st already.   55
HORATIO: So Guildenstern and Rosencrantz go to 't.
HAMLET: Why, man, they did make love to this employment;
They are not near my conscience; their defeat
Does by their own insinuation° grow:
'Tis dangerous when the baser nature comes   60
Between the pass° and fell incensed° points
Of mighty opposites.
HORATIO: Why, what a king is this!
HAMLET: Does it not, think thee, stand° me now upon —
He that hath kill'd my king and whor'd my mother,
Popp'd in between th' election° and my hopes,   65
Thrown out his angle° for my proper life,
And with such coz'nage° — is 't not perfect conscience,
To quit° him with this arm? and is 't not to be damn'd,
To let this canker° of our nature come
In further evil?   70
HORATIO: It must be shortly known to him from England
What is the issue of the business there.
HAMLET: It will be short: the interim is mine;
And a man's life's no more than to say "One."
But I am very sorry, good Horatio,   75
That to Laertes I forgot myself;
For, by the image of my cause, I see
The portraiture of his: I'll court his favours:
But, sure, the bravery° of his grief did put me
Into a tow'ring passion.
HORATIO: Peace! who comes here?   80

Enter a Courtier [Osric].

OSRIC: Your lordship is right welcome back to Denmark.
HAMLET: I humbly thank you, sir. *[To Horatio.]* Dost know this water-fly?°
HORATIO: No, my good lord.
HAMLET: Thy state is the more gracious; for 'tis a vice to know him. He hath
much land, and fertile: let a beast be lord of beasts,° and his crib shall stand   85
at the king's mess:° 'tis a chough;° but, as I say, spacious in the possession of
dirt.

---

54 **sequent**: Subsequent.   59 **insinuation**: Interference.   61 **pass**: Thrust;   **fell incensed**:
Fiercely angered.   63 **stand**: Become incumbent.   65 **election**: The Danish throne was
filled by election.   66 **angle**: Fishing line.   67 **coz'nage**: Trickery.   68 **quit**: Repay.
69 **canker**: Ulcer, or possibly the worm which destroys buds and leaves.   79 **bravery**:
Bravado.   82 **water-fly**: Vain or busily idle person.   85 **lord of beasts**: See Genesis 1:26, 28.
85–86 **his crib . . . mess**: He shall eat at the king's table and be one of the group of persons
(usually four) constituting a *mess* at a banquet.   86 **chough**: Probably, chattering jackdaw;
also explained as *chuff*, provincial boor or churl.

OSRIC: Sweet lord, if your lordship were at leisure, I should impart a thing to
you from his majesty.

HAMLET: I will receive it, sir, with all diligence of spirit. Put your bonnet to his   90
right use; 'tis for the head.

OSRIC: I thank you lordship, it is very hot.

HAMLET: No, believe me, 'tis very cold; the wind is northerly.

OSRIC: It is indifferent° cold, my lord, indeed.

HAMLET: But yet methinks it is very sultry and hot for my complexion.   95

OSRIC: Exceedingly, my lord; it is very sultry,—as 'twere,—I cannot tell how.
But, my lord, his majesty bade me signify to you that 'a has laid a great wager
on your head: sir, this is the matter,—

HAMLET: I beseech you, remember°—   *[Hamlet moves him to put on his hat.]*

OSRIC: Nay, good my lord; for mine ease,° in good faith. Sir, here is newly come   100
to court Laertes; believe me, an absolute gentleman, full of most excellent
differences, of very soft° society and great showing:° indeed, to speak
feelingly° of him, he is the card° or calendar of gentry,° for you shall find in
him the continent of what part a gentleman would see.

HAMLET: Sir, his definement° suffers no perdition° in you; though, I know, to   105
divide him inventorially° would dozy° the arithmetic of memory, and yet but
yaw° neither, in respect of his quick sail. But, in the verity of extolment, I
take him to be a soul of great article;° and his infusion° of such dearth and
rareness,° as, to make true diction of him, his semblable° is his mirror; and
who else would trace° him, his umbrage,° nothing more.   110

OSRIC: Your lordship speaks most infallibly of him.

HAMLET: The concernancy,° sir? why do we wrap the gentleman in our more
rawer breath?°

OSRIC: Sir?

HORATIO *[aside to Hamlet]:*   Is 't not possible to understand in another tongue?°   115
You will do 't, sir, really.

HAMLET: What imports the nomination° of this gentleman?

OSRIC: Of Laertes?

Horatio [aside to Hamlet]:   His purse is empty already; all 's golden words are
spent.   120

HAMLET: Of him, sir.

---

94 indifferent: Somewhat.   **99 remember:** I.e., remember thy courtesy; conventional phrase
for "Be covered."   **100 mine ease:** Conventional reply declining the invitation of "Remember
thy courtesy."   **102 soft:** Gentle; **showing:** Distinguished appearance.   **103 feelingly:**
With just perception;   **card:** Chart, map;   **gentry:** Good breeding.   **105 definement:** Definition;   **perdition:** Loss, diminution.   **106 divide him inventorially:** I.e., enumerate his
graces;   **dozy:** Dizzy.   **107 yaw:** To move unsteadily (of a ship).   **108 article:** Moment or
importance;   **infusion:** Infused temperament, character imparted by nature.
108–109 dearth and rareness: Rarity.   **109 semblable:** True likeness.   **110 trace:** Follow;
umbrage: Shadow.   **112 concernancy:** Import.   **113 breath:** Speech.   **115 Is 't . . . tongue?:**
I.e., can one converse with Osric only in this outlandish jargon?   **117 nomination:** Naming.

OSRIC: I know you are not ignorant—

HAMLET: I would you did, sir; yet, in faith, if you did, it would not much approve° me. Well, sir?

OSRIC: You are not ignorant of what excellence Laertes is—   125

HAMLET: I dare not confess that, lest I should compare with him in excellence; but, to know a man well, were to know himself.°

OSRIC: I mean, sir, for his weapon; but in the imputation° laid on him by them, in his meed° he's unfellowed.

HAMLET: What's his weapon?   130

OSRIC: Rapier and dagger.

HAMLET: That's two of his weapons: but, well.

OSRIC: The king, sir, hath wagered with him six Barbary horses: against the which he has impawned,° as I take it, six French rapiers and poniards, with their assigns, as girdle, hangers,° and so: three of the carriages, in faith, are   135 very dear to fancy,° very responsive° to the hilts, most delicate° carriages, and of very liberal conceit.°

HAMLET: What call you the carriages?

HORATIO [*aside to Hamlet*]:   I knew you must be edified by the margent° ere you had done.   140

OSRIC: The carriages, sir, are the hangers.

HAMLET: The phrase would be more german° to the matter, if we could carry cannon by our sides: I would it might be hangers till then. But, on: six Barbary horses against six French swords, their assigns, and three liberal-conceited carriages; that's the French bet against the Danish. Why is this   145 "impawned," as you call it?

OSRIC: The king, sir, hath laid, that in a dozen passes between yourself and him, he shall not exceed you three hits: he hath laid on twelve for nine; and it would come to immediate trial, if your lordship would vouchsafe the answer.   150

HAMLET: How if I answer "no"?

OSRIC: I mean, my lord, the opposition of your person in trial.

HAMLET: Sir, I will walk here in the hall: if it please his majesty, it is the breathing time° of day with me; let the foils be brought, the gentleman willing, and the king hold his purpose, I will win for him as I can; if not, I will gain nothing   155 but my shame and the odd hits.

OSRIC: Shall I re-deliver you e'en so?

HAMLET: To this effect, sir; after what flourish your nature will.

OSRIC: I commend my duty to your lordship.

---

124 **approve:** Command.   127 **but . . . himself:** But to know a man as excellent were to know Laertes.   128 **imputation:** Reputation.   129 **meed:** Merit.   134 **he has impawned:** He has wagered.   135 **hangers:** Straps on the sword belt from which the sword hung.   136 **dear to fancy:** Fancifully made;   **responsive:** Probably, well balanced, corresponding closely;   **delicate:** Fine in workmanship.   137 **liberal conceit:** Elaborate design.   139 **margent:** Margin of a book, place for explanatory notes.   142 **german:** Germane, appropriate.   153–154 **breathing time:** Exercise period.

HAMLET: Yours, yours. *[Exit Osric.]* He does well to commend it himself; there   160
    are no tongues else for 's turn.
HORATIO: This lapwing° runs away with the shell on his head.
HAMLET: 'A did comply, sir, with his dug,° before 'a sucked it. Thus has hey —
    and many more of the same breed that I know the drossy° age dotes on —
    only got the tune° of the time and out of an habit of encounter;° a kind of   165
    yesty° collection, which carries them through and through the most fann'd
    and winnowed° opinions; and do but blow them to their trial, the bubbles
    are out.°

Enter a Lord.

LORD: My lord, his majesty commended him to you by young Osric, who
    brings back to him, that you attend him in the hall: he sends to know if your   170
    pleasure hold to play with Laertes, or that you will take longer time.
HAMLET: I am constant to my purposes; they follow the king's pleasure: if his fit-
    ness speaks, mine is ready; now or whensoever, provided I be so able as now.
LORD: The king and queen and all are coming down.
HAMLET: In happy time.°   175
LORD: The queen desires you to use some gentle entertainment to Laertes
    before you fall to play.
HAMLET: She well instructs me.   *[Exit Lord.]*
HORATIO: You will lose this wager, my lord.
HAMLET: I do not think so; since he went into France, I have been in continual   180
    practice; I shall win at the odds. But thou wouldst not think how ill all 's here
    about my heart: but it is no matter.
HORATIO: Nay, good my lord, —
HAMLET: It is but foolery; but it is such a kind of gain-giving,° as would perhaps
    trouble a woman.   185
HORATIO: If your mind dislike any thing, obey it: I will forestall their repair
    hither, and say you are not fit.
HAMLET: Not a whit, we defy augury: there's a special providence in the fall of a
    sparrow. If it be now, 'tis not to come; if it be not to come, it will be now; if it
    be not now, yet it will come: the readiness is all:° since no man of aught he   190
    leaves knows, what is 't to leave betimes? Let be.

*A table prepared. [Enter] Trumpets, Drums, and Officers with cushions; King,
Queen, [Osric,] and all the State; foils, daggers, [and wine borne in;] and Laertes.*

KING: Come, Hamlet, come, and take this hand from me.

[The King puts Laertes' hand into Hamlet's.]

---

162 lapwing: Peewit; noted for its wiliness in drawing a visitor away from its nest and its
supposed habit of running about when newly hatched with its head in the shell; possibly
an allusion to Osric's hat.   **163 did comply . . . dug:** Paid compliments to his mother's
breast.   **164 drossy:** Frivolous.   **165 tune:** Temper, mood;   **habit of encounter:** Demeanor
of social intercourse.   **166 yesty:** Frothy.   **166–167 fann'd and winnowed:** Select and refined.
167–168 blow . . . out: I.e., put them to the test, and their ignorance is exposed.   **175 In happy
time:** A phrase of courtesy.   **184 gain-giving:** Misgiving.   **190 all:** All that matters.

HAMLET: Give me your pardon, sir: I have done you wrong;
　　　　But pardon 't as you are a gentleman.
　　　　This presence° knows,   195
　　　　And you must needs have heard, how I am punish'd
　　　　With a sore distraction. What I have done,
　　　　That might your nature, honour and exception°
　　　　Roughly awake, I here proclaim was madness.
　　　　Was 't Hamlet wrong'd Laertes? Never Hamlet: 200
　　　　If Hamlet from himself be ta'en away,
　　　　And when he's not himself does wrong Laertes,
　　　　Then Hamlet does it not, Hamlet denies it.
　　　　Who does it, then? His madness: if 't be so,
　　　　Hamlet is of the faction that is wrong'd;   205
　　　　His madness is poor Hamlet's enemy.
　　　　Sir, in this audience,
　　　　Let my disclaiming from a purpos'd evil
　　　　Free me so far in your most generous thoughts,
　　　　That I have shot mine arrow o'er the house,   210
　　　　And hurt my brother.
LAERTES: I am satisfied in nature,°
　　　　Whose motive, in this case, should stir me most
　　　　To my revenge: but in my terms of honour
　　　　I stand aloof; and will no reconcilement,
　　　　Till by some elder masters, of known honour,   215
　　　　I have a voice° and precedent of peace,
　　　　To keep my name ungor'd. But till that time,
　　　　I do receive your offer'd love like love,
　　　　And will not wrong it.
HAMLET: I embrace it freely;
　　　　And will this brother's wager frankly play.   220
　　　　Give us the foils. Come on.
LAERTES: Come, one for me.
HAMLET: I'll be your foil,° Laertes: in mine ignorance
　　　　Your skill shall, like a star i' th' darkest night,
　　　　Stick fiery off° indeed.
LAERTES: You mock me, sir.
HAMLET: No, by this hand.   225
KING: Give them the foils, young Osric. Cousin Hamlet,
　　　　You know the wager?
HAMLET: Very well, my lord;
　　　　Your grace has laid the odds o' th' weaker side.

---

195 presence: Royal assembly.   **198 exception:** Disapproval.   **211 nature:** I.e., he is personally satisfied, but his honor must be satisfied by the rules of the code of honor.   **216 voice:** Authoritative pronouncement.   **222 foil:** Quibble on the two senses: "background which sets something off," and "blunted rapier for fencing."   **224 Stick fiery off:** Stand out brilliantly.

KING: I do not fear it; I have seen you both:
    But since he is better'd, we have therefore odds.   230
LAERTES: This is too heavy, let me see another.
HAMLET: This likes me well. These foils have all a length?

[They prepare to play.]

OSRIC: Ay, my good lord.
KING: Set me the stoups of wine upon that table.
    If Hamlet give the first or second hit,   235
    Or quit in answer of the third exchange,
    Let all the battlements their ordnance fire;
    The king shall drink to Hamlet's better breath;
    And in the cup an union° shall he throw,
    Richer than that which four successive kings   240
    In Denmark's crown have worn. Give me the cups;
    And let the kettle° to the trumpet speak,
    The trumpet to the cannoneer without,
    The cannons to the heavens, the heavens to earth,
    "Now the king drinks to Hamlet." Come begin: *Trumpets the while.*   245
    And you, the judges, bear a wary eye.
HAMLET: Come on, sir.
LAERTES: Come, my lord.   *[They play.]*
HAMLET: One.
LAERTES: No.
HAMLET: Judgement.
OSRIC: A hit, a very palpable hit.

Drum, trumpets, and shot. Flourish. A piece goes off.

LAERTES: Well; again.
KING: Stay; give me drink. Hamlet, this pearl° is thine;
    Here's to thy health. Give him the cup.   250
HAMLET: I'll play this bout first; set it by awhile.
    Come. *[They play.]* Another hit; what say you?
LAERTES: A touch, a touch, I do confess 't.
KING: Our son shall win.
QUEEN: He's fat,° and scant of breath.
    Here, Hamlet, take my napkin, rub thy brows: 255
    The queen carouses° to thy fortune, Hamlet.
HAMLET: Good madam!
KING: Gertrude, do not drink.
QUEEN: I will, my lord; I pray you, pardon me.   *[Drinks.]*
KING *[aside]*:   It is the poison'd cup: it is too late.

---

239 union: Pearl.   **242 kettle:** Kettledrum.   **249 pearl:** I.e., the poison.   **254 fat:** Not
physically fit, out of training. Some earlier editors speculated that the term applied to the cor-
pulence of Richard Burbage, who originally played the part, but the allusion now appears
unlikely. *Fat* may also suggest "sweaty."   **256 carouses:** Drinks a toast.

HAMLET: I dare not drink yet, madam; by and by.   260
QUEEN: Come, let me wipe thy face.
LAERTES: My lord, I'll hit him now.
KING: I do not think 't.
LAERTES *[aside]:*   And yet 'tis almost 'gainst my conscience.
HAMLET: Come, for the third, Laertes: you but dally;
    I pray you, pass with your best violence;   265
    I am afeard you make a wanton° of me.
LAERTES: Say you so? come on.   *[They play.]*
OSRIC: Nothing, neither way.
LAERTES: Have at you now!

*[Laertes wounds Hamlet; then, in scuffling, they change rapiers,° and Hamlet
wounds Laertes.]*

KING: Part them; they are incens'd.
HAMLET: Nay, come again.   *[The Queen falls.]*
OSRIC: Look to the queen there, ho!   270
HORATIO: They bleed on both sides. How is it, my lord?
OSRIC: How is 't, Laertes?
LAERTES: Why, as a woodcock° to mine own springe,° Osric;
    I am justly kill'd with mine own treachery.
HAMLET: How does the queen?
KING: She swounds° to see them bleed.   275
QUEEN: No, no, the drink, the drink,—O my dear Hamlet,—
    The drink, the drink! I am poison'd.   *[Dies.]*
HAMLET: O villany! Ho! let the door be lock'd:
    Treachery! Seek it out.   *[Laertes falls.]*
LAERTES: It is here, Hamlet: Hamlet, thou art slain;   280
    No med'cine in the world can do thee good;
    In thee there is not half an hour of life;
    The treacherous instrument is in thy hand,
    Unbated° and envenom'd: the foul practice
    Hath turn'd itself on me; lo, here I lie,   285
    Never to rise again: thy mother's poison'd:
    I can no more: the king, the king's to blame.
HAMLET: The point envenom'd too!
    Then, venom, to thy work.   *[Stabs the King.]*
ALL: Treason! treason!   290
KING: O, yet defend me, friends; I am but hurt.
HAMLET: Here, thou incestuous, murd'rous, damned Dane,
    Drink off this potion. Is thy union here?
    Follow my mother.   *[King dies.]*

---

266 wanton: Spoiled child; **in scuffling, they change rapiers:** According to a widespread
stage tradition, Hamlet receives a scratch, realizes that Laertes's sword is unbated, and accordingly forces an exchange.   **273 woodcock:** As type of stupidity or as decoy; **springe:** Trap,
snare.   **275 swounds:** Swoons.   **284 Unbated:** Not blunted with a button.

LAERTES: He is justly serv'd;
   It is a poison temper'd° by himself.   295
   Exchange forgiveness with me, noble Hamlet:
   Mine and my father's death come not upon thee,
   Nor thine on me!   *[Dies.]*
HAMLET: Heaven make thee free of it! I follow thee.
   I am dead, Horatio. Wretched queen, adieu!   300
   You that look pale and tremble at this chance,
   That are but mutes° or audience to this act,
   Had I but time — as this fell sergeant,° Death,
   Is strict in his arrest — O, I could tell you —
   But let it be. Horatio, I am dead;   305
   Thou livest; report me and my cause aright
   To the unsatisfied.
HORATIO: Never believe it:
   I am more an antique Roman° than a Dane:
   Here 's yet some liquor left.
HAMLET: As th' art a man,
   Give me the cup: let go, by heaven, I'll ha 't.   310
   O God! Horatio, what a wounded name,
   Things standing thus unknown, shall live behind me!
   If thou didst ever hold me in thy heart,
   Absent thee from felicity awhile,
   And in this harsh world draw thy breath in pain,   315
   To tell my story.   *A march afar off.*
          What warlike noise is this?
OSRIC: Young Fortinbras, with conquest come from Poland,
   To the ambassadors of England gives
   This warlike volley.
HAMLET: O, I die, Horatio;
   The potent poison quite o'er-crows° my spirit: 320
   I cannot live to hear the news from England;
   But I do prophesy th' election lights
   On Fortinbras: he has my dying voice;
   So tell him, with th' occurrents,° more and less,
   Which have solicited.° The rest is silence.   *[Dies.]* 325
HORATIO: Now cracks a noble heart. Good night, sweet prince;
   And flights of angels sing thee to thy rest!
   Why does the drum come hither?   *[March within.]*
Enter Fortinbras, with the [English] Ambassadors [and others].
FORTINBRAS: Where is this sight?

---

295 temper'd: Mixed.   **302 mutes:** Performers in a play who speak no words.   **303 sergeant:**
Sheriff's officer.   **308 Roman:** It was the Roman custom to follow masters in death.   **320 o'er-
crows:** Triumphs over.   **324 occurrents:** Events, incidents.   **325 solicited:** Moved, urged.

HORATIO: What is it you would see?
  If aught of woe or wonder, cease your search.   330
FORTINBRAS: This quarry° cries on havoc.° O proud Death,
  What feast is toward in thine eternal cell,
  That thou so many princes at a shot
  So bloodily hast struck?
FIRST AMBASSADOR: The sight is dismal;
  And our affairs from England come too late: 335
  The ears are senseless that should give us hearing,
  To tell him his commandment is fulfill'd,
  That Rosencrantz and Guildenstern are dead:
  Where should we have our thanks?
HORATIO: Not from his mouth,°
  Had it th' ability of life to thank you: 340
  He never gave commandment for their death.
  But since, so jump° upon this bloody question,°
  You from the Polack wars, and you from England,
  Are here arriv'd, give order that these bodies
  High on a stage° be placed to the view;   345
  And let me speak to th' yet unknowing world
  How these things came about: so shall you hear
  Of carnal, bloody, and unnatural acts,
  Of accidental judgements, casual slaughters,
  Of deaths put on by cunning and forc'd cause,   350
  And, in this upshot, purposes mistook
  Fall'n on th' inventors' heads: all this can I
  Truly deliver.
FORTINBRAS: Let us haste to hear it,
  And call the noblest to the audience.
  For me, with sorrow I embrace my fortune: 355
  I have some rights of memory° in this kingdom,
  Which now to claim my vantage doth invite me.
HORATIO: Of that I shall have also cause to speak,
  And from his mouth whose voice will draw on more:°
  But let this same be presently perform'd,   360
  Even while men's minds are wild; lest more mischance,
  On° plots and errors, happen.
FORTINBRAS: Let four captains
  Bear Hamlet, like a soldier, to the stage;
  For he was likely, had he been put on,
  To have prov'd most royal: and, for his passage,°   365

---

331 **quarry:** Heap of dead;   **cries on havoc:** Proclaims a general slaughter.   339 **his mouth:** I.e.,
the king's.   342 **jump:** Precisely;   **question:** Dispute.   345 **stage:** Platform.   356 **of memory:**
Traditional, remembered.   359 **voice . . . more:** Vote will influence still others.   362 **On:** On
account of, or possibly, on top of, in addition to.   365 **passage:** Death.

The soldiers' music and the rites of war
Speak loudly for him.
Take up the bodies: such a sight as this
Becomes the field,° but here shows much amiss.
Go, bid the soldiers shoot.   370

*Exeunt [marching, bearing off the dead bodies; after which a peal of ordnance is
shot off].*   [c. 1600]

369 **field:** I.e., of battle.

FOR THINKING AND WRITING

1. Hamlet takes a long time to act on his father's request. Why does he delay?
   Should he have acted sooner, for example, when Claudius is praying?

2. In act 3, scene 4, Hamlet confronts his mother. After rereading this scene,
   what is your view of Hamlet's feelings toward his mother? Why do you
   think he uses such lurid imagery?

3. Contrast the relationship of Laertes and Polonius with that of Hamlet and
   his father. Is Laertes a more loyal son? Is Hamlet less devoted?

4. Some critics think that Hamlet idealizes his father's memory because he
   unconsciously resents his father. They also suggest that he cannot attach
   himself emotionally to Ophelia because he has not fully transferred his
   affection from his mother. Do you agree with these psychological interpretations? Why, or why not?

5. Make a list of all the family relationships in the play and characterize
   them as positive or negative, as healthy or troubled. Which relationship
   seems to you to be the most modern? The most ambiguous?

16

A Gallery of Essays

DIANE ACKERMAN
Plato: The Perfect Union

Diane Ackerman was born in 1948 in Waukegan, Illinois. She graduated from Pennsylvania State University and later received an M.F.A. and a Ph.D. from Cornell University. Ackerman has received the Academy of American Poets' Lavan Award as well as grants from the National Endowment for the Arts and the Rockefeller Foundation. Critics praised her book A Natural History of the Senses *(1990) for being wide-ranging, informed, and charming. She is the author of more than twenty books of poetry and nonfiction, including the recent* An Alchemy of Mind *(2004). The following essay is from* A Natural History of Love *(1994). She has taught at Columbia and Cornell and is currently a staff writer for* The New Yorker.

Proust's *Remembrance of Things Past* begins with a child waiting in bed for his mother to come and give him a good-night kiss. Sensitive and lonely, he grows anxious and unhinged, and the rest of the novel (more the mosaic of a life than a work of fiction) chronicles his attempts to bridge the gap between himself and the rest of humanity. He could not feel more separate, isolated, and alone. The passage shows the eternal quest of the child, who must learn to be separate from his mother even while he longs to reunite with her. One of the keystones of romantic love—and also of the ecstatic religion practiced by mystics—is the powerful desire to become one with the beloved.

This vision of love has its wellsprings in ancient Greek thought. To Plato, lovers are incomplete halves of a single puzzle, searching for each other in order to become whole. They are a strength forged by two weaknesses. At some point, all lovers wish to lose themselves, to merge, to become one entity. By giving up their autonomy, they find their true selves. In a world ruled by myth, Plato tried to be rational, often using myths as allegories to make a point. His investigations of love in the *Symposium* are the oldest surviving attempts to systematically understand love. In the *Symposium*, he advises people to bridle their sexual urges, and also their need to give and receive love. They should concentrate all that energy on higher goals. He understood perfectly well that people would have to struggle hard to redirect such powerful instincts; it would produce much inner warfare. When, almost 3,000 years later, Freud talks of the same struggle, using words like "sublimation" and "resistance," he is harking back to Plato, for whom love was a great predicament and a riddle. This was no doubt in part because Plato was confused about his own sexual identity; as a younger man, he wrote in praise of homosexual love, and as an older man he condemned it as an unnatural crime.

At the *Symposium*'s banquet staged in honor of Eros, Socrates — who was a teacher and companion of Plato — and his friends exchange ideas about love. Actually, Socrates' job is to poke holes in everyone else's ideas. The banqueters are not present just to praise love, but to fathom it, to dive through its waves and plumb its depths. One of their first home truths is that love is a universal human need. Not just a mythic god, or a whim, or madness, but something integral to each person's life. When it is Aristophanes' turn, he relates a fable — one that has influenced people for thousands of years since. He explains that originally there were three sexes: men, women, and a hermaphroditic combination of man and woman. These primitive beings had two heads, two arms, two sets of genitals, and so on. Threatened by their potential power, Zeus divided each one of them in half, making individual lesbians, homosexual men, and heterosexuals. But each person longed for its missing half, which it sought out, tracked down, and embraced, so that it could become one again — and thereby Aristophanes arrives at an astonishing definition of love:

> Each of us when separated, having one side only, like a flat fish, is but the indenture of a man, and he is always looking for his other half. . . . And when one of them meets with his other half, the actual half of himself, whether he be a lover of youth or a lover of another sort, the pair are lost in an amazement of love and friendship and intimacy, and will not be out of the other's sight, as I may say, even for a moment: these are the people who pass their whole lives together; yet they could not explain what they desire of one another. For the intense yearning which each of them has towards the other does not appear to be the desire of lover's intercourse, but of something else which the soul of either evidently desires and cannot tell, and of which she has only a dark and doubtful presentiment. Suppose Hephaestus,° with his instruments, were to come to the pair who are lying side by side and say to them, "What do you people want of one another?" They would be unable to explain. And suppose further, that when he saw their perplexity he said, "Do you desire to be wholly one; always day and night to be in one another's company, for if this is what you desire, I am ready to melt you into one and let you grow together . . ." There is not a man of them who when he heard the proposal would deny or would acknowledge that this meeting and melting into one another, this becoming one instead of two, was the very expression of his ancient need. And the reason is that human nature was originally one and we were a whole, and the desire and pursuit of the whole is called love.

Hephaestus: Greek god of fire (also called Vulcan).

It is an amazing fable, saying, in effect, that each person has an ideal love waiting somewhere to be found. Not "There's a lid for every pot," as my mother has sometimes said, but that each of us has a one-and-only, and finding that person makes us whole. This romantic ideal of the perfect partner was invented by Plato. It appealed so strongly to hearts and minds that people believed it in all the following centuries, and many still believe it today. As Freud discovered, Plato took his fable from India, where some gods were bisexual. Indeed, the original human in the Upanishads° is as lonely as Adam in the Bible, and like Adam he asks for company and is pleased when a female is made from his own body. In each case, all the people of the earth are born from their union. Evolutionary biologists tell us that our ultimate ancestor almost certainly was hermaphroditic, and something about that news feels right, not just in our reason but in the part of us that yearns for the other. John Donne° wrote magnificently about this passion for oneness, which takes on a special piquancy in his poem "The Flea." One day, sweetly loitering with his mistress, he notices a flea sucking a little blood from her arm and then from his. Joyously, he observes that their blood is married inside the flea.

Why should the idea of oneness be so compelling? Love changes all the physics in the known universe of one's emotions, and redraws the boundaries between what is real and what is possible. Children often believe in magic and miracles, and when they grow up they naturally believe in the miraculous power of love. Sometimes this is depicted in myths or legends by having the lovers drink a love potion, as Tristan and Isolde° do; be stung by Cupid's arrows; be enchanted by music as Eurydice° is; or receive a reviving kiss à la Sleeping Beauty.

In many eastern and western religions, the supplicants strive for a sense of unity with God. Although this is not supposed to be an erotic coupling, saints often describe it as if it were, dwelling in orgasmic detail on the sensuality of Christ's body. Religious ecstasy and the ecstasy of lovers have much in common—the sudden awareness, the taking of vows, the plighting of troths, the all-consuming fire in the heart and flesh, the rituals leading to bliss, and, for some Christians, a cannibalistic union with the godhead by symbolically drinking his blood and eating his flesh. Whether we fall in love with a human demigod or with a deity, we feel that they can return us to a primordial state of oneness, that then our inner electric can run its full circuit, that we can at last be whole.

How bizarre it is to wish to blend blood and bones with someone. People cannot actually literally become one, of course; it's a physical impossibility. The idea is preposterous. We are separate organisms. Unless we are Siamese twins, we are not merged with another. Why should we feel incomplete, anyway? Why believe that uniting our body and thoughts and fate with another person's will cure our sense of loneliness? Wouldn't it make more sense to believe that when love brings two people together they are a community of two, not a compound of

5

Upanishads: Texts from circa 900 B.C.E. that form the basis of Hindu religion.
John Donne: British poet (1572–1631).
Tristan and Isolde: Characters in a German opera (1865) by Richard Wagner celebrating romantic love.
Eurydice: In Greek mythology Orpheus tries in vain to rescue his wife, Eurydice, from Hades.

one? The idea of merging is so irrational, so contrary to common sense and observation, that its roots must strike deep into our psyche. Because a child is born of a mother, and lives as a separate entity, we think of the child as an individual. But in biological terms that is not precisely true. The child is an organic part of the mother that is expelled at birth, but it shares much of her biology, personality, even scent. The only and absolute perfect union of two is when a baby hangs suspended in its mother's womb, like a tiny madman in a padded cell, attached to her, feeling her blood and hormones and moods play through its body, feeling her feelings. After that perfect, pendent, dependent union, birth is an amputation, and the child like a limb looking to attach itself to the rest of its body. I am not saying this consciously occurs to anyone, but that it may explain the osmotic yearning we all feel, at one time or another, to blend our heart and body and fluids with someone else's. Only the thinnest rind of skin stands between us, only events slender as neurons. Only the fermenting mash of personality keeps us from crossing the boundary that organisms cherish to become one appetite, one struggle, one destiny. Then, when we finally reach that pinnacle, we feel more than whole: we feel limitless. [1994]

FOR THINKING AND WRITING

1. Do you think Ackerman is making a claim about true love or the about the desire for wholeness? What support does she provide? Is there an opposition? Does she give it?

2. Ackerman suggests that the desire for wholeness is fairly common. Have you felt something similar to an "osmotic yearning" (para. 7)? Is it primarily physical or spiritual?

3. Ackerman begins with an anecdote from Marcel Proust's *Remembrance of Things Past*, which seems to describe something different from romantic love. Does she justify opening in this way?

4. Many of the essay's examples are from literature. Should Ackerman have given more factual examples? Should she have consulted scientists? Sociologists? Psychologists?

5. At the end, Ackerman suggests that the pinnacle can be, and is, reached. Do you agree? How can we account for so many failed relationships then? Should we keep trying to find our perfect mate no matter how disenchanted we are?

BELL HOOKS
Inspired Eccentricity

Writer, professor, and social critic, bell hooks, born Gloria Jean Watkins in 1952, adopted the name of her maternal great-grandmother, a woman known for speaking her mind. Her books reflect her position as a bold interpreter of contemporary culture in terms of race, class, and gender: Ain't I a Woman *(1981),* Talking Back: Thinking Feminist, Thinking Black *(1989),* Yearning: Race, Gender and Cultural Politics *(1990),* Outlaw Culture: Resisting Representation *(1994), among others. She recently published a memoir,* Bone Black: Memories of Girlhood *(1996). Her most recent book is* Remembered Rapture: The Writer at Work *(1999). She has taught literature, women's studies, and African American studies at Yale University, Oberlin College, and City College of New York and continues to teach and to write poetry and social criticism. The selection that follows is from* Family: American Writers Remember Their Own *(1996), edited by Sharon Sloan Fiffer and Steve Fiffer.*

There are family members you try to forget and ones that you always remember, that you can't stop talking about. They may be dead — long gone — but their presence lingers and you have to share who they were and who they still are with the world. You want everyone to know them as you did, to love them as you did.

All my life I have remained enchanted by the presence of my mother's parents, Sarah and Gus Oldham. When I was a child they were already old. I did not see that then, though. They were Baba and Daddy Gus, together for more than seventy years at the time of his death. Their marriage fascinated me. They were strangers and lovers — two eccentrics who created their own world.

More than any other family members, together they gave me a worldview that sustained me during a difficult and painful childhood. Reflecting on the eclectic writer I have become, I see in myself a mixture of these two very different but equally powerful figures from my childhood. Baba was tall, her skin so white and her hair so jet black and straight that she could have easily "passed" denying all traces of blackness. Yet the man she married was short and dark, and sometimes his skin looked like the color of soot from burning coal. In our childhood the fireplaces burned coal. It was bright heat, luminous and fierce. If you got too close it could burn you.

Together Baba and Daddy Gus generated a hot heat. He was a man of few words, deeply committed to silence — so much so that it was like a religion to him. When he spoke you could hardly hear what he said. Baba was just the opposite. Smoking an abundance of cigarettes a day, she talked endlessly. She preached. She yelled. She fussed. Often her vitriolic rage would heap itself on Daddy Gus, who would sit calmly in his chair by the stove, as calm and still as the Buddha sits. And when he had enough of her words, he would reach for his hat and walk.

Neither Baba nor Daddy Gus drove cars. Rarely did they ride in them. They preferred walking. And even then their styles were different. He moved slow, as though carrying a great weight; she with her tall, lean, boyish frame moved swiftly, as though there was never time to waste. Their one agreed-upon passion was fishing. Though they did not do even that together. They lived close but they created separate worlds.

In a big two-story wood frame house with lots of rooms they constructed a world that could contain their separate and distinct personalities. As children one of the first things we noticed about our grandparents was that they did not sleep in

5

the same room. This arrangement was contrary to everything we understood about marriage. While Mama never wanted to talk about their separate worlds, Baba would tell you in a minute that Daddy Gus was nasty, that he smelled like tobacco juice, that he did not wash enough, that there was no way she would want him in her bed. And while he would say nothing nasty about her, he would merely say why would he want to share somebody else's bed when he could have his own bed to himself, with no one to complain about anything.

I loved my granddaddy's smells. Always, they filled my nostrils with the scent of happiness. It was sheer ecstasy for me to be allowed into his inner sanctum. His room was a small Van Gogh–like space off from the living room. There was no door. Old-fashioned curtains were the only attempt at privacy. Usually the curtains were closed. His room reeked of tobacco. There were treasures everywhere in that small room. As a younger man Daddy Gus did odd jobs, and sometimes even in his old age he would do a chore for some needy lady. As he went about his work, he would pick up found objects, scraps. All these objects would lie about his room, on the dresser, on the table near his bed. Unlike all other grown-ups he never cared about children looking through his things. Anything we wanted he gave to us.

Daddy Gus collected beautiful wooden cigar boxes. They held lots of the important stuff—the treasures. He had tons of little diaries that he made notes in. He gave me my first wallet, my first teeny little book to write in, my first beautiful pen, which did not write for long, but it was still a found and shared treasure. When I would lie on his bed or sit close to him, sometimes just standing near, I would feel all the pain and anxiety of my troubled childhood leave me. His spirit was calm. He gave me the unconditional love I longed for.

"Too calm," his grown-up children thought. That's why he had let this old woman rule him, my cousin BoBo would say. Even as children we knew that grown-ups felt sorry for Daddy Gus. At times his sons seemed to look upon him as not a "real man." His refusal to fight in wars was another sign to them of weakness. It was my grandfather who taught me to oppose war. They saw him as a man controlled by the whims of others, by this tall, strident, demanding woman he had married. I saw him as a man of profound beliefs, a man of integrity. When he heard their put-downs—for they talked on and on about his laziness—he merely muttered that he had no use for them. He was not gonna let anybody tell him what to do with his life.

Daddy Gus was a devout believer, a deacon at his church; he was one of the right-hand men of God. At church, everyone admired his calmness. Baba had no use for church. She liked nothing better than to tell us all the ways it was one big hypocritical place: "Why, I can find God anywhere I want to—I do not need a church." Indeed, when my grandmother died, her funeral could not take place in a church, for she had never belonged. Her refusal to attend church bothered some of her daughters, for they thought she was sinning against God, setting a bad example for the children. We were not supposed to listen when she began to damn the church and everybody in it.

Baba loved to "cuss." There was no bad word she was not willing to say. The improvisational manner in which she would string those words together was awe-

10

some. It was the goddamn sons of bitches who thought that they could fuck with her when they could just kiss her black ass. A woman of strong words and powerful metaphors, she could not read or write. She lived in the power of language. Her favorite sayings were a prelude for storytelling. It was she who told me, "Play with a puppy, he'll lick you in the mouth." When I heard this saying, I knew what was coming—a long polemic about not letting folks get too close, 'cause they will mess with you.

Baba loved to tell her stories. And I loved to hear them. She called me Glory. And in the midst of her storytelling she would pause to say, "Glory, are ya listenin'. Do you understand what I'm telling ya." Sometimes I would have to repeat the lessons I had learned. Sometimes I was not able to get it right and she would start again. When Mama felt I was learning too much craziness "over home" (that is what we called Baba's house), my visits were curtailed. As I moved into my teens I learned to keep to myself all the wisdom of the old ways I picked up over home.

Baba was an incredible quilt maker, but by the time I was old enough to really understand her work, to see its beauty; she was already having difficulty with her eyesight. She could not sew as much as in the old days, when her work was on everybody's bed. Unwilling to throw anything away, she loved to make crazy quilts, 'cause they allowed every scrap to be used. Although she would one day order patterns and make perfect quilts with colors that went together, she always collected scraps.

Long before I read Virginia Woolf's *A Room of One's Own* I learned from Baba that a woman needed her own space to work. She had a huge room for her quilting. Like every other space in the private world she created upstairs, it had her treasures, an endless array of hatboxes, feathers, and trunks filled with old clothes she had held on to. In room after room there were feather tick mattresses; when they were pulled back, the wooden slats of the bed were revealed, lined with exquisite hand-sewn quilts.

In all these trunks, in crevices and drawers were braided tobacco leaves to keep away moths and other insects. A really hot summer could make cloth sweat, and stains from tobacco juice would end up on quilts no one had ever used. When I was a young child, a quilt my grandmother had made kept me warm, was my solace and comfort. Even though Mama protested when I dragged that old raggedy quilt from Kentucky to Stanford, I knew I needed that bit of the South, of Baba's world, to sustain me.

Like Daddy Gus, she was a woman of her word. She liked to declare with pride, "I mean what I say and I say what I mean." "Glory," she would tell me, "nobody is better than their word—if you can't keep ya word you ain't worth nothin' in this world." She would stop speaking to folk over the breaking of their word, over lies. Our mama was not given to loud speech or confrontation. I learned all those things from Baba—"to stand up and speak up" and not to "give a good goddamn" what folk who "ain't got a pot to pee in" think. My parents were concerned with their image in the world. It was pure blasphemy for Baba to teach that it did not matter what other folks thought—"Ya have to be right with yaself in ya own heart—that's all that matters." Baba taught me to listen to my heart—to

15

follow it. From her we learned as small children to remember our dreams in the night and to share them when we awakened. They would be interpreted by her. She taught us to listen to the knowledge in dreams. Mama would say this was all nonsense, but she too was known to ask the meaning of a dream.

In their own way my grandparents were rebels, deeply committed to radical individualism. I learned how to be myself from them. Mama hated this. She thought it was important to be liked, to conform. She had hated growing up in such an eccentric, otherworldly household. This world where folks made their own wine, their own butter, their own soap; where chickens were raised, and huge gardens were grown for canning everything. This was the world Mama wanted to leave behind. She wanted store-bought things.

Baba lived in another time, a time when all things were produced in the individual household. Everything the family needed was made at home. She loved to tell me stories about learning to trap animals, to skin, to soak possum and coon in brine, to fry up a fresh rabbit. Though a total woman of the outdoors who could shoot and trap as good as any man, she still believed every woman should sew — she made her first quilt as a girl. In her world, women were as strong as men because they had to be. She had grown up in the country and knew that country ways were the best ways to live. Boasting about being able to do anything that a man could do and better, this woman who could not read or write was confident about her place in the universe.

My sense of aesthetics came from her. She taught me to really look at things, to see underneath the surface, to see the different shades of red in the peppers she had dried and hung in the kitchen sunlight. The beauty of the ordinary, the everyday, was her feast of light. While she had no use for the treasures in my granddaddy's world, he too taught me to look for the living spirit in things — the things that are cast away but still need to be touched and cared for. Picking up a found object he would tell me its story or tell me how he was planning to give it life again.

Connected in spirit but so far apart in the life of everydayness, Baba and   20
Daddy Gus were rarely civil to each other. Every shared talk begun with goodwill ended in disagreement and contestation. Everyone knew Baba just loved to fuss. She liked a good war of words. And she was comfortable using words to sting and hurt, to punish. When words would not do the job, she could reach for the strap, a long piece of black leather that would leave tiny imprints on the flesh.

There was no violence in Daddy Gus. Mama shared that he had always been that way, a calm and gentle man, full of tenderness. I remember clinging to his tenderness when nothing I did was right in my mother's eyes, when I was constantly punished. Baba was not an ally. She advocated harsh punishment. She had no use for children who would not obey. She was never ever affectionate. When we entered her house, we gave her a kiss in greeting and that was it. With Daddy Gus we could cuddle, linger in his arms, give as many kisses as desired. His arms and heart were always open.

In the back of their house were fruit trees, chicken coops, and gardens, and in the front were flowers. Baba could make anything grow. And she knew all about herbs and roots. Her home remedies healed our childhood sicknesses. Of course she thought it crazy for anyone to go to a doctor when she could tell them just what they needed. All these things she had learned from her mother, Bell Blair Hooks, whose name I would choose as my pen name. Everyone agreed that I had the temperament of this great-grandmother I would not remember. She was a sharp-tongued woman. Or so they said. And it was believed I had inherited my way with words from her.

Families do that. They chart psychic genealogies that often overlook what is right before our eyes. I may have inherited my great-grandmother Bell Hook's way with words, but I learned to use those words listening to my grandmother. I learned to be courageous by seeing her act without fear. I learned to risk because she was daring. Home and family were her world. While my grandfather journeyed downtown, visited at other folks' houses, went to church, and conducted affairs in the world, Baba rarely left home. There was nothing in the world she needed. Things out there violated her spirit.

As a child I had no sense of what it would mean to live a life, spanning so many generations, unable to read or write. To me Baba was a woman of power. That she would have been extraordinarily powerless in a world beyond 1200 Broad Street was a thought that never entered my mind. I believed that she stayed home because it was the place she liked best. Just as Daddy Gus seemed to need to walk — to roam.

After his death it was easier to see the ways that they complemented and completed each other. For suddenly, without him as a silent backdrop, Baba's spirit was diminished. Something in her was forever lonely and could not find solace. When she died, tulips, her favorite flower, surrounded her. The preacher told us that her death was not an occasion for grief, for "it is hard to live in a world where your choicest friends are gone." Daddy Gus was the companion she missed most. His presence had always been the mirror of memory. Without it there was so much that could not be shared. There was no witness.

Seeing their life together, I learned that it was possible for women and men to fashion households arranged around their own needs. Power was shared. When there was an imbalance, Baba ruled the day. It seemed utterly alien to me to learn about black women and men not making families and homes together. I had not been raised in a world of absent men. One day I knew I would fashion a life using the patterns I inherited from Baba and Daddy Gus. I keep treasures in my cigar box, which still smells after all these years. The quilt that covered me as a child remains, full of ink stains and faded colors. In my trunks are braided tobacco leaves, taken from over home. They keep evil away — keep bad spirits from crossing the threshold, like the ancestors they guard and protect.   [1996]

FOR THINKING AND WRITING

1. Do you think hooks is right, that we learn specific life lessons from people in our families? What lessons were you explicitly taught? Are there other, more indirect lessons that you learned from members of your family?

2. Explain the title. What attitude does hooks take toward her grandparents? Does she convince you? What would you think if they were your grandparents?

3. Hooks begins her memoir with a generalization that Baba and Daddy Gus gave her a "worldview that sustained [her] during a difficult and painful childhood" (para. 3). Does she adequately support this idea? How?

4. Writers use specific details about their characters to make them come alive. What are some concrete details or images that you remember about Baba or Daddy Gus? Do these details seem authentic? Is that important?

5. Often a tension exists in families between the roles and personalities members present in their public lives and those they have in their families. Is that the case in this memoir? In what ways might these tensions be good or bad for individual family members? For our culture?

MARTIN LUTHER KING JR.
Letter from Birmingham Jail[1]

A native of Atlanta, Martin Luther King Jr. (1929–1968) was the son of a Baptist minister and a schoolteacher. After graduating from Morehouse College in Atlanta, he studied at several universities before receiving a Ph.D. in theology from Boston University. He married Coretta Scott in 1955 and had four children. In 1959 he resigned his position as pastor of a church in Alabama to move back to Atlanta to direct the activities of the Southern Christian Leadership Conference. From 1960 until his death, he was copastor with his father at Ebenezer Baptist Church in Atlanta.

Dr. King was a central figure in the civil rights movement. Pivotal in the successful Montgomery bus boycott in 1956, he was arrested over thirty times for his participation in nonviolent demonstrations. His charismatic leadership and eloquent speeches stirred and inspired the conscience of a generation. Dr. King's idea of "somebodiness" gave black and poor people a new sense of worth and dignity, and his philosophy on nonviolent direct action helped change the nation's attitudes and priorities. His famous "I Have a Dream" speech at the Lincoln Memorial in 1963 and the classic "Letter" printed here are among the most important documents in American history. At thirty-five, he was the youngest person to win the Nobel Peace Prize. His assassination in 1968 set off riots in over one hundred cities. Today most of the country honors his birthday as a holiday.

[1] This response to a published statement by eight fellow clergymen from Alabama (Bishop C. C. J. Carpenter, Bishop Joseph A. Durick, Rabbi Hilton L. Grafman, Bishop Paul Hardin, Bishop Holan B. Harmon, the Reverend George M. Murray, the Reverend Edward V. Ramage, and the Reverend Earl Stallings) was composed under somewhat constricting circumstances. Begun on the margins of the newspaper in which the statement appeared while I was in jail, the letter was continued on scraps of writing paper supplied by a friendly Negro trusty, and concluded on a pad my attorneys were eventually permitted to leave me. Although the text remains in substance unaltered, I have indulged in the author's prerogative of polishing it for publication. [King's note]

My Dear Fellow Clergymen:

While confined here in the Birmingham city jail, I came across your recent statement calling my present activities "unwise and untimely." Seldom do I pause to answer criticism of my work and ideas. If I sought to answer all the criticisms that cross my desk, my secretaries would have little time for anything other than such correspondence in the course of the day, and I would have no time for constructive work. But since I feel that you are men of genuine good will and that your criticisms are sincerely set forth, I want to try to answer your statement in what I hope will be patient and reasonable terms.

I think I should indicate why I am here in Birmingham, since you have been influenced by the view which argues against "outsiders coming in." I have the honor of serving as president of the Southern Christian Leadership Conference, an organization operating in every southern state, with headquarters in Atlanta, Georgia. We have some eighty-five affiliated organizations across the South, and one of them is the Alabama Christian Movement for Human Rights. Frequently we share staff, educational, and financial resources with our affiliates. Several months ago the affiliate here in Birmingham asked us to be on call to engage in a nonviolent direct-action program if such were deemed necessary. We readily consented, and when the hour came we lived up to our promise. So I, along with several members of my staff, am here because I was invited here. I am here because I have organizational ties here.

But more basically, I am in Birmingham because injustice is here. Just as the prophets of the eighth century B.C. left their villages and carried their "thus saith the Lord" far beyond the boundaries of their home towns, and just as the Apostle Paul left his village of Tarsus[2] and carried the gospel of Jesus Christ to the far corners of the Greco-Roman world, so am I compelled to carry the gospel of freedom beyond my own home town. Like Paul, I must constantly respond to the Macedonian call for aid.[3]

Moreover, I am cognizant of the interrelatedness of all communities and states. I cannot sit idly by in Atlanta and not be concerned about what happens in Birmingham. Injustice anywhere is a threat to justice everywhere. We are caught in an inescapable network of mutuality, tied in a single garment of destiny. Whatever affects one directly, affects all indirectly. Never again can we afford to live with the narrow, provincial "outside agitator" idea. Anyone who lives inside the United States can never be considered an outsider anywhere within its bounds.

You deplore the demonstrations taking place in Birmingham. But your statement, I am sorry to say, fails to express a similar concern for the conditions that brought about the demonstrations. I am sure that none of you would want to rest content with the superficial kind of social analysis that deals merely with effects and does not grapple with the underlying causes. It is unfortunate that demonstrations are taking place in Birmingham, but it is even more unfortunate that the city's white power structure left the Negro community with no alternative.

5

---

[2] St. Paul was born in Tarsus, in present-day Turkey.
[3] The Christian community in Macedonia often called upon St. Paul for aid.

In any nonviolent campaign there are four basic steps: collection of the facts to determine whether injustices exist; negotiation; self-purification; and direct action. We have gone through all these steps in Birmingham. There can be no gainsaying the fact that racial injustice engulfs this community. Birmingham is probably the most thoroughly segregated city in the United States. Its ugly record of brutality is widely known. Negroes have experienced grossly unjust treatment in the courts. There have been more unsolved bombings of Negro homes and churches in Birmingham than in any other city in the nation. These are the hard, brutal facts of the case. On the basis of these conditions, Negro leaders sought to negotiate with the city fathers. But the latter consistently refused to engage in good-faith negotiation.

Then, last September, came the opportunity to talk with leaders of Birmingham's economic community. In the course of the negotiations, certain promises were made by the merchants—for example, to remove the stores' humiliating racial signs. On the basis of these promises, the Reverend Fred Shuttlesworth and the leaders of the Alabama Christian Movement for Human Rights agreed to a moratorium on all demonstrations. As the weeks and months went by, we realized that we were the victims of a broken promise. A few signs, briefly removed, returned; the others remained.

As in so many past experiences, our hopes had been blasted, and the shadow of deep disappointment settled upon us. We had no alternative except to prepare for direct action, whereby we would present our very bodies as a means of laying our case before the conscience of the local and the national community. Mindful of the difficulties involved, we decided to undertake a process of self-purification. We began a series of workshops on nonviolence, and we repeatedly asked ourselves: "Are you able to accept blows without retaliating?" "Are you able to endure the ordeal of jail?" We decided to schedule our direct-action program for the Easter season, realizing that except for Christmas, this is the main shopping period of the year. Knowing that a strong economic-withdrawal program would be the by-product of direct action, we felt that this would be the best time to bring pressure to bear on the merchants for the needed change.

Then it occurred to us that Birmingham's mayoral election was coming up in March, and we speedily decided to postpone action until after election-day. When we discovered that the Commissioner of Public Safety, Eugene "Bull" Connor, had piled up enough votes to be in the run-off, we decided again to postpone action until the day after the run-off so that the demonstrations could not be used to cloud the issues. Like many others, we waited to see Mr. Connor defeated, and to this end we endured postponement after postponement. Having aided in this community need, we felt that our direct-action program could be delayed no longer.

You may well ask, "Why direct action? Why sit-ins, marches, and so forth? Isn't negotiation a better path?" You are quite right in calling for negotiation. Indeed, this is the very purpose of direct action. Nonviolent direct action seeks to create such a crisis and foster such a tension that a community which has constantly refused to negotiate is forced to confront the issue. It seeks so to dramatize the issue that it can no longer be ignored. My citing the creation of tension as part   10 of the work of the nonviolent-resister may sound rather shocking. But I must confess that I am not afraid of the word "tension." I have earnestly opposed violent tension, but there is a type of constructive, nonviolent tension which is necessary for growth. Just as Socrates[4] felt that it was necessary to create a tension in the mind so that individuals could rise from the bondage of myths and half-truths to the unfettered realm of creative analysis and objective appraisal, so must we see the need for nonviolent gadflies to create the kind of tension in society that will help men rise from the dark depths of prejudice and racism to the majestic heights of understanding and brotherhood.

The purpose of our direct-action program is to create a situation so crisis-packed that it will inevitably open the door to negotiation. I therefore concur with you in your call for negotiation. Too long has our beloved Southland been bogged down in a tragic effort to live in monologue rather than dialogue.

One of the basic points in your statement is that the action that I and my associates have taken in Birmingham is untimely. Some have asked: "Why didn't you give the new city administration time to act?" The only answer that I can give to this query is that the new Birmingham administration must be prodded about as much as the outgoing one, before it will act. We are sadly mistaken if we feel that the election of Albert Boutwell as mayor will bring the millennium to Birmingham. While Mr. Boutwell is a much more gentle person than Mr. Connor, they are both segregationists, dedicated to maintenance of the status quo. I have hoped that Mr. Boutwell will be reasonable enough to see the futility of massive resistance to desegregation. But he will not see this without pressure from devotees of civil rights. My friends, I must say to you that we have not made a single gain in civil rights without determined legal and nonviolent pressure. Lamentably, it is an historical fact that privileged groups seldom give up their privileges voluntarily. Individuals may see the moral light and voluntarily give up their unjust posture; but, as Reinhold Niebuhr[5] has reminded us, groups tend to be more immoral than individuals.

We know through painful experience that freedom is never voluntarily given by the oppressor; it must be demanded by the oppressed. Frankly, I have yet to engage in a direct-action campaign that was "well timed" in the view of those who have not suffered unduly from the disease of segregation. For years now I have heard the word "Wait!" It rings in the ear of every Negro with piercing familiarity. This "Wait" has almost always meant "Never." We must come to see, with one of our distinguished jurists, that "justice too long delayed is justice denied."

We have waited for more than 340 years for our constitutional and God-given rights. The nations of Asia and Africa are moving with jetlike speed toward gaining political independence, but we still creep at horse-and-buggy pace toward gaining a cup of coffee at a lunch counter. Perhaps it is easy for those who have never felt the stinging darts of segregation to say, "Wait." But when you have seen vicious mobs lynch your mothers and fathers at will and drown your sisters

[4] The Greek philosopher Socrates (469–399 B.C.) would feign ignorance to expose the errors in his opponent's arguments.
[5] Reinhold Niebuhr (1892–1971), American theologian.

and brothers at whim; when you have seen hate-filled policemen curse, kick, and even kill your black brothers and sisters; when you see the vast majority of your twenty million Negro brothers smothering in an airtight cage of poverty in the midst of an affluent society; when you suddenly find your tongue twisted and your speech stammering as you seek to explain to your six-year-old daughter why she can't go to the public amusement park that has just been advertised on television, and see tears welling up in her eyes when she is told that Funtown is closed to colored children, and see ominous clouds of inferiority beginning to form in her little mental sky, and see her beginning to distort her personality by developing an unconscious bitterness toward white people; when you have to concoct an answer for a five-year-old son who is asking, "Daddy, why do white people treat colored people so mean?"; when you take a cross-country drive and find it necessary to sleep night after night in the uncomfortable corners of your automobile because no motel will accept you; when you are humiliated day in and day out by nagging signs reading "white" and "colored"; when your first name becomes "nigger," your middle name becomes "boy" (however old you are) and your last name becomes "John," and your wife and mother are never given the respected title "Mrs."; when you are harried by day and haunted by night by the fact that you are a Negro, living constantly at tiptoe stance, never quite knowing what to expect next, and are plagued with inner fears and outer resentments; when you are forever fighting a degenerating sense of "nobodiness"—then you will understand why we find it difficult to wait. There comes a time when the cup of endurance runs over, and men are no longer willing to be plunged into the abyss of despair. I hope, sirs, you can understand our legitimate and unavoidable impatience.

You express a great deal of anxiety over our willingness to break laws. This is   15
certainly a legitimate concern. Since we so diligently urge people to obey the Supreme Court's decision of 1954 outlawing segregation in the public schools, at first glance it may seem rather paradoxical for us consciously to break laws. One may well ask: "How can you advocate breaking some laws and obeying others?" The answer lies in the fact that there are two types of laws: just and unjust. I would be the first to advocate obeying just laws. One has not only a legal but a moral responsibility to obey just laws. Conversely, one has a moral responsibility to disobey unjust laws. I would agree with St. Augustine that "an unjust law is no law at all."

Now, what is the difference between the two? How does one determine whether a law is just or unjust? A just law is a man-made code that squares with the moral law or the law of God. An unjust law is a code that is out of harmony with the moral law. To put it in the terms of St. Thomas Aquinas: An unjust law is a human law that is not rooted in eternal law and natural law. Any law that uplifts human personality is just. Any law that degrades human personality is unjust. All segregation statutes are unjust because segregation distorts the soul and damages the personality. It gives the segregator a false sense of superiority and the segregated a false sense of inferiority. Segregation, to use the terminology of the Jewish philosopher Martin Buber, substitutes an "I-it" relationship for an "I-thou" relationship and ends up relegating persons to the status of things. Hence segregation is not only politically, economically, and sociologically unsound, it is morally wrong and sinful. Paul Tillich has said that sin is separation. Is not segregation an existential expression of man's tragic separation, his awful estrangement, his terrible sinfulness? Thus it is that I can urge men to obey the 1954 decision of the Supreme Court, for it is morally right; and I can urge them to disobey segregation ordinances, for they are morally wrong.

Let us consider a more concrete example of just and unjust laws. An unjust law is a code that a numerical or power majority group compels a minority group to obey but does not make binding on itself. This is *difference* made legal. By the same token, a just law is a code that a majority compels a minority to follow and that it is willing to follow itself. This is *sameness* made legal.

Let me give another explanation. A law is unjust if it is inflicted on a minority that, as a result of being denied the right to vote, had no part in enacting or devising the law. Who can say that the legislature of Alabama which set up that state's segregation laws was democratically elected? Throughout Alabama all sorts of devious methods are used to prevent Negroes from becoming registered voters, and there are some counties in which, even though Negroes constitute a majority of the population, not a single Negro is registered. Can any law enacted under such circumstances be considered democratically structured?

Sometimes a law is just on its face and unjust in its application. For instance, I have been arrested on a charge of parading without a permit. Now, there is nothing wrong in having an ordinance which requires a permit for a parade. But such an ordinance becomes unjust when it is used to maintain segregation and to deny citizens the First-Amendment privilege of peaceful assembly and protest.

I hope you are able to see the distinction I am trying to point out. In no sense   20
do I advocate evading or defying the law, as would the rabid segregationist. That would lead to anarchy. One who breaks an unjust law must do so openly, lovingly, and with a willingness to accept the penalty. I submit that an individual who breaks a law that conscience tells him is unjust, and who willingly accepts the penalty of imprisonment in order to arouse the conscience of the community over its injustice, is in reality expressing the highest respect for law.

Of course, there is nothing new about this kind of civil disobedience. It was evidenced sublimely in the refusal of Shadrach, Meshach, and Abednego to obey the laws of Nebuchadnezzar, on the ground that a higher moral law was at stake.[6] It was practiced superbly by the early Christians, who were willing to face hungry lions and the excruciating pain of chopping blocks rather than submit to certain unjust laws of the Roman Empire. To a degree, academic freedom is a reality today because Socrates practiced civil disobedience. In our own nation, the Boston Tea Party represented a massive act of civil disobedience.

We should never forget that everything Adolf Hitler did in Germany was "legal" and everything the Hungarian freedom fighters did in Hungary was "illegal." It was "illegal" to aid and comfort a Jew in Hitler's Germany. Even so, I am sure that, had I lived in Germany at the time, I would have aided and comforted my Jewish brothers. If today I lived in a Communist country where certain

---

[6] See the Book of Daniel in the Old Testament (1:7–3:30).

principles dear to the Christian faith are suppressed, I would openly advocate disobeying that country's anti-religious laws.

I must make two honest confessions to you, my Christian and Jewish brothers. First, I must confess that over the past few years I have been gravely disappointed with the white moderate. I have almost reached the regrettable conclusion that the Negro's great stumbling block in his stride toward freedom is not the white Citizen's Counciler[7] or the Ku Klux Klanner, but the white moderate, who is more devoted to "order" than to justice; who prefers a negative peace which is the absence of tension to a positive peace which is the presence of justice; who constantly says, "I agree with you in the goal you seek, but I cannot agree with your methods of direct action"; who paternalistically believes he can set the timetable for another man's freedom; who lives by a mythical concept of time and who constantly advises the Negro to wait for a "more convenient season." Shallow understanding from people of good will is more frustrating than absolute misunderstanding from people of ill will. Lukewarm acceptance is much more bewildering than outright rejection.

I had hoped that the white moderate would understand that law and order exist for the purpose of establishing justice and that when they fail in this purpose they become the dangerously structured dams that block the flow of social progress. I had hoped that the white moderate would understand that the present tension in the South is a necessary phase of the transition from an obnoxious negative peace, in which the Negro passively accepted his unjust plight, to a substantive and positive peace, in which all men will respect the dignity and worth of human personality. Actually, we who engage in nonviolent direct action are not the creators of tension. We merely bring to the surface the hidden tension that is already alive. We bring it out in the open, where it can be seen and dealt with. Like a boil that can never be cured so long as it is covered up but must be opened with all its ugliness to the natural medicines of air and light, injustice must be exposed, with all the tension its exposure creates, to the light of human conscience and the air of national opinion, before it can be cured.

In your statement you assert that our actions, even though peaceful, must be   25
condemned because they precipitate violence. But is this a logical assertion? Isn't this like condemning a robbed man because his possession of money precipitated the evil act of robbery? Isn't this like condemning Socrates because his unswerving commitment to truth and his philosophical inquiries precipitated the act by the misguided populace in which they made him drink hemlock? Isn't this like condemning Jesus because his unique God-consciousness and never-ceasing devotion to God's will precipitated the evil act of crucifixion? We must come to see that, as the federal courts have consistently affirmed, it is wrong to urge an individual to cease his efforts to gain his basic constitutional rights because the quest may precipitate violence. Society must protect the robbed and punish the robber.

I had also hoped that the white moderate would reject the myth concerning time in relation to the struggle for freedom. I have just received a letter from a

---

[7] White Citizen's Councils resisted desegregation after the Supreme Court declared segregated education unconstitutional in 1954.

white brother in Texas. He writes: "All Christians know that the colored people will receive greater equal rights eventually, but it is possible that you are in too great a religious hurry. It has taken Christianity almost two thousand years to accomplish what it has. The teachings of Christ take time to come to earth." Such an attitude stems from a tragic misconception of time, from the strangely irrational notion that there is something in the very flow of time that will inevitably cure all ills. Actually, time itself is neutral; it can be used either destructively or constructively. More and more I feel that the people of ill will have used time much more effectively than have the people of good will. We will have to repent in this generation not merely for the hateful words and actions of the bad people, but for the appalling silence of the good people. Human progress never rolls in on wheels of inevitability; it comes through the tireless efforts of men willing to be co-workers with God, and without this hard work, time itself becomes an ally of the forces of social stagnation. We must use time creatively, in the knowledge that the time is always ripe to do right. Now is the time to make real the promise of democracy and transform our pending national elegy into a creative psalm of brotherhood. Now is the time to lift our national policy from the quicksand of racial injustice to the solid rock of human dignity.

You speak of our activity in Birmingham as extreme. At first I was rather disappointed that fellow clergymen would see my nonviolent efforts as those of an extremist. I began thinking about the fact that I stand in the middle of two opposing forces in the Negro community. One is a force of complacency, made up in part of Negroes, who, as a result of long years of oppression, are so drained of self-respect and a sense of "somebodiness" that they have adjusted to segregation; and in part of a few middle-class Negroes who, because of a degree of academic and economic security and because in some ways they profit by segregation, have become insensitive to the problems of the masses. The other force is one of bitterness and hatred, and it comes perilously close to advocating violence. It is expressed in the various black nationalist groups that are springing up across the nation, the largest and best-known being Elijah Muhammad's Muslim movement.[8] Nourished by the Negro's frustration over the continued existence of racial discrimination, this movement is made up of people who have lost faith in America, who have absolutely repudiated Christianity, and who have concluded that the white man is an incorrigible "devil."

I have tried to stand between these two forces, saying that we need emulate neither the "do-nothingism" of the complacent nor the hatred and despair of the black nationalist. For there is the more excellent way of love and nonviolent protest. I am grateful to God that, through the influence of the Negro church, the way of nonviolence became an integral part of our struggle.

If this philosophy had not emerged, by now many streets of the South would, I am convinced, be flowing with blood. And I am further convinced that if our white brothers dismiss as "rabble-rousers" and "outside agitators" those of us who employ nonviolent direct action, and if they refuse to support our nonviolent efforts, millions of Negroes will, out of frustration and despair, seek solace and

[8] Elijah Muhammad (1897–1975), led the Nation of Islam, a Muslim religious group that called upon African Americans to reject integration and establish their own nation.

security in black-nationalist ideologies—a development that would inevitably lead to a frightening racial nightmare.

Oppressed people cannot remain oppressed forever. The yearning for free- 30 dom eventually manifests itself, and that is what has happened to the American Negro. Something within has reminded him of his birthright of freedom, and something without has reminded him that it can be gained. Consciously or unconsciously, he has been caught up by the *Zeitgeist*,[9] and with his black broth- ers of Africa and his brown and yellow brothers of Asia, South America, and the Caribbean, the United States Negro is moving with a sense of great urgency toward the promised land of racial justice. If one recognizes this vital urge that has engulfed the Negro community, one should readily understand why public demonstrations are taking place. The Negro has many pent-up resentments and latent frustrations, and he must release them. So let him march; let him make prayer pilgrimages to the city hall; let him go on freedom rides[10]—and try to understand why he must do so. If his repressed emotions are not released in non- violent ways, they will seek expression through violence; this is not a threat but a fact of history. So I have not said to my people, "Get rid of your discontent." Rather, I have tried to say that this normal and healthy discontent can be chan- neled into the creative outlet of nonviolent direct action. And now this approach is being termed extremist.

But though I was initially disappointed at being categorized as an extremist, as I continued to think about the matter I gradually gained a measure of satisfaction from the label. Was not Jesus an extremist for love: "Love your enemies, bless them that curse you, do good to them that hate you, and pray for them that despitefully use you, and persecute you." Was not Amos an extremist for justice: "Let justice roll down like waters and righteousness like an ever-flowing stream." Was not Paul an extremist for the Christian gospel: "I bear in my body the marks of the Lord Jesus." Was not Martin Luther an extremist: "Here I stand; I cannot do otherwise, so help me God." And John Bunyan: "I will stay in jail to the end of my days before I make a butchery of my conscience." And Abraham Lincoln: "This nation cannot survive half slave and half free." And Thomas Jefferson: "We hold these truths to be self-evident, that all men are created equal. . . ." So the question is not whether we will be extremists, but what kind of extremists we will be. Will we be extremists for the preservation of injustice or for the extension of justice? In that dramatic scene on Calvary's hill three men were crucified. We must never forget that all three were crucified for the same crime—the crime of extremism. Two were extremists for immorality, and thus fell below their environ- ment. The other, Jesus Christ, was an extremist for love, truth, and goodness, and thereby rose above his environment. Perhaps the South, the nation, and the world are in dire need of creative extremists.

I had hoped that the white moderate would see this need. Perhaps I was too optimistic; perhaps I expected too much. I suppose I should have realized that

---

[9] The spirit of the age.

[10] In 1961, the Congress of Racial Equality (CORE) directed activists to flout race laws in the south that mandated segregation in buses and bus terminals.

few members of the oppressor race can understand the deep groans and passionate yearnings of the oppressed race, and still fewer have the vision to see that injustice must be rooted out by strong, persistent, and determined action. I am thankful, however, that some of our white brothers in the South have grasped the meaning of this social revolution and committed themselves to it. They are still all too few in quantity, but they are big in quality. Some—such as Ralph McGill, Lillian Smith, Harry Golden, James McBride Dabbs, Ann Braden, and Sarah Patton Boyle—have written about our struggle in eloquent and prophetic terms. Others have marched with us down nameless streets of the South. They have languished in filthy, roach-infested jails, suffering the abuse and brutality of policemen who view them as "dirty nigger-lovers." Unlike so many of their moderate brothers and sisters, they have recognized the urgency of the moment and sensed the need for powerful "action" antidotes to combat the disease of segregation.

Let me take note of my other major disappointment. I have been so greatly disappointed with the white church and its leadership. Of course, there are some notable exceptions. I am not unmindful of the fact that each of you has taken some significant stands on this issue. I commend you, Reverend Stallings, for your Christian stand on this past Sunday, in welcoming Negroes to your worship service on a nonsegregated basis. I commend the Catholic leaders of this state for integrating Spring Hill College several years ago.

But despite these notable exceptions, I must honestly reiterate that I have been disappointed with the church. I do not say this as one of those negative critics who can always find something wrong with the church. I say this as a minister of the gospel, who loves the church; who was nurtured in its bosom; who has been sustained by its spiritual blessings and who will remain true to it as long as the cord of life shall lengthen.

When I was suddenly catapulted into the leadership of the bus protest in   35
Montgomery, Alabama, a few years ago, I felt we would be supported by the white church. I felt that the white ministers, priests, and rabbis of the South would be among our strongest allies. Instead, some have been outright opponents, refusing to understand the freedom movement and misrepresenting its leaders; all too many others have been more cautious than courageous and have remained silent behind the anesthetizing security of stained-glass windows.

In spite of my shattered dreams, I came to Birmingham with the hope that the white religious leadership of this community would see the justice of our cause and, with deep moral concern, would serve as the channel through which our just grievances could reach the power structure. I had hoped that each of you would understand. But again I have been disappointed.

I have heard numerous southern religious leaders admonish their worshipers to comply with a desegregation decision because it is the law, but I have longed to hear white ministers declare: "Follow this decree because integration is morally right and because the Negro is your brother." In the midst of blatant injustices inflicted upon the Negro, I have watched white churchmen stand on the sideline and mouth pious irrelevancies and sanctimonious trivialities. In the midst of a mighty struggle to rid our nation of racial and economic injustice, I have heard many ministers say: "Those are social issues, with which the gospel has no real concern." And I have watched many churches commit themselves to a completely otherworldly religion which makes a strange, unBiblical distinction between body and soul, between the sacred and the secular.

I have traveled the length and breadth of Alabama, Mississippi, and all the other southern states. On sweltering summer days and crisp autumn mornings I have looked at the South's beautiful churches with their lofty spires pointing heavenward. I have beheld the impressive outlines of her massive religious-education buildings. Over and over I have found myself asking: "What kind of people worship here? Who is their God? Where were their voices when the lips of Governor Barnett dripped with words of interposition and nullification? Where were they when Governor Wallace gave a clarion call for defiance and hatred? Where were their voices of support when bruised and weary Negro men and women decided to rise from the dark dungeons of complacency to the bright hills of creative protest?"

Yes, these questions are still in mind. In deep disappointment I have wept over the laxity of the church. But be assured that my tears have been tears of love. There can be no deep disappointment where there is not deep love. Yes, I love the church. How could I do otherwise? I am in the rather unique position of being the son, the grandson, and the great-grandson of preachers. Yes, I see the church as the body of Christ. But, oh! How we have blemished and scarred the body through social neglect and through fear of being nonconformists.

There was a time when the church was very powerful—in the time when the early Christians rejoiced at being deemed worthy to suffer for what they believed. In those days the church was not merely a thermometer that transformed the mores of society. Whenever the early Christians entered a town, the people in power became disturbed and immediately sought to convict the Christians for being "disturbers of the peace" and "outside agitators." But the Christians pressed on, in the conviction that they were "a colony of heaven," called to obey God rather than man. Small in number, they were big in commitment. They were too God-intoxicated to be "astronomically intimidated." By their effort and example they brought an end to such ancient evils as infanticide and gladiatorial contests. 40

Things are different now. So often the contemporary church is a weak, ineffectual voice with an uncertain sound. So often it is an archdefender of the status quo. Far from being disturbed by the presence of the church, the power structure of the average community is consoled by the church's silent—and often even vocal—sanction of things as they are.

But the judgment of God is upon the church as never before. If today's church does not recapture the sacrificial spirit of the early church, it will lose its authenticity, forfeit the loyalty of millions, and be dismissed as an irrelevant social club with no meaning for the twentieth century. Every day I meet young people whose disappointment with the church has turned into outright disgust.

Perhaps I have once again been too optimistic. Is organized religion too inextricably bound to the status quo to save our nation and the world? Perhaps I must turn my faith to the inner spiritual church, the church within the church, as the true *ekklesia*[11] and the hope of the world. But again I am thankful to God that some noble souls from the ranks of organized religion have broken loose from the paralyzing chains of conformity and joined us as active partners in the struggle for freedom. They have left their secure congregations and walked the streets of Albany, Georgia, with us. They have gone down the highways of the South on tortuous rides for freedom. Yes, they have gone to jail with us. Some have been dismissed from their churches, have lost the support of their bishops and fellow ministers. But they have acted in the faith that right defeated is stronger than evil triumphant. Their witness has been the spiritual salt that has preserved the true meaning of the gospel in these troubled times. They have carved a tunnel of hope through the dark mountain of disappointment.

I hope that the church as a whole will meet the challenge of this decisive hour. But even if the church does not come to the aid of justice, I have no despair about the future. I have no fear about the outcome of our struggle in Birmingham, even if our motives are at present misunderstood. We will reach the goal of freedom in Birmingham and all over the nation, because the goal of America is freedom. Abused and scorned though we may be, our destiny is tied up with America's destiny. Before the pilgrims landed at Plymouth, we were here. Before the pen of Jefferson etched the majestic words of the Declaration of Independence across the pages of history, we were here. For more than two centuries our forebears labored in this country without wages; they made cotton king; they built the homes of their masters while suffering gross injustice and shameful humiliation—and yet out of a bottomless vitality they continued to thrive and develop. If the inexpressible cruelties of slavery could not stop us, the opposition we now face will surely fail. We will win our freedom because the sacred heritage of our nation and the eternal will of God are embodied in our echoing demands.

Before closing I feel impelled to mention one other point in your statement that has troubled me profoundly. You warmly commended the Birmingham police force for keeping "order" and "preventing violence." I doubt that you would have so warmly commended the police force if you had seen its dogs sinking their teeth into unarmed, nonviolent Negroes. I doubt that you would so quickly commend the policemen if you were to observe their ugly and inhumane treatment of Negroes here in the city jail; if you were to watch them push and curse old Negro women and young Negro girls; if you were to see them slap and kick old Negro men and young boys; if you were to observe them, as they did on two occasions, refuse to give us food because we wanted to sing our grace together. I cannot join you in your praise of the Birmingham police department. 45

It is true that the police have exercised a degree of discipline in handling the demonstrators. In this sense they have conducted themselves rather "nonviolently" in public. But for what purpose? To preserve the evil system of segregation. Over the past few years I have consistently preached that nonviolence demands that the means we use must be as pure as the ends we seek. I have tried to make clear that it is wrong to use immoral means to attain moral ends. But now I must affirm that it is just as wrong, or perhaps even more so, to use moral

[11] The Greek New Testament term for the Christian church.

means to preserve immoral ends. Perhaps Mr. Connor and his policemen have been rather nonviolent in public, as was Chief Pritchett in Albany, Georgia, but they have used the moral means of nonviolence to maintain the immoral end of racial injustice. As T. S. Eliot[12] has said, "The last temptation is the greatest treason: To do the right deed for the wrong reason."

I wish you had commended the Negro sit-inners and demonstrators of Birmingham for their sublime courage, their willingness to suffer, and their amazing discipline in the midst of great provocation. One day the South will recognize its real heroes. They will be the James Merediths,[13] with the noble sense of purpose that enables them to face jeering and hostile mobs, and with the agonizing loneliness that characterizes the life of the pioneer. They will be old, oppressed, battered Negro women, symbolized in a seventy-two-year-old woman in Montgomery, Alabama, who rose up with a sense of dignity and with her people decided not to ride segregated buses, and who responded with ungrammatical profundity to one who inquired about her weariness: "My feets is tired, but my soul is at rest." They will be the young high school and college students, the young ministers of the gospel and a host of their elders, courageously and nonviolently sitting in at lunch counters and willingly going to jail for conscience' sake. One day the South will know that when these disinherited children of God sat down at lunch counters, they were in reality standing up for what is best in the American dream and for the most sacred values in our Judaeo-Christian heritage, thereby bringing our nation back to those great wells of democracy which were dug deep by the founding fathers in their formulation of the Constitution and the Declaration of Independence.

Never before have I written so long a letter. I'm afraid it is much too long to take your precious time. I can assure you that it would have been much shorter if I had been writing from a comfortable desk, but what else can one do when he is alone in a narrow jail cell, other than write long letters, think long thoughts, and pray long prayers?

If I have said anything in this letter that overstates the truth and indicates an unreasonable impatience, I beg you to forgive me. If I have said anything that understates the truth and indicates my having a patience that allows me to settle for anything less than brotherhood, I beg God to forgive me.

I hope this letter finds you strong in the faith. I hope that circumstances will soon make it possible for me to meet each of you, not as an integrationist or a civil-rights leader but as a fellow clergyman and a Christian brother. Let us all hope that the dark clouds of a racial prejudice will soon pass away and the deep fog of misunderstanding will be lifted from our fear-drenched communities, and in some not too distant tomorrow the radiant stars of love and brotherhood will shine over our great nation with all their scintillating beauty.

Yours for the cause of Peace and Brotherhood,
Martin Luther King Jr.   [1963]

50

---

[12] Thomas Stearns Eliot (1888–1965), American-born poet and literary critic.
[13] James Meredith was the first African American student to be admitted to the University of Mississippi.

FOR THINKING AND WRITING

1. At its simplest level, this letter articulates Martin Luther King Jr.'s answer to the question "Why are you in Birmingham?" Briefly state Dr. King's answer and the basic assumption behind his claim.

2. Dr. King combines appeals to authority with appeals to logic and emotion. Cite an example of each, commenting on their effectiveness.

3. One of the most famous sections of this letter focuses on laws (paras. 16–22). What distinction does Dr. King make between just and unjust laws? Which of his examples seem the most compelling? Can you think of other laws he might have broken? Are there some laws you think should not be obeyed? On what basis?

4. Dr. King uses a number of rhetorical devices, especially metaphors (e.g., "cup of endurance," "abyss of despair"). What other metaphors does he use? Are they rhetorically effective? Why?

5. Among other matters, this letter focuses on issues of social policy. After identifying an issue of social policy you would like to address, write an argument to your classmates for or against nonviolently protesting this particular policy. Try to include appeals to authority, to logic, and to emotion. Be sure to anticipate and answer objections to your argument.

6. Read over the section The Elements of Argument (pp. 16–29). Write a brief essay that analyzes the ways in which Martin Luther King Jr.'s "Letter from Birmingham Jail" does or does not conform to this discussion.

N. SCOTT MOMADAY
The Way to Rainy Mountain

Born in 1934 into a Native American family in Oklahoma next to Rainy Mountain, Momaday grew up on a family farm and later on several reservations. Momaday graduated from the University of New Mexico and earned his Ph.D. at Stanford University. He has taught writing at the University of California at Berkeley and at Stanford, and currently teaches at the University of Arizona. Momaday is a poet and novelist as well as an accomplished essayist and painter. He won the Pulitzer Prize in 1969 for House Made of Dawn. *Momaday's work celebrates his Native American heritage, about which he writes with reverence and artistic subtlety. His more recent books include* The Man Made of Words *(1998) and* In the Bear's House *(1999). The following essay appeared as the introduction to* The Way to Rainy Mountain *(1969), a collection of Kiowa legends.*

A single knoll rises out of the plain in Oklahoma, north and west of the Wichita range. For my people, the Kiowas, it is an old landmark, and they gave it the name Rainy Mountain. The hardest weather in the world is there. Winter brings blizzards, hot tornadic winds arise in the spring, and in summer the prairie is an anvil's edge. The grass turns brittle and brown, and it cracks beneath your feet. There are green belts along the rivers and creeks, linear groves of hickory and pecan, willow and witch hazel. At a distance in July or August the steaming foliage seems almost to writhe in fire. Great green and yellow grasshoppers are everywhere in the tall grass, popping up like corn to sting the flesh, and tortoises crawl about on the red earth, going nowhere in the plenty of time. Loneliness is an aspect of the land. All things in the plain are isolate; there is no confusion of objects in the eye, but *one* hill or *one* tree or *one* man. To look upon that landscape in the early morning, with the sun at your back, is to lose the sense of proportion. Your imagination comes to life, and this, you think, is where Creation was begun.

I returned to Rainy Mountain in July. My grandmother had died in the spring, and I wanted to be at her grave. She had lived to be very old and at last infirm. Her only living daughter was with her when she died, and I was told that in death her face was that of a child.

I like to think of her as a child. When she was born, the Kiowas were living the last great moment of their history. For more than a hundred years they had controlled the open range from the Smoky Hill River to the Red, from the headwaters of the Canadian to the fork of the Arkansas and Cimarron. In alliance with the Comanches, they had ruled the whole of the Southern Plains. War was their sacred business, and they were the finest horsemen the world has ever known. But warfare for the Kiowas was pre-eminently a matter of disposition rather than of survival, and they never understood the grim, unrelenting advance of the U.S. Cavalry. When at last, divided and ill provisioned, they were driven onto the Staked Plains in the cold of autumn, they fell into panic. In Palo Duro Canyon they abandoned their crucial stores to pillage and had nothing then but their lives. In order to save themselves, they surrendered to the soldiers at Fort Sill and were imprisoned in the old stone corral that now stands as a military museum. My grandmother was spared the humiliation of those high gray walls by eight or ten years, but she must have known from birth the affliction of defeat, the dark brooding of old warriors.

Her name was Aho, and she belonged to the last culture to evolve in North America. Her forebears came down from the high country in western Montana nearly three centuries ago. They were a mountain people, a mysterious tribe of hunters whose language has never been classified in any major group. In the late seventeenth century they began a long migration to the south and east. It was a journey toward the dawn, and it led to a golden age. Along the way the Kiowas were befriended by the Crows, who gave them the culture and religion of the Plains. They acquired horses, and their ancient nomadic spirit was suddenly free of the ground. They acquired Tai-me, the sacred sun-dance doll, from that moment the object and symbol of their worship, and so shared in the divinity of the sun. Not least, they acquired the sense of destiny, therefore courage and pride. When they entered upon the Southern Plains they had been transformed.

No longer were they slaves to the simple necessity of survival; they were a lordly and dangerous society of fighters and thieves, hunters and priests of the sun. According to their origin myth, they entered the world through a hollow log. From one point of view, their migration was the fruit of an old prophecy, for indeed they emerged from a sunless world.

Though my grandmother lived out her long life in the shadow of Rainy Mountain, the immense landscape of the continental interior lay like memory in her blood. She could tell of the Crows, whom she had never seen, and of the Black Hills, where she had never been. I wanted to see in reality what she had seen more perfectly in the mind's eye, and drove fifteen hundred miles to begin my pilgrimage.

A dark mist lay over the Black Hills, and the land was like iron. At the top of a ridge I caught sight of Devil's Tower upthrust against the gray sky as if in the birth of time the core of the earth had broken through its crust and the motion of the world was begun. There are things in nature that engender an awful quiet in the heart of man; Devil's Tower is one of them. Two centuries ago, because of their need to explain it, the Kiowas made a legend at the base of the rock. My grandmother said:

"Eight children were there at play, seven sisters and their brother. Suddenly the boy was struck dumb; he trembled and began to run upon his hands and feet. His fingers became claws, and his body was covered with fur. There was a bear where the boy had been. The sisters were terrified; they ran, and the bear after them. They came to the stump of a great tree, and the tree spoke to them. It bade them climb upon it, and as they did so, it began to rise into the air. The bear came to kill them, but they were just beyond its reach. It reared against the tree and scored the bark all around with its claws. The seven sisters were borne into the sky, and they became the stars of the Big Dipper." From that moment, and so long as the legend lives, the Kiowas have kinsmen in the night sky. Whatever they were in the mountains, they could be no more. However tenuous their well-being, however much they had suffered and would suffer again, they had found a way out of the wilderness.

My grandmother had a reverence for the sun, a holy regard that now is all but gone out of mankind. There was a wariness in her, and an ancient awe. She was a Christian in her later years, but she had come a long way about, and she never forgot her birthright. As a child she had been to the sun dances; she had taken part in that annual rite, and by it she had learned the restoration of her people in the presence of Tai-me. She was about seven when the last Kiowa sun dance was held in 1887 on the Washita River above Rainy Mountain Creek. The buffalo were gone. In order to consummate the ancient sacrifice — to impale the head of a buffalo bull upon the Tai-me tree — a delegation of old men journeyed into Texas, there to beg and barter for an animal from the Goodnight herd. She was ten when the Kiowas came together for the last time as a living sun-dance culture. They could find no buffalo; they had to hang an old hide from the sacred tree. Before the dance could begin, a company of soldiers rode out from Fort Sill under orders to disperse the tribe. Forbidden without cause the essential act of their faith, having seen the wild herds slaughtered and left to rot upon the ground, the Kiowas backed away forever from the tree. That was July 20, 1890, at the great bend of the Washita. My grandmother was there. Without bitterness, and for as long as she lived, she bore a vision of deicide.

Now that I can have her only in memory, I see my grandmother in the several postures that were peculiar to her: standing at the wood stove on a winter morning and turning meat in a great iron skillet; sitting at the south window, bent above her beadwork, and afterwards, when her vision failed, looking down for a long time into the fold of her hands; going out upon a cane, very slowly as she did when the weight of age came upon her; praying. I remember her most often at prayer. She made long, rambling prayers out of suffering and hope, having seen many things. I was never sure that I had the right to hear, so exclusive were they of all mere custom and company. The last time I saw her she prayed standing by the side of the bed at night, naked to the waist, the light of a kerosene lamp moving upon her dark skin. Her long black hair, always drawn and braided in the day, lay upon her shoulders and against her breasts like a shawl. I do not speak Kiowa, and I never understood her prayers, but there was something inherently sad in the sound, some merest hesitation upon the syllables of sorrow. She began in a high and descending pitch, exhausting her breath to silence; then again and again — and always the same intensity of effort, of something that is, and is not, like urgency in the human voice. Transported so in the dancing light among the shadows of her room, she seemed beyond the reach of time. But that was illusion; I think I knew then that I should not see her again.

Houses are like sentinels in the plain, old keepers of the weather watch. 10
There, in a very little while, wood takes on the appearance of great age. All colors wear soon away in the wind and rain, and then the wood is burned gray and the grain appears and the nails turn red with rust. The window panes are black and opaque; you imagine there is nothing within, and indeed there are many ghosts, bones given up to the land. They stand here and there against the sky, and you approach them for a longer time than you expect. They belong in the distance; it is their domain.

Once there was a lot of sound in my grandmother's house, a lot of coming and going, feasting and talk. The summers there were full of excitement and reunion. The Kiowas are a summer people; they abide the cold and keep to themselves, but when the season turns and the land becomes warm and vital they cannot hold still; an old love of going returns upon them. The aged visitors who came to my grandmother's house when I was a child were made of lean and leather, and they bore themselves upright. They wore great black hats and bright ample shirts that shook in the wind. They rubbed fat upon their hair and wound their braids with strips of colored cloth. Some of them painted their faces and carried the scars of old and cherished enmities. They were an old council of warlords, come to remind and be reminded of who they were. Their wives and daughters served them well. The women might indulge themselves; gossip was at once the mark and compensation of their servitude. They made loud and elaborate talk among themselves, full of jest and gesture, fright and false alarm. They went abroad in fringed and flowered shawls, bright beadwork and German silver. They were at home in the kitchen, and they prepared meals that were banquets.

There were frequent prayer meetings, and nocturnal feasts. When I was a child I played with my cousins outside, where the lamplight fell upon the ground and the singing of the old people rose up around us and carried away into the darkness. There were a lot of good things to eat, a lot of laughter and surprise. And afterwards, when the quiet returned, I lay down with my grandmother and could hear the frogs away by the river and feel the motion of the air.

Now there is a funereal silence in the rooms, the endless wake of some final word. The walls have closed in upon my grandmother's house. When I returned to it in mourning, I saw for the first time in my life how small it was. It was late at night, and there was a white moon, nearly full. I sat for a long time on the stone steps by the kitchen door. From there I could see out across the land; I could see the long row of trees by the creek, the low light upon the rolling plains, and the stars of the Big Dipper. Once I looked at the moon and caught sight of a strange thing. A cricket had perched upon the handrail, only a few inches away. My line of vision was such that the creature filled the moon like a fossil. It had gone there, I thought to live and die, for there, of all places, was its small definition made whole and eternal. A warm wind rose up and purled like the longing within me.

The next morning, I awoke at dawn and went out on the dirt road to Rainy Mountain. It was already hot and the grasshoppers began to fill the air. Still, it was early in the morning, and birds sang out of the shadows. The long yellow grass on the mountain shone in the bright light, and a scissortail hied above the land. There, where it ought to be, at the end of a long and legendary way, was my grandmother's grave. She had at last succeeded to that holy ground. Here and there on the dark stones were ancestral names. Looking back once, I saw the mountain and came away.   [1969]

FOR THINKING AND WRITING

1. Momaday wants to "see in reality" the things his grandmother described, so he travels "fifteen hundred miles to begin [his] pilgrimage" (para. 5). Is he successful in this quest? What does it mean to see as someone else has seen? How would you know if you had succeeded?

2. Momaday mixes memoir, folklore, myth, history, and personal reflections in this essay. Does he successfully blend these genres? What is Momaday's aim in each? How does he achieve coherence?

3. Critics claim that Momaday treats his grandmother's memory with tenderness and reverence. Can you cite specific examples of this attitude?

4. What specific attitudes or values of his grandmother's world does Momaday seem to miss? Does he share some of these values? Would our culture benefit from adopting the attitudes of the Kiowas, or is that impossible now?

5. How would you describe Momaday's attitude in the beginning of the penultimate paragraph?

BRENT STAPLES
The Runaway Son

As an editorial writer for the New York Times, *Brent Staples (b. 1951) is an influential commentator on American politics and culture. A proponent of individual effort, Staples resists being reduced to a symbol of African American progress, remembering his childhood as economically stable until marred by his father's alcoholism. After a chaotic family life during his high-school years, he had such little hope of attending college that he did not take the SAT; however, a special program at Philadelphia Military College and Penn Morton College provided needed skills. He earned a B.A. with honors from Widener University (1973) and received a Danforth Fellowship for graduate study at the University of Chicago, where he earned a Ph.D. in psychology (1977). "The Runaway Son" comes from Staples's memoir,* Parallel Time: Growing Up in Black and White *(1994).*

The mother at the beach was supernaturally pale, speaking that blunt Canadian French with a couple on the next blanket. At the market, she wore a business suit and was lost in a dream at the cheese counter. At the museum, the mother was tan and grimly thin, wearing ink-black shades and hissing furiously into a pocket phone. I was watching when each of these women let a small child wander away. The events were years and cities apart, but basically the same each time. I shadowed the child and waited for its absence to hit home. A mother who loses her cub—even for a moment—displays a seizure of panic unique to itself. Those seizures of panic are a specialty of mine. I guess you could say I collect them.

This morning I am walking to the doctor's office, brooding about mortality and the yearly finger up the butt. Today's mother has flaming red hair and is standing on the steps, riffling her bag for keys. Her little girl is no more than four—with the same creamy face, trimmed in ringlets of red. The mother's hair is thick and shoulder length, blocking her view as she leans over the bag. The child drifts down the steps and stands on the sidewalk. Idling as children do, she crosses to the curb and stares dreamily into traffic. Three people pass her without breaking stride. A pair of teenagers with backpacks. A homeless man pushing a junk-laden shopping cart. A businessman, who glances up at the woman's legs and marches onward.

For some people a four-year-old beyond its mother's reach is invisible. For me that child is the axis of the world. Should I run to her, pull her back from the curb? Should I yell in crude Brooklynese, "Hey lady, look out for the friggin' kid!" Nearing the child, I croon in sweet falsetto, "Hey honey, let's wait for Mommy before you cross." The mention of Mommy freezes her. Up on the steps, the red mane of hair whips hysterically into the air. "Patty, get back here! I told you: Don't go near the street!" The woman thanks me and flushes with embarrassment. I smile—"No trouble at all"—and continue on my way.

Most men past forty dream of muscle tone and sex with exotic strangers. Mine is a constant fantasy of rescue, with a sobbing child as the star. What I tell now is how this came to be.

♦   ♦   ♦

My parents were children when they married. She was eighteen. He was   5
twenty-two. The ceremony was performed in the log house where my mother was
born and where she, my grandmother Mae, and my great-grandmother Luella
still lived, in the foothills of the Blue Ridge Mountains. I visited the house often
as a small child. The only surviving picture shows a bewildered toddler sitting in
the grass, staring fixedly at an unknown something in the distance. My great-
grandmother Luella was a tall, raw-boned woman with a mane of hair so long she
had to move it aside to sit down. Her daughter, my Grandma Mae, wore tight
dresses that showed off her bosoms and a string of dead foxes that trailed from her
shoulder. The beady eyes of the foxes were frightening when she bent to kiss me.

The log house had no running water, no electricity. At night I bathed in a
metal washtub set near the big, wood-burning stove. Once washed, I got into my
white dressing gown and prepared for the trip to the outhouse. My grandmother
held a hurricane lamp out of the back door to light the way. The path was long
and dark and went past the cornfield where all the monsters were. I could tell
they were there, hidden behind the first row, by the way the corn squeaked and
rustled as I passed. Most feared among them were the snakes that turned themselves into hoops and rolled after you at tremendous speed, thrashing through the
corn as they came.

The outhouse itself was dank and musty. While sitting on the toilet I tried as
much as possible to keep the lamp in view through cracks in the outhouse wall. The
trip back to the log house was always the worst; the monsters gathered in the corn to
ambush me, their groaning, growling reaching a crescendo as they prepared to
spring. I ran for the light and landed in the kitchen panting and out of breath.

My father's clan, the Staples of Troutville, had an indoor toilet. My paternal
great-grandparents, John Wesley and Eliza Staples, were people of substance in
the Roanoke valley. In the 1920s, when folks still went about on horseback, John
Wesley burst on the scene in a Model T Ford with all the extras—and let it be
known that he paid for the car in cash. Though not an educated man, he could
read and write. He was vain of his writing: he scribbled even grocery lists with
flourish, pausing often to lick the pencil point. There was no school for black
children at that time. And so John Wesley and his two immediate neighbors built
one at the intersection of their three properties. Then they retained the teacher
who worked in it.

The Pattersons were rich in love, but otherwise broke. This made my
mother's marriage to a Staples man seem a fine idea. But domestic stability was
not my father's experience, the role of husband and father not one that he could
play. His own father, John Wesley's son Marshall, had routinely disappeared on
payday and reappeared drunk and broke several days later. He abandoned the
family at the start of the Depression, leaving Grandma Ada with four children in
hand and one—my father—on the way. Ada had no choice but to place her children with relatives and go north, looking for work.

The luckiest of my uncles landed with John Wesley and Eliza. My father   10
came to rest in hell on earth: the home of Ada's father, Tom Perdue. Three wives
preceded Tom into the grave and the family lore was that he worked them to
death. He hired out his sons for farmwork and collected their pay, leaving them
with nothing. My father was beaten for wetting the bed and forced to sleep on a

pallet under the kitchen sink. He left school at third grade and became part of Tom's dark enterprise. Birthdays went by unnoted. Christmas meant a new pair of work boots—if that. Had it not been for my father and a younger cousin, Tom would have died with no one to note his passing.

This childhood left its mark. My father distrusted affection and what there was of it he pushed away. He looked suspicious when you hugged or kissed him—as though doubting that affection was real. The faculty for praising us was dead in him. I could choose any number of examples from childhood, but permit me to skip ahead to college. I was obsessed with achievement and made the dean's list nearly every semester. My father was mute on the subject—and never once said "good job." Finally, I achieved the perfect semester—an A in every subject—with still not a word from him. Years later, I found that he had carried my grades in his wallet and bragged on them to strangers at truck stops.

My father worked as a truck driver; he earned a handsome salary, then tried to drink it up. My mother mishandled what was left. How could she do otherwise when money was a mystery to her? She grew up in a barter economy, where one farmer's milk bought another's eggs and the man who butchered the hogs was paid in port. She stared at dollar bills as though awaiting divine instruction on how to spend them.

I grew up in a household on the verge of collapse, the threat of eviction ever present, the utilities subject to cutoff at any moment. Gas was cheap and therefore easy to regain. The water company had pity on us and relented when we made even token efforts to pay. But the electric company had no heart to harden. We lived in darkness for weeks at a time. While our neighbors' houses were blazing with light, we ate, played, and bathed in the sepia glow of hurricane lamps. My mother made the darkness into a game. Each night before bed, she assembled us in a circle on the floor, with a hurricane lamp at the center. First she told a story, then had each of us tell one. Those too young to tell stories sang songs. I looked forward to the circle and my brothers' and sisters' faces in the lamplight. The stories I told were the first stirrings of the writer in me.

On Saturday night my father raged through the house hurling things at the walls. Sunday morning would find him placid, freshly shaven, and in his favorite chair, the air around him singing with Mennon Speed Stick and Old Spice Cologne. At his feet were stacked the Sunday papers, *The Philadelphia Bulletin* and *The Philadelphia Inquirer*. I craved his attention but I was wary of him; it was never clear who he would be.

On a table nearby was a picture of him when he was in the navy and not yet twenty years old. He was wearing dress whites, with his cap tilted snappily back on his head, his hand raised in a salute. He smiled a rich expansive smile that spread to every corner of his face. A hardness had undermined the smile and limited its radius. His lips—full and fleshy in the picture—were tense and narrow by comparison. The picture showed a carefree boy—free of terrible Tom—on the verge of a life filled with possibility. Ten years later those possibilities had all been exhausted. He was knee-deep in children, married to a woman he no longer loved but lacked the courage to leave. The children were coming fast. We were three, then five, then nine.

15

Our first neighborhood was called The Hill, a perfect place for a young mother with a large family and an unreliable husband. The men went to work at the shipyard and brought home hefty paychecks that easily supported an entire household. The women stayed home to watch and dote on the children. Not just their own, but all of us. Many of these women were no happier than my mother. They had husbands who beat them; husbands who took lovers within full view of their neighbors; husbands who drove them crazy in any number of ways. The women submerged their suffering in love for children. There was no traffic to speak of, and we played for hours in the streets. A child five years old passed easily from its mother's arms into the arms of the neighborhood. Eyes were on us at every moment. We'd be playing with broken glass when a voice rang out from nowhere: "Y'all stop that and play nice!" We'd be transfixed by the sight of wet cement, ripe for writing curse words, when the voice rang out again: "Y'all get away from that cement. Mr. Prince paid good money to have that done!" Women on errands patroled the sidewalks and made them unsafe for fighting. Every woman had license to discipline a child caught in the wrong. We feigned the deepest remorse, hopeful that the report would not reach our mothers.

Everyone on The Hill grew some kind of fruit; my gang was obsessed with stealing it. We prowled hungrily at people's fences, eyeing their apples, pears, and especially their peaches. We were crazed to get at them, even when they were tiny and bitter and green. We turned surly when there was no fruit at all. Then we raided gardens where people grew trumpet flowers, which gave a sweet nectar when you sucked them. The flowers were enormous and bright orange. When the raid was finished, the ground would be covered with them.

I lost The Hill when my family was evicted. We landed miles away in the Polish West End. The Poles and Ukrainians had once ruled much of the city. They had surrendered it street by street and were now confined to the westernmost neighborhood, their backs pressed to the city limits.

My family had crossed the color line. The people who lived in the house before us had been black as well. But they were all adults. After them, my brothers and sisters must have seemed an invading army.

The Polish and Ukrainian kids spelled their names exotically and ate unpronounceable foods. They were Catholics and on certain Wednesdays wore ashes on their foreheads. On Fridays they were forbidden to eat meat. When you walked by their churches you caught a glimpse of a priest swinging incense at the end of a chain. I wanted to know all there was to know about them. That I was their neighbor entitled me to it.

The Polish and Ukrainian boys did not agree. The first week was a series of fights, one after another. They despised us, as did their parents and grandparents. I gave up trying to know them and played alone. Deprived of friends, I retreated into comic books. My favorite hero was the Silver Surfer, bald and naked to his silver skin, riding a surfboard made of the same silver stuff. The comic's most perfect panels showed the seamless silver body flashing through space on the board. No words; just the long view of the Surfer hurtling past planets and stars.

My fantasies of escape centered on airplanes; I was drunk with the idea of flying. At home, I labored over model planes until the glue made me dizzy. At school,

20

I made planes out of notebook paper and crammed them into my pockets and books. I was obsessed with movies about aerial aces and studied them carefully, prepping for the acehood that I'd been born to and that was destined to be mine. I planned to join the air force when I graduated from high school. The generals would already have heard of me; my jet would be warming up on the runway.

My favorite plane was a wooden Spitfire with British Air Force markings and a propeller powered by a rubber band. I was flying it one day when it landed in the yard of a Ukrainian boy whose nose I had bloodied. His grandfather was gardening when the plane touched down on the neatly kept lawn. He seized the plane, sputtered at me in Ukrainian, and disappeared into the house. A few minutes later one of his older grandsons delivered what was left of it. The old man had destroyed it with malevolent purpose. The wings and fuselage were broken the long way, twice. The pieces were the width of popsicle sticks and wrapped in the rubber band. This was the deepest cruelty I had known.

My mother suffered too. She missed her friends on The Hill, but we were too far west for them to reach us easily. She was learning how difficult it was to care for us on her own, especially since there were few safe places to play. The new house sat on a truck route. Forty-foot semis thundered by, spewing smoke and rattling windows. My mother lived in terror of the traffic and forbade us to roller-skate even on the sidewalk. On The Hill, she had swept off on errands confident that we would be fine. In the Polish West End, she herded us into the house and told us to stay there until she got back.

The house had become a prison. My eldest sister, Yvonne, was thirteen years old — and the first to escape. She stayed out later and later and finally disappeared for days at a time. My mother strapped her. My father threatened her with the juvenile home. But Yvonne met their anger with steeliness. When they questioned her she went dumb and stared into space. I knew the look from prisoner-of-war movies; do your worst, it said, I will tell you nothing. She lied casually and with great skill. But I was an expert listener, determined to break the code. The lie had a strained lightness, the quality of cotton candy. I recognized that sound when she said, "Mom, I'll be right back, I'm going out to the store." I followed her. She passed the store and started across town just as I thought she would. I trotted after her, firing questions. "Where do you think you're going? What is on your mind? What are you trying to do to yourself?" I was my mother's son and accepted all she told me about the dangers of the night. Girls became sluts at night. Boys got into fights and went to jail. These hazards meant nothing to Yvonne; she ignored me and walked on. I yelled "Slut! Street dog!" She lunged at me, but I dodged out of reach. "Slut" I had gotten from my mother. But "street dog" was an original, I'd made it up on the spur of the moment. I had become the child parent. I could scold and insult — but I was too young and ill-formed to instruct. I relished the role; it licensed me to be judge and disparage people I envied but lacked the courage to imitate.

Yvonne was wild to get away. You turned your back and — POOF! — she was gone. Finally she stayed away for days that stretched into weeks and then months. There was no sign or word of her. My mother was beaten up with worry. By night she walked the floors, tilting at every sound in the street.

25

What is it like to be one of nine children, to be tangled in arms and legs in bed and at the dinner table? My brothers and sisters were part of my skin; you only notice your skin when something goes wrong with it. My youngest brother, Blake, got infections that dulled his hearing and closed his ears to the size of pinholes. Bruce broke his arm — while playing in the safety of our treeless and boring backyard. Sherri began to sleepwalk, once leaping down a flight of stairs. Every illness and injury and visit to the hospital involved me. I was first assistant mother now, auxiliary parent in every emergency.

My five-year-old sister Christi was burned nearly to death. Her robe caught fire at the kitchen stove. I was upstairs in my room when it happened. First I heard the scream. Then came thunder of feet below me, and soon after the sound of the ambulance. The doctors did the best they could and gave the rest up to God.

The sign at the nurses' station said that no one under sixteen could visit. I was only eleven; with Yvonne missing, I was as close to sixteen as the children got. I knew that Christi had been brought back from the dead. What I saw the first day added mightily to that awareness. A domed frame had been built over the bed to keep the sheets from touching the burns. Peering under the dome, I saw her wrapped in gauze, round and round the torso, round and round each leg, like a mummy. Blood seeped through the bandages where the burns were deepest. The burns that I could see outside the bandages didn't look too bad. The skin was blackened, but bearable.

Eventually she was allowed to sit up. I would arrive to find her in her bright white gauze suit, sitting in a child's rocking chair. I got used to the gauze. Then they took it off to air out the wounds. Her body was raw from the breast to below the knee. The flesh was wet and bloody in places; I could see the blood pulsing beneath what had been her skin. The room wobbled, but I kept smiling and tried to be natural. I walked in a wide circle around her that day, afraid that I would brush against her. I got past even this, because Christi smiled interminably. The nerve endings were dead and she felt nothing. In time I grew accustomed to flesh without skin. 30

Christi's injuries were the worst on the ward. Next to the burns everything else was easy to look at. I was especially interested in the boy with the steel rods jutting out of his leg. He'd been hit by a car, and the bone was shattered. He didn't talk much, but the rods in his legs were fascinating. The skin clung to them like icing to the candies on a cake.

The children's ward was sparsely visited on weekdays. I cruised the room, cooing at toddlers and making jokes with frightened newcomers. On weekends the ward filled up with parents, highlighting the fact that I was eleven years old — and that my own parents were elsewhere. When real parents visited, I felt like a fraud. I clung to Christi's bedside and did not stray. I wished that the scene at Christi's bed was like the scene around the other beds: fathers, mothers, relatives. But that was not to be.

Christi's accident made the world dangerous. When left in charge, I gathered the children in the living room and imprisoned them there. Trips to the bathroom were timed and by permission only. Now and then I imagined the smell of gas and trotted into the kitchen to check the stove. I avoided looking out of windows for fear of daydreaming. Staring at the sky, I punched through it into space and roamed the galaxy with my hero, the Silver Surfer.

I was daydreaming one day when my brother Brian cried out in pain. He had taken a pee and gotten his foreskin snarled in his zipper. He had given a good yank, too, and pulled it nearly halfway up. Every step tugged at the zipper and caused him to scream. I cut off the pants and left just the zipper behind. To keep his mind off his troubles and kill time until my parents got home, I plunked out a tune on the piano. The longer they stayed away the more crazed I became.

The days were too full for an eleven-year-old who needed desperately to   35
dream. The coal-fired boiler that heated our house was part of the reason. The fire went out at night, which meant that I built a new fire in the morning: chop kindling; haul ashes; shovel coal. Then it was up from the basement, to iron shirts, polish shoes, make sandwiches, and pack the school lunches. My mother tried to sweeten the jobs by describing them as "little": "Build a little fire to throw the chill off of the house." But there was no such thing as a "little" fire. Every fire required the same backbreaking work. Chop kindling. Chop wood. Shovel coal. Haul ashes. One morning she said, "Put a little polish on the toe of your brother's shoes." I dipped the applicator into the liquid polish and dabbed the tiniest spot on the top of each shoe. Yvonne's departure had left my mother brittle and on the edge of violence. I knew this but couldn't stop myself. She was making breakfast when I presented her with the shoes, which were still scuffed and unpolished. "I told you to polish those shoes," she said. "No, you didn't," I said, "you said 'put a little polish on the toe.' " She snapped at me. I snapped back. Then she lifted the serving platter and smashed it across my head.

My father was drinking more than ever. Debt mounted in the customary pattern. We pushed credit to the limit at one store, then abandoned the bills and moved on to the next. Mine was the face of the family's debt. I romanced the shop owners into giving us food and coal on time, then tiptoed past their windows to put the bite on the next guy. When gas and electricity were cut off, I traveled across town to plead with the utility companies. The account executives were mainly women with soft spots for little boys. I conned them, knowing we would never pay. We were behind in the rent and would soon be evicted. Once settled elsewhere, we would apply for gas and electricity, under a fictitious name.

The only way to get time to myself was to steal it. During the summer, I got up early, dressed with the stealth of a burglar, and tiptoed out of the house. The idea was to get in a full day's play unencumbered by errands or housework. Most days I escaped. On other days my mother's radar was just too good, and her rich contralto came soaring out of the bedroom. "Brent, make sure you're back here in time to . . ." to go shopping, to visit Christi at the hospital, to go a thousand places on a thousand errands.

Inevitably I thought of running away — to Florida. In Florida you could sleep outside, live on fruit from the orange groves, and never have to work. I decided to do it on a snowy Saturday at the start of a blizzard. Thought and impulse were one: I took an orange from the fruit bowl, grabbed my parka from the coat rack, and ran from the house.

I did not get to Florida. In my haste, I had grabbed the coat belonging to my younger brother Brian. It was the same color as mine but too small even to zip up. The freight train I planned to take never left the rail yard. The snow thickened and began to freeze. Numb and disheartened, I headed home.

Five years later I succeeded in running away—this time to college. Widener   40
University was two miles from where my family lived. For all that I visited them, two miles could have been two thousand. I lived at school year round—through holidays, semester breaks, and right through the summer. Alone in bed for the first time, I recognized how crowded my life had been. I enjoyed the campus most when it was deserted. I wandered the dormitory drinking in the space. At night I sat in the stadium, smoking pot and studying the constellations. I never slept with my brothers again.

Years later youngest sister, Yvette, accused me of abandoning the family. But the past is never really past; what we have lived is who we are. I am still the frightened ten-year-old tending babies and waiting for my parents. The sight of a child on its own excludes everything else from view. No reading. No idle conversation. No pretending not to see. I follow and watch and intervene because I have no choice. When next you see a child beyond its mother's reach, scan the crowd for me. I am there, watching you watch the child.   [1994]

FOR THINKING AND WRITING

1. If you hadn't read the first and last sections (paras. 1–4, 41), what would you say Staples's theme is? What generalizations does his narrative evidence point to?

2. Race and class figure in this essay in varying degrees. Explain. Do they figure in your experiences? In those of your friends?

3. Staples begins with three anecdotes about mothers and children, then concludes his first section with his "fantasy of rescue" (para. 4). Is his last paragraph a satisfactory conclusion to this idea?

4. Re-creating the past in nonfiction often involves the same techniques as fiction writing: using the five senses. Find examples of creative touches that you think make the essay real.

5. Do you agree that "the past is never really past" (para. 41)? Are you still somehow a ten-year-old? Is Staples's idea of having "no choice" one you identify with? Since the last paragraph cannot be literally true, what is Staples driving at?

JONATHAN SWIFT
A Modest Proposal

FOR PREVENTING THE CHILDREN OF POOR PEOPLE
IN IRELAND FROM BEING A BURDEN TO THEIR PARENTS
OR COUNTRY, AND FOR MAKING THEM
BENEFICIAL TO THE PUBLIC

*Jonathan Swift (1667–1745) was an eminent clergyman in his native Ireland, ris-
ing to the position of dean of St. Patrick's Cathedral in Dublin. But he also wrote
many essays, political pamphlets, poems, and works of fiction, his best-known text
being his 1726 prose satire* Gulliver's Travels. *"A Modest Proposal," written in
1729, also continues to be widely read and much discussed. It reflects Swift's concern over the poverty and food shortages then afflicting Ireland. To him, the country
suffered in part because of the narrow-minded policies of its ruler, England. Swift
also faulted British owners of property in Ireland, many of whom were absentee
landlords indifferent to their tenants' woes. Although "A Modest Proposal" is often
classified as an essay, it contains a significant element of fiction: the real-life Swift
surely did not agree with his narrator's remedy for Ireland. Indeed, this work is regarded as a classic example of irony. Through his narrator's absurd proposal, Swift
aimed to shock readers into thinking about genuine solutions to his country's plight.*

It is a melancholy object to those who walk through this great town or travel
in the country, when they see the streets, the roads, and cabin doors, crowded
with beggars of the female sex, followed by three, four, or six children, all in rags
and importuning every passenger for an alms. These mothers, instead of being
able to work for their honest livelihood, are forced to employ all their time in
strolling to beg sustenance for their helpless infants: who as they grow up either
turn thieves for want of work, or leave their dear native country to fight for the
Pretender in Spain, or sell themselves to the Barbadoes.

I think it is agreed by all parties that this prodigious number of children in the
arms, or on the backs, or at the heels of their mothers, and frequently of their
fathers, is in the present deplorable state of the kingdom a very great additional
grievance; and, therefore, whoever could find out a fair, cheap, and easy method of
making these children sound, useful members of the commonwealth, would
deserve so well of the public as to have his statue set up for a preserver of the nation.

But my intention is very far from being confined to provide only for the children of professed beggars; it is of a much greater extent, and shall take in the
whole number of infants at a certain age who are born of parents in effect as little
able to support them as those who demand our charity in the streets.

As to my own part, having turned my thoughts for many years upon this
important subject, and maturely weighed the several schemes of our projectors,°

---

projectors: Those who devise plans.

have always found them grossly mistaken in their computation. It is true, a child just dropped from its dam may be supported by her milk for a solar year, with little other nourishment; at most not above the value of 2s.,° which the mother may certainly get, or the value in scraps, by her lawful occupation of begging; and it is exactly at one year old that I propose to provide for them in such a manner as instead of being a charge upon their parents or the parish, or wanting food and raiment for the rest of their lives, they shall on the contrary contribute to the feeding, and partly to the clothing, of many thousands.

There is likewise another great advantage in my scheme, that it will prevent 5 those voluntary abortions, and that horrid practice of women murdering their bastard children, alas! too frequent among us! sacrificing the poor innocent babes I doubt more to avoid the expense than the shame, which would move tears and pity in the most savage and inhuman breast.

The number of souls in this kingdom being usually reckoned one million and a half, of these I calculate there may be about 200,000 couples whose wives are breeders; from which number I subtract 30,000 couples, who are able to maintain their own children (although I apprehend there cannot be so many, under the present distress of the kingdom); but this being granted, there will remain 170,000 breeders. I again subtract 50,000 for those women who miscarry, or whose children die by accident or disease within the year. There only remain 120,000 children of poor parents annually born. The question therefore is, how this number shall be reared and provided for? which, as I have already said, under the present situation of affairs, is utterly impossible by all the methods hitherto proposed. For we can neither employ them in handicraft or agriculture; we neither build houses (I mean in the country) nor cultivate land; they can very seldom pick up a livelihood by stealing, till they arrive at six years old, except where they are of towardly parts; although I confess they learn the rudiments much earlier; during which time they can, however, be properly looked upon only as probationers; as I have been informed by a principal gentleman in the county of Cavan, who protested to me that he never knew above one or two instances under the age of six, even in a part of the kingdom so renowned for the quickest proficiency in that art.

I am assured by our merchants, that a boy or a girl before twelve years old is no salable commodity; and even when they come to this age they will not yield above 3£.° or 3£. 2s. 6d.° at most on the exchange; which cannot turn to account either to the parents or kingdom, the charge of nutriment and rags having been at least four times that value.

I shall now therefore humbly propose my own thoughts, which I hope will not be liable to the least objection.

I have been assured by a very knowing American of my acquaintance in London, that a young healthy child well nursed is at a year old a most delicious, nourishing, and wholesome food, whether stewed, roasted, baked, or broiled; and I make no doubt that it will equally serve in a fricassee or a ragout.

I do therefore humbly offer it to public consideration that of the 120,000 10 children already computed, 20,000 may be reserved for breed, whereof only one-fourth part to be males; which is more than we allow to sheep, black cattle, or

2s.: Two shillings.   **3£.:** Three pounds sterling.   **6d.:** Six pence.

swine; and my reason is, that these children are seldom the fruits of marriage, a circumstance not much regarded by our savages; therefore one male will be sufficient to serve four females. That the remaining 100,000 may, at a year old, be offered in sale to the persons of quality and fortune through the kingdom; always advising the mother to let them suck plentifully in the last month, so as to render them plump and fat for a good table. A child will make two dishes at an entertainment for friends; and when the family dines alone, the fore or hind quarter will make a reasonable dish, and seasoned with a little pepper or salt will be very good boiled on the fourth day, especially in winter.

I have reckoned upon a medium that a child just born will weigh twelve pounds, and in a solar year, if tolerably nursed, will increase to twenty-eight pounds.

I grant this food will be somewhat dear, and therefore very proper for landlords, who, as they have already devoured most of the parents, seem to have the best title to the children.

Infant's flesh will be in season throughout the year, but more plentiful in March, and a little before and after: for we are told by a grave author, an eminent French physician, that fish being a prolific diet, there are more children born in Roman Catholic countries about nine months after Lent than at any other season; therefore, reckoning a year after Lent, the markets will be more glutted than usual, because the number of popish infants is at least three to one in this kingdom: and therefore it will have one other collateral advantage, by lessening the number of papists among us.

I have already computed the charge of nursing a beggar's child (in which list I reckon all cottagers, laborers, and four-fifths of the farmers) to be about 2s. per annum, rags included; and I believe no gentleman would repine to give 10s. for the carcass of a good fat child, which, as I have said, will make four dishes of excellent nutritive meat, when he has only some particular friend or his own family to dine with him. Thus the squire will learn to be a good landlord, and grow popular among the tenants; the mother will have 8s. net profit, and be fit for work till she produces another child.

Those who are more thrifty (as I must confess the times require) may flay the carcass; the skin of which artificially dressed will make admirable gloves for ladies, and summer boots for fine gentlemen. 15

As to our city of Dublin, shambles° may be appointed for this purpose in the most convenient parts of it, and butchers we may be assured will not be wanting: although I rather recommend buying the children alive, and dressing them hot from the knife as we do roasting pigs.

A very worthy person, a true lover of his country, and whose virtues I highly esteem, was lately pleased in discoursing on this matter to offer a refinement upon my scheme. He said that many gentlemen of this kingdom, having of late destroyed their deer, he conceived that the want of venison might be well supplied by the bodies of young lads and maidens, not exceeding fourteen years of age nor under twelve; so great a number of both sexes in every country being now ready to starve for want of work and service; and these to be disposed of by their

shambles: Slaughterhouses.

parents, if alive, or otherwise by their nearest relations. But with due deference to so excellent a friend and so deserving a patriot, I cannot be altogether in his sentiments; for as to the males, my American acquaintance assured me from frequent experience that their flesh was generally tough and lean, like that of our schoolboys by continual exercise, and their taste disagreeable; and to fatten them would not answer the charge. Then as to the females, it would, I think, with humble submission be a loss to the public, because they soon would become breeders themselves: and besides, it is not improbable that some scrupulous people might be apt to censure such a practice (although indeed very unjustly), as a little bordering upon cruelty; which, I confess, has always been with me the strongest objection against any project, how well soever intended.

But in order to justify my friend, he confessed that this expedient was put into his head by the famous Psalmanazar° a native of the island Formosa, who came from thence to London about twenty years ago: and in conversation told my friend, that in his country when any young person happened to be put to death, the executioner sold the carcass to persons of quality as a prime dainty; and that in his time the body of a plump girl of fifteen, who was crucified for an attempt to poison the emperor, was sold to his imperial majesty's prime minister of state, and other great mandarins of the court, in joints from the gibbet, at 400 crowns. Neither indeed, can I deny, that if the same use were made of several plump young girls in this town, who without one single groat to their fortunes cannot stir abroad without a chair, and appear at the playhouse and assemblies in foreign fineries which they never will pay for, the kingdom would not be the worse.

Some persons of a depending spirit are in great concern about the vast number of poor people, who are aged, diseased, or maimed, and I have been desired to employ my thoughts what course may be taken to ease the nation of so grievous an encumbrance. But I am not in the least pain upon that matter, because it is very well known that they are every day dying and rotting by cold and famine, and filth and vermin, as fast as can be reasonably expected. And as to the young laborers, they are now in as hopeful a condition: They cannot get work, and consequently pine away for want of nourishment, to a degree that if at any time they are accidentally hired to common labor, they have not strength to perform it; and thus the country and themselves are happily delivered from the evils to come.

I have too long digressed, and therefore shall return to my subject. I think the   20
advantages by the proposal which I have made are obvious and many, as well as of the highest importance.

For first, as I have already observed, it would greatly lessen the number of papists, with whom we are yearly overrun, being the principal breeders of the nation as well as our most dangerous enemies; and who stay at home on purpose to deliver the kingdom to the Pretender, hoping to take their advantage by the absence of so many good Protestants, who have chosen rather to leave their country than stay at home and pay tithes against their conscience to an Episcopal curate.

Psalmanazar: In 1704, the Frenchman George Psalmanazar (c. 1679–1763) wrote *An Historical and Geographical Description of Formosa* (now Taiwan). He claimed to be a Formosan native, but his hoax was exposed soon after the book's publication.

Secondly, The poor tenants will have something valuable of their own, which by law may be made liable to distress and help to pay their landlord's rent, their corn and cattle being already seized, and money a thing unknown.

Thirdly, Whereas the maintenance of 100,000 children from two years old and upward, cannot be computed at less than 10s. a-piece per annum, the nation's stock will be thereby increased £50,000 per annum, beside the profit of a new dish introduced to the tables of all gentlemen of fortune in the kingdom who have any refinement in taste. And the money will circulate among ourselves, the goods being entirely of our own growth and manufacture.

Fourthly, The constant breeders beside the gain of 8s. sterling per annum by the sale of their children, will be rid of the charge of maintaining them after the first year.

Fifthly, This food would likewise bring great custom to taverns, where the vintners will certainly be so prudent as to procure the best receipts for dressing it to perfection, and consequently have their houses frequented by all the fine gentlemen, who justly value themselves upon their knowledge in good eating; and a skilful cook who understands how to oblige his guests, will contrive to make it as expensive as they please.

Sixthly, This would be a great inducement to marriage, which all wise nations have either encouraged by rewards or enforced by laws and penalties. It would increase the care and tenderness of mothers toward their children, when they were sure of a settlement for life to the poor babes, provided in some sort by the public, to their annual profit instead of expense. We should see an honest emulation among the married women, which of them would bring the fattest child to the market. Men would become as fond of their wives during the time of their pregnancy as they are now of their mares in foal, their cows in calf, their sows when they are ready to farrow; nor offer to beat or kick them (as is too frequent a practice) for fear of a miscarriage.

Many other advantages might be enumerated. For instance, the addition of some thousand carcasses in our exportation of barreled beef, the propagation of swine's flesh, and improvement in the art of making good bacon, so much wanted among us by the great destruction of pigs, too frequent at our table; which are no way comparable in taste or magnificence to a well-grown, fat, yearling child, which roasted whole will make a considerable figure at a lord mayor's feast or any other public entertainment. But this and many others I omit, being studious of brevity.

Supposing that 1,000 families in this city would be constant customers for infants' flesh, besides others who might have it at merry-meetings, particularly at weddings and christenings, I compute that Dublin would take off annually about 20,000 carcasses; and the rest of the kingdom (where probably they will be sold somewhat cheaper) the remaining 80,000.

I can think of no one objection that will possibly be raised against this proposal, unless it should be urged that the number of people will be thereby much lessened in the kingdom. This I freely own, and it was indeed one principal design in offering it to the world. I desire the reader will observe, that I calculate my remedy for this one individual kingdom of Ireland and for no other that ever was, is, or I think ever can be upon earth. Therefore let no man talk to me of other expedients: of taxing our absentees at 5s. a pound; of using neither clothes

25

nor household furniture except what is of our own growth and manufacture; of utterly rejecting the materials and instruments that promote foreign luxury; of curing the expensiveness of pride, vanity, idleness, and gaming in our women; of introducing a vein of parsimony, prudence, and temperance; of learning to love our country, in the want of which we differ even from Laplanders and the inhabitants of Topinamboo; of quitting our animosities and factions, nor acting any longer like the Jews, who were murdering one another at the very moment their city was taken; of being a little cautious not to sell our country and conscience for nothing; of teaching landlords to have at least one degree of mercy toward their tenants; lastly, of putting a spirit of honesty, industry, and skill into our shopkeepers; who, if a resolution could now be taken to buy only our native goods, would immediately unite to cheat and exact upon us in the price the measure, and the goodness, nor could ever yet be brought to make one fair proposal of just dealing, though often and earnestly invited to it.

Therefore I repeat, let no man talk to me of these and the like expedients, till   30
he has at least some glimpse of hope that there will be ever some hearty and sincere attempt to put them in practice.

But as to myself, having been wearied out for many years with offering vain, idle, visionary thoughts, and at length utterly despairing of success, I fortunately fell upon this proposal; which, as it is wholly new, so it has something solid and real, of no expense and little trouble, full in our own power, and whereby we can incur no danger in disobliging England. For this kind of commodity will not bear exportation, the flesh being of too tender a consistence to admit a long continuance in salt, although perhaps I could name a country which would be glad to eat up our whole nation without it.

After all, I am not so violently bent upon my own opinion as to reject any offer proposed by wise men, which shall be found equally innocent, cheap, easy, and effectual. But before something of that kind shall be advanced in contradiction to my scheme, and offering a better, I desire the author or authors will be pleased maturely to consider two points. First, as things now stand, how they will be able to find food and raiment for 100,000 useless mouths and backs. And secondly, there being a round million of creatures in human figure throughout this kingdom, whose subsistence put into a common stock would leave them in debt 2,000,000£. sterling, adding those who are beggars by profession to the bulk of farmers, cottagers, and laborers, with the wives and children who are beggars in effect; I desire those politicians who dislike my overture, and may perhaps be so bold as to attempt an answer, that they will first ask the parents of these mortals, whether they would not at this day think it a great happiness to have been sold for food at a year old in the manner I prescribe, and thereby have avoided such a perpetual scene of misfortunes as they have since gone through by the oppression of landlords, the impossibility of paying rent without money or trade, the want of common sustenance, with neither house nor clothes to cover them from the inclemencies of the weather, and the most inevitable prospect of entailing the like or greater miseries upon their breed for ever.

I profess, in the sincerity of my heart, that I have not the least personal interest in endeavoring to promote this necessary work, having no other motive than the public good of my country, by advancing our trade, providing for infants, relieving the poor, and giving some pleasure to the rich. I have no children by which I can propose to get a single penny; the youngest being nine years old, and my wife past childbearing.   [1729]

FOR THINKING AND WRITING

1. Analyze this essay as an argument that the narrator makes. What are his main claims? What support does he provide for them? What are some of his key warrants or assumptions?

2. What is the narrator's attitude toward the Irish poor? Identify various words he uses that indicate his judgments of them.

3. A word often associated with Swift's piece is *irony*. What are possible meanings of this term? What meaning of it seems most appropriate to Swift's work?

4. At what point in the piece do you realize that it is ironic? How would you describe the narrator's personality and tone before you get to this moment? List several adjectives for him.

5. Do you think Swift's piece would have succeeded in making many people more determined to solve Ireland's problems? Why, or why not?

APPENDIX

Making Arguments Using Critical Approaches

Exploring the topics of literary criticism can help readers understand the various ways literature can matter. One popular way to investigate critical approaches to literature is to group critics into schools. Critics who are primarily concerned with equality for women, for example, are often classified as feminist critics, and those concerned with the responses of readers are classified as reader-response critics. Likewise, critics who focus on the unconscious are said to belong to the psychoanalytic school, and those who analyze class conflicts belong to the Marxist school.

Classifying critics in this way is probably more convenient than precise. Few critics like to be pigeonholed or thought predictable, and many professional readers tend to be eclectic — that is, they use ideas from various schools to help them illuminate the text. Nevertheless, knowing something about contemporary schools of criticism can make you a more informed reader and help literature matter to you even more.

There is a commonsense belief that words mean just what they say — that to understand a certain passage in a text a reader simply needs to know what the words mean. But meaning is rarely straightforward. Scholars have been arguing over the meaning of passages in the Bible, in the Constitution, and in Shakespeare's plays for centuries without reaching agreement. Pinning down the exact meaning of words like *sin*, *justice*, and *love* is almost impossible, but even more daunting is the unacknowledged theory of reading that each person brings to any text, including literature. Some people who read the Bible or the Constitution, for example, believe in the literal meaning of the words, and some think the real meaning lies in the original intention of the writer, while others believe that the only meaning we can be sure of is our own perspective. For these latter readers, there is no objective meaning, and no absolutely true meaning is possible.

Indeed, a good deal of what a text means depends on the perspective that readers bring with them. Passages can be read effectively from numerous points of view. A generation ago most English professors taught their students to pay attention to the internal aspects of a poem and not to the poem's larger social and political contexts. So oppositions, irony, paradox, and coherence — not gender equality or social justice — were topics of discussion. Proponents of this approach were said to belong to the New Critical school. In the last twenty years or so, however, professors have put much more emphasis on the external aspects of interpretation, stressing social, political, cultural, sexual, and gender-based perspectives. Each one of these perspectives can give us a valuable window on a text, helping us see the rich possibilities of literature. Even though each approach can provide insights into a text, it can also be blind to other textual elements. When we read in too focused a way, we can sometimes miss the opportunity to see what others see.

In Making Arguments Using Critical Approaches, however, we want to present our interpretation in a clear, logical, and reflective manner as we take a position and try to persuade others of its reasonableness. Since there are many possible lenses to see a text through, you can be sure your classmates will see things differently. Part of the excitement and challenge of making arguments that matter is your ability to analyze and clarify your ideas, gather and organize your evidence, and present your claim in carefully revised and edited prose.

Contemporary Schools of Criticism

The following eight approaches are just a few of the many different literary schools or perspectives a reader can use in engaging a text. Think of them as intellectual tools or informed lenses that you can employ to enhance your interpretation of a particular literary text:

* New Criticism
* Feminist criticism
* Psychoanalytic criticism
* Marxist criticism
* Deconstruction
* Reader-response criticism
* Postcolonial criticism
* New Historicism

NEW CRITICISM

New Criticism was developed over fifty years ago as a way to focus on "the text itself." Although it is no longer as popular as it once was, some of its principles are still widely accepted, especially the use of specific examples from the text as evidence for a particular interpretation. Sometimes called *close reading,* this approach does not see either the writer's intention or the reader's personal response as relevant. It is also uninterested in the text's social context, the spirit of the age, or its relevance to issues of gender, social justice, or oppression. These critics are interested, for example, in a poem's internal structure, images, symbols, metaphors, point of view, plot, and characterizations. Emphasis is placed on literary language — on the ways connotation, ambiguity, irony, and paradox all reinforce the meaning. In fact, *how* a poem means is inseparable from *what* it means. The primary method for judging the worth of a piece of literature is its organic unity or the complex way all the elements of a text contribute to the poem's meaning.

Critics often argue that their interpretations are the most consistent with textual evidence. A popular approach is to note the oppositions in the text and to focus on tensions, ironies, and paradoxes. Typically a paradox early in the text is shown at the end not to be that contradictory after all. The critic then argues that all the elements of the text can be seen as contributing to this resolution.

FEMINIST CRITICISM

Feminist criticism developed during the 1970s as an outgrowth of a resurgent women's movement. The goals of the feminist critic and the feminist political activist are similar — to contest the patriarchal point of view as the standard for all moral, aesthetic, political, and intellectual judgments and to assert that gender roles are primarily learned, not universal. They hope to uncover and challenge essentialist attitudes that hold it is normal for women to be kept in domestic, secondary, and subservient roles, and they affirm the value of a woman's experiences and perspectives in understanding the world. Recently both female and male critics have become interested in gender studies, a branch of theory concerned with the ways cultural practices socialize us to act in certain ways because of our gender. Primarily focused on issues of identity, gender criticism looks at the ways characters in literary texts are represented, or how they are constructed in a particular culture as feminine or masculine. Like the broader area of feminism, many gender specialists hope that studying the arbitrary ways we are expected to dress, walk, talk, and behave can help us widen the conventional notions of gender.

PSYCHOANALYTIC CRITICISM

Psychoanalytic criticism began with Sigmund Freud's theories of the unconscious, especially the numerous repressed wounds, fears, unresolved conflicts, and guilty desires from childhood that can significantly affect behavior and mental health in our adult lives. Freud developed the tripart division of the mind into the ego (the conscious self), the superego (the site of what our culture has taught us about good and bad), and the id (the primitive unconscious and source of our sexual drive). Psychoanalytic critics often see literature as a kind of dream filled with symbolic elements that often mask their real meaning. Freud also theorized that young males were threatened by their fathers in the competition for the affection of their mothers. Critics are alert to the complex ways this Oedipal drama unfolds in literature.

MARXIST CRITICISM

Marxist criticism is based on the political and economic theories of Karl Marx. Marxists think that a society is propelled by its economy, which is manipulated by a class system. Most people, especially blue-collar workers (the proletariat), do not understand the complex ways their lives are subject to economic forces beyond their control. This false consciousness about history and material well-being prevents workers from seeing that their values have been socially constructed to keep them in their place. What most interests contemporary Marxists is the way ideology shapes our consciousness. And since literature both represents and projects ideology, Marxist critics see it as a way to unmask our limited view of society's structures.

DECONSTRUCTION

Deconstruction is really more a philosophical movement than a school of literary criticism, but many of its techniques have been used by Marxist and feminist literary critics to uncover important concepts they believe are hidden in texts. Made famous by the French philosopher Jacques Derrida, deconstruction's main tenet is that Western thought has divided the world into binary opposites. To gain a semblance of control over the complexity of human experience, we have constructed a worldview where good is clearly at one end of a continuum and bad at the other. Additional examples of binary opposites include masculine and feminine, freedom and slavery, objective and subjective, mind and body, and presence and absence. According to Derrida, however, this arbitrary and illusory construct simply reflects the specific ideology of one culture. Far from being opposed to one another, masculinity and femininity, for example, are intimately interconnected, and traces of the feminine are to be found within the masculine. The concepts need each other for meaning to occur, an idea referred to as *differance*. Derrida also notes that language, far from being a neutral medium of communication, is infused with our biases, assumptions, and values—which leads some of us to refer to sexually active women as "sluts" and to sexually active men as "studs." One term ("sluts") is marginalized, and the other ("studs") is privileged because our culture grants men more power than women in shaping the language that benefits them.

Thus, language filters, distorts, and alters our perception of the world. For deconstructors or deconstructive critics, language is not stable or reliable, and when closely scrutinized, it becomes slippery and ambiguous, constantly overflowing with implications, associations, and contradictions. For Derrida, this endless freeplay of meaning suggests that language is always changing, always in flux—especially so when we understand that words can be viewed from almost endless points of view or contexts. That is why deconstructionists claim that texts (or individuals or systems of thought) have no fixed definition, no center, no absolute meaning. And so one way to deconstruct or lay bare the arbitrary construction of a text is to show that the oppositions in the text are not really absolutely opposed, that outsiders can be seen to be insiders, and that words that seem to mean one thing can mean many things.

READER-RESPONSE CRITICISM

Reader-response criticism is often misunderstood to be simply giving one's opinion about a text: "I liked it," "I hate happy endings," "I think the characters were unrealistic." But reader-response criticism is actually more interested in why readers have certain responses. The central assumption is that texts do not come alive and do not mean anything until active readers engage them with specific assumptions about what reading is. New Critics think a reader's response is irrelevant because a text's meaning is timeless. But response critics, including feminists and Marxists, maintain that what a text means cannot be separated from the reading process used by readers as they draw on personal and literary experiences to make meaning. In other words, the text is not an object but an event that occurs in readers over time.

Response criticism includes critics who think that the reader's contribution to the making of meaning is quite small as well as critics who think that readers play a primary role in the process. Louise Rosenblatt is a moderate response critic since she thinks the contributions are about equal. Her transactive theory claims that the text guides our response, like a printed musical score that we adjust as we move through the text. She allows for a range of acceptable meanings as long as she can find reasonable textual support in the writing.

Response critics like Stanley Fish downplay individual responses, focusing instead on how communities influence our responses to texts. We probably all belong to a number of these interpretive communities (such as churches, universities, neighborhoods, political parties, and social class) and have internalized their interpretive strategies, their discourse, or their way of reading texts of all kinds. Fish's point is that we all come to texts already predisposed to read them in a certain way: we do not interpret stories, but we create them by using the reading tools and cultural assumptions we bring with us. Our reading then reveals what is in us more than what is in the text. We find what we expect to see.

POSTCOLONIAL CRITICISM

Postcolonial criticism, like feminist criticism, has developed because of the dramatic shrinking of the world and the increasing multicultural cast of our own country. It is mainly interested in the ways nineteenth-century European political domination affects the lives of people living in former colonies, especially the way the dominant culture becomes the norm and those without power are portrayed as inferior. Postcolonial critics often look for stereotypes in texts as well as in characters whose self-image has been damaged by being forced to see themselves as Other, as less than. As oppressed people try to negotiate life in both the dominant and the oppressed cultures, they can develop a double consciousness that leads to feelings of alienation and deep conflicts.

Literary critics often argue that being caught between the demands of two cultures—one dominant and privileged, the other marginalized and scorned—causes a character to be "unhomed," a psychological refugee who is uncomfortable everywhere.

NEW HISTORICISM

New Historicism was developed because critics were dissatisfied with the old historicism, a long-standing traditional approach that viewed history simply as a background for understanding the literary text. History was thought to be an accurate record of what happened because the professional historian used objective and proven methods. But most literary critics no longer hold to this view of history. Instead, history is now thought to be just one perspective among many possibilities, inevitably subjective and biased. Influenced by the theorist Michael Foucault, history is seen as one of many discourses that can shed light on the past. But the dominant view is that all of us, including historians, writers, and critics, live in a particular culture and cannot escape its influences. And since these social, cultural, literary, economic, and political influences are all interrelated, all texts can tell us something important. Stories, histories, diaries, laws, speeches, newspapers, and magazines are all relevant. Culture permeates all texts, influencing everyone to see society's view of reality, of what's right and wrong and which values, assumptions, and truths are acceptable. Critics and historians try to interpret a vast web of interconnected discourses and forces in order to understand an era. Naturally, since many of these forces are competing for power, critics are always looking for power struggles among discourses. Think of the present struggle over the amount of influence religion should have in politics or who has the right to marry. Literature is one of the texts in a culture that shapes our views and which critics investigate to unearth these competing ideas.

Working with the Critical Approaches

Keep these brief descriptions of the critical approaches in mind as you read the following story by James Joyce, one of the most important writers of the twentieth century. Joyce (1882–1941) was born in Ireland, although he spent most of his life in self-imposed exile on the European continent. "Counterparts" is from *Dubliners* (1914), a collection of stories set in the Irish city of his childhood years. (For more on James Joyce, see his story "Araby" on p. 263.)

JAMES JOYCE
Counterparts

The bell rang furiously and, when Miss Parker went to the tube, a furious voice called out in a piercing North of Ireland accent:

— Send Farrington here!

Miss Parker returned to her machine, saying to a man who was writing at a desk:

— Mr Alleyne wants you upstairs.

The man muttered *Blast him!* under his breath and pushed back his chair to   5
stand up. When he stood up he was tall and of great bulk. He had a hanging face, dark wine-coloured, with fair eyebrows and moustache: his eyes bulged forward slightly and the whites of them were dirty. He lifted up the counter and, passing by the clients, went out of the office with a heavy step.

He went heavily upstairs until he came to the second landing, where a door bore a brass plate with the inscription *Mr Alleyne*. Here he halted, puffing with labour and vexation, and knocked. The shrill voice cried:

—Come in!

The man entered Mr Alleyne's room. Simultaneously Mr Alleyne, a little man wearing gold-rimmed glasses on a cleanshaven face, shot his head up over a pile of documents. The head itself was so pink and hairless that it seemed like a large egg reposing on the papers. Mr Alleyne did not lose a moment:

—Farrington? What is the meaning of this? Why have I always to complain of you? May I ask you why you haven't made a copy of that contract between Bodley and Kirwan? I told you it must be ready by four o'clock.

—But Mr Shelley said, sir—   10

—*Mr Shelley said, sir.* . . . Kindly attend to what I say and not to what *Mr Shelley says, sir.* You have always some excuse or another for shirking work. Let me tell you that if the contract is not copied before this evening I'll lay the matter before Mr Crosbie. . . . Do you hear me now?

—Yes, sir.

—Do you hear me now? . . . Ay and another little matter! I might as well be talking to the wall as talking to you. Understand once for all that you get a half an hour for your lunch and not an hour and a half. How many courses do you want, I'd like to know. . . . Do you mind me, now?

—Yes, sir.

Mr Alleyne bent his head again upon his pile of papers. The man stared   15
fixedly at the polished skull which directed the affairs of Crosbie & Alleyne, gauging its fragility. A spasm of rage gripped his throat for a few moments and then passed, leaving after it a sharp sensation of thirst. The man recognised the sensation and felt that he must have a good night's drinking. The middle of the month was passed and, if he could get the copy done in time, Mr Alleyne might give him an order on the cashier. He stood still, gazing fixedly at the head upon the pile of papers. Suddenly Mr Alleyne began to upset all the papers, searching for something. Then, as if he had been unaware of the man's presence till that moment, he shot up his head again, saying:

—Eh? Are you going to stand there all day? Upon my word, Farrington, you take things easy!

—I was waiting to see . . .

—Very good, you needn't wait to see. Go downstairs and do your work.

The man walked heavily towards the door and, as he went out of the room, he heard Mr Alleyne cry after him that if the contract was not copied by evening Mr Crosbie would hear of the matter.

He returned to his desk in the lower office and counted the sheets which   20
remained to be copied. He took up his pen and dipped it in the ink but he continued to stare stupidly at the last words he had written: *In no case shall the said Bernard Bodley be* . . . The evening was falling and in a few minutes they would be lighting the gas: then he could write. He felt that he must slake the thirst in his throat. He stood up from his desk and, lifting the counter as before, passed out of the office. As he was passing out the chief clerk looked at him inquiringly.

—It's all right, Mr Shelley, said the man, pointing with his finger to indicate the objective of his journey.

The chief clerk glanced at the hat-rack but, seeing the row complete, offered no remark. As soon as he was on the landing the man pulled a shepherd's plaid cap out of his pocket, put it on his head and ran quickly down the rickety stairs. From the street door he walked on furtively on the inner side of the path towards the corner and all at once dived into a doorway. He was now safe in the dark snug of O'Neill's shop, and, filling up the little window that looked into the bar with his inflamed face, the colour of dark wine or dark meat, he called out:

— Here, Pat, give us a g.p., like a good fellow.

The curate brought him a glass of plain porter. The man drank it at a gulp and asked for a caraway seed. He put his penny on the counter and, leaving the curate to grope for it in the gloom, retreated out of the snug as furtively as he had entered it.

Darkness, accompanied by a thick fog, was gaining upon the dusk of Febru-   25
ary and the lamps in Eustace Street had been lit. The man went up by the houses until he reached the door of the office, wondering whether he could finish his copy in time. On the stairs a moist pungent odour of perfumes saluted his nose: evidently Miss Delacour had come while he was out in O'Neill's. He crammed his cap back again into his pocket and re-entered the office assuming an air of absent-mindedness.

— Mr Alleyne has been calling for you, said the chief clerk severely. Where were you?

The man glanced at the two clients who were standing at the counter as if to intimate that their presence prevented him from answering. As the clients were both male the chief clerk allowed himself a laugh.

— I know that game, he said. Five times in one day is a little bit. . . . Well, you better look sharp and get a copy of our correspondence in the Delacour case for Mr Alleyne.

This address in the presence of the public, his run upstairs and the porter he had gulped down so hastily confused the man and, as he sat down at his desk to get what was required, he realised how hopeless was the task of finishing his copy of the contract before half past five. The dark damp night was coming and he longed to spend it in the bars, drinking with his friends amid the glare of gas and the clatter of glasses. He got out the Delacour correspondence and passed out of the office. He hoped Mr Alleyne would not discover that the last two letters were missing.

The moist pungent perfume lay all the way up to Mr Alleyne's room. Miss   30
Delacour was a middle-aged woman of Jewish appearance. Mr Alleyne was said to be sweet on her or on her money. She came to the office often and stayed a long time when she came. She was sitting beside his desk now in an aroma of perfumes, smoothing the handle of her umbrella and nodding the great black feather in her hat. Mr Alleyne had swivelled his chair round to face her and thrown his right foot jauntily upon his left knee. The man put the correspondence on the desk and bowed respectfully but neither Mr Alleyne nor Miss Delacour took any notice of his bow. Mr Alleyne tapped a finger on the correspondence and then flicked it towards him as if to say: *That's all right: you can go.*

The man returned to the lower office and sat down again at his desk. He stared intently at the incomplete phrase: *In no case shall the said Bernard Bodley be* . . . and thought how strange it was that the last three words began with the same letter. The chief clerk began to hurry Miss Parker, saying she would never have the letters typed in time for post. The man listened to the clicking of the machine for a few minutes and then set to work to finish his copy. But his head was not clear and his mind wandered away to the glare and rattle of the public-house. It was a night for hot punches. He struggled on with his copy, but when the clock struck five he had still fourteen pages to write. Blast it! He couldn't finish it in time. He longed to execrate aloud, to bring his fist down on something violently. He was so enraged that he wrote *Bernard Bernard* instead of *Bernard Bodley* and had to begin again on a clean sheet.

He felt strong enough to clear out the whole office singlehanded. His body ached to do something, to rush out and revel in violence. All the indignities of his life enraged him. . . . Could he ask the cashier privately for an advance? No, the cashier was no good, no damn good: he wouldn't give an advance. . . . He knew where he would meet the boys: Leonard and O'Halloran and Nosey Flynn. The barometer of his emotional nature was set for a spell of riot.

His imagination had so abstracted him that his name was called twice before he answered. Mr Alleyne and Miss Delacour were standing outside the counter and all the clerks had turned round in anticipation of something. The man got up from his desk. Mr Alleyne began a tirade of abuse, saying that two letters were missing. The man answered that he knew nothing about them, that he had made a faithful copy. The tirade continued: it was so bitter and violent that the man could hardly restrain his fist from descending upon the head of the manikin before him.

—I know nothing about any other two letters, he said stupidly.

—*You*—*know*—*nothing*. Of course you know nothing, said Mr Alleyne. Tell   35
me, he added, glancing first for approval to the lady beside him, do you take me
for a fool? Do you think me an utter fool?

The man glanced from the lady's face to the little egg-shaped head and back again; and, almost before he was aware of it, his tongue had found a felicitous moment:

—I don't think, sir, he said, that that's a fair question to put to me.

There was a pause in the very breathing of the clerks. Everyone was astounded (the author of the witticism no less than his neighbours) and Miss Delacour, who was a stout amiable person, began to smile broadly. Mr Alleyne flushed to the hue of a wild rose and his mouth twitched with a dwarf's passion. He shook his fist in the man's face till it seemed to vibrate like the knob of some electric machine:

—You impertinent ruffian! You impertinent ruffian! I'll make short work of you! Wait till you see! You'll apologise to me for your impertinence or you'll quit the office instanter! You'll quit this, I'm telling you, or you'll apologise to me!

He stood in a doorway opposite the office watching to see if the cashier   40
would come out alone. All the clerks passed out and finally the cashier came out
with the chief clerk. It was no use trying to say a word to him when he was with
the chief clerk. The man felt that his position was bad enough. He had been

obliged to offer an abject apology to Mr Alleyne for his impertinence but he knew what a hornet's nest the office would be for him. He could remember the way in which Mr Alleyne had hounded little Peake out of the office in order to make room for his own nephew. He felt savage and thirsty and revengeful, annoyed with himself and with everyone else. Mr Alleyne would never give him an hour's rest; his life would be a hell to him. He had made a proper fool of himself this time. Could he not keep his tongue in his cheek? But they had never pulled together from the first, he and Mr Alleyne, ever since the day Mr Alleyne had overheard him mimicking his North of Ireland accent to amuse Higgins and Miss Parker: that had been the beginning of it. He might have tried Higgins for the money, but sure Higgins never had anything for himself. A man with two establishments to keep up, of course he couldn't. . . .

He felt his great body again aching for the comfort of the public-house. The fog had begun to chill him and he wondered could he touch Pat in O'Neill's. He could not touch him for more than a bob—and a bob was no use. Yet he must get money somewhere or other: he had spent his last penny for the g.p. and soon it would be too late for getting money anywhere. Suddenly, as he was fingering his watch-chain, he thought of Terry Kelly's pawn-office in Fleet Street. That was the dart! Why didn't he think of it sooner?

He went through the narrow alley of Temple Bar quickly, muttering to himself that they could all go to hell because he was going to have a good night of it. The clerk in Terry Kelly's said A *crown!* but the consignor held out for six shillings; and in the end the six shillings was allowed him literally. He came out of the pawn-office joyfully, making a little cylinder of the coins between his thumb and fingers. In Westmoreland Street the footpaths were crowded with young men and women returning from business and ragged urchins ran here and there yelling out the names of the evening editions. The man passed through the crowd, looking on the spectacle generally with proud satisfaction and staring masterfully at the office-girls. His head was full of the noises of tram-gongs and swishing trolleys and his nose already sniffed the curling fumes of punch. As he walked on he preconsidered the terms in which he would narrate the incident to the boys:

—So, I just looked at him—coolly, you know, and looked at her. Then I looked back at him again—taking my time, you know. *I don't think that that's a fair question to put to me,* says I.

Nosey Flynn was sitting up in his usual corner of Davy Byrne's and, when he heard the story, he stood Farrington a half-one, saying it was as smart a thing as ever he heard. Farrington stood a drink in his turn. After a while O'Halloran and Paddy Leonard came in and the story was repeated to them. O'Halloran stood tailors of malt, hot, all round and told the story of the retort he had made to the chief clerk when he was in Callan's of Fownes's Street; but, as the retort was after the manner of the liberal shepherds in the eclogues, he had to admit that it was not so clever as Farrington's retort. At this Farrington told the boys to polish off that and have another.

Just as they were naming their poisons who should come in but Higgins! Of   45
course he had to join in with the others. The men asked him to give his version of

it, and he did so with great vivacity for the sight of five small hot whiskies was very exhilarating. Everyone roared laughing when he showed the way in which Mr Alleyne shook his fist in Farrington's face. Then he imitated Farrington, saying, *And here was my nabs, as cool as you please,* while Farrington looked at the company out of his heavy dirty eyes, smiling and at times drawing forth stray drops of liquor from his moustache with the aid of his lower lip.

When that round was over there was a pause. O'Halloran had money but neither of the other two seemed to have any; so the whole party left the shop somewhat regretfully. At the corner of Duke Street Higgins and Nosey Flynn bevelled off to the left while the other three turned back towards the city. Rain was drizzling down on the cold streets and, when they reached the Ballast Office, Farrington suggested the Scotch House. The bar was full of men and loud with the noise of tongues and glasses. The three men pushed past the whining matchsellers at the door and formed a little party at the corner of the counter. They began to exchange stories. Leonard introduced them to a young fellow named Weathers who was performing at the Tivoli as an acrobat and knockabout *artiste.* Farrington stood a drink all round. Weathers said he would take a small Irish and Apollinaris. Farrington, who had definite notions of what was what, asked the boys would they have an Apollinaris too; but the boys told Tim to make theirs hot. The talk became theatrical. O'Halloran stood a round and then Farrington stood another round, Weathers protesting that the hospitality was too Irish. He promised to get them in behind the scenes and introduce them to some nice girls. O'Halloran said that he and Leonard would go but that Farrington wouldn't go because he was a married man; and Farrington's heavy dirty eyes leered at the company in token that he understood he was being chaffed. Weathers made them all have just one little tincture at his expense and promised to meet them later on at Mulligan's in Poolbeg Street.

When the Scotch House closed they went round to Mulligan's. They went into the parlour at the back and O'Halloran ordered small hot specials all round. They were all beginning to feel mellow. Farrington was just standing another round when Weathers came back. Much to Farrington's relief he drank a glass of bitter this time. Funds were running low but they had enough to keep them going. Presently two young women with big hats and a young man in a check suit came in and sat at a table close by. Weathers saluted them and told the company that they were out of the Tivoli. Farrington's eyes wandered at every moment in the direction of one of the young women. There was something striking in her appearance. An immense scarf of peacock-blue muslin was wound round her hat and knotted in a great bow under her chin; and she wore bright yellow gloves, reaching to the elbow. Farrington gazed admiringly at the plump arm which she moved very often and with much grace; and when, after a little time, she answered his gaze he admired still more her large dark brown eyes. The oblique staring expression in them fascinated him. She glanced at him once or twice and, when the party was leaving the room, she brushed against his chair and said *O, pardon!* in a London accent. He watched her leave the room in the hope that she would look back at him, but he was disappointed. He cursed his want of money and cursed all the rounds he had stood, particularly all the whiskies and Apollinaris which he had stood to Weathers. If there was one thing that he hated it was a sponge. He was so angry that he lost count of the conversation of his friends.

When Paddy Leonard called him he found that they were talking about feats of strength. Weathers was showing his biceps muscle to the company and boasting so much that the other two had called on Farrington to uphold the national honour. Farrington pulled up his sleeve accordingly and showed his biceps muscle to the company. The two arms were examined and compared and finally it was agreed to have a trial of strength. The table was cleared and the two men rested their elbows on it, clasping hands. When Paddy Leonard said *Go!* each was to try to bring down the other's hand on to the table. Farrington looked very serious and determined.

The trial began. After about thirty seconds Weathers brought his opponent's hand slowly down on to the table. Farrington's dark wine-coloured face flushed darker still with anger and humiliation at having been defeated by such a stripling.

— You're not to put the weight of your body behind it. Play fair, he said.   50

— Who's not playing fair? said the other.

— Come on again. The two best out of three.

The trial began again. The veins stood out on Farrington's forehead, and the pallor of Weathers' complexion changed to peony. Their hands and arms trembled under the stress. After a long struggle Weathers again brought his opponent's hand slowly on to the table. There was a murmur of applause from the spectators. The curate, who was standing beside the table, nodded his red head towards the victor and said with loutish familiarity:

— Ah! that's the knack!

— What the hell do you know about it? said Farrington fiercely, turning on   55
the man. What do you put in your gab for?

— Sh, sh! said O'Halloran, observing the violent expression of Farrington's face. Pony up, boys. We'll have just one little smahan more and then we'll be off.

A very sullen-faced man stood at the corner of O'Connell Bridge waiting for the little Sandymount tram to take him home. He was full of smouldering anger and revengefulness. He felt humiliated and discontented; he did not even feel drunk; and he had only twopence in his pocket. He cursed everything. He had done for himself in the office, pawned his watch, spent all his money; and he had not even got drunk. He began to feel thirsty again and he longed to be back again in the hot reeking public-house. He had lost his reputation as a strong man, having been defeated twice by a mere boy. His heart swelled with fury and, when he thought of the woman in the big hat who had brushed against him and said *Pardon!* his fury nearly choked him.

His tram let him down at Shelbourne Road and he steered his great body along in the shadow of the wall of the barracks. He loathed returning to his home. When he went in by the side-door he found the kitchen empty and the kitchen fire nearly out. He bawled upstairs:

— Ada! Ada!

His wife was a little sharp-faced woman who bullied her husband when he   60
was sober and was bullied by him when he was drunk. They had five children. A
little boy came running down the stairs.

—Who is that? said the man, peering through the darkness.

—Me, pa.

—Who are you? Charlie?

—No, pa. Tom.

—Where's your mother?   65

—She's out at the chapel.

—That's right. . . . Did she think of leaving any dinner for me?

—Yes, pa. I —

—Light the lamp. What do you mean by having the place in darkness? Are
the other children in bed?

The man sat down heavily on one of the chairs while the little boy lit the   70
lamp. He began to mimic his son's flat accent, saying half to himself: *At the
chapel. At the chapel, if you please!* When the lamp was lit he banged his fist on
the table and shouted:

—What's for my dinner?

—I'm going . . . to cook it, pa, said the little boy.

The man jumped up furiously and pointed to the fire.

—On that fire! You let the fire out! By God, I'll teach you to do that again!

He took a step to the door and seized the walking-stick which was standing   75
behind it.

—I'll teach you to let the fire out! he said, rolling up his sleeve in order to
give his arm free play.

The little boy cried O, *pa!* and ran whimpering round the table, but the man
followed him and caught him by the coat. The little boy looked about him wildly
but, seeing no way of escape fell upon his knees.

—Now, you'll let the fire out the next time! said the man, striking at him
viciously with the stick. Take that, you little whelp!

The boy uttered a squeal of pain as the stick cut his thigh. He clasped his
hands together in the air and his voice shook with fright.

—O, pa! he cried. Don't beat me, pa! And I'll . . . I'll say a *Hail Mary* for   80
you. . . . I'll say a *Hail Mary* for you, pa, if you don't beat me. . . . I'll say a *Hail
Mary.* . . .   [1914]

A thorough critical analysis of "Counterparts" using any one of these
approaches would take dozens of pages. The following are brief suggestions for
how such a reading might proceed.

NEW CRITICISM

A New Critic might want to demonstrate the multiple ways the title holds the
narrative together, giving it unity and coherence — for example, Farrington and
his son Tom are counterparts since Tom is the victim of his father's bullying just

as Farrington is bullied by Mr. Alleyne at work. You can also probably spot other counterparts: Farrington and his wife, for example, trade off bullying each other and their means of escaping from the drudgery of their lives, the bar and the church, are also parallel. And naturally when Weathers, the acrobat, defeats the much larger Farrington in arm wrestling, we are reminded of the verbal beating Farrington must endure from his equally diminutive boss, Mr. Alleyne. New Critics are fond of finding the ways all the elements of a text reinforce each other.

A New Critic might argue that these counterparts or oppositions introduce tensions into the story from the first few lines when the "bell rang furiously" for Farrington to report to Mr. Alleyne for a dressing down. The irony is that Farrington is big and Alleyne small, that Farrington is powerful and Alleyne is fragile as an egg. But it is Mr. Alleyne who breaks Farrington, it is Farrington who is weak. Throughout the story, tensions, oppositions, and ironies continue, for example, when Farrington is defeated by the smaller Weathers. In the last scene, the tension is finally resolved when the larger Farrington beats his small son, making him a counterpart to both Alleyne and Weathers in oppressing the weak. The final evidence that Farrington is ethically powerless is cruelly obvious as the son promises to pray for his abusing father.

FEMINIST CRITICISM

Feminist critics and their first cousins, gender critics, would naturally be struck by the violent masculinity of Farrington, his fantasies of riot and abuse, his savage feelings of revenge, and his "smouldering anger" (para. 57). Farrington is depicted not only as crude and brutish but also as a kind of perverse stereotype of male vanity, self-centeredness, and irresponsibility. His obsession with obtaining money for drinking completely disregards his role as the provider for a large family, and, of course, the beatings of his son are a cruel parody of his role as paternal protector. And if he had not wasted his money on drink, Farrington would also be a womanizer ("Farrington's eyes wandered at every moment in the direction of one of the young women," para. 47). Gender critics would be interested in the social and cultural mechanisms that could construct such primitive masculinity.

A reasonable argument might focus on the representation of women in the story. Miss Parker, Miss Delacour, Farrington's wife, and the performer Farrington sees in the bar are marginal characters. One student made the following claim: "The women in Farrington's world, and Irish society in general, have no agency: they are prevented from taking an active part in determining their lives and futures." Another student argues differently, saying, "While women in general are oppressed by the raw and brutal masculinity represented by Farrington, the women in this story do hold a degree of power over men." Based on their own analysis and interpretations, these students demonstrated that there was reasonable textual evidence to support their claims.

PSYCHOANALYTIC CRITICISM

A psychoanalytic critic would first notice the extreme pattern of behavior Farrington exhibits, as he repeatedly withdraws from his adult work responsibilities and as he fantasizes about being physically violent against his supervisors. Critics would argue that such behavior is typical of Farrington's repressed wounds and his unresolved conflicts with his own father. Farrington seems to be playing out painful childhood experiences. Given the violent displacement (taking it out on someone else) visited on Tom, we can imagine that Farrington is beating not only his boss, Mr. Alleyne, but also perhaps his own abusive father. The fantasies at work in Farrington also suggest the psychological defense of projection, since Farrington is blaming his problems on Mr. Alleyne and his job. Although his tasks do seem to be tedious, they certainly cannot account for his "spasm of rage" (para. 15) nor his desire "to clear out the whole office single-handed" (para. 32). When Farrington feels "humiliated and discontented" (para. 57), it is only in part because of his immediate context. It is the return of the repressed that plagues Farrington, a resurfacing of a buried pain. These ideas should also be tied to Farrington's death wish, especially his stunningly self-destructive behavior at work. Freudian critics would also argue that these specific actions are related to other core issues that would include intense loss of self-esteem, fear of intimacy, and betrayal.

MARXIST CRITICISM

A Marxist critic would be interested in focusing on the specific historical moment of "Counterparts" and not on Farrington's individual psyche, which can only distract us from the real force that affects human experience — the economic system in which Farrington is trapped. Economic power — not the Oedipal drama or gender — is the crucial human motivator. Farrington's material circumstances and not timeless values are the key to understanding his behavior. The real battle lines are drawn between Crosbie and Alleyne (the "haves") and Farrington (a "have-not") — that is, between the bourgeoisie and the proletariat, between those who control economic resources and those who perform the labor that fills the coffers of the rich. In a Marxist analysis, critics would argue that Farrington is a victim of class warfare. His desperation, his humiliation, his rage, his cruel violence are all traceable to classism — an ideology that determines people's worth according to their economic class. Although Farrington does appear shiftless and irresponsible, it is not because of his class; it is because of the meaninglessness of his work and the demeaning hierarchy that keeps him at the bottom. In his alienation, he reverts to a primitive physical masculinity, a false consciousness that only further diminishes his sense of his worth.

Marxists are often interested in what lies beneath the text in its political unconscious. Like a psychoanalytic critic, to get at the unconscious Marxists look for symptoms on the surface that suggest problems beneath. Typically, such symptomatic readings reveal class conflicts that authors are sometimes unaware of themselves. Marxists critics might argue whether Joyce himself understood that the root cause of Farrington's aberrant behavior was economic and not psychological. This makes sense since for Marxists both reader and writer are under the sway of the same ideological system that they see as natural.

One student made the following claim: "Farrington's role as proletarian results in his feelings of inferiority, resentment over lack of entitlement, and an expectation of disappointment." This same student, like many Marxist critics who see the function of literature through a pragmatic lens, concluded her essay with an appeal toward change, arguing that "The remedy does not lie in changing Farrington's consciousness, but rather in changing the economic and political discourse of power that has constituted him."

DECONSTRUCTION

One of many possible deconstructions of "Counterparts" would involve focusing on a troubling or puzzling point called an *aporia*. Some deconstructive critics have looked at the incomplete phrase that Farrington copies, *"In no case shall the said Bernard Bodley be . . ."* as an aporia, an ambiguous and not completely understandable textual puzzle but one that might be a way into the story's meaning. The oppositions that are being deconstructed or laid bare here are *presence* and *absence, word* and *reality.* Working off the implications of the title "Counterparts," Bernard Bodley can be seen as a double or counterpart for Farrington, a character like Bodley whose existence is in doubt. Although Farrington's size suggests that he is very much physically present, his behavior might suggest otherwise. He spends his time copying other people's words and has a compelling need to repeat the narrative of his encounter with Mr. Allyne, as if he must demonstrate his own existence through repetition. He does not have a viable inner life, an authentic identity. Farrington's essence is not present but absent. His identity is insubstantial. He tries to fill the emptiness at the center of his being with camaraderie and potency, but his efforts produce the opposite— escape, loneliness, and weakness. In other words, the said Farrington does not really exist and cannot be. In this way, we can deconstruct "Counterparts" as a story where presence is absence, where strength is weakness, where Farrington's actions lead only to paralysis and repetition, where Farrington's frustration with his impotence makes his oppressors more powerful.

One student working with similar interpretations of "Counterparts" noted other oppositions, especially between male and female, escape and confinement. She argues that Farrington spends most of his time trying to avoid being thought of as stereotypically feminine. However, the more exaggerated his masculine aggression, drinking, violence, and irresponsibility become, the weaker, the more stereotypically feminine he becomes. Similarly, the more Farrington tries to escape, the more ensnared he is. In this way, the student argues, our conventional understandings of these opposing terms are deconstructed, so that we are no longer confident about the meaning of escape, masculinity, or strength.

READER-RESPONSE CRITICISM

Willa Ervinman, a student, was asked to respond to the story by using Stanley Fish's ideas and noting the conflicts between the interpretive or discourse communities Willa belonged to and those depicted in the story. The following are excerpts from her response journal:

> I was upset by Farrington's lack of responsibility at
> work. He is completely unreliable and demonstrates very
> little self-esteem. He must know that the people he works
> with consider him a slacker and a fake. I was raised in a
> middle-class home where both my parents worked hard in a
> bank from 9 to 5. Just the idea that they would sneak out
> of work to drink in dark bars is absurd. My belief in the
> discourse of middle-class responsibility or perhaps the
> Protestant work ethic makes it almost impossible for me
> to see Farrington with sympathy even though I can see
> that his work is probably completely mechanical and
> unfulfilling. . . .
>
> Farrington's domestic violence against his son is
> such a violation of the discourse of domesticity that it
> is hard to understand any other response. Someone in my
> response group thought that Farrington was a victim of
> his working-class discourse of masculinity. I can see
> how he was humiliated by the smaller men, Mr. Alleyne
> and Weathers, but beating his innocent son as a kind
> of revenge cannot be forgiven. My grandmother tells me
> that it was common for children to be physically pun-
> ished in her day, but in the interpretive community I
> was raised in, there is no excuse for domestic violence.
> It is more than a character flaw; it is criminal behav-
> ior, and I judge Farrington to be a social menace, beyond
> compassion.

Willa went on to argue that Farrington's violent behavior is inexcusable, interpreting our current understandings of domestic violence and responsible masculinity as evidence. She blended this personal view with textual support. Her warrant for her claim is that historical circumstances and norms should not be used to excuse reprehensible behavior.

POSTCOLONIAL CRITICISM

"Counterparts" was written in the early twentieth century at a time when the Ireland Joyce writes about was still a colony of the British empire. Farrington is, then, a colonial subject and subject to political domination. At the story's open-ing, Farrington, a Catholic from the south of Ireland, is summoned by a "furious voice" from Northern Ireland, a stronghold of British sympathy and Protestant domination. The tension is announced early because it is crucial to Farrington's behavior and his internalized and colonized mindset. Many colonials have a negative self-image because they are alienated from their own indigenous culture. Indeed, Farrington seems completely ill suited to the office copying task he is relegated to. He seems more suited to some physical endeavor, but given the difficult economics of Dublin, he probably has few career options.

Farrington is the Other in the discourse of colonialism, and he is made to seem inferior at every turn, from the verbal lashing of Mr. Alleyne to the physical defeat by Weathers, who is probably British. Symbolically, Farrington tries to resist his subjugation by the British establishment but fails. He is what postcolonial theorists refer to as *unhomed* or *displaced*. He is uncomfortable at work, in the bars where he seeks solace, and finally in his ultimate refuge, a place unprepared even to feed him. Indeed, in an act likely to perpetuate abuse upon future generations, Farrington turns on his own family, becoming, through his enraged attack on his child Tom, a metaphor for the conflicted, tormented, and defeated Ireland. When a colonial is not "at home" even in his own home, he is truly in psychological agony and exile. Joyce represents the trauma of British domination through one subject's self-destructive and self-hating journey, a journey made even more cruelly ironic by Farrington's attack — in a mimicry of British aggression and injustice — on his own subjected son.

HISTORICISM

A critic influenced by Foucault might argue that Farrington is a victim of an inflexible discourse of masculinity, that he has been socialized by working-class norms of how a man should behave to such an extent that he cannot change. Growing up in a working-class culture, Farrington would have received high marks among his peers for his size and strength, just as Mr. Alleyne would be diminished in status for his. And in another context, say, on a construction site, Farrington's sense of masculinity might be a plus. But in an office, his aggressive masculinity is a liability. In all cultures, people are subject to multiple discourses that pull us one way then another. Farrington's sarcasm, his drinking, his longing for camaraderie, and his resorting to violence to solve problems are the results of being too enmeshed in a discourse of masculinity from working-class Dublin and not enough in the middle-class business assumptions about discipline, responsibility, and concentration. Farrington is defeated at work, in the pubs, and at home because he is unable to move from one discourse to another. He is stuck in a subject position that only reinforces his powerlessness. His self-esteem is so damaged by the end of the story that he even violates his own code of masculinity by beating a defenseless child.

Sample Student Essay

The following essay was written by a first year student using postcolonial perspective.

Molly Frye

Prof. Christine Hardee

English 102

A Refugee at Home

It is difficult to argue that Farrington, the main
character in James Joyce's "Counterparts," should be seen
in a sympathetic light. After all, he seems an extreme
stereotype of an aggressive, irresponsible drinker.
Although his character traits certainly do not conform
to our modern standards of mature masculinity, I want to
argue that although we do not want to condone Farrington's brutal behavior, we can find it understandable. As
an Irish subject in the British empire, Farrington is
more sinned against than sinner, more victim than victim-
izer. Farrington is not simply an obnoxious male since
his actions can be understood as stemming from his colonial consciousness in struggling vainly against his
powerlessness. His frustrations are especially clear in
the three spaces Farrington inhabits: his office, the
bars, and his home.

Farrington's first appearance is telling. Because of
his poor job performance, his boss demands to see him:
"Send Farrington here!" Farrington, who most often is
referred to as "the man," mutters his first words, "Blast
him!" This typical antagonistic relationship in a colonial context foreshadows the rest of the story. Farrington is the working-class subject caught in a menial and
unsatisfying job he can never complete under a boss who
has social and cultural power. This counterpart relationship is similar to the positions of Ireland and England
where the colony is disparaged and oppressed by the
empire. In his office run by Protestants loyal to the
British, Farrington is ironically "tall and of great
bulk," while his boss, Mr. Alleyne, is "a little man"
whose head, "pink and hairless," resembles a "large egg."
Farrington's only asset, his size and strength, is irrelevant because he is so economically and socially weak.

This disparity only increases Farrington's frustration and precipitates fantasies of violence against his oppressor. When Mr. Alleyne rebukes him, "Do you mind me now," Farrington is sent into a "spasm of rage." He cannot, of course, act on his aggressive urges, so he represses these feelings by rationalizing that he must have a "good night's drinking." Thus begins a pattern of self-destructive behavior that only increases Farrington's marginal position in society.

Farrington is so uncomfortable at work, a postcolonial condition known as being unhomed, that he cannot concentrate on anything but drinking. He seems quite unsuited for the tedious task of copying legal documents, staring "stupidly at the last words he has written," knowing he will never finish his task, never advance, never get anywhere. Farrington is paralyzed by his alienation. He feels his only recourse is sneaking out to drink, which only exacerbates his poverty and powerlessness. When he attempts to cover up his inability to concentrate and finish copying letters for Mr. Alleyne, he is caught and confronted. Instead of acknowledging his underling position, he attempts a witticism which, of course, backfires. Even though he is forced to apologize, his job now seems in jeopardy. Mr. Alleyne humiliates him by calling him an "impertinent ruffian," a status that seems to him the most he can hope for. As a colonial subject, Farrington is plagued by a double consciousness. He longs for the masculine status his physical strength should give him in his working-class culture, but he must suffer indignities at the hands of Mr. Alleyne because of his inability to perform a simple task a competent child could do. Farrington should probably be working in construction as a laborer, not an office worker where discipline, patience, and mental concentration are necessary.

When Farrington finally leaves work, he expects to find some solace in the Dublin pubs. He has hocked his

watch for drinking money, a clear indication of how desperate he is to escape the confines of regimented office
work. The camaraderie of Paddy Leonard and Nosey Flynn is
temporary, and Farrington is not at home in these public
spaces either. He runs out of money he would have spent
drinking and womanizing, and he is finally humiliated by
another small British man. Called upon to "uphold the
national honour," Farrington's loss in an arm wrestling
contest with Weathers leaves him "full of smoldering
anger and revengefulness. He is humiliated and discontented . . . His heart swelled with fury. . . ." His longing
for escape from the confinement and disappointment of
work has taken a disastrous turn. Farrington's already
damaged self-esteem is degraded and his repressed anger
at his oppressor is near the breaking point. Perhaps his
self-destructive behavior can be redirected at his home,
his last possibility for comfort and acceptance.

  For the unhomed colonized, however, this is not to
be. Farrington enters the kitchen to find it symbolically
empty, "the fire nearly out." His wife is at chapel, his
five children in bed, and his dinner is cold. His agonies
continue. Having internalized the humiliations suffered
at work and in the pubs, Farrington has no resources
left. And so in a bitter irony, he beats his son for not
attending to the fire, "striking at him viciously with a
stick. Take that, you little whelp!" Farrington the
oppressed becomes Farrington the oppressor. His role as
provider and protector is cruelly turned upside-down.
Farrington compensates for his defeats at the hands of
Mr. Alleyne and Weathers by beating his son, and in doing
so, mimics the cycle of oppression prevalent in countries
dominated by the empire. Farrington is not only a cog in
the bureaucratic wheel at work; he is also a pathetic,
but understandable cog crushed by the wheel of power even
in his own home.

FOR THINKING AND WRITING

1. Using a feminist critique of Joyce, one student claimed that "Joyce's text indulges dominance over submission." Do you think there is textual evidence to support this assertion?

2. How might various critics (postcolonial, feminist, Marxist, psychoanalytical) interpret these lines from "Counterparts":
   - "The man passed through the crowd, looking on the spectacle generally with proud satisfaction and staring masterfully at the office girls."
   - "His heart swelled with fury and, when he thought of the woman in the big hat who had brushed against him and said Pardon! his fury nearly choked him."
   - "What's for my dinner?"

3. Influenced by New Critical ideas, one student wrote, " 'Counterparts' is filled with parallel scenes and emotions that reflect one another." What textual evidence would help support this notion?

4. As evidence for a Marxist critique, one student wrote "His unfair work conditions so distract him that he does not even know the names of his children." What do you think this student's claim is? What is the warrant behind such an assertion?

5. Using a new historicist approach, what might you learn about this story from doing research on the elementary school curriculum in Dublin, the pay scale in a law office, the legal rights of women, the laws on domestic violence, the unemployment rate? What other practices and texts do you think would illuminate the story?

A WRITING EXERCISE

Now you try. After reading the following story, construct an argument influenced by one or more of the following critical approaches: postcolonial, Marxist, reader-response, or feminist.

ANN PETRY
Like a Winding Sheet

Ann Lane Petry (1908–1997) consciously wrote in a long tradition of African American storytellers; for this she has been recognized by writers like Toni Morrison, Alice Walker, and Gloria Naylor. Unlike most of her literary ancestors, however, she grew up with the advantages of the middle class, including access to education. Born in Old Saybrook, Connecticut, she earned a degree from the University of Connecticut in 1934 and worked in the family drugstore until her marriage in 1938. Petry then became a journalist for Harlem newspapers and began to see her short stories published in magazines. In 1945, she won a fellowship for work on her first novel, The Street, *which was published the next year. In 1946, the short story* "Like a Winding Sheet" *was included in the annual anthology* The Best American Short Stories, *which was also dedicated to Ann Petry. Her* Miss Muriel and Other Stories *(1971) was the first collection of short stories by a black woman published in the United States. Her last novel was* The Narrows *(1988). In addition to her novels and stories, she wrote children's literature.*

He had planned to get up before Mae did and surprise her by fixing breakfast. Instead he went back to sleep and she got out of bed so quietly he didn't know she wasn't there beside him until he woke up and heard the queer soft gurgle of water running out of the sink in the bathroom.

He knew he ought to get up but instead he put his arms across his forehead to shut the afternoon sunlight out of his eyes, pulled his legs up close to his body, testing them to see if the ache was still in them.

Mae had finished in the bathroom. He could tell because she never closed the door when she was in there and now the sweet smell of talcum powder was drifting down the hall and into the bedroom. Then he heard her coming down the hall.

"Hi, babe," she said affectionately.

"Hum," he grunted, and moved his arms away from his head, opened one eye.   5

"It's a nice morning."

"Yeah." He rolled over and the sheet twisted around him, outlining his thighs, his chest. "You mean afternoon, don't ya?"

Mae looked at the twisted sheet and giggled. "Looks like a winding sheet," she said. "A shroud—" Laughter tangled with her words and she had to pause for a moment before she could continue. "You look like a huckleberry—in a winding sheet—"

"That's no way to talk. Early in the day like this," he protested.

He looked at his arms silhouetted against the white of the sheets. They were   10 inky black by contrast and he had to smile in spite of himself and he lay there smiling and savoring the sweet sound of Mae's giggling.

"Early?" She pointed a finger at the alarm clock on the table near the bed and giggled again. "It's almost four o'clock. And if you don't spring up out of there, you're going to be late again."

"What do you mean 'again'?"

"Twice last week. Three times the week before. And once the week before and—"

"I can't get used to sleeping in the daytime," he said fretfully. He pushed his legs out from under the covers experimentally. Some of the ache had gone out of them but they weren't really rested yet. "It's too light for good sleeping. And all that standing beats the hell out of my legs."

"After two years you oughta be used to it," Mae said.   15

He watched her as she fixed her hair, powdered her face, slipped into a pair of blue denim overalls. She moved quickly and yet she didn't seem to hurry.

"You look like you'd had plenty of sleep," he said lazily. He had to get up but he kept putting the moment off, not wanting to move, yet he didn't dare let his legs go completely limp because if he did he'd go back to sleep. It was getting later and later but the thought of putting his weight on his legs kept him lying there.

When he finally got up he had to hurry, and he gulped his breakfast so fast that he wondered if his stomach could possibly use food thrown at it at such a rate of speed. He was still wondering about it as he and Mae were putting their coats on in the hall.

Mae paused to look at the calendar. "It's the thirteenth," she said. Then a faint excitement in her voice, "Why, it's Friday the thirteenth." She had one arm in her coat sleeve and she held it there while she stared at the calendar. "I oughta stay home," she said. "I shouldn't go outa the house."

"Aw, don't be a fool," he said. "Today's payday. And payday is a good luck day   20 everywhere, any way you look at it." And as she stood hesitating he said, "Aw, come on."

And he was late for work again because they spent fifteen minutes arguing before he could convince her she ought to go to work just the same. He had to talk persuasively, urging her gently, and it took time. But he couldn't bring himself to talk to her roughly or threaten to strike her like a lot of men might have done. He wasn't made that way.

So when he reached the plant he was late and he had to wait to punch the time clock because the day-shift workers were streaming out in long lines, in groups and bunches that impeded his progress.

Even now just starting his workday his legs ached. He had to force himself to struggle past the outgoing workers, punch the time clock, and get the little cart he pushed around all night, because he kept toying with the idea of going home and getting back in bed.

He pushed the cart out on the concrete floor, thinking that if this was his plant he'd make a lot of changes in it. There were too many standing-up jobs for one thing. He'd figure out some way most of 'em could be done sitting down and he'd put a lot more benches around. And this job he had—this job that forced him to walk ten hours a night, pushing this little cart, well, he'd turn it into a sitting-down job. One of those little trucks they used around railroad stations would be good for a job like this. Guys sat on a seat and the thing moved easily, taking up little room and turning in hardly any space at all, like on a dime.

He pushed the cart near the foreman. He never could remember to refer to   25 her as the forelady even in his mind. It was funny to have a white woman for a boss in a plant like this one.

She was sore about something. He could tell by the way her face was red and her eyes were half-shut until they were slits. Probably been out late and didn't get enough sleep. He avoided looking at her and hurried a little, head down, as he passed her though he couldn't resist stealing a glance at her out of the corner of his eye. He saw the edge of the light-colored slacks she wore and the tip end of a big tan shoe.

"Hey, Johnson!" the woman said.

The machines had started full blast. The whirr and the grinding made the building shake, made it impossible to hear conversations. The men and women at the machines talked to each other but looking at them from just a little distance away, they appeared to be simply moving their lips because you couldn't hear what they were saying. Yet the woman's voice cut across the machine sounds — harsh, angry.

He turned his head slowly. "Good evenin', Mrs. Scott," he said, and waited. "You're late again."   30

"That's right. My legs were bothering me."

The woman's face grew redder, angrier looking. "Half this shift comes in late," she said. "And you're the worst one of all. You're always late. Whatsa matter with ya?"

"It's my legs," he said. "Somehow they don't ever get rested. I don't seem to get used to sleeping days. And I just can't get started."

"Excuses. You guys always got excuses," her anger grew and spread. "Every guy comes in here late always has an excuse. His wife's sick or his grandmother died or somebody in the family had to go to the hospital," she paused, drew a deep breath. "And the niggers is the worse. I don't care what's wrong with your legs. You get in here on time. I'm sick of you niggers—"

"You got the right to get mad," he interrupted softly. "You got the right to cuss   35
me four ways to Sunday but I ain't letting nobody call me a nigger."

He stepped closer to her. His fists were doubled. His lips were drawn back in a thin narrow line. A vein in his forehead stood out swollen, thick.

And the woman backed away from him, not hurriedly but slowly—two, three steps back.

"Aw, forget it," she said. "I didn't mean nothing by it. It slipped out. It was an accident." The red of her face deepened until the small blood vessels in her cheeks were purple. "Go on and get to work," she urged. And she took three more slow backward steps.

He stood motionless for a moment and then turned away from the sight of the red lipstick on her mouth that made him remember that the foreman was a woman. And he couldn't bring himself to hit a woman. He felt a curious tingling in his fingers and he looked down at his hands. They were clenched tight, hard, ready to smash some of those small purple veins in her face.

He pushed the cart ahead of him, walking slowly. When he turned his head,   40
she was staring in his direction, mopping her forehead with a dark blue handkerchief. Their eyes met and then they both looked away.

He didn't glance in her direction again but moved past the long work benches, carefully collecting the finished parts, going slowly and steadily up and down, and back and forth the length of the building, and as he walked he forced himself to swallow his anger, get rid of it.

And he succeeded so that he was able to think about what had happened without getting upset about it. An hour went by but the tension stayed in his hands. They were clenched and knotted on the handles of the cart as though ready to aim a blow.

And he thought he should have hit her anyway, smacked her hard in the face, felt the soft flesh of her face give under the hardness of his hands. He tried to make his hands relax by offering them a description of what it would have been like to strike her because he had the queer feeling that his hands were not exactly a part of him anymore — they had developed a separate life of their own over which he had no control. So he dwelt on the pleasure his hands would have felt—both of them cracking at her, first one and then the other. If he had done that his hands would have felt good now—relaxed, rested.

And he decided that even if he'd lost his job for it, he should have let her have it and it would have been a long time, maybe the rest of her life, before she called anybody else a nigger.

The only trouble was he couldn't hit a woman. A woman couldn't hit   45
back the same way a man did. But it would have been a deeply satisfying thing to have cracked her narrow lips wide open with just one blow, beautifully timed and with all his weight in back of it. That way he would have gotten rid of all the energy and tension his anger had created in him. He kept remembering how his heart had started pumping blood so fast he had felt it tingle even in the tips of his fingers.

With the approach of night, fatigue nibbled at him. The corners of his mouth drooped, the frown between his eyes deepened, his shoulders sagged; but his hands stayed tight and tense. As the hours dragged by he noticed that the women workers had started to snap and snarl at each other. He couldn't hear what they said because of the sound of machines but he could see the quick lip movements that sent words tumbling from the sides of their mouths. They gestured irritably with their hands and scowled as their mouths moved.

Their violent jerky motions told him that it was getting close on to quitting time but somehow he felt that the night still stretched ahead of him, composed of endless hours of steady walking on his aching legs. When the whistle finally blew he went on pushing the cart, unable to believe that it had sounded. The whirring of the machines died away to a murmur and he knew then that he'd really heard the whistle. He stood still for a moment, filled with a relief that made him sigh.

Then he moved briskly, putting the cart in the storeroom, hurrying to take his place in the line forming before the paymaster. That was another thing he'd change, he thought. He'd have the pay envelopes handed to the people right at their benches so there wouldn't be ten or fifteen minutes lost waiting for the pay. He always got home about fifteen minutes late on payday. They did it better in the plant where Mae worked, brought the money right to them at their benches.

He stuck his pay envelope in his pants' pocket and followed the line of workers heading for the subway in a slow-moving stream. He glanced up at the sky. It was a nice night, the sky looked packed full to running over with stars. And he thought if he and Mae would go right to bed when they got home from work they'd catch a few hours of darkness for sleeping. But they never did. They fooled around—cooking and eating and listening to the radio and he always stayed in a big chair in the living room and went almost but not quite to sleep and when they finally got to bed it was five or six in the morning and daylight was already seeping around the edges of the sky.

He walked slowly, putting off the moment when he would have to plunge   50
into the crowd hurrying toward the subway. It was a long ride to Harlem and tonight the thought of it appalled him. He paused outside an all-night restaurant to kill time, so that some of the first rush of workers would be gone when he reached the subway.

The lights in the restaurant were brilliant, enticing. There was life and motion inside. And as he looked through the window he thought that everything within range of his eyes gleamed—the long imitation marble counter, the tall stools, the white porcelain-topped tables and especially the big metal coffee urn right near the window. Steam issued from its top and a gas flame flickered under it—a lively, dancing, blue flame.

A lot of the workers from his shift—men and women—were lining up near the coffee urn. He watched them walk to the porcelain-topped tables carrying steaming cups of coffee and he saw that just the smell of the coffee lessened the fatigue lines in their faces. After the first sip their faces softened, they smiled, they began to talk and laugh.

On a sudden impulse he shoved the door open and joined the line in front of the coffee urn. The line moved slowly. And as he stood there the smell of the coffee, the sound of the laughter and of the voices, helped dull the sharp ache in his legs.

He didn't pay any attention to the white girl who was serving the coffee at the urn. He kept looking at the cups in the hands of the men who had been ahead of him. Each time a man stepped out of the line with one of the thick white cups the fragrant steam got in his nostrils. He saw that they walked carefully so as not to spill a single drop. There was a froth of bubbles at the top of each cup and he thought about how he would let the bubbles break against his lips before he actually took a big deep swallow.

Then it was his turn. "A cup of coffee," he said, just as he had heard the others say. 55

The white girl looked past him, put her hands up to her head and gently lifted her hair away from the back of her neck, tossing her head back a little. "No more coffee for a while," she said.

He wasn't certain he'd heard her correctly and he said "What?" blankly.

"No more coffee for a while," she repeated.

There was silence behind him and then uneasy movement. He thought someone would say something, ask why or protest, but there was only silence and then a faint shuffling sound as though the men standing behind him had simultaneously shifted their weight from one foot to the other.

He looked at the girl without saying anything. He felt his hands begin to 60 tingle and the tingling went all the way down to his finger tips so that he glanced down at them. They were clenched tight, hard, into fists. Then he looked at the girl again. What he wanted to do was hit her so hard that the scarlet lipstick on her mouth would smear and spread over her nose, her chin, out toward her cheeks, so hard that she would never toss her head again and refuse a man a cup of coffee because he was black.

He estimated the distance across the counter and reached forward, balancing his weight on the balls of his feet, ready to let the blow go. And then his hands fell back down to his sides because he forced himself to lower them, to unclench them and make them dangle loose. The effort took his breath away because his hands fought against him. But he couldn't hit her. He couldn't even now bring himself to hit a woman, not even this one, who had refused him a cup of coffee with a toss of her head. He kept seeing the gesture with which she had lifted the length of her blond hair from the back of her neck as expressive of her contempt for him.

When he went out the door he didn't look back. If he had he would have seen the flickering blue flame under the shiny coffee urn being extinguished. The line of men who had stood behind him lingered a moment to watch the people drinking coffee at the tables and then they left just as he had without having had the coffee they wanted so badly. The girl behind the counter poured water in the urn and swabbed it out and as she waited for the water to run out, she lifted her hair gently from the back of her neck and tossed her head before she began making a fresh lot of coffee.

But he had walked away without a backward look, his head down, his hands in his pockets, raging at himself and whatever it was inside of him that had forced him to stand quiet and still when he wanted to strike out.

The subway was crowded and he had to stand. He tried grasping an overhead strap and his hands were too tense to grip it. So he moved near the train door and stood there swaying back and forth with the rocking of the train. The roar of the train beat inside his head, making it ache and throb, and the pain in his legs clawed up into his groin so that he seemed to be bursting with pain and he told himself that it was due to all that anger-born energy that had piled up in him and not been used and so it had spread through him like a poison — from his feet and legs all the way up to his head.

Mae was in the house before he was. He knew she was home before he put   65
the key in the door of the apartment. The radio was going. She had it tuned up loud and she was singing along with it.

"Hello, babe," she called out, as soon as he opened the door.

He tried to say "hello" and it came out half grunt and half sigh.

"You sure sound cheerful," she said.

She was in the bedroom and he went and leaned against the doorjamb. The denim overalls she wore to work were carefully draped over the back of a chair by the bed. She was standing in front of the dresser, tying the sash of a yellow housecoat around her waist and chewing gum vigorously as she admired her reflection in the mirror over the dresser.

"Whatsa matter?" she said. "You get bawled out by the boss or somep'n?"   70

"Just tired," he said slowly. "For God's sake, do you have to crack that gum like that?"

"You don't have to lissen to me," she said complacently. She patted a curl in place near the side of her head and then lifted her hair away from the back of her neck, ducking her head forward and then back.

He winced away from the gesture. "What you got to be always fooling with your hair for?" he protested.

"Say, what's the matter with you anyway?" She turned away from the mirror to face him, put her hands on her hips. "You ain't been in the house two minutes and you're picking on me."

He didn't answer her because her eyes were angry and he didn't want to   75
quarrel with her. They'd been married too long and got along too well and so he

walked all the way into the room and sat down in the chair by the bed and stretched his legs out in front of him, putting his weight on the heels of his shoes, leaning way back in the chair, not saying anything.

"Lissen," she said sharply. "I've got to wear those overalls again tomorrow. You're going to get them all wrinkled up leaning against them like that."

He didn't move. He was too tired and his legs were throbbing now that he had sat down. Besides the overalls were already wrinkled and dirty, he thought. They couldn't help but be for she'd worn them all week. He leaned farther back in the chair.

"Come on, get up," she ordered.

"Oh, what the hell," he said wearily, and got up from the chair. "I'd just as soon live in a subway. There'd be just as much place to sit down."

He saw that her sense of humor was struggling with her anger. But her sense of humor won because she giggled.

"Aw, come on and eat," she said. There was a coaxing note in her voice. "You're nothing but an old hungry nigger trying to act tough and—" she paused to giggle and then continued, "You—"

He had always found her giggling pleasant and deliberately said things that might amuse her and then waited, listening for the delicate sound to emerge from her throat. This time he didn't even hear the giggle. He didn't let her finish what she was saying. She was standing close to him and that funny tingling started in his finger tips, went fast up his arms and sent his fist shooting straight for her face.

There was the smacking sound of soft flesh being struck by a hard object and it wasn't until she screamed that he realized he had hit her in the mouth—so hard that the dark red lipstick had blurred and spread over her full lips, reaching up toward the tip of her nose, down toward her chin, out toward her cheeks.

The knowledge that he had struck her seeped through him slowly and he was appalled but he couldn't drag his hands away from her face. He kept striking her and he thought with horror that something inside him was holding him, binding him to this act, wrapping and twisting about him so that he had to continue it. He had lost all control over his hands. And he groped for a phrase, a word, something to describe what this thing was like that was happening to him and he thought it was like being enmeshed in a winding sheet—that was it—like a winding sheet. And even as the thought formed in his mind, his hands reached for her face again and yet again.   [1946]

80

FOR THINKING AND WRITING

1. There is a French expression that says to understand all is to forgive all. Given the ending of "Like a Winding Sheet," argue for or against this idea.

2. Compare "Counterparts" and "Like a Winding Sheet" (see "Writing a Comparative Paper," pp. 70–77), arguing whether the authors have or have not prepared us for the endings.

Stephen Dunn. "Hard Work." From *New and Selected Poems: 1974–1994* by Stephen Dunn. Copyright © 1994 by Stephen Dunn. Reprinted by permission of the author and W.W. Norton & Company, Inc.

Cornelius Eady. "Who Am I?" From *Cornelius Eady: The Gathering of My Name* by Cornelius Eady. Copyright © 1991 by Cornelius Eady. By permission of Carnegie Mellon University Press.

Alan Ehrenhalt. Excerpt from *The Lost City* by Alan Ehrenhalt. Copyright © 1995 by Alan Ehrenhalt. Reprinted by permission of Basic Books, a member of Perseus Books, LLC.

T. S. Eliot. "The Love Song of J. Alfred Prufrock." From *Collected Poems 1909–1962* by T. S. Eliot. Reprinted by permission of Faber & Faber, Ltd.

Louise Erdrich. "Fleur." From *Tracks* by Louise Erdrich. Copyright © 1988 by Louise Erdrich. Reprinted by permission of Henry Holt and Company, LLC.

William Faulkner. "A Rose for Emily." From *Collected Stories of William Faulkner* by William Faulkner. Copyright © 1930 and renewed 1939 by William Faulkner. Reprinted by permission of Random House, Inc.

Carolyn Forché. "The Colonel." From *The Country Between Us* by Carolyn Forché. Copyright © 1981 by Carolyn Forché. Originally appeared in *Women's International Resource Exchange*. Reprinted by permission of HarperCollins Publishers, Inc.

Karen Gershon. "Race." From *Selected Poems* by Karen Gershon. Reprinted by permission of Val Tripp, Executor of the Estate of Karen Gershon.

Nikki Giovanni. "Legacies." From *My House* by Nikki Giovanni. Copyright © 1972 by Nikki Giovanni. Reprinted by permission of HarperCollins Publishers, Inc.

Louise Glück. "The School Children." From *The First Four Book of Poems* by Louise Glück. Copyright © 1968, 1971, 1972, 1973, 1974, 1975, 1976, 1977, 1978, 1979, 1980, 1985, 1995 by Louise Glück. Reprinted by permission of HarperCollins Publishers, Inc.

Lorraine Hansberry. A *Raisin in the Sun* by Lorraine Hansberry. Copyright © 1958 by Robert Nemiroff, as an unpublished work. Copyright © 1959, 1966, 1984 by Robert Nemiroff. Reprinted by permission of Random House, Inc. "Letter to the *New York Times* editor, April 23, 1964." From *To Be Young, Gifted and Black: Lorraine Hansberry in Her Own Words*, adapted by Robert Nemiroff. © 1969 by Robert Nemiroff and Robert Nemiroff as Executor of the Estate of Lorraine Hansberry.

Robert Hayden. "Those Winter Sundays." From *Angel of Ascent: New and Selected Poems* by Robert Hayden. Copyright © 1966 by Robert Hayden. Reprinted by permission of Liveright Publishing Corporation.

Seamus Heaney. "Punishment." From *Opened Ground: Selected Poems 1966–1996* by Seamus Heaney. Copyright © 1966 by Seamus Heaney. Reprinted by permission of Farrar, Straus and Giroux, LLC. From *New Selected Poems 1966–1987* by Seamus Heaney. Reprinted by permission of Faber & Faber Limited.

Essex Hemphill. "Commitments." From *Ceremonies* by Essex Hemphill. Copyright © 1992 by Essex Hemphill. Used by permission of Dutton, a division of Penguin Putnam, Inc.

Linda Hogan. "Heritage." From *Calling Myself Home* by Linda Hogan. Copyright © 1991 by Linda Hogan. First appeared in *Red Clay* by Linda Hogan. Reprinted by permission of The Greenfield Review Press.

bell hooks. "Inspired Eccentricity: Sarah and Gus Oldman." Reprinted by permission of the author.

A. E. Housman. "Loveliest of trees, the cherry now." From *Collected Poems of A. E. Housman*. © 1939, 1949, 1965 by Holt, Rinehart & Winston. © 1967, 1968 by Robert E. Symons. Reprinted by permission of The Society of Authors, as literary representatives of the Estate of A. E. Housman.

Pam Houston. "How to Talk to a Hunter." From *Cowboys Are My Weakness* by Pam Houston. Copyright © 1992 by Pam Houston. Reprinted by permission of W.W. Norton & Company, Inc.

Langston Hughes. "Theme for English B." From *Collected Poems* by Langston Hughes. Copyright © 1994 by the Estate of Langston Hughes. Reprinted by permission of Alfred A. Knopf, a division of Random House, Inc.

Lynda Hull. "Night Waitress." From *Ghost Money* by Lynda Hull. Copyright © 1986 by Lynda Hull. Reprinted by permission of the University of Massachusetts Press.

June Jordan. "Many Rivers to Cross." From *On Call: Political Essays* by June Jordan. Copyright © 1985 by June Jordan. Reprinted with the permission of the author.

Linda Pastan. "Ethics." From *Waiting for My Life, Poems by Linda Pastan.* Copyright © 1981 by Linda Pastan. Reprinted by permission of W.W. Norton & Company, Inc.

Ann Petry. "Like a Winding Sheet." From *Miss Muriel and Other Stories* by Ann Petry. Originally appeared in *The Crisis,* November 1945. Copyright © 1945 by Ann Petry. Renewed 1973 by Ann Petry. Reprinted by the permission of Russell & Volkening as agents for the author.

Marge Piercy. "To Be of Use." From *Circles on the Water* by Marge Piercy. Copyright © 1982 by Marge Piercy. Used by permission of Alfred A. Knopf, a division of Random House, Inc.

Sylvia Plath. "Daddy." From *Ariel* by Sylvia Plath. Copyright © 1963 by Ted Hughes. Reprinted by permission of HarperCollins Publishers, Inc. From *The Collected Poems* by Sylvia Plath, edited by Ted Hughes. Reprinted by permission of Faber & Faber, Ltd.

Sidney Poitier. Excerpt from *The Measure of a Man: A Spiritual Autobiography* by Sidney Poitier. Copyright © 2000 by Sidney Poitier. Reprinted by permission of HarperCollins Publishers, Inc.

Minnie Bruce Pratt. "Two Small-Sized Girls." From *Crime Against Nature* by Minnie Bruce Pratt. Copyright © 1990 by Minnie Bruce Pratt. Reprinted by permission of Firebrand Books.

Henry Reed. "Naming of Parts." From *Henry Reed: Collected Poems,* edited by Jon Stallworthy. Copyright © 1991 by the Executor of Henry Reed's Estate. Reprinted by permission.

Alberto Ríos. "Mi Abuela." First printed in *Whispering to Fool the Wind* by Alberto Ríos. © 1982 by Alberto Ríos. Published by Sheep Meadow Press, 1982. Reprinted by permission of the author.

Tomás Rivera. "Richard Rodriguez's *Hunger of Memory* as Humanistic Antithesis." Published in *Melus,* vol. II, 1984. Copyright © 1984 MELUS, The Society for the Study of Multi-Ethnic Literature of the United States. Reprinted by permission.

Richard Rodriguez. "Aria: Memoir of a Bilingual Childhood." Copyright © 1980 by Richard Rodriguez. Originally appeared in *The American Scholar.* Reprinted by permission of Georges Borchardt, Inc., Literary Agency, for the author.

Theodore Roethke. "My Papa's Waltz." Copyright © 1942 by Hearst Magazines, Inc. From *The Collected Poems of Theodore Roethke* by Theodore Roethke. Used by permission of Doubleday, a division of Random House, Inc.

Nelly Sachs. "A Dead Child Speaks." From *O the Chimneys* by Nelly Sachs, translated by Ruth and Matthew Mead. Translation copyright © 1967 and translation copyright renewed © 1955 by Farrar, Straus, and Giroux, LLC.

Ramón Saldívar. Excerpt from *Chicano Narrative* by Ramón Saldívar. © 1990. Reprinted by permission of The University of Wisconsin Press.

Scott Russell Sanders. "Doing Time in the Thirteenth Chair." From *Paradise of Bombs* by Scott Russell Sanders. Copyright © 1983 by Scott Russell Sanders. Originally published in *The North American Review.* Reprinted by permission of the author and the Virginia Kidd Agency, Inc.

Anne Sexton. "After Auschwitz." From *The Awful Rowing Toward God* by Anne Sexton. Copyright © 1975 by Loring Conant Jr., Executor of the Estate of Anne Sexton. Reprinted by permission of Houghton Mifflin Co. All rights reserved.

Anne Sexton. "The Farmer's Wife." From *To Bedlam and Part Way Back* by Anne Sexton. Copyright © 1960 by Anne Sexton. Renewed 1988 by Linda G. Sexton. Reprinted by permission of Houghton Mifflin Company. All rights reserved.

William Shakespeare. *Hamlet, Prince of Denmark,* including footnotes, from *The Complete Works of William Shakespeare,* 4th edition, edited by David Bevington. Copyright © 1997 by Addison-Wesley Educational Publishers, Inc. Reprinted by permission.

Leslie Marmon Silko. "Yellow Woman." Copyright © 1974 by Leslie Marmon Silko. Reprinted by permission of The Wylie Agency.

Stevie Smith. "Not Waving but Drowning." From *Collected Poems of Stevie Smith* by Stevie Smith. Copyright © 1972 by Stevie Smith. Reprinted by permission of New Directions Publishing Corp.

Cathy Song. "The Grammar of Silk." From *School Figures* by Cathy Song. Copyright © 1994. Reprinted by permission of the University of Pittsburgh Press.

Sophocles. "Antigone." From *Three Theban Plays* by Sophocles, translated by Robert Fagles. Copyright © 1982 by Robert Fagles. Used by permission of Viking Penguin, a division of Penguin Putnam, Inc.

Gary Soto. "Behind Grandma's House." From *Gary Soto: New and Selected Poems* by Gary Soto. Copyright © 1995 by Gary Soto. Reprinted by permission of Chronicle Books, San Francisco.

William Stafford. "Travelling Through the Dark." From *The Way It Is: New and Selected Poems*. Copyright © 1962, 1998 by the Estate of William Stafford. Reprinted with the permission of Graywolf Press, Saint Paul, Minnesota.

Maura Stanton. "Shoplifters." From *Cries of Swimmers* by Maura Stanton. Copyright © 1984 by Maura Stanton. Reprinted by permission of the University of Utah Press.

August Strindberg. *The Stronger.* From *Six Plays* by August Strindberg, translated by Elizabeth Sprigge. Copyright © 1955 by Elizabeth Sprigge. Reprinted by permission of Curtis Brown Ltd.

Wislawa Szymborska. "On Death Without Exaggeration." From *View with a Grain of Sand* by Wislawa Szymborska. Copyright © 1993 by Wislawa Szymborska. English translation by Stanislaw Baránczak and Clare Cavanagh. Copyright © 1995 by Harcourt, Inc. Reprinted by permission of the publisher.

Amy Tan. "Two Kinds." From *The Joy Luck Club* by Amy Tan. Copyright © 1989 by Amy Tan. Reprinted by permission of Putnam Berkley, a division of Penguin Putnam, Inc.

Dylan Thomas. "Do Not Go Gentle Into That Good Night." From *Collected Poems* by Dylan Thomas (J.M. Dent, Publishers). Reprinted by permission of David Higham Associates. From *The Poems of Dylan Thomas*. Copyright © 1952 by Dylan Thomas. Reprinted by permission of New Directions Publishing Corp.

Kitty Tsui. "A Chinese Banquet." From *The Words of a Woman Who Breathes Fire* by Kitty Tsui. Reprinted by permission of the author.

John Updike. "A & P." From *Pigeon Feathers and Other Stories* by John Updike. Copyright © 1962 by John Updike. Reprinted by permission of Alfred A. Knopf, a division of Random House, Inc.

Victor Villanueva, Jr. Excerpt from "Whose Voice Is It Anyway? Rodriguez's Speech in Retrospect." From *English Journal*, 1987. Copyright © 1987 by the National Council of Teachers of English. Reprinted with permission.

Alice Walker. "Everyday Use." From *In Love and Trouble: Stories of Black Women* by Alice Walker. Copyright © 1973 by Alice Walker. Reprinted by permission of Harcourt, Inc. "In Search of Our Mothers' Gardens." From *In Search of Our Mothers' Gardens: Womaist Prose* by Alice Walker. Copyright © 1974 by Alice Walker. "Women." From *Revolutionary Petunias & Other Poems* by Alice Walker. Copyright © 1970 by Alice Walker.

Rosanna Warren. "In Creve Coeur, Missouri." From *Stained Glass* by Rosanna Warren. Copyright © 1993 by Rosanna Warren. Reprinted by permission of W.W. Norton & Company, Inc.

Bruce Weigl. "Spike." From *The Circle of Hanh: A Memoir* by Bruce Weigl. Copyright © 2000 by Bruce Weigl. Used by permission of Grove/Atlantic, Inc.

Eudora Welty. "A Visit of Charity." From *A Curtain of Green and Other Stories* by Eudora Welty. Copyright © 1941 and renewed 1969 by Eudora Welty. Reprinted by permission of Harcourt, Inc.

William Carlos Williams. "The Last Words of My English Grandmother." From *Collected Poems: 1909–1939*, Volume I. Copyright © 1938 by New Directions Publishing Corp. "The Use of Force." From *The Collected Stories of William Carlos Williams*. Copyright © 1938 by William Carlos Williams. Reprinted by permission of New Directions Publishing Corp.

James Wright. "Lying in a Hammock at William Duffy's Farm in Pine Island, Minnesota." From *Above the River: The Complete Poems* by James Wright. Copyright © 1990 by Anne Wright. Reprinted by permission of Wesleyan University Press.

William Butler Yeats. "The Second Coming." From *The Collected Works of W. B. Yeats, Volume I: The Poems*, revised and edited by Richard J. Finneran. Copyright © 1924 by The Macmillan Company. Copyright renewed 1952 by Bertha Georgie Yeats, Michael Butler Yeats, and Anne Yeats. Reprinted by permission of Scribners, a division of Simon & Schuster, Inc.

Yevgeny Yevtushenko. "Babii Yar." From *Collected Poems 1952–1990* by Yevgeny Yevtushenko.

Adam Zagajewski. "Try to Praise the Mutilated World." From *Without End: New and Selected Poems* by Adam Zagajewski, translated by Clare Cavanagh, Renata Gorczynski, Benjamin Ivry, and C. K. Williams. Copyright © 2002 by FSG, LLC. Reprinted by permission of Farrar, Straus & Giroux, LLC.

Index of Authors, Titles, First Lines, and Terms

The boldfaced page references indicate where a key term is highlighted in the text.

Index of Rhetorical Terms